LATIN AMERICA'S WARS

ALSO BY ROBERT L. SCHEINA

Santa Anna: A Curse upon Mexico

Latin America: A Naval History: 1810–1987

American Battleships: 1886–1923 with John C. Reilly

U.S. Coast Guard Cutters and Craft of World War II

U.S. Coast Guard Cutters and Craft: 1946–1990

Latin America's Wars
The Age of the *Caudillo*, 1791–1899
Volume 1

Robert L. Scheina

Brassey's, Inc.
Washington, D.C.

Copyright © 2003 by Robert L. Scheina

Published in the United States by Brassey's, Inc. All rights reserved. No part of this book may be reproduced in any manner whatsoever without written permission from the publisher, except in the case of brief quotations embodied in critical articles and reviews.

Library of Congress Cataloging-in-Publication Data

Scheina, Robert L.
   Latin America's wars / Robert L. Scheina.—1st ed.
      v. cm
Includes bibliographical references and index.
Contents: v. 1. The age of the *caudillo*, 1791-1899
   ISBN 1-57488-449-2 (cloth : v. 1 : alk. paper—ISBN 1-57488-450-6 (pbk. : v. 1 : alk paper)
   1. Latin America—History, Military—19th century. 2. *Caudillos*—Latin America—History—19th century. I. Title.
   F1413 .S34 2003
   355'.0098—dc21

                                                                                                      2002008029

Printed in the United States of America on acid-free paper that meets the American National Standards Institute Z39-48 Standard.

Brassey's, Inc.
22841 Quicksilver Drive
Dulles, Virginia 20166

First Edition

10 9 8 7 6 5 4 3 2 1

*This work is dedicated to my two mentors
for their enormous sacrifices on my behalf
Dr. Richard Greenleaf
Father Antonine Tibesar*

CONTENTS

Illustrations and Maps	xi
Preface	xiii
Acknowledgments	xvii
Abbreviations	xxi
Introduction: What Were the Causes for War in Nineteenth-Century Latin America?	xxiii

Part 1. Wars for Independence against the Monarchs of Europe

1.	Haiti (Saint Domingue), 1791–1803	1
2.	Viceroyalty of New Granada and the Captaincy-General of Venezuela, 1810–23	20
3.	Viceroyalty of Rio de la Plata, 1810–24	41
4.	Viceroyalty of Peru, 1810–31	54
5.	Viceroyalty of New Spain, 1810–29	71
6.	Brazil, 1822–23	85

Part 2. Early Border Wars in Spanish America

7.	The United Provinces against Brazil and Uruguayan Independence, 1825–28	93
8.	Peru against Gran Colombia, 1828–29	105

Part 3. Wars of Separation versus Union—Spanish and Portuguese America

9.	Buenos Aires versus the Provinces, 1820–61	113
10.	Central American Union, 1826–40	126
11.	The Peru-Bolivia Confederation and its Aftershock, 1836–41	132

12. Guayaquil versus Quito, 1830–1911	140
13. Brazil, 1831–49	149

Part 4. Wars of Conquest by the United States and Great Britain

14. Texas Independence, 1835–36	157
15. *Caudillos* and the Second Texas-Mexican War, 1836–44	166
16. The United States and Mexico, 1846–48	179
17. Central America, 1834–59	198

Part 5. Wars of Conquest (Do-It-Yourself Manifest Destiny)—Filibustering

18. Filibustering against Mexico, 1819–1911	205
19. Filibustering against Cuba, 1849–50	214
20. Filibustering against Central America, 1855–60	221

Part 6. The Age of the *Caudillo* in Mid-America

21. The Struggle among Venezuela's *Caudillos*, 1830–1903	235
22. Mini-Wars among *Caudillos* of Central America, 1844–1907	250
23. The Misrule by Bolivian *Caudillos*, 1841–99	262

Part 7. Mid-Nineteenth-Century Intraclass Struggles

24. Colombia and Sixty-three Years of Intraclass Conflict, 1839–1902	271
25. Uruguayan Intraclass Conflict, 1832–1904	281
26. Chilean Intraclass Conflicts, 1851 and 1859	289
27. War of the *Reforma*, 1857–60	295
28. French Intervention in Mexico, 1861–67	303

Part 8. Mid-Nineteenth-Century Attempted Territorial Conquest and Reconquest

29. The War of the Triple Alliance, 1864–70	313
30. The Pacific War, 1865–66	333

Part 9. Late Wars for Independence

31. Captaincy-General of Santo Domingo, 1838–65	341
32. Captaincy-General of Cuba, 1868–98	351

Part 10. Wars of Conquest against Native Americans

33. The Indians, 1819–1927	365

Part 11. An Economic War

    34.   The War of the Pacific, 1879–83   375

Part 12. Late-Nineteenth-Century Intraclass Struggles

    35.   Argentine "Revolutions" of 1890 and 1893   391

    36.   The Chilean "Revolution" of 1891   397

    37.   The Brazilian "Revolution" of 1893–94   405

Part 13. Political Intervention by the United States

    38.   The Spanish-American War, 1898   415

Postscript: What Were the Surprises?   426

Notes   428

Index to Full Bibliographical Citations   532

Index   541

About the Author   570

ILLUSTRATIONS AND MAPS

ILLUSTRATIONS

1. Black prisoners being drowned by their French captors during the Haitian Revolution	17
2. Black leader Dessalines hanging French prisoners outside of Cap Haitian	19
3. Revolutionary Gen. Francisco Miranda lands at La Vela de Coro, Venezuela on August 3, 1806	22
4. Battle of La Victoria	28
5. Simón Bolívar	32
6. José de San Martín	59
7. Capture of the Brazilian naval brig *Cacique* by the Argentine privateer *General Brandzen* on September 9, 1827	103
8. Manuel Rosas	115
9. Giuseppe Garibaldi	122
10. Lance-armed cavalry on the Argentine pampas	124
11. Antonio López de Santa Anna	184
12. The Battle of San Pascual	187
13. The Battle of Cerro Gordo	191
14. Panoramic view of projected Nicaraguan canal	222
15. William Walker	224
16. The Battle of Rivas	226
17. Miguel Miramón	300
18. Foreign volunteers fighting for Maximilian on the march	306
19. Francisco Solano López	315
20. Paraguayan cavalry unit under attack	316
21. Paraguayan soldier on sentry duty at López' headquarters	317

22.	Brazilian monitors battle the Paraguayan battery at Tebicuary	322
23.	The Battle of Abtao	336
24.	An Armstrong cannon at the Santa Rosa battery, Callao, Peru	338
25.	General Calíxto García's army on the march	354
26.	A Mexican soldier stands ready to march against the Yaqui Indians	372
27.	The Battle of Angamos	380
28.	Chilean troops land at Arica following its capture on June 5, 1880	384
29.	A Chilean battery of Krupp artillery	387
30.	The Battle of Concepción	389
31.	The battleship *Blanco Encalada* under attack by torpedo boats	401
32.	*Gobiernista* troops awaiting an attack by the *Congresionalistas*	403
33.	The *Aquidabã*, backbone of the rebel fleet during the Brazilian Intraclass War	412
34.	U.S. troops land at Daiquiri on June 22, 1898	421
35.	The USS *Texas* returns to New York following the Battle of Santiago	423

MAPS

1.	Latin America before Independence, 1784	xxii
2.	Hispañola, 1802	xxx
3.	Latin America after the Early Wars for Independence, 1828	112
4.	Brazilian Empire, 1828	148
5.	Mexico, 1835	156
6.	Central America, 1855	220
7.	Gran Colombia, 1828	270
8.	Rio de la Plata Region, 1865	312
9.	Cuba, 1867	350
10.	Southwest Coast of South America, 1878	374

PREFACE

> It is a grandiose idea to think of consolidating the New World into a single nation. . . . It is reasoned that, as these parts have a common origin, language, customs, and religion, they ought to have a single government. . . . But this is not possible. Actually, America is separated by climatic differences, geographic diversity, conflicting interests, and dissimilar characteristics.
>
> —Simón Bolívar, "The Jamaica Letter," September 6, 1815

WHAT IS LATIN AMERICA?

Latin America is the "un-united" thirty-three countries to the south of the United States. The political, social, and economic differences among the nations are dramatic, significantly outweighing their similarities. Unfortunately, the adoption of the term "Latin America" has helped cause stereotyping which does a disservice to all the nations of the region. And yet, I can find no alternative but to use the term myself.[1]

WHY STUDY NINETEENTH-CENTURY LATIN AMERICAN MILITARY OPERATIONS?

War was pervasive throughout Latin America during the nineteenth century. Some fine books focus on the major conflicts. However, even by immersing oneself in all of these works, it is not possible to gauge the impact of war upon the region as a whole. In fact, no general history of Latin American military operations exists. This book endeavors to fill that void.[2]

HOW TO MEASURE THE IMPACT OF MILITARY OPERATIONS?

Many yardsticks may be used to measure the magnitude of military operations.

Death and Injury

Although death and casualty statistics are notoriously inaccurate, they can give a sense of the size of national sacrifice. Throughout the nineteenth century the number of Latin American war-related deaths and casualties dwarfs the experience of the United States. During its Revolutionary War (1775–1783), the United States and its allies lost (killed and missing) approximately 35,000 men and the British and those in their employment perhaps another 30,000.[3] By comparison, some 350,000 persons died in the Haitian War for Independence (1791–1803): 200,000 blacks and *affranchis* (people of mixed blood), 75,000 French soldiers, 45,000 British soldiers, and 25,000 white colonists.[4] Six times as many Haitians as Americans died during their respective wars for independence, and more British and French soldiers died fighting in Haiti than in North America. Edmund Burke, the noted British statesman, wrote concerning the Haitian campaign, "It is not an enemy we have to vanquish but a cemetery to acquire."[5]

During the War of the Triple Alliance (1864–1870), Paraguay lost perhaps 300,000 individuals from a population of 525,000 and the allies (Argentina, Brazil, and Uruguay) 180,000 persons from a total population of 10,850,000.[6] Comparing the deaths of the U.S. Civil War, North America's bloodiest conflict, with those of the War of the Triple Alliance shows that the loss of life in Latin American was almost as great as in North America despite the huge population difference. The United States (North and South) lost 650,000 persons from a population of 35 million.[7]

Percentage of Population Lost

During their wars for independence (1810–1824), the populations of Ecuador, Mexico, and Venezuela all decreased by over 25 percent.[8] During the War of the Triple Alliance, Paraguay lost almost 60 percent of its entire population and four out of five males between the ages of fifteen and fifty. By comparison the most severe North American loss was the 13 percent of the Union army during the U.S. Civil War.[9]

Admittedly, these comparisons have been between wars fought by a variety of Latin American nations as opposed to those fought by the United States alone. But comparing the percentage of casualties along purely national lines reveals that during the nineteenth century Cuba, the Dominican Republic, Ecuador, Haiti, Mexico, Paraguay, and Venezuela all lost a higher percentage of their population to war than did the United States.

Politics and Power

Another way to measure the influence of military operations upon a region is to see how many individuals have won the "presidency" because of their success on the battlefield. Many write that a common route to the office of president in Latin America led through the army barracks. Within Latin America, warriors made history through their exploits on the battlefield; however, most scholars choose to focus upon their political deeds. What is less appreciated is that throughout the nineteenth century individuals such as Jorge Montt (of Chile), Juan Manuel de Rosas (of Argentina), Pedro Santana (of Santo Domingo), and Cipriano Castro (of Venezuela) secured and maintained their position through *skills* on the battlefield and not merely political intrigue. To this we could add presidents who died on the battlefield—Peruvian Agustín Gamarra (November 18, 1841) and Guatemalan Justo Rufino Barrios (April 2, 1885)—and a former president who was killed fighting while he manipulated an individual who was merely keeping the presidential chair warm—Venezuelan Joaquín Crespo (April 16, 1898).

Conquests

Yet another measure of the influence of war upon Latin America was the quantity of territory that changed hands as a consequence of military operations, the most prominent example being the lands lost by Mexico to the United States between 1835 and 1848. Argentine Minister of Foreign Affairs Mariano Varela, when asked for his nation's territorial demands following the War of the Triple Alliance, responded, "Victory gives no rights."[10] Perhaps not, but typically victors took what they wanted.

Social Change

War profoundly altered the social structure of Latin America during the nineteenth century. The Haitian War for Independence may be the only successful slave revolution in modern history. The War of the Triple Alliance created two new social elements within Brazilian society: the professional military officer and the freed black who became the backbone of the Army. These elements played major roles in the downfall of the Brazilian monarchy in 1889 and in establishing a republic.

Economic Power

Military operations also profoundly altered the economic potential of some Latin American nations. The wars between Mexico and the United States (1835–1848) helped determine which would have the potential to become a world power. The War of the Pacific (1879–1883) made Chile the dominant economic power on the west coast of South America.

These various methods of measure demonstrate that military operations significantly influenced the development of Latin America during the nineteenth century.

HOW TO CONVEY AN APPRECIATION OF GEOGRAPHY?

Frequently, I reference the distance and direction "as the crow flies" (unless otherwise stated) of important sites to a strategic location, most often the capital, in order to convey an appreciation of size. Interpreting these numbers is difficult, for distance is not easily equated to travel time since mountains, rivers, and deserts can cause significant variations. Also, during the second half of the nineteenth century, technology increasingly impacted on travel time, over first water and then land. How these factors impacted on military operations is addressed within the chapters.

WHAT IMAGES DO WORDS OF VIOLENCE CONVEY?

Conflict terminology has been loosely applied to events in Latin America. But words are important for they convey images. Therefore, a revolution should be more traumatic than a rebellion, and a rebellion on a larger scale than a revolt. The same discrimination should be used when labeling wars, conflicts, and clashes. Such discrimination frequently has not been employed in the writings about violence in Latin America. So historians have written about "wars" which were not truly wars and "revolutions" which were not revolutions, and yet these classifications are continually mimicked in today's writings.

The fighting between France and Mexico in 1838 is commonly called the "Pastry War." True, Mexico declared war on France but only six hundred casualties were sustained and the fighting was brief. This event more accurately should be called the "Pastry Intervention." If it merely takes a declaration by one side to have a war, then we need to recognize the "war" declared by Honduras against the United States in 1847 which possibly has yet to be officially terminated.

Writings concerning Latin America are filled with this or that "revolution." If we accept Mr. Webster's definition of a revolution, a "fundamental change in political organization . . . ,"[11] there were few "fundamental" changes caused by war during the nineteenth century in Latin America. Even when examining the Wars for Independence, one is struck by the fact that Spain of 1821 was more Revolutionary than its rebellious colony Mexico, and that in 1823 Portugal was more Revolutionary than its rebellious colony Brazil. The commonly labeled "revolutions" of 1891 in Chile and of 1893 in Brazil are more accurately rebellions or civil wars since no fundamental political change occurred.[12]

Within this text I have endeavored to convey magnitude by choosing the word which I believe conveys the most accurate image. This frequently differs from that which these events have traditionally been called. Of course my choice is subjective; a magnitude of violence that I would call a war in small Ecuador might not justify my using the term for a similar event in large Mexico.

The views expressed in this book are those of the author and do not reflect the official policy or position of the National Defense University, the Department of Defense, or the U.S. Government.

ACKNOWLEDGMENTS

First and foremost, I want to thank Azad Ajamian, president of Brassey's Inc., for having the courage to undertake the publication of this mammoth work. In an age when the first question from a potential publisher is, How can it be reduced? Mr. Ajamian's question was, What will it take to do the subject justice? I also want to thank the acquisitions editor, Rick Russell, who tirelessly championed this effort from beginning to end. Thank you also to my agent, Fritz Heinzen, whose advice was always right on the mark.

I am deeply indebted to the following individuals for their substantive research, face-saving corrections, and thoughtful additions. They have persevered through a decade of research and a second of writing. Without their help, this book would have failed to meet my expectations.

Name	Contributions
Eduardo Alimonda Professor of Economics and Captain (ret.) Argentine Navy	Argentina and translations throughout
Reginaldo J. da Silva Bacchi Military Analyst and Journalist	Brazil
Robyn Scheina Brown Attorney at Law	Editorial review; troubleshooter
Carlos Hernández González Attorney at Law	Venezuela
David Mahan Medical Doctor and Bibliophile of Chilean Naval History	Chile
Jurg Meister Historian and author	Entire book

I wish to thank the following individuals for their contributions, which have strengthened specific chapters of this book. Without their help, my work would have been significantly less complete. For those in the military, the rank cited was that held when they made their contribution. Some have since been promoted.

Roxanne Andersen	Troubleshooter
Researcher

Melitón Carvajal Pareja	Peru
Rear Âdmiral (ret.) Peruvian Navy

Carlos Chavarria	Guatemala
Colonel, Guatemalan Army

Hugo Contreras	Colombia
Colonel (ret.), Colombian Army

Andres Duarte	Paraguay
Colonel, Paraguayan Air Force

Adrian English	Entire book
Scholar and author

Patricia Falconi	Argentina
Universidad de Belgrano

Nancy Westfall de Gurrola	Mexico
Professor, Universidad Iberoamericana

Julio Hang	Argentina
Brigadier General, Argentine Army

Terry Hooker	Texas War for Independence
President, El Dorado Society

Robert Hughes	Panama
Professor, Industrial College of Armed Forces

John Klingemann	Nineteenth-century Mexico
Scholar

Carlos López	Chile
Professor, Menlo College

Daniel Masterson	Peru
Professor, U.S. Naval Academy

Diego Mantilla Jaramillo	Ecuador
Captain, Ecuadorian Navy

Jay Mallin	Cuba
Journalist for major newspapers

Guillermo Montenegro	Argentina
Professor, Escuela de Guerra Naval

Acknowledgments

Jaime de Ojeda Spanish-American War, 1898
Spanish Ambassador to United States

Jorge Ortiz Sotelo Peru
Secretary General, Thalassa Society

Eduardo Pesce Brazil
Scholar, Universidade do Estado do Rio de Janeiro

Sergio Reyes El Salvador
Colonel, Salvadoran Army

Guadalupe Antonio Reythel Honduras
Professor, Colegio de Defensa Nacional

Patrick Roth Nineteenth-century U.S. interventions
Captain (ret.), U.S. Navy

Linda Scheina Editorial review
Confidante

Barbara Tenenbaum Nineteenth-century Mexico
Hispanic-American Division, Library of Congress

Miguel Viviani Buenos Aires, 1829–1861
Colonel, Argentine Army

Paul Walsh Entire book
Bibliophile of Latin American Military

Thom Whigham War of the Triple Alliance
Professor, University of Georgia

Catherine Wilson Troubleshooter
Researcher

César de Windt Lavandier Dominican Republic
Rear Admiral (ret.), Dominican Navy

ABBREVIATIONS

ca.	about
E	east
ed.	editor or edition
ft	feet
mi	miles
N	north
n.d.	no date of publication cited
n.p.	no publisher cited
OAS	Organization of American States
S	south
unk	unknown
vol.	volumes
W	west

Map 1. Latin America before Independence, 1784.

WHAT WERE THE CAUSES FOR WAR IN NINETEENTH-CENTURY LATIN AMERICA?

> There is no good faith in America, nor among the nations of America. Treaties are scraps of paper; constitutions, printed matter; elections, battles; freedom, anarchy; and life, a torment.
>
> —an 1829 anonymously published article attributed to Simón Bolívar

The causes for wars in Latin America during the nineteenth century are numerous and create a vivid, plaid tapestry. Patterns are difficult to discern; however, threads do stand out and some even transverse the entire cloth. The most vivid threads have been the race war, the ideology of independence, the controversy of separation versus union, boundary disputes, territorial conquests, *caudilloism*, resource wars, intraclass struggles, interventions caused by capitalism, and religious wars.

RACE WAR

The Haitian War for Independence (1791–1803) began as a struggle between the privileged white planters and the less privileged *affranchis* (those of mixed blood) and rapidly became an all-out race war when the third and largest racial element, the pure blacks, ultimately dominated. In 1791 the *affranchis* sought the liberties given to all citizens by the French Revolution. During the early years of the bloody warfare, some wealthy plantation owners were able to escape from Haiti with their slaves, contributing to the spread of race as a cause for conflict, particularly in neighboring Cuba. Conflicts in other areas of Latin America have also had racial overtones, but none equaled the extremes of the Caribbean experience.

IDEOLOGY OF INDEPENDENCE

Latin American wars for independence were an outgrowth of deep-seated political, economic, and social frustrations. Within colonial Latin America a class system existed which exalted the Europeans, gave lesser privileges to the American-born, pure-blooded whites, and repressed all others. Each class of Americans had its own irritants. For the *criollos* (persons of pure Spanish blood born in the New World), the principal frustration was the lack of political opportunities. The overwhelming majority of political, military, and ecclesiastical appointments went to *peninsulares* (persons born in Spain, also called *godos* in Buenos Aires and the Caribbean and *gachupines* in Mexico).

Complementing this political frustration was an economic system which also favored the *peninsulares* and strangled the development of the colonies. Mercantilism, an economic system which held that colonies existed for the benefit of the motherland, stagnated economic development throughout the New World. Trade was exclusive and monopolistic, conducted by Europeans in European ships. Further down the class ladder were the *mestizos*, Indians, and blacks, and each was treated progressively worse. They were heavily taxed. Many additional irritants unique to geographical regions compounded these frustrations.[1]

Events in Europe and North America were additional catalysts for independence, although not pervasive. The American Revolution (1775–1783), which had had the support of Spain, and the French Revolution (1789–1799) provided models. These influenced some of the privileged of the New World, the two most important being Simón Bolívar of New Granada and Miguel Hidalgo of Mexico.[2]

Spain had also changed. Carlos III, who came to the throne in 1759, initiated reforms that were contrary to Spanish traditions and practices. In 1807 Ferdinand, the presumptive successor to the throne of Spain, unsuccessfully attempted to take control of the crown. His father, Carlos IV, had abdicated because of a popular rising in Aranjuez and the hostility of the Spanish people toward his prime minister Godoy, who was also the queen's lover. Members of the entourage of the abdicated king turned to Napoleon Bonaparte for help. Skillfully taking advantage of the situation, Napoleon forced Carlos to sign the Treaty of Bayonne which ceded the throne to Napoleon.

This decapitated the head of the colonial, hierarchial government. Napoleon then invaded Spain in order to put his brother Joseph on the throne. In April 1810 the Spaniards created a *Junta* to govern in the name of Ferdinand VII.[3] After a period of turmoil within Spain, a Supreme *Junta* emerged and then a regency was created to govern in the name of the captive Ferdinand VII. For the most part, the legitimacy of these governments was not accepted in the Americas.[4] Latin American wars for independence were fought primarily between 1791 and 1824, with notable exceptions such as those in Santo Domingo (1820–44) and Cuba (1868–98).

Ferdinand VII's dream of regaining territory in the Americas died hard in spite of its improbability of success. His aspirations were aided by counterrevolutionary forces in Europe. Following Ferdinand's restoration the crowned heads discussed extending aid to the Spanish king so he might retake his lost empire in the Americas. Although this alliance did not endure, Spain persisted in its dream of reconquest. It invaded Mexico in 1829; welcomed the invitation to reintroduce colonial rule in Santo Domingo in 1861; and fought Chile and Peru (and also nominally Bolivia and Ecuador) in 1865–66. To some degree these adventures were motivated by the desire to reconquer lost colonies.

Spain was not the only nation that was inspired to renew the wars for independence. Fear of Spain caused a few Latin American nations to consider an attack against the remaining empire. In 1826 Colombia and Mexico toyed with the idea of forging a coalition in order to liberate Cuba from Spanish rule. During the Pacific War (1865–66), Peruvian President Ignacio Prado hired a former officer of the Confederate States Navy to command an attack against Cuba. Although none of these efforts to reignite the wars for independence were ever serious threats to their opponents, they nonetheless absorbed treasure.

Not all wars for independence within Latin America were against the European monarch. Some were caused by the heterogeneity within the vast viceregal governments. For example, Asunción and its surroundings had evolved very differently from Buenos Aires, the viceregal capital. When Spain abandoned its interests in this remote, relatively poor, but self-sufficient colony, Asunción perceived no threat from Spain and no advantage to remaining politically aligned to Buenos Aires. Therefore, Asunción's brief fight for independence was against Buenos Aires and not Spain.

Another factor that caused regions within a viceregal colony to seek independence from the colonial seat of power was economic competition within that colony. This competition had been successfully suppressed by mercantilism during most of the colonial era. But the Bourbon reforms and the wars for independence brought free trade. As a result, Montevideo became a competitor of Buenos Aires. This competition is one reason why Montevideo chose first to remain loyal to Spain and then once declaring independence to break with Buenos Aires.

SEPARATION VERSUS UNION

During the colonial era, many administrative entities within the Spanish colonial empire had been held together primarily through their loyalty to the King; he was the glue. Formidable geographical barriers of mountains, jungles, deserts, rivers, and vast distances created isolated pockets of population. Once this European monarch had been forced to abandon his Latin American supporters, a prime issue became whether these vast but sparsely populated colonial entities would become a single nation or whether they would break up—separation versus union.

The potential of the young nation breaking apart dominated Argentine politics and military operations for almost six decades (1816–61). Colombia was subjected to nearly eighty years of on-again, off-again civil wars between Centralists and Federalists; between 1828 and 1871 some fifty revolts occurred.[5] Liberal José Antonio Gamboa argued at the 1857 constitutional convention that Mexico's second most important problem (the Roman Catholic Church being the first) was the potential of national disintegration because of a lack of identity.[6]

BOUNDARY DISPUTES

The poorly defined boundaries of the newly independent nations caused wars. The Spanish king's inadequate knowledge of the geography transferred vast areas from one administrative entity to another in attempts to improve political, social, and economic control.[7] This gave almost every post-independence Spanish-speaking nation some basis to claim lands also cherished by a neighbor. The colonial boundaries in Spanish South America were particularly complex because the continent had been administratively reorganized in 1776, thus further confusing historical ties.[8] Also, the kings of Spain and Portugal were occasionally at war during the colonial era and the same held true for their colonies. Not surprisingly, a golden rule of Latin America power politics became: Relations between nations which share a common border are cool and those which do not are warm. Boundary wars began immediately after the wars of independence and continued throughout the nineteenth century.

WARS OF TERRITORIAL CONQUEST

The post-independence wars of territorial conquest against the native Americans (the Indians) were an extension of the colonial experience. Unassimilated tribes inhabited the more inhospitable regions throughout Latin America, and the new nations conducted campaigns against these Indians which continue in some places today.

Only a few wars for territorial conquest were initiated within Latin America in the years following independence. True, a border dispute may have been the excuse to begin the conflict, but in a war for territorial conquest, the aggressor had aspirations from the beginning of winning land well beyond any of those in dispute. The clearest example of wars for territorial conquest were the United States confrontations with Mexico (1835–48) and British expansion in Central America (1821–56).

In 1837, while Texas was an independent country, its representative in Washington, William H. Wharton, wrote to that new nation's secretary of state, John Forsyth, "Genl. [Andrew] Jackson says that Texas must claim the Californias on the Pacific in order to paralyze the opposition of the North and East to Annexation."[9] And, as late as 1858 President James Buchanan recommended to the U.S. Congress the occupation of northern Mexico—Sonora and Chihuahua in particular.[10]

The American desire to expand permeated its society. Even private citizens took it upon themselves to initiate Manifest Destiny, or the self-anointed right to territorial expansion. Armed expeditions of private citizens, known as filibusters, invaded Mexico, Cuba, and Nicaragua—all more than once—for the purpose of conquering their territory. Local representatives of the British government initially acting on their own initiative attempted to block the expanding influence of the United States in Central America by seizing Honduran and Nicaraguan territory.

The War of the Triple Alliance (1864–70) was also a war for territorial conquest. Francisco Solano López probably dreamed of an "Empire of the Rio de la Plata" composed of Paraguay, parts of Argentina and Brazil, plus Uruguay. Although no documentation exists outlining his plan, it is hard to draw any other conclusion from his actions, and López did have a wooden model of an imperial crown made in Paris.

CAUDILLOISM

The desire to rule in order to satisfy one's ambitions has also led to war in Latin America. Strong-willed individuals, known as *caudillos*,[11] routinely used force to achieve their personal ends. Throughout the nineteenth century hundreds of *caudillos* existed, most never rising above the local level and controlling only a handful of men. A few climbed to be "giants," the utterance of their names—Antonio López de Santa Anna of Mexico and Justo José de Urquíza of Argentina—delivered thousands to a cause. A few *caudillos* were motivated purely by patriotism for the fatherland (*la Patría*) and a few by purely selfish desires. Most were motivated by a combination of these and other factors.

Although *caudillos* generally professed political ideologies, many willingly sacrificed these when they conflicted with their quests for power. This explains how the Mexican Antonio López de Santa Anna could alternately profess allegiance to liberal and then conservative ideologies in order to achieve power. The Venezuelan *caudillo* Antonio Guzmán Blanco wrote: "I don't know where people have got the idea that Venezuelans love federalism, when they don't even know what the word means. The idea of federation came from me and some others who said to ourselves: Since every revolution has to have a slogan . . . let's invoke the idea of federation. For if our opponents, gentlemen, had said *federalism*, we should have said *centralism!*"[12]

The power of a *caudillo* was his ability to deliver his followers to the cause of his choice. Their loyalty was to him personally and could be lost if the *caudillo* were defeated in battle, or unable to deliver the spoils which his followers expected. In 1814 the monarchist José Tomás Boves was killed in battle and many of his followers joined the Revolutionary José Antonio Páez because of his military prowess. In 1860 the followers of republican Ignacio Mejía Fernández joined the monarchist Leonardo Márquez because the Mexican government had stopped paying them.[13]

RESOURCE WARS

The cause for the War of the Pacific (1879–83), sometimes called the "Nitrate War" between Chile against Peru and Bolivia, was the arbitrary taxation and duties imposed by Bolivia upon Chilean-owned nitrate firms, provoking Chile to intervene militarily and ultimately leading to war. Without the nitrates, the Chileans may never have attempted to conquer the desert.[14]

INTRACLASS WARS

In the decades following independence, the unresolved struggle between conservatives, who favored a monarchy, and liberals, who wanted a republic, led to wars. The most bloody were the French intervention in Mexico (1861–67) in support of the Mexican Conservatives and the Brazilian Civil War of 1893–94. Other political ideologies, such as federalism versus centralism, as well as economic disputes among the ruling class also sparked intraclass wars. The scale of these conflicts ranged from palace *coups* involving a few dozen people to full-scale wars involving armies of many thousands.

INTERVENTIONS CAUSED BY CAPITALISM

The commercial nations (principally the United States and Great Britain) frequently intervened within Latin America because they believed their investments or status vis-a-vis another commercial power was threatened. Latin American nations emerged from the wars for independence bankrupt, indebted, and devastated. In many of the new countries, agriculture, ranching, mining, manufacturing, and the population itself had been decimated. In Venezuela the "War to the Death" (*guerra a muerte*) reduced livestock by more than one half.[15]

The wars had brought trade to a standstill almost everywhere. Although many Latin American nations won their independence by 1824, few were politically cohesive. For decades regionalism and factionalism dominated. Within these environments, precarious oligarchies and dictatorial *caudillos* agreed to usurous loans from private American and European investors who insisted upon exorbitant profits to justify the risk. And many foreign merchants flocked to Latin America to exploit commercial opportunities. These individuals were frequently endangered by the lack of political stability. Normally, both the investor and the borrower claimed to be the victim (one of usurpation and the other of default). This combination of usurous rates and political immaturity led to defaults which, in turn, invited military interventions. The military advantage almost always rested with the more industrialized nation.

Other interventions were motivated by the competition between Great Britain and the United States over transit across Central America. Nineteenth-century interventions, although numerous, were generally on a small scale—perhaps one gunboat and a detachment of marines.

The Monroe Doctrine of 1823 did outline a policy for intervention in Latin America in order to prevent a monarchic counterrevolution against republican governments and to deter the expansion of European colonies in the New World. The first threat never materialized and the second too frequently was carried out by Great Britain, the world's dominant military power. Looking back over the nineteenth century, only on rare occasions did the United States threaten military intervention to enforce the Monroe Doctrine.[16]

More than one hundred interventions took place in Latin America during the nineteenth century. Virtually no country was immune.[17] And, not all interventions were initiated by nations. Many were the acts of individuals. British, Irish, and French fought in significant numbers against Spain during the wars for independence. Americans and British fought on both sides in the 1826–28 war between the United Provinces of Río de la Plata (the future Argentina) and Brazil. French and Italians fought in the siege of Montevideo against the forces of Manuel Rosas. Belgians and Austrians fought against Mexicans during the French intervention. Swiss, Germans, and Italians fought as volunteers and mercenaries in the Argentine army against Francisco Solano López during the War of the Triple Alliance.

Seemingly, North Americans rarely missed an opportunity to join in a fight. Lt. J. M. Gilliss, U.S. Navy, wrote in 1856 concerning the Battle of Loncomilla (December 8, 1851) during a Chilean rebellion: "the United States consul at Talchuano . . . notified our minister . . . that twenty-one Californians had left a ship . . . and joined the Revolutionaries. To their credit be it told they were 'volunteers without pay, who offered themselves from a hatred of oppression, and spirit of adventure,' characteristic of the race."[18]

RELIGIOUS WARS

Religion played an important role in Latin American wars. Fathers like Miguel Hidalgo and José Morelos, who led the War for Independence in Mexico, are but the most prominent examples of a significant number of clerics who took up the saber. Rafael Carrera's army, which controlled Guatemala for the Conservatives in the mid-nineteenth century, was a product of the Roman Catholic Church. Ecuador under Gabriel García Moreno (1860–95) was an almost theocratic state; those who fought the civil war which ended his policies were significantly motivated by anti-religion. Religion was a prime motivator during the intraclass struggles that plagued Colombia during the last seven decades of the nineteenth century.

These ten causes for war in Latin America—race war, the ideology of independence, the controversy of separation versus union, boundary disputes, territorial conquests, *caudilloism*, resource wars, intraclass struggles, interventions caused by capitalism, and religious wars—were intertwined and profoundly influenced the region throughout the nineteenth century. And war was pervasive.

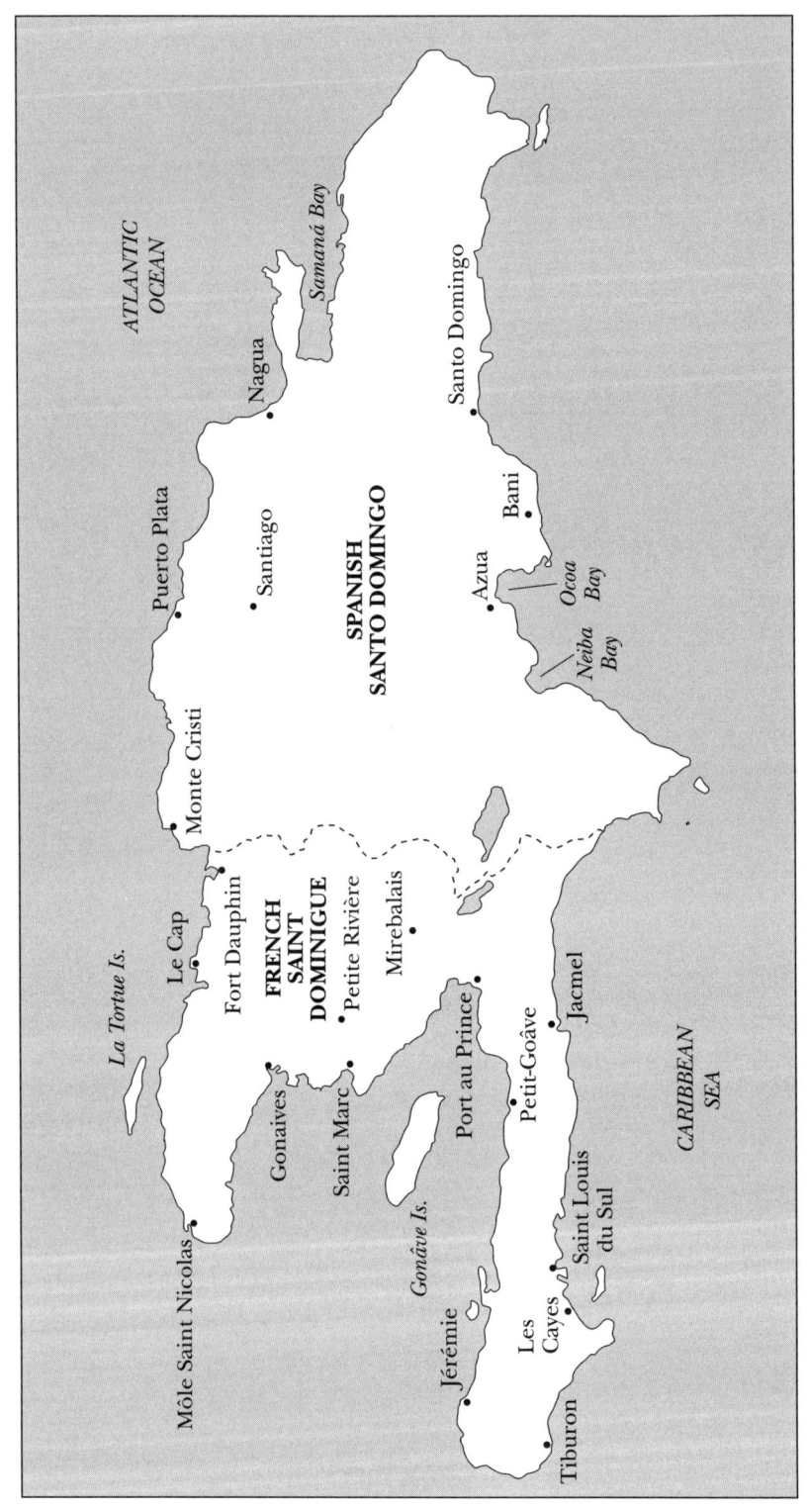

Map 2. Hispañola, 1802.

PART 1

WARS FOR INDEPENDENCE AGAINST THE MONARCHS OF EUROPE

CHAPTER ONE

HAITI (SAINT DOMINGUE) 1791–1803

> [T]hey [the blacks] now come on in regular bodies, and a considerable part of them are well armed with muskets, swords, etc., which they have taken and purchased. They fight under the bloody flag having on it a motto, denouncing "death to all Whites!"
> —a correspondent of the *Boston Independent Chronicle and the Universal Advertiser*, November 3, 1791

THE SPARK

On August 22, 1791, a slave rebellion ignited a race war in Haiti that endured for twelve years.

BACKGROUND

Racial injustice was the underlying cause for the Saint Domingue or Haitian Revolution. Slavery was practiced throughout the New World, but nowhere more brutally than in French Saint Domingue.[1] This produced acute class hatred.

The wealth of the colony was sugar cane and to a lesser degree coffee and cotton, all of which could most economically be harvested by slave labor. And these riches were great. By the late eighteenth century the value of exports from Saint Domingue exceeded those from the young United States. Saint Domingue accounted for almost one-third of France's overseas trade.[2]

The early pronouncements of the French Revolution (1789–99) offered political promise for all Frenchmen regardless of color. On October 5, 1789, the "Declaration of the Rights of Man and of Citizen" proclaimed that, "All men are born and live free and equal in their rights." And, on March 28, 1790, the French National Assembly granted the franchise in Saint Domingue to "all persons aged 25, owning property, or failing property ownership, to taxpayers of ten years standing."[3] However, declarations made in white, Revolutionary France were not easily enforced in black, reactionary Saint Domingue. For, if the *affranchis* (those of mixed blood) with wealth were granted equal rights with the whites, then what of the black slaves?

OPPOSING FORCES

For decades many on Saint Domingue feared the eruption of race warfare. Society was divided into classes based upon race—the whites, the *affranchis*, and the blacks. These classes were further subdivided by wealth which could provide limited social mobility.

The whites, which totalled about 38,000, were divided into three groups, the *grand blanc*, the middle class, and the *petit blanc*. The *grand blanc* were the wealthiest planters and the privileged of society, holding the high civil and military positions. The middle class were the shopkeepers, many of whom were concentrated around the capital of Port-au-Prince. The *petit blanc* were the plantation overseers, small farmers, and the minor civil and military officials. To be noble, rich, white, and born in France was the top of the social order. The *grand blanc* and the *petit blanc* held each other in contempt.

The *affranchis* were liberated slaves, many of whom were *mulattes* (those of mixed blood). They owned perhaps one-third of the land and of the slaves in Saint Domingue. In 1791 there were some 30,000 *affranchis*. At that time numerous political, social, and economic restrictions limited their ability to advance. They were allowed to serve in the militia but with distinct uniforms and strict social morays.

The blacks, who numbered about 422,000, were about 90 percent of the total population, and almost all were slaves. Most were from West Africa and the Congo. The planters, constantly preoccupied with the fear of insurrection, worked to destroy tribal identity.[4]

OPENING STRATEGIES

The rapid successes of governments that ruled France from 1789 through 1793 issued radically divergent political and economic policies. And with France so far away, frequently those representing the European nation in Saint Domingue pursued their own agenda. The one consistent objective of France was to maintain Haiti's colonial status. In Haiti the three racial groups—whites, *affranchis*, and blacks—violently competed for power. Initially, the French strategy was to maintain Saint Domingue with a few thousand European troops and political compromise. For the blacks, the immediate goal was revenge and freedom from slavery. Lacking leadership, the strategy of the blacks was to rape, kill, pillage, and burn. For the *affranchis* the issue was to achieve equality with the whites without further diffusion of power, freedom, and wealth to the blacks. The *affranchis* tried to bribe the French assembly; failing this they unsuccessfully sought a coalition with the whites against the blacks. For the whites the objective was to maintain the prerevolution status quo. The whites initially tried to use European troops and white officered, colonial troops to suppress the *affranchis* and the blacks.

WHITES AND AFFRANCHIS CLASH

By late 1790 whites and *affranchis* clashed as the latter group endeavored to win in fact what the Revolutionary French national legislature granted in theory. Vincent Ogé and Jean-Baptiste Chavannes emerged as *affranchis* leaders. Ogé obtained money from abolitionists in England, purchased arms in Charleston, South Carolina, and landed on the northern coast of Saint Domingue on October 21, 1790. After unsuccessfully petitioning the governor for political rights, Ogé armed *affranchis* in the north. During a confrontation, a white planter was shot and killed and Ogé declared a rebellion. He marched on Le Cap (175 mi NNE of Port-au-Prince),[5] the colony's principal port, with a force of about three hundred men. The *affranchis* won their first encounter but were soon overwhelmed by 1,500 white militia and black volunteers. Ogé and Chavannes were cruelly executed by being broken on the wheel; twenty-two others were hanged, including a white priest; and thirteen were sentenced to life in the galleys. Thus, the whites crushed the *affranchis* in the north and possibly their one potential ally against a slave revolution. Saint Domingue was rife with unrest.

THE SLAVES REVOLT

While the 38,000 whites and 30,000 *affranchis* struggled for control of the island, some 422,000 black slaves watched and waited.[6] On August 22, 1791, a general slave uprising erupted throughout the northern part of the island. Slaves armed with farm tools raped, killed, plundered, and burned. Those whites fortunate enough to escape the slaughter sought refuge in Le Cap. The town, rapidly fortified by ditches, palisades, and barricades, was attacked by some 15,000 slaves who unsuccessfully threw themselves against cannon and musket volleys.[7]

On August 30 André Rigaud,[8] with his *affranchis*, joined in the rebellion and defeated some local militia at la Croix des Bouquets. Throughout the north country innumerable atrocities were committed by both sides. Bodies of opponents were used as decorations. Some 10,000 slaves and 2,000 whites were slaughtered and over 200 sugar and 1,200 coffee plantations were burned.

In an unsuccessful attempt to confine the uprising to the north, the whites established three defensive cordons. The eastern cordon covered Trou du Nord, Fort Dauphin, and Vallière. The southern cordon protected Goncaives and Saint Raphael. The third cordon denied access to the northwest peninsula. These cordons were patrolled by planters and militia who would, on occasion, launch search-and-destroy missions. The local whites were supported by the veteran regiment "Le Cap." This was reinforced by two Irish battalions, perennial mercenaries of the Kings of France. Marquis de Rouvray, a veteran of the American Revolution who had successfully defended Le Cap against marauding blacks, took charge of the eastern cordon. He described the tactical problems for the whites: "We are up against an enemy whose principal, I would even say only, resource is his ability to keep ahead of us. Only by snapping at their heels with flying columns that threaten them every minute and run them down everywhere, can you hope to subdue them."[9]

The whites patrolled by day, but by night the countryside belonged to the blacks. Many *affranchis* in the north joined in the uprising against the whites. A carnage equal to that of the north followed in the west. Rigaud emerged as the principal *affranchis* leader.

THE WEST EXPLODES

In the west around the capital, Port-au-Prince, the three groups struggled for advantage. The rich whites allied themselves with the well-to-do *affranchis* when threatened by the poor whites but disavowed the alliance as soon as the threat subsided. In late October 1791 word reached Saint Domingue that the French National Assembly had disenfranchised the *affranchis*.

The west exploded. Port-au-Prince and Jacmel were left in ruins. Smaller towns were completely overrun. Rape, murder, and pillage were rampant. In the south the *affranchis* captured Saint Luis du Sud in December. By now both the whites and the *affranchis* in the south were arming their slaves, many of whom slipped away into the hinterland when the opportunity for freedom presented itself. By late 1791 the situation was chaotic. In the north the whites controlled the ports and ineffectively held their cordons against the blacks. In the west fighting raged between whites and *affranchis*, but both sided tenuously held down their black slaves.

THE FIRST FRENCH COMMISSION

To bring matters under control, the Revolutionary French National Assembly sent three commissioners to Saint Domingue. Their authority rested upon six thousand soldiers who came with them, a third of the number that had been promised. Arriving in the north on November 29, 1791, they were able to open a dialogue with the blacks. An amnesty had almost been concluded with the black leaders, who were promised their freedom in exchange for a return to slavery for their followers, when the blacks learned that the white colonists planned to slaughter them once they laid down their arms. The French commissioners had been betrayed by the island's whites, the very group they were trying to save. The blacks lashed out. Jean-François stormed the eastern cordon, sacking Fort Dauphin and Ouinaminthe during January 1792. The northwest peninsula, previously undisturbed, erupted in violence.

THE SECOND FRENCH COMMISSION

On April 4, 1792, the French National Assembly once again granted equality to all *affranchis* in an attempt to regain control over Saint Domingue. Three new commissioners and six thousand politically reliable troops under Gen. Etienne-Maynard Laveaux were sent to the island to restore order and enforce the decree which would not be favorably received by the whites.

On September 18 the commissioners and their army landed at Le Cap. Commissioner Léger Félicité Sonthonax gained control over the French delegation and allied himself with the *affranchis*. He was a Revolutionary zealot. He perceived the whites as would-be Royalists and counterrevolutionaries. Sonthonax cleverly wrestled political power from the whites and recognized only two classes, free men and slaves. The French force under Sonthonax's control fleetingly subjugated the north and west by January 1793 but failed in the south where the white planters, supported by their armed slaves, held control and refused to recognize the April 4 decree.

The pace of the French Revolution quickened when on February 1, 1793, France proclaimed the "war of all peoples against all kings," having beheaded its own king ten days earlier. Appreciating that rich, troubled Saint Domingue lying between Spanish Santo Domingo and English Jamaica was vulnerable to attack from these colonial rivals, the French National Assembly sent Gen. Thomas-François Galbaud, a professional soldier who had recently inherited property in Saint Domingue, as governor with orders to defend the island and leave politics to the commissioners.

GOVERNOR GALBAUD ARRIVES

Arriving at Le Cap on May 7, 1793, Galbaud found the north in chaos, the treasury empty, and troops unpaid. Galbaud's actions to restore order and his need for funds to pay his troops allied him with the white planters and alienated the *affranchis*. The French commissioners, who were at Port-au-Prince dealing with problems in the West, were disturbed by Galbaud's arrival. Commissioners Etienne Polverel and Sonthonax marched north with two hundred French infantry, four hundred *affranchis* troops, and a detachment of Orleans Dragoons. On June 10 the force was warmly welcomed by *affranchis* and received with suspicion by the whites as it entered Le Cap. The commissioners examined Galbaud's credentials and declared them invalid on the basis that the decree of April 4, which had given free blacks political equality, disqualified anyone owing property in the Americas from governing Saint Domingue. At that time, a French squadron of three ships of the line, six frigates, three smaller warships, and supporting auxiliaries lay off Le Cap. Sonthonax arrested Galbaud and sent him to a transport for passage home to France.

The rejected governor presented his case to the fleet and won its support. At noon on June 20, twelve hundred sailors and marines supported by eight hundred Royalist deportees launched the fleet's boats and stormed Le Cap. The bitter fighting which ensued all day ebbed and flowed. Many of the sailors broke into wine cellars and lost interest in the fight. The next day Galbaud landed his reserves and carried the arsenal and harbor fortifications. The artillerists from these batteries joined with Galbaud and the commissioners' forces were pushed from the city.

During the night of June 20, the commissioners had communicated with the slaves, offering freedom to anyone who would join their cause. Approximately ten thousand slaves burst upon Le Cap on June 21. To escape the slaughter, surviving whites sought refuge at the water's edge where they were protected by guns of the fleet and the remnant of Galbaud's force. The alliance between the commissioners and the slaves delivered Le Cap to the blacks; thus, the white refugees and the entire French naval establishment sailed for the Chesapeake. On August 29, 1793, Commissioner Sonthonax declared all slaves in the north to be free, a declaration of the existing reality. Thus ended slavery and white supremacy in Saint Domingue, although these changes would not go unchallenged.[10]

Due to its weakened condition, the French colony lay vulnerable to its Spanish neighbor with which it shared the island and to nearby English Jamaica. If protecting the sanctity of kings weren't enough motivation for the English and Spanish to seize Saint Domingue, there was always the added inducement of the colony's wealth.

SPAIN AND GREAT BRITAIN ATTACK SAINT DOMINGUE

Spain and Great Britain had long been meddling in the affairs of Saint Domingue. During the recent fighting, Spain had supplied and helped arm French Royalists on the island. The Spanish governor of Santo Domingo purchased the allegiance of important black leaders and their personal armies.[11]

In July 1793, more than a thousand white French planters deserted from the north to the sanctuary of Spanish Santo Domingo. Their exodus, the recently acquired loyalty of significant black armies to Spain, and the departure of the French navy from Le Cap virtually placed northern Saint Domingue at the mercy of the Spanish. In July Spanish forces, including former slaves led by, among others, Toussaint Louverture,[12] crossed the border and pushed back the disheveled French forces before them. Toussaint swept through and captured Goncaives. His success rested in part upon the capabilities of key subordinates. Among the most cunning and vicious were Jean Jacques Dessalines[13] and Moyse.[14] Fort Libérté (formerly Fort Dauphin), one of the last French strongholds in the north, fell on January 28, 1794.

In a desperate attempt to stem the invasion, Sonthonax abolished slavery throughout northern Saint Domingue on August 29. When extended to the west on September 21, many whites and *affranchis* turned against Revolutionary France.[15]

In the west a British force from Jamaica occupied Jérémie (140 mi W of Port-au-Prince) on September 20, 1793, with the support and jubilation of the white planters. Three days later the

British accepted the surrender of the massive fortification at Môle St. Nicolas (190 mi NW of Port-au-Prince) from the remaining 150 "Wild Geese" of the Dillon Irish Regiment, which no longer had a French king to serve. On October 4 the British failed to take Cap Tiburon (240 mi W of Port-au-Prince) from the sea. However, by December reinforcements arriving from Jamaica and white refugees sufficiently swelled British ranks to permit the capture of Léogane and St. Marc (60 mi NW of Port-au-Prince) in the west. When Sonthonax tried to counterattack, the British navy blockaded the French force in Port-au-Prince. The British now converged on Port-au-Prince, capital of Saint Domingue.[16]

Although the British controlled the seas and met little resistance on land, they were losing the battle "in the air." Soldier and sailor alike were dropping at an astonishing rate to yellow fever. Gen. Adam Williamson, Governor General of Jamaica, had assured the English crown that he could carry off the affair with his 877 troops. He now made the first of numerous calls for reinforcement.

On February 2–3, 1794, the British stormed the fort at Cap Tiburon. Its capitulation and the earlier capture of Môle St. Nicolas gave the British control of the Windward Passage and the approaches to Jamaica. On the nineteenth the British captured Fort l'Acul causing Grand Gôave to declare in support of Great Britain. By now the British held about one-third of Saint Domingue, but their advance had ground to a halt due to a shortage of troops. The French took heart. They raided British-controlled areas, burning Royalist plantations. In March the French regained the town of Jean Rabel, near the Môle St. Nicolas. On April 16 Bombarde, the source of most provisions for the Môle, also fell to the French. The British failed to retake Bombarde during a marine assault. French forces led by the *affranchis* Rigaud tried to retake Cap Tiburon on April 16 but failed. On May 3 Fort l'Acul was attacked by blacks.

By mid-1794 a stalemate settled in. The French still held Le Cap and Port-au-Prince in the north, and Les Cayes (120 mi WSW of Port-au-Prince) in the south. But all were under siege and blockade and in desperate straits. Laveaux at Port-au-Paix (220 mi NNW of Port-au-Prince) recorded, "We have been reduced to six ounces of bread a day. . . . If we had powder we would rest easier. We have no shoes, shirts, clothes, soap, or tobacco. Our soldiers mount guard barefooted. We have not even a flint to issue."[17] The English also had their problems. Their troops were stretched to the breaking point and the French Royalists were growing restless under British control.

TOUSSAINT CHANGES SIDES

The French received relief from an unexpected quarter. Toussaint, the black leader who had sold his allegiance to the Spanish, now literally cut their throats at the joint headquarters, Marmelade, and rejoined the French cause on May 24, bringing with him his personal following of 4,600 men. Toussaint's decision to once again switch sides allowed him to increase his power through concessions made by the French to regain his loyalty. Toussaint was not just one of the black leaders. Militarily, he was the "first among equals." Months earlier, following the collapse of the north but prior to the Spanish invasion, Toussaint had employed French deserters to teach his followers the rudiments of tactics, drill, and discipline. Aside from a few hundred European professionals shared between the two sides, Toussaint's troops were the best trained on the islands. And, they were better acclimated than the Europeans. Toussaint immediately went on the offensive; he began recapturing for France much of what he had previously taken for Spain.

On May 19, there arrived 1,683 British reinforcements, bringing their strength on Saint Domingue to 2,967 men. These reinforcements permitted the British to renew their offensive. Objectives abounded. Jean Rabel and Bombarde could be recaptured, thus securing the Môle, the northern gateway to the Windward Islands. In the south Les Cayes and Jacmel could be seized, thus eliminating privateering that was preying upon the Jamaican trade routes. In the north, Cap François and Port-au-Paix could be attacked; these were the principal French military and naval bases. And in the west lay Port-au-Prince, the capital and principal commercial port. All held rewards as well as dangers.

THE CAPTURE OF PORT-AU-PRINCE

The British chose to attack Port-au-Prince. A strike force of 1,465 men supplemented by over one thousand French Royalists and supported by four ships of the line, three frigates, and three sloops captured the city between June 1 and June 4. Only thirteen men were killed and nineteen wounded. The French commissioners barely escaped into the interior. Some of the British soldiers and sailors shared in 400,000 pounds in prize money for the 45 merchant ships captured in the bay. In addition, the British took 131 guns and large quantities of stores.[18]

The British made no effort to pursue the retreating French force or attack the French elsewhere. The window of opportunity proved very narrow. Within 60 days of the victory, the British counted 40 officers and 600 troops dead of yellow fever. From Martinique came 518 replacements. By the time they landed on June 8, only 290 were alive, most of whom soon died ashore from the yellow death.

By now no central authority remained on the French side. Laveaux, who was nominally governor, was at Port-au-Paix in the north but exercised no control over the other factions. Black and *affranchis* leaders were the real representatives of French power. Villatte held Le Cap in the north, Toussaint the center, and Rigaud Les Cayes in the south. These factions rarely cooperated, choosing to independently attack the British.

In September 1794 the *affranchis* revolted against British rule at Saint Marc due to discriminatory treatment; the uprising was suppressed with difficulty. In October French forces led by Rigaud were invited back into Léogane. In December Fort Bizothon was successfully defended by the British. On December 5 Rigaud attacked Port-au-Prince; repulsed, he then attacked Cap Tiburon on Christmas Day and drove the British out after the British armed transport *King George* blew up. The *affranchis* rebelled at Jérémie late in the year and were suppressed. The British also suppressed plots at Môle St. Nicolas, Saint Marc, and Port-au-Prince during early 1795.[19]

By the end of 1794, only 750 British soldiers were fit for service while a like number lay sick. Adam Williamson, now the British governor of Saint Domingue as well as Jamaica, began recruiting slaves into the army. Hundreds were promised their freedom in exchange for five years of service.

While the British slowly increased their strength at horrendous costs, Toussaint strengthened his position by rescuing the French governor, Laveaux, at Cap François from a plot contrived by the *affranchis* to seize power during November–December 1794. Toussaint was rewarded with the post of lieutenant governor and permission to raise even more troops—two horsed regiments, three on foot, and a personal bodyguard. Laveaux was now dependant upon Toussaint. This made Toussaint the most powerful man in French-controlled Saint Domingue.

THE BRITISH OFFENSIVE OF 1794–95

After numerous delays caused by French military victories in Europe and disastrous weather, significant British reinforcements began to arrive. Between April of 1795 and April of the following year, almost 5,000 British troops were sent to Saint Domingue. Among them were the 900-man 82nd Foot, selected because British authorities erroneously believed that regiment's normal station, Gibraltar, had acclimated it to tropical conditions. Within ten weeks, 630 men of the regiment had died. By September the 96th Foot, another replacement regiment, ceased to exist, another victim of yellow fever. The dying continued and the reinforcements kept coming—Dutch artillerymen, French emigre cavalry, and even Hanoverians—all in the service of King George.[20]

Although the Spanish had had much their own way in northern Saint Domingue, such had not been the case in Europe, and on July 22, 1795, the French republic and Spanish crown signed the Treaty of Basle. Frenchmen were to return to their side of the Pyrenees in Europe and Santo Domingo, the Spanish half of Hispañola, was to be ceded to France! Toussaint was a beneficiary of these terms, for as the bands of former slaves who had fought for Spain disbanded, many joined with him. He seized the Spanish colony, but for the most part, Toussaint was inactive because he lacked munitions. In an attempt to solve his dilemma, Toussaint traded rum and coffee to North American blockade runners in exchange for gunpowder.[21]

By August 1795 the British had tenaciously rebuilt their force to nearly 3,400 men and Williamson could boast that he had "literally saved the colony by the black corps that I have founded."[22] These blacks fighting for the British had repulsed Toussaint at Saint Marc in April 1795.

By mid-1795 much of Saint Domingue lay in ruins. Sugar exports had plummeted by 90 percent and coffee by half. Only remote regions protected by mountains temporarily escaped the massive destruction.[23]

THE BRITISH OFFENSIVE OF 1795–96

During the winter of 1795–96, a British army of almost 19,000 men sailed in a fleet of over two hundred ships with the goal of seizing the initiative throughout the West Indies. Like the preceding expedition, this one was badly battered by storms. Maj. Gen. Gordon Forbes, commanding British forces in Saint Domingue, was led to believe that he could expect over 15,000 men in November–December 1795 and another 4,000 to 5,000 soldiers somewhat later. He was ordered to prepare to attack the French stronghold in the north. To facilitate these plans, Forbes actively fostered defections among the blacks and *affranchis*. He was authorized to promise full civic equality. Aided by the rumor of a pending great expedition, Forbes had some successes. Blacks led by the former slaves Pompe and Pierre Dieudonné deserted the French land blockade of Port-au-Prince, and Forbes temporarily restored the capital's main water supply. In January 1796 these blacks attacked the *affranchis* garrisons at Jacmel and Léogane. Also during the month, Titus, another former slave who had a significant following, signed treaties with the British.

Forbes received 2,000 reinforcements from Gibraltar on February 9, 1796, and on February 22 received new orders informing him that the operations in Saint Domingue were to be given a low priority.

In March 1796 Forbes began a new offensive. The general launched an attack against the *affranchis* under Rigaud at Léogane with 750 British troops supported by French Royalists. On

March 21 the British navy bombarded Léogane, the gateway to the south. This was followed by a two-pronged assault over land. To the surprise of the British, the *affranchis* had circled Léogane with a deep palisaded ditch. The British had brought no siege artillery. Unable to secure ordnance from the fleet in adequate time, the British substituted six-pounders. These were ineffective against the *affranchis'* defenses. On March 22 Forbes decided to evacuate the attackers by sea. The *affranchis* cut their way through the rear guard formed by French white colonists and wreaked havoc upon the retreating British army. And the yellow fever now took its tool on the recent arrivals from Gibraltar. By June 1 the 1,000-man 66th Regiment was reduced to 198 fit and the 1,000-man 69th to 515 fit.[24]

Between May 1 and June 20, Forbes received more reinforcements: 2,000 British infantry; 1,200 British cavalry; 1,500 foreign cavalry; 200 Dutch artillerymen; and some miscellaneous for an approximate total of 6,500 men. Most of these were ill-suited to his needs. For the most part, these troops were units that Gen. Sir Ralph Abercromby, Forbes' superior, found unfit for service in the Windward Islands due to illness, poor outfitting, or poor training. Most of the cavalry were horseless and the foreign cavalry refused to serve as infantry since it was not in their contract. Also, cavalry had limited utility in the heavily fenced plains and extensive mountain region. In addition, Forbes was paralyzed by the news of the arrival of French reinforcements.[25]

THE THIRD FRENCH COMMISSION

On May 11, 1796, yet another set of French commissioners, five this time, arrived with orders to reestablish control over Saint Domingue and to lay claim to Spanish Santo Domingo.[26] They brought with them 3,000 troops, a large quantity of muskets and ammunition, and Generals Donatien Rochambeau[27] and Edmé-Etienne Borne Desfourneaux. Also, Forbes' fears were fueled by the rumor that French Rear Adm. Richard de Richery was expected with 10,000 more troops.

Although Forbes' sick-list was 2,500 soldiers long, he now possessed the largest British force assembled in Saint Domingue—7,000 troops with 1,200 recently arrived horses and supported by 10,000 French Royalists. His opponents together were perhaps twice as numerous, but their leaders were badly divided along racial lines and their troops poorly trained for conventional warfare. Twice in August, Forbes' cavalry caught Toussaint's blacks in the open and cut down large numbers.

THE BRITISH OFFENSIVE OF 1796–97

During the winter of 1796–97, Great Britain launched yet another offensive in the Caribbean. This time they attempted to seize the possessions of their former allies Holland and Spain. The islands of Trinidad and Puerto Rico were the primary objectives. Troops were drawn away from Saint Domingue to support the second objective. Trinidad was taken but the British were repulsed at Puerto Rico in May 1797. By the end of the healthy season, British troops were spread dangerously thin throughout the West Indies, and for that matter the world. Also, Great Britain's finances were severely strained.

Saint Domingue had grown horrendously expensive for the British to administer. Costs had escalated from 296,000 pounds in 1794 to 2,211,000 pounds in 1796.[28] Three problems stood in the way of quitting the island: the promises to the French planters who had accepted British rule; the bargaining value that the colony had at any peace negotiations with the French; and the protection afforded to Jamaica by occupying the forts along Saint Domingue's west coast. In February Lt. Gen. John Graves Simcoe[29] was selected to replace Forbes. He was ordered to maintain control of the Môle and to get the colonists to assume as much of the cost of maintaining the colony as possible. Forbes believed that British goals could best be achieved through aggressive action. Through sound administration and new taxes, Simcoe was able to reduce the annual cost to the crown to 744,000 pounds, but this was still too much for those in London. The British hold on Saint Domingue rested upon their defenses at Port-au-Prince, Mirebalais, and Jérémie.

While British attention had been diverted to Trinidad and Puerto Rico, Toussaint had eliminated many black and *affranchis* rivals in the north, and in February 1797 he attacked Mirebalais while his allies attacked Jérémie. He threw Moyse and Dessalines against Fort Borough and Fort Escahobe. On March 7 Escahobe collapsed after thirty-five assaults in twenty days, and Borough fell two days later. These victories cut off Port-au-Prince from its source of food and its land communications with Spanish Santo Domingo. However, French forces failed to capture Jérémie.

In May Simcoe attacked Mirebalais. He caught Toussaint, who was at Goncaives (100 mi NNW of Port-au-Prince) preparing to attack St. Marc, by surprise. Mirebalais was recaptured with few casualties. Simcoe then rushed his cavalry back to St. Marc in order to repulse Toussaint's attack on June 3. The seasonal rains then began along with malaria. Although Simcoe had moderate success in the field, opposition to the continued occupation of Saint Domingue continued to grow in London due to the extravagant costs. On June 9 Simcoe received a sharp letter reminding him of his instructions to withdraw to the Môle.[30]

On January 1, 1798, a new commander was appointed, Major General [first name unknown] Nesbitt, and he was ordered to withdraw to Môle St. Nicolas and Jérémie (which were desired to control the Windward Passage and for a foothold in Saint Domingue); he was to limit expenditure to 150,000 pounds per year; and if threatened by overwhelming forces, he was authorized to withdraw to Jamaica. The French colonists who supported the British were given one more chance to bear a greater share of the costs. Failing this, they were to be offered help in finding asylum. However, Nesbitt fell mortally ill and died in transit to Saint Domingue.

Maj. Gen. John Whyte, commanding in Simcoe's absences, remained on the defensive. This allowed Toussaint time to eliminate more rivals. In early 1798 Toussaint captured Grand Bois and Mirebalais. Laplume, another black general, carried important heights above Port-au-Prince. And Rigaud once again besieged Irois.

THE BRITISH EVACUATE

Acting Brig. Gen. Thomas Maitland (a thirty-eight-year-old lieutenant colonel), General Nesbitt's chief of staff, landed at Môle St. Nicolas on March 21. Maitland, who had gone ahead of his superior, was unaware that Nesbitt had died. Maitland, who was politically well connected, had long argued for the very instructions which Nesbitt had been given. However, Maitland had no authority to act on those orders and he chose not to share them with Whyte. Whyte wanted out; he retired to the Môle and ultimately sailed to England, leaving Maitland in *de facto* command.[31]

Within a few days of his landing, Maitland was followed by 520 men of the 40th Regiment and the Irish Brigade. This allowed him to drive the French from Cul de Sac and restore some security to the British position at Port-au-Prince. Maitland could muster 2,000 European troops and perhaps 8,000 islanders of dubious military value. He faced three formidable enemies. In the west and northwest, Toussaint had 20,000 men which included 700 Frenchmen, all that remained of the 12,000 French soldiers who had been sent to the island since 1791. Captain Rainsford, described a demibrigade loyal to Toussaint in early 1798: "At the whistle a whole brigade ran three or four hundred yards and then, separating, threw themselves flat on the ground . . . and all the time keeping up a strong fire. . . . This movement is executed with such facility and precision as totally to prevent cavalry from charging them in bushy and hilly countries."[32]

Laplune, at Léogane, threatened Port-au-Prince. In the south Rigaud had 12,000 followers and the countryside was teeming with armed men who owed allegiance to no one save themselves. Toussaint moved to encircle Port-au-Prince and Rigaud to tighten the siege of Jérémie. On April 20 Rigaud attacked the port of Irois. Two passing British frigates destroyed Rigaud's assault craft and forced him to withdraw. Maitland sent 1,000 troops from garrison duty to Grande-Anse to block Rigaud.

Twelve days after landing, Maitland secretly proposed to Toussaint that the British would evacuate the west including Port-au-Prince if allowed to do so peacefully and if Toussaint would suspend operations against the Môle and Grande-Anse during the truce. Toussaint agreed. Maitland chose to negotiate with Toussaint because his power base was in the north most distant from Jérémie, the weaker of the two positions Maitland was instructed to hold. By May 10 the British and their followers had carried out the withdrawal from the West.[33]

Maitland attempted to carry out his orders by going on the defensive at the Môle and taking the offensive in the west to protect Jérémie from Rigaud. A British force from Jérémie drove the *affranchis* into Cap Tiburon, which was besieged by land and sea. Toussaint rushed reinforcements to Rigaud, who quickly launched an offensive. Toussaint also attacked the Môle to take pressure off Rigaud. The weak British attack collapsed.

On July 30 Maitland received word of Nesbitt's illness and was charged to carry out his orders. Maitland, over the objections of the British navy, spent the next three months negotiating secret agreements with Rigaud and Toussaint and extracting the remaining British forces from the island. On August 31 Maitland and Toussaint concluded an agreement. The British would not attack any part of Saint Domingue under Toussaint's control, or meddle in Saint Domingue's internal affairs, plus they would lift the blockade of those ports controlled by Toussaint. In exchange, Toussaint agreed not to meddle in Jamaica, which was then experiencing a slave revolt.[34] Back in London, the government was having a change of heart—perhaps Saint Domingue could be held after all. But matters were moving faster in Saint Domingue than in London. On October 2, 1798, Adm. William Bligh (of *Bounty* notoriety) embarked the last of the British and their followers.[35]

The British attacks against Saint Domingue had been part of a grand scheme to win control of the West Indies. In this effort the British had taken Martinique, St. Louis, Tobago, Dutch Guinea, and Trinidad—modest gains.[36]

WAR OF THE KNIVES

Republican France made yet another attempt to subjugate Saint Domingue to its rule. Gabriel-Theodore-Joseph Hédouville was sent to pacify the island. Bringing few troops, his one hope lay in playing off Toussaint and Rigaud, the personifications of black and *affranchis* power, against each other. The commissioner proved no match for Toussaint in political intrigue and was forced to leave the island.

If Toussaint were to win total control, he had two more adversaries with which to deal, the French Commissioner Hédouville at Le Cap and Rigaud in the south. The Commissioner erred by rapidly demobilizing black regiments and sending them to the fields to work. Rumors spread that France was trying to reinstate slavery. Riots broke out and Hédouville had to call on Toussaint for help. Toussaint marched north with a picked regiment and put down the unrest. Hédouville, realizing that he was without power, embarked for France on October 22 along with 1,800 refugees. The Commissioner did get one last lick in before leaving: He promoted Rigaud to a rank equal with Toussaint and made Rigaud independent commander of the south.[37]

To maintain appearance as a loyal French subject, Toussaint invited Roume, the French commissioner in former Spanish Santo Domingo, to replace Hédouville as the representative of French authority in Saint Domingue and to mediate his dispute with Rigaud, well appreciating Rigaud's violent temper and lack of tact. To strengthen his economic and military position in the upcoming struggle against Rigaud, Toussaint entered into agreements with Great Britain and the United States, both of whom saw support of Toussaint as a blow to Revolutionary France. The predictable civil war ensued.[38]

Toussaint possessed considerably more manpower than Rigaud, but it was less homogeneous and not as well trained or armed. Toussaint's most dependable troops were blacks, but his force included some *affranchis* and a few whites. Rigaud's strength rested almost exclusively upon the *affranchis*.

Rigaud, a man of precipitous action, crossed the bridge at Miragoane (60 mi WSW of Port-au-Prince), the traditional boundary dividing the East and West, thus invading Toussaint's domain, on June 18, 1799. The *affranchis* took no prisoners, neither black nor white; the "War of the Knives" had begun. With this outbreak of civil war, many *affranchis* in the north and west declared for Rigaud, including many at the Môle, Port-au-Prince, and Le Cap. Toussaint reacted immediately. He rushed south to Léogane and placed his most loyal lieutenant, the brutal Jean-Jacques Dessalines, in charge of 20,000 men with orders to block Rigaud's advance. Toussaint then rode north executing thousands of *affranchis*, some of whom had betrayed him and some of whom had not. From July through September 1799 he raised the siege at Port-au-Paix and Le Cap and recaptured the Môle. With the north now secure, Toussaint went south to deal with Rigaud.

Toussaint had some 30,000 men and Rigaud 2,500 soldiers plus approximately 6,000 reserves. The opposing forces were not as uneven as the numbers suggest. Toussaint's force was mostly composed of black militia but did include a small corps of well-disciplined black troops. Pamphile de Lacroix, who had fought against Toussaint's best, described them as follows: "Officers commanded, pistol in hand, and had the power of life and death over their subordinates. It was remarkable to see these Africans with bare torsos and equipped only with cartridge pouch, sword and musket, give an example of perfect self-control. . . . To have succeeded in disciplining these barbarians was Toussaint's supreme triumph."[39]

Rigaud's 2,500-man force was well seasoned from fighting the British, well equipped, and valiantly led by officers who knew that the only mercy the loser could hope for would be a quick death.

Henry Christophe[40] led one wing of Toussaint's army against Jacmel, a strongly fortified port which would threaten his rear if bypassed. From November 1799 through early March

1800, Toussaint tightened the siege carrying the outer defenses one by one. Meanwhile the U.S. Navy, ordered "to scour the south side of the island," destroyed Rigaud's barges, transported blacks to the front, and bombarded Jacmel.[41] Reduced to eating rats and firing rocks, the surviving garrison of 1,400 men, led by Alexandre Pétion,[42] fought their way through Toussaint's lines into the mountains, sustaining heavy losses. On March 11 Toussaint's troops entered Jacmel and the slaughter that followed raised the casualties, military and civilian, to over 5,000 persons. Dessalines led the other wing of Toussaint's army against Grand and Petit Gôave (45 mi WSW of Port-au-Prince). Rigaud retreated; torrential rains prevented him from interposing scorched earth between his and Toussaint's troops.

Toussaint's assault was temporarily halted with the arrival of three new French commissioners, this time sent by First Consul Napoleon Bonaparte. Toussaint rapidly isolated them from power. Meanwhile, Rigaud continued to retreat across the south to Les Cayes fighting stubbornly for a lost cause. On July 31 Rigaud, most of his officers, and seven hundred of his troops sailed into exile rather than face Toussaint's vengeance; Rigaud fled to France.[43]

TOUSSAINT SEIZES THE SPANISH HISPAÑOLA

Against Bonaparte's orders, Toussaint decided to invade the Spanish half of the island. Toussaint intimidated Roume, the hollow representative of French authority, into supporting the seizure of the Spanish colony Santo Domingo. Toussaint then demanded that the Spanish authority surrender. When this was refused he sent two columns, one with 3,000 men and the other with 4,500, across to the eastern side of the island. After a skirmish, the Spanish governor surrendered on January 26, 1801, and, along with most of the garrison, sailed for Cuba. After nine years of warfare, Toussaint was master of the entire, now devastated, island.

NAPOLEON ATTEMPTS TO CONQUER SAINT DOMINGUE

For too brief a time, Toussaint was able to devote his energies to rebuilding the island. For Toussaint international events moved too fast; France was temporarily ending its struggle against England and the United States. Great Britain now feared the spread of revolutionary ideas to Jamaica, and the United States no longer needed to be concerned with French privateers in the West Indies and was happy to end its awkward arrangement with a rebellious black.[44]

If Toussaint were a student of duplicity, Napoleon Bonaparte was its master. The First Consul's ambitions now turned toward recreating an American empire and the first step was reconquering the once-rich colony of Saint Domingue. By early December 1801 an army of 21,175 veterans under Gen. Victor-Emmanuel Leclerc,[45] carried in 67 ships, sailed from France for the New World. The plan had many weaknesses. During their first six months, newcomers to the West Indies frequently contracted malaria or yellow fever. If they survived, their immunity increased and generally they were not susceptible the following fever season. Also, Napoleon looked to Jamaica and the United States as sources for provisions. This proved to be folly given his volatile relations with Great Britain and the United States.

Leclerc's instructions were pure Machiavelli. He was to seize the coastal towns by duplicity and deceit; smash organized resistance by winning over Toussaint's principal lieutenants through bribery; and once disunited, send all black leaders to France in chains. The interior was to be pacified through the use of mobile flying columns. When the time was correct, Leclerc was then to restore slavery.[46]

Leclerc's fleet arrived in Samaná Bay piecemeal due to bad weather and was further delayed due to improper loading for amphibious assault. After putting his force in order, Leclerc sent detachments by sea to seize the cities of Santo Domingo, Fort Libérté (formerly Fort Dauphin), Le Cap, Port-au-Paix, and Port-au-Prince, using bravado or force. Those ashore would have none of that ruse, so force proved necessary. Toussaint's strategy was time-tested. Retreat, kill the whites, scorch the earth, wait for the climate to decimate the French, and then kill the survivors.

While the French assembled their invasion force in France, a fact that could not be hidden from Toussaint, the self-proclaimed governor-general was busy suppressing a mutiny by Moyse. Toussaint was shaken by this event, for Moyse was his heir apparent. Some 2,000 persons including Moyse were executed.

Toussaint, not knowing where the French might land, hid supplies in the interior and divided his army among the important ports. On February 2 Leclerc arrived off Le Cap in twenty-three warships carrying 5,000 soldiers. For three days Leclerc, from the haven of the fleet, and Henry Christophe, from the safety of the city, tried bluffing each other into submission. Appreciating his increasing vulnerability, Chirstophe torched Le Cap on February 4. This scene was repeated at Port-au-Paix and throughout the north and west, Toussaint's traditional strongholds. At Port-au-Prince the blacks decided to fight rather than torch the city and then retreat. They proved no match for the French veterans. The south, the *affranchis* stronghold, and the east, the old Spanish colony, yielded peacefully to the French demands.

Toussaint's instructions to Dessalines left no room for interpretation: "The only resources we have are destruction and fire. Annihilate everything and burn everything. Block the roads, pollute the wells with corpses and dead horses. Leave nothing white behind you."[47]

By mid-February, Leclerc had won most of the strategic ports. In spite of severe shortages of boots, mess gear, and hospital supplies—all attributable to incompetence or graft in France—Leclerc took the offensive and struck inland from Fort Libérté, Le Cap, and Port-au-Prince. Two of his forces converged on Toussaint at Ravine-à-Couleuvre, a defilé, flanked by brush-covered mountains, a little over seven miles from Goncaives. On February 23 a bloody six-hour battle ensued. Toussaint, losing 800 dead, was defeated and retreated.

The only territory that remained under Toussaint's control was the mountainous terrain due east of Saint Marc. Toussaint's strategy was to hold up in the mountains and harass the French. At Petit Riviere de l'Artibonite stood the fort La Crête-à-Pierrot, which had been built by the English. At this formidable position, the French cornered Toussaint and forced him to make his stand. At first only 1,200 blacks faced the 12,000 French, but black strength increased as reinforcements arrived. On March 4 the French made contact with the blacks' outposts. As the French pressed on, the blacks fell back under the guns of the fort, which had the desired effect. Time after time the French tried to carry the fort by assault, but to no avail. Three generals, fifty other officers, and 600 veteran troops were killed or wounded. The French, failing to storm the fort, now lay siege. French mortars, commanded by Alexandre Pétion and manned by *affranchis*, who had returned to the island as part of Leclerc's force, lobbed shells into the fort day and night. The defenders' ammunition ran low and casualties mounted. Silently during the night of March 24, the fort was evacuated. Pamphile de Lacriox, a French participant, observed: "The retreat the commander of La Crête-à-Pierrot conceived and evacuated is a remarkable feat of arms. We had more than 12,000 men surrounding him. He got away with the bulk of his garrison and left us only the dead and wounded."[48]

The blacks lost 1,200 dead and wounded while 250 men escaped; the total French losses amounted to 2,000 troops. For Leclerc, the siege of La Crête-á-Pierott was costly, but a victory. The battle marked the end of organized opposition, although guerrilla warfare continued unabated. By the end of March 1802, Leclerc had 7,500 European and 7,000 black soldiers fit for duty, while another 4,500 white soldiers were sick. Altogether Leclerc had lost 4,000 men in only two months of offensive operations. Leclerc asked Paris to send him 6,000 men plus 2,000 soldiers every month as replacements. During the year he did receive 11,000 reinforcements.

Toussaint and Christophe independently opened secret negotiations with Leclerc. Only Dessalines would not immediately sue for peace. On April 28, 1802, Leclerc met with Christophe at Le Cap where the black's rank and command were confirmed. Eleven days later Toussaint entered Le Cap and agreed to retire to his plantation. His closest followers who wished to retire with him were allowed to do so and the remainder were allowed to join the French army if they wished. Finally, Dessalines came over to the French and was pardoned and given a command, although many of the secondary black leaders remained in the field against the French.

On June 7 Toussaint was lured to a meeting, arrested, and abducted to France to die in a prison, soon to be followed by hundreds of his most loyal followers.[49] Leclerc, whose force now numbered 8,000 men fit for service, did not feel secure enough to reintroduce slavery, which French forces were doing elsewhere in the Caribbean.

THE YELLOW FEVER DEFEATS LECLERC

What Toussaint had failed to do, defeat the French, the "Yellow Jack" now cruelly accomplished. By May Leclerc was losing thirty to fifty men a day, and by July it was 160 men a day. Attempting to conceal the losses, the dead were carted away at night and military funerals were suspended. But Leclerc could not hide his growing weakness. Also, rumors spread throughout Saint Domingue concerning the French desire to reinstate slavery. Perceiving the French predicament, the surviving black leaders, one by one, retired into the hinterland, organized, and armed themselves with some of the 140,000 muskets that had found their way to Saint Domingue since 1791. Among the last to join the rebels were Christophe and Dessalines.

Between May and November 1802, the French unsuccessfully attempted to find and destroy the weapons the blacks held. To rescue the deteriorating situation, Leclerc resorted to increasing brutality and as a result black opposition increased. In August Leclerc made the soldiers of the black 7th Colonial Brigade, who had mutinied, witness the public executions of their wives before he executed the entire brigade. As a consequence, the black 8th Colonial Regiment went over to the rebels. On October 13, Pétion mutinied with over three regiments and seized Haut-de-Cap. Christophe rebelled the following day.

Leclerc desperately concentrated his European troops. Under attack, Fort Liberté was evacuated by sea and the survivors joined the defenders at Le Cap. Leclerc now distrusted all black troops. He had hundreds drowned in the harbor along with their families. By October 16, Leclerc had defeated the black attack against Le Cap, but by the end of November, only Le Cap, Port-au-Prince, and Les Cayes remained under French control. The French retreated into St. Marc, Port-au-Prince, and the Môle.

Back in Europe, Napoleon had lost interest in the "jewel of the Antilles" so neither reinforcements nor supplies were forthcoming. And, the "Yellow Jack" gave no quarter. On September 13 Leclerc wrote to the Minister of the Marine, Duc de Decrés,

All my corps commanders save two are dead, and I have no qualified people to replace them. To convey an idea of my losses, the 7th of the Line arrived here 1395 strong; today there are 83 half-sick men on duty, 107 in the hospital; the rest are dead. The Eleventh Light Infantry debarked 1900 strong; today they have 163 fit for duty and 200 on the sick list. The Seventy-first of the Line, originally 1,000 strong, has 17 men on duty and 133 sick.[50]

In a letter to Napoleon dated September 16, Leclerc concluded that, to this point, the occupation of Saint Domingue had cost 20,000 men, and in a little over a month he too fell victim to yellow fever and died.

General Rochambeau succeeded to command. Leclerc described him as "a brave and skilled fighter with no tact or political sense whatsoever, no character, and easily led."[51] His brutality rivaled that of Dessalines. Rochambeau recaptured Fort Libérté to safeguard the shipment of Spanish cattle from the east and Port-au-Paix to safeguard the yellow fever hospitals on the island of La Tortue. Early in 1803 the south joined in the rebellion against the French and soon Dessalines emerged as the new leader of the blacks.

NAPOLEON'S FINAL ATTEMPT

In March 1803 things began to look up for the French. Rochambeau had 11,000 effective troops and only 4,000 sick. The Yellow Jack had passed and those still alive were now immune. Napoleon had renewed interest in Saint Domingue and 15,000 new troops arrived in March, plus a like number were scheduled to be sent in the fall. Rochambeau had no plans to practice the subtleties of Leclerc. Rather, he attempted to reduce the blacks by unspeakable brutalities. Dessalines responded in kind and the war became one of racial extermination.

Rochambeau's atrocities, the fear of reenslavement, and loss of rights by the *affranchis* united the blacks and *affranchis*. Dessalines, who was capable of matching Rochambeau atrocity for atrocity, became the embodiment of the struggle. Rochambeau's hopes, which had been nurtured by Napoleon's renewed interest, were dashed when the Peace of Amiens was broken on May 19, 1803, and France and Great Britain were again at war.

Now aided by the British navy, Dessalines captured the French-held ports one by one. Fort Libérté fell in September; Port-de-Paix on October 3; Port-au-Prince on the ninth of that month; and Les Cayes on the tenth. Only Môle St. Nicolas, held by a small number of troops under Gen. Louis Marie d'Arpajon, Vicomte de Noailles, and Le Cap, held by 5,000 men under Rochambeau, remained in French hands.

Dessalines besieged Le Cap with 16,000 men. Lacking siege artillery, he decided to storm Le Cap. During the morning of November 18 as the French trumpets sounded reveille, the Haitians attacked. French guns tore gaping holes in the advancing lines to no avail. The Haitians carried the outer fortifications and the heights commanding the city, forcing the French to retreat into the inner city. Rochambeau surrendered. He received ten days to embark the remnants of his army and sail into the arms of the waiting English blockade. Dessalines granted that the French wounded might remain behind until they were well enough to travel. The shattered army embarked. The French squadron unsuccessfully tried to elude the British warships, fired a token broadside, and surrendered. On November 29 Dessalines entered Le Cap. Three days later, the blacks took 800 wounded Frenchmen out to sea and drowned them.[52]

At the Môle, Vicomte de Noailles wrote a brighter chapter in French military history. Secretly spiking his guns so they could not be used by his enemy, he sailed in seven ships, evaded the blockaders, and boldly took station on the captured Rochambeau squadron unobserved by

Figure 1. Haiti (Saint Domingue), 1791–1803. Thousands of black prisoners, and sometimes even their families, were drowned by the French in an attempt to demoralize its enemy. *Copied from Marcus Rainsford,* A Memoir of Transactions that Took Place in the Spring of 1799 *(London: R. B. Scott, 1802).*

the British as it passed by. At an opportune moment, he tacked clear and escaped to Havana. The French were able to maintain control of Spanish Santo Domingo under Gen. Marie-Louise Ferrand (1753–1808) for another six years, a notable feat of arms and politics.[53]

OBSERVATIONS

The only successful slave revolution in modern history was over. Saint Domingue became the first Latin American colony to win its independence, although it was not declared until June 1, 1804, when the name Haiti was adopted. Saint Domingue, the richest Caribbean colony of the eighteenth century, emerged as Haiti, the most impoverished nation of the Americas. Dessalines crowned himself emperor in 1805. One year later he was assassinated. Thus began a parade of brutal strongmen who ruled Haiti for almost 200 years. Throughout these years the road to power ran through the barracks of the illiterate soldiers.[54]

Years later at St. Helena, Napoleon said to his chamberlain, Emmanuel Comte de Las Cases, "I must reproach myself for the attempt on Saint Domingue during the Consulship. It was a grave mistake. I should have been satisfied to govern by means of Toussaint Louverture."[55] Napoleon Bonaparte sent 55,131 soldiers to Saint Domingue, of which perhaps 10,000 men returned. Captain [first name unknown] Sorrell of the British navy observed, "France lost there one of the finest armies she ever sent forth, composed of picked veterans, the conquerors of Italy and of German legions. She is now entirely deprived of her influence and her power in the West Indies."[56]

Another 10,000 sailors from Napoleon's fleet also died in the attempt to hold the island. To this must be added the tens of thousands of European soldiers who fought and died in Saint Domingue during the earlier days of this fourteen-year revolution. Not least, there were the Haitians. Apparently some 350,000 or more Haitians had died during the course of the revolution.[57]

Tactically, Leclerc's military and political actions were sound. The mistakes were Bonaparte's, the French navy's, and the shortcomings of the supply organization. It is somewhat surprising with what ease the French sent ships and troops to Saint Domingue, notwithstanding the British naval supremacy.

This was the bloody beginning of the wars for independence in Latin America.

Figure 2. Haiti (Saint Domingue), 1791–1803. The black leader Dessalines hanged five hundred French prisoners outside of Cap Haitien in an attempt to force the French barricaded within the port to sail away. *Copied from Rainsford,* A Memoir.

CHAPTER TWO

VICEROYALTY OF NEW GRANADA AND THE CAPTAINCY-GENERAL OF VENEZUELA, 1810–23

> The hatred that the Peninsula [Spain] has inspired in us is greater than the ocean between us. It would be easier to have the two continents meet than to reconcile the spirits of the two countries.
> —Simón Bolívar, "The Jamaica Letter," September 6, 1815

THE SPARK

On Maundy Thursday, April 19, 1810, a mob inspired by the preaching of Chilean Canon José Cortés de Madariaga deposed the Captain-General of Venezuela, Field Marshal Vicente de Emperán. He was accused of favoring the "usurper" Joseph Bonaparte in his claim to the Spanish throne. A *Cabildo Abierto* (town meeting)[1] seized the Captaincy-General in the name of Ferdinand VII.[2]

BACKGROUND

In 1810 the Viceroyalty of Nueva Granada was composed of the provinces of Santa Fé (Bogotá), Cartagena, Antioquía, Popayán, Portobelo (Panama), and the Audiencia of Quito. In 1742 the Captaincy-General of Venezuela had been removed from the viceroyalty and reported directly to Spain. The Caribbean coasts of Colombia and Venezuela were collectively known as the *Tierra Firme*.

The activities of the Venezuelan Francisco de Miranda[3] were an important precursor to revolution in Venezuela. In 1797 Field Marshal Miranda, having earned that rank while serving in the French Revolutionary army, met in Paris with two South American dissidents, expelled Jesuits José del Pozo y Sucre and Manuel José de Salas. Boldly assuming the title of Commissioners of the *Junta* of the Deputies of the Towns and Provinces of South America, they wrote the Manifesto of December 22, 1797, which projected the independence of South America and a defensive alliance between Great Britain, the United States, and the South American provinces.[4]

Miranda then traveled to England, which in August 1796 had declared war on Spain, and met with Prime Minister William Pitt. Miranda offered future commercial concessions in exchange for immediate British financial and military help. Pitt was sympathetic and intimated that Great Britain would support a postulated 10,000-man expedition dispatched from the United States. Next, Miranda wooed Secretary of the Treasury Alexander Hamilton, but President John Adams did not wish to enmesh the United States in a war. Thus, Miranda's scheme came to naught.[5]

Miranda took renewed hope in October 1804 when war broke out again between Great Britain and Spain. Miranda's plan was again brought to the attention of the British cabinet. Sir Hume Popham was very much in favor of the idea and volunteered to accompany any expedition. But, due to the tremendous strain on the resources of the British Empire caused by Napoleon's activities, ultimately the British were unwilling to make the commitment. Miranda traveled to the United States once more but again failed to win support of government officials.[6]

Realizing that he could expect no aid from the U.S. administration, Miranda turned to private citizens. Two businessmen from New York City, Col. William S. Smith (son-in-law of John Adams) and Samuel Ogden, agreed to help. Colonel Smith recruited 200 volunteers (including his son) and outfitted two armed corvettes, *El Leandro* and *El Emperador*. The *El Emperador* (18 guns) sailed on February 3, 1806, to Santo Domingo where it was to join Miranda. The Spanish Minister to the United States learned of the enterprise and protested vigorously. Odgen and Smith were arrested and brought to trial but acquitted. The *El Emperador* now refused to join Miranda. Finally, with a force of 200 men (mostly Americans) carried in *El Leandro* and the schooners *Bacchus* and *Bee*, Miranda attempted to take Puerto Cabello, Venezuela's principal seaport. Alerted, the Spanish defenders easily beat off the attack on March 23, 1806. On April 27 the Revolutionaries arrived off Ocumare (40 mi E of Puerto Cabello). The following day, Spanish naval forces intercepted them and captured the schooners. However, Miranda escaped in *El Leandro*.

With his companions, Miranda wandered among the British Antilles, landing first at Trinidad and then at Barbados. In that port he met Rear Adm. Sir Alexander Cochrane, commander of the British forces in the region. Great Britain and Spain were at war. On June 9, 1806, Cochrane and Miranda made the following agreement: The future liberated provinces would give British commerce the same privileges enjoyed by the natives; these privileges could not be enjoyed by any other nation except the United States. This agreement was to last until a formal commercial treaty could be negotiated. In return, Cochrane agreed to aid Miranda in landing troops in Venezuela and allowed Miranda to recruit men in Barbados and Trinidad.

Miranda raised a force of 400 volunteers, many of them English. The expedition carried in eight warships, one transport, and a supply ship sailed from Trinidad on July 27. On August 3, 1806, Miranda landed at Vela de Coro, Venezuela (282 mi WNW of Caracas), under the protection of the British navy and routed the Spanish garrison. However, Miranda found the city deserted as the Spanish governor, Manuel de Guevara, convinced the people that Miranda was a pirate in British employment. Appreciating that the Royalists were gathering a large force, Miranda again withdrew to Trinidad and in December 1807 sailed for Aruba.[7]

While Miranda was unsuccessfully attempting to spark a revolution, the Spanish king's hold over his American empire was being destroyed in Europe. In March 1808 Charles IV abdicated and his son Ferdinand VII became king. Both were lured to Bayonne, France, by Napoleon

Figure 3. Viceroyalty of New Granada and the Captaincy-General of Venezuela, 1810–23. Revolutionary Gen. Francisco Miranda lands at La Vela de Coro, Venezuela, on August 3, 1806. Many consider this to be the beginning of the fight for independence in northern South America. Miranda reached the rank of field marshal while fighting for Revolutionary France, earning his name a place on the Arc de Triomphe. *Courtesy Venezuelan Army.*

Bonaparte who forced them to renounce the throne. In July Joseph Bonaparte entered Madrid claiming to be king, but within three weeks he was chased out by a Spanish army. In September a Central *Junta* claimed power in the name of Ferdinand VII. By the end of 1808, Napoleon had restored his brother Joseph to Madrid and chased the Central *Junta* across Spain. By January 1810 the *Junta* took refuge on the island city of Cádiz protected by the British navy. Soon the French overran Andalucia and in February 1810 the Central *Junta* was dispersed, thus allowing the Revolutionaries to argue that since the monarchy had been destroyed the constitutional link between Spain and the Americas had been broken.

The *Junta*, before dissolving, created a *Cortes* (Congress) to represent Spain and Spanish America. Within the *Cortes*, seventy-seven seats were allocated to Spain, which had a population of ten million, and thirty seats to Spanish America, which had a population of thirteen million. For this and other reasons, the idea of the *Cortes* received only a lukewarm reception in Spanish America. It appointed a regency of three to rule in Ferdinand's absence. Meeting in September, the *Cortes* ultimately drew up the Constitution of 1812.[8]

After Napoleon had placed his brother on the throne in Madrid, he sent representatives to the New World to win the support of the colonies. In Caracas, as elsewhere, they were politely asked to leave and the colonial government announced its support for Ferdinand VII.[9]

The events in Europe created shock waves in the New World. Some Venezuelan *criollos*, including the young, wealthy Simón Bolívar,[10] began to take an increasingly active role in politics. Bolívar and his compatriots, who opposed colonial status, were aided by the events in Europe. In May 1809 the new governor of Venezuela, Field Marshal Emperán, appointed Bolívar's cousin-in-law, Col. Fernando Rodríguez del Toro,[11] as the new Inspector General of the Militias. Through him the future Revolutionaries were able to learn of every military order.

As a consequence of the April 19, 1810, deposing of the Captain-General, the Spanish regency ordered the Venezuelan coast blockaded. Also, Spain had its supporters within the Captaincy-General. The towns of Coro, Maracaibo, and Angostura refused to follow the lead of Caracas. Caracas sent an expedition to subjugate Coro to its position, but the force was repulsed.

It soon became apparent to the Revolutionaries that they would need the support of a major power, so the Caracas *junta* sent Simón Bolívar and Luis López Méndez as agents to Great Britain. They were to solicit help and at the same time to profess loyalty to Ferdinand VII, with whom the British were allied. Great Britain still harbored the desire to break the monopoly of Spanish trade policy and to open new markets to British industry, but the *real politick* dictated that this be tempered by the need to retain Spain as an ally. England wanted the Revolutionaries to recognize the regency council; however, they refused to do so. Bolívar, disobeying instructions, met Miranda in London and invited him to return to Venezuela.

Until the calling of the *Cortes* in Spain on September 25, 1810, the *peninsulares* (those born in Spain) and the majority of the clergy had not publicly taken sides; this now changed.[12] They openly supported the government in Spain. Some *criollos*, Bolívar included, were displeased at the indecision of those governing. The Society for the Improvement of Economics became the vehicle for political debate among the Revolutionaries. Under pressure of the society, a Congress meeting in Caracas declared independence on July 5, 1811, the first Spanish-American colony to do so, and it adopted a constitution instituting a federal republic.

OPPOSING FORCES

Although eventually all elements of society were forced to choose sides during the War for Independence, initially the war was between the franchised members of society. Many Latin American *criollos* (particularly the descendants of the *Conquistadores*, the offspring of Spanish nobility born in the New World, and the large landholders) wanted to exercise the political power which had hitherto been hoarded by Spaniards.[13]

During the early years of the revolution, those of mixed races who did participate favored the crown. Eventually, they were influenced by Revolutionary members of the clergy and charismatic Revolutionary leaders; little by little, they changed sides. By 1810 bands of horsemen (mostly of mixed blood) known as *llaneros* roamed the great plain called the *llanos* which dominated southwestern Venezuela. The region had evolved into a "badlands" infested by those who were wanted by the authorities. These rugged individuals were recruited by both sides as irregular cavalry.[14]

Indians had looked upon the King as their protector against corrupt officials of state and church. It was immaterial to the Indians whether they were governed by *gachupines* or *criollos*. These were the officials who had abused the Indians and whom they mistrusted. The Indians frequently flocked to the banner of the King, which during the early years of the war (1810–1814) was raised with seemingly equal enthusiasm by both sides. Thus, frequently the Indian served the cause of Independence during the early years even when he believed that he was fighting for the King.[15]

In 1810 the black man was indifferent toward the revolution. Regardless, he was soon swept along in its current. Early on, some blacks served in the armies of both sides because their masters commanded them to do so. Soon, both sides offered the black his freedom in exchange for military service. Some, like Simón Bolívar, freed their slaves before an emancipation law was passed. Many blacks fought for the revolution and some for the King.[16]

Initially, neither side possessed a regular army. As throughout Spanish America, few Spanish troops were quartered in the Viceroyalty of Nueva Granada and the Captaincy-General of Venezuela at the outbreak of the revolution. There was a large militia whose loyalty to Spain was suspect since the overwhelming majority of its officers were *criollos*.[17]

Francisco de Paula Santander described the Revolutionary army in 1817:

> [W]e were forced to make war like Tartars. What times! . . . There were times when it was necessary to convert the system into disorder and to entice recruits with booty and looting. What discipline could you expect to have in troops composed of such men? There was only one law which obligated us; to fight the *godos* [Spaniards], and to obey it we could not worry about the means.[18]

Initially, as elsewhere, the crown (as represented by the regency) had to rely on the *peninsulares*, some *criollos*, and the Spanish Navy. And the Royalist blockade had some immediate effect. Trade was almost entirely cut off by the Spanish blockade and in a few months the entire savings of the colonial era were spent. The initial strength of the Revolutionaries was the dedication of many of the *criollos* officers in the militia.

Firearms and munitions were in short supply for both sides. As the war spread into the mountains, frequently guns were melted down to provide much-needed iron for horseshoes. The favorite weapon was the lance. John Miller described the use and effectiveness of the weapon:

The Colombian lance, twelve or fourteen feet long, is formed of a strong tough sapling, headed in the usual manner. The lancers fix the reins of their bridles above the knee, so as to be able to guide their horses, and, at the same time, leave both hands free to weild the lance. They frequently struck their opponents with such force, when at a gallop, as to lift them two to three feet above the saddle.[19]

OPENING STRATEGY

Initially Spain attempted to blockade the rebels into submission. The Revolutionaries attempted to create a credible government that could win recognition and ultimately protection from Great Britain.

THE FIRST CAMPAIGN FOR QUITO

The *Audiencia* of Quito (modern-day central Ecuador) was the first administrative entity in the Viceroyalty of New Granada to rebel. On August 10, 1809, a *junta* of leading citizens deposed the Spanish President, Conde de Ruiz de Castilla, and declared independence. The Viceroy in neighboring Peru, Fernando de Abascal, immediately dispatched an army under Lt. Col. Manuel Arredondo. The Viceroy gave overall responsibility for the campaign to the Governor of Guayaquil, Bartolomé Cucalón y Villamayor. Weapons were sent to the town of Cuenca in southern Ecuador to arm the Royalists there. As the Royalist columns advanced from Cuenca and Guayaquil toward Quito, the rebellion collapsed and the *junta* reinstated the royal authorities. The Revolutionaries were imprisoned where many of them died.[20]

On August 2, 1810, a second rebellion broke out in Quito and the Revolutionaries defeated the Royalist troops led by Arredondo. However, the Revolutionaries argued among themselves concerning the leadership of the movement. Abascal again dispatched troops to Guayaquil, this time under Gen. Toribio Montes. Once more Cuenca provided reinforcements. The Royalist army entered Quito on November 8, 1812, and the last Revolutionary stronghold, Ibarra, surrendered on December 10. The revolution did not spread and the Royalists retained uninterrupted control of Quito for a decade.[21]

THE FIRST CAMPAIGN FOR GUAYANA

In June 1810 the Province of Guayana (southeastern Venezuela), which had initially recognized the Revolutionary government in Caracas, retracted its recognition and permitted the Royalists to gain control. The Revolutionaries dispatched a force under Col. Francisco González Moreno to regain control of this province which was dominated by the Orinoco River and its tributaries. By the end of March 1811 the Revolutionaries had captured Barranca and Soledad on the north bank of the Orinoco. On April 13 a Royalist flotilla of ten small ships, supported by the artillery on the south bank, attacked the Revolutionaries but were driven off after heavy losses. Although the Revolutionaries were able to gain control of the Orinoco, they were not able to capture Angostura (now Ciudad Bolívar), the provincial capital. On March 25, 1812, a Royalist flotilla surprised a Revolutionary fleet and during the Battle of Sorondo the Revolutionaries lost twenty-eight boats and 200 men were killed. The Revolutionary land forces were forced to retreat. Guayana and the Orinoco were now securely in the hands of the Royalists.[22]

THE FIRST VENEZUELAN REPUBLIC

In December 1811 Congress adopted a federal constitution modeled after that of the United States. Among its members was Francisco Miranda, who had returned to Caracas on December 11, 1810, following a forty-year absence. He was made commander-in-chief of the Revolutionary army and ordered to immediately reestablish Revolutionary authority in the city of Valencia. Royalists, incited by the Capucin monks, had revolted.[23]

In March 1812 Commander Domingo de Monteverde,[24] commanding a company of Spanish marines, landed in Coro from Cuba. He immediately organized a 1,500-man force composed of marines, the small Spanish garrison in Coro, and Royalist volunteers. As it advanced, the force grew. On March 26, Holy Thursday, and the first anniversary of the Declaration of Independence, an earthquake destroyed half of Caracas killing some 10,000 persons. Four thousand more died in other towns held by the Revolutionaries while the Royalist towns were spared. The clergy loyal to Spain preached divine vengeance to the lower classes. The movement for independence suffered significant reverses.[25]

To meet this threat, Miranda was named *Generalísimo* and dictator and given command of 4,000 troops, which exceeded the force of his opponent.[26] An old man, he showed little initiative. From Coro to Maracaibo the Royalists attacked under the command of Monteverde. As a consequence of Miranda's timidity, the Royalists scored victories at Carora, Barquisimeto, and Valencia. Miranda drew back to Victoria where he repulsed Monteverde's attack, but the pleas of his officers to counterattack the disorganized enemy fell on deaf ears.

Bolívar had been given the task of defending the important port of Puerto Cabello, where some of the wealthy political prisoners were being held. On June 30 the Revolutionaries in San Felipe Castle were bribed and they declared themselves Royalists. The prisoners rebelled and the Royalists, beseiging the stronghold, continuously bombarded it. The small garrison finally surrendered on July 6, 1812, although Bolívar escaped by ship to La Guayra.[27]

Desertion and anarchy were rife among the 5,000-man Revolutionary force. Finally, on July 30, 1812, Miranda surrendered to the Royalists in Caracas. The conditions were amnesty to all and freedom to depart for all who wished to go. Miranda, along with most of the Revolutionary leaders, chose to leave. Bolívar and other officers, believing that Miranda had betrayed the revolution, arrested him. The Royalists found him in prison when they entered the city; Miranda was sent to Spain where he died in a dungeon four years later. The counterrevolution apparently had triumphed. Monteverde, under the flimsiest of pretexts, broke the amnesty and threw some 1,500 persons into dungeons where many died.[28]

Following the defeat, Bolívar, through the intercession of a Spanish friend, was released and given a passport, although his considerable properties were confiscated. He fled to Curaçao (then under British control) and then he and a small band of Revolutionaries went first to Curuçao and then to Cartagena which was in the hands of another group of Revolutionaries.[29]

BOLÍVAR MOVES ON TO CARTAGENA

The independence movements among the major towns in the Audiencia of Santa Fé (Colombia) paralleled the events in Venezuela. Cartagena and Bogotá, professing loyalty to Ferdinand VII, deposed their Spanish authorities and created governing *juntas*, as did many smaller towns. None, however, was willing to submit to a central government.

Cartagena had declared its independence on November 11, 1811, the first city and province in New Granada to do so, and was besieged by a Royalist army operating from the port of

Santa Marta (145 mi E of Cartagena), to which the Viceroy had fled. Such was the state of affairs when Bolívar arrived in November 1812, a refugee from Venezuela. Bolívar was given a minor command. He was charged with the defense of Barranca (today Calamar), a small town (80 miles ESE of Cartagena) on the left bank of the Magdalena River. Contrary to orders, on December 21 Bolívar, embarking 200 men in ten rivercraft, ascended the Magdalena River, surprised and captured the 500 enemy troops at Tenerife on December 23, 1812. He successfully repeated this tactic at Mompós on December 26 and later at Guamal, El Banco, Chiriguaná, and other towns. Bolívar occupied Ocaña (424 mi SSE of Cartagena), a provincial capital, on January 8, 1813. These successes forced the Royalists to retire from the interior of New Granada to Venezuela. Pierre Labatut, commander of Cartagena's forces, was furious at Bolívar's audacity but the city was wild with rejoicing. The *junta* in Cartagena awarded Bolívar citizenship and the rank of brigadier.[30]

THE ADMIRABLE CAMPAIGN (*CAMPAÑA ADMIRABLE*)

Notwithstanding the fact that Bolívar and other Revolutionaries had been driven from Venezuela, fighting continued there. Santiago Mariño,[31] leading a small band of Revolutionaries, established a base on Margarita Island. In early 1813 these Revolutionaries returned to the mainland and won some minor skirmishes.

In the meantime, Bolívar convinced the Congress of New Granada, meeting at Tunja, and the *junta* in Cartagena that the reconquest of Venezuela was essential to the independence of New Granada. In April 1813 they gave him permission to attack the Royalist-held, western Venezuelan provinces of Mérida and Trujillo. Bolívar assembled some 550 men, seven cannons, five mortars, and 1,400 extra muskets (to arm volunteers and conscripts) at Cúcuta, New Granada (403 mi N of Bogotá) on the border with Venezuela. The Royalist commander, Col. Ramón Correa, adandoned Mérida for Trujillo. Bolívar entered Mérida on May 23, 1813. Here he learned that Revolutionary General Mariño had returned to the mainland and was fighting in eastern Venezuela.[32]

Bolívar struck quickly before the dispersed, numerically superior Royalists could unite. Col. Atanasio Girardot,[33] leading 400 men, marched over 13,000-foot mountains which plunged into 2,500-foot valleys. He defeated Correa and entered Trujillo on June 10. Next, Girardot defeated 500 Royalists 25 miles north of Trujillo, capturing 100 prisoners and significant war materials.[34]

On June 15, 1813, Bolívar, due to the continuing atrocities committed by the Royalists, issued the "War to the Death Proclamation":

> Spaniards and Canary Islanders, count upon death, even though you are neutral, unless you work actively for the liberty of America! Americans, count on life, even though you are guilty![35]

Through his declaration he attempted to clarify who was the enemy and to encourage the Americans fighting for the King (many of whom had been impressed) to seize the opportunity to change sides without reprisals.[36]

A Neogranadian congressional committee ordered Bolívar to halt, but he pushed on defeating the Royalists at Niquitao and Barinas. The Spaniards decided to retreat to Valencia but Bolívar cut off their retreat at Taguanes. There, on July 31, after a few hours of fighting, the Royalists endeavored to escape into the foothills of the Andes. Bolívar ordered 200 infantrymen to mount horses behind the cavalrymen and this force reached the foothills first and

Figure 4. Viceroyalty of New Granada and the Captaincy-General of Venezuela, 1810–23. The Battle of La Victoria occurred on February 12, 1814, in north-central Venezuela. Royalist General Boves, leading 2,500 cavalry and 900 infantry, charged 800 defenders nine times but was driven off. Many of the Revolutionaries were students from the university and Catholic seminary of Caracas. As a consequence of this Revolutionary victory, February 12 has become the "Day of the Youth" (*Dia de la Juventud*) in Venezuela. *Courtesy Venezuelan Army.*

blocked the Royalists' escape. Following a bloody fight, the Royalists surrendered *en masse*. As Bolívar's 600-man army marched toward Caracas, Royalists deserted the King in droves. He entered Caracas on August 6, 1813. Bolívar's campaign had taken 93 days and covered some 800 miles.[37]

THE SECOND VENEZUELAN REPUBLIC

In October 1813 Bolívar was proclaimed "Liberator" and "Captain-General of the Armies of Venezuela" in Caracas and in January 1814 was named dictator. However, he was unable to persuade Santiago Mariño, who had defeated the Royalists at Maturín and evicted their remaining forces from Margarita Island, to submit to his authority.

Meanwhile, Monteverde, refusing all terms of surrender and reinforced by 1,200 men from Spain on September 14, 1813, tried to push out from Puerto Cabello but was defeated at Barbula and had to retire to the city again. In addition to Puerto Cabello, the Royalists still held Maracaibo, Coro, San Fernando, and Guayana. The fighting was bloody. At the Battle of Araure in December, the "Dragoons of Caracas" formed the Revolutionary army's rear guard and had orders to kill any of their own soldiers who ran from the fight.[38]

THE *LLANEROS* RESCUE THE CROWN

The *llaneros*, rugged, semicivilized plains cowboys, many of whom had mixed blood, were inspired by two Spaniards, José Tomás Boves[39] and Francisco Tomás Morales,[40] to declare for the King. These 1,200 plainsmen (only 200 of whom were Spaniards) were appropriately called "the Legion of Hell." They murdered for pleasure and tortured for pastime. Bolívar's position was very difficult since he did not have enough troops to fight the Royalists on all fronts.[41]

Following the Royalist victory at La Puerta on February 3, 1814, Boves divided his force into three columns and marched toward Caracas. As Boves approached the town of La Victoria, the inhabitants, fearing his cruelty, abandoned their homes. Boves was opposed by General José Félix Ríbas[42] who commanded 800 men. Many of the Revolutionary soldiers were students from the university and Catholic seminary in Caracas. On February 12 Boves, leading 2,500 cavalry and 900 infantry, attacked. Between 8 A.M. and 5 P.M., the Royalists unsuccessfully charged the Revolutionaries' position nine times. Late in the day, a Revolutionary cavalry unit commanded by Lt. Col. Vicente Campo Elías arrived and broke the Royalist center. No prisoners were taken by either side. The Revolutionaries lost 100 dead and 400 wounded; the Royalists' losses were much higher. The Royalists temporarily withdrew.[43]

Throughout March and April, fortunes favored first one side and then the other. At the Battle of Valencia in late March, Mariño shot one in every five Revolutionary deserters to prevent a mass exodus. On May 28 Bolivar defeated the Royalists on the plains of Carabobo, but on June 15, 1814, his army was routed at La Puerta (72 mi SW of Caracas) by Boves. Some 1,200 Revolutionaries died. Many were captured and executed, including Col. Diego Jalón y Dochagavia. His head was cut off and exhibited as a trophy. Bolívar escaped to Caracas and his army melted away under the ferocity of the *llaneros*.[44]

Bolívar did not believe that he could defend the city. He abandoned Caracas and some 10,000 inhabitants and, fearing the *llaneros*, fled with the army in the "Emigration of 1814" to Barcelona, 467 miles away. On August 17 Francisco Tomás Morales, Boves' second in command, defeated Bolívar at Cumaná. Bolívar was arrested by the Revolutionaries, tried for treason, and acquitted. But, Bolívar and Mariño were forced to flee Venezuela. The towns of

Venezuela, once again, were in the hands of the Royalists, although Revolutionary guerrillas were still active in the countryside.[45]

FERDINAND VII RETURNS

On March 22, 1814, Ferdinand VII was placed back on the throne of Spain. On May 4, 1814, he declared the liberal constitution of 1812 null and void. By a decree of May 24, he directed those ruling in Spanish America to submit to royal authority since the cause for division no longer existed; he promised to recall the *Cortes* as soon as possible to establish a modern monarchy.[46]

In December Spain dispatched a 10,640-man army, mostly Napoleonic War veterans, under the command of Lt. Gen. (Marine Corps) Pablo Morillo,[47] to reconquer the rebellious colonies. The fleet's destination was rumored to be Buenos Aires. However, Morillo carried secret instructions to sail to the *Costa Firme*. He was ordered to first reestablish the King's authority on Margarita Island and then at Cumaná on the mainland. From there he was to reconquer the remainder of New Granada. Following the campaign in northern South America, Morillo was instructed to first aid Peru and then Mexico.[48]

BOLÍVAR COMMANDS AGAIN IN NEW GRANADA

Bolívar, accompanied by Mariño and a small band of Venezuelans, sailed to Cartagena where they received a hero's welcome on September 25, 1814. There he found the Revolutionaries divided into feuding factions. Bolívar was employed by one of these factions, the Congress of the Federation, and ordered to subjugate the provinces of Cundinamarca and Santa Marta. Bolívar was promoted to General of Division and given command of the expedition. Bolívar rapidly advanced from Tunja, the provisional seat of the Congress, and captured Bogotá on December 12, 1814, thus forcing the province of Cundinamarca into the federation. As a reward, he was made Captain-General of the Armies of New Granada. Next, Bolívar marched against the coastal province of Santa Marta in the north. However, the Revolutionary commander of the port of Cartagena, Col. Manuel del Castillo, refused to let Bolívar enter the port let alone provide any help. To avoid a civil war among the Revolutionaries, Bolívar resigned. On May 11, 1815, Bolívar and a few dedicated followers chose exile and sailed for Jamaica.[49]

THE SPANISH ARMY FINALLY LANDS

Morillo's 10,640-man army, carried in forty-two transports and escorted by eighteen warships, arrived off Puerto Santo on April 5, 1815. Morillo conferred with Morales, who had replaced Boves as head of the *llaneros* following his death in battle. On April 10 the Royalists landed on Margarita which had evolved into a Revolutionary stronghold. The Revolutionaries, led by Juan Bautista Arismendi,[50] recognizing the futility of resistance, negotiated a reconciliation whereby they pleaded allegiance to Ferdinand VII in exchange for a pardon. On April 20 Morillo landed at Cumaná, where early in 1815 there had been a conspiracy among those of mixed race to kill all the whites; again, the Spanish force was met peacefully. Morillo moved on to Caracas where, pursuing his policy of clemency, he declared an end to the "War to the Death" on May 2. He had peacefully reestablished Spanish rule over Venezuela. Morillo also dispatched 2,000 men to Peru by sea.

Morillo had his problems. First, General Morales, the leader of Royalists' *llaneros*, felt alienated; his horsemen had expected to receive a considerable reward for their services. Second, the ship *Pedro Alcántara*, which carried much of the Spanish army's equipment and supplies, was lost due to an accident. This disaster forced Morillo to make good his loss through levees against the war-torn colony. Most was paid for by confiscating property belonging to individuals suspected of being Revolutionaries.[51]

Next, Morillo moved against Cartagena. On July 12, 1815, he embarked 5,000 European soldiers and 3,000 Royalists under Morales in fifty-six ships at Puerto Cabello. On July 22 Morillo disembarked at Santa Marta, a Royalist stronghold, and by August 20 he had blockaded Cartagena by land and sea. On December 5 Venezuelan naval captain Luis Brión,[52] commanding the corvette *Dardo* (twenty-four guns), broke through the blockade escorting two small ships. The ships carried 12,000 muskets and munitions. However, this help was too late. With the city on the verge of surrender, many of the Revolutionaries chose to run the Spanish blockade that same day on board the ships trapped in the harbor. Most were killed at sea, and only a few safely reached Jamaica or Haiti.[53]

Cartagena surrendered on December 6 following a 108-day siege. The Royalists lost 3,125 men during the siege, mostly to disease. Morillo continued to show leniency to the captured Revolutionaries in sharp contrast to the conduct of Morales, who was brutally suppressing the rebellion in the interior. Morillo did, nonetheless, execute nine Revolutionaries.[54]

Morillo now marched on Bogotá, the viceregal capital. On February 22 the Revolutionaries commanded by Gen. Custodio García Robira attempted to block the Royalist advance into the central highlands at Cachirí. The Revolutionaries were decisively defeated and no prisoners were taken. Morillo entered Bogotá in May. He reversed his policy of conciliation and adopted one of repression. Suspected Revolutionaries were brutally treated and Morillo no longer attempted to restrain Morales. Morillo was probably influenced by the fact that Arismendi, who had been pardoned, led Margarita into rebellion once again and by the guerrilla tactics adopted by the remaining Revolutionaries.[55] The one remaining organized Revolutionary force in New Granada, led by Francisco de Paula Santander, fled across the Andes and joined the Revolutionary irregulars in Venezuela now led by José Antonio Páez.[56]

Páez gradually won the *llaneros* away from the Royalists by demonstrating superior leadership on the battlefield and personal bravery. His growing force lived off the land—beef and water; everything else was acquired by stripping the enemy. These lance-wielding horsemen could almost make themselves invisible behind the neck and mane of their horses as they charged the enemy. Expert swimmers in a land of floods and rivers, they could disappear on the vast plains.[57]

THE FIRST EXPEDITION FROM LOS CAYOS

Bolívar, during his six-month stay in Jamaica, attempted to organize a relief expedition for Cartagena but the port fell to the Royalists. When Bolívar was unsuccessful in gaining the support of Great Britain, he moved on to Haiti. Here he was received by President Alexandre Pétion who became his protector and benefactor. Bolívar also won the personal loyalty of Brión; as a result, Bolívar gained a small fleet sufficient to maintain communications with Venezuela and to transport a small army. Once Bolívar learned of the revolt on Margarita Island, he devoted his energies to creating a force to reenter the fighting. On April 16, 1816, Bolívar sailed from Los Cayos de San Luis with 250 men, 4,000 muskets, and a few canon in a squadron of seven small ships.[58]

On May 2 the Revolutionary squadron encountered a Royalist fleet off eastern Venezuela. After a sharp fight in which Brión was wounded, the Revolutionaries captured the brigantine

Figure 5. Viceroyalty of New Granada and the Captaincy-General of Venezuela, 1810–23. Simón Bolívar wears the typically heavily embroidered tunic of the Napoleonic era. Bolívar's opponent, Royalist Gen. Pablo Morillo wrote, "Nothing is comparable to the restless activity of this man. His daring and talents are his best credentials, entitling him to maintain himself at the head of the revolution and the war . . . Bolivar is THE REVOLUTION." *Copied from William Miller,* Memoirs, *2 vols. (London: Longeman, Rees, Orme, Brown, and William Miller Green, 1829).*

Interpido and the schooner *Rita*. The remainder of the Royalist squadron escaped to Cumaná. The Revolutionary army landed on Margarita on May 3. Besieged by land and sea, the Royalist garrison withdrew to Cumaná in July. Morillo, still in Bogotá, reacted to these events by dispatching Morales, commanding 1,200 men, back to Venezuela.[59]

Next, Bolívar landed at Ocumare (20 mi E of Puerto Cabello) on July 6, 1816. Here he issued a decree liberating the slaves and announcing the end of the "War to the Death." This undermined the Royalists hold on the blacks and those of mixed blood and fulfilled a promise to Petión, the black President of Haiti. Bolívar fought his way eastward. He united with General Manuel Carlos Píar[60] and defeated the Royalists at Júncal. However, on July 13 the outnumbered Royalists attacked and defeated Bolívar at Los Aguacates. Bolívar lost one third of his force and was forced to retreat to Ocumare. Unable to gain the recognition and support from Revolutionary generals Mariño and José Francisco Bermúdez,[61] Bolívar again sailed for Haiti on 22 August.[62]

THE SECOND EXPEDITION FROM LOS CAYOS

On December 21, 1816, Bolívar once again returned to the mainland at the head of a small army. Brión landed the force near Margarita on the twenty-eighth. Incorporating the Revolutionaries under General Arismendi, Bolívar, now commanding 300 men, captured the port of Barcelona on the mainland. Next, he advanced against Caracas but was driven back to Barcelona by Royalist forces. Bolívar was then besieged by land and sea for two weeks. The Royalists abandoned their siege in early March and fell back to Cumaná.[63]

While Bolívar had been absent from the continent, José Antonio Páez, Santiago Mariño, José Francisco Bermúdez, and Manuel Píar—had carried on the fight. A number of the Revolutionary leaders who had remained in Venezuela when Bolivar had taken refuge in Haiti felt that they had a more legitimate right to head the revolution than Bolívar. General Píar, who was a mulatto, represented the greatest challenge to Bolívar's authority.

Píar, commanding 1,800 Revolutionaries (including 200 native archers), won a major victory at San Félix (671 mi SE of Caracas) on April 11, 1817, when he defeated 1,500 Royalists under Nicolás María Cerruti. The Royalists lost 593 dead and 497 captured, of whom 160 were *peninsulares*. All of the Spaniards were decapitated. The Revolutionaries lost 31 killed and 65 wounded.[64] Bolívar met with Píar and at least temporarily defused the problem.

Bolívar decided to move south into the valley of the Orinoco against the Royalists in the Province of Guayana. On July 7 a numerically inferior Revolutionary squadron, commanded by Admiral Brión, defeated a Royalist fleet of small craft at Pagayos, exposing Angostura to a riverine assault. On July 17 thirty ships evacuated 4,000 Royalists and the next day General Bermúdez occupied the provincial capital. Gen. Miguel de la Torre,[65] commanding the Royalist flotilla, fought his way to the British colony of Grenada, losing half his fleet along the way. Royalist casualties were 280 killed, 300 wounded, and 1,731 captured. The Revolutionaries lost 32 killed and 31 wounded. By the end of September, the Revolutionaries had won control of the Orinoco River and established a provisional government at Angostura.[66]

After Angostura had been taken, Bermúdez informed Bolívar that Píar planned an insurrection. Píar fled to the eastern provinces but was captured on September 27, tried by court-martial, and shot on October 16.[67]

THE THIRD VENEZUELAN REPUBLIC

Following the capture of Angostura, Bolívar united his forces in the east with the *llaneros*, led by Páez, on the plains of Apure in the southwest. On January 31, 1818, the two leaders met at Caujaral. Bolívar began operations on the south bank of the Apure River. On February 6 a Royalist squadron of armed canoes blocked his advance against Santa Fé. A group of lance-wielding *llaneros*, led by Col. Francisco Aramendi, charged into the shallow river and captured the Royalist boats, thus permitting the capture of the riverine port.[68]

While Bolívar was operating in the south, Morillo dispatched a force to capture Margarita Island, but, although it gained a foothold, the Revolutionaries fighting from behind every bush made life hell for his forces. Morillo successfully retreated to Valencia.

Bolívar now carried the war from the sparcely populated east into the north-central heartland. He suddenly appeared south of Calabozo (160 mi S of Caracas) leading 5,200 Revolutionaries. Morillo, leading 1,800 Royalists, rushed to join the city's 650-man garrison. He arrived on February 10, 1818. Lacking siege guns, Bolívar took up position north of the city. However, the Royalists escaped from Calabozo initially undetected and marched northeast, with Bolívar belatedly in pursuit. Bolívar's force dwindled to 2,200 men as various *caudillos*, including Páez, preferred to pursue other objectives.

Bolívar soon realized that Royalist forces under Morillo, Morales, and La Torre were closing on his force from three different directions. Bolívar reversed his march but he was overtaken at the ravine of El Semen. On March 17 the opposing forces fought a bloody three-hour battle. The Revolutionaries got the worst of it, losing 400 dead and an equal number wounded, most of whom died from lack of medical attention. Additionally, Bolívar lost all his baggage, 1,500 muskets, numerous flags, and his correspondence; the Royalists penetrated the Revolutionaries' camp and nearly killed Bolívar. The Royalists lost about 600 dead and wounded.[69]

During May, June, and July of 1818, Bolívar attempted to penetrate into Royalist-held territory in the north without much success. On August 23 a combined expedition, led by Admiral Brión and General Bermúdez, expelled the Royalists from Guitia. The Revolutionaries captured five warships.

THE INFLUX OF NAPOLEONIC VETERANS

The cessation of hostilities in Europe with the ending of some thirty years of almost constant warfare between the two most powerful nations in the world, France and England, changed the nature of the wars for independence in Spanish America. Luis López Méndez vigorously recruited for Bolívar's army in England over the objections of the Spanish ambassador. The terms (or more accurately, promises) of service were very attractive, especially to out-of-work, experienced soldiers. Every officer was given a higher rank than that held during the Napoleonic wars; pensions were promised in case of injury; each soldier was promised that he would not be transferred without his permission to a unit other than the one for which he volunteered; 40 pounds were advanced to outfit each officer and 15 pounds for each enlisted soldier. But many important details were overlooked. Troops were not trained or outfitted for tropical service. Rarely were maps, interpreters, or medicines provided. And, not surprisingly given the vast stocks available, second-hand and, too frequently, poorly manufactured arms were issued.[70]

The first expedition embarked in November 1817 but did not sail for a month due to poor planning. When twenty-four hours at sea, the six-ship expedition carrying 720 men was struck by a storm. The *Britannia* went down taking 211 of 220 soldiers to their graves. By the time the expedition reached the British Caribbean colony of Grenada it had degenerated to near-mob rule. The artillery regiment sold its guns and the captain of the *Emerald* sold his ship to recover money they both claimed was owed to them. Of the original 750 volunteers, only 150 ill-equipped survivors reported to Bolívar's headquarters for duty.

Over the next two years, some 4,000 to 6,000 soldiers sailed from British ports to South America. Most landed at Margarita Island, and a few at Angostura or San Fernando on the Apure River. Yellow fever, malaria, and dysentery decimated their numbers. These foreign troops were, for the most part, detested by the native troops. They were better paid and frequently committed excesses that would not have been tolerated if they had been carried out by the native troops. On the other hand, the foreign troops were the best fighting units in Bolívar's army.[71]

THE WAR IN VENEZUELA BECOMES A STALEMATE

Bolívar, unable to dislodge Morillo from the north, adopted guerrilla warfare. The fighting degenerated to skirmishes and harassments. Bolívar controlled the eastern and southern regions and Morillo held most of the more densely populated north. Neither seemed to be able to make permanent inroads into the other's domain. In February 1819 Bolívar called a congress at Angostura which duly elected him president on February 16. Elsewhere, General Santander had succeeded by the end of April in clearing the Royalists from the plains of Casanare, which was the only part of New Granada that had resisted Spanish restoration. The struggle in Venezuela had settled into a stalemate.

At sea, Revolutionary Admiral Brión, commanding nine small warships, drove a seventeen-ship Royalist squadron into Cumaná during March. This permitted him to capture a number of prizes.

CROSSING THE ANDES

In mid-1819 Bolívar abandoned his strategy of trying to penetrate northern Venezuela and chose to strike across the Andes into New Granada which was held by some 4,000 Royalists. This was a bold move because it placed the entire army at risk. He united his 1,850 soldiers with the 1,200 Neogranadians (future Colombians) commanded by Santander. Páez refused to lead his 4,000 *llaneros* out of the plains. He feared that the mountainous terrain would neutralize the saddleless lancers by denying them the opportunity to maneuver. He claimed that the *llaneros* would desert rather than cross the Andes. Bolívar, as a consequence, ordered Páez to hold the attention of the enemy on the plains. This was not the first time nor the last that Páez acted independently of Bolívar's desires. Bolívar ordered Generals Bermúdez and Rafael Urdaneta[72] to attack the enemy at Calabozo and Barcelona, respectively.[73]

Poorly clad and ill-shod, the 3,000-man army, which included only 300 *llaneros*, began its march on May 26 from Mantecal. The rainy season had just begun, and Bolívar's army crossed by wading or in improvised canoes seven major rivers; it rained day and night. For hours on end Bolívar's men were in water up to their waists. Bolívar chose the steeper but shorter route through the 13,000-foot-high Pisba Pass to achieve the greater surprise. He crossed the *páramo*, a high, cold plateau, which inflicted additional suffering upon his troops. By July 6, 1819, Bolívar reached the village of Socha, 9,000 feet above the sea and on the west slope of the mountains. Bolívar lost 30 percent of his army—1,000 men—and all of the horses to exposure, oxygen starvation (mountain sickness known as *sorochs*), or accidents. But through superb organization and leadership, Bolívar recruited 3,000 Neogranadians, obtained enough horses to mount the 300 *llaneros* who had crossed the Andes, and gathered sufficient food.[74]

BATTLE OF PANTANO DE VARGAS

On July 25 the Royalists took up a strong defensive position. The fighting began at 11 A.M. and raged for six hours. Lt. Col. José María Barreiro, believing victory was within his grasp, committed his reserves. As the sun was setting, Bolívar committed the "British Legion," which drove the Royalists from the high ground. Next, Bolívar's freshly mounted *llaneros* charged the Royalists who broke and ran. In the darkness, Barreiro covered the retreat and saved most of his army. The Royalists lost about 500 killed and wounded and 200 to 300 as prisoners; Bolívar lost 140 killed and wounded. Additionally, the Revolutionaries captured 1,200 rifles and large quantities of equipment. Due to their exhausted condition and the poor medical services available, most of the wounded later died, including Col. James Rooke, commander of the "British Legion."[75]

The inhabitants of the Savana (Santa Fé's highlands), who had previously hesitated to support the independence movement, now threw in their lot with Bolívar. In some cases, they had little choice. He ordered the forced enlistment of local men between the ages of fourteen and forty on pain of death. These levees received very hasty training. On August 3 Bolívar again crossed the Sogamoso River at night and took Paipa (134 mi N of Bogotá), and two days later Tunja, where he was warmly received.

BATTLE OF BOYACÁ

Colonel Barreiro attempted to reform his shattered 3,000-man force and fall back upon the capital, Bogotá. On August 7, 1819, the Royalist officer was caught at the bridge crossing the swollen Boyacá River some sixty miles north of the capital with his army split between the two banks. The Royalist advanced guard had crossed over and taken up position on the far side. Barreiro permitted the main body to halt for a meal before crossing; it had been on the march in constant rain for two days.

Bolívar, commanding 3,200 men (of which 1,200 were raw conscripts), advanced behind the cover of a ridge and surprised the Royalists. The "Venezuelan Rifles" and the "British Legion" blocked the Royalists from reuniting. The remainder of the Revolutionary army, led by General Santander, attacked the main body of Royalists. The Royalists counterattacked against the "Venezuelan Rifles" and the "British Legion." The foreign mercenaries held their ground and Barreiro was forced back to an indefensible position which was dominated by enemy fire. The battle had lasted barely two hours. Barreiro surrendered; 200 Royalists were killed and more than 1,600 taken prisoner, including most of the senior officers. Less than 50 Royalists escaped. Bolívar lost 13 killed and 53 wounded. When the news of the Royalist defeat reached Bogotá, the Viceroy fled. On August 10, 1819, Bolívar entered Bogotá, securing the liberation of New Granada from Spanish rule. Leaving Santander as Vice-President at the head of the provisional government in Bogotá, Bolívar returned to Angostura.[76]

Upon his return, Bolívar first had to deal with factionalism among the Revolutionaries. On December 17, 1819, solely through the force of his will, Bolívar imposed the creation of the Republic of Gran Colombia. In addition to Cundinamarca (Colombia), it included Venezuela and Quito (Ecuador), which remained unliberated and was ignorant of its inclusion in the new nation.

THE COLOMBIAN COASTAL CAMPAIGN

On January 22, 1820, a twenty-six-craft Revolutionary squadron commanded by Lt. Col. José Antonio Mayz defeated an eleven-gunboat Royalist squadron commanded by naval Capt. Joaquín de Mier y Benitz at Barbacoas Cliff on the Magdalena River. In March Bolívar dispatched 1,300 men under Gen. Mariano Montilla, carried in a fleet of eighteen ships commanded by Admiral Brión, against Royalists forces on the Hache River. Once the Revolutionary squadron had sailed, the Royalists blockaded the mouth of the Orinoco. Another Revolutionary squadron was dispatched from Angostura, and by the time they reached the mouth of the river, the Royalists had withdrawn to Cumaná. On June 25 a seven-boat riverine squadron commanded by Comdr. Hermogenes Maza surprised eleven Royalist craft commanded by Vicente Villa at Tenerife on the Magdalena River. Nine of the craft were captured and all but twenty-nine of the 300 Royalists killed. Villa blew himself up rather than surrender. With the victory the Revolutionaries won control of the river.[77] A fleet under Brión blockaded Cartagena and the Revolutionary army took Santa Marta by assault on November 10.[78]

BACK IN SPAIN

Ferdinand VII had assembled another expeditionary force at Cadiz but the troops waited a year for shipping to be assembled. On January 1, 1820, Cols. Rafael de Riego and Antonio Quiroga led a rebellion in the Spanish army and demanded that the King take an oath to the Liberal Constitution of 1812 which he did on March 9. The new Spanish constitutional government wished to end the war which was ruining Spain, so in mid-April it ordered Morillo to treat for terms.

Finally, on November 25 Morillo and Bolívar agreed to a six-month armistice which froze their positions throughout New Granada and Venezuela. This worked to the benefit of the Revolutionaries. Bolívar had time to organize, train, and gather new recruits; the Royalists had no remaining source of manpower within the Americas. Morillo, who had petitioned many times to be relieved, turned over his command to Miguel de la Torre and returned to Spain.[79]

On January 28, 1821, Maracaibo, long a Royalist stronghold, revolted against Spanish rule and while Bolívar was in Bogotá, General Urdaneta marched into the province. The Spanish pronounced that this broke the armistice and hostilities were renewed on April 28, 1821.[80]

The war at sea began immediately. On May 24 Capt. José Prudéncio Padilla,[81] commanding a Neogranadian squadron of small warships, boldly sailed into Cartagena Harbor and blockaded the city. In a few days the Spanish corvette *Ceres* broke the blockade and escorted a North American merchantman through.[82]

BATTLE OF CARABOBO

Some 10,000 Royalist troops under General La Torre remained in northern Venezuela where they controlled the majority of the population and most of the wealth. Bolívar planned a massive envelopment of the Royalists to destroy this force. He pulled together his scattered forces. The reunited Revolutionary army of 6,300 men advanced toward Valencia.[83]

On June 24 General La Torre, commanding 5,000 troops, chose to make his stand where the road entered the plain of Carabobo (114 mi W of Caracas). There, rolling hills, dense thickets, and rushing streams restricted maneuverability. Bolívar tried to flank the Royalist position with his *llaneros* led by Páez. La Torre spotted the maneuver and blocked the way with three battalions. Initially, the Revolutionaries were driven back. The "British Legion" renewed the attack, halting briefly for lack of ammunition. Supplied and supported by General Páez' *llaneros*, the "British Legion" punched a hole through the enemy's line. The attack cost the "British Legion" one-third of its men and its two senior officers. Páez led his horsemen into the gap. La Torre attempted to plug the hole with his 1,000-man cavalry led by General Morales. But this failed and Páez fell on the Royalist rear.

La Torre was forced to abandon the road where he had been successfully holding Bolívar's frontal assault and retreated. The 1,000-man "Valencey" Battalion, which had been on the southwest corner of the battlefield, fought an orderly rear-guard action which permitted some 2,000 demoralized Royalists to escape into heavily fortified Puerto Cabello. The Royalists lost 2,786 killed, wounded, and captured, and the Revolutionaries lost 200 killed, mostly among the "British Legion."[84]

THE WAR AT SEA

In early 1821 a Spanish naval force, composed of two frigates, a corvette, two brigantines, and four transports, delivered a considerable quantity of military stores to Venezuela. This permitted the Royalists to operate along the coast for two more years.

On June 25, 1821, Revolutionary Commodore José Padilla sailed into Cartagena's harbor and made off with eleven prizes while the port's garrison was drawn to the landward defenses by a feint attack led by a Swedish count, Col. Friedrich de Adlercreutz. Cartagena surrendered on October 1, 1821. Brig. Gen. Gabriel de Torres and his 700 men were permitted to sail to Cuba.[85]

Two years later, on July 24, 1823, a Revolutionary squadron commanded by Admiral Padilla defeated a Royalist squadron commanded by Capt. Angel Laborde in the Battle of Lake Maracaibo. On August 3 General Morales surrendered the city of Maracaibo and on November 8 Puerto Cabello surrendered to General Páez. On November 23, 1823, the Royalists marched out of Puerto Cabello, flags flying and drums beating, boarded ships, and sailed for Cuba. The fight for the independence of New Granada and Venezuela ended.[86]

Bolívar convened a congress in order to write a constitution for his creation, Gran Colombia. Meeting at Cúcuta near the Santa Fé–Venezuelan border, the congress created a united, Centralist republic with theoretical states' rights and balance of powers. Bolívar was elected president and Santander vice president. Bolívar would continue the war while Santander governed.

THE SECOND CAMPAIGN FOR QUITO

On October 9, 1820, the Province of Guayaquil (modern coastal Ecuador) declared its independence from Spain and dispatched an army against the Royalists in the highland *Audiencia* of Quito. Some 1,000 veteran Royalists led by Col. Francisco González defeated 1,800 Revolutionaries at Huachi on November 22; 1,500 were killed, wounded, or missing. On December 20 the Revolutionaries were again defeated, this time at Verdeloma, and the Royalists regained control of the highlands. The badly shaken Revolutionaries requested help from both Bolívar in Venezuela and San Martín in Peru. Bolívar sent Gen. Antonio José de Sucre,[87] with 400 Gran Colombians by sea, to support the revolution at Guayaquil and to annex Ecuador to Colombia. Landing in May 1821, he placed the Province of Guayaquil under the protection of Gran Colombia. Sucre then marched toward Quito. He was victorious at Yaguachi on August 19 but the Royalists crushed him at Guachi on September 12. The Revolutionaries lost 800 men—only

100 escaped. The two sides signed the Armistice of Babahoyo and retired to their respective strongholds to prepare for the next campaign.[88]

On January 11, 1822, the Spanish frigates *Venganza* and *Prueba* switched sides in Guayaquil in exchange for the back pay of 80,000 pesos. Under orders of José de San Martín, they were incorporated into the Peruvian navy.[89]

In December 1821 Bolívar started overland for Quito. On April 7, 1822, Bolívar, commanding 3,000 troops, met 2,200 Royalists led by Col. Basilio García at Bomboná. The Royalists were well entrenched and their flanks were protected by high ground and a river. The battle dissolved into confusion and resulted in a draw. The Royalists sustained 250 dead and wounded and the Revolutionaries 116 dead and 343 wounded.[90]

BATTLE OF PICHINCHA

While Sucre's campaign against Quito was faltering, San Martín dispatched 1,500 men under Andrés de Santa Cruz via a land route to Cuenca. These troops were on the march when fighting broke out in Guayaquil among Revolutionaries favoring annexation to Gran Colombia, those wanting incorporation into Peru, and those desiring independence. San Martín, fearing a civil war between his supporters and those of Simón Bolívar, on March 13, 1822, ordered Santa Cruz to withdraw to the frontier. Shortly, he reversed the order and the troops under Santa Cruz joined those under Sucre.[91]

Sucre now marched against Quito with an army composed of Argentines, Colombians, Ecuadorians, Peruvians, and Venezuelans. Sucre made a night march and threatened Quito from the north. This forced the Royalists to abandon their positions to the south and move to block Sucre's access to the city. On May 24, 1822, the Revolutionaries attacked in the foothills of the Pichincha volcano (20 mi N of Quito), and after a sharp fight complicated by mist and rough terrain, the Revolutionaries won. The Royalists lost 400 dead and 200 wounded; the Revolutionaries lost 91 dead and 67 wounded. The following day Quito surrendered and Ecuador's independence was secured. On July 26, 1822, Simón Bolívar and José de San Martín met in Guayaquil to discuss their differences.[92]

North of Peru, only the Conservative stronghold of Pasto (in modern Colombia) remained in the hands of the Royalists. On December 23, 1822, Sucre commanding 1,500 men attacked and seized the high ground from the 2,000-man garrison and captured the city. Three days of looting took place before Sucre restored order and proclaimed an amnesty. The Royalists lost 300 dead and the Revolutionaries 8 dead and 32 wounded.[93]

PANAMA

On November 28, 1821, a council of officials, army officers, and clergy met and declared Panama free and announced its desire to unite with Gran Colombia.

OBSERVATIONS

The Revolutionaries succeeded in their primary objective, breaking the colonial bondage. However, they failed to transform the Viceroyalty of New Granada and the Captaincy-General of Venezuela into a nation. What temporarily united these colonies into the single nation of Gran Colombia was the fear of the common enemy—the Royalists—and the will of Simón Bolívar. Both were fleeting.

The War for Independence was initially between the *criollos* and the *peninsulares*. Both sides sustained heavy losses and each needed to find replacements. During the nine years of fighting, the American Royalists in northern South America were reinforced by some 20,000 Spanish soldiers sent from the Old World; however, disease and combat killed 16,000 to 17,000 of these soldiers. The primary assassin was the mosquito. Spanish Gen. Pablo Morillo wrote:

> The mere bite of a mosquito often deprives a man of his life, or causes an ulcer that first incapacitates him for a long time, and then leaves him an invalid. . . . The local diet causes every type of illness in Europeans, and very few are able to resist its fatal influence. The immense wildernesses in which the war is conducted, the lack of any sort of assistance, the contaminated water which it is often necessary to drink, and the extraordinary fatigue suffered by the soldiers, who are obliged to march over such considerable distances through such diverse climate: all this contributes to our destruction, and the annihilation of the troops.[94]

As the war progressed, the Revolutionaries increasingly conscripted and recruited from among those of mixed blood, particularly the mulattos. This need of men provided for social mobility which had not existed prior to the revolution. The Latin American aristocracy did not make good its dream of supplanting the *peninsulares*. It was decimated, ruined, and submerged by the incessant war of independence.[95]

This constant fighting ingrained many future leaders with the belief that violence offered a solution to political problems. On February 5, 1823, confidential agent Charles S. Todd wrote to U.S. Secretary of State John Q. Adams:

> A faithful narrative of this struggle can never be published—and for the sake of humanity and civilization, it is well that it cannot—a detail will thus be saved to the world, of savage barbarities and oppressions. . . . The progress of this war had been so destructive in every portion of the country whether occupied by friends or foes, that peace is demanded in a short time, or a development of its resources may be postponed for ages.[96]

Venezuela lost about one-fourth of its one million population; banditry was extensive; and Revolutionary Generals Páez and Juan de Escalona were openly hostile toward each other.

Colombia was nearly bankrupted by the war. Pay to military officers and civilian officials was in arrears. Ecuador's population decreased from 600,000 inhabitants to 480,000.[97]

As was true throughout Spanish America, the war for the independence in New Granada and Venezuela was a civil war. Francisco Miranda, Simón Bolívar, Santiago Mariño, Juan Bautista Arismendi, and many other Revolutionaries had been trained within the Royalist militia. But there are some glaring differences between these individuals and those who had been trained by the Crown and yet secured the independence of Mexico, Central America, Peru, and Bolivia. In general, those from New Granada and Venezuela joined the revolution during its early years (1810–1813) and many held relatively junior ranks (below colonel) when serving the King. The opposites were true for those from Mexico, Central America, Peru, and Bolivia.[98]

Also, the civil war for independence helped spawn the *caudillo* tradition—the toughest of the tough placed himself above the law and held his following by rewarding it from the wealth of the nation. Such men would rule much of Latin America for the next two centuries. Símon Bolívar lamented, "The tyrants of my country have taken it from me, and I now have not even a *patría* for which to sacrifice myself."[99]

By mid-1822 the Spanish were driven out of the Viceroyalty of Nueva Granada. This was achieved in large measure by the military skills of Bolívar, Santander, and Páez. Also, the cause was greatly aided by foreign soldiers and money. However, as long as the Spaniards held Peru, they could easily return to Gran Colombia.

CHAPTER THREE

VICEROYALTY OF RÍO DE LA PLATA, 1810–24

The hour of all true patriots is at hand. The ultimate crisis of freedom, with no alternative but victory or death.
       —Proclamation issued by José de San Martín, Mendoza, 1815

THE SPARK

During the early morning hours of May 22, 1810, a *cabildo abierto* (open town meeting) composed of 251 prominent citizens (450 had been invited) seized power from the Spanish Viceroy Baltasar Hidalgo de Cisneros and voted to create a *junta* to rule in the name of King Ferdinand VII. By the 25th, a nine-man *junta* dominated by Cornelio Saavedra, Manuel Belgrano,[1] and Mariano Moreno refused to recognize the authority of the Spanish Council of Regency which claimed to rule in the name of Ferdinand VII. These events were a *de facto* declaration of independence which would formally be proclaimed six years later.[2]

BACKGROUND

The Viceroyalty of Río de la Plata was but thirty-two years old in 1808. Until the administrative reforms of the late eighteenth century, the region had been a remote province governed overland from Peru. At least to the degree to which Spain could enforce the law, trade between Río de la Plata and the rest of the world had to move through Lima, a 3,000-mile trek over the Andes which took a mule train at least three months to travel. By the early part of the nineteenth century, Buenos Aires, long among the poorest cities in Spanish America, showed promise of becoming one of the wealthiest.

The Viceroyalty of Río de la Plata was divided into eight *Intendencias* and four *Gobernaciones*. These administrative entities made up modern-day Argentina, Bolivia (then called Upper Peru), Paraguay, and Uruguay. The viceroyalty had a population of approximately one million inhabitants. The Viceroyalty of Río de la Plata had two centers of political power. First were the young trading ports of Buenos Aires and Montevideo, whose populations were 55,000 and 15,000 respectively. Immediately outside these cities was the wild frontier where brigandage, cattle rustling, and vagrancy abounded until one reached the older, interior provincial capitals of the northwest such as Chuquisaca (now Sucre, Bolivia) and Potosí (983 mi NW of Buenos Aires).³ These had been founded overland from Peru during the early days of the conquest and were the heart of Spain's waning mining operations and wealth.⁴

Shortly after Spain went to war with Napoleon in 1808, Buenos Aires and the other Spanish-American ports were opened to British shipping. Great Britain, the world's greatest mercantile power, expanded upon its already active but illicit trade. Many in Buenos Aires grew to desire independence so that they might freely trade with the rest of the world.⁵

Great Britain also played a role in bolstering the military confidence of those of Buenos Aires, who were known as *Porteños*. At the end of 1805, Great Britain sent an expedition, commanded by Sir Home Popham, to capture the Dutch colony at the Cape of Good Hope.. Accomplishing this on January 18, 1806, Popham decided on his own to add Río de la Plata to the British Empire. Popham dispatched Gen. William Carr Beresford with 1,640 men across the South Atlantic. On June 25, 1806, the English troops disembarked at Quilmes (11 mi S of Buenos Aires), and entered the city two days later. Rafael Sobremonte, the Spanish Viceroy, had paid no attention to rumors that English ships had appeared off the coast. The night the British landed the Viceroy was attending a gala ball. Learning of the landing, Sobremonte fled to Córdoba, unsuccessfully endeavoring to take his wealth with him. The *Porteños* were outraged at the Viceroy's cowardliness. On June 27 Beresford took possession of the city's citadel.⁶

Following the loss of the city, the *Porteños* plotted its recapture. Juan Martín de Pueyrredón collected 1,000 *Porteños* a few miles outside the city, but the British dispersed them on August 1. The second attempt was led by Santiago Liniers, a Frenchman who was employed by the Spanish Crown as the captain of the port of Ensenada. He obtained 1,300 men from the Spanish Governor of Montevideo. Under cover of night, Liniers landed his army at Tigre (40 mi NE of Buenos Aires). The remnants of Pueyrredón's force joined him in San Fernando along with other volunteers and together the 2,500 marched on Buenos Aires. On August 11 Liniers attacked, driving the British into the central plaza and then the citadel. The following day Beresford surrendered 1,200 men, 35 cannon, 1,600 muskets, and his flags having lost 300 men. The British agreed to withdraw from Buenos Aires but their fleet remained in the Río de la Plata estuary. The *Porteños* proclaimed Liniers the commander of the local military forces. The Viceroy, who was slowly advancing from Córdoba at the head of 3,000 men, at first refused to acknowledge this *fait accompli*.⁷

The *Porteños* were flush with victory and immediately raised a militia. All inhabitants between the ages of sixteen and fifty were required to enlist. The militiamen elected their officers who in turn chose their commanders. Ten infantry battalions were created: five composed of Spaniards, three of *Porteños*, one of blacks and mulattos, and one of those from the interior. The cavalry was predominantly formed by *criollos*. The *Porteños* requested help from Spain but were told that they would have to get along the best they could. By October 1806 they raised an 8,151-man militia, of whom only 3,000 were Spaniards.⁸

Because communications between the continents moved at the speed on a sailing ship, those in London were frequently reacting to events that had been superseded. London enthusiastically welcomed the news of the conquest of Buenos Aires. Gen. Samuel Auchmuty commanding 2,000 men was dispatched to reinforce Beresford. A second force of 4,700 men under Gen. Robert Craufurd was to be sent to conquer Valparaíso in the Captaincy-General of Chile, but never sailed. At about the same time, aware of the British loss of Buenos Aires, Popham dispatched 1,300 reinforcements from Capetown; these occupied the port of Maldonado (98 mi

E of Montevideo) in Banda Oriental. London, now learning of the loss of Buenos Aires, ordered Craufurd to subordinate his command to Auchmuty. Admiral Charles Stirling was sent to replace Popham. In January 1807 General Auchmuty arrived with 4,000 fresh troops carried in 90 transports and escorted by 20 warships. On February 6 the British assaulted Montevideo by land and sea and captured it after a bloody fight. Once again, Viceroy Sobremonte, who was in Montevideo, fled; in Buenos Aires the *Cabildo* and the Royal *Audiencia* (the highest court in the colony) charged him with cowardice and deposed him. Mobs in Buenos Aires clamored for the expulsion of the British.

In May General Craufurd arrived at Montevideo with 4,000 troops, and by June British troops in Montevideo had swollen to 12,000 soldiers. On June 28, 1807, the British navy landed 7,822 troops under Gen. John Whitelocke some thirty-six miles south of Buenos Aires, leaving the general to conduct a difficult four-day march through swamps. Liniers led 7,000 men out of Buenos Aires to fight the British and was defeated on July 2. In the meantime, Martín Alzaga, the *alcalde* (mayor), was busy fortifying the city and on July 5 Whitelocke attacked. He divided his forces into thirteen columns which advanced down parallel streets toward the river. Only two of the columns succeeded in reaching the water. The others were cut to pieces from ambush and surrendered. On July 6 Whitelocke surrendered the remainder and accepted the terms imposed by Liniers, which included the immediate evacuation of Montevideo.[9]

These successful military operations created an air of self-confidence in Buenos Aires. The reconquest in 1806 and the defense in 1807 had been the work of the *Porteños* and gave them an awareness of their capabilities. Also, these attacks helped to create the *criollo* party headed by Liniers.[10]

As throughout Spanish America, the detention of Ferdinand VII by Napoleon Bonaparte in 1808 and the subsequent occupation of Spain by French troops ultimately caused the *criollos* to break with Spanish rule. On May 13, 1810, a British ship brought news that Seville had fallen to the French four months earlier and that the Central *Junta*, the source of Viceroy Cisneros' authority, had collapsed. The *Cabildo Abierto* removed the Viceroy and appointed a *junta* to rule in the name of the King. As elsewhere, the pretense of loyalty to the King was maintained while denying the authority of those in Spain who claimed to rule for him.

Evicting Viceroy Cisneros from Buenos Aires in May 1810, the Revolutionary *junta* notified other population centers of its actions and its claim to the viceregal boundaries. In response, the Royalists in Upper Peru (future Bolivia), Córdoba, and Montevideo declared themselves enemies of the revolution. The answer of the leaders of the province of Paraguay was evasive.[11]

A unique twist to the struggle for independence within Río de la Plata was that Doña Carlota, daughter of Carlos III (and sister of Ferdinand VII) and wife of the Prince Regent of Portugal, claimed the territories in Spanish America as heir to the possessions of her deposed father; the most accessible of these to Portuguese power (then concentrated in Brazil) was La Plata. Carlota was supported in this claim by the Portuguese crown which had long contested Spain's right to the Banda Oriental (future Uruguay) and the Province of Paraguay in particular.[12]

OPPOSING FORCES

The Spanish navy, although formidable on paper, was in abominable condition. Ships were in ill-repair, undermanned, and rarely put to sea. Corruption was rife and morale very poor. Perhaps two-thirds of the seventy-five or so ships of the line (battleships of their day) were not capable of getting underway. In addition to the ships of the line, the Spanish navy possessed some 40 frigates, 100 sloops, and numerous minor craft. These also were in very poor condition. In 1810 the following Spanish naval units were at Montevideo: frigates *Flora* and *Prosperina*; corvette *Mercurio*; brigs *Belén*, *Cisne*, and *Gálvez*; and small craft *Aranzazú*, *Carlota*, *Fauna*, *San Carlos*, *San Luis*, and *San Martín*.[13]

There were less than 2,400 Spanish soldiers in Río de la Plata at the beginning of the nineteenth century and, given events in Spain, few reinforcements could be expected.[14] The crown could count on the *peninsulares* and some *criollos*; however, apparently a smaller percentage of *criollos* fought for the King within the Viceroyalty of La Plata than elsewhere in Spanish America.

The principle strength of the Revolutionaries was among the *criollos*.[15] A number of *criollo* officers serving in the Spanish army and navy throughout the world returned to fight for their homeland. Among the most experienced were Carlos de Alvear[16] and José de San Martín.[17]

Portugal had significant forces in Brazil. When Dom João and the royal family escaped from Lisbon, they were accompanied by much of the Portuguese navy, the entire Marine Corps, and some Army units.

OPENING STRATEGY

The Revolutionary government of Buenos Aires potentially faced many threats. Foremost was Spain as represented by a new viceroy who established his seat in Montevideo (125 mi E of Buenos Aires). Next was the militancy by the Presidencies of Charcas and Chuquisaca (Upper Peru). This was the once silver-rich backyard and former dependency of the Viceroyalty of Peru. Third, the interior cities of the Viceroyalty of Río de la Plata such as Asunción, Córdoba, and Salta, at one time or another, challenged Buenos Aires' claim to the viceregal boundaries. Lastly, Portugal, through its surrogate Brazil, presented a threat to the provinces of Banda Oriental and Paraguay.

Buenos Aires' initial strategy was to seek reconciliation with the interior provinces, to subjugate by force the remote presidencies, and to create land and naval forces to deal with the Spanish and Portuguese threats.[18]

Spain's strategy was to buy time by blockading Buenos Aires. Even though Spanish sea power was grossly overcommitted throughout the world, it held an initial advantage, because the Revolutionaries had no navy. Also, Montevideo was closer to the mouth of the Río de la Plata than Buenos Aires, thus giving the Spanish navy a geographical advantage. The Viceroy of Peru, Fernando Abascal, devised a strategy to create an army in Upper Peru and another in southern Chile. The first was to drive south and capture Buenos Aires and the other was to go north and take Santiago. Whichever succeeded first was to go to the aid of the other.[19]

Portugal watched and waited for an opportunity to seize territory.

PARAGUAY SEPARATES ITSELF FROM RÍO DE LA PLATA

Paraguay was perhaps the most remote and among the poorest wealth-exporting provinces in Spanish America. That is not to say wealthless, for if one were content with a provincial lifestyle, Paraguay's fertile land produced all of its necessities. Paraguay was accessible only by the Paraná/Paraguay River complex. Its remoteness and austerity made Paraguay very difficult to conquer and provided little financial incentive for undertaking the task.

When the news of the May 25, 1810, revolution reached Paraguay, the Spanish governor, Bernardo de Velasco, called an assembly of notable citizens on July 24. It refused to submit to the rule of Buenos Aires. In order to persuade Paraguay to declare allegiance to the revolution and Buenos Aires, the *junta* dispatched Col. José de Espínola. Unpopular because of his arrogance and ineptitude, he failed to win over Paraguay.[20]

Next, the *junta* tasked General Belgrano with finding a solution to the Paraguay problem. Engaged in raising an army to fight the Royalists in Banda Oriental, Belgrano decided first to use the fledgling army to intimidate Paraguay into submission. On December 18, 1810, Belgrano's 950-man force, half of whom were raw recruits and poorly equipped, landed at the Paraná River port of Encarnación. Belgrano defeated Velasco's vanguard at Campichuelo, so he decided not to wait for 400 militiamen and two cannon coming from Misiones. Belgrano then marched slowly toward Asunción (570 mi N of Buenos Aires). On January 19, 1811, some 2,000 Paraguayans overwhelmed Belgrano at Paraguarí (60 mi S of Asunción). The Paraguayans lost 70 dead and wounded; Belgrano lost 14 dead, 126 prisoners, 2 guns, and 150 rifles.[21]

The *Junta* in Buenos Aires decided to challenge the Royalist ships which were blockading the port and controlled the Paraná and Uruguay Rivers. Three former merchant ships, commanded by Juan Bautista Azopardo, were armed and renamed the *25 de Mayo* (18 guns), *Americana* (3 guns), and *Invincible* (12 guns). Six hundred soldiers, reinforcements for Belgrano, went on board. However, on March 2, 1811, the small squadron was overwhelmed by twelve Royalist ships commanded by Jacinto de Romarate at the Battle of San Nicolás after a bitter fight. Only a quarter of those manning the Revolutionary ships escaped injury or death.[22]

On March 9 Belgrano's small force was surprised by a *criollo* army at Río Tacuarí just north of the eastward bend in the Paraná River. Some 1,400 Paraguayans defeated Belgrano's 550 infantrymen, 400 cavalry, and 50 gunners (6 cannons) forcing the surrender of General José Machain and capturing 150 men, 130 rifles, and 3 cannon. Col. Manuel Anastacio Cabañas granted Belgrano generous terms and the *Porteño* army slipped across the river.

Meanwhile, within the province of Paraguay, the Governor, whose popularity had plummeted due to his conduct at Paraguarí where he fled the battle, attempted to disband the *criollo* army fearing its political potential. On February 3, 1811, the Governor wrote to Portuguese authorities requesting their help in sealing the southern border against Revolutionaries. In May a Portuguese emissary, Lt. José de Abreu, told the Royalists in Asunción that the price of Portuguese help would be the recognition of Carlota Joaquina as heir to the Spanish throne. In the meantime a Revolutionary *junta* declared Paraguayan Independence on May 14 and overthrew Governor Velasco on June 19. By 1813 José Gaspar Rodríguez Francia gained control of Paraguay through political intrigue. He declared Paraguayan independence from Spain *and* Buenos Aires being in the advantageous position of allowing the *Porteños* to fight Paraguay's war for independence down river.

THE FIRST REVOLUTIONARY CAMPAIGN IN BANDA ORIENTAL (URUGUAY)

During the late colonial period, as Spain moved from a mercantile-based economy to one of free trade, Montevideo increasingly became a competitor of Buenos Aires. However, as long as

Montevideo remained administered from Buenos Aires the playing field would never be even. A number of factors encouraged Montevideo to pursue independence from Buenos Aires. First was the brief British occupation in 1806–07, which demonstrated the advantages of unlimited free trade. The second was the trade advantages acquired after becoming the viceregal capital following the expulsion of Spanish authority from Buenos Aires in May 1810. When the *Porteños* seized power in Buenos Aires, the authorities in Montevideo refused to recognize the Revolutionary government. As a consequence, the new viceroy sent by the Spanish regency in January 1811 to rebellious Río de la Plata, Francisco Javier de Elío, established his viceregal capital in Montevideo.[23]

Soon after the *Porteños* declared local rule in the name of Ferdinand VII, a Royalist squadron operating out of Montevideo blockaded Buenos Aires. The on-scene British squadron commander, Vice Adm. Michael de Courcy, recognized the legality of the blockade but this was soon repudiated by Lord Percy Strangford, the British minister in Río de Janeiro. As a consequence, Lt. Robert Ramsay, commanding the British schooner *Mistletoe* (8 guns), broke the blockade.[24]

In spite of becoming the viceregal capital, many in Banda Oriental favored independence from Spain, among them José Gervasio Artigas,[25] a *gaucho* (plains cowboy). On February 15, 1811, he offered his services to the Revolutionary *junta* in Buenos Aires. Commissioned a commander of militia, he led 150 followers back into the Banda Oriental. Within a month, his force had swollen to 1,000 men (mostly irregular cavalry). The Revolutionary *junta* ordered General Belgrano, who had withdrawn from Paraguay with 867 men, to lead the fight in Banda Oriental. Col. José Rondeau, who had succeeded Belgrano, named Artigas commander of the vanguard.

On April 24 the Revolutionary *gauchos* defeated 1,340 Royalists at San José. This forced Viceroy Elío to draw his troops back to Montevideo. In order to fight Artigas and the *Porteños*, Spanish Viceroy Elío asked the help of the Portuguese court (Spain's traditional enemy) then in residence in Río de Janeiro. On July 17, five thousand Portuguese troops commanded by Gen. Diogo de Sousa would cross to Cerro Largo (now Melo) into Uruguay.[26]

On May 18, 1811, Artigas, commanding 1,100 Revolutionaries, defeated Spanish naval commander José Posadas, commanding 1,200 Royalists at Las Piedras Mill (12 mi N of Montevideo). The Revolutionaries lost 70 and the Royalists 100 dead, 60 wounded, and 500 captured. As would become common, many of those captured changed sides. The defeated Royalists fell back to Montevideo; the Revolutionaries lay siege to the city.[27]

In the far northwest, the Revolutionary defeat in Upper Peru at Huaqui and the subsequent advance of the Royalist army toward Buenos Aires forced the Revolutionaries to abandoned the siege of Montevideo just when success appeared near. On October 21, 1811, the *Porteños* compromised with the Viceroy residing in Montevideo. They withdrew from Banda Oriental and the Portuguese did the same. However, Artigas refused to accept the truce and withdrew behind the Río Negro.[28]

THE FIRST REVOLUTIONARY CAMPAIGN AGAINST UPPER PERU (BOLIVIA)

The creation of the Viceroyalty of Río de la Plata in 1776 influenced those in the interior as profoundly as it had in the growing port cities. The older elites in the interior resented the changing economic reality of the decline of mining and mercantilism and the rise of free trade which, for them, meant a loss of wealth and power. Although the administration of Upper Peru was transferred from the Viceroyalty of Peru to that of Buenos Aires in 1776, socially, economically, and geographically Upper Peru had more in common with the northwest than with the southeast. It was populated by an Indian peasantry, whereas Buenos Aires and Río de la Plata's interior provincial capitals were mostly populated by *criollos*. Upper Peru's economy was dominated by mining, whereas that of the southeast was agrarian and trade. Upper Peruvians lived on high plateaus, while southeasterners resided in the lowlands.

La Paz, in fact, was the first Spanish-American city to declare independence. On May 25, 1809, the prominent citizens of Chuquisaca deposed the president of the *audiencia* and seized power in the name of Ferdinand VII. In July a *criollo junta* in the neighboring city of La Paz declared independence! On July 27 the *junta* issued a proclamation stating: "Now is the time to organize a new system of government, founded upon the interests of our country which is greatly depressed by the bastard policies of Madrid."[29]

The King's authorities reacted quickly. The Viceroy of Peru, José Fernando de Abascal y Souza, hastily dispatched 5,000 men under Gen. José Manuel de Goyeneche, a *criollo* from Arequipa, despite the fact that Upper Peru was no longer under his jurisdiction. Viceroy Cisneros of Río de la Plata sent 1,000 men of the *Porteño* militia under Marshal Vicente Nieto as well. Goyeneche arrived first and easily restored royal authority, beheading the leaders. Second to arrive, the militarily senior Nieto declared himself president of the *audiencia*. Soon learning of the May 1810 revolution in Buenos Aires, Nieto asked Abascal to re-annex Charcas to Peru and the Viceroy did so in July.[30]

The Revolutionary *junta* in Buenos Aires was eager to reunite mineral-rich Upper Peru to Río de la Plata, and it anticipated the help of those in Charcas who had supported the 1809 revolution. On July 9, 1810, a 1,150-man army commanded by Col. Francisco Ortíz de Ocampo marched north. First, it captured the loyalist stronghold of Córdoba (434 mi NW of Buenos Aires) where former Viceroy Liniers, hero of the defense of Buenos Aires against the British, was taken prisoner along with four other Royalists. Liniers was attempting to organize a counterrevolution against the *junta* in Buenos Aires. Ocampo refused to execute the prisoners as ordered. He was replaced by Juan José Castelli, a member of the ruling *junta*, who carried out the executions.[31]

Now commanded by Castelli, 1,500 Revolutionaries pushed northward but were defeated at Cotagaita (Upper Peru—240 mi N of Jujuy) by 2,000 Royalists under Gen. José de Córdoba on October 27, 1810. The Royalists pursued the retreating Revolutionaries, overtaking them at Suipacha. There, 800 Revolutionaries defeated 600 Royalists on November 7. Córdoba and two Royalist governors were captured and executed.[32]

Turning northward again, the Revolutionary army triumphantly marched through Potosí, Oruro, and La Paz. Castelli showed no mercy to the captured Royalists. Looting, rape, and murder followed in the wake of the army, creating an image of a conquest and not a liberation. While the reign of terror moved northward, Royalist General Goyeneche waited behind the Desaguadero River (the boundary between the viceroyalties of Río de la Plata and Peru) gathering strength. Camped on opposite sides of the river, the Revolutionary Castelli and the Royalist Goyeneche agreed to a forty-day truce on May 16.[33]

Violating the agreement by attacking eight days prior to its expiration, Goyeneche, leading 6,500 Royalists, surprised the 5,000 Revolutionaries supported by a few thousand Indian allies at Huaqui on June 20, 1811, and completely routed them.

While the Revolutionary Army in Upper Peru was being defeated, Juan Martín de Pueyrredón, who had remained in Córdoba as governor, had enough time to sack the *Casa de Moneda* (the royal treasure house) in Potosí. The shaken Revolutionary army was again defeated in mid-August at Amiraya. The remnants, some 800 men, fled southward, not stopping until they reached Tucumán (583 mi NW of Buenos Aires). By October 1811 the Revolutionary army in the northwest possessed neither guns nor munitions; only Güemes' *gauchos* remained to oppose the Royalists.[34]

THE EXODUS OF THE PEOPLE OF BANDA ORIENTAL

Following the truce between the *Porteños* and Viceroy Elío on October 21, 1811, Artigas and his followers, which now included many townspeople, were driven across the plains by Portuguese soldiers (who had not immediately withdrawn) and the Royalists. Crossing the Uruguay River into the Province of Entre Ríos, the 16,000 fugitives lived like nomads. In mid-July 1812, the Portuguese, under diplomatic pressure from Great Britain, withdrew their army from Uruguay.[35]

THE SECOND REVOLUTIONARY CAMPAIGN IN BANDA ORIENTAL

On October 20, 1812, a *Porteño* army joined José Culta commanding 350 *Orientales* in the second siege of Montevideo. On December 31 Captain-General Gaspar Vigodet (who had succeeded Viceroy Elío) led, 2,300 Royalists with 8 cannon out of the city and attacked the besiegers. Rondeau, commanding the Revolutionaries, defeated Vigodet at El Cerrito and held the siege. The Revolutionaries lost 90 killed and 40 prisoners while the Royalists had 100 killed, 146 wounded, and 30 taken prisoner.[36]

Gen. Manuel de Sarratea, overall commander of the Revolutionary forces in Banda Oriental, removed *Porteño* troops from under Artigas' authority. The furious Artigas helped Rondeau secure Sarratea's position through intrigue, and the *junta* in Buenos Aires acquiesced to the power grab.[37]

José de San Martín helped tighten the siege on Montevideo by defeating the Royalists at San Lorenzo on February 3, 1813. This victory earned him prestige and stopped the Royalists' raids along the river banks. Nevertheless, the Royalists tenaciously held on to the port.[38]

POLITICAL STRIFE WITHIN BUENOS AIRES

For five years the military efforts of the Revolutionaries in Buenos Aires were hampered by ineffective governments. The *junta*, which had been formed in May 1810, lost its popular support with the departure of its two ablest members, Manuel Belgrano and Mariano Moreno. It evolved into the *Junta Grande*, whose membership changed frequently. In September 1811, discredited by the defeat in Upper Peru, the *Junta Grande* was replaced by a triumvirate that badly stumbled through one year. The Triumvirs were evicted by a *coup d'etat* led by Alvear and San Martín and replaced by three more individuals who called the Congress of 1813. The Congress chose Alvear as Supreme Director.[39]

THE SECOND REVOLUTIONARY CAMPAIGN AGAINST UPPER PERU

General Belgrano persuaded his Revolutionary colleagues that the subjugation of Upper Peru must be given priority over that of Montevideo. Belgrano proposed to capture Salta (810 miles NW of Buenos Aires), advance into Upper Peru, secure it as a base of operations, and then attack lower Peru.[40]

In March 1812 Belgrano took command of the dispirited 1,200 Revolutionaries at Tucumán; they possessed 580 muskets, many of which were unserviceable. Assisted by Baron Edward Kaillitz von Holmberg, a German who had arrived in Buenos Aires on board the same ship as San Martín, he improved the morale and discipline of the army.[41]

Meanwhile in Upper Peru, Royalist General Goyeneche persisted in the strategy of driving south, uniting with Royalists in Córdoba, and then marching east and joining forces with the Royalists in Banda Oriental. The united Royalist force would then attack Buenos Aires.[42]

The 3,000-man Royalist army commanded by General Pío Tristán overran the provinces of Jujuy and Salta. However, on September 24, 1812, Belgrano, commanding 800 regular infantry and supported by 1,000 *gauchos*, defeated the 3,400 Royalists in front of Tucumán. Belgrano commanding 3,700 Revolutionaries crushed 3,400 Royalists at Salta on February 20, 1813, in spite of being severely ill. The Royalists lost 480 dead, 114 wounded, and the remainder were taken prisoner. The Revolutionaries lost 103 dead and 433 wounded.[43]

Belgrano continued to push north. He occupied Potosí and Cochabamba. While Belgrano was marching deep into Upper Peru, the new Royalist commander, Gen. Joaquín de la Pezuela, was collecting forces. The two armies fought at Vilcapugio on October 1, 1813. The 3,500 Revolutionaries were soundly defeated by 4,000 Royalists; the Revolutionaries lost many experienced officers and their entire train. Belgrano commanding 3,400 Revolutionaries unsuccessfully attempted to make a stand at Ayohuma on November 14 but was crushed by 3,500 Royalists; only 400 Revolutionaries escaped. The Revolutionaries fled back to Tucumán; Pezuela reoccupied Salta; and the second campaign in Upper Peru ended in a disaster for the Revolutionary cause.[44]

In January 1814 José de San Martín replaced Belgrano as the commander in the north. San Martín's appointment may have been facilitated by his membership in the influential secret Lautaro Lodge, founded by Francisco Miranda in London. San Martín spent four months transforming Tucumán into a fortified camp and rebuilding the shattered army. He then resigned, claiming ill health but in fact believing the strategy of attacking Royalist power through Upper Peru to be ill-conceived. Following his resignation, San Martín solicited and obtained the appointment as Governor of Cuyo, which comprised the provinces of Mendoza, San Juan, and San Luis. This remote region, far from the fighting, seemed insignificant to many. Here San Martín constructed the Army of the Andes which would soon conquer Chile (see chapter 4).[45]

THE THIRD REVOLUTIONARY CAMPAIGN IN BANDA ORIENTAL

By 1814 the threat to the *de facto* independence of Buenos Aires significantly increased. The King had been restored to his throne and was busy gathering an army, the destination of which was rumored to be Río de la Plata. The Royalists in Upper Peru defeated all attempts to subjugate them and were marching south. Buenos Aires' hold over the interior provinces was, at best, tenuous. In November 1813 the Royalists seized the Island of Martín García on La Plata River (23 mi N of Buenos Aires). Spanish naval forces operating out of Montevideo were destroying the commerce of Buenos Aires. It became critical to capture Montevideo in order to eliminate it as a base of operation for the Spanish navy, as a possible port of disembarkation for a Spanish Army, and as a potential supply center for the Royalist army moving southward from Upper Peru.[46]

As 1814 began, Rondeau commanding 4,000 men still held Montevideo under siege. However, in August 1813 Vigodet had received significant reinforcements and he now commanded

5,000 men. In late 1813 Buenos Aires called a general congress and Artigas sent five delegates. Their proposals, which were in fact demands by Artigas, were unacceptable to Buenos Aires. The Congress attempted to avoid a confrontation; it refused to seat the *Orientales* arguing that they had not been duly elected. Artigas was furious. He withdrew his troops from the siege of Montevideo under cover of darkness thereby endangering the entire Revolutionary army. Artigas also declared Uruguayan independence. Buenos Aires declared him a traitor and placed a price on his head.[47]

Capt. Guillermo Brown,[48] commanding the Revolutionary squadron of ten small warships manned by "sailors of fortune," many of whom were English and Irish, began a new offensive against the Royalists on March 11, 1814, when he attacked their positions on the Island of Martín García. Driven off with heavy losses by a Royalist squadron commanded by Jacinto Romarate, Brown managed to return on the fifteenth and captured the island. On April 20 Brown established a blockade of Montevideo with seven ships, complementing the land siege of 4,000 Revolutionaries. On May 14 thirteen Royalists' ships commanded by Miguel Sierra sortied; after a three-day running fight near El Buceo Bank, most of the Royalist ships were captured while the remainder returned to Montevideo. Through intrigue, Revolutionary General Alvear displaced Rondeau on the seventeenth and on the twentieth Montevideo surrendered. The Revolutionaries captured 7,000 prisoners, 500 cannon, 9,000 muskets, and 99 merchant ships.[49]

The full consequence of the Revolutionary victory was not immediately apparent. Pezuela, commanding the Royalist forces in Upper Peru, was advancing against Tucumán when he learned of the fall of Montevideo; he chose to turn back. Although the Spanish expedition led by General Morillo ultimately sailed to the *Tierra Firme* and not Río de la Plata, the threat of another expedition sailing south seemed real. Buenos Aires dispatched a commission to London to purchase arms and sent Bernardino Rivadavia to Europe to negotiate a settlement with Spain. Both failed; also, the instability of the Revolutionary government continued. In May 1815 the Supreme Directorship collapsed and Alvear fled. The provinces of Santa Fé, Corrientes, and Entre Ríos broke away from the union and formed a loose confederation which recognized Artigas as its titular head.

Artigas and his *Orientales* were not a party to the capture of Montevideo. His forces did control most of the Banda Oriental outside the port. A series of clashes now took place between two Revolutionary factions, the *Orientales* and the *Porteños*. On January 15, 1815, Gen. Fructuoso Rivera, commanding 1,200 Uruguayans (including Indians), decisively defeated *Porteño* Gen. Manuel Dorrego commanding 800 men (including 200 recently defected Spaniards) at Guayabos. The *Porteños* lost 200 dead and wounded plus 400 prisoners. Following negotiations between Artigas and the *Porteños*, the latter withdrew from Montevideo on February 25, 1815.[50]

THE THIRD REVOLUTIONARY CAMPAIGN AGAINST UPPER PERU

Following the defeat of Belgrano in late 1813, Gen. Martín Güemes,[51] with *gauchos* and other irregulars, defended the north against the Royalists. On May 25, 1814, he defeated a Royalist force at La Florida.

General Rondeau then led the third Revolutionary incursion into Upper Peru. Once again, Potosí was occupied. On November 29, 1815, Royalist Gen. Joaquín de la Pezuela, commanding 5,100 Royalists, defeated General Rondeau, commanding 3,500 Revolutionaries, at the

Battle of Sipe Sipe, and once again the Revolutionaries retreated in disorder. The Revolutionaries lost 1,000 men (dead, wounded, and prisoners), all their artillery (9 pieces), and 1,500 muskets. The Royalists lost 32 killed and 198 wounded. Contributing to the Revolutionary disaster were the ill-feelings between Rondeau and the local *caudillo*, Martín Güemes.[52]

Belgrano's return as the commander of the army restored harmony. For six years the defense of the north now fell to Güemes and his *gauchos*. Spanish Brig. Gen. Andres García Camba described this irregular cavalry:

> The *gauchos* were people of the land with good horses, all being armed with knives or sabres, guns or cavalry carbines, which they used alternately without dismounting. Of surprising swiftness, they would encicle our troops with so much confidence, grace and gallantry that our European soldiers could not help but admire these extraordinary horsemen.[53]

On November 15, 1816, three thousand Royalists, commanded by Gen. Josè de la Serna, surprised six hundred Revolutionaries, commanded by General Campero, at Yavi. The Royalists seized the horses belonging to the Revolutionaries and captured Campero and three hundred men.[54]

Attempting to exploit their perceived advantage in the north, the Royalists launched an offensive in January 1817, the objective of which was to destroy the army San Martín was creating in Mendoza. The political orientation of key Royalist officers had changed. The previous commanders had been devoted Monarchists; now the commander was the Liberal and veteran of the war against Napoleon, José de la Serna. Liberals José Canterac and Gerónimo Valdés joined his staff. The introduction of these Liberals caused friction with Conservative *criollos* who were fighting for absolutism![55] The *gauchos* harassed La Serna's advance at every step. La Serna managed to fight his way to Salta, still more than 528 miles from San Martín's camp in Mendoza. By early May La Serna's strength was spent and he was forced to retreat.[56]

THE CONGRESS OF TUCUMÁN

The Revolutionaries selected the northwest provincial capital of Tucumán as the site for a national congress to demonstrate strength on the doorstep of the Royalist army concentrated in Upper Peru (Bolivia) and to draw the rebellious provinces back into the union. However, Banda Oriental, Santa Fé, Corrientes, and Entre Ríos did not send delegates. The thirty-two delegates represented ten cities of Río de la Plata and regions within Upper Peru. The Congress elected the *Porteño* Juan Pueyrredón as Supreme Director, thus ending the succession of weak governments. On July 9, 1816, its members unanimously proclaimed the independence of the United Provinces of South America, formalizing the events of May 1810. Beyond this, the congress was unable to reach consensus on pressing political, economic, and social issues.

PORTUGAL WINS CONTROL OF BANDA ORIENTAL

In August 1816 a 10,000-man Portuguese army, led by Gen. Carlos Federico Lecor, the Barão de Laguna, invaded Banda Oriental from Rio Grande do Sul. Many of the troops were veterans who had fled Portugal in 1810 along with the royal family.[57]

On September 18 Lecor occupied Maldonado. While Lecor advanced into Banda Oriental, *gauchos* from Corrientes and Entre Ríos loyal to Artigas advanced into Rio Grande do Sul but were repulsed at San Borja (October 5) and Ibiracahy (October 19). On October 27 Col. Joaquim Curado Oliveira Alvares, commanding 800 men, defeated Artigas, commanding 500 infantry and 700 lancers, at Carumbé. Artigas lost half his force. Three weeks later, on November 19, Portuguese Brigadier Sebastião Pinto de Araujo, leading 900 men, soundly defeated 1,000 led by Gen. Fructuoso Rivera at India Muerta.[58]

Hard-pressed by the Portuguese, two members of Montevideo's *cabildo* negotiated an agreement with Pueyrredón, Supreme Director of the United Provinces. Buenos Aires agreed to provide help and Banda Oriental agreed to obey the General Congress of the United Provinces and send deputies to the body. Artigas renounced the agreement.

During early 1817 the fighting was intense in northwestern Banda Oriental. The Portuguese defeated the *Orientales* at Arapey (January 3) and Calalán (January 4). On January 19 the Marqués de Alegrete led 600 men supported by five cannon across the Uruguay River into Corrientes to take reprisal against the towns that had supported Artigas. Opposed by 500 men, the Marqués was soundly defeated at Aguapey on January 19.[59]

On January 20, Lecor commanding 8,000 men entered Montevideo. The *Orientales* besieged the city. Their forces suffered numerous setbacks during late 1817 and throughout 1818. In October Col. Rufino Bauzá abandoned the siege and joined the United Provinces. In July Manuel Artigas and Bernabé Rivera were defeated.[60]

In December 1819 Artigas invaded Rio Grande do Sul in an attempt to draw the Portuguese out of Banda Oriental. He defeated a Portuguese force at Santa María in Rio Grande do Sul. Finally, on January 22, 1820, Count Filgueira's 3,000 Portuguese soundly defeated the 2,000 *Orientales* commanded by Andrés de Latorre at Tacuarembó Chico. Artigas fled Uruguay, ultimately receiving sanctuary in Paraguay where he died in poverty in 1850. Portugal annexed Banda Oriental on July 18, 1821, as the Cisplatine Province.[61]

THE LATE YEARS OF THE WAR

Annually between 1817 and 1822 the Royalists in Upper Peru invaded Río de la Plata. In 1820 and again in 1821 they penetrated as far as Salta. The Revolutionaries of Río de la Plata felt, therefore, seriously threatened by Royalist forces. The war did grind on and the Royalists had their share of victories (see chapter 4).

OBSERVATIONS

The Revolutionaries within the coastal area of the Viceroyalty of Río de la Plata won their war against the Royalists more rapidly than the Revolutionaries in any other region. Ferdinand VII apparently had fewer supporters here than anywhere else in Spanish America. These Royalists were defeated before Spain was free from Napoleon's intrigues. The capture of Montevideo by the Revolutionaries in 1814 proved to be a decisive turning point because it eliminated the Royalist base of operation on the east coast of South America. After the fall of Montevideo, no Royalist army ever approached within 800 miles of Buenos Aires. However, inland it was another matter. The opposing armies surged back and forth between the old settlements in northwestern Argentina and the highlands of Bolivia for some fifteen years, with neither gaining a decisive advantage.

Although the *Porteños* won independence for themselves and others, they could not hold the Viceroyalty of Río de la Plata together. Upper Peru was too distant and too different—politically, socially, and economically. Paraguay was too inaccessible, which helped to give it a unique identity from that of Buenos Aires. Banda Oriental was coveted by Brazil, a competitor too strong to be easily defeated. The war in Banda Oriental had evolved into a quadrangular struggle among the Spaniards, Portuguese, *Porteños*, and *Orientales*. Once one side appeared to have victory within grasp, some combination of the others temporarily united to prevent it from happening. The *Porteños* were barely able to hold onto the northeastern territories.

The winning of independence by the peoples of the Viceroyalty of Río de la Plata was not synonymous with peace and union. Before the war for independence had even ended for the former Viceroyalty of Río de la Plata, a titanic struggle lasting five decades began over the question of federalism versus unionism, which frequently went to the extreme and became separation versus union (see chapter 9).

CHAPTER FOUR

VICEROYALTY OF PERU, 1810–31

> This treaty of only five articles [between Chile and Argentina] is memorable not only because it was the first in which they celebrated their recently acquired sovereignty by force of arms, but because of the great objective which they had in view, to carry liberty to Peru and to consummate the Independence of the whole American continent.
> —Historian Diego Barros Arana

THE SPARK

On September 18, 1810, the prominent citizens of Santiago, Chile, named a seven-man *junta* to govern in the name of Ferdinand VII. Although this did not provoke an immediate response from the Viceroy of Peru, it was the first in a series of decisions which led to war.

BACKGROUND

The Viceroyalty of Peru had been the center of Spanish power within South America for more than 250 years. It, like the Viceroyalty of New Spain (Mexico), had sent much wealth back to Spain and, not surprisingly, had received more attention from the motherland than the less wealthy colonies. As revolutions were spreading throughout Spanish America, Lima, the heart of the Viceroyalty, remained loyal.

The Viceroyalty of Peru was composed of more or less modern Peru and had a limited degree of oversight responsibility for the Captaincy-General of Chile.[1] In 1810 the population of Peru was 1.5 million and that of Chile 800,000 persons. Within Peru 100,000 individiuals lived in Lima and Callao, while within Chile 36,000 persons lived in Santiago, 5,000 in Concepción, and 4,000 each in Valparaíso and La Serena.[2]

As the Napoleonic Wars raged in Europe, the Spanish king ordered the Captaincy-General of Chile and the Viceregalty of La Plata to open their ports in order to raise enough money to defend themselves against the King's foes. This became a direct threat to the merchants of Lima but the Viceroy of Peru could do little to reestablish Lima's monopoly.

Among the seven Chileans appointed to rule in the name of Ferdinand VII was the republican Juan Martínez de Rozas. Principally through his efforts an army was created and trade was opened to the world. This *junta* was short-lived and was followed by an elected congress which met in Santiago on July 4, 1811. In August the Congress created a new three-man *junta* and passed a number of laws, which included the prohibition of the slave trade and the emancipation of the children of Chilean slaves. The Congress evolved into three factions: those who supported the King; those who were openly for independence; and those who secretly worked for independence. The faction that favored independence became frustrated and ultimately gave its support to José Miguel Carrera,[3] who led a revolt on September 4, 1811. Not satisfied with the outcome, Carrera led a second *coup* in November. This time he seized power and organized a *junta*. Among other actions, Carrera increased the army and purchased armaments. By now independence was openly discussed.[4]

OPPOSING FORCES

Spain was probably stronger relative to the Revolutionaries along the west coast than anywhere else in South America. It had a dominant (although admittedly small) naval force. Spain, from her strongly fortified harbor at Callao (3 mi W of Lima), projected naval power along the west coast of the Americas. Ships were the only practical means of long-distance transportation along the west coast of South America. The principal cities were isolated pockets of population separated by geographical barriers. These included the formidable Atacama Desert separating Peru from Chile.

The revolutionary cause received little sympathy within Peru during the early years of the fighting. Some of the vast wealth of Spanish America, which had flowed through Lima on its way to Spain, was retained to administer the colonial system. As a consequence, those who shared the wealth preferred the *status quo*. Here, perhaps more than elsewhere in Spanish America, the Indians looked upon the King as their protector. Once it became clear that the Revolutionaries were fighting for independence, many Indians chose to fight for the counter-revolution. However, in remote Chile, revolutionary sentiments were strong.[5]

OPENING STRATEGY

The initial strategy of the Revolutionaries was to seize control of the government in the name of Ferdinand VII, while preparing to defend themselves against attack from the Royalists in Peru. The Royalists' strategy was to blockade Valparaíso in order to buy time. Viceroy Fernando Abascal planned to attack Río de la Plata and Chile simultaneously. A Royalist army was to be sent through Upper Peru against Buenos Aires and officers, sergeants, and munitions were to be sent by sea to the island of Chiloé (1,916 mi S of Lima), an army created from the garrison and inhabitants, and Santiago attacked from the south. Whichever army succeeded first was to aid the other.

THE VICEROY MOVES TO CRUSH THE REBELLION

Viceroy Abascal dispatched two ships that had been captured while smuggling (the *Vulture* and *Warren* out of Baltimore), to blockade Valparaíso (1,306 mi S of Callao). At the end of 1812, the Viceroy dispatched Brigadier Antonio Pareja (who had commanded the *Argonauta* at Trafalgar) commanding five brigs which were carrying arms, money, and some soldiers to Chiloé in order to raise an army. Within two months Pareja created a 1,400-man force. He sailed to Valdivia which had declared for the Royalists, where he recruited 2,000 more men. Pareja then sailed to the Bay of San Vicente, near Talcahuano. The patriots were taken by surprise. In short order the Spanish general captured Talcahuano, Concepción, and marched as far north as Chillán (242 mi S of Santiago). By the end of March 1813, the southern half of Chile was retaken by the Royalists with almost no fighting. While these events were transpiring, the

Revolutionaries continued to squabble. Finally, they raised an army of 4,000 poorly armed men and placed General Carrera in change.[6]

The Revolutionaries also attempted to piece together a naval squadron. In Valparaíso, Francisco de la Lastra (a former midshipman in the British navy) chartered the merchant frigate *Perla* (formerly the *Pearl*) and the brig *Portillo* (ex-*Colt*), and on May 2 he sailed to engage the *Warren*. However, the Royalists had successfully bribed the crews of the Revolutionary warships and they joined the Royalists.[7]

BATTLE OF SAN CARLOS

In May 1813 the two armies clashed south of the Maule River, but the battle was inconclusive. The Royalists retired to Chillán where Brigadier Pareja died and was succeeded by Juan Francisco Sánchez. The Revolutionaries recaptured Concepción and Talcahuano and besieged Chillán. Gabriel Pointsett, the American consular agent, volunteered to assist Carrera in the siege. He even suggested the placement of the artillery. However, this was to no avail because the Revolutionaries' magazine blew up. The soldiers on both sides stopped fighting to watch the fireworks. The siege failed. Before long the Royalists returned to the offense. Aided by the weather, Sánchez defeated Carrera. The war was now six months old and without results. During the conduct of this fratricidal war, both sides treated their prisoners with unusual cruelty.

The Viceroy sent reinforcements and a new commander, Spanish Gen. Gavino Gaínza. They joined the Royalists at Chillán during the beginning of 1814. The authorities in Santiago accused Carrera of having failed in his duty and replaced him with Bernardo O'Higgins[8] who had distinguished himself in combat. The Royalists now captured Talca. This created alarm among the Revolutionaries who were separated geographically. Part of the army was at Concepción under O'Higgins and the remainder at El Membrillar under Juan Mackenna O'Reilly. The Revolutionaries hurried to unite their forces. The Royalists, aware of the situation, attacked Mackenna but were repulsed at the Battle of El Membrillar by 300 volunteers from the Río de la Plata Provinces. As a consequence, the Revolutionaries were able to unite. Both sides now raced for unprotected Santiago. O'Higgins crossed the Maule River first and blocked the Royalists' advance at Quechereguas on the bank of the Claro River. After two unsuccessful attacks, Gaínza fell back to Talca. Although Santiago was saved, most of southern Chile once again fell to the Royalists. Both sides were exhausted and Commodore James Hillyar of the British navy negotiated a cease-fire; the combatants signed the Treaty of Lircay in May 1814.[9]

CARRERA REGAINS CONTROL

While the treaty was being negotiated, the Carrera brothers, who had been captured by the Royalists in early 1814, were allowed to escape; the Royalist commander wished a pretext for not fully complying with the treaty. On July 23, 1814, José Carrera and his followers captured the barracks at Santiago and organized a new *junta*. O'Higgins marched north to reestablish the deposed government. On August 12, 1814, the Revolutionary armies of Luis Carrera and O'Higgins fought at Maipú and O'Higgins was forced to retreat.

After disavowing the Treaty of Lircay, the Viceroy appointed a new commander, Gen. Mariano Osorio, to renew the fight. General Osorio arrived at Talcahuano with 5,000 men, including the 800-man Spanish Talavera Regiment, which had recently arrived on board the ship of the line *Asia*; the remainder were Peruvian Royalists. In view of the threat posed by the Spanish offense, O'Higgins desisted from his plan to continue the fight with Carrera. The two feuding Revolutionaries met at Tres Acequias. O'Higgins recognized Carrera as the general in chief and O'Higgins and his army submitted to Carrera's command. At the end of August, hoping to take advantage of the discord among the Revolutionaries, Osorio marched north. He delayed at Talca after learning of the reconciliation of the Revolutionary factions. Osorio now prepared to attack Santiago.[10]

BATTLE OF RANCAGUA

On October 1, 1814, some 5,000 Royalists led by Gen. Gavino Gaínza attacked O'Higgins and his 1,900 men entrenched at Rancagua (52 mi S of Santiago). Juan José Carrera, José Miguel's older brother, commanded some 2,000 ill-disciplined Revolutionaries just outside the city. The more numerous Royalists vigorously attacked O'Higgins, ever tightening the encirclement. The fighting was extremely bitter throughout the first day. On the second day Luis Carrera attempted to lead his command to O'Higgins' rescue and was easily routed by the Royalists. A few hundred of the weary defenders of Rancagua, including O'Higgins, finally succeeded in cutting their way out and escaped to Santiago. O'Higgins' defeat marked the temporary eclipse of Chilean independence. Some 3,000 Revolutionaries, including the Carrera brothers, the volunteers from Río de la Plata, and O'Higgins, fled across the Andes Mountains through the Uspallata Pass and ultimately to Mendoza, in Río de la Plata.[11]

The capital, Santiago, received the Royalists with great adulation. After a month Osorio began persecuting those Revolutionaries who had remained. Spanish Capt. Vicente San Bruno, a former Franciscan who had joined the Spanish Army to fight the French on the Iberian Peninsula, executed numerous prisoners. Prominent citizens who had supported the revolution were deported to the island of Juan Fernández 364 miles west in the Pacific Ocean where they lived in poverty. Their property was seized and special taxes were levied to pay the expenses of the royal army. Adding insult to injury was the arrival of the new royal governor, Francisco Casimiro Marcó del Pont, whose incapacities became legendary. Thus, Chile was restored to Spanish rule. However, the Royalists' repressive policies did drive many to support the guerrilla activities of Manuel Rodríguez who kept the Revolutionary cause alive within Chile.[12]

SAN MARTÍN ENTERS THE SCENE

Mendoza, on the eastern slope of the Andes, now became the focal point for the reconquest of Chile. The region had been settled from Chile and transferred to Río de la Plata in 1776. The city had been a haven for those exiled by Carrera while he ruled Chile and it was where many of those defeated at Rancagua sought refuge. José de San Martín chose to transform this sanctuary into the birthplace of the Army of the Andes. Following Belgrano's defeats in Upper Peru (future Bolivia), San Martín was given command of the northern army from which he soon asked to be relieved, feigning illness. San Martín did not believe that the Royalists in Peru could be successfully attacked through Upper Peru as had General Belgrano. San Martín outlined his strategy in a letter to Nicolás Rodriguez Peña dated April 22, 1814:

> The Fatherland will not make any progress on the northern front, unless it is in defensive battle and nothing else: and for this the gallant gauchos of Salta, supported by two good veteran squadrons, are enough. To think anything else is to throw men and money down a rathole. That's the way it is, I will not move [from Tucumán] nor will I attempt any expedition whatsoever. Now I have told you my secret—a small well disciplined army in Mendoza in order to invade Chile and to finish off the Goths there, to support a government of solid

friends in order to eliminate the anarchists ruling in Chile. Allying our forces we will pass by sea to take Lima. That is the road, not the other one, my friend. Convince yourself that the war will not end until we are in Lima.[13]

This was a bold plan with numerous obstacles. First, an army would have to be created. Then it would have to cross the Andes and arrive in Chile prepared to fight. After defeating the Royalists in Chile, a navy would have to be created to win control of the seas. Once these goals were achieved, San Martín could attack Peru, the seat of Royalist power.[14]

CARRERA IS EXPELLED

Carrera exhibited in Mendoza the same arrogance that had lost him much support in Chile. He insisted on being called the Chilean Head of State. Many of the Chilean refugees in Mendoza had been expelled from Chile by Carrera during his days in power. In contrast, O'Higgins entered Mendoza modestly. Also, O'Higgins was a "brother" of San Martín in the secret Lautaro Lodge; Carrera was not a member. San Martín tried to reduce the tensions between the Chilean factions by asking Carrera to leave Mendoza and settle in San Luis. Ten days later, on October 30, 1814, O'Higgins surrounded the barracks that housed Carrera's followers, disarmed them, and arrested Carrera. On November 3 Carrera was taken under guard to San Luis where he was to await the orders of the government in Buenos Aires.[15]

SAN MARTÍN INITIATES HIS PLAN

Awaiting San Martín in Mendoza when he arrived in mid-1814 were twenty-eight poorly trained and poorly equipped militiamen. The United Provinces immediately dispatched two companies of artillery and 220 Horse Grenadiers, the force San Martín had raised when he joined the Revolutionary cause in 1812, to protect the town. San Martín conscripted all males between the age of fourteen and forty-five. He also ordered that all Spanish-owned slaves between seventeen and twenty be sent to Mendoza.

At the same time, San Martín began to improve the infrastructure of the region so that it might support the creation of an army. Old roads were repaired and new ones built; irrigation ditches were dug to increase food production; textile factories were built to make uniforms; a gunpowder mill was established; and blacksmith shops were built to manufacture the necessary accouterments for crossing the Andes. Horses and mules were trained to climb while carrying burdens on their backs. Of special concern were horseshoes; these were not worn by horses on the Pampas but were essential for crossing the Andes.[16]

San Martín also attracted talented subordinates. Manuel Rodriguez, the son of a Spaniard living in Santiago, crossed the Andes three times spying for San Martín. His great knowledge of geography and his dedication to the Revolutionary cause made him singularly qualified for the task. San Martín also sent Álvarez Condarco, an engineer on his staff, over the Los Patos Pass ostensibly to present a copy of the declaration of independence adopted by the Congress at Tucumán to the Royalist leader, Marcó del Pont. While the royal governor was burning the document before a large crowd in Santiago, Condarco was returning to San Martín via the Uspallata Pass, all the while collecting valuable intelligence.[17]

Events in far-off Buenos Aires had the potential to doom San Martín's efforts. In January 1815, Alvear, a friend of Carrera, with whom San Martín had differences, became Supreme Director. San Martín, anticipating dismissal, resigned. The people of Mendoza refused to accept San Martín's replacement and insisted that he continue.

Figure 6. Viceroyalty of Peru, 1810–31. José de San Martín was ill during much of the campaign in Peru and weighed significantly less than shown in this illustration. The historian Bartolomé Mitre wrote, "few times was the intervention of a man in human destinies more decisive than his, both in the direction of events, and in the logical unfolding of the consequences." *Copied from Miller, Memoirs.*

In December 1815, following Rondeau's defeat at Sipe Sipe, San Martín announced his strategy to his officers at a banquet. The election in 1816 of Juan Martín de Pueyrredón as Supreme Director of the United Provinces of Río de la Plata gave San Martín the political support necessary to execute his plan. In May 1816, 450 infantrymen and substantial war supplies were sent from Buenos Aires.

San Martín attached great secrecy to his plans. Misleading information was leaked to the enemy. Presses were hauled from Buenos Aires to Mendoza and propaganda printed. Forays were made into Chile to confuse the Royalists. San Martín sent parties to explore passes which, in fact, would be only used by small parties. The Royalist Governor believed that the Revolutionaries would use a multitude of passes. Therefore, he distributed his 5,500-man army from Concepción to Copiapó, a distance of 792 miles, and tried to defend everywhere. The Governor even guarded some ports anticipating a possible attack from the sea.

A *PORTEÑO* PRIVATEERING SQUADRON INVADES THE PACIFIC

In late 1815 Capt. Guillermo Brown sailed a squadron of three warships—the frigate *Hércules* (29 guns), brigantine *Trinidad* (16 guns), and sloop *Halcón* (18 guns)—around Cape Horn into the Pacific. His mission was to disrupt the enemy's communications and commerce, rescue the Chilean patriots exiled on the island of Juan Fernández, and measure the sentiments of the populace for the Revolutionary cause. The *Hércules* was sent to the island but, damaged in a storm, had to abandon the mission. On January 20, 1816, Brown blockaded Callao and attacked the port from small craft. On January 23 he captured the Spanish merchant frigate *Consecuencia* and added her to his force as the *Argentina*. Abandoning the blockade on January 30, Brown sailed north. In February Brown attempted to attack Guayaquil at night by sailing the *Trinidad* up the Guayas River. The remainder of the squadron drew too much water to participate. The *Trinidad* grounded and Brown was forced to surrender. Those in the Revolutionary squadron were able to effect an armistice and an exchange of prisoners on February 16 which included Brown. Brown, after sailing north to the coast of Gran Colombia, returned to the Atlantic as well. This small squadron significantly stressed Spain's Pacific defenses.[18]

SAN MARTÍN CROSSES THE ANDES

In December 1816 San Martín reviewed his army of 5,350 soldiers, 1,600 horses, and a great number of mules.[19] The army began its assent on January 9, 1817, the height of the summer, and used six passes along a 500-mile front. San Martín advised his commanders of the routes selected only seventy-two hours before the advance began, and subordinates learned the route only on the day of the march. The main body and practically all of the artillery and animals used the north-central Los Patos Pass which is 11,705 feet high while the remainder of the bulk of the army traversed the Andes just to the south through the Uspallata Pass.[20] The mission of these forces was to divide the enemy's force, defeat it piecemeal, and capture Chile's capital, Santiago. Two small detachments of 200 men each passed through the northern passes of Azufre and Caballos; their objective was the conquest of northern Chile. Two other small detachments crossed through the Planchon and Portillo passes; their primary objective was to convince the Royalists that they were the vanguard of the main body. In early February 1817 San Martín and his army descended from the Andes and easily gained control of northwestern Chile. The main force united at San Felipe (53 mi N of Santiago).[21]

BATTLE OF CHACABUCO

San Martín's program of misinformation had been successful. The Royalist army was scattered along the *cordillera*. By mid-January, the Royalist governor, Marshal Marcó del Pont, learned that San Martín was crossing the Andes in strength but had no idea where Martín's force was concentrated. Finally on February 10 the Governor dispatched General Rafael Maroto from Santiago with 1,400 men, all that he could scrape together, to Chacabuco (34 mi N of Santiago), a place that offered good ground to defend. Maroto joined some 1,000 Royalists at Chacabuco, a one-day march from the capital. He took up a defensive position on a ridge overlooking the road to Santiago.

San Martín possessed good intelligence concerning the size of Maroto's force and the enemy's prospects concerning reinforcements. He chose to attack on the morning of February 12 and divided his force in two. Col. Estanislao Solar was to attack the enemy's left flank along the protected road. The other division under O'Higgins was to advance along the unprotected road and attack once Soler had engaged the enemy. Upon coming out of a ravine, O'Higgins found his force confronted by massed Royalist troops. Ambrosio Cramer [Kramer], a former officer of Napoleon's army, recognized the danger and suggested a bayonet charge to O'Higgins, who gave the order. At that moment the Mounted Granadiers, the unit San Martín had raised years earlier, charged the right flank of the Royalists and decided the battle in favor of the Revolutionaries. Solar attacked too late to take part in the deciding action.[22]

The demoralized Royalists withdrew with the Revolutionary cavalry in pursuit. The Royalists lost 600 dead, 550 captured, and their artillery; San Martín lost 11 dead and 110 wounded. Among the prisoners was San Bruno; he was executed.[23]

The defeated Royalists escaped to Valparaíso. Those who were fortunate managed to get on board one of the Spanish ships in the harbor; those who were not remained behind and many committed atrocities before being dealt with by the Revolutionaries. The Spanish ships sailed to Callao, where those on board were harshly received by the Viceroy and ordered to join the Royalist forces in Talcahuano.[24]

On February 13, 1817, San Martín entered Santiago, the Royalists having already abandoning the city. In keeping with his Spartan character, he refused a festive reception. On the eighteenth the notables met to organize a government. They nominated San Martín governor of Chile with full authority; he refused to accept.[25] He suggested that they meet again; this time they chose O'Higgins and bestowed the title of Supreme Director.

San Martín recrossed the Andes and rode to Buenos Aires seeking reinforcements. Col. Juan Gregorio de Las Heras led 1,300 Revolutionaries into southern Chile to attack the Royalist stronghold at Talcahuano (319 mi S of Santiago). The Revolutionaries captured Concepción and the Royalist retreated back to Talcahuano.[26]

On February 12, 1818, the first anniversary of the Battle of Chacabuco, O'Higgins, the Bishop of Santiago, and San Martín swore an allegiance to independence. The O'Higgins government controlled Chile north of Talcahuano. It had two cardinal principles: to maintain the Río de la Plata–Chilean alliance and to continue the war against Spain.

BATTLE OF CANCHA RAYADA

While San Martín and O'Higgins were attending to political matters, the largely undefeated Royalist army was coming together from many scattered locations. All attempts by the Revolutionaries to capture the port of Talcahuano by land had failed. The port stubbornly remained in Royalists hands which allowed General Osorio, the victor at Rancagua, to land there in January 1818 with 3,276 men, 10 cannon, and extra weapons from Peru. Osorio marched north, assimilating Royalists until his army numbered 5,000 men and crossed the Maule River. O'Higgins, who had advanced from Santiago, abandoned Talca, which was occupied by Osorio on March 4.

The now reinforced Revolutionaries, whom San Martín had rejoined, marched to the Plain of Cancha Rayada a few miles northeast of Talca (155 mi S of Santiago) which had been occupied by the Royalists. At 9 P.M. on March 19, Osorio's 4,612 men and 14 cannon attacked the 8,011 Revolutionaries with 33 cannon while they were repositioning their forces. The Revolutionaries were surprised, perhaps because they were celebrating San Martin's Saints Day. O'Higgins' horse was shot from under him and he was wounded. Although the Revolutionaries fled in disarray, the 2nd Division under Gregorio las Heras and the artillery under Blanco Encalada escaped without significant loss. The Royalists did captured 22 pieces of artillery, but their casualties were higher than those of the Revolutionaries. Osorio lost 300 men and San Martín 120 plus hundreds of deserters and much of his train. The initial news to reach Santiago exaggerated the scale of the Revolutionary defeat and caused near panic. Rumors circulated that San Martín had been killed. Manuel Rodríguez convincingly exhorted mobs of citizens not to abandoned the revolution. Finally, the return of San Martín and O'Higgins to Santiago restored confidence and order. Osorio cautiously advanced toward Santiago.[27]

BATTLE OF MAIPÚ

On April 5, 1818, Revolutionaries numbering 4,900 from the Río de la Plata and Chilean provinces with 21 cannon commanded by San Martín confronted 5,300 Royalists with 14 cannon led by General Osorio on the plain of Maipú some 25 miles outside Santiago. Osorio placed his army to command the road between Santiago and Valparaíso. The opposing armies each held high ground separated by distances ranging between 150 and 300 yards. The Revolutionary artillery opened the battle at about noon. The Revolutionaries to the northwest drove the Royalists back, but in the southeast the Royalists initially were successful against units which included many blacks. San Martín committed his reserves against the Royalists in this sector and the Royalists' position collapsed. By 2 P.M. the Royalists were driven from the field and tried to fortify the village of Del Espejo; the Revolutionaries gave no quarter and the entire Royalist army was destroyed—2,000 killed, 2,432 captured, the entire train lost, and only 600, including General Osorio, escaped back to Talcahuano. The Revolutionaries lost 1,000 men. This victory eliminated Spanish influence within Chile except for the south. Once again San Martín returned to Buenos Aires to seek resources. Only through the threat of his resignation was he able to secure at least part of what he wanted.[28]

EVENTS AT SEA

In the meantime, Chilean Revolutionaries were organizing a naval force in order to carry the war to Peru. First they needed to break the blockade that Osorio had established with the ships that had landed his army at Talcahuano. In February 1818, they captured a former smuggler, the brigantine *Aguila*, when it anchored in Valparaíso. The arrival of the former East Indianman *Windham*, which was renamed the *Lautaro* (44 guns), allowed the Revolutionaries to challenge the blockade. On April 26 the *Lautaro* fought a draw with the Spanish frigate *Esmeralda* (44 guns) and broke the blockade. Meanwhile, Chilean and *Porteño* agents, relying solely upon personal assets, were also busy acquiring warships in Great Britain and the United States. The *Lautaro* captured the *San Miguel* (unk guns) and recaptured the *Perla* (unk guns). The arrival of the 64-gun *San Martín* (ex-*Cumberland*), sloop *Chacabuco* (20 guns), and smaller warships gave the Chilean patriots a formidable squadron.[29]

In 1818 Spain sent some 2,000 troops along with extensive munitions to reinforce the Royalists at Talcahuano, Chile, and Callao, Peru. The eleven transports were escorted by the 50-gun frigate *María Isabel*, one of the old ships acquired from Russia. During the passage from Spain, the crew of the transport *Trinidad* killed the chief of the expedition and some of the officers and sailed the ship to Buenos Aires. Thus, the *Porteños* learned full details of the expedition (including its secret signals) from the mutineers and sent word to Chile. The foreign-built squadron, made up of the *San Martín*, *Lautaro*, and *Chacabuco*, and commanded by Manuel Blanco Encalada,[30] intercepted the enemy at Talcahauno on October 25. After a brief fight the *María Isabel* surrendered. Only one of the crowded transports carrying about 100 soldiers reached safety at Callao, Peru; the remainder were captured.[31]

COCHRANE TAKES COMMAND OF THE FLEET

Lord Thomas Cochrane,[32] a British officer who had won fame as a frigate captain during the Napoleonic Wars, was recruited by Álvarez Condarco to command the Chilean navy. His first expedition against Callao did not accomplish anything significant. In his second expedition, which sailed from Valparaíso on September 9, 1819, he reconnoitered Callao but then turned south, and on February 3–4, 1820, he surprised and captured Valdivia (575 mi S of Valparaíso). This victory incorporated that territory into Chile and yielded a large amount of munitions, deprived the Royalists of their heavily fortified southern harbor, and helped secure British loans.[33]

In 1819 Spain again tried to send reinforcements to Peru. The expedition, which left Cadiz in May, was composed of the 74-gun *San Telmo*, the 74-gun *Alejandro I* (acquired from Russia), the frigate *Prueba*, and various merchant ships. The *Alejandro I* was taking on so much water that she had to turn back after reaching the equator. The *San Telmo* was lost in a storm in Antarctic waters on September 2 with all hands (some 800 men).[34] The frigate *Prueba*, with some of the surviving transports, arrived off Callao only to find it blockaded by the Chilean squadron. Finally, the shattered squadron found safe haven to the north at Paita, Peru.

THE UNITED LIBERATION ARMY

While these events were unfolding, the Revolutionaries had been working hard at Valparaíso to prepare a force with which to invade Peru. All did not go well.

Carrera pursued his own plan to free Chile from Spanish rule. In Buenos Aires he attempted to interest the government in his plan, but in vain. He then sought help in the United States but came away only with some support from private individuals. He sailed for Buenos Aires in the corvette *Clifton* which was accompanied by other ships loaded with arms. Arriving in Buenos Aires, he learned of San Martín's victory at Chacabuco (February 12, 1817). The government in Buenos Aires, fearing that Carrera might divide those serving the Revolutionary cause, did not give him permission to continue his voyage around Cape Horn. Carrera attempted to sail regardless, for which he was imprisoned. Carrera and his brothers escaped to Montevideo. They then fought in the internal wars of Argentina (see chapter 9). All were captured and shot between 1818 and 1821.[35]

Buenos Aires, distracted by internal strife and another threat of invasion from Spain, lost enthusiasm for the amphibious invasion of Peru. San Martín was ordered to return with his army and Chile was bordering on bankruptcy. San Martín chose to disobey his orders and O'Higgins decided that Chile would assume the costs of the expedition. On August 20, 1820, sixteen transports carrying 4,642 men (about 2,300 from Río de la Plata and 1,800 from Chile), 35 pieces of artillery, 650 horses, armaments and equipment for an additional 15,000 men, and supplies for four months sailed north escorted by the 64-gun *San Martín*, 50-gun *O'Higgins* (the captured *María Isabel*), 46-gun *Lautaro*, 28-gun *Independencia*, and fourteen smaller warships. They were opposed by 23,000 Royalists scattered throughout Upper and lower Peru of whom 8,000 men were in the vicinity of Lima.[36] The Spanish squadron was too weak to oppose the escorts. San Martín's plan was to land at Pisco (1,159 mi N of Valparíso and 147 mi S of Lima) and attract the Royalists to the south then move by sea to the north of Lima. This had been suggested to him by some Peruvian patriots in 1818. San Martín sent 1,100 men under Col. Juan Álvarez de Arenales on a raid into the interior to recruit followers and to keep the Royalists guessing. He also conscripted Peruvians and slaves, much as he had done in Mendoza. San Martín suffered from a stomach disorder and became incapacitated by the strong drugs used to fight the illness. San Martín reembarked the army and landed at Huacho (71 mi N of Lima) on November 9. The Revolutionaries, ravaged by an epidemic, confined their efforts to besieging Lima.

Cochrane blockaded Callao. On the night of November 5, he led fourteen boats (carrying 160 seamen and 80 marines) into the harbor and boldy captured in 15 minutes the most powerful Spanish warship on the coast, the frigate *Esmeralda* (44 guns), from under the guns of the Spanish forts at Callao. The Revolutionaries lost 11 dead and 30 wounded; the Royalists sustained 160 casualties and 200 captured. Between February and late May 1821, Cochrane, commanding three warships with 500 Marines under William Miller,[37] raided Peru's southern ports.

San Martín and Cochrane continued to quarrel frequently over strategy. San Martín, greatly outnumbered by the Royalists, refused to risk a general engagement in Peru, which the admiral advocated. Cochrane wanted San Martín to attack Lima at once. San Martín preferred to try to involve Peruvians in the process of winning independence.[38] Therefore, San Martín remained near the coast of Peru while sending emissaries throughout the country to prepare public opinion in favor of a national uprising against the Spaniards. During the night of December 2, the 675-man Royalist Numanica Battalion (which had been raised in Venezuela) mutineed and joined San Martín's army.[39]

BACK IN SPAIN

The Royalists also suffered from internal dissensions. In May 1820, far away in Spain, Ferdinand VII was forced to adhere to the liberal Constitution of 1812. In Peru the liberal Royalists overthrew Viceroy Joaquin de la Pezuela and replaced him with La Serna on January 29, 1821. In May of that year, peace commissioners arrived in Peru from Spain and open unsuccessful negotiations with San Martín. La Serna evacuated Lima which the Revolutionaries occupied on July 9. A *Cabildo Abierto* declared the independence of Peru and on the twenty-eighth San Martín assumed the title and functions of Protector of Peru. Influential Peruvian *criollos*, thinking that San Martín had personal ambitions, opposed him.

In August Royalist General Canterac leading 3,200 men slipped around 5,900 Revolutionaries and joined the defenders in Callao. On September 16 Canterac abandoned Callao carrying with him its large quantity of munitions, and on the nineteenth the Royalist General La Mar switched sides and surrendered the port's defenses. San Martín was completely occupied with political matters and the Royalist army avoided major engagements, choosing to concentrate on rebuilding its strength, successfully recruiting among the peasantry of southern Peru and Upper Peru.[40]

COCHRANE SAILS OFF

The intensity of the quarreling between San Martín and Cochrane increased—the Admiral's flamboyant character clashed with the General's austere one. Cochrane insisted that the squadron be paid immediately. Finally, on October 6 Cochrane seized the treasury, which was kept on board the *Lautaro*, and paid his men. Some of the officers chose to join the newly created Peruvian navy and sided with San Martín. In October Cochrane, commanding the *O'Higgins*, *Independencia*, and *Valdivia* (former *Esmeralda*), sailed north in search of two Spanish frigates on his own authority. The squadron sailed as far as the Gulf of Cortez off Mexico without encountering the enemy warships. Numerous Royalist ports were attacked. When Cochrane returned to Peru, he learned that the two Spanish frigates had surrendered to San Martín and that Peruvian ports were closed to his squadron. Cochrane then sailed for Chile and subsequently contracted his services to the new Brazilian government.[41]

Cochrane's successes had swept the Spanish navy from the Pacific. His landings had terrorized the Royalist-held ports. This domination of the sea had allowed San Martín's army to sail north to Peru and Bolívar's army to sail south to Guayaquil. Furthermore, Chilean privateers had brought Royalist commerce to a standstill from Cape Horn to California.[42]

On land, the military campaign against the Royalists was lagging. Gen. Domingo Tristán, commanding 1,600 men, occupied Ica (175 mi SSE of Lima). His mission was to block the Royalists' path to Lima. On April 7 General Canterac leading 2,000 men surprised the Revolutionaries at 1:00 A.M., almost annihilating the Revolutionary force. The Royalists withdrew southeast to their stronghold.

THE MEETING

On July 26, 1822, José de San Martín and Simón Bolívar met in Guayaquil to discuss their differences. At issue were three main points: the future of Guayaquil; the number of Bolívar's troops to serve in Peru; and the future type of government in Peru (Bolívar wanted a republic and San Martín a monarchy). Unable to reach an accommodation, San Martín returned to Lima. While the Revolutionaries were struggling to resolve their political differences, the Royalists were unharassed as they rebuilt their army from the peasant stock of southern Peru and Upper Peru.

THE FOURTH REVOLUTIONARY CAMPAIGN AGAINST UPPER PERU

San Martín's political and military positions were growing weaker by the day. Cochrane had quit and Bolívar had refused substantive help. Before leaving for Guayaquil, San Martín devised a new strategy to destroy the Royalists in the *Altiplano* and thereby end the struggle in Spanish South America. This would be the first real offensive against Upper Peru since Rondeau's disastrous campaign in 1814 launched from northern Río de la Plata. San Martín conceived a plan which attacked the enemy simultaneously at numerous, widely dispersed locations. Gen. Juan Álvarez de Arenales, commanding 3,000 men, was to drive southeast from Lima thereby pinning down the forces under Canterac in the cities of Jauja (108 mi E of Lima) and Huancayo (126 mi E of Lima). The army along the southern frontier of Upper Peru was to push northward from Salta thereby holding Olañeta in Potosí Province. Gen. Rudecindo Alvarado leading 4,000 men was to sail south from Callao, disembark in Arica, and drive to Arequipa (465 mi SE of Lima) and on to Cuzco (348 mi SE of Lima). Thus, under pressure from the north, south, and west, the Royalists would not be able to take advantage of their interior lines and concentrate their forces. After returning from Guayaquil, San Martín, frustrated and ill, called a congress in Lima and resigned his command. He retired from the struggle and ultimately from the Americas, accepting self-imposed exile in France.[43]

The remnants of the United Liberation Army commanded by Alvarado sailed from Callao on October 17, 1822, landed at Arica (593 mi S of Callao) on December 6, and marched inland. Canterac ignored Álvarez' advance from Lima and hurried to join Valdés in southern Peru. The united Royalists defeated Alvarado at Torata (528 mi SE of Lima) on January 19, 1823. The Revolutionaries lost 500 men and the Royalists 250. Two days later the Royalists attacked the disorganized and demoralized Revolutionaries at Moquegua (528 mi SE of Lima). One thousand Revolutionaries were captured. Alvarado retreated to the port of Ilo (528 mi SE of Lima). Only 500 survivors escaped by sea to Callao. This disastrous campaign cost the Revolutionaries more than 1,700 casualties. The army that had conquered Chile and captured Lima no longer existed as an effective fighting force.[44]

Meanwhile, Peru's First Congress appointed a triumvirate to rule, but the new leaders argued among themselves. The financial system collapsed and trade was paralyzed. Therefore, Congress elected Col. José de la Riva Agüero as president on February 28, 1823. Following the disastrous campaign against Upper Peru, Riva Agüero asked Bolívar for military assistance. Bolívar sent 6,000 men under General Sucre who arrived in May. Within a short period of time, Sucre was enmeshed in the web of Peruvian politics.[45]

THE FIFTH REVOLUTIONARY CAMPAIGN AGAINST UPPER PERU BEGINS

Again in 1823 the Revolutionaries conceived a plan to simultaneously attack the Royalists from three directions. Santa Cruz would land along the coast and drive toward La Paz (624 mi SE of Lima). The Colombian army in Lima would march toward Jauja in order to pin down Canterac. The Revolutionary army along the southern frontier would advance into Upper Peru in order to hold Olañeta's attention.

Santa Cruz embarked 5,095 men and 8 cannon at Callao in mid-May 1823. Part of this force disembarked at Arica and part at Ilo. Gen. Agustín Gamarra, commanding the force that landed at Arica, captured Tacna (30 mi N of Arica). Those at Ilo under Santa Cruz occupied Moquegua by mid-June. On July 23 both columns renewed their advance toward La Paz. On August 8 Santa Cruz captured La Paz and Gamarra occupied Viacha some 18 miles to the southwest. On the twelfth Gamarra marched south to confront Olañeta who was advancing against him. In the meantime Santa Cruz marched northwest around the southwest corner of Lake Titicaca to meet the advance of Viceroy La Serna. Santa Cruz and La Serna fought the inconclusive battle of Zepita (600 mi SE of Lima) on August 25.

THE ROYALISTS RECAPTURE LIMA

While the Revolutionaries were beginning to execute their fifth campaign against Upper Peru, the Royalists took advantage of the weakened defenses of Lima. On June 18 generals Canterac and Valdez, commanding 9,000 men and 24 cannon, surprised and reoccupied Lima. The Revolutionaries panicked, voted Sucre dictatorial powers, and fled to Callao. In the capital the Royalists collected forced contributions to their cause. They remained until July 16, by which time Santa Cruz's operation threatened to defeat their armies in Upper Peru piecemeal. The evacuation of Lima freed Sucre so that he could move south and aid Santa Cruz.[46]

THE FIFTH REVOLUTIONARY CAMPAIGN AGAINST UPPER PERU CONTINUES

In August Sucre, commanding 3,000 men, sailed from Callao and disembarked west of Arequipa which he occupied on August 31. He offered to aid Santa Cruz, who refused to accept. On September 8 the forces under Santa Cruz and Gamarra reunited some 18 miles northwest of Oruro and occupied Sora Sora; their combined force numbered 4,500 men. On September 14 the Royalist forces under La Serna and Olañeta united near the same city, giving them a total of 6,500 men. Also on the fourteenth, Santa Cruz rapidly marched north to unite with Sucre, whom he expected to find near Lake Titicaca. The Royalists followed the Revolutionaries to Ayo Ayo. Santa Cruz wanted to turn on the Royalists but his artillery became separated from the army due to the pace of the march, and he chose not to risk a battle without it. The decision not to fight broke the morale of his weary troops and the Revolutionary army's withdrawal turned into a rout. The Royalists took 2,000 prisoners and most of the train. The remnants of the Revolutionary army reembarked at Ilo in late September. Sucre, who had remained near Arequipa, also withdrew his forces by sea on October 12. The campaign was again disastrous for the Revolutionaries. They failed to engage the Royalists piecemeal and were unable to effect their own union.[47]

BOLÍVAR TAKES COMMAND

Finally, in August 1823, after numerous refusals, the Congress in Bogotá gave Bolívar permission to take command in Lima where he was voted full political and military powers on September 10. When Bolívar arrived in Peru, four Revolutionary armies were in the field—those of Peru, Chile, and Colombia, and Río de la Plata; each obeyed a different authority. The fleet, now commanded by Adm. Martín Guise, was answerable to the Peruvian government. And, the Peruvian government was just as fragmented as the Revolutionary armies. In addition to the Peruvian Congress in Lima, there was a new president in Lima and a deposed one in Trujillo (274 mi N of Lima). The rebellious ex-president, Riva Agüero, opened negotiation with the Royalists. He proposed to unite their forces and drive Bolívar out of Peru; the plot was exposed and Riva Agüero was allowed to go into exile.[48]

Once again, events in Europe altered the course of the war in the Americas. In late 1823 a French-supported counterrevolution overthrew the liberal Spanish government, abrogated the Constitution of 1812, and restored Ferdinand VII to absolute power. This restoration reverberated throughout Peru.

THE REVOLUTIONARIES IN CALLAO MUTINY

Between February 4 and 6, 1824, the Río de la Plata troops garrisoning Callao, who had not been paid for months, declared for the King and released the Spanish prisoners! On the tenth the Peruvian Congress voted Bolívar dictatorial powers. On February 29 Royalist Gen. Antonio Monet entered Callao, securing the work begun by the mutineers. Next the Royalists advanced on Lima. Bolívar ordered the city evacuated and it was reoccupied by the Royalists. The city of Trujillo and its immediate surroundings were the only Peruvian territory still controlled by the Revolutionaries. Bolívar's position was desperate. He pleaded with Revolutionary governments as far away as Mexico for reinforcements.[49]

But, the Royalists also suffered from factionalism. General Olañeta, a *criollo* absolutist, became increasingly incensed by his subordinate position to a liberal Spaniard, Viceroy La Serna, and finally took matters into his own hands. Controlling most of Upper Peru, Olañeta evicted those office holders who were Liberals and on June 20, 1824, declared himself "Protector of Religion and Absolutism." The Viceroy was furious and decided to first suppress this insubordination before dealing with Bolívar. La Serna dispatched a force under Gen. Gerónimo Valdés against Olañeta. After some minor skirmishes, Valdés and Olañeta reached an agreement which gave the latter *de facto* independence of action.[50]

THE SIXTH REVOLUTIONARY CAMPAIGN AGAINST UPPER PERU

Learning of the discord among the Royalists caused by Olañeta, Bolívar, in spite of being ill, transformed an ill-disciplined, heterogeneous collection of units into an army. The city of Trujillo was converted into an arsenal, duplicating the feat accomplished by San Martín at Mendoza.

BATTLE OF JUNÍN

The Revolutionary army began its march from northern Peru on July 15, 1824, and by early August reached the high plains of Cerro de Pasco. General Canterac was taken by surprise. However, on August 6, 1824, the Royalist cavalry caught that of the Revolutionaries led by General Miller emerging from a narrow defile. The Royalists forced the head of the column, General Miller and 250 riders, onto swampy ground. The remainder of the Revolutionaries rallied and drove the Royalists from the field. Reputedly, not a shot was fired; the Battle of Junín (130 mi NE of Lima) was fought entirely with steel. The Royalists lost 364 killed and 80 captured; the Revolutionaries lost 50 killed and 91 wounded. This Royalist defeat profoundly affected the morale of the troops; some 3,000 men were lost to the cause through desertion and illness. Canterac retreated southward to Cuzco.[51]

August and September were spent preparing for the next clash. Bolívar, leaving Sucre in command, set out for the coast on October 1 and reoccupied Lima (which had been abandoned by the Royalists on March 28). The Colombian Congress, under the influence of Santander, now rescinded Bolívar's powers as President, but he paid little attention to the legislators.

THE WAR AT SEA

Admiral Guise, commanding a five-ship Peruvian squadron manned by English, American, and Peruvian sailors, fought an indecisive engagement with a Spanish squadron which included the *Asia* (74 guns) off Callao on October 7, 1824.[52]

BATTLE OF AYACUCHO

Back in the highlands, Viceroy La Serna took the initiative. He planned to outflank Sucre to the west, thereby cutting off the Revolutionaries from their support in the north and their route of escape by the sea. On October 22 La Serna began his march from Cuzco circling south of Sucre. Sucre, perceiving the viceroy's intentions, paralleled his march northward. By December 8 the Royalists gained a position to the north of the Revolutionaries on the plains of Ayacucho (207 mi SE of Lima) at an altitude of 11,600 feet. Sucre took up a defensive position with both his flanks protected by deep ravines. Sucre commanded 5,780 men (4,500 men from Gran Colombia, 1,200 from Peru, and 80 from Río de la Plata) and 2 cannon and La Serna 9,310 men (mostly American Royalists) and 11 cannon.

The battle began at dawn. William Miller reported, "The battle of Ayacucho was the most brillant ever fought in South America. The troops on both sides were in a state of discipline which would have been creditable to the best European armies."[53]

The Royalist division led by Mariscal Villalobos attacked the Revolutionary right composed of Colombians commanded by Gen. José María Córdoba. They were repulsed with heavy losses. In the center, the Royalists led by General Monet advanced but were met by *húsares* (heavily armed cavalry) and thrown into disorder. On the left a Royalist division led by General Váldes drove back the Peruvian division under General La Mar. As the fighting continued the Colombians mounted a bayonet charge against Monet's division, and the Revolutionary cavalry led by General Miller dispersed that of the Royalists as it tried to come to his rescue. The Royalist reserves advanced but were surrounded and the Viceroy captured. Canterac attempted to take command and execute an orderly retreat, but the surviving troops wanted no part of it and surrendered.

The Royalists lost 1,400 killed, 700 wounded, and 2,500 captured. In addition to the Viceroy, these included 15 generals, 16 colonels, and 68 lieutenant colonels; the roster read like the roll call of preeminent Royalists. The only missing name was Olañeta. The Revolutionaries lost 309 dead and 607 wounded. The composition of the royal army, mostly Americans, reflected what had taken place elsewhere during the fourteen-year-old struggle. Ayacucho was the death knell of the Royalist cause throughout Spanish South America, although the end was not immediately perceived. The Royalists in Callao, Chiloe, and Alto Peru refused to obey the surrender order issued by Viceroy La Serna.[54]

UPPER PERU (FUTURE BOLIVIA) FALLS

The Revolutionaries besieged and captured Cuzco, Peru, on December 24. From there, they cautiously advanced into Upper Peru, defeating General Olañeta at Tumusla on April 2, 1825; Olañeta was killed by his own troops. On August 6, 1825, an assembly declared Upper Peru independent and named the new nation Bolivia in honor of Simón Bolívar. On January 23, 1826, Gen. Jose Rodil surrendered Callao, the last Royalist stronghold in Peru.[55]

However, while Spain retain possession of the Island of Chiloé (2,016 mi SSE of Lima) off the southwestern coast of Chile, it had the potential to reintroduce its forces back into the Pacific Coast. The new Peruvian government, led by Bolívar, considered attacking this remaining Royalist stronghold, which had become part of Peru in the late 1700s and was more closely tied (ideologically and logistically by sea) to Peru than to Chile. Adm. Manuel Blanco Encalada, commanding the Chilean-Colombian-Peruvian squadron blockading the Royalists in Callao, withdrew the Chilean ships perceiving that an expedition launched from Peru against Chiloé was not in the best interest of the new Chilean government.

The Spanish garrison at Callao surrendered on January 23, 1826, after a stubborn defense. Due to growing political problems in Colombia, Bolívar resigned supreme authority over Peru in September 1826 and returned to Bogotá. Still, no formal peace treaty was signed. So, the new South American republics talked of war, issued letters of marque, and harassed Spanish ships while the Spanish fleet, in turn, periodically blockaded their ports.

The fighting in the southern part of Chile continued for two long years after Ayacucho. The archipelago of Chiloé remained in the hands of the Royalists and served as a base of operations by land and sea. The remnants of the Royalist forces defeated at Maipú (April 5, 1818) had found refuge in the south where they joined with the Araucanian Indians. Also, the

Spanish governor of Chiloé, Antonio de Quintanilla, issued letters of marque. Ships carrying these charters preyed upon the commerce of the new republics. As a result, there was no public security in the southern region.

Finally, in late 1825, a Chilean squadron commanded by Blanco Encalada landed an army under Gen. Ramón Freire on Chiloé and then blockaded the island. On January 12, 1826, that Royalist force surrendered, thus ending three centuries of Spanish rule in South America.

On the mainland the Araucanians and a few die-hard Royalists continued a guerrilla war. The Chilean government had to maintain an army in the south to contain these raids. This resistance was finally broken by General Manuel Bulnes in 1831.

OBSERVATIONS

Independence was won in the Viceroyalty of Peru primarily due to the military genius of San Martín and Bernardo O'Higgins plus those who assumed their task, Simón Bolívar and José Sucre. San Martín's analysis that the Spaniards could not be decisively defeated in South America until driven from Peru proved correct; however, he was not able to complete the task primarily due to illness.

O'Higgins created the Chilean navy, without which San Martín and later Bolívar could not execute their strategies. O'Higgins governed in Chile until January 28, 1823. The assassination of Manuel Rodríguez, the shooting of the Carrera brothers, the high taxes needed to support the fleet and liberation army, and O'Higgins' unwillingness to share power contributed to his downfall. Under pressure, O'Higgins yielded his authority to a *junta* and ultimately went into voluntary exile to Peru.[56]

Even in the Viceroyalty of Peru, the center of Spanish power in South America, the majority of officers and men in the Royalist army were Americans. During the tenure of Viceroy Pezuela, more than two-thirds of the officers were Americans and the American Royalist Goyeneche commanded an exclusively American army in Upper Peru. The Royalist army captured after the Battle of Ayacucho was composed of 1,512 Americans and only 751 Spaniards. Apparently, most of the Indians remained loyal to the King. The Arucanians continued to fight for the Crown until 1827 and felt betrayed when the Spaniards finally withdrew.[57]

Following the defeat at Ayacucho and the loss of Peru, many Spaniards and some American Royalists fled to the Caribbean islands, principally Cuba, where Spain clung to the remnants of her colonial empire in the Americas until 1898.

Although the precise number of Spanish troops sent to fight the independence movement in the Americas is still open to debate, it was probably less than 50,000 men. Of these, only some 6,000 men successfully reached Peru directly from Spain, although others found their way there from neighboring theaters of operations.[58]

On December 27, 1826, the British Consul-General to Peru, Charles Milner Ricketts, described to the Foreign Secretary, George Canning, the destruction caused by the War for Independence:

> Commanding officers of Spanish and Revolutionary armies were ready to despoil the wealth [of Peru]; there were some confiscations with frivolous purposes, and church ornaments were stolen to pay for troop expenses. So the wealth of Peru disappeared progressively; part of it was absorbed by Spain, part went to England, and the remaining part was distributed between payment of naval armaments, and for troops from Buenos Aires, Chile and Colombia which joined to help Peru in its fight for freedom.[59]

CHAPTER FIVE

VICEROYALTY OF NEW SPAIN, 1810–29

> [a] hydra reborn as fast as one cuts off its head.
> —Spanish Brigadier Félix Calleja, 1811

THE SPARK

About eight o'clock in the morning on September 16, 1810, Father Miguel Hidalgo[1] exhorted a crowd of some 600 men who had come for Mass at the hamlet of Dolores where he was the curate to join him in rebellion; most did. This event, known as the *Grito de Dolores* (the Cry of Dolores), began the eleven years war for Mexican independence.

BACKGROUND

According to Alexander von Humboldt, the population of Mexico in 1803 was at least 5.8 million persons. Of these individuals, 3 million were *mestizos*; more than 2.5 million were Indians; 112,000 were *criollos*; and, 80,000 were *peninsulares*.[2]

Those few *peninsulares* and *criollos* in Mexico (or New Spain, as it was then called) who were politically empowered reacted to Napoleon Bonaparte's seizure of the Spanish King in 1808. The *peninsulares* sought to preserve the King's empire and their privileges. Many *criollos* wanted to increase their privileges. Within this second group was a small element, some of whom had been significantly influenced by the Enlightenment, and who first sought home rule and eventually independence. The masses had no political voice or goal.

The *peninsulares* and mainstream *criollos* struggled for control of Mexico, each ostensibly in the name of the imprisoned King. On September 15, 1808, 300 armed *peninsulares* seized the opportunistic Viceroy of New Spain, José Iturrigaray, in order to forestall a threat from Iturrigaray and the *criollos*. They replaced him with the eighty-year-old marshal (*mariscal de campo*) Pedro de Garibay.

Over the next two years, the *peninsulares* controlled the office of viceroy and the two groups clashed verbally and, on occasion, with arms. Intrigue abounded. In December 1809 the captain of the Valladolid militia, José María Obeso, and a Franciscan, Fray Vicente de Santa María, conspired to revolt against the *peninsulares* but were betrayed. Elsewhere, Father Miguel Hidalgo and the more liberal *criollos* made their own plans to rebel.[3]

OPPOSING FORCES

While the *peninsulares* and mainstream *criollos* wrestled over who was to be the King's representative in Mexico, a small group of Liberal *criollos* plotted to establish home rule. Professed allegiance to a king, who in 1810 appeared to have little chance of regaining his throne, gave the liberal-*criollo* plot respectability and broadened its appeal while a seemingly powerless monarch could not prejudice their actions. At this time most of those involved in the plot sought home rule and had no thought of declaring an independent nation.[4]

Lacking confidence in their ability to field a *criollo* army in a timely manner, the rebels planned to raise a peasant army. These *criollos* chose Father Hidalgo as the spokesman for their cause because of his popularity among the poor. The number of peasant Indians available to the Revolutionaries was limited only by logistics. They were armed with clubs and homemade edged weapons. The liberal *criollos* did not appreciate the peasants' ignorance of the martial arts. Apparently, many of the Indian peasants were so naive that they believed that a mere sombrero placed over the muzzle of a cannon would prevent its firing.[5]

Opposing Hidalgo and the liberal *criollos* were the *peninsulares* and overwhelming majority of the *criollos*, who were conservative. They perceived that the Hidalgo-led revolt was a class struggle so they presented a united front against it. The Royalist military, loyal to the King, in theory numbered some 33,000 men in 1810 and compared to its opponent was well armed. Less than one-third of the military units were regulars, the remainder militia.[6] In reality, the royal colonial army was a hollow force. In 1831 Hipólito Villarroel wrote concerning that army: "Without exaggeration, the King has more officers than privates; it being evident that most of the former purchased their places to mock justice, to escape paying their debts, to indulge in gaming and live a life of libertinage under the protection of their epaulettes."[7]

The Royalist army was scattered throughout the viceroyalty and unprepared for a major class struggle. The only projected enemies were Europeans invading Vera Cruz, North Americans attacking the north, and the unassimilated Indian tribes. Hurriedly, a Royalist army (the "Army of the Center") commanded by *peninsular* Félix Calleja[8] gathered at San Luis Potosí. With the exception of a few senior officers, there were no Spanish soldiers in New Spain in 1810. The rank and file of the royal army were colonials, or Mexicans. The officers were *criollos* and the enlisted were *mestizos* and *mulattos*. Indians were exempted from military service. Numbering some 5,500 men, the army's second in command was the *criollo* Manuel de Flon.[9]

OPENING STRATEGY

Hidalgo believed that he could use the Indian masses to overthrow the *peninsulares* and drive them from Mexico. His strategy was to establish local *juntas* in the name of Ferdinand VII in the principal towns that he captured to undermine the authority of the *peninsulares*.

The conspirators planned to proclaim their rebellion at the San Juan de los Lagos annual fair, which was to be held December 1–15, 1810. Given Father Hidalgo's oratory skills, it was perceived to be an easy matter for the priest to incite the pilgrims to seize the Spanish merchants and their goods and ignite a religious crusade.[10]

Apparently influenced by their capability to manufacture arms, the liberal *criollos*' confidence in their ability to raise a peasant army increased prior to the fair. Therefore, the conspirators moved the date of the rebellion up to October 2. Two events occurred in August and September that caused the conspirators to expedite their plans. First, rumors were spreading concerning the plot. This is not surprising considering the increasing number of people who were becoming involved. Second, on September 11 a new viceroy took charge of Mexico. Francisco Javier de Venegas was a career soldier who had distinguished himself in the Peninsular Campaign against Napoleon's armies. This honest and hard-working officer replaced the inept pawn of the *peninsulares*.[11]

GRITO DE DOLORES

At two o'clock in the morning on September 16, Father Hidalgo and other conspirators, who happened to be visiting him at Dolores (275 mi NW of Mexico City), were awakened with the news that they were betrayed. Among those present was Ignacio Allende,[12] the senior military person involved in the conspiracy. The leaders decided to rebel immediately. At morning Mass Father Hidalgo exhorted a crowd to follow him in rebellion and these converts were armed. The local prison was emptied and used to house captured *peninsulares*.[13]

The insurgents advanced south through the hamlet of Atotonilco where Hidalgo adopted the banner bearing the image of the Virgin of Guadalupe, the dark-skinned patron saint of the Indian, as a Revolutionary symbol. They reached San Miguel at dusk and easily captured the town. During the night the first acts of violence were committed against *peninsulares*. However, Allende, a resident of the town, was able to restore order by threatening prompt retribution against his followers. Hidalgo marched against the wealthy town of Celaya (180 mi NW of Mexico City). Here, Hidalgo threatened to execute his captive *peninsulares* should the town not surrender. This and his large following persuaded the leaders of Celaya not to resist. The rebel force, more akin to a mob than an army, entered the town on September 21 and pillaged it. Hidalgo now attempted to organize his army which had grown to 25,000 men and women. According to a Royalist agent, the rebel army was composed of 9,000 Indians armed with bows and arrows, slings and clubs; 4,000 Indians possessing lances and machetes; and 12,000 mounted men including some from the Queen's Cavalry Regiment who had followed their commander, Allende, into rebellion. The rebel army included less than 1,000 regulars. At this time Hidalgo was proclaimed the "Captain-General of America."[14]

THE SACKING OF GUANAJUATO

On September 23 the rebel army turned west and then north. Its objective was the rich mining center of Guanajuato (250 mi NW of Mexico City), which was at that time the third-largest city in Spanish America with a population of some 60,000 (only Mexico City and Havana, Cuba, were larger). The local Intendant chose to resist. He gathered the *peninsulares*, the treasury, and royal supporters in the fortress-like public granary. On the twenty-eighth the rebels stormed the granary. The fighting raged for five hours; some 300 defenders and 2,000 attackers died. The rebels massacred most of the survivors and sacked the city.[15]

Hidalgo dedicated much of the next week to organizing a rebel government at Guanajuato. To his growing army Hidalgo now added many miners and domestic workers. Hidalgo and Allende split their growing force and within a few weeks they captured Zacatecas and Valladolid (now Morelia). These early successes and the size of the rebel horde, which now numbered some 80,000 persons, encouraged the rebel leaders to move directly against the viceregal capital, Mexico City.[16]

Elsewhere, the Royalists were collecting themselves. The viceroy ordered General Calleja to march with all dispatch to the protection of the capital. A price of 10,000 pesos was placed on the heads of the rebel leaders. The tribute paid by the lower classes was abolished in an attempt to hold their loyalty. The government's printing press began a propaganda campaign and church authorities attempted to demonize the insurrectionists. In spite of the government's activities, new recruits flocked to Hidalgo's banner. By October 29 the rebel army passed through Toluca (40 mi W of Mexico City) without stopping. The only obstacles between Hidalgo's army and Mexico City were a range of low mountains and some 7,000 Royalist troops under Spanish Lt. Col. Torcuato Trujillo.[17]

BATTLE OF MONTE DE LAS CRUCES

Colonel Trujillo chose to block Hidalgo's advance in the mountain pass near Monte de las Cruces (a place where bandits were crucified). There at the narrows the two armies fought from 8:00 in the morning until 5:30 in the afternoon on October 30. The disciplined soldiers supported by well-served artillery held the high ground against an opponent twenty times their number. Although Trujillo's force was badly mauled losing 2,500 men dead and wounded, it was able toward nightfall to fight its way out of an encirclement and retreat toward Mexico City. The army's reception was less than enthusiastic, and the Viceroy seriously considered fleeing to Vera Cruz.[18]

Hidalgo sustained some 2,000 killed, and many more were wounded. More importantly, large numbers deserted the cause. Some 40,000 followers faded away. The rebel army was demoralized by this encounter with disciplined troops. The following day Hidalgo led his battered army over the mountains toward the capital as far as Cuajimalpa. There the army lingered for three days as the rebel leaders quarreled over their next move. Allende argued that the march on the capital should be continued. Hidalgo sent out agents to recruit new followers from the local villages but they were without success. The Viceroy ignored Hidalgo's call to surrender while a royal army led by Calleja rushed to rescue the capital. The cumulative weight of these factors probably caused Hidalgo to turn away from Mexico City.[19]

BATTLE OF ACULCO

On November 3 the rebel army, now 40,000 men, moved northwest and captured Guadalajara (424 mi WNW of Mexico City) without opposition and then marched toward Querétaro. Four days later the rebel army and 15,000 Royalists, ignorant of the other's approach, fought a meeting engagement (both armies on the move) at Aculco. The rebels had enough time to take up a defensive position on a hill. Calleja attacked. Realizing the poor morale of their army, Hidalgo and Allende sacrificed their train (baggage and livestock) and artillery in a vain attempt to prevent a general engagement. However, their retreat rapidly disintegrated into a rout. Hundreds of rebels were captured and thousands more deserted; Calleja shot the prisoners. The Royalists lost only one man killed and another wounded.[20]

Hidalgo and Allende quarreled and split the rebel army. Hidalgo marched to Valladolid to reorganize and recruit new followers; however, he remained for only a few days before returning to Guadalajara. Allende marched back to Guanajuato where he hoped to create a stronghold and manufacture cannons and munitions, but on November 24 he was driven out by the approaching Calleja. Both sides executed hundreds as these towns changed hands.[21]

By the time Hidalgo reached Guadalajara, his army was reduced to 7,000 men. However, he was heartened by rebel successes in the west under Father José María Mercado and in the south under Father José María Morelos. Also, Calleja moved cautiously awaiting reinforcements. Here at Guadalajara, Hidalgo was busy rebuilding his army and giving form to the rebel government. On December 9 Allende arrived from Guanajuato.

By the thirtieth a Royalist spy estimated the rebel army to number 36,000 men—6,000 cavalry armed with lances, 5,000 archers, and 25,000 peasants armed with lances, clubs, and slings. Of this huge army the spy estimated that only 200 formerly served in the militia and that the rebels had only 600 muskets. The rebels developed steel-tipped rockets, probably derived from the type used at church celebrations, in an attempt to compensate for their lack of fire power. The rebels managed to gather 122 cannon, most of which were small caliber and poorly manufactured.[22]

By January 1811 the Royalists were advancing on Guadalajara from two quarters. José de la Cruz was closing from Querétaro with 2,000 veterans, and Calleja was moving from León with 6,000 well-disciplined troops, half of which were cavalry, and ten professionally served field pieces. The rebels held a council of war which aggravated the deep division between Hidalgo and Allende. Hidalgo wanted to risk everything on a single battle; he argued that only by preserving the army's unity and defending Guadalajara could its morale be maintained. Allende wished to divide the massive army into six or more parts and commit it piecemeal; he argued that it was too poorly disciplined to be employed in a single mass. Hidalgo prevailed and in mid-January 1811 he led his army of some 80,000 followers, which included 20,000 horsemen and 95 cannons, out of Guadalajara to battle. Only 1,000 Revolutionaries were well armed and properly trained.[23]

BATTLE OF CALDERÓN

On January 17, 1811, the two armies met some twenty miles from Guadalajara. The mammoth Revolutionary army was arrayed advantageously on hilltops; Calleja attacked without waiting for Cruz. The battle raged undecided until a cannon shot hit a rebel ammunition wagon. The resulting explosion ignited a grass fire that a strong wind drove upon the rebels. The horde panicked and the rebel army disintegrated. More than 1,000 Revolutionaries were killed during the ensuing rout and all of their artillery and train was captured. Hidalgo, Allende, and other rebel leaders escaped. The Royalists lost 49 killed, 134 wounded, and 10 missing. Among their dead was Flon, who was cut down while leading a charge on the rebel artillery.[24]

Calleja appreciated that he had inadequate forces to confront each and every uprising. Hence, he adopted a policy of brutality to intimidate would-be Revolutionaries. Exemplary punishment included summary executions. Villages were also burned to the ground.[25]

Although the Revolutionary cause still flourished to the north and in the south, Hidalgo's force had represented the heart of the rebellion. Its destruction left the tentacles to slowly wither. The Revolutionary leadership retreated northward toward the United States, but this was ended by treason, prison, and execution for Hidalgo, Allende, and others by mid-1811. Ignacio López Rayón[26] took charge of the remainder of Hidalgo's army, although few of the surviving rebel leaders were willing to acknowledge him as their chief. The first phase of the war, which was fought primarily in central Mexico and northward into Sinaloa and Texas, ended badly for the Revolutionaries. In spite of his military failures, Miguel Hidalgo is justly honored as being the father of Mexican independence.[27]

MORELOS IN COMMAND

The mantel of rebel leadership now evolved upon José María Morelos.[28] Morelos and Hidalgo had shared common experiences. Both were members of the clergy, both had studied at San Nicolás College in Valladolid where their paths had crossed, and both had developed a close relationship with the lower classes. However, in more respects they were dissimilar. Morelos was a mestizo and not a *criollo*. He did have a university degree but did not possess Hidalgo's intellectual background. Morelos had spent eleven years working among the indigenous people. Morelos had sought out Hidalgo as he marched from Valladolid and on October 20, 1810, the two men had a two-hour interview. Morelos chose to join the rebellion and Hidalgo commissioned him as *lugar-teniente* (a person who exercises political and military power in lieu of the individual granting the authority) and directed him to spread the revolution to the west coast.[29]

SIEGE OF ACAPULCO

On November 12, 1810, Morelos and approximately twenty followers armed with less than a dozen old firearms set out for the rich port city and Spanish stronghold of Acapulco (284 mi S of Mexico City).[30] By December 12 Morelos' army, which had grown on the march to 2,000 men and several cannons, occupied Aguacatillo, on the outskirts of Acapulco, and besieged the port. Here, Morelos issued a decree outlawing slavery and caste distinctions.

On January 4, 1811, some 1,000 Revolutionaries defeated 3,000 Royalists at Tres Palos, outside Acapulco. The Royalists lost 400 men and 700 prisoners plus 700 muskets. The Revolutionaries lost 200 killed.[31]

A month later, on February 7, Morelos tried to take the port through trickery. At four in the morning the rebels advanced on the fortress after sighting a prearranged signal from a royal artillery officer who had agreed to change sides. As they neared they were suddenly greeted by heavy artillery fire from the fort and the warships in the harbor. Morelos fell back to Las Iguanas and renewed the siege. For nine days he bombarded the enemy; however, on the nineteenth the Royalists attacked from the fort and captured most of his artillery.[32]

Unable to continue the attack against Acapulco, Morelos abandoned the siege and marched north, winning a series of battles. Morelos entered Chilapa on August 18, where he remained for three months. During these months Morelos rebuilt an army of some two to three thousand and attracted many who would become Mexico's future Liberal leaders.[33]

Morelos believed the most effective force to be a small, disciplined army. Promotion should be based on performance and merit. Officers lacking in courage or leadership were to be dismissed. Morelos prescribed the death penalty for anyone found guilty of insubordination, cowardice, treason, "or any disturbance which is opposed to the law of God, the peace of the Kingdom, and the progress of our arms."[34]

Beginning in 1811 Calleja attempted to create a tiered defensive system. Towns, cities, and provinces were to raise their own militias for self-defense, thus freeing the royal army from garrison duty and allowing it to take the offensive against the largest of the rebel forces. No one outside military service was allowed to possess firearms. Only wealthier communities could comply.[35]

MORELOS' SECOND CAMPAIGN

In mid-November 1811 Morelos began his second campaign. His immediate goal was to distract enemy forces that were threatening Zitácuaro and ultimately to encircle and isolate Mexico City and Puebla. On December 4 he defeated Royalist forces under Mateo Musitú at Chiaulta (180 mi SSE of Mexico City). Musitú was captured and executed; this was the fate of important prisoners taken by either side. Lesser Royalist prisoners were imprisoned in Zacatula where the heat and heavy labor usually caused the same fate.[36]

Morelos now divided his force into three columns. Miguel Bravo marched south against Ometepec. Hermenegildo Galeana moved west against Taxco, and Morelos pushed north threatening Izúcar and the road to Puebla. Taxco and Izúcar were taken. Morelos then captured Cuautla Amilpas (65 mi SSE of Mexico City) on Christmas Day. Although the way to Puebla, the stronghold of conservatism, seemed open, for unknown reasons Morelos turned west and joined Galeana in Taxco.[37]

During January 1812 Morelos drove the Royalists under Rosendo Porlier back to Toluca and then retired to Cuautla Amilpas. Here he reunited his forces, now numbering about 3,000 men; they included a number of well-disciplined units. Once again he planned to attack Puebla and threatened the capital. Alarmed, Viceroy Venegas ordered Calleja's army to attack the rebels in the south.

THE DESTRUCTION OF ZITÁCUARO

Calleja, commanding 5,000 men, advanced against Zitácuaro (100 mi SW of Mexico City) where the Revolutionary *junta* met. Finally on January 2, 1812, Calleja captured and methodically destroyed Zitácuaro and eleven nearby Indian villages. Calleja lost 2,000 men and the Revolutionaries some 7,000. Next, he returned to Mexico City to a hero's welcome. However, jealousy had developed between the General and the Viceroy and within a few days Calleja was on the march to fight Morelos at Cuautla Amilpas. The pending clash was apparent to both sides, so each called in all the reinforcements he could find. Calleja wrote to the Viceroy, "with the fate of Cuautla [Amilpas] will be decided the fate of this kingdom."[38]

SIEGE OF CUAUTLA AMILPAS

Cuautla Amilpas was a good defensible position. Thick groves of trees grew to the edge of the town. A road ran north and south through the town connecting the convents of San Diego and Santo Domingo. A thick wall existed along most of the west side of the town and a broad, swift river flowed along the east side. Morelos linked the strong points with a system of trenches. The Royalists numbered about 9,000 men and the rebels 3,300 men (1,000 infantry and 2,300 cavalry). Each side had about 25 cannon of various calibre.[39]

Calleja tried to take the town by assault on February 19, 1812, but due to the bravery and leadership of Hermenegildo Galeana was repulsed with heavy losses. The Royalists now laid siege. On March 1 Brigadier Ciriaco de Llano arrived with 1,500 reinforcements (the "Army of the South") but he brought few supplies, little ammunition, and no money. On March 10 the Royalists began a vigorous bombardment which lasted for four days but had little effect on the spirit of the defenders. The Royalists also attempted to cut off the town's water supply by diverting the river, but this also failed. The siege became a test of endurance. The Revolutionaries were threatened by diminishing provisions while the Royalists were afflicted by dysentery and endemic fever. During March, the Revolutionaries still had bread, corn, and beans, although meat was scarce. By the middle of April only corn remained. Henry G. Ward wrote, "a cat sold for six dollars, a lizard for two, and rats for one."[40] By late April, twenty-five to thirty people a day were dying from starvation. Calleja wrote, "if the devotion and activity of the defenders of Cuautla [Amilpas] were with morality and directed to a just cause, they would merit some day a distinguished place in history."[41] On the other side, heavy rains tormented the besiegers and turned their campsite into a swamp and made their artillery unserviceable. The Royalists went unpaid, further undermining morale. However, the advantage lay with the besieger, for only he could receive outside help and only he could disengage without risking battle.⁴²

As Calleja was writing to the Viceroy declaring that he must break off the siege because of his failing health, Morelos felt compelled to break out. At two in the morning on May 2, 1812, after enduring seventy-two days of siege, the rebel army and townspeople assembled in the plaza and began the march north. Galeana led the advanced guard of a thousand infantry. Morelos and the Bravo brothers commanded 250 cavalry, a body of troops armed with slings and lances, and the townspeople. Arzures commanded the rear composed of infantry and artillery. The Royalists guarding the road north were overpowered and the columns marched north, their departure going undetected for two hours. Finally aware of what had transpired, the Royalist cavalry fell on the exposed flank of the rebels, slowing the enemy and allowing Calleja's infantry to catch up. Resistance was hopeless, so Morelos gave the order to disperse and rendezvous at Izúcar. A melée followed and the Royalists killed perhaps 3,000 individuals, many being townspeople—men, women, and children. The rebels lost their artillery, their archives, and Leonardo Bravo, who was captured and later executed. Morelos, thanks to the sacrifices of almost his entire personal guard, escaped with two crushed ribs; also the Revolutionary army escaped total destruction. The Royalists had spent almost two million pesos but had neither captured Morelos nor destroyed his army. Although Cuautla Amilpas was a defeat for the rebels, it was not the decisive victory sought by the Royalists.⁴³

CAPTURE OF OAXACA

During the next six months the rebels regained some of the countryside they had lost during the siege of Cuautla Amilpas. In early October 1812 Morelos gathered the elements of his army, 5,000 men and 40 cannons, and secretly planned to attack Oaxaca (342 mi SE of Mexico City), a provincial capital and the most important city in the south. He caught by surprise 2,000 Royalists possessing 36 guns and they offered a feeble resistance. Morelos entered the city on October 25. The Bishop of Oaxaca fled with the approach of the rebels. The rebels, long starved for a victory and having captured the city of one of their most outspoken opponents, sacked Oaxaca and executed numerous prisoners. The victory at Oaxaca confirmed Morelos as the foremost rebel leader. Also, he captured 1,000 muskets, 60 cannon, and 3 million pesos' worth of bounty which allowed him to rebuild his army and attend to civil affairs such as organizing a government. These matters occupied Morelos for the next few months.⁴⁴

On March 4, 1813, Calleja replaced Venegas as viceroy. Spanish merchants had influenced the removal of Venegas because they believed he had been ineffective. Calleja immediately sought to improve his financial position by extracting loans from merchants and by creating new taxes so that he could afford to refit the army. He also paid special attention to improving the collection of clandestine intelligence. Calleja dissolved the Army of the Center and created smaller elements which he placed in charge of Spanish officers; these were sent to seek out and destroy the larger rebel bands. He immediately conscripted and armed much of the male *criollo* population and incorporated them into the militia to protect the major population centers.⁴⁵

SECOND SIEGE OF ACAPULCO

Morelos next chose to attack Acapulco, his original commission from Hidalgo. He wanted to deprive the Royalists of this important seaport and gain a site through which he might conduct foreign affairs.⁴⁶ His 1,500-man army arrived in April 1813. Subordinates were dispatched to complete the subjugation of the surrounding countryside. By August the Royalists were confined to fortress "San Diego" on the east side of the harbor. On August 16 Morelos began a heavy bombardment in preparation of a direct assault. Four days later the Royalists chose to surrender rather than face the attack. Morelos was now the master of most of southern Mexico except for the cities of Mexico City, Puebla, and Vera Cruz. However, the siege had cost seven months during which time the Royalists regained control over much of central and northern Mexico.[47]

Morelos turned to civil affairs. He called for a national congress to meet at Chilpancingo in September. On September 15 that body named Morelos *Generalísimo* (the commander of the army) and on November 6 it declared independence. While Morelos was attending to civil matters and successfully besieging Acapulco, the Royalists were reforming their military structure.[48]

Morelos chose not to unify his forces but rather to pressure the capital from numerous directions. Rayón commanded the force in the east; minor chiefs such as "El Manco" ("the one handed") Albino García commanded those in the northwest; and Morelos commanded those in the south. The rebels won many minor skirmishes in the rural areas.[49]

DEFEAT AT VALLADOLID

Once again Morelos called together scattered elements, uniting those commanded by Nicolás Bravo, Hermenegildo Galeana, and Mariano Matamoros with his own. On November 7 Morelos marched north in command of his largest force, more than 6,000 men and 30 cannon, to attack the city of Valladolid (228 mi W of Mexico City), the wealthy capital of Michoacán. To the north lay territory dominated by the Royalists and to the south that controlled by the rebels. The 800-man garrison refused to surrender; so, as threatened, Morelos attacked on December 23. As the battle raged, 3,000 Royalists commanded by Gen. Ciriaco Llano arrived and drove the rebels from the city's gates. The Viceroy had guessed Morelos' intentions. Stunned by this turn of events, Morelos placed Mariano Matamoros in command of a night assault. Apparently, Morelos' order for the attackers to blacken their faces so that they would not be mistaken for the enemy was intercepted. Accordingly, several hundred Royalists led by Col. Agustin de Iturbide, second in command of the Royalist forces, blackened their faces and attacked the rebels. Pandemonium broke out in the rebel ranks and Morelos sustained a major defeat.[50]

BATTLE OF PURUARÁN

Morelos retreated a short distance; in spite of the advice of his subordinates, he chose to make a stand. On January 5, 1814, 3,000 Royalists with 23 cannon attacked at Puruarán with its artillery controlling the outcome. The fleeing rebels were driven into a river and cut down by the hundreds. The rebels lost 600 dead and 700 captured. Morelos continued his retreat and the rebel cause began to fall apart. The Congress was then forced to flee Chilpancingo as the Royalists approached, running from place to place never finding a safe haven. Morelos in disgrace was forced to surrender his executive power and retained only the empty title of *Generalissimo*. Morelos was captured by Iturbide on November 5, 1815, near Tesalaca while escorting Congress through enemy territory to Tehuacán. He was executed on December 22. Morelos had tried to give the Revolutionary forces discipline, which had eluded Hidalgo.[51]

DEFEAT IN THE NORTH

In March 1811 Bernardo Gutiérrez had been sent to Washington by Hidalgo to obtain recognition and help. Failing, Gutiérrez went to New Orleans and recruited 450 men and crossed into Texas. Through some hard fighting he won control of Nuevo León and Texas. Alvarez de Toledo, who had been appointed to succeed Gutiérrez in Washington, betrayed his compatriot to the Spanish minister to the United States. The insurgents were defeated at San Antonio de Bejar (now San Antonio, Texas) on March 15, 1814.[52]

FERDINAND VII IS RESTORED

Far away in Spain, Napoleon's forces were defeated at Victoria and Salamanca. In March 1814 the liberated Ferdinand VII recrossed the Pyrennes and successfully reestablished absolute rule in Spain and attempted to regain control over the rebellious colonies.[53]

GUERRILLA WARFARE

Morelos' death had ended the second phase of the war during which the Revolutionaries had won and then had lost practically all of Mexico south of Mexico City. By now 80,000 Royalists (mostly *criollo* militia) were under arms. Lesser Revolutionary leaders, scattered throughout Mexico, continued the struggle. The most competent were Vicente Guerrero,[54] who had 1,000 men in Oaxaca, and Guadalupe Victoria,[55] who commanded 2,000 men scattered between Puebla and Vera Cruz. Although they were not strong enough to directly confront the Royalist army, the rebels did seriously disrupt economic life and civil order, particularly in the rural regions. Other rebels resorted to banditry. They fortified themselves in mountain strongholds and preyed on locals and passing convoys. The years between 1814 and 1821 were bleak for the Mexican insurgents. Although a number of Hidalgo's and Morelos' lieutenants remained in the field, none rose to the stature of their mentors.[56]

The Royalist army created *estacamentos volantes* (flying detachments) to hunt down the highly mobile bands of insurgents. They summarily executed suspected insurgents and torched towns that sympathized with the rebels.[57]

THE MINA EXPEDITION

In 1817 the Royalists in New Spain were attacked by a Revolutionary from an unexpected quarter. Francisco Javier Mina,[58] who had championed constitutional reform in Spain, recruited some 300 men during his trek from Liverpool to Norfolk, Baltimore, Saint Thomas, Port-au-Prince, Galveston, and finally New Orleans. On April 15, 1817, Mina captured Soto la Marina (650 mi NNE of Mexico City) on the Gulf of Mexico. Mina was aided in the invasion by Commodore Luis d'Aury, a French sailor of fortune who held a rebel commission as "governor of Texas."

The invasion alarmed the government in Mexico City, for if not dealt with swiftly and successfully, it might serve as an example for others in the United States. The Royalists dispatched the Spanish frigate *Sabina* (40 guns) and two armed tenders from Vera Cruz in mid-May. They sank two of Mina's ships and drove the third off. In the meantime, Mina, leaving 100 men to guard Soto la Marina, marched for Guanajuato where he believed the Revolutionary activities to be centered. En route, commanding 300 followers, Mina defeated a 2,000-man Royalist force at Armiñán on June 15 through reckless abandonment. Finally the Royalists tracked Mina down and captured him at the ranch of El Venadito on October 27. He was shot at Los Remedios on November 11, 1817.[59]

BACK IN SPAIN

Events in Spain began the third phase of the war for independence, sometimes called the "National War" (*La Guerra Nacional*). On January 1, 1820, Rafael Riego, commander of a battalion of Asturian soldiers stationed at Cadiz, proclaimed for the liberal constitution of 1812. Thus, the *Gran Expedición*, which had been preparing since 1818 to strike a decisive blow against the Revolutionaries in Spanish America, was thwarted. The revolt rapidly spread throughout Spain and on March 7, 1820, Ferdinand VII reluctantly stated that he supported the organic law. In the Americas pardon was offered to the rebels and by April thousands in Mexico had accepted. Vicente Guerrero, however, was not among them. In order to bring Guerrero to terms, the Viceroy recalled retired colonel Agustín de Iturbide[60] and promoted him to brigadier.[61]

THE PLAN OF IGUALA

In late November 1820 Iturbide led 2,500 men southward from Mexico City. Iturbide's campaign against the insurgents was indecisive at best. Instead of vigorously pursuing the enemy, he subtly sought support among influential *criollos* concerning the prospects of his declaring independence while at the same time he was writing to the Viceroy that operations were proceeding well. On February 16, 1821, Iturbide wrote to the Viceroy that Guerrero had placed himself and his 1,200 men under his orders. Adding that negotiations were not complete, he painted a rosy picture. In fact, Iturbide had written to Guerrero on January 10 outlining a plan for independence under one of the members of the Spanish royal family. Guerrero replied, independence or death, but agreed to talk.

On February 24 Iturbide and Guerrero issued the Plan of Iguala. A unique feature of the plan was that it praised the Spaniards for their contributions to Mexico. The plan successfully preserved the privileges of the upper class. Mexico was to become an independent kingdom with Ferdinand VII or some other European prince as a constitutional monarch; the Catholic Church was to keep its privileges; the *peninsulares* and *criollos* were to be equal. In order to guarantee the success of the plan, the formerly hostile forces were forged into the Army of the Three Guarantees (*Ejército de las Tres Garantes*) with Iturbide as its commander.[62]

On March 3, 1821 the Viceroy denounced Iturbide. To help assure that his plan would succeed, Iturbide seized a convoy of silver valued at 525,000 pesos, which was being carried from Mexico City to Acapulco to pay for the cargo of a galleon which had recently arrived from Manila.[63]

In March 1821 Iturbide had perhaps 1,800 men under his command, including those of Guerrero. The Viceroy had about 6,000 loyal troops stationed in the vicinity of the capital but he procrastinated. Initially, the two sides conducted an intense propaganda campaign. Unit after unit, city after city, and province after province declared for the plan. Although some blood was spilled at numerous sites, it was more peaceful than violent.[64]

Iturbide marched against Valladolid. On May 12 he called for the city to surrender. This was initially rejected. After the Army of the Three Guarantees breached the defenses on the same day, the Royalists surrendered and were given generous terms. Unlike his earlier campaigns, Iturbide was humane to his enemy. He next marched against Guanajunto. From Acámbaro he marched to San Juan del Río, key to Querétaro, which surrendered in June. The Royalist garrison at Querétaro, significantly reduced by desertion, surrendered on June 28. Once again, terms were generous. They were to embark for Havana as soon as possible.[65]

Meanwhile, Viceroy Venadito gathered his resources to defend the capital. On June 1 he called for all able-bodied males between seventeen and forty to join the army. On July 5 a revolt in the capital forced the Viceroy to surrender his authority to Marshal Francisco Novella. By early August, the Army of the Three Guarantees controlled all of Mexico except Acapulco, Mexico City, Fort San Carlos at Perote, Vera Cruz, and the Castle of San Juan de Ulúa. Iturbide in large measure won the day through a policy of conciliation and generosity.[66]

Puebla (80 mi E of Mexico City) was besieged by José Joaquin de Herrera and Nicolás Bravo, who had recently been released from the Vera Cruz dungeon. A relief column from Mexico City and a sortie from the besieged city failed to raise the siege. Puebla surrendered on August 2.[67]

On July 30, 1821, Juan O'Donojú, the recently appointed Captain-General of New Spain and Superior Chief Political Marshal, landed at Vera Cruz (285 mi E of Mexico City). The port was besieged by Iturbide's followers, and members of O'Donojú's family and escort began dying from yellow fever. Also, Novella refused to recognize O'Donojú's authority and O'Donojú had no forces at his disposal. While the Army of the Three Guarantees neared Mexico City, O'Donojú and Iturbide met on August 24 at Córdoba. They signed the Treaty of Córdoba which slightly modified the Plan of Iguala. Mexico should be independent and a constitutional monarchy. On September 13, Iturbide, O'Donojú, and Novella met at the Hacienda of Patera near the Shrine of Guadalupe. On September 27 the 16,000-man Army of the Three Guarantees marched into Mexico City. Only Vera Cruz and its harbor's castle, San Juan de Ulúa, remained in the hands of the Royalists. The "Act of the Independence of the Mexican Empire" was signed the next day by the *criollos* and *peninsular* members of the *Junta*.[68]

THE AFTERSHOCK

The decade of the 1820s was chaotic. Iturbide made himself Emperor Agustín I, but his rivals deposed him in 1823 and shot him the next year when he tried to return from exile. Although a republic had been created, Ferdinand VII dreamed of reconquering his former colony. Mexican officials, absorbed in their domestic problems, paid little attention to Spanish preparations to invade.[69]

On July 6, 1829, a substantial, but poorly outfitted, invasion force sailed from Cuba. Rear Adm. Ángel Laborde commanded a small fleet carrying some 3,000 troops. One transport wrecked in a heavy storm off Louisiana. On July 16, in the heat of summer, 2,600 Spanish troops commanded by Brigadier Isidro Barradas landed at Cabo Rojo some 60 miles south of Tampico (452 mi NE of Mexico City). The fleet immediately returned to Cuba as ordered. The troops marched into the port on August 6 expecting a friendly reception and supplies; instead, they got yellow fever.[70]

The opportunistic Gen. Antonio López de Santa Anna, governor of Vera Cruz, seized the moment. Anticipating the invasion, he gathered 2,000 troops and supplies at Vera Cruz. Once Santa Anna learned that the Spanish had landed, he extracted a forced loan of 20,000 pesos from the merchants, chartered some ten ships, and embarked his 1,000 infantry. He sailed north without any warships for escort, brashly ignoring the possibility that the Spanish fleet might be patrolling the coast. Santa Anna ignored the fact that he required congressional approval to take his troops into another state. He also ordered 1,000 cavalrymen north by land.[71]

While Santa Anna was sailing north, Barradas had moved 2,000 men north of Tampico, seeking healthier ground. Santa Anna landed at Tuxpán, 90 miles south of Tampico, in early August. On August 12 Santa Anna sent his cavalry by land and his infantry and artillery in canoes across Tamiahua Lagoon and by August 16 the force reunited below Tampico. On August 21 Santa Anna attacked the 600 Spaniards south of the port. At 2 P.M. the Spaniards asked for a truce. While these talks were going on, General Barradas returned with 2,000 Spanish soldiers who had been sent north of the city. Although Santa Anna and his staff were in an awkward position, Barradas honored the truce and permitted them to withdraw.[72]

Meanwhile, Mexican Gen. Manuel Mier y Terán was methodically assembling other Mexican troops at Altamira, some 20 miles north of Tampico. On September 7 Mier's force of 1,000 regulars, 1,000 militia, and 3 cannons joined that of Santa Anna. Time was on the side of the Mexicans, who grew stronger as the Spaniards grew weaker. However, Santa Anna would not be denied his glory and insisted that the Spanish be attacked. Late in the afternoon on September 10, the combined forces of Santa Anna and Mier y Terán attacked and the fighting continued into the night. By now the Spanish had lost 908 men (including to disease) and the Mexicans 135 dead and 151 wounded. Santa Anna permitted the Spaniards to surrender the next day. They were allowed to withdraw from Mexico after surrendering their weapons and supplies. Only 1,792 Spaniards were left to sail for Cuba. Santa Anna emerged as a war hero. He would deviously manipulate Mexican politics for most of the next twenty-five years.[73]

Matters did not end here. In retaliation against Spain, Mexico commissioned Gen. José Ignacio Basadre to recruit blacks in Haiti to infiltrate Cuba and instigate a slave revolt; however, the plan was never acted upon. Also, the army assembled at Jalapa to deal with the Spanish threat was used by Vice-President Anastasio Bustamante to overthrow President Guerrero in December 1829.[74]

OBSERVATIONS

As throughout Spanish South America, the war for independence in Mexico was a struggle between Latin Americans fighting to liberate themselves from colonial rule and Latin Americans, led in many cases by senior Spanish officers, fighting to remain under the rule of Ferdinand VII. Throughout the eleven years of fighting, Spain sent only 9,685 troops to Mexico.[75]

The *criollo*-dominated Royalist army in Mexico became the creator of the nation. As a consequence, the new Mexican army rewarded itself with a superior status within society which was protected by the retention of the colonial *fuero militar* (a separate legal system). Former Royalists dominated the new Mexican army of 1823. The only lieutenant general was Pedro Celestino Negrete, a Spaniard by birth. The Minister of War and Marine was another Spaniard, Antonio Medina. Iturbide created five marshals of which only one, Vicente Guerrero, had been a Revolutionary prior to 1821. He also promoted nine officers to brigadiers, only one of which, Nicolás Bravo, had been a longtime Revolutionary. Of the 188 generals and colonels on the army register in 1840, eighty-one had begun their careers in the Spanish army.[76]

And, in the future, men such as Antonio López de Santa Anna, Valentín Canalizo, José Joaquin de Herrera, Mariano Paredes, Mariano Salas, and Pedro María Anaya, who had fought against Hidalgo and Morelos but pledged their loyalty to Iturbide in 1821 and the Army of the Three Guarantees, would eventually become presidents of Mexico during the 1830s and 1840s, some more than once.[77]

Many of these officers were young, ambitious, and had already demonstrated their willingness to sell their loyalty. Many had risen four ranks within the Army—captains to generals—by changing sides more than once during the war, particularly in its last days.[78]

In addition to the Army, the Church, which retained all of its colonial property and privileges, as well as the landowners, the merchants, and the wealthy middle class, whose property was now more secure than it had been during the colonial era, were also winners. The losers were the Mexican masses and Spain. What little hope for change, the masses had embodied in Hidalgo and Morelos. Following their deaths early in the war no one of sufficient stature remained to champion their cause.[79]

Although similarities existed between the war in Mexico and those in South America, one difference is striking. The war in Mexico was at times closer to a class war than the contests in Spanish South America. In Mexico the overwhelming majority of the *criollos* fought for the King and most of the *mestizos* and Indians who did fight, fought for the Revolutionaries. Many wealthy *criollos* were won over to the independence movement only after the Liberals in Spain had seized power from Ferdinand VII. Others contributed money to both sides in order to protect their interests. Aside from now desiring independence, these *criollos* shared little politically, socially, and economically with their republican countrymen.[80]

The limitations placed upon Ferdinand VII's power by the Spanish rebellion of 1820 caused the Mexican War for Independence to end with the Conservatives in control. As a result, the ultraconservatives intellectually, and, on occasion, militarily, opposed the Liberals for decades and generally dominated. They drew their support from many in the Church, those who had remained loyal to Ferdinand VII (both Spaniards and *criollos*), the Mexican nobility (owners of the vast estates), and the army whose officers were nearly all *criollos* and for the most part belonged to the landed families. An important consequence of the war for independence in Mexico would be the inability of this politically divided nation to defend the territory it claimed through exploration and weak colonization from the United States.[81]

James Smith Wilcocks, the future U.S. consul to Mexico City, wrote to Secretary of State John Quincy Adams on October 25, 1821, describing the devastation caused by the war:

> Before the insurrection of the year 1810, the Kingdom contained six millions of inhabitants . . . the royal revenue exceeding $20,000,000, and the money coined at the mint of this city upwards of $28,000,000 annually; it has, however, ever since been on the decline, in consequence of the devastations committed by both parties in the long and cruel war between the Europeans and Americans, so that the population cannot now be computed at more than four millions, the revenue at more than half of what it was, and the money coined yearly at from $5,000,000 to $8,000,000; this year it will probably not exceed $4,000,000.[82]

Estimates of the number killed range from 250,000 to 500,000 individuals. Additionally, a large number of people fled Mexico.[83]

CHAPTER SIX

BRAZIL, 1822–23

> "Independence or Death"
> The Cry of Ypiranga
> –by Dom Pedro

THE SPARK

On September 7, 1822, Pedro I declared Brazil an independent empire (*grito do Ypiranga*), separating it from Portugal and formally beginning Brazil's war for independence.

BACKGROUND

On November 27, 1807, the Portuguese royal family, escorted by a British squadron, fled the Napoleonic invasion of their country and sailed to Brazil; that colony then became the temporary seat of the Portuguese government. Accompanying or trailing the royal family were some 15,000 court followers and most of the small Portuguese navy (8 ships of the line, 4 frigates, 5 corvettes, and 3 schooners) and marine corps.[1]

Brazil immediately experienced significant social, economic, and political change. It was transformed from a backwater colony to the seat of an empire almost overnight. Brazilian ports were immediately opened to trade with those nations allied with Portugal; Great Britain was the primary beneficiary.

Brazil soon became involved in military adventures. French Guiana was briefly occupied (1808–17), and more significantly the *Banda Oriental* (Uruguay) was added to the empire as the Cisplantine Province in 1821 (see chapter 3).[2]

After years of procrastination, João VI, King of Portugal and Brazil (which had been elevated to equal status with Portugal in 1815), reluctantly sailed back to Europe on April 26, 1821, with 3,000 followers, leaving his son Pedro, the prince regent, in charge. It is speculated that João's parting advice to his son was "Pedro, Brazil will, I fear, ere long separate herself from Portugal; and if so place the crown on thine head, rather than allow it to fall into the hands of any adventurer."[3]

The departure of João VI removed much of the glue that had held Brazil to the Portuguese empire. Many Brazilians held animosities toward the Portuguese. Mercantilism had created a gulf between the two societies. Those who returned to Portugal with João carried off everything they could, including the specie out of the Bank of Brazil.

With the return of the King to Europe, the Portuguese *Côrtes* (legislature) was determined to reduce Brazil back to colonial status and resubjugate it to numerous restrictions. Pedro's presence in Brazil was an obstruction to the *Côrtes'* plan. In September 1821 it unsuccessfully tried to recall Pedro, who at first could not make up his mind whether to go or to stay. Pedro ordered back to Lisbon the Portuguese squadron sent to carry him home; this infuriated the *Côrtes*.[4]

Next, in September 1821 the *Côrtes* attempted to revive an old administrative system which would divide Brazil into captaincies with each directly responsible to Portugal, thus making Pedro's status in Rio de Janeiro irrelevant. Such a bureaucratic change was slow moving and not suited to solving the problem.[5]

On January 9, 1822, Pedro proclaimed, *"Fico"* ("I shall remain"). As a consequence, on January 11, the 2,000-man Portuguese garrison in Rio de Janeiro known as the "Auxiliary Division" occupied the Morro do Castelo which dominated the city. The division had recently returned from fighting in Uruguay. The commanding officer, Lt. Gen. Jorge d' Avilez, wanted to force Pedro to return to Portugal. Soon Avilez realized that his action was opposed by most of the residence in Rio so, finally, his command sailed for Europe on February 15. Shortly after Avilez' departure, reinforcements under Gen. Maximiano de Souza arrived from Portugal and these too were persuaded to return to Europe.[6]

While these events were transpiring, the young prince was being advised by his wife, Leopoldina, an Austrian-born archduchess, and by José Bonifacio de Andreda e Silva, a Brazilian scholar who would become his chief minister, on how to achieve independence. Many Brazilians, particularly those with wealth, were witnessing the decade-long destructive Wars for Independence in Spanish America, and wanted to avoid a similar fate. After a formal declaration of independence on September 7, 1822, the prince became Pedro I, Constitutional Emperor and Perpetual Defender of Brazil.[7]

OPPOSING FORCES

The population of Brazil at the turn of the century was about 3.6 million. Within Brazil about three-fifths were free people, the majority being of mixed African, Indian, and European blood. Whites born in Portugal were called *Reinols* and whites born in Brazil were *Mazombos*. The small minority of whites, mostly those born in Portugal, held all the political power and most of the economic power. The remaining two-fifths of the population were Negro slaves.[8]

It is difficult to judge how many *Reinols* were living in Brazil in 1822 since all living there were classified as Portuguese. The *Reinols* were mostly found in the ports, which controlled access to the interior. The majority of the Brazilians lived close to the sea and were concentrated in the provinces of Pernambuco, Bahia, and Minas Gerais. These three regions dominated the economic and political life of Brazil, so controlling these was essential. Pernambuco, occupying the northeast hump, was a rich sugar-producing region, a crop of great value during this era. To the south the Bahia region produced sugar, cotton, molasses, and tobacco. This was the most densely populated and wealthiest region in Brazil. Farther south was the region of Rio de Janeiro which included the gold-yielding hills of Minas Gerais.

Both sides viewed the Portuguese warships scattered throughout Brazil (mostly in a state of disrepair) as the military instrument by which they would achieve victory. In early 1822 the Portuguese navy controlled one ship-of-the-line, two frigates, four corvettes, two brigs, and four other armed warships in Brazilian waters. There were perhaps 10,000 Portuguese soldiers and reliable Royalist troops along the Atlantic seaboard. About 3,000 troops were under siege at Montevideo by Brazilians, a similar number were also under siege at Salvador, and the remainder scattered throughout the region.[9]

The warships immediately available to the new Brazilian navy were more numerous but in very poor condition. Although the carcasses of many of the ships which carried João VI to the New World littered Rio de Janeiro, they were worm-eaten and of little value. The Brazilian agent in London, the Marquis de Barbacena (Marshal Felisberto Caldeira Brant), was ordered to purchase fully outfitted and manned warships on credit; however, no suppliers were willing to take the risk. Finally, public subscription was resorted to and the new emperor purchased 350 shares, thus inspiring others. Eventually the young government succeeded in raising money to support its fleet.[10]

Manning the fleet was also a difficult problem. Significant numbers of Portuguese senior officers and crews volunteered to serve the new nation and swore allegiance. However, their loyalty was suspect, so British junior officers and seamen were recruited to make up the shortage and to relieve the fleet's dependence on the Portuguese. Seamen were in so short a supply that on occasion prisoners were pardoned to serve in the fleet.[11]

The Brazilian colonial army was composed of regulars and militia. All officers were nominated by the court in Lisbon. In 1817 a republican revolt had taken place in Pernambuco. As a consequence, some 2,000 additional Portuguese soldiers known as the "Auxiliary Division" were sent to Brazil. Following the arrival of these Portuguese troops, native Brazilian officers were not given significant responsibilities.[12]

OPENING STRATEGIES

Portugal's hold on Brazil was maintained by garrisons at strategic ports. Portuguese strategy to regain Brazil was to withdraw its garrison from Montevideo (1,140 mi SW of Rio de Janeiro) and use it to reinforce the one at Salvador (750 mi N of Rio de Janeiro). These troops would then reconquer the region of Bahia while the Portuguese navy blockaded Rio de Janeiro. Pedro's strategy was to isolate the Portuguese garrisons and force them, one by one, to sail for home.

SEPARATING

Throughout 1822 those inhabiting Brazil began to take sides as political events unfolded in Rio de Janeiro and Lisbon. The Portuguese-Brazilian army occupying Cisplantine (Uruguay) split. Portuguese regiments withdrew into Montevideo and were besieged by their former brethren, the Brazilians led by Barão de Laguna. In the remote, sparsely populated north of Pará and Maranhão, pro-Portuguese *juntas* declared their loyalty to the motherland. Pernambuco favored independence but in Bahia a consensus among the population had not yet taken shape.

THE SIEGE OF SALVADOR

Portuguese Brigadier Inácio Luiz Madeira de Melo, who had arrived with reinforcements from Portugal on February 19, 1822, seized and controlled the fortified city of Salvador, the capital of the province of Bahia, while the Brazilians held the surrounding countryside. The rag-tag 10,000-man Brazilian army could hold Madeira in Salvador but could not intimidate Madeira's 3,000 men into leaving. Pedro tried commanding Madeira to withdraw but he was ignored. Next Pedro ordered Chief of Division (*Chefe-de-Divisão*, a one-star rank) Rodrigo Delamare, commanding a small Brazilian squadron, to land reinforcements led by French-born

Gen. Pedro Labatut and then blockade Salvador. Delamare was fortunate just to get the troops there and return to Rio de Janeiro given the questionable loyalty of his Portuguese-born sailors.[13]

Initially Madeira's position grew stronger while that of the Brazilians weakened. In March 1822 he received 205 well-equipped troops. Six hundred Portuguese troops arrived from Europe on August 27, and on September 8 another 1,200 men and a new commander for the naval forces, Chief of Division João Felix Pereira de Campos, followed. On February 16, 1823, an additional 1,600 troops sailed for Bahia.[14]

By mid-1822 Labatut had secured the neck of the Peninsula upon which Salvador is situated, thus cutting Madeira off from the land side. In October Madeira unsuccessfully attacked the Brazilians defending the island of Itaparica in an attempt to protect his water-borne supply route. Reinforced, Madeira tried again in January 1823 but was repulsed after two days of hard fighting. The stranglehold around Salvador tightened. The Brazilian army besieging Salvador swelled to 12,000 men. Although Madeira's force had increased to something less than 5,000 men, his troops went unpaid and supplies were running short. Also, Madeira was forced to strip the warships of their crews in order to man the defenses. In late January 1823 all of the Brazilian warships then ready—two frigates, two corvettes, and two schooners—escorted a convoy carrying 700 picked troops and supplies to the besiegers of Salvador.[15]

WAR AT SEA

The new Brazilian navy experienced an ominous event in January 1823 when the first lieutenant of the naval schooner *Maria Theresa* arrested the captain and delivered to the Portuguese garrison at Montevideo the ship and the cargo of ordnance she was escorting. This event, plus the lack of a distinguished flag officer among the Portuguese who chose to serve Brazil, made Bonifacio, Pedro's principal advisor, look outside the navy for his commander-in-chief. Thomas Alexander Cochrane was the obvious choice. He was *the* most distinguished naval warrior of his day. Cochrane, who was then quarreling with José de San Martín in Peru, immediately accepted the invitation.

COCHRANE TAKES COMMAND

Cochrane, who arrived on March 13, 1823, brought many trusted naval officers who had served in the Chilean navy.[16] The rank of First Admiral was created in order to satisfy Cochrane's demands. He was paid three times that of the second most senior Brazilian admiral and 500 pounds more a year than the commander-in-chief of the British fleet![17]

On April 1, 1823, a Brazilian squadron, commanded by Cochrane and composed of the ship-of-the-line *Pedro I* (74 guns), frigates *Piranga* (62 guns) and *Niterói* (38 guns), corvettes *Maria da Glória* (26 guns) and *Liberal* (20 guns), brig *Guarani* (14 guns), and brigantine *Imperial* (fitted as a fireship), sailed from Rio de Janeiro with much ceremony. Cochrane's orders were to route the Portuguese out of Salvador, 800 miles to the north.

In the meantime, Madeira had been reinforced with 1,800 fresh troops from Portugal. This allowed him to return his sailors, who were manning the defenses, to the ships. Now the Portuguese fleet could take the offensive. Commodore Felix de Campos was ordered to break the blockade of Montevideo, thus freeing the Portuguese warships trapped there. Adding these to his force, the Commodore was then to blockade Rio de Janeiro. However, on April 19 the British frigate *Tartar* (36 guns) entered Salvador and spread the news of Cochrane's arrival in Rio and his orders to attack Salvador. The Portuguese fleet at Salvador was slightly more numerous than Cochrane's and had a much heavier broadside weight (the fleet's firepower). The Portuguese fleet sailed on April 29—the ship-of-the-line *Dom João VI* (74 guns); the frigates *Consltluçāu* (52 guns) and *Perola* (46 guns); corvettes *Regeneração* (18 guns), *Principe* (22 guns), *10 de Fevereiro* (24 guns), and *Calipso* (22 guns); armed ships *Activo* (22 guns), *Restauração* (22 guns), *Gaulter* (26 guns), and *Princeza Real* (22 guns); plus two scout vessels.[18]

The two fleets sighted each other on May 4 and formed battle lines. Cochrane planned to cut the Portuguese line at the eighth ship and overwhelm the last four before the remaining seven could come to their aid. Only Cochrane's flagship, the *Pedro I* (74 guns), successfully broke through the line. The two squadrons carried on a running gun battle; however, the fire from the Brazilian ships was sporadic and ineffective. Many of the Portuguese sailors serving in the Brazilian warships would not fulfill their duties. Cochrane found it prudent to retire. Felix de Campos chose not to press the fight in spite of the favorable circumstances.[19]

Cochrane sought haven in the small harbor of Morro de São Paulo some 30 miles south of Salvador. Cochrane wrote a secret letter to José Bonifacio outlining his problems—the sailcloth was inferior, the gunpowder weak, the ships incompatible because of differences in speed, the Marines useless, the Portuguese mutinous, and the Brazilians inexperienced. Cochrane advocated a new strategy. He would blockade Salvador with his two fastest ships manned by picked crews and attack the enemy with fireships.[20]

Cochrane began his blockade on May 18 with the *Pedro I* (74 guns) and the *Maria da Glória* (26 guns). Within two weeks he had taken six prizes in spite of the presence of the Portuguese squadron to the east of the port and cut off most of the *farinha* (coarse flour) coming from São Matheos.[21]

International and national news was encouraging for the new empire of Brazil. In Europe a French Royalist army was poised to invade Spain and restore Ferdinand VII's absolute authority; this had ominous overtones for the constitutional Portuguese *Côrtes*. Both the Monarchists and Liberals in Brazil viewed the *Côrtes* as the primary opponent of their independence. Also, the provinces of Piauí and Ceará declared for the new empire. And more former British officers and sailors plus naval stores arrived from England. By mid-1823 over 500 former British sailors were serving in the Brazilian navy.[22]

Cochrane's naval blockade completed the encirclement of Salvador. Matters were becoming desperate for the trapped Portuguese. On May 25 the timid Felix de Campos sailed out to attack Cochrane's base at Morro de São Paulo. Once again he backed away.[23]

On June 3 the Brazilian Army commanded by Gen. José Joaquim de Lima e Silva aggressively attacked the Portuguese defensive positions at Salvador. On the twelfth Cochrane attempted to sail into Salvador with the *Pedro I* (74 guns), *Maria da Glória* (26 guns), and the recently arrived *Real Carolina* (44 guns) disguised as a British squadron and cut out the Portuguese frigate *Constitução* (52 guns). Frustrated by the lack of a land breeze, which was required to escape, the attack had to be aborted. However, the attacks from the land side and the failed naval attempt contributed to the demoralization of the starving Portuguese. On June 20 the Portuguese decided to evacuate Salvador.[24]

As Cochrane was readying a fireship attack, the *Maria da Glória* brought word that the Portuguese were preparing to evacuate. On July 2 the Portuguese evacuation flotilla emerged from Salvador—seventeen warships and seventy merchantmen—and sailed north. Cochrane's instructions to his captains were to captured as many troopships and as much military equipment as possible and to prevent the Portuguese from landing in the northern provinces which had declared for Portugal. On July 3 Cochrane took up the chase with the *Pedro I* (74 guns), *Maria da Glória* (26 guns), *Niterói* (38 guns), and the *Bahia* (unk guns). The Brazilian warships were like hounds at the heels of a wounded animal. In spite of the stormy weather which helped cloak the Portuguese flight, Cochrane's squadron captured sixteen ships carrying some 2,000 men by July 9. Among the prizes was the *Grão Pará* which yielded the Portuguese signal book and the admiral's orders. Part of the transports were to sail to Maranhão and the remainder were to rendezvous at the island of Fernando de Noronha. Cochrane sailed to the island. He harassed the Portuguese by floating primitive mines into their mist. By mid-July it was apparent that the Portuguese ships that had sought haven at the island were sailing for Europe.[25]

THE CRUISE OF THE NITERÓI

Under orders from Cochrane, Capt. John Taylor, commanding the frigate *Niterói* (38 guns), sailed across the Atlantic during August. Disguised as a British warship, the frigate boldly watered in the Portuguese Azores before proceeding to the coast of Portugal. Patrolling off Tagus, the *Niterói* captured prizes, some being escapees from Salvador. Learning that the Portuguese squadron had arrived in Lisbon, Taylor set sail for Brazil. The cruise had lasted four months and the *Niterói* had taken eighteen prizes.[26]

WAR IN THE NORTH

The northern provinces had remained loyal to the Portuguese *Côrtes*. However, the eastern population of the province of Piauí was less dominated by the Portuguese merchants and in October 1822 the port of Paraiba (now João Pessoa—1,210 mi N of Rio de Janeiro) declared for Pedro I. Those loyal to Portugal sent troops and the brig *Infante D. Miguel* (12 guns) to blockade and attack the rebellious port. Outnumbered and outgunned, the Brazilians fled eastward to Ceará where those loyal to Pedro were in control. As the Portuguese departed Oeiras in Piauí province to attack Parnaiba, townspeople in Oeiras (1,095 mi N of Rio de Janeiro) declared for Pedro. Reacting, patriot troops from Ceará marched to their support.[27]

THE BATTLE OF JENIPAPO

On March 13, 1823, Maj. João José da Cunha Fidié, a veteran of the European Peninsular Campaign, led elements of his 1,000-man force (mostly Brazilians loyal to Portugal) toward the Jenipapo River. He planned to retake the city of Oeiras from the rebels. Some 2,000 Revolutionaries were hiding among the trees along both banks. Led by Col. Luis Rodrigues Chaves and Commander [first name unknown] Alecrim, they were poorly armed and disorganized. Fidié's cavalry discovered the awaiting ambush. The Portuguese commander surprised the two groups of Brazilians from the rear. The Brazilians twice charged the Portuguese but were repulsed both times. After five hours of fighting Fidié was victorious. Some 600 Brazilians (mostly from the provinces of Ceará and Piauí) were killed, 80 wounded, and 542 taken prisoner. The remainder escaped through the *caatinga* (brushwood, typical in mid-eastern Brazil). Portuguese casualties were light.[28]

This defeat proved to be only a temporary setback for the rebels. Towns throughout the north began to declare for Pedro. And, the half-breed *vaqueiros* (cowboys) of the northern plains began to join Pedro's army. Fidié retreated to Caxias (1,240 mi N of Rio de Janeiro), in the province of Maranhão, which he fortified. Soon, only the Caxias, São Luiz (1,390 mi N of Rio de Janeiro), and the adjacent areas remained in Portuguese hands.[29]

By May 1823 an 8,000-man Brazilian army began to march on Caxias. In July news arrived that the Portuguese *Côrtes* and constitution had been overthrown and João VI had been restored as an absolute monarch. The news broke the will of many of the Portuguese to continue the fight. On July 15 the Portuguese schooner *Emilia* (unk guns), escorting six transports that had escaped from Salvador, entered São Luiz. This was just when the port was debating changing alliance to Pedro. Portuguese General [first name unknown] de Fara, now with 325 additional troops at his command, made it clear that no change in allegiance would be permitted.[30]

THE RUSE IN SÃO LUIZ

As the Brazilians tightened the siege of São Luiz, General de Faria's only hope of additional reinforcements lay in those who escaped from Salvador due to the chaos in Portugal. On July 26 a large warship flying the Portuguese flag appeared off the port and the brig *Infante D. Miguel* (12 guns) was sent to investigate. The ship-of-the-line proved to be Cochrane's flagship, the *Pedro I*. Once under the guns of the *Pedro I*, the *Infante D. Miguel* could not escape and surrendered. Cochrane convinced Lt. Francisco Salema Freire Garção, commanding the brig, that the entire Brazilian army and navy, which had captured Salvador, were about to descend on São Luiz, and the rebels were very upset over the treatment of those who supported independence in the north. Cochrane coolly explained that the only way to escape the wrath of these forces was to unconditionally surrender. São Luiz did so on July 28. Cochrane hurriedly readied transports to carry the loyalists to Portugal before they discovered that his threat was hollow. General de Faria and 421 troops sailed on August 1 and those loyal to Pedro I easily gained control of São Luiz. Cochrane seized all Portuguese property, public and private, as prizes of war. This soon put him at odds with the local Brazilians who argued that the public property had always belonged to Brazil and not Portugal, and therefore could not be taken as a prize.[31]

THE RUSE IN BELÉM

Aside from Montevideo, only the vast Province of Pará remained in the hands of the Portuguese. As elsewhere throughout the north, the interior favored the new empire but the ports, gateway to the outer world, were controlled by the Portuguese merchants and garrisons. Cochrane attempted the same *ruse* in Pará that had worked so well in São Luiz. He commandeered the brig *Infante D. Miguel* and renamed her the *Maranhão* and placed her under the command of Lt. John Grenfell.[32] On August 11 Grenfell arrived off Belém (1,505 mi N of Rio de Janeiro). Armed with a letter written by Cochrane, which spelled out the fate of those who opposed the rapidly approaching Brazilian army and navy, Belém declared for Pedro I.[33]

Within six months, Cochrane had expelled the Portuguese from Brazilian soil. Only Montevideo remained in Portuguese hands and it had open negotiations to surrender. On November 9 Cochrane sailed into Rio and was honored for his services which included capturing seventy merchantships. However, the warm feelings soon cooled as Cochrane and the new Brazilian empire argued over what was subject to prize money.[34]

AFTERSHOCK

Cochrane performed one more service for the new Brazilian emperor. In August 1824 Cochrane blockaded Recife, the capital of Pernambuco. A separatist republican rebellion had broken out. The port was captured by 1,200 imperial troops in September and the leaders of the rebellion were executed.[35]

OBSERVATIONS

In 1825 British mediation secured Portugal's recognition of Brazil as an independent kingdom. In one respect, the Brazilian War for Independence was the antithesis of the Spanish-American wars for independence. Pedro perceived this to be a war between the Emperor of Brazil and the "Portuguese parliamentary forces."[36] The loss of enthusiasm for the war by the Portuguese forces in Brazil after the overthrow of the constitutional *Côrtes* by the Royalists would support his conclusion.

Pedro's seizing power was a continuation of government rather than a revolution. Keeping the transfer of power "within the family" in the short term significantly decreased the threat of Brazil splintering apart as was occurring throughout the Spanish viceroyalties. It was Pedro's father, Dom João VI, who had initiated a peaceful social, economic, and political revolution through his thirteen-year stay in Brazil.

Although a significant quantity of property and a considerable number of lives were lost during the Brazilian War for Independence, apparently no one has hazarded a guess as to how much and how many.

In 1825 the Brazilian Empire signed a treaty with Portugal whereby Portugal recognized Brazilian independence and Brazil agreed to pay two million pounds sterling to Portugal. The money went unpaid until 1852 when the principal and interest inflated the amount to over six million pounds sterling.

Gaining nationhood was far less traumatic for Brazil than it had been for the former Spanish colonies.

PART 2

EARLY BORDER WARS IN SPANISH AMERICA

CHAPTER SEVEN

THE UNITED PROVINCES AGAINST BRAZIL AND URUGUAYAN INDEPENDENCE, 1825–28

> ... it is an undisputed fact that the Orientalists [Uruguayans] dislike being subject to Buenos Aires *only less* than being subject to Brazil, and that independency is their dearest wish.
> —Lord J. Ponsonby, British Minister to the United Provinces, to Prime Minister George Canning, October 2, 1826

THE SPARK

On August 25, 1825, an assembly of Uruguayans at the town of Florida voted to unite with the United Provinces (today's Argentina), and on October 25 a congress in Buenos Aires accepted this request. As a consequence, Brazil, which had annexed Uruguay in 1821, declared war on the United Provinces on December 10, 1825, and the United Provinces reciprocated on January 1, 1826.[1]

BACKGROUND

From their colonial origins the new nations of the United Provinces of la Plata and Brazil each had historical claims to the province of *Banda Oriental* (today's Uruguay). And, during the Wars for Independence, they both sent troops into Uruguay beginning in 1811. Between then and 1821 a three-way fight raged in Uruguay among those from the United Provinces (principally *Porteños*), the Uruguayans (as personified by Manuel Artigas), and the Portuguese Brazilians (see chapter 3). In spite of their common Spanish heritage, seldom did the Uruguayans and those from the United Provinces unite for long against the Brazilians, and, as a result, Brazil won.[2]

Within Brazil two factions developed. Gen. Federico Lecor led those favoring the annexation of Uruguay and Alvaro da Costa led the Portuguese faction which favored relinquishing Uruguay.[3] On July 18, 1821, Brazil annexed the Banda Oriental as the Cisplatine Province. By the early 1820s, the United Provinces were wrestling with a threat to national cohesion, and this took priority over continuing the struggle for Uruguay.

Brazil was also searching for cohesion during the early 1820s. At first glance one is left with the impression that Pedro I, the first emperor of Brazil, replaced his father Joäo VI, Emperor of the Kingdoms of Portugal and Brazil, on the throne after a short tiff (see chapter 6). In fact, the newly created Brazil was far from united behind its first emperor. Republicanism ran strong particularly in the sugar-growing states of Pernambuco, Ceará, Rio Grande do Norte, Parahyba, and Maranhão. In 1825 Manoel de Carvalho attempted to create the breakaway Confederation of the Equator from among these states. The emperor sent Lord Cochrane and the Brazilian navy to suppress the uprising.

Also, the long colonial rivalry between Portugal and Spain made it difficult for the Portuguese-born Brazilian emperor and court not to want to take advantage of the turmoil within the disintegrating Spanish empire. As Bolivar's army climbed into the *Altiplano* following its victory at Ayacucho (December 9, 1824), the province of Chiquitos in Upper Peru (today's Bolivia) sought to preserve its attachment to Spain. Spanish Royalists requested that the imperial authorities of the adjacent Brazilian state of Mato Grosso provide protection until the Spanish king could reconquer his possessions. Accordingly, Brazilian troops marched into Chiquitos where they were welcomed. The imperial government in Rio feared this might be an open invitation to Simón Bolívar to invade Brazil. Given the strong republican sentiments in parts of Brazil, such a prospect could prove dangerous. As a consequence, Rio ordered the troops to withdraw.[4]

Uruguay was far from united. Independence, as well as union with either Brazil or the United Provinces, all had their advocates. Following the Portuguese victory in 1821, many Uruguayans favoring the Spanish heritage sought sanctuary in Buenos Aires. Inspired by the defeat of the Spanish Royalists at Ayacucho, thirty-three *Orientales* known as the *inmortales* (actually eleven were from the United Provinces) led by Juan Antonio Lavalleja crossed the mouth of the Uruguay River in an open boat during the stormy night of April 19, 1825, and landed near Colonia (66 mi W of Montevideo) in southwestern Uruguay. Six days later the *inmortales* declared independence and called for Uruguayans to rise up against Brazil.[5]

Uruguay's society was similar to that of Argentina. Montevideo controlled the trade but the *gauchos* ruled the countryside. The *gauchos* of the hinterland immediately took up their lances to fight the Brazilians, and Buenos Aires supplied weapons and munitions. The *caudillo* Fructuoso Rivera, who fought at the side of José Artigas, deserted the Brazilians and joined his countrymen with his following. Perhaps to ensure the continuation of aid from Buenos Aires, Lavalleja convened an assembly which declared Uruguay joined to the United Provinces (thus recanting the pledge of independence); this Buenos Aires endorsed, which in turn led to war between the United Provinces and Brazil.

OPPOSING FORCES

Brazil had a significant population advantage over its enemies. Brazil's population was about 4.5 million (which included 1.1 million slaves), the United Province 600,000, (150,000 in the Province of Buenos Aires), and Uruguay about 60,000.[6] However, population was not an adequate measure of strength. Many Brazilians were physically and emotionally remote from the struggle. Within the United Provinces, only the *Porteños* were enthusiastic about the fight. Although the majority of Uruguayans fought with the *Porteños*, some sided with the Brazilians.

Both Brazil and the United Provinces had difficulty creating national armies. The backbone of the Brazilian Army, which had fought in Uruguay between 1811 and 1821, had been Portuguese. After Brazil declared its independence in 1822, the Portuguese troops in Montevideo returned to Europe in March 1824 and were replaced by recently recruited Brazilian troops. Beginning in 1822 the Emperor of Brazil started to create a national army around those Brazilian units that did exist, but much needed to be done.

However, these troops fell far short of the numbers needed and the government turned to impressment. John Armitage wrote, "Notwithstanding their abhorrence of a military life, they [the free peasantry] were seized like malefactors, and after being bound and crammed into the holds of filthy ships, were sent off to the bleak and dreary plains of the south, there to contend with the rigours of the inhospitable clime, and the tactics of a pitiless enemy."[7] Because of the difficulty of inducing Brazilians to serve in the army, mercenaries were recruited in Germany and Ireland, but these troops offered no immediate help.[8]

The Brazilian Army of 1826 numbered about 10,000 men, 6,000 of whom were in the Banda Oriental: 2,500 at Montevideo; 1,100 at Colonia; 1,100 scattered in garrisons along the Uruguay and Negro Rivers; and the remainder here and there. Many of these 6,000 men were local recruits.[9]

The United Provinces also had problems raising an army. Juan de las Heras,[10] the *caudillo* and governor of the Province of Buenos Aires (the two being synonymous at this time) raised an army of 800 men under General Martín Rodriguez near Concepción del Uruguay, in Argentina. The flower of the city's manpower had been sent to the west coast of South America to fight the Royalists and the interior provinces did not have the same enthusiasm for the war against Brazil as the *Porteños* and did not send troops.[11]

Although Uruguay's population was small compared to those of Brazil and the United Provinces, it had less difficulty raising an army. Most Uruguayans lived on the interior plains and were well suited to be irregular cavalry. Armitage described the typical frontiersman: "Equipped only with his bolas, his lasso, and the knife invariably stuck in his girdle, every Gaucho is from his habits a soldier; animated by the spirit of nationality, and ever eager to engage in corporeal strife."[12]

Navies were another matter. Although Lord Cochrane had departed for England, the Brazilian navy, which he created and manned mostly by some 1,200 English, Irish, and American mercenaries, remained fairly intact. One-third of the Brazilian naval officers were British. The navy did suffer from a shortage of junior officers. In 1826 the Brazilian navy possessed one ship of the line, six frigates, five corvettes, eighteen brigs and brigantines, and some thirty-five lesser warships.[13]

The Buenos Aires navy was decidedly inferior to that of Brazil. Initially, it consisted of the brigs *General Belgrano* (14 guns) and *General Balcarce* (14 guns) and a few gunboats. Also, a number of merchant ships were purchased and armed, the most important being the corvette *Comercio de Lima*, which became the *25 de Mayo* (28 guns). The United Provinces also purchased three Chilean warships that had been laid up for some time—the frigate *O'Higgins* (44 guns) which it renamed the *Buenos Aires*, corvette *Independencia* (28 guns), and corvette *Chacabuco* (20 guns). The ships would sail from Valparaíso on May 25, 1826; however, the *Buenos Aires* foundered off Cape Horn in a storm with the loss of 500 lives and the *Independencia* ran aground and was a total loss. Over one half of the fifty-six officers were either British or American. Regional trade was booming and the potential for prize money was great. Therefore, encouraging privateers was an easy matter.[14]

OPENING STRATEGIES

Brazil hoped that a naval show of force prior to hostilities would temper the actions of the *Porteños* and that they would back away from their support of the Uruguayans. Beginning in late April 1825, Brazil began dispatching significant reinforcements to its small squadron in the Plate River. Vice Adm. Rodrigo Ferreira Lobo was given command.[15]

This show of force failed to deter war, so Brazil hoped that a blockade of Buenos Aires would subdue the *Porteños*. However, Buenos Aires was a most difficult port to blockade. The waters immediately outside the harbor were too shallow for the heavier Brazilian warships and the channel into the harbor was narrow and windy. Also, very few landmarks were distinguishable from sea to aid in navigation. For these same reasons a naval bombardment of Buenos Aires was extremely difficult to achieve.[16]

The United Province's initial strategy was to break the blockade through hit-and-run attacks against the blockaders by smaller, more agile warships. The shallow-draft *Porteño* warships would sally forth from Buenos Aires and attempt to draw the Brazilian blockaders into shallow water, where hopefully they would ground. Once grounded, they could be successfully attacked by small warships. Also, Buenos Aires' plan was to aggressively supply the Uruguayan *gauchos*, appreciating their greater motivation to fight than the occupying Brazilian troops.

INITIAL BATTLES

On land, Lavalleja raised an army of 2,000 men. The most important acquisition was the defection of Fructuoso Rivera, a Uruguayan *caudillo* who had loyally served the Brazilian emperor. The Uruguayans fought and won a series of skirmishes, the most important being Arroyo del Aguila (September 4), Rincón de las Gallinas (September 24) and Sarandí (October 12). The Uruguayans avoided pitched battles, preferring to use hit-and-run tactics. These successes drove the Brazilians out of the countryside and into the ports of Colonia and Montevideo where they could be supported by the Brazilian navy.[17]

On January 12, 1826, Commodore William Brown sailed out of Buenos Aires, which lay 125 miles southeast of Montevideo across the Río de la Plata; cut off the new Brazilian gunboat *Araçatuba*; and towed it back to port to the cheers of the *Porteños* who had climbed to their rooftops to witness the action.

BATTLE OF CORALES

On February 9 Brown sailed forth again in the *25 de Mayo* supported by three brigs, a schooner, and a host of gunboats. The opposing fleets sighted each other and maneuvered for advantage. The *25 de Mayo* outdistanced the other Argentine warships and came under fire from the more numerous and heavier Brazilian squadron. The two-hour Battle of Corales was indecisive; the *25 de Mayo* sustained 26 dead and wounded.[18]

BATTLE OF COLONIA DE SACRAMENTO

On February 26 Brown, commanding six warships, sailed for Colonia on the north bank of the Plate River. The defenses of the port, which were under siege by Argentine troops and Uruguayan *gauchos*, were strong: 1,500 troops supported by the brig *Real Pedro* (10 guns) and three schooners. Brown attempted to bombard the port into submission, but, the brig *General Belgrano* grounded and was lost. Not deterred, Brown brought six shallow-draft gunboats from

Buenos Aires, and during the night of March 1 they crossed the sandbar that had prevented the larger *Porteño* warships from getting in close. The *Porteños* boarded the *Real Pedro* and set her afire. Next, they landed and tried to carry the port by assault. They were repulsed and lost five gunboats plus 200 dead, wounded, or captured. On March 3 Brown again bombarded the port. Finally, a very cautious Admiral Lobo came to relieve the blockaded port on March 6 but Brown successfully escaped.[19]

Although Brown had little tangible to show for the battles of Corales and Colonia, the audacity of these attacks made the careful Admiral Lobo even more conservative. He wanted to wait to take the offense until he possessed overwhelming superiority and ordered the island of Martín García, which dominated the entrance to the Uruguay River, evacuated.[20]

On April 9 Brown, commanding six warships, sailed out of Buenos Aires. Three warships under Brown sailed east for Montevideo and three others sailed north for Colonia. On April 10 Brown captured the schooner *Isabel Maria* (5 guns). The next day the *25 de Mayo*, with Brown on board, boldly sailed into Montevideo's outer harbor, while the other two warships remained farther off. The *25 de Mayo* gave chase to a small craft within clear view of the Brazilian frigate *Niterói* (36 guns), which was taking on stores, and a hoist of smaller Brazilian warships in port. The Brazilians scrambled to recall their crews and get underway. Soon, the chase was on. Brown hoped that the larger and faster Brazilian warships would outdistance the smaller ones and he could attack them individually. However, the Brazilian fleet maintained good discipline and chased Brown back to Buenos Aires.[21]

THE ATTACK ON THE *IMPERATRIZ*

Brown, commanding seven warships, sailed again on April 26. His plan was to surprise and capture by boarding the small Brazilian frigate *Niterói* while at anchor in Montevideo harbor. Brown sneaked into the harbor while most of the Brazilian squadron rode quietly at anchor to the south. Unable to determine which of the warships in the inner harbor was the *Niterói*, Brown attacked the larger frigate *Imperatriz* (50 guns) in error. The disciplined Brazilian crew responded well and drove off the attackers. The Argentines also suffered a few casualties. The superior Brazilian fleet chased the audacious Brown back into Buenos Aires. Once again, Brown had little tangible to show for his actions, but his boldness played well in the press.[22]

Due to Lobo's timidity, command of the Brazilian squadron was now vested in Adm. Rodrigo Pinto Guedes[23] on May 13, 1826. His first order was to replace five timid captains, most with Britons who had served Cochrane. He reorganized the Brazilian fleet into four divisions. The first division was to patrol the mouth of the Plate River, which was fifty miles wide; the second was to continue the blockade of Buenos Aires; the third was to patrol the Uruguay and Paraná Rivers; and the fourth was held in reserve.[24]

BATTLE OF LOS POZOS

Adm. Pinto Guedes decided to carry the fight to Brown. He ordered Capt. James Norton,[25] commanding the first division and supported by the second division (31 warships of all sizes), to attack the Argentine anchorage at Los Pozos (3 mi NW of Buenos Aires). On June 10 Brown detected the approach of the Brazilians. He anchored his eight warships and gunboats across the mouth of the channel rigged on springs so they could pivot. Only the smaller Brazilian warships could bring the Argentine defenses under fire due to the shallow waters. The cannonade from both sides was ineffective. But once again, Brown won a public relations victory as the population of Buenos Aires witnessed Brown beating off an enemy many times his size.[26]

BATTLE OF QUILMES

During the late evening of July 29, Brown, commanding eighteen small warships, once again slipped out of port and unsuccessfully attempted to surprise the Brazilians. The next day, as the Argentine squadron approached the Brazilians at a right angle, Norton split his force, catching the Argentine between two fires. Brown in the *25 de Mayo* reversed course. Those ships in the Argentine van came under heavy fire. After three hours of fighting, the Argentine fleet escaped into shallow water. The *25 de Mayo*, a floating wreck, was towed into Los Pozos and capsized in a strong southwester. The Brazilian lost six dead and twenty wounded; among this latter group was John Pascoe Grenfell who lost an arm. Argentine losses might have been as high as one hundred dead and one hundred wounded.[27]

THE SIEGE OF MONTEVIDEO

The fighting on land settled into a stalemate. The Brazilians held up in the principal ports and the allies roamed the countryside. In July the *Porteños* began to besiege Montevideo. General Lecor refused to be drawn out of the capital. In September, officers commanding the Brazilian troops in Rio Grande do Sul mutinied due to Lecor's inactivity but were suppressed. In late October the *Porteños* lifted the siege, finally realizing that with the tight Brazilian blockade of Buenos Aires, Montevideo had clandestinely become their primary commercial outlet.[28]

In November Pedro I traveled to Rio Grande do Sul and attempted to personally take command of the military operations. However, by the time he reached the south the feud between the ailing, pregnant empress and the Emperor's mistress publicly erupted, and the Emperor returned to Rio. Before departing, Pedro replaced General Lecor with a court favorite, the Felisberto Brant, Marquis de Barbacena. He was a skilled diplomat but an untested soldier. The shabbily treated empress died before Pedro reached Rio.[29]

BROWN RAIDS BRAZILIAN COMMERCE

The effectiveness of the Brazilian blockade caused Brown to change his strategy. On October 26 Commodore Brown slipped through the Brazilian blockade with the schooner *Sarandí* (9 guns), joining the corvette *Chacabuco* (20 guns) at sea which had arrived from Chile. These two ships, sailing up the Brazilian coast, captured fourteen merchantmen and bombarded offshore Brazilian islands. Commodore Brown in *Sarandí* slipped back into Buenos Aires on Christmas Day and the *Chacabuco* returned to Patagonia on January 1, 1827.[30]

BROWN'S URUGUAY RIVER EXPEDITION

Remaining in port for only two days, Brown next sailed up the Plate River, commanding a shallow-draft, riverine squadron, which had been assembled in his absence. Brown's objective was to destroy the Brazilian 3rd Division, operating on the Uruguay River. On December 28, 1826, the two squadrons encountered each other. One paper, they were equal—17 ships, 69 guns, and about 740 men each. The Argentine warships were manned by more experienced officer and sailors. Aware of this, Pereira took up a defensive position behind a sandbar off the mouth of the Negro River. Unable to break the Brazilian defensive line, Brown left a battery commanded by Capt. Tomas Espora behind at Punta Gorda which commanded some narrows, thus trapping the Brazilian force up the Uruguay River.[31]

BATTLE OF JUNCAL

Next, Brown fortified the island of Martín García at the mouth of the Uruguay River. Adm. Pinto Guedes decided to catch Brown between two forces. He ordered Pereira to come down the Uruguay River and created a nine-ship squadron under Capt. Frederick Mariath to go up the Plate River. Immediately, Brown was privy to the plan through a superb spy system. Brown and Mariath clashed off Martín García on January 18 but neither was able to gain an advantage.

Brown then sailed up the Uruguay River and attacked the Brazilian 3rd Division at dawn on February 8, 1827. The action was interrupted by a fierce storm. The following day Brown led his squadron toward the Brazilians. Pereira ordered his squadron to form a line and drop anchor; chaos followed. Soon the superior seamanship of the Argentine squadron won the day. Only three of the seventeen ships escaped destruction or capture; ten of these small warships were added to the Argentine navy.[32]

Mariath's squadron attempted to aid the 3rd Division. However, the schooner *Maceió*, sent to sound the channel, grounded. Mariath chose to bombard Martín García at long range and finally retired to Colonia. The loss of these shallow draft warships significantly hampered the Brazilian navy's potential to interdict the supplies being carried across the River Plate and up the Uruguay River to the growing allied army in Uruguay.

THE WAR ON LAND

Throughout 1826 Brazil dispatched additional troops to Uruguay and by early 1827 controlled the coastal areas and the region bordering Rio Grande do Sul. Brazil had 12,000 men on the Brazil-Uruguay frontier; 5,000 in Montevideo; 1,000 in Colonia; 1,000 on Gorriti Island; and 500 on Lobos Island.[33]

The *Porteños* and their Uruguayan allies set up camp in the Río Negro Valley. This location permitted the growing army under Gen. Carlos Alvear (who had replaced Rodríguez) to be supplied by shallow-draft craft from Buenos Aires. By mid-January the allied army (*porteños* and Uruguayans) numbered about 5,500 men and began to march toward the town of Bage just across the Brazilian border, a distance of some 250 miles.[34] Arriving there on January 26, they surprised the defenders and captured the town without resistance. The Brazilian commander, Marquis de Barbacena, marched from his headquarters at Santa Anna do Livramento to block any deeper penetration into Rio Grande do Sul.

BATTLE OF ITUZAINGÓ (PASO DEL ROSARIO)

The allies continued their advance toward San Gabriel, fighting a number of skirmishes. By February 19 Barbacena closed to within striking distance. He believed that the allies were fording the Santa María River, so he ordered his First Division to attack the enemy's center at 8 o'clock in the morning on the twentieth. The armies were about equal in strength. The allies had 7,700 men—5,400 cavalry, 1,800 infantry, and 500 artillerymen serving 16 guns. The Brazilian army was composed of 6,300 men—3,700 cavalry, 2,300 infantry, and 300 artillerymen serving 12 guns. After a hard fight, the allied cavalry drove the Brazilians back. The allied cavalry then attacked the Brazilian flank but was repulsed. By 2 P.M. both sides were comfortable with the terrain they held. Finally, Barbacena ordered a withdrawal which was orderly. The Brazilians lost some 200 dead, 90 wounded, 150 prisoners, and 800 missing. The allies lost 147 dead (one of whom was Col. Hollander Brandsen,[35] a veteran of the 1812 Russian campaign) and 256 wounded. Practically all of the allied casualties were among the cavalry.[36]

Gen. José Paz, a participant and an admired tactician, stated that Ituzaingó "could be called the battle of disobediences: there all of us commanded, all of us fought, and all of us triumphed, directed by our own inspirations."[37] The allied army withdrew into Uruguay due to the poor condition of their horses and lack of supplies. Both commanders were reprimanded for their lack of aggressiveness. Initially relieved, General Alvear was returned to command; the Marquis do Barbacena was replaced by General Lecor, who again took command.[38]

BRAZIL'S DISASTER AT CARMEN DE PATAGONES

On February 16, 1827, Adm. Pinto Guedes dispatched four warships carrying 340 soldiers and marines (including 260 British mercenaries) under the command of Capt. James Shepherd[39] to destroy the *Porteños'* privateering base at Carmen de Patagones (425 mi SSW of Buenos Aires) some 15 miles up the Río Negro. The port was protected by a shallow, winding channel and some small gun batteries.

Arriving off the mouth of the river, the Brazilians fought their way past the fort guarding the narrow channel on February 28. However, in the process, the corvette *Duqueza de Goias* (20 guns) grounded; three days later the corvette broke up in a storm. A few miles up the river, the corvette *Itaparica* (20 guns) also grounded and was left behind while the brigantine *Escudeira* (5 guns) and the schooner *Constança* (3 guns) carrying the troops proceeded.

On March 6, six miles below the port, some 320 men disembarked and proceeded over land. Shepherd expected his enemy to be a few hundred poorly trained militia. What he did not know was that in addition to the local forces were 330 seasoned privateers led by three of the boldest privateer captains—the Frenchmen Pierre Dautant and François Fourmantine and the Englishman James Harris.

After a tiring march, the Brazilians attacked Carmen at dawn on the seventh. Shepherd was shot dead almost immediately and the Brazilians were driven off by the numerically superior defenders. George Bynon (the commander of the *Chacabuco*) commanded a force that sailed down the river in the privateer *Oriental Argentina* and three prize ships which seized the Brazilian warships while *gauchos* harassed the retreating Brazilians. Their ships captured, the Brazilians surrendered. The Argentines captured 600 men and three warships. Although the victory was acclaimed in Buenos Aires, it had little impact on the balance of naval power which greatly favored the Brazilians.[40]

BATTLE OF MONTE SANTIAGO BANK

On March 27 Brown selected his best four warships to attack Brazilian shipping along the coast. During the night of April 5, the brigs *República Argentina* (16 guns) and *Independencia* (22 guns), plus the corvette *Congreso Nacional* (18 guns) and the schooner *Sarandí* (9 guns), slipped out of Los Pozos. Less than ten miles from port, Brown was discovered by the Brazilian blockaders, again commanded by Cmdr. James Norton. Brown hugged the southern shore hoping to elude the Brazilians in the darkness. At 2:30 A.M. on the sixth, the *República Argentina* and the *Independencia* grounded off Ensenada Spit. Throughout the next day Norton, unable to approach too closely due to the shallow water, carried out an ineffective long-range bombardment. By April 8 the Brazilians had brought up four shallow-draft schooners; also, the frigate *Dona Paula* (50 guns) was carefully towed to within range. After a hard fight, the heavier, more numerous Brazilian guns shattered the two stranded brigs.

The *Sarandí* and *Congreso Nacional* escaped back to Buenos Aires after taking numerous hits. Brown's personnel losses were significant. Capt. Francis Drummond,[41] commanding the

Independencia, was killed; Capt. Guillermo Granville, commanding the *República Argentina*, lost an arm; and Brown was slightly wounded. The crews sustained 54 dead and 160 wounded out of a total of 400 men. Following these losses, Brown confined his activities to the River Plate and its tributaries.[42]

BRAZIL'S DISASTER AT SAN BLAS

Admiral Pinto Guedes decided on a second raid against the privateer havens south of Buenos Aires. In September 1827 he dispatched the corvette *Marceió* (18 guns) and the brigs *Indêpendencia ou Morte* (16 guns) and the *Caboclo* (16 guns) under Capt. William Eyre to recapture the merchant ship *Condessa de Ponte* lying in the Bay of San Blas (394 mi SSW of Buenos Aires). Entering the bay on the twenty-first, the *Marceió* and the *Indêpendencia ou Morte* immediately grounded. Soon, both ships were smashed by deteriorating weather before they could free themselves. Only the *Caboclo* escaped. The Argentines captured 83 Brazilian sailors (including Eyre) as they came shore and approximately 40 drowned.[43]

FIGHTING ON LAND

Following the Battle of Ituzaingó (Paso del Rosario), General Alvear withdrew to Corrales in central Uruguay and Brazil regained control of the north. Also, reinforcements and supplies from Buenos Aires slowed to a trickle because of the loss of revenue caused by the blockade and the need to defend the Argentine frontier against Indian attacks. By mid-1828 the allied army was reduced to some 4,000 poorly outfitted men. The Brazilian army had also been reduced to 4,000 men due to internal problems.[44]

Rivadavia ordered General Alvear to take the offensive in order to create a more favorable environment for peace talks. He began moving north on April 13 and an advanced unit occupied Bage in southern Brazil on the sixteenth. At night Alvear attacked 1,600 Brazilians at Camacuá Chico, some 21 miles from Bage. Although the Brazilians offered a spirited fight, they were surprised and overwhelmed. Alvear sent three columns north during May but ultimately had to withdraw due to lack of support from Buenos Aires.

PRIVATEERING

Throughout the entire war privateering wreaked havoc upon commerce, particularly that of Brazil. Initially, the environment was ideal. Buenos Aires could not be closely blockaded due to the shallow water surrounding its entrance. Prior to the outbreak of fighting, Brazilian trade was booming, particularly with Great Britain making the potential of prizes abundant. And maritime mercenaries from Great Britain, Ireland, the United States, and elsewhere were plentiful.

The United Provinces and Uruguay commissioned 57 privateers during the war. Of these, 27 were captured and 18 wrecked. They captured 405 prizes of which 139 ships reached Argentine ports to be condemned by prize courts.[45]

Among the most successful privateers was the *Lavalleja*, commanded by the Frenchman François Fourmantine. Flying the Uruguayan flag, he captured twenty-one Brazilian prizes before being driven aground early in the war. In June 1826 the tiny *Hijo de Mayo*, commanded by the Englishman James Harris, captured two Imperial transports loaded with stores and munitions. In October the tiny *Hijo de Mayo*, commanded by Fourmantine, captured six prizes. In March 1827 the *Sin Par*, commanded by the Swede [first name unknown] Tidblon, captured nine ships. Other successful privateers were the *Oriental Argentina*, commanded by the Dutchman Pierre Dautant; the *Union Argentina* under the Englishman Thomas Prouting; and the *General Mancilla* commanded by the American Thomas Beazley.[46]

The privateers were so bold that on occasion they attacked Brazilian warships. On June 26, 1827, the American George DeKay,[47] commanding the brig *General Brandzen* (8 guns), attacked the naval lugger *Príncipe Imperial* (14 guns) and the naval schooner *Isabella* (5 guns). The *Príncipe Imperial* fled and, after an hour-and-a-half battle, the *Isabella* surrendered. On September 9 DeKay boarded and captured the naval brig *Cacique* (18 guns) off Pernambuco after a hard fight. The *Cacique* sustained six dead and seventeen wounded; the *General Brandzen* lost one dead and fourteen wounded, including DeKay.[48]

On January 25, 1828, the American John Coe,[49] commanding the privateer *Niger* (11 guns), attacked the Brazilian naval corvette *Maria Isabel* (28 guns) while she was escorting twelve merchant ships from Santos to Rio de Janeiro. The privateer attempted to board the *Maria Isabel* three times before quitting the fight.

The English commercial newspaper *The British Packet* described the impact of the privateers in May 1827:

> The damage inflicted is immense. Many of the corsairs, and probably all, have made successful voyages to the coast of Brazil and, if the war continues, the commerce of that country will be shaken to its foundation. It is useless to talk of convoys; even if the Brazilian navy had five times as many ships as it has, it could not give adequate protection to its commerce.[50]

TALK OF PEACE

Rivadavia, confronted by rebellious provinces and an empty treasury, sent Manuel García to Rio to negotiate an end to the war. The minister, ignoring his instructions, returned with a treaty which recognized the independence of Brazil and renounced the claims of the United Provinces to Uruguay![51] Rivadavia rejected the treaty but was forced to resign in July 1827 regardless. Manuel Dorrego, who had organized the provinces against Rivadavia, continued the war against Brazil.

The terms of the rejected treaty injected a fresh enthusiasm for the war on both sides. As the war wore on, Commodore Brown led his squadron of small warships out of Buenos Aires' inner roads and dueled with the Brazilian squadron commanded by now Admiral Norton. Nonetheless, the Brazilian blockade grew tighter and its convoy system continually reduced the threat from privateers.[52]

The United Provinces once again dissolved into a condition where the Governor of Buenos Aires retained the authority over war and foreign relations but all others rested with provincial leaders. The economies of both Brazil and the United Provinces were being ruined, the first primarily by privateers and the second by a blockade. Also suffering greatly were British commercial interests.

REGIONAL *CAUDILLOS* SEIZE THE INITIATIVE

Fructuoso Rivera, who had remained inactive due to a feud with Lavalleja, raised some 1,000 *gauchos* in the Province of Santa Fé. In February 1828 he marched north, crossed the Uruguay River, and defeated a Brazilian force at Ibicuí just inside Rio Grande do Sul, Brazil, on April 21. Estanislao López, another *caudillo*, organized some horsemen at the river port of

Figure 7. The United Provinces against Brazil and Uruguayan Independence, 1825–28, was in large measure fought at sea between the British-influenced Brazilian navy and the "sailors of fortune"-dominated Argentine navy and privateers. Here the Argentine privateer *General Brandzen* (8 guns), commanded by the American George DeKay, captures the Brazilian naval brig *Cacique* (18 guns), commanded by the Englishman George Manson, on September 9, 1827. *Courtesy U.S. Naval Historical Center.*

La Cruz, in the province of Corrientes. He planned to attack Porto Alegre, Brazil. This threatened to extend the war deep into Rio Grande do Sul.[53]

MUTINY IN RIO DE JANEIRO

In Brazil many of the 2,000 German and Irish quartered in Rio de Janeiro mutinied on June 11, 1828, due to numerous grievances. At the request of the Brazilian government, 224 British marines and 500 French sailors landed from the foreign squadrons and the militia from Minas Gerais called up. Following three days of savage fighting, order was restored. Approximately sixty German and Irish were killed as well as a few hundred Brazilians.[54]

Brazil and the United Provinces now found it within their interests to accept British mediation. On October 27, 1828, Brazil, Uruguay, the United Provinces, and the Great Britain signed a treaty that created the Oriental State of Uruguay. Great Britain guaranteed the sovereignty of the new nation for five years.[55]

OBSERVATIONS

The winners of the war were the Uruguayans, who achieved independence in large measure thanks to the internal problems of Brazil and of the United Provinces and thanks to the threat this war posed to British commercial interests. After almost three years of fighting, both Brazil and the United Provinces needed to end the war in order to deal with internal threats. For Brazil, it was the threat of republicanism in the northeast. For the United Provinces, it was the struggle between the port of Buenos Aires and the interior provinces.

Like Americans, the Brazilians were imbued with "Manifest Destiny" which drove them to expand westward. However, this war was viewed by many Brazilians as an extension of the imperial policies of João VI and the aspirations of the Portuguese Empire and not those of Brazilians. As a consequence, the war farther undermined the popularity of Pedro I.[56]

The morale of the allied army's officers and men proved superior to that of the Brazilians. John Armitage noted, "General Lecor . . . had from his dilatory policy received the general appellation of 'Fabius secundis;' and his young officers were, with few exceptions, too well satisfied with the attractions of Montevideo, to be at all anxious to quit it for the plains."[57] Also, the allied soldiers, as volunteers, outperformed those of Brazil who were conscripts or mercenaries. Armitage wrote: "With regard to precision of movements, watch-words, signals, and all the formalities and minutiae of military science, which the Gauchos in their unsophisticated ignorance affected to despise they [the Brazilians] had attained a proficiency truly astonishing; yet even this proficiency proved at times but a feeble guarantee against the irregular assaults of the enemy."[58]

One casualty of the war was the national army of the United Provinces. It disappeared. Upon returning from Uruguay, the Pacific, and the Bolivian frontier, those wishing to serve in the military found employment in the provincial and *Porteño* armies.[59]

Buenos Aires had created two navies—Brown's squadron and the privateers. Brown constantly pressured the Brazilian navy to concentrate while the privateers required it to disperse. They complemented each other during the early part of the war. However, Buenos Aires did not have the naval establishment—shipyards and naval arsenals—to sustain such an effort. In the end, the weight of the Brazilian naval establishment wore Buenos Aires down.

CHAPTER EIGHT

PERU AGAINST GRAN COLOMBIA, 1828–29

> The termination of these events [the Peruvian invasion of Bolivia to force the removal of Gran Colombian troops] disproves the slanders of General Bolívar; and convinces [us] that Peru did not carry war there [to Bolivia] but rather independence; not conquest and oppression, but rather liberty and tranquility.
> –José de la Mar, President of Peru, 1828

THE SPARK

The two sides in this conflict believed that the leadership of the other was responsible for starting the war. Peruvians believed that Simón Bolívar exploited greviances against Peru in an attempt to bolster his waning internal support. Colombians believed that Peruvian leaders José de la Mar[1] and Agustín Gamarra[2] held animosities against Simón Bolívar for dismembering the former Viceroyalty of Peru.[3]

BACKGROUND

The Liberator Simón Bolívar dreamed of uniting the Spanish-American nations. He had already succeeded in forcing the modern nations of Colombia, Venezuela, and Ecuador into a single country—Gran Colombia. And in 1826, when he called the Congress of Panama, he still had hopes of incorporating Peru and Bolivia even though most influential citizens in those nations were opposed to Bolívar's dream. In September of that year, Bolívar was forced to return from Peru to Gran Colombia to deal with mounting internal opposition. He left trusted lieutenants in charge of Peru and Bolivia, each supported by Gran Colombian military units—the Bolivian Andrés de Santa Cruz in Peru and the Venezuelan Antonio Sucre in Bolivia. Neither Santa Cruz nor Sucre was able to stem the awakening of nationalism within these new countries.[4]

The independence of Peru had—in significant measure—been fought for and won by foreigners like Bolívar, and now they governed in the person of Santa Cruz, who was backed by Gran Colombian soldiers. It is difficult to calculate the number of Peruvians who had participated in the war for independence. Although the 1,200 men in the Peruvian units that fought at Ayacucho (December 9, 1824) represented only 24 percent of the Revolutionary army, it is unclear how many Peruvians had been used to replace casualties in other national armies before the battle. This practice of conscripting Peruvians into the Gran Colombian army became a source of friction between the two young nations.⁵

Before the guns were cold, Peruvians began plotting the removal of Bolívar's influence. The political atmosphere was confused; neither Peruvian Liberals nor Peruvian Conservatives could lay clear title to having won independence. Adding to the political turmoil was the decimation of the Peruvian economy. Although fighting on Peruvian soil had been brief (1820–24) when compared to other areas in South America, it had been particularly destructive. Callao, the principal seaport, lay in ruins, and many of the agricultural estates had been ravaged by the opposing armies.

On January 26, 1827, the 2,400 Gran Colombian troops in Peru, inspired by locals and wanting to go home, mutinied. Santa Cruz, hoping to be chosen president by the Peruvians, arranged for the withdrawal of the Gran Colombian soldiers and on June 4 called a new congress. Soon Santa Cruz and Congress, led by the Liberal Francisco Javier de Luna Pizarro, were at loggerheads; and Congress chose the more pliable José de la Mar as president. La Mar, born in southern Ecuador, had one driving ambition: to incorporate parts of Ecuador, which had been annexed by Bolívar to Gran Colombia in 1822, back into Peru where they had been off and on during the colonial period.⁶

The Peruvian Liberals supported La Mar's aspirations and maneuvered Congress toward war with Gran Colombia. Led by Luna Pizarro, they were motivated by ideology. The defeat of the increasingly conservative Bolívar would promote liberalism in Colombia and increase its strength in Peru and Ecuador.⁷

One element of the mutinous Gran Colombian garrison, led by Col. Juan Francisco Elizalde, landed at Guayaquil. There, Juan joined his brother Antonio, a local official, and together they led an insurrection on April 16, 1827, that briefly gave control of the province of Guayaquil to Peru.⁸

At about the same time, Gen. Agustín Gamarra, who commanded the Peruvian army in the south, bore his own grudge against Bolívar. An extreme nationalist, Gamarra blamed Bolívar for the creation of Bolivia and wanted to reunite this former province of Upper Peru into Peru as it had been for much of the colonial period.⁹

Gamarra conspired with prominent Bolivians to eject the 5,000-man Gran Colombian garrison in Bolivia and to overthrow Sucre. They demanded the repatriation of the Gran Colombians to which Sucre agreed. Most of the troops departed via the port of Arica. On April 18, 1828, a handful of conspirators attacked the small Gran Colombian barracks at Chuquisaca, Bolivia, and killed the commanding officer. The homesick Gran Colombians mutinied and joined in the rebellion against the government. Sucre suppressed the rebellion but was wounded in the head and right arm in the process. Gamarra and Sucre met on the banks of the Desaguadero River which separated Bolivia and Peru. Sucre declined Gamarra's offer to use the Peruvian army to restore peace. Regardless, Gamarra invaded Bolivia on May 1 with an army of 5,000 men.¹⁰

This initiative by Gamarra complemented the plans of La Mar and the Liberals in Peru. The president of Bolivia, Antonio Sucre, was an ardent supporter of Simón Bolívar, president of Gran Colombia, and probably would not have remained neutral in a war between Peru and Gran Colombia. The Bolivians offered little resistance to Gamarra and capitulated in early July. Sucre resigned and left for Ecuador, then known as Gran Colombia's Southern Departments. Peru and Bolivia signed the Treaty of Piquiza on July 6 which provided for the departure from

Bolivia of all foreign-born troops, for Bolivia to pay the expenses of the Peruvian army, and for Bolivia to abrogate its constitution.[11]

Gamarra met with Generals Antonio Gutierrez de la Fuente and Santa Cruz, who was returning to his native Bolivia from Peru hoping to take advantage of Sucre's downfall at Arequipa. The three conspired to gain control of Peru and Bolivia and join them in a confederation under the leadership of Santa Cruz. Gamarra would march north, join President La Mar in the now *defacto* war with Gran Colombia, and await the opportunity to betray and seize him. La Fuente would proceed to Lima and be ready to act against the vice president. And Santa Cruz would gain control of Bolivia.

Gran Colombia also had its claims against Peru. It wanted the regain control of disputed lands in the *selva*. Also, Gran Colombia wanted Peru to pay back the loans it received during the Wars for Independence. As a consequence of Peru's activities to remove Colombian influence from Peru and Bolivia, its control of the disputed territories, and its delay in paying the war debts, Bolívar declared war on Peru on July 3, 1828, although Peru, in turn, never formally declared war on Gran Colombia.[12]

OPPOSING FORCES

Gran Colombia was about one-and-a-half times the size of Peru. More importantly, the population of Gran Colombia (2.9 million) was almost double that of Peru (about 1.5 million). However, the population of Gran Colombia's Southern Departments (Ecuador) was only some 600,000 inhabitants, and two-thirds of these lived in the northern highlands, 200 miles from the contested southern provinces. And many in the contested areas were sympathetic to Peru.[13]

The war matched the victors of the final struggle for independence in South America against each other. The Gran Colombian army in Ecuador numbered 4,200 men (3,800 infantry and 400 cavalry). Most of the soldiers were veterans of the campaigns in Peru during the War for Independence. Bolívar gave regional command to Antonio Sucre, the most decorated hero of the Wars for Independence, excepting only the two Liberators, José de San Martín and himself. Bolívar wrote to Sucre, "All my powers, good and bad, I delegate to you. Whether you make war or peace, whether you save or lose the South, you are the arbiter of its fate, and it is in you that I have placed all my hopes!"[14] Sucre's second in command was Juan José Flores[15], an Ecuadorian by choice.[16]

The 8,000-man Peruvian army was commanded by José de la Mar and his second was Agustín Gamarra.[17] Sucre thought well of the Peruvian soldiers but was disdainful of the officers:

> The infantry is good to hold any position and fight shot by shot. It can resist a lot of fire, especially if it has the slightest shield. In contrast, if they are attacked violently, if they are charged with the bayonet in accessible terrain, they do not resist one minute. The cavalry is only of medium value; in Junín one squadron performed well and so did another in Ayacucho because they were under good command. But now the officers and chiefs, which it had back then, have been replaced by parade officers.[18]

The Peruvian navy, commanded by Vice Adm. Martin Guise,[19] was composed of the frigate *Presidente* (52 guns), the armed merchantman *Monteagudo* (12 guns), the sloop *Libertad* (22 guns), the brigantines *Congreso* (20 guns) and *Arequipeño* (13 guns), and the schooners *Limeña* (1 gun) and *Peruviana* (1 gun).[20]

Although Gran Colombia possessed a respectable navy, most of its warships were in the Caribbean Sea. Three warships were in the Pacific: the sloop *Pichincha* (10 guns), the schooner *Guayaquileña* (12 guns), and the brigantine *Adela* (18 guns) which was being completed at Guayaquil. With the outbreak of hostilities, the new American-built frigate *Colombia* (62 guns) was prepared and ordered around Cape Horn into the Pacific. The trip took five months, and the ship arrived off Ecuador in February 1830, long after the fighting had ended.[21]

OPENING STRATEGIES

Bolívar confronted numerous threats. In addition to the Peruvian blockade, individuals rebelled in Pasto (today, southwestern Colombia) and in Guayas (today, south coastal region of Ecuador) seeking to separate themselves from Gran Colombia. Bolívar's strategy was to have Sucre remain on the defensive until he could suppress the rebellion in Pasto and then reinforce Sucre. Sucre chose to concentrate his army at Cuenca (183 mi SE of Quito), which lay on the road from Peru to the capital. This left Guayaquil undefended; but given Peru's naval superiority, the port was virtually undefensible.[22]

La Mar's strategy was to seize control of the sea in order to deny its use to Gran Colombia. Next he would invade Ecuador and seek a decisive battle before Bolívar could pacify the rebellious Pasto Province and come to the relief of Sucre. The leaders on both sides knew the local terrain. La Mar was a native, and Sucre had campaigned over these same grounds in 1821 and 1822.[23]

THE WAR AT SEA

On August 31, 1828, the Peruvian sloop *Libertad* (22 guns) and the Gran Colombian corvette *Pichincha* and schooner *Guayaquileña* exchanged broadsides off Punta Malpelo, both sides sustaining significant casualties. On September 9 Peru declared a blockade of all Gran Colombian ports in the Pacific.[24]

CAPTURE OF GUAYAQUIL

In late September Vice Admiral Guise, commanding a Peruvian squadron of five warships and eight armed launches, arrived off Guayaquil (712 mi NNW of Callao, Peru), which was once again in the hands of Gran Colombia. On November 6 the crew of the Gran Colombian corvette *Pichincha* mutineed and turned the ship over to the Peruvian navy.[25]

On November 22 Admiral Guise began to bombard Guayaquil. The city's defenses included a chain stretched across the river protected by the battery *Cruces* (ten guns), the schooner *Guayaquileña*, four armed launches, and the nearly complete brigantine *Adela*. The battery *Cruces* was caught by surprise and fell silent and the Peruvian frigate *Presidente* broke the chain. Nonetheless, the remaining guns ashore, the flotilla, and marksmen continued the fight. The city's defenses were under the command of Col. John Illingworth. The Peruvian bombardment continued throughout November 23. At 2 A.M. on the twenty-fourth, the *Presidente* grounded. The clearness of the night allowed the Gran Colombians to immediately attack with cannons ashore and the flotilla of small craft commanded by Lt. Francisco Calderón. At 9 A.M. the *Presidente* was refloated and the attackers beaten off when one of the last shots fired in the engagement killed the Admiral. Shortly thereafter, Illingworth received orders to send the bulk of his troops defending Guayaquil to Cuenca, 183 miles to the southeast. Apparently, the combination of the attacks by the Peruvian navy and the reduction in his forces caused Illingworth to surrender the city on January 13, 1829. The *Guayaquileña* and two of the armed launches were taken into the Peruvian navy.²⁶

BATTLE OF PORTETE DE TARQUI

On November 11, La Mar, leading 4,500 men, occupied the frontier. On the twenty-eighth, in coordination with the naval assault on Guayaquil, he advanced toward Cuenca (636 mi N of Lima). The march was slow—nine miles a day—because of the rugged terrain. La Mar advanced as far as the town of Nabón, several miles from the town of Cuenca. On January 28, 1829, Sucre arrived at Cuenca. He maneuvered to Tarqui in an attempt to draw the Peruvians into combat on unfavorable ground. La Mar ordered Col. Pedro Raulet, commanding 250 infantry and 50 cavalry, to flank Sucre and capture Cuenca. On February 10 he captured Cuenca taking many prisoners and 1,200 muskets. In order to quicken his march, Raulet had left his baggage in Saraguro under the protection of the rear guard. On the thirteenth a Gran Colombian unit led by Colonel [first name unknown] Jiménez surprised the rear guard and captured most of the Peruvian train.²⁷

Sucre returned to Cuenca. Gamarra, commanding 3,500 men, joined La Mar. Unaware of Gamarra's hidden agenda of replacing him as president, La Mar was delighted to receive the reinforcements and made Gamarra second in command. Gamarra ordered a Peruvian division under Gen. Leónidas Plaza Gutiérrez with only the ammunition in their cartridge belts to occupy Portete de Tarqui, some seven miles from the main body. Portete de Tarqui was a deep ravine in the Andes through which the road between Tarqui and Cuenca passed. During the night of February 26, 1829, Sucre ordered a rapid night march by the 1st Gran Colombian Division. The following morning, while still dark, this 1,500-man force fell upon the advanced Peruvian position. It seized a hill in the midst of the Peruvians. Sucre reinforced the First Division with the 1,500-man 2nd Gran Colombian Division when it arrived on the field of battle. When the main body of the Peruvian army arrived, it was boxed in a gorge and could not spread out effectively to support General Plaza's division. The Peruvians could not dislodge the Gran Colombians from their defensive positions on high ground. Gamarra ordered a retreat, perhaps prematurely.²⁸ The Gran Colombians lost 360 men and the Peruvians lost 613 plus much of their equipment.²⁹

La Mar was forced to sign the Treaty of Girón on February 28, one day after the battle. Peru was required to evacuate all territory in dispute with Gran Colombia including Guayaquil; to return all of the captured ships; and to pay Gran Colombia 150,000 pesos to cover Gran Colombia's expenses in the conflict. Each nation was to reduce its army in northern Peru and southern Gran Colombia to 3,000 men each; to appoint commissioners to settle the boundary dispute based upon the limits of the viceroyalities of New Granada and Peru in August 1809; to respect each other's independence; and to refrain from interfering in the other's domestic politics. However, the treaty was repudiated by the Peruvian Congress on April 2, claiming it was signed *en el campo* (in the field) under duress.³⁰

Of the 8,000-man Peruvian army which invaded Gran Colombia, 4,500 men returned to Peru. The remainder were casualties of battle, disease, or desertion. Nonetheless, military operations dragged on. The Peruvian navy raided the Gran Colombian coast as far north as Panama. The Peruvian garrison at Guayaquil was reinforced. Due to the riverine environment surrounding Guayaquil and the lack of a Gran Colombian naval force, Bolívar found it difficult to attack the city.³¹

Back in Peru, believing that La Mar had been sufficiently discredited, Gamarra notified La Fuente to seize the Vice President, and on June 7 Gamarra took La Mar prisoner and exiled him to Central America.[32]

On August 31 the Liberals in the Peruvian Congress bowed to the *fete a campi* and named Gamarra provisional president and La Fuente vice president. On September 22, 1829, Peru and Gran Colombia signed the Treaty at Guayaquil (also know as the Larrea-Gual Treaty), which conceded much of the disputed territory to Gran Colombia.[33]

OBSERVATIONS

Both sides were disappointed with the results of the war. For the Peruvian Liberals, the war had the opposite effect for which they had hoped. La Mar's defeat led to the collapse of the weak Peruvian executive and the seizure of power by the domineering Gamarra. Also, Sucre's victory helped Bolívar to suppress the Liberals in Gran Colombia.[34]

The war did not achieve Gamarra's desires of reassembling the old Viceroyalty of Peru. But both he and Andrés de Santa Cruz succeeded in gaining the presidencies of their respective homelands, Peru and Bolivia. Following the Peruvian defeat by Gran Colombia, Gamarra and La Fuente chose to ignore their agreement with Santa Cruz to unite Peru and Bolivia (see chapter 11).[35]

Gran Colombia was unable to occupy the disputed territory in the *selva*. In 1830 Gran Colombia dissolved into New Granada, Venezuela, and Ecuador. Now Ecuador fell heir to this territorial dispute with Peru.[36]

Sucre, once again, demonstrated his superior skills as a strategist. His task was made easier by Gamarra's duplicity. Gen. Juan Flores distinguished himself as chief of staff of the Gran Colombian army during the Battle of Portete de Tarqui and was promoted to division general; this enhanced his political stature within Ecuador.[37]

The war was too short to permit Peru's superior navy to influence its outcome.

Map 3. Latin America after the Early Wars for Independence, 1828.

PART 3

WARS OF SEPARATION VERSUS UNION—SPANISH AND PORTUGUESE AMERICA

CHAPTER NINE

BUENOS AIRES VERSUS THE PROVINCES, 1820–61

> "Death to the filthy, loathsome, savage Unitarians."
> —slogan of Juan Manuel de Rosas

THE SPARK

On February 1, 1820, some 1,600 Provincials from Santa Fé and Entre Ríos led by Estanislao López defeated 2,000 *Porteños* (those inhabiting the port of Buenos Aires) led by José Rondeau at the Battle of Cepeda (120 mi NW of Buenos Aires). Only 900 *Porteños* escaped death or capture. The Provincials compelled the *Porteños* to sign the Treaty of Pilar on February 23 which created a federation within modern Argentina. In fact, between 1820 and 1824 no federation existed; each province was sovereign.[1]

BACKGROUND

The struggle between the *Porteños* and those in the provinces (including the province of Buenos Aires) over the destiny of today's Argentina was deeply rooted in the colonial and independence era. Although frictions existed among the provinces, they could agree upon one point: the Provincials did not want to be governed by the *Porteños*.

Even before independence had been secured, the overriding political issue for the United Provinces (the former Spanish viceregalty of Río de la Plata) was into how many countries would it fragment. Bolivia and Paraguay began to break away as early as 1810 and Uruguay in 1816. Even within what is now Argentina, significant friction existed between the older population centers in the interior, such as Córdoba and Santa Fé, and the upstart port of Buenos Aires.[2]

The vast space in between was dominated by the *gauchos*. Their enemies saw them as "Christian savages . . . whose principal furniture consists of the skulls of horses, whose food is raw meat and water, and whose favorite pastime is running horses to death," as described by

Sir Walter Scott.³ Their friends saw rugged individualists who cherished freedom. "What other troops in the world are so independent? With the sun for their guide, mare's flesh for food, their saddle-cloths for beds; as long as there is a little water, these men would penetrate to the end of the world." Thus wrote Charles Darwin.⁴ The *gaucho* was a fierce fighter who gave his allegiance only to those who were even tougher. And the toughest of the tough were the *caudillos*.⁵

In 1816 the Congress of Tucumán belatedly declared independence of the United Provinces of South America from Spain. The name itself was a contradiction. Notably absent from the Congress were the province of Banda Oriental (today's Uruguay), and northeastern, modern-day Argentina—the provinces of Santa Fé, Corrientes, and Entre Ríos. And, those who were present at Tucumán could not agree on many major issues, including the form of government to be adopted. Nevertheless, for the short term the Congress did create a strong executive in Buenos Aires, which successfully supported General San Martín's war against the Royalists in faraway Chile. But those in the interior provinces viewed the Congress as divisive; it threatened their independence. For three years (1816–19), Martín Pueyrredón ruled from the port with an iron fist.⁶

In 1819 the Congress in Buenos Aires dominated by the *Porteños* (having earned the enmity of the provinces by migrating from Tucumán) drafted a Unitarian, Centralist constitution which was opposed by the *caudillos* who ruled in the provinces—Estanislao López in Santa Fé; Pedro Ramírez in Entre Ríos; Martín Guemes in Salta; and Bernabé Araóz in Tucumán. José Rondeau, who had replaced Pueyrredón as the governor of the port of Buenos Aires, ordered General San Martín to return from Chile with the Army of the Andes and rescue the central government from the *caudillos*; San Martín refused, believing that the defeat of the Royalists was the supreme business at hand.⁷ Rondeau also ordered General Belgrano, commanding the Army of the North, to come to his aid. However, this army mutinied at Arequito (165 mi WNW of Buenos Aires) and disintegrated. The Provincials defeated the *Porteños* at Cepeda and imposed the Treaty of Pilar.⁸

OPPOSING FORCES

Many participated in the fighting over the next four decades—the Provincials or Federalists, the *Porteños* or Unitarians, the opposing *Blanco* and *Colorado* parties in Uruguay, and, on occasion, the Bolivians, Paraguayans, Brazilians, British, and French, plus assorted collections of "citizens of the world."

In the 1820s, the population of today's Argentina was about 600,000 people. About one-quarter lived in the province of Buenos Aires (about the size of today's Uruguay); it was stronger than any other province but not equal to their combined weight. Of the 150,000 people living in the province of Buenos Aires, many lived in the port. The southern half of today's Argentina was empty except for nomadic Indians. And this distribution of the Argentine population remained constant over the next few decades; immigration was not encouraged. As a consequence, by the early 1850s, the population had increased only by some 200,000 people.⁹

The Provincials primarily relied on the *gauchos* to form their armies. Typically, such armies had three times as many cavalry as infantry. Future Argentine President Domingo Sarmiento wrote, "he [the *gaucho*] and his horse are but one person. He lives on horseback; trades, buys, and sells on horseback; drinks, eats, sleeps, and dreams on horseback."¹⁰

Once Manuel Rosas¹¹ dominated the Provincials beginning in the late 1820s, he added a new element to the Provincial army: the poor from the port of Buenos Aires. He maintained an army

Figure 8. Buenos Aires vs. the Provinces, 1820–61. Manuel Rosas dominated the Río de la Plata from the late 1820s through the early 1850s. To this day, he is characterized as a "saint" by some and a "devil" by others. Those who laud this *caudillo* dwell on his opposition to the incursions of European nations into the region. Those who demonize Rosas focus on his brutality. His armies usually included an individual with the "rank" of executioner. Those executed typically had their throats slit. *Copied from* Harper's New Monthly Magazine, *Vol. 61 (July 1880).*

camp just outside the port. Both the poor and the *gaucho* disdained the more affluent Unitarians, hence the slogan "Death to the filthy, loathsome, savage Unitarians."[12] Rosas' army did not require much logistical support. The *gauchos* were used to living off the fertile countryside, and the poor, who made up the infantry, were used to doing without.[13]

Although armed with muskets and rifles, native weapons were favored due to the scarcity of gunpowder. Much of the cavalry was armed with lances which frequently were the most lethal weapons on the battlefield. Most men carried a knife, a lazo, and a *boleadora* (also known as "the three Marys"). A *boleadora* was three stones or lead balls attached to rawhide thongs about five feet long which were tied together. When throwing, the user held one ball and swung the others to gain momentum before releasing it.[14]

Another force at Rosas' disposal for maintaining internal security was the *Mazorca* (ear of corn, so called because of the cohesion of its members). During Rosas' brief absence from politics (1832–35), his wife worked through a society for his restoration (*La Sociedad Popular Restauradora*) which evolved into the secret support group, the *Mazorca*. The *Mazorca* created a cult that deified Rosas. His portraits found their way near the altars of the churches. Even the color blue, associated with the Unitarians, vanished from view and everyone was required to wear the scarlet of the federation.[15]

The Unitarians initially drew their support from the commercial class. Once driven into exile in Montevideo, their numbers were swelled by Europeans who abandoned their homelands frequently following failed revolutions against conservative governments.

OPENING STRATEGIES

Both sides employed brutality on and off the battlefield to intimidate or eliminate opponents. Frequently, armies would not take prisoners. Rosas elevated this to an art form. Those captured were executed by having their throats cut (*pasado a degüello*). Executioners (*degolladores*) held the rank of noncommissioned officers and were feared and respected.[16]

Rosas controlled the littorial provinces through shifting alliances with *caudillos*, maintaining a balance of power in his favor. Since Rosas controlled the custom houses through which eighty percent of all revenues passed, including those of the interior provinces, the *caudillos* could not ignore Rosas' desires. No national constitution existed, only Rosas' word. As governor of the province of Buenos Aires, he conducted foreign affairs, including the making of war.

Those who opposed Rosas agreed that he needed to be deposed, but each favored a different strategy, usually driven by his own goals and resources. The *émigré Porteños* favored the direct approach—attack the city of Buenos Aires—but never had enough strength to carry through. The Uruguayan *Colorados* preferred to attack Rosas through Entre Ríos and Corrientes, hoping to detach these provinces from the United Provinces and add them to Uruguay. When involved, the British and French preferred to use the indirect approach of the blockade, because their primary strength was naval power and their prime motivation was commerce. Frequently, the forces opposed to Rosas would politically unite but seldom abandoned their own military strategies in favor of their allies.

THE UNEASY TRUCE BETWEEN PROVINCIALS AND *PORTEÑOS*

In February 1826 the Congress at the port of Buenos Aires elected Bernardino Rivadavia president to lead the United Provinces in war against Brazil (see chapter 7). The Provincial *caudillos* did little to support the war against Brazil. Toward the end of the war, Rivadavia was forced to resign and Manuel Dorrego, the *caudillo* of the province of Buenos Aires, took charge.[17]

On December 1, 1828, Gen. Juan Lavalle, leading troops that had just returned from the war against Brazil, seized the seat of government in the port of Buenos Aires. Governor Dorrego attempted to flee, was captured by Lavalle at Navarro on December 13, and within two hours was shot by Lavalle's order without a trial.[18]

In April 1829 the provinces led by Estanislao López and Juan Manuel de Rosas, the *caudillos* of the provinces of Entre Ríos and Buenos Aires, defeated Lavalle who fled to Uruguay. On December 8 Rosas was elected governor of the province of Buenos Aires, thus beginning his direct and indirect rule over the future Argentina which lasted until 1852.[19]

THE UNITARIAN LEAGUE

Unitarian Gen. José M. Paz, a one-armed War for Independence veteran and a superior tactician, was the first to seriously challenge Rosas' authority. In 1829 Paz assembled an army of 1,000 men, marched inland to Córdoba (434 mi NW of Buenos Aires), and defeated Gov. Juan Bautista Bustos commanding 1,600 Provincials at San Roque on April 22.[20]

Facundo Quiroga ("the tiger of the *llanos*"), the *caudillo* from Rioja, joined Bustos and formed a new Provincial army of 5,000 men. Paz, leading 1,650 Unitarians, defeated Quiroga on June 22–23, 1829, at La Tablada, northeast of the city of Córdoba. Paz, commanding 4,000 Unitarians, again defeated the Provincials on February 25, 1830 at Oncativo. The Provincials lost 1,000 dead and 500 prisoners, and the Unitarians sustained only 80 dead and wounded. As a result, Paz won control of nine interior provinces uniting them in the Unitarian League (*Liga Unitaria*) on August 30, 1830.[21]

Control of today's Argentina was divided among Paz who held the interior, Estanislao López the littoral, and Rosas the province and port of Buenos Aires. Paz demanded that Rosas and López submit to his authority. As a consequence, on January 4, 1831, Rosas and López created the Littoral League (*Liga del Litoral*) and in February declared war on Paz.

On May 10 Paz, while reconnoitering a potential battlefield with a small escort, was unhorsed by *boleadoras* and captured. The Unitarian cause collapsed on November 4, 1831, when 1,650 Provincials crushed 1,950 Unitarians at Ciudadela de Tucumán. Some thirty-three Unitarian officers were executed.[22]

Between 1832 and 1835 Rosas chose to go off and fight the Indians because the *junta* (his local power base) refused to extend his dictatorial powers. During his absence, his wife carried on a successful campaign for his recall.

WAR AGAINST THE PERU–BOLIVIA CONFEDERATION

In 1837 Rosas joined Chile to make war on the Peru-Bolivia Confederation (see chapter 11). Numerous factors motivated Rosas to declare war on May 19, 1837. Most important was a boundary dispute over the province of Tarija. Also, Rosas perceived the unification of Peru and Bolivia as creating a strong neighbor and a possible threat. And finally, Unitarian refugees had found haven in Bolivia from Rosas' terror. Throughout the first year the fighting was inconclusive, but on June 24, 1838, the Bolivians defeated troops from the United Provinces at the Battle of Montenegro (495 mi NW of Buenos Aires and 495 mi SSE of La Paz, Bolivia), and Rosas withdrew from the war.[23]

FRENCH BLOCKADE

On March 28, 1838, the French consul announced the blockade of the port and province of Buenos Aires. Superficially, the cause was Rosas' treatment of a consular agent who had protested the impressment of French citizens into Rosas' army. The motivation was more complex. Rosas, France, and Great Britain were all competing for domination of the region's commerce. The center of anti-Rosas Unitarian activity was Montevideo. At the same time, an on-again, off-again civil war raged in Uruguay between the *Blancos* headed by Manuel Oribe and the *Colorados* led by Fructuoso Rivera (see chapter 25).

An alliance was forged among the commander of the French fleet, Admiral Luis LeBlanc; exiled Unitarians; and the out-of-power Uruguayan *Colorado* Rivera. On June 15, 1838, Rivera, leading an army composed of Rosas' enemies, defeated Oribe at El Palmar (130 mi NW of Montevideo). Oribe retreated into Montevideo.[24]

Next, the allies captured the Island of Martín García (23 mi N of Buenos Aires) on October 11, 1838, following a stout defense by 125 defenders. The capture of the island gave them control of the Paraná and Uruguay Rivers. As a consequence, Rosas' custom house receipts plummeted.[25]

THE GREAT WAR, 1839–52

The victorious anti-Rosas allies besieged Montevideo and forced the Uruguayan *Blanco* Oribe to flee on October 24, 1838. Rosas received Oribe in Buenos Aires as Uruguay's president in exile and placed him in command of an army. In Montevideo the anti-Rosas Unitarians formed an Argentine government in exile. The Uruguayan Congress now led by Rivera declared war against Rosas (and not Argentina, to gain the participation of the Unitarians) on February 24, 1839.[26]

The fighting intensified in the littoral provinces (Santa Fé, Entre Ríos, and Corrientes). Gen. Estanislao López, the "Patriarch of the Federation," *caudillo* of Entre Ríos, and ally of Rosas, had died on June 15, 1838. Initially, he was succeeded by Domingo Cullen, who did not support Rosas. On December 31, 1838, Berón de Astrada, Governor of Corrientes, pronounced against Rosas and joined the Uruguayan *Colorado* Rivera to fight Rosas. Their plan was to invade Entre Ríos and cross the Paraná River into Santa Fé.

Rosas succeeded in replacing Cullen with Gen. Juan Pablo López, Estanislao's brother. Gen. Pascual Echagüe, an ally of Rosas, invaded Corrientes and crushed Berón de Astrada at the Battle of Pago Largo (290 mi N of Buenos Aires) on March 31, 1839. Echagüe's vanguard was commanded by the talented Justo José de Urquíza.[27] Echagüe commanded 5,500 cavalry, 360 infantry, and two cannon; Berón de Astrada had 4,500 cavalry, 450 infantry, and three cannon. The Unitarians lost 2,000 men, which included 800 prisoners whose throats were slit. Among those was Astrada. Echagüe lost 55 dead and 104 wounded.[28]

REBELLION IN THE SOUTH

Col. Ramón Maza (son of the president of Rosas' rubber-stamp assembly in the port of Buenos Aires), General Lavalle in Montevideo, and anti-Rosas would-be *caudillos* in the southern part of the province of Buenos Aires, conspired to depose Rosas. The plan was discovered. Maza and his followers in the city (including his father) were executed.[29]

THE UNITARIANS RETURN

On August 2, 1839, General Lavalle, leading 550 men, sailed from Montevideo in French warships. His initial strategy was to disembark south of the port of Buenos Aires. However, he changed his plan because of the difficulty of receiving support along the open coast and the pressure on northern Uruguay by Rosas' ally General Echagüe. Thus, without support from Lavalle, on October 29, 1839, would-be *caudillos* in the south of Buenos Aires Province rebelled. Rosas dispatched an army under his brother Prudencio who defeated the rebels at Chascomús (62 mi SSE of Buenos Aires) on November 7. Their heads were used to decorate the local plaza.[30]

Turning north, Lavalle disembarked in Entre Ríos on September 2. Lavalle defeated Governor Echagüe at Yeruá (330 mi N of Buenos Aires) on the twelfth. From Entre Ríos Lavalle marched north into Corrientes. Juan Pablo López, Governor of Santa Fé and supporter of Rosas, crossed the Paraná River with 2,500 men and sought battle which Lavalle successfully evaded. On December 29, 1839, Rivera, leading 4,800 Uruguayans (4,000 cavalry and 800 infantry) defeated Echagüe leading 5,000 Argentine Provincials. Echagüe lost 480 dead and 1,000 prisoners; Rivera lost 323 dead and 190 wounded.

In early 1840 Lavalle turned south but was defeated in a series of battles by Echagüe. Evacuated by the French navy, Lavalle now landed near Buenos Aires. He marched to Merlo (12 mi W of Buenos Aires). Support did not materialize so, perhaps losing his nerve, he retreated northward to join the "Coalition of the North" (the provinces of Tucumán, Salta, La Rioja, and Juyuy) which had declared against Rosas.[31]

Rosas sent Gen. Gregorio Aráoz de la Madrid to fight the Unitarians; however, when he arrived at Tucumán he changed sides. Undeterred, Rosas gathered an army of 10,000 men and placed it under Oribe. On November 28 these forces met at Quebracho Herrado (280 mi NW of Buenos Aires) in Santa Fé. Defeated, Lavalle split major units from the main body. Oribe did the same and Rosas' forces triumphed in the subsequent actions between these elements. The main forces met again at Famaillá on September 19, 1841. The Unitarian army was composed of 1,300 cavalry, 70 poorly armed infantry, and three cannon. The Provincials had 1,700 cavalry, 700 infantry, and three cannon. The Unitarians were crushed losing 600 killed and 480 prisoners. José Cubas, Governor of Catamarca, and 600 of his followers had their throats cut. Lavalle was shot in October while trying to flee to Bolivia.[32]

By October 29, 1840, the French wearied of the struggle and Great Britain, concerned that it might lose commercial advantage to its European rival, pressured the French to end the fighting. France raised the blockade which had never been effectively pursued.[33] French claims were submitted to arbitration. The island of Martín García was returned to Rosas. He agreed to respect the independence of Uruguay "so long as the rights, honour and security of the Argentine Confederation were not endangered."[34] Rosas emerged as a national hero for having conceded virtually nothing to the European power.

FIGHTING ON THE RIVER

Following the lifting of the French blockade of Buenos Aires, Rosas ordered his squadron to attack the Unitarians and Uruguayans. During the second half of 1841, Admiral Brown fought four battles (May 24, August 3, and December 9 and 21) against John Halstead Coe and won control of the lower river for Rosas.[35]

Giuseppe Garibaldi, who had fled from Rio Grande do Sul following the defeat of the separatists by the Brazilian empire, was given command of three small Uruguayan warships. Brown caught Garibaldi at Costa Brava near the Corrientes-Entre Ríos border on August 15, 1842, and forced him to abandon his ships.[36]

PAZ RETURNS

In the meantime, General Paz escaped from Rosas' control after eight years of captivity and gathered an army in Corrientes. He was joined by Unitarians who had been defeated at Famaillá and trekked through the forests of the Chaco to return home. Rosas once again called upon General Echagüe of Entre Ríos to oppose this new threat. Paz crossed the Corrientes River at night and took Echagüe's army by surprise, defeating it on November 28, 1841, at Caaguazú (324 mi N of Buenos Aires).[37]

Internal dissension among the anti-Rosas forces caused the command of the army to change from Paz to the Uruguayan President Rivera. On December 6, 1842, Oribe, commanding 6,500 cavalry, 2,500 infantry, and 18 guns, crushed Rivera, commanding 5,500 cavalry, 2,000 infantry, and 16 guns at the Battle of Arroyo Grande (165 mi N of Buenos Aires). Oribe lost 300 dead and wounded. Rivera lost 2,000 dead and 1,400 prisoners. The captured officers and sergeants had their throats cut.[38]

BRITISH AND FRENCH INTERVENTION

There was still no peace between Uruguay and Rosas. Rosas knew well that in addition to encouraging exiles, Rivera coveted Corrientes and Entre Ríos for Uruguay. In 1841 Uruguay offered trade concessions, first to Great Britain and then to France, in exchange for protection against Rosas. They refused but decided to intervene in order to safeguard their commercial interests. Following Rivera's defeat at Arroyo Grande, Oribe crossed the Uruguay River and marched against Montevideo. The French and British ministers in Buenos Aires issued formal declarations that the belligerents must cease fighting. On January 3, 1843, Admiral Brown sailed from Buenos Aires to blockade Montevideo and by mid-February General Oribe began a siege that would last for nine years.

A 7,000-man militia dominated by foreigners (2,000 French led by Juan Thiébaut, 600 Italians led by Garibaldi, and 500 Unitarians led by Eustaquio Díaz Vélez) and led by Paz saved the city.[39]

The British Commander of the South East Coast of America, Adm. John Purvis, who disliked the Irish, ordered Brown to withdraw, citing as his authority the British Foreign Enlistment Act of 1819 which prohibited British subjects from bearing arms in wars in which Great Britain was neutral. Brown sailed back to Buenos Aires where, through diplomacy, the British disavowed Purvis' actions and, in the middle of June, Brown once again established a blockade of Montevideo.[40]

The siege of Montevideo continued throughout 1844 and 1845. On April 24, 1844, Paz led 7,800 troops out of the city in an attempt to surprize Oribe. The 2,000 attackers sent by boat up the Río de la Plata to outflank the besiegers made so much noise disembarking at Arroyo Pantanoso that they alerted the enemy and foiled the attack. On July 4 Paz resigned as the garrison's commander and emigrated to Rio de Janeiro.[41]

On March 27, 1845, Urquiza decisively defeated Rivera at India Muerta (80 mi NE of Buenos Aires). Both armies were about 3,000 strong and Rivera lost 400 dead and 500 prisoners. Rivera fled to the safety of the Brazilian province Rio Grande do Sul.[42]

"THE STEALING OF THE FLEET"

In May 1845, the British and French ministers in Buenos Aires feared a Rosas victory. On July 31 their squadrons, commanded by Adm. Samuel Hood Inglefield and Adm. Pierre Jean Honorat Lainé,[43] seized Brown's command—one corvette, two brigs, and two schooners—and forced the numerous English, Irish, and French sailors fighting for Rosas to abandon the siege. These sailors were forced to sign a document promising not to take part in a war against the nation of their origin or they would be considered traitors. At this time, Brazil joined the European powers and made its warships available. On September 18 France and Great Britain declared a blockade of Buenos Aires.[44]

GARIBALDI'S OFFENSIVE

Free from opposition from Brown's squadron, the Uruguayan navy, commanded by Garibaldi and aided by the British and French fleets, took action. Garibaldi, commanding 1,000 men which included 700 Italian volunteers, captured Colonia (66 mi W of Montevideo) on August 31, 1845, and the island of Martín García on September 6. Proceeding up the Uruguay River, he sacked Gualeguaychu, Argentina, on September 20 and captured Salta, Uruguay, in late October.[45]

BATTLE OF VUELTA DE OBLIGADO

Meanwhile, in November 1845 Great Britain and France chose to force the passage of the Paraná River which Rosas had closed to all foreign navigation. They dispatched six British and five French warships convoying fifty merchant ships. Rosas' forces erected batteries composed of twenty-one assorted medium-calibre guns on the bluff of Tonelero at Vuelta de Obligado (90 mi NW of Buenos Aires and 60 mi SE of Rosario) and blocked the river by placing chains across.

The defenses were overcome after a nine-hour fight by the heavier guns in the fleet on November 20. Rosas' forces lost 150 dead, 93 missing, and 90 wounded; the British lost nine killed and 24 wounded, and the French lost 20 killed and 60 wounded. In spite of the defeat, Rosas was acclaimed the defender of national sovereignty against foreign intervention.[46]

THE NORTH REBELS AGAIN

The province of Corrientes, which had been brought into the Argentine Confederation following the Battle of Arroyo Grande, rebelled. The rebels chose General Paz to lead the Corrientes' troops. Also, Paraguayan President (for life) Carlos López declared war on Rosas and sent 4,000 troops under his son Francisco Solano López to support the Madariaga brothers and Paz. On February 4, 1846, Urquiza defeated the vanguard of the Corrientes' army led by Juan Madariaga at Laguna Limpia (225 mi N of Buenos Aires). The Corrientes signed the Treaty of Alcaraz on August 15 which required them to adhere to the federal pact.

However, Rosas rejected the treaty and ordered Urquiza to depose the leaders. A resentful Urquiza nevertheless complied. Urquiza, commanding 6,500 men (6,000 cavalry, 500 infantry, and seven guns), defeated Joaquin and Juan Madariaga commanding 5,000 men (4,100 cavalry, 900 infantry, and twelve guns) at Potrero de Vences (240 mi N of Buenos Aires) on November 27, 1847.[47]

Concerned by the 1848 Revolutionary movements in Europe and the U.S.-Mexican War in North America, the British and French reached an accommodation with Rosas. The British

Figure 9. Buenos Aires vs. the Provinces, 1820–61. Giuseppe Garibaldi was one of many displaced European revolutionaries who fought against Rosas and Argentina. Garibaldi commanded anti-Rosas forces both on land and at sea. Ironically, because of his ultimate stature as a hero of Italian independence, the Argentine navy named a number of its most important warships for Garibaldi, beginning in the late nineteenth century. The choice of his name was undoubtedly influenced by the very large number of Italians who migrated to Argentina at that time. *Copied from* The Century Magazine, *Vol. 24 (1882).*

raised their blockade of Buenos Aires in July 1847. In June 1848 the French gave up their blockade of Buenos Aires but continued to blockade the ports in Uruguay controlled by Oribe.

On November 24, 1849, and August 31, 1850, respectively, Great Britain and France signed peace treaties with Rosas. The British and French returned Martín García and the seized warships, and disarmed and evacuated the foreign legion from Montevideo. In exchange, Rosas withdrew his troops from Uruguay. The British and French intervention had been particularly injurious to Rosas' source of revenue. However, the loose siege of Montevideo by Oribe commanding Uruguayan *Blancos* continued.[48]

BATTLE OF CASEROS

By 1851 Urquiza had evolved into the strongest *caudillo*, now even stronger than the aging Rosas, whom he had supported. On May 1 Urquiza issued a *pronunciamiento*, which declared that Entre Ríos resumed the power it had delegated to Rosas — a virtual declaration of independence. On May 29, representatives of Entre Ríos, Corrientes, Brazil, and the *Colorados* of Uruguay signed a pact at Montevideo against Rosas.

Urquiza led his 6,500-man army across the Uruguay River into Uruguay and forced Oribe to surrender, thus lifting the nine-year siege of Montevideo. Reacting, Rosas declared war against Brazil on August 16. Meanwhile, the allied army grew to 28,189 men (10,670 from Entre Ríos, 5,260 from Corrientes, 4,240 from Buenos Aires, 4,040 from Brazil, 1,907 from Uruguay, and 2,072 more men in the artillery and train).

In December 1851 Urquiza, aided by Brazilian Rear Admiral Grenfell,[49] crossed the Paraná River into Santa Fé and advanced on Buenos Aires. Santa Fé joined the rebellion. On February 3, 1852, the opposing armies met at Caseros (7 mi W of Buenos Aires). Rosas' army was composed of 12,000 cavalry and 10,000 infantry supported by thirty guns. In the middle of the battle, General Urquiza chose to lead cavalry charges, leaving his surprised adjutant with the responsibility of issuing battle orders. Although the wings of Rosas' army were easily put to flight, the artillery which formed the center fought tenaciously. Rosas lost 1,400 killed and 7,000 prisoners; Urquiza lost 600 killed and wounded. Defeated, Rosas fled to England.[50]

On May 31, 1852, the governors of the provinces agreed to the Pact of San Nicolás. This provided for a national congress, eliminated provincial trade barriers, and made Urquiza provisional director of the nation.[51]

BUENOS AIRES VERSUS THE PROVINCES

With the defeat of Rosas, the province and port of Buenos Aires began to atone. Many of the Unitarians returned from exile and now helped to expel the Provincials who supported Rosas. On September 11, 1852, the port of Buenos Aires declared independence from the confederation. Reacting, Col. Hilario Lagos led the *gauchos* of the Province of Buenos Aires against the city and besieged it between December 1852 and July 1853. Urquiza supported the besiegers and used the provincial squadron to blockade Buenos Aires. The commander of the squadron, Commodore John Coe, sold out to the city for 26,000 ounces of gold, and the siege collapsed. On January 8, 1855, Buenos Aires and the United Provinces signed a peace treaty, but it was not well observed, and both sides carried on a trade war against the other.[52]

Thus, two nations began to evolve. The frontier nation of the Argentine Confederation (minus Buenos Aires) had a population of about one million, with few of the social and economic developments associated with a modern, mid-nineteenth-century nation. The other was the province of Buenos Aires whose 400,000 population included the vast majority of the educated.[53] Almost all foreign trade passed through Buenos Aires, thereby giving it control over most revenues. In order to raise revenue and promote trade, the United Provinces passed a tax upon European goods which were shipped through Buenos Aires. This and subsequent economic retaliations by Buenos Aires led again to war.

BATTLE OF CÉPEDA

On May 29, 1859, the Confederation authorized Urquiza to resubjugate Buenos Aires. On July 7 Buenos Aires dispatched the steamers *General Pinto* and *Buenos Aires* up the Paraná

SAN LUIS.—RETURN OF THE VIDETTES.

Figure 10. Buenos Aires vs. the Provinces, 1820–61. During the first seven or eight decades of the nineteenth century lance-armed cavalry, like these pictured on the Argentine *pampas*, dominated Latin American battlefields in Argentina, southern Brazil, eastern Colombia, western Cuba, northern Mexico, eastern Santo Domingo, Uruguay, and most of Venezuela. These twelve-foot lances were wielded with great agility and inflicted lethal wounds. *Copied from* Harper's New Monthly Magazine, *Vol. 17 (1858).*

River to prevent the confederation from using the river as an avenue of advance. However, the marines on board the *General Pinto* mutinied and switched sides. In October a Confederation squadron fought its way past the Buenos Aires' battery on the island of Martín García and then aided Urquiza's movement down the Paraná River.[54]

The two sides met at Cépeda (117 Mi NW of Buenos Aires) on October 23, 1859. General Urquiza, commanding 10,000 men (6,000 cavalry, 3,000 infantry, 1,000 gunners) defeated Mitre commanding 8,300 men (4,000 cavalry, 4,000 infantry, and 300 gunners). Urquiza lost 300 men. Mitre escaped with 2,000 men and a few cannon, but Urquiza captured 2,000 *Porteños*, 20 cannon, and most of the enemy's supplies.[55]

Urquiza marched toward Buenos Aires and the Governor resigned. Through the mediation of Francisco Solano López of Paraguay, Buenos Aires reunited with the Confederation on November 11. The 1853 Constitution was amended to give Buenos Aires greater representation.

BATTLE OF PAVÓN

Again in 1861 war broke out between Buenos Aires and the United Provinces over the sharing of power. On September 17, 1861, 16,000 troops (9,000 infantry, 6,000 cavalry, 35 cannon) from Buenos Aires led by Mitre met the 16,000-man Provincial army (5,000 infantry, 11,000 cavalry, and 42 guns) led by Urquiza at Pavón (146 mi NW of Buenos Aires). Urquiza's cavalry defeated that of Buenos Aires but his infantry was routed and most of his artillery captured. Urquiza chose not to continue the fight, led his cavalry from the field, and did not stop until he reached Entre Ríos even though he had lost fewer men to this point. Mitre captured 1,650 prisoners, 37 guns, and the enemy's entire train.[56]

The result was the triumph of Buenos Aires by default and the unification of Argentina. Mitre occupied the city of Paraná, the capital of the United Provinces, dissolved the federal Congress, and assumed national authority.[57]

Not everyone peacefully accepted the union and over the next two decades force was necessary to suppress rebellious *caudillos*. Between 1870 and 1876 *caudillos* led three separate insurrections.

OBSERVATIONS

By 1861 modern Argentina began to emerge from this long and chaotic struggle as the age of the *caudillo* was ending. The incessant fighting which had taken place between 1820 and 1861 was as much social in character as political and economic. In the early years, it was the port of Buenos Aires against the provinces; the educated against the uneducated; the city dwellers against those of the country; the upper class against the lower; and the democrats and anarchists of the provinces against the Monarchists and aristocrats of Buenos Aires. In short, the way of life was at stake.[58]

Between 1829 and 1851 Manuel Rosas dominated today's Argentina. There is possibly no more controversial figure in Latin American history, savior to some and archvillain to others. Recounting his brutalities is easy. He ruled as an absolute dictator. His armies seldom showed mercy to the defeated but frequently the same could be said for the other side. In the port of Buenos Aires, perhaps 20,000 people died at the hands of the *Mazorca* by poisoning, beheading, strangulation, and the like. Socially, economically, and politically Rosas unsuccessfully attempted to prevent change.[59]

Citing Rosas' successes is more difficult because one can only guess at the alternative outcomes. At the least, Rosas left Argentina no less united than when he took control in spite of the intentions of many powerful men, Argentine and foreign, to break it apart. A very kind evaluation might be that Rosas was a heavy-handed caretaker.[60]

Rosas' rule had been dependent upon his physical qualities, which made him a *caudillo* (toughest of the tough), the help of the other *caudillos*, and the support of the port's poor. If nothing else, aging undermined his physical prowess and as a consequence his hold over the other *caudillos*. Rosas last appeared on the field of battle in 1840. Also, the free-spirited Urquiza eventually believed that Rosas' policy of personalized anarchism was counterproductive.[61]

Between 1851 and 1861, Justo Urquiza attempted to dominate Argentina as Rosas had done in the previous decades. A *caudillo* perhaps no less brutal than Rosas, Urquiza may be credited with having been the catalyst for Argentina's transition from neofeudalism to an emerging nation.[62]

CHAPTER TEN

CENTRAL AMERICAN UNION, 1826–40

"Long Live Religion, and Death to the Foreigners"
—Battle Cry of Rafael Carrera

THE SPARK

Throughout 1826 tensions increased between the Liberals and Conservatives in the recently proclaimed United Provinces of Central America. On October 13 the acting chief of state of Guatemala, Cirilo Flores, was killed by an Indian mob because of his anticlerical position. As a consequence, the Liberal Salvadorian delegation to the national legislature withdrew from Guatemala City. Both the Liberals and Conservatives prepared to impose their will by force.[1]

BACKGROUND

Spaniards first set foot in Central America in 1502 and within thirty years they had subdued the isthmus (but never completely conquered it). The isthmus' first government, an *audiencia*, was established in Panama City in 1533 and within ten years it was superseded by the *audiencia* in Guatemala City which evolved into the Captaincy-General of Guatemala. Initially, the Captaincy-General was composed of the provinces of Chiapas (today part of Mexico), Guatemala, Honduras, Nicaragua, and Panama (which in 1751 was transferred to the Viceroyalty of New Granada). El Salvador (originally called San Salvador) gained provincial status in the eighteenth century. The Captaincy-General of Guatemala was the last Spanish mainland dependency to declare independence, doing so on September 15, 1821.

A number of political factions emerged within Central America. The Conservatives were split between the *Serviles*, mostly centered in Guatemala, and the *Provincianos*, who were scattered throughout the remaining provinces. The *Serviles* favored a government based upon traditional institutions (particularly the Roman Catholic Church) and dominated by Guatemala, as had been the political situation during colonial days. The *Provincianos* favored a similar political agenda without the dominance of Guatemala. The Liberals (also called Radicals) favored significant institutional changes particularly as they related to the role of the Roman Catholic Church. Their strength was in El Salvador and Honduras but they also had followers throughout other parts of Central America.

At the invitation of Mexican Gen. Agustín de Iturbide (soon to become Emperor Agustín I), the former Captaincy-General of Guatemala, then dominated by the Conservatives, chose to be annexed to Mexico on January 5, 1822. However, the decision was far from unanimous. The Liberals in the town of San Salvador declared their independence. They raised an army in order to subdue those towns in El Salvador which had declared for union with Mexico. To prevent this, the Conservatives in Guatemala sent an army under Col. Manuel Arzú which captured San Salvador; however, the Conservatives soon withdrew and San Salvador reasserted its independence.[2]

Agustín I dispatched Gen. Vicente Filísola, commanding 600 Mexicans, to Guatemala City to ensure that the Central Americans did not change their minds. In November he led 2,000 troops against El Salvador, which had refused to accept the union with Mexico. El Salvador unilaterally declared its annexation to the United States of America in a futile attempt to prevent its subjugation by Mexico. The provincial capital, San Salvador (140 mi SE of Guatemala City), fell to the Mexican-led army on February 10, 1823.[3]

Also during this brief Mexican rule, a civil war broke out in Nicaragua when the city of Grenada and the surrounding area attempted to secede from the province. This provincial struggle within Nicaragua was soon overtaken by events in Guatemala City.[4]

The union with Mexico was short; on July 1, 1823, the former Captaincy-General of Guatemala declared its independence and became the United Provinces of Central America (Chiapas remained part of Mexico). Filisola was in no position to oppose the independence declaration because he knew that Iturbide had been overthrown in February 1823. Thus, independence came to Central America with little bloodshed, notwithstanding that European incursions continued along its coasts.[5]

On September 14, 1823 the first "palace *coups*" in Central America occurred when Capt. Rafael Ariza y Torres attempted to extract a promotion and payment for his troops from Congress. Reacting, 750 Salvadorians commanded by the *peninsular* José Rivas marched on Guatemala City and Ariza fled. The troops supported the Liberal legislators. Shortly, 200 Guatemalan troops arrived from Quezaltenango who, along with 50 Mexican soldiers temporarily left behind, favored the Conservatives. The Conservative-controlled legislature used these 250 troops as the backbone of a 1,000-man, rag-tag army. After some street brawls, both forces agreed to simultaneous withdrawals. This incident demonstrated the severity of the animosity which existed between the Liberals and Conservatives.[6]

On April 21, 1825, the Congress of the United Provinces chose the Liberal Manuel José Arce as president. He attained the presidency by compromising with the Conservatives whereby he agreed not to support a separate bishopric in the Liberal-controlled El Salvador. The compromise alienated the more radical Liberals in Honduras and El Salvador. The murder of Cirilo Flores by the Indian mob on October 13 brought matters to a head.[7]

OPPOSING FORCES

Although united by declaration, Central America was in fact fragmented. El Salvador was very suspicious of the power of Guatemala. Nicaragua and Honduras were almost evenly split between the Conservatives and Liberals. Costa Rica was isolated and frequently chose to remain aloof from Central American politics. In Guatemala, the capital dominated to the point that those in the hinterland talked of secession. Adding to the confusion, Liberals in one province had more in common with Liberals in another than they had with their own Conservatives. The same could be said for the relationship among the Conservatives.[8]

The first national congress estimated the population of Central America to be 1,270,000 inhabitants. Deputies, each representing 30,000 people, were distributed as follows: Guatemala 18, El Salvador 9, Honduras and Nicaragua 6 each, and Costa Rica 2. This distribution clearly recognized that Guatemala was home to 40 to 45 percent of the region's population. The Provincials hoped that Chiapas would rejoin the Central American union and that the separatists of Los Altos within the Guatemalan highlands around Quezaltenango would succeed, join the union, and thus weaken Guatemala's strength.[9]

The people of Central America were probably more racially stratified than anywhere else in Spanish America. Two-thirds of the population were Indians and most of the remaining were *mestizos*. Some 20,000 Negroes and mulattos and less than 100,000 whites rounded out the population. Many people lived in hamlets in the valleys isolated by the rivers, jungles, and mountains.[10]

Initially, both the Liberal and Conservative armies were very similar in composition. The officers and sergeants were associated with the appropriate political party and the conscripts were gathered from the peasant class, at times by force. Conditions within the army were poor. On both sides the civil authorities were nearly bankrupt. Troops were unpaid and some sold their weapons to buy food. Military service was so unpopular that desertions went unpunished for fear of causing mass desertions.[11]

The composition of the Conservative army would change after Rafael Carrera[12] rose to prominence in the late 1830s. His army was composed of ignorant Indians. They were armed with anything that would serve as a weapon. Carrera began with thirteen men armed with old muskets which had to be fired by touching a cigar to the flash pan.[13] With the help of the Roman Catholic Church and wealthy landholders, Carrera soon recruited thousands of fanatical followers.

OPENING STRATEGIES

Much (but not all) of the fighting was between the Conservatives in Guatemala against the Liberals in El Salvador and those of Honduras. El Salvador, Guatemala, and Honduras collectively are slightly smaller than Oregon.

For the Conservatives in Guatemala, their first concern was suppressing the elements within their province opposed to their domination, principally their Liberals and the separatists of Los Altos. The Salvadorian Liberals' initial strategy was building a coalition with Liberals throughout Central America strong enough to defeat the more numerous Guatemalans.

CIVIL WAR OF 1826–29

By 1826 both the Salvadorian and Honduran Liberals invaded Guatemala but were defeated by the Guatemalan and Honduran Conservatives led by the former Liberal, President Arce. He in turn invaded Liberal-dominated El Salvador but was repulsed. Francisco Morazán[14] emerged as the most capable Liberal field commander. Morazán defeated the invading Conservatives at La Trinidad, Honduras, on November 10, 1827. In March 1828 the Conservatives won a bloody battle at Chalchuapa, Honduras. However, by the end of 1828 Morazán drove the Conservatives out of Honduras and El Salvador. Leading a 2,000-man Liberal army composed of Hondurans, Nicaraguans, and Salvadorians, he invaded Guatemala in early 1829. Morazán lay siege to Guatemala City in February and after more than two months of resistance the city surrendered to Morazán on April 12.[15]

Many Conservatives were exiled, their property confiscated, and numerous antichurch measures were enacted. Following Morazán's election as president of the United Provinces of Central America in May 1832, Congress announced that all religions would be tolerated; priests were encouraged to marry, and Protestants were welcomed.

SPAIN THREATENS TO RETURN

The invasion of Mexico by Spain in 1829 alarmed the Liberals and encouraged the Conservatives to believe that a reconquest of Central America was at hand (see chapter 5). The Liberals prepared to repel an invasion while the Conservatives rallied behind Arce, then in exile in Mexico.[16]

The Conservative plan was complex. Arce was to invade Los Altos of Guatemala from Mexico. Conservatives in Honduras were to seize the Atlantic ports of Omoa and Trujillo and then seek help through the Guatemalan Archbishop Ramón Casáirs who remained exiled in Cuba. Initially, their plan went well. Omoa was seized and a ship sent to Cuba for help. Trujillo was captured and the force marched into the interior. El Salvador, momentarily in the hands of the Conservatives, seceded from the union. However, by March 1832 Morazán defeated these threats one by one, including the Conservatives reinforcements sent from Cuba.[17]

In 1834 Morazán moved the federal capital from Guatemala City to San Salvador in an attempt to reduce the influence of the Guatemalan Conservatives. His government was plagued by economic problems.

WAR OF PRINCIPLES

Although the Liberals gained control of Guatemala in 1831, they were soon arguing among themselves. In 1836 Liberals Mariano Gálvez, Governor of Guatemala, and José Francisco Barrundia, responsible for judicial reform, became alienated when Gálvez suspended the extension of new liberal codes. These would have given greater autonomy to the Indian-populated regions of the province. Simultaneously, a cholera epidemic broke out in Belize and spread to El Salvador and Guatemala. In order to contain the epidemic, Gálvez attempted to cordon off the region to prevent the Indians from migrating. The Governor also sent the limited medical aid available into the region. Roman Catholic priests, who supported the Conservative cause, told the Indians that the Liberals sent the doctors to poison their drinking water. This sparked an Indian uprising in the Mita district and Gálvez assumed dictatorial powers.[18]

Among those who were sent to enforce the quarantine was Rafeal Carrera, commanding a platoon of government soldiers. However, he deserted the Liberal-controlled army and championed the Indian cause. Carrera forged the previously apathetic Indians into fanatical guerrillas, primarily through his personal example. Although frequently defeated, Carrera's resiliency became legendary. Indian uprisings occurred throughout the isthmus.[19]

Liberals Gálvez and Barrundia sought allies in their feud. Gálvez turned to the Guatemalan Conservatives. Morazán, governing the union from San Salvador, lost confidence in Gálvez. By 1837 Gálvez was forced to spend one-third of the province's revenues on fighting the war.

Barrundia struck an alliance with Carrera, now known as the "king of the Indians," incorrectly believing that he could control the semi-illiterate Carrera. In early February 1838 Carrera's peasant army of 4,000 men entered Guatemala City, and only through promises,

1,000 muskets, and an $11,000 bribe was he convinced to return to the hinterland. Initially, Barrundia was able to forge a fragile coalition among the Liberals and Conservatives. However, all were preoccupied with Carrera's possible reactions to their decisions.[20]

Los Altos took advantage of this indecision, declared its independence from Guatemala and its loyalty to the Morazán-led union.[21] In March 1838 Carrera once again began guerrilla warfare against those governing in Guatemala City. Barrundia called on Morazán for help and the President of Central America marched into Guatemala with 1,000 Salvadorian soldiers.[22]

BREAKUP OF THE UNION

Morazán carried out an aggressive campaign against Carrera and successfully weakened his following. Once again, fighting spread throughout the region. Atrocities by one side were answered by those from the other. Morazán took control of the Guatemalan government. In Morazán's absences from San Salvador the union began to dissolve. On April 30, 1838, Nicaragua seceded and on May 30 the Congress in San Salvador declared that the provinces could go their separate ways if they wished. Morazán returned to San Salvador in an attempt to stop the exodus, but failed.[23]

When Morazán left Guatemala the Conservatives once again gained control of the government. However, they continued the fight against Carrera. By September Carrera occupied Antigua and threatened Guatemala City. However, Gen. Carlos Salazar (a Liberal in the employment of the Conservatives) decisively defeated Carrera at Villa Nueva. Under the Treaty of El Rinconcito (December 23, 1838), Carrera agreed to lay down his arms and recognize those governing in exchange for his restoration as the military commander of Mita.[24] By the end of 1838 Costa Rica and Honduras had also seceded. Only three provinces adhered to the union: El Salvador, Los Altos, and Guatemala.

With Carrera temporarily out of the way, Morazán reentered Guatemala, deposed the Conservative government, and placed General Salazar in charge on January 30, 1839. As this was taking place, the Conservatives took control of Honduras and Nicaragua and prepared to invade El Salvador. Once again Morazán withdrew to deal with the threat. On March 24, 1839, Carrera declared an alliance with Honduras and Nicaragua against Morazán. Carrera reoccupied Guatemala City at the head of a large Indian army, driving the Liberals into exile and declared independence from the union. In late January 1840 Carrera marched into Los Altos and crushed the Liberals at Quezaltenango and reintegrated the region back into Guatemala.[25]

Elsewhere, a 1,200-man Horduran-Nicaraguan army led by Honduran Francisco Ferrera invaded El Salvador which had a 1,300-man army. Morazán commanding 700 men defeated the invaders at El Espíritu Santo on April 5 and 6, 1839. The Horduran-Nicaraguan army lost over 200 men while the Salvadorians' losses were less than 30 casualties.[26]

Carrera's allies defeated, Morazán seized the initiative and invaded Guatemala in March 1840. Outmaneuvering Carrera, Morazán entered Guatemala City on the eighteenth. Carrera's Indian hordes stormed the city and surrounded Morazán in the city's main plaza. The fighting raged for three days with barricades being constructed out of dead bodies. Finally, by concentrating his surviving force against one point, Morazán and 500 followers broke out on the twenty-first. Those captured were executed. Morazán fled first to Costa Rica, then Panama, and finally, in 1841, Peru, where he was invited to serve in the army.[27]

MORAZÁN'S RETURN

On April 7, 1842, Morazán returned from exile to El Salvador. Leading a few hundred recruits and commanding a small squadron, he overthrew the Costa Rican dictator Braulio Carillo without opposition. Morazán then tried to raise an army in Costa Rica for the reunification of Central America. However, on September 11, 1842, the population of San José Heredia y Alhajuela, Costa Rica, rose up against Morazán and defeated him. He was captured and shot on the fifteenth.[28]

OBSERVATIONS

Many factors worked against the union of Central America. Although the provinces shared common Spanish and Indian heritages, the racial mixtures within each province differed significantly.[29] Therefore, the Conservative-Liberal struggle over the fate of the union came close to being a race war pitting the *criollos* and *mestizos*, who were generally liberal, against the Indians, who were overwhelmingly conservative, supported by the church and the aristocracy.

Also, mountains and jungles isolated many population centers from one another, contributing to the provincialism that had evolved centuries before independence. These geographical barriers were penetrated only by burro paths. The degree of ideological separation between the Liberals and Conservatives could best be measured by their differing attitude toward the Roman Catholic Church.

One historian estimates that 7,088 men died in battles fought between 1824 and 1842.[30] This does not take into account the numerous deaths caused by disease or among the civilians.

Carrera's victory permitted the Conservatives to assert themselves throughout the isthmus for many decades. He formed an alliance with the Honduran Conservative Francisco Ferrera and imposed his lieutenant Francisco Malespín on El Salvador.[31]

Although numerous attempts were made to revive the Union of Central America, particularly during the nineteenth century, all would fail miserably (see chapter 22).

CHAPTER ELEVEN

THE PERU-BOLIVIA CONFEDERATION AND ITS AFTERSHOCK, 1836–41

> Chile's position in relation to the Peru-Bolivian Confederation is untenable. It can be tolerated neither by the people nor by the government, for it would be equivalent to suicide.
> —Chilean Minister Diego Portales, 1836

THE SPARK

On July 7, 1836, a group of Chilean exiles led by former president Ramón Freire sailed from Callao, Peru, in two ships, the former merchant frigate *Monteagudo* (12 guns) and brig *Orbegoso* (6 guns). These were inactive Peruvian warships which had been leased to the exiles through a third party. The Peruvian government did nothing to encourage or to prevent the well-armed expedition from sailing. The ships were separated by a storm. The *Orbegoso* sailed into and captured San Carlos de Ancud, the principal port on the island of Chiloé, on August 4. However, the crew of the *Monteagudo* mutinied, carried her into Valparaíso, and surrendered. The Chilean government then dispatched the *Monteagudo*, crewed by those loyal to the government, to Chiloe, where they surprised the rebels and crushed the uprising.[1]

Meanwhile, Chile sent the brig *Aquiles* (20 guns) to Callao. During the night of August 21, l836, Victoriano Garrido led 80 men in five boats into the harbor where they quietly seized the unmanned Peruvian warships *Santa Cruz* (12 guns), *Arequipeño* (13 guns), and *Peruviana* (1 gun). The ships were then sailed to Chile. These events, coupled with the creation of the Peru-Bolivia Confederation on October 28, led to war between Chile and the Confederation.[2]

BACKGROUND

Within Latin America a number of individuals aspired to recapture the greatness that once belonged to their homeland during colonial times. Among these individuals was Andrés de Santa Cruz,[3] the president of Bolivia. He aspired to unite Bolivia and Peru, which had been elements of the Viceroyalty of Peru throughout much of the colonial era.

In 1828 Santa Cruz conspired with Peruvian generals Agustín Gamarra and Antonio Gutierrez de la Fuente to establish a Peru-Bolivia Confederation under his leadership. However, once Gamarra seized the presidency of Peru, he chose to ignore the deal with Santa Cruz (see chapter 8).

Relations between Santa Cruz and Gamarra were seriously strained in the late 1820s and early 1830s as both men saw themselves as the future unifiers of Bolivia and Peru. In 1830 Gamarra wanted to declare war on Bolivia but the Peruvian Congress rejected the idea. Chile mediated the dispute between the two nations. This temporarily quieted matters.[4]

In 1833 Peru once again slipped into political chaos. Gamarra, who had governed since 1828, was barred from reelection by the constitution. Influenced by his domineering wife Francisca Zubiaga de Gamarra (known as *La Mariscala*—"the female marshal"), Gamarra chose Pedro Pablo Bermúdez to be his successor. The Liberal Francisco Luna Pizarro, who was once again back from exile, preferred Gen. Luis José de Orbegoso and Congress chose Orbegoso as president. *La Mariscala* helped persuade her husband to impose Bermúdez by force. On January 4, 1834, Bermúdez seized Lima, and army units in Cuzco, Puno, Ayacucho, and Huancavelica declared their support. However, those in Arequipa remained loyal to Orbegoso and with these troops he drove the rebels southward. As the civil war raged during the early months of 1834, Orbegoso asked Bolivia for help. Santa Cruz responded that he would help if Orbegoso accepted his plan of federation. However, Bolivian help was not needed. On April 24, 1834, the two warring Peruvian factions met on the Plains of Maquinhuayo. Much to Gamarra's astonishment, his men simply walked over to the other side and laid down their arms in what is now called the "Embrace of Maquinhuayo." Gamarra was exiled to Bolivia.[5]

Gamarra and President Santa Cruz found it to mutual advantage to conspire once again. Gamarra would seize Cuzco in southern Peru, pronounce against Orbegoso, and proclaim the Peru-Bolivia Confederation to be headed by Santa Cruz. On May 20, 1835, Gamarra recrossed into Peru at the head of a hastily gathered an army of 3,000 men.[6]

Unrelated to the conspiracy, the youthful conservative Gen. Felipe Santiago de Salaverry[7] rebelled against Orbegoso on February 23, 1835, and drove him and his Liberal supporters out of Lima. Gamarra, who seized Cuzco (348 mi SE of Lima), was now caught between proclaiming the confederation, which he had promised Santa Cruz, or making a deal with Salaverry. Santa Cruz made the decision for him. Abandoning Gamarra, Santa Cruz formed an alliance with Orbegoso. Santa Cruz promised to support Orbegoso against both Gamarra and Salaverry in exchange for Orbegoso's support of a plan of confederation. Hence, Gamarra agreed to support Salaverry and fight the Orbegoso-Santa Cruz alliance.[8]

On June 16, 1835, 5,000 Bolivian soldiers crossed the Desaguadero River into Peru. Gamarra commanded 4,000 Peruvian soldiers and 6,000 Indians armed principally with slings. On August 13 Gamarra disobeyed Salaverry's orders not to engage Santa Cruz's superior army and, as a consequence, Gamarra was defeated at the two-hour battle of Yanacocha; Santa Cruz took 915 prisoners. Gamarra escaped to Lima where Salaverry, not trusting him, exiled Gamarra to Costa Rica but he found his way to Chile instead. In the meantime, Salaverry declared a war to the death against Santa Cruz. All who killed Bolivian soldiers were declared "meritorious of the fatherland" (*benemérito de la patria*) and exempted from taxes for five years.[9]

Salaverry transported his army down the coast and landed at Islay (468 mi SE of Lima). Santa Cruz drew Salaverry away from the ocean which the Peruvian navy controlled. In February 1836 Santa Cruz and Salaverry fought at Socabaya a few miles south of Arequipa (467 mi

SE of Lima), and the latter sustained a crushing defeat. Santa Cruz captured 1,500 men including Salaverry; Salaverry was executed. The surviving Conservatives fled to Chile.[10]

On March 17 and August 6, 1836, South Peru and North Peru declared themselves independent nations, each with its own president, and they joined with Bolivia to form the Confederation of the Andes. Santa Cruz was chosen as "Protector" for ten years while remaining president of Bolivia. Great Britain, France, and the United States recognized the Confederation but its neighbors refused to do so.[11]

The establishment of the Confederation increased tensions in the already strained relations between Peru and Chile. In the late days of the War for Independence, Chile had loaned Peru 1.5 million pesos. Peru, in constant political turmoil, ignored the debt. Also since independence, Valparaíso increasingly rivaled Callao as the preeminent commerical port on the west coast of South America. Soon Santa Cruz passed a discriminatory tariff which favored ships coming around Cape Horn that bypassed Valparaíso and went directly to Callao.

Chile and Bolivia disputed the ownership of the Atacama Desert. Now that Peru and Bolivia were united, this became a Confederation matter. In August 1835 Chilean exiles, possibly protected by Peru, had attempted to seize Chiloé. The Peruvian government's participation was never proved. Nevertheless, on August 21 the Chilean navy had carried out a preemptive strike by seizing the three Peruvian warships.[12]

Santa Cruz was most anxious to preserve peace in order to gain time to consolidate the Confederation. On the other hand, Portales was just as eager to have war. Santa Cruz invited an envoy from Chile. The Chilean terms for peace included the dissolution of the Confederation. These were rejected by Santa Cruz and on December 28, 1836, Chile declared war.[13]

Juan Manuel de Rosas, the President of United Provinces (future Argentina), declared war on the Confederation on May 19, 1837. He had many reasons. Rosas saw a foreign war as being a unifying factor in the far-from-united United Provinces. He believed that Santa Cruz was attempting to undermine Buenos Aires' influence among its provinces bordering Bolivia. Rosas knew that Santa Cruz was giving asylum to his enemies, the Unitarians. He saw this as an opportunity to settle the sovereignty dispute with Bolivia over the province of Tarija. And, if that were not enough, Rosas simply did not like Santa Cruz.[14]

OPPOSING FORCES

The population of the Confederation was 4 million inhabitants and that of Chile 1.1 million. The annual revenues of the Confederation were about three times that of Chile.[15]

Because of the vast Atacama Desert which stretches from northern Chile, across Bolivia, and into southern Peru, the only practical avenue for invasion, whether northward or southward, was by sea. In the months leading up to the war, the Chilean navy grew from two warships (the brigantine *Aquiles* and the schooner *Colo Colo*) to eight. The government purchased the French merchant frigate *Valparaíso* and armed her with 20 guns. In addition, it incorporated the two Peruvian warships leased to Freire and the three Peruvian warships captured in Callao.[16]

The Confederation navy (in fact, the old Peruvian navy) consisted of three corvettes—the *Confederación* (20 guns), *Socabaya* (24 guns), and *Libertad* (24 guns); three brigs—the *Junín* (6 guns), *Fundador* (20 guns), and *Flor del Mar* (unarmed); and two schooners—the *Limeña* (1 gun), and *Yanacocha* (10 guns). The navy had been poorly funded during the early 1830s, a victim of the internal strife which drained away resources.[17]

Following the creation of the Confederation, a number of these warships were manned only by skeleton crews. This was due in part to economy and in part because Santa Cruz did not politically trust the naval officers, many of whom had recently supported Salaverry. Some of the active warships were manned principally by foreign seamen. Two Chileans on board the *Libertad* led a conspiracy which seized the ship and sailed it to Valparaíso, arriving on December 8, 1836. Not a single officer was Peruvian.[18]

Significant differences existed among the armies. The Bolivian army, which numbered about 3,000 men, had been administratively reformed by Santa Cruz. The infantry served six-year enlistments and the cavalry and artillery eight. A national guard supplemented the army. The Peruvian army numbered about 8,000 men. However, perhaps only about 5,000 of these men were subordinate to individuals loyal to the Confederation. The remainder supported *caudillos* who chose not to side with either the Confederation or the Chileans. All these troops were raised principally through impressment. Santa Cruz had introduced reforms into the Peruvian Army but few had taken hold before the war.[19]

The Chilean army numbered about 3,000 men and the national guard 4,500 men. However, much of this force was needed to contain the Araucanian Indians in the South (see chapter 33), to man fortifications, and to preserve domestic tranquility (the last serious rebellion being in 1829–30). And the populace was not enthusiastic about the war. Therefore, the government had to resort to impressment. On June 2, 1837, the men being assembled for the expeditionary force at Quillota mutinied but were suppressed by some 2,000 loyal troops from Valparaíso. Even as defeat was apparent, the mutineers killed Minister Diego Portales (politically the most powerful individual in Chile). Many Chileans believed that Santa Cruz had instigated the rebellion and the subsequent assassination of Portales, and this helped temporarily to forge a national consensus against Santa Cruz.[20]

OPENING STRATEGIES

Chilean Minister Portales wrote, "The navy should act before the army, dealing decisive blows. We must rule forever in the Pacific."[21] Next, an expedition was to be landed in southern Peru, where, according to the Peruvian exiles in Chile, the population was waiting to rise up against Santa Cruz. The Chilean army, supplemented by Peruvians, would then advance through Puno into Bolivia while the United Provinces attacked Bolivia from the south. Santa Cruz perceived that his enemies did not have the support for a prolonged war, so his initial strategy was to avoid a crushing defeat and not to enrage his adversaries.[22]

THE FIRST EXPEDITION FOR "THE RESTORATION OF PERU"

President Joaquín Prieto dispatched the 2,682-man (2,280 Chileans and 402 Peruvian exiles) Expedition of Restoration, commanded by Adm. Blanco Encalada, on September 15. The force landed at Aranta and Quilca in October 1837 and marched to Arequipa, arriving on the twelfth. The advance was difficult. Supplies and equipment had been lost in the landing and smallpox broke out among the troops. The uprising against Santa Cruz, which the Peruvian exiles had predicted, never materialized. Blanco Encalada barracaded himself in Arequipa. Santa Cruz pulled together some 5,000 troops to oppose the invaders. The poorly outfitted and supplied Chilean expedition was soon surrounded and under siege by Santa Cruz. Blanco Encalada grew weaker as the besiegers grew stronger. Finding himself in a deteriorating position, Blanco Encalada negotiated the Treaty of Paucarpata on November 17, 1837, without firing a shot.

Santa Cruz granted generous terms, including the peaceful withdrawal of the expedition; however, he insisted that Chile recognize the Confederation. Back in Chile, the government denounced the treaty and notified Santa Cruz that a state of war still existed.[23]

In order to escort this expedition from central Chile to southern Peru, the Chilean warships blockading Callao had to be withdrawn. As a consequence, a Confederation squadron composed of the *Socabaya*, *Confederación*, and *Fundador* with 400 soldiers embarked and, commanded by the Colombian Trinidad Morán, sailed from Callao on October 15 and cruised in the waters off Chile. In November Morán captured the island of Juan Fernández. There he seized munitions and freed Chileans opposed to Prieto who were being held as prisoners on the island. On October 23 he arrived off Talcahuano. Believing the defenses too strong, he was content to seize the merchant brigantine *Feliz Inteligencía* near San Antonio before sailing north. Morán landed the liberated Chileans at Huasco in hopes of fomenting problems for Prieto. The squadron then sailed to Callao.[24]

CHASE OFF ISLAY

Freed from supporting the failed invasion of southern Peru, the Chilean navy renewed its offensive. On January 10, 1838, a Chilean squadron (the *Aquiles*, *Libertad*, *Valparaíso*, *Monteagudo*, and *Arequipeño*) commanded by Roberto Simpson arrived off Arica, Peru (593 mi S of Lima). A single, unarmed vessel entered the port while the remainder of the squadron remained over the horizon. An officer went ashore carrying a sealed envelope to be forwarded to Santa Cruz. The officer told the local Peruvian commander that the Treaty of Paucarpata had been accepted. In fact, the message inside the envelope stated that it had been rejected. Through this ploy the Chilean squadron hoped that Peruvian ships would lower their guard. However, the local Peruvian commander opened the envelope.

The Chilean squadron sailed to Islay. On the twelfth it encountered a Confederation squadron (the *Socabaya*, *Fundador*, and *Junín*) commanded by Juan José Panizo. Following a running duel, Panizo broke away in foggy weather from the superior Chilean squadron and escaped into Islay.[25]

The Chilean navy did score a major success on January 18 when the *Libertad* captured the *Confederación* south of Callao. The *Confederación* was carrying Bolivian Gen. José Ballívan to Arica. He was an accomplished officer. The Chilean squadron attempted to blockade Callao, but the British and American warships on scene refused to recognize its legality to do so.[26]

FIGHTING WITH ARGENTINA

Throughout the second half of 1837 Argentina and the Confederation fought a few minor battles. All were indecisive. Chile endeavored to persuade the United Provinces to increase its war efforts but to no effect. In late May and June 1838 the Conferation army defeated Rosas' forces in a series of small engagements and he withdrew his troops from the war.[27]

INTERNAL OPPOSITION TO THE CONFEDERATION

Santa Cruz anticipated a second Chilean expedition. He declared martial law and increased the army to 17,000 men—7,000 in North Peru, 5,000 in South Peru, and 5,000 along the frontier with Argentina.

While Santa Cruz was preparing to meet the Chilean threat, elements within the Confederation plotted its dissolution. Paramount among these was one in North Peru led by former president Orbegoso. On July 30 Orbegoso declared the independence of North Peru but pledged to continue the war against Chile.

THE SECOND EXPEDITION FOR THE "RESTORATION OF PERU"

While these events were transpiring, the government of Chile was raising a new army. Now that the United Provinces was out of the war, Chile abandoned its southern strategy and planned to attack Lima. The command was given to Gen. Manuel Bulnes,[28] who had recently commanded the frontier army against the Araucanian Indians. Bulnes was concerned that the government was not fully committed to the expedition. Once again, the expedition was not well outfitted. Officers of the expedition confided to a Swiss traveler, Johann Jakob von Tschudi, "they, together with the majority of their conrades, were yet unprovided with arms, and knew not where to procure them."[29] The common soldiers were worse off. Von Tschudi observed: "I was standing on the *muele* [sea wall] when the Santiago battalion was shipped. The soldiers, who were in wretched uniforms, most of them wearing ponchos, and unarmed, were bound together two-and-two by ropes, and absolutely driven into the boats."[30] Nonetheless, the expedition sailed on June 16, 1838, carried in 23 transports and escorted by 4 warships. They too were poorly manned and outfitted. A week after Orbegoso's declarations in northern Peru, some 5,400 troops, including only 60 Peruvian dissidents (Gamarra and La Fuente among them), landed at Ancón on August 7 and 8.[31]

Once the Chilean army had landed, the Chilean navy possessed enough ships to blockade Callao. At 11:30 P.M. on August 19, long boats from the Chilean fleet seized the *Socabaya* from under the Peruvian guns protecting the harbor.[32]

Orbegoso, who held the fortified port of Callao, at first refused to cooperate with either Bulnes or Santa Cruz and demanded that both withdraw from Peru. Bulnes defeated Peruvian troops at Guías, some of whom supported Orbegoso, and occupied Lima on August 21. The spilling of Peruvian blood by the expeditionary force dampened the enthusiasm of many Peruvians to support those opposed to the Confederation. Bulnes declared Gamarra president of Peru; in fact, eight individuals claimed to be president of Peru, each holding sway over some part of the nation. Gamarra abolished the double tariff on foreign goods that first touched at a Pacific port before Callao and agreed that Peru would pay for the war against Santa Cruz. These events drove Orbegoso into an alliance with Santa Cruz.[33]

Bulnes found his position in Lima untenable. Sickness broke out among his troops due to the hot climate and poor sanitation. Bands of guerrillas harrassed his outposts. By November 3, 1838, Santa Cruz had arrived from the Sierra with a numerically superior army at Santa Eulalia, some 30 miles from Lima. Bulnes decided to seek more defensible ground. He reboarded his fleet with the infantry and sailed north to Huacho (71 mi N of Lima). Santa Cruz, aided by Orbegoso, reentered Lima on November 10, 1838, to a tumultuous welcome. Santa Cruz then pushed Orbegoso into exile.[34]

THE BATTLE OF CASMA

In order to transport and to protect the Chilean army north to Huacho, the Chilean fleet once again lifted the blockade of Callao. To offset the superior Chilean navy, Santa Cruz recruited privateers. He offered to pay them 200,000 pesos for the destruction of the Chilean squadron. Accepting such an offer was an extremely bold decision.[35]

These privateers, led by the Frenchman Jean Blanchet (a former lieutenant in the French navy), now successfully escaped from Callao. On January 12, 1839, four privateers—the *Edmond* (5 guns), *Arequipeño* (6 guns), *Peru* (10 guns) and *Mexicana* (12 guns)—in a most daring move, attacked three Chilean warships—the *Confederación* (22 guns), *Santa Cruz* (20 guns), and *Valparaíso* (20 guns)—under Commodore Roberto Simpson, which were loading firewood in Casma Bay. The Chilean ships got underway and fought a sharp engagement. They captured the privateer *Arequipeño*. The Chileans sustained eight dead and eight wounded. The privateers, in their smaller, more lightly constructed ships, lost many times that number, including Blanchet. The remaining privateers, flying French flags, escaped. They were intercepted by a French warship which ended their privateering careers. Both sides claimed victory. Santa Cruz' "navy" was disbanded following the battle.[36]

BATTLE OF YUNGAY

The Chilean Army set up headquarters in the Department of Huaylas in northern Peru. Bulnes wanted time to retrain his troops. He planned to remain on the defensive, hoping to draw Santa Cruz to him. On November 24 Santa Cruz began his march northward. On January 6, 1839, he attacked the Chilean First Infantry Battalion at Puente de Buin, who stoutly defended their position. The Chileans lost 93 dead and 220 wounded, which was twenty percent of those engaged. The Confederation lost 70 dead and 150 wounded.[37]

On January 20, 1839, Bulnes, commanding 5,267 men (4,467 Chileans and 800 Peruvians), attacked Santa Cruz commanding 6,100 men at Yungay, nestled in the Andes Mountains some 312 miles north of Lima. Santa Cruz took up a strong defensive position anchored by a hill called Pan de Azúcar; Bulnes immediately attacked the hill and the fighting spread along the entire line. By the end of the day, Bulnes defeated Santa Cruz in one of the bloodiest battles in South American history. The Confederation lost 1,400 dead; 1,600 prisoners; and many others were wounded. The Chilean losses were almost as grave as those of the Confederation. Santa Cruz fled. He resigned as President of Bolivia and Protector of the Confederation. The Peruvian electoral college chose Gamarra to serve a four-year term as president on July 10, 1840.[38]

THE AFTERSHOCK

With the exile of Santa Cruz, Bolivia fell into anarchy. On June 10, 1841, Col. Sebastián Agreda deposed Gen. José Miguel de Velasco, who had seized the government, and proclaimed Santa Cruz to be president once more. A civil war errupted among the followers of Velasco, Santa Cruz, and Gen. José Ballivián. Peruvian President Gamarra believed the time was now ripe for him to unite Bolivia and Peru. Gamarra agreed to support Ballivián and allowed him to use Tacna (600 mi SE of Lima) as a base of operations. On September 24 Ballivián invaded Bolivia and was soon proclaimed acting president. Gamarra then invaded Bolivia, which united behind Ballivián against the Peruvians, and occupied La Paz.[39]

BATTLE OF INGAVI

The Peruvian army of 5,377 men and the Bolivian army of 4,136 met at Ingavi (390 mi NNE of La Paz) on November 18. Gamarra was decisively defeated in less than one hour. Some 174 Peruvian officers and 3,200 soldiers were captured. The total casualties between the two sides were 708 men dead and 856 wounded. Gamarra was among the dead, the first nineteenth-century Latin American head of state to die on the battlefield.[40]

In order to pressure the Peruvian government to come to terms, Ballivián invaded its neighbor with an army of 6,000 men. He occupied the Peruvian cities of Puno, Arequira, and Moquegua. Peru finally signed a peace treaty on June 7, 1842.[41]

OBSERVATIONS

Santa Cruz' administrative and diplomatic skills, aided by chaos in Peru, enabled Bolivia to swallow Peru even though Bolivia possessed a smaller population and less economic potential than its northwestern neighbor. However, the dissension within Peru, which allowed Santa Cruz to forge the confederation, combined with the fears of Chile and to a lesser degree those of the United Provinces, spelled the doom of the Confederation.

Given the poor condition of the Chilean expeditions, how was it possible for Chile to have won? Due to the constant warfare with the Araucanian Indians, Chile maintained the only standing army on the continent. Apparently, enough of the men of the second expedition of the "Restoration of Peru" were experienced soldiers to make a difference. As the war dragged on, Santa Cruz increasingly had to rely on Peruvian Indian forced-conscripts to fill out his army. They were not as motivated as the well-disciplined Bolivian troops.[42]

Also, the War of the Confederation reconfirmed the strategic lesson from the War of Independence for the Viceroyalty of Peru. Whoever controlled the sea held the initiative.[43]

CHAPTER TWELVE

GUAYAQUIL VERSUS QUITO, 1830–1911

And in 1830 it constituted itself as a Republic, not with the name of Republic of Quito, which bound it to the glorious tradition of the Kingdom of Quito of Atahualpa and his predecessors, but incurred a grave error . . . calling itself the Republic of Ecuador because the equatorial, geographic demarcation which divides the world passes in the proximity of the city of Quito.

—Ecuadorian historian Pío Jaramillo Alvarado

THE SPARK

On May 13, 1830, Gen. Juan José Flores,[1] a Venezuelan whom Simón Bolívar had left behind in command in Quito, declared the Departments of Azuay, Guayas, and Quito independent of Gran Colombia. Playing it safe, he also declared that this new nation would reunite with other states of northern South America to recreate Gran Colombia as the "Republic of Colombia." On August 14 a Conservative constitution, vesting extensive power in the executive branch, was written; Flores was declared president; and the name Ecuador was chosen in an attempt to allay the rivalry between the cities of Quito and Guayaquil. As Delazon Smith wrote from Ecuador in 1845, "A settled spirit of animosity and rivalship [sic], has always existed between the Citizens of Guayaquil and those of Quito."[2]

BACKGROUND

Ecuador had less tradition of unity than either of its Spanish-speaking neighbors, Colombia or Peru. It possessed an ill-defined sense of nationhood, which was fueled by the rivalry between its two leading cities, and vague boundaries, which brought it into protracted disputes with neighbors, particularly Peru (see chapter 8 and companion volume). These problems created fertile ground for the rise and fall of *caudillos*.[3]

Like Uruguay, Ecuador in part owed its creation and survival to the fact that it possessed two more powerful neighbors, in this case Colombia and Peru, neither of which was strong enough to overcome the other and absorb this buffer area. However, both would continue to try for decades, adding to the turmoil within Ecuador.[4]

Ecuador was also the poorest of the three nations created from the former Gran Colombia. In December 1834 Ecuador assumed 21.5 percent of the debt of the former confederation.

It had no money to pay, thus creating decades of friction with creditors, primarily British investors.

Ecuador's mountainous terrain and unhealthy lowlands dictated that armies would remain small and slow moving. The 300-mile wagon road between Guayaquil and Quito was not completed until 1872, and the last spike in the rail line between the two cities was finally driven on June 17, 1908. Prior to the completion of the wagon road, the two rival cities were almost inaccessible to one another during the rainy season (late December through mid-April), being connected only by an Indian trail.[5]

Guayaquil was one of the most unhealthy cities in the entire world. Frequently, it was ravaged by long epidemics of bubonic plague and yellow fever. Delazon Smith observed in 1845, "The port of Guayaquil is not approachable on account of the yellow fever, which rages constantly, having destroyed one half of her former citizens within the three years last past."[6] Guayaquil was not successfully sanitized until 1920.[7]

OPPOSING FORCES

In 1830 the population of Ecuador was estimated to be 600,000 individuals, which was overwhelmingly Indian and *mestizo*. The nation's political, economic, and social life was dominated by its two largest cities, Quito and Guayaquil. The population of the province of Quito was about 358,000 persons and that of the province of Guayaquil about 94,000. Those from the highlands (Quito) were known as *serranos* (people from the sierra), and their leaders were typically from the Conservative party; those from the lowlands (Guayaquil) were called *costeños* (people from the coast), and their leaders most often were Liberals. In general, the Conservatives could count on the support of the Roman Catholic Church and the Liberals that of the mercantile class.[8]

Many political factions existed. Some individuals favored a republic dominated by the highlands and others favored a republic dominated by the lowlands. A faction in the sierra, significant though a minority, favored union with Gran Colombia while another minority, mostly on the coast, favored union with Peru.[9]

The army, particularly the officer corps, was bloated with idle and unpaid foreigners (Venezuelans, Colombians, British, and Irish) since Ecuador had been one of the last battlegrounds of the wars for independence.[10] A future president of Ecuador, Vicente Rocafuerte, wrote to the President of Nueva Granada, Francisco de Paula Santander:

> [O]ur revolutions . . . have all arisen from the military spirit that General Bolívar created against all political rule and that Ecuador is now experiencing the disastrous effects of his aberrations. To swell his ranks, he took from the prisons . . . the prisoners and all the criminal leaders, and in ten years of war and political tumult they have risen out of the lower ranks and have reached the high commands and colonels. When the army of Colombia returned from Peru to Nueva Granada and to Venezuela, these great villains remained in Ecuador, . . . they have been constant promoters of civil strife.[11]

The soldiers were drawn from the indegenous peasantry frequently by force or by the promise of spoils.[12]

OPENING STRATEGIES

For those in the rival cities of Quito and Guayaquil, the goal was at the least to maintain independence and at the most to capture the others' seat of power.

GRAN COLOMBIAN ARMY REBELS

On November 29 Gen. Luis de Urdaneta,[13] who commanded the Gran Colombian troops in Guayaquil, declared in favor of maintaining Gran Colombian union. In December leaders in Cuenca and some in Quito joined the movement. Since Guayaquil had not paid all of the $500,000 levy that Urdaneta had placed upon the port to pay his troops, on December 28 he burned down a section of the city as punishment. Urdaneta then ordered the town of Saraguro to be burned for the same reason. These harsh acts, combined with the news of Bolívar's death which occurred on December 17, caused Urdaneta's following to disappear. He and twenty-five other army officers, including two generals and eight colonels, were exiled to Panama.[14]

CONFLICT WITH NUEVA GRANADA

In 1830 various towns in the Department of Cauca (183 mi NW of Quito) rebelled against the authority of the dissolving Gran Colombia. As a consequence, on December 20 President Flores declared these towns incorporated into Ecuador. Nueva Granada (the former Gran Colombia and future Colombia) protested, to which Flores responded that the province of Pasto and part of the province of Buenaventura were annexed to Ecuador and the remainder of the department was free to choose its fate. On July 22, 1831, the Granadian Congress authorized the President to reintegrate the Department of Cauca into the nation.[15]

In October, Nueva Granada dispatched troops under Gen. José Hilario López to Popayán. Soon, the Granadian president, Gen. José María Obando, took command of the army which had increased to 6,000 men. Flores marched north to take charge of Ecuadorian operations. In the meantime, some 1,500 Ecuadorian soldiers, who were poorly clothed and fed, occupied the city of Pasto. The local Ecuadorian commander, Gen. Juan Otamendi (who was a Granadian by birth), subverted the Ecuadorian troops and they mutinied at Latacunga and Ambato, killing their officers and sacking the towns. Flores found it impossible to hold Pasto with his hungry soldiers and abandoned the town. Pasto was occupied by Granadian troops. Many of the Ecuadorian troops who were from the disputed region went over to the Granadian army. In December 1832 Nueva Granada and Ecuador signed a treaty in Pasto which gave the upper Cauca Valley to Nueva Granada. The Carchi River became the boundary between the two nations.[16]

GUAYAQUIL REBELS

In October 1833 rebels in Guayaquil freed the Liberal Vicente Rocafuerte, who was then being escorted under guard into exile by orders of Flores. Rocafuerte was declared "supreme chief." However, the Liberals neglected to protect Guayaquil adequately and it was easily captured by Flores on November 24. Rocafuerte still commanded the Ecuadorian navy composed of the heavy frigate *Colombia* (67 guns), six schooners, and five armed launches. He retreated to Puná Island and declared the port under blockade. For the next ten months his forces were supported by the coastal towns in what was known as the "War of the Chihuahuas (*Guerra de las Chihuahuas*)."[17] Then, Rocafuerte was betrayed in mid-April 1834 by José María Sáenz (brother of Bolívar's mistress Manuelita), and he was captured by Flores. Flores, appreciating Rocafuerte's talent, cut a deal with his prisoner. In July Rocafuerte was freed and made the Supreme Chief of Guayas (the department in which Guayaquil is found) under Flores as president.[18]

ÉMIGRÉS INVADE ECUADOR

In the meantime, Ecuadorian refugees from Nueva Granada, led by José Félix Valdivieso and Gen. Isidoro Barriga,[19] invaded their homeland and captured the capital. Two of the three departments (Azuay and Quito) declared in favor of the invaders. Flores, leading 1,000 veterans and supported by Rocafuerte, crushed 2,000 rebels under General Barriga at Minarica on January 18, 1835. Many of the rebels were butchered in the late stages of the battle; 900 men died between the two sides. When Flores' term as president ended in 1835, Rocafuerte became president; Flores became commander-in-chief of the army.[20]

ECUADOR MEDDLES IN NUEVA GRANADA

In 1840 Flores, once again president, sent military assistance to Granadian Conservatives in Pasto ostensibly to aid in suppressing a revolt. In reality he was hoping to incorporate the province of Pasto into Ecuador, but the scheme failed. In 1843 a new Ecuadorian constitution was adopted which lengthened the presidential term from four to eight years; the primary purpose of its authors was to prolong Flores' rule. Flores became increasingly dictatorial, and Rocafuerte fled to Peru.[21]

ECUADOR MEDDLES IN PERU

At this time, Flores secretly aided Peruvian exile Col. Justo Hercelles. Hercelles, commanding a small force, sailed from Guayaquil in December. The forces landed at Tumbes, Peru, and advanced toward Amotape where they were forced to surrender.[22]

THE "MARCH" CIVIL WAR

On March 6, 1845, Guayaquil Liberals, led by Rocafuerte and Gen. Antonio Elizalde,[23] revolted against Flores and the domination of the military by foreigners. An 1844 rebel *manifesto* declared, "In Ecuador there are three commanding generals. . . . The commander at Cuenca is a Venezuelan general, at Guayas an Irish general, and at Pichincha an English general. The Inspector General of the Army is a Frenchman."[24] To this it could been have added that the president was a Venezuelan general; twelve out the fifteen generals were foreign born; the 1st and 2nd Battalions were commanded by Venezuelans; plus the 1st Cavalry Regiment was commanded by a Spaniard and the 2nd Cavalry Regiment by a Venezuelan.[25]

Flores entrenched his 1,500 well-armed veterans at "La Elvira" hacienda near Babahoyo (188 mi SW of Quito and 117 mi NE of Guayaquil). On May 9 and 10 General Elizalde attacked with 700 men and after significant losses was driven away. Next, Gen. John Illingworth[26] surrounded Flores. Rather than risk an assault, he dispatched units to the surrounding countryside, cutting off Flores' source of supplies. Flores appreciated that he soon would be overwhelmed by the constantly increasing rebel force. As a consequence, on June 17, 1845, he surrendered at the Hacienda de la Virginia. Flores agreed to a two-year exile with titles. Rocafuerte became president. Soon both sides accused the other of having violated the terms of the surrender.[27]

FLORES' FILIBUSTERING EXPEDITION OF 1846

Flores did not quietly retire. In Spain the Bourbon Queen María Cristina underwrote with two million pesos Flores' projected filibustering expedition against Ecuador in anticipation of acquiring a throne for one of her young sons. Flores was able to recruit at least 1,400 adventurers in Spain and an additional 900 men in England and Ireland. He purchased the ships

Glenelg, Monarch, and *Neptune* in England. However, in November 1846 the British Foreign Secretary, Lord Palmerston, ordered the ships seized, and the plot collapsed.[28]

ECUADOR AGAIN MEDDLES IN NUEVA GRANADA

Tensions ran high between Ecuador and Nueva Granada in 1846. Nueva Granada believed that the new Ecuadorian government might attempt to conquer disputed territory. Also, Rocafuerte granted asylum to Granadian Gen. José María Obando. Nueva Granada sent soldiers to the frontier, and its senate authorized war with Ecuador. However, the problem was defused when the two nations signed an agreement on May 29, 1846, to negotiate their boundaries.[29]

Three years later, Conservative Diego Noboa and Liberal Antonio Elizalde disputed the 1849 presidential election, and Ecuador plunged into chaos. Finally, in February a national convention chose Noboa. He wanted to reattach Ecuador to Nueva Granada. First, this would require ousting Nueva Granada's Liberal president, José Hilario López. Noboa conspired with Jesuits who had been expelled from Nueva Granada to organize a revolt. Noboa also provided money and arms to Conservatives in the Nueva Granadian province of Pasto. Reacting, López prepared for war. Meanwhile, Liberals in Guayaquil, led by Generals José Urbina,[30] Francisco Robles,[31] and Guillermo Franco, rebelled and deposed Noboa in July 1851.[32]

FLORES' FILIBUSTERING EXPEDITION OF 1852

Flores was observing these events from Peru and decided to take advantage of the chaos in Ecuador during 1852. In late March he appeared off Guayaquil commanding 700 men on board the steamer *Chili*, the barkentine *Almirante Blanco*, and three schooners. Apparently intimidated by some Ecuadorian soldiers led by Illingworth and José de Villamil,[33] Flores dropped some 40 miles down the Guayas River to the island of Puná and established a blockade. As the days dragged on, Flores' force grew weaker. Many of his followers were Chileans who believed that they had signed on to be transported directly to the gold fields in California. The Ecuadorian government began to assemble a small flotilla under the direction of Illingworth to fight Flores. On July 4 Flores attacked Guayaquil but was repulsed. Flores again sailed down the river and captured the village of Machala. On the seventeenth some 120 men deserted Flores, sailed up the river, and surrendered the steamer *Chili*. Soon, others quit Flores, taking his remaining vessels. This forced Flores and his last faithful 150 followers to march to Tumbes in northern Peru. There the force was disarmed. While these events were transpiring, support for Noboa collapsed, and Urbina became president of Ecuador.[34]

CHAOS IN MID-CENTURY

By 1860 no national government existed; petty *caudillos* ruled throughout the country. One of these, Guillermo Franco, signed the Treaty of Mapasingue with Peru ceding the province of Guayaquil to Peru. Ever-ready Flores rushed back to Ecuador and, along with Gabriel García Moreno, a lawyer, captured Guayaquil on September 24, 1860. They crushed the *caudillos*, restored the central government, and denounced Franco's agreement with Peru. García Moreno seized the presidency in 1860 and reshaped Ecuador into a "Christian State" or a "Theocratic Despotism" depending upon one's belief in church/state relations.[35]

FIGHTING WITH NUEVA GRANADA

In 1860 and again in 1863, Ecuadorian and Granadian troops clashed. At the heart of both incidents were the egos of *caudillos* on both sides who wanted to recreate Gran Colombia—of course, under their direction. In both cases the Ecuadorian army was defeated (see chapter 24).³⁶

LIBERALS FROM GUAYAQUIL REBEL

On June 5, 1864, Liberals in the coastal province of Manabi just north of Guayaquil rebelled. Two months later General Urbina landed in the province of El Oro and occupied Machala. García Moreno temporarily relinquished the presidency and took command of the armed forces to fight the former president. García Moreno acquired the English merchant steamer *Anne*, and armed and renamed it the *Guayas*. Along with the steamer *Smyrk* and schooner *Salado* (5 guns), these ships defeated a small rebel squadron. One victim of the campaign was General Flores, who died from an undetermined, violent illness.³⁷

Again in 1865, Liberals from Guayaquil rebelled on May 31 and seized the steamer *Guayas*. Two ships loyal to General Urbina, the *Bernardino* and *Washington*, joined the *Guayas* in the Guayas River. García Moreno traveled to Guayaquil, chartered the English steamer *Talca* with its crew, and, together with the *Smyrk*, attacked the rebels in the Jambelí Channel on June 26. The *Talca* sank the steamer *Guayas* and captured the *Bernardino*. The *Smyrk* captured the rebel ship *Washington*. Twenty-six of the prisoners from the three ships, including General Franco, Capt. José Marcos (the rebel commanding officer of the *Guayas*), and Col. José María Vallejo, were shot in spite of numerous protests.³⁸

CHAOS IN THE MID-1870S

García Moreno was hacked to death with a machete on August 6, 1875, and this plunged Ecuador into a new era of chaos fueled by the Guayaquil/Quito rivalry. Liberal Gen. José Veintemilla,³⁹ the military commander of Guayaquil, revolted against Conservative President Antonio Borrero on September 8, 1876. Veintemilla marched toward Quito, and on December 14 he defeated the government's troops near Galte. Borrero was exiled.⁴⁰

"RESTORATION"

In 1883 Veintemilla, who was neither a Liberal nor a Conservative but simply an opportunist, completed his elected term but tried to remain in power. This provoked a civil war known as the "Restoration." In January Liberal José Eloy Alfaro⁴¹ landed in Esmeraldas and gathered support. In the highlands a rebel army composed of both Liberals and Conservatives drove Veintemilla from the capital, and he retreated to Guayaquil. His best subordinate proved to be his wife, Marieta, who took charge of the troops and directed the artillery fire against the rebels.⁴²

On July 9, 1883, a "Restoration" flotilla composed of the river steamers *Quito* (unk guns), *Huáscar* (unk guns), *Bolívar* (unk guns), and *Victoria* (unk guns) defeated Veintemilla's flotilla composed of the river steamers *Santa Lucía* (3 guns), *Huacho* (3 guns), *Manabí* (2 guns), *América* (unk guns), and *Chimborazo* (unk guns). Veintemilla sought sanctuary on board an English ship.⁴³

For a brief period both factions, Liberals and Conservatives, claimed to be the legal government. A compromise was reached and José Caamaño was elected president on February 7, 1884. Nonetheless, disturbances continued. The ever-rebellious Eloy Alfaro returned from Panama and fought the naval battle of Manabí. Appreciating that the battle was lost, he set fire to his ship, the *Pichincha*, and escaped to Panama.⁴⁴

CIVIL WAR OF 1895

In a bizarre set of circumstances, the Ecuadorian government of Dr. Luís Cordero fell due to its role in the sale of a Chilean warship. Japan, then at war with China, wanted to buy warships. Chile eagerly wanted to sell the cruiser *Esmeralda* but appreciated that selling it to Japan would be a breach of international law. The Chileans, giving President Cordero a substantial payment, induced him to have Ecuador accept the cruiser and then turn it over to the Japanese in Ecuadorian waters. The flagrant abuse of the Ecuadorian flag sparked the Liberals to rebel.[45]

In April 1895 Liberal leaders in Carchí declared Alfaro, then in exile in Nicaragua, as the head of the nation. This was followed on June 4 by the rebellion of the Guayaquil garrison. Since his participation in early revolts, Alfaro had educated himself in strategy and tactics.[46] Alfaro arrived on June 18 and assembled an army. The rebel government decreed that the Indians were no longer subject to a head tax or work details; this won them recruits. Alfaro defeated government troops at San Miguel de Chimbo on August 6 and at Gatazo near Riobamba on August 13 and 14. Eloy Alfaro entered Quito on September 1, 1895, and controlled the government for sixteen years (1895–1911).[47]

CIVIL WAR OF 1911

In 1911, shortly before his term was to expire, Alfaro resigned as president. Within a few months the new president, Emilio Estrada, died of a heart attack on December 22, and Gen. Pedro Montero proclaimed himself president. Alfaro returned from self-imposed exile in Panama and subverted the Guayaquil garrison on December 28. However, Alfaro was decisively defeated at Huigra on January 14, 1912, by his old nemesis, Gen. Leónidas Plaza Gutiérrez,[48] and imprisoned in Quito. On January 28, a mob stormed the prison and hacked Alfaro into pieces.[49]

OBSERVATIONS

Separation versus union caused by the competition between those in Quito and those in Guayaquil and compounded by *Caudillismo* and border disputes kept Ecuador in turmoil for more than one hundred years.

As a consequence of the nineteenth-century Quito-Guayaquil rivalry, Guayaquil evolved institutions such as the Benevolent Society (*Junta de Beneficencia*) which were independent of the central government. These institutions would become issues of contention during the late twentieth century.[50]

By the end of the War for Independence, a new social elite had emerged in Ecuador, the foreign military officers. These men displaced the indigenous civilians and retarded the development of a bureaucratic class capable of leading the young republic.[51]

On occasion both Liberal and Conservative leaders lost control of their soldiers, who most frequently were Indians who had not been assimilated into modern society, and they committed savage cruelties.[52]

Map 4. Brazilian Empire, 1828.

CHAPTER THIRTEEN

BRAZIL, 1831–49

> Woe to the land whose king is a child.
> —Ecclesiastes 10:6

SPARK

At 2 A.M. on April 7, 1831, without consulting anyone, Dom Pedro I, Emperor of Brazil, abdicated in favor of his four-year-old son, Dom Pedro de Alcantara, and sailed to Europe. Those wanting greater local autonomy, those seeking to secede from the Brazilian empire, and those desiring a republican form of government all perceived that the opportunity was now at hand to achieve their goals.[1]

BACKGROUND

Although Brazil emerged from its War for Independence as an entity, it was far from united. After all, the Portuguese Cortes had worked hard to undermine Brazil's loyalty to the errant Portuguese King João VI, who long delayed returning to Portugal from Brazil (see chapter 6). His son, Dom Pedro I, the first emperor of Brazil, was soon at odds with many in the Brazilian Constituent Assembly over the issue of power sharing. The opposing political groups polarized. The remaining Portuguese and Royalists clung to the emperor and the nationalists and republicans supported the Andrada brothers, José Bonifacio and Martim Francisco.[2]

The emperor's absolutist ideology and quick temper ill-suited him to compromise. And Dom Pedro I was supported by many in the army due to the large number of Portuguese officers and soldiers serving within it. Following the successful siege of Bahia during the War for Independence, the captured Portuguese soldiers had been incorporated into the new *imperial* Brazilian Army and became ardent supporters of the new emperor.

The citizens of Rio de Janeiro remained awake throughout the night of November 11, 1823—the "night of agony" (*noite de agonia*)—as tension mounted between the political factions. At noon of the following day, Gen. José Manuel de Morais, commanding a few artillerymen with their cannon and a cavalry squadron, surrounded the Assembly. An officer delivered to the Assembly's secretary the decree of the Emperor accusing the representatives of disloyalty, closing the Assembly, and sending the representatives home. Six deputies were exiled to France, including the three Andrada brothers.[3]

Although this action temporarily solved the Emperor's political problems in the capital, he was soon confronted by a series of international and national crises, most of which he handled poorly. Technically, Brazil was still at war with Portugal. In order to end the war, the Emperor sought British mediation. But many in Brazil thought the settlement price paid to Portugal and the commercial concession made to Great Britain for its good offices were too high. Also, the Emperor led the nation into a disastrous war against Buenos Aires over the recently annexed Cisplatine Province, the future Uruguay (see chapter 7). Many blamed Dom Pedro I for the ensuing defeat.[4]

Internally, the Emperor's policies were no more successful. Many provinces perceived that the central government was insensitive to their needs. The first major revolt against his absolutism occurred in June 1824 when separatists in the provinces of Pernambuco, Paraíba, Rio Grande do Norte, Alagoas, Piauí, and Ceará declared the Confederation of the Equator. Headed by Manuel Paes de Andrade, it adopted the Constitution of Gran Colombia. Like an earlier rebellion in Pernambuco during 1817, it was suppressed by the fleet under the British naval hero Thomas Cochrane and troops loyal to the Emperor. On August 14, 1824, some 1,200 troops landed at Jaguarão (990 mi SW of Rio de Janeiro) south of the city of Pernambuco (today Recife) and easily captured it. The other rebellious provinces were pacified later in the year.[5]

When the Emperor's father, Dom João VI, died in Europe and Dom Pedro became heir to the Portuguese throne, he delayed in renouncing the European throne, causing Brazilian nationalists to question his commitment to Brazil. Also, Dom Pedro delayed in assembling a parliament until 1826; the assembly was required under the new 1824 constitution. Once the assembly was called, Dom Pedro was soon at odds with its members.

The influence, openly exercised, by the Emperor's mistress, significantly increased the resentment of the populous against the Emperor. This was due in part to their affection for Empress Leopoldina whose death in 1826, many believed, had been hastened by the Emperor's infidelity.[6]

An underlying frustration of many Brazilians was their accurate perception that the numerous Portuguese who remained within the Brazilian Empire continued to hold special privileges. On March 13 a bloody riot known as the "night of the bottles" (*noite das garrafadas*) broke out in Rio de Janeiro between native Brazilians and Portuguese.[7]

On April 6, 1831, the Emperor dismissed his cabinet and nominated six nobles to take its place. The population of the capital and some in the army rose up. The next morning, Dom Pedro I, abdicated. Thus began a nine-year regency (1831–1840) for his young son. The immediate consequence of the abdication was a wave of anarchy, which unsurprisingly was at its worst in the extreme north and south in the provinces farthest from the seat of power of the empire.[8]

OPPOSING FORCES

During the early years of the regency, it became apparent that the new Brazilian Army, mostly composed of Portuguese, mercenaries, and Royalists, could not be trusted to maintain discipline when suppressing dissidents. As a consequence, Father Diogo Antonio Feijó, then the Minister of Justice and soon to be the regent, cashiered the insubordinate elements and created a national guard or citizen militia. However, to forge an efficient militia force took time and much energy.[9]

Those opposed to the power of the empire were a heterogeneous lot. Most had little or no military experience so they fought mostly as mobs. The primary exception were the *gauchos* from the southernmost province of Rio Grande do Sul. On October 23, 1839, their army numbered 9,372 men (6,903 cavalry, 2,247 infantry, and 222 artillerymen). This cavalry-dominated army had access to some 20,000 remounts from the neighboring provinces in Uruguay and Rio de la Plata. These mounted, rugged plainsmen ignored political boundaries and fought in Uruguay, the Río de la Plata provinces, and Rio Grande do Sul. Also among the separatists were a few European republican Revolutionaries who, as a consequence of the Peace of Vienna (1815), had been forced to flee their homelands.[10]

The empire had a much greater pool of manpower than the rebels but also had many more commitments. Typically, the imperial troops outnumbered the rebels, at times as many as three to one.

In general, both sides were armed with European-manufactured muskets which had been accumulated during the colonial era. Frequently, the long lance was the dominate battlefield weapon. The rebels' source of artillery was guns captured from the imperial army.[11]

OPENING STRATEGIES

Most of the rebellious provinces were seeking greater autonomy but not separation from Brazil. Their strategy was to seize and defend the provincial capital in an attempt to dissuade the empire from reestablishing complete control. Initially many in Rio Grande do Sul only sought greater autonomy but this evolved into a separatist movement. They preferred to fight on the open plains where their cavalry held significant advantages over infantry and artillery.

PARÁ PROVINCE (1832–36)

Shortly after Dom Pedro I's abdication, Pará, the large province through which the Amazon River empties into the Atlantic, slipped into anarchy as provincial republicans and Monarchists came to blows. Finally, Col. Felix Antonio Clemente Melcher, an opportunist, seized control of the republican movement and defied the imperial authorities. The local imperialists captured and imprisoned him toward the end of 1834. Freed by his soldiers, they then went on a rampage. Melcher, who declared himself "President of Pará," was murdered by one of his followers, Pedro Vinagre, who in turn was also assassinated. In early 1835 an imperial squadron blockaded the provinical capital, Belém (1,505 mi N of Rio de Janeiro). Reinforced by seven warships and two transports, expeditions were sent ashore to reestablish imperial control. On September 20, 1836, the squadron bombarded and a landing force carried by assault against the last rebel stronghold of Oeiras (1,095 mi N of Rio de Janeiro). Martial law was established and harsh punishments handed out.[12]

RIO GRANDE DO SUL, THE FIRST PHASE (1835–40)

Citizens of Rio Grande do Sul, the southernmost province in Brazil, sought greater autonomy and this ultimately evolved into the "War of the Ragamuffins" (*Guerra dos Farrapos*). In fact, this name was misleading because many of the well-to-do of the province also wanted greater autonomy. The term referred to the fringed leather clothing worn by the rebels.[13]

Rio Grande do Sul was awash with political agitators from neighboring Uruguay and the unruly provinces of Río de la Plata which were in an almost perpetual state of political chaos. These circumstance exposed the *Riograndenses* to republican ideas and made the acquisition of arms easy.

On September 19, 1835, partisans of the imperial provincial president, Fernandez Braga, clashed with the followers of the commander of the national guard, Col. Bento Gonçalves da Silva, who favored more autonomy. On September 21 Gonçalves marched into Porto Alegre (700 mi SW of Rio de Janeiro), the provincial capital, and chased Braga out. The regency, which had just committed its limited resources to suppress the anarchy in Pará, was without the ability to militarily enforce its will in Rio Grande do Sul. As a consequence, the regency sent José de Araújo Ribeiro as the new provincial president to replace Braga. He was supported by an imperial squadron commanded by John Grenfell.[14] Nonetheless, Ribeiro was rejected in early 1836 by the Assembly of Rio Grande do Sul.[15]

The selection of Ribeiro was nonetheless fortuitous because it detached from the ranks of the rebels his relative, Bento Manuel Ribeiro, who was their ablest military leader, and brought him to the side of the empire. The imperial squadron immediately blockaded the coast. On August 28, 1836, a landing party from the fleet captured Fort Itapoã, which allowed the imperial troops to recapture Porto Alegre from those wanting greater autonomy. Winning a series of battles, the Royalists chased the rebels, led by Bento Gonçalves, into the interior. A loyalist flotilla of small craft controlled Lagoa dos Patos (the huge, brackish-water lake that parallels the coast, bordered by Porto Alegre on the north and Rio Grande on the south) and the interior rivers, thus making Gonçalves' position more difficult.[16]

Bento Gonçalves possessed important allies in his struggle against the central government. Fructuoso Rivera, the leader of the Uruguayan Federalists (the *Colorados*), had earlier sought refuge in Rio Grande do Sul after being evicted from Uruguay by Manuel Oribe, the leader of that nation's Unitarians (the *Blancos*). As was the case with *caudillos*, a band of *gauchos*, akin to a small nomadic hord, followed Rivera into exile. Also, the "outs" of La Plata, the Argentine Unitarians, allied themselves with the exiled Uruguayan Federalists and the rebel *farrapos*, notwithstanding the seemly ideological contradiction.[17]

Aided by Rivera, the rebel *farrapos* defeated the loyalists at Rio Pardo some 70 miles west of Porto Alegre on September 10, 1836. The imperial navy stopped a complete route by preventing the insurgents from crossing the São Gonçalo River. However, the following month, the insurgents suffered a major setback. On October 4 the imperial shallow-draft flotilla, cooperating with the loyalist troops commanded by Bento Manuel Ribeiro, defeated the *farrapos* at the Isle of Fanfa on the Jacuí River. Bento Gonçalves, his entire staff, and 900 men were captured.[18]

Notwithstanding, in November the *farrapos* declared the Priatinim republic and chose the captive Bento Gonçalves as president. José Gomes Vasconcellos Jardim was selected as interim president. The decision to secede from the empire and not just to seek greater autonomy was influenced by the ruthlessness of the imperial troops as they sacked towns and executed prisoners.[19]

However, the empire's greatest disaster in Rio Grande do Sul was self-inflicted. In early 1837 the regency dismissed Araujo Ribeiro as its primary administrator in Rio Grande do Sul. As a consequence, the *caudilho* Bento Manuel Ribeiro changed sides again. Much of the territory controlled by the imperialists was now won back by the *farrapos*. The regency in Rio de Janeiro despaired as the administrators dispatched from the capital failed to woo back the errant province and the imperial assembly refused to fund new military expeditions.[20]

Due to his failure to solve the problems in Rio Grande do Sul, Father Feijó resigned as regent on September 19, 1837, and Pedro de Araujo Lima took his place. The parliament now granted the military the wherewithall, which it had refused to Feijó, to forcefully subjugate Rio Grande do Sul.[21]

The insurgents also had new leadership. The Italian Revolutionary, Giuseppe Garibaldi,[22] was placed in charge of Rio Grande do Sul's modest naval forces. The rebels established a small naval base at Camaquã (765 mi SW of Rio de Janeiro) and armed four small topsail schooners. This allowed Garibaldi to disrupt the empire's use of Lagoa dos Patos. On October 25, 1837, Capt. Frederick Mariath replaced Grenfell as the commander of the imperial naval forces. During Mariath's short tenure, the rebels destroyed two gunboats and a lighter belonging to the imperial navy, so Grenfell resumed control in May 1838. Grenfell attacked Camaquã with thirty small vessels. He captured a number of rebel craft; however, Garibaldi escaped.[23]

The empire also had its problems on land. On April 30, 1838, Antônio de Souza Netto defeated imperial troops commanded by Sebastião Barreto at Rio Pardo. Once again, the central government tried conciliation by offering a general amnesty on January 1, 1839. The *farrapos* interpreted this as a sign of weakness. The only remaining imperial stronghold in Rio Grande do Sul was the provincial capital of Porto Alegre and it was under siege.[24]

In the summer of 1839, the *farrapos* expanded the war by invading the province to their north, Santa Catharina. Garibaldi used carts, each pulled by fifty oxen, to move two lighters over 54 miles. These were launched on Lake Tramandaí which gave them access to the sea. One of the lighters, the *Farroupilha*, sank in bad weather, however, and the other, the *Seival* commanded by the North American John Griggs, played an important role in the capture of the little port of Laguna (518 mi SW of Rio de Janeiro) on July 22. In Laguna, Garibaldi seized a few small vessels. With these he sailed to Imbituba which he captured. Finally on November 15, 1839, Garibaldi was trapped by a superior imperial squadron commanded by Mariath and defeated off Laguna; Griggs was among the dead.[25]

Late in the year the empire was able to mount a combined land and sea attack which drove the *farrapos* back into their province. The central government did not follow up on this success. In 1840 Bento Manuel Ribeiro, and those who followed the *caudilho*, abandoned the insurgency and accepted an amnesty.[26]

THE SALVADOR INTERLUDE (1837-38)

While the struggle against the *farrapos* dragged on, newspaper editor Francisco Sabino Álvares de Rocha Vieira led a successful rebellion in Brazil's second largest city, Salvador (750 mi N of Rio de Janeiro). On November 17, 1837, he drove those loyal to the Emperor out of the port and declared a republic. By the end of November, 1,900 loyalists besieged the port while the imperial navy established a blockade. On March 12 and 13, 1838, the imperialists stormed the city. Sabino surrendered on the sixteenth. Hundreds died and thousands were condemned to hard labor.[27]

THE MARANHÃO INTERLUDE (1839-40)

Next, anarchy broke out in Maranhão in the north. The most important consequence of the empire's success in restoring order was the emergence of Col. Luis Alves de Lima e Silva[28] as a promising military leader.

RIO GRANDE DO SUL, THE SECOND PHASE (1840-42)

By 1840, the empire's attempt to subdue the *farrapos* showed little promise for success. As a consequence, the ruling Liberal Party began an effort to have the fifteen-year-old Dom Pedro

II declared of age and, therefore, capable of assuming the throne even though this was unconstitutional (the Constitution placed the minimum age of an emperor at thirty-five years old). Dom Pedro declared, "I will it at once" (*quero já*),[29] and he began his reign on July 23, 1840. Dom Pedro's ascendancy did not produce immediate successes on the battlefield as his new cabinet acted indecisively against the separatists.[30]

Alvares Machado was now named the imperial president of the province of Rio Grande do Sul, and Gen. João Paulo dos Santos Barreto was given command of military operations. The two did not work well together and Barreto refused to seek out the separatists, blaming his inactivity on a shortage of resources. He preferred to concentrate his troops along the frontier in an unsuccessful endeavor to cut off the insurgents from outside help. Finally, in March 1841 Machado was recalled.[31]

The failure of imperial policy in Rio Grande do Sul caused another ministerial crisis in Rio de Janeiro and Jose Clemente Pereira now became the minister of war. He dispatched reinforcements and additional supplies to subdue the separatists. The troops were recruited in the North, brought to Rio de Janeiro for training, and then dispatched to the South. However, the new commander, the Conde de Rio Pardo, remained in Porto Alegre, allowing the separatists to control the countryside.[32]

THE SÃO PAULO INTERLUDE (1842)

On May 17, 1842, a revolt broke out in the province of São Paulo. The basic cause was the growing belief that the decisions of the imperial government were arbitrary and capricious. Rafael Tobias de Aguiar was proclaimed president of the province and he established his government in his native town of Sorocaba (273 mi SW of Rio de Janeiro). The rebels soon fled before the imperial army commanded by the Baron of Caxias and Sorocaba fell on June 20. Captured rebel leaders were deported to Espirito Santo and their followers were impressed into the army. The bishop of Marianna invited Caxias to a *Te Deum* (a high Mass) in celebration of the empire's victory. Caxias replied that the clergy should pray for the dead and not rejoice in a victory over fellow countrymen.[33]

MINAS GERAIS (1842)

Teófilo Benedito Ottoni led a rebellion in the central province of Minas Gerais. Like the rebellion in São Paulo, it was sparked by seemingly capricious imperial policies. The rebels captured a few small towns and planned to attack the provincial capital, Ouro Preto (174 mi N of Rio de Janeiro). Caxias, who had just returned to Rio de Janeiro from crushing the rebellion in São Paulo, easily subdued the rebels in Minas Gerais.

RIO GRANDE DO SUL, THE THIRD PHASE (1842–45)

The third and final phase of the war in Rio Grande do Sul began when the *farrapos*' Uruguayan ally, Fructuoso Rivera, who had regained power in Uruguay, was badly defeated at the Battle of Arroyo Grande on December 6, 1842 (see chapter 25). The remains of the Uruguayan Federalist army retreated into Montevideo where it was besieged by the Uruguayan Unitarians, supported by Manuel Rosas of Buenos Aires. The immediate consequence for the *farrapos* was the loss of the munitions, horses, and volunteers that had flowed across the border from their Uruguayan allies whenever needed.[34]

In late 1842 Gen. Luis Alves de Lima e Silva, the Baron of Caxias, was placed in charge of restoring to the empire those areas of Rio Grande do Sul still held by the rebels. He commanded some 11,500 troops; the *farrapo* force numbered about 3,500 men.[35]

Caxias' strategy was to gain control over the Uruguayan resources now lost to the *farrapos*. Caxias was able to purchase the services of these foreigners through negotiations with Rosas of Buenos Aires and Oribe of Uruguay. With his newly purchased cavalry, Caxias relentlessly pursued the *farrapos*. Since the *farrapos* lacked infantry and artillery, even when they did win battles, they were incapable of exploiting them because they could not occupy and hold territory.[36]

Also, Bento Manuel Ribeiro, now fighting for the empire again, became the principal Royalist field commander. By 1843 the rebellious *farrapos* were forced to break into small, nomadic bands as the imperial cavalry detachments hunted them down. The end came when Manuel Marques de Souza (the future conde de Porto Alegre) captured the rebel capital Piratini (918 mi SW of Rio de Janeiro) in late 1844. The rebel cause was now irretrievably lost. In return for surrender and acceptance of imperial authority, the life and property of the former rebels were safeguarded. In February 1845, some 1,200 rebels laid down their arms.[37]

PERNAMBUCO (1848–49)

The last serious separatist movement during the reign of Pedro II occurred in the easternmost province of Pernambuco and became known as the Praieira Revolt (the Liberal newspaper which spearheaded the revolt was published on the Rua da Praia). The immediate cause of the conflict was the smoldering hostilities between the remaining Portuguese and the Brazilians.

The Liberal deputies in the imperial chamber in Rio de Janeiro sympathized with the revolt. The imperial deputies from Pernambuco, led by Joaquim Nunes Machado, issued a manifesto on December 31, 1848, calling for rebellion. The rebels attacked Recife (1,160 mi NE of Rio de Janeiro) on February 2, 1849, but Machado was killed during the assault. The uprising was soon quelled.[38]

OBSERVATIONS

Three primary factions coexisted during the regency: the Monarchists who advocated the return of Pedro I; the Monarchists who wanted the government placed in the hands of his presumptive heir; and the provincial republicans. Once the two Monarchist factions coalesced behind Dom Pedro II, they became strong enough to deal with the republicans, one province at a time. This struggle between union versus separation did not surface again in Brazil until the abdication of Pedro II in 1889. This may be attributed in large measure to the wisdom of his rule.

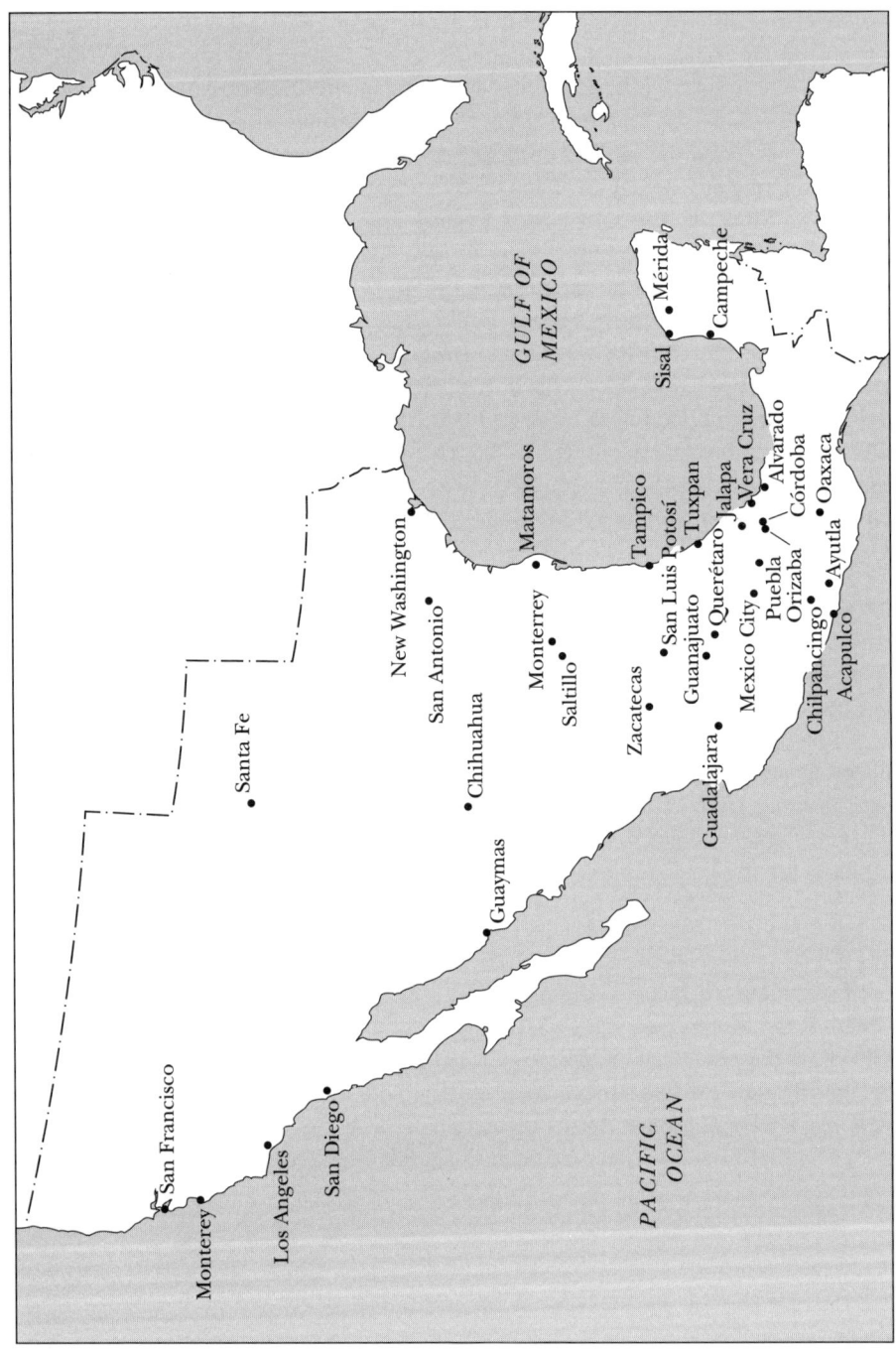

Map 5. Mexico, 1835.

PART 4

WARS OF CONQUEST BY THE UNITED STATES AND GREAT BRITAIN

CHAPTER FOURTEEN

TEXAS INDEPENDENCE, 1835–36

> Our country found itself invaded not by an established nation . . . nor by Mexicans. . . . The invaders were all men who . . . wished to take possession of that vast territory extending from Béxar [or Béjar, present-day San Antonio] to the Sabine belonging to Mexico. . . . All the existing laws . . . marked them as pirates and outlaws.
>
> —Antonio López de Santa Anna

THE SPARK

On October 2, 1835, some 150 Texans (who at the time preferred "Texians") led by militia colonel John W. Moore dispersed an eighty-man Mexican squad that had been sent to Gonzales, Texas (70 mi E of San Antonio), a province of Mexico, to repossess an old cannon. One Mexican soldier was killed.[1]

BACKGROUND

The United States and its citizens had long shown a desire to acquire the territory of Texas. Although titled to Mexico, Texas, and for that matter the lands bordered by the Louisiana Territory on the east, the Pacific on the west, Canada to the north, and old Mexico to the south, had been sparsely colonized and poorly administered. And, the United States had a history of expansionism. It purchased Florida from Spain in 1795, the Louisiana Territory from France in 1803, east Florida from Spain in 1819, and made its first offer for Texas in 1826. By the 1830s the contemporary American parlance describing its appetite for more territory became "Manifest Destiny"; nonetheless, the drive to acquire more land had existed prior to the coining of the term.

Spain and subsequently Mexico were not oblivious to this American predilection. For the most part foreign immigration into this wilderness had been prohibited until 1821. In the waning days of Spanish rule over Mexico, King Ferdinand VII awarded to the Missourian Moses

Austin the right to bring 300 American families to colonize and granted to him a large tract of land on the condition that the settlers accept Spanish rule and the Roman Catholic religion. This was an ill-advised attempt to develop a corridor of loyal settlers from among those who possessed the threat. The contracting parties almost immediately changed to Stephen Austin (Moses' twenty-two-year-old son) and the new emperor of Mexico, Agustín Iturbide, but the terms remained basically the same. Additional grants were soon issued.[2]

Mexico, governed by Conservatives, soon realized that this had opened a floodgate. Brig. Gen. Manuel de Mier y Terán, an engineer, was sent to Texas to investigate the problem in 1828. He reported that the Americans were pouring into Texas and that they already controlled Nacogdoches. His recommendations became the basis for the Law of April 6, 1830. The law rescinded grants not yet filled; established new *presidios* (forts) manned by individuals who had chosen military service over a penitentiary sentence; and prohibited the importation of slaves.[3]

Within Mexico, the struggle between Liberals and Conservatives had raged unabated following independence (1821). In January 1833 the Liberal ticket of Antonio López de Santa Anna[4] and Valentín Gómez Farías won, a promising event for regions like Texas which sought greater autonomy. Soon Santa Anna tired of the drudgery of the office and retired to his ranch. Gómez Farías then began to execute an extremely liberal program which focused on limiting the powers of both the Roman Catholic Church and the military.[5]

In the meantime, the Texans held a convention at San Felipe on October 1, 1832, the purpose of which was to gain greater autonomy from the central government, and sent Stephen Austin to Mexico City to represent their cause. The Texans believed that the new Liberal Santa Anna administration would champion federalism and that the time was right to promote their cause. However, on January 2, 1834, Austin was arrested and imprisoned.[6]

On April 24, 1834, Santa Anna led a Conservative revolt against the Liberals and arguably his own presidency! As a consequence, the states of Jalisco, Nuevo León, San Luís, Zacatecas, and Coahuila[7] (which then included Texas) rebelled against the Conservatives. Most were readily subdued except for Zacatecas. There, Governor Francisco García raised an army of 5,000 untrained civilians. Santa Anna marched against these Liberals with 3,500 men. He convinced the general leading the Liberal militia to lead his men into a trap, and Santa Anna decisively defeated them on May 11, 1835. All arms and public treasure were seized. One-fifth of the state's territory was broken away, out of which the new state of Aguascalientes was created. Santa Anna also permitted his army to loot, murder, and rape, attempting to intimidate Liberals elsewhere.[8]

On May 31 Santa Anna dissolved the national congress, abolished the Constitution of 1824 (thus doing away with states' rights), and proclaimed himself dictator. In September Santa Anna sent his brother-in-law, Gen. Martín Perfecto de Cós,[9] with 500 reinforcements to Texas. Santa Anna directed him to maintain order but not to antagonize the population until Santa Anna could complete the subjugation of the Liberals in old Mexico.

A few Liberals did persist in the struggle. General José Antonio Mejía had fled to New Orleans, Louisiana. There he recruited 200 adventurers and in November 1835 arrived off Tampico in three ships. He succeeded in capturing the fort on the sixteenth, but the town's garrison remained loyal to the central government and defeated Mejía. During this time Gen. Juan Álvarez led the Federalists in the south against Santa Anna, but he was also defeated.[10]

While the Liberals were being suppressed in old Mexico, Texas had not remained peaceful. On June 30, 1835, William Barret Travis (a South Carolinian lawyer) leading 25 "war hawks"[11] supported by an old cannon evicted the Mexican garrison at Anahuac (184 mi NE of San Antonio). Cós demanded that the Texans turn over Travis so he could be tried as a traitor, but they refused. Four months later the Mexican squad under General Ugartechea was repulsed at Gonzales on October 2.[12]

OPPOSING FORCES

By the mid-1830s many distinct societies had evolved in the Mexican territory of Texas. There were 7,800 Mexicans (mostly *mestizos*) who, for the most part, gave their loyalty to the distant and often apathetic government in Mexico City; some 20,000 to 30,000 recently arrived colonists and adventurers, calling themselves "Texans," whose close ties with the United States made their loyalty to Mexico suspect; some 5,000 black slaves; perhaps 4,500 "settled" Indians, and 10,000 "wild" Indians.[13]

Following General Cós' arrival, the Mexican Army in Texas numbered a mere 1,400 men. Theoretically, the Mexican Army in Texas was organized into battalions and regiments, but in reality it functioned at the squad level. The bulk of the Mexican army was garrisoned at San Antonio de Béxar (today's San Antonio). Mexican soldiers did not like serving in Texas; it was too far from home and troops stationed there were always the last to be paid. In addition, the work could be dangerous (from Indians and outlaws) and frequently unappreciated (by the Texans). Apparently, the Mexican army was armed with rifles and possibly carbines manufactured by Ezekiel Baker in London. These weapons were probably surplus or discarded models, having been well worn in British service.[14]

Some Texans and *Tejanos* (those of Hispanic decent) possessed militia experience. Typically, the Texans served in a defensive capacity and fought on foot against marauding Indians. The *Tejanos* fought on horseback, conducting forays into Indian territory.[15]

The Texan army, or more accurately armed mob, which gathered at Gonzales, was some 300 men strong; and as it marched to San Antonio its number doubled. Most were recent arrivals from the United States. Perhaps five percent were *Tejanos*; they were employed primarily as scouts and in the cavalry.[16]

The army included everyone from farmers with neither military experience nor weapons to wily Indian fighters who were armed to the teeth. This group elected Stephen Austin as their titular head in spite of his poor health and ignorance of military matters. In 1835 Noah Smithwick, a volunteer, described the army:

> Buckskin breeches were the nearest approach to [a] uniform. . . . Boots being an unknown quantity, some wore shoes and some moccasins. Here a broad-brimmed sombrero overshadowed the military cap at its side. Here a big American horse loomed up above a nimble Spanish pony, there a half-broke mustang pranced besides a sober, methodical mule.[17]

OPENING STRATEGY

The Texans did not agree among themselves as to their ultimate objective. The volunteer Noah Smithwick observed, "some were for independence, some were for the Constitution of 1824, and some were for anything, just so long as it was a row."[18] The initial Texan plan was to force Cós to leave Texas. Many of the decisions made by the Texans during the early days of the revolt were based upon voice votes.

Also, the Texans feared a slave rebellion and some exploited this to foster solidarity. Rumors of an uprising spread which caused the seizing of lands belonging to free blacks, whippings, and hangings.[19]

Cós announced that he intended to drive out of Texas all American settlers who had been there less than five years. He dismissed the Legislature of Coahuila (of which Texas was then a part). He ordered that no quarter be given to the rebels. All military prisoners were to be shot, and all farms, ranches, and towns owned by Americans burned.

EARLY FIGHTING AT SEA

On September 1, 1835, the Mexican schooner *Correo de Mejico* (unk guns) seized an American-owned merchant ship that possessed improper papers. Some Texans put to sea in the unarmed steamer *Laura* and liberated the merchant ship when the *Correo de Mejico* was becalmed. The following day the *Correo de Mejico* unsuccessfully attempted to seize the merchant ship *San Felipe* which was returning from Vera Cruz with Stephen Austin (who had been released from jail under an amnesty) and arms to fight the government of Santa Anna. After both were off-loaded, the *San Felipe* sailed out to fight the *Correo de Mejico*. The two ships inconclusively exchanged fire throughout September 3. In mid-December the Mexican schooner *General Bravo* (unk guns) chased aground off Paso Caballo the American schooner *Hannah Alexander*, which was carrying arms. It was recaptured a few days later by the first warship of the Texas navy, the schooner *William Robbins* (6 swivels).[20]

THE EARLY FIGHTING ON LAND

Events moved rapidly after the fight for the Gonzales gun on October 2, 1835. On the ninth Capt. George M. Collinsworth, leading fifty Texans, attacked and captured the forty-man garrison at Goliad. This cut Cós off from seaborne reinforcements. The Texas army attacked Cós at San Antonio. First, the Texans defeated the outlying Mexican garrisons. On October 28, 1835, some 300 Texans, led by Col. James Bowie and Capt. James W. Fannin, routed a 275-man Mexican force at Concepción Mission, two miles south of San Antonio. The Texan force, which had grown to 1,000 men, was still too small to storm San Antonio so they lay siege to the town.[21]

Meanwhile, the leaders of the Texans met in San Felipe and on November 5 declared their loyalty to the Mexican Constitution of 1824 by a vote of 33 to 15, which granted extensive autonomy to the states. They denounced the rights of Mexican federal authorities then in Texas to govern, and asserted Texas' right to secede from Mexico, if necessary. This was a conditional declaration of independence. The convention also appealed to the United States government and its people for assistance. Volunteers and private donations continued to pour in, particularly from the southern United States. Within the diplomatic world, the United States government professed strict neutrality. The U.S. War Department did order Gen. Edmund Gaines to proceed to the western border of Louisiana on January 23, 1836, to protect American lives and property.

The besiegers at San Antonio were significantly reinforced by volunteers from the United States, including two companies of "New Orleans Greys." These were volunteers who had organized and outfitted themselves prior to entering Mexico illegally. The Mexican defenses were relatively strong. The garrison, numbering about 1,700 men, was composed of the "Morelos"

Battalion and about five presidial companies. The strongest position was the fortified mission, the Alamo.

On November 26 James Bowie leading some forty horsemen intercepted a 1,000-man Mexican relief column one mile southwest of San Antonio. Following a sharp fight the Texans captured forty pack animals carrying fodder and not the anticipated silver to pay the Mexican garrison; thus the skirmish became known as the "Grass Fight."[22]

On December 5, in a somewhat spontaneous event, Ben Milam[23] led the "New Orleans Greys" (who were quickly renamed the "San Antonio Greys") in an attack. After four days of house-to-house fighting in San Antonio, General Cós surrendered. The Mexican lost about 150 dead and missing and the Texans 4 dead and 14 wounded. The garrison was permitted to march out carrying enough weapons to defend itself against Indians. In turn, the Mexicans agreed not to take up arms against the 1824 Constitution.[24]

Following the victory at San Antonio, the Texans sent a fifty-man expedition against Matamoros (258 mi SSE of San Antonio) in search of war materials (as well as loot) and an alliance with Federalists in old Mexico against Santa Anna. On February 27 General José Urrea,[25] leading 400 Mexicans, caught the Texans at San Patricio and killed or captured practically all. Notwithstanding this setback, a convention of Texans meeting at Washington, Texas, declared complete independence on March 2 and appointed Sam Houston[26] the new commander of the army.[27]

While the Texans were moving toward formally declaring independence, Santa Anna assembled an army of 6,018 men with 20 cannon at San Luis Potosí in old Mexico (616 mi SSW of San Antonio) by late 1835. More than half of the Mexican soldiers were raw recruits.[28] Typical of the self-proclaimed "Napoleon of the West," his supply system was abominable and his administration corrupt. However, since Santa Anna was sufficiently financed through a usurious loan from European bankers at 48 percent per year, enough money trickled down to permit some sustenance to reach the common soldier. The Mexican soldiers who marched north under Santa Anna were only slightly better prepared than those in Texas. The army, although on paper organized into companies, battalions, and regiments, was poorly trained; and many units were incapable of more complex offensive or defensive maneuvers.[29]

Meanwhile, Sam Houston's strategy was to retreat before the overwhelming Mexican force, hoping that Santa Anna would disperse his strength. Also, such a retreat would bring Houston closer to his primary source of men and supplies, the United States, and Santa Anna further from his, old Mexico. Houston planned to attack only when an opportunity afforded him the prospect of success.

In January 1836 he sent Bowie and thirty volunteers to the Alamo with orders to destroy the facility and withdraw. Bowie, in council with the commanding officer of the poorly fed, unpaid garrison, James Neill, decided that the Alamo must and could be defended. Others also chose to ignore Houston's authority including Colonel Fannin at Goliad (83 mi SE of San Antonio) with 400 men and Colonel Johnson and Dr. Grant at Refugio (112 mi SE of San Antonio). Additionally, many of the Texas settlers had returned to their ranches and farms, leaving an army mostly composed of recently arrived American adventurers. Houston attempted to resign since his subordinates refused to obey orders; this was refused but he was granted a leave of absence.[30]

Back in old Mexico, Santa Anna's army departed San Luis Potosí in December 1835. Ramón Martínez Caro, Santa Anna's secretary, later described the march: "They set out on their long march over deserts, in the middle of winter, which is very severe in those regions, without sufficient clothes, particularly among the wretched recruits who in the main were conscripts and were practically naked."[31]

THE ALAMO

By February 10, 1836, the Alamo garrison had swollen to at least 183 men. Recent arrivals included William Travis with thirty men, David Crockett and the Tennessee Company of Mounted Volunteers, and those members of the "San Antonio Greys" who had not joined the disastrous Matamoros expedition. Travis, the senior officer present, allowed the men to choose a post commander. They elected Bowie who was ill, most likely with typhoid.[32]

Santa Anna's ill-provisioned army arrived in San Antonio on February 23, a month before expected. Santa Anna began his loose siege and indicated that no quarter would be given. On the twenty-fifth the Mexicans began a sustained bombardment with their field artillery; the heavier siege guns were still en route. Initially, the Texas guns responded but before long had to withhold fire to conserve ammunition. On March 3 Santa Anna was reinforced by General Gaona's Brigade.

At 5:30 A.M. on March 6, Santa Anna began his assault with some 1,400 troops. Santa Anna attacked on all sides with four columns of troops. The defenders shot down the leading soldiers, mostly conscripts carrying ladders. The Texans forced those attacking from the east and west to pinch toward the north wall. After a brief lull, Santa Anna committed his reserves and renewed the attack from the north and south. The Mexicans carried the fortified mission at 6:30 A.M. True to his word, Santa Anna gave no quarter. The Texans lost about 182 men with 6 survivors who were executed the following day. The Mexicans sustained 78 dead (26 officers and 52 men) and 251 wounded (18 officers and 233 men), many of whom died in the days following. Losses were particularly heavy among sergeants and corporals because they led the attacks.[33]

Although the event was of little military consequence, politically it had profound repercussions. It solidified support for independence among the Texans as well as many in the United States. In fact, on March 2, 1836, four days before the Alamo fell, Texas declared its independence and Houston was elected the new commander-in-chief of the army.

Texan setbacks continued. At 10:30 A.M. on March 2, Gen. José Urrea ambushed forty-one Texans under Dr. Grant at Los Cuantes de Agua Dulce (50 mi SE of San Antonio). Six were taken prisoner and most of the rest were killed; the Mexicans sustained no losses.[34]

Santa Anna believed that the rebellion was broken. He dispersed his army in order to root out the American settlers. Gen. Antonio Gaona's division (700 men) was sent northeast from San Antonio to Bastrop; Gen. José Urrea's division (about 500 men) was sent southeast from Goliad to Matagorda and Brazoria; Santa Anna took 750 men of Joaquín Ramírez Sesma's reinforced command and pursued the fleeing Texan government.[35]

THE GOLIAD MASSACRE

Meanwhile, about 300 Texans under James Fannin had gathered at Goliad. On March 13 or 14 Houston ordered Fannin to march to Guadalupe Victoria but he delayed. Finally, on the nineteenth Fannin began his march taking 1,000 muskets and nine cannon but few vitals and little water. That same day Fannin's force was caught in the open nine miles east of Goliad by an advanced element of General Urrea's command. The 360 Mexican infantry and 80 heavy cavalry drove the Texans into some heavy woods. They then assaulted the position throughout the day. During the early morning of the twentieth, Urrea received badly needed munitions and reinforcements from Colonel [first name unknown] Garáy. As Urrea's recently arrived artillery opened fire, the Texans asked for terms. Urrea informed them that he did not have the power to grant anything but unconditional surrender, which Fannin accepted. The Texans lost 7 killed and 60 wounded; the Mexicans lost 11 killed and 49 wounded at the battle of Coleto.[36]

Urrea wrote to Santa Anna urging clemency. By express order of Santa Anna, most were executed (approximately 390 men) on March 27, Palm Sunday, outside Goliad; twenty-seven managed to escape.[37]

THE CONTINUING WAR AT SEA

During early 1836 the Texans put four small warships to sea—the *Independence*, *Brutus*, *Liberty* (formerly *William Robbins*), and *Invincible*. In January and February the *Independence* (unk guns) cruised as far south as Tampico, capturing numerous small Mexican craft. On March 3 the *Liberty* captured the Mexican schooner *Pelicano* off the Yucatan. Although her manifest showed that she was carrying flour, it proved to be 420 kegs of gun powder for Santa Anna's army; it was delivered to that of Houston instead. On March 25 the *Liberty* captured the American-owned brig *Durango* which was carrying supplies for the Mexican army. On April 3 the *Invincible* (8 guns) broke off a gun duel with the *General Bravo*, chased, and captured the U.S. merchant brig *Pocket* which was carrying a false manifest, Americans seeking service in the Mexican navy, and a contract to carry Mexican troops to Texas.[38]

THE RUNNING SCRAPE

By now Houston's command, the only remaining organized body of Texans, was in retreat. On March 17 it reached the Colorado River and camped at Burnhams. Houston found the ford choked with civilians fleeing Santa Anna's advance. For three days the Texas army was forced to wait in order to protect the crossing of the refugees. The day after Houston crossed the swollen river, 800 Mexican cavalry and infantry under Gen. Joaquín Ramírez y Sesma arrived at the ford. For six days the two armies stared at each other from opposite banks. Finally, Houston continued his eastward trek, attempting to organize and to train his force into an army as it retreated. Houston also received the gift of two 6-pounders, courtesy of the citizens of Cincinnati, Ohio. Throughout the retreat, Houston ignored his critics and threats of his removal.

By April Santa Anna, tired of the chase, made plans to return to Mexico City by sea. First he would make a demonstration near the border with the United States and then turn command of the army over to Gen. Vicente Filísola. However, the senior officers were not so confident that victory was at hand and persuaded Santa Anna to delay his departure.[39]

Santa Anna pressed on in an attempt to capture the Texan representatives at Harrisburg (219 mi ENE of San Antonio) but arrived too late on April 15. Burning Harrisburg, Santa Anna hurried to New Washington on Galveston Bay just in time to see the Texas president board a schooner and sail away. Burning New Washington on April 20, Santa Anna turned northwest to rendezvous with reinforcements and hunt down Houston's army.

On April 18 Houston's scouts intercepted dispatches between General Vicente Filísola[40] and Santa Anna. Houston learned that Santa Anna was in New Washington with 1,000 men, and he had outdistanced his subordinates. In two and one half days, Houston's army closed the 60 miles separating it from Santa Anna's force. On April 20 Houston positioned his 800 men in the woods by the San Jacinto River (207 mi ENE of San Antonio) and waited for Santa Anna's force. The armies skirmished. Santa Anna, believing that Houston was trapped between the two swollen rivers, was content to await the arrival of his reinforcements. Fearing an attack, Santa Anna had his troops stay up all night.

BATTLE OF SAN JACINTO

On the morning of April 21, Santa Anna was reinforced by General Cós and 400 men, bringing his strength to about 1,500 men, one field gun, and a few cavalry. As the day wore on, apparently Santa Anna became convinced that the Texans would not seek a battle. During the afternoon of April 21 Houston sent seven scouts to destroy Vince's Bridge. This prevented further reinforcements from reaching Santa Anna but also cut off the Texans' prime avenue of retreat.

At 4:30 P.M. Houston attacked, literally catching the Mexicans napping. Initially the Texan line, some 900 yards long and two ranks deep, advanced silently. Then, shouting "Remember the Alamo" and "Remember Goliad," the Texans fell on the Mexicans. The Mexicans had neglected to station pickets. The advancing Texan line almost immediately broke down into a charging, angry mob. They burst upon the Mexicans before the Mexicans could form up their ranks. Santa Anna lost all control. Eventually, he fled like the rest. The Texans slaughtered whoever did not escape. Although the battle lasted but eighteen minutes, the killing went on for hours. Two of the 783 attackers were killed and 23 wounded (six later died). Six hundred fifty Mexicans were killed and some 730 taken prisoner.[41]

Santa Anna was captured the following day disguised as a private. Probably fearing for his life, Santa Anna signed the Treaties of Velasco which recognized Texas' independence and required the Mexican army to withdraw from Texas, which it did. Although the Mexican Congress repudiated the agreed on July 29, it had no means to enforce its will.[42]

THE UNITED STATES MAKES ITS PRESENCE KNOWN

On April 25 Gen. Edmund Gaines, commanding U.S. forces along the border, advanced to Nacogdoches (276 mi NE of San Antonio). Between July and December 1836, United States troops occupied the town. Also, Gaines permitted his troops to carry out punitive attacks into Mexican territory against the hostile Indians.

OBSERVATIONS

For the most part, the War for Texas Independence was between Santa Anna, primarily supported by Mexican Conservatives, and the United States citizens, who had recently arrived in Texas. The majority of those who fought for Texas at San Antonio (December 1835), the Alamo (March 1836), and San Jacinto (April 1836) were North Americans who had been in Texas but a short period of time.

Ironically, Mexican Liberals were blamed for the disastrous Texas campaign more than the Conservatives. After all, the Texans had initially professed that they were fighting as Mexican Liberals for the 1824 Constitution and not for independence.

Mexico's greatest shortcoming was Santa Anna's poor leadership. He brashly wasted his men in a frontal assault against those hopelessly trapped in the Alamo. A more prudent strategy would have been to wait for the arrival of his siege artillery and he could have then pounded the enemy into submission. During the Texas Campaign, he dispersed his army before defeating the enemy's main force. Santa Anna blamed his disastrous defeat on fate and his subordinates. He wrote, "It was fate, and fate alone that clipped the wings of victory that was about to crown our efforts."[43]

Throughout the campaign the Mexican army dominated in the western prairies when their more numerous infantry could mass musket fire supported by their superior cavalry and artillery. On the other hand, the Texans dominated in the eastern woodlands, where their rifle-armed infantry could exploit their tactical independence.[44]

One author estimates Mexican casualties at 1,000 dead, 700 prisoners, and 400 wounded. Desertion and noncombat deaths would significantly increase these numbers. The Texans lost about 600 killed and 350 wounded.[45]

CHAPTER FIFTEEN

CAUDILLOS AND THE SECOND TEXAS-MEXICAN WAR, 1836–44

> The enemies of our national integrity, who today by some mistake occupy the fertile soil of Texas, and who tried to extend from there the limits of that territory . . . have met with the intrepid and bellicose nature of the New Mexicans.
>
> —General Manuel Armijo, Mexican Governor of New Mexico

THE SPARK

The Battle of San Jacinto on April 21, 1836, ended the War for Texas Independence and began the Second Texas-Mexican War.

BACKGROUND

Following the Battle of San Jacinto, Gen. Vicente Filísola, second in command of the Mexican army in Texas, carried out Santa Anna's orders to withdraw. This was in spite of the fact that Santa Anna was a captive of the Texans when he issued the orders, and that some senior officers including Gen. José Urrea were opposed to its execution. On July 29 the Mexican Congress repudiated Santa Anna's concessions to the Texans and his orders to the Mexican army; however, by now it was too late to reverse the army's withdrawal. Nevertheless, Mexico refused to recognize the Republic of Texas and continued to consider it a rebellious state. The issue of slavery prevented Texas from being admitted to the Union so it had little choice but to become an independent nation.[1]

OPPOSING FORCES

Immediately following the news of San Jacinto, Interim Mexican President José Justo Corro ordered the Secretary of War, Gen. José María Tornel y Mendivil, to prepare a 3,000-man expedition commanded by Gen. Gabriel Valencia[2] to reinforce the "Army of Operations" (Santa Anna's Texas Expedition). While the new force was being assembled, Mexico City learned the full extent of the disaster in Texas. Taking into consideration its political and economic difficulties as well as the approaching yellow fever season, the government decided to delay sending reinforcements. The surviving elements of the Army of Operations were instructed to take up a defensive position along the Rio Grande and wait for reinforcements. Finally, on November 21, 1836, some 2,000 troops marched north out of Mexico City for Matamoros (842 mi N of Mexico City). The army trekked northward across inhospitable terrain during the harsh winter months, finally arriving at Matamoros on January 18, 1837. United with the survivors of the Texas campaign, the new "Army of the North" consisted of 3,500 men, half of whom had just marched from the south and the other half of whom had been quartered under miserable conditions in Matamoros for the past six months.[3]

Adding to the army's problems, Gen. Nicolás Bravo,[4] the commanding officer, was ill and resigned on February 3, 1837. The interim president offered the command to Gen. Anastasio Bustamante[5] who declined, citing his candidacy for the office of president as the reason. Finally, General Filísola was appointed commander of the Army of the North. At about this time Mexico began to rebuild its navy by purchasing five warships.

Following its victory at San Jacinto, Texas feared another invasion by Mexico. However, the new country was almost bankrupt and could not afford to maintain a standing army for a long period. Also, since the battle of San Jacinto, the army had shrunk from 2,000 men to less than 1,000 (mostly unruly volunteers). By mid-1837 the four-ship Texas navy ceased to exist.[6]

OPENING STRATEGY

The prime objective of Mexico was to restore Texas to its dominion. The Mexican leadership believed that if Texas independence went unchallenged, other states would follow suit. Mexico soon concluded that it could not immediately dedicate sufficient resources to the Texas problem because of the continuing internal Conservative-Liberal struggle; therefore, it devised a hit-and-run strategy. Mexican officials believed that Texans were vulnerable in pitched battles: "the Texans were like *ladino* (wild) cattle, brave and light in mountainous and wooded terrain, but crippled and frightened in the plains."[7]

Texas' primary objective was to maintain its independence. The Texas strategy was in flux between two extremes. President Samuel Houston (1836–38 and 1841–44) believed that Texas could not financially afford a war with Mexico or, for that matter, with the "wild" Indians; so he worked to prevent confrontation, and he reduced government spending. On the other hand, President Mirabeau Bonaparte Lamar (1838–41) believed in a policy of expansion. This required building up the army and the navy and supporting military adventurism to the west and to the south.[8]

MUTINY OF THE "FOUR ONE-ARMED AMPUTEES"[9]

Before Mexico could launch an offensive against Texas, revolts by Liberals against the Conservative government broke out throughout the country. Many of these required the government to draw troops away from the Army of Operations. On November 3, 1836, Juan Bautista Alvarado seized Monterey, California, and on the seventh declared Alta California a sovereign state until the Mexican government restored the Constitution of 1824; this revolt was suppressed.

A more serious revolt occurred in San Luís Potosí (327 mi NNW of Mexico City). On April 14, 1837, Lt. Col. Ramón Ugarte rebelled in favor of a federal form of government. Hearing of the approach of government troops, the rebels fled to the town of Río Verde and joined Gen. Esteban Moctezuma, who had also rebelled. Gen. Mariano Paredes[10] led 1,000 men drawn from the Army of the North, together with a group of Bajio plains troops and 400 men from Jalisco, against the rebels. Paredes decisively defeated the rebels at the town of Santa Elena (now Fernández City) on May 26, 1837.

THE WAR AT SEA

Mexico's first success against Texas was at sea. On April 17, 1837, the brigs *Vencedor del Alamo* and *Libertador* intercepted the Texas warship *Independence* off the Brazos River and after a six-hour chase forced it to surrender; the *Independence* was added to the Mexican navy as the *Independencia*.[11]

The Texas navy struck back. The Texas Secretary of the Navy, S. Rhodes Fisher, ordered the *Brutus* (4 guns) and *Invincible* to attack Mexican commerce in spite of Sam Houston's instructions (elected president on October 22, 1836) to the contrary. The ships sailed on June 11, 1837, with Fisher on board as a volunteer. First, the squadron claimed Mujeres Island off the east coast of the Yucatan for Texas. Then, landing parties went ashore along the Yucatan coast until being forced out by some Mexican cavalry. In reprisal, the Texans burned two villages and tried to force the town of Sisal to pay a $25,000 tribute. Returning to the high seas, the squadron captured six merchant ships, the last being the British *Eliza Russel*. This did not set well with the English. Then, sailing for home, the squadron was intercepted at Galveston Harbor by the Mexican brigs *Iturbide* and *Libertador*. Both Texan warships were run aground on August 29 and broke up that night by the tides. Temporarily, the Texas navy ceased to exist.[12]

NEW MEXICO REBELS

On August 1, 1837, Mexican Liberals (most of whom were Federalists) rebelled against the central government. Col. Albino Pérez, the governor, was defeated; he and his top aides were captured and murdered. The rebels occupied Santa Fé; however, on January 28, 1838, Gen. Manuel Armijo led the Conservatives (most of whom were Centralists) and retook control of New Mexico.

GENERAL URREA REBELS AGAINST CENTRALISM

In December 1837 Gen. José Urrea, the Commandant-General of Sonora, declared in favor of federalism and in early 1838 led a force into Sinaloa in order to subjugate that state. Mexican President Bustamante sent a superior force under General Paredes to crush the rebellion. Urrea evaded battle for months; finally, Paredes defeated him near Mazatlán (780 mi NW of Mexico City) in May 1838. Urrea escaped to Tampico where he joined Gen. José Antonio Mejía who was also conspiring against the central government.[13]

THE PASTRY INTERVENTION

Also in 1837, the French claimed 600,000 pesos from Mexico for damages suffered by French citizens living in Mexico, among them a baker, Rémontel, at Tacubaya near Mexico City.

In order to put pressure on the Mexicans, France sent a naval squadron to the Gulf of Mexico. Two 60-gun frigates and four bricks (small sailing craft) under Capt. François Bazoche arrived at Isla Sacrificios, a few miles south of Vera Cruz on March 21, 1838, but failed to impress the Mexicans. The French squadron was weak, badly supplied, and suffering from yellow fever. On April 16 Bazoche declared Mexico's ports in a state of quarantine. However, Bazoche died from yellow fever (*vomitó*) and was replaced by the energetic one-armed, Rear Adm. Charles Baudin with instructions to use force if necessary. His squadron of four frigates, two corvettes, eight bricks, two bombardes, and two steamers reached Isla Sacrificios on October 26, 1838. Baudin delivered an ultimatum to the Mexican government on November 17, which increased by $200,000 the indemnity demanded to cover the cost of his naval expedition and trade concessions. On the twenty-seventh the Mexicans rejected the proposal.[14]

That same afternoon two of the frigates were towed into position by the two steamers, while the third maneuvered under sail alone; and all anchored at distances of between 1,000 and 1,650 yards from the fortress San Juan de Ulúa at a location where only nineteen of the 193 Mexican cannons could be brought to bear. The French bombardment started at 2:35 P.M. After 5 P.M. the Mexican guns fell silent; and the French ships ceased at 9 P.M., after the bombardment had torn holes in the soft, poorly maintained coral walls of the fortress, knocked several guns off their carriages, and exploded two powder magazines. The French lost 4 killed and 29 wounded, while Mexico sustained over 200 casualties. The commanders of the fortress San Juan de Ulúa and the town of Vera Cruz capitulated.

Mexican President Bustamante was furious at these events. He declared war on France, ordered all French citizens expelled from Mexico within two weeks, and placed Santa Anna in command of Mexican forces in the vicinity of Vera Cruz. In the meantime, General Mariano Arista arrived at the port from Matamoros with a detachment from the Army of the North.

On December 5, 1838, Admiral Baudin landed several hundred marines and gunners at three points along the waterfront. Their objective was to capture Santa Anna and Arista. A column led by François Ferdinand d'Orleans, Prince of Joinville, just missed capturing Santa Anna, who escaped over the rooftops in his underclothes. It did capture Arista, whom the French found asleep. The raiding party then attacked the Merced Barracks. Arriving on the scene, Admiral Baudin ordered his men to withdraw. In the meantime, Santa Anna rallied some troops and attacked the withdrawing French. While pursuing the French, Santa Anna was hit by grapeshot fired from one of the light guns in a French longboat which was covering the withdrawal of the French troops. The shot killed Santa Anna's horse and shattered his left leg, which had to be amputated below the knee.

France obtained some satisfaction through documents signed on March 9, 1839, which gave France and its nationals a $600,000 indemnity, granted most-favored-nation status to both France and Mexico, and restored fortress San Juan de Ulúa to Mexican control. French casualties were less than 100 men and Mexico's perhaps five times that number.[15]

Most importantly for Mexico's struggle with Texas, the "Pastry War" began the restoration of Santa Anna's stature as a military hero and the French captured and retained virtually the entire Mexican navy. Now neither Mexico nor Texas possessed navies.[16]

GENERAL MEJÍA REBELS AGAINST CENTRALISM (AGAIN)

Another rebellion by Liberals occurred on October 7, 1838, at Tampico (452 mi NE of Mexico City). Within a short time General Mejía, who had returned from exile in New Orleans, emerged as its leader. Again, the government sent a significant detachment from the Army of the North—1,100 men—under Gen. Valentín Canalizo, to unite with loyal units from Mexico City under Gen. Martín Perfecto Cós. This combined force attacked Tampico on November 20 but was beaten back, losing 500 men. The rebellion spread throughout Tamaulipas and contiguous states.

As a consequence, President Bustamante raised an army at San Luís Potosí. However, Mejía and Urrea did not remain in Tampico. Instead, they marched south by separate routes and threatened the National Road which linked Mexico City with Vera Cruz (285 mi E of Mexico City). Interim President Santa Anna ordered 500 troops from the Federal District to block Urrea's advance. He called out the 1,600-man Puebla garrison to oppose Mejía's force. On May 3 Santa Anna decisively defeated Mejía near the town of Acajete. The two sides sustained 600 casualties. Mejía was captured and summarily shot. Urrea fled to Tampico. However, on June 5 a 3,000-man government force captured the port, so Urrea fled by sea. Finally, he was captured in Tuxpán in October and was imprisoned in Mexico City.

Although Santa Anna had not directly participated in the fighting, he had positioned the government's forces to defeat the threat. He knew how to reap more than his share of the credit.[17]

REBELLION OF THE NORTHERN TOWNS

Yet another rebellion occurred in old Mexico; it began on November 9, 1838, in the pueblo of Camargo and was led by attorney Antonio Canales. The rebellion spread until it threatened Matamoros harbor. Between December 10 and 12, 1839, Gen. Pedro de Ampudia[18] successfully defended the harbor. General Arista, now commanding the "Army of the North Corps" (formerly the Army of the North), defeated the rebels at the town of Santa Rita, Morelos, on March 24 and 25, 1840.

Thus, during the years immediately following the defeat at San Jacinto, the Army of the North Corps could do no more than maintain a defensive posture along the Rio Grande, try to prevent the incursions into old Mexico by Texans and hostile Indians, and respond to internal crises. No money was available for recruiting, training, equipment, or fortifications.[19]

THE YUCATAN REBELS

In May 1838 Capt. Santiago Iman of the state militia led a Liberal rebellion against the central government of Mexico. Although initially defeated, he took refuge in the jungle. He was soon joined by Yucatecans from his old battalion who seized the ship that was carrying them northward to fight the Texans for the central government. Even with these new recruits, Iman was again defeated.

Iman then appealed to the massive Indian population and promised them relief from forced conscription to fight Mexico's wars and from compulsory church contributions. Many Indians flocked to his cause. In February 1840 he captured Valladolid, which encouraged those in Mérida (1,211 mi ENE of Mexico City) to join in the rebellion. The Yucatan declared independence until the federal system should be reestablished, although the leaders of the rebellion probably had no intention of rejoining Mexico. The Conservatives took refuge in the port of Campeche (820 mi E of Mexico City) which was then besieged. Gen. Joaquín Rivas y Salas surrendered on June 6, 1840, leaving the Liberals in control of the entire peninsula.[20]

REBIRTH OF THE TEXAS NAVY

In 1838 Texas embarked on rebuilding its navy. On November 13 it contracted Frederick Dawson of Baltimore, Maryland, to build six warships for $280,000. The ships were delivered between June 1839 and April 1840. In addition, in 1839 Texas purchased the large paddle-wheel steamer *Charleston* and renamed her the *Zavala*.[21]

When James Treat's diplomatic mission to Mexico failed, Commodore Edwin Moore[22] blockaded the Mexican coast. The Yucatecans, with the help of the Texas navy, extended their rebellion into Tabasco. On November 19, 1840, the steamer *Zavala* towed the *Austin* and *San*

Bernard seventy miles up the Tabasco River and, supported by 150 Yucatecans, captured San Juan Bautista (now Villahermosa). On the twentieth the squadron returned to Texas after losing the schooners *San Jacinto* and *San Antonio* to heavy weather. Texas now sent another emissary to Mexico City, James Webb, but this overture also failed.[23]

URREA LEADS ANOTHER REBELLION

On July 15, 1840, the Fifth Infantry Regiment and the "Comercio de Mexico" Regiment quartered near Mexico City rebelled. They freed General Urrea who was being held in the former Inquisition building. Then they seized the National Palace and captured President Bustamante. However, General Valencia, who commanded the capital's garrison, refused to support the movement and occupied the *ciudadela* (arsenal) some ten blocks from the National Palace. At 2 P.M. the two sides began exchanging artillery fire which lasted for twelve days. Hundreds of casualties occurred, most of whom were civilians.

During the subsequent night, President Bustamante escaped from Urrea. Few joined the rebellious general. On July 27 Urrea sought surrender terms. Generous terms were accorded in spite of the casualties and damage inflicted. The ease with which President Bustamante had been captured significantly damaged his reputation.[24]

JORDAN'S EXPEDITION

In 1840 Col. S. W. Jordan led some 110 Texans into Mexico with the objective of creating the "Republic of the Río Grande" out of northern Mexican states. He was soon besieged by a much larger Mexican force commanded by General Arista. The Texans fought their way back across the Río Grande.[25]

THE FIRST SANTA FÉ EXPEDITION

During the summer of 1840 Texas President Lamar sent agents into New Mexico to proclaim the inhabitants as fellow citizens of Texas. If New Mexico could be incorporated into Texas, the growing overland trade between the east and west coasts would have to pass through Texas' custom houses. In early 1841 Lamar decided to go on the offensive both on land and at sea against Mexico. Newspapers detailed the preparations of an expedition to invade New Mexico.[26]

Some 320 men under Col. Hugh McLeod departed Texas on June 20, 1841. They suffered from poor leadership and a lack of discipline. Not knowing the terrain, the Texans trekked over 1,000 miles to cover a distance which should have required closer to 500 miles. Governor Armijo, forewarned, mobilized the militia. By August 30, 1841, the Texas expedition had deteriorated, and McLeod divided his command. Capt. William Cooke took the strongest 100 men and pressed ahead to San Miguel; McLeod followed as best he could with the remainder. On September 16 Capt. Damasio Salazar, commanding sixty-eight Mexicans, captured the first of the Texans, an advance party of five men. The next day Salazar captured the remainder of Cooke's party at Antón Chico. On October 4 General Armijo, commanding some 1,500 men, found McLeod at Laguna Colorada. The remaining 233 Texans surrendered the next day without a fight. They were marched off for imprisonment in Mexico City suffering starvation and exposure. President Lamar was publicly censured by the Texas Congress, and the disaster contributed to Houston's reelection.[27]

The disastrous outcome of the Santa Fé expeditions impacted upon the outlook of the future. Texas' inability to occupy territory that it claimed weakened its financial credibility in

Europe and decreased the flow of immigration coming from the United States. Also, the Santa Fé expedition increased apprehension in Mexico City concerning Texas desires to conquer additional territory. As a result, Mexico's desire to reconquer Texas was rekindled and a new offensive planned.[28]

PLAN OF POLITICAL REGENERATION

Yet another rebellion occurred in Mexico. On August 8, 1841, General Paredes, military commander of Jalisco, mutinied against the government of General Bustamante and proclaimed his "Plan of Political Regeneration." This was one Centralist rebelling against another. The movement spread rapidly. General Valencia, still in command of Mexico City's garrison, supported the rebels as did regional *caudillos*, one by one. Finally, Santa Anna seized the fortress at Perote (110 mi E of Mexico City) and declared against the government. Bustamante was driven out of the capital on September 20 and was compelled to resign as president on the twenty-ninth.[29]

THE VÁZQUEZ EXPEDITION

The ever-alert Santa Anna seized power as a result of the *Estranzuela* Convention. He decided to carry the war to Texas. Three days after assuming power, on December 9, 1841, he ordered General Arista, commanding the Army of the North Corps, to dispatch a raiding expedition of 500 well-mounted and equipped troops against San Antonio. The departure of the expedition was delayed until February 23, 1842. Finally, 391 soldiers, commanded by Brevet Gen. Rafael Vázquez, trekked across 188 miles during ten days of uninterrupted marching from San Ferrando de Rosas to San Antonio. There the invaders were met by 260 Texans, who chose to surrender the city. The garrison, one company of Texas Rangers, fled. On March 5, 1842, Vázquez took possession of the town, symbolically appointed an *alcalde* (mayor), proclaimed Mexican law to be in effect, and withdrew across the Rio Grande.[30]

In support of the Vázquez expedition, on February 19 Capt. Ramón Valera led 153 Mexican cavalry from Mier toward Texas; within a few days he was joined by Capt. Agatón Quinones with fifty more men. On February 28, some 132 men (the remainder having deserted) reached the Nueces River. Most of the force was on foot, having lost their horses crossing the rough terrain. This force crossed the Nueces River, but it marched less than 30 miles over the next two days due to the shortage of mounts. Using forty of the best mounts, Valera sent Brevet Capt. Miguel Aznar ahead to surprise the town of Goliad. The town surrendered, and Aznar rejoined Valera during the night of March 3. The next day Aznar led fifty-five men against Refigo Mission which he captured without a fight. Having received no news of General Vázquez and due to the poor state of his horses, Captain Valera decided to return to the Nueces River. On March 10, while camped at Santa Gertrudis, Valera was attacked by 300 Lipan and Tancahue Indians. The Mexicans suffered sixteen badly wounded and the Indians over forty.[31]

Santa Anna was highly dissatisfied with Mexico's attack on San Antonio, stating that General Vázquez failed in his primary task "to take by surprise and capture or put the knife to the garrison of adventurers."[32] In order to counteract possible rumors that General Vázquez had retreated out of fear of the Texans, Santa Anna ordered General Arista to dispatch a force of some 800 men under the command of Gen. Adrian Woll.[33] Under the pretext of poor health, General Arista, disgusted with the authorities in Mexico City, surrendered command of the Army of the North Corps to Brigade Gen. Isidro Reyes, Commandant-General of Coahuila.

Just prior to this change in command, the Secretary of War notified the Commander of the Army of the North Corps that some 3,000 Texas adventurers aided by United States citizens would strike from New Orleans against Matamoros. The Commander was ordered to transfer his headquarters to Mier and to concentrate his forces between Mier and Matamoros. General Ampudia was ordered to work day and night on the defenses of Matamoros. Some 500 Mexican reinforcements were sent from Tampico. The Commander of the Army of the North Corps was further ordered to harass any enemy force that reached the Nueces River. However, this invasion never materialized.[34]

SNIVELY'S EXPEDITION

In the spring of 1842 Col. Jacob Snively led 180 men northward to attack the transcontinental trade caravans with the consent of the Texas government. The Texans routed 400 Mexican cavalry which were riding eastward to join and to escort the caravan. However, when the Texans did intercept the caravan, it was under the escort of 200 U.S. dragoons. The American commander, Capt. Philip St. George Cooke, told the Texans that they were trespassing on U.S. territory and disarmed them (except for ten muskets). They returned to Texas humiliated.[35]

THE BATTLE OF LIPANTITLAN

On June 17, 1842, Col. Antonio Canales, commanding the Mexican garrison at Camargo, learned that a force of some 200 Texans were camped near the mouth of the Nueces River, approximately 112 miles to the northeast. He approached the enemy with 354 local militia and 185 regulars, while others had been ordered to retire due to poor mounts. Shortly after daybreak on July 7, the Texans discovered the Mexican force attempting to encircle them before attacking. After some brief musketry, the Texans sought refuge in dense woods, deserting their camp. The Mexicans attacked the Texans but were repulsed. They chose not to continue the fight; so they gathered up 11 rifles, 42 pistols, 2 flags, and a standard, all of which had been abandoned in the Texans' haste. Both sides claimed the other lost about 30 men dead and that they only lost a handful. Emotions ran high in Texas. On June 27 the Texas Congress declared a war of invasion against Mexico, but this was vetoed by Houston, who was once again president.[36]

At sea, the Texans were more successful. Yucatan agreed to purchase the protection of the Texas fleet for $8,000 a month. Four Texas warships set sail on December 13, 1841. The squadron primarily operated off of Vera Cruz, capturing four merchant ships. In August 1842 the fleet returned to Texas when Yucatan and Mexico agreed to a truce, and Yucatan suspended its monthly payments.[37]

MEXICO RETURNS TO THE OFFENSIVE

Now confronted with two rebellious provinces—Texas and the Yucatan—Mexico began a land and sea offensive. On July 5, 1842, Commodore Tomás Marín,[38] leading fifty-seven men, surprised those guarding the Yucatecan brigantine *Yucateco* at Campeche and took her into the Mexican navy as the *Mexicano*. Taking on board army troops under Gen. Juan Morales, the *Mexicano* proceeded to the island of Carmen where he attacked the remainder of the Yucatecan navy—the brig *Iman* and the armed canoes *Campecheano* and *Sisalino*—on August 22. More ominous for the Texas navy, Mexico purchased the two modern side-wheel steamers *Guadalupe* and *Moctezuma* from British builders. The ordnance on board each included one 68-pound Paixhans pivot gun which easily outranged any cannon in the now dilapidated Texas fleet.[39]

In October, General Morales, receiving 1,000 reinforcements, landed at Champotón and advanced into the Yucatan Peninsula but had little success against the rebels. Gen. José Vicente Miñón reinforced him with the 2,720-man Second Brigade which also bogged down.[40]

GENERAL WOLL'S EXPEDITION AGAINST TEXAS

Carrying out Santa Anna's orders, on August 31, 1842, Gen. Adrian Woll led 1,082 handpicked troops, two artillery pieces, twelve carts loaded with corn for fodder, fifty young bulls for fresh meat, and 213 mules loaded with 30,000 rations of flour and dry meat—enough for forty-six days out of Nogal. This undoubtedly was the best provisioned Mexican expedition during the long struggle over Texas.

General Woll avoided the well-traveled roads and cut across the desert in order to avoid detection. On September 10 he camped some seven miles from San Antonio. Woll ordered the roads leading from the town blocked. That evening a delegation from San Antonio approached the Mexican camp. Woll immediately advanced closer to the town. At daybreak Woll led the troops into San Antonio. Once the force had penetrated the center, it was fired upon. Some 150 Texans had hastily constructed a redoubt in front of a house which they chose to defend. After a thirty-minute fusillade, fifty-two Texans unconditionally surrendered. The remainder escaped through the back door and into the woods. The Texans lost twelve dead and three wounded and the Mexicans one dead and eighteen wounded.[41]

As Woll was preparing to fall back across the Rio Grande on September 18, 1842, thirty-eight mounted Texans were discovered just to the east of the town. The Mexicans immediately gave chase, and they were led toward an ambush where 300 Texans under Col. Matthew Caldwell were waiting seven miles northeast of San Antonio. Woll discovered the trap. Although ordered by Santa Anna not to attack Texans who were protected by woods, Woll did so taking into consideration his numerical superiority. He could not dislodge the Texans from their defensive position. About a mile from this engagement, some 500 Mexican cavalry overwhelmed 53 Texans at Salado Creek. Woll chose not to continue the fight. Both sides reported widely differing casualty numbers. At the least, the Mexicans lost 29 dead and 58 wounded and the Texans 36 dead and 15 captured.[42]

On September 20 General Woll began his withdrawal. The next day he learned that a 150-cart caravan of Mexican townspeople, fearing reprisals, was following his tracks. He delayed his column during the twenty-first, allowing them to catch up. On the twenty-second the column was attacked by some 100 Texan horsemen, but they were scattered. On October 1 they entered the town of Rio Grande, having completed a 640-mile trek.[43]

TEXAS STRIKES BACK

These raids created a public outcry in Texas to invade Mexico and eliminate the threat. President Sam Houston was privately opposed to such a military adventure, believing it to be folly; however, the public outcry was so great that he felt compelled to humor it. The Texas Congress had met in the interlude between the two raids and had authorized offensive operations against Mexico. Houston ordered militia Brig. Gen. Alexander Somervell to march the 750 volunteers, who had gathered at San Antonio following the second raid, to the Rio Grande. On December 8 he occupied the small town of Laredo on the east bank; Somervell could not maintain discipline and pillaging took place. Among the volunteers were several Texan ex-generals and ex-colonels who were spoiling for a fight. Calling for volunteers, Somervell crossed the Rio Grande with some 500 men and occupied the town of Guerrero on December 17, 1842. Somervell then ordered a withdrawal to San Antonio. One hundred eighty-nine men obeyed; the remaining 300 chose a new commander, William S. Fisher, and followed the Río Grande southeast to the town of Mier.

THE BATTLE OF MIER

While the Texans were trekking southeast, the Mexicans were hurriedly collecting their scattered forces at Mier. The Texans arrived first on December 22, 1842. Awaiting a tribute to be paid by the town, the Texans withdrew, spending the night at Casas Blancas ranch 9 miles northeast of Mier. At this point the Texans captured a Mexican who told them that General Ampudia now occupied Mier with a few hundred men. The Texans decided to attack before Ampudia could receive reinforcements. Finally, during Christmas evening the 300 Texans attacked the 635 Mexicans commanded by General Ampudia. They succeeded in winning a foothold on the south edge of the town. On the twenty-sixth Ampudia seized the initiative. His cavalry seized the ford across the Rio Bravo thereby cutting the Texans off from their train which had been left at the Casas Blancas ranch while the Mexican infantry pressured the Texans holding the edge of town. Ampudia then used his superior numbers to compress the Texans against the river. Finally, the Texans saw the hopelessness of their fight and surrendered. Two hundred forty-two Texans were captured along with all of their weapons and supplies. The Mexicans lost 30 dead and 66 wounded.[44]

THE BLACK BEAN INCIDENT

The prisoners then began their march to Mexico City. On February 10, 1843, the majority, led by Capt. Ewen Cameron, rushed and overpowered their Mexican guards. The senior Texan officers had been taken ahead, in part to ensure the good conduct of the men. The 193 escapees (three died and eighteen wounded were left behind) began marching home. They were recaptured by the Mexican cavalry. Mexico City ordered that one in ten of the escapees be executed. Seventeen black beans were mixed in a jar with 157 white beans. Those drawing black beans were shot.[45]

Back in Texas the disaster at Mier only intensified the enthusiasm for offensive operations against Mexico. Houston publicly increased his enthusiasm for such an endeavor while privately he held against it. Volunteers came from the United States but were not in large enough numbers to create problems for Houston.

JONES SEIZES MONTEREY

While General Woll was raiding San Antonio and the Texans were counterattacking, an ominous event occurred for Mexico. On October 20, 1842, American Commodore Thomas A. C. Jones, believing that war had broken out between the United States and Mexico, seized Monterey, California. Learning of his mistake, he withdrew and was reprimanded by President John Tyler. However, this was a clear signal that the Americans were ready to seize ports in California.[46]

THE SECOND SANTA FÉ EXPEDITION

Following the disastrous operations in the lower Rio Grande valley, Texas turned its attentions again toward the northwest. Commissions were issued to individuals to raise groups of armed men to attack Mexican territory and property. An added enticement was the trade that moved over the Santa Fé Trail, the principle commercial route between the United States and the West Coast.[47]

First to act was Charles A. Warfield. Commanding twenty-one men he surprised the Mexican outpost at Mora, killing five soldiers. He was then driven to Bent's Fort by superior Mexican forces. On May 29, 1843, Warfield disbanded his group.[48]

SEA BATTLE OF YUCATAN

Commodore Moore chose not to let the naval imbalance deteriorate any further and put to sea with the *Austin* and *Wharton*. He had received a renewed $8,000 monthly payment from the Yucatan plus contributions from American and Texan businessmen. However, offensive action was contrary to the desires of President Houston, who had succeeded Lamar on January 1, 1842, thus entering his second term. Privately, he worked for a negotiated settlement with Mexico; publicly he frequently made war-like utterances in order to placate the hawks in Texas.

Moore learned from an American merchant ship that the *Moctezuma* was embarking troops at Telchac. Seeking to catch the steamer alone, he set sail from New Orleans (more frequently the home port of the Texas navy than any site in Texas) on April 19, 1843. On the thirtieth Moore found the *Moctezuma* at Lerma coaling and five other Mexican warships—the *Guadalupe, Aguila, Mexicano, Iman,* and *Campechana*—ten miles to the south. The Texas warships tried to get to the *Moctezuma* before she could rejoin the others but failed. Both fleets maneuvered for tactical advantage. The Texans were handicapped by lack of steam. The Mexicans were handicapped by the ravaging effects of yellow fever upon their crews. The commanding officer of the *Moctezuma* had died the night before from the disease, and yellow fever had reduced the crews of the Mexican ships to barely enough to sail and steam them, let alone efficiently work their guns. The ensuing fight was inconclusive. This was the first engagement where exploding shells were used by opposing warships. The Texas squadron entered Campeche and broke the Mexican blockade of Yucatan.

SEA BATTLE OF CAMPECHE

Both sides prepared to renew the fight. Commodore Marín, who had relieved Commodore Francisco de Paula López, laid up the *Mexicano* in order to use its crew to round out the crews in his other warships. When the British serving in the Mexican fleet refused to continue, they were replaced by inexperienced soldiers from the army. On the Texan side, Moore borrowed two long 18-pounders for the *Austin* and a long 12-pounder for the *Wharton* from Campeche's defenses in order to increase the range of his ordnance.[49]

On May 16, 1843, the Texans, finding adequate wind, sailed to give battle. Becalmed three miles from the Mexicans, the *Guadalupe* and *Moctezuma* steamed close enough to take advantage of their longer-range artillery. Then a breeze returned the advantage to the shorter-range, but heavier, broadside of the *Austin* (the *Wharton* never found sufficient wind to close the enemy). The battle raged for three hours and was finally broken off by the Mexican steamers. The Texas ships returned to Campeche, thus preventing a new Mexican blockade. By early June, Moore learned that Houston had declared his cruise illegal and a piratical act. The *Austin* and *Wharton* returned to Galveston on June 14. Moore was later exonerated by a court-martial. Once again Yucatan and the central government of Mexico agreed to an armistice. The Yucatan was granted virtual autonomy.[50]

TABASCO REBELS

The state of Tabasco, which lies west of the Yucatan on the Gulf of Mexico, declared its independence. In July 1843 a force led by General Ampudia suppressed the secessionists. Rebel Gen. Francisco Sentmanat fled to the United States.[51]

A SHORT ARMISTICE WITH TEXAS

On July 7, 1843, the British Minister to Mexico informed the President that Texas was interested in discussing peace. Representatives met at Sabinas, Mexico, and signed an armistice on February 15, 1844, which provided for further negotiations, suspended military operations, and prohibited trespassing by either side. Mexico did not recognize Texas independence nor did Texas admit to subservience. However, within a short time President Santa Anna ordered General Woll, now commanding the "First Brigade of the North" (the new name for the Army of the North Corps) to notify the "so-called President of Texas" that the armistice was over.[52]

GENERAL SENTMANAT RETURNS TO TABASCO

On May 27, 1844, General Sentmanat, along with 70 followers transporting 200 extra rifles, sailed from New Orleans on board the U.S. schooner *William A. Turner*. The would-be secessionists landed on a Tabasco beach. General Ampudia sent 100 infantry and 22 cavalry to hunt down the invaders. Most of the intruders were captured on June 13 near the village of Jalapa. Thirty-eight of the forty-two men were captured, including Sentmanat, and summarily shot. Sentmanat and fourteen others had their heads cut off, boiled in oil, and hung in iron cages from the walls in San Juan Bautista. While in exile, Sentmanat had married an American and made many friends. His fate angered many in New Orleans.[53]

GENERAL PAREDES REBELS

In November 1844 General Paredes, commanding 2,000 men, rebelled against the government of Santa Anna. Santa Anna, once again semiretired at his ranch while others ran his government, rushed to the capital. There he gathered 7,000 infantry, 1,500 cavalry, and 20 cannons. On the twenty-second Santa Anna set out for Querétaro (167 mi NNW of Mexico City) to deal with Paredes but left a very hostile Congress behind. Culminating a long series of grievances, Congress argued that Santa Anna as president had violated the Constitution by placing himself at the head of the army. On December 2, 1843, the Congress voted a protest of Santa Anna's dictatorial conduct. On the fifth the capital's garrison declared for the Congress. Interim President Valentín Canalizo (Santa Anna's proxy) ordered the army to suppress the mutiny but it refused. A mob then went on an anti-Santa Anna rampage; they disinterred his leg lost at Vera Cruz in 1838 which had been buried at great pomp and expense, and dragged it through the streets. Congress named José Joaquin Herrera[54] as the new executive.[55]

Santa Anna found his position increasingly difficult. His army was beginning to shrink through desertions; Paredes' army now at Guadalajara (424 mi WNW of Mexico City) had swollen to 4,000 men, and Herrera controlled the capital with 8,000 men commanded by Generals Bravo and Valencia. The anti-Santa Anna uprising spread to the east and south. Believing Mexico City too strong to attack, Santa Anna marched against Puebla (80 mi E of Mexico City) in order to secure a base of operations. The city would not peacefully welcome him so on January 2, 1845, he attacked. Although Santa Anna carried some outposts, those in Puebla refused to surrender, anticipating help from Mexico City. Perhaps losing his nerve, Santa Anna permitted the enemy's reinforcements to enter Puebla unmolested. He then attempted to flee and was caught by some Indians who planned to cook him (literally) before collecting the price on his head. A parish priest intervened. Finally in June Santa Anna was exiled.[56]

OBSERVATIONS

Mexico began and ended the era in political chaos caused by the competing Conservative and Liberal ideologies and selfish *caudillos*, practically all of whom were former Royalist officers. This made military victory over Texas almost impossible.

Mexico had not improved the quality of its army. Numerous reforms were legislated, but the sacrifices in treasure, talent, and time necessary for implementing them were never made.[57] Mrs. Frances Calderón de la Barca described General Paredes' troops in September 1841: "The Infantry, it must be confessed, was in a very ragged and rather drunken condition—the cavalry better, having *borrowed* fresh horses as they went along."[58]

On the other side, Texas produced neither officers capable of leading a campaign against Mexico nor the disciplined troops necessary for fighting. Neither side could financially sustain a naval force long enough to do serious damage to the other.

By 1844 the danger to Texas independence had passed, not because of success on the battlefield but because of the U.S. decision to admit it into the Union and Texas' growing economy. The Mexican raids into Texas had ceased, and the Indians were temporarily at peace. The Texan population had grown from some 30,000 individuals to 212,000 by 1850, thanks primarily to immigration from the United States. Also, Texans made Texas more "anglo"; many Mexican families were driven out. The currency had stabilized and was at a par with gold. The public debt had not increased.[59]

Chapter 16

THE UNITED STATES AND MEXICO, 1846–48

> I . . . to this day regard the war . . . as one of the most unjust ever waged by a stronger against a weaker nation.
> —Ulysses S. Grant

THE SPARK

Mexicans and Americans would probably choose different events as the spark that ignited the war. For the Mexicans, the American annexation of Texas on July 4, 1845, was tantamount to a declaration of war.[1] On April 25, some 1,600 Mexican cavalry attacked sixty-three U.S. dragoons north of the Río Grande but south of the Nueces River. President James Polk denounced this as an act of war against the United States; war was declared on May 13.[2]

BACKGROUND

Since 1836 Texas had maintained by force its independence from Mexico. For almost ten years Texas attempted to join the Union; however, the issue of slavery delayed its annexation. In the 1844 U.S. presidential election, Democrat James Polk campaigned on a platform that included the annexation of Texas and the settlement of the Oregon issue. Also, following the election, President Polk confided to a friend that he also wanted to acquire California.[3]

On March 1, 1845, Congress pass a joint resolution favoring the immediate annexation of Texas. The House voted overwhelmingly for the resolution; in the Senate the vote was 27 senators in favor and 25 opposed. On March 6 the Mexican minister in Washington, outraged, asked for his passport, and the Mexican government broke diplomatic relations on March 28. The Texas Congress voted favorably for annexation on June 23, and on July 4 the Texas people in convention accepted the terms. On July 20 the Mexican President recommended to Congress a declaration of war should annexation occur or Texas be invaded by U.S. troops.[4]

On June 15 Polk ordered Gen. Zachary Taylor[5] to advance his 3,922-man army into Texas. By August Taylor established his headquarters on the west bank of the Nueces River, near Corpus Christi, about 135 miles from the Río Grande. On January 13, 1846, Secretary of War William L. Marcy ordered Taylor to occupy the disputed area between the Nueces and the Río Grande (Mexico claimed that the Nueces River was the boundary between the rebellious province of Texas and Mexico, and the United States claimed the Río Grande to be the boundary between the recently admitted state of Texas and Mexico).[6]

Among the numerous factions within Mexico, opposition to the annexation of Texas by the United States became the measure of political virility. Since the War for Independence (1810–21) central-conservatism and federal-liberalism had struggled for domination.[7] With the exception of 1833–34, the Conservatives had controlled the government. On December 4, 1844, the moderate Conservatives overthrew the dictatorial Antonio López de Santa Anna and packed him off to exile in Venezuela. Gen. José Joaquin Herrera was made president; however, his weakly executed, middle-of-the-road policies pleased neither political extreme. On December 14, 1845, Gen. Mariano Paredes again successfully revolted and restored the Conservatives to power. Each of these new governments, brought on by the rapid succession of *coups*, found it necessary to be increasingly committed to a military solution to the Texas problem in an attempt to enhance its survival within the chaotic politics of Mexico.[8]

OPPOSING FORCES

Mexico's population was about eight million and that of the United States twenty-one million. The two armies differed significantly in character. The Mexican army numbered 29,377 troops. They were scattered throughout Mexico in garrisons. Most of the Mexican infantry were conscripts, many of whom had been impressed through the *leva*. They came from the lower economic classes and were predominantly of Indian origin. Many did not even speak Spanish, making indoctrination extremely difficult. A majority of the Mexican officers held their commissions as a result of family ties. Most were *criollos*, those of pure Spanish ancestry. The pride of the Mexican army was its cavalry. Its primary weapon was still the lance. As throughout Latin America, gun powder was typically in short supply and of poor quality. The Mexican artillery was composed of 140 guns, many of which were locally cast to pre-Independence design. They were dispersed throughout the country.[9]

Perhaps worse for Mexico, it was bankrupt. In September 1846 the national treasury housed a pitiful 1,839 pesos! During the decades of political chaos caused by the struggle between the Conservatives and Liberals, many unscrupulous men had held the purse strings of the army with dire consequences. The pitiful state of the army in early 1846 may be surmised by the surprise of José Fernando Ramírez, a member of the national legislature, at seeing the army actually drilling:

> Today [January 7] Mexico City witnessed a spectacle which it perhaps can not recall having seen before: a General who took the trouble to review in detail all the various bodies of troops in the division. Paredes did just that, and furthermore, saw to it that all the soldiers received the pay due them from funds that were more than enough to suffice.[10]

Unfortunately for the Mexican cause, this attention to discipline and training was the exception and short lived.

On the eve of war, the strength of the U.S. Army was 8,500 men. When Congress declared war on Mexico on May 13, 1846, it authorized an army of 17,800 men and appropriated $10 million to fight the war. About half of the soldiers were regulars, or professionals, and the other half volunteers. Although some officers in the U.S. Army held their appointment because of political connections, particularly among the volunteers, most were professionals having been trained at the U.S. Military Academy or having had extensive experience in the Indian Wars.

The U.S. Army possessed four artillery regiments each having ten batteries. Each battery consisted of six bronze smoothbore 6-pounders. One battery in each regiment was designed "horse artillery." Commonly known as "flying batteries," the artillerymen rode on either horses or the gun caissons (wagons).[11]

Contemporary opinion differed sharply on the question of who would win a war between Mexico and the United States. Those predicting a Mexican victory pointed to its larger army, three times that of the United States; to its numerically superior light cavalry; to its significantly shorter supply lines; to its knowledge of national terrain; to the emotional advantage of fighting on its own soil; to the divisiveness of the slavery and states' rights issues in the United States; to the poor performance of the U.S. Army in its last major war (1812); and to the possible support of Great Britain for Mexico as a consequence of its territorial disputes with the United States elsewhere. Even the U.S. Secretary of State, James Buchanan, was among those who believed that England and France would join Mexico in war against the United States. President James Polk wrote in his diary, "Then, said Mr. Buchanan, you will have war with England as well as Mexico, and probably France also, for neither of these powers will ever stand by and see California annexed to the United States."[12]

Those believing that the United States would win called attention to its significantly greater wealth and industrial capacity; to its dominant navy; to its army's superb horse-drawn artillery; and to the weaknesses of the Mexican army caused by class stratification and political chaos.

OPENING STRATEGIES

President Polk's opening strategy was to seize population centers in the coveted northern territory. Polk hoped this would lead to negotiations.[13] On May 26 President Polk proposed to his cabinet that an expedition be sent from Independence, Missouri, to Sacramento to seize California before the winter set in. The territories were so vast and mid-nineteenth-century communications so slow that, in order to be victorious, commanders had to demonstrate initiative and forces had to live off the land.[14]

The Mexican strategy was to reinforce its long-ignored garrison at Matamoros, cross the Río Grande, destroy the American army, and capture its general. To that end President José Joaquin de Herrera had ordered an army raised at San Luis Potosí (327 mi NW of Mexico City). However, in early 1846 General Paredes led this army south to Mexico City and overthrew the Herrera government instead of going north to confront the Americans. There, Paredes found it necessary to retain part of the army in the capital to assure the continuance of the new government. Paredes ordered the politically reliable general Pedro Ampudia[15] to lead a 2,200-man force to reinforce the 3,000-man garrison at Matamoros.[16]

The selection of Ampudia did not find favor with the officers at Matamoros, and, as a result, Gen. Mariano Arista[17] replaced Ampudia as the commanding officer, but Ampudia was retained as the second in command. Controversy also surrounded the selection of the American general. In the United States, President Polk had searched for a qualified member of the Democratic Party to lead the troops but could find none. Polk settled upon the seemingly politically benign Republican Zachary Taylor so that he would not have to give the command to the politically ambitious and arrogant Republican Winfield Scott.[18]

THE BATTLES OF PALO ALTO AND RESACA DE LA PALMA

On April 25, 1846, General Arista ordered 1,600 cavalrymen commanded by Gen. Anastasio Torrejón to cross the Río Grande. Torrejón was ordered to interdict American communications between Port Isabel and General Taylor's army. The Mexican cavalry attacked sixty-three American dragoons (mounted infantry). Eleven were killed, six wounded, and most of the remainder captured.[19]

Next, Arista crossed the river with his main body. However, the anticipated fleet of boats needed to ferry the troops across turned out to be but two, and the frustrating operation took twenty-four hours to complete. Also, Torrejón's cavalry had failed to prevent Taylor from reaching Port Isabel. Arista now decided to block Talyor's path back to Fort Texas, which lay across the Río Grande from Matamoros some twenty-six miles from the Gulf of Mexico. In order to draw Taylor to the fort, Arista ordered General Ampudia to invest the fort with a 1,230-man brigade. Mexican artillery south of the Río Grande began bombarding Fort Texas (later renamed Fort Brown to honor Major Jacob Brown killed while commanding the fort) from Matamoros.[20]

On May 8, Arista, receiving word that Taylor was approaching, arrayed his remaining 3,270 troops in a double line across a mile-wide front. A swamp protected his left and a wooded knoll his right. When Taylor, commanding 2,200 troops, advanced to within 700 yards, the Mexican artillery opened fire. The quality of the powder was, however, so poor that the flights of the cannon balls were easily seen, allowing the American troops to dodge them. Taylor ordered his "flying artillery" forward, and it fired into the Mexican line with devastating effect. A 1,000-rider Mexican cavalry charge against the American right was broken up. This was followed by a strong infantry attack on the American left and a renewed cavalry attack on the American right. Firing canister (cans filled with shrapnel), the "flying artillery" tore large holes in the tight formations of the attacking Mexican infantry and cavalry. A Mexican officer later wrote,

> The artillery of the Americans, much superior to ours, made horrid ravages in the ranks of the Mexican army. The soldiers yielded, not overwhelmed in a combat in which they might deal out the death which they received—not in the midst of the excitement and gallantry which the ardor of a battle brings forth, but in a fatal situation in which they were killed with impunity, and decimated in cold blood.[21]

Both sides were forced to disengage as night fell because of the prairie fires started by their rifles' muzzle fire. The Mexican army was in disarray; it lost 252 men killed, wounded, and captured. The United States lost 5 men killed, 48 wounded, and 2 missing.[22]

Arista withdrew seven miles to the dense chaparral of Resaca de la Palma—a 200-foot-wide, four-foot-deep dry channel of the Rio Grande—in an attempt to protect his troops from the devastating fire of the American artillery. At 4:30 P.M. on May 9, the Americans attacked. Once again the "flying artillery" opened the American attack. The fighting was intense, but finally the Mexicans yielded. Arista at first thought that it was no more than harassment, and by the time he appreciated the seriousness of the threat, it was too late. He personally led a late charge by his lancers, but it was unsuccessful. The Mexican force, already dispirited from the previous encounter, panicked, abandoning weapons and baggage. Arista fled across the Río Grande to Matamoros (842 mi N of Mexico City), ordered it abandoned, and retreated to Linares, 180 miles to the south. Taylor followed for about sixty miles and then returned to Fort Brown to await reinforcements. Arista lost 160 killed, 228 wounded, and 159 missing. By the time Arista reached the haven of Linares, only 2,638 men of his 4,000-man force remained, and the news of his disaster was sweeping through Mexico. Taylor lost 33 killed and 89 wounded at Resaca de la Palma. As a result of these battles, Arista was stripped of his command and General Ampudia was elevated to the top position.[23]

THE OVERTHROW OF PAREDES AND THE RETURN OF SANTA ANNA

While the war with the "Gringos"[24] held Paredes' attention, the Liberals led by Valentín Gómez Farías planned his overthrow. Gómez Farías corresponded with Antonio López de Santa Anna. This demagogue par excellence convinced Gómez Farías that he had seen the light and had become a Federalist; and if he were allowed to return to Mexico and lead the *coup*, he would champion that cause. Gómez Farías agreed. On February 13, 1846, Col. Alejandro Atocha, Santa Anna's confidential agent, visited and ultimately convinced President Polk that it was in America's best interest to permit Santa Anna to pass through the American blockade and return to Mexico from exile.[25]

The Liberal-led revolt began on July 31. Its success was immediately assured when on August 5 Gen. José Mariano Salas, commanding the Mexico City garrison, declared in favor of the revolt. Santa Anna passed through the American blockade on August 12 and arrived in Mexico City on September 14. He accurately perceived that Mexico was in no mood for capitulation, so he decided to head the war effort and forsake any commitment to President Polk. Santa Anna immediately set out to raise a large army at San Luis Potosí, not quite midway between Mexico City and Monterrey, which Taylor was threatening. Santa Anna marched north with the troops that had remained in the capital to protect the Paredes government, arriving at San Luis Potosí on October 14.[26]

BATTLE OF MONTERREY

While Santa Anna was politicking in Mexico City, General Ampudia had moved the "Northern Army" northwest to Monterrey (625 mi N of Mexico City), the most important city in the northern region of old Mexico. He assembled an army of 7,303 men and prepared defenses. Elsewhere, Taylor crossed the Río Grande but was delayed at Matamoras for three months while he gathered his supporting train of 1,900 pack mules. Dysentery and an epidemic of measles killed several thousand of his men. It took an additional month for Taylor's force of over 6,000 men to cover the 150 miles to Monterrey.[27]

The city is situated in a fertile valley protected on the south side by a river and surrounded at some distance by mountains. Almost half of the American army had recently joined Taylor and were green volunteers, many of whom were undisciplined. Ampudia constructed numerous strong points. However, he constantly changed his plans, wasting resources and causing anxiety among his officers. The overthrow of his patron, General Paredes, must have distracted his attention. Additionally, Santa Anna urged Ampudia to withdraw to Saltillo, stating that Monterrey was not defensible.[28]

Ampudia ordered General Torrejon's cavalry to harrass the American advance. However, upon the approach of the 6,220-man American army, Torrejon retreated to Monterrey. Taylor began his assault on September 19. He attacked the eastern defenses for two days and sustained heavy casualties. The Americans discovered that the supply route from Saltillo was poorly protected. On the twenty-first in a heavy rain, Gen. William Worth led 2,000 men around to the west side of the city in order to cut the road leading to Saltillo. There, led by the Texas Rangers, his force attacked and captured gun emplacements in hand-to-hand combat.[29]

Figure 11. The United States and Mexico, 1846–48. Antonio López de Santa Anna was recalled from exile in Cuba by the Mexican Liberals to lead their fight against the Mexican Conservatives and the United States. Although he demonstrated bravely at a number of battles, his operational strategies were frequently flawed and his tactics lackluster. *Courtesy Naval Historical Foundation.*

On the twenty-second the Americans captured and mounted artillery in the Obispado Heights; this permitted them to fire down into Monterrey. As a consequence, Ampudia abandoned the outer defenses. The next day Worth's men began to penetrate Monterrey from the west; Taylor threw Twiggs' and Maj Gen. William Butler's divisions against the north and east sides of the city. Once inside the city, the fighting became house to house. To escape the fire of Mexican sharpshooters stationed on rooftops, the Americans broke through the interior rock and adobe walls which interconnected the houses as they advanced toward the center of the city.[30]

The Mexican army, and a large number of civilians, was trapped within a shrinking perimeter. Ampudia appreciated his increasingly dangerous location as well as the mounting American casualties. On September 24 he offered Taylor an armistice whereby the Mexican army should retain their arms, six cannon, and a limited amount of munitions. All other war materials were to be left behind, and Ampudia and his army were to honorably march out of the city. Taylor's command was reduced to about 5,000 effective soldiers, many of whom were exhausted. He was short of munitions and provisions. The Mexicans held a strong defensive position. Taylor lost 120 killed and 368 wounded; Mexico's casualties were 367 men. Undoubtedly taking these factors into consideration, Taylor agreed to the Mexican proposal plus an eight weeks' armistice. In fact, Taylor had exceeded his orders. On September 25 Ampudia began the long trek to San Luis Potosí where he arrived in November. Back in Washington, President Polk was furious with the armistice and ordered Taylor to resume hostilities.[31]

The war south of the Río Grande came to a standstill as the American leadership contemplated how to strike a lethal blow that would cause Mexico to sue for peace. Immediately south of Taylor's army lay 200 miles of inhospitable desert. Initially, Polk favored an attack against the port of Tampico (452 mi NE of Mexico City) while keeping Taylor on the defensive. Then, the capture of Vera Cruz (285 mi E of Mexico City) was added to the list of objectives. Only after it became apparent that even the capture of these ports would not force Mexico to capitulate was an attack on Mexico City contemplated.[32]

MEXICO LOSES NEW MEXICO

While Arista and Taylor were fighting along the Río Grande, on May 14 Polk ordered Col. Stephen W. Kearny to lead 1,700 dragoons and volunteers from Fort Leavenworth, Kansas, to Santa Fé, New Mexico, a distance of 856 miles. The Mexican governor, Manuel Armijo, raised a force of some 3,000 poorly armed civilians to block the American advance at Apache Canyon; but with the approach of the Americans, he disbanded the force and fled south. After capturing Santa Fé on August 18 and claiming New Mexico by conquest, Kearny left a small garrison in Santa Fe and set out for California.[33]

Marching south from Santa Fe, Kearny detached the 856-man 1st Missouri Mounted Volunteers under Col. Alexander W. Doniphan when he reached Socorro, New Mexico, on December 14, 1846. This force marched south toward Chihuahua, routing two small Mexican forces at Sacramento and Brazito. Doniphan captured Chihuahua on March 1, 1847. He occupied the city for two months, during which time his men acted so badly that he reported that they were "wholly unfit to garrison a town or city."[34] On April 25 Doniphan evacuated Chihuahua and joined Taylor at Saltillo.[35]

Just west of Socorro, Kearny, whose command was now reduced to 300 mule-mounted dragoons, happened upon Christopher "Kit" Carson, who was carrying Commodore Robert

Stockton's message reporting the seizure of California by the U.S. Navy. Back in Santa Fé, Mexicans belatedly rebelled against the American invaders, but to little avail. Kearny, retaining two mountain howitzers, cut his force in half. He sent one group back to Santa Fé carrying the message; and Kearny, guided by Carson, proceeded to California with 150 dragoons.[36]

THE FIGHT FOR CALIFORNIA

During 1845 Lt. John C. Fremont led an "exploring expedition" of sixty armed men from the Oregon Territory into northern California. This frontiersman had led two previous western expeditions prior to the Polk presidency. Fremont was politically well connected, married to the daughter of Senator Thomas Benton who was at this moment one of Polk's closest confidants. During the winter of 1845, Fremont camped in an isolated location, preventing possible confrontation with the Californians, who, lest we forget, were Mexicans. In the spring of 1846, the Californians threatened to attack so Fremont began to withdraw toward Klamath Lake in Oregon Territory. Marine Lt. Archibald Gillespie overtook Fremont on the trail and delivered letters from home and the news that war was eminent. Fremont reversed his march and returned to Sacramento where he took charge of a group of Americans who declared California an independent republic.[37]

Commodore John Sloat, commanding the U.S. Pacific Squadron, seized Monterey on July 7; he heard rumors concerning the fighting along the Río Grande but had hesitated to act earlier, being unsure that war had been declared. On July 9 a subordinate, U.S. Navy Capt. John Stockton, seized San Francisco. Next, Stockton landed 360 sailors at San Pedro on August 7. Joined by Fremont and eighty followers, they entered Los Angeles unopposed on the twelfth. However, within weeks, 500 Californian Mexicans led by Capt. José María Flores rallied against the American invaders and in October drove them out of Los Angeles. The following month, the Americans were repulsed by 150 Californians as they tried to retake the port. The Californians also besieged Stockton at San Diego.[38]

By December 1846, Kearny's "Army of the West," now 150 dragoons strong, reached California. On December 6 he was surprised at San Pascual, 35 miles northwest of San Diego, by about 500 Californians led by Andrés Pico. The American forces mounted on worn-out mules and half-broken horses were hard pressed to hold off the lance-wielding Californians. The superior firepower of the Americans was nullified because their powder was wet. Kearny lost 18 killed and 13 wounded; the Mexicans' losses were about 30 men. The Americans retreated, buying enough time for a rescue column to be sent by Stockton. Two hundred Marines and soldiers broke out of besieged San Diego and escorted Kearny back to the port, arriving on December 12.[39]

Within a few weeks Kearny and Stockton, commanding 600 men, marched against Los Angeles. The California Mexicans under Flores made a stand at the San Gabriel River on January 9, 1847. The subsequent American victory was heavily influenced by the guns from the fleet which were brought along. On January 13, the Californians surrendered to Fremont, who had reached Los Angeles from the north. Late in February the Americans again defeated the Mexicans, this time at Sacramento, and won control of California.[40]

Gen. John E. Wool, commanding some 4,000 regulars and volunteers, departed Fort Leavenworth in the fall of 1846. However, Wool was diverted to Parras, Mexico, to protect Talyor's west flank.[41]

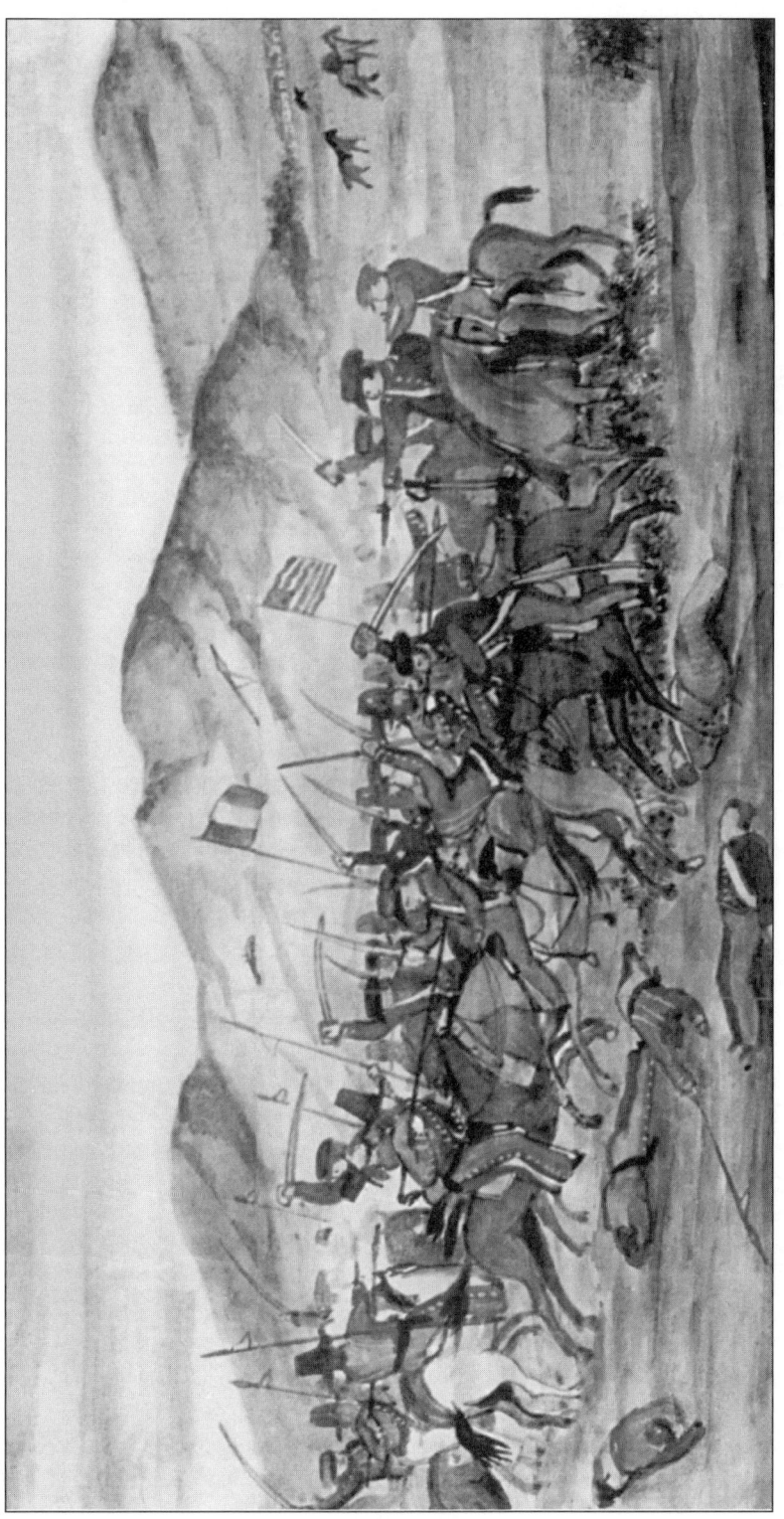

Figure 12. The United States–Mexico (1846–48). At the Battle of San Pascual, California (December 6, 1846), five hundred Mexican lancers defeated one hundred fifty American dragoons. This minor clash was one of the few battlefield successes for Mexican arms during the war. Prior to the war, Mexico's large irregular cavalry was perceived to be one of the advantages it would possess in a war against the United States. In fact, these mounted irregulars proved to be too lightly armed to be employed in battle and the American troops too well led and disciplined to be found at disadvantage at other times. At San Pascual the Americans were caught with wet gunpowder and riding worn-out mules. *Courtesy Franklin D. Roosevelt Library.*

BUILDING A NEW MEXICAN ARMY AT SAN LUIS POTOSÍ

While the United States was winning control of Mexico's northern provinces, Santa Anna was building a new army at San Luis Potosí. Levies for men, arms, clothing, and other war material were assessed against each of the Mexican states. Only five central states and the federal district responded. Everything was in short supply, particularly winter clothing. Too much of Santa Anna's time was spent on political intrigue and fulfilling an extravagant lifestyle and too little on preparing and providing for his army. Manuel Balbontín described the Mexican army at San Luis Potosí:

> The troops were drilled with frequency. The infantry, by brigades, under the command of its respective generals; but they never saw a general drill, not even by division. The cavalry maneuvered only by regiments. The artillery were rarely accustomed to maneuver and never fired blanks. The general-in-chief never appeared in the camp of instruction, by luck, because he could not appreciate the respective quality of the corps which were under his command. . . .
>
> During the months of November and December, reinforcements arrived for the army. Also, the troops raised in the states of Guanajuato and Jalisco arrived. These troops were in general badly armed; there were corps in which were seen arms of all sizes, and a large part of them without bayonets, one noted many guns held together with leather straps or with cords instead of braces.[42]

Back in Mexico City, Gómez Farías orchestrated laws (January 11 and February 4) allowing the government to raise 5 million pesos through the sale of church property.[43]

BATTLE OF BUENA VISTA

On January 6, 1847, Santa Anna obtained captured messages. These revealed that all of Taylor's regulars, the quality half of his force, had marched southeast to join Gen. Winfield Scott at Tampico and were to be used for the assault on Vera Cruz. Santa Anna decided to strike at Taylor's weakened army. In the dead of winter, while riding in a carriage drawn by eight mules, he marched his ill-equipped 21,533-man army, dragging 21 guns, north across 240 miles of inhospitable desert, which separated him from the Americans. Some 4,000 men died or deserted on the march north.[44]

Although Taylor had been ordered by Polk to remain on the defensive, he disobeyed and advanced to Saltillo, southwest of Monterrey. On February 20 American scouts discovered the Mexican army approaching. Taylor fell back 14 miles to a narrow ravine through which the road passed near a ranch named Buena Vista and began to concentrate the 5,000 men under his command. Mexican scouts came upon American supplies that had not been burned due to the haste of the American withdrawal. Santa Anna erroneously concluded that the American army was in full flight. He ordered his army, which had just crossed the last 35 miles of desert within the last twenty-four hours, to make a forced march over the 48 miles separating the two armies. But instead of fleeing, Taylor took up a strong defensive position.[45]

The Mexicans attacked at 3:30 P.M. on February 22. Santa Anna hurled Ampudia's *cuerpo ligero* against the American left and drove the Americans back in a pouring rain. The corps held its position throughout the night without campfires or food. At 8 A.M. the next day, the reinforced light infantry continued its assault against the American left. Then, the divisions commanded by Gen. Manuel María Lombardini and Gen. Francisco Pacheco attacked Taylor's center; these were driven back while sustaining heavy casualties. The Illinois Regiment charged in an attempt to capture the Mexican artillery. Santa Anna led a counterattack which overran some American positions. Reacting, General Wool swung his artillery to cover the hole in the American center. Maj. William Bliss reported to Taylor that the battle was lost. Taylor responded, "I know it, but the volunteers don't know it. Let them alone, we'll see what they do."[46]

Elsewhere, the Mexican light infantry and Torrejón's cavalry turned the American left flank and rushed through heading for the American train. Taylor shifted forces from the right to support the left and committed the reserves, the First Mississippi volunteers led by Col. Jefferson Davis, Taylor's estranged son-in-law. Davis broke up a Mexican cavalry charge. Also, the Mexican cavalry suffered terrible losses from the American "flying artillery."[47]

In spite of an absence of food and sleep, the Mexican troops continued to press the attack as a heavy rain fell; however, the American defenses were sufficiently deep to prevent the Mexicans from breaking through. By 5:00 P.M. on the second day, both sides were exhausted and disengaged. The United States lost in the fighting 267 men killed, 456 wounded, and 23 missing, plus two guns and some flags. The Mexicans lost 591 men killed (which included 21 officers), 1,037 wounded, and 1,854 missing.[48]

Unexpectedly, Santa Anna ordered his army to fall back ten miles, abandoning hundreds of wounded. To the surprise of most, Santa Anna chose not to continue the battle.[49] Instead, he ordered the campfires to be kept burning throughout the night while he ordered his exhausted army on a disastrous trek back across the desert. Santa Anna went on ahead. His battered army staggered across the desert back to San Luis Potosí. An officer described the march:

> The food in the days before had been reduced to detestable and putrid meat, and the water which they drank was brackish. Those who had taken these unhealthy aliments were attacked with a violent dysentery, which spread with a gloomy prevalence until very few were free from it. . . . The army seemed made up of dead men: the miserable condition to which the sick were reduced caused the skin of many to stick to their bones, and its shrinking exposed their teeth, giving to the countenance the expression of a forced laugh, which filled one with horror.[50]

The beleaguered army that staggered into San Luis Potosí on March 12 was less than half the size of the one that had gone forth to fight at Buena Vista. The army lost more than 10,000 men through casualties and desertions.[51]

Having proceeded his shattered army to San Luis Potosí, Santa Anna learned that the Americans were off Vera Cruz *and* that a revolt had occurred in Mexico City. On February 28 some national guard battalions, recruited from among the skilled and upper classes of Mexico City (known as *Polkos* because allegedly they enjoyed dancing the polka), revolted. They were angered by an order issued by the Vice President on February 22 telling them to march within twenty-four hours to the defense of Vera Cruz. The revolt was well financed by the church, which was threatened with the confiscation of property by the current administration. Santa Anna rushed to Mexico City to deal with the crisis while dispatching the majority of his remaining reliable troops to block the American advance toward the capital. After betraying Gómez Frías and placing the government in the hands of Brig. Gen. Pedro María Anaya, Santa Anna joined the army to confront General Scott.[52]

THE ROAD TO MEXICO CITY

In order to bring stubborn Mexican leaders to the negotiating table, President Polk decided to attack the Mexican capital. Initially, the American plan called for the American forces to assemble at the mouth of the Río Grande and sail for Vera Cruz and from there march inland to the Mexican capital. However, Santa Anna ordered the defenses at Tampico abandoned, thus allowing the Americans to use that port as their base of operations and cut the distance to their objective, Vera Cruz, to 170 miles.[53]

General Winfield Scott, leading some 13,000 soldiers, landed on March 9, 1847, two months behind schedule, a few miles south of Vera Cruz, the gateway to the Mexican capital, 285 miles inland over the National Road.[54] The ideal date, in January, would have allowed the American fleet to escape the severe storms known as "Northers" and the army to escape the beginning of yellow fever season. Heavy guns brought ashore from the fleet pounded the port into submission. After a surprisingly short siege, Vera Cruz's garrison surrendered on March 27. Scott accepted its parole not to take up arms again. He lost nineteen dead and fifty-seven wounded. The timely capture of Vera Cruz allowed Scott's army to attempt to escape from the lowlands before the beginning of the yellow fever season. Scott's first objective was Jalapa, which lay just above the fever zone.[55]

BATTLE OF CERRO GORDO

Santa Anna chose to fight Scott at a narrow pass called Cerro Gordo, 4,680 feet above sea level, through which the National Road passed before reaching Jalapa (35 mi W of Vera Cruz and 250 mi E of Mexico City). If Santa Anna could hold the pass, the Americans would be trapped in the increasingly unhealthy lowlands.[56]

Santa Anna blocked the National Road with nineteen pieces of artillery and 1,800 of his best troops; the remaining 8,000 were held in reserve some miles away. He fortified the nearby 500-foot hill *El Telégrafo* with four 4-pounders and one hundred of his best troops. On *La Atalaya*, a spur 1,000 yards to the northeast, he chose to place only a few men. South of the road, Santa Anna placed 900 men supported by six cannon.

The first American troops, 2,600 men under Gen. David Twiggs, arrived on April 12. Twiggs ordered a precipitous attack which escaped disaster only due to the overeagerness of the Mexican gunners. Scott arrived on the fourteenth with an additional 3,900 men. The Mexican position was formidable, and Scott ordered a reconnaissance. Engineer officers Capt. Robert E. Lee and Lt. George Derby explored to the left and the right. Lee discovered a path around the Mexican position. Santa Anna had been informed of this possibility by his engineers, but he brashly ignored their report.[57]

Scott ordered Twiggs to advance along the trail and cut off the Mexican avenue of retreat. James Shields' and William Worth's commands were to follow. Brig. Gen. Gideon Pillow was to attack the Mexican right flank in order to hold the attention of the Mexicans. Before reaching the enemy's rear, Twiggs in error cut in and attacked *La Atalaya* and *El Telégrafo* at noon on the seventeenth. This fight raged for three hours before the defenders were driven off.

Early on the morning of the eighteenth, Scott opened a general assault. This time the American troops under Shields using the trail reached the road in the rear and opened fire on the Mexicans. However, they were too late to cut off the retreat of the Mexican left and center. Pillow mismanaged his responsibility by closing the Mexican artillery before it had been silenced. However, Shields' advance and Twigg's attack broke the morale of the Mexican army, and it

Figure 13. The United States and Mexico (1846–48). At the Battle of Cerro Gordo (April 18, 1847), Santa Anna endeavored to block the American advance toward Mexico City. His battle plan was poorly conceived. He placed a number of his units on isolated promenades where they were easily defeated piecemeal by the less numerous, but better trained and equipped, American army. Santa Anna gave away whatever advantage he might have accrued from possessing a larger army than the Americans. Many of his troops were camped miles from the battlefield that he had chosen and never took part in the fight. *Copied from* Harper's New Monthly Magazine, *Vol. 11 (1855).*

fled in disarray; Santa Anna barely escaped capture. By 10:00 A.M. resistance collapsed. The Mexicans lost approximately 3,000 men, while another 3,000, including five generals, were captured along with 40 guns and a large quantity of munitions. The Americans lost 63 dead and 367 wounded.[58]

José Ramírez, a member of the Mexican legislature, wrote, "Everything is lost. Absolutely nothing was saved; not even hope."[59] Cerro Gordo was a critical defeat for Mexico. The Americans escaped from the unhealthy lowlands, and the destruction of the Mexican army begun in the north was practically completed at Cerro Gordo. Only a few effective units remained. Scott's army already reported one thousand men who were too ill to go on and had to be sent back to Vera Cruz.[60]

Santa Anna returned to Mexico City to rebuild the army one more time; however, his defeats at Buena Vista and Cerro Gordo significantly undermined his credibility. On April 20 the Mexican Congress gave him the administrative power to continue the war, but he was prohibited from making peace or ceding territory. Santa Anna was faced with a Herculean challenge. Representative Ramírez observed on April 25, "Strictly speaking, the army does not exist. What today bears that name is only a mass of men without training and without weapons."[61]

On the other side, Scott advanced slowly toward Puebla (80 mi E of Mexico City). Generals Worth and J. A. Quitman entered Puebla unopposed on May 15.[62]

Both armies had their problems. On May 11 Ramírez wrote, "S.A. [Santa Anna's] division consisting of about 4,500 men is in a serious condition, especially in the case of the cavalry. Álvarez was coming to their support with 3,000 men, but these troops cannot be relied upon because they know how to carry on only a guerrilla warfare and this only in their own districts."[63] On the other side, the unacclimated Americans suffered from diarrhea and dysentery caused by the local food and water. While at Puebla the terms of 3,000 twelve-month volunteers expired. Only four officers and sixty-four soldiers volunteered to continue and, reluctantly, Scott allowed the others to go home.[64] In spite of his numerous victories, Scott was unpopular with his troops because of his strict discipline. At this time Santa Anna secretly corresponded with Scott stating he would negotiate peace terms, but first the American had to send $10,000 so that Santa Anna could buy political support within the Mexican Congress. Scott became one more victim of Santa Anna's duplicity.[65]

With the departure of the volunteers, Scott had too few troops to advance while protecting his lengthy supply line at the same time. Scott made a bold decision: He decided not to protect his supply routes and concentrated his remaining 6,000 men at Puebla; for three months his forces lived off the land. By August Scott's army had swelled to 10,738 men through reinforcements; no more could be expected, so on the seventh he began his advance on Mexico City.[66]

DEFENDING MEXICO CITY

Mexico City, inhabited by 200,000 souls, sat in a 7,000-foot-high elliptical bowl (32 by 46 miles) on an old lake bed surrounded at a distance on all sides by mountains. Nearer the city were numerous shallow lakes, hills, lava fields, and marshes. Access into the city was provided by causeways. Where each causeway entered the capital, there was a *garita* (fortified customs house). Santa Anna supplemented these nautral barriers with man-made fortifications and positioned his troops to defend the access avenues.[67]

Santa Anna raised a new army of some 25,000 men, although it was of the poorest quality yet fielded. The army was so ill prepared that it could not execute offensive maneuvers.

Therefore, Santa Anna chose a defensive strategy. He would position his militia in strong points and use his few remaining regular troops as a mobile reserve. Santa Anna chose to center his defense at *El Penón*, a 450-foot-high fortified hill to the east of the city.[68]

Maj. Gen. Gabriel Valencia, commanding approximately 5,000 men, circled around Texcoco to the northeast of Mexico City in an attempt to flank the Americans. By the eleventh, the Mexican trap was set. Santa Anna was at *El Penón* with about 7,000 men; Valencia at Texcoco with 5,000; Álverez' irregular cavalry of 3,000 maintained contact with the American rear guard; and the Mexican reserves were in Mexico City. In the continuing Liberal-Conservative struggle, the Governor of the State of Mexico refused to allow the state's artillery and troops to be used by the central government, arguing that he needed them for the defense of the state.[69]

While the Mexicans were preparing their defenses, Scott neared the capital. On the fifteenth he skirted *El Penón* by using a 30-mile route through rough terrain discovered once again by his engineers. On August 17 the advanced guard under General Worth captured the village of San Agustín some eight miles south of Mexico City. Scott had successfully flanked Santa Anna's exterior lines of defense. Scott ordered Worth to advance north to San Antonio which he found heavily defended. The American engineers reconnoitered to the west. They discovered that with difficulty it would be possible to cut a road through the rocky lava field called the *Pedregal*. Scott ordered Worth to make a show of force at San Antonio while the remainder of the army crossed the lava field.[70]

THE BATTLE OF CONTRERAS

Santa Anna hastily repositioned his forces. He intended to defend the approaches to the capital, San Antonio and San Angel. He ordered General Valencia, commanding 4,000 men and 23 guns, to occupy San Angel. In an act of insubordination, General Valencia moved forward to the isolated hill position at Contreras. On September 19 General Pillow's advancing division came upon Valencia's command and was driven back by the Mexican artillery. Santa Anna ordered Valencia to fall back. However, the overconfident subordinate ignored the order.

On the nineteenth the American army exploited a ravine which ran to the rear of Contreras. Scott ordered Gen. Franklin Pierce to feint a frontal attack. On August 20 the Mexican artillery opened a heavy fire in the direction of Pierce while American troops attacked from the rear. The battle lasted 17 minutes. The Mexicans sustained 700 casualties and 813 prisoners, including four generals, plus twenty cannon. The American losses were 60 dead and wounded. Santa Anna advanced with 7,000 men from Toro Hill but arrived only in time to meet the fleeing fugitives of the battle. Santa Anna then ordered all Mexican troops to fall back to the inner defenses close to Mexico City.[71]

THE BATTLE OF CHURUBUSCO

Santa Anna ordered the fortified bridge across the Churubusco River, five miles south of Mexico City, to be held at all costs. Gen. Francisco Pérez prepared to defend the bridge, and Gen. Manuel Rincón prepared to defend the nearby Convent of San Mateo with 1,400 men. The defenders included poorly trained and inadequately armed militia from Mexico City. The Mexican artillery was served by the "Saint Patrick" Battalion, many of whom were Irish-Catholic deserters from the American army. They could expect no clemency if taken prisoners. The troops occupying the fortified positions were supported by a large militia force under Gen. Pedro Maria Anaya.[72]

On August 20 the Americans attacked the bridge. Repeatedly, Perez' command, supported by the "Saint Patrick" Battalion, drove the Americans back. The fighting raged for three hours before some of the American troops were able to ford the river and outflank the convent, the defenders of which had exhausted the ammunition for their British-manufactured Baker flintlocks. Ironically, the defenders did have ammunition for a larger calibre weapon which would not fit into their guns. The bridge finally fell in vicious hand-to-hand fighting. General Anaya, dying from his wounds, surrendered to General Twiggs. Twiggs demanded the surrender of the remaining ammunition. Anaya replied, "If there was [sic] ammunition, you would not be here, General."[73]

Both sides sustained serious causalities. The Mexicans lost approximately 3,500 men, which included the last of their remaining trained troops. Among the 1,259 Mexican prisoners were 85 men from the San Patricio Battalion.[74] In addition, perhaps 3,000 men deserted the Mexican army. Since leaving Puebla, Scott had lost in combat 273 killed and 865 wounded, leaving him about 7,359 men. And, the survivors continued to suffer from diarrhea and dysentery. Santa Anna lost 4,200 men dead and wounded; 2,000 captured; and 3,000 deserters, leaving him some 13,000 men. The American army was now but three miles from Mexico City, and Scott ordered the siege guns brought up.[75]

Santa Anna, commanding a badly shaken army, asked for and was granted an armistice in order to conduct negotiations. During that time Santa Anna called in outlying units and strengthened the *garitas* with earthworks; Scott reorganized his army. The actions of both sides were contrary to the terms of the armistice. Finding after two weeks that the two sides could not come to terms, Scott terminated the truce on September 6.[76]

THE BATTLE OF MOLINO DEL REY

Two fortified positions, separated by 1,000 yards, helped block Scott's approach from the southwest, Molino del Rey and Chapultepec. The first, a cluster of stone buildings, had been the principal cannon foundry in the country since colonial times. Scott received erroneous information that cannon were still being forged. The second was the old Chapultepec Castle, then being used as the Mexican military academy. On the morning of September 8, Scott attacked Molino del Rey. After a brief cannonade, Worth led 500 hand-picked men against the position at 5:45 A.M. and succeeded in capturing Molino del Rey and the stone building Casa Mata 500 yards to the west. Once again Santa Anna was not obeyed by a subordinate. General Álvarez would not charge the Americans as ordered. The battle was costly to both sides. In all Scott lost 116 killed, 865 wounded, and 18 missing while the Mexicans sustained 2,000 casualties plus 683 prisoners.[77]

THE BATTLE OF CHAPULTEPEC

Concerned over mounting casualties, Scott pressed on to Chapultepec. To draw the Mexican troops away from the castle, divisions under Quitman and Worth attacked the Belén and San Cosmé gates, and Twigg's division made a feint against the San Antonio *Garita*. Chapultepec, set atop a crag some 200 feet above the valley floor, was defended by the ancient warrior Gen. Nicolás Bravo commanding 832 national guard troops and 43 cadets, some as young as thirteen years of age. Although called a "castle," it had been constructed as the summer residence for the colonial viceroy and its walls were relatively thin.[78]

Throughout the day of September 12 and into the next morning, the Americans bombarded the castle with their heavy siege guns. At 8 A.M. on the thirteenth, General Pillow's division began the climb through a cypress grove to the base of the castle. It was temporarily halted by stiff resistance and only regained its momentum once reinforced. The American troops were delayed a second time by the lack of scaling ladders. At this point an American soldier discovered a canvas tube fuse which led to land mines; this was cut before it could be lit by the Mexicans. The Mexicans were handicapped by the poor quality of their powder. After fierce hand-to-hand fighting, General Bravo attempted to surrender, but the cadets fought on. One cadet, Juan Escutia, reportedly wrapped himself in the academy's flag and leaped from the highest rampart rather than surrender. The United States lost 130 killed, 703 wounded, and 29 missing; Mexico sustained more than 1,800 casualties. These included 6 cadets killed, 3 wounded, and 37 captured. By 9:30 A.M. the fighting was over.[79]

Scott immediately advanced on the city; Quitman's division was sent along the Belén causeway and Worth's over the San Cosmé causeway. By nightfall the gates of the city were in American hands. On September 14 the city surrendered and the remains of the Mexican army, 9,000 men, retreated north for four miles to the village of Guadalupe Hidalgo.[80]

Back in Washington, President Polk, ignorant of the capture of Mexico City, grew increasingly frustrated with the apparent lack of progress. He wrote, "[I]f Mexico continued obstinately to refuse to treat, I was decidedly in favor of insisting on the acquisition of more territory than the provinces named [New Mexico, the Californias, and the right of Passage across the Isthmus of Tehuantepec]."[81]

Santa Anna, having resigned as president, was not ready to stop fighting. He unsuccessfully attacked the U.S. garrison at Puebla with a small force, attempting to cut the American supply line. Driven off, he next tried to intercept Brig. Gen. Joseph Lane's column marching from Vera Cruz to Mexico City with reinforcements. Once again, he was unsuccessful. By this time a Mexican field army ceased to exist, and guerrilla warfare began to spread. However, the wealthy *criollos* feared the consequences of a guerrilla war more than the concessions needed to get the Americans to withdraw.[82]

The negotiations at Guadalupe-Hidalgo did not go smoothly. The Mexican government was in chaos and the American President had lost confidence in his commander and negotiator. Polk wrote, "Mr. Trist had exceeded his instructions and had suggested terms to the Mexican commissioners which I could not have approved if they had agreed to them."[83] On October 4, 1847, Polk recalled Trist and followed it with a reprimand and repeated the order. These were received by Trist on November 16. While Trist was awaiting an escort, the Mexican government appointed peace commissioners and pressed for negotiations. Trist, fearing the collapse of the Mexican peace party, assumed the extraordinary responsibility of negotiating without portfolio (the power to negotiate) and while under reprimand. On February 2, 1848, Trist and Mexican representatives signed the Treaty of Guadalupe-Hidalgo ending the war. Mexico recognized the Río Grande as the international boundary between the two countries and ceded more than one-third of its territory to the United States. In consolation, the United States paid Mexico $15 million and assumed the responsibilities for $3.5 million in claims by American citizens against the Mexican government.

OBSERVATIONS

Above all else, the outcome of the Mexican War guaranteed the United States the resources to develop into a world power and conversely deprived Mexico of the potential to become a first-rate power.

The United States did not suffer a single significant defeat throughout the entire war. This stunning success may be attributed to an abstract quality. The more stable form of political order that existed in the United States fostered the evolution of a military where seniors did not perceive initiative on the battlefield by juniors as a threat to their personal interests. Foremost among the American advantages was superior leadership.[84] Both Taylor and Scott recognized the talents of many younger officers and gave them the opportunity to use their abilities.[85]

On the Mexican side, military success bred political ambition. Therefore, those at the top, Santa Anna in particular, viewed ambitious and talented subordinates as a threat. When a talented Mexican officer did have command, fate always seemed to match him against a more skillful American. American senior officers who gained their rank due to political favor always seemed to escape disaster in spite of themselves.[86]

Undoubtedly, on the battlefield Winfield Scott was the master of all. The Duke of Wellington, who had earlier announced Scott's doom, proclaimed of the American, "His campaign was unsurpassed in military annuals. He is the greatest living soldier."[87] And yet, the extremely bad relations between President Polk and his two principal generals, Taylor and Scott, might have been exploited by the Mexicans if they had known their enemy. President Polk's diary is filled with contempt for the two generals. On January 14, 1847, Polk wrote, "The truth is neither Taylor or Scott are fit for the command of the army in the great operations in progress and which are contemplated."[88] Scott reciprocated, "Mr. Tyler . . . was weaker in office than Mr. Polk, whose little strength lay in the most odious elements of the human character—*cunning and hypocrisy*."[89] Additionally, "instead of a friend in the President, I had, in him, an enemy more to be dreaded than Santa Anna and all his hosts."[90]

Santa Anna was neither a gifted strategist nor tactician. However, his plans were generally sound, and he deserves credit as the man who was able to raise several armies and find the money, the weapons, and at least some logistics to fight the invader. The insubordination of Valencia at the battle of Contreras and Álvarez at Molino del Rey significantly contributed to Santa Anna's defeat before Mexico City.[91]

The United States also possessed almost insurmountable technological advantages, the magnitude of which was not clearly perceived before the war. The American artillery proved to be far superior to Mexico's whether it be the "flying artillery" used so effectively in the north or the heavier seige guns used in the assault on the central valley. The Mexican guns were antiquated, the powder of poor quality, and the gunners inadequately trained.[92]

Some of the American infantry was using a new Model 1841 muzzle-loading flintlock rifle which fired a long "sugar-loaf" bullet and used a percussion cap for ignition. The improved ramrod, possessing a cup-shaped head, more accurately seated the bullet, improving accuracy to 400 yards, frequently eight times that of the Mexican weapons. The most common Mexican weapons were second-hand European discards, which had seen their best years of service in some other army. Frequently, they were more lethal as clubs than as firearms.[93]

The American regulars performed very well. The volunteers were spirited but initially not well disciplined. The Texas Rangers earned a gruesome reputation as *Los Diablos Tejanos* among the Mexicans because they raided villages, destroyed farms, took no prisoners, and shot civilians.[94]

Contrary to prewar speculation, frequently it was the United States that gained operational and tactical advantage through a better knowledge of local geography due to its superior reconnaissance. For the most part, the Mexican cavalry was ineffective throughout. Its tactical experience was as an irregular guerrilla force and not as a *coup de maitre*. Its lightness, which was the source of its agility, prevented it from being used in direct combat against the better disciplined American regulars.[95]

Mexico's internal struggle between Conservatives and Liberals significantly contributed to the nation's inability to defend its territory against the United States. Each accused the other of complicity with the enemy. Yucatan declared its neutrality in the war. This confrontation would not be settled until 1867 and cost Mexico dearly in lives, territory, and treasure.[96]

Contemporaries marveled at the ability of the Mexican soldier to withstand hardship and, at the same time, his inability to win battles against inferior numbers. This is not a contradiction in his character. When it came to combat, the Mexican soldier could not comprehend his stake in the battle, whereas he obviously understood survival. Many had been impressed into service against their will, and a significant number did not even speak Spanish but rather one of a number of Indian dialects. These soldiers typically were poorly trained and, therefore, could only carry out the most elementary maneuvers. They were easily discouraged and frequently in need of direction, which all too often was not provided. The officer corps was riddled with men who held their position because of favoritism and not ability. This was particularly true in the higher ranks. Magnifying these problems was the corruption that permeated any army led by Santa Anna.[97]

The United States lost 1,192 men killed in action, 529 dead of wounds, 362 accidental deaths, and 11,155 dead of disease. The number of Mexican casualties is unknown, but undoubtedly it was many times that of the Americans. As in all previous wars, disease was the greatest killer—yellow fever (called the black vomit), dysentery, and diarrhea were the most common causes. The military expenditures for the United States totaled about $100 million. For that plus the expenses of the Treaty of Guadalupe-Hidalgo, the United States acquired almost one million square miles including Texas.[98]

The United States' conquest of Mexican territory, particularly California, sent tremors of fear into Latin America. In June 1847 Honduras declared war on the United States; the United States took no notice. And in the far south, Peruvian President Ramón Castilla warned against American expansionism.[99]

CHAPTER SEVENTEEN

CENTRAL AMERICA, 1834–59

> But almost simultaneously with the dissolution of the [Central America] confederation in 1839, and the consequent loss of power of united resistance, appeared a greater jealousy of American designs, which overcame the earlier hesitation, and the policy of the [British] government became as aggressive as its agents could desire.
>
> —Historian Mary Wilhelmine Williams

THE SPARK

Beginning in July 1834 the British consul to Central America, Frederick Chatfield, took it upon himself to strengthen British claims in the region and to secure for the Crown transit routes across the isthmus, potentially the world's most important highway. Chatfield's actions first brought him into conflict with the disintegrating Central American union and later the equally expansionistic representatives of the United States.[1]

BACKGROUND

British interests in Central America dated from the early colonial days. Its activities were centered in Belize, the islands of Honduras Bay, and the Mosquito Coast. The British had been involved in log cutting in Belize since 1662; had occupied Bay Islands in 1642 (and subsequently abandoned them); and had maintained commercial outposts on the Mosquito Coast since the 1680s. Between 1783 and 1814 Great Britain signed treaties with Spain acknowledging that Great Britain had commercial but not territorial rights in these regions. Britain had not claimed sovereignty over any of these areas prior to the declaration of the Monroe Doctrine in 1823 but did maintain such *de facto*. During the first few decades of the nineteenth century, on-scene diplomats took it upon themselves to expand British territorial claims.[2]

OPPOSING FORCES

Three forces were in conflict. First, on-site British diplomats were on occasion able to convince those governing in London into backing their aggressive territorial expansion. Second, the North American diplomats also engaged in a free-lance policy. When they were able to attract the interest of those in Washington, these diplomats could call upon a significant navy, many of whose officers frequently acted boldly and even brazenly. Third, the United Provinces of Central America were dissolving into five tiny nations. Each could muster only a few hundred poorly trained and equipped soldiers on those rare occasions when each was free from internal strife.

OPENING STRATEGY

On-scene British diplomats encouraged British settlers and business interests to expand their activities beyond those boundaries recognized during the colonial era. Once this was achieved, these diplomats recognized the claims of these citizens and extended protection. The Central American union and later the separate nations had no military options. Diplomatically, they sought the protection of the United States. U.S. diplomats sought to tie the protection of boundaries to commercial concessions.

ON-SCENE BRITISH INITIATIVES

By 1821 the British settlers in Belize had pushed south of the Sibún River, the previously agreed-to southern limits of their commercial enclave, and soon reached the Sarstoon River. Tensions increased between the British settlers and the United Provinces as the government in Guatemala City attempted to pressure the British into retreating by placing a discriminatory tariff on goods passing through Belize. The British settlers reacted by changing the name of their enclave from Belize to British Honduras and in November 1834 petitioning London for colonial status. This and similar requests throughout this era were rejected by London. Regardless, in 1840 the Superintendent of the Settlement, Alexander Macdonald, proclaimed that the "Law of England is and shall be the Law of the Settlement or Colony of British Honduras."[3]

Chatfield, while pursuing his personal interpretation of British interests, soon became caught up in the Central American Liberal-Conservative struggle. Shortly after the Liberal Morazán seized the government of the United Provinces in 1829, he demanded that the British pull back to the Sibún River. As a consequence, Chatfield chose to support the Conservatives who were less concerned about British expansionism. By the 1840s the British settlers of Belize controlled an area three to five times greater than that which had been agreed to between Great Britain and Spain but a few decades earlier.[4]

In 1830 the Superintendent of Belize, Macdonald, took it upon himself to seize Ruatán Island using as a pretext the United Provinces' refusal to return fugitive slaves. This, the largest of the Bay Islands (approximately 30 by 8 miles in size, and 40 miles off the coast) possessed good anchorages and dominated the Caribbean approach to Guatemala. London disavowed the initiative, openly censured Chatfield, and ordered the island evacuated. However, the British government did not renounce its claim to the islands.[5]

In 1838 a group of liberated slaves from the Grand Cayman Islands migrated to Ruatán. The Honduran island commandant (the United Provinces were in the process of dissolving) informed the liberated slaves that they required the permission of the Honduran government to remain. Some refused and appealed to the British superintendent in Belize. Macdonald again landed on Ruatán, hauled down the Central American flag, and hoisted that of Britain. This act of replacing the other side's flag repeated itself a number of times. Finally, in 1841 London informed the governor of Jamaica that he had the authority and responsibility without recourse to London to forcibly eject any foreigners who attempted to occupy the islands.[6]

While the British settlers and local representatives were expanding the size of Belize and attempting to bring the Bay Islands under their control, they were also slowly extending their influence along the Mosquito Coast. Beginning in 1816, the "King of the Mosquitos," Robert Charles Frederick, was crowned in Belize wearing the uniform of a British major. This formalized a tutelary relationship between the "king" and the British government which had existed for some time. In August 1841 a British ship carried Macdonald and the Mosquito "King" to San Juan del Norte at the mouth of the San Juan River, a certain terminus of any interoceanic canal through Nicaragua. There, on August 12, they raised the Mosquito flag, claimed the port, announced a protectorate over the Indians, kidnapped the Nicaraguan commander of the port, and abandoned him on a deserted beach. The British ordered the other Central Americans to leave by March 1842, and departed. Macdonald's actions began without the knowledge of London, and the British government did not support him. The Nicaraguans protested, but the British ignored this, although they did not evict the remaining Central Americans as threatened.[7]

In 1842 the Mosquito "King" unexpectedly died, causing anarchy. By 1844 the British had appointed Patrick Walker as consul-general of the Mosquito Coast, the Mosquitos were made British subjects, the name of the region was changed to Mosquitia, and a new flag patterned upon the Union Jack was given to the Indians.[8]

LONDON BECOMES DIRECTLY INVOLVED

The predictable absorption of Texas into the United States helped spark Great Britain to strengthen its position *vis-a-vis* the Mosquito Coast. In 1845 the government in London now claimed that the Mosquito dependency extended from Cape Honduras to the mouth of the San Juan River. In reaction, Nicaragua forcefully took possession of the port San Juan del Norte in 1846.[9] In October 1847 the new Mosquito "King" ordered the Nicaraguans to withdraw from the port of San Juan del Norte by January 1, 1848, or they would be evicted. The Nicaraguan government replied that if the Mosquitos under British protection occupied the port, they risked war. The Nicaraguans also appealed to the United States for help, but their appeals went unanswered.[10]

On New Year's Day the Mosquito superintendent, Patrick Walker, accompanied by the Mosquito "King" and backed by the sloop *Alarm* (28 guns) and the steam sloop *Vixen* (6 guns), hauled down the Nicaraguan flag and hoisted the Mosquito flag. The British renamed the port Greytown to honor Sir Charles Grey, Governor of Jamaica. A small party was left behind and the Nicaraguan customs officials were given a short time to clear out. On the ninth, the Nicaraguan garrison returned, seized the British officials, and took them to the port of Serapaqui. On February 12 the two British warships and 250 men returned and retook Greytown and destroyed Serapaqui. A British force then marched to Lake Nicaragua. Walker accidently drowned during the operation. On March 7 Great Britain and Nicaragua signed a treaty whereby Greytown was returned to the control of the Mosquito "King" and those individuals taken prisoner on the eighth by Nicaragua were freed.[11]

UNITED STATES CHALLENGES BRITISH EXPANSION

Before the close of the war with Mexico, President Polk dispatched Elijah Hise to Guatemala as chargé d'affaires.[12] Prior to that, the United States had intermittently sent representatives to Central America but they accomplished little. Hise was instructed to support the reunification of Central America and block British expansion. By the time Hise arrived in early November 1848, the union was dead. On his own initiative, Hise signed the Hise-Selva Treaty (still needing the approval of the U.S. Senate) with Nicaragua on June 21, 1849. The treaty would grant the United States the right of transit across Nicaragua in perpetuity and the right to fortify the route. In exchange, the United States would protect Nicaraguan "rightful territories." Obviously to the Nicaraguans, their territory included the Mosquito Coast.[13]

While Hise was negotiating with the Nicaraguans, the American-owned Atlantic and Pacific Ship-Canal Company was formed and in March 1849 signed a contract with Nicaragua for use of the San Juan River. Learning of this, the British government notified Nicaragua and the American company that the San Juan River, from its mouth to the Machuca Rapids, was the property of the Mosquito King and any use needed British approval. The company turned to the U.S. government for help.[14]

In mid-1849 Hise was recalled and Ephraim George Squier was appointed to succeed him. Squier was instructed to negotiate a treaty for access across Nicaragua (the Hise-Selva Treaty was never submitted to the U.S. Senate) but not to guarantee Nicaragua's borders in exchange. This new treaty was submitted to the U.S. Senate on March 19, 1850, but was never acted upon. Squier also worked to unite Honduras, Nicaragua, and El Salvador, all of whom distrusted the British. However, Chatfield blocked this through diplomacy. Squier succeeded in inducing Nicaragua to grant the Americans a concession to build a canal along the line of the San Juan River.[15]

Meanwhile, Chatfield worked to acquire for Great Britain Tigre Island in the Gulf of Fonseca from Honduras in order to secure the Pacific terminus of any canal route. He threatened to confiscate the island should Honduras not pay its debts to British subjects, a payment which he knew was beyond the means of the Honduran government. At the same time, Chatfield wrote to Palmerston in London arguing the wisdom of this initiative. Palmerston had little enthusiasm for the undertaking, since he did not believe that Parliament would assume the debt owed by the Hondurans.

Squier, learning of Chatfield's plan, negotiated a treaty on September 28 with Honduras which leased the Tigre Island to the United States for eighteen months. On October 16, one week before that treaty was to go into effect (the U.S. Senate did not know of its existence), Commander James Paynter of the British navy seized the island. However, Adm. Phipps Hornby, Commander in Chief of Pacific Squadron, ordered the island restored to Honduras. Both Chatfield and Squier were reprimanded by their governments.[16]

CLAYTON–BULWER TREATY

On April 18, 1850, Great Britain and the United States signed the Clayton-Bulwer Treaty in an attempt to resolve their differences in Central America. Each side interpreted the treaty differently. Great Britain perceived that the treaty applied to only future activities and that existing claims and activities were still valid. The United States believed that the treaty placed the two nations on equal footing and that neither would fortify, colonize, or exercise domain over *any* part of Central America. Regardless of the interpretation, the treaty did compromise the Monroe Doctrine, which in 1823 declared that in the future the Americas were only for the Americans. British and American subjects continued to clash over trade and transit.[17]

GREAT BRITAIN AND THE UNITED STATES RENEW THEIR STRUGGLE

Almost immediately the United States and Great Britain renewed their competition in Central America. On November 21, 1850, a British warship fired upon the U.S. passenger steamer *Prometheus* as it was departing Greytown. The commanding officer of the British warship charged that the U.S. ship had not paid the port tariffs. None other than Cornelius Vanderbilt was on board. He had come to Nicaragua to oversee the development of the Atlantic and Pacific Ship-Canal Company. The U.S. government vigorously objected, arguing that the British warship was exercising "dominion" to which it was not entitled. The United States dispatched the steam sloop *Saranac* (15 guns) and sail sloop *Albany* (20 guns) under Commodore Foxhall A. Parker to Greytown. In this case the British government backed down and apologized.[18]

On March 20, 1852, Great Britain declared Ruatán and five neighboring islands the Colony of the Bay Islands. On August 10 Great Britain formally occupied the islands. Many in the United States, particularly Democratic senators, interpreted this a direct violation of the Clayton-Bulwer Treaty. The British argued that the treaty had recognized the islands as part of Belize.[19]

Tension between Great Britain and the United States in Central America continued to escalate, due in part to the initiatives of the new U.S. Minister to Central America, Solon Borland. He was an ardent Southern expansionist and announced that the Clayton-Bulwer treaty should be abrogated because the British violated the terms, and then he proceeded to act as if it had been abrogated. Apparently, his personal agenda was to annex Central America to the United States. Squier, who was now in Nicaragua as a private citizen, shared Borland's objectives. Tension ran high as Guatemala, diplomatically supported by Great Britain, and Honduras, with the diplomatic support of the United States, fought over their border.[20]

In early 1853 the U.S.-owned Accessory Transit Company (an outgrowth of the Atlantic and Pacific Ship-Canal Company) and British authorities of Greytown became engaged in a dispute over the company's misuse of leased land. The company exceeded its concession to establish a coaling depot at Point Arenas by constructing warehouses and hotels, thus depriving the citizens of Greytown the opportunity to participate in the profits from the growing trans-Isthmus traffic. In retaliation, armed men from Greytown destroyed some of the company's buildings; however, on March 12, U.S. Marines from the American sloop *Cyane* (22 guns) prevented them from completing their work. As a consequence, townspeople hampered the company's operations and stole its property.[21]

A more serious confrontation occurred in 1854. Capt. T. T. Smith, commanding the Transit Company's river steamer *Routh*, shot and killed a black citizen of Greytown. Greytown authorities attempted to arrest Smith for murder. Borland, who had resigned as minister due to a rebuke from the American Secretary of State because of Borland's denouncement of the Clayton-Bulwer Treaty, witnessed the incident. He defended Smith telling the marshal that the United States did not recognize his authority over U.S. citizens. A few minutes later Borland, seizing a rifle from a bystander, ordered the marshal and his supporters off the *Routh*. Borland persuaded fifty American passengers bound for New York to remain behind to protect U.S. interests while he sailed on the company's ocean steamer *Northern Light* to the United States to seek help.

Once again the sloop *Cyane*, commanded by George N. Hollins, was dispatched. Hollins demanded that the town pay $24,000 in damages for the stolen property, an apology to the United States, and a pledge of its good behavior in the future. When these terms were not met, the *Cyane* bombarded Greytown on July 13. Those buildings still standing were burned by a landing party. Amazingly, no one was killed.[22] In spite of the harshness of the American actions, the British only protested and demanded an apology which it never received. Even taking into consideration the fact that Great Britain was engaged in the Crimean War (1854–55), its weak response to the American aggression demonstrated a lack of commitment to its protectorate.

Rumors of filibustering expeditions from the United States continued to strain U.S.-British relations. In early 1854 the British government received reports concerning the Central American Agricultural and Mining Association, headed by Col. H. L. Kinney of Philadelphia. He held an 1839 grant from the Mosquito King for land south of San Juan del Norte.[23] This was yet another extension of the territory claimed by the "King." However, the real challenge would come from the Pacific and William Walker, who militarily seized Nicaragua in 1855 (see chapter 20).

By the close of 1856, Great Britain began to back away from its confrontation with the United States in Central America. British politicians failed to back these activities because the British populace did not perceive Central America to be important enough to jeopardize relations with Great Britain's most important trading partner, the United States.[24] As the London *Times* observed, "we see no reason why we should resist the process [of American expansionism], except where a British community is established and demands our aid, or where some real interest can be shown to be at stake."[25]

In 1859 Great Britain and Guatemala signed a treaty whereby Guatemala recognized British sovereignty over Belize in exchange for the British construction of a road between Guatemala City and the Caribbean, a distance of some 150 miles. The construction was long delayed and in 1940 Guatemala abrogated the treaty. Also in 1859, Great Britain relinquished part of the Mosquito Coast to Honduras and the following year returned the Bay Islands to that Central American nation. And, in 1860 Great Britain surrendered Greytown and part of the Mosquito Coast to Nicaragua under the Treaty of Managua.[26]

OBSERVATIONS

The United Provinces and the subsequent nations of Central America were in a near-defenseless position against British power as executed by its local representatives. The only potential hope for Central America was to secure the help of the United States to offset the strength of the British. Prior to 1847 the United States showed little interest in the region. After that year American interests awakened; however, too frequently for the good of Central Americans, the execution of U.S. foreign policy was in the hands of Americans whose desires for territorial acquisitions were no less greedy than those of their British counterparts.

PART 5

WARS OF CONQUEST (DO-IT-YOURSELF MANIFEST DESTINY)—FILIBUSTERING

CHAPTER EIGHTEEN

FILIBUSTERING AGAINST MEXICO, 1819–1911

> The British and the North Americans are the Phoenicians and the Carthagenians of modern times.
> —Antonio José de Irisarri, Nicaraguan Plenipotentary to the United States, 1856

THE SPARK

Greedy soldiers of fortune anointed themselves with the right to conquer parts of northern Mexico and to determine the future of these weakly defended lands.

BACKGROUND

Filibustering was older than the Latin American republics and not exclusively a "Gringo" enterprise.[1] But most frequently, filibusters were American citizens who militarily intervened in Latin America in order to conquer territory. These filibusters would then seek to join their conquests to the Union either formally or in a fraternal relation; it was a do-it-yourself "Manifest Destiny." The three most coveted prizes by American filibusters were northern Mexico, Cuba (see chapter 19), and Central America (see chapter 20).

The Age of Revolution gave birth to modern filibustering. In 1805 the former vice president of the United States, Aaron Burr, was involved in a plot which possibly included seizing parts of the Spanish Southwest, later if not sooner. Gen. James Wilkinson, commander of the U.S. Army in the Southwest, conspired with Spanish officials to detach Kentucky and Tennessee from the United States and attach them to Spanish Louisiana. Apparently, he also conspired with American filibusters to detach Texas from Spain and create an independent country.[2]

In another conspiracy, Gregor MacGregor sailed from Savannah, Georgia, in 1817 with a band of adventurers and captured the town of Fernandina on Amelia Island off Spanish East Florida. Having insufficient resources to attack St. Augustine, he sailed off to seek his fortune in Central America. MacGregor was succeeded by Luis Aury, who, apparently more interested in privateering under charter from a Latin American republic, claimed East Florida for Mexico, thus causing intervention by American troops.[3]

OPPOSING FORCES

Typically, the leaders of filibustering expeditions recruited the toughest adventurers who came from the four corners of the world. Many were recklessly brave, accustomed to hardships, and unscrupulous. The filibusters only required the promise of good pay and adventure. Generally, filibusters armed themselves, and since surrender was not an attractive perspective, they tended to buy the best weapons available.

Since filibustering expeditions against northern Mexico were launched when that government was under duress, few disciplined Mexican troops could be found in the remote reaches of the nation to confront the invaders. Therefore, frequently the Mexicans who opposed the filibusters were irregular troops, civilians, and bandits. Most were poorly armed (some not at all) and possessed little if any military training.

OPENING STRATEGIES

The filibusters relied on surprise to seize a strategic site and then claim a vast region. They would then rely on their maternal nation, most frequently the United States, to recognize and defend that claim. Often the Mexican government had little or no forewarning of these incursions. Remote, sparsely populated provinces could expect little and slow help from the central government.

LONG'S EXPEDITION OF 1819

In early June 1819 James Long[4] and seventy-five followers started from Natchez, Mississippi, for Nacogdoches in the then-Spanish province of Texas. They were motivated by the terms of the Transcontinental Treaty of 1819 in which the United States conceded any claim to Texas in exchange for the Floridas. By the time they reached their destination, their numbers had swelled to over 300 men. These filibusters established a civil government and chose Long as their president. On June 23 they declared independence.[5]

Long dispersed small bodies of men to gain control over the province. The Spanish authorities reacted swiftly and sent 700 men, under Col. Ignacio Pérez, to drive out the invaders. Long endeavored to reassemble his force at the Cochattee village on the Trinity River. Colonel Pérez was able to intercept the invaders before they could unite and defeated them piecemeal. The remaining filibusters at Nacogdoches, including Long, fled to safety across the Sabine River into the United States.[6]

In the spring of 1821, Long, commanding fifty-one men, led a second expedition into Texas. Professing loyalty to the independence movement then gaining momentum in central Mexico (see chapter 5), Long captured La Bahía (renamed Goliad in 1829) on October 4 unopposed. However, within a few days his entire force was captured by Colonel Pérez and Long was sent to Mexico City as a prisoner. He was released when Mexican independence was declared.[7]

MOREHEAD'S EXPEDITION OF 1851

By the early 1850s the Mexican government was preoccupied with internal disorder. The struggle between the Liberals and Conservatives, ignited by the compromise solution ending the Wars for Independence, still raged (see chapter 27). Plus, Mexico had recently been emasculated in a series of wars against the citizens of the United States (see chapters 14–16). And,

Apaches ravaged the northern frontier. Joseph C. Morehead led several hundred filibusters into northwest Mexico with the objective of seizing Baja California and Sonora. Once in Mexico, the expedition fell apart.[8]

RAOUSSET'S FIRST EXPEDITION OF 1852

In the spring of 1852 Count Gaston de Raousset de Boulbon[9] negotiated a contract with Mexican authorities which permitted him to establish a colony in Sonora. The Frenchmen were given a mining concession in exchange for creating a barrier against the Apaches. Originally, these 200 Frenchmen had come to California in search of gold.[10]

On May 19 they sailed from San Francisco on the *Archibald Gracie*, down the Pacific, up the Gulf of California, and landed at Guaymas, Sonora (925 mi NW of Mexico City), on June 1. Upon landing, the count became embroiled with local politicians who did not share the same objectives as the bureaucrats in Mexico City. Raousset ignored the order of the local military commander, Gen. Miguel Blanco, to march through his headquarters at Arispe on the Count's way to Saric, his base of operation. As a consequence, Blanco demanded that the Frenchmen take an oath of allegiance to Mexico and reduce their number to fifty men. This the Count refused to do.[11]

Exasperated, Raousset marched against the town of Hermosillo. He arrived on October 14, having been delayed at Magdelena by a romantic interlude. Anticipating the Count's move, the delay gave Blanco enough time to ocupy Hermosillo with one thousand militiamen. Ordered to surrender, instead the Count attacked and routed the Mexicans. The Frenchmen lost 17 killed and 25 wounded; the Mexicans lost some 200 killed and wounded.[12]

Next, Raousset unsuccessfully endeavored to instigate an uprising by the local populace, claiming to be the champion of an independent Sonora. He then decided to capture the port of Guaymas to improve his communications with California, the possible source of reinforcements and supplies. As the Count marched toward the port, Mexican irregulars seriously harassed his advance and the Count was stricken with fever. Raousset, under an armistice, was carried into Guaymas for medical treatment. His remaining 182 men lost contact with their commander, and appreciating the weak position in which they now found themselves, surrendered to Brigade General Blanco at the ranch of San José de Guaymas. These adventurers gave up their arms for 11,000 pesos and were permitted to return to the United States. The Count began preparation for a second expedition but this was overshadowed by William Walker's activities.[13]

WALKER'S EXPEDITION OF 1853-54

Following the acquisition of California by the United States under the 1848 Treaty of Guadalupe-Hidalgo, Baja California became a favorite quest of North American filibusters. The frontier that divided the slender peninsula from upper California was purely artificial. And, the territorial capital, Ensenada, lay at the northern end of the Baja California Peninsula on the Pacific side, only 80 miles from San Diego, California, and some 1,400 miles from Mexico City.

William Walker became interested in leading a filibustering expedition into northern old Mexico during 1852. Having failed to secure a concession for a mining colony (a ploy to gain entry into Mexican territory) during a visit to Guaymas in 1853, Walker returned to San Francisco where he gathered a band of mercenaries, raised money, and purchased arms and munitions.[14]

Walker chartered the brig *Arrow*. However, on September 30, 1853, a U.S. marshal seized the ship. More secretive the next time, Walker and forty-five followers successfully sailed during the night of October 16 on board the bark *Caroline*. In the haste, he had to abandon one-third of his men, the weapons and munitions stored on the *Arrow*, and a considerable quantity of supplies on the wharf as the *Caroline* was towed out of San Francisco harbor.[15]

Walker arrived off Cape San Lucas at the southern tip of Baja California on October 28. He paused briefly to await reinforcements, which failed to arrive. Anticipating that his colleagues were not coming or had sailed past them, Walker sailed to La Paz, a seaport to the north inside the Gulf of California. On November 3, Walker entered the port flying the Mexican flag and captured La Paz and Territorial Governor (*Principal Gobernador*) Rafael Espinosa. Following a looting spree, Walker called a mock election, and his followers chose him "President of the Republic of Lower California." The Civil Code of Louisiana, which permitted slavery, was declared the law of the land. Just as Walker was preparing to sail from La Paz, a newly appointed Mexican territorial governor, Col. Juan C. Rebolledo, arrived on board the *Neptune* and fell into Walker's hands. Walker learned that Mexican troops were on the way. While departing, the townspeople attacked Walker's band and both sides sustained casualties.[16]

Next, Walker sailed out of the Gulf of California, trying to decide where to establish his "capital." He again landed at Cape San Lucas on November 8 but after a few weeks' delay sailed northward up the Pacific coast to Ensenada where he arrived on the twenty-ninth. Walker sustained a major blow when the first mate of the brig *Caroline* seized control of the ship and deserted the filibusters, sailing off with many of their arms and much of their supplies.[17]

Walker commandeered horses from local ranches and dispatched some mounted men against the pueblo and military colony at Santo Tomás, 30 miles south of Ensenada. Forewarned, the Mexican garrison repulsed the filibusters, pursued them to their camp, and laid siege. The attacking Mexicans were led by Guadalupe Melendres, a local *caudillo* and bandit. On December 14, Walker successfully drove off the attackers.[18]

Meanwhile, back in California, Walker's friends openly recruited reinforcements. Many were willing to go and the local representatives of the U.S. government were unable or unwilling to enforce the antifilibustering laws. The bark *Anita* sailed from San Francisco on December 7 with 230 mercenaries on board. After a rough voyage, the new filibusters landed at Ensenada on December 20. These reinforcements were well armed but brought no supplies. So Walker had them forage the countryside "paying" for what they took with worthless promissory notes of the "new" republic.[19]

On January 18, 1854, Walker declared the annexation of Sonora (without even having set foot in the state) and changed the name of his "new" country from the "Republic of Lower California" to the "Republic of Sonora." In the meantime, the Mexican navy schooner *Iturbide* (3 guns) arrived off Ensenada and in early February it was joined by the U.S. sloop of war *Portsmouth* (20 guns).[20]

Not all of the filibusters were satisfied with Walker's leadership. A group of discontents plotted to blow up the magazine and desert with what they could plunder. Walker learned of the plot, tried two of the ringleaders by court-martial, and summarily shot them. Two others were publicly whipped. Walker then mustered the men. He asked who was still willing to follow him. All of the original forty-five and a few of the *Anita*'s group chose to go with Walker. He disarmed the remainder and permitted them to leave.

On February 13, 1854, leaving his sick and wounded at Ensenada (for the *Portsmouth* to rescue), Walker marched his "army" of some 130 men south and captured Santo Tomás without a fight. Next he took San Vicente, some twenty miles farther south, and unsuccessfully tried to recruit a Mexican auxiliary force. His army dwindled through desertions.[21]

Walker now reversed his line of march, heading up the peninsula and toward Sonora. His army, numbering less than one hundred men, drove along a herd of cattle for sustenance. They crossed the Colorado River on rafts at a point where it was 400 yards wide and very deep. Most of their cattle drowned. Half of his force deserted, making its way up the Colorado River for 70 miles to Fort Yuma. The filibusters were harassed by savage Indians and Mexican irregulars. Ambush and disease thinned their ranks, and the army shrank to thirty-five starving men. Three days into Sonora on April 4, Walker held a council of war, and the survivors decided to return to San Vicente.[22]

While recrossing into Baja California on April 6, Walker was attacked on three sides by the Indians. Hiding twelve men in a clump of bushes under Lt. P. S. Veeder, Walker retreated only to find that the Indians had closed off his line of escape as well. The Indians on the flanks and those guarding the pass charged Walker's group. When the Indians passed the hiding place of Veeder's men, the filibusters shot down twelve of them. At the same time, Walker wheeled and delivered an accurate volley. The dispirited enemy fled. After this experience the Indians kept their distance, preferring to rob the graves of the filibusters as they died from their wounds.[23]

The "army," now reduced to thirty-five men, finally returned to San Vicente on April 17 only to find that the eighteen-man garrison that had been left behind had either deserted or been tortured to death by Meléndrez. There was no hope of reinforcements. Walker led his weary followers toward the California border. Three miles short of the frontier, Meléndrez, leading a large band of ill-trained Mexicans and their Indian allies, confronted Walker and demanded his surrender. Leaving six men in hiding, the remainder of Walker's force was able to draw the Mexicans to within range of their rifles. The Mexicans had no desire to fight these desperate marauders and galloped off. Walker lost only one man whose judgment was clouded by too much *aguardiente* (local liquor). On May 8, 1854, thirty-year-old William Walker and thirty-three followers surrendered to Maj. Justus McKinstry of the U.S. Army at San Diego, California. All were paroled on the pledge that they present themselves for trial in San Francisco where they were acquitted in October. Walker then became the editor of the *San Francisco Commercial Adventurer*.[24]

Walker had been defeated by the Indians, Mexican irregulars, and the harsh terrain. Nonetheless, he became an instant hero among Southern expansionists. Walker proved that he was brave and was willing to act decisively.

RAOUSSET'S SECOND EXPEDITION OF 1854

The Mexican government, once again headed by Santa Anna (for the eleventh and final time), was disturbed by the actions of the American filibusters. Santa Anna decided to invite itinerant foreigners (excluding North Americans), who were stranded in California, to Mexico. He hoped to create a barrier against North American incursions. Santa Anna gave permission for 3,000 foreigners to immediately land at Guaymas, Sonora. He planned to stifle any political initiative on their part by disbursing them in small bands among the coastal states. The Mexican consul in San Francisco asked the French consul, who in turn asked Count Raousset, to recruit the men. The count, who had been conspiring to return to Mexico, was delighted to help. On April 2, 1854, he dispatched 350 individuals, mostly Frenchmen from San Francisco, on board the British ship *Challenge*, the Count remaining behind. Raousset apparently had shared his scheme of conquest only with the leaders.[25]

The Count slipped out of San Francisco on the pilot-boat *Belle*. In addition to the two-man crew, the Count, and four associates, the tiny boat carried 180 rifled carbines, bayonets, and supplies. After thirty-five rough days at sea, Raousset landed at Guaymas, Sonora, on June 28.[26]

A cat-and-mouse game then ensued between Raousset, who was endeavoring to take command and seize the port, and Mexican Gen. José María Yañez, who was trying to win time for reinforcements to arrive from the central government. Matters came to a head on July 13 when the Frenchmen attacked the port's barracks. The Mexican troops held their ground for three hours while the ammunition-deficient Frenchmen, led by Raousset, repeatedly charged their position. The Mexican victory was complete. Forty-six Frenchmen were killed and 60 wounded; 50 Mexicans died and 100 were wounded. At sunrise on August 12, a firing squad shot the Count in Guaymas' La Mole Square. Sixty of the Frenchmen were pardoned and permitted to sail to San Francisco. The remainder were marched under harsh conditions to the Perote fortress (110 mi E of Mexico City). With the intervention of the French government, the survivors were released by the end of 1854.[27]

CRABB'S EXPEDITION OF 1857

Henry A. Crabb[28] led the next filibustering expedition, calling it the Gadsden Colonization Company, into northern Mexico. Apparently he had been invited by a prominent Mexican family into which he had married. On January 22, 1857, Crabb and fifty-five followers sailed from San Francisco to the Gadsden Purchase territory on board the *Sea Bird*. This was far short of the thousand men he had promised to raise. The party landed and camped at El Monte, California, a short distance from San Pedro. They were joined by others which increased their number to about 140 men. The party then marched to Fort Yuma, Arizona, which took a month. During this trek about one-third of the men deserted.[29]

The expedition continued up the Gila Valley for about 45 miles and then turned southeast toward the Mexican border town of Sonoita. In order to speed his march, Crabb ordered his wagons, containing most of his ammunition and guarded by twenty men, to follow as best they could as he proceeded to Sonoita with sixty-eight men. On March 21 Crabb and nine others entered Sonoita to purchase food. There, he learned that Mexican forces were being assembled to evict him. Crabb wrote a threatening letter to the local *prefect* (mayor) and marched southward.[30]

The seventy filibusters were strung out as they entered the village of Caborca south of Sonoita. Two hundred Mexicans attacked from ambush on the morning of April 1. Six hundred more Mexicans, commanded by Commandant Hilario Gabilondo, soon joined the fight. The filibusters fought their way into the pueblo and held out for six days. On April 6 Crabb surrendered. The Mexicans sustained about 35 killed and 18 wounded; Crabb sustained about 10 dead and seriously wounded. The next day 59 filibusters, all Americans, were executed. One fourteen-year-old boy was spared. Although rumors of mutilations and atrocities were common, there appears to be little or no truth to these.[31]

On April 17 Gabilondo dispatched patrols to round up scattered elements of Crabb's expedition. One Mexican patrol crossed into Arizona to a ranch north of Sonoita. It captured one individual and killed four. Altogether ninty-three filibusters were killed. Both governments accused the other of violating its sovereignty and tempers flared on both sides of the border.[32]

MULKEY'S ABORTED EXPEDITION OF 1888

Although numerous border incidents occurred following Crabb's expedition, no major filibustering schemes were hatched for the next thirty years. In July 1888 Col. J. K. Mulkey helped organize the "Order of the Golden Field," a secret filibustering society whose objective was to seize Baja California and proclaim the "Republic of Northern Mexico." Cells were established in California, Arizona, and Texas. The scheme was leaked to the public by the San Francisco *Chronicle* and, as a consequence, abandoned.[33]

SMITH'S ABORTED EXPEDITION OF 1890

Two years later, as economic conditions in Baja California worsened, another filibustering scheme surfaced and Walter Gifford Smith, editor of the San Diego *Sun*, emerged as its leader. This time the Mexican Land and Colonization Company, an English syndicate with a large investment in the peninsula, backed the conspiracy. They pledged $100,000 to support a filibustering expedition.[34]

The conspirators' strategy was similar to the one that would succeed in Panama in 1903 (see companion volume). Local Mexican officials would be invited to a fiesta in the Hotel Iturbide in Ensenada. There, they would be overpowered or bibbed and the filibusters would seize the port. A "declaration of independence" was drafted and Smith was to be named "president." However, Smith unwisely granted an interview to a Los Angeles newspaper, his wealthy investors got "cold feet," and the exposed plan unraveled.[35]

THE EXPEDITIONS OF 1911

In 1910 the dominant twentieth-century event in the history of Mexico, a great seven-year revolution, began (see companion volume). One of the numerous sideshows was a series of incursions into Baja California. Although initially not filibustering expeditions, they evolved into such. The individuals participating in these invasions were strange bedfellows. Initially, the supporters of the Flores Magón brothers, long-time opponents of Porfírio Díaz, dominated giving the early incursions a "revolutionary" character. As events transpired North Americans became increasingly involved, changing the character of these operations into filibustering expeditions. Overlaying these two groups were unemployed members of the International Workers of the World; some of them wanted to establish a socialist republic. These invaders grew from a score to a few hundred. This was possible because U.S. border guards did not interfere with the trickle of men and supplies flowing across the border. Mexican forces defending the peninsula initially numbered 112 men. Twenty-two police patrolled the frontier from the Colorado River to the Pacific Ocean and ninety troops were garrisoned in Ensenada.[36]

In early 1911 Mexicans Simón Berthold and José María Leyva led fifteen other expatriates and two North Americans across the border into Baja California. On January 29 they captured the border village of Mexicali. After taking what they wanted, these individuals extorted protection money from business interests. Mexican Col. Celso Vega, commanding less than 100 men, marched northward from Ensenada on January 30 and arrived at Mexicali in mid-February. His exhausted, poorly equipped troops attacked the reinforced and entrenched invaders and were defeated. The wounded Mexicans, including Colonel Vega, were taken into the United States for medical care.[37]

The invaders, who could increasingly be characterized as filibusters, now attacked the border town of Algodones which lies east of Mexicali on the Colorado River. The town was unsuccessfully defended by the local magistrate and twelve citizens. Next, the filibusters, who were now probably about one hundred individuals, divided into two columns. The one commanded by Berthold marched south against Ensenada and the other commanded by Leyva headed west against the border town of Tecate, where more filibusters under Luís Rodríguez were waiting.

In the meantime, the Mexican government sent the 8th Infantry Battalion (500 men) by sea from Guadalajara to Ensenada. It arrived on March 8. Col. Miguel Mayol, the battalion's commanding officer, and Colonel Vega, who had returned from the United States by sea, concurred on a plan of action. Colonel Mayol dispatched a company under Capt. Justino Mendieta to attack the filibusters at Tecate. On March 13 Mendieta defeated the group headed by Rodríguez before Leyva had arrived. On the twentieth he defeated Leyva at Tecate and the surviving filibusters from this band fled into the United States.[38]

Colonel Mayol, with the remainder of the 8th Infantry Battalion, marched from Ensenada on April 8 toward the mouth of Colorado River. Near Mexicali he defeated a band of filibusters led by Stanley Williams (alias William Stanley, [first name unknown] Cohen, Robert Lober), a deserter from the U.S. Army. Most of the surviving filibusters retreated to Mexicali and the remainder escaped back into the United States. Mayol did not attack Mexicali; rather, he continued his march toward the Colorado. Later he explained that a shortage of ammunition dictated his actions.[39]

Carl Rhys Pryce now took charge of the filibusters along the border and marched toward the Colorado River to confront the 8th Infantry Battalion, but then he changed his mind and occupied Tecate. He sent a message to Berthold asking him to join in the fight against Mayol. At the time Berthold was some fifty miles north of Ensenada, his march having been delayed by three Mexican sharpshooters. On March 23 these filibusters sacked the pueblo of El Alamo. On April 14 Berthold died of wounds sustained at El Alamo and was succeeded by Jack Mosby (a deserter from the U.S. Marine Corps).[40]

Mosby countermarched to join Pryce at Tecate. As these fifty filibusters passed by the village of El Carrio, they were attacked by fifteen Mexicans led by Lerdo González. Mosby was among the wounded; he and the other injured returned to the United States. The remaining filibusters, now led by Sam Wood, joined Pryce at Tecate. Additional filibusters from the United States joined the force and together they planned to attack Tijuana.[41]

Tijuana (1,480 mi NW of Mexico City) was defended by fifty-six Mexicans (thirty soldiers and twenty-six volunteers). Ammunition was in short supply since it had been embargoed by the United States. On April 8, two hundred filibusters led by Pryce and Wood attacked but the defenders held out. In a bold move, Sub-lieutenant [first name unknown] Guerrero, leading thirty Mexicans, attacked the filibuster camp a little after midnight. The filibusters panicked and fled back into the United States. Sam Wood was among the dead.[42]

The filibusters, led by Pryce, were not ready to quit. Reinforced from the United States, they attacked and captured Tijuana. Twenty of the Mexican defenders escaped to Ensenada but the remainder were killed or wounded. Pryce raised the American flag and other filibusters wanted to declare a socialist republic. The Flores Magón brothers released a proclamation in San Diego, California, on April 30, which announced the capture of the town; guaranteed liberty and justice; denounced the despotism of Porfírio Díaz and Francisco Madero; and did not condemn

Pryce's actions. The filibusters chose Jack Mosby, who had recovered from his wounds, as their new military leader, and on June 3 Richard Ferris proclaimed himself "Provisional President of Lower California."[43]

In the meantime, the Mexican citizens of Baja California formed the Defenders of the National Integrity (*Defensores de la Integridad Nacional*) headed by Dr. Horacio E. López. The "Defenders" assembled 140 volunteers and a large quantity of cartridges at Ensenada. On June 18 Vega began the march north at the head of 600 men. They attacked the one hundred filibusters camped at Tijuana on June 22. The fighting was brief. The filibusters lost 31 dead; the Mexicans lost 3 dead and 6 wounded. The filibusters fled across the border and surrendered to Capt. Frank A. Wilcox, U.S. Army, of the Thirteenth Infantry Division.[44]

OBSERVATIONS

Even in the somewhat lax framework of nineteenth-century international laws, filibustering was illegal and should have been condemned by U.S. tribunals, but this was not the case. These filibustering expeditions were a major source of the ill feelings and mistrust that Mexicans held toward the government of the United States. Mexicans, whose political experience had been with a governmental structure where power emanates from the top down, found it difficult to believe that filibustering activities could be undertaken without the active participation of the American government.

Throughout this century-long era, many highly-placed American officials wanted to exploit the activities of filibusters to add to American territory. Shortly after the Crabb Filibustering Expedition, the American Minister to Mexico, John Forsyth, wrote to President James Buchanan in April 1857, "You want Sonora? The American blood spilled near its line would justify you seizing it."[45]

CHAPTER NINETEEN

FILIBUSTERING AGAINST CUBA, 1849–50

> There are laws of political as well as of physical gravitation; and if an apple severed by the tempest from its native tree cannot choose but fall to the ground, Cuba, forcibly disjoined from its own unnatural connection with Spain, and incapable of selfsupport, can gravitate only towards the North American Union which by the same law of nature cannot cast her off from its bosom.
> —John Q. Adams, 1822

THE SPARK

In June 1848 Secretary of State James Buchanan betrayed to the Spanish Minister in Washington, Angel Calderón de la Baca, that Narciso López[1] planned a revolution against Spanish rule in Cuba. Ironically, this sent López fleeing across the island to safety in the United States.[2]

BACKGROUND

Cuba had been the object of North America's aspirations since the earliest days of the young republic. In 1805 President Thomas Jefferson told the British Minister that the United States might seize the island should there be war with Spain. Three years later the President sent Gen. James Wilkinson to Cuba to see if Spain would sell the island to the United States; it would not. In 1818 Spain opened Cuban ports to international trade and within two years over half of that trade was with the United States. The U.S. delegates to the 1826 Congress of Panama were instructed to oppose any attempt by the Latin American nations to free Cuba from Spanish rule, preferring it to remain under the domination of a weak Spain and still available for annexation. In particular, the United States feared British intervention. Since the days of President Monroe, the United States had adopted a "no-transfer" policy to Cuba—Spain must not cede the island to a third party.[3]

And Cubans had long sought the help of the United States, some wanting independence and others annexation. Two primary groups existed among those seeking annexation. First, there were the wealthy Cuban planters who wished to preserve slavery. They aligned themselves with Southern Democrats who championed Manifest Destiny. Second, there were the Liberals who opposed slavery and believed in the incorporation of Cuba into the United States as a free state. General Narciso López, the President of the Spanish Permanent Executive Military Commission on the island, was an important leader among the annexationists.[4]

In 1842 when Spain replaced the Liberal Gen. Gerónimo Valdés with the Conservative Gen. Leopoldo O'Donnell as the governor of Cuba, López, along with other Valdés supporters, was swept out of office. Following his removal, López, through the business connections of his Cuban wife's family, traveled freely throughout the island, winning followers. Although not a successful businessman, López used his freedom of travel to win supporters and at his Cuban Rose Mines, the workers secretly forged machetes and pikes.[5]

In mid-1844 Captain-General O'Donnell discovered a plot by those advocating independence. He brutally stamped out this "Conspiracy of the Ladder" (*Conspiración de la Escalera*).[6] This temporarily terrorized the independence movement.[7]

By 1850 Cuba's wealth was founded on sugar which in turn was based on slavery. Sugar comprised 83 percent of Cuban exports, 40 percent of which went to the United States. By this time over half of Cuba's 800,000 population was black slaves. Those wealthy Cuban planters who feared that López might free the slaves during his attempt to forcibly annex Cuba to the United States rallied around the more conservative Havana Club (*Club de la Havana*) which had been formed in 1848 by Cubans living in New York. Working through John L. O'Sullivan,[8] they successfully convinced President James Polk to attempt to purchase the island for $100 million.[9]

Next, the Havana Club sent its agent Rafael de Castro to Jalapa, Mexico, where he offered Gen. William Worth $3 million for his services and those of 5,000 American veterans of the U.S. Mexican War. Unexpectedly, de Castro died on May 20, 1849.[10]

López decided to rebel on June 24, 1848. However, the Havana Club told him of their plans to bring Worth and 5,000 American veterans to the island so López agreed to wait. On June 2 O'Sullivan told Polk of López' planned uprising and of the Worth expedition. Polk ordered the Secretary of War to prevent Worth from sailing to Cuba. Secretary of State Buchanan betrayed the López conspiracy (known as the Rose Mine Conspiracy) to the Spanish Minister in Washington. This was done to prove to Spain that the United States was not attempting to secure the island through devious means. The Polk administration hoped that this action and the $100 million offer for the island would cause Spain to sell it to the United States. The Spanish reply was that "they would prefer seeing it sunk in the Ocean."[11]

As time wore on, the annexation of Cuba was caught up in the raging slavery controversy within the United States. In general, the Democratic administrations favored annexation and those of the Whigs opposed it.

OPPOSING FORCES

The few thousand filibusters who participated in López' first expedition were soldiers of fortune, cutthroats, and a few veterans of the recent U.S. Mexico War. One observer described the recruits as the "most desperate looking creatures as ever were seen would murder a man for ten dollars."[12] To this core López expected to rally hundreds if not thousands of Cuban Liberals who wished the island annexed to the United States. In 1849 the Spanish army in Cuba was small, perhaps 25,000 men. More importantly, the Spanish authorities could count on a large number of ill-disciplined irregulars who were controlled by the wealthy, conservative land owners.

OPENING STRATEGY

López planned to invade the island with a filibustering expedition from the United States. This expedition would be led by a Southern hero from the U.S. Mexican War and composed primarily by veterans of that war. Once in Cuba, López would then call for a general uprising.

Spain planned to intercept the filibusters at sea. Failing this, it would concentrate overwhelming forces at the point of the landing.

THE ROUND ISLAND FIASCO

In late 1848 López founded the Cuban *Junta* (*Junta Cubana*) in New York City. He unsuccessfully sought to involve the new Zachary Taylor administration in the expedition. Failing this, López turned to Southern Democrats and offered command of the expedition first to Jefferson Davis and then to Robert E. Lee, but both men declined. Hence, by default, López became the commander of the expedition. The ranking Americans were Col. W. F. Briscoe and Col. E. D. White, who had commanded a Louisiana Company in the U.S. Mexican War.[13]

Some 1,300 filibusters were recruited in New York and then sailed to Cat and Round Islands near Pass Christian on the Mississippi River in the steamers *New Orleans* and *Sea Gull*. The steamer *Fanny* carried 200 men recruited in New Orleans to the islands, arriving on July 31, 1849. President Taylor ordered the U.S. Navy to prevent the expedition from sailing. Commander Victor M. Randolph blockaded Round Island with six warships. Finally, in early September the isolated filibusters surrendered to the Navy. The filibusters were allowed to keep their weapons and stores. After a brief interment, their two ships, the *Sea Gull* and the *New Orleans*, were returned to them as well.[14]

THE CÁRDENAS EXPEDITION

A primary result of the failed Round Island expedition was the break in relations between López and the Cuban Conservatives who favored annexation. As a consequence, the Conservatives withheld all the resources they had gathered including the ships and weapons used in the failed Round Island expedition. López took a new approach. He openly organized the next expedition as "emigrants" to California via Panama. The men would sail without weapons or training to avoid seizure under the 1818 Neutrality Act. They would land on an uninhabited Mexican island where they would be armed and trained. Once again, López offered the command of the expedition to a Southern hero of the Mexican War, Gen. John A. Quitman,[15] but he refused.[16]

The recruits of the Cárdenas Expedition were significantly different from those of the Round Island fiasco. Veteran officers of the U.S. Mexican War raised "regiments" which bore states' names. Col. Theodore O'Hara commanded the Kentucky Regiment, Col. W. T. Bunch the Mississippi Regiment, and Col. Chatham R. Wheat the Louisiana Regiment. The filibusters were to be paid and given the same allowances as those of the U.S. Army. At the end of one year or when the campaign was completed (whichever came first) each soldier would receive a $4,000 bounty or its equivalent in lands in Cuba. The officers were to receive a $10,000 bounty. Only five of the filibusters were Cubans; all the rest were North Americans. Some of the arms were obtained from the Mississippi state arsenals. Three ships were purchased, the sailers *Georgiana* and *Susan Loud* and the steamer *Creole*.[17]

During late April and early May 1850, the three ships sailed independently to the Mexican island of Contoy off the coast of Yucatan, carrying López and approximately 1,000 filibusters disguised as emigrants. There they organized and proceeded to Cuba in the steamer *Creole*. Narrowly missing the overloaded steamer, the Spanish paddle-wheel frigate *Pizarro* (6 guns) and the sail brigantine *Habanero* (20 guns) captured the two sail ships as they were returning to New Orleans carrying some fifty men who had changed their minds.[18]

López planned to land at Cárdenas (85 mi E of Havana) at night and then take the town by surprise. Next, he would proceed to Matanzas, some thirty miles to the west of Cárdenas and capture it. Then one hundred men would proceed to within nine miles of Havana and destroy a key bridge on the road leading to the east. While this was being carried out, Cubans would be recruited to fill out the three skeleton regiments. Within a few days, López planned to be leading 30,000 men against Havana.[19]

López landed at Cárdenas during the evening of May 18, 1850. In the early morning hours of the nineteenth, Col. John T. Pickett (who had a $25,000 reward on his head placed there by the Captain-General of Cuba) led twenty-five men of the Kentucky "Regiment" and seized the railroad station that connected Cárdenas and Matanzas. Once the town's garrison awoke it made a stout fight until charged. The battle lasted three hours. With the town secured, López called upon the townspeople to join with them to drive the Spaniards from the island. Not a single Cuban volunteered. Spanish forces could be seen collecting on the outskirts of the town; López judged that without the anticipated uprising the cause was hopeless. His party successfully repulsed its attackers as it reboarded the *Creole*. At nine in the evening, they steamed out of the harbor, only to ground in Cárdenas Bay and be stranded helplessly for five hours.

Finally, they refloated the steamer by throwing some of their arms overboard and they made their escape. López wanted to attempt another landing, this time west of Havana, but the men were opposed. Reluctantly, López sailed for Key West, Florida (92 mi NNE of Havana). The *Creole* barely escaped into Key West, Florida, on May 20 with the Spanish war steamer *Pizarro* in hot pursuit. The citizens of Key West helped the filibusters escape from their ship and the captain of the *Pizarro* had to be content with seizing the *Creole*. The filibusters lost fourteen killed and sustained thirty wounded during the fighting on Cuba.[20]

López surrendered himself to the U.S. Attorney in Savannah, Georgia, appreciating where Southern sympathies lay; he was released on the grounds that insufficient proof existed of a conspiracy to violate U.S. neutrality laws. The legal proceedings repeated themselves in New Orleans, Louisiana, with the same result. López gained much free publicity from these court proceedings.

In response to these filibustering expeditions, Spain attempted to revive a tripartite pact proposal whereby France, Great Britain, and the United States would guarantee Spain's sovereignty over Cuba. British Foreign Secretary George Canning had made a similar proposal in 1825. The United States would have no part of this.[21]

THE BAHÍA HONDA EXPEDITION

Millard Fillmore, who succeeded to the U.S. presidency with the death of Zachary Taylor on July 9, 1850, was strongly opposed to filibustering expeditions. In a December 2 message to Congress, he declared, "We instigate no revolutions, nor suffer any hostile military expeditions to be fitted out in the United States to invade the territory or provinces of a friendly nation."[22]

Yet rumors abounded of another expedition to be led by López. In April 1851 two vessels belonging to López were seized and some Hungarian and Polish recruits arrested in New York harbor, but they were released after a mistrial. In Cuba a group of dissidents proclaimed independence on July 4, and they sought to place the island under the protection of the United States. The instigators hoped that their actions would coincide with López' return to the island.

They were premature. López, delayed by the seizures, hurriedly assembled an expedition in an attempt to take advantage of the events in Cuba. The hastily assembled filibusters were armed with condemned muskets. Many did have personal revolvers and knives. A "regiment" being raised in Kentucky had not yet arrived in New Orleans. Regardless, in early August 453 men, most of whom were ruffians, sailed from New Orleans on board the overly crowded, small steamer *Pampero*. There were Hungarian and German "regiments," thanks to the ill-fated European revolutions of 1848. López' *aide-de-camp* was the famed Hungarian soldier of fortune Maj. Louis Schlesinger.[23]

Once again, the expedition included some prominent Americans including William S. Crittenden, nephew of the Attorney General and a West Point graduate. Unaware that the Revolutionaries in Cuba had been eliminated, López sailed from New Orleans on August 3 and landed at Bahía Honda (50 mi W of Havana) on the twelfth. López chose the landing site based upon false information planted by the Spanish Captain-General.[24]

López immediately sent the *Pampero* back to Key West for reinforcements and then led 323 men inland toward Los Pozos (20 mi SW of Bahía Honda) where he anticipated that *criollos* would flock to the cause. While the *Pampero* was steaming northward, she was sighted by the *Pizarro* which rushed to Havana to spread the alert. The Spanish embarked 800 men and dispatched the *Pizarro* to Bahía Honda.[25]

In the meantime, López had proceeded inland to Los Pozos with 323 men. Colonel Crittenden, commanding 130 men, was to follow with the baggage as best he could. It took him the better part of a day to find oxen and carts before he set out to join López. The 800 Spanish troops, led by Gen. Manuel Enna, landed at Bahía Honda. They intercepted Crittenden's force on the road before it could reunite with López. Enna scattered these filibusters and then attacked López. López was driven from Los Pozos and on August 14 retreated into the mountains. Finally, he was captured on August 31. Once again, López had been disappointed by the Cubans, none of whom joined his force.[26]

The remainder of Crittenden's command tried to flee Cuba in four small fishing boats but were captured by the *Habanero*. On the orders of the Governor-General, José de la Concha, Crittenden and some fifty under his command were court-martialed and shot on August 16. López was garroted on September 1. Back in the United States, General Quitman frantically attempted to prepare the relief expedition. Those in New Orleans hesitated awaiting news from Cuba. When it did arrive, it reported the disaster which befell López. The remainder of the Cuban and American prisoners were imprisoned in Spain. Although there was a public outcry for intervention in Cuba within the United States, particularly in the South, the Filmore Administration wished to be free of the entanglement.[27]

As a result of the López expeditions, Spain in 1852 once again unsuccessfully sought to create a tripartite pact (France, Great Britain, and the United States) to guarantee Spain's sovereignty over Cuba.

OBSERVATIONS

Just prior to his execution, López shouted, "My death will not change the destiny of Cuba."[28] The inability of López to rally a Cuban following during either of his landings on Cuba suggests that annexation to the United States was not as popular among the common folk as he and a small numbers of *criollos* believed.

Americans did not abandon their quest to acquire Cuba. In October 1854 the U.S. ministers to Spain (Pierre Soulé), France (J. Y. Mason), and Great Britain (James Buchanan) wrote the Ostend Manifesto which recommended the purchase of Cuba to the American administration. They wrote that if Spain would not sell the island it should be taken. Although President Franklin Pierce rejected the manifesto, it helped elect Buchanan the fifteenth president of the United States.[29]

López' death, combined with the approaching American Civil War, did temporarily stop American citizens from attempting to change the government of Cuba by force. The filibusters failed in part because Cuba was not a weak Central American republic or a remote province of war-torn Mexico. Cuba was the most important Spanish colony in the New World and, as a consequence, was crowded with Spanish soldiers who were supported by many Cuban Conservatives and tolerated by Cubans who wished for independence and bided their time.

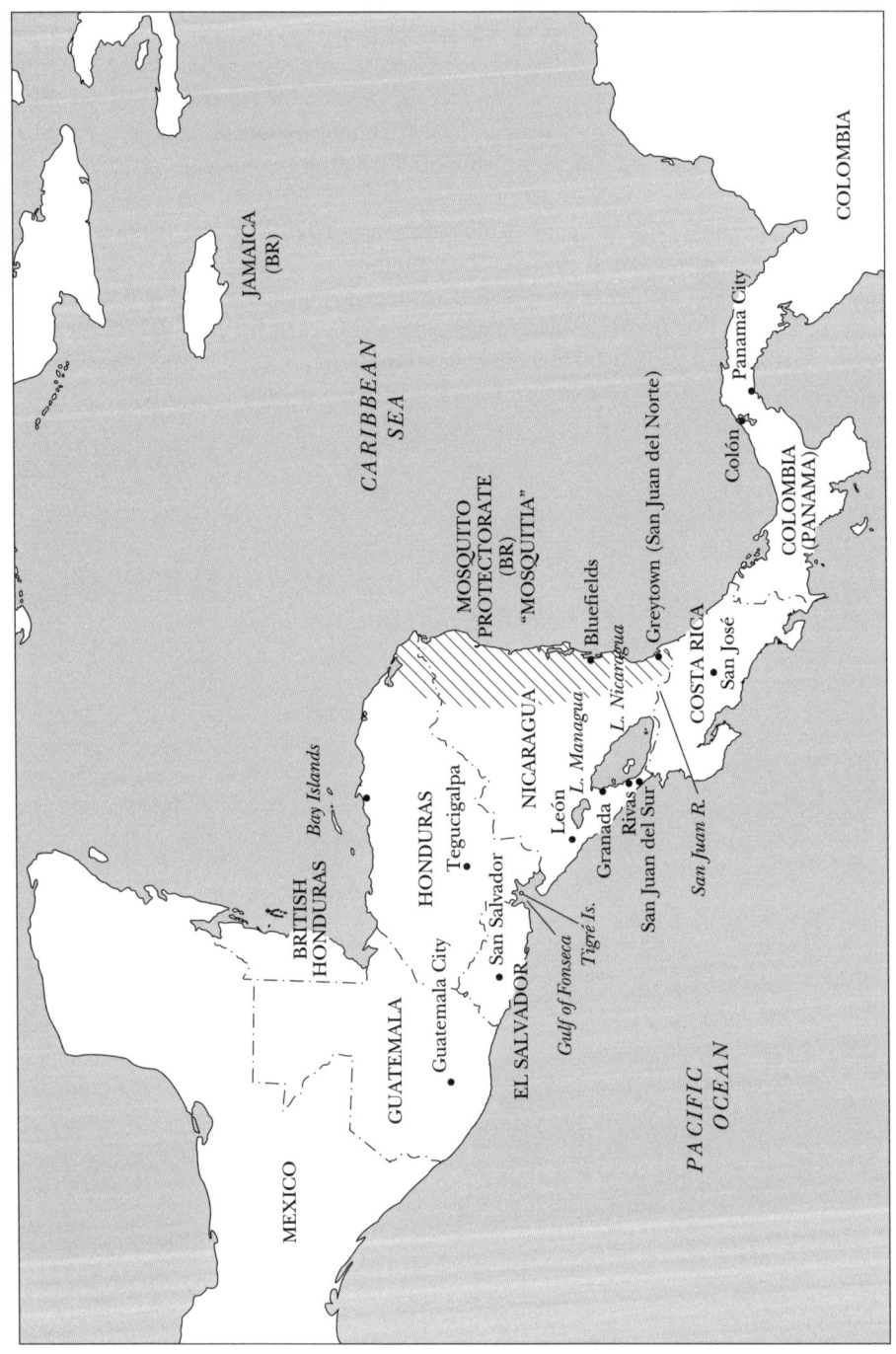

Map 6. Central America, 1855.

CHAPTER TWENTY

FILIBUSTERING AGAINST CENTRAL AMERICA, 1855–60

> Yes, citizens, I appeal to all of you, in the name of your memories of the past, and your hopes for the future, to carry on and perfect the [North] Americanization of Central America.
> —William Walker

THE SPARK

In early February 1855 Nicaraguan Liberal President Francisco Castellon contracted William Walker[1] to bring 300 "colonists" to Nicaragua whose rights included "forever the privilege of bearing arms."[2] Their presence changed the fighting in Nicaragua from a struggle between the nation's Liberals and Conservatives to one between North American filibusters and native Central Americans.

BACKGROUND

Nicaragua was the best location for a trans-isthmus crossing during the nineteenth century. By using the San Juan River and Lake Nicaragua, one could travel to within about thirty miles of the Pacific Ocean entirely by canoes and steamers. The land leg required a stagecoach ride over a macadamized road from La Virgin across the low plain of Leon to San Juan del Sur.[3] The discovery of gold in California in 1848 caused a tremendous increase in the traffic to the Pacific Coast of North America, making the control of a trans-isthmus route very lucrative. In 1849 Cornelius Vanderbilt and associates formed the Atlantic and Pacific Ship-Canal Company. When it proved impossible to dig a canal within the twelve years allocated by the contract, the agreement was modified in 1851 by which the Accessory Transit Company was awarded the concession for the transit privileges. Some 24,000 travelers used the route in 1852, the first year of its operation.[4]

Following independence, Nicaragua had not produced a stable government. The Conservatives (also called the Legitimists or the Servile party) with their southern stronghold in Granada were perpetually in conflict with the Liberals (also called the Democrats) based at Leon in the North. The two cities lay some eighty miles apart. Granada did hold a geographical advantage since the trans-isthmus route lay south of that city, which meant that in order for the Liberals from Leon to control the crossing, they had to first neutralize Granada.

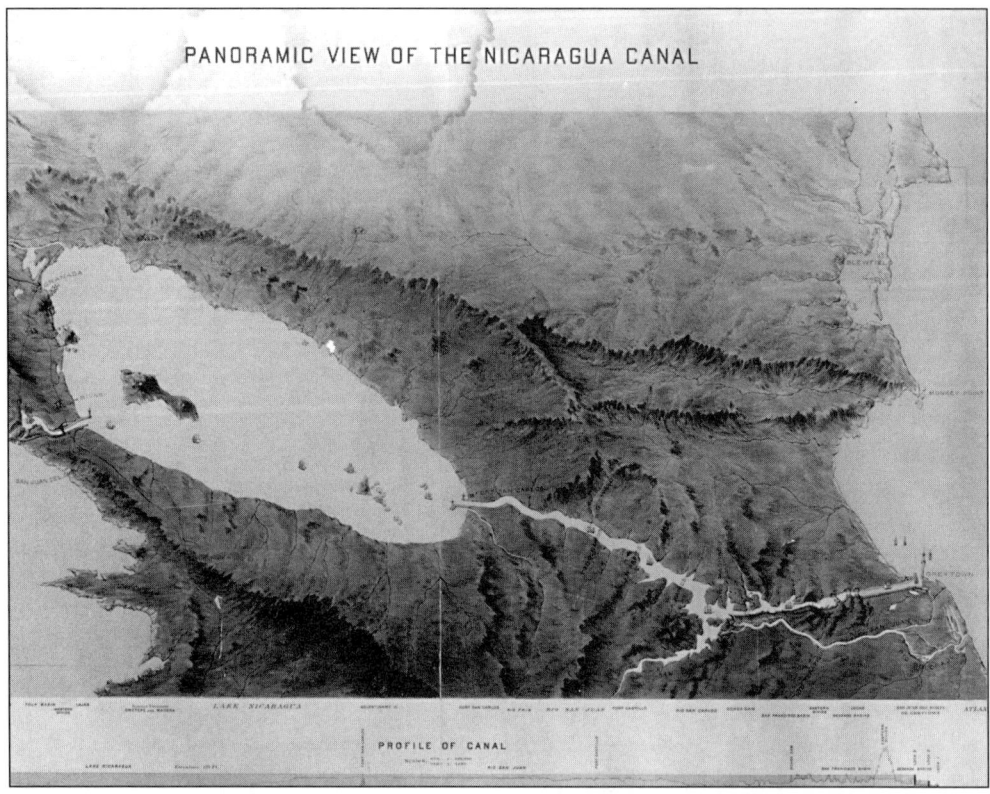

Figure 14. Filibustering against Central America, 1855–60. This panoramic view of a projected Nicaraguan canal immediately reveals the potential of a transit route across the isthmus of Central America. The San Juan River flowed from Lake Nicaragua into the Caribbean. It would need to be enhanced and the water route from the lake into the Pacific Ocean, shown on this projection, would need to be dug. One must remember that most merchant ships of the 1850s were less than 200 feet long and drew less than 8 feet of water. Such small ships would require a more modest canal that the one finally dug in Panama fifty years later. *Courtesy Library of Congress.*

The labels *Liberals* and *Conservatives* more accurately described the animosity between the two groups than their political philosophies; both groups were politically and socially conservative. Adding to regional instability and confusion was the fact that each neighboring country also had Liberal and Conservative parties which were frequently at war with each other. The "outs" in Nicaragua could find sanctuary and clandestine help from their political counterparts in Honduras or Costa Rica should they be in power, thus drawing them into Nicaragua's internal affairs and vice versa (see chapter 22).[5]

In 1854 Francisco Castellon (a Liberal) and Fruto Chamorro (a Conservative) both claimed to be president based upon their interpretation of the 1853 election. Chamorro exiled Castellon to Honduras. On April 30, 1854, Chamorro proclaimed himself president for two two-year terms. Within a week Castellon landed at Realejo with thirty-six followers. Shortly, forces loyal to Castellon drove Chamorro into the Conservative stronghold of Granada. The Liberal army was commanded by Gen. José Trinidad Muñoz, who has served under the Mexican Antonio López de Santa Anna. The Liberals seized control of Lake Nicaragua and the San Juan River and laid siege to Granada.[6]

Among those besieging Granada was an American adventurer, C. W. Doubleday, leading some thirty foreign mercenaries. By the time the siege was raised, this group had been reduced to four, primarily through disease. Doubleday then organized a native contingent of sharpshooters who covered the Liberal retreat to Leon. These mercenaries and the effectiveness of their rifles made a lasting impression upon Central American leaders.

In 1854 Byron Cole, a previous owner of the San Francisco newspaper *Commercial Adventurer* which had employed William Walker, traveled to Central America seeking business opportunities. He met with Castellon and proposed that the Liberals increase their strength by inviting a 300-man company of North Americans headed by Walker. Returning to California, Cole showed the agreement to Walker who stated that, as written, it violated the Neutrality Act of 1818 and did not provide adequate reward for the risks to be taken.

In October 1854 Cole returned to Nicaragua and Castellon agreed to increase the land grant from 21,000 to 52,000 acres and that those contracted should be called "colonists" so that Walker and his men would agree to come.[7]

OPPOSING FORCES

As with the Mexican adventure, William Walker recruited from among those who flocked to California in search of easy wealth. Although the initial number of filibusters was small—fifty-eight—Walker could expect many recruits if he were initially successful. Each of the mercenaries was responsible for his own weapons. Typically, each carried a rifle, at least one pistol, and the ubiquitous American Bowie knife. These weapons made the North Americans significantly better armed than their opponents. The filibusters did not wear uniforms. They only had a red ribbon around their hats; this made them hard to distinguish from legitimate passengers using the transit route across Nicaragua.

The Conservative and Liberal armies were each composed of a few hundred veterans; they were fit, uniformed, and armed with muskets but not rifles. The remainder were at best poorly trained militiamen.[8]

OPENING STRATEGIES

Walker intended to fight the Conservative forces immediately in open battle in order to take advantage of his highly motivated and better armed men. Apparently, the Conservatives made no preparations to confront filibusters.

CONDITIONS IN 1855

By 1855 the Liberals were hard pressed. Although the Conservative President Chamorro died on March 12 of that year and was succeeded by Senator José María Estrada, not a particularly dynamic leader, the Conservatives continued to win. They had raised the nine-month siege of Granada. Castellon's Honduran allies had abruptly departed to confront an invasion of their own country from Guatemala. The Conservatives now controlled the lakes and river. The Conservative army, commanded by Gen. Ponicano Corral, isolated the Liberals in Leon.[9]

(After an Engraving by J. C. BUTTRE, of New York)

Figure 15. Filibustering against Central America, 1855–60. William Walker—the infamous filibuster—was a gray-eyed, small, slight man (5 ft. 5 in., 140 pounds). He had sandy hair and wore it closely cut which contributed to his boyish appearance. He assumed the title of "colonel," not an uncommon practice for southern "gentlemen." In frontier California such titles earned through bravado were as acceptable as those conferred by Congress. Walker was self-confident, fearless, and a strict disciplinarian. He was short on words and long on action, winning the loyalty of "free spirits" who rarely gave it. Walker abhorred drunkenness, debauchery, and profanity. *Copied from James Roche,* The Story of the Filibusterers *(New York: Macmillan, 1891).*

WALKER SAILS FOR NICARAGUA

Unknowingly, Walker purchased a debt-incumbered, leaky brig, the *Vesta*; borrowed a thousand dollars from businessman Joseph Palmer; and recruited fifty-seven men. Outwitting a deputy sheriff who was charged with preventing his departure due to outstanding liens against the ship, Walker and his self-proclaimed "Immortals" sailed from San Francisco at one o'clock in the morning on May 4, 1855.[10]

FIRST BATTLE OF RIVAS

The 2,700-mile voyage was stormy and the filibusters arrived at Realejo, Nicaragua, on June 16. Walker was met by Liberal representatives and escorted to Leon. Walker's contingent was organized as a separate corps, *La Falange Americana* (the American Phalanx). The Americans and 100 Nicaraguans, all irregulars under Colonel [first name unknown] Ramírez, were ordered to retake Rivas, a city of 11,000 inhabitants, which was held by 600 Conservative troops. The city was located on Lake Nicaragua (50 mi S of Leon) and straddled the transit route. The Liberal force was carried down the coast in the *Vesta* and landed near the town of Brito. After a two-day march they overwhelmed the enemy pickets at the village of Tola. On June 28 the Americans attacked Rivas, while the Nicaraguans under Colonel Ramírez were held in reserve. The Americans successfully fought their way to the central plaza. Walker, now hard pressed, called for the reserves only to find that those under Colonel Ramírez had fled. The enemy perceived the defection and drove the filibusters into some adobe huts where they held out for three hours. Walker, finding his casualties mounting, ordered a retreat. The Conservatives chose not to pursue. The mercenaries lost six dead. Among the dead were the second in command Lt. Col. Achilles Kewen, who had been with López in Cuba, and the third in command Maj. Timothy Crocker, who had been with Walker in Mexico. Also, a dozen were wounded, among them Doubleday. The Conservatives lost 150 killed and wounded.[11]

Returning to Realejo on board the *Vesta*, Walker's band then proceeded to Leon. There, Walker demanded better guarantees of support, upon which the Liberal cabinet could not agree. Complicating Castellon's position, Gen. J. Trinidad Muñoz was openly hostile toward the filibusters. Hence, Walker withdrew to Realejo. He embarked in the *Vesta* under the pretext of sailing for Honduras to offer his services to President José Cabañas.

Meanwhile, the Conservatives under Ponciano Corral with their Honduran allies led by Santos Guardiola[12] were nearing Leon. Muñoz, leading 600 men, defeated the Conservatives at the Battle of Sauce, but Muñoz was killed.[13]

The Liberal leadership pleaded with Walker to return. He was accompanied by Byron Cole, the person who had suggested the expedition, and Baron Bruno von Natzmer, a former Prussian cavalry officer. Shrewdly, Cole negotiated a new contract which Walker then interpreted to his advantage. Without the permission of the Liberal leadership, Walker began a second campaign to capture the transit route. Among those joining Walker were the Nicaraguan *mestizo* José María Vallé and his 120 followers. On August 23 the *Vesta* sailed for San Juan del Sur, the Pacific terminus of the Accessory Transit Company's route, arriving on the twenty-ninth. The Conservatives fled without fighting.[14]

About this time Walker captured Parker H. French, a Californian apparently in the employment of the Conservatives. Claiming to be a spy working against the Conservatives and boasting of great influence with the American entrepeneur Cornelius K. Garrison, Walker accepted

Figure 16. Filibustering against Central America, 1855–60. In this drawing of the Battle of Rivas, Nicaragua (June 28, 1855), Walker's American filibusters appear to be wearing uniforms. The prime source for the illustration, and many others of nineteenth-century Latin American battles, was the artists' imaginations. In fact, Walker's followers had no distinctive dress. Their only uniformity was red ribbons tied around their black "slouch" hats. In spite of the hot, humid climate, they wore woolen shirts, usually blue or red; coarse trousers; and heavy boots. Each was armed with at least a rifle, a revolver, and a Bowie knife. *Copied from Frank Leslie's Illustrated Newspaper, May 17, 1856.*

French's offer to help without questioning French's motivation. Walker sent French back to California to gather money and recruits.[15]

BATTLE OF VIRGIN BAY

After a four-day delay at San Juan del Sur, Walker started toward Rivas where he believed Guardiola waited with 600 Conservatives. Guardiola instead made a forced march and fell upon Walker on September 3 from the front and flank at Virgin Bay on Lake Nicaragua. Outnumbered five to one, Walker took up a defensive position and the Nicaraguans loyal to Vallé fought well. Although Guardiola's men fought bravely, they finally gave way under the accuracy of the American marksmanship. The battle that took place on September 3 lasted only two hours. The Conservatives lost 60 killed and 100 wounded. On the Liberal side, three Nicaraguans were killed and a few Americans wounded, including Walker and Doubleday. Guardiola fell back to Rivas.[16]

On October 3, 1855, French returned from San Francisco to San Juan del Sur on board the Accessory Transit steamer *Cortes* bringing thirty-five volunteers. Among these were the one-legged Col. Charles Gilman, who had lost the limb under Walker in the Sonora expedition, and Capt. George R. Davidson, another veteran of that campaign. Also on board was C. J. McDonald, the confidential agent of Cornelius Garrison, the San Francisco manager of the Accessory Transit Company. What agreement McDonald made with Walker is unknown. Walker did get immediate possession of the company's steamer *La Virgin*, which had been assembled on Lake Nicaragua and drew too much water to be able to sail down the San Juan River to the Caribbean.[17]

BATTLE OF GRANADA

Walker now learned of the death of Castellon from cholera; Castellon was succeeded by Masario Escoto. The new Liberal president congratulated Walker on his victory at Virgin Bay and promised help. Through intercepted letters, Walker learned that the Conservative capital, Granada, was almost defenseless. On October 11 Walker began his advance along the Transit road to Virgin Bay with 150 Americans and 250 Nicaraguans supported by two small cannons. The Conservatives were in disarray; Guardiola and Corral quarreled over command. Corral, who won control, believed that Walker was marching into a trap and devoted his energies to blocking Walker's route of retreat back to San Juan del Sur.

Walker's force boarded the transit steamer *La Virgin*. While Granada slept following a fiesta, *La Virgin* steamed slowly toward the lakeside city. Finally, the city awakened, but it was too late. Walker and Vallé led the assault. The surprised garrison made a fleeting stand in the plaza, but was soon swept aside. Apparently the only casualty on either side was a drummer boy! Walker now held the families of many prominent Conservatives hostage. Restraining his men from plundering, Walker organized a provisional government.[18]

Meanwhile, Parker French seized one of the lake steamers and led a freelance attack on Fort San Carlos at the head of the San Juan River. The filibusters were easily repulsed. In reprisal, Conservative soldiers attacked New York-bound passengers awaiting transit at Virgin Bay; a half-dozen people were killed. Shortly afterward, Fort San Carlos fired into a westbound steamer, killing more passengers. Perhaps the soldiers mistook these passengers for filibusters. The Conservatives, who still held Rivas and the fort, ignored protests from the U.S. government. In retaliation, Walker court-martialled the Conservative secretary of state, Mateo

Mayorgo, who had been captured at Granada, and executed him. The message was not lost upon Conservative General Corral, and he immediately sued for peace.[19]

WALKER FORMS A NEW ADMINISTRATION

Walker and Corral, with the nominal sanctions from the Liberal and Conservative presidents, came to terms on October 23, 1855. Patricio Rivas (a moderate Conservative) was named president; Parker French, Minister of *Hacienda*; Ponciano Correl, Minister of War; and William Walker *generalissimo* of the army. The army was composed of 1,200 men, mostly filibusters. Five hundred men were stationed at Leon and the reminder at Virgin Bay, Granada, Rivas, and other strategic points.[20]

Within a few days Walker intercepted letters written by Corral to Conservative refugees and Guardiola imploring them to take up arms against the Americans; Walker consequently executed Corral on November 7. This caused many Conservatives to flee from Nicaragua.[21]

Walker needed money and replacements. McDonald immediately advanced him $20,000 in gold. This was accomplished by extracting the amount from a shipment of bullion bound from California. Every steamer from California brought in a handful of recruits. The Accessory Transit Company steamers carried recruits from New York and San Francisco without charge. These volunteers swelled Walker's force by hundreds and further indebted him to the company.[22]

By early 1856 the Falange contingent had grown to some 1,200 men. Among them were some 300 Cubans led by Francisco Alejandro Laine and D. Domingo de Goicouria. Walker promised the Cubans that he would allow them to use Nicaraguan territory to organize an expedition against the Spanish in Cuba.[23]

By now the filibusters were organized into two battalions, the "Rifles" and the "Light Infantry." No uniforms were prescribed but insignias were sewn on the left shirt pocket. Many in the Rifles battalion were armed with Sharps repeaters, and typically those in the Light Infantry carried smoothbore muskets. Most were also armed with Colt revolvers and Bowie knives.[24]

Walker unknowingly became entangled in a power struggle within the Accessory Transit Company. The Company's agents who had financed him, J. P. Morgan and Garrison, wanted to take control of the company from Vanderbilt. Making Walker a partner, they convinced him to persuade Rivas to revoke the company's charter and issue a new one to the conspirators.[25] Vanderbilt was furious. First he sought the help of the U.S. government, which refused to become involved. Next he sent Hosea Birdsall to seize transit property in Greytown, but Walker's influence was too great.[26]

Back in the United States, the Franklin Pierce administration issued a proclamation warning Americans against filibustering in Nicaragua, but this had little effect.[27] The Pierce administration refused to recognize the first representative of the Rivas government, Parker H. French, because of the transparency of his allegiance,[28] as well as the second, Fiamin Ferrer. By now, President Rivas was merely a figurehead and Walker was making major decisions. Incensed at the U.S. decision, Walker severed diplomatic dealings with the American Minister in Granada.

Those opposed to Walker began to unite. Walker intercepted a letter from the Costa Rican consul-general in London to that nation's president, José Rafael Mora, stating that Great Britain would sell Costa Rica 2,000 muskets at a nominal price for the purpose of "kicking Walker and his associates out of Nicaragua." And Vanderbilt helped finance the campaign.[29]

Walker, now appreciating the need for the Nicaraguan representative in Washington to at least appear to represent the Nicaraguans, chose Father Augustín Vijil (former curate at

Granada) as the next envoy to be sent to Washington. Pierce, under domestic pressure in part caused by the British offer to supply arms to Costa Rica, accepted his credentials although Father Vijil soon returned from Washington due to its diplomatic coolness.[30]

COSTA RICA DECLARES WAR

On February 26, 1856, Costa Rica declared a war of "no quarter" on Nicaragua expressly to drive the filibusters out. Peru, sympathizing with the action, loaned $100,000 to Costa Rica.[31] Nicaraguan President Rivas immediately declared war on Costa Rica. Col. Louis Schlesinger led 200 recently recruited filibusters across the border into Costa Rica on March 19.[32] The next day, 500 Costa Ricans led by the Costa Rican President, General Mora, and the Prussian Baron Bruno von Natzmer, surprised the filibusters at Hacienda of Santa Rosa some 30 miles from the town of Liberia, Costa Rica, and easily defeated them. Those filibusters captured were executed including the wounded. The filibusters lost fifty men.[33]

SECOND BATTLE OF RIVAS

Misfortunes mounted for Walker. The news of the defeat disheartened the Nicaraguan Liberals and sparked the Conservatives to plot against Walker. The Honduran Guardiola began to amass troops along Nicaragua's northern border. Walker came down with the fever. Some 2,500 Costa Ricans overran southern Nicaragua. On April 11 Mora attacked Rivas, catching Walker by surprise. The filibusters defended a number of well-fortified positions, including a large house known as the "War Inn" (*Mesón de Guerra*). The Costa Rican soldier Juan Santamaría rushed the building, setting it on fire; he was shot dead, but the filibusters were forced to retreat. They took refuge in a church, and that night managed to escape. The Costa Ricans sustained 800 casualties in the assault. Costa Rican soldiers executed nine employees of the Transitory Company and burned the company's warehouses. The Transit Company steamers suspended operations, and Walker lost communication with California. No longer required to protect the transit route, Walker retreated to Granada.[34]

A few days after the Battle of Rivas, cholera broke out in the Costa Rican army and spread into its homeland. President Mora immediately returned to the capital, San José, leaving Gen. José María Cañas in charge. In April Cañas retreated back to Liberia, Costa Rica, abandoning the campaign. Only 400 men out of the 2,500 who had invaded Nicaragua lived to return home. Some 10,000 Costa Ricans out of a population of 112,000 died from the epidemic.[35]

WALKER ELECTS HIMSELF PRESIDENT

On June 29, 1856, Walker elected himself President of Nicaragua and the U.S. Minister, John H. Wheeler, immediately recognized the new government. The Pierce administration censured the minister and refused to receive Walker's representative.[36] Walker repealed the Constitution of 1838, thereby abrogating the abolishment of slavery and gaining additional support from proslavery elements within the United States.

THE NATIONAL WAR AGAINST WALKER

In late 1856 El Salvador, Guatemala, and Honduras joined forces to depose Walker. They recognized Rivas, who had fled Nicaragua, as the provisional Nicaraguan president. The allies advanced against Walker's capital, Granada. Walker chose not to defend the well-fortified city of Masaya which lay just northwest of Granada, and withdrew into the capital. He then changed his mind and led a frontal assault against Masaya, which the allies had occupied. Walker then learned that the allies had slipped behind him and had captured Granada on October 13. Walker abandoned the attack on Masaya and recaptured Granada instead.

At this time the famous soldier of fortune Charles Frederick Henningsen[37] joined Walker. Henningsen brought with him several thousand Minié rifles and some howitzers, gifts from his wife, the niece of Senator John Berrien of Georgia. This bolstered the moral of the filibusters. Walker made Henningsen second in command! Within a month Walker rebounded. The Salvadoran and Guatemalan leaders argued over future operations. Also, the allies failed to cut the transit route across Nicaragua, thus, Walker continued to receive reinforcements.[38]

COSTA RICA REJOINS THE FIGHT

With the ending of the cholera epidemic, President Mora renewed the fight against Walker. General Cañas led 400 men into Nicaragua, capturing San Juan del Sur and Rancho Grande from Nicaraguan Liberals who supported Walker in November 1856 where he was joined by Nicaraguan Conservatives opposed to Walker. With lightning speed, Walker counterattacked at Rancho Grande and Cañas was abandoned by his Nicaraguan Conservative allies. The Costa Rican soldiers retreated in disarray, failing to hold either San Juan del Sur or Rivas.[39]

THE WAR AT SEA

While these events were transpiring on land, Walker's lone warship, the schooner *Granada* (2 guns), commanded by Lt. Callender Irvine Fayssoux[40] intercepted on November 22 the Costa Rican brigantine *Once de Abril* (4 guns) in the Gulf of Fonseca. It was crowded with men and supplies for General Cañas' army ashore. After a four-hour fight, the magazine of the *Once de Abril* exploded, destroying the schooner.[41]

VANDERBILT TAKES HIS REVENGE

At this point Vanderbilt interceded against Walker, having failed to eliminate Walker by indirect means. Vanderbilt sent a mercenary force under R. C. Webster, an Englishman, and Sylvannius H. Spencer, an American, to interrupt the trans-isthmus traffic. This would compel the transit company to suspend operations and cut off Walker's source of reinforcements. On December 16, 1856, some 120 mercenaries and Costa Ricans commanded by [first name unknown] Barillier descended in canoes and rafts the San Carlos River to its junction with the San Juan River. There, they surprised a garrison of fifty men. Then the attackers continued down the San Carlos River to Greytown, which they captured on December 22 along with four river steamers. Subsequently, they steamed up the San Carlos River with 800 more Costa Ricans on board, commanded by the Costa Rican President, General Mora, and armed with state-of-the-art Minié muskets using fixed ammunition. These had been supplied by Vanderbilt. Mora captured Forts Castillo Viego and San Carlos which guarded the east entrance to Lake Nicaragua. He also seized two lake steamers at Hipps Point. This cut Walker off from the Caribbean.[42]

BURNING GRANADA

By November 3,000 Guatemalans, Salvadorans, and Nicaraguans gathered at Masaya (10 mi NW of Granada) and were preparing to attack Granada again. Walker marched north from the capital with 560 men. Halfway to Masaya, Walker learned that some of the enemy were sent south to join the remnants of the Costa Rican army to attack Rivas. This threatened to cut the transit route once again. Walker split his force, sending half south, and with the remainder he continued against Masaya. For two days Walker unsuccessfully attacked Masaya, losing to death and wounds some 150 men. Walker then retreated to Granada.[43]

Walker next decided to burn Granada to the ground and retreat southward where he could better defend the transit route. Walker sent his sick and wounded to Ometepe Island and left 227 filibusters commanded by Henningsen behind to destroy the capital, home of 70,000 Nicaraguans. In the process of doing so, Henningsen's men stopped to drink confiscated liquor, and soon became trapped by the advancing allies. The filibusters fought their way into the church of Guadalupe, a strong structure which dominated the potential escape avenue to Lake Nicaragua. For seventeen days the filibusters held out against almost uninterrupted attacks. All Walker could do was watch from on board his lake steamer, *La Virgin*.[44]

Serendipitously in early December, 300 well-armed recruits joined Walker from New Orleans and San Francisco. Col. John Waters led 160 men back into Granada. The filibusters created an escape corridor to the lake. On December 14 Henningsen escaped with 111 men, many of whom were wounded.[45]

By January 1, 1857, Walker's position was stalemated. He held Rivas with about 1,000 filibusters, of whom only 200 were not on the sick list. But Vanderbilt and Mora controlled the San Carlos River, the route to the Caribbean.

In February, 500 well-armed filibusters landed at Greytown and attempted to fight their way across the isthmus to join Walker. First they attacked La Trinidad defended by Costa Ricans under Máximo Blanco, but were repulsed. Next they attacked Castillo Viejo defended by 37 men under Col. George Cauty. Cauty held on until reinforcements arrived from Fort San Carlos. The filibusters were unable to fight their way through the Costa Ricans.[46]

Also in February, President Mora of Costa Rica offered protection and passage home to all who would desert Walker. In April Garrison and Morgan suspended ocean steamer service to the coasts since Vanderbilt's mercenaries controlled the lake steamers.[47]

The Central American allies persistently harassed Walker's position at Rivas. On April 11 the allies attempted an all-out attack but were repulsed. Meanwhile, a steamer captured by Vanderbilt's mercenaries anchored near the Ometepe Volcano in full view of Walker's forces at Rivas. Walker still had the transit company's steamer *Granada* at San Juan del Sur on the Pacific Ocean and believed he could escape on that ship if the situation became untenable. However, Capt. Charles H. Davis, commander of the U.S. sloop *St Marys* (20 guns), threatened to seize the *Granada*, potentially eliminating the escape ship. Walker's following now numbered only 463 men, half of whom were either sick or wounded. Walker surrendered to Davis on May 1, 1857, and was taken back to the United States for trial. Thus ended Walker's first Nicaraguan filibustering expedition.[48]

Six armies were now afoot in Nicaragua: those of Guatemala, El Salvador, and Honduras in the North; Costa Rica in the South; and those of the Nicaraguan Liberals and Conservatives. The Conservatives led by Gen. Tomás Martínez and the Liberals led by Maximo Jeréz were preparing to renew their civil war. However, Costa Rica, led by General Mora, refused to evacuate the south bank of the San Juan River. Martínez and Jeréz agreed to a joint dictatorship and prepared for war against Costa Rica; this was forestalled by Walker's return to Nicaragua.[49]

WALKER RETURNS TO NICARAGUA

In September 1857 the representatives of Costa Rica, Guatemala, and El Salvador in Washington informed Secretary of State Lewis Case that William Walker was preparing another filibustering expedition. Walker was arrested; soon released on bail, he and 270 filibusters sailed from New Orleans for Nicaragua on November 14, 1857. This time his financial support came from proslavery Southerners.[50]

On November 24 Walker landed a detachment below Greytown. Commanded by Col. Frank Anderson, within a few weeks these filibusters surprised the Costa Ricans manning the forts guarding the entrance to Lake Nicaragua. In the meantime, Walker dashed into Greytown on the steamer *Fashion* and landed the remainder of his men right under the guns of the American sloop *Saratoga* (20 guns). However, on December 6 the U.S. steam frigate *Wabash* (40 guns), commanded by Commodore Hiram Paulding, arrived. Paulding, using his overwhelming force, arrested Walker and brought him back to the United States. President James Buchanan, caught on the horns of the slavery dilemma, censured Commodore Paulding for violating Nicaraguan sovereignty but stated also that Walker's expedition was a crime and a hinderance to the conduct of foreign affairs in Central America.[51]

WALKER FILIBUSTERS AGAINST HONDURAS

Although this ended Walker's filibustering against Nicaragua, he attempted another expedition, this time against Honduras. Early in 1860 an inhabitant of one of the Bay Islands invited Walker to prevent the island's transfer from Great Britain to Honduras. Upon arriving with a small band, Walker found that the British flag was still flying. After a few weeks of waiting, Walker seized the fortress Trujillo on the mainland from Honduran troops. During the confusion, $3,000 of British custom's receipts disappeared. Within a few days, Commander Norvell Salmon of the British wooden steam sloop *Icarus* (11 guns) sent Walker a note telling him that his occupation was not in the best interests of the British government and that he must withdraw. Walker tried to escape but was soon surrounded by the Hondurans. On September 5 Walker surrendered to the British on the condition that he be turned over to American authorities. Salmon broke his promise and Walker was given to the Hondurans at Trujillo. He was executed on September 12, 1860, by firing squad.[52]

OBSERVATIONS

William Walker's name will live in infamy throughout Central America, having become synonymous with North American arrogance and greed. Although the underlying cause for Walker's activity was unrestrained do-it-yourself American expansionism, the significant degree of his success may be attributed to the rivalry among financial giants such as Cornelius Vanderbilt for the control of the transit across Nicaragua. The Walker expeditions demonstrated the unrestrained political and military activities of these industrialists. Following Walker's demise, the hostile competition among the industrialists effectively prevented the reopening of the Nicaraguan route and it was soon superseded in importance by the trans-Panama railroad which had begun service in 1855.

Walker's activities also showed the influence of the slavery issue upon U.S. foreign policy. Although the United States had adequate laws to prevent and to punish filibustering, they were unenforceable because many in the South chose to ignore them.

U.S. expansionism during the mid-nineteenth century, including Walker's activities, caused representatives of Chile, Peru, and Ecuador to meet in Santiago, Chile, during 1856 to discuss how to deal with the United States. However, they could not find a solution.

Out of perhaps 2,500 mercenaries who fought under Walker's leadership, more than 1,000 died, mostly from disease. The number of deaths sustained by the Central Americans due to Walker's activities was undoubtedly many times greater.[53]

The image of the Nicaraguan Liberal party was so badly tarnished by its association with Walker that the Conseratives held power until 1893. Nicaragua conceded disputed territory to Costa Rica, giving it the south bank of the San Juan River, and thus joint interest in any trans-isthmus route using that river, in consideration for future aid against filibusters.[54]

PART 6

THE AGE OF THE *CAUDILLO* IN MID-AMERICA

CHAPTER TWENTY-ONE

THE STRUGGLE AMONG VENEZUELA'S *CAUDILLOS*, 1830–1903

> The nations of our America will fall into the hands of vulgar, petty tyrants.
> —Simón Bolívar

THE SPARK

The inability of *caudillos* to subordinate their personal ambitions to the good of the new Venezuelan nation, which had been created on January 13, 1830, when it seceded from Gran Colombia, kept the nation in almost perpetual turmoil for the next seventy-four years.

BACKGROUND

The War for Independence (see chapter 2) within Venezuela broke the political ties to Spain; annihilated the dominant *criollo* class; created *caudillos* who considered themselves the creators and definers of the nation; and devastated the economy. Mines were flooded, farms burned, and the population displaced throughout the nation as Revolutionaries, royalists, and neutrals alike tried to find havens from reprisals and banditry. Immediately following independence, merchants engaged in export began to financially recover but by 1840 an economic crisis again gripped the entire country.[1]

Caudillos emerged as the fundamental power brokers of the new republic. They competed for power through shifting alliances with groups such as the merchants, large landholders, the ecclesiastic hierarchy, and the new military. The strongest *caudillo* to emerge from the War for Independence was José Antonio Páez. Among many successes, he was the hero of the decisive Battle of Carabobo (June 24, 1821). He was handed control of the government. Within Venezuela he was the great patriarch of independence, a status enhanced with the death of Simón Bolívar on December 17, 1830. Páez governed through his reputation, his prowess with the lance, and coalitions among the regional *caudillos*, the Conservatives (also known as *Godos*[2]) and Liberals (also called *Amarillos* or Yellows) who mostly lived in Caracas.

Venezuela's geography made national cohesion difficult during the nineteenth century. The tropical coast, which was home to the majority of the people, was the center of economic life during the early decades while cacao remained the dominant export. The sparsely populated Andean highlands in the southwest became increasingly important beginning in the 1830s with the development of coffee plantations. The central third of Venezuela, the great treeless plains known as the *llanos*, was home to cattle and fiercely independent plainsmen (*llaneros*). The south, known as Guayana, made up almost half of Venezuela and was mostly unpopulated jungle.[3]

OPPOSING FORCES

Young Venezuela had many enemies. The most brazen *caudillos* wanted to become "king of the hill" and make themselves presidents. Local *caudillos*, possessing only regional appeal, championed secessionist movements. And, foreign nations coveted Venezuelan wealth and territory.

The population of Venezuela in 1831 was about one million people. About fifty percent were mixed blood, thirty percent white, and the remainder black of whom about 50,000 were slaves. By the beginning of the twentieth century the population had increased to about 2.5 million persons. The population was concentrated along the coast and in the highlands bordering New Granada (the name adopted by Gran Colombia following the secession of Venezuela and Ecuador). Strong feelings of regionalism existed among the dispersed population pockets.[4]

The Constitution of 1830, which promoted a central government, established an army, a navy, and a national militia. All were very weak. The force totalled a mere 2,683 men.[5]

The army lacked cohesion due to class stratification and regionalism. Soldiers were conscripted and obligated to work. Those who did not comply were brutally punished. Their food was awful and uniforms and equipment were almost nonexistent. In 1827 and 1828 food mutinies occurred at a number of barracks.[6]

The weapons used until the middle of the nineteenth century were those employed during the War for Independence, most of which had their origins in the colonial era. Possibly the most common flintlock musket was the British Baker Model 1802. By the early 1860s the percussion-cap muskets showed up on the battlefields. The "needle" rifle was introduced in 1870 in small numbers. And, in about 1890 the government chose the 8mm Mauser as the standard rifle. The cavalry remained the dominant arm well into the nineteenth century and continued to use the lance as its primary weapon. The cannons were a hodge podge of indigenously produced ordnance intended to be mounted in coastal fortifications. Modern ordnance did not appear on the battlefield until the late 1860s.[7]

In 1830 the navy possessed bases at Puerto Cabello, Maracaibo, and Guayana on the Orinoco River, and seventeen warships.[8] This was a hollow force since the ships were poorly maintained and their skeleton crews inadequately trained. By 1845 the navy had deteriorated to the point that the Minister of War and Navy was humorously referred to as "the Minister of War and Schooner."[9]

The national militia was the reserve for the army. Additionally, it provided local defense, and recruited and trained men for the army. The militia was divided into active and local units. By 1834 there was a marine militia made up of four companies.[10]

The real military power rested with the *caudillos* and their lance-wielding, mounted frontiersmen. The *caudillos* jealously held onto the top military ranks, rewards they had earned during the War for Independence. The *llaneros*, like the Argentine *gauchos* and the Mexican *vaqueros*, were excellent horsemen accustomed to living off the land and to settling disputes by force. A *caudillo* could add to his following by defeating a rival and absorbing his followers. Armies rarely exceeded a few thousand men until the 1860s.[11]

OPENING STRATEGIES

Typically, a rebellious *caudillo* would rally lesser *caudillos* and their plainsmen to his banner and then ride to Caracas to depose the president. The president, also a *caudillo*, would also rally his *caudillos* and plainsmen and ride out to defeat the rebels before they could threaten the capital. Since there were many *caudillos*, and therefore many small armies, decisive battles were difficult to orchestrate.[12]

THE "BOLIVARIANS" REBEL

Páez' leadership was almost immediately challenged by the "Bolivarians," who professed Bolívar's concept of a federation among the new republics. Many "Bolívarians" were veterans who had fought in the War for Independence beyond the boundaries of their native provinces.

On January 15, 1831, local *caudillos* led the inhabitants of the city of Aragua de Barcelona (196 mi ESE of Caracas) into rebellion against the new government, demanding the reestablishment of Gran Colombia and the return of ecclesiastical and military privileges. Influenced by the powerful, local *caudillos*, the brothers José Tadeo Monagas[13] and José Gregorio Monagas,[14] the rebels limited their demands to reestablishing the special privileges.[15]

By April, when José Antonio Páez was sworn in as president, the rebels remained defiant. Accordingly, Páez ordered the Secretary of War, Gen. Santiago Mariño,[16] to lead a campaign first through the Tuy Valley and then against the city of Aragua de Barcelona. Mariño, without consulting Páez, marched directly against the city. There, Mariño confronted a force led by José Gregorio Monagas. Suspicious of Mariño's motives, Páez took command of the army away from Mariño.[17]

On May 13 Mariño deserted the government and joined the Monagas brothers. They declared that before they would recognize the government of Venezuela and the authority of Páez, the Venezuelan Congress would have to agree to a new "independent" state within eastern Venezuela called "Colombia" (not to be confused with the former Gran Colombia or the future nation of Colombia) in which Mariño would be governor (more accurately, chief executives of states were called presidents) and José Tadeo Monagas second in command. Also, the military and ecclesiastical privileges and all military promotions, which had been granted during the War for Independence, would have to be reinstated. The Congress rejected the proposal and dismissed Mariño. José Tadeo Monagas, appreciating the weakness of his position, negotiated a truce on June 23, 1831, in the Valle de la Pascua. The rebels recognized the constitution and the government guaranteed their lives and property.[18]

WAR OF THE "REFORMS"

In April 1834 a civilian, Dr. José María Vargas, won the presidency, defeating General of the Division Carlos Soublette,[19] the candidate sponsored by Páez. In February of the following year, Páez peacefully handed over the reigns of government and retired to his ranch. In the meantime, the *caudillos* had further polarized into two political camps, the "Anti-Bolivarians" and the "Bolivarians," now called "Reformers." The Reformers sought to restore the federation with New Granada (formerly Gran Colombia); to reorganize Venezuela into federal states; to recognize Catholicism as the state religion; and to declare that only those who had fought in the War for Independence should be employed by the government.

On June 7, 1835, the Reformers rebelled in Maracaibo (416 mi W of Caracas) and declared General Mariño their leader; within a few days the government successfully crushed the rebellion. However, on July 7 "Reformer" Generals Diego Ibarra, Pedro Briceño Méndez, and Justo Briceño led an uprising in Caracas; that night Lt. Col. Pedro Carujo,[20] leading the presidential guard and the Anzoátegui Battalion, arrested President Vargas. On the tenth the President and Vice President, Andrés Narvarte, were exiled to the island of St. Thomas.

The revolt spread rapidly. Garrisons in Valencia, Maracaibo, Puerto Cabello, Cumaná, and Barquisimeto declared for the "Reformers." General José Tadeo Monagas led the rebels in the east. Within the navy, the sailors at Puerto Cabello rebelled but those at Maracaibo and Guayana remained loyal to the government.[21]

Before being captured, Vargas had designated Páez as the commander of the army and navy and had charged him with the responsibility of reestablishing constitutional order. On July 15 Páez rode out of his ranch at the head of fifty men. As he trekked the 120 miles to Caracas, his following swelled and the Reformers abandoned the capital, which Páez entered on the twenty-eighth. One month later, on August 28, Vargas returned to Caracas and resumed the presidency. However, the east and the ports of Maracaibo and Puerto Cabello remained in the hands of the rebels.[22]

In the east the government's ground forces, led by Páez, and its naval forces, commanded by Capt. Pedro Dautant, defeated the rebels within two months. General Monagas and his followers were pardoned on November 3, 1835. This left the ports of Maracaibo and Puerto Cabello in the hands of the rebels.[23]

At Maracaibo the rebels controlled the land and the government the sea. Commander Felipe Baptista enforced a rigorous blockade which closed the port and Lake Maracaibo. At the end of October, the rebels, led by Col. Francisco María Faría, dislodged the fleet's toehold ashore. Also, numerous sailors deserted to the Reformers. In early November Baptista attacked the rebels' fortifications and small flotilla but was beaten back. A new government fleet of three warships, commanded by Capt. Sebastián Bouguier and carrying 500 infantry commanded by General of the Division Mariano Montilla, recaptured Maracaibo on January 1, 1836.[24]

This left only Puerto Cabello (121 mi W of Caracas) in the hands of the Reformers. General Páez, who was at Valencia, marched to Puerto Cabello and placed it under siege on December 17, 1835. A government naval squadron composed of the former American brigantine *Stag* and three armed schooners under the command of Capt. Nicolás Joly,[25] blockaded the port. During an engagement on December 24, Colonel Carujo was severely wounded, captured, and soon died. General Mariño, appreciating that the rebels were losing control of the port, decided to carry the fight to the government. Commanding a fleet of four small craft, he ran the blockade. However, during the night of January 8, 1836, three of the rebel craft deserted and surrendered to the government. Marino fled to Curaçao on board the schooner *Eloisa*. Back in Puerto Cabello, rebel generals Diego Ibarra and Francisco Carabaño y Ponce and Rear Adm. Renato Beluche[26] surrendered on March 1 along with 23 political chiefs, 38 officers and 447 soldiers. The rebellion had lasted 267 days.[27]

Most of the rebellious junior officers, sergeants, soldiers, and sailors were pardoned and some were re-incorporated into the military service. All of the leaders were exiled for life. Other officers, who were sympathetic to the Reformers but had not participated in the revolt, were removed from public office. Due to the light punishment handed out to the rebels and his disagreements with Congress, Vargas renounced the presidency in April 1836 and Vice President Narvarte completed his term, which ended on January 20, 1837.

Peace did not come to Venezuela. In April 1836 Col. Francisco Farfán rebelled at Apure, but Páez defeated him on July 9. In January 1837 the garrison in Guayana rebelled, proclaimed a Reformist agenda, and chose General Mariño, then in exile, as its leader. The leaders of the Reformers, who were exiled throughout the Caribbean, sailed for Venezuela on board the schooners *Ana Celestina* (unk guns) and *Petit Canal* (unk guns) with the intention of landing on the western coast.[28] However, the government schooners *Constitución* (unk guns) and *Carlota* (unk guns) drove them off. Subsequently, Páez defeated the rebels from Guayana at the battle of Payara on April 26.[29]

Following the defeat of the Reformers, the military branches were significantly reduced. In 1836 the Congress decreed that the army should be composed of 105 officers and 2,530 men. In fact it only reached 1,595 men. Fortifications were ordered demolished since they had provided havens for the rebels and were expensive to maintain. One artillery detachment was maintained in Caracas to defend the city. By February 1838 the navy operated only four ships, the brigantine *Páez* and the schooners *Constitución*, *Urica*, and *28 de Julio*.[30]

Despite armed uprisings, which were put down without undue brutality, generally the nation was at peace (except on the *llanos* where banditry continued) during the next ten years. Administration was honest, did not violate the constitution (which was conservative), and was not repressive. By 1846 the Venezuelan army was reduced to insignificance. Although 1,050 officers and men were authorized, only 423 were in service. Venezuela had a one-ship navy manned by less than sixty men. Although the military received 21.5 percent of the budget, this percentage was relatively high because insignificant amounts were being spent on other government programs.[31]

THE MONAGAS ERA

In 1846 Antonio Leocadio Guzmán, who was the Liberal (then also known as *Colorados* or Reds) candidate for president, revolted against Páez but was defeated.

In 1847 the former rebel José Tadeo Monagas won the presidency with the backing of Páez, thus beginning the rule of the Liberal oligarchy. Soon Monagas deserted his alliance with the Conservatives and Páez. On January 24, 1848, a Monagas-sanctioned mob attacked the Congress and killed five parliamentarians and wounded numerous others, thus successfully intimidating Congress to Monagas' will. On the first anniversary, Monagas declared a national holiday to keep memories of the event alive![32]

Páez denounced the attack and declared against the government on February 4. The rebellion spread rapidly. *Caudillos* Carlos Soublette, Col. Agustín Codazzi, Gen. Judas Tabeo Piñango, and Gen. Ezequiel Zamora[33] declared against Monagas. Páez, leading 3,000 men, took control of the state of Coro. At a critical moment General Zamora and 1,300 of his followers deserted Páez, and Páez was defeated at Los Araguatos in the state of Apure in March by his former lieutenant José Cornelio Muñoz. Páez escaped to New Granada; nevertheless, the Conservatives fought on. General Muñoz led 1,000 Liberals against a somewhat smaller force of

Conservatives under Gen. Judas Tadéo Piñango at Taratara. General Piñango was unhorsed and wounded and the Conservative army fled to Maracaibo. Páez, sailing from Puerto Cabello, briefly joined the wounded Pinañgo at Maracaibo but soon sailed to St. Thomas from where he tried to supervise the war.[34]

Shortly before the Battle of Taratara, the commanding officer of the government schooner *Constitución* (unk guns) defected to Páez. The warship—half of the Venezuelan navy—was carrying 6,000 muskets and $23,000 in specie. The Conservatives also commandeered a number of coastal craft. Monagas reacted quickly to this creation of a Conservative navy. He acquired the brigantine *Presidente* (unk guns), the schooners *Independencia* (unk guns), *Fama* (unk guns), and *Democracia* (unk guns), and two gunboats. This squadron blockaded Maracaibo. In May the Liberals attacked in launches but were beaten back, losing fourteen 60-foot launches and some 1,000 men. On the thirtieth the Liberals forced the less numerous Conservatives to evacuate Maracaibo and to seek refuge on San Carlos Island whose fort guarded the entrance to Maracaibo Bay.

The besieged Conservatives went on the offensive. In June their squadron, manned by 344 men and composed of eight small craft, none carrying more than seven guns and most carrying only one, raided coastal towns and briefly hesitated off Puerto Cabello. On June 10 the Conservative squadron caught the Liberal squadron peacefully at anchor at Capana. The *Independencia* was intentionally run aground so that government troops ashore could prevent its capture. The cruise accomplished little.[35]

While the Conservatives held out at San Carlos, which gave them the control of Maracaibo Bay and Lake and little else, the Liberals were purchasing ships and arms in the United States. On September 2 the rebels engaged a rebuilt government squadron composed of the brigantines *Presidente* (unk guns) and *Manzanares* (unk guns) and the schooners *Avila* (unk guns), *Diana* (unk guns), *Boliviana* (unk guns), *Democracia* (unk guns), *Intrépida* (unk guns), *Fama* (unk guns), and *Estrella* (unk guns) and escaped into Maracaibo. On September 17 the Conservatives, temporarily laying up their tiny warships, attacked 300 Liberals at Quisiro on the east side of Maracaibo Bay. However, the Conservatives were defeated, suffering significant losses, and retreated back to San Carlos. In September the opposing squadrons fought an indecisive battle.[36]

In October the American steamer *Augusta*, chartered by the Liberals, arrived off Puerto Cabello. Renamed the *Libertador* and armed, she joined the Liberal squadron besieging the Conservatives at San Carlos. Not to be outclassed, the Conservatives purchased two American steamers. The *Scourge* (unk guns), sailing from Aruba to Maracaibo, ran short of fuel and was captured by the Liberals. The smaller steamer, *General Jackson* (3 guns), successfully ran the Liberal blockade and crossed the Maracaibo Bar.[37]

Although the Conservative squadron exchanged fire with the Liberals, time was running out for the Conservatives. They could find few new recruits while bottled up on San Carlos and their forces were getting weary of fighting. On December 23, loading 400 men on the small *General Jackson*, the Liberals abandoned San Carlos. The steamer proceeded up the Escalante River to the Zulia River where the Liberals occupied the village of San Carlos (not to be confused with the recently deserted island). Here their numbers swelled to 1,200 men as fresh recruits joined. During the night 363 Liberals surprised and defeated the Conservatives on December 31. The *General Jackson* was captured the next day by the *Libertador* as it tried to escape down the river. Among the 300 Conservatives captured were Páez' three sons. Attempting to end the rebellion, Monagas proclaimed a general amnesty on January 20, 1849.[38]

Páez was not yet ready to concede defeat. On June 24 the Conservatives unsuccessfully attempted to assassinate Monagas in Caracas. On July 2 Páez landed with a new force in La Vela de Coro (268 mi WNW of Caracas). However, the rebellion was poorly coordinated. Páez' followers, while trying to flee into the *llanos*, were overtaken by 2,000 Liberals led by Monagas and captured at Macapo Abajo on August 15. Captured along with Páez were 89 officers and 560 men. Imprisoned at the Castle of San Antonio de Cumaná, Páez was shackled and confined in a small cell in the stifling heat. Public pressure forced Monagas to honor the terms of Páez' surrender, and in July 1850 he was exiled to the United States.[39]

The Monagas dynasty lasted for twelve years as José Tadeo Monagas passed the presidency to his brother, José Gregorio, who returned the favor. These were turbulent years. A short-lived rebellion favoring Páez broke out in May 1853. The following June, another rebellion calling for Páez to return occurred. In May 1856 Gen. Trinidad Brache returned from exile and unsuccessfully attempted to lead yet another rebellion.[40]

In 1857, in order to secure his own immediate reelection, José Tadeo Monagas dictated a new constitution.[41] This, plus the fact that he was accused of giving into British demands for territory along the Guiana border, led to his overthrow. On March 5, 1858, Julián Castro, the Governor of Carabobo, led a coalition of Conservatives and Liberals in revolt. On December 31, 1858, a new constitution, adopting a federal structure, was promulgated which satisfied neither the Liberals (most of whom became Federalists and were identified by the color yellow) nor the Conservatives (most of whom became Constitutionalists and were identified by the color blue) and led to the Federal War.[42]

CONFRONTING THE MAJOR POWERS

Even before the Federalists and Constitutionalists took up arms against each other over the Constitution, Venezuela faced a major crisis with France and Great Britain. The new Castro government guaranteed to the foreign diplomats Monagas' safe passage out of the country. However, adverse popular reaction forced the resignation of the cabinet minister who had signed the document and the Castro government retracted its guarantee and refused to pay the debts of the Monagas regime. As a consequence, French and British warships blockaded La Guayra and Puerto Cabello in May 1858. They seized the small Venezuelan squadron and sank one schooner. Although the constitutional convention agreed to let Monagas leave the country as soon as the blockade was lifted, the convention soon suspected that the foreign legations were encouraging the Federalists in Congress to plot against Castro. As a consequence, Castro was given dictatorial powers.

The British and French *chargés d'affaires* retreated to their warships. The Federalist Juan Falcón[43] revolted against Castro in La Guaira but was defeated by the old warrior Gen. Carlos Soublette. On August 27 the blockaders and the government agreed that Monagas would be allowed to leave and normal relations were resumed.[44]

On June 7, 1858, the most prestigious Federalists were exiled; they plotted their return and the overthrow of the new constitution. The principal conspirators were Falcón in St. Thomas, Monagas in Trinidad, and Zamora in Curaçao. The three factions met in St. Thomas in October 1858 and agreed on a strategy and a federal agenda. Falcón was chosen as the leader.

THE FEDERAL WAR (*LA GUERRA LARGA*)

On February 20, 1859, forty Federalists captured the village of Coro (not to be confused with La Vela de Coro) on the shores of Lake Maracaibo. When Zamora learned of this, he hurried from exile. Landing on the twenty-second, he proclaimed a provisional federal government in La Vela de Coro. Leading 800 men, Zamora marched against Puerto Cabello, but his departure allowed the Constitutionalists to recapture La Vela de Coro. Meanwhile, Gen. Juan Antonio Sotillo, another Federal *caudillo*, invaded the east and was welcomed.[45]

Zamora turned southward toward the *llanos*. By the middle of April, his following had increased to 3,000 men, many of whom were undisciplined, some even criminals. The towns of Guanare and Barinas were burned to the ground. Now the seasonal rains came and lasted until October, making military operations on the plains impractical. Zamora dispatched a 700-man expedition southwest into the Andean states, but it was driven back. On August 18, 1859, he declared a war "to the death."

Meanwhile, Falcón returned to Venezuela on July 24 to provide political direction of the Federalists. The war spread throughout Venezuela; many minor clashes occurred and it became difficult to distinguish these from banditry.[46]

Back in Caracas, the more conservative Constitutionalists ousted Castro as president on August 1 and replaced him with Pedro Gual. Gual, defeated on the battlefield, was replaced by Manuel Felipe de Tovar, a member of the upper class. This caused some *caudillos* to desert the Constitutionalist cause and join the Federalists. The city of Barquisimeto fell to the Federalists after a victory at the battle of Sabana de la Cruz.

On December 10, 1859, Zamora defeated the Constitutionalists under Pedro Ramos at San Inés. The battle lasted nineteen hours and the Constitutionalists lost 800 men and the Federalists 200. Zamora pressed the retreating Constitutionalists. While attacking San Carlos, Zamora was killed by a rifle shot on February 10, 1860; thus, the Federalists lost their most successful field commander. The Federal army was now 5,400 men strong.[47]

Falcón turned toward the *llanos*. On February 17, 1860, some 5,000 Constitutionalists (almost all infantry) under Gen. León de Febres Cordero overtook the Federalists at Coplé. During a fifty-minute battle, the Federalists were badly defeated, losing 2,200 men dead, wounded, or captured. The shattered army disbanded. Most of the *caudillos* and their followers sought refuge in their home states. Falcón and a few other leaders fled to New Granada (the future Colombia). Arguments among the leaders on both sides prevented either from taking advantage of the other's discord. Guerrilla bands roamed the countryside, causing devastation but without gaining military advantage for either side.[48]

In March 1861 the Constitutionalists invited Páez, now seventy-one years old, to return from exile in the United States and take command of their army. He immediately began to plot against Tovar. Disgusted, Tovar resigned in May in favor of Pedro Gual. On September 10 Páez easily ousted Gual who was eighty years old.[49]

While Páez was reacquiring power, Falcón was roaming the Caribbean gathering supporters. In July 1861 Falcón landed in Coro and was joined by the local Federal *caudillo* José González. On December 8, 1861, Falcón and Páez met face to face at Carabobo but could not reach an agreement.[50]

In August 1862 Gen. Antonio Guzmán Blanco[51] opened a successful Federalist campaign in central Venezuela. On December 26 and 27, 1862, González severely defeated the Constitutionist *caudillo* Col. Facundo Camero at Buchivcoa in a continuous twenty-five-hour battle. The 2,500-man Constitutional force was almost completely destroyed. Following this Federal victory a number of *caudillos* defected to the Federal side.[52]

By early 1863 the Federalists held all but the region immediately around the capital. Between April 14 and 17, 1863, the Federalists won a series of battles gaining control of the Federal District. On May 23 Guzmán Blanco (representing Falcón) and Pedro Manuel Rojas (representing Páez) signed the Treaty of Coche. This ended hostilities, caused Páez to resign, and created an assembly equally nominated by the chiefs of both parties. On June 17 the assembly appointed Falcón president and Guzmán Blanco vice president. Páez once again returned to exile.[53]

Although the Federalists had defeated the Constitutionalists, unrest continued throughout the nation for the next four years. In August 1863 Falcón issued a "Decree of Guarantees" in an unsuccessful attempt at reconciliation. In that month Falcón had to subdue Constitutionalists in Puerto Cabello. In 1864 uprisings occurred in Trujillo, Táchira, Cagua, Guárico, and Carabobo. On March 28, 1864, a new federal constitution was adopted for the United States of Venezuela but in fact it differed little from the 1858 document.[54]

In September Guayana declared its independence; the central government blockaded the mouth of the Orinoco River and within a month the state accepted the new constitution. Then Gen. Venancio Pulgar rebelled in Maracaibo against Falcón in July 1865; this too was rapidly suppressed. Finally, Falcón's own party, the Federalists, revolted against him and he resigned in favor of Brigade Gen. Ezequiel Bruzual.[55]

THE BLUE REVOLUTION (THE RECONQUEST)

In 1868 the aging, former Liberal José Tadeo Monagas now led the Constitutionalists in revolt. After some sharp fighting, Bruzual was wounded, fled to Curaçao, and died. José Tadeo Monagas entered Caracas on June 26 and once again became president. However, Monagas died on November 18 and was succeeded by his son, Gen. José Ruperto Monagas, in February 1869. The younger Monagas was soon challenged by Federalist Gen. Antonio Guzmán Blanco who had been in Europe on a diplomatic mission when Falcón was overthrown.[56]

GUZMÁN BLANCO SEIZES POWER

Guzmán Blanco, who was exiled by Monagas, organized an expedition in Curaçao. He had amassed a fortune while vice president. With this and borrowed money (which he later repaid out of the Venezuelan treasury), Guzmán Blanco purchased fifty-two ships and craft of every description and lots of munitions. Crewing his vessels with mercenaries, Guzmán Blanco landed in La Vela de Coro on February 14, 1870, where he raised an 18,000-man army. On April 27, 1870, after a bloody three-day battle, Guzmán Blanco defeated Monagas in Caracas fighting from house to house. Guzmán Blanco achieved complete control when he defeated former supporters during the next eighteen months. His victories in part could be attributed to superior weapons—"needle" rifles and German manufactured artillery.[57]

Guzmán Blanco ruled Venezuela directly and indirectly for the next eighteen years. He reduced the presidential term to two years and alternated himself with cronies. Guzmán Blanco frequently traveled to Europe, living opulently.[58]

Minor uprisings continued. In January 1880 Gen. José Pío Rebolledo rebelled in Ciudad Bolívar. Situated 366 miles southeast of Caracas by land, the most convenient route to the river port was by sailing east along the coast and then up the Orinoco River. Guzmán Blanco immediately dispatched 12,000 troops in a squadron—the steamers *República* (unk guns), *Reinvindicador* (unk guns), *Remolcador* (unk guns) and schooners *Ricaurte* (unk guns), *Sucre* (unk guns), and *3 de Agosto* (unk guns)—under Gen. Venancio Pulgar. On February 16 Rebolledo was defeated and imprisoned.

In June 1885 Generals Venancio Pulgar and José Ignacio Pulido rebelled. Unable to attract a sufficient following, they fled to Santo Domingo on board the steamer *Justice*.[59]

In 1888 Dr. Juan Rojas Paúl, supported by Guzmán Blanco, was elected president. Rojas did not prove to be his dupe. Rojas repudiated many of Guzmán Blanco's shady financial concessions and reinstated numerous freedoms. Gen. Joaquín Crespo,[60] who had been in Curaçao planning an uprising, sailed for the coast of Coro but was intercepted at sea and imprisoned. Rojas then persuaded Crespo that his fight was with Guzmán Blanco and not him. Crespo agreed not to act against Rojas and was set free. In October, while Guzmán Blanco was in Paris, mobs rioted in the Caracas against the dictator and torn down his statues. Appreciating that his time was up, Guzmán Blanco remained abroad.[61]

Rojas then became enamored of an Italian opera singer. After a tumultuous affair, he retired from public life and was succeeded by Dr. Raimundo Andueza Palacio. In 1892 he refused to step down as president and General Crespo rebelled. The lesser *caudillos* chose sides and most joined Crespo. The decisive battles took place at Mataruca and Peña Blanca in August 1892. Crespo victoriously entered Caracas on October 7 and Palacios fled Venezuela. General Crespo threw out the old congressmen and brought in new ones who elected him to a four-year term as president.[62]

Crespo chose his cronie Gen. Ignacio Andrade as his successor. Two powerful *caudillos*, Gen. José Manuel Hernández ("the Maimed"[63]) and Ramón Guerra who had supported Crespo when he ousted Palacio, refused to accept this decision and rebelled in February 1898. Crespo took command of the government's forces. Hernández surprised Crespo at Mata Carmelera on the *llanos* and killed him in the first charge on April 16. Andrade now bribed Guerra to take command of the government's forces and he captured Hernández. But when Andrade named Guerra governor of the state of Guárico, Gen. Lorenzo Guevera rebelled. Andrade then freed Hernández and, as a consequence, Guerra revolted. In October 1899, leaving Gen. Victor Rodríguez as president, Andrade fled to Colombia.[64]

CASTRO SEIZES POWER

On May 23, 1899, Gen. Cipriano Castro,[65] the "Lion of the Andes," led sixty "mountainmen" from exile in Colombia into Venezuela. By the second day their numbers swelled to 600 men and within a few weeks to 2,000. Castro surrounded San Cristobál (536 mi SW of Caracas), the state capital of Táchira. He then slipped away and destroyed an advancing relief column under Gen. Leopoldo Sarría. Castro then returned and surprised the defenders of San Cristobál, capturing it on the twenty-eighth.[66]

Castro learned that a government force led by Gen. Rafael González Pacheco was advancing from the mountainous state of Médida against him. Castro rushed forward, caught González Pacheco at the foot of Zumbador Mountain, where on June 11 the government's troops were exhausted from filing down the steep, narrow trail, and defeated them. Another government force, 5,000 men, marched from Maracaibo to do battle. Again, Castro rushed forward from San Cristobál. His force, including his supply train, covered thirty miles over the rocky terrain on the first day. On the third day, Castro split his army in two. The train (including many women and children) with a small escort marched northeast. Castro and most of the fighters rode northwest toward the advancing enemy. He led his men over the high Codillera de Tovar, through the Yegüines Pass, and fell upon the enemy's advanced guard. He drove it back into the main column. Then Castro rapidly withdrew through the Yegüines Pass, leaving the stunned enemy slowly pursuing. Now Castro turned northeast toward Caracas and not southwest toward San Cristobál as his pursuers believed.[67]

Castro's reunited column was opposed by 700 men outside the city of Mérida (404 mi SW of Caracas); he brushed these aside. Gen. Leopoldo Baptista, commanding 2,500 government troops, awaited Castro in the Trujillo Valley but Castro skirted around him and passed through the state capital, Trujillo. At the Lara state border, Castro left the main trail and took a little-known path, again eluding his pursuers. As he emerged at Parapara, he captured the supply train of a force that was waiting to attack him back along the main trail.[68]

Castro skirted the town of Barquisimeto (211 mi SW of Caracas) and continued into the Yaracuy Valley. By now his force had swollen to 3,000 men. At the town of Nirgua, Castro defeated 800 men led by Gen. Rosendo Medina, and many of the survivors joined his force. Castro now arrived at the city of Valencia, only eighty-five miles from Caracas. He was caught between two forces—by now 5,000 government troops were chasing him and a significant body of troops lay between him and the capital. Castro marched southeast, away from Caracas, looking for a site to fight a decisive battle. Nine miles from Valencia he found a place where barbed wire paralleled either side of the trail and created a funnel. There at Tocuyito, 4,000 government troops hurried unsuspectingly into the trap on September 12 and sustained 2,000 casualties before fleeing back through Valencia to La Victoria. Castro himself became a casualty that day, having broken his leg during a cavalry charge.[69]

Now many of the lesser *caudillos* deserted Andrade. The President and his principal supporters fled to Curaçao. On October 22, 1899, General Castro triumphantly entered Caracas, accompanied by his chief lieutenant Juan Vicente Gómez,[70] at the head of his Andean troops and was elected president. The trek had covered 750 miles and had taken six months; it started with sixty men and may have swelled to 10,000.[71]

During the next six months, lesser *caudillos* rebelled and all were suppressed. While these events were transpiring, the State of Táchira rebelled and seceded from Venezuela. In February 1900 Castro sent his most trusted lieutenant, General Gómez, to deal with the problem. Gómez subdued the movement principally through persuasion.[72]

CONFRONTING THE MAJOR POWERS AGAIN

Financially, Venezuela was prostrate, caused by the decades of fighting and exasperated by the fall in the price of coffee, now the nation's dominant export.[73] The country was near financial ruin and neither the internal nor external debts were being paid. Foreigners were demanding compensation for damage to their property that had occurred during the numerous rebellions. Castro arrested the foreign ministers who pressed the claims of their countrymen and defied the European powers to act.

On December 9, 1902, British and German warships captured four small Venezuelan warships, sinking three and retaining one; they also began to blockade the coast. On the thirteenth the German heavy cruiser *Vineta* and two torpedo launches plus the British second-class cruiser *Charybdis* and two torpedo-gunboats bombarded the *Castillo "Libertador"* in Puerto Cabello. On December 20 Italy joined in the blockade, which was declared officially enforced by the three powers on that same day. Four days after Christmas the Argentine Foreign Minister, Luís Drago, sent a memorandum to the American governments, including the United States, declaring that the use of force to collect debts was contrary to international law.[74]

In retaliation, Castro declared war on the European powers. Theodore Roosevelt, the President of the United States, stepped in and told Kaiser Wilhelm II that if his warships were not withdrawn within forty-eight hours, the U.S. Navy would fire on them. As a consequence, the European powers stated that the United States had to be responsible for collecting the debt. On February 13, 1903, the three European nations agreed to submit their dispute to the Hague Tribunal. On February 22, 1904, the Hague Tribunal judged that thirty percent of Venezuela's custom duties would be used to pay the foreign debts and that the citizens of Germany, Great Britain, and Italy would be paid first.[75]

"THE LIBERATION" (*LA LIBERTADORA*) REBELLION BEGINS

While the major powers were blockading Venezuela, a banker, Manuel Antonio Matos, rebelled. He had been imprisoned briefly by Castro for not producing funds on demand. The European blockading nations permitted Matos, who was operating out of Trinidad, to introduce arms along the coast to numerous opportunistic, lesser *caudillos*. Luciano Mendoza, the Governor of Aragua, rebelled on December 19, 1901. Mendoza was the most threatening of these *caudillos* to Castro due to his proximity to Caracas. Also, he possessed a substantial reputation because he had been the *caudillo* who had defeated the legendary José Antonio Páez. Matos purchased the old merchantship *Banright*, renamed it the *Libertador*, and armed it. Loading the ship with men and arms, Matos landed at La Vela del Coro.

Castro, preoccupied by debauchery, ordered Gómez to destroy Mendoza. Gómez questioned (probably not out loud): "How am I going to fight Mendoza with these *tres gatos* [three cats, or a few men]? Well, I'd go out for him even alone. If he [Mendoza] beats me, I'll be beaten by the best man in the country."[76] Gómez loaded his men on railroad cars which carried them to San Mateo. They attacked Mendoza the same day at Cagua, taking him by surprise. Gómez pursued Mendoza to La Puerta, a bottleneck pass that separated coastal Venezuela from the *llanos*. Gómez seized the high ground and fired down into Mendoza's trapped horsemen. The battle lasted one hour before Mendoza broke and ran. Gómez chased Mendoza into the *llanos* for 75 miles and cornered him at San José de Tiznados. Mendoza's force was destroyed but the *caudillo* escaped.[77]

Now Gómez dropped back to La Puerta and there on December 30 ambushed another rebellious force led by Gen. Antonio Fernández. In the meantime, Mendoza raised another force in Sierra de Carabobo. Gómez immediately attacked him at El Barro on January 5, 1902, and defeated him again. Gómez then defeated two more of the rebellious *caudillos*. Within sixty-five days Gómez had crushed the "Liberation" rebellion in central Venezuela; however, the rebels were winning in the west and in the east. In the west the rebels had won control of the states of Falcón and Lara. In the east the government's forces had been defeated at Guanaguana and most of their troops were being held as prisoners. Now Castro ordered Gómez to deal with these problems.[78]

In mid-March 1902 Gómez led a force, carried on board the gunboat *Restaurador* (7 guns) and two schooners, to La Vela de Coro; this was his first time he had seen the Caribbean Sea! He sent two expeditions inland but both were defeated by the rebels. Next, he personally led the attack and defeated the rebels at Urucure. He again caught them at Sabaneta and scattered their force. On April 15 Gómez was recalled to Caracas to deal with the rebellion in the east. In his absence, the rebels attacked and recaptured La Vela de Coro, taking the governor of the state as prisoner.[79]

On April 29 Gómez sailed from La Guayra eastward. In early May he landed near the town of Cumaná (251 mi E of Caracas) that was held by the rebels. He attacked and the rebels withdrew. Next, he sailed with 850 men to Carúpano, which was held by 2,000 rebels. At six o'clock in the morning on May 6, he attacked. The fighting was still raging at 5:30 in the afternoon when Gómez was shot through the thigh. Carried off the field, his troops abandoned the attack in confusion.[80]

Castro himself now took the field, leaving the recuperating Gómez as provisional president. Castro, commanding 3,000 men, drove 5,000 rebels out of Barcelona to Aragua on the edge of the *llanos*. There, the rebels turned on him and inflicted sufficient casualties to escape into the plains. Castro had had enough and returned to Caracas and its women. However, the rebels soon threatened the capital. So, once again, Castro took the field. He assumed a defensive position in the valley of the Tuy. This gave the rebels an opportunity to unite. Meanwhile, Gómez kept Castro's lifeline, the railroad from Caracas, operating.[81]

By October 1902 Castro, commanding 6,000 men, was nearly surrounded by 12,000 rebels at the city of La Victoria (40 mi S of Caracas). They had been led there by the most influential of the rebel *caudillos*—Gregorio Segundo Riera, Luciano Mendoza, Nicolás Rolando, Rafael Montilla, and Amábile Solagnie—and joined by Matos. This would be a clash between the *caudillo*-created army and an embryonic national army. The rebellious *caudillos* chose Mendoza as their commander. He ordered the surrounding hills occupied and defensive positions prepared. While these preparations were dragging on, Castro summoned help from Gómez, who seized the initiative.[82]

Gómez and the reinforcements arrived the next day by train. Mendoza did nothing to block his uniting with Castro. Each night, for fifteen days, Gómez feigned a general attack and the rebels rushed to arms and wasted ammunition. Then, in the middle of the night on November 2, Gómez attacked and the rebels, caught now unprepared, were driven from their positions and retreated southward in disarray and scattered.[83]

Castro returned to Caracas and engaged in his amorous diversions. Once again the rebels pulled themselves together. Rebellious *caudillo* Nicolás Rolando threatened the capital with 3,000 men and some of Castro's supporters defected to the rebels. At this point Gómez intercepted a letter from Matos to a *caudillo* in the state of Zulia whereby Matos promised not to release "El Mocho" Hernández from prison (placed there by Castro) once he, Matos, came to power. Gómez published the letter and released the popular, old *caudillo* in exchange for his support.[84]

In early April Gómez departed Caracas to confront Rolando, who, commanding 3,000 men, had entrenched himself at El Guapo (95 mi E of Caracas). Outnumbered and outgunned, Gómez attacked on April 11. Following a three-day bloody fight, Rolando fled deep into the *llanos* to Ciudad Bolívar some 400 miles east of the capital.[85]

Castro then ordered Gómez to the west where the rebels had regained control. Gómez sailed from La Guayra and on May 1 landed at Tucuas, which he captured before the rebels realized that he had disengaged from Rolando in central Venezuela. Gómez then rapidly advanced along the railway line which ran to Barquisimeto, driving the enemy before him. On May 23 he captured Barquisimeto and pressed on after the retreating enemy the same day. On June 2 Gómez and Matos fought at Mata Palo. The fighting began at 8 o'clock in the evening and continued until 6 o'clock the following afternoon. The rebel forces were destroyed and Matos fled to Curaçao. This left only Rolando now in the east with whom to deal.[86]

Gómez sailed from La Guayra on June 27, commanding the gunboats *Restaurador*, *Zamora*, and *Bolívar* and 3,000 troops. On July 1 he landed at Soro while the enemy fired down upon his troops from nearby hills. The following day Gómez defeated 500 rebels at Campo Claro, clearing the way to Ciudad Bolívar. On July 5 Gómez reboarded the gunboats and sailed up the Orinoco River. On the thirteenth he disembarked at Santa Anna (48 mi SE of Ciudad Bolívar). At three o'clock on July 19 the gunboats began bombarding the river port and Gómez' troops attacked the outer defenses. The city was stubbornly defended, street by street, but by early in the morning of the twenty-first, Rolando was beaten and surrendered. The rebels lost 800 men dead and wounded and the remainder captured. Gómez lost 250 men dead and 400 wounded. Throughout the "Liberation Rebellion," Gómez consistently acted faster than his opponents.[87]

Castro, anticipating that rebellions would continue, spent more than half of his first two budgets on modern weapons—Mauser rifles, Krupp artillery, and Hotchkiss machine guns. He sent General Gómez back to Táchira in the Andes to recruit more loyal followers; this freed him from the traditional dependence on plainsmen supplied by *caudillos* from the *llanos*.[88] On September 12, 1904, Norman Hutchinson, the American Minister to Venezuela, wrote, "The army . . . seems to be on his side. He has treated it better than it has ever been treated before, especially the rank and file, and he takes good care who his officers are."[89] To further improve his army, Castro created a general staff.[90]

GÓMEZ ASSUMES POWER

In late 1908 Castro became ill due to his indulgences and on November 23 temporarily turned over the government to General Gómez, by now nicknamed "the wizard" (*El Brujo*). Although it was not Castro's intention, this evolved into the first "Andean succession" and Gómez ruled dictatorially until his death in 1935. Castro repeatedly plotted to return and regain power, but foreigners and nationals alike had been sufficiently affronted by Castro's abrasive personality and social excesses to prevent his return.[91]

OBSERVATIONS

Venezuela found itself immersed in political and economic crises at the end of the War for Independence from which it did not emerge during the nineteenth century. One author states that between January 1, 1830, and December 31, 1903, Venezuela sustained thirty-nine revolutions and 127 armed uprisings. He adds that throughout these seventy-four years, fighting was occurring somewhere in Venezuela one out of every three days.[92]

This turbulent era in Venezuelan history opened with the struggle between the "Bolivarians" and Páez over the issue of separation versus union with Gran Colombia. This soon gave way to struggles among the *caudillos* over who would rule. The composition of the "army" in 1901 bears witness to the domination of these *caudillos*, who persistently rewarded themselves and their followers with military ranks and privileges. Apparently, the Venezuelan "army" was made up of four generals-in-chief (including the President and Minister of War), twenty-eight presidentially nominated generals-in-chief, 1,439 generals, 1,462 colonels, 2,302 majors, 3,230 captains, 2,300 lieutenants, 1,000 ensigns and 4,000 soldiers.[93]

Those who decided the fate of Venezuela during the nineteenth century were *caudillos* and not the military. The *caudillos* won or lost followings based on their ability to enforce their wills and not because of their political agendas. Many of them died on the field of battle—Joaquín Crespo, Julio Monagas, Judas Tadeo Piñango, Andrés Avelino Pinto, and Ezequiel Zamora, to name only the most prominent. *Caudillos* who governed honored two of their nineteenth-century compatriots by having states' renamed for them—Coro became Falcón in 1874 and Maturín became Monagas in 1909. These facts alone did not entitle the *caudillos* to be labelled as the Venezuela military.[94]

Caudillos continued to rule Venezuela through six decades of the twentieth century (Generals Juan Vicente Gómez, 1908–35, and Maros Pérez Jiménez, 1950–58, being the most durable). However, the twentieth-century *caudillos* brought peace (but not democracy) by creating and controlling professional militaries which allowed them easily to defeat the nineteenth-century practice of calling the plainsmen to arms.[95]

Throughout the seventy-four-year struggle, the professional military was more frequently a victim of conflict than either an instigator or participant. Early during this era, the military was reduced to near extinction by the *caudillos*, including Páez, and did not recover during the nineteenth century. The *caudillos* preferred to build militias out of plainsmen, which in practice were their private armies. On June 17, 1872, the miniscule regular army was disbanded and replaced by a 3,000-man force whose officers were chosen by President Guzmán based upon personal loyalty. The act was repeated on March 2, 1877, by the new president, Gen. Linares Alcántara.[96]

Although the Federal War resulted in the adoption of a federal constitution, the ideological overtones of the document did not matter as much as the *caudillo* who would interpret it. Although labeled Federalists (or Liberals) and Constitutionalists (or Conservatives), these opposing forces more accurately might be called decentralists and centralists. Although the Liberals did emancipate the slaves in 1854, their social agenda differed little from the Conservatives.[97]

The decades of fighting destroyed the national economy. Successive governments accumulated a huge external debt.

One researcher estimates that during these seventy-four years of conflict some 300,000 combatants and 700,000 civilians were killed directly (battlefield deaths and assassinations) or indirectly (wounds, sicknesses, starvation, and imprisonment). Another author estimates that between 30,000 and 50,000 individuals died in combat during the Federal War and that 100,000 died from all causes related to the fighting.[98]

CHAPTER TWENTY-TWO

MINI-WARS AMONG *CAUDILLOS* OF CENTRAL AMERICA, 1844–1907

> We [Central America] shall never be a great country until we are a united country.
> —Justo Rufino Barrios, President of Guatemala, 1873–85

THE SPARK

The immediate cause of these wars among the young Central American nations was the ambition of one national *caudillo* or another, each of whom at the least wanted to dominate his neighbors and at the most wanted to recreate the short-lived Central American Union under *his* rule (see chapter 10).[1]

BACKGROUND

By 1840 the Central America Union had dissolved into five independent nations. The ultra-Conservative Guatemalan Rafael Carrera, who had destroyed the union in the earlier wars, imposed Conservative governments on El Salvador and Honduras, while Nicaragua and Costa Rica already possessed Conservative governments. Almost immediately two feeble political attempts were made to reconstruct the union. In 1842 Honduras, Nicaragua, and El Salvador declared a loose confederation; however, it was never implemented. In 1849, influenced by British territorial ambitions, the same three nations again tried to unite in matters related to foreign policy, but this fell apart by 1852.[2]

Two underlying causes plunged the young Central American nations into ceaseless fighting for more than sixty years. First, Conservatives in one country made common cause with those in another; no less could be said for the Liberals. This guaranteed that national borders would be crossed with impunity. The two parties represented elites seeking power and had less to do with political ideology. The measure of how liberal or conservative a government might be was its policies toward the Roman Catholic Church. The second underlying cause for conflict was the internal struggle for power within the republics. Frequently this pitted family-elites against each other and at other times the old rich (cattle barons) against the new rich (banana and coffee growers).[3]

As the nineteenth century slipped by, two economic factors increasingly influenced events in Central America. The first was the growing importance and practicality of a trans-isthmus railway (and later canal) and the second was Central America's growing agricultural importance, based first upon bananas and later coffee as well. In spite of these economic developments, Central America remained one of the most isolated regions in the hemisphere.[4]

OPPOSING FORCES

The national *caudillo* (who, not coincidentally, was also the president) primarily depended on lesser *caudillos* (local autocrats) and their followers. Sometimes he also had a small cadre of mercenaries, who most frequently were North Americans, to provide specialized skills.[5] National armies were akin to pre-Independence, feudal armies and typically fielded a few hundred men at most. Armies were mostly infantry; they possessed few cannons and even fewer shells. Rarely was their cavalry deserving of the name; when present, it was more akin to mounted infantry due to the lack of good horses. The soldiers were frequently gathered by force, poorly armed, poorly trained, poorly led, poorly outfitted, poorly fed, and poorly treated. In the late nineteenth century, a Nicaraguan recruiter wrote to his superior, "I send you forty volunteers. Please return the ropes."[6]

What mattered most in raising a feudal army was the size of a nation's population. This made Guatemala, which possessed three times the population of El Salvador, and El Salvador, which had at least two times the population of any one of the three remaining republics (Costa Rica, Honduras, and Nicaragua), potentially the strongest nations in Central America.[7] Although ethnic and racial composition varied among the Central American nations, these factors rarely influenced the fighting quality of the troops.

During these six decades (1844–1907) there were exceptions to these feudal armies, most notably in Guatemala. During the twenty-five-year rule (1840–65) of Rafael Carrera, the Guatemalan army was usually well armed and well paid by regional standards. During the fourteen-year rule (1871–85) of Justo Rufino Barrios, steps were taken to professionalize the force, including the founding of a military academy on September 1, 1873.[8]

OPENING STRATEGIES

The ultimate goal of the competing national *caudillos* was the reunification of Central America under their leadership. The immediate objective for each side was to force the neighboring president (or presidents) from power and impose his successor. This could be accomplished by a variety of strategies: one could help his opponent's internal opposition to overthrow him; one could seize territory belonging to his opponent and refuse to surrender it until he stepped down; one could defeat his opponent on the battlefield. Typically, such a defeat would cause regional *caudillos* to withdraw their support from the national *caudillo* and he would fall from power.

Geography played an influential role in each nation's strategy. The rugged terrain and rigid caste system of northernmost Guatemala encouraged separatist movements which occupied much of Guatemala's military energy. El Salvador lay in the shadow of the regional giant, Guatemala. Honduras' "crossroads" location between more powerful northern and southern neighbors frequently forced it to fight. A geographical depression in the Cordillera in southern Nicaragua (a possible canal route) made it the envy of its neighbors, not to mention the world's maritime powers. Geographical isolation afforded southernmost Costa Rica some protection.

(Panama would not be considered a Central American nation until after its 1903 separation from Colombia.)

GOVERNING CONSERVATIVE SALVADORIANS DEFEAT DISSIDENT CONSERVATIVE SALVADORIANS, 1844

Following Rafael Carrera's destruction of the Central American Union in 1840, he placed Francisco Malespín at the head of the Salvadorian army to watch over those who governed. On February 1, 1844, Malespín seized control of the Salvadorian government. The Conservative aristocracy, believing Malespín to be too difficult to control, backed exiled Liberal-turned-Conservative Manuel José Arce's attempt to return to power. Arce invaded El Salvador from Guatemala at the head of an army that included Guatemalans (possibly filibusters) and penetrated ten miles, as far as Atiquizaya. Arce proved even less popular with the Salvadorian people than Malespín, so they rallied around the latter. Malespín defeated Arce at Ocotepeque (50 mi N of San Salvador). The victorious 4,000-man Salvadorian army pursued Malespín's defeated force into Guatemala, arriving at Jutiapa (75 mi SE of Guatemala City) on May 20, 1844. Reacting to the invasion, Carrera led a Guatemalan army toward the invaders. Malespín had second thoughts about provoking Carrera into a war and negotiated a peace in August.[9]

CONSERVATIVE SALVADORIANS AND HONDURANS DEFEAT LIBERAL NICARAGUANS, 1844–45

Salvadorian President Malespín and Honduran President Francisco Herrera placed the blame for their internal unrest on dissidents who had been given haven in León, Nicaragua, a Liberal stronghold. Nicaraguan Liberals, acting before Conservative Salvadorians and Hondurans could join forces, attacked Nacaome, Honduras (42 mi S of Tegucigalpa), on October 23, 1844, but were repulsed following two hours of fighting. As a consequence, Nicaragua unsuccessfully sued for peace.

On October 25 Malespín took personal command of the Salvadorian army, marched through Honduras assimilating its army, and invaded Nicaragua. One month later, on November 26, 1844, the combined army known as "The Protector of the Peace" (*Ejército Protector de la Paz*) began the attack on León. The defenses were under the command of Senator Emiliano Madrid. At 3 A.M. on the twenty-seventh, Malespín ordered an assault while intoxicated. The attackers were badly mauled and the Hondurans wanted to quit. With difficulty, Malespín persuaded them to remain. In the meantime, the Nicaraguan Conservatives deserted the besieged Nicaraguan Liberals in León and supported Malespín. In a stroke of luck, Malespín intercepted a shipment of arms on board a ship at Realejo that was intended for the besieged Nicaraguan Liberals. The weapons included 1,000 muskets and 200 rifles, plus powder, lead, and flints. With these arms Honduran Gen. José Santos Guardiola led the Honduran and Salvadorian troops in the storming of León on January 24, 1845. The siege had lasted fifty-nine days. Malespín showed the town no mercy; he executed prominent citizens, including Senator Madrid, and allowed the army to rape and pillage. However, while campaigning in Nicaragua, Malespín was deposed by Liberals in El Salvador on February 2.[10]

LIBERAL SALVADORIANS DEFEAT CONSERVATIVE HONDURANS, 1845

Conservative Hondurans rallied to reimpose their ally, Conservative Malespín, as president of El Salvador. On June 2, 1845, Honduran General Guardiola, commanding a small army, landed at La Union, El Salvador, while another force led by Gen. Indalecio Cordero marched over land. The new Salvadorian president, Joaquín Eufracio Guzman, did not immediately declare war on Honduras, hoping to negotiate a settlement. Nonetheless, the Honduran army continued to advance. The Hondurans defeated the Salvadorians commanded by General Cabañas at Comayagua on June 2 and at Sensenti on June 10. Guardiola executed the captured Salvadorian wounded, which enraged the Salvadorian population. On August 15 the Salvadorians routed 900 Hondurans at the hacienda Obrajuelo near San Salvador. The Hondurans lost some 600 men and most of their supplies. The two sides negotiated a peace on November 27; Malespín was exiled. In November 1846 Malespín again attempted to return to power in El Salvador but was killed.[11]

CONSERVATIVE SALVADORIANS AND NICARAGUANS RESTORE CONSERVATIVE HONDURANS, 1849

The Honduran vice president supported by Liberals and some Conservatives attempted to overthrow Conservative President Juan Lindo Zelaya. As a consequence, Conservatives from El Salvador and Nicaragua restored him to power.[12]

CONSERVATIVE GUATEMALANS DEFEAT LIBERAL SALVADORIANS AND HONDURANS, 1850–51

Salvadorian President Doroteo Vasconcelos aspired to recreate the Central American Union. Diplomatically he worked to join El Salvador, Guatemala, and Los Altos (a separatist region in Guatemala) into a union. When it became apparent that this could not be achieved peacefully, a 1,500-man Salvadorian and Honduran army (which also included Liberal Nicaraguans and Guatemalans) invaded Guatemala in November 1850. Guatemalan Conservative Carrera, commanding a smaller force, met the invaders at San José la Arada near Chiquimula, Guatemala (95 mi SE of Guatemala City), on February 2, 1851. Vasconcelos, who possessed no military experience, ordered his four columns to attack Carrera when they heard three cannon blasts. However, because all did not hear the signal, the attack was poorly coordinated and Carrera won. Threatening to invaded El Salvador, Carrera forced the Salvadorian Congress to remove Vasconcelos from office and installed Francisco Dueñas.[13]

CONSERVATIVE COSTA RICANS AND HONDURANS HELP DEFEAT LIBERAL NICARAGUANS, 1851

On August 4 Liberal Nicaraguans led by Gen. José Trinidad Muñoz revolted against the Conservative government. Conservative Nicaraguan troops reinforced by Conservatives from Honduras and Costa Rica forced Muñoz to surrender.[14]

CONSERVATIVE GUATEMALANS DEFEAT LIBERAL HONDURANS, 1852–55

In 1852 Honduran Conservative President Lindo, perhaps out of exhaustion, relinquished the government to Liberal José Trinidad Cabañas. Guatemalan President Carrera was displeased by this turn of events and supported dissident Honduran Conservatives led by Gen. Santos Guardiola while Cabañas aided Guatemalan separatists in Los Altos. On October 31, 1852, a Guatemalan army led by Gen. Joaquín Solares invaded the Honduran Department of Copán. In February 1853 the Honduran army commanded by President Cabañas blocked the invaders in the Department of Garcias and on April 19 they agreed to a truce. Attempting a preemptive strike, the Honduran army invaded Guatemala but was defeated at Chiquimula (95 mi SE of

Guatemala City) on July 6, 1853, and at Jalapa (90 mi E of Guatemala City) on the twelfth. Responding, the Guatemalan army invaded Honduras and captured Omoa (115 mi NW of Tegucigalpa) on August 24. It then withdrew.[15]

Making matters worse for Honduras, it entered into a dispute with El Salvador while still at war with Guatemala. Guatemala sent troops to help defend El Salvador and continued to aid Conservative Honduran General Guardiola. The Honduran Conservatives defeated the Honduran Liberals on October 6 at the hamlet of Masaguara and overthrew Cabañas. On February 13, 1856, a treaty was signed ending the war and Guardiola then served as Carrera's dupe.[16]

CONSERVATIVE GUATEMALANS AND NICARAGUANS DEFEAT LIBERAL SALVADORIANS AND HONDURANS, 1863

Gerardo Barrios[17] succeeded to the Salvadorian presidency in 1858. Although he had been a confidant of Guatemalan Conservative Carrera throughout the 1850s, he pursued an aggressive Liberal agenda. Among his initiatives, he began to create a modern, national army and established a military academy. A Liberal government also came to power in Honduras when in 1862 Conservative President Santos Guardiola was assassinated by the presidential guard. Liberal Victoriano Castellanos took power. In early 1863 Carrera invaded El Salvador in order to depose the Liberal government. Some 6,500 Guatemalans attacked 5,000 Salvadorians at Ocotepeque. The battle lasted two days (February 22–23) but the Guatemalans were unable to drive the Salvadorians from their strong defensive positions. The Guatemalans lost 900 dead and 1,500 wounded as well as 9 cannon and 2,000 rifles. The Salvadorian losses were much smaller. Carrera was not deterred by this defeat. In March he sent a 500-man raiding party into El Salvador which attacked and sacked the town of Ahuachapán (72 mi E of San Salvador). The following month another 500-man raiding party attacked and sacked Metapán (70 mi NE of San Salvador).[18]

Following the victory at Ocotepeque, El Salvador and Honduras declared war on Nicaragua in order to break Nicaragua's alliance with Guatemala. El Salvador sent a force under Gen. Eusebio Bracamonte which united with a Honduran force and together they invaded Nicaragua. On April 28, 1863, a 1,500-man Nicaraguan force commanded by Col. Salvador Galarza defeated the invaders at San Jacinto a few miles outside León.[19]

Back in the north, Carrera again invaded El Salvador, occupied Chalchuapa on June 21, and advanced toward Santa Ana (38 mi E of San Salvador). On the twenty-seventh dissident Conservative Salvadorian Francisco Dueñas, leading sixty followers, invaded El Salvador from Guatemala and seized the town of Izalco. There he declared himself provisional president. On the following day, in a conspiracy unrelated to the Carrera-Dueñas connection, José Antonio González unsuccessfully tried to subvert the garrison in San Salvador, the capital, against President Barrios. Nonetheless, rumors spread within the Salvadorian army that Barrios had been overthrown and caused much confusion. At this point, Liberal Gen. Santiago González, José Antonio's brother, attempted to negotiate a deal with Carrera. Carrera insisted that González recognize Dueñas as President of El Salvador and surrender the town of Santa Ana which was occupied by forces under González' command. González chose to fight Carrera, but by now the force defending the town had dwindled to 700 men through desertions. On July 4, some 3,000 Guatemalans attacked Santa Ana. During a stout defense, General González and other senior officers deserted their troops. The soldiers continued to fight for a few more hours but were defeated. Those captured by the Guatemalans were executed. In addition to the human losses, the Salvadorians lost 8 cannon, 2,000 rifles, and 10,000 *pesos* (the army's war chest). Barrios withdrew into San Salvador where he withstood a four-month siege before fleeing the country in October. Conservative Dueñas, supported by Carrera, became the new Salvadorian president. Honduran President Victoriano Castellanos, who had supported Barrios, was also forced out of office and replaced by Conservative José María Medina.[20]

CONSERVATIVE HONDURANS HELP DEFEAT *CONSERVATIVE* SALVADORIANS, 1871

At the heart of this conflict was the animosity between Conservative Presidents José María Medina of Honduras and Francisco Dueñas of El Salvador. The immediate cause was the sanctuary that El Salvador and Honduras were giving to each other's dissidents. On March 5, 1871, Honduras declared war on El Salvador. Salvadorian Liberals supported by Honduran troops invaded El Salvador through Sensuntepeque while a Honduran army invaded through the east. On March 5 Salvadorian Gen. Florencio Xatruch defeated the Hondurans at the hamlet of Pesaquina. Undeterred, the Salvadorian Liberals declared Santiago González provisional president at Sensuntepeque and marched on to Santa Ana. These fatigued troops found themselves confronted by a 5,000-man Salvadorian army commanded by Gen. Tomás Martínez, the former Conservative President of Nicaragua. In order to buy time, Honduran Col. Felipe Ochoa, commanding fifty soldiers, attacked the Salvadorian position. Driven back, Ochoa had four horses shot from under him before being shot dead. This bought enough time for the Liberals to prepare for battle. This raged between April 7 and 11 and was decided in favor of the rebels and Honduras by a flanking attack led by Gen. Emilio Delgado commanding 600 machete-men (*macheteros*). General González marched on to the capital, arriving on April 15. The Salvadorian Congress deposed Dueñas and González became president; Honduras and El Salvador signed an alliance.[21]

LIBERAL SALVADORIANS AND GUATEMALANS DEFEAT CONSERVATIVE HONDURANS, 1872–74

In an ideological "about-face," Guatemala went from the rule of an ultra-Conservative (Rafael Carrera, 1840–65) to an ultra-Liberal (Justo Rufino Barrios,[22] 1871–85)! This demonstrated how volatile *caudillo*-driven Central American politics could be. The introduction of repeating rifles (Remingtons and Winchesters) by the Guatemalan Liberals had helped them to win a civil war which had raged between 1871 and 1874.[23]

At the same time that Guatemalan President Barrios was emerging as the champion of the Liberals, Honduran President Medina was becoming the champion of Conservative Salvadorian and Guatemalan dissidents. In addition to supporting these rebels, Medina claimed an indemnity from El Salvador for his help in the overthrow of President Dueñas. On March 25, 1872, Medina severed diplomatic relations with El Salvador. El Salvador and Guatemala declared war on Honduras.

Three columns invaded Honduras—one commanded by Gen. Miguel Espinosa via the Nacaome road, one commanded by Gen. Ricardo Streber over the Gulf of Fonseca, and the third commanded by Salvadorian President Santiago González via the Chalatenango Road. Streber's force occupied Amapala on April 8. The force under Espinosa defeated the Hondurans at Sábana Grande and occupied Tegucigalpa on May 9. The troops commanded by President González drove Honduran troops commanded by President Medina out of Gracias (65 mi

W of Tegucigalpa). There, González set up a provisional Honduran government under Céleo Arias. Guatemalan troops led by their president, Garcia Granados, joined their Salvadorian allies at Gracias. The Guatemalan army turned over 700 Remington repeating rifles to the Salvadorians. In the meantime, Honduran President Medina retreated to Trujillo and then embarked for Omoa. Salvadorian troops defeated Medina at Santa Cruz on July 12 and at Santa Bárbara (55 mi NW of Tegucigalpa) on the twenty-eighth. Shortly afterward, he was taken prisoner.[24]

However, Arias proved incapable of suppressing Guatemalan and Salvadorian Conservatives who were operating from Honduras, so the Guatemalans and Salvadorians asked him to step down, which he refused to do. They now championed Ponciano Leiva for the presidency. The allies laid siege to Comayagua, Honduras, on January 6, 1874; Arias surrendered on the thirteenth and Leiva became president.[25]

LIBERAL GUATEMALANS DEFEAT CONSERVATIVE HONDURANS, 1876

The Honduran government still did not satisfy Guatemalan Liberal Barrios. Between 1863 and 1876 eighteen Conservatives had governed in Honduras and Honduran President Leiva was moving in that ideological direction. Barrios (and the new Liberal president of El Salvador, Andrés Valle) encouraged former Honduran President Medina, who he had overthrown two years earlier, to rebel. Medina, supported by 1,500 Guatemalan soldiers, won early victories. At this time, the President of El Salvador changed sides and Salvadorian and Honduran troops defeated General Medina at Los Navanjos on February 22. Just as matters seemed settled in Leiva's favor, a new contestant, Marco Aurelio Soto, entered the fray. A Honduran by birth, Soto was then serving as the Guatemalan Minister of War and commanded the Guatemalan troops in Honduras. The Guatemalan army succeeded in making Soto president of Honduras.[26]

LIBERAL GUATEMALANS AND HONDURAS DEFEAT *LIBERAL* SALVADORIANS, 1876

Guatemalan President Barrios cut diplomatic relations with El Salvador as a consequence of its having changed sides during the February 1876 intervention into Honduras. El Salvador declared war on Guatemala on March 10. Two theaters of operations evolved at opposite ends of El Salvador.

In the west, the Salvadorian army advanced into Guatemala but was defeated by Barrios at the plantation of "El Platanar" (35 mi SE of Guatemala City) on the twenty-fifth. As a consequence, Barrios occupied Ahuachapán and Chalchuapa, El Salvador. On April 14 the Salvadorians successfully recaptured Apaneca but failed in an effort at Chalchuapa two days later. Both sides sustained heavy casualties during these engagements.

In the east, 2,000 Honduran troops led by Gen. Gregorio Solares and 500 Salvadorian dissidents following Gen. Indalecio Miranda (as well as a Guatemalan contingent) invaded El Salvador through the departments of San Miguel and La Unión. Solares occupied the town of Pasaquina, while Miranda occupied the port of La Unión. On April 17–19, General Solares defeated 1,500 Salvadorians at Pasaquina. Some 600 men died in the fighting.

The decisive battle came in the west at Ahuachapán (40 mi SW of San Salvador) on April 18–21. Salvadorian Gen. Francisco Menéndez took up defensive positions in the town of Ahuachapan. Barrios threw 4,000 Guatemalans at the enemy. Both sides maintained an artillery bombardment. The defenders were being worn down by the superior numbers of the Guatemalans. A temporary truce began on the twenty-first, and four days later Salvadorian

President Valle resigned and Barrios' cronie, Liberal Rafael Zaldívar, became president of El Salvador.[27]

LIBERAL COSTA RICANS DEFEAT DISSIDENT COSTA RICANS AIDED BY GUATEMALA, 1877

Guatemalan Barrios was also displeased by the return to power of Costa Rican Liberal President Tomás Guardia[28] who had executed a successful *coup d'etat* against the recently elected Aniceto Esquivel on September 16, 1877. Guardia was a strong executive and could have thwarted Barrios' ambitions for a united Central America. Also, Barrios suspected Guardia's involvement in an unsuccessful plot to overthrow his government by Conservatives led by Enrique Palacios among others. In January 1879 Federico Mora led a small band, most of whom were Nicaraguans, into Costa Rica; he had the support of Guatemalan Barrios. Mora was defeated at both El Zapote and Matina and fled to Nicaragua. The campaign lasted eight days.[29]

CONSERVATIVE NICARAGUANS AND LIBERAL COSTA RICANS AND SALVADORIANS DEFEAT LIBERAL GUATEMALANS AND HONDURANS, 1885

On February 28, 1885, President Barrios unilaterally proclaimed the reestablishment of the Central American Union and declared himself "General-in-chief of the Central American forces." On March 22 Costa Rica, Nicaragua, and El Salvador (representing both Liberal and Conservative governments) entered into an alliance against Guatemala, whereas Honduras chose to side with Guatemala. Each side readied their armies. A 500-man Nicaraguan army commanded by Gen. Florencio Xatruch marched north to join its Salvadorian ally. The Honduran army under Gen. Longino Sánchez prepared to oppose its march through Honduras.

On March 3 a 14,500-man Guatemalan army led by President Barrios invaded El Salvador. Two days later it won the Battle of El Coco (50 mi W of San Salvador), although the Salvadorians were able to effect an orderly retreat. The Guatemalan army then marched toward Chalchuapa (35 mi W of San Salvador) where a 3,000-man Salvadorian army entrenched itself. On April 1 the opposing sides exchanged artillery fire. On the second the Guatemalan infantry attacked. At about ten o'clock in the morning President Barrios personally led an attack and was shot dead! The Guatemalans, carrying off Barrios' body, retreated in disorder. The Hondurans, Nicaraguans, and Costa Ricans did not arrive in time to participate in the fighting. With Barrios' death, peace was restored.[30]

GUATEMALA AND EL SALVADOR FIGHT TO A DRAW, 1890

On June 22, 1890, Salvadorian Gen. Carlos Ezéta attacked the national palace and President Francisco Menéndez died of a heart attack. Guatemala and Honduras refused to recognize the new Ezéta government. Also, Salvadorian Gen. Doroteo Fuentes declared against the new government and marched from the department of San Miguel toward the capital at the head of 2,000 men, but this force disintegrated along the way. On June 28 Guatemalan President Barillas declared war on El Salvador and border fighting erupted on July 16.

The next day Guatemala seized small arms purchased by El Salvador which were being transferred between the U.S. merchant steamers *Colima* and *City of Sidney* in the harbor of San José, Guatemala. In fact, the U.S. Minister to Central America, Lansing B. Mizner, had arranged the transfer so that the arms would not be delivered to El Salvador.[31]

On July 21 and 22, Guatemalan forces defeated those of El Salvador at El Coco and advanced toward Chalchuapa. At the same time a Salvadorian force invaded Guatemala in order to help Guatemalan Conservatives opposed to Barillas. Forces loyal to Barillas blocked their progress and forced them to retreat.

Exiled Salvadorian Gen. Jose Maria Rivas declared his desire to fight against Guatemala and was permitted to return from exile in Honduras. As a reward, General Ezéta armed some 2,200 troops loyal to Rivas. When Rivas reached the city of Santa Tecla, he changed sides and marched against the Salvadorian capital. The battle for the government house, "La Casa Blanca" (the White House) raged for fourteen hours. The defenders, significantly outnumbered, finally surrendered. Rivas declared the First Vice President Rafael Ayala, who was then a refugee in Honduras, to be president of El Salvador. President Ezéta, who was in Santa Ana directing operations against Guatemala, ordered his brother, Antonio, to retake the capital, which he did on July 30–31. Rivas was captured and executed. On August 26 U.S. Minister Mizner helped negotiate a solution whereby Carlos Ezéta relinquished control of the government but was eligible to run for the presidency, which he won.[32]

HONDURAN DISSIDENTS AIDED BY EL SALVADOR AND NICARAGUA FAIL TO BRING DOWN THEIR GOVERNMENT, 1891–93

In 1891 Conservative Ponciano Leiva once again became president of Honduras. This was perhaps the eleventh time (counting very brief interim periods) that he held the position. This attested to his ideological agility but also earned him Conservative as well as Liberal enemies. On November 27, 1891, three days before Leiva took office, dissatisfied Conservative Hondurans invaded from El Salvador. The rebels rapidly captured the town of La Ceiba and the port of Trujillo. Exiled Conservative Gen. Manuel Bonilla reentered Honduras from Guatemala and took command. However, the government was able to isolate and defeat the rebels.

While this was transpiring, Liberals in Tegucigalpa rebelled against Leiva. They were joined by other Liberals who had sought refuge in Nicaragua. The opposing armies fought on September 7 and 8, 1892, and the government troops were able to drive the Liberals back into Nicaragua. On February 9, 1893, Leiva stepped down but the new president, Rosendo Agüera, could not reach an accommodation with the Liberals who were now led by Gen. Policarpo Bonilla. The opposing armies met at Tatumbla in an indecisive engagement which lasted thirty-two days. On March 26 the Liberal army broke off the fight and marched on the capital. Between March 28 and April 2, the armies fought another indecisive battle outside Tegucigalpa. Finally, the Liberals retreated back into Nicaragua.[33]

LIBERAL NICARAGUANS DEFEAT CONSERVATIVE HONDURANS, 1893–94

For thirty years moderate Conservatives had governed Nicaragua in relative tranquility. In April 1893 coffee planters revolted against Conservative Roberto Sacasa and brought Liberal José Santos Zelaya[34] to power, which he would retain for sixteen years. He began a Liberal agenda (in particular the suppression of the Roman Catholic Church) and rapidly evolved into a ruthless despot. Zelaya also reorganized and modernized the army.[35]

In late 1893 recently elected Conservative Honduran President Domingo Vásquez threatened Zelaya that if he did not expel dissident Liberal Hondurans from Nicaragua, Vásquez would declare war on Nicaragua. Zelaya formed an alliance with Honduran Liberal Policarpo Bonilla. On December 23 Bonilla invaded Honduras at the head of Honduran Liberals and Nicaraguan troops. Between December 30, 1893, and January 3, 1894, the Liberals won the bloody battle of Choluteca (38 mi SE of Tegucigalpa). Following the battle, the captured commander of the Conservative forces, Gen. Vicente Williams, was executed. President Vásquez, commanding the Honduran army, attacked the Liberals at Choluteca on January 15 through 17 but was repulsed. The Liberals then laid siege to Tegucigalpa from January 24 through February 22. Finally, Vásquez fled into El Salvador and ardent Liberal Policarpo Bonilla became president. Some 700 soldiers died in the fighting.[36]

On June 20, 1895, El Salvador, Honduras, and Nicaragua again tried to revive the Central American union and agreed to conduct a united foreign policy. In December 1896 the United States recognized the union; however; El Salvador broke with the agreement on November 29, 1898, and the union dissolved.[37]

HONDURAN ARMY AIDS NICARAGUAN ARMY IN THE DEFEAT OF NICARAGUAN CONSERVATIVES, 1896

Liberal Nicaraguan President Zelaya asked Liberal Honduran President Policarpo Bonilla to send his army, which was led by Gen. Manuel Bonilla (a Conservative), into Nicaragua to help defeat a Conservative seaborne invasion from New York led by Enrique Soto. On April 13, 1896, the Conservatives captured Puerto Cortés and then marched toward San Pedro Sula and Villanueva. Nicaraguan Conservatives operating from El Salvador captured Copán and other towns. However, within one month Gen. Terencio Sierra, commanding the Nicaraguan army, crushed the rebellion.[38]

GUATEMALA REPULSES A SALVADORIAN INVASION, 1906

On May 27 exiled Guatemalan Gen. Manuel Barillas invaded Guatemala from El Salvador with the objective of overthrowing President Manuel Estrada Cabrera but was defeated at Ayutla (40 mi SE of Guatemala City) on June 11. On July 9 Gen. Tomás Regalado, the Salvadorian Minister of War who was frequently inebriated, spontaneously led a second invasion; he was killed in the first engagement four days later. Guatemala then invaded El Salvador. Some 7,000 Guatemalans attacked 2,000 Salvadorians in bloody, indecisive fighting near the haciendas of "El Platanar" and "Las Escobas" between July 12 and 17. Mexico and the United States intervened and restored peace. On July 20 a truce was signed on board the U.S. cruiser *Marblehead*. A regional peace conference was convened in Costa Rica; however, Nicaraguan President Zelaya refused to be represented and the gathering accomplished little as all parties prepared for renewed fighting.[39]

LIBERAL NICARAGUANS DEFEAT CONSERVATIVE HONDURANS AND SALVADORIANS, 1907

On February 1, 1903, Honduran Conservative Manuel Bonilla rebelled against Liberal President Juan Angel Arias who had been recently elected. Following a series of victories, Bonilla seized the capital, Tegucigalpa, on April 10 and was declared the president. In turn, Liberal General Dionisio Gutiérrez, supported by Liberal Nicaraguan President Zelaya, rebelled against Conservative Bonilla on December 23, 1906. The Honduran army chased the Liberal rebels into Nicaragua. As a consequence, Nicaraguan Liberal President Zelaya demanded reparations, which Honduras refused. Now, the Honduran Liberals *plus* the Nicaraguan army invaded Honduras in February 1907. On February 25 the invaders seized San Marcos, capturing 200 rifles, 10,000 cartridges, and a Krupp field gun.[40]

Zelaya dispatched a second force, 600 men on board two steamers. Their objective was to seize the Honduran Caribbean banana ports, an important source of revenue. The United States, wanting to restrain Zelaya's ambitions, landed Marines at Puerto Cortés, La Ceiba, and Trujillo to protect U.S. financial interests. The U.S. naval commander, Capt. William F. Fullam, extracted a promise from the Nicaraguans that American property would not be violated. In exchange, he permitted the Honduran troops to land at La Ceiba and Puerto Cortés. Fullam also arranged the surrender of the sole Honduran warship, the dilapidated *Marietta*.[41]

On March 11, some 5,000 Salvadorians commanded by Gen. José Dolores Preza joined 1,500 Hondurans. Together they met the Nicaraguans at the town of Nacaome (35 mi SE of Tegucigalpa). The battle raged for five days (March 18–23). It opened with a bombardment by the Krupp-made, Nicaraguan artillery. On the second day the Salvadorians and Hondurans attacked into fire from Maxim machine guns (used for the first time in Central America). As the fighting raged, almost half of the Honduran army deserted to the enemy's side. The Conservative Salvadorians and Hondurans were cut to pieces, losing more than 1,000 men. In large measure the Nicaraguan victory could be attributed to superior weapons. Zelaya reported, "The number of dead which they left on the field [was] so great that we were unable to bury all."[42]

Bonilla and 500 followers fled to the fort on the Island of Amapala in the Gulf of Fonseca. Appreciating the hopelessness of his position, Bonilla sought refuge on board the U.S. cruiser *Chicago*. The U.S. *chargé d'affaires*, Phillip Brown, in collaboration with the Nicaraguan and Salvadorian chancellors, supported Terencio Sierra for the Honduran presidency. However, a Liberal provisional government had declared Miguel R. Dávila president. Dávila dispatched troops against Sierra's followers, who were defeated. Although a Liberal, Dávila was distrusted by Nicaraguan President Zelaya.[43]

Next, Zelaya attempted to foster a revolution in El Salvador. In 1906 Guatemala and El Salvador had signed a friendship pact which Zelaya interpreted as being anti-Nicaraguan. At this point, Guatemala prepared to intervene to prevent Zelaya from succeeding. Mexico and the United States again stepped in to prevent the conflict from spreading.[44]

OBSERVATIONS

The most important event *vis-a-vis* late-nineteenth-century Central America was the reawakening of U.S. interests in the region following decades of Civil War reconstruction. As a consequence, the sixty-three years of feuding within and among the Central American countries became increasingly suppressed by American imperial ambitions.

The most important consequence of the fighting in the early years of the twentieth century was the 1907 Washington Treaty signed by Costa Rica, El Salvador, Guatemala, Honduras, and Nicaragua, plus Mexico and the United States. It forbade the use of one nation's territory to foment revolution against another. It declared Honduras neutral; this nation had been the most frequent battlefield during these conflicts; in return, Honduras pledged not to participate in future wars. The treaty declared that any government that came to power through force would not be recognized by the other states. It established the Permanent Central American Court of Justice to deal with regional disputes.[45]

The treaty was not an instant success. Neither Nicaraguan President Zelaya nor Guatemalan President Cabrera honored the agreement. Zelaya continued to send armed men into El Salvador. The United States and Mexico talked of establishing a joint naval patrol, the objective of which would have been to intercept the infiltrators, but this was never implemented.

Guatemala and El Salvador aided Conservative Hondurans who attempted to overthrow Liberal President Dávila. Thereupon, Nicaraguan President Zelaya supported Honduras. The United States and Mexico forced the Honduran issue to come before the Central American Court of Justice. The tribunal absolved Guatemala and El Salvador, although the evidence suggested otherwise. This decision helped to destroy the court's credibility.[46]

In 1916 the court heard claims by El Salvador and Costa Rica to rights in any future Nicaraguan canal. Both Nicaragua and the United States refused to accept the decision and the court never met again. The United States became the enforcer of the 1907 treaty when it chose to do so.[47]

No attempts have been made to quantify the impact of these "mini-wars" upon Central America. The destruction was most visible to those who traveled to El Salvador and Nicaragua where the geographical concentration of economic development made it more obvious.[48]

CHAPTER TWENTY-THREE

THE MISRULE BY BOLIVIAN *CAUDILLOS*, 1841–99

[T]he barracks was the schoolroom.
—Bolivian historian and politician Alcides Argüedas

THE SPARK

Geographical isolation, which significantly contributed to the lack of political, economic, and social development, created a "hot-house" for growing indigenous *caudillos* who would rule Bolivia throughout the nineteenth century.

BACKGROUND

Bolivia is the third-largest country in South America and in the mid-nineteenth century was about three times the size of Texas. The dominant factor in the national and international evolution of Bolivia is that practically all of the nation's population is isolated on a high plateau (*altiplano*) far from its own borders and even farther from the rest of the world. Sandwiched between the eastern and western *cordilleras* of the Andes Mountains is the Bolivian *altiplano*, some 500 miles long and 80 to 100 miles wide. The altitude ranges between 5,500 and 16,000 feet, with the average being 10,000 feet. The *altiplano* is cold and dry much of the year, despite the fact that it lies within the tropics. La Paz, the principal city, sits at 13,000 feet.[1]

The census of 1846 placed the population in the *altiplano* at 1.4 million persons. Perhaps 20 percent of these were pure-blooded Indians (most of the Quechua and Aymará groups), more than 70 percent were *mestizos* (called *cholos* in Bolivia), and the few remaining were white. These statistics could be misleading because race within Bolivia was determined as much by wealth as by ethnic origin. There were an estimated 700,000 "ungoverned" Indians in the eastern lowlands. The populations of the principal cities were: La Paz 40,000; Cochabamba 30,000; Sucre (formerly Chuquisaca) 12,000; Santa Cruz 9,000; and Oruro 4,600.[2]

These same four cities were also Bolivia's four political centers, and all lay in the *altiplano*. Most of the few poor roads that existed in Bolivia connected these cities. Sucre was the constitutional capital; however, Congress met alternately in the north (La Paz), the center (Cochabamba and Oruro), and south (Sucre) as a concession to regionalism. The greatest distance by land travel between any of these cities was 464 miles.[3]

Financially, the principal sources of money for the government were taxes imposed upon the Indians (a head tax and a tax on coca leaves), which initially accounted for some 60 percent of the revenue; those collected at the mines; and, as the nineteenth century progressed, those related to the export of nitrates from the Atacama Desert. These did not provide much revenue. When necessary, which was frequent, those who ruled levied contributions from whomever could be forced to pay.[4]

OPPOSING FORCES

Liberal and Conservative factions struggled for control of Bolivia; however, these labels merely indicated the degree of their disagreement and possessed little ideological significance. Real political parties did not begin to coalesce until the end of the nineteenth century. In general, the Conservatives represented a small aristocracy and were Centralists. The Liberals were more tolerant of those who had achieved high political status by whatever means possible, and were anticlerical Federalists.[5]

As with armies elsewhere in Latin America, Bolivia's was bloated with officers. During the War for Independence (see chapter 4) and the War of the Confederation (see chapter 11), those in power liberally gave out commissions to reward and to assure loyalty. By 1841 there was one general for every one hundred soldiers. However, the number of soldiers (frequently forced conscripts) was small. Following the Battle of Ingavi (August 14, 1841), the size of the army was reduced to less than 2,000 men. Typically, the Bolivian troops, which opposed each other in the intraclass battles of the nineteenth century, numbered but a few hundred men on each side.[6]

Horses do not thrive on the *altiplano*. Therefore, cavalry units were small and most frequently rode mules. Artillery pieces were holdovers from the colonial era and were used well past the middle of the nineteenth century.[7]

OPENING STRATEGIES

More often than not, the primary objective of individuals in conflict was to eliminate a rival, and this often could be achieved most expeditiously by assassination. Therefore, military operations, which could be expensive, frequently were not the first option when dealing with an enemy. Also, having four "capitals" instead of the normal one made starting rebellions easier and ending them more difficult.

THE RULE OF BALLIVIÁN (1841–47)

Because of his victory at the Ingavi on November 18, 1841, Gen. José Ballivián[8] emerged as the new strongman in Bolivia. The 1843 Constitution (the third of the young nation) gave the President an eight-year term and extensive powers. In an attempt to reduce the influence of the army, Ballivián established "military colonies" in the eastern lowlands and reduced the size of the army. Yet, about one-half of the government's small budget still went to paying military salaries and pensions.[9]

Ballivián's actions fueled discontent within the army. Three officers who were supporters of exiled former President Andrés de Santa Cruz plotted his return; they were discovered, tried, and shot. In spite of this, Santa Cruz attempted to regain power. He obtained a promise of help from Peruvian Gen. Manuel Vivanco. On October 15, 1843, Santa Cruz attempted to secretly land at Mejillones, Bolivia (500 mi SSW of La Paz). He was arrested and taken to Tacna, Peru, never again to set foot in Bolivia.[10]

On October 10, 1847, Gen. José Miguel de Velasco rebelled in Sucre (275 mi SE of La Paz). Ballivián defeated him at Vitichi on November 7. Then General Manuel Belzú[11] rebelled, assembled a 2,000-man army at Oruro (146 mi SE of La Paz), and marched against Ballivián. Rather than fight a civil war, Ballivián resigned on December 23 and retired into voluntary exile. General Velasco became president and Belzú secretary of war. Belzú, whose wife had had an illicit affair with Ballivián, now began a vendetta against Ballivián's supporters which lasted for years.[12]

THE RULE OF BELZÚ (1848–55)

On October 6, 1848, Belzú secretly left La Paz and joined rebels at Oruro. He decisively defeated Velasco, who commanded 1,500 infantry and 500 cavalry, at the village of Yamparáez after one hour of fighting on December 6, 1848. Between the opposing armies some sixty-five soldiers were killed and one hundred wounded.[13]

President Belzú immediately appealed to class hatred and encouraged the "have not" *cholos* to attack the great landlords. Mobs in La Paz and Cochabamba rose up in support of the regime. Guerrilla bands roamed the countryside stealing, raping, and murdering almost at will; this environment fueled endless conspiracies to oust the *caudillo* particularly by influential *criollos*. Captured enemies were brutally punished.[14]

In March 1849 followers of Ballivián rebelled in Oruro. The President's brother, Francisco de Paula Belzú, mobilized the "have nots." After three hours of street fighting, the troops deserted their rebellious chiefs who then fled to Peru, taking part of the nation's treasury with them. While this fighting was taking place, President Belzú marched from La Paz toward Oruro. In his absence, General Ballivián subverted the "*Batallón de Carabineros*" and captured the city. At midday the populace rose up and attacked the rebellious soldiers. Leaving 300 dead in the streets, the rebels escaped. Belzú returned to La Paz and received a tumultuous welcome.[15]

Soon, former President Velasco, who had been exiled to Argentina, together with José María Linares,[16] raised 2,000 men, invaded Bolivia, and captured Tarija (430 mi SE of La Paz). Belzú dispatched 1,700 men under Gen. José Gabriel Téllez who defeated the rebels on July 1, 1849; Velasco and Linares fled back into Argentina.[17]

On September 6, 1850, a student shot Belzú in the face, seriously wounding him. Gen. Agustín Morales was behind the plot. Belzú's popularity with the masses preserved his regime during a long convalescence. Those involved in the attempted assassination were shot along with other political enemies, including the President of Congress.[18]

Once again, Velasco and Linares invaded from Argentina with 2,000 followers and captured the town of Cotagaita (450 mi SE of La Paz). Belzú sent a force under Col. Jorge Córdova. These government troops defeated the invaders at the Battle of Mojo near the Argentine frontier on July 10, 1853. Once again, the rebels fled back across the border. Fighting at the battle were four men who had been or would be president of Bolivia—Velasco, Linares, Córdova, and Gregorio Pacheco.[19]

Émigrés continued to attack Belzú. On July 22, 1853, exiled Bolivian Gen. Sebastián Agreda, supported by Peruvian troops, landed and occupied the Bolivian port of Cobija (475 mi SSW of La Paz). Anticipated help from the exiled José María Linares that did not arrive, coupled with the possibility of an attack from Bolivian forces, caused the invaders to withdraw.[20]

Rebellions against Belzú continued. Col. Mariano Melgarejo[21] rebelled in Quinoni in December 1853 and was defeated and captured. Almost simultaneously Linares and General Ballivián, leading some one hundred rebels afoot and thirty on horseback, invaded Bolivia from Peru and captured the town of Escoma on January 12, 1854. The local inhabitants rose up and evicted the invaders. As a consequence of the incursions from Peru, Bolivian troops occupied the Peruvian towns of Zepita, Pomata, and Yunguyo but soon withdrew. In December Col. José María Cortés rebelled in Cotagaita and was defeated by Col. José María Suárez in Mocomoco. Tired of this constant fighting, Belzú voluntarily stepped down on August 15, 1855, in favor of his son-in-law, Gen. Jorge Córdova.[22]

THE RULE OF LINARES (1857–61)

José María Linares, who had led countless unsuccessful attempts to overthrow Belzú, rebelled against Córdova in Oruro on September 8, 1857. Soon, other cities joined the rebellion and Córdova fled to Peru. Linares attempted to reform Bolivia's fiscal program. Among other actions, he reduced the size of the army, which had grown to 6,000 men, to 1,200 troops and created a militia. Linares' rule became increasingly capricious.[23]

For the next three years one uprising after another occurred. Although they were successfully repressed, these rebellions took their toll on the government. In November 1860 the government massacred rebellious Indians at the shrine of Copacabana on Lake Titicaca. Also, Linares had a priest shot for conspiracy; as a consequence, two of his ministers resigned in protest and the public was outraged.[24]

On January 14, 1861, on the eve of presidential elections, Government Minister Ruperto Fernández and Generals José María de Achá, Minister of War, and Manuel Antonio Sánchez, commander of the garrison in La Paz, executed a *coup d'etat*. Congress elected General Achá president.[25]

The rebellions continued. On October 23 a group of Belzú supporters unsuccessfully attempted to seize La Paz while President Achá was out of the city. The conspirators were captured. Sixty of the prisoners, including former President Córdova, were massacred that same day by order of the city's military commander, Col. Plácido Yáñez. A mob rose up and quartered Yáñez.[26]

On March 7, 1862, Gen. Mariano Torrelio rebelled in Sucre. The rebels advanced to Potosí which they ransacked, including the Mint (*Casa de Moneda*), for fifteen days. Finally, a government force led by Gen. Gregorio Pérez chased the rebels back to Sucre and defeated them on April 4.[27]

Now it was General Pérez' turn to rebel, and he was supported by troops in Oruro and La Paz. Pérez gathered his forces on the Plain of San Juan, twelve miles from Oruro. On September 15, 1862, Achá approached with an inferior force and hesitated. Col. Mariano Melgarejo, commanding one of the divisions, said, "My General, it is necessary to attack, and I attack."[28] Without waiting for a response, he led his division in a charge. Pérez' army was defeated and retreated to La Paz. Achá recaptured the city which sustained significant damage. More than 1,000 Bolivians died in the fighting between Achá and Pérez.[29]

THE RULE OF MELGAREJO (1864–70)

On December 28, 1864, General Melgarejo seized the presidential palace in Cochabamba (140 mi SE of La Paz), made Achá his prisoner, and proclaimed himself president the next day.

He abrogated the Constitution, ruled by decree, and made sergeants ministers within his government.[30]

In March 1865 former President Belzú returned from exile and entered into La Paz to popular acclaim. Melgarejo marched from Oruro and attacked the city in eight columns on the twenty-seventh. The fighting was intense and Melgarejo led reckless charges while many of his soldiers deserted to Belzú. Undeterred, Melgarejo forced his way into the national palace with a handful of men, killed the guards, and shot Belzú with his own pistol while he was preparing to give a victory speech.[31]

Melgarejo's increasingly tyrannical rule inspired numerous rebellions. He created the elite "Colorado" Battalion, fanatically loyal to him personally. He crisscrossed the *altiplano* cutting down his opponents. Such grueling campaigning seemed to make Melgarejo stronger.[32]

Rebellions against Melgarejo did not end. In September 1865 Gen. Nicanor Flores rebelled. He occupied a hill called the Cantería near Potosí (265 mi SE of La Paz) and waited for Melgarejo's attack, who did so on September 5 in three columns. Flores' men stood out on the hillside and were easy targets. The rebels were easily defeated, sustaining many casualties. Melgarejo shot many of the prisoners, including the wounded. In June 1869 Col. Leonardo Antezana massacred Indians while carrying out Melgarejo's policy of seizing indigenous lands. When not fighting, Melgarejo devoted himself to liquor, women, gambling, gluttony, and brawling, while his mistress, Juana Sánchez, emulated his debaucheries.[33]

On November 24, 1870, *criollos* allied with Col. Hilarión Daza,[34] whose loyalty had been purchased for 10,000 pesos, rebelled. Now Daza commanded the Colorado Battalion which was stationed in La Paz. Melgarejo, who was in Oruro, did not go quietly. He defeated Gen. José Manuel Rendón at Potosí. As Rendón retreated to Cotagaita, Melgarejo marched against the rebels in La Paz. Col. Narciso Campero, who was returning from Buenos Aires with arms, joined forces with Rendón. Together they returned to Potosí where they defeated one of Melgarejo's supporters, Gen. Sebastián Agreda.[35]

Meanwhile, Melgarejo attacked La Paz. At 9 A.M. on January 15, 1871, Melgarejo, leading 2,100 men, attacked the barracks occupied by the rebels. Bloody street fighting raged until 8 P.M. when Melgarejo abandoned the attack and fled into exile. In all, 1,087 Bolivians died.[36]

Congress declared Col. Agustín Morales president on January 21. Morales' relations with Congress deteriorated to the point that on November 25 he dissolved the assembly. Two days later Morales was killed in a quarrel with a nephew. In May 1873 Congress chose Adolfo Ballivián, son of the victor of Ingavi, as president; however, he died of illness on February 14, 1874. His place was taken by Tomás Frías.[37]

Numerous rebellions occurred during Frías' tenure. In November 1874 the 3rd Battalion rebelled in Cochabamba but was suppressed. On December 23 the "Verdes" Battalion rebelled in La Paz and went on a three-day rampage. Frías and Daza took to the field. On January 18, 1875, Frías defeated Gen. Quintin Quevedo commanding 1,300 rebels. Frías lost three dead and seven wounded; Quevedo lost more than 100 dead and wounded plus 583 captured. Captured leaders were shot. On March 25, Frías and 716 government soldiers defeated 1,200 rebels led by Miguel Aguirre at Cochabamba.[38]

Another rebellion occurred, this time on the Pacific coast. Daza traveled to Arica, Peru. He embarked in a ship with 116 men and landed at the open roadstead of Cobija, Bolivia. This show of force was enough to quell the uprising. More revolts broke out in La Paz, Oruro, and

Cochabamba. The government palace in La Paz was burned. However, throughout these uprisings the government prevailed.[39]

THE RULE OF DAZA (1876–79)

On the eve of presidential elections, now-General Hilarión Daza, one of the candidates, seized the government and Congress proclaimed him president on May 4, 1876. Almost immediately, rebellions broke out in Potosí, Santa Cruz, and on the Pacific coast; they were all crushed.[40]

A poorly conceived law that taxed all nitrate exported from the Bolivian littoral, in spite of treaty obligations with Chile to the contrary, led to the War of the Pacific between Bolivia and Peru against Chile (see chapter 34). Daza led the Bolivian army to the coast but the war was disastrous for Bolivia, in part due to Daza's poor leadership. Daza received reports of unrest back in La Paz, and prepared to march back from Tacna to the capital and restore his authority. The Bolivian army in the Littoral mutinied and declared Colonel Camacho its leader. He was proclaimed president by those in La Paz and yet another constitution was adopted. These events could not prevent the loss of the war and on April 4, 1884, Chile and Bolivia signed the Treaty of Valparaiso, whereby Bolivia lost its lands bordering the Pacific Ocean and became a landlocked nation. The loss of the war did significantly reduce the influence of the army.[41]

The four presidents who succeeded Camacho and governed between 1884 and 1899 were all civilians. Although there were fewer rebellions during these decades, they did still occur. On October 8, 1888, President Aniceto Arce, commanding 2,500 men, fought an indecisive battle at Caricari against Col. Eliodoro Camacho leading 800 men. Following the fight, the rebels disagreed among themselves and the rebellion fell apart. Camacho led another unsuccessful attack against the government in May 1890.[42]

In January 1892 a major Indian insurrection occurred at Tiahuanacu (35 mi WSW of La Paz) over the issue of land ownership. The government reacted harshly, indiscriminately killing Indians throughout the *altiplano* for many months.[43]

THE RULE OF PANDO (1899–1904)

In early December 1898 the Conservative-dominated Congress voted to make Sucre the permanent capital. On the twelfth the citizens of La Paz, led by Col. José M. Pando,[44] rebelled against President Severo Alonso; this is commonly called the "Federal Revolution." The Conservatives, known as Constitutionalists, were supported by the silver interests (and as a consequence their miners) and the large landowners around Sucre and Potosí. The Liberals, known as Federalists, drew their support from the tin interests (and their miners), the masses in La Paz, and wealthy entrepreneurs from the eastern frontier.[45]

Immediately President Alonso led his forces from Sucre toward La Paz. They were armed with new Mauser rifles but lacked supplies. Their advance stalled at Viacha (26 mi SW of La Paz). In the meantime, the rebellious Federalists attempted to buy modern rifles in Peru. Also, for the first time, the Federalists armed the Indians and encouraged them to fight. The principal chief, Pablo Zárate, mobilized thousands of Indians. President Alonso dispatched foraging parties from Viacha to find supplies, but these patrols were attacked by the Indians. Some of these small units were killed to the man.[46]

In January 1900 the Federalists supported by Indians defeated a company of Constitutionalists at Cosmini. Twenty-four wounded Constitutionalists were interned in the church at Ayoayo.

There, they were attacked by Indians led by Villca Zárate and one by one tortured to death. The Constitutional army was demoralized by these events and retired to Oruro.[47]

The brothers Carlos and Lino Romero, who owned vast territory in the eastern lowlands, raised a force and defeated a numerically superior government force at Camargo (400 mi SE of La Paz) in the province of Cinti on February 24. As a consequence, they retained control over their vast holdings.[48]

On March 1, some 130 rebels led by Dr. Auturo Eguino occupied the hamlet of Mohoza. An Indian mob, probably mistaking them for government troops, surrounded the rebels and then locked them in the town's church. During the night the Indians began torturing their prisoners to death, one by one. The gruesome killings were prolonged over ten days.[49]

The Federalists attacked Cochabamba on March 14 but were driven off by well-entrenched Constitutionalists. Ten days later 600 Federalists led by Dr. Anibal Capriles captured Cochabamba from 150 Constitutionalists. On April 6 Gen. Pedro Vargas, commanding infantry, cavalry, and four Krupp guns, attempted to recapture the city. The fighting raged for six hours but the rebels tenaciously held onto the city. The following day government artillery bombarded Cochabamba for seven hours but to no avail.[50]

In April the opposing main armies began advancing toward each other, Alonso from Oruro and Pando from La Paz. Both planned to rest at Paria. They met on the road near the hamlet on the tenth. The Battle of Segundo Crucero lasted two hours. Alonso's army broke and ran, abandoning its artillery and baggage. In all, more then 600 men died. That same night Alonso escaped by train to Antofagasta, Chile. The power of the long-dominating Conservative oligarchy was broken by the Federalists and the Liberal Party came to power. Sucre continued as the constitutional capital but the government's offices were moved to La Paz.[51]

The Indians proved difficult to resubjugate: they reoccupied land, seized goods, and attacked the establishment. The civil war that had just ended had the potential to spark an interclass revolution. Pando reneged on his promises to the Indians. Their leadership was seized and executed. The Indians were beaten back into submission.[52]

OBSERVATIONS

Throughout the nineteenth century, Bolivia sustained some sixty civil wars and rebellions. Six individuals who served as president were assassinated—Pedro Blanco, Belzú, Córdova, Morales, Melgarejo, and Daza. And of these, Blanco (six days into his term) and Morales were murdered while serving. During the same period ten constitutions were promulgated and largely ignored.[53]

While repression and chaos alternated as the order of the day throughout the nineteenth century, Bolivia lost one territorial dispute after another, costing the nation its sparsely populated outlands. In 1867 Melgarejo ignorantly ceded to Brazil almost without challenge some 180,000 square miles bordering the Madeira and Paraguay Rivers. In 1879 Chile occupied and kept Bolivia's Pacific coast during the War of the Pacific (see chapter 34). In 1899 Argentina occupied the Chaco between the Bermejo and Pilcomayo Rivers. In 1903 Brazil defeated Bolivia in the Arce War and won a vast jungle region (see companion volume). In 1909 Peru was awarded by arbitration a small area along the Ucayali River. And in 1935, as a result of the Chaco War, Bolivia lost vast lands in the east (see companion volume). By the mid-twentieth century, Bolivia was about half the size it had claimed to be a century earlier.[54]

During the twentieth century, Bolivia would sustain few destructive intraclass rebellions and civil wars. The military would professionalize to the point that fighting among the elites would involve only their closest supporters, resulting in *coup d'etats* such as those in 1930 and 1934.

By the beginning of the twentieth century, the army became increasingly involved in maintaining the social and economic status quo, which meant holding down the Indians and miners. This lasted until 1952 (see companion volume).

Map 7. Gran Columbia, 1828.

PART 7

MID-NINETEENTH-CENTURY INTRACLASS STRUGGLES

CHAPTER TWENTY-FOUR

COLOMBIA AND SIXTY-THREE YEARS OF INTRACLASS CONFLICT, 1839–1902

> They [elections] were never orderly or fair. They were bloody combats in which voters risked their lives.
> —Historian J. Fred Rippy

THE SPARK

The single greatest spark to conflict was geographical isolation.

BACKGROUND

No country in the Western Hemisphere possesses greater geographical barriers to national cohesion than Colombia. As the 20,000-foot-high Andes Mountains entered southwestern Colombia and expanded northward, they forked into three major ranges which divided Colombia into four regions. Nestled among these ranges were steaming jungles, lush valleys, and grassy plains. Almost 90 percent of the population lived in the hills and valleys of the three Andean ranges, leaving the coastal Pacific sparsely populated and the large eastern *llanos* (plains) and *selva* (jungle) almost uninhabited.

To travel from one region to another during the nineteenth century required herculean effort if one did not take the long way around. The long route was to use one of the rivers that flowed into the Caribbean and then another river, or the Pacific Ocean, to come back southward to your destination. Traveling any distance east to west was almost impossible due to the mountain ranges. Even the long route was not easy because the mighty Magdalena and other rivers were difficult to navigate due to their shallows and rapids. Bogotá was the most inaccessible capital in the Americas. It cost less to ship goods from Southampton, England, to Medellín, Colombia (a distance of 6,170 miles), than from Medellín to Bogotá (a distance of 337 miles via burros and river steamers). As the nineteenth century closed, very little infrastructure had been constructed to overcome these geographical barriers.[1]

Following the breakup of Gran Colombia into Colombia (at first called Nueva Granada, then the Granadine Confederation in 1858, and finally Colombia in 1863), Venezuela, and Ecuador in 1830, the Colombian army was held in low esteem by the public because of the economic burden it placed on the young republic. In 1828 the Colombian army possessed 90 generals and 200 colonels, and military expenses consumed two-thirds of the national budget.[2]

Also, the composition of the Colombian army was very different from those found elsewhere within Latin America. The army was dominated by senior Venezuelan officers, holdovers from the War for Independence, thus providing little social mobility for the few native officers. Only a few Colombians had received land grants for military service, and therefore, no new landed aristocracy was created by the War for Independence as elsewhere. As a consequence of being land-poor, the native officers had little prospect of marrying into influential families, which would have improved their social standing.[3]

In 1831 over 200 Venezuelan officers (including 13 generals and 26 colonels) were expelled from Colombia, thus beginning the disintegration of the national army which continued for decades.[4] As a consequence, Colombia developed a tradition of civil dominance over the military, but that would not equate to peace or prosperity.[5]

OPPOSING FORCES

Two political parties evolved as the century progressed, and by the 1850s they were distinguished by sharp differences. The Liberal Party was composed of merchants (known as *Gólgotas*)[6] who wanted free trade, artisans and manufacturers who wanted protectionism, and junior military officers (known as *Draconianos*). The Liberals favored separation of church and state and initially greater autonomy for the provinces and a weak executive. The Conservatives drew their support from the large landowners and the Roman Catholic Church. They wanted a state religion, the Roman Catholic Church, and initially a strong, central government.

In general, Pasto and Medellín were Conservative strongholds, and Bogotá and the Caribbean coast, those of the Liberals. The peasants generally obeyed their *patrones*. Therefore, raising an army was almost feudal in nature. The struggle between the Liberals and Conservatives concerned only who among the franchised would rule the nation; therefore, all of these conflicts were interclass struggles.[7]

OPENING STRATEGY

Most frequently, both sides accurately perceived that capturing the enemy's capitals was the best strategy. Also, control of the Magdalena River was important because it was the only practical avenue for acquiring weapons and munitions by those who governed in Bogotá. Given the shortage of firearms and gun powder within Colombia during the middle decades of the nineteenth century and the feudal nature of the opposing armies, the generals had limited operational and tactical options. Massed frontal assaults and fighting with edged weapons were frequently the order of the day. In the last decades of the century, both sides were most commonly armed with weapons manufactured in the United States. The Remington rifle, Winchester carbine, and Gatling machine gun could be found on both sides. Typically, artillery was obsolete.[8]

PRELUDE TO CHAOS

Following the death of Simón Bolívar in 1830, moderately conservative presidents governed Colombia for twenty years in relative peace. On July 22, 1833, Gen. José Sardá, a Spaniard who had fought for the Revolutionaries in Mexico and Colombia, led a short-lived barracks rebellion against the government of Francisco de Paula Santander.[9] This uprising was ruthlessly suppressed. In 1837 the moderately Conservative José Ignacio de Márquez was elected president. Less tactful than his predecessors, he seized four virtually deserted convents in the province of Pasto in the southwestern corner of Colombia with the intention of using the proceeds from their sales to promote public education in Pasto.[10]

WAR OF THE SUPREMES (WAR OF THE CONVENTS)[11]

In June 1839 hard-line Conservatives in Pasto rebelled in protest to the closing of the convents. Although crushed by July 1840, the rebellion was revived by the Liberal José María Obando.[12] Soon he was joined by other regional *caudillos*. Obando's main goal was to oust President Márquez. Additional rebellions occurred in the northeast, and in November 1840 other rebels in Panama declared independence which they maintained until 1842. The Liberals attacked Bogotá but were repulsed by the city's militia. All seemed lost for the government when it won battlefield victories in October 1840 and April 1841, which turned the tide in its favor. By mid-1841 the rebellion had collapsed, and General Pedro Alcántara Herrán,[13] one of the government's most successful commanders, was inaugurated president on May 2, 1841. The war produced a conservative, Centralist backlash which was formalized in the Constitution of 1843. The Church regained much of the power and privilege that it had lost during the War for Independence. Ecclesiastical courts were restored and the Jesuits (expelled by the King in 1767) were allowed to return. Thousands died during the fighting.[14]

THE CIVIL WAR OF 1851

In 1849, using intimidation, the Liberal José Hilario López[15] was elected president. In May 1851 the Conservatives in the province of Pasto rebelled, and this spread to the provinces of Antioquía, Mariquita, Neiva, Pamplona, and Tunja. The largest insurgency force was 3,000 men under Gen. Eusebio Borrero in the province of Cauca. This force was defeated at Buesaco by Gen. Manuel María Franco. Within a few months, the new Liberal government regained control. To consolidate their power, the Liberals promoted the adoption of the Constitution of 1853. This replaced the unitary state with a federal union. Many of the social issues championed in the failed European revolutions of 1848 were adopted. The church and state were separated, the tithe outlawed, ecclesiastical courts abolished, and the Jesuits once again expelled.[16]

THE BARRACKS REBELLION (*GOLPE DE CUARTEL*) OF 1854

On April 17, 1854, a group of disgruntled radical Liberals (*Draconians*), angered over the failure of Congress to dismantle the national army, overthrew the Liberal President Gen. José María Obando, whom they had helped elect. The new Liberal president, José María Melo,[17] who was the commander of the Bogotá garrison, drove many members of Congress and government officials out of the capital. He formed workers' battalions to defend the new government. The mainstream Liberals united with Conservatives against Melo, calling themselves Constitutionalists (*Constitucionalistas*).

Three former presidents, leading their private armies, converged on Bogotá.[18] On November 22 Melo attacked the force led by General López at Bosa; the seven-hour battle was indecisive. On December 3 the 11,000-man *Constitucionalista* army battled Melo's 7,000-man force at Tres Esquinas. On the fourth the *Constitucionalistas* fought their way into Bogotá. Overall, 800 men died including three generals. Three hundred individuals were imprisoned or deported to Panama. In an about-face, the Conservatives now professed federalism, seeking a diffusion of power into the provinces as a method of insulating themselves against the Liberals who controlled the national government.[19]

The Liberals were ousted by the election of Conservative Mariano Ospina Rodríguez in 1857. The adoption of the Constitution of 1858, which again restored numerous privileges to the Roman Catholic Church, reduced the size of the national army. During the preceding years, the army had increasingly aligned itself with the moderate Liberals. Also, the Conservatives attempted to increase their control over the state militias; this alienated the regional *caudillos*.[20]

In 1859 fighting broke out between the Liberals and the Conservatives within numerous states (the Constitution of 1858 had reorganized Colombia into states). The Conservatives in Santander revolted against the Liberal state government but were defeated. Liberals in Bolívar overthrew their Conservative state government. Liberals and Conservatives in the states of Magdalena and Cauca were waging a bitter fight with each other. Public order disintegrated in the state of Santa Marta where those who challenged the honesty of the elections went on a rampage; the national army garrisons were too weak to intervene.

THE CIVIL WAR OF 1860

On September 13, 1859, President Ospina declared a state of emergency and designated General Herrán, then in the United States, as the commander of the national army. Congress passed a law making state officials criminally liable for breaches of the peace. In May 1860 officials in Cauca, Bolívar, Magdalena, and Santander each declared their states independent from Colombia and chose Gen. Tomás Cipriano de Mosquera,[21] now a Liberal (he had served as a Conservative president in 1845–49), as "Supreme Director of War." They were referred to as the Confederationists (*Confederacionistas*), and the government's forces were called the Legitimists (*Legitimistas*). Initially, the fighting went badly for the *Confederacionistas*. On August 15 the Conservatives of Santander won the Battle of Oratorio, taking control of the state. On the twenty-sixth, Mosquera, commanding 3,500 men from Cauca, was defeated by 3,000 *Legitimistas*. Appreciating his vulnerability, he negotiated a truce to buy time.[22]

Mosquera concluded a new military pact with the leaders in the other rebellious states. On November 19, 1860, commanding 3,000 men, he defeated 770 *Legitimistas* in Segovia, capturing half of the enemy, many of whom were executed. This victory gave Mosquera control of the Magdalena River and permitted him to establish contact with the *Confederacionistas* along the Atlantic Coast.[23]

As the fighting continued, the *Confederacionistas* won control of the areas along the Caribbean while Mosquera tied down the government's principal force in the Magdalena River valley near Bogotá. On March 13, 1861, Mosquera negotiated another local cease fire with the government, allowing his 3,500-man army from Cauca to temporarily avoid combat with a *Legitimista* force almost twice its size. Twelve days later, 5,000 *Legitimistas* commanded by Gen. Joaquín París defeated 2,700 *Confederacionistas* commanded by Mosquera in a fourteen-hour battle at Santa Bárbara. In all, 1,100 casualties were sustained, the majority being

Confederacionistas. Again, Mosquera negotiated a three-day truce to bury his dead and attend to his wounded. This gave him time to reorganize his army.[24]

On May 3, some 800 *Confederacionistas*, commanded by Col. Santos Gutíerrez, arrived from the north reinforcing Mosquera's command. This brought his army to 3,000 men (2,300 infantry and 700 cavalry). At 6 A.M. on July 18, Mosquera attacked the outer defenses of Bogotá. Following an eight-hour battle, the *Legitimistas* were defeated. Two hundred were killed and twice as many wounded. In spite of this victory, guerrilla warfare continued in the countryside for another two years.[25]

Once again the political process was reversed, and liberal constitutions were adopted in 1861 and 1863. The Jesuits were expelled once more. No priests were permitted to exercise rites without the consent of the government, and the archbishop of Bogotá was imprisoned for his failure to enforce the new liberal constitution among the clergy.[26]

FIGHTING WITH ECUADOR

While the Civil War of 1860 raged, a group of Colombian Liberals led by Julío Arboleda sought refuge in Tulcán, Ecuador. They were pursued by Conservative Capt. Matías Rosero, and fighting soon broke out inside Ecuador. Among the injured was Vicente Fierro, the local Ecuadorian *caudillo*, who supported the Colombian Liberals. Ecuadorian President Gabriel García Moreno raised an army of 1,900 men (1,500 Ecuadorians and 400 Colombian Liberals) and advanced toward the frontier. In the meantime Colombian Gen. Julío Arboleda crossed into Ecuador and routed its army, capturing the Ecuadorian President and his general staff (*Estado Mayor*). Arboleda advanced deeper into Ecuador when on November 12 he was fatally wounded by an assassin, dying the next day.[27]

In 1863 President Mosquera, wishing to recreate Gran Colombia, contacted Ecuador and Venezuela; but neither was interested. Mosquera encouraged Ecuadorian dissidents to overthrow García Moreno. Fighting broke out in border areas and Ecuador sent armed launches and the armed merchant schooner *Flor de Avante* (2 guns) to its northeastern province of Esmeraldas. Recklessly, Ecuadorian Gen. Juan José Flores invaded Colombia at the head of 6,000 men (5,300 infantry and 700 cavalry). Mosquera commanding 3,880 men (mostly state troops from Cauca) marched southward. On December 6, 1863, they fought the Battle of Carlosama (called Cuaspud or Guaspud by the Ecuadorians). The Ecuadorians lost 96 dead and 2,200 prisoners; the Colombians lost 52 dead. A generous peace restored the status quo.[28]

THE *COUP D'ETAT* OF 1867

In 1866 Mosquera returned to the presidency. He sought to increase the power of the national government over the states. He endeavored to reorganize the "Colombian Guard" (the national army) and to disarm the states' armies. Mosquera privately concluded a secret agreement with Peru without the knowledge of Congress whereby Colombia would purchase for Peru with Peruvian money the ship *Rayo* to be used in Peru's war against Spain (see chapter 30). This was an attempt by Peru to circumvent U.S. neutrality laws. On April 29, 1867, Mosquera seized dictatorial powers. Outraged by these events, on May 23 the Conservatives and Radical Liberals temporarily united and overthrew Mosquera.[29]

THE CIVIL WAR OF 1876

The Liberals held the presidency from 1861 into the 1880s. Throughout these years, frequent near-anarchy reigned in the countryside. Nine states became virtually independent, each possessing its own army. The most serious rebellion against the central government occurred in 1876 when, shortly after the Liberal Aquileo Parra assumed the presidency, the Conservatives in the states of Cauca, Antioquia, and Tolima rebelled.[30]

In July 1876 Conservative Col. Francisco de Paula Madriñán captured the city of Palmira, Cauca (307 mi SW of Bogotá), and began fratricide in the name of the Roman Catholic Church. On the twenty-sixth national troops recaptured the city. On July 31 Liberal Gen. Julián Trujillo, leading 3,000 men, defeated Conservative Gen. Joaquín María Córdoba, commanding 4,000 men, at the bloody Battle of Los Chancos in Tolima. The Conservatives lost 770 men and the Liberals 500. Trujillo advanced into Antioquía. Between November 20 and 22, some 5,000 Liberals and 7,000 Conservatives fought the Battle of Garrapata, another bloody engagement during which neither side gave quarter. The Liberals lost 970 men and the Conservatives 500. The Conservatives negotiated a sixteen-day truce and retired to Manizales.[31]

The Liberal government in Bogotá dispatched additional troops under Gen. Daniel Aldana to reinforce Trujillo. Some 5,000 Liberals and 4,000 Conservatives met again at La Donjuana on January 27, 1877. The Liberals won the field sustaining 500 dead and 680 wounded; the Conservatives lost 250 dead and 300 wounded. They met again at Manizales on April 5. Once again the Liberals took the initiative, attacked, and were victorious. The Conservatives lost 250 dead and the Liberals 140. This battle completed the destruction of the Conservative army. On April 6 the Conservative guerrillas in Cundinamarca surrendered, bringing organized fighting to an end. In spite of its victory, the Liberal central government was almost powerless to subdue the independence of the Conservatives within many states. Also, throughout the decade of the seventies, Panama was frequently in revolt.[32]

THE CIVIL WAR OF 1884

In 1880 Rafael Núñez won the presidency as a Liberal. Abandoning his old party, he created the National Party, successfully drawing together moderate Liberals and Conservatives. In late 1884 bands of Liberals in the states of Santander, Boyacá, Cundinamarca, Magdalena, Bolívar, and the province of Panama rebelled. Those in Panama acquired the English vessel *Morro* and the coastal steamer *Alajuela*. The national government placed Conservative Gen. Leonardo Canal in command of the national army and recalled to service numerous regional Conservative *caudillos*. Within three months, they had raised an 8,000-man army. Many Liberal officers within the national army deserted, taking with them their men and equipment.[33]

Within central Colombia numerous engagements took place throughout late 1884 and 1885. Rarely did the opposing forces number more than a few hundred men and most frequently those representing the national government were victorious.[34]

The rebellious Liberals did not have much better success in the north, their traditional stronghold. The Liberal commanders of garrisons in Panama declared against the national government. They were supported by some who had come to dig the canal, many of whom were the dregs of society. On March 31, 1885, Liberal Col. Pedro Prestán torched Colón rather than let it fall into the hands of the government, leaving 15,000 persons homeless.[35] Civil order completely broke down, and landing parties from British, French, and United States warships worked to restore order. On April 27 Conservative Gen. Rafael Reyes landed in Panama and restored the province to national control.[36]

While the Liberals were experiencing disaster in Panama, they met a similar fate at Cartagena (983 mi NNW of Bogotá). During the night of May 7, Liberal Gen. Ricardo Gaitán

Obeso unsuccessfully attempted to storm the city's defenses with 2,800 men. After ten hours of fighting, the attackers lost 300 dead and 278 prisoners, plus 297 Remington and Peabody rifles and 20,000 cartridges; the government's losses were but a handful of men. Next, the Liberals half-heartedly besieged the city; this was broken when a rag-tag, government relief force arrived on the twentieth having traveled over 500 miles from the south.[37]

On June 17 the opposing sides fought the bloody Battle of La Humareda (or El Hobo). Government troops held the port of La Gloria on the left bank of the Magdalena River not far from the Caribbean Sea. At nine o'clock in the morning, a Liberal flotilla made up of the small steamers *Bismarck*, *Confianza*, *María Emma*, *Isabela*, *Cometa*, and *El Vigilante* (armed with 12 cannon and 3 machine guns) attacked.

While the steamers held the enemy's attention, Liberal forces flanked the government troops to the north and south. In order to inspire their men, Liberal generals led the attacks against the entrenched enemy, and fighting became hand to hand. By 4:30 P.M., the outnumbered defenders began to retreat. Coincidentally, both sides had ordered their troops to wear green bandanas for identification. This caused confusion and worked to the advantage of the government troops, permitting many to escape. It was a Pyrrhic victory for the Liberals. They lost 300 dead and 250 wounded, including six generals. Also, a crewman on board the *María Emma* accidentally set the ship afire, destroying it and valuable munitions. The government lost 230 dead, 180 wounded, and 100 prisoners, including three generals.[38]

Following the Battle of La Humareda, the Liberals made a stand at Calamar. Inhabited by 1,000 persons, this Magdalena River port was the terminus of the Dique Canal which connected Cartagena with that river. The fighting began on June 6, and finally on July 21 the Liberal defenses collapsed as their small steamers sailed downriver to Barranquilla (950 mi N of Bogotá) where they ultimately surrendered. On August 26, 1885, the national government declared the civil war at an end.[39]

Following the defeat of the Liberals, Núñez championed the Constitution of 1886, which restored the power of the Roman Catholic Church, reconstructed a strong regular army, and reserved to the central government the right to possess arms and munitions. States lost much of their independence and were now called departments. These circumstances split the Liberal Party into peace and war factions.[40]

THE CIVIL WAR OF 1895

On January 22, 1895, the "war" Liberals in Bogotá unsuccessfully attempted to seize Nationalist President Miguel Antonio Caro. Other Liberals in the departments of Cundinamarca, Tolima, Santander, and Boyacá, and the province of Panama joined the rebellion. The national government declared an emergency. The "war" Liberals in Santander were reinforced by Venezuelan mercenaries and those in Panama by adventurers led by the Mexican Catarino Garza. President Caro appointed the self-made dynamo Rafael Reyes[41] as commander of the national army.

After quelling the rebellion in the central region, Reyes arrived in the coastal port of Barranquilla on February 19 and organized the government's forces in the north. On March 15, some 1,500 government troops led by Reyes defeated 2,500 rebels (Colombian and Venezuelans) led by Gen. José María Ruiz at the Battle of Enciso. The Liberals lost 300 dead (including Venezuelan Colonel [first name unknown] Entrena) and a large number of prisoners. The government lost 200 men. The following day government troops surprised 2,000 rebels at

Capitanejo and they surrendered. During April rebel forces in Panama were defeated and Garza killed. By early November the national government was once again in total control.[42]

WAR OF A THOUSAND DAYS

The last civil war of the nineteenth century, the War of a Thousand Days, was the bloodiest. It began on October 17, 1899, when the "war" Liberals in Santander seized the towns of El Socorro and San Gil. Within a few days the entire North was in rebellion. On the nineteenth Liberals in the river port of Barraquilla seized eight merchant craft and the gunboats *Hércules* and *Colombia*. This success gave them control of the Magdelana River. On the twenty-fourth government troops (known as *Legitimistas*) stormed the craft while at dock and recaptured them. The Liberals lost 204 men and the government losses were minimal.[43]

Undeterred, 2,500 Liberals led by Gen. Rafael Uribe attacked 1,200 *Legitimistas* defending Piedecuesta on October 28. The better disciplined government troops repulsed the attackers. Next, Uribe attacked Bucaramanga (285 mi NNW of Bogotá) on November 12–13 with a slightly larger force, and again was beaten back, losing 1,000 dead (including 3 generals) and 500 wounded. The *Legitimistas*' losses were significantly less, but the government did not aggressively follow up these victories.[44]

For the next few weeks the two sides gathered their scattered forces. Between December 15 and 17, some 4,000 Liberals commanded by Uribe fought 5,610 *Legitimistas* commanded by *Generalísimo* Vicente Villamizar at the Battle of Peralonso. The fighting turned when Uribe charged with only fourteen followers over a contested bridge and the *Legitimistas* panicked. The government lost 700 dead and wounded, 900 prisoners, and 2,000 deserters; the Liberals lost 750 dead and wounded. The victorious Liberal army entered the city of Cúcuta, thus preserving its source of weapons and munitions across Colombia's frontier with Venezuela. Now it was the Liberals who failed to exploit a major victory as they did not immediately march on Bogotá.[45]

On February 2, 1900, Liberals captured the government fort at Gramalote. The same day Liberals led by Uribe surprised some *Legitimistas*, capturing 700 men (including 3 generals) and their train. While the Liberals were winning local victories, the government was rebuilding its army. Also, the Liberals received additional weapons and munitions from Venezuela, following Gen. Cipriano Castro's military victory over Venezuelan President Ignacio Andrade in October (see chapter 21).[46]

On April 23 a Liberal army, calling itself the "Restorer" (*Restaurador*), marched southward toward Bogotá, arriving at Palonegro on the twenty-ninth. There, between May 11 and 29, some 8,000 Liberals led by Gen. Gabriel Vargas Santos battled 21,600 *Legitimistas* commanded by Gen. Próspero Pinzón. The battle line extended ten miles. On the thirteenth Liberal Generals Uribe and Benjamín Herrera led violent attacks and machetes were frequently used against the government's center and left. A Liberal victory seemed within grasp, but Gen. Vargos Santos failed to provide reinforcements to exploit the success. On the fourteenth the Liberals renewed their attacks as a heavy rain began to fall. Finally, the Liberals lost the initiative as the unburied dead decomposed in the rain and contaminated the water.

On the twenty-sixth of May, the Liberals abandoned the battlefield and retreated northward to their traditional stronghold without being harassed by the *Legitimistas*. The government lost 2,600 men dead and wounded; 2,300 to illness; and 1,290 to desertion. The Liberals lost 2,000 men dead (including many officers), 1,000 prisoners, 1,100 to desertion, and many wounded.[47]

The Liberals had sought to rebuild their power. They had acquired the small ships *Peralonso* and *General Gaitán*. Under the command of Gen. Siervo Sarmiento, the ships carried 1,800 rifles and 200,000 cartridges to Riohacha on the Caribbean on May 8, 1900. There the general died of yellow fever, and the Mexican adventurer Francisco Ruiz Sandoval betrayed the Liberals and sailed the ships to Venezuela, where they were interned by President Castro.[48]

Back in Bogotá, the traditional Conservatives, seeking a political solution to the fighting, supported a successful *coup* by Vice President José Manuel Marroquín against President Manuel Antonio Sanclemente, a nationalist, on July 31, 1900. Marroquín proved to be more hardline than his predecessor and prosecuted the war with new vigor.[49]

About this time, Colombians and Venezuelans clashed at Riohacha. On September 13, 1901, government troops defeated a Liberal force which included many Venezuelans. The *Legitimistas* took 200 prisoners. As a consequence, Colombia broke diplomatic relations with Venezuela. Additionally, the president of Ecuador, Eloy Alfaro, financially supported the "war" Liberals who had been driven from Buenaventura and Tumaco into Ecuador.[50]

The Liberals shifted the focus of their activity to Panama with the support of the Nicaraguan president, José Santos Zelaya. The Liberals purchased the Salvadoran-built cattle boat *Iris*, armed it, and renamed the ship the *Almirante Padilla*. Liberal General Herrera, commanding 1,500 soldiers, captured Tonosí, Panama, on December 24, 1901. In Panama, the *Legitimistas* seized the Chilean merchant ship *Lautaro* on January 20, 1902, which with the gunboats *El Chucuito* and *Boyacá* prepared to seek out the *Almirante Padilla*. However, on that same day, the *Almirante Padilla*, disguised as a merchant ship, sailed into Panama Bay and sank the *Lautaro*, killing many of the crew including Gen. Carlos Albán, the governor. The *Almirante Padilla* then escaped.[51]

Liberal General Herrera, who was well informed by spies in Panama City, attacked the town of Aguadulce (120 mi WSW of Panama City and 2 miles inland from the Pacific Ocean). On February 23, 1901, some 4,000 Liberals here defeated 1,500 *Legitimistas*. The Liberals lost 339 men dead and wounded and the government 300 men dead and wounded plus 200 desertions. Herrera then occupied the town of David near the frontier with Costa Rica in order to reorganize his army, rest his men, and improve communications with Nicaragua.[52]

In mid-1902, the new *Legitimista* governor of Panama, Gen. Víctor M. Salazar, dispatched the gunboat *Próspero Pinzón* to the waters off Nicaragua in order to interrupt the support being provided to the Liberals throughout that country. The gunboat forced the ships *San Jacinto* and *La Rosita* to seek refuge in Nicaraguan ports. Next, the *Legitimistas* reoccupied Aguadulce on July 30. However, on that day, they sustained a catastrophic naval defeat off the Pacific coast of Panama. The *Almirante Padilla* destroyed the government's squadron. It drove off the gunboat *El Chucuito*, captured the gunboat *Boyacá*, and seized the transport *Campo Serrano*. On board the latter were three generals, five colonels, three lieutenant colonels, six sergeant majors, 65 junior officers, 250 troops, three cannons, 350 rifles, 50,000 cartridges, plus other war supplies.[53]

Now the 8,000 Liberals commanded by Herrera besieged the 5,000 *Legitimistas* under Col. Luís Morales Berti in Aguadulce. The *Legitimistas* held out for one month, surrendering on August 27. Many of the prisoners joined the Liberal army, making it the strongest fielded by them during the entire war. The Liberals controlled all of Panama with the important exceptions of Colón, Panama City, and the railroad that ran between them. However, they were unable to carry the fight to those important cities.

Commander Thomas C. McLean, captain of the U.S. cruiser *Cincinnati*, notified both sides that he would not permit any military operations that would interfere with the railroad. Soon, the Colombian government acquired the gunboat *Bogotá*, a warship far superior to the *Almirante Padilla*; thus the Liberals' control of the Pacific was in serious jeopardy. The Liberals held Panama (except for the transit corridor) and the *Legitimistas* the remainder of Colombia. Neither side was capable of changing the status quo in the short term.[54]

Finally, on October 24 Liberal General Uribe surrendered the Liberal forces in Panama in exchange for amnesty and some political reforms. A formal peace treaty was signed on board the U.S. battleship *Wisconsin* on November 21, 1902. Some Liberals in the interior of Colombia continued to fight, eventually being crushed by the national government.[55]

OBSERVATIONS

The endless fratricidal rebellions, some of which grew into full-scale civil wars, were the norm within Colombia throughout six decades of the nineteenth century. The severity of the ultimate struggle, the War of a Thousand Days, discredited the extremists in both parties. As a consequence, moderate, Conservative presidents would govern Colombia from 1902 until 1930 and would appoint bipartisan cabinets.[56]

Due to the decades of fighting by armies based upon feudal-like obligations, the new, more moderate leadership began the process of creating a modern, professional military.[57]

How many individuals died as a consequence of sixty-three years' turmoil is unknown. An 1843 census calculated the population at 1,931,684 individuals; by 1885 the population was about 3,000,000; and at the end of the century between 3,500,000 and 4,000,000.[58] Between 25,000 and 40,000 soldiers died in combat during the War of a Thousand Days. Jesús María Henao and Gerardo Arrubla calculated:

> This three-year struggle caused incalculable losses. On the battlefields 100,000 men or more perished; thousands were maimed for life; commerce was ruined; communications were very difficult; production almost negligible; and paper money, issued in increasing quantities to meet the needs of the government, depreciated so much that a paper peso was worth less than one *centavo* in gold.[59]

The nation had stagnated. Railroad miles, a measure of industrial progress during the second half of the nineteenth century, provide some insight into the failure to develop infrastructure within Colombia. In 1893 Colombia possessed only 218 miles of track. Peru, a country possessing a similar population, resources, and geographical barriers, plus its share of civil disorder, had 883 miles.[60]

Another consequence of the six decades of fighting was Colombia's inability to prevent the loss of Panama (see companion volume). Throughout much of the War of a Thousand Days, Panama was governed by the port of Cartagena and not the capital of Bogotá.[61]

CHAPTER TWENTY-FIVE

URUGUAYAN INTRACLASS CONFLICT, 1832–1904

> I am retiring to private life being discouraged to the point of believing that our country is an ungovernable country.
> —President Lorenzo Latorre upon his resignation, March 13, 1880

THE SPARK

The rivalry between the *caudillos* Fructuoso Rivera[1] and Juan A. Lavalleja,[2] each of whom represented political factions nearly equal in strength, sparked seven decades of fighting between these factions.[3]

BACKGROUND

Two political parties appeared shortly after Uruguayan independence in 1830, the *Blancos* (Whites) and the *Colorados* (Reds). Although they both professed differing ideologies with laudable goals, what really distinguished them from each other were the agendas of their members. The *Blancos* drew their strength from the large ranchers (*estancieros*), merchants, and high clergy. Externally, the *Blancos* were supported by Juan Manuel de Rosas of Argentina (had ideology really mattered, Rosas would have been a strange bedfellow for these Centralists). The *Colorados* were supported by the Uruguayan *gauchos*, the intellectuals, the "have-nots" of society, the Argentine *émigrés*, and the dispossessed European Liberals. Externally, the *Colorados* were supported by the Argentine provinces opposed to Rosas and by Brazil. In general, one was born into his party and rarely changed allegiance.[4]

Two political centers emerged within Uruguay by the 1830s. One was Montevideo, which lay on the mouth of the Río de la Plata. Roads and trails projected northward from the port like spokes on a wheel, penetrating to the Uruguay River in the west, the Brazilian border in the north, and the Atlantic Ocean in the east. The other political center was the fertile, grassy prairie which dominated the remaining Uruguayan landscape.

The population of Uruguay in 1828 was about 60,000 inhabitants, and about 15,000 of these individuals lived in Montevideo. The population rapidly increased throughout the nineteenth century due to immigration, prominently from Spain and Italy, and initially most of these people settled in Montevideo. By 1900 the population of Uruguay reached 1,000,000 inhabitants.[5]

Another contributor to conflict during Uruguay's turbulent century was the fact that Uruguay was a buffer state between two powerful neighbors, Argentina and Brazil. Both coveted the "*La Banda Oriental*" (the Eastern Shore of the Uruguay River) as one of their own provinces. Also, Uruguay and Brazil disputed the demarcation of their boundary.[6]

In 1830 Uruguay was far from a modern, cohesive nation. Brazilian coins were the common currency, Charrúa Indians pillaged the frontier, slavery was still indiscriminately practiced in spite of the laws which freed some blacks, and the titles to ranches in the backlands were typically decided by force.[7]

OPPOSING FORCES

To varying degrees, both the *Blancos* and the *Colorados* drew upon the same elements of society to fill the ranks of their armies. *Guachos*, *émigrés*, displaced European Liberals, slaves seeking freedom, and the "have-nots" needed little encouragement to fight. *Caudillos* had perfected manipulating these elements into an art form. And, the mere mention of Manuel Rosas' name frequently inspired one of two extreme emotions—love or hate—and could fill the ranks on either side.[8]

Initially, arms left over from the War for Independence were plentiful. Within the cavalry the lance remained the favorite weapon throughout most of the century. In 1876 the Uruguayan army began to standardize its arms. It purchased Remington rifles and carbines and Krupp cannons.[9]

OPENING STRATEGIES

The initial objective for both sides was to control the capital, Montevideo. Once accomplished, the goal then became to eliminate the external support for the opposing political party. Until 1852, for the *Colorados* this meant the defeat of Rosas of Argentina and for the *Blancos* the defeat of his enemies who were numerous.

RIVERA VERSUS ORIBE

Uruguay won its independence as a consequence of the 1825–28 war between Argentina and Brazil (see chapter 7). Two strong *caudillos*, Rivera and Lavalleja, emerged from the fighting as the leading contenders for the presidency. The Uruguayan Congress chose Rivera on November 6, 1830.[10]

In June 1832 supporters of Lavalleja unsuccessfully attempted to assassinate Rivera. Then on July 3 troops in Montevideo, led by Col. Eugenio Garzón,[11] rebelled calling for Lavalleja to be made commander of the army. Rivera, who included exiled Argentine Unitarians in his army, defeated Lavalleja at Tupambaé (230 mi NNE of Montevideo) on September 18 and Lavalleja fled to Brazil. Rivera arrested Lavalleja's supporters (including his wife) and confiscated their property.[12]

Lavalleja solicited and received the support of Argentine leader Juan Manual de Rosas who hoped to reincorporate Uruguay into Argentina. Lavalleja also received help from separatists in the Brazilian province of Rio Grande do Sul which bordered Uruguay. They expected Rivera to return the favor in the future. Lavalleja invaded Uruguay from Argentina in March 1834. He was defeated at the Battle of Perico Flaco and fled back into Brazil.[13]

On March 1, 1835, Gen. Manuel Oribe,[14] another Revolutionary war hero and friend of Lavalleja, succeeded Rivera as president; however, Rivera retained command of the army. Oribe began to investigate finances during Rivera's tenure and passed a series of laws affecting the interior, a region Rivera considered his private domain. In January 1836 Oribe removed Rivera as commander of the army.[15]

Rivera rebelled on July 16, 1836. Oribe gathered an army and ordered them to wear a white piece of apparel bearing the words "Defenders of the laws" (*Defensores de las leyes*). Rivera countered by having his troops wear a red item. This was the origin of the colors associated with the two sides—*Blancos* and *Colorados*.[16]

Lavalleja, who had been given an amnesty by Oribe, led Argentine troops into Uruguay to aid Oribe in his fight against Rivera, while Rivera's followers were aided by Argentine Unitarians led by General Lavalle. On September 19 Oribe defeated Rivera at the Battle of Carpintería (200 mi N of Montevideo) and Rivera fled to Brazil. There his men fought with the separatists' army of Rio Grande do Sul in its war with the Brazilian Empire while Rivera reconstituted his force (see chapter 13). Rivera, leading 800 men, reentered Uruguay and defeated Oribe at the Battle of Yucutujá near the Brazilian border (425 mi NNW of Montevideo) on October 22, 1837. Most of the survivors from Oribe's army joined Rivera, raising his following to 2,000 men. Rivera decisively defeated Oribe at the Battle of Palmar (250 mi NNW of Montevideo) on June 15, 1838, and Oribe fled to Montevideo. The French navy, which at that time was fighting Rosas over commercial issues, helped Rivera take control of the Paraná and Uruguay Rivers. On October 11 they captured the island of Martín García from 121 Argentine soldiers. Together, they besieged Oribe in Montevideo. On October 24 Oribe resigned and fled to Argentina.[17]

THE GREAT WAR, 1839–52

On February 24, 1839, Rivera and his allies (the Argentine province of Corrientes, Argentine *émigrés*, and France) declared war on Rosas but not the Argentine people. After twenty months the French quit the fight against Rosas. Between 1843 and 1851 the *Blancos*, aided by Rosas, besieged in Montevideo the *Colorados*, who were helped by Rosas' numerous enemies. Finally, when the *caudillo* of Entre Ríos, Justo José Urquíza, broke with Rosas on May 1, 1851, the *Blancos* and Rosas could no longer maintain the siege. On May 29, 1851, Uruguay, Brazil, and Entre Ríos signed an alliance against Rosas. The allies decisively defeated Rosas at the Battle of Monte Caseros on February 3, 1852, and shipped him off to permanent exile in Europe (see chapter 9).[18]

In the meantime, on October 12, 1851, Uruguay made major concessions to Brazil in exchange for its help against Rosas. Uruguay renounced its territorial claims north of the Río Cuareim and made numerous commercial concessions.[19]

"MUSICAL" PRESIDENTS

Juan Francisco Giró, a *Blanco*, was elected president. He unsuccessfully endeavored to reorganize the war-torn nation. On July 18, 1853, troops in Montevideo mutinied, reigniting the *Blanco-Colorado* feud. In September Giró fled to the French legation. A *Colorado* triumvirate composed of the ancient *caudillos* (and former enemies) Lavalleja and Rivera, plus Col. Venancio Flores,[20] were chosen to complete Giró's term. Lavalleja and Rivera soon died of natural causes, leaving Flores as sole executive. In 1854 Flores asked the help of Brazil to restore order in Uruguay. Emperor Dom Pedro II sent 4,000 troops (known as the Auxiliary Army) which occupied the principal cities from mid-1854 until early 1856. Flores was overthrown by his own party on August 28, 1855, which led to more turbulence.[21]

THE CIVIL WAR OF 1863–65

On April 19, 1863, following the slaughter of *Colorado* prisoners at the Quinteros prison, Venancio Flores landed in Uruguay with a small following from Argentina. For eighteen months he dominated the plains while President Bernardo Berro controlled Montevideo. However, the *Blancos* soon alienated both Argentina and Brazil while Flores won their favor. Aided by 5,000 Brazilian troops, Flores captured Montevideo in February 1865. The *Colorados*, beholding to Argentina and Brazil, joined them in their war against Francisco Solano López of Paraguay (see chapter 29).

THE FAILED *COUP'D ETAT* OF 1868

As the War of the Triple Alliance against Paraguay was drawing to a close, Flores returned to Montevideo. Flores chose not to seek another term as president. In order to force him to change his mind, his sons, Fortunato and Eduardo Flores, led the Montevideo garrison into rebellion on February 7, 1868. The senior Flores persuaded the rebels to lay down their arms. The *Blancos*, believing that the government was undefended, chose this moment to rebel.[22]

On February 19, 1868, *Blancos*, led by former President Berro, seized the government palace and others, led by Colonel [first name unknown] Freire, and attacked the barracks of the "Libertad" Regiment. The regiment's commanding officer, Colonel [first name unknown] Olave, cut down Freire with his sword, rallied his soldiers, and recaptured the government buildings. While these events were transpiring, General Flores was assassinated when his carriage was stopped on Juncal Street. Berro and other *Blanco* leaders were captured and shot the same day.[23]

On March 1, 1868, the *Colorados* elected another soldier, Gen. Lorenzo Batlle, as president. Turbulence continued. Máximo Pérez and Gen. Francisco Caraballo each led separate, unsuccessful rebellions. Illustrative of the shifting loyalties among the *caudillos*, Pérez was defeated by Caraballo for the Uruguayan government and, conversely, Caraballo was later defeated by Pérez for the same government.[24]

REBELLION OF "THE LANCES"

In the meantime, Col. Timoteo Aparicio Saravia, a *Blanco*, assembled significant war materials in the Argentine provinces of Corrientes and Entre Ríos. On March 5, 1870, Saravia, leading seventy men, crossed into Uruguay and declared a rebellion. His army soon swelled to some 5,000 men. He defeated the *Colorados* led by Gen. José Suárez at Severino (60 mi N of Montevideo) on September 12. Saravia immediately marched against Montevideo and captured an outer fortification, the "Hill" (*Cerro*), in November.[25]

In the meantime, the *Colorado* forces in the interior regrouped. Saravia, appreciating that he would be seriously threatened should the *Colorado* forces unite, chose to fight General Caraballo before he could join with General Suárez. The armies fought at Corralito (130 mi NNW of Montevideo) on September 29, both sustaining heavy casualties. Saravia, confident that he had won, opened negotiations with Caraballo. The *Colorados* took advantage of the pause in the fighting to escape by carrying out a nighttime forced march over thirty-six miles. Steamers awaited the *Colorado* army on the Río Negro and transported it to Paysandú (298 mi NNW of Montevideo) where Caraballo and Suárez joined forces.[26]

Saravia, whose army had grown to 7,000 men, once again advanced toward Montevideo. On November 28 the *Blancos* again captured the fortress at the *Cerro*, following a bloody fight.

The next day the *Blancos* assembled some river steamers above Montevideo which they planned to use for an assault. *Colorado* President Lorenzo Batlle surprised the *Blancos* on the twenty-ninth and sortied from the city. The *Blancos* abandoned Villa de la Unión and the steamers but held their ground elsewhere, so Batlle retired back to Montevideo. Between the two sides more than 300 Uruguayans died.[27]

Suárez, who had been given command of the *Colorado* forces in the interior, marched from Paysandú toward Montevideo. He successfully crossed the Río Negro unopposed. In the meantime, President Batlle dispatched reinforcements for Suárez; these were sent by sea and were to land at Puerto del Inglés. Not to be outmaneuvered, Saravia seized the port and the expedition had to return to Montevideo. Suárez was now in a dangerous position. Saravia was advancing toward him with a superior force. On December 23 Suárez boldly marched around Saravia's flank and by forced marches won the race to Montevideo. The now-united *Colorado* army, some 5,000 men, and the *Blancos*, of equal number, fought a bloody Battle of Sauce (20 mi N of Montevideo) on Christmas Day. One thousand men died. The *Blancos* were defeated; Savaria had to abandon his artillery and train to save the rest of his army. Fortunately for him, the *Colorados* did not aggressively follow up their success.[28]

By June 1871 Saravia had rebuilt the *Blanco* army to 2,500 men at Manantiales (110 mi NW of Montevideo). However, a *Colorado* division under Gen. Enrique Castro decisively defeated the yet demoralized *Blancos* on July 17. Only some cavalry escaped. With these men Saravia pursued a guerrilla campaign. On April 6, 1872, through the mediation of Argentina, the protagonists signed a truce. The *Blancos* were to become *jefes politicos* of four departments—Canelones, San José, Florida, and Cerro Largo. This began a process of partitioning Uruguay between the *Blancos* in the north and the *Colorados* in the center and south.[29]

THE *COLORADOS* FIGHT AMONGST THEMSELVES

The *Colorados* now split into two factions: the *Principistas*, who wanted limited reform and some accommodation with the *Blancos*, and the *Netos*, who favored no concessions. Unexpectedly, in the 1873 presidential election, the *Netos*, appreciating their candidate could not win, threw their support to a "dark horse," Dr. José Ellauri, and he won. The new President, appreciating that he had no political power base, attempted to resign. The army demonstrated in front of the government building and told Congress that his resignation was unacceptable. Ellauri reluctantly remained in office. His first act was to restore Maj. Lorenzo Latorre[30] to the command of the 1st Regiment of *Cazadores*. Former President Tomás Gomensoro had dismissed Latorre for interfering in elections.[31]

Soon, the two *Colorado* factions were fighting each other. In late 1874 *netos* assassinated Col. Romualdo Castillo, a supporter of Ellauri, in Paysandú. And, Col. Máximo Pérez led an unsuccessful revolt in the Department of Soriano. In January 1875 street fighting broke out between the two *Colorado* factions in Montevideo over the mayoral elections. After five days of rioting, troops occupied Constitution Plaza and declared Ellauri's term at an end on January 15. Ellauri sought asylum on a Brazilian warship. The *Blancos* rallied at Florida in Uruguay, placing themselves under the command of Colonel Saravia. Saravia offered Ellauri the assistance of the *Blancos* but he refused. So, Saravia recognized the *Colorado* provisional government and was promoted to general.[32]

In February new President Pedro Varela, supported by the *Netos*, rounded up fifteen *Principistas*, placed them on the barely seaworthy barque *Puig*, and instructed the Captain to take them to Cuba; however, they were not permitted to land there. They disembarked in Charleston, South Carolina, after many arduous weeks at sea. Eventually these exiles found their way to Buenos Aires where they plotted against the *Netos*.[33]

THE TRICOLOR REBELLION[34]

In May 1875 Col. Julián de la Llana, a *principista*, rebelled in the department of Maldonado. He was soon joined by many prominent *principistas caudillos*. An expedition from Buenos Aires, led by Col. Julio Arrúe, landed in the department of Colonia and its troops occupied the town of Mercedes. The National Guard was called up to fill out the ranks of the rebel army. Many *Blancos* joined the rebellion; however, General Saravia, true to his word, remained loyal to the government. In fact, he took command of one of the government's army corps and gave the rebels little rest. In the north government forces were commanded by Minister of War Latorre. Although the rebels won the Battle of Perseverano (120 mi NW of Montevideo) on October 7, they were crushed in early 1875 at the Battles of Guayabos and Palomas. By December the rebels retreated into Argentina and Brazil.[35]

On January 15, 1876, Col. Lorenzo Latorre, commander of Montevideo's garrison, deposed President Ellauri. His rule was dictatorial. He started the process of creating a national army by improving training, equipment, and weapons. But on March 13, 1880, Latorre declared Uruguay "ungovernable" and emigrated to Argentina.[36]

Gen. Máximo Santos ruled between 1882 and 1886. He was crude, extravagant, and impractical. He kept caged jaguars in his garden, which fed rumors as to the fate of political rivals who quietly disappeared. Crises mounted due to his inept rule. On March 28, 1886, an expedition from Argentina led by Generals Enrique Castro and José Miguel Arredondo landed at Guaviyú. Poorly organized, the rebels were defeated by Gen. Máximo Tajes[37] on the thirtieth at Quebracho (325 mi NNE of Montevideo) and again the following day at Puntas de Soto. Some 200 rebels were killed and 600 captured. The government's losses were light.[38]

On August 17 President Santos was shot, the bullet breaking his lower jaw. This plus mounting domestic problems caused Santos to retire on February 14, 1887. Congress chose General Tajes as president. He attempted to remove the army's political influence by disbanding several regiments whose officers had been particularly active.[39]

THE "NATIONALISTS" REBELLION

In 1897 the *Blancos*, now calling themselves "Nationalists," revolted. They believed that the Congressional elections of November 1896 were fraudulent. Also, the *Blancos*, who had been promised control over four departments in the 1872 pact, had received control over only three. In February 1897 some 300 men, led by Saravia,[40] crossed into northern Uruguay from Brazil and another small band, led by Diego Lamas,[41] entered southern Uruguay from Argentina. Soon the Nationalist armies swelled to 3,000 men. Most were irregular cavalry armed with revolvers and lances; as in past decades, they lived off the rich, abundant land.[42]

The government's press-gangs swept through Montevideo gathering up reluctant conscripts. In March the government dispatched troops from Montevideo northward. Lamas defeated a government force at Tres Arboles (250 mi NNW of Montevideo) on March 17, 1897. Other government troops found Saravia at Arbolito (260 mi NNE of Montevideo) upon carefully selected ground. On March 17 Saravia fought the government troops to a stalemate and then slipped away. Next, Saravia fought two indecisive engagements with the government at Cerros

Colorados (120 mi NNE of Montevideo) on April 16 and at Cerros Blancos (350 mi N of Montevideo) near the Brazilian border on May 14.[43]

Over the next few months both sides energetically worked to increase their forces. The government built its army to over 10,000 men. Although the rebels had fewer resources on which to draw, they succeeded in winning good relations with the plainspeople of the north and west. These individuals provided them with timely intelligence. The fighting on the plains dragged on through June and July; the rebels fought only when it was to their advantage.[44]

In June 400 rebels boarded the commercial steamer *Venus* in Buenos Aires disguised as passengers for Montevideo. Once outside the harbor, the rebels seized the steamer and ordered its captain to take them to a point on the Uruguayan coast. However, an Argentine warship noticed the irregular behavior and required the ship to return to Buenos Aires. The rebels were detained for a few days and then released. However, the discovery betrayed the element of surprise.[45]

The two sides agreed to an armistice throughout much of August but could not come to terms. On August 25, 1897, Independence Day, President Juan I. Borda was shot dead while leaving the cathedral following a special *Te Deum*. The new president, Juan Cuestas, initiated new peace talks with the rebels which succeeded in producing *El Pacto de la Cruz* on September 18. The ruling *Colorados*, appreciating the increasing sympathy for reforms, conceded that in six of the nineteen departments (states) the governor should be a member of the Nationalist or *Blanco* party; Nationalists were to be fairly represented in Congress; and $200,000 was to be distributed to the rank and file of the rebel army. In exchange, the rebels were to surrender their weapons and return to their homes. This furthered the reality of a partitioned Uruguay.[46]

Cuestas' conciliations to the *Blancos* and his governmental reforms, which included a reduction of the military, brought him into conflict with the *netos*. On February 10, 1898, the President suspended the Constitution and assumed dictatorial powers. On July 1, 1899, the 4th Regiment of Artillery mutinied in Montevideo. Two days of fighting left 200 dead and wounded, but Cuestas' government survived.[47]

REBELLION OF 1904

On March 1, 1903, José Batlle y Ordóñez succeeded Cuestas as president. Tensions continued to increase between the *Colorados* and *Blancos*. The *Blancos* accused the new president of violating the *Pacto de la Cruz*. Saravia proclaimed a rebellion on March 16. However, this was nipped in the bud by a new agreement. The *Pacto de Nico Pérez* was reached on March 22.[48]

During this time, fighting occurred between Uruguayan and Brazilian partisans in the department of Rivera which bordered Brazil. The Uruguayan government sent two cavalry units into the department which was the political domain of the *Blancos*. On January 1, 1904, Saravia rebelled again. The fighting ebbed and flowed. The government won at Mansavillagra (120 mi NNE of Montevideo) on January 14, but lost at Fray Marcos (60 mi NNE of Montevideo) on January 30, and fought to a draw at Tupambaé (210 mi NNE of Montevideo) on June 22. The rebellion came to a sudden end when Saravia was mortally wounded at the Battle of Masoller (400 mi N of Montevideo) near the border with Brazil on September 1. He died three days later in the Brazilian province of Rio Grande do Sul.[49]

The Treaty of Aceguá ended the coparticipation politics which had begun in 1872 and terminated the cycle of *Colorado* and *Blanco* confrontation. The rebellious *Blancos* were given a general amnesty, $100,000 to pay their officers and men plus permission for the officers to be incorporated into the national army, and the promise of political reforms. However, the *Blancos* were deprived of the guaranteed control of specific departments and of their weapons.[50]

OBSERVATIONS

Uruguay, like Costa Rica, earned its reputation as being politically one of the most stable nations in Latin America only during the twentieth, but not the nineteenth century. From independence through the early 1900s, Uruguay was in perpetual turmoil. Of the twenty-five presidents who served between 1830 and 1904, nine were overthrown by force, two were assassinated, and one was so severely injured that he had to step down. And only three of the twenty-five presidents served without a serious rebellion. Nonetheless, Uruguay was consolidated as an independent nation surviving through turbulent decades.[51]

Until the middle of the nineteenth century, the *Blancos* and the *Colorados* were nearly equal in strength and the loser in presidential contests frequently resorted to the sword. By mid-century the *Colorados* gained the upper hand over the *Blancos*, in large measure due to the shift in power caused by ever-increasing immigration from Europe, which concentrated in Montevideo, and the fall of Rosas in Argentina. Toward the end of the nineteenth century, the *Blancos* made a comeback, in part due to the introduction of family farms on the prairie, which increased their numbers through immigration, and the rising value of beef on the European market, which benefited the *Blanco* ranchers of the north.[52]

This endless fighting gave blacks a way out of slavery. Both the *Blancos* and the *Colorados* always needed more men for their armies. Freedom was a compelling inducement to fight.

Finally, the battlefield victory over the *caudillo* Saravia afforded President Batlle the opportunity to introduce significant political, social, and economic reforms which helped transform Uruguay into a modern nation.[53]

CHAPTER TWENTY-SIX

CHILEAN INTRACLASS CONFLICTS, 1851 AND 1859

> Long Live the Democratic Republic
> Long Live the Society of Equality
> Valor against Tyranny
> —inscribed on the Chilean flag by Equalitarians, 1850

THE SPARK

On April 20, 1851, members of the liberal Society of Equality (*Sociedad de la Igualdad*) bribed soldiers from the "Valdivia" and "Chacabuco" regiments and together these 600 individuals attacked the capital's artillery barracks. Some 700 loyal troops defeated the rebels in bitter street fighting. More than 100 persons died before the government could reestablish order. This led to Gen. José María de la Cruz'[1] rebellion in September.[2]

BACKGROUND

Chile had been ruled by the Conservative party since the end of the War for Independence in the 1820s. Beginning in 1850, the ruling Conservatives quarreled amongst themselves over their presidential succession. The traditional choice would have been Gen. José María de la Cruz; however, President Manuel Bulnes preferred the civilian Manuel Montt Torres. The Liberals saw this as an opportunity to gain influence. The Society of Equality, a creation of the socialist Francisco Biblao, led the opposition to the government's candidate. In August 1850 government sympathizers attacked a gathering of the society. This inspired the society to become more public and violent. By the end of the year, the *intendant* (governor) of Santiago ordered the society disbanded and its leadership first imprisoned and then exiled. These actions inflamed the society's followers. On April 20, 1851, street fighting broke out in the capital but was suppressed. The Liberals then chose Conservative Gen. de la Cruz, outgoing President Bulnes's cousin, as their candidate. But the constitutional process favored the government's candidate and Manuel Montt was elected president.[3]

OPPOSING FORCES

The 1854 census placed the Chilean population at 1.5 million people. Chile was in the very early stages of industrialization and far ahead of any other Latin American nation. Railroads, telegraph lines, public schools, and port improvement projects were beginning, particularly in the Central Valley where the capital was located. The population in the major cities exploded—Santiago had grown to 150,000 persons and Valparaiso to 60,000—as did squalor and poverty. As experienced elsewhere, the new riches brought about by the California gold-rush market and indigenous industrialization were unevenly shared.[4]

The Chilean army was composed of 2,266 men—1,398 infantry in four battalions, 525 cavalrymen in two regiments, and 343 artillerymen. The army was distributed throughout the nation, focusing on three potential threats—the Peruvians in the north, the Argentines in the east, and the Araucanian Indians in the south. On paper, the militia (*Guardia Nacional*) possessed 66,241 men. Quality among these troops varied significantly. The best trained and armed were those in the south due to the Indian threat.[5]

The rebels were an amalgamation of old and new elements of society, each with their own grievances. Some entrepreneurs, particularly wealthy miners, were frustrated by the government's favoritism toward the old landed aristocracy. The old rivalry between those in the capital, Santiago, and Concepción, gateway to the south, became volatile. Concepción was the headquarters of the commander in chief of the Army of the South, the frontier force opposing the Araucanian Indians. In early 1851 General de la Cruz, the losing presidential candidate, was its commander. Chile had been the only Latin American nation that had evolved a permanent frontier army during the colonial era due to the threat from the Araucanians Indians, a problem that still persisted (see chapter 33). Some rebel soldiers were German immigrants, who had fled the aftermath of the failed "Revolution of 1848" (an attempt to create a liberal German national state) and settled mostly in southern Chile. Others were mine workers from the booming copper, silver, and coal mines. Still others were artisans from the cities. The intellectual voices of the rebels were the poet José Victorino Lastarria and Biblao, both of whom were exiled to France from Chile.[6]

The governing Conservatives had the support of the powerful landed aristocracy and most of the regular army. However, some of these troops were in the south under the command of General de la Cruz. As a consequence, in June many of these soldiers were ordered north to Santiago. Also, the government promoted Col. Benjamín Viel, a French veteran of Waterloo, to general and made him *Intendente* of Concepción. It was hoped that this would make him more loyal to the government than to his old friend de la Cruz.[7]

OPENING STRATEGIES

Due to the new and unpredictable social forces at work in Chile, the government could not be content to wait on the rebels at the capital. Its army needed to immediately march and destroy the rebels before the rebellion could gain momentum. The rebels needed to immediately demonstrate viability. This could be achieved by fielding and maintaining a strong army. Ultimately, its objective was to capture the capital.[8]

THE 1851 REBELLION

Liberals rebelled throughout the country. The first insurrection was in Valparaíso (71 mi ENE of Santiago) on September 5; this was immediately suppressed. Next, on September 7 the Liberals in La Serena (283 mi N of Santiago) rebelled; then those in Coquimbo (275 mi N of Santiago) rose up; and on the nineteenth Liberals in Concepción (309 mi S of Santiago) revolted. The Liberals chose General de la Cruz as their leader.[9]

The new president called up the militia but the response was poor. Montt immediately chose former President General Bulnes to command the government's forces, and this restored the confidence of the military. Bulnes rushed southward to Chocoa on September 2 escorted by fifty grenadiers commanded by Capt. Manuel Baquedano, where he gathered local army units and munitions to keep them from being subverted to the rebellion. Of the two regular regiments stationed near Concepción, one joined de la Cruz and the other Bulnes. Santiago and Valparaíso were stripped of soldiers, including the presidential escort, and sent to join Bulnes. On October 21 he reviewed his army—1,909 infantry, 1,330 cavalry, and nine pieces of artillery.[10]

At sea the rebels seized the initiative. They captured the small commercial steamers *Firefly* and *Arauco*. The rebels in Coquimbo used the *Firefly* to ship government funds, which they had seized, to their compatriots in Concepción. Most of the Chilean navy was laid up to save money; only the brigantine *Meteoro* (8 guns) was immediately available for service. And, it was sail- powered and had no way to force the outgunned rebel steamers to fight. The government purchased the merchant ship *Cazador* to transport troops.[11] More importantly, it also induced the British naval squadron off its coast to hunt down the rebel ships by labeling them as pirates. In this process, the British, with the permission of the Chilean government, blockaded the Bay of Coquimbo, which infuriated the U.S. representative to Chile, Balie Peyton, because of its impact on his nation's commerce.[12]

Back on land in the south, Bulnes, commanding 3,335 men, began to march south to meet the rebels on November 2. General de la Cruz, commanding 1,800 infantry, 1,000 cavalry, and five pieces of artillery, waited at the Cocharcas Ford across the Maule River. His force was composed mostly of provincial militia. Additionally, some 2,000 Araucanian Indians, inspired by their hatred for Bulnes, joined the rebels. De la Cruz burned the crops along Bulnes' line of march to prevent him from living off the land. Bulnes chose not to force a crossing, but instead marched east. Cruz paralleled his march on the opposite bank, resolved to take up a defensive position in Los Guindos and block Bulnes' approach to Chillán (245 mi S of Santiago). On the morning of the nineteenth, Bulnes marched toward Chillán; he exposed his left flank to the rebels. Instead of attacking, de la Cruz solicited a truce, wanting to discuss new elections. De la Cruz believed that there was sufficient dissension among the government troops to induce them not to fight. Without answering, Bulnes continued past the rebels to Monte de Urra, two miles outside of Chillán. There, his march-weary troops took up defensive positions. Later that day the opposing cavalries and artillery units engaged each other in a bloody but indecisive fight.[13]

BATTLE OF LONCOMILLA

Bulnes abandoned Chillán on November 29 and marched toward Talca where the government was assembling 1,500 reinforcements. By December 4 he reached the Loncomilla Valley and took up a defensive position. General de la Cruz, commanding 3,411 men, including 21 North American filibusters, followed. Bulnes attacked at three o'clock in the morning on December 8. The battle lasted seven hours. During the first phase of the battle the cavalry on both sides were decimated being trapped in deep ravines along the Loncomilla River. During the second phase the government troops launched a bloody infantry assault. By the end of the day, only a third of either army was fit to continue the fight. Two thousand died and 1,500 were wounded. De la Cruz initiated talks but no agreement was reached. Following the battle, which both sides claimed to be a victory, the odds began to shift in favor of the government.

Apparently, the "Carampangue" Battalion was bribed to desert de la Cruz and come over to the government. Also, Bulnes received some reinforcements. As a consequence, de la Cruz retreated southward and surrendered on December 14, receiving generous terms under the Treaty of Purapel.[14]

FIGHTING IN THE NORTH

Pockets of Liberals rebelled in the north as well, principally in the province of Coquimbo. The rebels sent an expedition to Huasco (427 mi N of Santiago) where they seized 2,000 rifles and 30,000 pesos which belonged to the Bolivian government of General Ballivián. Garrisoning La Serena, Carrera, and Arteaga, 1,000 rebels marched southward toward the capital. They were met at the hamlet of Petorca by an equal number of government soldiers. The rebels were decisively defeated by Col. Juan Vidaurre Leal on October 14 during a three-hour battle. The rebels lost 70 killed and 364 captured; the government losses were much less.[15]

Coquimbo received news of the surrender of de la Cruz and was abandoned by the rebels. However, on December 26, a hundred other rebels, unaware of de la Cruz' defeat and the loss of Coquimbo, seized the mining town of Copiapó. There, 1,000 rebels, mostly mine workers, assembled. On January 8, 1852, seasoned government troops defeated the miners. Lt. J. M. Gilliss, U.S. Navy, described the battle:

> Thus the miners, becoming disgusted with weapons they found so difficult to manage, flung them away very soon after the action commenced, and rushed into the combat with only stones and knives—an inequality they fought under for more than two hours, against troops entrenched and barricaded with all the skill a regularly educated soldier could devise.[16]

The government lost five men dead and twenty wounded. The rebels lost fifty men dead, fifty wounded or prisoners, and the remaining 450 fled. The rebels surrendered at Copiapó on January 9.[17]

During the fighting Montt had hired 150 Argentine mounted mercenaries, which caused bitter feelings throughout the north toward the President for having involved Chile's historical enemies.[18]

The consequences of the 1851 rebellion altered the political environment for both the Liberals and the Conservatives. A general amnesty was declared. A new civil code, written by noted Venezuelan scholar Andrés Bello, the head of the University of Chile, was published and became very influential. But in March 1852 a law was passed that deprived those convicted by court-martial of the right to appeal.[19]

THE ELECTION OF 1859

During Montt's second five-year term (1854–59) as president, tensions increased between the Liberals and the Conservatives. Leading Liberals were exiled. Additionally, Conservative solidarity began to dissolve. The immediate cause for this was a dispute between Montt and the archbishop of Santiago over the removal of a sacristan (a caretaker), although the underlying issue was the right of patronage (the government's approval of clerical appointments). The most devout Catholics and Conservatives, who were opposed to the law abolishing entailed estates (the right of the firstborn to inherit the entire estate), joined with the rebellious Liberals.[20]

THE 1859 REBELLION ("THE CONSTITUENT REVOLUTION")

On January 5, 1859, rebellions broke out simultaneously in San Felipe, Valparaíso, Concepción, Talca, and Copiapó (482 mi N of Santiago). It was rapidly suppressed everywhere but in Copiapó. There the Liberals, who controlled the militia, drove out the government's representative, Lt. Col. José María Silva Chávez. This mining town was isolated from the south by the Atacama Desert. These rebels could neither immediately aid those elsewhere nor could they readily be threatened.[21]

The rich miner Pedro León Gallo[22] methodically recruited and armed 1,000 men. His officers included only three individuals who had served in the Chilean army, and one of these had been expelled from the Military Academy (*Escuela Militar*) for disciplinary reasons. Some of the soldiers came from upper- and middle-class families and others were miners. Gallo rehabilitated an abandoned railroad workshop and turned it into an ordnance foundry. His first cannon was forged on March 1 and by the end of the month he possessed ten serviceable guns. His mechanics mounted 5mm-thick iron plates on railroad cars to afford the occupants protection from rifle fire. He also minted silver *pesos* to help finance the cause.[23]

The government dispatched 1,200 soldiers to the north and placed them under the command of Lt. Col. Silva Chávez. They landed at Coquimbo. Anticipating León's move, Chávez, overconfident, force-marched to Los Loros where on March 14 his exhausted troops were defeated. The government lost about 60 men dead, 100 wounded, and 250 prisoners. The rebel losses were significantly less. This permitted Gallo to capture the city of La Serena.[24]

BATTLE OF CERRO GRANDE

The government's control of the sea allowed it to recover rapidly from this defeat. A 3,000-man army commanded by now-General Vidaurre Leal disembarked at Tongoy on April 16. It then traveled by rail to Peñuelas, three miles south of La Serena. Gallo's force occupied a defensive position at the foot of a hill between the Bay of Coquimbo and the city of La Serena. He had 1,800 men armed primarily with rifles captured at Los Loros and 900 unarmed men who were to pick up and use the weapons of any comrade who fell in action. The battle raged for five hours on April 29 before the rebels exhausted their ammunition and were defeated. Many rebels were killed or wounded and 500 men were taken prisoner. They government lost five dead and ninety-five wounded. Gallo fled to Argentina and later to the United States and Europe. As during the failed 1851 rebellion, other rebel leaders fled to Araucanian-controlled territory and incited the Indians against the government.[25]

OBSERVATIONS

The intraclass rebellions that had taken place throughout Latin America during the first half of the nineteenth century had been struggles between power elites over sharing the spoils of sovereignty. The 1851 and 1859 Chilean rebellions were far more complex, involving a greater diversity of actors and objectives.

Not since independence had the Chilean government faced such serious armed challenges. Initially, the government reacted repressively. A new law extended the inability to appeal convictions for rebellion from the military into the civil courts. The "Law of Civil Responsibility" was enacted which provided that citizens who participated in riots or revolts should be held accountable for the resulting property damage.[26]

As a consequence of the strong showing by the Liberals throughout the decade, both Montt and his first choice as successor, Antonio Vargas, believed that it was prudent to choose a moderate. José Joaquín Pérez, who was acceptable to the Liberals, became president. Chile entered a period known as "the Liberal republic." These nineteenth-century Liberals championed economic growth and the expansion of public education. They also protected the rights of the landholders and were reluctant to extend political participation to the masses.[27]

Some 4,000 individuals died and $2 million were expended by the government in the 1851 rebellion and another 5,000 died persons in the rebellion of 1859.[28]

CHAPTER TWENTY-SEVEN

WAR OF THE *REFORMA*, 1857–60

> Cruelest . . . civil war in the history of Mexico.
> —Historian A. Teja Zabre

THE SPARK

The promulgation of the *Ley Juárez* on November 23, 1855, which suppressed all ecclesiastical and military courts, and the *Ley Lerdo* on June 25, 1856, which limited the real estate owned by the Roman Catholic Church, helped ignite a civil war known as both the "War of the *Reforma*" and the "Three Years War" between Liberals and Conservatives throughout Mexico.

BACKGROUND

By 1848 Mexico was in chaos. It had been crushed in a catastrophic war with the United States, having to sacrifice one-third of its national territory in order to get the invaders to leave (see chapter 16). Many of the northern states were in rebellion and talking of secession, and the Yucatan seceded for a second time. Banditry was common throughout the distressed nation and French and American filibusters invaded the north (see chapter 18). Ignoring these ills, the Liberals and Conservatives continued to fight for control of Mexico, resulting in shortlived governments, a lack of central control, and continued civil disorder.

In early 1853 the Mexican Conservatives recalled Antonio López de Santa Anna from exile to restore order. They hoped that their patriarch, Lucas Alamán, would be able to prevent Santa Anna from abusing power. However, Alamán died on June 1, and on December 16 Santa Anna abolished the Congress and adopted the title of "His Most Serene Highness."[1]

While consolidating into his own hands political power, Santa Anna also needed to find money to guarantee the loyalty of his supporters. As a consequence, he sold to the United States the Mesilla Valley (30,000 square miles) for $10 million. Known as the Gadsden Purchase, the Mexican public was outraged.[2]

On March 1, 1854, Liberals in the state of Guerrero proclaimed the "Plan of Ayutla" to overthrow "His Most Serene Highness."[3] Santa Anna marched south at the head of 5,000 men to put down the rebellion; however, Ignacio Comonfort, who controlled Acapulco (284 mi S of Mexico City), withstood an attack and refused to surrender the port on April 20, leaving Santa

Anna without a supply base. Santa Anna burned some Indian villages, shot the few Liberals he caught, and then returned to Mexico City proclaiming that the rebellion had been crushed.[4]

Meanwhile, the Liberals slowly gained control, first over the south, then the west and north, and finally over the east. Santa Anna twice marched out of Mexico City and twice precipitously returned. On August 4, 1855, Santa Anna resigned and five days later fled into exile, first to Cuba and then to Colombia.[5]

The old liberal Gen. Juan Álvarez, a full-blooded Indian who had fought with Morelos during the War for Independence, was swept into power. He was demagogic but supported liberal reforms imposed upon the Church. The Chief Justice Minister of the new government, Benito Juárez,[6] guided a series of laws through Congress known as the *Ley Juárez* and *Ley Lerdo*. As a consequence, Conservatives sparked uprisings in San Luis Potosí and Guanajuato against the antiChurch policies and caused Álvarez' resignation. He was replaced by the more moderate Ignacio Comonfort on December 11, 1855. Before resigning, Álvarez had recreated a national guard drawn from civilians as a counterbalance to the Conservative-dominated, regular army and called a constitutional congress.[7]

On December 12, 1855, Conservatives in the mountain village of Zacapoaxtla, Puebla, rebelled against the Liberal government. The regular army cavalry units sent to suppress the rebellion defected to the Conservatives. These desertions from the regular army were traced to the work of a Conservative agent, Antonio Haro y Tamariz, who was arrested in the capital on January 2, 1856, but soon escaped. On January 5, an army infantry unit, commanded by Gen. Ignacio de la Llave, was sent, but most of these men defected as well. Seven days later, on January 12, a 1,500-man army brigade under General Severo del Castillo was dispatched against the rebels and it, too, defected, General and all. These events raised serious questions as to the loyalty of the regular army to the Liberal government.[8]

On January 17, some 3,000 Conservatives from Zacapoaxtla, now commanded by Haro, attacked the Liberal, regular-army garrison at Puebla, a city that was a Conservative bastion and strategically located on the road between Mexico City and Vera Cruz. Commanding a small garrison, Liberal Gen. Juan B. Traconis put up a stout defense, finally surrendering on the twenty-third. He was permitted to march out with honors.[9]

Comonfort was now in a difficult position. A Conservative army was but eighty miles away in Puebla. Following the deactivation of regular army units in November of the previous year, 800 army officers of questionable loyalty were idle in Mexico City. Plus, Comonfort's revenue flow from the Vera Cruz customhouse was now cut off. Comonfort immediately posted these army officers to towns outside the capital, forcing them to choose sides. Most went to Puebla and formed the Conservative *Legión Sagrada* (Sacred Legion).[10]

As the Conservatives hesitated at Puebla, Comonfort's force began to come together. General Traconis and the expelled Puebla garrison blocked the road leading to the capital at the bridge over the Río Frío. An army brigade led by Gen. Luis Ghilardi, which had previously rebelled, asked to be allowed to prove its loyalty to the Liberal government. It was sent to reinforce Traconis. Also, national guard units slowly began coming into the capital from Guanajuato, Querétaro, Vera Cruz, Zacatecas, Oaxaca, and Morelos.[11]

As Comonfort gathered his forces in Mexico City, the towns of Del Valle, Tulancingo, Pachuca, Chalchicomula, and Huehuetla declared for the Conservative cause. However, national guard units easily put these uprisings down.[12]

On February 23, 1856, President Comonfort led his 12,000 troops, primarily inexperienced national guards, out of Mexico City. General Parrodi's force was added to their numbers as they passed through Río Frío, giving the Liberals nearly a two-to-one advantage over the Conservatives in Puebla. As the Liberal force approached Puebla, some of the advanced Conservative units defected to Comonfort. During the morning of March 8, the Conservatives, numbering about 5,000 men, attempted a surprise attack; however, the Liberals were well dug in and prepared. The Battle of Ocotlán raged for only two hours. The Conservatives mistook a cloud of dust caused by Comonfort's headquarters moving forward as Liberal reinforcements and asked for a cease fire. They used this time to return to their defensive positions in Puebla. During the battle the national guard proved its courage, while the Conservative tactic of abandoning its defenses in favor of an attack in the open caused them heavy losses.[13]

Comonfort attacked and captured the city's outer defenses the day after the battle. The demoralized Conservatives withdrew into the center of the city. Comonfort offered clemency for those who surrendered but not for those who continued to fight. However, only a few gave up, while some 2,600 Conservatives held out. On March 14 Comonfort began a fifteen-day assault against the Conservative positions. Their numbers dwindled through casualties and desertion while the Liberal force grew to 16,000 men as reinforcements continued to arrive. Haro resigned in favor of Gen. Carlos Oronoz since Comonfort would no longer negotiate with him. General Oronoz agreed to an unconditional surrender. Comonfort confiscated enough Church property to pay for the expedition and on May 12 exiled the bishop of Puebla.[14]

On October 20, 1856, the Conservatives rebelled yet again, this time in Puebla, San Luis Potosí, Michoacan, and Tlaxcala. Comonfort sent Gen. Tomás Moreno to suppress the revolt in Puebla. After a stubborn defense, the Conservatives surrendered on December 3. By March 1857 the other uprisings had been extinguished throughout the country and Comonfort pardoned the rebels.[15]

On February 5, 1857, the Constitutional Congress created the liberal Constitution of 1857 which proclaimed individual liberty and freedom of speech and press, but remained silent on the relationship between the Church and state, thereby eliminating any special relationship. In fact, the document cast the Roman Catholic Church against government officials. The Church declared anyone who took an oath of obedience to the Constitution was automatically excommunicated!

President Comonfort, who sought compromise between the extreme positions of the Liberals and Conservatives, soon found himself without supporters. On December 17 Brig. Gen. Félix María Zuloaga, commander of the Mexico City garrison, mutinied and declared the Conservative "Plan of Tacubaya." This called for the nullification of all Liberal reforms, a new constitutional convention, but recognized Comonfort as President. On the nineteenth Comonfort announced his support of the plan and had thereby joined the rebellion against his own Liberal government! Soon again reversing his position, Comonfort attempted to raise an army to fight the Conservatives, but it was now too late. He fled into exile to the United States on January 21, 1858.[16]

Juárez, as Chief of the Supreme Court, became acting President, while Conservative Félix Zuloaga was elected President by a nominated congress. Thus, by January 1858 Mexico had two governments, the Conservative Félix Zuloaga and the Liberal Benito Juárez.

OPPOSING FORCES

President Zuloaga, who controlled Mexico City thanks to the military successes of Gen. Miguel Miramón,[17] had the support of most of the army's officer corps—and therefore, by default, most of the rank and file—the Church with its wealth, and the Conservative politicians. As in the past, the Army officers were mostly Conservative *criollos* while the common soldiers were drawn (sometimes by force) from the poor.

President Juárez, who tentatively controlled the outlying states through their Liberal governors, was supported by the inexperienced national guard and the remnants of the Liberal Congress. The Liberal army numbered 7,500 men with 30 cannon and was commanded by Anastasio Parrodi.[18]

Comonfort had begun the process of deemphasizing the regular army and of building the national guard. He had reduced Mexico City's garrison; had cut the number of civilians working for the army almost in half; had transferred arms from the army to the governors for use by the national guard; and had appointed only those loyal to the Liberals as officers in the national guard. The Liberal officers, for the most part, were merchants, shopkeepers, and professional men such as Santos Degollado, Ignacio de la Llave, Pedro Ogazón, and González Ortega, all of whom were lawyers.[19]

OPENING STRATEGIES

The Conservatives, controlling the regular army, wanted to force the Liberals into large battles. Also, they needed to capture a port, preferably Vera Cruz. The nation's prime source of revenue was the tax collected at the customhouses. As long as the ports remained in the hands of the Liberals, the Conservatives were completely dependent upon the Roman Catholic Church for their revenue.[20]

The Liberals, whose strength was in the national guard and bands of guerrillas, preferred numerous small actions. So, the Conservatives sought to achieve victory on the battlefield and the Liberals sought to avoid defeat there.[21]

THE CHASE

Conservative forces chased Juárez northwest across Mexico. He fled to Queretaro (167 mi NNW of Mexico City) on January 21, 1858, which proved impossible to defend; then to Guadalajara (424 mi WNW of Mexico City), where his troops mutinied. Juárez and his cabinet faced a firing squad but the eloquence of Minister Guillermo Prieto saved their lives. Finally, the fleeing President arrived at Manzanillo (842 mi N of Mexico City) on the Pacific Ocean. There on April 11 he and four cabinet ministers embarked in the U.S. merchant steamer *John L. Stevens* which carried him to Panama. His trek took him later to Havana, Cuba, and then on to New Orleans, Louisiana. Before departing Mexico, Juárez named Santos Degollado as commander of the Liberal "Army of the North and West" to succeed Parrodi.[22]

THE CONSERVATIVE OFFENSIVE OF 1858

Miguel Miramón, the youngest and ablest of the Conservative generals, and Leonardo Márquez, their most brutal, marched north from Mexico City, occupied San Luis Potosí, and drove the Liberal Gen. Santiago Vidaurri back into Nuevo León. The Conservative force then marched westward where Márquez captured Guadalajara in July and Miramón advanced to the Pacific Coast. Yet, as soon as the Conservative army passed through an area, the Liberal guerrillas filtered back into the territory.[23]

LAWS OF THE REFORMA

Meanwhile, Juárez had arrived at Vera Cruz on May 4, 1858, by steamer from New Orleans where he reestablished his Liberal government. In July Juárez promulgated by decree the Laws of the *Reforma*, which confiscated church property (except for the actual worship building) without compensation; suppressed all monasteries; closed convents once their occupants had died; nationalized all cemeteries; and made marriage a civil contract.[24]

THE SIEGE OF VERA CRUZ

On February 2, 1859, Miramón was elevated to the presidency by the Conservatives and decided to attack Vera Cruz, a traditional Liberal stronghold. Miramón was unable to take the port by storm, probably due to the lack of heavy artillery, so he began a siege. However, yellow fever broke out among his troops and Liberal Gen. Santos Degollado threatened the capital from the north, so Miramón abandoned the coast and sought relief in the highlands closer to Mexico City.[25]

THE BATTLE OF TACUBAYA

While Miramón confronted Vera Cruz, Liberal General Degollado advanced from Michoacán with 4,000 men against Mexico City with Conservative General Márquez, also with 4,000 men, in pursuit of him from Guadalajara. Degollado delayed outside the capital, waiting for the city's Liberals to rebel. They did not and Márquez caught Degollado at Tacubaya just south of Mexico City on April 10.

The following day, the eleventh, the Liberals sustained a crushing defeat. They lost all their artillery and their train. Those who survived fled into the mountains. Miramón, who returned to Mexico City while the battle was in progress, ordered all captured Liberal officers executed. Márquez not only shot the officers but also the physicians and medical students who had come from Mexico City to attend to the Liberal wounded, earning for himself the nickname "Tiger of Tacubaya" from his Conservative admirers. However, many of the physicians were from prominent families, thus alienating them from the Conservative cause.[26]

By this time the war had become one of vengeance. Haciendas were sacked by both sides as well as by bandits. Towns were forced to pay tribute to both sides to prevent looting. Troops barracked in cities mutinied; buildings were destroyed and churches and convents broken into. Monks fought in the ranks of the Conservatives. Priests refused to give sacraments to Liberals, for which they were frequently shot, and Liberals sacked the Cathedral at Morelia.[27]

THE "JECKER" DEAL

In October 1859, short on funds, Miramón sold Jean Baptiste Jecker, a Swiss banker, Mexican bonds with a face value of 15 million pesos for 750,000 pesos in cash. This was a usurious rate even by mid-nineteenth century, Latin American Revolutionary standards and would haunt Mexico's future![28]

SPAIN AND THE UNITED STATES TAKE ADVANTAGE OF THE WAR

Spain negotiated the Mon-Almonte Treaty with the Conservatives on November 26, 1859, which removed the threat of immediate intervention in exchange for the reinstating of some previously canceled debts. However, this did nothing to improve the financial crisis confronting the Conservatives.

Figure 17. War of the *Reforma*, 1857–60. One of Mexico's most talented generals, Miguel Miramón, was rarely defeated on the battlefield and when it did occur, he was overwhelmed by superior numbers. Unfortunately for his reputation, he fought for the Conservatives with whom historians have not been sympathetic. On June 19, 1867, he, Ferdinand Maximilian Habsburg, and Tomás Mejía were shot at Queretaro by the Liberals. Maximilian thought so highly of Miramón that he relinquished to him the place of honor in the middle. *Copied from Victor Daran,* Le Général Miguel Miramon *(Rome: Imprimerie de L'Editeur Edoardo Perino, 1886).*

The United States negotiated the McLane Ocampo Treaty with the Liberals which gave the United States rights across the Isthmus of Tehuantepec and the right to intervene by force, if necessary (however, the treaty was never ratified by the U.S. Senate). In exchange, the United States recognized the Juárez government on December 14, 1859, which significantly strengthened its ability to borrow money.[29]

In general engagements the Conservatives continued to triumph. On November 13, 1859, Miramón defeated Degollado at La Estancia de las Vacas, Jalisco (170 mi NNW of Mexico City). The Conservatives captured 30 cannon and 43 wagons with supplies. Miramón turned south and again defeated the Liberals.[30]

THE NAVAL BATTLE FOR VERA CRUZ

Now Miramón marched against the Liberal stronghold at Vera Cruz, this time with an army of 5,000 men. While he besieged the port, a Conservative squadron composed of the steamers *General Miramón* (unk guns) and *Marqués de la Habana* (unk guns) under the command of Capt. Tomás Marín, appeared off the port on March 6. The senior U.S. naval officer present, Capt. Joseph Jarvis, had orders not to recognize any blockade of Mexican ports by Conservative forces. Jarvis assigned an officer and about eighty men to each of the merchant steamers *Indianola* and *Wave*, which were under charter to the Juárez government. Those officers took command of the steamers and proceeded to tow the U.S. sloop-of-war *Saratoga* (20 guns) to where the Conservative steamers had anchored. A short fight ensued. The *General Miramón*, trying to defend itself while fleeing, ran aground. The *Marqués de la Habana* surrendered without a fight.

The two prize ships were sent to New Orleans along with the squadron's commander, Tomás Marin, for adjudication. The U.S. district court declared the captures illegal and ordered the ships to be returned. The Conservatives took little consolation in the decision because they were deprived of the services of the two makeshift warships plus their cargoes of two mortars, 4,000 muskets, munitions, and supplies on board at a critical time. Once again Miramón was forced to retire to higher, healthier ground, this time defeating a Liberal army at Jalisco.[31]

BATTLE OF SILAO

However, the Conservative army was suffering the effect of being deprived of the revenue from the Vera Cruz customhouse. Its revenue, supplied by the Roman Catholic Church, was dwindling. At the same time, the Liberal army was learning discipline and finding new, more capable officers. On August 10, 1860, Liberal generals González Ortega, Ignacio Zaragoza, and Santiago Doblado, commanding 8,000 men with 38 cannon, defeated Miramón leading 3,282 men with 18 cannon at Silao. The Liberals then occupied Guanajuato (250 mi NW of Mexico City). This was Miramon's first defeat. The Liberals captured four generals, 66 other officers, and some 2,000 men. Demonstrating compassion and confidence, the Liberals released most on parole.[32]

SEIZING MONEY

Both sides, desperate for revenue, seized money belonging to British merchants. The Liberals took one million pesos' worth of silver bullion belonging to British mine-owners in San Luis Potosí with a promise to pay it back. The Conservatives seized 700,000 pesos from the British legation in Mexico City, making no promises.[33]

THE SIEGE OF GUADALAJARA

The money came too late to aid the Conservatives. On September 22 the Liberals besieged Guadalajara (424 mi WNW of Mexico City). On November 1 Conservative General Márquez was defeated at nearby Zapotlanejo, losing 3,000 men and 18 cannons. Márquez fled into the mountains. As a consequence, the Conservative garrison of Guadalajara surrendered on November 3.

BATTLE OF SAN MIGUEL CALPULALPAN

Miramón, cutting his way through guerrillas who were harassing Mexico City, confronted Liberal General González, leading 20,000 men, at San Miguel Calpulalpan, Tlaxoala, on December 22. The 8,000-man Conservative army was destroyed in a two-hour battle. The Conservatives lost 800 dead, 1,200 wounded, and some 6,000 captured. Miramón fled ultimately to France and on January 1, 1861, Ortega entered Mexico City at the head of a 25,000-man army composed of national guardsmen and guerrillas and was given a hero's welcome. Juárez' arrival, eleven days later, attracted little notice.[34]

Juárez proclaimed amnesty for all except a few Conservative generals, but he expelled the Spanish and Guatemalan ministers, the Papal delegate, and three prelates for their support of the Conservatives. Many of the Conservative leaders, including Zuloaga (who claimed to be President), Márquez, and Mejía now took up guerrilla warfare against the victorious Liberals.[35]

OBSERVATIONS

Although the Mexican Liberals and Conservatives had taken up arms against each other in the past, the lives lost and property destroyed in previous fighting paled in comparison to losses during the "War of the *Reforma*."

The degree of savagery and destruction had not been experienced in Mexico since the Hidalgo uprising of 1810. Many on both sides ignored any moral restraints upon their conduct. Accurate figures as to the casualties and property loss are not available. However, some 200,000 men bore arms in a war in which very few large battles occurred.[36]

As before, both Liberals and Conservatives were willing to make concessions to foreigners for aid to fight their national rival.[37]

The War of the *Reforma* was the first armed struggle that the Liberals won against the Conservatives. Also, for the first time, Mexico had a truly civilian president, Benito Juárez. Prior to and throughout the war, Juárez attempted to change the social and economic relationship between the rich and poor through a series of legislative acts, a new constitution, and presidential decrees. These did not accomplish that goal.

CHAPTER TWENTY-EIGHT

FRENCH INTERVENTION IN MEXICO, 1861–67

[I]t is not to our interest that she [the United States] should grasp the whole Gulf of Mexico, rule thence the Antilles as well as South America, and be the sole dispenser of the products of the New World.

—Napoleon III to General Elie Forey, July 3, 1862

THE SPARK

Napoleon III's decision during 1861 to intervene in Mexico in order to make Archduke Ferdinand Maximilian[1] of Austria its emperor reignited the still simmering conflict between Mexican Liberals and Conservatives.

BACKGROUND

The government of Benito Juárez emerged from the War of the *Reforma* (1857–60) almost destitute. It owed 82.2 million pesos to foreign interests (70 million to British, 9.4 million to Spanish, and 2.8 million to French). The sale of the confiscated church property produced a pittance due to poorly written legislation, naivete, mismanagement, waste, and fraud. The Liberal government was burdened not only by mistakes of its own overzealous supporters but also by those of the defeated Conservatives. For example, Great Britain expected to be fully compensated by Juárez' Liberal government for the funds seized by Miramón's Conservative government inside the British legation. Financially strapped, in July 1861 the recently reelected Juárez requested and Congress approved the unilateral suspension of interest payments on the foreignowed debt for two years.[2]

Although the Conservatives had been defeated during the War of the *Reforma* (see chapter 27), two significant guerrilla bands remained at large, that under Gen. Tomás Mejía in the mountains in Querétaro, and that under Leonardo Márquez in central Mexico. Between June and August 1861, Márquez caught three prominent Liberals, Melchor Ocampo, Santos Degollado, and Leandro Valle, and shot them all. He even raided San Cosme on the outskirts of Mexico City.[3]

On October 31, 1861, Great Britain, France, and Spain signed (and Austria and Belgium approved) the Convention of London wherein they agreed to send a joint expedition to seize Vera Cruz. The tariffs collected at the custom house were to be used to pay their citizens. The

United States was invited to participate, the Europeans well knowing it was caught up in a civil war and could not interfere in their plans.[4]

On December 14, 1861, a contingent of 6,243 Spanish troops commanded by Gen. Manuel Gasset y Mercader landed unopposed at Vera Cruz (285 mi E of Mexico City). They were followed by 3,000 French troops and 700 British marines on January 8, 1862. The Spanish and British objective was to collect the money claimed by their nationals. The French had more clandestine motives: They wanted an excuse to place Archiduke Maximilian on the "throne" of Mexico, so they claimed an exorbitant amount that, if paid, would have made Mexico completely destitute and left nothing for the British and Spanish citizens.[5]

Juárez' position was most difficult. His nation was in shambles, his treasury empty, and his army (mostly national guardsmen) exhausted. He responded to the foreign presence by decreeing that any Mexican who aided the invaders would be tried by court-martial, and if found guilty, executed as a traitor. He also ordered a defense prepared. However, he did not want to prod the invaders to action.

The allies had their own problem—yellow fever. By February 1862, some 300 Frenchmen were hospitalized and 800 Spaniards had been sent back to Havana for convalescence. Juárez agreed to allow the unwelcome "guest" to move from the unhealthy coast at Vera Cruz to higher ground near Orizaba (199 mi E of Mexico City). For this concession, he wanted recognition of his government and the promise of the British, French, and Spanish to return to the coast before beginning hostilities should a settlement not be reached. Soon, the Spanish and British accurately perceived the French intentions and withdrew in April 1862.

However, Napoleon III was also a victim of deceit. Napoleon's bastard half-brother (Duc de Morny), his wife (Empress Eugénie), the French ambassador to Mexico (Comte de Saligny), European bankers, and Mexican exiles, all for their own reasons, misled Napoleon into believing that the Mexican population was just waiting for the right moment to overthrow the "hated" Liberals.[6]

OPPOSING FORCES

On March 5, 1862, some 4,000 French reinforcements commanded by Gen. Guillaume Latrille de Lorencez landed at Vera Cruz, bringing French strength to some 6,500 men. The French army had performed well in the Crimea (1854–56) and in Italy (1859) and still carried its Napoleonic reputation—man for man, it was perceived to be the equal of the best. Also, the French initially had high expectations of support from their Conservative Mexican allies, a number of whom had accompanied the French from their exiles.[7] The French were well armed. Most of the infantry carried the muzzle-loading, Model 1857, rifled-percussion muskets, and the remainder carried the older smoothbore-percussion muskets.[8]

The Mexican Liberal army was no match for the French. The officers and men were still amateurs; their victories during the War of the *Reforma* were more the result of superior numbers and reckless courage than their understanding of tactics and discipline. During the War of the *Reforma*, Juárez had been dependent upon guerrillas whose loyalty was difficult to maintain. And, many of these guerrillas went over to the conservative side, when following the War of the *Reforma*, the Liberal government precipitously disbanded their units giving each soldier a meager five pesos, a horse, and the weapons in his possession to safely see him home through bandit-infested countrysides. Many of these men knew nothing but fighting.[9]

Juárez had no money for the national guard, so it had to do with old equipment and armaments that were in its possession. Most firearms were castoffs from an earlier Napoleonic era (1798–1815) and were obsolete and worn out. Some soldiers were armed with smoothbore muskets, while others were armed with old flintlocks, and still others had no firearms at all.[10]

OPENING STRATEGIES

The French army naively believed that it had come to Mexico to tip the scales in favor of the majority of Mexicans who were waiting to overthrow the Liberals. Initially, their generals believed that this could easily be accomplished by capturing Juárez and, failing this, taking Mexico City.

Juárez had no illusion as to the difficulty of his task. His first strategy was to prevent the French army from reaching Mexico City. Should he be unsuccessful, Juárez could escape to the north to ensure the survival of the Liberal government. Compounding the problems within his military was the considerable political dissension within the Liberal party. His prime rival was the popular Gen. González Ortega. Should Mexico City be captured by the French, Juárez would fight a war of attrition against the invader by relying on the guerrilla bands.[11]

FIRST BATTLE OF PUEBLA OR 5 DE MAYO

General de Lorencez, the French commander, now unrestricted by the reluctance of Great Britain and Spain, broke his promise to return to the coast and occupied the town of Orizaba. He was joined by General Marquéz, the Mexican Conservative who had turned guerrilla following the War of the *Reforma*. Together the French and Mexican Conservatives routed the Liberals attempting to hold the heights of Acultzingo, which dominated the road to Mexico City, on April 28, 1862.[12]

The 6,500-man French army expected to be warmly welcomed at the Conservative stronghold of Puebla (80 mi E of Mexico City), which lay along the route to Mexico City. Instead, de Lorencez found the city well fortified by 3,791 Liberals who were commanded by Gen. Ignacio Zaragoza. Without hesitating, on May 5 de Lorencez threw his force at the center of the Mexican defenses, the *Cerro* (Hill) of Guadalupe. This force was repulsed so he attacked the enemy's right. Here, Gen. Porfirio Díaz, commanding the 2nd Brigade, again pushed the French back. The French army expended half of its ammunition and sustained 476 casualties. The Liberals sustained only 227 casualties. The Mexicans tried to follow up their success but were defeated at Cerro del Borrego. Lorencez retreated back to Orizaba.[13]

SECOND BATTLE OF PUEBLA

The results of the first Battle of Puebla shocked the French army. Napoleon III was too committed to back down, plus now the considerable reputation of the French army was at stake. During September and October 1862, some 26,000 more French troops, many of them veterans of the Crimean and Italian campaigns, landed at Vera Cruz. General Forey replaced Lorencez in command. Forey remained on the coast for some time trying to convert Mexicans to the French cause.[14]

Meanwhile, Juárez, deprived of the revenue from the Vera Cruz customs house, imposed new taxes, forced loans, and issued a *levée en masse* (a product of the French Revolution, this decree assigned *every* citizen a task in fighting the enemy). But all that could be gathered by war-weary Mexico was some 30,000 fighters (national guard and regulars). Most of the manpower was divided between the "Army of the East," commanded by Gen. González Ortega

Figure 18. French Intervention in Mexico, 1861–67. Foreign volunteers fighting for Maximilian are on the march. Foreign mercenaries—on land, at sea, and in the air—have fought in many Latin American wars. They have come from Austria, Belgium, England, France, Germany, Holland, Ireland, Italy, Portugal, Russia, Scotland, Spain, the United States, and elsewhere. *Courtesy of Musée Royal de l'Armée et d'Histoire Militaire, Brussels, Belgium.*

who was charged with defending Puebla (General Zaragoza had died from typhoid on September 8) and the "Army of the Center," commanded by Ignacio Comonfort (who had returned from exile to fight the invader), who was to defend Mexico City should the French bypass Puebla.[15]

The 31,000-man French army (which included about 3,000 Mexican Conservatives) began its march toward Puebla early in 1863. Defending the city were 23,930 men under Ortega supported by another 8,000 men under Comonfort. The attack against Puebla began on March 16. Initially, the defenses proved strong enough to hold the French at bay. On the twenty-ninth the French stormed Fort Iturbide and the fighting entered the city. For a week the French advanced slowly, capturing one house at a time with losses of some 600 men in the process.

On May 10 a French detachment ambushed a Mexican relief force under General Comonfort at San Lorenzo, killing 1,000 soldiers and capturing 1,000 prisoners as well as 20 loaded supply wagons and 8 cannon. By May 17 every animal had been eaten and every bullet fired in Puebla. General Ortega ordered all remaining military equipment destroyed, and some 12,000 Mexican soldiers surrendered. Of these some 5,000 men now embraced the Conservative cause. The 868 officers were to be taken to Martinique and France as prisoners of war. Notwithstanding, 336 of them, including Porfirio Díaz and Ortega, escaped while still in Mexico.[16]

Mexico City, having few natural defenses, was abandoned by Juárez, his cabinet, and the remnants of the Mexican army on May 31; they fled north to San Juan Potosí (327 mi NNW of Mexico City). The French army entered Mexico City during early June to a well-orchestrated reception. General Forey, contributing to the charade that the public supported the French intervention, wrote, "The entire population of the capital welcomed us with an enthusiasm verging on delirium. The soldiers of France were literally crushed under the garlands and nosegays."[17]

THE FOREIGN LEGION AT CAMERONE

While General Forey was reducing Puebla, elements of the French Foreign Legion were landing at Vera Cruz. The General chose to use the Legion to protect his lines of communications, reasoning, "I preferred to leave foreigners rather than Frenchmen to guard the most unhealthy area, the tropical zone from Vera Cruz to Córdoba, where the malaria reigns."[18]

On April 30 a company of sixty-five Legionnaires, commanded by one-armed Capt. Jean Danjou, were caught in the open by some 2,400 Mexicans. For ten hours the fight raged at the "Camerón" farm. The Legionnaires refused to surrender in spite of thirty dead and thirty-two severely wounded. Finally, a Foreign Legion relief column arrived the next day. Although this action had little effect on the outcome of the French intervention, it significantly contributed to the reputation of the Legion.[19]

MAXIMILIAN CHOSEN EMPEROR

In July, General Forey gathered an "Assembly of Mexican Notables" (those Conservatives willing to cooperate with the French) who voted for a monarchy. A delegation of Conservative Mexicans offered the throne to Maximilian. He accepted, conditional upon a free vote by the entire population of Mexico. Marshal François-Achille Bazaine,[20] who had replaced General Forey on October 1, 1863, orchestrated the desired result, and the naive Maximilian formally accepted on April 9, 1864, arrived in Vera Cruz on May 28, and entered Mexico City on June 12.[21]

THE CHASE

While these events were occurring, more than 27,000 French and 8,000 Conservative troops chased Juárez northward and defeated the Mexican army every time it stood and fought. Querétaro, Guanajuato, Guadalajara, Oaxaca, Chihuahua, and other important cities and towns were lost by the Liberals. On November 14 General Comonfort, now commanding the Liberal army, was ambushed and killed by Conservatives, notwithstanding being escorted by fifty soldiers! Juárez was chased from San Luis Potosí to Saltillo, and then to Monterrey (635 mi N of Mexico City).[22]

While Juárez was at Monterrey, a number of important Liberals defected. Santiago Vidaurri, who almost independently ruled the north, refused to give Juárez the revenues from the customs house at Piedras Negras and declared his loyalty to Maximilian. Doblado and Ortega also deserted Juárez. The Liberal President was driven to Paso del Norte (today's Ciudad Juárez, 1,221 mi NW of Mexico City) where he reestablished his government. By late 1863, Juárez tentatively controlled the far north, the ancient soldier Álvarez the state of Guerrero, and Porfirio Díaz the city of Oaxaca and its surroundings. The French won the large cities and towns. The guerrillas, mostly loyal to Juárez, some only to themselves, and others in the pay of the French, held the countryside.[23]

The army supporting Maximilian was at its peak of strength. There were some 36,000 Frenchmen, 8,500 foreign volunteers (mostly Austrians and Belgians), about 7,000 Conservative regulars, and perhaps 20,000 guerrillas. Juárez had only a few thousand regulars remaining and these were split between the region along the border with the United States and southern Mexico. The real strength of the Liberals were the innumerable guerrilla bands that supported Juárez.[24]

FRENCH NAVAL OPERATIONS

While the French army was chasing Juárez, the French navy landed garrisons at Tampico, Matamoros, Minatitlan, Campeche along the Gulf coast, and Mazatlan in the Pacific. The navy also had the most difficult task of preventing arms from being smuggled into Mexico without the ability to proclaim a blockade, since France was not at war with Mexico. While carrying out these assignments, the gunboat *Lance* stranded off Tampico in November 1862 and the frigate *Montezuma* off Minatitlan in July 1863. Both ships were lost.

On the Pacific Coast a French squadron under Adm. Louis Edouard Bouët-Willaumez bombarded Acapulco (284 mi S of Mexico City) for three days (January 10–12, 1863), landing sailors who were replaced later by Algerians. Throughout these operations, the fleet suffered from yellow fever, losing over fifty officers and 2,000 sailors.[25]

MAXIMILIAN'S GROWING PROBLEMS

In spite of numerous military victories, Maximilian's problems compounded daily. The increasing cost of the war forced him to become more dependent upon his benefactor, Napoleon III.[26] The French collected the revenue at the customs houses and Marshal Bazaine freely spent it to execute Napoleon's policies. Far from blameless, Maximilian spent money recklessly on endless balls and banquets, extravagant gifts to loyal followers, and for the restoration of Chapultepec Castle, his residence. Maximilian's policy of conciliation toward Liberals who swore allegiance to him alienated many Conservatives. His refusal to restore Church property seized by the Juárez government angered the clergy, including the Pope. His cancellation of peon debts and abolition of the use of the whip upset the large landowners.[27]

By September 1864 Marshal Bazaine occupied the states of Nuevo León and Coahuila, thus increasing the French control over north-central Mexico. On February 8, 1865, an army of 4,780 French soldiers and 500 Conservatives captured Porfirio Díaz and his army as well as the city of Oaxaca (342 mi SE of Mexico City).[28] By now, Juárez was reduced to only a few mountain strongholds. And by the spring of 1865, it appeared as if Maximilian was on the threshold of victory. Most of Juárez' regular troops had been destroyed and only isolated guerrillas continued the fight.[29]

But international events turned against Napoleon, and consequently Maximilian. The North finally defeated the South in the American Civil War during the spring of 1865. The reunited United States began leaving stocks of "unattended" weapons and ammunition along its border with Mexico for the Liberals to "find." Some 3,000 former Union soldiers, promised good pay and land, joined the Liberal army.[30] Also, the United States massed 50,000 veteran troops under Gen. Philip Sheridan on the border. In February 1866 the United States told the French to leave Mexico. In Europe Prussia defeated Austria in the fall of 1866. France now felt eminently threatened by the potential unification of the Germans. Napoleon instructed Bazaine to make one last concerted effort to destroy Juárez and then come home.[31]

At Bazaine's urging, Maximilian, misled to believe that Juárez had fled the country, decreed on October 3, 1865, "that all persons carrying arms against the Empire, as well as all persons aiding them by selling them arms or supplies, were to be tried by courts-martial and condemned to death."[32] On October 21 Conservative Col. Juan Méndez shot five senior Liberal officers at Uruapan, Michoacan, where the said decree had yet to be promulgated. The decree and Mendez' actions enraged the Liberals and increased the brutalities committed by both sides.[33]

By March 1866 the new French offensive had run its course and Juárez proved as elusive as ever. As the French withdrew from Monterrey, Saltillo, and Tampico, the followers of Juárez moved in behind them. Meanwhile, Porfirio Díaz had escaped from his prison in the city of Oaxaca and began organizing guerrillas in the southern mountains.[34]

Slowly, Maximilian came to the realization that Napoleon was going to desert him. Initially, Maximilian chose to abdicate, but Carlotta, his wife, declared that this would be cowardly; a letter from his mother advised him to persevere; and his advisors persuaded him that victory was still possible. Maximilian worked to create a native army, held together by the pressgangs, requisitions, and extortion, and given backbone by the few Austrian and Belgian volunteers who remained behind.[35] The new army was outfitted and funded by Marshal Bazaine, contrary to Napoleon's instructions. Carlotta rushed to Europe to urge Napoleon III and the Pope for help.[36]

By early 1867 Maximilian controlled only Mexico City, Puebla, Querétaro, Vera Cruz, and little else. Learning that Carlotta had gone insane, he prepared to abdicate. Napoleon instructed Bazaine to negotiate with any Liberal except Juárez for the transfer of government in exchange for recognition of the debt to French citizens; but there were no takers. Maximilian was persuaded by ultra-Conservatives, who now had his ear, that victory was still possible. Conservative Generals Márquez and Miramón had returned to Mexico from exile and were preparing to fight Juárez.[37]

As instructed by Napoleon, Bazaine made one last effort to persuade Maximilian to abdicate. When this failed, Bazaine destroyed those war supplies he could not carry off, hoping this would change Maximilian's mind. The French army marched out of Mexico City on February 5, 1867. It had to negotiate safe passage through the countryside with Liberal General Porfirio Díaz. The last French troops sailed from Vera Cruz on March 12.[38]

THE SIEGE OF QUERÉTARO

The principal element of the new imperial army, some 10,000 men, and the most prominent Conservative leaders assembled at Querétaro (167 mi NNW of Mexico City). The Conservatives convinced Maximilian to join the army, thus lessening any thoughts he might have of abdicating. The Emperor took command; Márquez was made chief of staff; Miramón commanded the infantry; Mejía the cavalry; Méndez the reserves; Manuel Ramírez Arellano the artillery; and Prince Felix von Salm Salm the Sharpshooters (*Batallón de Cazadores*).[39]

Three Liberal armies converged on Querétaro. The 25,000-man "Army of the North," commanded by Gen. Mariano Escobedo, arrived first on March 6. It was the best trained and equipped of the Liberal armies, being the primary beneficiary of the arms received from the United States. Many of its units were better outfitted than even Maximilian's European mercenaries, some having Spencer repeating rifles. And, the bulk of the American-supplied artillery was manned by former Union soldiers. Miramón wanted to immediately attack. However, Maximilian had greater confidence in Márquez, who advised waiting. Throughout March the "Army of the Center" and the "Army of the West" united with the "Army of the North." Now some 40,000 Liberals tightened the siege on Querétaro.[40]

On March 27 General Márquez, leading 1,200 cavalry, cut his way out of Querétaro, with instructions to go to Mexico City, take command of the Conservative garrison, and attack the besieging Liberals in the rear so that Maximilian's army could escape. Arriving in Mexico City, he decided instead to march southeast with 5,000 men and relieve the Conservatives besieged in Puebla by Porfirio Díaz. Learning of Márquez' approach on April 2, the Liberal General immediately stormed Puebla. Porfirio Díaz, who had been reinforced by those besieging Querétaro, then caught Márquez in the open on the tenth and defeated him. Márquez fled to Mexico City and ultimately to Cuba.[41]

Meanwhile, the siege tightened at Querétaro. Maximilian planned a breakout for May 14, the goal of which was to take refuge in the Sierra Gorda with General Mejía's tribesmen; the attempt was postponed one hour before its scheduled execution. During that night Col. Miguel López betrayed Maximilian and allowed elements of the Liberal army through the trenches he commanded; they took the town almost without firing a shot. Maximilian joined Mejía on the *Cerro de las Campañas* (Hill of the Bells) where they were captured on May 15. Maximilian was tried by a court-martial of junior officers and condemned to death. On June 19, in spite of appeals for mercy by many (but not Maximilian), he and Conservative Generals Miramón and Mejía were shot. Two days later, General Porfirio Díaz led a Liberal army into Mexico City. Benito Juarez returned to Mexico City on July 15.[42]

OBSERVATIONS

The war against the French and Maximilian ended the Mexican Liberal-Conservative struggle, but only for thirty-three years. Ironically, the Liberals lost most of the battles, won the war, and then lost the peace. True, the Monarchist element within the Mexican Conservative movement was crushed; however, the Liberals did not hold power for long. In 1871 Congress declared Juárez president for another term. The unsuccessful candidate, Porfirio Díaz, failed in an attempt to overthrow Juárez. Juárez died in 1872 and the Chief of the Supreme Court, Sebastián Lerdo, succeeded him. Lerdo's forces were defeated in a second *coup* attempt by Porfirio Díaz in 1876. Although a cunning and courageous Liberal general during the War of the *Reforma* and the fight against the French and Maximilian, Porfirio Díaz evolved into an ultra-Conservative and ruled Mexico from 1876 to 1911.

Archduke Maximilian proved to be a very poor choice by Napoleon III and the Mexican Conservatives. The Archduke was more the enlightened romantic than the aristocratic monarch that they had wanted. Maximilian did not even repeal the *Reforma* Laws. As a consequence, he forfeited Conservative support but won over few of the Liberals.[43]

The intervention was disastrous for Napoleon III. He lost popular support at home, frivolously sapped the strength of the French army, alienated the United States, spent 900 million francs, and in general, lost prestige.[44]

With the ending of decades of on-again, off-again warfare, many Mexicans skilled in the art of guerrilla warfare were turned loose on a land whose productivity had largely been destroyed. Juárez reduced the Liberal army from 90,000 men to 30,000 men. Also, the thousands who had fought for the Conservatives were without employment. As a result, banditry and social unrest became chronic.[45]

Taking into consideration the six-year duration of the war, the presence of yellow fever, the lack of sanitation and medical services, and the brutality practiced on both sides, one might estimate that the French lost 10,000 men (6,000 from the army; 2,000 from the foreign legion; and 2,000 from the navy); the Austrian and Belgian mercenaries lost 3,000 men; and the Mexican Conservatives lost 20,000 men. And, the more poorly trained and initially more poorly armed Liberals undoubtedly lost more men than the 33,000-plus of their adversaries.[46]

Map 8. Río de la Plata Region, 1865.

PART 8

MID-NINETEENTH-CENTURY ATTEMPTED TERRITORIAL CONQUEST AND RECONQUEST

CHAPTER TWENTY-NINE

THE WAR OF THE TRIPLE ALLIANCE, 1864–70

> ... waged by hundreds against thousands, a battle of [Napoleonic] Brown Bess [rifles] and poor old flintlocks, against Spencer and Enfield rifles; of honeycombed carronades, long and short, against Whitworths and La Hittes; and of punts and canoes against ironclads.
> —Richard F. Burton

THE SPARK

On November 12, 1864, the Paraguayan warship *Tacuarí* seized the Brazilian mail steamer *Marquês de Olinda* at Curuzú Chica near Antequera (85 mi N of Asunción) on the Paraguay River inside Paraguay. Although formal declarations of war were delayed, this event started the attempt by the Paraguayan dictator Francisco Solano López[1] to extend by force his influence in the Río de la Plata Basin.[2]

BACKGROUND

The War of the Triple Alliance (1864–70) pitted Paraguay against Argentina, Brazil, and Uruguay. For decades the diplomatic and military struggle for the domination of Uruguay, and therefore the Platine basin, had been between Argentina and Brazil, with political elements of Uruguay seeking help from one or the other of their giant neighbors. In 1862 Francisco Solano López, with his Irish mistress Eliza Lynch[3] at his side, emerged as the ruler of Paraguay and involved his nation in the contest. Some within the *Blanco* party of Uruguay increasingly looked to Paraguay, which they possibly perceived to have the strongest military force in South America,[4] to support their cause against the *Colorado* party, which for once had the help of both Argentina and Brazil. The ruling *Blancos* alienated Argentina and ignored Brazil's demands, possibly believing that Paraguay would come to their aid in case of war.

In 1863, following Uruguay's seizure of weapons being carried by an Argentine merchant ship, the Argentine navy blockaded the Uruguay River. The blockade allowed the *Colorado* rebels to land troops and ammunition unmolested by the Uruguayan navy.[5] A year later, on October 12, 1864, Brazil invaded northern Uruguay, being motivated by land disputes and having failed to receive satisfaction through diplomacy for numerous border violations. The Uruguayan army retired and the Brazilian troops halted, hoping that the *Blancos* now appreciated their display of resolve.

While the two armies were facing off in northern Uruguay, Brazil sent three warships under Adm.[6] Joaquim Tamandaré to blockade Montevideo. While ascending the Paraná River, the squadron met the Uruguayan warship *Villa del Salto*. A fight ensued. The Uruguayan warship was forced to seek refuge in Argentine waters, and later, when the Uruguayans tried to run past the Brazilian ships, the *Villa del Salto* was forced ashore and burned.

Six hundred *Colorados* led by Venancio Flores[7] and supported by a few thousand Brazilian soldiers and marines, as well as the warships under Admiral Tamandaré, captured the Uruguay River port of Paysandú (298 mi NW of Montevideo) from 1,500 *Blanco* defenders on January 2, 1865, following a fifty-two-hour bombardment. They shot Leandro Gómez and other *Blanco* defenders. The victors marched against Montevideo, and the Admiral sailed to blockade the Uruguayan capital.

In an attempt to draw Paraguay into the war, Uruguay invaded the Brazilian province of Rio Grande do Sul, a region possibly desired by López. However, López did not send the anticipated aid, and the Uruguayans were soon forced to retreat. In February 1865 Montevideo fell to the *Colorados* and their Brazilian allies. Before going into exile, the embittered Uruguayan Blanco president, Atanasio Aguirre, denounced Paraguay's lack of timely support.

In fact, López had taken action, but it did not relieve the pressures building against the Uruguayan *Blancos*. The Paraguayan warship *Tacuarí* seized the *Marquês de Olinda*, and she was taken into the Paraguayan navy. Then two Paraguayan columns invaded Brazil's Mato Grosso do Sul to the north; one split in two after crossing the frontier. A 2,440-man riverine expedition led by Col. Vicente Barrios pushed up the Paraguay River on board six steamers, two *chatas* (lowlying, flat-bottomed barges), and three towed sailing ships. Col. Francisco Isidoro Resquín led 1,450 and Maj. Martin Urbieta led 365 men, both on foot, toward Dourados and Brilhante in Brazil. The Brazilians defended Coimbra for forty-eight hours, but Corumba fell without a fight. Although Paraguay did seize some old guns, munitions, and other booty in this sortie to the north, it gained no strategic advantage and squandered time that the allies desperately needed in order to prepare to fight.[8] Communications with the interior were poor; it took forty-seven days (February 22, 1865) before the Brazilian government in Rio de Janeiro heard the first rumors of the attack, and confirmation was not received by mail until March 17.[9]

OPPOSING FORCES

The Paraguayan peacetime army was of moderate size, notwithstanding exaggerated contemporary reports. It was composed of about 9,000 men (589 of which were officers) and the navy consisted of 668 (25 officers). In addition, there was a police battalion of 500 men, the overwhelming majority of which were stationed in Asunción. On March 20, 1865, the Paraguayan army had 38,173 men under arms. Potentially another 35,100 were available; these included those not yet trained and those awaiting arms, many of whom were either very young or very old. The army was organized into battalions which ranged in size between 600 and 1,000 men.[10]

Figure 19. War of the Triple Alliance, 1864–70. Francisco Solano López, perceiving himself to be a military genius, led Paraguay into a disastrous war against overwhelming odds—Argentina, Brazil, and Uruguay. Historians still debate the magnitude of the losses sustained by Paraguay but most agree it was between 60 and 80 percent of the male population. *Copied from George Thompson,* The War in Paraguay *(London: Longmans, Green, 1869).*

Francisco Solano López had purchased a very limited amount of the best European military hardware money could buy (and a lot of junk); however, these did not go far among his troops. The army's rifles were a gun collector's dream and a quartermaster's nightmare. Three battalions were armed with Witton rifles; another three or four with percussion rifles; and the remainder with an assortment of flintlocks, which had been manufactured worldwide.[11] In 1864 López had about twenty modern artillery pieces, four of Prussian origin, four of British, eight of French, and at least one breechloader for the navy. The remainder of his artillery was a conglomeration of Spanish colonial pieces, some dating to the seventeenth century, many of which had arrived in Paraguay as ships' ballast. López also purchased some Congrêve rockets which in combat proved to be mostly "sparkle." Most of the modern European war material purchased by López was not delivered, either because he had not paid for it in time or because the neutrality of some states forbade delivery.

INROAD OF THE CAVALRY.

Figure 20. War of the Triple Alliance, 1864–70. A Paraguayan cavalry unit (left) is attacked by that of the allies (right). After the first few years of the war, the Paraguayans had to eat their horses in order to survive. By the late years of the conflict they also ran out of men. *Copied from* Harper's New Monthly Magazine, *Vol. 40 (1870).*

López had built a naval yard run by British technicians and a small naval squadron of seventeen ships built around one warship, the gunboat *Tacuarí*.[12] He had expanded a foundry at Ibicuí and had found ingredients locally for the manufacture of gunpowder. The army had little combat experience. The true strength of the Paraguayan army rested in its homogeneity of language (Guaraní and Spanish) and race,[13] its fanatical loyalty to López, and its strict discipline.[14]

Brazil's standing army, upon which the brunt of the fighting for the allies would fall, was of modest size. Almost the entire regular army was in Rio Grande do Sul when the war broke out. However, its potential was overwhelming when compared to that of Paraguay's. The Brazilian army of 1864 was 16,834 strong with a reserve of some 20,000—the *Guarda Nacional*; however, the *Guarda Nacional* was constitutionally prohibited from fighting outside of Brazilian territory. Therefore, new battalions, *Voluntários do Pátria*, were formed; many of the recruits were black freedmen and slaves. Enticements such as freedom, money, and land were offered; when these failed to fill the quotas, impressment became necessary.[15] The army reached its maximum field strength of 67,000 men in April 1866. The soldiers were drawn from the lower

Figure 21. War of the Triple Alliance, 1864–70. A Paraguayan soldier late in the war on sentry duty at López' headquarters was lucky to have a worn-out musket. As the war dragged on, some Paraguayan soldiers entered combat without weapons and were expected to arm themselves from those of fallen comrades. *Copied from* Harper's New Monthly Magazine, *Vol. 40 (April 1870).*

class and socially were considered repugnant. On the whole, morale and training were poor. This weakness was offset by a superior officer corps that received training at the *Escola Militar* in Rio de Janeiro.

The standard rifles used percussion caps or were center-fire weapons. As the war progressed the army purchased a substantial number of modern rifles, including repeaters.[16] The Brazilian artillery had a substantial number of modern weapons including 32-pounder English-made rifled Whitworth guns; however, much of the ammunition for the artillery was faulty, especially during the first years of the war.[17]

Brazil was the only one of the allies to possess a real navy. It numbered some forty-five vessels; however, the vast majority were ill suited for riverine operations. Brazil was soon able to purchase four monitors and two lightly-armored gunboats which had been ordered by López in Europe.[18] Like the army, the naval officers were drawn from the upper class and were well educated.[19]

The Argentine army may have been the largest among the allies at the start of the war. There were some 8,500 regulars making up six infantry battalions and nine cavalry regiments, and some artillery. An additional 9,500 troops forming nineteen battalions had been raised throughout the provinces. Also, the provinces of Entre Ríos and Corrientes had mobilized their national guard units, which on paper represented an additional 10,000 men although in reality probably comprised only a fraction of that number and were of poor quality. At least 4,000 troops were needed to guard the southern frontiers against Indian attacks and the country against rebellion.[20]

The smallest of the allies, Uruguay, had been the victim of a long civil war. As to be expected, its numerical contribution was small, being some 1,500 men led by General and now provisional President Flores. Although few in number, they were well seasoned.

OPENING STRATEGIES

Paraguay did not possess a blue water fleet capable of attacking Brazil along its Atlantic seaboard. Thus, if Paraguay wished to carry the war to Brazil, only two practical avenues lay open. The first would be to continue to advance north into the sparsely populated Mato Grosso, which offered no prospect of being decisive, and the second to march southeast through Argentina without its permission which it had denied.[21]

Brazil's strategic objective became the removal of Francisco Solano López as the ruler of Paraguay. To accomplish this, Brazilian leaders correctly assumed that it would be necessary to invade Paraguay. Again, the most practical route lay across Argentina and it refused Brazil permission to cross its territory in order to make war on Paraguay; Argentina did, however, state that the Paraná and Uruguay Rivers were open to both parties. Territorial acquisition was a secondary motivation for Brazil as well.[22]

In preparation for the invasion through Argentina, Paraguay attacked and captured the Argentine river port of Corrientes (430 mi N of Buenos Aires), thus bringing Argentina into the war. Once into the war, Argentina saw the conflict as an opportunity to obtain territory it disputed with Paraguay. In Uruguay the ruling *Colorado* party encouraged both Argentina and Brazil to go to war because it helped cement the Rio de Janeiro–Buenos Aires alliance upon which they depended.

Once Argentina joined Brazil and Uruguay in war against Paraguay, the traditional invasion route into Paraguay—through Misiones, crossing the Paraná River at the port of Encarnación, and then over dry ground into central Paraguay—became unencumbered by issues of neutrality. This was the route that General Belgrano had taken in 1811. However, this route would not allow the Brazilians to employ their superior navy. Instead, the allies chose an approach up the Paraguay River.

LÓPEZ ATTACKS ARGENTINA

On Good Friday, April 13, 1865, a Paraguayan squadron of five warships attacked and took the river port of Corrientes (170 mi S of Asunción).[23] The Paraguayan army then advanced down the east bank of the Paraná River. López had hoped for the support of Gen. Justo José de Urquíza, the powerful *caudillo* of Entre Ríos and a political opponent of Argentine President Bartolomé Mitre.[24] In fact, López' invasion of Argentina had the opposite effect. Urquíza and many other Argentine Federalists had sympathized with the Uruguayan *Blancos*. The murder of the *Blanco* Gen. Leandro Gómez by the *Colorados* following his gallant defense of Payasandú against the Brazilians and *Colorados* in January 1865 had piqued their emotions. But now the actions of López gave the Argentine Federalists only two choices: fight against the invader or remain neutral. Urquíza initially promised to fight López.

TRIPLE ALLIANCE FORMED

On May 1, 1865, after but one day of official meetings, Argentina, Brazil, and Uruguay formed the Triple Alliance to oppose Paraguay. Under the terms of the agreement, Gen. Bartolomé Mitre, President of Argentina, was made chief commander of operation on Argentine and Paraguayan soil. Should the fighting move to Brazilian or Uruguayan soil, then the chief commander would come from the appropriate country. Vice Admiral Tamandaré was given command of all naval operations. The allies agreed not to withdraw from the war until López had been defeated, and then only by common consent. The independence of Paraguay was to be respected. Free navigation of the Paraná and Paraguay Rivers was to be established while Paraguay was to be held liable for the costs of the war. And, Argentina and Brazil awarded to themselves all of the territory they disputed with Paraguay. These terms were to be kept a secret, a secret which proved to be poorly held by Uruguay.

The three allies were ill-prepared for a protracted war and required time to get ready. Each struggled to raise an army. The few Argentine troops immediately available concentrated in Entre Ríos, south of the Paraguayan border. The Brazilian fleet, under Admiral Tamandaré, was sent up the Paraná River to provide support. General Urquíza was to raise an irregular cavalry force in Entre Ríos. The Brazilian and Uruguayan armies were to form and march up the Uruguay River, crossing near Candelaria. However, they were not prepared to advance until June 1865.

THE ALLIES TEMPORARILY RECAPTURE CORRIENTES

A small, 3,846-man allied force under Argentine Gen. Wenceslao Paunero shadowed the enemy's activity. Seeing that the Paraguayans had left Corrientes poorly defended as they marched down on the east bank of the river, the General embarked his Argentine troops along with 364 Brazilians plus some 500 European mercenaries in the Brazilian squadron, proceeded up the Paraná River, and on May 25 (the Argentine national holiday) recaptured Corrientes after some heavy fighting.[25]

López immediately sent troops to recapture the town, while the allied raiding force withdrew, holding Corrientes for less than twenty-four hours. The allied victory, although short-lived, boosted morale. Also, the attack demonstrated to López how vulnerable were the lines of communication of his invading army.

BATTLE OF RIACHUELO

In order to regain the initiative, López attempted to destroy the Brazilian squadron anchored at the mouth of the Arroyo Riachuelo five miles downriver from Corrientes. On June 11, 1865, a Paraguayan makeshift fleet of eight steamers (mounting 30 guns) towing six *chatas*, each mounting one 8-inch gun, attacked nine Brazilian warships carrying 59 guns including a few modern 32-pound Whitworths. As it passed the Brazilian anchorage, the Paraguayan fleet fired, then anchored under twenty-two camouflaged guns of the 2nd Paraguayan Horse Artillery Regiment which had been moved secretly into place; these ranged from 4- to 18-pounders. The Brazilians counterattacked, and the battle raged at close range for several hours with victory seemingly within the grasp of the Paraguayans. At this point Brazil's flagship, the frigate *Amazonas*, successfully rammed four enemy ships and gave the Brazilians a clear victory. The Brazilian superior fire power, better maneuverability, and greater discipline overcame the element of surprise and the ferocity of the Paraguayan attack. The Paraguayans lost three steamers, all six *chatas*, and several hundred men.[26]

The Paraguayan leader, Commander Pedro Ignacio Meza, died later of wounds at Humaitá, thus cheating the executioner who had his orders should he survive. The Brazilians lost one ship and sustained heavy damage to a second one. Admiral Tamandaré was absent at the time of the attack, so the Brazilian fleet was commanded by Commodore Francisco Manoel Barroso da Silva.[27] Paraguay lost a naval battle which ultimately would lead to the Brazilian control of the rivers, but it was able to retrieve its surviving warships and tow them to Humaitá because the Brazilian fleet withdrew to Esquina for repairs and due to the critical shortage of coal.

PARAGUAY INVADES RIO GRANDE DO SUL

Simultaneous with the naval attack, a 10,000-man Paraguayan force crossed the Argentine province of Misiones. Reaching the Uruguay River, the force split into two columns and turned southward, marching down both banks of the river. Lt. Col. Antonio de la Cruz Estigarribia, the overall commander, led the almost 7,500 troops of the east bank and Maj. Pedro Duarte commanded the 2,500 troops on the west.[28] The Paraguayans met little opposition from the Argentines on the west bank or the Brazilians on the east. López believed that if he could gain control of Rio Grande do Sul and invade Uruguay, then the Brazilian slaves would rise up and the recently ousted *Blancos* of Uruguay would again take up arms. Also, Paraguayan emissaries had successfully stirred up sedition among the irregulars being raised by Urquíza in Entre Ríos. Urquíza, who had been given command of the allied vanguard, volunteered to return to the province and restore order. Instead, he retired to his ranch, increased his wealth by selling horses to the allies, and the irregulars deserted to their farms and ranches.

By August 1865, Colonel Estigarribia arrived just north of Uruguayana, Brazil, a few miles north of the Uruguayan frontier. His contact with Major Duarte was intermitted due to the harassment of two armed Brazilian vessels, commanded by Lt. Floriano Peixoto and the swamps that lay between them.[29]

BATTLES OF YATAÍ AND URUGUAYANA

Uruguayan President Flores, camped at Concordia, Uruguay, chose to attack the smaller Paraguayan force under Major Duarte. He ordered General Paunero, then in southwest

Corrientes, to join him in haste. Through a series of forced marches, the Argentines joined the Uruguayans on August 15. Two days later, the Allied force of 8,581 men with 32 guns decisively defeated the Paraguayan force of 3,220 men without a single gun on the west bank.[30] The Paraguayans lost between 1,000 and 1,700 killed, 1,700 wounded and captured, and 200 escaped. The Allies lost 300 to 600 men. When Colonel Estigarribia learned of Duarte's defeat, he occupied Uruguayana, which had been evacuated by the Brazilians, and awaited orders from López.[31] Given the distances involved, Estigarribia was either foolish or on a very short "leash" to think that waiting for orders was a practical course to follow. During the next month the allies amassed an overwhelming besieging force. Following some negotiations, a desultory bombardment began on September 18. Just minutes before the Allied attack was scheduled to begin, Estigarribia unconditionally surrendered his surviving forces of 59 officers and 5,515 men, for which López declared him a traitor.

The Paraguayan offensive to the south had been disastrous. Politically, López lost any hope of winning Rio Grande do Sul and the possibility of aid from the beaten Uruguayan *Blancos*.[32] Perhaps more importantly, he also lost the initiative which he never regained. Militarily, his losses were substantial. More than 20,000 men were lost (most to sickness); this was between a third and a half of the manpower available at that time. Most of the losses consisted of newly formed units of reservists and recruits. Also, at least 13,000 rifles and five old cannon were lost.[33]

THE ALLIES INVADE PARAGUAY

The Allies now decided on the strategy of invading Paraguay from the south and attacking Humaitá, a heavily fortified, double bend on the Paraguay River (134 mi S of Asunción). López countered by concentrating his forces in the delta between the Paraguay and Paraná Rivers at the fortified Paso de Patria. It was November before the Allied army of 40,000 men was ready to advance toward its initial objective, the Argentine city of Corrientes. López ordered the city evacuated without a fight.[34] Gen. Francisco Isidoro Resquín then replaced General Robles as commander of the Paraguayan forces in Argentina. He executed a well-planned retreat from the south. This need to concentrate forced López to withdraw the few troops that remained in Mato Grosso in the north.

Argentine and Uruguayan enthusiasm for the war began to wane. Neither was now threatened by Paraguay. Andean countries such as Chile and Peru, plus the great powers of the day, Great Britain, France, and the United States, favored negotiations but for different reasons. Brazil would have none of it and reminded its allies of their obligations to continue the fight. The Allied armies assembled at Corrientes in preparation for the invasion. On several occasions, the Paraguayans crossed the Paraná in strength and raided the Allies. During these actions José Díaz,[35] the former police chief of Asunción, first distinguished himself. The Brazilian navy remained passive.[36]

While the Allies prepared to cross at the fork of the Paraguay and Paraná Rivers, the recently arrived, new Brazilian ironclads *Brasil* and *Tamandaré* dueled with Paraguayan batteries. During the night of April 5, 1866, a Brazilian force of 900 seized the sandbank Banco de Itapirú and fortified it with a battery of La Hitte cannon and four mortars.[37] Five days later at four in the morning, José Díaz sent 1,200 handpicked Paraguayans in an unsuccessful attempt to retake the sandbank. Díaz was expressly forbidden by López to lead the assault. The Paraguayans were driven back at the point of bayonets, losing some 800 men; the Brazilians lost 153 men.

Figure 22. War of the Triple Alliance, 1864–70. Brazilian monitors battle the Paraguayan battery at Tebicuary. The Allied strategy was to advance up the Paraguay River to capture the Paraguayan capital of Asunción. This would permit the Allies to employ the superior Brazilian navy. Paraguayan ingenuity made this a most difficult undertaking. The Paraguayans planted underwater mines, manufactured crude but reasonably effective cannon, attacked in canoes, and even floated down upon the Brazilians on river plants. Brazilian warships forced passage of the battery on a number of occasions and some ships sustained considerable damage. *Copied from L'Illustration Universel (1868)*.

Since mid-April, the Brazilian squadron had bombarded the Paraguayan Fort Itapirú as a diversion. A Brazilian advanced guard under Gen.[38] Manuel Luis Osório[39] landed on April 26, 1866, near Tres Bocas on the Paraguay River, and this force was followed by the Argentines under General Mitre. This river landing was the largest in Latin American history. Some 42,000 men and 90 guns were transported on 65 steamers and 50 sailing vessels and *chatas* (barges). After a brief fight the Paraguayans abandoned their position after destroying all of the potential value to the allies.[40]

In spite of having gained the Paraguayan side of the Paraná River, the allies still faced formidable geographical barriers. Between the allies and the strongly fortified position of Humaitá was a heavily wooded region; the west bank of the Paraguay River was thick with undergrowth; and to the east lay the inhospitable Estero Bellaco swamp.

THE BATTLE OF ESTERO BELLACO

Perhaps overconfident due to the ease with which they crossed the Paraguay River, the Allies poorly guarded their camp from attack. López saw that many of the Allied pickets were placed in wooded areas where observation was difficult and too distant from the main body. He attacked with 6,000 men through a number of clearings. By midday of May 2, the Allies' outposts were cut to pieces. The Uruguayan brigade was the first to perceive the danger and put up a stout defense. Its "Florida" Battalion counterattacked with fixed bayonets. However, they were soon surrounded and not relieved by the main body for over an hour. As the Allies pursued their enemy, they came face to face with extensive Paraguayan entrenchments known as the "Lines of Rojas." During the battle the Paraguayans lost some 3,000 men and the Allies 1,100.

THE FIRST BATTLE OF TUYUTÍ

The Allies' advance began on May 20 under the command of General Mitre. Four days later, while they were throwing up entrenchments, 18,000 Paraguayans attacked in three columns, one each against the Argentines on the right, the Uruguayans in the center, and the Brazilians on the left. López selected this date because he knew that the Allies planned to attack him on the twenty-fifth, the Argentine national day. His aim was to frustrate the Allied preparations for that attack. López' plan was to have the two wing columns break through the lines of the Allies and encircle the center. Only the 19th Cavalry Regiment succeeded in breaking through to the rear of the Allies, and those who survived—about twenty—reached the Paraguayan lines in the Sauce Forest. General Flores, who had been given command of the Allied vanguard when Urquíza withdrew, detached two Uruguayan battalions from the center and with them stabilized the left. Finally, the Paraguayans were repulsed, 7,000 men killed in action and 7,000 more wounded, most of whom reached their own lines. Of these, 2,000 men later died of their wounds. The Allies lost about 4,000 men killed, wounded, and missing. Here and at Estero Bellaco, López lost the flower of his army. For the first time in the war, Paraguay's new 40th Battalion was virtually annihilated.[41]

General Osório, commanding the Brazilians, wanted to pursue the fleeing Paraguayans, but Mitre was hesitant. As a result of this difference of opinion, Osório retired to Rio Grande do Sul.[42]

The strategy of both sides was somewhat surprising. López had left well-prepared defensive positions and initiated two major battles with officers possessing inadequate training to carry out a complex offensive maneuver, regardless of how courageous they might be—this by a leader who was literally beginning to run out of men and weapons.[43] The Allies chose to cut across country expecting to find little opposition before reaching Humaitá, instead of advancing up the river where the fleet could afford some support. The lack of geographical information and the fear of mines and hidden batteries might have influenced their decision.

"LINES OF ROJAS"

After having fought two battles, the Allies now confronted an extensive system of trenches prepared by George Thompson and the other British on López' payroll at some distance from the river. A council of war determined that politically it was unwise to withdraw to the Paraná River and that the "Lines of Rojas" would need to be taken, preferably through bombardment. An assault was to be attempted once fresh troops arrived. On July 11 at Yataity Corá and again between July 16 and 18 at Boquerón del Sauce, the armies clashed as a result of provocations caused by fire initiated from newly dug Paraguayan trenches. On the eighteenth alone the Allies lost 2,670 men and the Paraguayans 1,500. The Paraguayans were able to hold most of their trenches while the Allies avoided walking into a trap which López had laid for them. General Mitre did not believe that his force was strong enough to continue the attack, already having lost some 2,000 men. Hence, the Allies fell into inactivity.

BATTLE OF CURUZÚ

The Allied reinforcements did not arrive until August, months overdue. A council of war decided that the best course of action would be to send a force up the Paraguay River, attack the fortifications of Curupaití (144 mi S of Asunción), thereby threatening Humaitá, and drawing the defenders away from the "Lines of Rojas." Six Brazilian warships escorting transports carrying 9,000 men started up the Paraguay River. However, their progress was soon blocked by a battery at Curuzú. The battery was bombarded by the fleet on September 1. On the second, 8,391 men landed at Las Palmas and they successfully stormed the battery.

During the fighting the new ironclad *Rio de Janeiro*, pride of the Brazilian navy, struck a mine and sank. Lacking watertight compartments, the warship sank in a few minutes. Practically its entire crew, including the captain and all the engineers, drowned. After a stout defense, the Paraguayans fell back on Curupaití, being badly outnumbered. The Allied victory was expensive—700 men were lost as well as the ironclad; the Paraguayans lost 832.[44]

The action at Curuzú divided the Allied military leaders as to their future course of action. General Porto Alegre and most Brazilian leaders wanted to move in force against Curupaití. General Mitre opposed weakening the army at Tuyutí which faced the "Lines of Rojas." Admiral Tamandaré believed that the fleet was not strong enough to face the fortifications at Curupaití, particularly following the loss of the *Rio de Janeiro*.

BATTLE OF CURUPAITÍ

López requested an armistice conference that was held at Yataity Corá on September 12, 1866. The Brazilian General, Polidoro da Fonseca Quintanilha Jordao, refused to meet with López. Flores was present for only a short time. The five-hour meeting was principally between Mitre and the Paraguayan leader. López offered peace with the Argentines and Uruguayans on the condition that he remain in power. He was well aware that the Brazilians would not discuss any terms. Mitre rejected the terms.[45]

Possibly the fact that López proposed talks exhibited a lack of confidence in his military position not previously shown and helped to end the Allies' indecision. Mitre now agreed to support the Brazilian plan to attack Curupaití. Gen. Polidoro da Fonseca Jordao was told to hold Tuyutí with a Brazilian detachment and attack the "Lines of Rojas" once the attack on Curupaití began. The Uruguayans under Flores were to open and protect communications between Tuyutí and Curuzú. The Argentines under Mitre were to join the Brazilians and the fleet at Curuzú, and together they would attack Curupaití.

The Allies' attack against Curupaití was postponed from September 18 until the twenty-second due to heavy rains that occurred on the seventeenth and raised the level of the river. Admiral Tamandaré requested the delay. This gave General Díaz time to complete his fortifications. The Paraguayan guns were positioned above the river bank, well camouflaged and protected by logs and sandbags. When the Brazilian navy attacked, it was unable to sufficiently elevate its guns in order to bring the Paraguayan batteries under fire. On land, the Argentine and Brazilian troops encountered a ditch 2,000 yards long, 6 feet deep, and 10 feet wide. Obstacles had been placed in front of the ditch. Behind it was a trench which attracted most of the fire from the Allies. In fact, it contained but few Paraguayans. Twentytwo Brazilian warships armed with 101 guns fired some 5,000 shells at Curupaití.[46]

Curupaití was then attacked by 10,000 Brazilians and 9,000 Argentines. The small Paraguayan Legion composed of political enemies of López also participated. The attack was a disaster for the Allies. They lost 4,000 men killed, wounded, or taken prisoner, half of whom were Brazilians. Those from the Paraguayan Legion who were captured were immediately hanged or flogged to death. The Paraguayans lost less than a hundred men.[47] The fact that the Paraguayans did not pursue the beaten enemy demonstrated López' lack of military talent. Nobody, not even Díaz, dared to act without orders. Making matters worse for the Allies, Jordao did not attack the "Lines of Rojas" because Flores never opened communications with Curuzú.

This Allied debacle resulted in the wholesale change of commanders and strategy. Marshal Caxias[48] was given command of the Brazilian forces on November 17, 1866, and Vice Adm. José Ignacio replaced the ailing Tamandaré. The Allies fell once more into inactivity while awaiting reinforcements.

At this time yet another rebellion occurred in the Argentine Province of Mendoza that threatened the existence of that Argentine federation. Initially, Gen. Bartolomé Mitre, who was after all also the President of Argentina, dispatched 3,000 men under General Paunero to deal with the problem, but soon Mitre was obliged to take the field himself against the Federalists. Also, General Flores returned to Uruguay to face similar problems.

BRAZIL ATTACKS IN THE NORTHWEST

In April 1867, a 1,680-man Brazilian expedition with four oxendrawn La Hitte guns crossed the Apa River and opened a second front from Mato Grosso. The expedition had been formed in Rio de Janeiro and had taken two years to reach the Mato Grosso, trekking across Brazil, a trip of over 1,250 miles. Even though the expedition was soon driven from Paraguay sustaining 980 dead, the Brazilians still managed to bring all four guns and their flags back in a thirtyfiveday operation that took its place among the prouder pages of Brazilian military history. Many of the Brazilian losses were due to cholera; the 980 deaths do not include a large number of Indians as well as women and children who marched with the army.[49]

ALLIES FLANK THE "LINE OF ROJAS"

Even more than before, the brunt of the fighting fell to the Brazilians. Marshal Caxias inherited an Allied army of 35,000 men, most of whom were Brazilians, and he expected 10,000 of his countrymen to reinforce him soon. In fact, only 7,000 men arrived, led by General Osório, having been delayed and reduced in number by Asiatic cholera. As in most wars, disease and desertion were taking a far heavier toll than enemy bullets.[50]

The material superiority of the Allies grew daily. The artillery corps was obtaining more and more Whitworth and La Hitte guns. Armored monitors were supplementing older warships.

Since entering Paraguay, the Allies had been handicapped by poor intelligence. In order to help solve this problem, Brazil contracted observation balloonists from the United States. They made numerous tethered ascents and mapped the terrain east of the Paraguayan fortifications.[51]

The Allied army had swelled to about 45,000 men—5,000 Argentines, a few hundred Uruguayans, and the remainder Brazilians. López could muster only about 20,000—15,000 infantry, 3,500 cavalry, and 1,500 artillerymen.[52] On July 22, 1867, Caxias, possessing fresh troops and improved intelligence, attacked.[53] A force of 9,000 under General Porto Alegre were left to guard Tuyutí. General Osório commanded the vanguard of 6,000, and Caxias followed with 22,000. Wading through swamps and cutting their way through thick underbrush, they outflanked the "Line of Rojas" to the east. The Paraguayans abandoned their trenches and marched east paralleling the Allies. By nightfall, Caxias reached the village of Río Hondo, a few miles north of Humaitá, and was able to cut the telegraph line and land communication between that stronghold and the Paraguayan capital. López was forced to abandon some of the outer defenses of Humaitá.[54]

THE SIEGE OF HUMAITÁ TIGHTENS

The Allies overoptimistically concluded that forcing passage of the Humaitá fortification and threatening the Paraguayan capital were the keys to ending the war. The Paraguayans were resolved to block the passage of the Brazilian squadron. In addition to the powerful fortifications, the way was blocked by three heavy iron chains stretching across the river. Even though the Brazilian navy operated on the Paraguay River as far north as Curupaití, the banks were in the hands of the Paraguayans except at sites where the Allies chose to put strong garrisons ashore.

It was impossible to move supplies in unescorted merchant ships since the Paraguayans controlled the river banks. In an attempt to gain control of the east bank of the Paraguay River, the Allies pushed westward from Tuyutí. The advance was slow, since not many troops could be spared from the investment of Humaitá, and the Paraguayans offered stiff resistance. To further isolate Humaitá, the Allies captured Villa de Pilar to the north of Río Hondo on September 24, 1867, and the river village of Tayí on November 2. General Barreto mounted batteries of heavy guns to command the river, thus cutting off Paraguayan water communications between Humaitá and Asunción. On January 11, 1867, the Paraguayans attempted to land 400 men at Tayí. This force was almost annihilated by General Barreto. The Paraguayans also lost the steamers *25 de Mayo* and *Olimpo*; the damaged *Ygurey* escaped downriver toward Humaitá. In all, the Paraguayans lost over 500 men killed and 150 taken prisoner while the Brazilians lost 31 killed and 57 wounded.[55]

THE SECOND BATTLE OF TUYUTÍ

López appreciated that the enemy was tightening its encirclement of Humaitá. However, the supplies for those besieging Humaitá still needed to be brought over land from Tuyutí, a distance of 13 miles. The Paraguayans frequently sortied from the Humaitá defenses to attack allied supply columns. In turn, the Allies attacked Paraguayan horses grazing just outside the fortress. In the end, the Paraguayans lost many men and almost all of their horses.

On November 2 and 3, some 9,000 Paraguayans under General Barrios attacked Tuyutí, achieving complete surprise. Only those Allied troops that managed to reach the central trenches survived. López gave an order to his troops to pillage should the enemy camp be captured. This proved to be the undoing of the attack. While the Paraguayans were eating, drinking, and collecting booty, General Porto Alegre checked his retreating, panic-stricken troops and successfully led a counterattack. Finally, the Paraguayans were forced to retire to Humaitá as Allied reinforcements arrived. The Paraguayans lost 2,743 killed, 155 taken prisoner, and at least 2,000 wounded. The Allies lost 249 killed, 435 missing, and 1,198 wounded.[56] The Brazilians lost one Whitworth gun and the Argentines, one Krupp and eleven others. The second battle of Tuyutí demonstrated that the Paraguayans were still capable of launching major attacks but also that López was so short of men that he could not take strategical advantage of tactical success.

Once again, political crises in Argentina and Uruguay diverted much of the support of those Allies from the war. General Juan Sa and others raised the standard of rebellion in Córdoba and demanded an end to the war. Again, Gen. Bartolomé Mitre was forced to return to Argentina. Also, Venancio Flores, who had been the provisional president of Uruguay when the war broke out, returned to Montevideo in 1867 and was assassinated there on February 15, 1868, only a few days after he handed over the presidency to his successor (see chapter 25). Weeks passed before the Allies were ready to renew the offensive.

THE FLEET PASSES HUMAITÁ

Finally, at 3 A.M. on February 19, 1868, the Brazilian fleet, composed of forty-three warships mounting 223 guns and manned by over 4,000 men, steamed toward the Humaitá fortifications. It was the Brazilian intention to pass the fortress with only six ships, the three armored ones each towing a monitor alongside. The Paraguayans detected their approach and lit bonfires along the west bank to help their gunners see the targets.[57]

Guns of the fleet concentrated on the two barges that supported the ends of the great chain which stretched across the river. The fire was so effective that the barges sank immediately, allowing five of the six ships to pass the forts by night. The cable with which the armored corvette *Buhia* towed the monitor *Alagoas* was shot away, and the latter drifted down below the batteries. The captain was signaled from the flagship not to attempt to force the batteries in daylight. The commanding officer nevertheless successfully ran the gauntlet, taking over two hundred hits in the hull and settling two inches each hour.

Capt. Delfim Carlos de Carvalho, the commander of the six-ship squadron, was made a baron (*Barão de Passagem*) for his bravery. The six ships, three monitors and three armored corvettes, received 380 hits. Amazingly, only four officers and eleven sailors were wounded in all six ships. The remainder of the fleet stayed below the fortifications.[58]

While the warships forced passage, the army tightened its encirclement. The Brazilians stormed the La Cierva redoubt two miles north of Humaitá while the Argentines drove in the

Paraguayan outposts in the east. Three thousand men under Marshal Caxias captured the town of Timbó without a fight.

The six successful warships took refuge at Tayí where they effected emergency repairs. Two armored craft were so badly damaged that they could not proceed. The *Bahia*, along with another armored corvette, the *Barroso*, and the monitor *Rio Grande do Sul*, steamed to Asunción and shelled the capital on February 20, firing some sixty rounds. Although they did little material damage, López ordered the evacuation of Asunción.

THE PARAGUAYANS ATTACK USING CANOES

López decided to attack the Brazilian fleet lying below Humaitá. At daybreak on March 2, 1868, a fleet of canoes fell on the *Lima Barros* while a rowing Brazilian guard boat sounded the alarm. The Paraguayans also boarded the ironclads *Herval* and *Cabral*, killed some men on deck, but were unable to force open the steel hatches before the remainder of the fleet riddled the decks of their sister ships with grapeshot at point blank range. Of the 220 men who participated, 175 were killed or drowned, 15 were taken prisoner, and only 30 escaped.[59]

HUMAITÁ FALLS

During March the Paraguayans abandoned some of the outer defenses of Humaitá and replaced one chain across the river. On March 2, López left for the Tebicuary River to construct another line of fortifications. He also erected a new riverside battery nearby at the confluence of the Tebicuary River and Paraguay River. Transiting ships had to pass within eighteen yards of the battery. It was armed with some of the remaining 8-inch and 32-pound cannons. Although Brazilian warships forced passage of the battery on a number of occasions, some ships sustained considerable damage.

Elsewhere, the Allies captured the remaining "Line of Rojas" as well as Curupaití. In April, the Allies began a steady bombardment of Humaitá which was to last for three months. At times the garrison would make forages against the besiegers; frequently these resulted in heavy casualties to both sides. But, the Paraguayans were unable to loosen the grip of the tightening siege. Late in the month, the two remaining Paraguayan warships operating near Humaitá were trapped and destroyed by Brazilian warships above the fortress.[60]

THE PARAGUAYANS ATTACK USING CAMALOTES

The situation for López was becoming desperate, and extraordinary measures were called for. López formed a special "Canoe Paddlers Corps" (*Cuerpo de Bogavantes*). Canoes were lashed to floating water plants called camalotes, common in those waters, and rowed in disguise down upon the Allied fleet. On July 9, the Paraguayans tried unsuccessfully to capture the monitor *Rio Grande do Sul* and the armored corvette *Barroso*. They reached and boarded the monitor undetected and wrought havoc among the crew before being driven off by other ships in the fleet. Of the 240 attackers, over 100 were killed or drowned, and 24 were taken prisoner.

The Allies tried to storm Humaitá on July 16. The Paraguayan garrison had been so reduced that defenders had to be spaced some 50 feet apart. They successfully beat back the Allies killing between 1,000 and 2,000 men while sustaining only 40 dead and 104 wounded.[61]

On the twenty-first three Brazilian warships once again forced passage of Humaitá. They came through relatively undamaged, revealing that the defenses were weakening. On July 26 the Paraguayan garrison abandoned their fortifications. In spite of the Brazilian domination of the river around Humaitá, the Paraguayans evacuated practically all of the defenders by canoes to the Chaco side of the river from where many escaped to the north, recrossing the river at Timbó. The last 1,800 men, surrounded on Isla Poi, finally surrendered on August 5, 1868, after a tenacious defense. Humaitá was razed, the great chains cut in three pieces and delivered to the seat of government in Argentina, Brazil, and Uruguay. Curupaití, Humaitá, and the outlying defenses of "Lines of Rojas" had held the Allies at bay for more than two years.[62]

THE MARCH TO ASUNCIÓN

Many in Argentina and Brazil believed that the war was now over, and it became increasingly difficult to obtain support for the effort. However, López showed no signs of capitulating. Upon the approach of the Allies, López ordered the population to abandon their homes and retire to the interior. On August 28 the Allies reached the fortified position at the mouth of the Río Tebicuary (93 mi S of Asunción). They advanced but, to their surprise, they took the site without a struggle. The Allies discovered that López had already evacuated the position. At his former headquarters, San Fernando, the Allies discovered hundreds of bodies of political and military prisoners whom López had ordered executed. López had discovered a real or imaginary plot and had taken his vengeance and then abandoned Tebicuary in favor of a position 140 miles to the north, near the small river town of Villeta. A new river battery was prepared at Angostura.[63]

The Allies advanced to the Paraguayan defenses at Angostura Villeta some 35 miles south of Asunción. Caxias was confronted by supply problems and appreciated the fact that yet another frontal attack would be slow, costly, and in all probabilty not result in the destruction of López. The Brazilian marshal planned, therefore, a flanking operation that should allow him to gain the enemy's rear.

Caxias ordered General Argolo to cross the Paraguay River into the Chaco with 2,000 men and to construct a road beyond Villeta to be used to outflank López. López, aware of this move, believed that it would take months to accomplish the work, given the terrain. He sent a small detachment to harass the workers but did not believe additional action was necessary. The Brazilian force constructed a six-and-one-half-mile road through the Chaco in twenty-three days. Many thousands of palm trees were felled to provide the corduroy road covering.[64]

Much to the surprise of López, the road was completed by the beginning of December, and Marshal Caxias concentrated 22,000 men (18,999 infantry, 926 cavalry, and 742 artillery) near San Antonio on November 5, 1868, 12 miles north of Villeta and flanking the right wing of the Paraguayan defensive position. Having met no resistance, the Brazilians then marched in the direction of the weakly fortified and poorly garrisoned Villeta. The Brazilians were forced to cross the Arroyo Itororo on a bridge that was not held but subject to heavy Paraguayan fire. Marshal Caxias personally led the third charge shouting, "Those who are true Brazilians follow me!" Osório's third corps had been misled by a scout and arrived too late to participate. The Brazilians lost 2,416 men and the Paraguayans between 400 dead and 800 wounded.[65] The Brazilians continued their advance toward the Lomas Valentinas. Villeta fell without a fight. López detailed General Cabellero with 5,443 men to hold yet another indefensible position at the Arroyo Avay where the armies battled in heavy rain on November 11, 1868. The Paraguayans were soundly defeated suffering 3,600 killed and 1,200 taken prisoner, most of whom were wounded. The 40th Paraguayan Battalion was completely destroyed for the second time. The Brazilians lost only 185 killed and 587 wounded.

THE SEVEN DAY BATTLE OF LOMAS VALENTINAS

Elsewhere, the Argentine General Gelly y Obes carried the outer defenses at Angostura, while General Osório captured the outlying positions near the Pikysyry River. Children fought in the ranks of the decimated Paraguayan army while, for at least some of the battle, López was nominally under the protection of the U.S. flag as he met with the North American envoy. The Allies won a series of bloody battles—Ytororo (on December 6), Avay (December 11), and in the Lomas Valentinas (December 21–27), destroying the Paraguayan army. Casualties were heavy. During the month of December, the Allies lost 9,000 dead, wounded, and missing (mostly Brazilians) and the Paraguayans lost 18,000, plus perhaps 2,000 desertions and executions. Among the Brazilian wounded were Generals Osório and Argolo. Among the Paraguayans, women and children, many of whom chose to fight in blind loyalty to López, fought to their deaths. On December 30, Angostura surrendered and the first Brazilian troops entered Asunción on January 1, 1869. Apparently they plundered the capital while the Argentines remained outside. López escaped into the interior with some ninety followers.

THE CAMPAIGN IN THE HILLS

Once again the Allies' hopes of ending the war, this time by the capture of López and the destruction of his army, proved a failure. Marshal Caxias was now fed up with the war, his allies, and the Brazilian navy; he declared victory and resigned his command.[66] Conde d'Eu,[67] who would not arrive until April 16, 1869, replaced Caxias as the Allied commander.

Gen. Guillermo Xavier de Souza, temporarily in charge, contented himself with strengthening his hold on the countryside. Barao do Rio Branco, a special representative of Brazil, organized a Paraguayan puppet government in opposition to López, formed in Asunción on August 15, 1869. Once the Conde d'Eu arrived, he prepared the army once again for field operations. The army was composed of 26,000 Brazilian veterans, a token Argentine force under Gen. Emilio Mitre, and a handful of Uruguayans. The inexperienced Conde d'Eu was ably supported by his two corps commanders, Osório, who was still suffering from his jaw wound sustained at the Battle of Avay, and Jordao, the former commandant of the military academy.

In the meantime, López rebuilt his army around the 2,500-man garrison that had escaped from Asunción. At Cerró Léon, López found 6,000 sick and wounded men. At least another 500 escaped from the Allies' prisoner camps following the Lomas Valentinas battles and reached him. By the end of January 1869, his army had grown to 13,000. Weapons were a major problem. Twenty light field guns had been cast at the makeshift arsenal at Caacupé. The sources for small arms were few—mostly former battlefields and some allied prisoners.[68] López established a defensive line along the Cordillera escarpment, the westward edge of the Paraná plateau, and the railroad. In April, López created a makeshift armored train and mounted a light field gun on a railway car; he unsuccessfully attacked the bridge near Areguá. He also sent out patrols to burn railroad bridges and crossties.[69]

The Conde d'Eu was surprised by the rejuvenation of the Paraguayan army. He decided to attack López' new capital, Piribebuy (37 mi N of Asunción). On August 12, the Paraguayans were defeated after a heroic defense. Even though the Allied artillery held commanding ground and continually fired into their defensive positions, the Paraguayans did not waver. The garrison made no effort to flee once defeat was obvious. Of the 1,800 defenders, 730 were killed, 600 wounded, and 400 taken prisoner. Boys as young as eight years of age were carrying guns.

The Brazilians executed the commanders of the Paraguayan forces and hundreds of the wounded. The Allies lost 550 men, including the popular Gen. João Manoel Mena Barreto.

Conde d'Eu continued to pursue López. On August 16, d'Eu defeated General Caballero at the battle of Campo Grande (called the battle of Los Niños or AcostaÑu by the Paraguayans) near the Yagarí River. On the eighteenth the opposing armies fought in the forest of Caguijuru. The Paraguayans lost 260 dead and 530 prisoners. The Brazilians captured the city of Caraguatí. López, retreating farther into northeastern Paraguay, remained in the field for another eight months, always outnumbered and harried.

On March 1, 1870, the war came to an anticlimactic end. A Brazilian force caught up with López at Cerró Corá (210 mi N of Asunción). With López were about 500 mostly sick, wounded, and hungry men, including well over one hundred officers. When the Brazilians attacked, López fled, escorted by a few officers who were killed trying to protect his flight. Seriously wounded by a Brazilian lancer, Gen. José Antônio Corrêa de Câmara (later Viscount of Pelotas) offered to spare López' life if he would surrender; López refused. Lying in an arroyo unable to move, López was killed, reportedly uttering the words, "I die with my country." Two of his sons were also killed. His oldest son, Panchito, a colonel and "chief of staff," age sixteen, was killed while escorting the oxen-drawn carriage his mother, Elisa Lynch, and three younger brothers were in while they attempted to escape into the bush. José Felix, son of another mistress, Juana Pabla Pesoa, age ten, was also killed, circumstances unknown. In this last action the Paraguayans lost 40 officers, 160 men, plus an unknown number of civilians killed. The Brazilians reported seven wounded.

A provisional Paraguayan government signed a preliminary treaty with the Allies on June 20, 1870. Brazil signed a separate peace with Paraguay in 1872 which caused much misunderstanding between Argentina and Brazil. Bartolomé Mitre, President of Argentina, negotiated an accord of November 19, 1872, which led to the pact of February 3, 1876, signed by the three allies. This finally settled all pending disagreements.

OBSERVATIONS

For Paraguay, the War of the Triple Alliance confirmed that it would remain a small, landlocked nation. It lost half of its 300,000 inhabitants and 36,000 square miles to Argentina and 24,000 square miles to Brazil. By 1870 Paraguay had degenerated into a state of near anarchy.[70]

For Brazil, it was the mainstay of the Allies—the primary source of men, money, and materiel.[71] The war accelerated the demise of slavery. Blacks had been the backbone of the Brazilian army, which had born the brunt of the fighting for the Allies. Their recruitment and service focused national attention on the issue. Also, the army became a political force. National heroes emerged who politically could not be ignored. The officer corps now included many of humble birth, thus broadening its political base. Brazil's total casualties were perhaps 100,000 men.[72]

For Argentina, the war was a catalyst, helping to forge a modern nation in spite of the remaining opposition of some important *caudillos*. Argentina probably lost about 20,000 men.[73]

For Uruguay, the war confirmed the Treaty of Rio de Janeiro of August 27, 1828, by which Argentina and Brazil had ended the open rivalry over the domination of that small nation. From now on, the contest would be more subtle. No official or otherwise reliable count exists concerning Uruguayan losses. Of the 3,000 to 4,000 real Uruguayans who served in the war, only 600 returned home. Perhaps 1,400 were killed in action or died of their wounds. Perhaps a similar number died of illness and many deserted. Many foreigners, including Paraguayan refugees and prisoners of war, served in Uruguayan units, making a count most difficult.

The war had evolved from one of pitched battles to one of assaults on fortified positions and sieges. This change in tactics was primarily due to the fact that Paraguay, running out of soldiers, had to remain behind defensive positions. Why López did not attempt guerrilla warfare, particularly after the fall of Asunción, is unclear. It is possible he feared losing control, particularly after the defeats of December 1868.

Only Brazil appreciated that the key to victory was the elimination of Francisco Solano López. The other allies believed that capturing strategic sites such as Corrientes, Humaitá, and Asunción would end the war. Therefore, Argentina and Uruguay experienced frustration and despair once they captured these places and López continued to fight.

Concerning leadership in Paraguay, the decisions of Francisco Solano López dominated all. He was arrogant, overconfident, and a coward. He rarely consulted advisors, domestic or foreign, and seldom if ever followed their advice in matters concerning strategy or tactics. But above all, López was one of the best propagandists of the nineteenth century; in this attribute (and only this one), he was the equal of Napoleon Bonaparte. Only second in importance to López was Eliza Lynch. This beautiful young lady was loyal to Francisco Solano to the end.[74] She was a good organizer and propagandist.

Paraguay had many brave officers, but they had almost no training in leadership nor were they given the opportunity to make important decisions. The strength of the Paraguayan army lay in its bravery and blind loyalty to López.

A number of allied leaders earned recognition for their conduct. Early in the war, generals Paunero (an Argentine) and Flores (a Uruguayan) aggressively defeated the Paraguayan offensive. During the advance on Humaitá, Marshal Caxias and General Osório (Brazilians) were the most capable. The capture of Asunción may be attributed to the skills of Caxias, ably supported by Generals Argolo, Mena Barreto, Osório (Brazilians), and Gelly y Obes (an Argentine). Gen. Bartolomé Mitre (Argentine) deserves credit for organizational and logistical skills but was not successful in combat. Admiral Tamandaré (Brazilian) successfully denied Paraguay the use of the river complex below Humaitá. But the Admiral never fully exploited the victory of Richuelo.

A number of Allied initiatives failed because of poor intelligence, the Battle of Curupaití being the most significant. Paraguayan intelligence was superior to that of the Allies, but López rarely knew how to exploit it. The First and Second Battles of Tuyutí, notwithstanding good Paraguayan intelligence, were disastrous for López.

The Paraguayans in particular demonstrated tactical skill and ingenuity. Paraguay's assault of a superior fleet at Richuelo with its warships supported by horsedrawn artillery was a complex plan that almost succeeded. Twice the Paraguayans came close to capturing a major Brazilian warship by surprise attacks.

On the whole, the production of war materiel by Paraguay was a most remarkable feat. Notwithstanding, the quantity and quality of arms and ammunition always fell short of needs. The Paraguayans, guided by their British technicians, cast some 150-pound field and siege guns of rather poor quality. Heavy ordnance was manufactured almost to the end of the war.[75] The Paraguayans successfully used mines to sink a major Brazilian warship and to hamper the movements of the enemy fleet.

CHAPTER THIRTY

THE PACIFIC WAR, 1865–66

The safety of this country, as well as that of all the Pacific States, is seriously threatened by the present hostilities of Spain.

—Alvaro Covarrubias, Chilean Minister of Foreign Affairs

THE SPARK

On August 4, 1863, a group of Spanish Basques working in northern Peru engaged in a brawl with locals at the hacienda "Talambo." One member of each group was killed and others injured.[1]

BACKGROUND

Peruvian and Spanish relations had remained strained following the War for Independence which had ended decades earlier (see chapter 4). Peru had been the seat of Spanish power within South America and the richest of all the colonies. Spain believed that its citizens had never been properly compensated for their property which had been confiscated during the War for Independence.[2]

In 1863 Spain sent a small naval squadron under Rear Adm. Luis Henández Pinzón to the west coast of South America, ostensibly for scientific purposes and exploration. It arrived off Peru in July. The brawl on August 4 caused the relationship between the two nations to disintegrate further.[3]

To negotiate the safety of its nationals, Spain sent Eusebio de Salazar y Mazarredo to Peru with the title "Special Royal Commissioner" because Spain had not yet formally recognized Peruvian independence. Peru found the title (but not the individual or his mission) objectionable because it was reminiscent of Spanish colonial titles which possessed arbitrary powers. The diplomat Salazar was rejected and in a huff he boarded the Spanish squadron. Salazar showed Admiral Pinzón his instructions which provided general guidelines for dealing with Peru. However, he neglected to tell the Admiral that he was also instructed not to use force.[4]

On April 14, 1864, the Spanish squadron overpowered the 200-man Peruvian garrison and seized the guano-rich Chincha islands (120 mi SSE of Callao), 12 miles off the coast of Peru. The sale of guano from these islands had become Peru's single most important source of revenue.[5]

333

The disagreement dragged on as both Peru and Spain hardened their positions. The Peruvian Congress authorized the purchase of warships and arms. Admiral Pinzón, whom Spain perceived as being too lenient, was relieved by Adm. José Manuel Pareja who had been born in Lima and whose father had died in Chile during 1813 fighting against the independence movement. He brought with him three frigates. On December 24, 1864, the Peruvian negotiator, Gen. Manuel Ignacio de Vivanco, agreed to the Spanish demands. These harsh terms included a three million gold pesos compensation for the expense of the intervention. The Spanish squadron returned to Callao adding a note of urgency to the proceedings through the implied threat of a bombardment. The Peruvian Congress refused to ratify the agreement before it adjourned. Caught in a difficult position, President Juan Antonio Pezet approved the terms by decree on February 2, 1865. As a consequence, Col. Mariano Ignacio Prado and others rebelled against the government. While the rebels were gaining strength, the Pezet administration was executing the agreement. Peru paid the indemnity and Spain returned the islands. A year later, Prado would triumph and would be empowered as the "Supreme Chief of the Republic."[6]

In the meantime, an uneasy peace was achieved. The Spanish squadron remained in the vicinity and tensions ran high. On February 5, 1865, street fighting broke out between enraged Peruvians and Spanish sailors who were on liberty in Callao and Lima. One Spaniard and a few Peruvians were killed. Also, tensions increased between Spain and Chile. Chilean citizens held public protests against Spanish actions against Peru. When the Spanish gunboat *Vencedora* (3 guns) stopped at Lota, Chile, Chilean authorities refused to sell it coal, declaring coal a war supply and Spain a belligerent nation even though neither Spain nor Peru had declared war. Also, Chilean volunteers, including the future naval hero Patricio Lynch, sailed north to join in the anticipated fight against Spain.[7]

The Chilean government feared that Spanish actions against Peru were a smokescreen to hide Spanish desires to reconquer its former colonies. Like Peru, Chile ordered warships from Europe. In May the Spanish minister to Chile demanded an apology from Chile for its "hostile acts." Chile responded in a conciliatory manner. However, on September 7 Admiral Pareja presented a new ultimatum which the Chilean government rejected. As a consequence, Pareja announced a blockade and Chile responded by declaring war on September 24 before its inception.[8]

OPPOSING FORCES

Once again, the inhospitable coastal desert—which stretched from southern Peru through Bolivia and into northern Chile—the vast distances involved, and the mid-nineteenth-century technology available to the combatants dictated that navies would play a leading role.

Throughout the events leading up to the war and during the fighting, Spanish warships came and went from the west coast of South America. Initially, the "scientific expedition" was composed of four warships: the steam frigates *Resolución* (44 guns) and *Triunfo* (44 guns) and the steam gunboats *Covadonga* (3 guns) and *Vencedora* (3 guns).[9] These "gunboats" in fact were dispatch boats and had little combat value. In mid-1866, when most of the fighting took place, the Spanish squadron was composed of seven warships: the new seagoing ironclad *Numancia* (40 guns); the steam frigates *Almansa* (40 guns), *Berenguela* (36 guns), *Blanca* (36 guns), *Resolución* (44 guns), and *Villa de Madrid* (46 guns); and the steam gunboat *Vencedora* (3 guns). The *Numancia* alone was more than a match for the entire allied squadron. Spain had no ground troops in South America.[10]

Chile's navy was in a state of disrepair. It possessed two warships, the steam corvette *Esmeralda* (18 guns) and the small steamer *Maipo* (4 guns). In late 1864, as tensions mounted with Spain, the Chilean navy sent Rear Adm. Roberto Simpson first to the United States and then to Europe to purchase warships. He found none suitable to Chilean needs. Hence, Chile contracted for the construction of two ironclad corvettes, the *O'Higgins* (3 heavy guns) and the *Chacabuco* (3 heavy guns) in England. However, since a state of war now existed with Spain, the prospect of these or any other warships being added to the fleet was not good, since many nations possessed neutrality laws which prohibited deliveries of war materials to belligerent nations.[11]

The unexpected revenues from the guano trade had allowed Peru to both build and purchase new warships. On hand in early 1866 were the old steam frigates *Amazonas* (36 guns) and *Apurímac* (30 guns); the schooner *Tumbes* (2 guns); the ironclad ram *Loa* (1 heavy gun); and the small monitor *Victoria* (1 heavy gun). These last two were completed in Lima and were armored with railorad rails; they were only suitable for harbor defense. Expected shortly from France were the corvettes *América* (12 guns) and *Unión* (12 guns). In addition, the newly built seagoing monitor *Huáscar* (2 very heavy guns) and armored frigate *Independencia* (2 very heavy guns and 12 heavy guns) were outfitting in England. The two steam frigates were in poor condition. And, Peru did not have enough sailors to man either its warships in national waters or those being built abroad.[12]

OPENING STRATEGIES

Chile was in a very poor strategic position. It possessed neither a fleet adequate to protect its commerce nor coastal defenses capable of defending its major ports. Chilean diplomats worked to secure allies and to rally all American nations against Spain. Prior to the outbreak of hostilities, Chile ordered its overmatched warships, crowded with extra hands, to depart Valparaíso so they would not be trapped by the superior Spanish squadron. Chile also began issuing letters of marque throughout the Americas and Europe. Although it had signed the 1856 Declaration of Paris which outlawed privateering, it argued that since Spain had not, Chile was not bound by the declaration. Great Britain and France agreed.[13]

At first even Peru was hesitant to join Chile in the fight against Spain. This reluctance in part was caused by lingering animosities toward Chile (see chapter 11). However, once Prado assumed power with the strong political backing of Chile, Peru also declared war on Spain. Peru delayed declaring war until January 13, 1866, wanting to be sure that the new ironclads *Huáscar* and *Independencia* had sailed from Europe so that they would not be interned. Its strategy and that of its ally Chile was to preserve their naval strength until the ironclads had arrived and then seek out the Spanish fleet.[14]

Ecuador and Bolivia declared war on Spain on February 27 and April 4, respectively. Chile and Peru demonstrated significant diplomatic skills to persuade Ecuador and Bolivia to join the alliance.[15]

Spain left its strategy in the hands of the on-scene fleet commander. The Admiral was authorized to take any action necessary to bring the war to a successful and speedy conclusion. Time was not the Admiral's ally. Once the four west coast nations joined in war against Spain, the nearest ports open to the Spanish fleet were in the Atlantic Ocean. Admiral Pareja believed that the west coast nations could be brought to terms through blockade and bombardment if necessary.[16]

Figure 23. The Pacific War, 1865–66. The Battle of Abtao (February 7, 1866) was between the Spanish and Allied fleets of Peru and Chile. The large warship in the foreground to the left is the Spanish flagship, the seagoing ironclad *Numancia*. The original oil is the Naval Museum, Callao, Peru. *Courtesy Archivo de Instituto de Estudios Histórico-Marítimos del Perú.*

THE CAPTURE OF THE *COVADONGA*

On November 26, 1865, the *Esmeralda*, commanded by Capt. Juan Williams Rebolledo, surprised and captured the Spanish gunboat *Covadonga* off Papudo Roads, thus depriving the Spaniards of their only shallow-draft warship and providing the Chileans with the Spanish signal book. Following the capture, Williams was ordered to go to the Chiloé archipelago and await the Peruvian squadron. The capture of the *Covadonga*, along with other setbacks, so distressed Admiral Pareja that he committed suicide. The commanding officer of the *Numancia*, Capt. Casto Méndez Nuñez, took charge of the Spanish squadron.[17]

BATTLE OF ABTAO

The Peruvian warships, which had many Chileans among their crews, joined the Chilean warships at Chiloé (2,016 mi SSE of Callao and 679 mi S of Valparaíso). There was much discord between the Chilean and Peruvian officers. The Spanish squadron blockaded Valparaíso, inflicting considerable damage on commerce by capturing more than thirty merchantmen, but it did not have enough warships to extend the blockade much beyond this port. In February, Méndez Nuñez dispatched the steam frigates *Villa de Madrid* and *Blanca* south to Chiloé to force a battle with the allied squadron. At about 2:30 P.M. on the seventh the Spanish warships discovered the Peruvian *Apurímac*, *América*, and *Unión* plus the Chilean *Covadonga* under the command of the Peruvian Capt. Manuel Villar at anchor in shallow water off Abtao. The Spaniards were afraid to risk their deep-draft warships by closing in on the weaker enemy. A two-hour, long-range cannonade ensued. The Spanish warships were forced to retire after receiving considerable material damage but no loss of life. The allies lost two killed and one wounded.[18]

The allies moved their fleet to Huitó, on Chiloé Island, where the shallow water and shore defenses prevented the Spanish warships from approaching to within gun range. There the allies awaited the arrival of the *Huáscar* and *Independencia* from Europe.[19]

CHILE TRIES NEW TECHNOLOGY

In an attempt to break the Spanish blockade of Valparaíso, Chilean President José Joaquín Pérez endorsed the construction and use of a submarine. Designed by inventor Carlos Flach, built at Duprat Shipyard in Valparaíso, and launched in 1866, the boat was less than 42 feet 6 inches (13 meters) in length, spindle-shaped, and crewed by a maximum of six persons who provided propulsion. A small cannon was installed for firing either above or below water. The President observed the launching of the craft. The submarine dove several times. In April 1866 the inventor, his son, and ten friends submerged. The overloaded craft nose-dived and was never seen again.[20]

Next, Chile attempted to devise a spar torpedo to be used against the blockaders. The British minister in Santiago advised against this on the grounds that the Chilean government would no longer be entitled to claim that Valparaíso was a defenseless port and, therefore, theoretically free from bombardment. In fact, Rear Admiral Méndez Nuñez, recently promoted, declared that any attempt to damage his ships would result in the bombardment of Valparaíso.

VALPARAÍSO BOMBARDED

On March 24, Admiral Méndez Nuñez, frustrated by the uncompromising attitude of the Chileans in spite of the blockade and his inability to force a fight with the inferior allied fleet, presented an ultimatum from Madrid. If Chile failed to meet Spain's demands, he would bombard Valparaíso. Over the strenuous objections of the international community, on March 31,

Figure 24. The Pacific War, 1865–66. An Armstrong cannon at the Santa Rosa battery, Callao, Peru, was one of many heavy guns at Callao. This port was the best-protected Pacific Coast seaport throughout the nineteenth century. During the War for Independence in Peru (1810–26) the port was not permanently captured by the revolutionaries until 1826. In the Pacific War (1865–66), the port's guns severely punished an attacking Spanish squadron and drove it off. And in the War of the Pacific (1879–83), the seaward defenses held the Chilean fleet out of the harbor until the port could no longer be defended from the land side. *Courtesy Archivo de Instituto de Estudios Histórico-Marítimos del Perú.*

1866, five Spanish warships bombarded the port for three hours, their principal targets being customs warehouses filled with merchandise. However, some of the 2,600 shells fired missed their targets, hitting churches and a hospital. The Chilean defenses did not return fire. The bombardment killed two persons and destroyed property estimated to be worth fourteen million gold pesos. Almost half of that property belonged to neutrals, mostly British. Méndez Nuñez then set fire to or sank thirty-three captured Chilean merchant ships.[21]

CALLAO BOMBARDED

The Spanish fleet next sailed to Peruvian waters, arriving off Callao on April 25. The Spanish Admiral immediately declared a blockade. Callao, the seaport for Lima, had been heavily fortified since early colonial times. In 1866 it was defended by 46 heavy guns: four new 450-pound Armstrongs, four new 300-pound Blakelys, one 68-pounder, two 48-pounders, one 38-pounder, and thirty-four 32-pounders. Although the fleet mounted 275 guns, none was equal in weight to the largest guns ashore. The fleet's guns could fire much more rapidly than those ashore, but the Spanish Admiral feared getting too close from which distance he could have used grapeshot (a shotgun-type shell) to drive the Peruvians from their guns because he feared that mines had been planted in the water to prevent his approach.[22]

Shortly after noon on May 2, 1866, six heavy and five light Spanish warships entered the harbor and a general melee ensued. The *Villa de Madrid* was so badly damaged by a hit from a Blakely that it had to be towed out of danger. The *Berenguela* was also hit by a heavy shell and briefly raised the distress signal. On shore, a shell exploded inside a tower and killed twenty-eight Peruvians including the Minister of War, José Gálvez. At 4:45 P.M. the Spanish fleet withdrew. Casualties were heavy on both sides. Approximately 200 Peruvians were killed or wounded. The Spanish did not report their losses but they were surely more than the Peruvians and might have been as high as 375 men. Méndez Nuñez was wounded nine times. All of the ships received damage. Two frigates intentionally were run aground on San Lorenzo Island to prevent their sinking. Property damage in Callao was very light.[23]

By May 9, 1866, Admiral Méndez Nuñez considered that he had fullfilled his duties to punish Peru and, taking into account his shortage of ammunition, he decided to sail for home. The Admiral's decision might have been influenced by the anticipated arrival of the two new Peruvian ironclads *Huáscar* and *Independencia*. Actually, both Peruvian armored ships were then still far off the east coast of South America, delayed by minor collisions, crew discontent, and all sorts of mechanical problems. The new Peruvian warships missed an opportunity to offer battle to several Spanish ships as they rounded Cape Horn, and they did not arrive off Callao until several months after the Spanish departure. An informal peace dragged on for years before the belligerents officially ended the conflict.[24]

OBSERVATIONS

Once again, sea power played a preeminent role in deciding the outcome of a war along the west coast of South America. The attempted Spanish blockade was unrealistic. The Admiral did not have nearly enough ships to execute such a strategy. Chile alone had an 1,800-mile coastline and 43 ports; Bolivia, Peru, and Ecuador possessed another 2,200 miles of coastline and more ports.[25]

Chile discovered how vulnerable it was without an adequate navy. Unlike the War of the Confederation in 1836–38 (see chapter 11) when Chile escaped the potential consequence for having neglected its navy, this time Valparaíso was significantly damaged and the surviving Chilean merchant marine was sunk, burned, or driven to foreign flag registration. Looking to the future the Chilean government ordered the construction of the ironclads *Almirante Cochrane* and *Valparaíso* (later renamed *Blanco Encalada*), the gunboat *Magallanes*, and the paddle steamer *Tolten* in 1872. The corvettes *O'Higgins* and *Chacabuco*, which had been embargoed by Great Britain while in the final phases of their construction, were released to Chile in 1868 following the end of the fighting. Just as important, the navy concerned itself with training Chileans to man the warships. These well-crewed warships would be the backbone of the Chilean navy during the War of the Pacific in 1879–83 (see chapter 34).[26]

Peru, in large measure, had to rely upon foreigners to man its warships. The victory achieved at Atbao and the perceived influence exerted upon Spain by the approach of the ironclads *Huáscar* and *Independencia* may have given Peru a false confidence in its warships.[27]

PART 9

LATE WARS FOR INDEPENDENCE

CHAPTER THIRTY-ONE

CAPTAINCY-GENERAL OF SANTO DOMINGO, 1838–65

> God, Country, and Liberty.
> —Creed of Juan Pablo Duarte

THE SPARK

On July 16, 1838, Juan Pablo Duarte[1] founded the secret movement known as *La Trinitaria* (The Trinity),[2] the purpose of which was to win independence for Santo Domingo from Haiti.[3]

BACKGROUND

The Captaincy-General of Santo Domingo, which prior to the mid-eighteenth century had encompassed all of the Spanish Caribbean islands, was limited to the oldest Spanish settlement in the New World by the beginning of the nineteenth century on the island of Hispañola.

By the time of the Treaty of Ryswick (1697), which gave the western one-third of the island to France, the population of Santo Domingo consisted of a few thousand whites, perhaps 30,000 black slaves, and a few Indians (who bordered on extinction). By 1789 the population had grown to 125,000 persons. But, by the late eighteenth century, Santo Domingo was among the least wealthy and least important of Spain's New World possessions. And in the Caribbean, the Spanish colony of Santo Domingo was strategically and economically less important than either Cuba or Puerto Rico.

The division of Hispañola between France and Spain in 1697 recognized a reality with which neither the Kings nor their Revolutionary successors were happy. Although the population of Spanish Santo Domingo was perhaps one-fourth that of French Saint Domingue, this did not prevent the Spanish King from launching an invasion of the French side of the island in 1793, attempting to take advantage of the chaos sparked by the French Revolution (1789–99).

Although the Spanish military effort went well on Hispañola, it did not so in Europe. As a consequence, Spain was forced to cede Santo Domingo to the French under the terms of the Treaty of Basle (July 22, 1795) in order to get the French to withdraw from Spain.

The ceding of Santo Domingo to France put Joaquín García, the Spanish Captain-General of Santo Domingo, in a very difficult position. Spanish colonists did not want to come under French rule. In 1801 Toussaint Louverture, who at least in theory represented imperial France, marched into Santo Domingo from Saint Domingue to enforce the terms of the treaty. To prevent the capital from being sacked, García surrendered the city on January 27, 1801. Notwithstanding, Toussaint's army committed numerous atrocities; as a consequence, the Spanish population fled from Hispañola in exodus proportions.[4]

French control of the former Spanish colony passed from Toussaint Louverture to Gen. Charles Leclerc when he seized the city of Santo Domingo in early 1802. Following the defeat of the French under Gen. Donatien de Rochembeau at Le Cap in November 1803 by the Haitians, their new leader, Dessalines, attempted to drive the French out of Santo Domingo. He invaded the Spanish side of the island, defeated the French-led Spanish colonials at Río Yaque del Sur, and besieged the capital on March 5, 1805. At the same time the Haitian General Christophe marched north through Cibao, capturing Santiago where he massacred prominent individuals who had sought refuge in a church. The arrival of small French squadrons off the Haitian coast at Goncaives and at Santo Domingo forced the Haitians to withdraw. As Christophe retreated across the island, he slaughtered and burned.[5]

In October 1808 the Spanish planter Juan Sánchez Ramírez, who had fled Santo Domingo during French rule to Puerto Rico, landed along the northeast coast and began a rebellion in the name of Ferdinand VII against the French colonial administrators in the city of Santo Domingo. The Spanish insurgents received aid from Spanish Puerto Rico, independent Haiti, and British Jamaica. The British blockaded the capital and occupied the port of Samaná. Sánchez defeated those loyal to France at Palo Hincado on November 7. On July 9, 1809, the British captured the city of Santo Domingo and as a consequence returned the eastern part of Hispañola to Spanish rule.[6]

The Spanish Council of Regency, ruling in the name of Ferdinand VII, confirmed Sánchez as governor and the liberal Spanish Constitution of 1812 granted Santo Domingo representation in the Spanish *Cortes*. However, when Ferdinand VII was restored to the throne in 1814, he revoked the constitution and most of the acts passed by the council in his name. Ferdinand began an era of despotism known as "Silly Spain" (*España Boba*) and Santo Domingo politically, socially, and economically stagnated and regressed.[7]

Spain's hold over Santo Domingo remained precarious. The arrival of the fugitive Simón Bolívar and his followers in Haiti in 1815 alarmed the Spanish authorities in Santo Domingo. Following the rebellion of the Army in Spain during 1820, which restored the liberal constitution, some of the colonial administrators in Santo Domingo broke with the mother country; and on December 1, 1821, the Spanish Lieutenant Governor, José Núñez de Cáceres, proclaimed the independence of "Spanish Haiti."[8]

Many in Santo Domingo, fearing that the Spaniards would return or that the Haitians would invade, attempted to annex themselves to Gran Colombia. While this request was in transit, Jean-Pierre Boyer, the ruler of Haiti, invaded Santo Domingo on February 9 with a 10,000-man army. Having no capacity to resist, Núñez de Cáceres surrendered the capital on February 9, 1822. For the next twenty-two years, Haiti ruled Santo Domingo (called *Partie de l'Est* by the

Haitians), treating it as a colonial possession. The occupying Haitian army, receiving no pay, lived off the Dominican people and land, taking without compensation whatever they wanted.⁹

OPPOSING FORCES

Haiti is about the size of the state of Maryland and the Dominican Republic is twice as large. Haiti's strength was its abundance of manpower and its willingness to expend it; the Haitian population in 1840 was about 600,000 persons. The Dominicans' military strengths were more potential than existent. The population of Santo Domingo in 1845 was approximately 230,000 persons (100,000 whites; 40,000 blacks; and 90,000 mulattoes).¹⁰ Haiti had formed two regiments composed of Dominicans from the city of Santo Domingo; potentially, these were the nucleus of a national army. And, the rough cowboys in the eastern plain, like their counterparts on the Argentine pampas and the Venezuelan llanos, had the makings of an outstanding light cavalry.

OPENING STRATEGIES

Throughout the period of occupation (1822–44), Haiti relied on the tried and proven strategy of intimidation through brutality. The Dominicans soon appreciated that their best possibility of winning independence was to take advantage of Haitian internal strife. Once Santo Domingo had achieved independence, Haiti's strategy was to invade along the northern and southern coastal roads with its forces converging on the capital, Santo Domingo. The Dominican strategy was to rely on *caudillos* to call up popular followings and to use its small naval squadron to disrupt Haitian movements along the coast.¹¹

LA TRINITARIA

La Trinitaria met for the first time on July 16, 1838. The Haitians discovered the movement and unsuccessfully tried to eliminate it. Most members of *La Trinitaria* escaped detection and reunited as members of *La Filantrópica* (The Philanthropy).¹² The *"Trinitarios"* took advantage of a Haitian rebellion against the dictator Jean-Pierre Boyer. The *Trinitarios* won the loyalty of the two Haitian regiments made up of Dominicans. They rose up on January 27, 1843, ostensibly in support of the Haitian Charles Hérard who was challenging Boyer for the control of Haiti. Known as "The Reform" (*La Reforma*), the rebellious Dominicans seized the capital, Santo Domingo, on March 24 in the name of Hérard. The movement soon discarded its pretext of support for Hérard and now championed Dominican independence. In the meantime, Hérard overthrew Boyer and marched against Santo Domingo in order to resubjugate the Dominicans. Hérard entered the capital on July 12, executed some Dominicans, and threw many others into prison; Duarte escaped.¹³

Upon returning to Haiti, Hérard, a mulatto, faced a rebellion by blacks in the continuing racial strife between those two elements within Haiti (see chapter 2). The two regiments of Dominicans were among those used by Hérard to suppress the uprising. Their loyal participation convinced Hérard that the Dominican troublemakers had been eliminated.¹⁴

DECLARATION OF INDEPENDENCE

Surviving members of the *La Trinitaria*, now led by Tomás Bobadilla, planned another uprising. Once again, the conspirators persuaded the two Dominican-manned regiments to participate. Also, a powerful rancher, Pedro Santana Familias,¹⁵ committed his personal followers;

these were the roughened cowboys from his estate in the east near El Seibo (60 mi NE of Santo Domingo).[16]

Duarte was persuaded to return from exile in Venezuela. While sailing north he became very ill and landed at Curaçao. Fearing that the plot might be discovered by the Haitians, the rebels launched their attack without Duarte. On February 27, 1844 (now Independence Day), some one hundred Dominicans seized the fortress of Puerta del Conde in the city of Santo Domingo, and the following day the Haitian garrison surrendered. As these Haitian troops withdrew to the west side of the island, they pillaged and burned.[17]

CAMPAIGN OF 1844

On March 7, 1844, the President of Haiti, Hérard, declared a blockade of the Dominican ports. On the tenth he sent three columns of Haitian troops, each numbering 10,000 men, marching into Santo Domingo. Hérard commanded the troops sent along the road toward Las Caobas; General [first name unknown] Souffront commanded those sent toward Neiba; and Luis Pierrot commanded those marching toward Santiago and Puerto Plata. At the same time, Santana, now a general, rode west at the head of his cowboys. A number of skirmishes took place; most frequently, the Haitians were victorious. On March 19 Santana defeated Hérard (Souffant's command had earlier merged with his) at the Battle of Azua. Rather than following up his victory, Santana fell back to Sabana Buey, a distance of ten miles. As a consequence, Hérard was able to occupy Azua.[18]

In the meantime in the north, Dominican Generals José María Imbert and Fernando Valerio defeated the Haitian column led by Pierrot at the Battle of Santiago (109 mi N of Santo Domingo) on the thirtieth, thanks to a warning of the pending attack by an Englishman, Stanley Theodore Heneken. As the Haitians retreated, they laid waste to land.[19]

Meanwhile at sea, the Dominican schooners *María Chica* (3 guns), commanded by Juan Bautista Maggiolo, and the *Separación Dominicana* (5 guns), commanded by Juan Bautista Cambiaso, defeated a Haitian brigantine *Pandora* (unk guns) plus schooners *Le Signifie* (unk guns) and *La Mouche* (unk guns) off Tortuguero on April 15. As a consequence of these Haitian defeats, Hérard was overthrown on May 3, thus causing the temporary suspension of Haitian military operations.[20]

A short power struggle for political control of Santo Domingo ensued between the enlightened Liberal Duarte, who championed democracy and complete independence, and the *caudillo* Santana, who was motivated by personal ambitions. The idealistic Duarte (later to be acclaimed father of Dominican independence) was no match for the despotic Santana, and Duarte was forced into exile.[21]

Now two protracted struggles raged in Santo Domingo, interrupted by periods of exhaustion. The first was the continuing war to maintain independence from Haiti, and the second was the struggle among *caudillos* to see who would govern Santo Domingo. Although those competing for power professed a variety of ideologies, their primary motivation was personal gain. The two most powerful *caudillos* were Santana and Buenaventura Báez Méndez.[22] Both favored the annexation of Santo Domingo to a major power, provided that they and their followers were well rewarded. Santana's power base was the ranchers and cowboys and Báez' the bourgeoisie of the capital. Although they shared the goal of annexation, neither man was willing to be a "bridesmaid to the other."[23]

CAMPAIGN OF 1845-46

While the Dominicans argued amongst themselves, Haitian troops attacked border settlements during July. On August 6 the new Haitian president, Luis Pierrot, ordered his army to invade Santo Domingo. On September 17 the Dominican Gen. José Joaquín Puello defeated the Haitian vanguard near the frontier at Estrelleta (90 mi WNW of Santo Domingo) where the Dominican "square" repulsed with bayonets a Haitian cavalry charge.[24]

On August 5 Pierrot issued "letters of marque" against ships trading with Santo Domingo and on September 27 he declared all Dominican ports closed to commerce, but had no navy to legally enforce such a declaration. The Haitian privateers were causing considerable damage to Dominican seaborne commerce. As a consequence, the people of Cibao contributed money for the purchase of the U.S. merchant ship *Alert* so that it might be fitted out as a warship. By February 14 of the following year, the Dominican navy had grown to ten small warships.[25]

On September 27, 1845, Dominican Gen. Francisco Antonio Salcedo defeated a Haitian army at the battle of "Beler," a frontier fortification. Among the dead were three Haitian generals, including the Army's commander, [first name unknown] Seraphin. On October 28 other Haitians attacked the frontier fort "El Invencible" and were repulsed after five hours of hard fighting. Events at sea also went poorly for the Haitians. The Haitian squadron, commanded by Admiral Cadet Antoine, which was carrying troops to be landed at Puerto Plata (150 mi NNW of Santo Domingo), was driven aground off that port by bad weather on December 21, and the admiral and 148 others were taken prisoner. Shortly after Pierrot announced a new campaign for 1846, he was overthrown on February 27.[26]

CAMPAIGN OF 1849

Faustin Soulouque, who now governed Haiti, launched a new invasion of Santo Domingo with an army of some 10,000 men.[27] On March 21, 1849, Haitian soldiers attacked the Dominican garrison at Las Matas (100 mi W of Santo Domingo). The demoralized defenders offered almost no resistance before abandoning their weapons.[28]

Soulouque pressed on, capturing San Juan. This left only the town of Azua (55 mi W of Santo Domingo) as the remaining Dominican stronghold between the Haitian army and the capital. Since a Dominican flotilla dominated the coastal road with its guns, Soulouque was forced to use the longer approach through El Número and Las Carreras to reach Azua and could not be supplied or reinforced from the sea.[29]

These circumstances forced the president of Santo Domingo, Manuel Jimenes, to call upon Santana, whom he had ousted as president, on April 2 to restore the confidence of the army and to lead the Dominicans against this new invasion. Santana hurried from El Seibo at the head of his mounted following, some 200 men. On the sixth, Azua fell to the 18,000 Haitians and a 5,000-man Dominican counterattack failed.[30]

Santana's force swelled to some 800 men as he advanced westward. On April 17 Gen. Francisco Domínguez defeated an element of the Haitian army at El Número, but, lacking supplies and potable water, he ordered a retreat to Las Carreras. Beginning on the twenty-first, Santana delivered the *coup de grace* to the Haitian army personally commanded by Soulouque at the two-day Battle of Las Carreras. The battle opened with a cannon barrage and devolved into a hand-to-hand blood bath. Neither side took prisoners. As the remnants of the Haitian army retreated along the southern coastal road, they were under fire from a small Dominican squadron. The Haitian's hastily burned the town of Azua and the hamlets of Neiba, San Juan, and Las

Matas. Following his victory at Las Carreras, Santana turned the army against President Jimenes and, on May 30, once again seized the reigns of government but soon lost them to his old rival Báez.[31]

Báez worked vigorously to get one of the major powers to assume a protectorate over Santo Domingo. The primary enticements were the magnificent bay of Samaná along the northern coast and trade concessions.[32] However, France, Great Britain, and the United States, each fearing that one of the others might gain an upper hand, settled for the *status quo*.[33]

In November 1849 Báez launched a naval offensive against Haiti to forestall the threat of another invasion. A Dominican squadron composed of the brigantine *27 de Febrero* (unk guns) and schooner *Constitución* (unk guns) and commanded by Capt. Charles J. Fagalde, a Frenchman, appeared off the Haitian coast taking prizes. On November 4 the squadron bombarded the village of L'Anse à Pitre and disembarked a landing party, seizing of booty. The next day the Dominican ships bombarded Les Cayes (120 mi WSW of Port-au-Prince) and captured the schooner *Charite*. Fagalde wanted to sail up the Windward Passage between Haiti and Cuba in search of more prizes. However, the Dominican crews mutinied so Fagalde returned to the port of Santo Domingo. On November 8 Soulouque declared the Dominicans pirates, but possessing no naval force at that time he could do little else. The Dominican squadron captured a schooner and sank some small craft.[34]

Following a Haitian rejection of a Dominican peace proposal, Báez dispatched a second naval expedition against Haiti. On December 3 the squadron composed of the brigantines *27 de Febrero* and *General Santana* (unk guns) and the schooners *Constitución* and *Las Mercedes* (unk guns) and commanded by Juan Alejandro Acosta,[35] bombarded and burned the town of Petit Rivière. Two days later Dominican and Haitian flotillas met off Les Cayes, but a storm broke up the battle. The Haitian squadron was composed of the corvette *Olive* (unk guns) and schooners *Picolet* (unk guns), *Avant-Garde* (unk guns), and *Le Signifie* (former *Virginia*, unk guns).[36]

As the fighting disrupted sea commerce, the great maritime powers became involved. On March 6, 1850, Great Britain and Santo Domingo signed a commercial treaty. And on December 19 of that year, France, Great Britain, and the United States declared to the Haitian government that if it persisted in invading Santo Domingo, they would take appropriate measures.[37]

CAMPAIGN OF 1855

Given the threat of the major powers, Haiti bided its time. Finally, Faustin I (Soulouque had elevated himself from President to Emperor on August 25, 1849) chose to invade Santo Domingo in November 1855 to preempt a possible annexation by the United States, a slave nation, of all or part of Santo Domingo and also to take advantage of the French and British preoccupation with the Crimean War.

Once again Santana was called upon to repel the invaders. The Haitian army, perhaps as many as 30,000 men, invaded Santo Domingo along three routes. One entered from the north, another in the center, and the third from the south. The Dominican frontier forces retreated in relatively good order and the Dominican navy prevented the Haitians from being supplied from the sea.[38]

Dominican Gen. José María Cabral defeated the southern column led by Soulouque at the Battle of Santomé on December 22. The Haitians lost 695 men, including Gen. Antonio Pierre. On the same day, the Haitian northern column was crushed at Cambronal by Gen. Francisco

Sosa y Lorenzo de Sena. On January 27, 1856, some 8,000 Dominicans defeated 22,000 Haitians at the battle of Sabana Larga near Dajabón (165 mi NW of Santo Domingo) after eight hours of fighting which came down to hand-to-hand combat. Thousands of dead or dying were abandoned on the battlefield. The Haitians retreated back across the border. Again Santana and Báez plotted against each other for political dominance, with Báez winning the first encounter and expelling Santana in 1857, and Santana winning the second and expelling Báez in 1859.[39]

WAR OF THE RESTORATION

Finally, on March 18, 1861, Santana pledged his loyalty and his country to Spain; Queen Isabella reannexed Santo Domingo to the motherland. Santana reportedly told a Spaniard, "I have made you an immensely valuable gift, for I have given you a people without journalists and devoid of lawyers."[40] The Queen appointed Santana governor and captain-general of the renewed colony.[41]

Spanish troops poured into Santo Domingo to support the "army" of Spanish bureaucrats and priests who displaced Dominicans as civil and religious servants. Within a few months, 6,000 Spanish troops occupied the island. Soon the number swelled to 30,000 soldiers supported by twenty-two warships. These were supplemented by battalions of Cuban and Puerto Rican volunteers. Additionally, more than 12,000 Dominicans, principally from the provinces of Azua, Santo Domingo, Sabo, and the town of Baní, served the Spanish queen.[42]

At first, only a few Dominicans opposed the Spaniards. This was more a result of the shortage of weapons than the will to fight. On May 2, 1861, Col. José Contreras led a group of Dominicans against the barracks at fortress Moca (80 mi NW of Santo Domingo). Santana, leading his cowboys, captured the ringleaders and executed them. Soon, Dominicans, who had fled to Haiti from Spanish rule, began raiding across the border. In June Gen. Francisco del Rosario Sánchez and Jose María Cabral began a better organized rebellion; however, Santana enticed Sánchez into a trap at El Cercado where Sánchez was captured. He and twenty-one followers were executed. A Spanish fleet was dispatched to Port-au-Prince and extracted an indemnity in retaliation for Haiti's meddling and a promise from the Haitians to prevent further crossings.[43]

Before long, tactics settled into a pattern. The Spanish, having superior artillery and rifles, preferred fighting at a distance. The more numerous Dominicans, knowing the terrain, preferred close quarters where they could employ lances and edged weapons.[44]

Santana, believing that his services and those of his followers were not adequately rewarded, resigned on March 28, 1862, as Spanish rule became increasingly unpopular. Santana was replaced as captain-general by the Caracas-born Spaniard Felipe Rivero y Lemoyne, an incredibly inept administrator.[45]

Compounding the problems of Spain, yellow fever broke out in the summer of 1862. On July 3 the U.S. Commercial Agent to Santo Domingo, William G. W. Jaeger, wrote to Secretary of State William Seward, "On July 1st, 1,000 troops arrived from Havana. Of the 5,000 troops previously landed, only 300 remain, all the rest having died of yellow fever, and of those left between twenty and thirty are dying daily."[46] And the dying continued is spite of the fact that the Spanish troops introduced into Santo Domingo had come from Cuba and Puerto Rico and were thought to be acclimated to the tropics.

By 1863 uprisings spread throughout Santo Domingo, and guerrilla warfare erupted. In February the Spanish authorities declared Santo Domingo under a state of siege. In April the

Spanish Army defeated the Dominicans led by Gen. Lucas de Peña at Cibao. In August Dominican dissidents in collaboration with the Haitian rebel Sylvain Salnave established sanctuaries along the Haitian-Dominican border to their mutual advantage.[47]

On August 16 fourteen dissidents led by Santiago Rodríquez, Benito Morción, and José Cabrera crossed the northeast frontier into Santo Domingo and called for the nation to rise up against the invaders (*Grito de libertad en Capotillo*). On that day, they routed a small Spanish detachment. Soon the insurrection had spread to the outskirts of the capital.[48]

On September 9 Spanish reinforcements of two battalions arrived at Puerto Plata on board the *Isabel la Católica* and the *El Pájaro del Océano*. Spain, believing it had no choice, once again turned to the elderly, wily *caudillo* Santana to salvage the situation. Perhaps unable to refuse the limelight, he led an army composed mostly of mercenaries against his countrymen at Cibao. When he reached Monte Plata, Santana discovered that the rebels had seized 6,000 rifles at Santiago. The rebels burned Santiago and Puerto Plata to delay his advance. On September 14 the insurgents established a provisional government led by Gen. José Antonio Salcedo Ramírez in Santiago de los Caballeros. It declared Santana a traitor and ordered that he be shot on sight.[49]

Santana's march stalled at Monte Plata (40 mi NNE of Santo Domingo). Rebel forces led by Gen. Gregorio Luperón harassed his troops and depleted his strength. The Dominicans captured Santana's entire supply train along with two Spanish generals and some one hundred Spanish soldiers at Yamasá. Many deserted Santana's army and the Spanish authorities refused to send reinforcements. Frustrated, Santana retired to El Seibo. In May 1864 the Spanish Captain-General ordered Santana to face court-martial. However, on June 14, 1864, he probably died from a stroke.[50]

The Captain-General of Santo Domingo, now the Spaniard José de la Gándara y Navarro, embraced a strategy of occupying the northern ports, thus cutting off the dissident Dominican government in Santiago from outside support. However, he did not take into consideration his lack of supplies and the poor equipment with which the Spanish forces were outfitted. The rifles and cannon were obsolescent and many of the navy's warships were unseaworthy. U.S. Commercial Agent Jaeger wrote to Secretary of State Seward on January 10, 1864:

> The Spanish war vessels are rotten. An American engineer in Spanish employ has told me that there are ten Spanish men-of-war lying in Cuba with their boilers burnt out, not fit to go to sea. One of the principal Spanish frigates, the *Blanca*, 51 guns, fired a salute at Port-au-Prince, which so completely disabled her that she had to proceed at once to Spain for repairs.[51]

Also, yellow fever continued to take a heavy toll. Of the 21,000 troops sent to the island, 9,000 had died of the fever or were incapacitated. Another 1,000 men had been killed in combat.[52]

In spite of these obstacles, La Gándara pulled together some men, which included impressed Dominicans, and joined a force of 6,000 men who sailed from Santiago de Cuba to Manzanillo Bay on board fourteen ships. The Spanish attacked and captured Monte Cristi (181 mi NW of Santo Domingo), but sustained heavy losses, including the wounding of Field Marshal Primo de Rivera. Next, La Gándara attempted to subdue the rebels between Monte Cristi and Santiago. This played into the hands of the Dominicans. They resorted to hit-and-run tactics and intercepted many of the supplies intended for La Gándara. The only victory in the campaign was the capture of Monte Cristi, and that at great cost.[53]

By 1865 the Dominican forces confined the Spaniards to the capital and they were afraid to venture out. Realizing that the reconquest of Santo Domingo would be costly and complicated due to the ending of the U.S. Civil War, the Queen authorized the abandonment of the colony on May 3, 1865. The last Spanish troops withdrew on July 11.[54]

OBSERVATIONS

Although the Wars for Independence against Haiti and the War of Restoration against Spain resolved once and for all that Santo Domingo would be independent, the rivalries among Dominicans *caudillos* over who would rule caused chaos for decades. The history of Santo Domingo (renamed the Dominican Republic in 1844) from the Wars for Independence until fairly recently has been mostly *caudillo* rule interrupted by periods of anarchy.

Apparently, no one has dared to guess as to the loss of lives and property incurred during the decades of fighting for independence by Santo Domingo against Spain, France, Haiti, and then Spain again. During the War of Restoration, Spain lost some 18,000 men. This number does not include the Dominicans, Cubans, and Puerto Ricans fighting on its side. The Dominicans fighting for independence against Spain lost more than 4,000 men. The Dominicans were better acclimated to local diseases, this explaining the large difference between the losses on the two sides.[55] To this day, the bitterness held by the Dominicans toward the Haitians suggests that during the fighting between them the loss of life and destruction of property were severe.

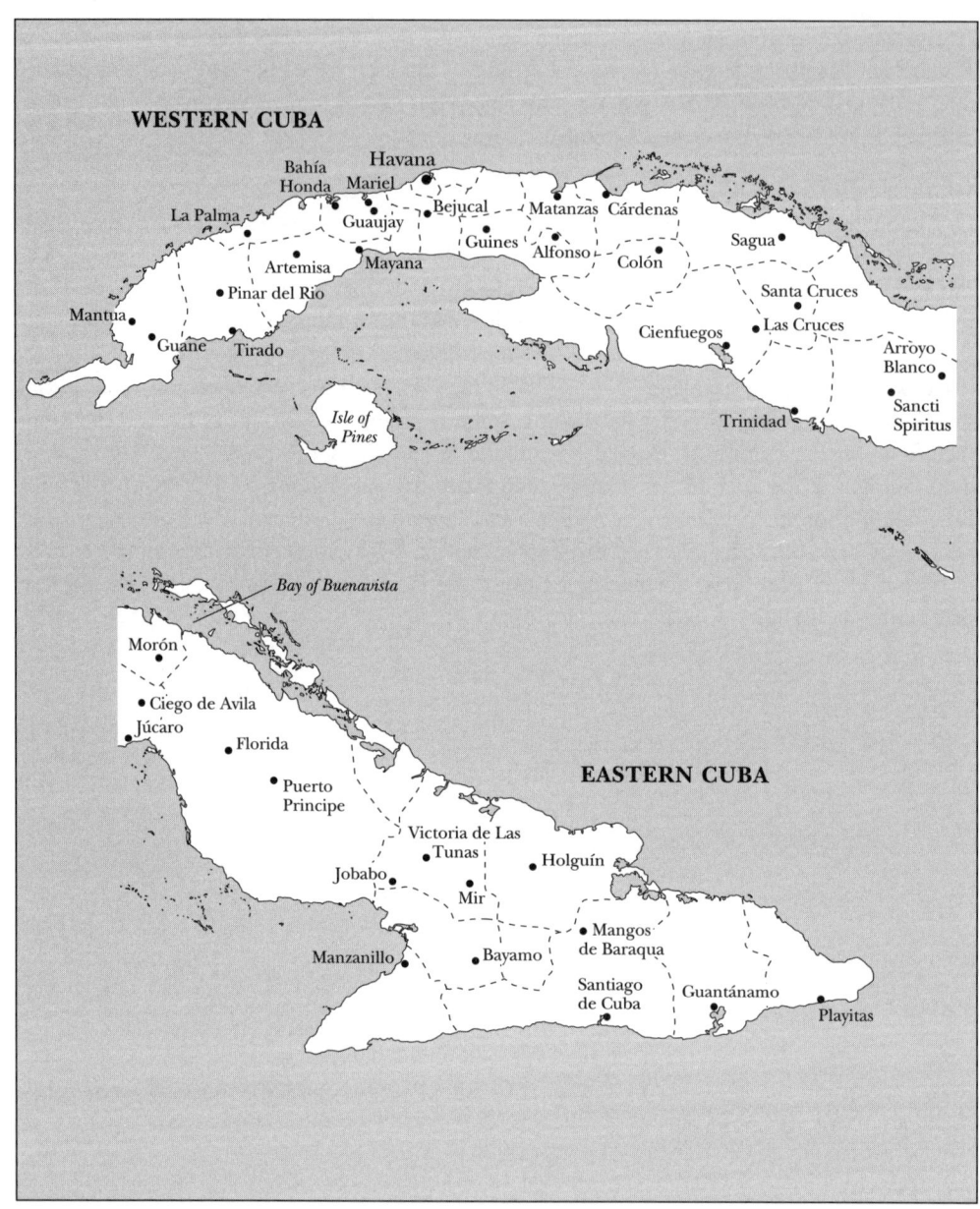

Map 9. Cuba, 1867.

CHAPTER THIRTY-TWO

CAPTAINCY-GENERAL OF CUBA, 1868–98

> Bolívar would see, with fist clenched against his bosom, the specters come and go through the air, and they can find no rest until his task is finished!
> —José Martí

THE SPARK

Late on October 9, 1868, thirty-eight Cuban planters revolted against Spain. Although many acts of rebellion had preceded this one (which today is celebrated on the tenth of October), the declaration at "La Demajagua" sugar mill located in Oriente Province in eastern Cuba (554 mi ESE of Havana and 113 mi WNW of Santiago) is considered the beginning of the wars for Cuban independence. Carlos Manuel de Céspedes, the owner of the plantation, became the commander of Revolutionary forces in the Bayamo area. He freed his thirty slaves (although he did not denounce slavery) and they joined the Revolutionary army which numbered 147 men.[1]

THE TEN YEARS WAR: BACKGROUND

The wars for Spanish-American independence in North and South America (1810–24—see chapters 2 through 5) made Cuba more "Spanish" than any of Spain's other New World possessions. Very early in the Napoleonic era, Cuba became a haven for *peninsulares* and *criollos* fleeing revolution in the other colonies. In 1801, when Toussaint Louverture demanded and obtained possession of Spanish Santo Domingo, thousands of white families abandoned their homes and fled to Cuba. Following the defeat of Rochambeau in 1803 in French Saint Domingue, thousands more whites fled to Cuba. In all some 30,000 persons emigrated (see chapter 1). And, throughout the Wars for Spanish-American independence, some 7,000 Spanish troops were sent to garrison Cuba. As Spain's hold on the South American and later the North American continents began to fail, other Royalists, mostly whites, fled to Cuba.

The number of slaves in Cuba also dramatically increased during this age of revolution. Some of the sugar planters who fled Saint Domingue brought their slaves with them. Also, with the destruction of Saint Domingue's sugar-growing capacity, Spain introduced vast numbers of Africans into Cuba to capture the sugar market.

Even before the Battle of Ayacucho (December 9, 1824), Cuban Revolutionaries unsuccessfully sought U.S. help to win independence from Spain. Secretary of State John Quincy Adams believed that Cuba's status as a vassal of a weak Spain best served U.S. interests until the time when the United States might take advantage of Spain's weakness and acquire Cuba. And Cuba was never far from America's thoughts. The island lay on its principal southern shipping routes and Cuba was becoming economically dependent upon the United States. Many Southerners coveted the island as a future slave state. And those championing "Manifest Destiny" saw the island as an essential addition to the Union.

Both the Spanish Royalists and Americans, North and South, viewed Cuba as the key to any attempted reconquest of Spanish America. Cuba was to be the center of operations for the defense of Florida against any possible attack by the upstart United States, and also for a military expedition that would be sent against rebellious Venezuela and New Granada. Therefore, Cuba had strategic importance to both Latin American nations and the United States. At the time of the Panama Conference (1826), President James Monroe worried that the Colombians and Mexicans might form a coalition and liberate the island.[2]

Cuba was not immune to the political, economic, and social factors that had shaped the movement for independence in the rest of Spanish America. The antagonisms between the *criollos* and *peninsulares* were as great in Cuba as they were in other parts of Spanish America. And, Cuba's nearness to the United States provided a safe haven for those working for the independence of the island. However, a number of other influences suppressed these urges for independence. The large number of recently displaced white colonists from colonial French and Spanish America feared that an independence movement would spark a slave rebellion. One had already taken place in 1812. A free Negro, José Antonio Aponte, conspired but the project was discovered and crushed.

On September 23, 1817, Great Britain finally forced Spain to suppress its slave trafficking. This meant that the Cuban economy needed to substitute white for black labor. The population in 1817 was 630,980 persons, of which 291,021 individuals were white; 115,691 free black; and 224,268 black slaves. The population had increased 132 percent since 1791 and the whites had become a minority. The Spanish government passed a number of laws trying to encourage the increase of the white population through immigration but this failed. By 1898 the population had increased to 1.6 million individuals.[3]

Cuba is the size of the state of Pennsylvania. Two "Cubas" existed. The east was primitive, mountainous, and poor. The west was fertile, metropolitan, and the source of wealth which supported those who governed.

Cubans could not agree on their political future—the most discussed options were independence, continued subservience to Spain, and annexation to either the United States or Great Britain. In 1822 a small faction of Cuban *criollos* asked the United States to annex the island. The proposition was sent to President James Monroe in September 1822 who rejected the advance out of fear of war with Great Britain. In 1850 and again in 1851, Narcisco López led filibustering expeditions to Cuba, unsuccessfully attempting to wrestle the island from Spain (see chapter 19). These all proved to be false starts in achieving separation from Spain.

CUBA'S TEN YEARS WAR: OPPOSING FORCES

The thirty-eight individuals who responded to the call for independence on October 9, 1868, had almost no military experience. They, and other Cubans, ignorant of the martial skills, were soon joined by a small band of political refugees from Santo Domingo. A number of these individuals had fought for Spain in Santo Domingo following its re-annexation (1861–65). When Spain quit Santo Domingo for the second time, some Dominican colonial officers immigrated to Cuba. Most were unable to find service in the Spanish army in Cuba. Some of these former soldiers joined the new Revolutionary army and provided its initial training and leadership.

The new Cuban army also included veterans of William Walker's adventures in Central America (1855–60), the Mexican Wars of the Reforma (1857–59), the U.S. Civil War (1861–65), and the French Maximilian adventure in Mexico (1861–67).[4] Soldiers of fortune came from Canada, Colombia, France, Mexico, Peru, Poland, Venezuela, and the United States. Two North Americans role to the rank of general—Thomas Jordan and Henry Earl Reeves. Numerous Chinese nationals, who had been brought to the island as indentured servants, joined the new army. All said and done, blacks comprised the bulk of the soldiers. The Cuban Revolutionary army never numbered more than 15,000 regular troops, to which must be added large numbers of irregulars.[5]

Cuban soldiers were poorly outfitted. Many were armed only with machetes and did not even have shoes. Therefore, a prime goal in any battle was to capture weapons and equipment, particularly shoes. On occasion, the Revolutionaries cut off the feet of dead Spanish soldiers and carried them off; the heat of battle did not permit a less gruesome method of acquisition.[6]

In 1868 the Spanish army in the island numbered about 7,000 regular troops. Over the next ten years, its size increased to almost 95,000 men. Supplementing these regulars were two distinct irregular forces. The Commercial Volunteers of Havana (*Cuerpo de Voluntarios del Comercio de La Habana*) numbered about 30,000 men in 1871. They were principally Spaniards residing on the island. This group had tremendous economic and political power. As a consequence, they could intimidate the Spanish Captain-General of Cuba into adopting their conservative policies. These irregulars were used for guard duty in order to free regular troops for offensive operations. However, the irregulars were undisciplined and difficult to control. The second group of irregulars were known as guerrillas (*guerrilleros*). These were mostly rural Cubans who remained loyal to Spain. Many made excellent scouts due to their knowledge of the terrain and the difficulty of distinguishing them from the Revolutionaries. By 1871 they numbered some 30,000 men.[7]

OPENING STRATEGIES

The Revolutionaries initially hoped to cause a spontaneous uprising and sweep across the island. Little thought was given to a prolonged struggle. Many of the Cuban Revolutionaries were mounted, which afforded them great mobility. Most frequently, they dismounted to fight, preferring to shoot at a distance. The most common rifles among the Revolutionaries were those of U.S. manufacture—Remingtons and Winchesters. These were not military issue and were significantly inferior in range and reliability to the Spanish-manufactured Mauser rifle. Also, the American-produced weapons fired black powder, which gave away the location of the riflemen. The preferred tactic was to remain on the defensive. Máximo Gómez wrote, "the advantage always goes to the one who waits and not the one who advances."[8] When the Revolutionaries ran short of ammunition they would resort to machete charges.[9]

The early Spanish strategy was to isolate and then eradicate the Revolutionaries. Initially, strategic sites were fortified in areas known to be sympathetic to the Revolutionaries. Then the region was saturated with troops. Captured Revolutionaries were executed and the property of

Figure 25. Captaincy-General of Cuba, 1868–98. Cuban Gen. Calixto García's army is on the march. These soldiers are carrying single-shot, Remington rolling-block rifles. These simplistic and rugged weapons were the late-nineteenth-century equivalent of the Soviet Union's "AK-47" of the more modern era. These Remingtons were sold to numerous revolutionary movements throughout the Americas. Once this war was "Americanized" following the destruction of the battleship *Maine*, the Americans relegated the Cuban army to other than combat roles for political and racial reasons. *Courtesy U.S. National Archives, SC-113540.*

suspected sympathizers confiscated or destroyed. All civilians in rural areas were forced to resettle near government-controlled towns in an effort to deny the Revolutionaries food and support. Civilians were often cruelly treated, particularly by the guerrillas loyal to Spain. In fact, both sides attempted to intimidate their enemy through terror. For example, the Revolutionary general Quintin Banderas[10] decapitated enemy soldiers with a machete during and after battle.[11]

The Spanish employed centuries-old military tactics that emphasized tight formations in order to mass gunfire. During the war the Spanish began arming their troops with repeating Mauser rifles that had a range of 2,400 yards—four times that of the rifles used by the Revolutionaries. These Mausers were not given to the troops until they reached Cuba for fear that the weapons might fall into the hands of dissident elements in Spain where civil wars ragged throughout much of the late nineteenth century. As a consequence, Spanish officers had little opportunity to develop doctrine as how to best employ these rifles and the soldiers received little training. These ultramodern rifles were employed as had been the flintlock muskets of an earlier century. The tactic of massing troops made them easier targets for the Revolutionaries.[12]

THE WAR IN THE EAST

The first rebel attack was a disaster. Céspedes and thirty-six followers entered the hamlet of Yara (565 mi ESE of Havana) during the dark of night only to discover 130 Spanish soldiers who were camping there. Twenty-four of Céspedes "army" fled without fighting.[13]

In spite of the fiasco at Yara, the Revolutionary army rapidly swelled to 12,000 men as it swept through Oriente Province, capturing the important town of Bayamo (575 mi ESE of Havana) on October 18, 1868. There the Revolutionaries established a provisional government and proclaimed their policy toward slavery. Slaves who escaped from the enemy's control would be accepted into the army; those who escaped from friendly control would not be permitted to join the army without the permission of their owners. At this time another Dominican, Máximo Gómez,[14] joined the rebel cause.[15]

Initially, Captain-General Francisco Lersundi could not respond to the uprising. He had but 7,000 troops on the island, and most were concentrated in the more prosperous western half of the island. Also, metropolitan Spain was experiencing political discord as the governments of Generals Francisco Serrano and Juan Prim searched for a monarch. In December 1868 Domingo Dulce became the new Captain-General of Cuba.[16]

In February 1869 a Revolutionary assembly from Camagüey (342 mi ESE of Havana) abolished slavery in the areas under their control. Two months later a constitutional convention at Guámairo declared all inhabitants absolutely free. The Guámairo Convention also declared in favor of annexation by the United States. Later, the newly created House of Representatives required former slaves to work for their former masters. This was an attempt to appease the wealthy western plantation owners, but it satisfied no one.[17]

The Spanish policy toward the rebels hardened in spite of Dulce's desires to find a negotiated settlement. On April 4 Gen. Blas Villate, Count of Valmaseda, ordered that all males over the age of fifteen in Oriente Province found away from their homes without cause would be shot. All women and children who had abandoned their homes were to be forced into fortified towns. All unoccupied houses were to be burned. In May Royalist volunteers forced their way into Dulce's residence and insisted that the Captain-General resign. The volunteers governed *de facto* until the arrival from Spain of a new captain-general, Gen. Caballero de Rodas. His hardline policies were compatible with those of the volunteers.[18]

By 1869 the struggle had disintegrated into guerrilla warfare. The rebels lived off the land. They relied on sabotage as their chief tactic and avoided general encounters with the Spanish army. The Spaniards fortified and garrisoned the cities and major towns. In the West the wealthy land owners converted their plantations into armed enclaves. In October Céspedes declared the policy of slash and burn. The rebel leader in the Escambray Mountains, Federico Cavada, began burning sugar plantations and fields of cane in the south-central part of the island.[19]

In a counteroffensive, the Spaniards drove Cavada westward out of the Escambray Mountains. More inhabitants were forced into concentration camps. Both sides executed individuals merely based upon suspicion and committed atrocities. A bloody stalemate took hold. Three hundred miles to the east of Havana, the Spanish began digging a thirty-mile ditch (*la trocha*), running the width of the island between Júcaro in the south to Morón in the north and then onto the Bay of Buenavista, to confine the rebels to the eastern half of the island. They fortified positions along the ditch and patrolled the intervals with infantry and cavalry. Out of frustration a rump meeting of the Revolutionary House of Representatives removed Céspedes as president and replaced him with Salvador Cisneros Betancourt.[20]

BLOCKADE RUNNING

Almost from the beginning of the war, adventurers, mostly Americans, attempted to run the Spanish blockade carrying arms, munitions, and mercenaries. On May 11 and 12, 1869, the *Perit* disembarked 100 Cubans, 85 adventurers, 2,300 rifles, 50 carbines, 200 Colt revolvers, 6 cannon, 410,000 cartridges, 800 pairs of shoes, and more. The *Anna* off-loaded on January 19, 1870; the *Hornet* on January 8, 1871; and the *Fannie* and the *Edgar Stewart* some time later. All told, more than fifty expeditions sailed from the United States and only a few were caught.[21]

One of those intercepted was the *Virginius*. On October 31, 1873, the Spanish steam corvette *Tornado* (5 guns) captured the blockade runner *Virginius* off Haiti.[22] Although flying the U.S. flag, the ship was owned by the Revolutionary *Junta* of New York (*Junta Revolucionario de Nueva York*). The *Virginius* was taken into Santiago. Four Revolutionary leaders were executed on November 4 and three days later thirty-seven more. These included Capt. Joseph Fry, a graduate of the U.S. Naval Academy, and other Americans. More might have been shot if it had not been for the arrival and threatened bombardment of Santiago by the captain of the British steam sloop *Niobe* (4 guns), Lambton Lorraine. A furor arose in the United States but was tempered by President Grant's moderation and an expression of regret by the Spanish government. The Spanish paid an $80,000 indemnity and agreed to punish Gen. Juan Nepomuceno Burriel who gave the orders.[23]

THE WAR MOVES WEST

The battles during 1873 proved indecisive. On May 11 the Spanish defeated the Cubans at Jumaguayu (18 mi S of Camagüey); among the dead was the Cuban Gen. Ignacio Agamonte. On December 2 the Cubans led by Máximo Gómez won at Palo Seco, Camagüey, killing over 500 Spaniards.[24]

Revolutionary Generals Gómez and Antonio Maceo[25] long advocated expanding the fighting and destruction to the wealthy western half of the island. Also, after April 14, 1872, Spain was in turmoil when Don Carlos revolted against Amadeo, brother of the King of Italy, who had recently been chosen King of Spain. Finally, in February 1874 the Revolutionary politicians gave their generals permission to invade the western half of the island. The Spanish commander learned of their intentions. The two armies met at El Naranjo (2 mi SE of Camagüey) on February 19, 1874. Outnumbered almost three to one, Gómez placed his 400 infantry and 300 cavalry in a defensive position. General [first name unknown] Bascones attacked the Revolutionaries but was unable to break their defensive position. In the battle the Spanish lost 100 dead and 200 wounded and the Revolutionaries a total of 150 dead and wounded.[26]

On March 7 Gómez renewed his march westward. He was reinforced by Gen. Manuel Suárez, increasing his army to 1,600 infantry and 450 cavalry. Gómez learned that a Spanish force of 3,000 men under Brigadier General [first name unknown] Arminan was advancing to Las Guásimas (8 mi SE of Camagüey).[27] Gómez blocked his advance. The Spanish cavalry was enticed into a trap and defeated. The Cuban force then enveloped the Spanish infantry. Following three days of heavy fighting, 2,000 fresh Spanish troops under General Bascones rescued the trapped soldiers on March 18. On the following day the Spanish army retreated. The Battle of Las Guásimas cost the Spanish 1,037 casualties and the Revolutionaries 174 casualties. However, the Revolutionaries had expended most of their munitions and exhausted most of their other supplies that had been collected for the offensive. They retired to the eastern half of the island.[28]

By June Gómez had gathered enough supplies to renew the offensive against the west. However, the Revolutionary political leaders were hesitant. Also, white Revolutionary leaders in the province of Las Villas feared the possible consequences of battlefield victories by the mulatto Maceo. Maceo was relieved as second in command and replaced by the less talented black Cecilio Gonzáles. Gómez did not cross "the ditch" back into the west until January 1875. He burned eighty-three plantations around Sancti Spiritus (232 mi ESE of Havana) within a six-week period and freed their slaves. However, the conservative Revolutionary leaders feared the consequences of these actions and diverted troops away from Gómez' army, causing the campaign to fizzle.[29]

By 1876 the Revolutionary cause was disintegrating due to racial prejudice. Gómez surrendered his command when he was told that the officers of Las Villas would no longer follow his orders since he was a Dominican. Whites intensified their campaign to discredit Maceo because he was a mulatto. Morale throughout the Revolutionary army was low.[30]

SPAIN CHANGES STRATEGY

By late 1876 the civil war in Spain had ended and the new Spanish monarch was firmly in place. Spain reinforced its army in Cuba which now numbered over 100,000 regulars. In 1877 Gen. Arsenio Martínez Campos[31] was appointed captaingeneral of Cuba, and he significantly altered the character of the war. Prisoners were no longer executed; the treatment of civilians improved; slaves (blacks and Chinese) were freed if they chose to fight for Spain; defecting Revolutionaries were paid five gold pesos for their weapons and twenty gold pesos if they also brought in a horse. Revolutionaries and deserters from the Spanish army were offered amnesty. Those accepting the terms were protected from Spanish persecution and reprisals. Cubans were also promised a greater degree of self-government.[32]

Also, the Revolutionaries sustained devastating losses. In October 1877 the Spanish captured Revolutionary president Estrada Palma. Shortly afterward Eduardo Machado, a leading conservative Revolutionary, was killed. The revolution collapsed on December 21, 1877, when a truce was reached. Among other reforms, Spain promised to end slavery which was finally abolished in 1886. Gen. Antonio Maceo and a few others wanted to continue fighting, but the conservative politicians and the populace, who had supported the Revolutionaries, had had enough. The pact of El Zanjón ended the Ten Years War on February 11, 1878.[33]

OBSERVATIONS CONCERNING THE TEN YEARS WAR

Spain succeeded in bringing the fighting to an end, at least temporarily, through a change in strategy. Spain sustained some 200,000 casualties, mostly from disease. At times, 60 percent of the Spanish Army was incapacitated due to illness. The Cuban Revolutionaries sustained between 100,000 and 150,000 dead and the island sustained over $300 million in property damage. The Spanish estimated that the war had cost $300 million and this sum was added to the debt that Spain claimed the colony owed to the mother country.[34]

The Revolutionaries suffered significantly from philosophical differences, regionalism, and racism. The struggle between the Liberals and Conservatives over the structure of the new government was divisive.[35] The revolution also suffered from strong regional animosities between the *Orientales* and the *Camagueyanos*. Racism was a significant problem. The revolution drew heavily upon the slave population and the Spanish were able to play on the fears of the more affluent whites. General Gómez concluded that the revolution failed because the war was not successfully carried to the west which was the source of the revenue for the Royalists. The Revolutionaries never built a disciplined army; at times anarchy prevailed.[36]

PUERTO RICAN AID CUBAN INDEPENDENCE

As early as 1866 the Puerto Rican independence movement became tied to that of Cuba. In that year Juan Manuel Macias, leader of the Republican Society of Cuba and Puerto Rico (*Sociedad Republicana de Cuba y Puerto Rico*), wrote that "the firm and only purpose of the society is the independence of the Antilles and the absolute freedom of all its inhabitants, without regard to race or colour."[37] The late 1860s were years of economic depression throughout the islands, in spite of which Spain imposed new taxes. In 1867 Puerto Ricans Ruis Rivera, Ramón Emeterio Betances, and José Francisco Basora founded the Revolutionary Committee of Puerto Rico (*Comite Revolucionario de Puerto Rico*), which called for a united effort by Cubans and Puerto Ricans to win independence from Spain.[38] In 1869 the Republican Society proclaimed revolution, "liberty for all the inhabitants of Cuba and Puerto Rico without distinction of race or color."[39]

A band of Puerto Ricans rebelled on February 3, 1868, in Lares, a town in central Puerto Rico, and the affair became known as *El Grito de Lares* ("The Cry of Lares"), but this was easily put down.[40]

Early in the Cuban Ten Years War (1868–78), the Revolutionary Committee of Puerto Rico, led by Ramón E. Betances, gave the Cuban Revolutionaries financial support and the modest collection of weapons it had hidden in Saint Thomas, Curaçao, and Haiti. These included 400 Enfield rifles, 45 Snider rifles, 110 carbines, 87 handguns, and one cannon (with 200 shells) plus small arms ammunition. A number of Puerto Ricans worked and fought for Cuban independence during the Ten Years War, the most notable being Ruis Rivera.[41]

AFTERSHOCK OF THE TEN YEARS' WAR

On March 16, 1878, General Maceo met with Gen. Martinez de Campos, a prime negotiator of the pact of El Zanjón, at Baraguá. Known as the "Protest of Baraguá," Maceo would accept no less than independence and freedom for the slaves. Maceo and his 1,500 followers soon found themselves fighting Cubans who had accepted the Pact of El Zanjón as well as the Spaniards. By May Maceo was overwhelmed and he sailed into exile.[42]

THE LITTLE WAR ("LA GUERRA CHIQUITA")

Gen. Calixto García, who had escaped from a Spanish prison, led a new uprising in the summer of 1879. The Spanish learned of the planned uprisings and arrested suspected conspirators. Fighting broke out in the eastern half of the island, but the Spaniards acted swiftly and decisively. General García was captured in August and the Little War dissolved into banditry and collapsed.[43]

Unsuccessful attempts to spark Cuba into rebellion continued during the 1880s. In 1883 Ramón Bonachea led a small band ashore at Manzanillo. He was captured and shot along with four of his followers. Two years later, Limbano Sánchez led another landing near Santiago. He was also killed and his followers shot or imprisoned.[44]

DISSIDENT CUBANS AND PUERTO RICANS UNITE

Many prominent Cuban Revolutionaries fled to New York City where they established the Cuban Revolutionary Party. More commonly referred to as "the New York *Junta*," its leaders were Tomás Estrada, Calixto García, and José Martí.[45] Between 1890 and 1891 the Puerto Rican Sotero Figueda Fernández founded the Club of Independence Supporters (*Club los Independentistas*) to aid the Cuban independence movement and a year later he established the Borinquen Club (*Club Borinquen*), the goal of which was Puerto Rican independence.

During 1891 the Cuban José Martí and Tómas Estrada Palma organized over 200 clubs throughout the United States, which financially supported the growing movement. On April 10, 1892, Martí, supported by the Puerto Rican Francisco Gonzalo Marin Shaw, founded the Revolutionary Cuban Party (*Partido Revolucionario Cubano*). Its chapter not only called for the independence of Cuba but also that of Puerto Rico.[46] The prime instrument of propaganda was Martí's newspaper *Pátria*. Martí stated, "The newspaper is born, because of the will and with the resources of Cubans and Puerto Riqueños '*independentistas*' in New York, to contribute, without wasting time and without rest to the organization of the free men of Cuba and Puerto Rico."[47] Martí wrote to Máximo Gómez on September 13, 1892, seeking his help in the fight for Cuban and Puerto Rican independence.[48] Martí also wrote to Ramón Betances, a leader of the Puerto Rican revolution and a veteran of the Ten Years' War, "I know that for you there is no sea between Cuba and Puerto Rico. . . . would you be willing to contribute you valuable assistance to organize in Paris a vigorous and active group of helpers for our serious and growing revolution?"[49]

THE SECOND CUBAN WAR FOR INDEPENDENCE: THE SPARK

On February 24, 1895, the Second War for Cuban Independence began. Numerous demonstrations were planned throughout Cuba, but many were forestalled when Spanish authorities arrested prominent agitators. Those demonstrations that did occur sparked within a few days uprisings throughout the island.

THE SECOND CUBAN WAR FOR INDEPENDENCE: BACKGROUND

Two Cuban political factions had grown out of the Ten Years' War: those who wished to achieve administrative autonomy from Spain by peaceful means and those who wanted to fight for complete independence. Martí emerged as the leader of the second faction. An excellent orator, he called on all Cubans to set aside their racial, economic, and regional prejudices and to fight for Cuban independence.[50] Martí successfully solicited the participation of Máximo Gómez (exiled in Santo Domingo) and Antonio Maceo (exiled in Costa Rica), the military heroes of the Ten Years' War.

In 1892 José Martí founded the Cuban Revolutionary Party *(El Partido Revolucionario de Cuba)*. At the end of 1893, Martí made plans to land in Cuba in February 1894; however, this was delayed. Early in 1895 the Spanish government learned of Martí's plans. Events in Cuba were unfolding so fast that on February 24, 1895, a revolution had broken out in a number of towns including Baire (420 mi ESE of Havana); these became known as the "Yell of Baire" *(Grito de Baire)* but the Spanish successfully put down the insurrections. Martí did not land in Cuba until early March.[51]

THE SECOND WAR FOR INDEPENDENCE: OPPOSING FORCES

Shortly after the new call for independence the Revolutionary Cuban army numbered 4,500 men, limited by the available arms. The army had a particularly large camp following because of the fear of Spanish reprisals. As during the Ten Years' War, blacks made up at least 70 percent of the Revolutionary army. This was double their percentage within the population at large. The army was completely integrated. By December 1895 the Revolutionary army numbered roughly 25,000 men.[52]

In June 1895, some 52,000 Spanish troops were in Cuba and by October the Spanish army had swelled to 120,000 regulars, 60,000 irregulars, and a large but weak naval force. Gen. Martínez Campos, the architect of the 1878 peace, returned to the island to deal with the new uprising.[53]

THE SECOND WAR FOR INDEPENDENCE: OPENING STRATEGY

Martí's overarching strategy was to keep the United States out of the fight. He wrote, "Through the independence of Cuba, it is my duty . . . to prevent the USA from spreading over the West Indies and falling with added weight upon other lands of Our America."[54] Militarily, Máximo Gómez and Antonio Maceo agreed that they must not be deterred from carrying the fight to the rich, conservative west. They planned on financing the revolution by charging farmers for permission to plant and harvest crops.[55] The Spanish strategy was to confine the revolution to the eastern half of the island and to prevent the gathering of large Revolutionary forces, but General Martínez Campos acknowledged, "If [Gomez] wants to pass, he will pass."[56]

THE REVOLUTIONARIES LAND

The landing of the Revolutionary leaders was almost catastrophic. Gen. Antonio Maceo, his brother José, and twenty followers landed at Playa de Duaba on the northern coast (620 mi E of Havana) on April 1, 1895. They were immediately chased and had to scatter. Martí, General Gómez, and four followers landed from a schooner at Playitas on the southern coast just west of the easternmost tip of Cuba on the eleventh. They had a rough time rowing ashore. Finally, the Revolutionary chiefs united at La Mejorana (35 mi NNW of Santiago). On May 19 Martí was killed in an ambush at Dos Ríos just east of Bayamo. However, the Revolutionaries had successfully established themselves in the eastern mountains.[57]

For the Revolutionaries the initial months were spent creating a political structure and training an army. An American observer described the Cuban army in 1895:

> In the whole island there were some twenty-five thousand insurgents under arms, all both infantry and cavalry, carrying the *machete* as a sidearm, and a rifle . . . usually a Remington.
>
> More rifles and ammunition are constantly being run into the country; and with the increased supply of arms the numbers in the field could be largely increased since those who desire to join in the struggle very largely exceed the number of rifles available.
>
> The rank and file of the rebels in the east are black, but farther west they are almost exclusively white. . . . The Negroes are fine fighting men, and able to endure every kind of hardship; they march thirty or forty miles in a day without great fatigue, and are able to go for long periods without food. . . . A few of the officers are black, but usually they are Cubans [white].[58]

In the meantime, the Spanish deployed forces to keep the rebels confined to the east and attempted to hunt down the rebel leaders. As the Spanish aggressively hunted the rebels in the interior, yellow fever took a heavy toll on their forces.

On July 13 Cuban Revolutionaries led by General Maceo ambushed 1,500 Royalists at Peralejo (560 Mi ESE of Havana). The rebel victory forced the Spaniards to move about in large formations to avoid being attacked. Also in July, Gómez ordered all farmers to stop growing crops and suspended commerce with towns occupied by the enemy. Those not complying would be tried for treason and their farms burned.[59]

THE ADVANCE WEST

General Maceo led 3,000 troops (mostly light cavalry) across the center of the island. General Banderas led 1,000 infantry along a more southerly route. Both easily breached *la trocha* and marched into the agriculturally rich west. The Revolutionaries avoided major battles, not wishing to have their strength sapped before reaching the western provinces as had happened to them during the Ten Years' War. The Spaniards attempted to use their artillery to slow the advance, but did not press for a major engagement. The Revolutionaries did have some problems with desertion as their troops marched farther from their homes and some white troops were reluctant to take orders from a black general. On December 3 the Revolutionaries ambushed the Spaniards at Iguará (240 mi ESE of Havana).[60]

The first major battle occurred at Mal Tiempo (180 mi ESE of Havana), in sugar cane fields on December 15, 1895. Generals Gómez and Maceo led a cavalry charge and the Spaniards formed a defensive square. The Spanish were defeated losing 100 dead and substantial munitions and supplies. The Cubans lost twenty-four dead.[61]

As the Cubans advanced, they burned cane fields (which were nearing harvest), as well as a number of small towns which they sacked. The two armies fought at Calimete (105 mi ESE of Havana) on December 29. The Spanish defensive square withstood three machete charges and the Revolutionaries sustained heavy casualties. The Cubans captured numerous hamlets but the Spaniards refused to be drawn out of the major towns.

In early January 1896, Maceo feinted an attack on Havana and many in the city panicked. Instead, he continued to march westward with 1,600 men. Gómez remained near Havana with 2,300 Revolutionaries protecting Maceo's rear. On January 22 General Maceo marched into Mantua at the western extreme of Cuba; the Revolutionaries had successfully spread the insurgency the entire length of the island. The Revolutionaries had brought economic devastation to the rich west. The sugar crop of 1894 had been 1.5 million tons; that of 1896 was 225,000 tons.[62]

On February 1 Maceo did sustain a major defeat at Paso Real (120 mi SSW of Havana) when he attacked 900 Spaniards in a strong defensive position with 2,000 men. The Revolutionary casualties were 262 men and the Royalists 46.

Spain decided to replace Martínez Campo with a more aggressive general. Valeriano Weyler,[63] arriving in Cuba on February 10, became the new captain-general of Cuba. Weyler reverted to the brutalities that had been used during the early years of the Ten Years' War. Some 300,000 Cubans, mostly farmers, were forced into concentration camps near the large, well-garrisoned towns in an attempt to deny the Revolutionaries food. By the end of 1896 few crops were being grown. Many on both sides died from hunger. In contrast, the Cuban army adopted a more humane approach. In an attempt to improve discipline, Gómez ordered that soldiers who did not obey orders were to be hanged regardless of their rank.[64]

Weyler worked to breathe new life into the Spanish army. He ordered built a second north-south defensive line. This was between Mayana on the southern coast and Mariel on the northern one, a distance of twenty-three miles. The new barrier was some twenty-five miles west of Havana. Weyler also reinforced the original *trocha*. He weeded out the less efficient cavalry units and required that the sabre be substituted for the machete; the sabre was a more lethal weapon. Patrolling the countryside was left to the loyal guerrillas while the Spanish troops were concentrated in larger towns and cities and prepared for offensive operations.[65]

RUNNING THE BLOCKADE

By 1896 the Cuban Revolutionaries also received increasing support from the United States. The Cuban Revolutionary government, headquartered in the United States, raised money, purchased weapons, outfitted expeditions, and even created a navy. Thirty-four out of forty small, well-organized expeditions successfully landed and joined the Cuban army. Numerous ships ran the Spanish blockade delivering desperately needed weapons and munitions. At least eight ships were purchased and used primarily as blockade runners. On March 24, 1896, the *Bermuda*, commanded by Johny O'Brian (an American), landed Gen. Calíxto García, some volunteers, a thousand rifles, one artillery piece, and several hundred thousand rounds of ammunition in Oriente Province. On November 28, 1897, the *Dauntless* disembarked men and supplies near the town of Banes in Oriente Province.[66]

FIGHTING IN THE WEST

Weyler now took the offensive west of the new *trocha*, seeking to destroy Maceo's force. Spanish Gen. Arsenio Linnes leading 3,000 men attempted to prevent Gómez and Maceo from joining forces not far from Havana. Maceo defeated Linnes at the Battle of Moralitos (28 mi SE of Havana) on February 19, 1896, but lost over 100 men. Gómez turned eastward as Maceo continued to operate in the west. Maceo destroyed everything in his path—plantations, crops, telegraph lines, locomotives, rolling stock, and railroad bridges.[67]

Maceo avoided general engagements as he continued his rampage. His 1,500-man force was trapped by a superior Spanish force at Cacarajícara (50 mi WSW of Havana) on August 30, 1896, and he lost some 200 dead. For a while Maceo's more mobile force was able to avoid any more direct encounters with the Spanish army. On September 18 Maceo made a successful stand at Ceja del Negro west of Havana in order to protect some 1,000 rifles, 500,000 rounds of ammunition, one artillery piece, and 2,000 pounds of dynamite which had arrived on board the blockade runner *Dauntless* on the eighth.[68]

Weyler escalated the intensity of the conflict on October 21 when he required the entire population of the province of Pinar de Río to the west of Havana, the region in which Maceo was then operating, to move inside the fortified towns within eight days or be declared rebels. Food was distributed only under Spanish supervision. Maceo's force escaped east of the new *trocha* by taking boats around the northern end.[69]

Notwithstanding, Weyler ruthlessly pursued the rebel bands. Spanish troops killed José Maceo on July 5 at the battle of Loma del Gato in the east. On December 7 a Spanish column surprised and killed Gen. Antonio Maceo and Máximo Gómez' son, Pancho, at Punta Bravo. Gómez and the political leaders of the revolution were increasingly arguing among themselves. And in New York, Estrada Palma resigned from the leadership of the "New York *junta*." Weyler believed he had turned the corner.[70]

Undeterred, the seventy-three-year-old Máximo Gómez recrossed the Morón-Júcaro ditch back toward the west with 3,000 men. However, Weyler concentrated 40,000 troops in the province of Las Villas under his personal command. General Gómez refused a general encounter with this grossly superior force and used his irregular cavalry to harass the Spaniards. Although disease, and to a lesser degree the Cuban cavalry, took a toll on the Spanish army, Gómez found the Spanish defenses too strong to attack. Again, Weyler believed that victory was near. Only a few important rebel commanders remained in the field. Quintín Banderas operated in the west but was isolated and Máximo Gómez had only a small force in Santa Clara Province. And poor, remote Oriente Province was still in rebellion.[71]

On August 25, 1897, the Cubans achieved a significant moral victory. Some 4,000 Revolutionaries beseiged the fortified town of Las Tunas (390 mi ESE of Havana). The seventy-nine-man garrison held out for three days but was finally subdued by two cannon and six machine guns manned by Americans. Finally, the Spaniards surrendered the prize of 1.5 million rounds of ammunition plus weapons and supplies.[72]

The influence of public opinion in the United States and the assassination of the Conservative President of the Spanish Council of Government, Antonio Cánovas del Castillo, by an anarchist in August 1897 led to Weyler's recall. Lt. Gen. Ramón Blanco Erenas replaced Weyler as captain-general. He was instructed to do away with the concentration camps and to adopt moderating policies, including home rule. The Revolutionaries refused to be conciliatory.[73]

THE TIDE SLOWLY TURNS

The Second War for Cuban Independence was slowly turning in favor of the Revolutionaries in spite of horrific casualties and destruction on both sides. The Spaniards were drawing back into the larger cities. By late 1897 and early 1898, the towns of Bayamo, Guisa, Guaimaxo, Jiguani, and Loma de Hierro had fallen to the rebels. The cities of Manzanillo and Santiago were being threatened. Both sides were carrying on intense guerrilla warfare. By 1898 the Cuban economy was near collapse.[74]

THE UNITED STATES TAKES OVER THE WAR

On February 15, 1898, the American secondclass battleship *Maine* blew up in Havana harbor, killing 260 sailors. This event cause the Second Cuban War for Independence to be swallowed by the Spanish-American War. On April 23 the United States declared war on Spain (see chapter 38). The U.S. Navy immediately began to escort Cuban blockade runners. At the request of the United States, the Cuban provisional government sent Brig. Gen. Enrique Collazo to Washington to coordinate war plans.[75]

OBSERVATIONS

The Cubans lost control of the war against Spain to the United States and as a consequence Cuba became a U.S. protectorate. Martí had warned, "Once the United States is in Cuba, who will get it out?"[76]

José Martí had been able to suppress the racial, social, and regional bias, which had significantly contributed to the defeat of the Cuban army during the Ten Years' War. However, his death early during the Second War for Independence left Cuba without its most effective politician. The conflict between the Cuban civilian and military leadership, so prominent during the Ten Years War, was in large measure avoided by a clear delineation of the responsibilities of each.

Some 300,000 Cubans died during the Second War for Independence. Of these, 200,000 civilians died from disease and famine created by the concentration camps. Two contemporary sources estimated that by December 1895 the rebel army had lost between 29,850 and 42,800 men. Many Cuban generals were killed in combat, strongly suggesting an active leadership. Of the 200,000 Spanish troops in Cuba during the Second War for Independence, less than one third were fit for duty in 1898.[77]

Many Cuban farms and plantations were destroyed. The extensive destruction of property facilitated its passing from Cuban ownership to that of North Americans. Following the two wars for independence and the Spanish-American War (see chapter 38), Americans invested $50 million, primarily in sugar and tobacco plantations but also in mining, giving them control over much of the Cuban economy.[78]

PART 10

WARS OF CONQUEST AGAINST NATIVE AMERICANS

CHAPTER THIRTY-THREE

THE INDIANS, 1819–1927

> Whenever two civilizations meet, one or the other becomes predominant.
> —Jose Vasconcelos, former Secretary of Education of Mexico

THE SPARK

The Indians of Latin America were largely conquered by the Europeans and their descendants during the colonial era. However, a few Indian groups did continue the fight after the wars for independence in the early nineteenth century or were sparked into action by abuses.

BACKGROUND

Only those tribes inhabiting regions that were inhospitable and did not possess immediate wealth, such as gold or silver, maintained their independence from colonial rule. Since these inhospitable areas were generally ill-suited to agriculture, the Indian inhabitants were, for the most part, nomadic hunters and few in number. Their social order produced numerous petty chiefs; no single individual controlled large followings. This was both a strength and a weakness when fighting the intruders. Few tribes could ever truly unite and threaten the existence of the Europeans and their descendants. On the other hand, seldom could a tribe be subdued in a single battle. As technology allowed settlements to be established farther into the hinterland, those Indians not subjugated by the Europeans became increasingly constricted and oppressed and, on occasion, lashed out at the "civilized" world.

OPPOSING FORCES

The nomadic Indian warriors were armed with preconquest hunting weapons such as lances, clubs, and stabbing and cutting weapons; a few were able to steal or capture firearms, but ammunition was always scarce. The long lance (approximately ten feet) and the *boleadora* (see page 116 for a description) were the preferred weapons of the Ranqueles Indians. The Mayan warriors, on the other hand, did have access to firearms.[1]

Lt. J. M. Gilliss, U.S. Navy, sent to South America on a scientific expedition during the middle of the nineteenth century, described the Araucanian warrior:

> Usually mounted bare-back on almost untamed horses, which the powerful bit of Chile enables them to control with the ease of thought, their dark and half-naked bodies painted in colors of many shades, their long hair streaming in the wind as they rush to the fight, waving lances of extraordinary length, and uttering such shrieks as only children of the forest can compass, they are objects that may well terrify. To strike them seems almost impossible. With the left arm clinging to the neck, and one foot only over the horse's back, they lie close along his side, and in this manner ride with such momentum that they will sometimes unhorse a rider and carry him several yards on the ends of their lances.[2]

Until the middle of the nineteenth century, the national troops (frequently militia) that opposed the Indians used lances and swords as their primary weapons. By mid-century firearms and ammunition were more plentiful, thus giving the national forces an advantage in fire power over most Indians.

OPENING STRATEGIES

Latin American Indians employed guerrilla tactics against the Conquistador and his descendants from the earliest days of the European invasion. And, the tactics of guerrilla warfare remained similar between 1791 and today, little influenced by the increasingly rapid advance of technology. Small mobile assault groups, operating without regard to battle lines, attacked the enemy where he appeared to be most vulnerable.[3] The European descendants relied principally upon forts built along the frontiers to bar the hostile Indians from raiding its settlements. On occasion, the national governments would raise armies, sometimes numbering as many as 6,000 men, to hunt down the Indians. Seldom was "quarter" given by either side.

Although numerous struggles continued into the nineteenth century, four Indian groups stand out as the most persistent. They were the Araucanians, the Ranqueles, the Mayans, and the Yaqui.

THE ARAUCANIANS

The Araucanian Indians inhabited modern-day southern Chile, bordered on the north by the Bío Bío and Laja Rivers, on the south by the Toltén River, on the west by the Pacific Ocean, and on the east by the Andes Mountains. The Spanish *Conquistadores* first made contact with the Araucanians in 1556 when they reached the bank of the Bío Bío River. For the next 330 years these Indians were frequently at war with the intruders. During the colonial era the colonists built forts along the Bío Bío River at Los Angeles, Nacimiento, San Carlos, Santa Bárbara, Chillán, and Arauco to force the Araucanians to remain south of the river, and created a standing army (probably the first in the Western Hemisphere). This defensive line collapsed during the Wars for Independence as many of the forts were abandoned and many Araucanians, fighting for the Spanish King, raided to the north. This created a condition of near chaos along the frontier. By the dawn of independence (1824), about 500,000 persons inhabited Chile, of whom about 100,000 individuals were the unassimilated Araucanians. The most southern major Chilean garrison was at Concepción (325 mi S of Santiago).[4]

Between 1819 and 1832 Araucanians loyal to Chief Francisco Mariluán and the remaining Spanish Royalists waged a bloody "War to the Death" against the Chilean army led by Gen. Manuel Bulnes and the Indians loyal to the new nation. In the end, Bulnes was able to reestablish the defensive line along the Bío Bío River. The Chilean government paid tribute to help insure the loyalty of important chiefs.[5]

Following the War of the Confederation (see chapter 11), Chile began expanding its control south of the Bío Bío River. In 1842 a military colony was created south of the river. Veteran soldiers were awarded land, thus extending control while reducing defense expenditures. In 1849 militias (*batallones cívicos*) were formed at San Carlos, Nacimiento, and Negrete.[6]

In 1851 dissident Araucanians joined forces with presidential candidate Gen. José María de la Cruz Prieto, who rebelled after losing the election to Manuel Montt. De la Cruz held the loyalty of the frontier troops, so the government ordered the Commissioner of Indians, Major [first name unknown] Zúñiga, to attack the rebellious Araucanians with loyal Indians in order to hold them in the south. However, on November 6, 1851, the rebellious Indians assassinated Zúñiga and his family. As a consequence, de la Cruz forged a 3,500-man army from the frontier garrison, the militia from Concepción, and hundreds of Araucanians. This force was defeated by a 3,700-man army led by General Bulnes at the Battle of Loncomilla on December 8, 1851 (see chapter 26).[7] Following this defeat, the Araucanians returned to their raiding and the Chilean government continued to push southward throughout the 1850s.

In 1859 the Araucanians joined another Chilean rebellion. They were sparked in part by pressure from immigrants, principally Germans, who wanted land south of the Bío Bío River where the climate was similar to northern Europe. The guerrilla fighting raged for the next two years. During the bloody campaign, the army pushed farther and farther into Indian territory. More forts were built and small towns grew up under their protection.[8]

In November 1860 the French trader Aurelio Antonio de Tounens anointed himself King Orelie Antoine I of Patagonia and encouraged the Araucanians to exert their independence. Tounens was captured in January 1862, declared insane, and expelled. However, his actions demonstrated the tenuousness of Chile's sovereignty over the region and caused the government to more aggressively bring the region under its control.[9] Throughout the next two decades, increasing numbers of soldiers and amounts of money were dedicated to winning control over the south.

In 1878 the War of the Pacific (see chapter 34) broke out and a significant part of the frontier army was sent north to fight the Bolivians and the Peruvians. As a consequence, rebellious Araucanians were able to capture some of the border forts and to raid deep into colonized areas beginning in 1880. The following year army units, returning from their victories, began to suppress the uprising. This campaign took two years to accomplish.[10]

In 1883 the Chilean government signed a treaty which gave the Araucanians a small reservation subject to laws enacted by the national government. This "concession" to the Indians did not stop the southward movement of European descendants as the Araucanian preserve became crisscrossed by railroads and telegraph lines. Later the Araucanians were given representation in the Chilean Congress. The 350-year struggle against the Arucanians ended in the late nineteenth century with their subjugation.

THE RANQUELES

The Ranqueles was the name commonly used for the tribes in central and southern Argentina. These Indians roamed freely over the Pampas (commonly called the "desert" because it was largely unpopulated) as nomadic hunters, raiding ranches and settlements and frequently enslaving or killing whites. One did not have to venture more than a few miles from a city, including Buenos Aires, to be in Indian territory. The only law in the Pampas was that which the individual could personally enforce. This environment helped create the tough *gaucho* (cowboy), and the "toughest of the tough" Manuel de Rosas.

Due to the struggle between the Centralists and Federalists (see chapter 9) and a war with Brazil (see chapter 7), the Indian problem was tolerated by the United Provinces (today's Argentina) until 1833. Throughout the 1820s, almost annual military expeditions numbering between one and two thousand men were dispatched into the Pampas, but these did little more than maintain the status quo.[11]

In 1833 the United Provinces launched a three-column expedition against the Indians, the objective of which was to push back the frontier. Brig. Gen. José Félix Aldao led 800 men from San Carlos, Mendoza (530 mi W of Buenos Aires), southward. Gen. Jose Ruiz Huidobro led 1,000 men from San José del Morro, San Luis (364 mi W of Buenos Aires), in the same direction. And Juan Manuel de Rosas led 2,000 men from San Miguel del Monte (52 mi S of Buenos Aires), near the port of Buenos Aires, toward the south. These three columns, driving the Indians before them, converged at the Colorado River.[12] Charles Darwin, who visited Rosas' camp near the Río Colorado, described the army: "The soldiers were nearly all cavalry; and I should think such a villanous, banditti-like army, was never before collected together."[13]

Rosas could forge such men into an effective army because he was "tougher" than they were and a strict disciplinarian. Rosas pushed back the frontier in the south and the west as far as the Colorado River. During the campaign his followers killed 6,000 Indians and freed 2,000 captive Christians. Rosas built new forts and attempted to garrison them with his followers, to whom he granted land; he also paid tribute to some Indian chiefs. Although this campaign further enhanced his already considerable reputation, its effects were short-lived since the United Provinces were unable to maintain this forward defensive line.[14]

Between 1834 and 1855 the Ranqueles routinely raided the settlements in the southern and western parts of the province of Buenos Aires. Meanwhile, the white settlers were busy fighting among themselves over the issues of federalism versus centralism. Forts fell into disrepair and were abandoned.

In 1855 the chief Calfucurá led 5,000 Indians against the town of Azul (145 mi SW of Buenos Aires) where 300 inhabitants were either killed or taken as slaves. The Ranqueles then defeated a series of expeditions sent against them. On March 30, 1855, they defeated a 700-man force led by Col. Bartolomé Mitre at the Battle of Sierra Chica. The Argentine troops escaped during the night on foot after having lost 16 dead, 234 wounded, and most of their equipment. In 1856 the Indians ambushed a force of 124 militia (*Guardias nacionales*), killing all but two men. Later in 1856 Calfucurá defeated a force of 3,000 men supported by 12 artillery pieces led by Col. Manuel Hornos at Tapalqué (130 mi SW of Buenos Aires). Hornos lost 270 dead and wounded.[15]

Between the late 1850s and early 1870s, Argentina (having assumed that name in 1853), sent over a dozen small expeditions against the Indians with little success. The continuing raids by the Indians were sparked by the ever-encroaching barbed-wire fences. In early 1872, some 3,500 Indians sacked the frontier towns of Alvear, 25 de Mayo, and 9 de Julio. Gen. Ignacio Rivas, commanding 1,800 men, overtook the raiders near San Carlos Fortress (170 mi SE of Buenos Aires) and defeated them.[16]

By the administration of President Nicolás Avellaneda (1874–80), it was clear that appeasement by tribute, the strategy frequently employed since Rosas' campaign of the 1830s, had failed to pacify the Indians. General Julio A. Roca, Minister of War, put forth a new strategy: "[T]he best system of finishing with the Indians, either exterminating them or pushing them back of the Río Negro, is an offensive war. . . . Forts established in the middle of the desert kill discipline, decimate troops, and dominate little or no space."[17] Such a campaign was now possible because the decades-old struggle between the interior and the port of Buenos Aires had finally ended.

Congress appropriated 1.5 million pesos and Roca led a 6,000-man army, in large measure *gauchos*, south in 1879; this was the last militia campaign in Argentine history. The army advanced in five columns, pushing the Indians beyond the Negro and Neuquén Rivers. Killing Indians was the easiest part of the campaign. Supplying the troops was another matter; frequently they ate their horses. Many died from pneumonia and one division was decimated by smallpox. Six Indian chiefs were eliminated, 1,600 Indians were killed or taken prisoner in skirmishes, and over 10,000 Indians were captured. The Indians who escaped were driven out of the fertile Pampas into bleak Patagonia. Many of those captured were sent to work colonies in semitropical Sante Fé and Entre Ríos in northern Argentina. Some were jailed, others confined on the Martin Garcia Island, and many youths were made indentured domestic servants, their masters pledging to teach them Christianity.[18]

Although the campaigns against the Indians did not end until 1911, the campaign of 1879 marked significant changes in Argentina. The Indian problem began to disappear rapidly as did the influence of the *gaucho*; no longer would the cowboy determine the fate of the nation. Roca was rewarded for his success against the Indians with the title of "the Conqueror of the Desert" and elected president in 1880. Domingo Sarmiento wrote in 1879 "one is ashamed to think that we needed a powerful military establishment and at times eight thousand men to fight off just two thousand [Indian] lances."[19]

THE MAYANS

The Mayan struggle for independence against the Mexican government was significantly different from those of the Araucanians and the Ranqueles. The Mayans, who lived primarily in the Yucatan Peninsula and Central America, were more numerous than the two South American groups since the Mayans were mainly farmers and not nomadic hunters. They were tenuously integrated into colonial New Spain and its successor, Mexico, through the *encomienda* and the *repartimiento* (forced labor systems) with all of their abuses.[20]

In 1840 the *ladinos* (*criollos* and *mestizos*) of the Yucatan began fighting the central government of Mexico for their independence (see chapter 15). To succeed, they armed the Mayans and organized them into militias. Prior to this time the Indians were forbidden to use firearms. In exchange for their military service, the Mayans were promised land and relief from church taxes; neither promise was kept.

In 1847 the *ladinos* in Yucatan again declared their independence from Mexico and declared their neutrality in the war between the United States and Mexico. The Mayans chose this moment to rise up against the *ladinos*. The revolt began in the town of Valladolid on January 15, 1847, thus starting what is commonly called the "Caste War." Both sides committed rape, murder, and pillage. Initially the Indians held the advantage due to surprise and superior numbers. The Mayans drove the *ladinos* from their haciendas and hamlets and within a year isolated them within the towns of Mérida (1,211 mi ESE of Mexico City) and Campeche (820 mi SE of Mexico City). By 1848 the Mayans were poised to capture Mérida, a town of 48,000 inhabitants; however, their attack was interrupted by the need to plant maize, their food staple, and Mérida escaped probable destruction. The death toll had to be in the thousands.[21]

The reprieve from Indian attacks gave the *ladinos* time to organize. They followed the retiring Mayans into their cornfields and killed many. International events also turned favorable for the *ladinos*. In March 1848 the *ladinos* purchased 2,000 rifles and some artillery from the Spanish colonial government in Havana and received 300,000 pounds of corn from charitable organizations in Vera Cruz and New Orleans.

By mid-1848 it became clear that the *ladino* separatists' initiatives to seek admission into the United States or come under its protection were doomed, so they sought reinstatement into Mexico. The central government, having just lost one-third of the nation to the United States, was willing to let bygones be bygones. Mexico accepted; on August 17, 1848, the Yucatecans declared their reunification. Mexico used some of the money paid by the United States for the northern territory to buy guns from the departing Americans. In mid-July five ships landed 28,000 pesos, 1,000 rifles, 100,000 bullets, and 300 tons of gunpowder at Campeche.[22]

By mid-August 1848 the Mayans completed the planting in spite of the harassment of the *ladinos* and the Indians assembled a 5,000-man army. However, they proved no match for the rejuvenated *ladino* army. It swept across the peninsula and drove the Mayans into the bush which was, however, unmapped and unknown to the *ladinos*. Only the port of Bacalar (1,350 mi E of Mexico City), which was the prime commercial link with Belize and a source of munitions, remained in the hands of the Indians. The Indians harvested their hidden cornfields and again returned to fight.[23]

As gunpowder carried over land from Belize on mules became more plentiful, the Indians laid siege to the towns of Tihosuco and Saban in the spring of 1849. Both sides sustained considerable losses. Once again, these sieges were interrupted by planting season and the Indian need for more gunpowder.[24]

On April 20, 1849, the *ladinos* dispatched an expedition against Bacalar, the objective of which was to cut off the Mayan source of gunpowder from Belize. Some 800 troops, including about 150 American mercenaries, sailed from Sisal on board the Spanish steamboat *Cetro*. The ship's services were paid for by selling Mayas as slaves to Spaniards in Cuba, thus beginning a slave trade which lasted off and on for decades. Bacalar was tenaciously defended but in the end the *ladinos* triumphed. However, they now became the besieged as fresh Mayan warriors were brought against them.[25]

The war settled into a stalemate. Each side had battlefield successes that ran up the death toll but did not change the balance of power. The *ladinos* held virtually every population center and the Indians the interior. Between 1846 and 1850 the population of the peninsula decreased by some 247,000 persons. Since the Yucatan's wealth was not only its land but the people to work it, these losses were economically devastating.

On September 16, 1853, the Yucatecan provincial government and a faction of Mayans calling themselves the "Peaceful Indians of the South" (*indios pacíficos del sur*), signed a peace treaty which recognized much of modern day Quintana Roo (which at that time was part of the state of Yucatan) as being "independent." In 1855 the Mexican government wishfully declared the "Caste War" over, although both sides continued to kill, pillage, and enslave.[26]

From the mid-1850s through much of the 1870s, the *ladinos* in the Yucatan were caught up in the War of the *Reforma*, the French Intervention (see chapters 27 and 28), and the anarchy that followed. They had few resources to devote to the Mayan problem. By January 1873 the Mayans had conquered many of the smaller villages and were threatening Merída.[27]

Within a decade circumstances changed. Porfirio Díaz brought political stability and economic promise to Mexico at the cost of rights of the individual. His advisors, "*cientificos*" became increasingly interested in the Yucatan. During the second half of the nineteenth century, the region developed from one of Mexico's poorest provinces to one of its richest, thanks to the increasing demand for henequen (used to make rope).

In 1899 the Mexican government dispatched a major expedition under Gen. Ignacio Bravo to "solve" the Mayan problem. Although seventy years old, Bravo was an energetic and competent soldier. First, Bravo captured Bacalar on March 20, 1901. A flotilla of thirty machine gun-armed small craft patrolled the rivers. Bravo then divided his force, advanced into the interior along numerous routes, and captured the Indian capital of Chan de Santa Cruz on May 4. By 1902 the conquest of the Mayans was complete. Fifty *criollo* plantation owners took control of the peninsula and some 100,000 Indians worked in slavelike conditions farming henequen and chicle (used to produce chewing gum).[28]

THE YAQUI

The Yaqui, who inhabited northwestern old Mexico, settled into fertile valleys in the state of Sonora. Following Mexico's independence (1821), the Yaqui and the Mexican government fought sporadically. In 1826 Juan Ignacio Jusacamea led his tribesman into a revolt which lasted for a year. Pardoned, he led a second uprising in the early 1830s, during which he was caught and executed.[29]

In 1842 the Yaqui again took up arms, this time to defend the land between the Yaqui and Mayo Rivers. This struggle for land being encroached upon by farmers lasted for half a century. In 1868 the Yaqui, led by Cajeme (José María Leyva), again rebelled, this time in part because of the lack of protection from marauding Apache Indians from the north. In May 1873 the government sent a major expedition that temporarily subdued the Yaqui by 1877.[30]

In the 1880s the "*cientificos*" decided that the Yaqui were not adequately exploiting their rich land and, believing that Indians were hopelessly inferior, dealt with them as if they were animals. The Yaqui were pushed off their land and it was sold to wealthy *criollos* and foreigners so that they could grow rice and cotton, export crops.

In 1885 the Yaqui, again led by Cajeme, retreated into the mountains and from there conducted guerrilla warfare. In March 1886 a 1,200-man force was sent against the Indians. The government soldiers encircled the Yaqui stronghold by fortifying key towns on its perimeter. On May 11 Col. Lorenzo Torres, leading 300 soldiers, attacked 4,000 Yaqui at their mountain fortress of Buatachive. The Yaqui were defeated, losing 200 dead and 2,000 captured. The Mexicans lost twenty-one dead and forty-eight wounded. Cajeme fled deeper into the mountains.

On June 21 Colonel Torres caught Cajeme in the open. The poorly armed Indians were again easily defeated. On April 12, 1887, Cajeme was betrayed, captured, and shot and his followers who were caught were sold for seventy-five pesos a head to the henequen plantation owners in Quintana Roo where most of them died. This practice continued until 1910 when the Mexican Revolution broke out.[31]

Figure 26. The Indians, 1819–1927. A Mexican soldier stands ready to march against the Yaqui Indians. Both cavalry and infantry were used to fight the Yaqui in northern Mexico. Typically, Mexican armies were not supported by logistical trains filled with the necessities for the campaign. Either the soldier or his family, which frequently followed him into the field, carried what was needed, or he did without. *Copied from* Harper's New Monthly Magazine, *Vol. 79 (November 1889).*

The Yaqui continued to resist. On May 15, 1892, Chief Juan Tabas, leading 3,000 Indians, attacked and captured Navojoa. Seven years later, on July 21, 1899, Yaqui chiefs sent an ultimatum to now-General Torres demanding that all whites leave the state of Sonora. In the fighting that followed, the Yaqui suffered numerous defeats. On January 18, 1900, Torres defeated the Yaqui at Mazocoda in hand-to-hand fighting. Some 400 Yaqui were killed and 1,800 captured. Half of the captives died during a forced march into captivity. The Mexicans lost 56 killed and 104 wounded. In spite of these losses, the Yaqui continued to resist. At each skirmish the government's losses were significantly less than those of the Indians. Following each defeat, the Yaqui were hunted down by government forces and those caught were sold into slavery. On August 31, 1900, the government declared the campaign at an end although skirmishes continued into 1902.[32]

These and other abuses made the Yaqui willing soldiers against Porfirio Díaz in the Mexican Revolution (1910–20). Yaqui Indians were the backbone of the force raised in 1912 by Alvaro Obregón to oppose the usurper Victoriano Huerta. Although promised much for their services, they received little.[33]

In September 1926 the Yaqui robbed a train in Sonora that was carrying former President Alvaro Obregón. On September 13 the Mexican government declared them in open rebellion and launched a campaign to suppress the Yaqui once and for all. Aircraft were used to track and bomb the Indians. The fighting, which took place in the Sierra Occidental, continued for a year. The Yaqui surrendered to Gen. Francisco Manzo on July 28, 1927.[34]

OBSERVATIONS

The "solution" to the "hostile" Indian problem in Latin America by extermination and confinement was no more cruel than that practiced in North America by the United States. The Araucanians, Ranqueles, and Yaqui were perceived to impede economic progress and to be threats to society.

The post-independence struggles against the Mayans were different. The Mayans were perceived to be a threat becuse they significantly outnumbered the *ladinos*. This perception was exacerbated when the *ladinos* further isolated themselves from their kinsman in Mexico City by proclaiming their independence. The struggle against the Mayans became a race war; success was measured in the numbers killed and not the amount of land conquered.

Eventually, the superior weapons of the government overwhelmed the Indians. Well into the latter decades of the nineteenth century, governments troops, like the Indians, frequently had to rely on edged weapons due to a shortage of firearms and gunpowder. Once machine guns and aircraft were employed by government forces, the Indians were doomed.

Map 10. Southwest Coast of South America, 1878.

PART 11

AN ECONOMIC WAR

CHAPTER THIRTY-FOUR

THE WAR OF THE PACIFIC, 1879–83

> The fundamental cause of the War of the Pacific was the mounting power and prestige, the economic and political stability of Chile on the one hand and the weakness, the political and economic deterioration of Bolivia and Peru on the other.
>
> —Fredrick Pike

THE SPARK

On February 23, 1878, Bolivia passed an export duty on nitrate in place of existing taxes. Chile perceived this to be a flagrant disregard of Bolivia's treaty obligations toward Chilean citizens in the nitrate-rich province of Atacama.[1]

BACKGROUND

The province of Atacama, or more accurately the desert by that name, was poorly administered for decades following the Wars for Independence by those who claimed it due to its seeming insignificance and inhospitality. Although both Bolivia and Chile claimed the territory, initially neither concerned themselves with establishing a boundary. In 1839 valuable guano deposits were discovered in the desert. In 1866 while Bolivia and Chile were allied in a war against Spain, they signed a treaty establishing their boundary at the 24th parallel, south latitude, and also providing that Chileans, who already owned land between the 23rd and 24th parallels, should be allowed to mine and export without increased taxation or hindrance by the Bolivian government.[2]

Diplomatic disputes soon occurred between Bolivia and Chile concerning the interpretation of this treaty. On February 6, 1873, Bolivia and Peru concluded a secret defensive treaty which provided that if either Bolivia or Peru were attacked by a foreign nation (obviously, it was directed against Chile), the other nation would go to the aid of the co-signer.

On February 23, 1878, Bolivia levied an export duty of ten centavos per each hundredweight on all nitrates, including those mined by Chileans between the 23rd and 24th parallels. When the Chilean government protested the tariff, the Bolivian government not only refused to rescind the export duty but declared it retroactive and further decreed that if it were not paid before February 14, 1879, the nitrates in the possession of the Chilean exporters would be sold by auction. Soon, Bolivia cancelled the concession with the Chilean companies, seized their properties, and confiscated the nitrates.

On February 14, 1879, a Chilean naval expedition seized the principal Bolivian nitrate port of Antofagasta. At the same time Chilean warships occupied the roadsteads of Cobija, Mejillones, and Tocopilla.[3]

On March 18 Bolivia declared war and confiscated all Chilean property in Bolivia and under the terms of a secret treaty asked for Peru's assistance against Chile. Initially, a strong antiwar movement emerged in Lima. In an attempt to head off war, Peruvian President Mariano Ignacio Prado sent the diplomat José Antonio Lavalle to Santiago, Chile, but, ultimately, Peruvian decision-makers feared that if they did not honor the secret treaty, Bolivia might join with Chile and seize Peru's Tarapacá nitrate fields.[4]

Peru acquiesced to Bolivia's request and began to prepare for war. President Prado sent José Arnaldo Márquez to Argentina in an attempt to draw that nation into a military alliance against Chile. However, Argentina's boundary dispute with Chile had lost much of its intensity since the early 1870s; therefore, Buenos Aires saw no advantage to an alliance.[5]

Chile, learning of the Peruvian preparations for war, wanted to know the reason for these activities and demanded that they stop. Chile was not satisfied with Peru's reply and, therefore, declared war on April 5 and let it be known that it was aware of the secret treaty. Peru declared war on Chile the same day.

OPPOSING FORCES

Naval power would play a critical role given the geographical barriers and the lack of railroads and roads. The Chilean navy was substantially superior to that of Peru. The backbones of the fleet were the two central battery ironclads *Almirante Cochrane* and *Blanco Encalada*. Built in the mid-1870s, they were newer, larger, and more heavily armed and armored than the Peruvian seagoing monitor *Huáscar* and the central-battery armored frigate *Independencia*.[6] The Peruvian ships had been built a decade earlier and this was an era when naval technology was rapidly improving. More important than the ships, following the Pacific War with Spain (see chapter 30), the Chilean navy had fostered the education of its officer corps and the training of the crews. Some of the officers had gained valuable experience in foreign service. Conversely, the Peruvian government had neglected its navy following the war with Spain. Most of the enlisted personnel and technicians were either Chileans or castoffs from foreign navies and merchant marines. Bolivia had no navy.[7]

The allies—Peru and Bolivia—had a significant manpower advantage. Peru's population was 2.7 million; Bolivia's about 2 million; and Chile's 2.1 million.[8]

Prior to the war, the Chilean standing army was composed of 2,694 men (1,660 infantry; 634 cavalry; and 400 artillerymen). Although small, it was better organized and better disciplined than that of Peru. Also, the Chileans had developed a mobilization plan. By April 5, 1879, the army swelled to six infantry regiments (6,800 men), an artillery regiment and group (470 men), and two cavalry regiments (636 men). In addition, the Chilean National Guard (militia) was composed of 6,687 men. The army was armed with a variety of weapons. The rifles were of foreign manufacture by Comblain, Grass, Minié, Beaumont, and Remington. Although produced by many manufacturers, most fired the same caliber cartridge (11 millimeter) and Chile operated a modern ammunition factory in Santiago. The Chilean army possessed seventy-five artillery pieces, most of which were Krupp and Limache manufacture, and six Gatling guns. The cavalry was armed with French sabers and Winchester and Spencer carbines.[9]

Prior to the war the Peruvian army was some 10,000 men strong—which included more than 3,000 national police and police in Lima. Of these, 2,679 were officers. The army was composed largely of Quechua Indians. After the declaration of war, all males between eighteen and thirty years of age were liable for conscription and those above the age of thirty were subject to service in the reserves. The most common rifle in the Peruvian army was the French Chassepot. At the beginning of the war Peru had no modern field artillery.[10] The army lacked specialists—commissariats and engineers—and a general staff. The mounts used by the Peruvian cavalry were small and inferior to those of the Chileans.[11]

When war broke out the Bolivian army had 2,232 infantry backed by a 54,000-man National Guard (militia) that existed on paper. The bulk of the soldiers were Aymará Indians. The *Colorados* Battalion was armed with Remington rolling-block rifles but the remainder was armed with odds and ends—including flintlock muskets. The artillery had three rifled 3-pounders and four machine guns. The cavalry—which rode mules because of the shortage of good horses—was armed with sabers and miscellaneous fire arms.[12]

Despite the apparent qualitative differences, some contemporary analysts believed that Bolivia and Peru could win a war against Chile. They reasoned that the combined armies of Peru and Bolivia were large enough to overwhelm the Chileans. Furthermore, because the two navies were equal in size—little attention was paid to the Chilean navy's technologically superior warships and better trained personnel—the edge was given to the allies.

OPENING STRATEGIES

Chilean President Aníbal Pinto wanted his navy to immediately attack Peru's principal port and naval base, Callao. Should the harbor defenses prove too strong to permit the destruction or capture of the Peruvian fleet, the President wanted the Chilean navy to blockade the Peruvian port. Adm. Juan Williams Rebolledo[13] believed that Callao was too far from the nearest safe port, Antofagasta, which was 813 miles to the south. The Admiral preferred to attack Iquique, the principal Peruvian port in the south and only 154 miles north of Antofagasta.[14]

The Peruvian strategy was to harass the Chileans with its navy but to refuse direct combat—and the risk of losing precious ships—thereby giving the nation adequate time to prepare its numerically superior army to confront the Chileans on land. Bolivia's strategy was to await an expected Chilean invasion of the Bolivian highlands, the *altiplano*. This would allow them to fight in the highlands to which they were acclimated and prevent them from having to make the long trek to the coast.[15]

PREPARATIONS FOR WAR

Following the Chilean occupation of the Bolivian ports, the belligerents spent the next few months carrying out naval operations and preparing for the land campaign. Each country took steps to raise new army units. In Peru, thousands of Indians were brought in from the interior to fill out the ranks.

The Chilean navy blockaded Iquique—Peru's principal port in the far south—and used its anchorage as a base of operations for its raids on Peruvian ports, beginning the destruction of that nation's economic and war potential. The Peruvian navy, by contrast, was not yet ready to fight. The *Huáscar* lay at Callao with her boilers removed for retubing, and it took more than a month to get her operational.

Bolivia decided to send its army to the coast as soon as it became obvious that the Chileans would not be so accommodating as to invade the *altiplano*. Two routes were available. The easier from La Paz was across Lake Titicaca to Puno, Peru, and then by rail to Mollendo. The more difficult route was by foot to Tacna. The Peruvians requested that the Bolivian army march to Tacna because of their weakness there. The Bolivian army marched out of La Paz on April 17, 1879, and arrived in Tacna on the thirtieth, a distance of 252 miles. Many of the soldiers were shoeless.[16] On May 2 Captain-General Hilarión Daza (the Bolivian President, although the Constitution required him to relinquish that office while at the head of the army) telegraphed to President Prado: "Nine thousand men of the Bolivian army [in fact, perhaps 3,000 men] under my command, badly dressed, poorly armed, but full of enthusiasm and valor, stand ready to receive your orders."[17] As previously agreed upon, Prado took charge because they were on Peruvian soil.

GRAU SEIZES THE INITIATIVE

Finally, on May 16, a Chilean squadron, composed of the *Blanco Encalada*, *Almirante Cochrane*, *O'Higgins*, *Chacabuco*, *Abtao*, and auxiliaries sailed north to reconnoiter Callao. Admiral Williams was seeking a decisive engagement with the Peruvian fleet. The old wooden corvette *Esmeralda* and the gunboat *Covadonga* were left behind to blockade Iquique. On the same day, Peruvian Capt. Miguel Grau[18] sailed south with the *Huáscar* and the *Independencia* escorting three transports carrying troops commanded by General Prado, the President of Peru, and arms for the Bolivians at Tacna and Arica. The two fleets did not sight each other.

Upon arriving at Arica, Captain Grau learned that the two Chilean ships were blockading Iquique, sixty miles south of Arica. He decided to attack. On May 21, 1879, the substantially superior *Huáscar* and *Independencia* fought it out with the Chilean warships *Esmeralda* and *Covadonga*. The *Huáscar* closed to within three hundred yards of the *Esmeralda*—which could only steam at four knots owing to the poor condition of her boilers. The main battery of the Peruvian seagoing monitor was so ineffective that Grau was finally forced to try to ram the Chilean warship with the *Huáscar*. During the first attempt Commander Arturo Prat,[19] the captain of the *Esmeralda*, with sword and pistol in hand, boarded the *Huáscar*; he was followed by 1st Sgt. Juan de Dios Aldea and a sailor, Arsenio Canave. All three were killed. During the second ramming attempt, Lt. Ignacio Serrano and about a dozen men again tried to take the *Huáscar* by boarding; the majority were killed or captured and a few escaped over the side of the Peruvian ironclad. After a four-hour fight, the *Huáscar* made a third attempt to ram. This time it was successful and the *Esmeralda* sank. Of the Chilean ship's two hundred officers and men, only fifty-four survived. One man on the *Huáscar* was killed. The Chilean blockade of Iquique was broken.

While the action between the *Huáscar* and the *Esmeralda* was taking place, the *Covadonga* enticed the larger *Independencia* onto some rocks, where she became stranded. Her loss was a severe blow to the Peruvian navy. Now it had but one armored ship, the *Huáscar*, which, because it was essentially a seagoing monitor, was inferior to either of the Chilean warships *Blanco Encalada* or *Almirante Cochrane*.

The *Covadonga* made her escape to Antofagasta. On May 26 Admiral Grau reconnoitered Antofagasta, but the *Covadonga* was protected by shore batteries so he sailed north to Callao.[20]

While the *Huáscar* was undergoing repairs after the battle, some of the gunners were replaced because of their overall poor performance. Grau was promoted to rear admiral. In the meantime, the Chilean navy had reinstituted the blockade of Iquique.

After her repairs were completed, the *Huáscar* cruised the coast, evading the Chilean squadrons, and made sudden and unexpected appearances at Carrizal, Chañaral, Huasco, Antofagasta, Tocopilla, Taltal, and Caldera along the Chilean coast. On July 23 the *Huáscar* captured the large transport *Rimac*, carrying a Chilean cavalry squadron and a large number of water skins intended for use during the march across the Atacama Desert. The *Huáscar*'s activities caused the Chilean navy to assign warships to convoy duty, practically paralyzed the seaborne movements of the Chilean army, and created a public outcry.[21]

The activities of the *Huáscar* could not be ignored, and the Chilean navy moved to end the threat. The blockade of Iquique was abandoned on August 2, and all major fleet units were sent to Valparaíso for reconditioning—except for the two ships protecting Antofagasta, the *Magallanes* and the *Abtao*, where the Chilean water supply was exposed to naval gunfire. On August 25, the *Huáscar* entered Antofagasta and attacked the Chilean warships. The ships saved themselves by seeking cover behind neutral merchant ships. Grau fired only one Lay torpedo at the *Abtao*. The weapon turned back on the *Huáscar* and Lt. Diaz Canseco jumped overboard and deflected its course.[22]

Grau's audacity heightened consternation in Chile and embarrassed the Chilean navy. Admiral Williams Rebolledo resigned because of "ill health" and Capt. Galvarino Riveros[23] replaced him as commander of the Chilean squadron. Chile overhauled its ironclads *Blanco Encalada* and *Almirante Cochrane* to improve their speed. This was a major undertaking because Chile had no dry dock. Divers painstakingly cleaned the ships' bottoms an inch at a time by hand. The ships' boilers needed new tubing and 1,800 boiler tubes were made by hand in Santiago. When the work was complete, the *Almirante Cochrane* could make 11 knots, still less than the *Huáscar*'s best top speed of 12.3 knots.[24]

BATTLE OF ANGAMOS

While the Chilean navy was finishing its preparations, President Prado ordered Grau to make another raid south. Grau advised against this because the *Huáscar*'s speed had in the meantime been significantly reduced due to fouling of her bottom. However, the Peruvian President was insistent. On September 3, the *Huáscar* and the sloop *Unión* sailed first to Iquique, then to Coquimbo and Antofagasta. Finding nothing, the Peruvian ironclad sailed south to Los Vilos, a small port to the north of Valparaíso. Then the *Huáscar* rejoined the *Unión* off Point Tetas and headed north.[25]

On October 1 the Chilean fleet, centered around the reconditioned ironclads *Blanco Encalada* and *Almirante Cochrane*, sailed from Valparaíso and headed north to hunt the *Huáscar*. After a visit to Arica, the squadron split in two, one ironclad assigned to each half. On the morning of October 8 the *Huáscar* and the *Unión* were trapped between the two Chilean squadrons. Admiral Grau ordered the *Unión* to escape, a feat she accomplished owing to her superior speed. The *Huáscar*, however, was unable to outrace her opponents; therefore, Grau decided to fight it out.[26] The Admiral was killed at the beginning of the fight and the steam system was also hit. The *Huáscar* became unmanageable and her speed fell off. After a

Figure 27. War of the Pacific, 1879–83. At the Battle of Angamos (October 8, 1879) the Chilean ironclads *Almirante Cochrane* and *Blanco Encalada* captured the Peruvian seagoing monitor *Huáscar*. The bloody battle lasted ninety minutes. Following the death of Admiral Miguel Grau, four other Peruvians succeeded to command only to be killed. The *Huáscar* is now preserved in Talcahuano, Chile. *Courtesy Chilean Navy.*

punishing ninety-minute battle, the Chileans captured the *Huáscar*. Admiral Grau, four succeeding commanding officers, and about thirty other Peruvians died. Of the 150 shots fired at the *Huáscar*, seventy-six hit the target.[27]

With the capture of the *Huáscar* the Chilean navy won control of the sea, gained unimpaired mobility, and tied Bolivian and Peruvian land forces to defensive positions in a barren and mountainous terrain not easily traversed. The Chilean navy still had to overcome Peruvian coastal fortifications.

THE CAPTURE OF IQUIQUE

On November 2 a Chilean expedition of 4,890 men carried in twenty ships and escorted by four warships attacked Pisagua, one hundred miles north of Iquique. Pisagua was a small nitrate port (in fact, an open roadstead) perched at the foot of a 1,200-foot-high bluff. Access to the interior could only be gained by a rail line and two narrow paths, and surrounding terrain afforded significant advantages to the defenders. Pisagua was defended by 895 Bolivians and 285 Peruvians (mostly untrained volunteers)—plus two 100-pound guns. By 9:30 in the morning, the Chilean warships had silenced the two big guns and a landing was attempted to the north of the town but was repulsed, while a second landing south of Pisagua succeeded and soon 1,940 men were ashore. This force was to hold the attention of the defenders while 2,175 Chileans landed at undefended Junín Cove, six miles south of Pisagua. Finally, these men seized the initiative and fought their way up the bluff. After two hours of hard fighting, they carried the heights. The allies lost some 200 men with 60 wounded, the Chileans lost 58 dead and 173 wounded. Many of the wounded later died because in the rush to load the expedition the ambulances had been left behind. The victory was so swift that the allies failed to destroy valuable rolling stock before fleeing.[28]

From Pisagua the Chileans marched east-southeast and captured Agua Santa on November 6. They then turned south and captured Dolores. This assured the Chileans of abundant fresh water and positioned the Chilean army between allied-held Iquique to the south and the source of the allies' supplies in central Peru.[29]

Reacting to the Chilean landing, President Prado decided to counterattack. Prado's plan was to have Captain-General Daza march south from Tacna with three thousand Bolivians and Gen. José Buendia, commanding 10,000 allied troops near Iquique, to march north. The two forces were to unite near the gorge of Camiña at the railroad line running from Pisagua. Daza was then to assume command of the combined force.

Daza marched out of Tacna on November 4 but lingered at Arica until the eleventh. He began to march across the desert in the heat of the day without adequate water supply (many of the canteens of the soldiers' were filled with wine) or a guide. By the time they reached Camarones on the fourteenth, the Bolivians were exhausted. After telegraphing Prado, the army turned back.[30]

Meanwhile, General Buendia had marched thirty miles across the desert in three days to Dolores. While preparing to attack the Chileans, the Bolivians in Buendia's army learned of Daza's withdrawal and became demoralized; however, Buendia persuaded them to remain. On November 19, the Peruvian advance guard precipitously attacked the Chilean artillery which had been mounted on Santiago Hill near the town. The Chileans rushed troops to defend the guns and the opposing forces collided at the gun emplacements. The Peruvians had been mauled by the Chilean artillery and were driven back by the Chilean infantry. Worse still, General Buendia, who was with the advance guard, lost contact with the remainder of the army and chaos followed. Apparently, Bolivians mistook Peruvians for the enemy—because of the similarity of their uniforms—and fired on them. The army fell back in confusion. By 5 P.M., the battle was over. The Chileans lost 208 killed and wounded (most of the wounded dying later) and the allies 220 killed, 76 wounded, and 100 prisoners. More critically, the surviving Bolivians quit the war and walked home. Unable to sustain his exposed position, Buendia abandoned his artillery and the Peruvian troops trekked back across the desert with little food or water. They found refuge at Tarapacá four days later.[31]

Buendia now believed his position at Iquique to be indefensible and evacuated the port. The Chileans occupied it on November 26, thus gaining control of the nitrate ports from which Bolivia and Peru derived a large percentage of their revenues.

BATTLE OF TARAPACÁ

The 1,182 allies who had evacuated Iquique joined Buendia's force, about 5,000 men, at Tarapacá. A 2,300-man Chilean force shadowed the retiring allies, which it incorrectly believed to be demoralized. The Chileans hoped to lure the Peruvians into a battle in which they could take advantage of their longer range artillery. On November 27, the Chilean force, its vision obscured by a thick desert mist, inadvertently advanced to within half a mile of the allies' position. The allies seized the initiative and quickly attacked. At close quarters, the Chileans lost the advantage of their superior artillery, and by the end of the day they were forced to retreat. The Chileans lost 516 killed, 179 wounded, and 52 prisoners—plus eight of their ten field guns. The allies lost 236 killed and 337 as wounded, among which were a significant number of officers. This victory temporarily rejuvenated allied morale. Also, Colonels Andrés Cáceres and Francisco Bolognesi emerged as national Peruvian leaders. Following this victory, Buendia chose to abandoned the south and he retired unmolested to Arica, where he arrived on December 18.[32]

COUPS D'ETATS ROCK PERU AND BOLIVIA

On November 26, President Prado gave command of the Peruvian army at Arica to Rear Adm. Lizardo Montero and returned to Lima. In the capital he found that Congress had refused to vote for taxes to pay for the war but instead had decided to rely on the old, easy practice of increasing the supply of paper money. Continuing the decadeslong struggle between Liberals and Conservatives, prominent members of the opposition refused to serve in Prado's cabinet. On December 17 the President shocked Lima when he sailed for Europe with the stated purpose—perhaps sincere—of raising money to purchase new ironclads. General La Puerta, the Vice President, took charge of the government. On December 21 Gen. Nicolas de Piérola—one of those who had refused to serve in Prado's cabinet—rebelled against the government. Supported by the majority in the capital who believed that Prado was running away, Piérola entered Lima the next day and declared himself Supreme Chief of the Nation. As if that were not enough with which to deal, on January 7, 1880, a landslide blocked the Oroya rail line, effectively closing communications between Lima and the interior.[33]

On December 25 Captain-General Daza said he would not recognize the Piérola government and would return to Bolivia to deal with growing unrest. However, while Daza was conferring with Admiral Montero on December 27 at Arica, the Bolivian army at Tacna revolted; this was followed the next day by a revolt in La Paz. A primary cause of the army's discontent was Daza's inept leadership—particularly his conduct during the illfated expedition south which became known as "the retreat of the shrimp" (*la retirada de Camarones*). On December 29 Gen. Narciso Campero[34] was named provisional president. Contrary to expectations, the events in Bolivia strengthened the alliance because the Peruvians had never trusted Daza fully.[35]

THE CAPTURE OF TACNA AND ARICA

While Peru and Bolivia were rocked by revolts, the Chileans were planning their campaign against the port of Arica and the town of Tacna (14,000 inhabitants). Arica was the Pacific terminus of the primary trade route to Bolivia's capital, La Paz. A rail line ran northward only as far as Tacna, a distance of thirty-five miles, and from there to La Paz one had to walk the ancient trail.

Arica's seaward defenses were formidable—twenty heavy guns, the monitor *Manco Capac*, and a small torpedo boat. The Chilean navy had been successful in stemming the flow of most materials to southern Peru. In an isolated success the Peruvian navy's *Union* did run out through the blockade to Callao and returned with munitions. The steam sloop again successfully ran out through the blockade on that same day and again escaped from Arica. Attacking

Arica from the rear, where its defenses were the weakest, was not feasible so long as the allies had a strong army at Tacna.[36]

Chilean Minister of War, Rafael Sotomayor, and Commander-in-Chief of the Army, Gen. Erasmo Escala, disagreed on the readiness of the army to attack Tacna and Arica. Escala demanded additional troops and only agreed to lead the expedition on the condition that he be absolved from any responsibility should the campaign fail. Some 10,000 troops landed at Ilo (100 mi NW of Arica) on February 26; the port offered no resistance. Sotomayor hoped that this invasion would cause the allied army to advance from Tacna and give battle. When this did not happen, the Chilean army attacked the port of Mollendo hoping to draw the allies from their stronghold.[37]

The environment around Ilo proved very inhospitable and within a short time the health of the army deteriorated. The senior officials continued to argue. General Escala renounced his command and he was replaced by the commander of the cavalry, Gen. Manuel Baquedano.[38] The army marched to Ite (69 mi NW of Arica). The advance on Tacna was delayed due to the shortage of wagons. On May 20 Sotomayor died of a stroke. By May 25 the Chileans were within six miles of Tacna.[39]

BATTLE OF TACNA

While the Chileans were isolating Tacna from the north, the new Bolivian Captain-General, Campero, arrived in Tacna on April 19 with between 2,000 and 3,000 men. Admiral Montero had already moved the Peruvian army from Arica to the town. Campero assumed command of the 13,650-man force (8,500 Peruvians and 5,150 Bolivians). He wanted to fall back twenty miles north of Tacna to the Sama Valley, a site that offered a strong defensive position and abundant water. However, the Peruvians thought the plan impractical because of the lack of draft animals, and they also opposed the idea of abandoning Tacna.[40]

Campero created a double defensive line to the southwest along the crest of a plateau with the flanks protected by deep ravines. The army was completely integrated—Bolivian and Peruvian units alternated across the battlefield. Campero learned from some captives that the Chileans would attack *en masse* on the twenty-sixth. So, he decided to launch a surprise attack the night before. The force got lost in the dark and staggered back into camp at 5 A.M.—two hours before the Chilean attack.[41]

On May 26 General Baquedano, commanding 14,000 men, opened the attack with his 12-pound Krupp guns which outranged those of the enemy and soon destroyed them. The one-hour bombardment was followed by a four-column Chilean attack along the entire front. By 2 P.M. those defending the northern part of the line fell back, causing a general retreat. The allies lost 2,500 killed and wounded which included 400 prisoners. The Chileans lost 687 killed and 1,032 wounded. Most of the surviving allies fled to the town where the Bolivians quit the fight and continued all the way back to La Paz. Baquedano captured Tacna and now turned his attention to Arica.[42]

THE BATTLE OF ARICA

Following the Battle of Tacna, Montero ordered Bolognesi, who commanded the garrison at Arica, to retreat north along the Andes Mountains. Montero, commanding the Peruvian survivors who had fought at Tacna, marched northward but Bolognesi, after consulting his officers, chose to defend Arica.

Figure 28. War of the Pacific, 1879–83. Chilean troops land at Arica following its capture on June 5, 1880. In the background looms the 1,200-foot-high rock, *El Morro*. Some of Peru's most capable officers, including Col. Francisco Bolognesi, fought to the death defending this high ground. *Courtesy Jesús Torres Chavera.*

The southern end of the port was dominated by the lofty rock *El Morro*, which rose to 1,200 feet, upon which the Peruvians mounted ten heavy guns. North of the port the Peruvians built three redoubts named *Dos de Mayo* (3 heavy guns), *Santa Rosa* (3 heavy guns), and *San José* (4 heavy guns). In addition, each had a Gatling gun. The open roadstead was protected by the U.S.-built monitor *Manco Capac* (two 380-pound guns) and a torpedo brigade with the torpedo boat *Alianza* stationed at Alacrán island to the south of *El Morro*. Colonel Bolognesi commanded 1,400 infantrymen, 300 artillery apprentices, 250 sailors from the wrecked *Independencia*, 50 poorly armed, mounted civilian volunteers, and a few Bolivian soldiers who had escaped after the battle of Tacna.[43]

On June 5, the Chileans opened a land and sea bombardment. By the end of the day, some eighty heavy shells had been fired by both sides. At daybreak on the seventh, the Chilean infantry simultaneously attacked the defenses at the rear of *El Morro* and the three redoubts. The Peruvians had planted dynamite in the landward approach to *El Morro* and detonated it under the feet of the first Chilean charge. The second wave was infuriated and took the heights at bayonet point. As defeat appeared imminent, Colonel Bolognesi called on his Peruvian troops to fight to their last cartridge and he sacrificed his own life as an example. When Capt. José Sánchez Lagomarsino perceived that the battle was lost, he scuttled the *Manco Capac*. The allies lost 700 killed, including Colonels Bolognesi and Ugarte plus Captain Moore and most of the defenders on *El Morro*, and 1,328 prisoners. The Chileans lost 473 killed and more than 200 wounded. Chile now controlled southern Peru and decided to carry the war to central Peru.[44]

BLOCKADING CALLAO

On April 10, 1880, the Chilean fleet appeared off Callao (1,306 mi N of Valparaíso), and its commander, Rear Admiral Riveros (promoted after the Battle of Angamos), declared a blockade of the port. Callao was Peru's chief seaport, lying eight miles seaward from Lima, the capital; therefore, since colonial days, it had been heavily fortified. In 1880 the port boasted twenty-seven heavy guns, numerous old 32-pounders, the monitor *Atahualpa*, the *Unión*, one U.S.-built Herreshoff torpedo boat, steam launches, a torpedo brigade, mines, and an experimental submarine. Initially, the Chilean blockading squadron was made up of the *Blanco Encalada*, *Huáscar*, *Angamos*, *Pilcomayo*, and transport *Matias Cousino*. As the blockade dragged on for nine months, most of the Chilean navy—including its recently acquired torpedo boats—saw service before Callao. The two sides dueled with artillery; both sides sustained damage.[45]

The Peruvian navy, having lost its major warships, had to attack the enemy with unconventional means. On May 25, the new Chilean torpedo boat *Janequeo* was sunk in Callao harbor when Lt. José Galvez[46] of the Peruvian navy floated a 100-pound case of gunpowder from a steam launch onto the *Janequeo* and detonated it with a pistol shot. Both launches went down. On July 3 the Chileans discovered an abandoned boat loaded with fresh vegetables at anchor sixteen miles north of Callao. The prize was towed into the Chilean anchorage and tied alongside the transport *Loa*. As the last of the boat's cargo was being unloaded, a tremendous explosion ripped a fifteen-foot gash in the side of the *Loa*. She sank and at least fifty of her crew perished. Some type of explosive had been hidden in the vegetable-filled ship. While blockading Chancay, the Chilean warship *Covadonga* discovered a launch with a fine gig astern. The *Covadonga*'s guns sank the launch and the seemingly harmless gig was brought alongside and hoisted on board. As it was being hauled up the davits, the gig exploded with such a force that the starboard side of the *Covadonga* was shattered and she sank. The Chileans retaliated for these losses by bombarding Chancay, Ancon, and Chorrillos.[47]

RAVAGING THE NORTH

Beginning on September 4, 1880, Capt. Patricio Lynch of the Chilean navy led a 3,000-man force that laid waste to the Peruvian coast between Callao and Payta, 505 miles to the north. The force landed at Huacho, Supe, Chimbote, Salaverry, Trujillo, Pascamayo, Chiclayo, Eten, Lambayeque, and Payta, destroying everything of potential value—factories, shops, dwellings, warehouses, water tanks, farms, crops, rolling stock, locomotives, and bridges. The expedition paralyzed the flow of commerce in northern Peru.[48]

THE PERUVIAN NAVY'S LAST HOPE

Peru's situation grew more desperate with each passing day. For the navy, an event of the previous year offered a flicker of hope. On October 12, 1879, four days after the *Huáscar* had been captured, Federico Blume Othon[49] launched in Paita his submarine, the *Toro Submarino* (underwater bull). On the surface, she was powered by a small steam engine; semisubmerged, the boat ran on a compressed air motor. Blume took her underwater for the first time on October 14. The craft semisubmerged to twelve feet (the two viewing towers and snorkels remaining above water), navigated at three knots, and remained down for thirty minutes. After eighteen more test dives, the submarine and her inventor were transported by sea to Callao about five hundred miles to the south, where, following much delay, Blume demonstrated his craft's submersible capability. President Piérola appointed a committee of naval officers and engineers to study the invention. The government dedicated 10,000 souls to the work of building an improved craft. The construction began at Cristobal del Tren.

Before the new boat was ready, the situation at Callao grew desperate. The blockade had been tightened and Callao and Lima were threatened. The Peruvian government decided to modify and use the original boat constructed by Blume. The two viewing towers were replaced by one amidships, the two snorkels were removed, and four Lay torpedoes, each carrying ten pounds of dynamite, were fitted externally, rigged to detonate on impact. The Lay torpedo of 1870 was a semisubmerged automobile torpedo controlled remotely by an electric cable. Whether these torpedoes were to be launched, dropped, or attached to spars is unclear. Midshipman Manuel Elias Bonnemaison tested the craft. The *Blanco Encalada* and the *Almirante Cochrane*, the backbone of the Chilean fleet, were chosen as targets. The attack was to be carried out at night, but before it could take place the Chilean warships retired, possibly alerted to the danger by a spy.[50]

THE UNITED STATES ATTEMPTS TO MEDIATE

After a futile series of peace talks on board the U.S. steam sloop *Lackawanna* in October 1880, Chile began to advance from Tacna to Lima. A force of 23,621 men and 63 guns disembarked at Pisco from November 22 through 24, 1880, and then moved by sea to another point some twenty-five miles south of Lima. The last naval engagement occurred on December 6 when Chilean torpedo boats attacked a Peruvian launch, sparking a general bombardment of Callao that lasted an hour and a half. Within six weeks the Chilean army was ready to march against Lima.

THE ATTACK ON LIMA

The army defending Lima was of uneven quality. The regular troops numbered about 26,500 men. In addition, every male resident of Lima between the ages of sixteen and sixty was required to fight. The younger ones were used to fill out the ranks of the regular units, but most were placed in the reserves. These 7,000 conscripts were of dubious value due to their age, training, and equipment. President Piérola chose to man two defensive lines. The first extended along a range of hills from Punta Chorrillos, near Callao, to Monterico Chico, in the shape of a crescent, a distance of about eight miles. The second line was about 4.5 miles behind the first and was manned by the reservists.[51]

On December 22 the bulk of the Chilean army disembarked at Curayacu just south of Lima. In early January 1881 the Chileans reconnoitered the Peruvian defenses south of Lima. The first Peruvian line lay within the range of the Chilean fleet, and the guns of the fleet were used to support the Chilean army attack on January 13, 1881. The flanks were probed but found to be secure so the Chilean commander, General Baquedano, ordered a frontal assault. The Peruvian artillery was ineffective and the troops, who were armed with two different calibre rifles, fre-

Figure 29. War of the Pacific, 1879–83. A Chilean battery of Krupp artillery poses for a photograph. In 1879 the Chilean army possessed seventy-five artillery pieces, most of which were modern Krupp and Limache manufacture. Peru possessed no modern field artillery at the start of the war. *Courtesy Museo Historico Nacional, Santiago, Chile.*

quently had the wrong ammunition.[52] The battle of Chorrillos ended in a complete Chilean victory. During the evening, Chilean troops sacked Chorrillos, the summer residence of prominent Peruvians, giving no quarter to either soldier or civilian. Sixty percent of the Peruvian soldiers were killed, wounded, or captured.[53]

Less than a quarter of the Peruvian regulars rallied behind the second defensive line. Two days later the Chileans attacked Miraflores. The Miraflores line was manned mostly by recently conscripted civilians. Piérola demonstrated great courage, frequently exposing himself to enemy fire. But not once did he issue an order. Some 6,000 reserves were never sent into the battle. In the bloody battles of Chorrillos and Miraflores, the Chileans lost 1,478 killed and 4,670 wounded. The Peruvians casualties were 7,850 killed and wounded—including many members of Peru's most prominent families.[54]

TRYING TO FIGHT ON

Following the defeat at Miraflores, Piérola retreated into the interior. Lima was occupied on January 17. When news of Lima's fall reached Callao, the Peruvian navy destroyed its remaining ships and Callao surrendered. Piérola attempted to instigate a guerrilla war against the Chilean occupiers, but before long Peruvian notables assembled in Lima chose Francisco García

Calderón as president. A Peruvian Congress, which met at Chorillos in March, declared Piérola's actions null and void.[55]

Between April 1881 and July 1883, the Chileans sent four major expeditions from Lima into the interior of Peru to ferret out the remaining Peruvian forces. On July 9, 1882, a force of 2,000 Peruvians surrounded the sixty-three-man Chilean garrison at La Concepción (120 mi SE of Lima). A twenty-hour battle raged before the garrison was massacred. But such Peruvian successes were rare. The final battle occurred at Huamachuco on July 9, 1883, where the Peruvians were defeated.[56]

The Treaty of Ancon (October 20, 1883) ended the fighting. Chile's victory was complete. From Bolivia, Chile received that nation's entire seacoast as well as financial concessions. From Peru, Chile obtained the territory of Tarapacá and the territories of Tacna and Arica were to remain subject to Chilean control for ten years, after which they were to have a plebiscite. Since the treaty did not specify the rules for the plebiscite, the issued dragged on for decades. Also, the victorious army took art, literary, and other treasures from Lima back to Chile, contributing to demands for revenge among Peruvians for decades.[57]

OBSERVATIONS

The war confirmed Chile as the dominant power on the west coast of South America. Chile won in large measure because it was politically and economically more mature than either Peru or Bolivia. This maturity endowed it with numerous advantages, such as the capacity to create a modern army and navy, and an economic foundation adequate to sustain an aggressive, amphibious campaign. Peruvian society, in many respects, remained in the eighteenth century as did many of the social, economic, and technological aspects of its army and navy. Bolivia lagged even farther behind. No amount of bravery could overcome such handicaps.[58]

In the post-Bonaparte era, the loser was forced to reward the winner and to bear the full cost of the war. Such was the fate of Peru and Bolivia. Abraham Koning, the Chilean Minister in Bolivia, observed on August 13, 1900: "Chile occupied the [Bolivian] littoral and has taken possession of it with the same right with which Germany annexed Alsace and Lorraine to its empire, with the same right with which the United States of North America took Puerto Rico."[59]

Chile and Peru had purchased technologically sophisticated warships. But neither nation had developed the industrial base necessary to maintain these ships. Therefore, the warships of both countries suffered from chronic mechanical problems and required herculean efforts to maintain them in operational condition.

The war also increased suspicions between the United States and Chile. U.S. diplomats were opposed to a Chilean victory because they perceived Chile as an expansionist power that would come into conflict with future U.S. aspirations in the region. Chile perceived the United States as endeavoring to steal its victory to ensure U.S. influence in Peru and future aspirations.

Also, this war left deeper scars on the relations among three Latin American nations—Bolivia, Chile, and Peru—than any other conflict within the region.[60]

Figure 30. War of the Pacific, 1879–83. The Battle of Concepción (July 8–9, 1882) between a company of the Chilean Chacabuco Regiment and a Peruvian force of some 3,000 irregulars. The badly outnumbered Chileans put up a heroic fight before being overwhelmed. *Courtesy Carlos López.*

PART 12

LATE-NINETEENTH-CENTURY INTRACLASS STRUGGLES

CHAPTER THIRTY-FIVE

ARGENTINE "REVOLUTIONS" OF 1890 AND 1893

> Each province was a factory and each public office a market stand. . . . the government expunged free elections all over the country, the municipal system and provincial autonomy; it encouraged a wild speculation; the ruin of the country was precipitated through bank operations and clandestine printing of currency; the administrators confused the public treasury with their own wealth.
>
> —Francisco A. Barroetaveña, 1886, member of the opposition

THE SPARK

On July 26, 1890, rebel forces seized the government arsenal at *Plaza de Artillería* (today's Lavalle Square), initiating hostilities with government forces.

BACKGROUND

Argentina, becoming a modern nation during the middle of the nineteenth century, had been ruled by an oligarchy of landlords, merchants, and bankers, an element of which was known as the "Córdoba Clique." Toward the end of the century, new political elements began to emerge. European immigrants wanted political rights; an *inteligencia* sought economic and social reform; and an embryonic, professional military officer corps desired a nation better able to create a modern military apparatus.[1]

The government of President Juárez Celman (1886–90), noted for its corruption and economic disasters, was increasingly pressured by these dissatisfied elements. The *Unión Cívica*, a recently formed, popular political party, created in large measure by Leandro Alem, forged an alliance with junior and midlevel army and naval officers, and together they conspired to rebel on July 21. The dissidents chose Gen. Manuel J. Campos to lead their military action. He and other leaders solicited the support of more and more military officers to aid in the *coup* attempt, and eventually the inevitable happened; the government learned of their plans. General

Campos was arrested on July 18 and troops suspected of disloyalty were posted outside the capital, Buenos Aires.

After this turn of events, the civilian members of the conspiracy convinced their military allies still at large to delay the uprising. After a few days General Campos was freed when the 10th Infantry Regiment, his jailor, switched loyalties. Campos again took command of the insurgent forces and decided to launch his uprising on July 26, 1890.

OPPOSING FORCES

In 1890 Argentina's population was estimated to be 3,500,000 of whom 1,000,000 were aliens. Most of the aliens were recent immigrants from southern Europe. The population of Buenos Aires City was some 500,000 individuals of whom 300,000 were aliens. These aliens had no legal status and the vast majority sympathized with the *Unión Cívica*.[2]

The rebels could muster many civilians, mostly aliens; some junior and midlevel officers, especially in the navy; and the following army units: one artillery regiment (the only one in the capital), two battalions of infantry and part of a third, one regiment of cavalry, a battalion of engineers, and the senior cadets from the Military Academy and the School for Corporals and Sergeants. In all, the rebels numbered about 1,500 men.[3]

The government controlled the overwhelming majority of the army: 8,000 regulars; 236,000 National guardsmen (ages fourteen to forty-five); and 68,000 reservists (ages forty-five to sixty); however, most regulars were posted far away in the interior.[4] Immediately available in the capital were two battalions of infantry and part of a third, two regiments of cavalry, and the city's police force, for a total of about 3,000 men.[5]

OPENING STRATEGIES

The rebel strategy confined the revolt to the capital. They planned to seize the arsenal at *Parque de Artillería*—which reportedly contained rifles, 550,000 rounds, and a battery of field guns—and subvert the fleet lying in Buenos Aires roadstead. Some of the leaders believed that the Celman administration would collapse following this demonstration of resolve.[6]

During the night of July 25, Lt. Eduardo O'Connor and five other naval officers crossed in a launch from the Boca del Riachuelo to the flagship, the protected cruiser *Patagonia*. The squadron commander was ashore, but the officer in charge agreed to join the rebels and the *Patagonia* was placed under the command of Lt. Ramón Lira. Next, the rebels summoned the officer of the day from the river gunboat *Paraná* to the flagship and invited him to join the rebellion. He refused and was detained. The rebels then took two launches to the *Paraná*, where the officer in charge pledged to support the rebels. When the torpedo boat *Maipú* was boarded, the commanding officer resisted and was wounded. The rebels did not try to incorporate the obsolete monitor *Los Andes* into their growing fleet.[7]

The government, which initially took the threat lightly, slowly assembled loyal army units at the *Retiro*, the Buenos Aires railroad station. The government, unaware that much of the fleet had already been subverted, ordered Rear Adm. Bartolomé Cordero to take command of the squadron. The admiral attempted to board the *Paraná* but was refused permission. He boarded the monitor and was soon arrested.

THE 1890 *COUP* ATTEMPT

In the early morning of July 26, some 1,500 rebels seized the *Parque de Artillería* and constructed barricades. The undefended seat of government, the *Casa Rosada* (the presidential residence), lay less than a mile away, but General Campos chose to wait and see how the government would react to the seizing of the arsenal.

The government's reaction was swift. Most of the limited forces immediately available were sent to *Plaza Libertad*, only one block from *Plaque de Artillería*. Another loyal force was stationed at *Plaza Victoria* in order to protect the *Casa Rosada*. Skirmishers were placed on rooftops and ordered to shoot the rebels on sight.

A little after 8 A.M. the government forces from *Plaza Libertad* attacked *Plaza de Artillería*. After a few artillery rounds, they tried to storm the barricades but were repulsed. Sporadic fighting continued between the land forces throughout the day.[8]

Meanwhile, the insurgent fleet commander, Lieutenant O'Connor, ordered his units to shell the concentration of government forces in the *Retiro* and the *Plaza de Mayo*, the park upon which the *Casa Rosada* faced. The rebels afloat and ashore developed an elaborate communications system. Those ashore were to release two paper globes if they wanted the fleet to bombard *Retiro*, and three, if the target were to be the *Plaza de Mayo*. As it turned out, the complicated signaling system didn't work. Moreover, the rebel ships were preparing to fight the monitor *Los Andes*, which they had not yet learned had already joined the rebellion. Precious time was lost. Meanwhile, government forces temporarily abandoned the *Retiro*, possibly fearing a naval bombardment.[9]

On July 27 government ground forces again attempted to storm the rebel's barricades and were again repulsed. However, the rebels discovered that they had only 30,000 rounds of rifle ammunition left. In fact, only 200,000 rounds were found in the arsenal, and the undisciplined civilian volunteers expended 170,000 cartridges in the two-day action![10]

Also on the twenty-seventh, the rebel squadron began bombarding suspected concentrations of government troops at *Retiro* and at the presidential palace. Ships maneuvered to within half a league of the shore, as close as they could get in the shallow water. In the afternoon the *Patagonia* captured a government transport after a short engagement while attempting to enter *La Boca* (the entrance to the southern harbor). Late in the day, higher tides permitted the warships to move closer to the city and the rebels renewed their naval bombardment, many of their rounds falling into parts of the city where foreign-owned businesses were located. At this point, foreign warships in port intervened to stop the bombardment.[11]

Around three in the afternoon, the Spanish *Infanta Isabel*, the Uruguayan *General Rivera*, and the British *Beagle* and *Bramble* steamed in column in pursuit of the *Patagonia* and the transport. The other rebels ships escaped to the north.[12] The *Patagonia* and the transport were overhauled by the foreign squadron. The commanding officers of the foreign warships appealed to the commander of the insurgent squadron to stop the bombardment. Lieutenant O'Connor responded that he would only obey the orders of the provisional government.[13] What accommodations were made is unclear. All of the rebel warships returned to Buenos Aires.

Meanwhile, additional army units loyal to the government began to arrive in the city. By the morning of the twenty-eighth, two thousand men arrived from Córdoba (where Marco Juárez Celman, the President's brother, was Governor) and 1,000 men from Tucumán. Later that day, General Campos, aware of the arrival of these reinforcements, opened negotiations with the government over the objections of the rebellious junior officers. The rebels demanded the resignation of the President and amnesty for those involved; the government rejected the terms.[14]

On the morning of July 29 the rebel warships took up position near the city once again. At 12:45 A.M. the *Los Andes*, joined by the *Maipú* and the *Patagonia*, opened fire on the city. Over one hundred shells were fired, most of which fell short and burst into the water. At the same time, heavy rifle fire opened in the city. At 2:55 P.M. the international code signal CGL ("peace has been proclaimed") was hoisted in the city but went unheeded by the rebel fleet.[15] An hour later a steamer carrying a flag of truce made its way to the rebel fleet and the firing ceased.[16]

A stalemate set in. The rebels were short on ammunition and the government forces were swelling. On the other hand, the rebels controlled the fleet and had significant popular sympathy.[17] Finally, the two sides agreed to terms. No reprisals were to be taken against those who participated in the rebellion; the insurgent army units were to be allowed to return to their barracks; the ships' crews were to be treated in the same manner as those ashore; and civilians were to disarm peacefully.[18] After the signing of the capitulation, the rebel fleet sailed to the provincial capital of La Plata, where the sailors disembarked.

The rebellion was successful enough to help cause some sixty congressmen to ask for President Celman's resignation; he did so on August 5. Senator Manuel D. Pizarro declared to the Congress, "The revolution is crushed, but the government is dead."[19] The junior officers felt betrayed by General Campos.[20]

Casualties were high on both sides, considering the brevity of the insurrection and the size of the forces involved. The government lost 700 men killed and wounded out of 3,000 engaged. And, the rebels sustained 400 men killed and wounded, mostly civilians, out of 1,500 engaged.[21]

THE 1893 COUP ATTEMPT

Although the *Unión Cívica* caused the downfall of Juárez Celman, the "Córdoba Clique" remained influential and Celman left the treasury empty. To help heal the country, Argentina's two most powerful personalities, Bartolomé Mitre (a *Porteño*) and Gen. Julio Roca (champion of the interior), agreed to support a compromise candidate for the 1892 election. Alem opposed *El Acuerdo* (The Agreement) and the *Unión Cívica* split over the issue, the majority following Alem into the new *Unión Cívica Radical*. The new party grew in popularity across the nation and openly opposed the government and *El Acuerdo*. *El Acuerdo* coalition nominated Dr. Luis Sáenz Peña for president. As Alem perceived that the election would not be fair, his rhetoric became more threatening. As a consequence, he and other *Unión Cívica Radical* leaders were arrested and exiled. In late 1892 Alem was permitted to return from exile and was elected to the national assembly.

President Sáenz Peña, possessing no personal following, found it very difficult to govern. He rejected pressure to resign and built a new cabinet around Dr. Aristóbulo del Valle, a member of the old *Unión Cívica* prior to 1890. The new cabinet was dominated by *porteños*, and this alienated many old-line politicans in the interior.

Discontent grew in the provinces of Buenos Aires, Corrientes, San Luis, Santa Fé, Santiago del Estero, and Tucumán. Alem and other radical members of the *Unión Cívica Radical* hoped to use this to spark a national revolution. Arms were smuggled into the provinces. The strategy called for naval officers to seize the ships and boats at the Tigre River torpedo boat base and assist those on land to capture the river port of Rosario (150 mi NW of Buenos Aires).[22] It was to serve as a provisional capital. Rosario lies on the banks of the Paraná River, which ran through the heart of the then rebel-infested interior.

The governors of Buenos Aires, Santa Fe, and San Luis raised provincial armies in defiance of the Constitution in an attempt to prevent popular uprisings.[23]

An uncoordinated series of revolts followed. On July 29, 1893, the radicals in the provincial capital of San Luis (400 mi W of Buenos Aires) successfully attacked the police *cuartel* (barracks), seized the governor, and declared a provisional government.[24]

On the thirtieth other radicals seized the Governor of Santa Fé in his provincial capital and captured the river port of Rosario, which lay approximately 220 miles up the Paraná from Buenos Aires.[25]

Also on July 30 uprisings occurred in eighty-eight locations throughout the province of Buenos Aires. Some 3,000 men commanded by Hipólito Yrigoyen concentrated at Témperley awaiting reinforcements before attacking the provincial capital, La Plata. The radicals demanded that the federal government remove Governor Julio Costa and that his provincial army be disbanded. President Sáenz Peña agreed and sent Costa an ultimatum; Costa stepped down on August 6.[26]

Meanwhile, two loyal regiments arrived in the city of Buenos Aires. On August 9 they occupied the town of La Plata (30 mi SE of Buenos Aires). The next day, the national legislature approved the military intervention into the province of Buenos Aires and subsequently into the other rebellious provinces.[27]

On August 14 rebellion broke out in Corrientes and by the twenty-second the insurgents controlled the province. This was suppressed by government troops by early September.[28]

On September 17 the radicals in Tucumán rebelled, and after three days of fighting controlled most of the province. The federal government dispatched 1,200 men under Gen. Francisco Bosch who successfully disarmed the rebels on the twenty-fifth.[29]

Next, rebellion broke out in the city of Santa Fe (215 mi NW of Buenos Aires) on September 24. Some 510 rebels (450 civilians and 60 members of the 3rd Battalion) occupied the customs house. They were opposed by 900 loyal troops from the 9th Regiment. Both sides suffered numerous casualties in the fighting. On the twenty-fifth, more federal troops arrived on board the steamers *Ceres* and *Quinto Misiones* from the province of Entre Ríos, and the rebels were defeated.[30]

On September 25 Col. Mariano Espiña and Commander Santiago Danuzzio led sailors and civilians manning the torpedo boat base at Tigre (13 mi NW of Buenos Aires) into revolt. They seized two torpedo boats. The next day, while the old coastal monitor *Los Andes* was steaming up the Paraná River, most of the officers and crew, led by Lts. Gerardo Valotta and Alberto Enciña, declared for the rebellion. The commanding officer, Commander Ramón Flores, was injured while resisting and later put ashore. The *Los Andes* joined the rebels at Rosario, bringing with her a valuable cargo of 1,800 Remingtons, 2,000 carbines, four 75mm cannons, and 600,000 rounds of ammunition—weapons and munitions destined for government forces in Entre Ríos.[31] The rest of the navy remained loyal to the government, which had changed those in key positions prior to the general uprising.[32]

The government's fleet reacted to the naval defections with speed. On September 26 the torpedo boat base was surprised by a government squadron composed of the coast-defense ships *Independencia* and *Libertad*, the old central battery corvette *Almirante Brown*, and the protected cruisers *Nueve de Julio* and *Patagonia*. This overwhelming force crushed the rebels.

Next, the government sent the torpedo-gunboat *Espora* up the Paraná River to find the *Los Andes*. Earlier the rebels had seized the tug *Victoria R.*, and she had been sent down the river to reconnoiter. The tug discovered the government warships near the Island of Martín García, evaded discovery, and alerted the *Los Andes*.[33]

Early in the morning of September 27 the coast-defense ship *Independencia* started up the Paraná River searching for the *Los Andes*. That night the *Independencia* anchored and the next morning was joined by the *Espora*. On the twenty-eighth they sailed together toward Rosario, with the *Espora* in the van. At 10:30 A.M. on the twenty-ninth, the *Espora* sighted the *Los Andes* with the *Victoria R.* in front of Espinillo Island off Rosario (1,130 mi N of Buenos Aires). Shallow water prevented the *Independencia* from closing the rebels. At 11:15 A.M. the *Los Andes* opened fire with her 9.45-inch guns at 2,000 yards on the *Espora*; the *Espora* returned the fire.[34] Partly because of poor-quality gunpowder, the *Los Andes'* seventeen shots had little effect. The two government ships, now under fire from the *Los Andes* and rebel batteries ashore, continued to maneuver toward the rebel ship. At half past noon the *Independencia* opened fire, soon joined by the *Espora*. The government ships fired 356 shots of various calibers, scoring numerous hits. The battered *Los Andes*, no match for her opponents, sought refuge among river traffic that included some foreign ships. At half past eight in the evening, the *Los Andes* raised the white flag and at 1:30 A.M. on September 30 government forces boarded her and found that she was sinking. The *Independencia* was only slightly damaged.[35]

While the naval units were fighting, federal troops under Gen. Luis María Campos advanced against Rosario, which fell on October 2.[36] The rebellion was crushed!

Casualties between the two sides probably numbered at least a few hundred. Alem and other rebel leaders were exiled to Isla de los Estados, a penal colony a few miles to the east of Tierra del Fuego. Hundreds fled to Montevideo, Uruguay. Alem, released under the amnesty law of 1895, returned to Buenos Aires and committed suicide the following year.[37]

OBSERVATIONS

Although the 1890 clash was an intraclass struggle initiated by those already sharing power, Leandro Alem and other radical leaders threatened to spark interclass warfare in 1890 and actually attempted to do so in 1893. If the rebels of 1890 were to have any chance of winning, they were required to act boldly and without hesitation. General Manuel Campos prevented this from happening. If the rebels of 1893 had any chance of victory, they needed to act simultaneously, which they did not. But the actions of the *Unión Cívica* heralded the emergence of a new political force in Argentina: the middle class.

CHAPTER THIRTY-SIX

THE CHILEAN "REVOLUTION" OF 1891

> They [the *Congresionalistas*] recognized a truth which is sometimes forgotten, that fleets cannot act on land.
>
> —W. H. Wilson

THE SPARK

In early January 1891 Captain Jorge Montt,[1] commander of the Chilean navy, learned that President José Manuel Balmaceda planned to order the fleet to sail from Valparaíso so that it would not become involved in his dispute with Congress. Balmaceda was too late.[2] During the early morning of January 7, the Chilean fleet left its anchorage in Valparaíso with the President of the Chamber of Deputies, the Vice President of the Senate, and several other congressmen on board, initiating what is commonly called the "Revolution of 1891."

BACKGROUND

A governmental crisis over presidential vice-congressional dominance split Chile in late 1890 between President Balmaceda and the Congress. President Balmaceda wanted a strict interpretation of the Constitution which would allow him to carry out changes that were opposed by Congress. As the President and Congress grew farther apart, Balmaceda acted independently of congressional authority.

The Congress wanted to remove Balmaceda and realized the need for military power. Balmaceda already had substantial support among the army. The Congress approached Gen. Manuel Baquedano, conqueror of Peru during the War of the Pacific (1879–83), and asked for support. The General's prestige was substantial and might have swung the army to their side, but he would not be drawn into the conflict.[3] The legislature then sought the help of the commander of the fleet, Captain Montt, who made his support conditional. The heads of both congressional chambers had to assume in writing the responsibility for a possible military action.[4] Congress did so and many sought refuge on board the warships.

President Balmaceda declared Captain Montt a traitor; informed foreign nations that acts committed by the fleet were not the responsibility of his government; informed the army and the intendents (governors) in the provinces that much of the Congress and navy had rebelled;

and ordered the imprisonment of the congressional majority (only one congressman was caught).

OPPOSING FORCES

During early 1891 both sides scrambled to gather military assets, which were plentiful as a consequence of the recent War of the Pacific. Almost the entire 5,500-man standing army declared for Balmaceda. Government warehouses were crammed full of war trophies and could have outfitted a 75,000-man army. The infantry used the same rifles as in the War of the Pacific—Grass, Beaumonts, and Comblains—and the artillery Krupp guns. Eventually a 40,000-man army was created.

The *Gobiernistas* (the supporters of the President) concentrated their army in four locations all connected by rail—a 6,000-man division at Santiago, a 7,000-man division at Valparaíso (71 mi WNW of Santiago), a 9,000-man division at Coquimbo (275 mi N of Santiago), and a 10,000-man division at Concepción (309 mi S of Santiago). If the Coquimbo division were attacked, its orders were to fight alone and if defeated fall back to Santiago. The other divisions were not to give battle until reinforced by a second division which could rapidly be accomplished by rail.[5]

The *Gobiernistas* did succeed in arming the fast merchant ship *Imperial* and intercepting the new torpedo gunboats *Almirante Lynch* and *Almirante Condell* which had been purchased in England. But by the time these two reached Valparaíso their boilers needed to be retubed and the necessary steelstock was not available in Chile. Instead, brass tubes were removed from locomotives and used as an expedient.[6]

The *Congresionalistas* (the supporters of the Congress) were busy shepherding stray warships, seizing merchant ships, establishing a blockade of the northern ports, and seeking a base of operations. The *Congresionalistas* succeeded in rounding up the entire navy except for the two torpedo gunboats and the old gunboat *Pilcomayo* on survey duties in the south. Almost the entire navy had been immediately available at Valparaíso—the central-battery ironclad *Blanco Encalada*, the former Peruvian seagoing monitor *Huáscar*, the corvette *O'Higgins*, and the gunboat *Magallanes*. The only other major warship, the central-battery ironclad *Almirante Cochrane*, lay eighteen miles north in Quintero Bay.

The *Congresionalistas* also had substantial sympathy from British bankers and the nitrate czars, a group from which they could reap money and manpower.[7]

OPENING STRATEGIES

Chilean geography afforded special opportunities to a naval force. In the 1890s, owing to the country's lack of rail transportation in the north and the south, a large body of troops could be transported by sea about twenty times as fast as it could be marched across land in all but the central region. Santiago, Valparaíso, and Coquimbo were joined by rail, as were the important population concentrations just south of the capital, but in the north, there were few lines and these ran from east to west to service the mines and in the deep south there were none. The sea, moreover, was a natural scene. Once a fleet was beyond the sight of land, its destination could not be predicted, an advantage compounded by the fact that, regardless of the size of the land forces, the land forces had a strategic tendency to disperse to meet the enemy wherever he might strike.

The navy, nonetheless, was faced with one enormous strategic problem. How could it exert pressure on the land forces? The ships had hesitated before Valparaíso, hoping that the mere sight of their guns would cause the enemy to be conciliatory. The fleet made no impression on the resolute opponent. Bombarding the nation's chief seaport, home of many of the sailors, was out of the question. And throwing a callow fleet landing party against an experienced army would have been disastrous.

In order to win, both sides had to create a counterforce to defeat the other's strength. The *Gobiernistas* needed a navy and the *Congresionalistas* an army. Balmaceda tasked his foreign minister to buy a fleet. He asked the British minister in Santiago to help the government purchase the British Pacific squadron's flagship, the armored cruiser *Warspite*. The request, dismissed, was only one of a series of aborted efforts made by the *Gobiernistas* to scratch together a navy.[8]

The *Congresionalistas* concluded early that a blockade alone would not bring victory. The warships could not entirely close Chilean ports to the outside world, a development, even if successful, not likely to enlist the sympathies of the population or to force the *Gobiernistas* to capitulate. First, the fleet was too small to enforce an effective blockade the entire length of Chile. Second, such an attempt might lead to a confrontation with a major naval power. And third, land routes over the Andes, although primitive, made a total blockade impossible. The defeat of the *Gobiernistas* could only be realized ashore and for this a sizeable landing force would be necessary. It would take time, money, and manpower—a landing force of 10,000 men. To round up this many troops from the fleet and the northern territories would have been a difficult task had the War of the Pacific not ended but seven years earlier, leaving most of the male population with valuable military experience.

THE WAR FOR THE NORTH

After lingering off Valparaíso, the fleet sailed north in order to capture lightly defended ports and collect booty that included nitrate revenues, volunteers for the naval brigade, and small arms. The *Congresionalistas* won their first permanent foothold when they captured Pisagua (1,145 mi N of Santiago) on February 6. There, the *Congresionalistas* threw together a 1,200-man ragtag army from the Pisagua garrison, the militia of Taltal Province, volunteers gathered in mining ports, and sailors from the fleet. The force was poorly armed and lacked experienced officers. This army set out by land to capture Iquique (1,114 mi N of Santiago). In the meantime, the *Imperial* had been busy running the blockaded northern ports and landing *Gobiernista* reinforcements. Between January 6 and 11, some 2,000 troops were carried to the north. Maurice Harvey, an English newspaper reporter, described the deck of the *Imperial* during one trip:

> [T]he spar deck, extensive as it was, was literally packed with humanity. Most of the soldiers appeared to have two or three wives, and each wife a liberal supply of children, so that what the total number of souls came to it was hard to guess within a few hundred.[9]

A 900-man veteran *Gobiernista* force defeated 1,200 *Congresionalistas* from Pisagua at Huara on February 17. The *Congresionalistas* lost 250 men and the *Gobiernistas* significantly fewer men. However, the *Gobiernistas* had left Iquique virtually unguarded and during their absence sailors from the fleet captured it on February 16. Two days later the victors of Huara marched back to Iquique and attacked. The *Congresionalistas* took refuge in the customs house and, supported by the guns of the fleet, refused to surrender. The stalemate was finally broken when Col. José M. Soto and his *Gobiernista* troops changed sides.

The *Gobiernistas* still had 1,300 regulars in the north at Calama (938 mi N of Santiago). The *Congresionalistas* at Iquique stripped their ships of what could be used in a land battle—boat guns and machine guns—and mounted them on railroad cars. The *Congresionalista* army then advanced north. The forces collided at Pozo Almonte. After two hours the *Gobiernistas* exhausted their ammunition and yielded. The *Congresionalistas* lost 45 percent of their men.

ARMING THE *CONGRESIONALISTA* SOLDIERS

By mid-April the *Congresionalistas* had occupied the northern third of the country and, controlling the sea, had time to import much-needed modern rifles and to train. Ten thousand Mannlicher repeating rifles were purchased in Europe. (The *Gobiernistas* were armed with the older style singleshot breechloaders.) The steamer *Maipo* picked these up in Tierra del Fuego. Eventually, she arrived safely at Iquique with her valuable cargo, which gave the *Congresionalistas*' soldiers an advantage over their opponents.

On April 8 the steamer *Itata* was sent north to the United States to pick up arms. The United States, which supported President Balmaceda, suspected her intentions and placed a deputy on board in San Diego. During the evening of May 6 the *Itata* slipped out of port, deposited the deputy on a remote beach, and loaded munitions outside the three-mile limit from a schooner. This created a furor within the United States; the U.S. Navy chased but did not catch the *Itata*. The cruiser *Charleston* entered Iquique, the *Congresionalistas*' principal base, on June 3 and sequestered the *Itata*. The incident further strained the relations between the *Congresionalistas* and the United States.[10]

The *Congresionalistas* grew stronger through support from the outside world while the *Gobiernistas* were unable to find similar help. The friendly neutrality of two key world powers, Great Britain and Germany, was almost guaranteed. The British navy had long regarded the Chilean navy as a favored grandchild. The embracing of the *Congresionalistas*' cause by army Capt. Emil Korner[11] assured the sympathies of Germany and brought to their side a brilliant tactician. He organized and trained the *Congresionalista* army. An English observer described the troops as "a rough, hard body of men, suitable to the climate and the work."[12]

TORPEDOING THE *BLANCO ENCALADA*

The *Gobiernistas* did have one stunning victory at sea. In the dark on the morning of April 22, the torpedo gunboats attacked the *Congresionalista* fleet at Caldera (498 mi N of Santiago). A torpedo from the *Almirante Lynch* struck the *Blanco Encalada* amidships. She sank in less than ten minutes and 182 men died. Five or six torpedoes had been fired, one had hit. This was the first verified successful use of an automotive torpedo.[13] When the *Congresionalistas* had sailed away from Valparaíso in January, one of the items they had to abandon was their torpedo nets. These were to be hung around a warship to protect it from such an attack.[14]

Ashore, they could but organize, train, and wait the time and place of attack chosen by the enemy. Typical of the tactical difficulties confronting the *Gobiernistas* was the experience of a 1,000-man force sent to reinforce Antofagasta under Col. Hermogenes Camus. These orders being countermanded, the force twice traversed 700 miles on foot in the winter, losing 200 men to the elements without ever sighting the enemy.

Figure 31. Chilean "Revolution" of 1891. The *Congresionalista* battleship *Blanco Encalada* was torpedoed and sunk on April 22, 1891, by torpedo-boats belonging to the *Gobiernistas*. The torpedo was perceived to be the great equalizer by those possessing inferior naval forces to their enemies. Historical "firsts" are always dangerous to declare but this was possibly the first time that a self-propelled torpedo sank a warship. The *Blanco Encalada* was at anchor when torpedoed. *Copied from Maurice H. Hervey, Dark Days in Chile (London: Edward Arnold, 1892).*

THE LANDING IN QUINTERO BAY

By July the *Congresionalistas* had assembled, equipped, and trained a naval brigade in the north at Caldera, Huasco, and Iquique behind the protection of the Atacama Desert. The *Gobiernista* forces had been busy strengthening fortifications. Descending from their harbor strongholds, the *Congresionalistas* carried out a well-executed amphibious assault just north of Valparaíso near Concón in the afternoon of August 20, 1891, landing their 9,184-man army. A U.S. intelligence report recounted the obsession with detail:

> Equally careful orders for disembarkation were issued on the trip down as those for embarkation. A great quantity of flatbottom bateaux had been made which were transported, lashed bottom out on the sides of the ships. They were each capable of landing 150 men in pleasant weather in one trip. . . . Ladders were also provided, one for each [of the] 150 men, and an officer detailed for each ladder at the upper end, with two seamen to receive the soldiers in the boats. Arrangements were made for buoys to be planted near the shores as guides, with lines running to the shore to haul out and in with. Each float was towed by a launch, and to go and return as quickly as possible. The cavalry were instructed to land with their saddles and bridles in one package, while the crews of the vessels look out for disembarkation of the horses. The horses were to be directed in the water to a suitable place on the beach for landing, where the troops were to assemble. The general officers and staff were to be landed in pulling boats.
>
> In case of being opposed on landing the commanders of transports and paymasters were to be responsible for landing the equipment as quickly as possible after the troops had secured a foothold. The men were to carry their pieces in their left hand at the height of the lower band on the ladders, and in case of landing through a surf the cartridge belts were to be worn around the neck. Commanders of transports were to provide an abundant warm meal to be given the men just before the formation for disembarkation.[15]

The *Congresionalistas* had chosen Concón as their landing site because the network of roads there would permit them to advance against either Santiago or Valparaíso. They tried with some success to deceive the *Gobiernistas* into believing that they would land at Coquimbo.

BATTLE OF CONCÓN

Balmaceda ordered the divisions at Santiago and Concepción to rush by rail to Valparaíso. Disobeying orders, Gen. José Miguel Alcérreca chose not to wait for the arrival of reinforcements and attacked the *Congresionalistas* with the 6,500 men under his command. His troops had only one hundred rounds each and the rough terrain negated the use of his cavalry. Once the two armies engaged on August 22, the *Gobiernista* positions were within range of the cruisers *Esmeralda* and *O'Higgins*. Their heavy artillery caused great destruction and panic among the *Gobiernistas*. By 4 P.M. the *Gobiernistas* were defeated. They lost 2,200 dead and wounded, 2,000 prisoners, and 1,000 deserters. The *Congresionalistas* lost 400 dead, 600 wounded, and 122 disappeared (possibly drowning victims).[16]

Although the Mannlicher repeating rifle had significantly contributed to the victory, the *Congresionalistas* had almost exhausted the ammunitions and for twelve hours remained impotent until resupplied. Also, the *Congresionalistas* failed to seize the rail line between Santiago and Concón, thus allowing 8,000 *Gobiernista* soldiers to reach Valparaíso from the capital. Balmaceda had been able to concentrate a fresh army in less than two days.[17]

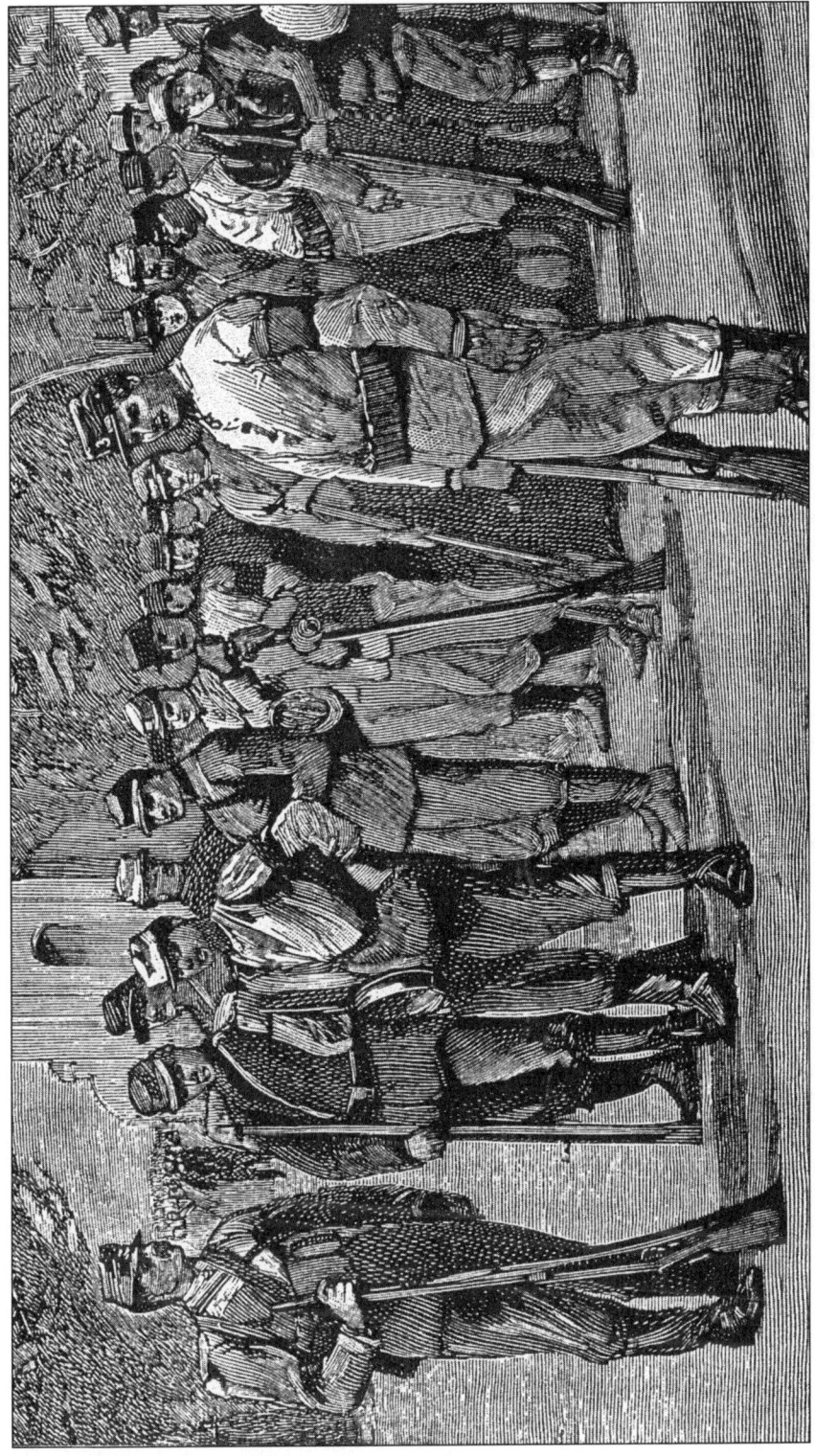

Figure 32. Chilean "Revolution" of 1891. *Gobiernista* troops await the attack of the *Congresionalistas*. Both sides developed sound strategies and both possessed plenty of arms, many of which were holdovers from the War of the Pacific a decade earlier. However, the *Congresionalistas* held the initiative. Control of the sea gave them the ability to choose the time and place of the battle and this proved decisive. *Copied from Maurice H. Hervey,* Dark Days in Chile *(London: Edward Arnold, 1892).*

BATTLE OF PLACILLA

Once resupplied with ammunitions, the *Congresionalistas* moved against Valparaíso. Believing that the defenses facing them were too strong, they maneuvered to approach the city from the east. This separated them from the direct support of the fleet. They endeavored to conceal this maneuver but were detected by the *Gobiernistas* who established a defensive position near Placilla. The two armies met there on August 28. Considerable dissention existed among the *Gobiernista* generals and they did not work well together. The battle raged for three hours and the *Congresionalistas* won. They lost 1,800 men and the *Gobiernistas* 3,000.[18]

After eight days of stubborn fighting, the *Congresionalistas* triumphantly entered Valparaíso, and Santiago soon followed. Montt established himself in *La Moneda* (the presidential palace). Balmaceda sought sanctuary in the Argentine embassy. The houses of his supporters were sacked; jails were filled with his supporters. For a time Balmaceda considered surrendering for trial. On September 18, 1891, he wrote his Political Testament (*El Testamento Político de Balmaceda*) in which he argued that Chile would remain divided as long as the legislative branch dominated, and then shot himself.

OBSERVATIONS

The Revolution of 1891 was an intraclass struggle between elements of society, each of which already exercised power.

Militarily, both sides decided upon credible strategies given their resources. The *Congresionalistas* appreciated that they could not win if they could not defeat the *Gobiernistas* on land. The *Congresionalista*'s plan allowed concentration of force when and where they desired, rendering the *Gobiernistas*' numerical superiority of more than three-to-one in men and equipment useless. On the other side, the *Gobiernistas*, failing to create a navy, did not unreasonably disperse their strength. They had the potential to reunite elements of their force to guarantee a two-to-one advantage. However, "the devil was in the details." The *Congresionalistas* executed their plan brilliantly, in particular the amphibious landing, and the *Gobiernistas* carried theirs out poorly.

This *Congresionalista* victory made the navy the preeminent military service within Chile, a position of political power it retained until the 1931 fleet mutiny. No other Latin American navy has ever achieved this status. The war also catapulted Adm. Jorge Montt into the presidency in 1891. He was the first naval officer to be elected president in Latin America.[19]

The conflict brought Chile and the United States closer to war. A series of incidents—the splicing of a cable around Iquique, the *Itata* affair, the unencrypted reporting of the landing at Quintero Bay, and the controversial actions of U.S. Ambassador Morris P. Egan—all contributed to a growing of animosities between Chile and the United States. Within a few months of the end of the revolution, the countries would go to the brink of war. On October 16, there were 177 sailors from the U.S. cruiser *Baltimore* who were given shore liberty in the post-revolution, electrified environment of Valparaíso. Two sailors were killed and several hurt.[20]

CHAPTER THIRTY-SEVEN

THE BRAZILIAN "REVOLUTION" OF 1893–94

> Practically the army and the navy are in open war with each other, each unable to invade the other's territory. The insurgent fleet has no men to land to hold possession of any point in this city; and the President has no naval force to meet the insurgents on water. Both have supplies to continue the struggle for some time to come, but meanwhile a great part of the burdens and losses must fall upon the noncombatants who are caught between them.
>
> —*Rio News*, September 14, 1893

THE SPARK

On September 7, 1893 (Brazilian independence day), Rear Adm. Custódio José de Mello, supported by a handful of politicians who had sought sanctuary on board the battleship *Aquidabã* in Rio de Janeiro harbor, issued a manifesto calling for the restoration of a constitutional regime without addressing the form the new government should take.[1] This began what is commonly called the "Revolution of 1893–94."

BACKGROUND

The political crisis in Brazil during the first years of the new republican regime, as well as the rivalry between the army and the navy—which became more serious after the ascension of Marshal Floriano Peixoto to the presidency—formed the background for the rebellion. The movement began in the name of the purity of republican ideals, but later acquired a monarchical character, especially after Custódio de Mello, anticipating the difficulties of reaching victory, established a link with the Revolutionary leader from Rio Grande do Sul, Gaspar da Silveira Martins, and after Rear Adm. Luís Felipe de Saldanha da Gama, who had remained neutral until December 7, 1893, joined the cause of the rebellion.[2]

Following the downfall of the monarchy on November 15, 1889, the first president, Marshal Manoel Deodoro da Fonseca, declared martial law and assumed dictatorial powers on November 3, 1891. Opposition was almost immediate. On November 23, 1891, Admiral Mello seized command of the warships in Rio de Janeiro harbor and trained the guns of the fleet on the city. Army units in the city soon declared their support for the fleet. Fonseca resigned, and the Vice President, Marshal Floriano Vieira Peixoto, assumed the reins of government. As a reward for his role, Admiral Mello was appointed Minister of Marine.

A split soon developed between acting President Peixoto and Admiral Mello. Peixoto continued Marshal Fonseca's preferential treatment of the army. Sporadic uprisings occurred in the states. Several state governments had not yet organized themselves along federal lines, even though they were required to adopt a state constitution patterned after the constitution of the republic by the end of 1892. A Federalist movement flared up again in the state of Rio Grande do Sul, and conditions were ripe for revolt throughout the nation. Peixoto retired thirteen generals and admirals who signed a political manifesto urging a presidential election. In April 1893 Admiral Mello, a senator, and Lt. Col. Serzedello Corrêa, Minister of Finance, resigned their portfolios and publicly criticized Peixoto. On May 23 Congressman J. J. Seabra accused the President of unconstitutional acts from the floor of Congress. An impeachment process was started but failed to obtain the necessary votes.[3]

For a second time in less than two years, the navy rebelled. The first rebellious act, an isolated incident (which would later be endorsed by Mello), occurred on July 6 when Rear Adm. Eduardo Wandenkolk seized the Brazilian merchant ship *Júpiter* in Montevideo, Uruguay (1,140 mi SW of Rio de Janeiro). The admiral proceeded to the city of Rio Grande (830 mi SW of Rio de Janeiro), arriving there three days later. He then seized two gunboats and several merchantmen. The seaward batteries were ominous and the Admiral's force was not strong enough to attack the city, and a hoped-for uprising among rebels ashore never materialized. Soon the government cruiser *República* captured the *Júpiter* with the rebellious Admiral on board. The rebels were taken to Rio de Janeiro and confined in Fort Santa Cruz, where Senator Ruy Barbosa attempted to obtain a writ of *habeas corpus* for Admiral Wandenkolk.[4]

On September 4 Peixoto vetoed a proposed law that would have prohibited him, a vice president acting as a president, from running in the next presidential election. On the evening of September 5 the naval battalion (marines) at Rio de Janeiro rebelled. On the sixth Admiral Mello took command of the rebellion and assumed the title of Commander of the Naval Insurgent Forces of the United States of Brazil. The Admiral, supported by thirty or forty officers, seized control of the fleet. The flagship, the battleship *Aquidabã*, had been removed from dry dock two days earlier.[5] A small group of officers, anticipating the revolt, had taken the torpedo warheads from storage and kept them on board the gunboat *Orion*. A few prominent citizens, including six or seven members of Congress, joined the Admiral on the *Aquidabã*. On September 7, from the safety of the battleship, Mello and his supporters issued the manifesto calling for the removal of Peixoto but left the fate of the republican form of government in doubt.[6]

OPPOSING FORCES

Practically the entire army, which numbered about 30,000 officers and men, sided with Peixoto; however, it was not available to protect Rio.[7] Most of the troops were needed in the south to protect the borders or suppress the Federalist movement in Rio Grande do Sul. Therefore, the government resorted to extraordinary measures to create an adequate force in the capital. The *Rio News* reported on September 27,

> Since the revolution began the old abuse of impressing recruits has been revived, and so injudiciously and mischievously has it been carried into effect that the greatest injuries to the country have resulted. Instead of picking up the stray vagabonds who haunt our streets, the pressgangs have directed their raids against the factories established in the city, where they could secure a large number of men at a stroke.[8]

Also, the President commanded eleven of the thirteen forts that protected Rio de Janeiro. Combined, they mounted over one hundred guns. Of these at least ten guns were large, modern, and capable of easily penetrating the armor of the *Aquidabã*.[9]

Admiral Mello's immediate military support came from all the naval units at Rio de Janeiro and many of the most experienced naval officers, but only one-fourth of the navy's active duty enlisted men. The rebel fleet included the second-class battleship *Aquidabã*, completed in England in 1885; the one-year-old protected cruiser *República*, also built in England; and numerous smaller warships and captured merchantmen.[10]

Significantly absent among the warships commandeered by Admiral Mello were the second-class battleship *Riachuelo* (undergoing repairs in Europe), the new gunboat *Tiradentes*, and the new training ship *Benjamin Constant* (completing in France), as well as smaller warships in Bahia and Montevideo, Uruguay.[11] These scattered units loyal to Peixoto gave the acting President a potentially stronger fleet than that of the rebels, but it would take considerable time to pull them together and not enough officers had remained loyal to be able to immediately man these units.

In addition to the protagonists, there was a powerful neutral: Rear Adm. Luís Felipe de Saldanha da Gama, a Monarchist sympathizer who commanded Fort Villegaignon, strategically located on an island off Rio de Janeiro, and was superintendent of the Naval Academy.

OPENING STRATEGIES

Admiral Mello apparently believed that the naval revolt would achieve an early success like the one of November 15, 1889, which dethroned the Emperor and the one of November 23, 1891, which removed Deodoro de Fonseca from office.[12]

Admiral Mello's initial strategy was to reduce the harbor forts by gunfire and intimidate Peixoto into resigning by bombarding Rio de Janeiro and Niterói, the mercantile port on the other side of the bay. President Peixoto's strategy was to diplomatically isolate Mello as a rebel, resist any attempt of the navy to gain a foothold ashore, and tenaciously create a naval force of his own.

THE EARLY GUN DUELS

For ten days during September, the fleet and army forts blasted away at each other with devastating effect on the population. Rio's English-language newspaper described the effects:

> Suddenly, about 10 o'clock, the firing began on the part of the fleet, although the guns of [Fort] Santa Cruz had been at work some time before. And then the stampede began! Men, women, and children, carts and carriages, people with bundles, boxes and parcels of every size and description, began pouring through the streets in search of some place of safety. It was a pitiful sight.[13]

FOREIGN INTERVENTION

The effects of the revolt abroad could not be worse. To European observers, Brazil's political and economic crises were part of a single widespread crisis that would include Brazil in the list of South American "banana republics," plagued by military *pronunciamientos*. Brazil's ability for self-government and the new republic's ability to enforce national unity were questioned.[14]

During that first week the government's new Minister of the Navy sent the loyal chief of the naval staff to the French cruiser *Aréthuse*, the British cruiser *Sirius*, the Italian cruiser *Giovanni*

Basan, and the Portuguese gunboat *Mindelo* to tell them that the fleet had rebelled and recommended that they take measures for their own protection. The Brazilian government also sent a letter to the Portuguese, British, French, German, United States, and Italian diplomats (who were then in Petrópolis) inviting them to discuss the protection of their citizens. To Peixoto's surprise, all of them refused the invitation.

On October 5 the foreign powers finally intervened in an attempt to protect Rio de Janeiro and their commercial interests. Foreign naval commanders informed Admiral Mello that they would not permit another bombardment of Rio, and they asked the government to refrain from acts that would encourage the fleet to retaliate with a general bombardment. Thus Mello, while he lost the power to bombard at will, unofficially gained recognition as a belligerent.

As the conflict spread, the major naval powers were unable to eliminate the threat to shipping by mines. The forces of President Peixoto sowed Rio de Janeiro's harbor with so many mines that crews from neutral warships attempted to clear the harbor of these devices out of sheer self-defense.

The city of Niterói was not spared under this arrangement extracted by the foreign powers. On October 5 the rebels exchanged fire with the battery on São Bento while attempting to capture the steamer *São Diogo*, tied up along the quay. A number of shells from the fleet fell into Niterói and inflicted heavy casualties upon civilians. Gunnery duels between the fleet and the gun emplacements added to the casualty list throughout October.

THE NAVY SAILS SOUTH

By late September Admiral Mello decided to extend the revolution to southern Brazil in hopes of widening his base of support. Admiral Mello seized Desterro (460 mi SW of Rio de Janeiro—now Florianópolis), located on an island off Santa Catarina. The acting governor of Santa Catarina surrendered on September 28 to Capt. Frederico Lorena commanding the cruiser *República*, the converted merchantman *Palas*, and the torpedo boat *Marcílio Dias*. Lorena established a provisional government in Desterro on October 14, unrealistically expecting foreign nations to recognize a rebel government controlling 12,000 people while the Peixoto government in Rio controlled 14 million.

THE GOVERNMENT CREATES A NAVY

In mid-October Peixoto placed the loyal Adm. Jerônimo Gonçalves in charge of the government's sea forces. On October 12 Gonçalves left for the south in the *Thames* with his officers and loyal troops, planning to take possession of the old coastal defense battleship *Bahia* and the gunboat *Tiradentes*, which then lay in Montevideo.

President Peixoto realized that he could not rely solely upon the scattered loyal remnants of the Brazilian navy, the most important warships of which could not be made ready to sail for more than a year. Additionally, he lacked experienced officers to man them. True, the rebellious navy could be held at bay by the forts protecting Rio de Janeiro, especially with the benevolent support of the major powers, but the rebel fleet might be able to provide the margin of victory for Federalists in the south, thus shattering the central government's hold on the country.[15]

Peixoto tasked his ambassadors in the United States and Europe to acquire naval forces. In North America the Brazilian government enlisted the services of Charles R. Flint, the flamboyant entrepreneur who once again charged headlong into the mission of creating a naval force for a Latin American nation. He realized that to create a fleet within a few weeks he would have to purchase ships that were immediately available and crew them principally with North Americans, while those coming from Europe would have to be crewed by Europeans.

Flint decided to buy ships with a fair speed and the recently invented dynamite gun. A fifty-foot-long cylinder with a fifteen-inch diameter threw a dynamite projectile to a distance of about 3,000 yards. But the aerial torpedo, which contained fifty pounds of dynamite, could not be pointed; the ship had to change course to train it. The problem was hitting the target. The performance of the gun was erratic and the velocity of the projectile very slow, making it difficult at best to hit anything that was moving. Despite these shortcomings, Flint hoped to intimidate the rebels by aggressively publicizing the presumed military capabilities of his new acquisitions. He set up a "literary bureau" to control information traveling between Brazil and the United States. For the consumption of the rebels, the imformation entering Brazil emphasized the ingenious character of the "dynamite fleet" and the destructive power of its new weapon. Dispatches released in the United States extolled the successes and virtues of the loyalists.[16]

Flint's fleet was composed of armed merchantmen and experimental craft. The flagship was the steamer *El Cid*, purchased from the Morgan Line. A fast merchantman, she was the only ship actually armed with the dynamite gun. Flint also purchased the *Destroyer*, a creation of the famed John Ericsson, more for her publicity value than for her military prowess.[17] He further acquired the Norwegian *Midnight Sun*, a fast tourist ship. These units were armed with guns that Flint bought off the floor of the Columbian Exposition in Chicago. He selected a former clipper ship commander to head the fleet. Indeed the dynamite fleet was more bravado than substance, whether those manning it knew so or not. President Peixoto's agents in Europe were much more practical. Their primary acquisitions were one large torpedo gunboat from Armstrong in England and five small ones from Schichau in Germany.[18]

ADMIRAL MELLO TAKES COMMAND IN THE SOUTH

Meanwhile, back in Rio de Janeiro, Admiral Mello decided to go south to aid the Federalists in Rio Grande do Sul. On December 1 the transport *Esperança* and the battleship *Aquidabã* with the Admiral embarked ran the gauntlet of forts protecting the harbor's entrance, receiving only slight damage.

ADMIRAL DA GAMA JOINS THE REBELLION

The departure of the Admiral raised speculation that Admiral da Gama was about to join the ranks of the rebels.[19] On the seventh, da Gama finally declared in favor of the revolution and took command of the units in the harbor. It was assumed that he wanted to restore the monarchy. However, the revolt was also supported by many ardent republicans, including Ruy Barbosa, then exiled in Argentina, and the congressmen who had embarked in the fleet back in September.

The Admiral's manifesto, dated two days later, contributed to the confusion over his political objectives. It condemned the administration and said that the nation should "solemnly choose" its form of government. It was published by both sides in slightly but significantly different wording. The government claimed that the manifesto proved da Gama wanted to restore the monarchy; the rebels argued that the Admiral favored self-determination. Straddling sides as it did, the manifesto had a negative effect on pro-republican rebels and neutrals and failed to gain pro-Monarchist support. Numerous false manifestos attributed to da Gama now appeared and added to the suspicions of the republicans and reluctance of some Monarchists.[20]

THE UNITED STATES INTERVENES

Devastating to the rebel cause was the refusal of the U.S. commander, Rear Adm. Andrew Benham, to recognize the zone in which Admiral Mello declared ships were not permitted to unload. Benham gave two U.S. merchant ships permission to discharge their cargoes at wharves there and informed the rebels that if they interfered American warships would open fire on the rebel fleet. The U.S. squadron, consisting of the armored cruiser *New York* and the protected cruisers *Charleston*, *Detroit*, *Newark*, and *San Francisco*, was far superior to the rebel fleet, and the threat went unchallenged. Because Admiral Benham refused to recognize the belligerent status of the rebellious navy, Admiral da Gama loosened the grip on the harbor blockade. This was an irreversible action, as he soon realized.[21]

THE AQUIDABÃ RETURNS

On January 16, 1894, the rebels in Rio received renewed confidence with the return of the battleship *Aquidabã*. However, she brought no provisions, munitions, or reinforcements for Admiral da Gama who was disappointed. *Aquidabã*'s big guns did force government troops from prepared positions. Admiral Mello remained with the *República* in the south.[22]

On February 9 Admiral da Gama made a supreme effort to take Niterói, attacking Ponta de Armação with 500 men. Although at first successful, he was eventually forced to retreat by superior numbers after sustaining considerable losses. The Admiral was wounded in the neck and right arm.[23]

THE GOVERNMENT'S FLEET ARRIVES

Meanwhile, in early 1894, the government's "dynamite fleet" and the torpedo gunboats arrived off the coast of Brazil from North America and Europe. Adm. Jerônimo Gonçalves, commander of the loyal forces afloat, sailed from Montevideo on January 19 to the rendezvous at Salvador (750 mi N of Rio de Janeiro), where he found some of the ships from North America and Europe on his arrival on the twenty-fifth. Over the next few days the remainder of the loyal warships staggered into port.[24]

On February 21 Admiral da Gama ordered the *Aquidabã* and the cruiser *República* to proceed to Bahia to confront the government's fleet. However, the *República* was hit by shore batteries and sustained severe engine-room damage. The two ships instead proceeded to Paranaguá, southwest of Rio de Janeiro, to effect repairs. The *República* could not be made ready for combat so the *Aquidabã* returned to Rio de Janeiro. The opportunity to seek a decisive engagement with the President's fleet was lost.[25]

On March 1 the government fleet sailed from Bahia for Rio de Janeiro and anchored outside that harbor a week later with great difficulty. The government ships were ill-equipped. They lacked boarding weapons, such as swords and cutlasses. No one knew how to operate the Sims-Edison torpedoes that were on board some of the ships. There were only a few rounds for the dynamite gun. Many of the ships had been improperly loaded. And some members of the crews were even suspected of being rebel sympathizers. In fact, the only reliable elements of the entire fleet were the European-built torpedo boats. On March 8 the tug *Audaz* brought orders from the President and took the Minister of the Navy Coelho Neto, who had traveled in Admiral Gonçlaves' flagship the *Niterói*, ashore.[26] The fleet dropped anchor in Rio's harbor on March 10.[27]

Admiral da Gama judged that he did not have sufficient force to meet a combined attack by forts and ships. The protected cruiser *Almirante Tamandaré* had only one engine room operational and could therefore make only six knots. In fact, for the last several months Admiral da Gama's charisma and professionalism had been all that had kept the revolt alive in Rio.[28]

On March 11 the Admiral tried without success to negotiate terms. He offered to surrender, provided that his officers were permitted to leave Brazil and that the lives of his men were spared. President Peixoto rejected the proposal on the grounds that a government could not accept terms offered by rebels. The next day the government announced that its forces would attack within forty-eight hours. Admiral da Gama and his supporters sought and received asylum on board two Portuguese warships.[29] The government forces, although aware that the rebel ships and strong points had been abandoned, still carried out its bombardment, which lasted for an hour and a half. By nightfall the government's forces occupied the rebel ships and positions in the harbor.[30]

Admiral da Gama had quit the fight. Whether Flint's propaganda concerning the dynamite fleet played a part in his decision is unclear. Probably the Admiral just succumbed to a more tenacious adversary. Luckily for the "dynamite fleet," the Admiral did not have enough strength left in Rio de Janeiro to confront it. The *Aquidabã* alone, had she been present, could have made it uncomfortable for the Yankeemanned fleet.

THE REBELLION CONTINUES IN THE SOUTH

The naval rebellion was not yet extinguished, though. Admiral Mello was in Curitiba still coordinating efforts with the rebels ashore, and he still had under his control the *Aquidabã*, *República*, *Iris*, *Meteoro Esperança*, two torpedo boats, and a few commandeered merchantmen. A half-hearted attempt to capture the state of Rio Grande do Sul failed and on April 16 the rebel cause received its *côup de grace* when Admiral Mello took his ships into Argentine waters and surrendered to local authorities. Under his command at the time were all rebel naval units except the *Aquidabã*.

TORPEDOING THE AQUIDABÃ

After gaining control of Rio's harbor, President Peixoto sent his expensive new navy south to deal with the remnants of the rebel fleet. A squadron of six armed merchantships and four torpedo craft found the *Aquidabã* in Santa Catarina Bay, near Desterro, the remaining rebel stronghold.[31] Her commanding officer had a line of buoys laid across the channel to simulate mines.[32] Apparently there were no small boats patrolling.

On the night of April 14–15, boats from the squadron reconnoitered and found the battleship anchored under the lee of fortified Santa Cruz. The torpedo boats *Gustavo Sampaio*, *Pedro Afonso*, *Pedro Ivo*, and *Silvado* attempted to attack, but they were discovered entering the bay. The *Aquidabã* was alerted and the torpedo boats retired. The following evening the *São Salvador* entered the bay and destroyed the lookout station with machine-gun fire. After the moon set, the torpedo boats started in a second time and passed through the simulated mines.

The night was dark. The torpedo boats entered the bay line abreast and, once in the harbor, turned in succession to starboard. They did not find the battleship where they believed her to be. Soon, however, the *Gustavo Sampaio* stumbled on the *Aquidabã* and drew her fire. The *Gustavo Sampaio* launched her first torpedo prematurely and without result. The second torpedo, fired at a distance of four hundred feet, struck the *Aquidabã* forward without seeming to damage her.

Figure 33. The Brazilian "Revolution" of 1893–84. The heavy guns of the *Aquidabã* were the backbone of the rebel fleet and although they could deliver tactical successes, they could not produce a strategic victory. *Aquidabã* proved to be a very unlucky ship. It was possibly the first warship to be hit by an automotive torpedo *while under way* (April 16, 1894). The *Aquidabã* was destroyed later by an internal explosion (January 21, 1906). *Courtesy Brazilian Navy.*

The exchange of fire drew the other torpedo boats to the battleship. The *Pedro Ivo* had boiler problems and abandoned the attack; the *Silvado* was driven off by a launch coming from shore; and the *Pedro Afonso* fired two torpedoes but apparently neither hit. The torpedo craft withdrew without knowing the extent of their success. In fact, the torpedo from the *Gustavo Sampaio* had ripped a 26-by-6-foot hole in the bow of the *Aquidabã*.[33] The crew got the battleship underway, beached it in relatively shallow water, and abandoned the ship. She was boarded by government forces on April 16, the same day Admiral Mello surrendered to Argentine authorities.

OBSERVATIONS

The conflict of 1893–94 was a struggle between the haves of society over sharing power. It was a classic intraclass struggle. Both sides talked about constitutional issues; however, for many this was more form than substance.

A succession of political and military blunders doomed the Brazilian naval revolt. First, the navy did not gauge the national will accurately. Although some of the population was opposed to President Peixoto, he still enjoyed the loyalty of a majority, at least in the capital. And the heterogeneity of the navy's supporters compounded the fleet's problems. This was painfully demonstrated by the growing rift between Admirals Mello and da Gama as the revolution wore on.

Second, Admirals Mello and da Gama could not agree on how to deal with the slowly forged navy of Peixoto, thus ignoring a primary tenant of sound naval strategy, namely eliminating the enemy's fleet. The government's sea force was slowly but surely pulled together, and it ultimately played a major role in defeating its enemy. The rebel navy failed to take advantage of one great opportunity: If the government's ships had been defeated as they arrived piecemeal, all of Flint's propaganda would have worked against them. Contemporary Brazilians who appreciated the weakness of Flint's "Dynamite Fleet" referred to it as the "Cardboard Fleet" (*Esquadra de Papelão*). Given the poor track record of the dynamite gun, a rebel victory is not inconceivable.

The insurgents also made other tactical errors. The blockade of Rio de Janeiro was inconsistently enforced, ultimately causing its collapse, and the reliance on the gun to pressure the government was a failure. The presence of the *Aquidabã*'s big guns often provided the margin of a tactical victory; however, it could not bring strategic success.

Whether a meaningful union with rebellious land forces in the south was possible is open to conjecture, but it is clear that only through such a union could the fleet have acquired what it needed most—a creditable land force.

As it turned out, the large number of ships available to the rebels was of little advantage. The rebels were unable to hold strategic points it seized such as Armação and Ilha das Cobras due to its shortage of men.[34] Manpower was so limited that the protected cruiser *Almirante Tamandaré* was crewed by only thirty-seven men during the height of the gun duels against the harbor forts; its normal complement was 400 men.[35]

PART 13

POLITICAL INTERVENTION BY THE UNITED STATES

CHAPTER THIRTY-EIGHT

THE SPANISH-AMERICAN WAR, 1898

> Please remain. You furnish the pictures and I'll furnish the war.
> —William Randolph Hearst to Frederic Remington

THE SPARK

During the evening of February 15, 1898, the U.S. second-class battleship *Maine* exploded in Havana Harbor. Of the 350 men on board, 252 were killed or missing and 8 more died in hospitals over the next few days. A U.S. naval court of inquiry which convened in March concluded that a submarine mine had set off the ship's magazine. American public opinion was inflamed by the press. The headlines of Hearst's *New York Journal* read "THE WARSHIP MAINE WAS SPLIT IN TWO BY AN ENEMY'S SECRET INFERNAL MACHINE."[1] The United States declared war against Spain on April 25, effective on the twenty-first.[2]

BACKGROUND

By the end of the nineteenth century, new world powers were beginning to emerge—Germany, Japan, and the United States. The United States' interest in Latin America was reawakened following some three decades of post-Civil War reconstruction. Concurrent with the renewed activity of the United States in the region, Great Britain found it militarily expedient to concede the Americas to Uncle Sam and concentrate its resources against the more threatening upstarts of Germany and Japan.

One place within Latin America had held the interest of the United States from the earliest days under the Constitution—Cuba. The acquisition of Cuba had been the objective of numerous diplomatic initiatives and many filibustering expeditions.

Cuba did not have its first serious independence movement until the late 1860s. The First War for Independence was fought between 1869 and 1879 and the Second War for Independence between 1895 and 1898—the latter having ground into a stalemate when the *Maine* exploded (see chapter 32).

The decade of the 1890s was also an era of intense newspaper competition within the United States. Americans, reawakened to the outside world, were hungry for news. Hearst and Pulitzer owned newspapers that were the leading rivals. These and other tabloids sent reporters to Cuba where wars had raged on and off since 1868. The hottest stories were Spanish "brutalities" verified by "eyewitnesses." The measure of successful journalism was the sale of newspapers and not the truth—this sensationalism became known as the "yellow press."[3] By 1896 the "yellow press" had made Cuba a presidential campaign issue. Newly elected U.S. President William McKinley sent the Spanish various proposals for solving the Cuban dilemma. Although not formally answering, the Spanish did replace the brutal Gen. Valeriano Weyler as the administrator of the island in October 1897 as a concession.

Then, a series of incidents brought the two nations to the brink of war. On January 12, 1898, rioting broke out in Havana in protest to Captain-General Blanco's proposed concessions for the autonomy of Cuba; these were staged by supporters of General Weyer who opposed any concessions. Although there was no threat to U.S. property, Consul-General Fitzhugh Lee requested the presence of a U.S. warship; the battleship *Maine* arrived on January 25.

On February 9 the Hearst newspaper the *New York Journal* published a private letter from the Spanish Minister Plenipotentiary to Washington, Enrique Dupuy de Lôme, to his friend. Dupuy de Lôme wrote, "McKinley is weak and catering to the rabble, and, besides, a low politician who desires to leave a door open to me and to stand well with the jingoes of his party."[4] Although Dupuy de Lôme resigned and the Spanish government apologized, this incident contributed to increasing tensions. Six days later, the battleship *Maine* exploded while at anchor. On March 28 President McKinley forwarded to Congress a Navy report which concluded incorrectly that a submarine mine had set off the ship's magazine.[5] Although this report was withheld, the public, influenced by the "yellow press," had already come to the same conclusion. A New York newspaper boasted on March 26, "The readers of the *Journal* knew immediately after the destruction of the *Maine* that she had been blown up by a Spanish mine."[6] The popular outcry became "Remember the *Maine!*"

The McKinley administration immediately requested additional money for national defense from Congress and demanded numerous concessions from Spain which ultimately included the abandonment of Cuba. Although Madrid did stop its *reconcentrado* policy and met other American demands, it would not yield on this issue of sovereignty. On April 11 McKinley asked Congress for the authority to end the fighting on Cuba. Between the eleventh and the nineteenth, Congress debated this request, split by the question of recognition for the Cuban insurgents. On April 21 Congress passed a joint resolution giving the President authority to intervene. The Spanish government declared that the resolution amounted to a declaration of war by the United States. In response, McKinley asked Congress for a declaration of war on the twenty-fifth. Congress declared war on that day but made it retroactive to the twenty-first to legalize any prizes the U.S. Navy had already seized since it had declared much of Cuba blockaded, effective the twenty-second. Before going to war, the United States renounced the annexation of Cuba (but reserved freedom of action with regard to Spain's other colonies—Puerto Rico, the Philippines, the Carolines, and the Marianas).[7]

OPPOSING FORCES

Navies would play the preeminent role in a war between Spain and the United States, because Cuba and the Philippines were islands and because of the vast distances between theaters of operations. Both navies in fact, although not in name, had general staffs. These were designed to direct the strategy of both protagonists. This was made feasible, at least in the minds of the staffs, by the advent of improved communications—the telegraph in particular. Warships did not possess radios yet. As a consequence, decision-makers sitting in their capitals telegraphed their fleets via ports of call.

Logistics was a major challenge for both countries. The biggest problem was supplying enough coal where it was needed for the fleets. A major warship carried about one thousand tons of coal. Coaling at sea could be accomplished only under ideal conditions and was rarely done. The sea had to be calm; the crews well trained; and an adequate number of sacks or baskets on hand which were normally carried by the collier (a coal-carrying ship). Therefore, it was important to secure coaling sites adjunct to protected waters near the war zone.

Preceding the war the Spanish navy had been influenced by the French *jeune école* (the young school). These naval theoreticians argued that the proper composition of a modern navy should be of commerce-raiding cruisers for offense and fortifications and torpedo boats for defense. Battleships were a thing of the past. A most appealing aspect of this theory was that a fleet based on the *jeune école* concept was significantly less expensive than one based on battleships. In 1898 the Spanish navy was composed of one old battleship, four armored cruisers, seven small destroyers, and seven torpedo-destroyer boats.[8] In addition, Spain had about seventy very small gunboats scattered throughout the empire. Of this entire collection only four armored cruisers, three destroyers, and a few gunboats were of much value.

Immediately before the war, Spain endeavored to purchase warships from abroad. A number of regional arms races were underway and a number of European yards were building warships on speculation. Spain only succeeded in buying the partially armed armored cruiser *Giuseppe Garibaldi* (future *Cristóbal Colón*) from the Italian navy.[9]

The U.S. Navy had been reborn in 1883 after the nation's disinterest in the sea service following the Civil War. In 1898 the U.S. Navy had four first-class battleships, one second-class battleship, six harbor defense monitors, fourteen protected cruisers, eight torpedo boats, and some twenty lesser craft. As with any new military force, some of these ships suffered from design and teething problems. In general the freeboard of the battleships was too low, making them very difficult to fight even in moderate seas. Also, the high-performance reciprocating steam engines in some U.S. battleships and cruisers proved cranky.[10]

Anticipating war, the U.S. Navy added over one hundred ships to its fleet through purchase or charter between March 16 and August 12. Most of these formed the train intended to provide logistical support. There were a few first-class warships. The U.S. Navy purchased the new cruisers *Amazonas* (future *New Orleans*) and the *Almirante Abreu* (future *Albany*) from the Brazilian navy to prevent the Spanish navy from buying the ships. The composition of the U.S. Navy was best suited to a general fleet action in relatively protected waters close to the United States.[11]

Meanwhile, the United States ordered the battleship *Oregon* to make the long trip from San Francisco around South America to the Caribbean, and recalled the cruiser *Cincinnati* and two gunboats from South American waters, as well as various gunboats from Central America.[12]

On paper the size of the Spanish army was impressive. In 1898 almost half a million men (regulars and volunteers) were under arms and many were in the right places to defend the 400-year-old empire: 278,447 men in Cuba; 10,005 men in Puerto Rico; 51,331 men in the Philippines; and 152,284 men in Spain. Due to the corruption within the army, these were grossly inflated numbers. Superiors were pocketing the allowances for the dead and missing. The true strength of the army in Cuba was about 80,000 men and proportionally reduced elsewhere.[13]

The Spanish infantry was armed with first-quality Mauser repeating rifles which fired cartridges using smokeless powder. The artillery was a mixed bag. The army possessed a few Krupp breachloaders. The remainder were old, muzzleloading guns of limited value.

On the other side of the Atlantic, the U.S. Army was ill-prepared for the war. It numbered 28,183 regulars, most of whom were serving in the western frontier. Although the regular army was doubled at the outbreak of the war, it was still grossly undersized to fight the Spaniards and at the same time continue its safeguarding of the frontier. Initially, the 100,000-man state militias were to be mobilized but this plan was abandoned in favor of calling for regiments of volunteers due to the popularity of the war. In some cases entire state militias joined as volunteer units. In all some 200,000 men volunteered. As to be expected, these volunteer regiments varied significantly in quality. Many officers were political appointees, but some were former regulars who had quit the army for the better pay and more relaxed discipline of the volunteers.[14]

The United States possessed only 53,000 Krag-Jorgeson repeating rifles (known as the new magazine rifle) and 15,000 Krag carbines. These weapons fired 7.62mm bullets and their magazines held five cartridges. These were adequate to supply the regulars, but the volunteers had to be armed with the singleshot "trapdoor" Springfield rifles which were a remanufactured Civil War design. This weapon fired a cartridge using black powder which produced clouds of smoke and gave away the position of the user. The American artillery was weak. The 3.25-inch breachloader was the standard gun. It also discharged clouds of smoke.[15]

OPENING STRATEGIES

The United States had a clear objective—the liberation of Cuba from Spanish rule—and its strategy was to land a 70,000-man army at Mariel and capture Havana, which it believed would force Spain to come to terms. There was some urgency to the issue. First, yellow fever was most intense during the rainy season (May through November). In the recent past this disease had virtually destroyed unacclimated European armies campaigning in the Caribbean within a few months. Second, the other major world powers were not anxious to see the strength of the upstart United States increase at the expense of weak, sick Spain. Although American diplomats did not believe any would come to the aid of Spain, this could not be guaranteed.[16] Third, long wars have never been popular in democracies.[17] How to capture Havana before the onset of the yellow fever season and who was to command the army was unclear. So, an interim step was taken.[18]

Many believed that the most logical candidate to lead the U.S. Army to Cuba was Maj. Gen. Nelson A. Miles,[19] Commander-in-Chief of the U.S. Army. However, he was a Democrat with political ambitions which made him unpalatable to a Republican administration. Instead, McKinley chose the grossly overweight, old wily Indian fighter William "Pecos Bill" Shafter[20] to lead a reconnaissance in force to the island in order to breathe new life into the Cuban Revolutionaries.

Publicly, Spain's objective was to preserve its sovereignty over Cuba, Puerto Rico, and the Philippines. Privately, at least some politicians concluded that this was impossible given the preponderance of U.S. forces. At least two strategies were discussed. The first was to establish a base of operations at San Juan, Puerto Rico, or Havana, Cuba, and raid U.S. convoys and commerce. The second strategy discussed was even less realistic. This called for combining the Cape Verde and Havana Squadrons and blockading the Yucatan Channel and the Straits of Florida. As reinforcements arrived, the blockade would be extended to the East Coast of the United States in order to bring about a decisive naval engagement.[21]

The Spanish military did believe that the United States had an "Achilles heel." An 1896 Spanish estimate of the U.S. military concluded,

> The North American Navy without doubt suffers from a serious defect . . . it is the lack of men for the ships' crews. . . . The system of recruiting in use is, as in the land forces, the admission of volunteers desiring to serve; and as the strength of the Regular Army is constantly seen to be diminishing by the plague of desertion.[22]

THE OPENING MOVES

Prior to the outbreak of war, Spain tried to practice a little gunboat diplomacy of her own. The armored cruiser *Vizcaya* was sent to New York on a goodwill tour to counter the *Maine*'s presence in Havana; the Spanish ship had the misfortune of arriving in the United States three days after the *Maine* exploded. And the armored cruiser *Oquendo* was sent to Havana to bolster Spanish presence. Appreciating that war might be imminent, these ships were ordered to rendezvous with a flotilla of destroyers and torpedo boats in the Atlantic on April 8. The force then proceeded to the Cape Verde Islands where it was joined by the armored cruisers *Colón* and *Teresa* from Spain. The squadron was in sad condition. The *Vizcaya* could make only fourteen knots due to the fouling of her bottom. Admiral Cervera was short of money, coal, and auxiliaries. The steamer *San Francisco* arrived with two thousand tons of coal, but this only temporarily eased the problem.[23]

Within days of declaring war, the U.S. Navy began to blockade Cuba; however, it was weeks before the entire island was subjected to a full blockade. The U.S. Navy also immediately began to escort ships running guns and supplies to the insurgents. On April 26 the fast steamer *Monserrat*, carrying 800 Spanish troops and arms, slipped into Cienfuegos ahead of the blockaders. A large number of ships were needed to maintain the blockade and this forced the U.S. Navy to disperse much of its force.

Lacking a clear strategy, Adm. Pascual Cervera y Topete sailed from the Cape Verde Islands for the Caribbean on April 29. On the same day, Rear Adm. William T. Sampson, commanding U.S. naval forces in the Caribbean, was notified by the War Department that Cervera had sailed destination unknown. Days passed with no news of the Spanish fleet. Erroneous sightings were reported along the length of America's Atlantic seaboard. In response to public outcry for protection, the U.S. Navy formed a flying Squadron composed of its fastest ships, created the Northern Patrol Squadron, and stationed old monitors in various ports. The Flying Squadron, commanded by Commodore Winfield Scott Schley, was stationed at Norfolk, Virginia. If the United States had been aware of the conditions in Cervera's fleet, the Americans would have rested more easily. *Colón*, recently purchased from Italy, did not mount her main battery. *Vizcaya* was in need of an overhaul. All three torpedo boats were found to be unseaworthy and sent home. The fleet was short of ammunition, coal, food, fresh water, and even charts of the American coast.[24]

SEARCHING FOR CERVERA

Guessing that Cervera would make for the nearest port in the Caribbean, the U.S. battle fleet arrived at San Juan, Puerto Rico, early on May 12. Frustrated at not finding Cervera, Sampson bombarded San Juan for two hours and then sailed for Havana.

On the same day, Cervera arrived at Martinique 385 miles to the southeast. He sent the destroyer *Furor* ahead to Fort de France to send and receive telegraph messages. The news could not have been worse: A state of war existed between Spain and the United States; no coal was available in Martinique; a powerful U.S. squadron was operating off Puerto Rico; two fast U.S. auxiliary cruisers (armed ocean liners) were near the island; the Spanish squadron in Manila had been destroyed; and the U.S. fleet was blockading Cuba but Santiago was unguarded. Desperate for coal, he sailed to his alternate rendezvous site, Curaçao, arriving on the fifteenth, but still no collier. Given his shortage of coal, he had two practical choices—Cienfuegos (121 mi ESE of Havana) or Santiago (580 mi ESE of Havana). Although he had been misinformed that no coal was available in Santiago, at least it was a haven. The Spanish squadron reached Santiago on May 19 without being detected.

The Americans were still unaware of Cervera's location. Schley and the Flying Squadron were ordered to Key West. On May 17 the War Board inaccurately informed Sampson that Cervera had orders to go to Havana or Cienfuegos. On the eighteenth Schley sailed for Cienfuegos, arriving four days later, and Sampson watched Havana. Schley could not immediately determine whether the ships' masts that could be seen were those of Cervera's fleet. Meanwhile, Sampson was notified that Cervera had been seen entering Santiago. He ordered Schley to proceed there to investigate. Schley, still unaware of the types of ships in Cienfuegos, delayed until the twenty-fourth but then sailed. He arrived off Santiago on May 26, talked to U.S. vessels stationed off the port which had no knowledge of Cervera's presence, and then sailed for Key West. One day out, Schley was intercepted by a dispatch boat which confirmed that Cervera was indeed in Santiago. Returning on the twenty-ninth, the *Colón* could been seen at the mouth of the harbor. On May 31 Schley's force dueled with the *Colón* and the coastal batteries at 7,000 yards. Neither side did damage. Sampson arrived with the remainder of the American major combatants on June 1 and took command. On June 2–3 the U.S. Navy failed in an attempt to scuttle the U.S. collier *Merrimac* in the narrow entrance to the harbor. On June 10 Sampson landed a battalion of Marines and seized Guantanamo Bay, fifty miles east of Santiago, as a coaling station.[25]

CREATING THE AMERICAN ARMY

While the naval cat-and-mouse game was going on, the United States struggled to create an army. Volunteers flooded in faster than they could be accommodated. Scandals of poor sanitation occurred in the camps as a result.

Regular Army units were sent to Tampa, Florida, the U.S. port closest to Cuba with a rail connection; its facilities proved completely inadequate to handle the task. Loading of the expedition did not begin until June 8 due to the poor organization. Prohibited from chartering a fleet train until the outbreak of war, the Army found poor pickings left behind by the Navy. It gathered together a conglomeration of coastal steamers and paddlewheel relics.

While the Army was being assembled, General Miles dispatched Lt. Andrew Rowan to Cuba to find General Calixto García and discuss possible strategies. Calíxto García sent Brig. Gen. Enrique Collazo and Lt. Col. Carlos Hernández back to Washington. Hernández soon re-

Figure 34. Spanish-American War, 1898. American troops land at Daiquiri on June 22, 1898. They were unopposed thanks to the initiative of the Cuban revolutionary army that had driven the Spaniards from the town. Amphibious landings were a very risky business during the nineteenth century and typically were poorly executed due to inadequate time to prepare and a lack of attention to detail. Two landings that were exceptionally well planned and executed were the American one at Vera Cruz in March 1847 and the Chilean one at Quintero Bay in August 1891. *Copied from* Harper's New Monthly Magazine, *Vol. 98 (May 1899).*

turned to Cuba with a note from General Miles asking Calíxto García to keep 5,000 soldiers in the vicinity of Santiago.[26]

LANDING IN CUBA

The 16,873-man expedition under Major General Shafter sailed on June 14. The 5th Corps was organized into two infantry divisions, a cavalry division, an independent brigade, and miscellaneous corps. Fortunately for the slow, barely seaworthy invasion flotilla, no storms occurred and no Spanish torpedo boats appeared. As Rear Adm. M. Plüddenmann of the German navy observed, "The voyage and the landing were effected in the most beautiful weather; the Americans had good luck, as they always did."[27]

Shafter believed that his immediate problem was getting his force safely to Cuba. He and Admiral Sampson disembarked from their respective flotillas and met ashore with the Cuban Revolutionary, General Calíxto García. Shafter decided to land at Daiquiri, some thirteen miles east of Santiago, over Sampson's objections that it was too far from that city. Cuban Gen. Demetrio Castillo Duany captured Daiquiri, clearing the way for the American landing.

Playing it safe, a ship bombardment preceded the landing on June 22. Following the landing, the Americans discovered that their naval gunfire had failed to hit any of the evacuated Spanish blockhouses. While the Americans were landing, Cuban Revolutionary General Duany secured the coast as far as Siboney.[28]

THE BATTLE OF LAS GUÁSIMAS

The Americans then advanced against Santiago in two columns, one along the main road and the other by way of a jungle path that paralleled it. These merged at Las Guásmas which was defended by 1,500 Spaniards supported by two Krupp guns. Spanish sniper fire pinned down the "Rough Riders," who had taken the trail. The Americans advanced and the Spanish quit without much of a fight. U.S. losses were sixteen dead and fifty-two wounded; the Spanish casualties were thirty-five. From the hills around Las Guásimas, one could see the rooftops in Santiago. The American Army could not advance because of a lack of ammunition and vitals, which had not yet been unloaded.[29]

THE LAND BATTLE OF SANTIAGO

Some 36,000 Spanish troops under Gen. Arsenio Linares defended Santiago province. He spread the city's 10,500-man garrison in a circle around Santiago, choosing to defend the entire perimeter with equal force. Three thousand Spanish reinforcements were on their way from Manzanillo, some 140 miles to the west over a poorly maintained road. However, they were delayed by the Cuban Revolutionaries.[30]

The Americans simultaneously attacked El Caney and San Juan Heights overlooking the city. Shafter believed that Brig. Gen. Henry Lawton's 5,400-man division could carry El Caney within three hours. The hill was defended by 600 Spanish troops commanded by Brig. Gen. Joaquin Vara del Rey, an experienced officer. In the early morning of July 1, the American artillery began firing on the Spanish troops entrenched at El Caney. However, the attacking American troops were soon pinned down and it took ten hours of hard fighting to take El Caney. The defenders, nearly out of ammunition, sustained 400 casualties, including General Vara del Rey. The attackers sustained 450 casualties. The attack on San Juan Heights also opened with an artillery bombardment. The Americans were met first by sniper fire and then by Krupp artillery. Fierce fighting continued throughout the day. By nightfall the Americans, bloodied and somewhat shaken, had taken the heights. They lost 205 dead and 1,180 wounded; the Spanish lost 215 dead and 376 wounded, including General Linares.

Although these two successes gave Shafter the heights that overlooked Santiago, he possessed no heavy artillery to fully exploit the advantage and he was overextended. Shafter sent a dispatch to Washington stating that he was considering withdrawal. However, the destruction of Cervera's fleet on the third placed the Spanish army defending Santiago in a hopeless position.[31]

THE SEA BATTLE OF SANTIAGO

The Spanish perceived their position in Santiago was deteriorating. The Americans were tightening their circle on the city. Insurgents were delaying the advance of the relief column. Supplies were running low. And, the fleet had orders to escape. During Sunday morning, July 3, the Spanish fleet sortied. Sampson had departed a half hour earlier with a battleship and two cruisers to recoal at nearby Guantanamo Bay and confer with General Shafter. The Spanish fleet steamed west hugging the coast. A general running melee ensued. The Spanish gunners

Figure 35. Spanish-American War, 1898. The second-class battleship *Texas* returns to New York following the Battle of Santiago. Her wartime grey paint scheme is well worn. The *Texas*' design and that of the ill-fated *Maine* were influenced by the design of the Brazilian armored cruiser *Aquidabã*. Ironically, the *Texas* suffered numerous "teething" problems early in her career and had the reputation of being a hard-luck ship whereas her near-sister, the *Maine*, was perceived to be a lucky ship. *Courtesy Naval Historical Foundation.*

overshot their targets but the Americans were more accurate. This combined with their greater speed and volume of fire and heavier ordnance soon wreaked havoc in the Spanish fleet. After a three-hour-and-forty-five-minute unequal gun duel, the entire Spanish fleet was destroyed. In all, 323 Spanish sailors died, 151 were severely wounded, and the remainder, some 1,813, were taken prisoner. The United States lost one dead and six wounded; the fleet sustained virtually no damage.[32]

As the siege of Santiago tightened, the relations between the mostly white American Army and the predominantly black Cuban army disintegrated. The Cuban army had taken little part in the attacks against Santiago's outer defenses. The Americans entrusted the Cubans with forty Spanish prisoners and the Cubans promptly cut off their heads. General Calíxto García did not use his forces to delay the Spanish relief column as it neared Santiago. Regardless, all worked out to the advantage of the Americans because the Spanish reinforcements brought no munitions or supplies. Thus, the relief column became part of the problem for the Spanish commander and was not the hoped-for solution.[33]

Following the U.S. naval victory off Santiago, Gen. José Toral, who had relieved Linares after he was wounded, unconditionally surrendered. The victory came none too soon because yellow fever had broken out among the U.S. troops. Relations between the U.S. and Cuban troops continued to sour. Shafter prohibited Cuban troops from entering Santiago. This was resented by the Cubans, who had to be restrained by Calíxto García.[34]

ENDING THE WAR

On July 23 Spain requested U.S. terms to end the war. McKinley demanded independence for Cuba and the cession of Puerto Rico and Guam. Manila would be held pending the peace treaty. On July 25, some 3,300 U.S. troops under General Miles landed at Guanica, on the southwest coast of Puerto Rico. The force swept northward toward San Juan. The American forces had captured the western half of the island when Spain agreed to terms and signed the protocols of peace on August 12, ending the fighting. The United States did not permit the Cuban Revolutionaries to take part in the peace conference. The war formally ended on December 10, 1898. On January 1, 1899, Captain-General Adolfo Jiménez Castellanos surrendered Havana to Gen. R. Brooke, ending four hundred years of Spanish rule over Cuba.[35]

OBSERVATIONS

Ambassador John Hay captured the American euphoria with the results of the war when he wrote to Theodore Roosevelt, "It has been a splendid little war; begun with the highest motives, carried on with magnificent intelligence and spirit, favored by that fortune that loves the brave."[36]

By the Treaty of Paris, Spain relinquished sovereignty over Cuba and ceded to the United States the Philippine Islands, Guam in the Marianas, Puerto Rico, and "other islands now under Spanish sovereignty in the West Indies." The United States promised the inhabitants of these islands "the free exercise of their religion" but their civil and political rights were to be determined by the U.S. Congress. The United States had become a true imperial power.[37]

The Spanish-American War heralded the emergence of the United States as a political and military world power, thus complementing its status as an economic power. A foreign diplomat in Washington stated three years after the war, "I have seen two Americas, the America before the Spanish-American War and the America since."[38]

The United States had intentionally taken the war effort away from the Cuban Revolutionaries in order to "Americanize" the outcome. Following the Spanish capitulation, Maj. Gen. Fitzhugh Lee, the new military governor of Havana and Pinar del Río provinces, feared that the Revolutionary soldiers might renew the fight, this time against the United States as was taking place in the Philippines, or they might resort to banditry. To prevent these possibilities, the new U.S. military government gave many Revolutionary officers civil appointments, began public works projects, and paid 33,950 Revolutionary veterans seventy-five pesos each for their weapons. These efforts were financed by a loan from private U.S. banks. By the end of 1899, the

Revolutionary army no longer existed. Whether the seventy-five pesos was fair compensation for their services remained the most volatile subject of Cuban politics for the next thirty years.[39]

As a consequence of the war, Cuba became a protectorate of the United States. For Latin America, the Spanish-American War was a clear, loud signal that the United States had renewed its interest in expanding its influence southward. For Chile in particular, with whom the United States had feuded during the 1880s and 1890s, the warning was that the northern giant had grown beyond Chile's military potential and possessed the will to use its recently forged muscle.

The American victory was one of brute force with little finesse. Many men died of disease first in the United States and later in Cuba; of the 5,462 U.S. deaths, only 379 fatalities were in combat. At times logistical planning was atrocious; for example, most U.S. troops fought on these semitropical islands in blue woolen uniforms. Cooperation among the senior officers left much to be desired. And politics frequently held sway over sound military judgment. The United States won so easily because she had chosen the right enemy. As Otto von Bismarck reportedly growled, "God takes care of drunken men, sailors, and the United States."[40]

Possibly the most significant military reform to take place in the United States was the creation of a general staff system to replace the commanding general and the chiefs of the army bureaus. Under this old system the relationship between the Commanding General and the Secretary of the Army was ill-defined and bureau chiefs had virtual life tenure which did not contribute to efficiency. The new Chief of Staff of the Army was selected by the President for a four-year tour.[41]

The poor Spanish showing can be attributed in large part to corruption. This had resulted in forged rosters, false inventories, and defective ammunition. On land, Spain was unable to take advantage of its better artillery and more abundant, quality rifles. At sea, Spain failed to evolve a strategy that offered any hope of victory.

Vice Admiral P. H. Colomb of the British navy concluded: "He [Cervera] was not only asked to make bricks without straw, but without even clay, and his failure was always certain. . . . Spain did nothing that she ought to have done and left undone everything that she ought to have done."[42]

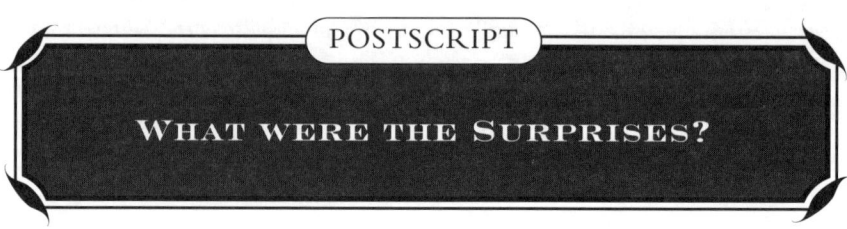

POSTSCRIPT

WHAT WERE THE SURPRISES?

> Human experience largely consists of surprises superseding surmises.
>
> —Humanist Ogden Nash

When I neared the end of a decade of writing, which followed a decade of research, I asked myself, "What were the surprises?" Experience tells me that these responses are either the shattering of inaccurate beliefs or the filling of important voids.

STRATEGIC SURPRISES

First, the early Latin American wars for independence (1810–24) were civil wars between Latin Americans and not wars against foreigners. And these conflicts were filled with all the horrors of civil wars—the horrendous destruction of life and property.

It would be a gross oversimplification to say that these civil wars evolved into intraclass struggles where competing elites fought for decades to determine who would decide the fate of their nation. Nonetheless, this gross overstatement does offer a starting point to comprehend the Latin American wars that followed those for independence.

Second, many nineteenth-century Latin American wars were fought by feudal armies. The lord was the *caudillo* and his vassals the peasants. The peasants were loyal to the *caudillo*, or vice versa, because he fulfilled their needs and they, like the *caudillo*, did not care much about ideology. One should not be surprised that when a Liberal *caudillo* was defeated and killed by a Conservative *caudillo*, many of the dead *caudillo*'s followers, both men and women, changed sides in spite of an apparent ideological contradiction.

Toward the end of the nineteenth century, the influence of the *caudillo* began to decline in South America but lingered much longer in Central America and the Caribbean. The era of the *caudillo* declined for many reasons. Some ruling *caudillos* realized that the system that had brought them to power would ultimately consume them when they became old and were no longer the "toughest of the tough." These *caudillos* began to professionalize their officer corps to preserve their rule against the likes of themselves. Thus, the era of the professional officer corps began to evolve in the late nineteenth century.

Third, many Latin American soldiers who become the "presidents" of their nations achieved that status through their successes on the battlefield and not just through political manipulation.

Since many survey histories are written from a political science perspective, many of these "presidents" are judged by their poor political skills and moral misconduct, frequently leaving one to wonder how these politically inept and morally bankrupt individuals ever became the leaders of their nations. In fact, their personal bravery and martial skills allowed them to seize and to retain the "right" to govern. Three individuals who exemplify this were Antonio López de Santa Anna of Mexico, Mariano Melgarejo of Bolivia, and Cipriano Castro of Venezuela.

OPERATIONAL SURPRISES

Most nineteenth-century Latin American wars were fought by "fleas" (very small armies) fighting on the back of an "elephant" (a large land mass). In 1846, for example, an American army of 150 men trekked more than 1,300 miles from Fort Leavenworth, Kansas, to San Diego, California, to carry the war to Mexico. No Latin American army approached the size of those commanded by Napoleon Bonaparte and his European opponents. This does not mean that Latin American military operations were less challenging, they were just different from the European experience.

During two wars, the War between the United Provinces and Brazil (1825–28) and the War of the Confederation where Bolivia and Peru fought against Chile (1836–41), privateers aggressively attacked larger warships. The privateers were inspired by prize money. Regardless, one should be impressed with the courage of these "sailors of fortune"—a trait not common among their brethren in other regions.

TACTICAL SURPRISES

The lack of industrialization within Latin America made the lance and edge weapons the dominant battlefield arms throughout much of the nineteenth century. When the fighting occurred in terrain favorable for horses (Argentina, southeastern Brazil, southern Chile, eastern Colombia, Uruguay, and Venezuela), the cavalry dominated. The dominance of the lance-armed horseman, at which the native American excelled, made it impossible to overwhelm the plains Indians in Latin America until firearms *and* ammunition became available in sufficient quantities, which did not occur until the late nineteenth century.

The exploitation of new weapons was dependent upon their maturity, the ability to service them, *and the local evolution of doctrine on how to employ them*. During the Wars for Cuban Independence (1868–98), the Spaniards used the ultramodern, multishot Mauser rifle as if it were a short-range, muzzle-loading musket. This was because they would not properly train their men for fear that the weapons might be used in Spain against those who governed. Therefore, Spain sacrificed significant battlefield potential.

Nineteenth-century wars profoundly affected the evolution of Latin America. The birth and perfection of *caudillo* rule significantly contributed to the stagnation of democratic evolution. Cannons and commerce did not mix and in many areas these seemingly endless wars never permitted economies to develop. This was particularly damaging since the world was in a period of accelerating economic integration caused by the decline of colonialism and the dawning of the industrial age. Socially, these wars were both an inhibitor and an accelerator of change depending on where and when their impact was measured. In many cases the gap between the socially enfranchised and disenfranchised widened, but in a few cases it narrowed. Overall, during the nineteenth century battlefields were more influential than congressional halls or the pulpits of churches.

NOTES

PREFACE

1. Barbara A. Tenenbaum, ed., *Encyclopedia of Latin American History and Culture*, 5 vols. (New York: Charles Scribner's Sons, 1996), 2: 620.

2. Hernâni Donato, *Dicionário das batalhas brasileiras* (São Paulo: IBRASA, 1987), 19–195.

3. Howard H. Peckham, *The Toll of Independence* (Chicago: University of Chicago Press, 1974), xi–xii, 132–33.

4. Martin Ros, *Night of Fire* (New York: Sarpedon, 1994), 197; Samuel Hazard, *Santo Domingo Past and Present* (London: Sampson Low, Marston, Low & Searle, 1873) 131; David Geggus, "The Cost of Pitt's Caribbean Campaigns, 1793–1798," in *The Historical Journal* 26: 3; 699–706 (1983) 702; Robert Debs Heinl and Nancy Gordon Heinl, *Written in Blood* (Boston: Houghton Mifflin Company, 1978), 121.

5. Heinl and Heinl, *Written in Blood*, 81.

6. The number of deaths sustained by Paraguay during the War of the Triple Alliance is hotly debated and some have placed the figure as high as one million. A recent study by Jurg Meister places the 1864 population at between 500,000 and 525,000 inhabitants. He estimates the postwar population at some 221,000, which means that about 300,000 either died or were killed during the war. Jurg Meister, *Francisco Solano López Nationalheld oder Kriegsverbrecher?* (Osnabrück: Biblio Verlag, 1987), 345, 355, 454–55.

7. Bureau of the Census, *Historical Statistics of the United States, Colonial Times to 1970*, 2 vols. (Washington, D.C.: Government Printing Office, 1975), 2: 7, 1140.

8. Antonio Arráiz, *Los días de ira* (Caracas: Vadell Hermanos, 1989) 98; Enrique Ayala Mora, ed. *Nueva historia del Ecuador*, 15 vols. (Quito: Corporación Editora Nacional, 1990–91), 6: 132; William R. Manning, ed., *Diplomatic Correspondence of the United States concerning the Independence of Latin-American Nations*, 3 vols. (New York: Oxford University Press, 1925), 3: 1600–1.

9. Peckham, *The Toll*, 133.

10. Pedro Henríquez-Ureña, *Literary Currents in Hispanic America* (Cambridge: Harvard University Press, 1945), 133. This quotation is also attributed to Domingo F. Sarmiento. Harold E. Davis, *The Americas in History* (New York: The Ronald Press Company, 1953), 511.

11. *Webster's New International Dictionary of the English Language*, 2d ed. (Springfield: G. & C. Merriam Company, Publishers, 1961), 2134.

12. "Particularly with reference to Latin America, the word [revolution] has been so often used that it has become synonymous with a range of changes from relatively insignificant trading of power between leaders at the pinnacle of a stable political pyramid to profoundly significant upheavals in which social and political institutions mutate to new and unexpected

forms." Richard W. Patch, "Bolivia: The Restrained Revolution," *Annals of American Academy of Political and Social Science* 123–32 (March 1961), 124.

INTRODUCTION

1. Hubert Howe Bancroft, *History of Mexico* (San Francisco: The History Company, Publishers, 1886), 4: 13–17; Mariano Torrente, *Historia de la revolución hispano-americana* 3 vols. (Madrid: La Imprenta de D. Leon Amarita and Imprenta de Moreno, 1829–30), 1: prolog 58–68.

2. Marius André, *La fin de l'empire espagnol d'Amérique* (Paris: Nouvelle Librairie Nationale, 1922), 36–37.

3. Cecil Jane, *Liberty and Despotism in Spanish America* (Oxford: Clarendon Press, 1929), 98.

4. André, *l'empire espagnol*, 45–46.

5. Gustavo Arboleda, *Revoluciones locales de Colombia* (Popayán: Martinez y Torres R., editores, 1907), 60.

6. Walter V. Scholes, *Mexican Politics during the Juárez Regime, 1855–1872* (Columbia: University of Missouri Press, 1957), 11–12.

7. On April 7, 1890, Sir Charles E. Mansfield, the British Minister resident in Lima, wrote to the Marques of Salisbury, the Secretary of State for Foreign Affairs, "There is not a good map of Peru and many of the mentioned points are but found in maps. It is possible without any difficulty to find the rivers and important cities, but indeed many of those names [found on maps] only represent temporary settlements or ancient explorations, abandoned or not existent Indian villages, or points or hills where some chapel existed or still exists." Heraclio Bonilla, *Gran Bretaña y el Peru: informes de los cónsules británicos: 1826–1900*, 5 vols. (Lima: Editorial Gráfica Pacific Press, S.A., 1975–77), 1: 201.

Félix Denegri Luna wrote, "Before independence, boundaries could be adjusted by internal administrative orders from the Spanish king." *Peru and Ecuador: Notes for the History of a Frontier* (Lima: Instituto Riva-Agüero, Pontifica Universidad Católica del Peru, 1996), xv.

8. Salvador de Madariaga, *The Fall of the Spanish-American Empire* (New York: Collier Books, 1963), 240–41; Charles Edward Chapman, *Colonial Hispanic America: A History* (New York: The Macmillan Company, 1933), 170–86; Bernard Moses, *Spain's Declining Power in South America* (Berkeley: University of California Press, 1919), 153–73.

9. George P. Garrison, ed., *Diplomatic Correspondence of the Republic of Texas*, 3 vols. (Washington, D.C.: Government Printing Office, 1908–11), 1: 193–94.

10. Scholes, *Mexican Politics*, 76–77; James Daniel Richardson, *A Compilation of the Messages and Papers of the Presidents*, 22 vols. (New York: Bureau of National Literature, 1897–1917), 7: 3045.

11. The term *caudillo* traces its roots to the Latin *capitellum*, meaning "a small head."

12. Guillermo Morón, *A History of Venezuela* (London: Allen & Unwin, 1964), 168.

13. R. B. Cunninghame Graham, *José Antonio Páez* (New York: Cooper Square Publishers, Inc., 1970), 116; Luís Garfías, *Generales mexicanos del siglo XIX* (Mexico: Secretaría de la Defensa Nacional, 1980), 190–91.

14. "The appearance of great wealth in new areas itself brought conflict, as in the case of the War of the Pacific (1879–1883)." Tulio Halperín Donghi, *The Contemporary History of Latin America* (Durham, N.C.: Duke University Press, 1993), 124.

15. Thomas E. Skidmore and Peter H. Smith, *Modern Latin America*, 2d ed. (New York: Oxford University Press, 1989), 37.

16. W. Stull Holt, "The United States and the Defense of the Western Hemisphere, 1814–1940," *Pacific Historical Review* 10:1; 29–38 (March 1941), 29.

17. Robert L. Scheina, *Latin America: A Naval History, 1810–1987* (Annapolis: U.S. Naval Institute Press, 1987), 304–20.

18. J. M. Gilliss, *The U.S. Naval Astronomical Expedition to the Southern Hemisphere, during the Years 1949–'50–'51–'52*, 4 vols. (Washington, D.C.: A.O.P. Nicholson, Printer, 1855–56), 1: 329; issued as House of Representatives Executive Document No. 121, 34d Congress, 1st Session.

CHAPTER ONE

1. During the colonial era the island Haiti shares with the Dominican Republic was known as Saint Domingue by the French and Santo Domingo or Hispañola by the Spanish. France had been ceded the western half of the island by Spain in 1697 under the Peace of Ryswick.

2. Michael Duffy, *Soldiers, Sugar, and Sea Power* (Oxford: Clerendon Press, 1987), 6, 11–12, 16–17, 155–56.

3. Heinl, *Written in Blood*, 40.

4. Henri Mézière, *Le Général LeClerc 1772–1802 et l'expédition de Saint Domingue* (éditions Tallandier, 1990), 132–36; Rayford W. Logan, *Haiti and the Dominican Republic* (New York: Oxford University Press, 1968), 17–23.

5. Le Cap Haitien, the most important city in northern Haiti, has been known by a variety of names. Throughout its history the city has often been called simply Le Cap.

6. Authors estimate the population of Haiti to be between 500,000 and 600,000. See J. N. Léger, *Haiti Her History and Her Detractors* (New York: The Neale Publishing Co., 1907), 41; Duffy, *Soldiers*, 26n; Logan, *Haiti*, 18–19.

7. David Marley, *Wars of the Americas* (Santa Barbara: ABC-CLIO, 1998), 350.

8. André Rigaud (1761–1811) was an *affranchis* born in Saint Domingue and educated in France. He served in the French West Indian expeditionary force led by Comte d'Estating against the British at Savannah, Georgia, during the American Revolution.

9. de Rouvray continued, "Where is the army that can do this? Where are you to find light cavalry for such a campaign? Troops properly acclimated, hardened against fatigue immune to the insalubrities of the air and climate—soldiers you can garrison, feed, equip, without difficulty and without special gear—*are any other such available except mulatres?*" The use of free *affranchis* against the slaves was unacceptable to the white aristocracy. Heinl, *Written in Blood*, 51.

10. Marley, *Wars*, 352.

11. Thus, former slaves leading black armies which were personally loyal to them changed sides from France, which had abolished slavery, to Spain, which still practiced slavery. Undoubtedly their goal was to increase their personal power in spite of the seemingly self-destructive nature of the decision.

12. Toussaint Louverture (1743–1803) was a literate black slave who had been a coachman and veterinarian prior to the revolution. His knowledge of herbs gave him the status of medicine man among some of the blacks. When he joined the revolution he was given the rank of "Physician-in-Chief of the Armies of the King of France."

13. Jean Jacques Dessalines (1758–1806) was a black slave who had been mistreated and hated both the whites and *affranchis*. The contemporary historian Pamphile de Lacroix described him as "one of the most ferocious beings ever born."

14. Moyse formerly Gilles Bréda (1772–1801)—along with Dessalines, represented the racial extreme of the black revolution. Toussaint affectionately referred to Moyse as his "nephew" and many considered him to be Toussaint's heir apparent.

15. Marley, *Wars*, 352–53.

16. ibid., 353.

17. Heinl, *Written in Blood*, 68.

18. Lt. Col. Thomas Maitland critically wrote in 1796: "H.M.'s cruisers had looked into all the Ports and finding the only large booty of shipping was to be met with at Port-au-Prince against it they determined to go contrary to every idea of military principle." Duffy, *Soldiers*, 100–1.

19. Marley, *Wars*, 354.

20. The French also had their sources of foreign soldiers. Switzerland was then a satellite of France and had to provide three demibrigades (regiments) to the French Army, of which one battalion was sent to Saint Domingue. Of the 840 Swiss soldiers who went to Haiti, only eleven returned home.

21. Marley, *Wars*, 354.

22. Duffy, *Soldiers*, 148.

23. David Geggus, *Slavery, War, and Revolution: The British Occupation of Saint Domingue 1793–1797* (Oxford: Clarendon Press, 1981), 234–48.

24. Duffy, *Soldiers*, 246; Marley, *Wars*, 355.

25. Duffy, *Soldiers*, 246–48.

26. Within fifteen months all of the commissioners were gone except Sonthonax who had once again returned as one of the five. Toussaint was rid of Sonthonax when he was elected to the French Corps Legislatiff (no longer the National Assembly). Marley, *Wars*, 355.

27. Donatien-Marie-Joseph de Vimeur Rochambeau (1750–1813), the son of the French general who won fame at the side of George Washington, had seen extensive service in the West Indies. He was known for his bravery and cruelty. During a critical moment at the Battle of Ravine-a-Couleuvre, he threw his hat into the midst of the blacks and shouted, "My comrades, you will not leave your General's hat behind." Leclerc to the Minister of Marine, February 26, 1802, published in the London *Times*, 2–3 (April 19, 1802), 3.

28. Duffy, *Soldiers*, 298.

29. John Graves Simcoe (1752–1806) served as a light cavalry commander during the American War for Independence and was captured with Cornwallis' army at Yorktown in October 1781.

30. Duffy, *Soldiers*, 303.

31. Michael A. Palmer, *Stoddert's War: Naval Operations during the Quasi-War with France, 1798–1801* (Columbia: University of South Carolina Press, 1987), 153.

32. Heinl, *Written in Blood*, 85.

33. Duffy, *Soldiers*, 306.

34. Jamaica experienced a number of slave revolts during the colonial era, possibly the first in 1678. The first war against runaway slaves, Maroons (derived from the Spanish *cimarrón*, meaning "wild"), lasted five decades (1690–1739). In 1760 slaves rebelled but this was sustained for a few months. In 1795 the Second Maroon War broke out but again did not last long. Many of the captured rebels were banished to Nova Scotia.

35. Palmer, *Stoddert's War*, 153–54; C. L. R. James, *The Black Jacobins: Toussaint L'Ouverture and the San Domingo Revolution*, 2d ed. (New York: Vintage Books, 1963), 211–12.

36. Heinl, *Written in Blood*, 81; Ott, *Haitian Revolution*, 81.

37. Somerset de Chair, ed., *Napoleon on Napoleon* (London: Cassell, 1992), 175.

38. Palmer, *Stoddert's War*, 160–64.

39. Heinl, *Written in Blood*, 85.

40. Henri Christophe (1767–1820) was a former black slave who as a boy worked as a cook on a plantation. In 1779 he served in the unsuccessful French expedition against Savannah, Georgia, during the American Revolution and was twice wounded. He also had served as a gunner in the force made up of white militia and black volunteers which had defeated the *affranchis* Ogé and Chavannes in 1789.

41. Heinl, *Written in Blood*, 86; Palmer, *Stoddert's War*, 162–64.

42. Alexandre Petion (1770–1818) was an *affranchis* born in Saint Domingue. As a boy he had been trained as a goldsmith. He enlisted in the French Army at the age of eighteen.

43. Marley, *Wars*, 355.

44. The Constitution of 1801 made Toussaint governor-general for life, gave him the power to appoint his successor, abolished slavery, made military service compulsory for males aged fourteen to fifty-five, recognized Catholicism as the state religion, and permitted the importation of blacks to augment the decimated population.

45. Charles Victor-Emmanuel Leclerc (1772–1802) was Napoleon Bonaparte's brother-in-law. Of lower-class origin, Leclerc served as Napoleon's ad*junta*nt-general in 1796 and 1797. On December 3, 1800, Leclerc led a successful surprise raid on Freising during the Battle of Hohenlinden. In 1797 he married Pauline, Napoleon's youngest sister. Bonaparte wrote, "Captain-General Le Clerc was an officer of the first merit, equally skilled in the labours of the Cabinet and in the manoeuvres of the field of battle." De Chair, *Napoleon on Napoleon*, 182.

46. Heinl, *Written in Blood*, 104–06. Bonaparte wrote that Leclerc had a set of secret orders "for securing the enjoyment of civil liberty to the blacks, and to confirm the orders of classification and labour that Toussaint-Louverture had established." De Chair, *Napoleon*, 182–83. Leclerc's actions did not conform to these instructions, if in fact they had been issued.

47. Heinl, *Written in Blood*, 104.

48. ibid., 106.

49. Toussaint Louverture was imprisoned at Fort de Joux near Pontarlier and permitted one servant. This was a deliberate death sentence to a man of failing health. Thomas O. Ott, *Haitian Revolution* (Knoxville: University of Tennessee Press, 1973), 160.

50. Heinl, *Written in Blood*, 112–13.

51. ibid., 114.

52. Rochambeau was captured by the British navy on November 30, 1803. He remained a prisoner of war until exchanged in 1811.

53. Joannès Tramond, *Manuel d'histoire maritime de la France des origines à 1815* (Paris, Société d'Éditions Géographiques, Maritimes et Coloniales, 1947), 702.

54. Selden Rodman, *Quisqueya A History of the Dominican Republic* (Seattle: University of Washington Press, 1964), 43.

55. Heinl, *Written in Blood*, 117–18.

56. The London *Times* 2 (January 27, 1804), 2.

57. See note 4, preface.

CHAPTER TWO

1. On the eve of the revolution, the *Cabildo Abierto* (town meeting) was a gathering of important people and was most frequently called by the king's representative. Víctor Andrés Belaúde, *Bolívar and the Political Thought of the Spanish-American Revolution* (Baltimore: The Johns Hopkins Press, 1938), 6.

2. André, *La fin de l'empire espagnol*, 132–33.

3. Francisco de Miranda (1750–1816) came from a wealthy Venezuelan family. He fought for Spain in Africa and in North America during the American Revolution, taking part in the Pensacola Campaign. Disgusted with Spanish service, he resigned and traveled to Cuba. He visited the United States and traveled throughout Europe, winning favor through his charm. In 1790 he tried to interest the British Prime Minister, William Pitt the Younger, in a scheme to create a great South American nation under an Inca prince. He then entered the service of Republican France. In 1792 and 1793 he distinguished himself in the war with Prussia, rising to the rank of field marshal and earning his name a place on the *Arch de Triomphe*. As a consequence of the failed blockade of Maestrict, the loss of the Battle of Neewinden where Miranda commanded the left wing of Dumouriez's army, the consequent defection of Dumouriez, and the fall from power of his Girondin friends, Miranda was imprisoned. After regaining his freedom, he traveled to London. Great Britain, wanting to be in touch with the revolutionary movements in Spanish America, picked up the living expenses for Miranda. Following his failed attempt to lead Venezuelan independence, Miranda died in the dungeon at Madrugada, Spain, on July 14, 1816.

4. André, *La fin*, 39–40; William Spence Robertson, "Francisco de Miranda and the Revolutionizing of Spanish America," in *Annual Report of the American Historical Association for the year 1907*, 2 vols. (Washington: Government Printing Office, 1908), 1: 318–20.

5. Robertson, "Francisco de Miranda," 1: 320–22; Ricardo Levene, ed., *Historia de América*, 14 vols. (Buenos Aires: W. M. Jackson, 1940–43), 6: 314–15.

6. Robertson, "Francisco de Miranda," 1: 355–57.

7. José Gíl Fortoul, *Historia constitucional de Venezuela*, 5th ed. (Caracas: Ediciones Sales, 1964), 174–75; Elío Arrechea Rodríguez, *Próceres y batallas de la independencia en la América bolivariana* (Caracas: Cardenal Ediciones, S.A., 1978), 88; Marley, *Wars*, 369.

8. Harold E. Davis, *History of Latin America* (New York: Ronald Press, 1968), 287.

9. Napoleon realized that he did not have the resources to gain control over Spanish America. He also knew that the income derived from the New World by Spain significantly contributed to its ability to conduct war against him. As a result, Napoleon attempted to ferment revolution in Spanish America in order to deprive Spain of the resources. André, *La fin*, 95–96; [Manuel Palacio Fajardo], *Outline of the Revolution in Spanish America* (New York: James Eastburn, 1817), 55–56.

10. Simón Bolívar (1783–1830) was born in Caracas, Venezuela, into one of the wealthiest and most prominent families of the *criollo* aristocracy. At an early age he inherited a vast cacao estate, over 1,000 slaves, and other assets which provided an income of 20,000 pesos a year. During his early years, Bolívar was greatly influenced by one of his teachers, Simón Rodríquez, who introduced him to Rousseau, and Bolívar became profoundly influenced by the Enlightenment and the ideas of reason, dignity, liberty, and humanity. His uncle (and guardian) sent him to Spain in 1799, when he was a second lieutenant in the militia, to be educated. Traveling via New Spain, he shocked the viceroy with his radical political ideas. In 1804 he fell in with a group of young South Americans who were in disfavor at court. Bolívar

and his friends were forced to leave the court on the pretext of a temporary food shortage. Bolívar then traveled to Paris and became a great admirer of Napoleon Bonaparte until the victor of Marengo had himself crowned emperor, a ceremony which Bolívar attended. Bolívar returned to Venezuela in 1807 by way of the United States. He immediately became involved in the revolutionary movement. Spanish General Morillo wrote concerning Bolívar, "Nothing is comparable to the restless activity of this man. His daring and talents are his best credentials. . . . Bolívar is THE REVOLUTION!" Daniel A. del Río, *Bolívar and the Liberating Crusade* (Washington, D.C.: Bicentennial of Simón Bolívar and the Embassy of Venezuela, 1980), 41.

11. Fernando Rodríguez del Toro e Ibarra (1761–1851) was born in Caracas. He was the cousin of María Teresa Rodríguez del Toro, Bolívar's wife, and his good friend. Rodríguez de Toro was one of the prime inspirers of the April 19, 1810, movement. He signed the Act of Independence on July 5, 1811.

12. José Manuel Restrepo, *Historia de la revolución de la república de Colombia*, 7 vols. (Bogotá: Pubicaciones del Ministero de Educación Nacional, 1942–50), 2: 148.

13. André, *La fin*, 75–77; *Cartas de Bolívar 1799 a 1822*, notes by Rufino Blanco-Fombona (Paris: Sociedad de Ediciones Louis-Michaud, 1913), 139.

14. Robert L. Gilmore, *Caudillism and Militarism in Venezuela, 1810–1910* (Athens: Ohio University Press, 1964), 70–71.

15. André, *La fin*, 89–94.

16. ibid., 94–95.

17. In about 1800 Spain maintained 13,126 men under arms in Venezuela. Of these some 1,700 were regulars from Spain, 3,500 militia in active service, and the remainder militia who were inactive. Gilmore, *Caudillism*, 106.

18. Francisco de Paula Santander, *Cartas y mensajes del general Francisco de Paula Santander*, compiled by Roberto Cortázar, 10 vols. (Bogotá: Talleres Editoriales de Libreria Voluntad, S.A., 1953–56), 2: 336.

19. John Miller, ed., *Memoirs of General Miller*, 2 vols. (London: Printed for Longman, Rees, Orne, Brown, and Green, 1829), 2: 164.

20. Marley, *Wars*, 378.

21. Fernando Díaz Venteo, *Las campañas militares del virrey Abascal* (Sevilla: Escuela de Estudios Hispano-Americanos, 1948), 81–125; Ayala *Nueva historia*, 6: 99–116.

22. Antonio R. Eljuri-Yunez S., "La primera campaña para la liberación de Guayana." *Revista de la Armada* 4, 51–54 (Caracas, December 17, 1984).

23. Among others, Bolívar believed that this federal form of government was a mistake for Venezuela. Frederick A. Kirkpatrick, *Latin America* (New York: The Macmillan Company, 1939), 55–56; Marley, *Wars*, 382.

24. Domingo de Monteverde (1773–1832), born in the Canarias Islands, entered the Spanish army at the age of twelve. Later he joined the Spanish navy. In 1812 with the rank of commander he was sent to the Americas and took command of the Royalist forces fighting in Venezuela. After the surrender of Francisco Miranda, Monteverde was designated Captain-General of Venezuela and President of the Royal Audiencia of Caracas. Monteverde returned to Spain and in 1817 was promoted to general of brigade in the Spanish marine corps.

25. Escuela Superior de Guerra [de Argentina], *Manual de historia militar*, 3d ed., 3 vols. (n.p.: n.p., 1975–80), 2: 185; Marley, *Wars*, 386; Kirkpatrick, *Latin America*, 55–56.

26. On April 23, 1812, the Venezuelan Congress meeting at Valencia named Francisco Miranda *General en Jefe de los Ejércitos de Tierra y Mar de la Confederación de Venezuela*.

Notes

27. Alberto Lozano Cleves, *Así se hizo la independencia*, 2d ed. (Bogotá: Biblioteca Popular, 1980), 23–33; Marley, *Wars*, 387.

28. Kirkpatrick, *Latin America*, 56; Marley, *Wars*, 387. Perhaps Miranda failed because he had lived far too many years abroad and had lost touch with the South American scene.

29. Lozano, *Así se hizo*, 35.

30. Eleazar López Contreras, *Bolívar conductor de tropas* (Caracas: Colección Carabobo, 1971), 28–29; Lozano, *Así se hizo*, 36; Del Río, *Bolívar*, 14–19; Escuela Superior, *Manual*, 2: 185; Alfred Hasbrouck, *Foreign Legionares in the Liberation of South America* (New York: Octagon Books, 1969), 20–21.

31. Santiago Mariño (1788–1854), born on the Island of Margarita, joined the royal militia at an early age. He fought for the Revolutionaries in the Guayana campaign in 1812 as a captain. The following year as a lieutenant colonel, he liberated the eastern provinces of Cumaná and Barcelona. In 1813 he fled to Trinidad Island. In 1814 Mariño and Simón Bolívar had a difference of opinion concerning the union of the provinces of the Viceroyalty of Nueva Granada into a single nation. Notwithstanding, they united their forces at various times to fight the Royalists. In May 1816 Mariño was proclaimed second in command of the revolutionary army under Bolívar. In 1821 Mariño was appointed chief of staff of the army.

32. Del Río, *Bolívar*, 22–23; Lozano, *Así se hizo*, 38.

33. Atanasio Girardot (1790–1813) was born in Medellín, New Granada. He joined the Revolutionaries in 1811 and fought throughout the "Admirable Campaign." He was killed at the Battle of Trincheras (September 30, 1813).

34. Del Río, *Bolívar*, 23–24.

35. Thomas Russell Ybarra, *Bolivar The Passionate Warrior* (New York: Ives Washburn Publisher, 1929), 80.

36. Del Río, *Bolívar*, 25–26, 37–38; Hasbrouck, *Foreign Legionares*, 20–21. Hasbrouck writes that this was a mistake because it contributed to the increasing brutality of the fighting. Most historians argue that this declaration made the choices clear to all and encouraged many Latin Americans to change sides.

37. Del Río, *Bolívar*, 31–36; Lozano, *Así se hizo*, 43; Hasbrouck, *Foreign Legionares*, 22.

38. López Contreras, *Bolívar*, 48–50; Arráiz, *Los días*, 137; Escuela Superior, *Manual*, 2: 186.

39. José Tomás Boves—real surname Rodríguez (ca. 1770–1814)—earned the nickname the "Attila of Spanish America" because of his cruelty. A tall redhead born in Oviedo (Asturias), Spain, Boves went to Venezuela at a very early age. He served as a sergeant in the Spanish Army but was dismissed for misconduct. He lived on the Venezuelan plains (*llanos*) as a shopkeeper. Initially, Boves favored the Revolutionaries but in 1812 was persuaded by Monteverde to change sides. By 1813 Boves grew increasingly independent of Spanish authority and in 1814 declared himself "Commanding General of the King's Forces in Venezuela." Boves was killed by a lance at the Battle of Úrica on December 5, 1814—ironically he won the battle.

40. Francisco Tomás Morales (ca. 1781–1845), born in the Canarias Islands, came to Venezuela at an early age. He joined the Royalist force of José Tomás Boves in 1813 and became his second in command. With the death of Boves in 1814, Morales took command of Royalist forces in Venezuela until the arrival of Mariscal Pablo Morillo in 1815. Morales took part in the siege of Cartagena and the resubjugation of Colombia. In 1816 he returned to

Venezuela to deal with the return of Bolívar. Morales was defeated at El Juncal in 1817. During the following two years, Morales participated in the successful Royalist campaigns in Guayana and Apure. In June 1821 he fought at Carabobo and retreated with elements of the defeated Royalist army to Puerto Cabello. In November 1821 Morales was promoted to *mariscal de campo*. In July 1822 he assumed the command of Royalist forces in Venezuela. Morales began a campaign to recapture Venezuela and by the end of 1822 dominated the area around Zulia. However, following the defeat of a Royalist flotilla in the Battle of Lake Maracaibo in August 1823, the Royalist effort collapsed. Morales went to Cuba and in 1827 he was appointed the Commandant General of the Canarias Islands and President of the Royal Audencia.

41. Torrente, *Historia de la revolución*, 1: 52.

42. José Félix Ríbas (1775–1814), born in Caracas, was married to Simón Bolívar's aunt. Ríbas participated in the April 19, 1810, overthrow of Spanish authority and became a member of the Supreme *Junta* formed by the Revolutionaries. He fought under Francisco Miranda against Monteverde in 1812. When the First Republic fell, Ríbas fled to Nueva Granada (Colombia). Ríbas joined Bolívar in Ocaña and fought in the Admirable Campaign, commanding a division. In September 1814 Ríbas was defeated at Urica and again at Maturín. Ríbas was captured at Tucupido and executed. His head was cut off and sent to Caracas in an iron cage.

43. Lozano, *Así se hizo*, 96. The 12th of February is celebrated as the "Day of Venezuela Youth" in memory of the students who fought in the battle of La Victoria.

44. Lozano, *Así se hizo*, 134–37; Arráiz, *Los días*, 137.

45. Ybarra, *Bolivar*, 111–24; Lozano, *Así se hizo*, 139–41; Hasbrouck, *Foreign Legionares*, 23–24.

46. Restrepo, *Historia de la revolución*, 2: 156–57; Marley, *Wars*, 395.

47. Pablo Morillo (1778–1837), born in Fuentesecas, Spain, into the lower class, entered the Spanish marine corps in 1791. Morillo fought against the Napoleonic forces which invaded Spain in 1808 and became an officer at the age of thirty for his actions at the Battle of Bailén. Rapidly advancing through the ranks, he was promoted to *mariscal de campo* following the Battle of Vitoria in 1813. After the defeat of Napoleon, Morillo was appointed Commander of the Expeditionary Army of *Costa Firme*. As a reward for capturing Cartagena in 1815, Morillo was made *Marques de la Puerta* and *Conde de Cartagena*. He was badly wounded at the Battle of El Semen (March 17, 1818). Morillo was impaled on a lance which had to be pulled out through his back. Late in the Latin American wars for independence, Morillo returned to Spain.

48. Restrepo, *Historia de la revolución*, 2: 222–23, 233, and 3: 8–9.

49. Lozano, *Así se hizo*, 149–52; Restrepo, *Historia de la revolución*, 3: 50–52; John B. Trend, *Bolivar and the Independence of Spanish America* (London: Hodder & Stoughton, 1946), 112–13; Del Río, *Bolívar*, 67–69. Bolívar established himself at Kingston and dedicated much of his time to writing his famous letter from Jamaica. On December 18 Bolívar sailed for Cartagena to take part in its defense. While at sea, he learned of the fall of the fortress to Morillo's army so he changed course for Haiti.

50. Juan Bautista Arismendi (1770–1841), born on Margarita Island, joined the local militia in 1790 and rose to the rank of captain in 1810. In that year the Revolutionaries commissioned Arismendi a colonel and he took part in the 1812 Guayana campaign. For the following two years, he fought under Bolívar. In 1815 he was designated the commander of revolutionary forces on Margarita Island. In September 1815 his second wife, Luisa Cáceres de Arismendi, then sixteen years old and pregnant, was taken hostage by the Royalists and jailed. The baby died at birth. General Arismendi made numerous unsuccessful attempts to

obtain his wife's release. She was sent to Caracas and ultimately to Cádiz, Spain, where she arrived in January 1817. While held in prison, she refused to sign a document acknowledging the legal authority of Ferdinand VII and renouncing the revolution. In March 1818, with the help of the English consul, she escaped on board an American ship bound for Philadelphia. She returned to Margarita Island in July 1818. *La señora* eventually died at the age of sixty-six and her remains were placed in the National Pantheon in Caracas. Following the War for Independence, General Arismendi was Vice President of Gran Colombia and later a Venezuelan senator.

51. Laura F. Ullrick, "Morillo's Attempt to Pacify Venezuela," *The Hispanic American Historical Review* 3: 4, 535–65, (November 1920), 540–41.

52. Luis Brión (1782–1821) was born on Curaçao. In 1795, while living in Holland, he fought in the battles of Bergen and Castricom against English forces where he was taken prisoner. In 1804 and again in 1805 he commanded the Curaçao militia against British assaults. In 1810 he joined the revolutionary movement in Venezuela, supporting it with his ships and money. Brión died in Amsterdam.

53. *Documentos del almirante Brión*, 2 vols. (Caracas: Ediciones del Congreso de la República, 1982), 1: 18; Arrechea Rodíguez, *Próceres y batallas*, 34; Francisco Alejandro Vargas, *Nuestros próceres navales* (Caracas: Imprenta Nacional, 1964), 220–22.

54. Lozano, *Así se hizo*, 213–17; Ullrick, "Morillo's Attempt," 542–43.

55. Marley, *Wars*, 398; Ullrick, "Morillo's Attempt," 543–45.

56. José Antonio Páez (1790–1873) was born in Curpa on the western plains of Venezuela. In 1810 he began his military career as a horseman in the insurgent army. Captured by the Royalists, he was freed by the Revolutionaries. By 1816 he was the leader of the *llaneros*, a status achieved through bravery and leadership. As a general of brigade he won the battles of Mata de la Miel, El Yagual, and Mucuritas. The following year, Páez campaigned in central Venezuela and in January 1819, as a general of division, he won the battle of Queseras del Medio where he attacked 6,000 Royalists with 150 *llaneros*. At the Battle of Carabobo in June 1821, Páez commanded the 1st Division which saw the heaviest fighting. For his bravery in battle, he was promoted to general in chief. In September 1823 the Royalists at Puerto Cabello, their last stronghold in Venezuela, surrendered to Páez. Páez emerged from the War for Independence as a wealthy landholder.

57. Kirkpatrick, *Latin America*, 64.

58. Lozano, *Así se hizo*, 153.

59. ibid.; Marley, *Wars*, 398.

60. Manuel Carlos Píar (1774–1817), born in Willhemstad, Curaçao, fought in defense of Curaçao against the English invasion in 1804. He took part in the 1807 unsuccessful conspiracy of Venezuelans Manuel Gual and José María España against the Royalists in La Guaira, Venezuela. In 1807 Píar participated in the Haitian Revolution commanding a warship. In 1813 he created the first Venezuelan naval squadron and temporarily drove Spanish shipping from the coast. In 1814, as a general of division, Píar took part in the expedition to Los Cayos and fought at the naval battle of Los Frailes. In April 1817 Píar defeated the Royalists at the Battle of San Félix and was promoted to general in chief. Following the Guayana campaign, Píar was among those who questioned Bolívar's right to be the overall commander. Píar was removed from command of troops and as a consequence, requested to retire. He conspired against Bolívar, was apprehended, was judged by a council of war, and condemned to death. He was shot in Angostura on October 17, 1817.

61. José Francisco Bermúdez (1782–1831) was born in San José de Aerocuar in eastern Venezuela. He joined the Revolutionaries in 1810 and in 1813 he took part in Mariño's campaign in eastern Venezuela. The following year, as a colonel, he fought under Bolívar in western Venezuela. Between 1816 and 1818 Bermúdez again served under Mariño and participated in the liberation of the Guayanas. In 1821 he fought in the actions leading up to the Battle of Carabobo but was ill at the time of the battle and did not participate. Notwithstanding, he was promoted to general in chief. Bermúdez retired from the army in August 1830 and was assassinated in December 1831.

62. Gíl Fortoul, *Historia constitucional*, 377–78; Lozano, *Así se hizo*, 154–55; Hasbrouck, *Foreign Legionares*, 25–26; Escuela Superior, *Manual*, 2: 187–88.

63. Lozano, *Así se hizo*, 155–60; Marley, *Wars*, 400–1; Francisco Alejandro Vargas, *Historia naval de Venezuela*, 2 vols. (Caracas: Publicaciones de la Fuerzas Navales de la República Venezuela, 1956–61), 2: 8–11.

64. Marley, *Wars*, 404.

65. Miguel de la Torre y Pando (1786–1843), born in Bernales, Spain, joined the Spanish army as a private. He fought against Napoleon's invasion of Spain in 1808. In 1815 Torre arrived in Venezuela in commanded of the "Victoria" Regiment, a unit within Morillo's expedition. Torre took part in the siege of Cartagena. In 1816 he was promoted to brigadier and commanded a company of *llanos* (American lancers) at Angostura. In 1820 Torre assumed command of the Royalist forces in Venezuela when Morillo returned to Spain. Torre was promoted to *mariscal de campo*. Following the defeat of the Royalists at Carabobo in June 1821, Torre took refuge in Puerto Cabello. In 1822 he went to Puerto Rico where he became governor and captain-general.

66. Hasbrouck, *Foreign Legionares*, 26–27; Vargas, *Historia naval*, 2: 21–47; Marley, *Wars*, 406.

67. Escuela Superior, *Manual*, 2: 188; Marley, *Wars*, 407.

68. Lozano, *Así se hizo*, 162–63; Hasbrouck, *Foreign Legionares*, 27; Vargas, *Historia naval*, 2: 61–62.

69. López Contreras, *Bolívar*, 131; Lozano, *Así se hizo*, 166–67; Vargas, *Historia naval*, 2: 66–69.

70. Hasbrouck, *Foreign Legionares*, 46–64.

71. The British Foreign Enlistment Bill, which prohibited service in foreign armies, did not pass Parliament until 1819. British and Irish volunteers mutinied more than once. Some 500 did so at Achaguas, Venezuela, on October 28, 1820, killing and wounding several officers. Philip Ziegler, "Bolívar's British Legion." *History Today* 17: 7; 468–74 (July 1967), 468–71; Marley, *Wars*, 408, 422.

72. Rafael Urdaneta (1788–1845), born in Maracaibo, Venezuela, joined the Revolutionaries in Bogotá on July 20, 1810. In 1813 he distinguished himself during the "Admirable Campaign." In 1814, commanding 280 men, he successfully defended Valencia against 3,000 Royalists. The following year he fought at El Yagual and Achaguas and in 1817 at Barinas. Urdaneta took part in the campaign leading to the Battle of Carabobo but was ill at the time of the battle. In 1822, Urdaneta became the Commandant General of the Department of Cundinamarca. He served as the president of the senate of Gran Colombia (1823–24) and president of Nueva Grenada (1830–31). Urdaneta returned to Venezuela and served as the Secretary of War and Marine in 1837–38 and 1843–45.

73. Hasbrouck, *Foreign Legionares*, 190–92; Lozano, *Así se hizo*, 248–50.

74. Hasbrouck, *Foreign Legionares*, 192–97; Lozano, *Así se hizo*, 299–307; Del Río, *Bolívar*, 51–52.

75. Del Río, *Bolívar*, 52–55; Hasbrouck, *Foreign Legionares*, 200–1; Escuela Superior, *Manual*, 2: 190.

76. Del Río, *Bolívar*, 63–64; Hasbrouck, *Foreign Legionares*, 204–9; Lozano, *Así se hizo*, 299–307.

77. Marley, *Wars*, 419–20.

78. Vargas, *Historia naval*, 2: 101–9.

79. Escuela Superior, *Manual*, 2: 190; Marley, *Wars*, 420.

80. Del Río, *Bolívar*, 78; Hasbrouck, *Foreign Legionares*, 229–30, 323; Escuela Superior, *Manual*, 2: 190.

81. José Prudéncio Padilla (1778–1828) born in Río Hacha, New Granada, enrolled in the Spanish navy at the age of fourteen. Captured at the Battle of Trafalgar (October 21, 1805), he was held prisoner until 1808 at which time he returned to Spain. He joined the revolutionary movement in New Granada in November 1811. In 1815 he began serving under Bolívar.

82. Vargas, *Historia naval*, 2: 118–20.

83. Del Río, *Bolívar*, 77–82.

84. ibid., 87–91; Hasbrouck, *Foreign Legionares*, 233–40; Lozano, *Así se hizo*, 323–34.

85. Marley, *Wars*, 428, 430.

86. Vargas, *Historia naval*, 2: 200–10; Hasbrouck, *Foreign Legionares*, 287–93; Marley, *Wars*, 435.

87. Antonio José de Sucre (1795–1830) was born in Cumaná, Venezuela, and could trace his ancestry to the *conquistadores*. A student of engineering, he served on Miranda's staff. Exiled by the Royalists, he first went to the West Indies and then to New Granada. He participated in the unsuccessful defense of Cartagena against Morillo's siege, escaping just prior to the surrender of the city. In late 1820 Sucre was one of Bolívar's representatives during the negotiations with Morillo. Sucre was murdered on Berruecos Mountain, Gran Colombia, on June 4, 1830.

88. Ayala, *Nueva historia*, 6: 120–23; Lozano, *Así se hizo*, 350–52; Marley, *Wars*, 429–30.

89. This suggests that late in the war the Spanish navy off the Americas, like the Spanish army in the Americas, was composed largely of Latin Americans. Marley, *Wars*, 431.

90. Lozano, *Así se hizo*, 342–45.

91. Bartolomé Mitre, *Historia de San Martín*, 3 vols. (Buenos Aires: Editorial Universitaria de Buenos Aires, 1977), 3: 254–57.

92. Ayala, *Nueva historia*, 6: 123–24; Lozano, *Así se hizo*, 352–61; Marley, *Wars*, 432.

93. Marley, *Wars*, 432.

94. Rebecca Earle, "'A Grave for Europeans'? Disease, Death, and the Spanish-American Revolutions," *War in History* 3: 4; 371–83 (November 1996), 376.

95. Julio Albi, *Banderas olvidades El Ejército realista en América* (Madrid: Ediciones de Cultura Hispánica, 1990), 404; André, *La fin*, 75–77; Brain Loveman, *For la Patria* (Wilmington: Scholarly Resources, Inc., 1999), 33.

96. Manning, *Dipl. Corrs. of the U.S. concerning*, 2: 1241–42.

97. Arráiz, *Los Días*, 94; Ybarra, *Bolivar*, 219; Gilmore, *Caudillism*, 72; Ayala, *Nueva historia*, 6: 132.

98. Torrente, *Historia de la revolución*, 1: prolog 74.
99. Loveman, *For la Patria*, 27.

CHAPTER THREE

1. Manuel Belgrano (1770–1820) was the son of a prosperous Italian merchant and a *criollo* mother. Born in Buenos Aires, he studied law in Spain from 1786 to 1794 and was influenced by the Physiocrats, Adam Smith, and the French Revolution. In 1806 he joined the defenses of Buenos Aires against the British and a year later served as a headquarters aide-de-camp during a second British invasion. Belgrano lamented, "I confess I was ignorant ... of even the rudiments of military service." Following the expulsion of the British, he was elected an officer in one of the newly formed militia regiments. In 1810 the revolutionary *junta* placed him in charge of military preparations. Manuel Belgrano, *Autobiografía y memorias sobre la expedición al Paraguay y batalla de Tucumán* (Buenos Aires: Emecé—editores, 1942), 17.

2. José María Rosa, *Historia Argentina*, 4 vols. (Buenos Aires: Editorial Oriente, S.A., 1993), 2: 173–98; Félix Best, *Historia de las guerras Argentina*, 2 vols. (Burzaco: GRAFICSUR S.R.L., 1983), 1: 162.

3. Caesar A. Rodney and J. Graham, *The Reports on the Present State of the United Provinces of South America* (London: Baldwin, Cradock, and Joy, 1819), 337.

4. Escuela Superior, *Manual*, 2: 97–98.

5. "The question of customs duties was more important to the exporters of the Plate than the *Rights of Man*." André, *La fin*, 77–78.

6. Rosa, *Historia*, 2: 25–41; Best, *Historia*, 1151–52.

7. Best, *Historia*, 1: 152–54; Marley, *Wars*, 368–69; Juan Carlos Christensen, *Historia Argentina sin mitos* (Buenos Aires: Grupo Editor Latinoamericana, 1990), 77–81.

8. Rosa, *Historia*, 2: 45–49, 162–63; Escuela Superior, *Manual*, 2: 97–99.

9. Christensen, *Historia*, 81–86; Best, *Historia*, 1: 152–54; Rosa, *Historia*, 2: 50–70; Marley, *Wars*, 370–71.

10. Rosa, *Historia*, 2: 43–49; Christensen, *Historia*, 81–86; Best, *Historia*, 1: 154–55; Comando en Jefe del Ejército, *Reseña historica y orgáncia del ejército argentine*, 3 vols. (Buenos Aires: Círculo militar, 1972), 1: 104–9.

11. Rosa, *Historia*, 2: 223–29.

12. Rosa, *Historia*, 2: 117–30.

13. Aldo N. Canceco, "La guerra naval antes de 1814. Primera escuadrilla" published in *Historia Naval Argentina*, 10 vols. (Buenos Aires: Departamento de Estudios Históricos Navales, 1981–93), 5: 129; Otto von Pivka, *Navies of the Napoleonic Era* (Newton Abbot, Devon: David & Charles Publishers, 1980), 203–5.

14. Manuel R. García, "Estudios sobre el período colonial," *Revista de Río de la Plata* 4: 14; 354–69 (Buenos Aires, 1872), 368. Of the 15,636 Spanish soldiers sent to the New World before Ferdinand VII regained the throne in 1814, only 4,524 men were dispatched to the Viceroyalty of Río de la Plata and they went to Montevideo.

15. André, *La fin*, 77–78.

16. Carlos de Alvear (1789–1853) was born in the Jesuit mission district (now Paraguay) and traveled to Spain as a child. He entered the Spanish army to fight the Napoleonic invasion. Alvear distinguished himself, earning the rank of ensign. He arrived in Buenos Aires on board the *George Canning* on March 9, 1812, along with San Martín.

17. José de San Martín (1778–1850), born in Yapeyú, Viceroyalty of Río de la Plata, was the son of a Spanish officer and a *criollo* mother. He was educated at the *Seminario de Los Nobles* in Madrid. At age twelve he joined the Spanish army as a cadet and served in the Spanish army for twenty-two years. San Martín distinguished himself at the Battle of Bailen (July 19, 1808) against the French and ultimately reached the rank of lieutenant colonel before resigning. He returned to Buenos Aires on March 9, 1812, on board the merchant frigate *George Canning* and offered his services to the revolution. San Martín immediately exhibited a concern for detail rarely found among his peers on either side. In the spring of 1812, he was authorized to raise a corps of mounted grenadiers. San Martín recruited 300 *criollos* from the interior and selected officers from among the best families of Buenos Aires. He enforced an extremely high level of discipline and training. Through public subscription, he raised funds to outfit the grenadiers. Bartolomé Mitre, *Historia de San Martín*, 3 vols., 2d ed. (Buenos Aires: Editorial Universitaria de Buenos Aires, 1977), 1: 61.

Vicuña characterized the differences between San Martín and Bolívar as follows: "San Martín is a Spartan. Bolívar a brilliant daredevil." Benjamin Vicuña Mackenna, *El general don José de San Martín*, 3d ed. (Buenos Aires: Editorial Francisco de Aguirre, 1971), 117.

18. Best, *Historia*, 1: 165–66; Rosa, *Historia*, 2: 194–95, 204–5, 220–21.

19. Best, *Historia*, 1: 165; Rosa, *Historia*, 2: 230–32.

20. John Hoyt Williams, "Governor Velasco, the Portuguese and the Paraguayan Revolution of 1811: A New Look." *The Americas* 28:4, 441–49 (April 1972), 441.

21. Some sources (such as Martín Suárez, *Atlas histórico militar argentino* (Buenos Aires: Circulo Militar, 1974), 39, cite the number of Paraguayans to be much larger. The arsenal in Asunción had only 500 firearms of all sorts; 4,600 cartridges; a little more than 1,000 sabres, lances, and daggers; 41 cannon; 2,954 roundshot; and 275 canister shot. This was hardly enough to arm 2,000 men. Meister, *Francisco Solano López*, 17; Rosa, *Historia*, 2: 245–46; Best, *Historia*, 1: 172–75.

22. Laurio H. Destéfani, *Manual de historia naval Argentina*, 3d ed. (Buenos Aires: Tall. Gráf. De la DIAB, 1980), 45; Teodoro Caillet-Bois, *Historia naval Argentina* (Buenos Aires: Emecé Editores, 1944), 52–56.

23. Rosa, *Historia*, 2: 267; Best, *Historia*, 1: 178–79.

24. Gerald S. Graham and R.A. Humphreys, *The Navy and South America 1807–1823* (London: Navy Records Society, 1962), 58–59; Suárez, *Atlas*, 41; Rosa, *Historia*, 2: 308–9.

25. José Gervasio Artigas (1764–1850) was a classic *caudillo*. He commanded a significant following because of his ability to physically enforce his will. He possessed great strength and a commanding presence. He rose to the rank of captain in the militia of Montevideo and was among those who fought the British in 1806 at Buenos Aires. The following year he took part in the unsuccessful defense of Montevideo against the British. Artigas, at best, was an insubordinate ally to Buenos Aires, and, at worst, an open rival for the loyalty of not only Banda Oriental but also the other provinces along the Río de la Plata.

26. Rosa, *Historia*, 2: 272–75.

27. ibid., 273; Suárez, *Atlas*, 43; Best, *Historia*, 1: 180–81; Marley, *Wars*, 384.

28. Suárez, *Atlas*, 43; Best, *Historia*, 1: 181.

29. Ricardo Levene, *A History of Argentina*, trans. by William Spence Robertson (New York: Russell & Russell, Inc., 1963), 216; Rosa, *Historia*, 2: 130–37.

30. Díaz Venteo, *Las campañas*, 59–76; Rosa, *Historia*, 2: 137–39.

31. Díaz Venteo, *Las campañas*, 127–39; Suárez, *Atlas*, 15; Best, *Historia*, 1: 166; Rosa, *Historia*, 2: 234–36.

32. Rosa, *Historia*, 2: 241; Suárez, *Atlas*, 16; Best, *Histora*, 1: 166–67; Escuela Superior, *Manual*, 2: 103.

33. Rosa, *Historia*, 2: 242; Suárez, *Atlas*, 16.

34. Rosa, *Historia*, 2: 301–2, 331; Díaz Venteo, *Las campañas*, 147–65; Suárez, *Atlas*, 17–19; Best, *Historia*, 1: 168–69.

35. Suárez, *Atlas*, 43; Marley, *Wars*, 385.

36. Suárez, *Atlas*, 44; Best, *Historia*, 1: 182–83.

37. Suárez, *Atlas*, 45–46.

38. ibid., 46–47; Best, *Historia*, 1: 183–86.

39. Rosa, *Historia*, 2: 314–15, 320–22; Marley, *Wars*, 389.

40. Federico A. Gentiluomo, "Los planes de campaña del general San Martín," *Actas del congreso nacional de historia del libertador San Martín*, 3 vols. (Mendoza: Universidad Nacional de Cuyo, 1950–53), 3: 323, 340–41; Suárez, *Atlas*, 20.

41. Rosa, *Historia*, 2: 377–78.

42. Gentiluomo, "Los planes," 3: 322.

43. Rosa, *Historia*, 2: 383–84; Suárez, *Atlas*, 21–25; Best, *Historia*, 1: 188–96; Escuela Superior, *Manual*, 2:104.

44. Rosa, *Historia*, 2: 280–81; Suárez, *Atlas*, 27–31; Best, *Historia*, 1: 196–202; Marley, *Wars*, 393–94.

45. "Vicuña, *El general*, 18–19; J. M. Paz, *Memorias póstumas del general José María Paz*, 2d ed., 3 vols. (La Plata: Impr. "La Discusión," 1892,) 1: 88; Best, *Historia*, 1: 207–8.

46. Suárez, *Atlas*, 47.

47. Suárez, *Atlas*, 47–48.

48. William "Guillermo" Brown (1777–1857) was born in Foxford, Ireland. He went to sea as a child and served in the North Atlantic trade. By the age of twenty, he commanded a merchant ship. He arrived in Buenos Aires in 1809.

49. Suárez, *Atlas*, 48–49; Best, *Historia*, 1: 203–6; Marley, *Wars*, 395–96.

50. Marley, *Wars*, 396–97.

51. Miguel Martín de Güemes (1785–1821) fought against the British during the invasions of 1805 and 1806. He led a group of Revolutionaries from Salta in the 1812 siege of Montevideo. When Rondeau seized power from Sarratea, Güemes retired from the siege. Returning to Salta, he commanded a large following of *gauchos* through his personal prowess.

52. Suárez, *Atlas*, 33–35; Best, *Historia*, 1: 218–19.

53. Terry Hooker and R. Poulter, *The Armies of Bolivar and San Martin* (London: Osprey Publishing Ltd., 1991), 13.

54. Suárez, *Atlas*, 69–70; Best, *Historia*, 1: 222–23; Marley, *Wars*, 400.

55. Lewis A. Tambs, "Seven Times against the Citadel: Mount Potosí, the Charcas Redoubt and the War for Independence," *Revista de Historia de América* 69, 63–83 (Enero-Junio 1970), 75.

56. Suárez, *Atlas*, 70–72.

57. ibid., 79; Best, *Historia*, 1: 228–29; Marley, *Wars*, 399.

58. Suárez, *Atlas*, 79–81; Best, *Historia*, 1: 229–31; Marley, *Wars*, 400.

59. Suárez, *Atlas*, 81–82; Best, *Historia*, 1: 232–33; Marley, *Wars*, 400–1.
60. Suárez, *Atlas*, 82; Best, *Historia*, 1: 234; Marley, *Wars*, 401.
61. Suárez, *Atlas*, 82–83; Best, *Historia*, 1: 235–36.

CHAPTER FOUR

1. Late colonial Peru included the *Intendencias* of Arequipa, Cuzco, Huamanga, Huancavelica, Lima, Puno, Tarma, Trujillo (including Guayaquil), as well as Maynas and Quijos (which had been transferred from New Granada by a royal order of 1802), and Chiloé plus other southern and western islands.

2. R. F. Menendez, *Las conquistas territoriales argentinas* (Buenos Aires: Circulo Militar, 1982), 37–38; Francisco Valdés Vergara, *Historia de Chile para la enseñanza primaria*, 6th ed. (Valparaíso: Sociedad "Imprenta y Litografía Universo," 1908), 91; Francisco Antonio Encina-Castedo, *Resumen de la historia de Chile redacción*, 3 vols. (Santiago: Zig-Zag, 1962), 3: 2011.

3. José Miguel Carrera (1785–1821) came from a distinguished family. Because of his aggressive spirit, José was sent to Spain to complete his education. He joined the Spanish army to fight Napoleon. Fighting in numerous battles, he reached the rank of sergeant major of cavalry when seriously wounded. When he learned of events in Chile, he left Spain, arriving in Valparaíso on July 25, 1811. He and his two brothers, Luis and Juan José, were ardent republicans.

4. Valdés Vergara, *Historia de Chile*, 101–3.

5. The great uprising of the Indians of Peru in 1780 under the leadership of José Gabriel Condorcanqui (1740–81) who called himself Tupac Amarú II, the last of the Incas, was the result of complaints against corruption and abuse. Initially, it was not nationalistic. Later, Tupac Amarú tried to direct the cause of the revolt toward establishing a national monarchy in Peru. André, *La fin*, 89.

6. Agustin Toro Dávila, *Sintesis histórico militar de Chile*, 3 vols. (Santiago: Fondo Editorial Educacion Moderna, 1969), 61; José Miguel Carrera, *Diario militar*, vol. 1 of *Coleccion de historiadoes i de documents relativos a la independencia de Chile* (Santiago: Imprenta Cervantes, 1900), 71–73; Valdés Vergara, *Historia de Chile*, 109–11.

7. Carlos López Urrutia, *Historia de la marina de Chile* (Santiago: Andrés Bello, 1959), 17–18.

8. Bernando O'Higgins y Riquelme (1778–1824), born in Chillán, was the illegitimate son of Ambrosio O'Higgins, Governor of Chile, and Doña Isabel Riquelme. Educated in a Franciscan convent in Chillán and a seminary in Lima, Bernando was sent to London with scant means to learn a profession. There he fell in with Francisco Miranda and other Spanish-American Revolutionaries. Upon his father's death, Bernando returned to Chile to look after his inheritance.

9. The Lircay Treaty was mediated by Commodore Sir James Hillyar of the British navy, who on February 8, 1814, had captured the American frigate *Essex* in Valparaíso.

10. Carrera, *Diario militar*, 366–95; Valdés Vergara, *Historia de Chile*, 115–18.

11. Marley, *Wars*, 396.

12. Valdés Vergara, *Historia de Chile*, 118–29; Luis Galdames, *A History of Chile*, trans. by Isaac Joslin Cox (Chapel Hill: University of North Carolina Press, 1941), 188–89.

13. Gentiluomo, "Los planes," 328–29.

14. Escuela Superior, *Manual*, 2: 104–9.

15. Fernando Campos Harriet, *José Miguel Carrera* (Santiago: Orbe, 1974), 73; Valdés Vergara, *Historia de Chile*, 130–33.

16. Mitre, *Historia de San Martín*, 1: 309–31.

17. Encina-Castedo, *Resume*, 1: 611; Valdés Vergara, *Historia de Chile*, 167–69; Suárez, *Atlas*, 91–95.

18. Luis Langlois, *Influencia del poder naval en la historia de Chile* (Valparaíso: Progreso, 1911), 105; Marley, *Wars*, 398; José Toribio Medina, *La Expedición de corso del comodoro Guillermo Brown en aguas del Pacifico* (Buenos Aires: Talleres s.a. Casa Jacobo Peuser, ltda., 1928).

19. Valdés Vergara, *Historia de Chile*, 138.

20. Passes used by San Martín to cross the Andes in 1817:

Date	Departed	Troops	Commander	Pass Height
Jan 9	Mendoza	200	Cabot Azufre	11,910 feet
Jan 9	Rioja	200	Zelada Caballos	17,071 feet
Jan 14	Mendoza	380	Freire Planchon	13,531 feet
Jan 18	Mendoza	800	Heras Uspallata	16,611 feet
Jan 19	San Carlos	130	Lemos Portillo	13,663 feet
Jan 19	Mendoza	1,783	San Martín Los Patos	11,794 feet

21. Valdés Vergara, *Historia de Chile*, 142–44; Mitre, *Historia de San Martín*, 1: 346, 350–51, 368; Marley, *Wars*, 401.

22. Escuela Superior, *Manual*, 2: 124–30; Marley, *Wars*, 402.

23. Suárez, *Atlas*, 91–95; Mitre, *Historia de San Martín*, 1: 368–77.

24. They arrived in Talcahuano on May 1, 1817, just in time to fight in the Battle of Gavilán. Defeated again, the Royalists found refuge in their fortified camp at Talcahuano. The Revolutionaries attacked the camp on December 6, 1817, but were beaten off. Jorge Beaucheff, *Memorias militares* (Santiago: Andres Bello, 1964), 103–10; Valdés Vergara, *Historia de Chile*, 156–61.

25. Guillermo Feliú y Cruz, "La elección de O'Higgins para director supremo de Chile," *Revista Chilena de Historia y Geografía* 23: 337–70 (1917), 338–40.

26. Marley, *Wars*, 404.

27. Toro, *Sintesis*, 1: 146–49; Valdés Vergara, *Historia de Chile*, 163–69; Galdames, *A History of Chile*, 198–99; Escuela Superior, *Manual*, 2: 136–40.

28. Mitre, *Historia de San Martín*, 2: 67–81; Escuela Superior, *Manual*, 2: 141–50.

29. López U., *Historia*, 33.

30. Manuel Blanco Encalada (1790–1876) was born in Buenos Aires. He entered the Spanish navy in 1806 and was educated at the Academia de Guardiamarinas de la Isla de León. In 1812 he returned to South America and joined the Chilean Revolutionary cause, rising to the rank of colonel of artillery. Blanco Encalada was captured at the Battle of Rancagua (October 1–2, 1814) and was interned on the Island of Juan Fernández. All Revolutionaries held on the island were freed following the Revolutionary victory at Chacabuco (February 12, 1817). In June 1818 he was promoted to rear admiral and given command of the Chilean navy.

31. Anjel Justiniano Carranza, *Campañas navales de la república Argentina*, 4 vols. (Buenos Aires: Departamento de Estudios Históricos Navales, 1962), 2: 154–57.

32. Lord Thomas Alexander Cochrane (1775–1860), born in Armfield, Scotland, was renowned as a daring and intrepid frigate captain during the Napoleonic wars. At the age of twenty, he commanded the brig *Speedy* and conducted a highly successful Mediterranean cruise. Cochrane ran for Parliament financing his campaign with prize money he had won while commanding a frigate. In 1814 he was dismissed from the British navy, accused of being involved in a stock exchange scandal. Cochrane was offered a position by the Spanish navy but accepted a Chilean offer instead. He was pardoned and reinstated in the British navy in 1832, after having served in the Greek navy as well.

33. Carlos López Urrutia, *Chile: A Brief Naval History* (privately published, 1983), 26; Beaucheff, *Memorias*, 126–33.

34. The remains of what is believed to be the *San Telmo* were recently found on one of the Antarctic Islands. Evidence suggests that some of the crew survived for several months.

35. Valdés Vergara, *Historia de Chile*, 154–56, 170–74.

36. Frederick A. Kirkpatrick, *A History of the Argentine Republic* (New York: AMS Press, Inc, 1969), 105.

37. William Miller (1795–1861) was born in Wingham, Kent, England. He fought as an officer in the Napoleonic Wars and in the United States during the War of 1812. Arriving in Buenos Aires in 1817, San Martín appointed him a captain. For rescuing the revolutionary artillery at the Battle of Cancha Rayada (March 19, 1818), Miller was promoted to major. Thrice wounded at Pisco, Peru, he was promoted to colonel. Following the war Miller was appointed Governor of Potosí and made a Gran Marshal of Peru. Between 1826 and 1834 Miller returned to England. In 1834, back in Peru, he became commanding general of the army.

38. San Martín wrote to O'Higgins on December 25, 1820, "Everything goes well. . . . In the end, with patience and without hurrying, all of Peru will be free within a brief time." Mitre, *Historia de San Martín*, 2: 291.

39. San Martín, through his emissary, proposed the independence of Peru with a monarchial form of government. Valdés Vergara, *Historia de Chile*, 189–92; Marley, *Wars*, 424.

40. Marley, *Wars*, 429.

41. See Carlos López Urrutia, *La escuadra chilena en Méjico* (Buenos Aires: Editorial Francisco de Aguirre, 1971).

42. Donald E. Worcester, *Sea Power and Chilean Independence* (Gainesville: University of Florida Press, 1962), 87.

43. Vicente Lecuna, *Crónica razonada de las guerras de Bolívar*, 3 vols. (New York: Colonial Press, 1950), 3: 221–33; and Mario Guillermo Saravi, "La misión Gutierrez de la Fuente: San Martín, Buenos Aires, y las provincias," *Revista de Historia Americana y Argentina*, 1: 1–2; 363–78 (Mendoza, Universidad de Cuyo, 1956–57), 363–64.

44. Suárez, *Atlas*, 139–41; Lecuna, *Crónica*, 3: 241–42; José Rodríguez Ballesteros, *Historia de la independencia del Peru desde 1818 hasta 1826*, 3 vols. (Santiago de Chile: Imprenta Cultura, 1949), 3: 86–104.

45. Hasbrouck, *Foreign Legionaries*, 295–97.

46. Suárez, *Atlas*, 141–43; Marley, *Wars*, 434.

47. Suárez, *Atlas*, 141–43; Hasbrouck, *Foreign Legionaries*, 297–99; Marley, *Wars*, 435.

48. Escuela Superior, *Manual*, 2: 233; Hasbrouck, *Foreign Legionaries*, 299–301.

49. Enrique de Gandía, "Las guerras de los absolutistas y liberales en América," *Revista de Indias* 14: 57–58 (July–December 1954), 411; Encina, *Bolívar*, 388–91; Rodríguez Ballesteros, *Historia*, 3: 396–405.

50. Gandía, "Las guerras," 412–17; Andrés García Gamba, *Memorias para la historia de las armas españoles en el Peru 1809–1825*, 2 vols. (Madrid: Soc. Tip. de Hortelano, 1846), 2: 325; Hasbrouck, *Foreign Legionaries*, 304–5.

51. Escuela Superior, *Manual*, 2: 238–41; Hasbrouck, *Foreign Legionaries*, 308–9; Marley, *Wars*, 436–37.

52. Spanish Commodore Roque Guruceta, after learning of the Royalist defeat at Ayacucho, sailed for Guam; however, the crews mutinied. They surrendered the *Asia* to Mexico and the *Aquiles* to Chile. José Valdizan Gamio, *Historia naval del Peru*, 4 vols. (Lima: Direcion General de Intereses Marítimos, 1980–87), 3: 121–23; Rosendo Melo, *Historia de la marina del Peru*, 2 vols. (Callao: Publicaciones del Museo Naval, 1980–81), 1: 156–57.

53. Miller, *Memories*, 2: 201–2; Hasbrouck, *Foreign Legionaries*, 311–12.

54. André, *La fin*, 98; Escuela Superior, *Manual*, 2: 242–52; Marley, *Wars*, 437–38.

55. Marley, *Wars*, 440.

56. Valdés Vergara, *Historia de Chile*, 221–23.

57. *Historia general del ejército peruano*, 4 vols. (Lima: Comision Permanente de Historia del Ejército del Peru, 1980–84), 4: 1185; Torrente, *Historia de la revolución*, 1: 66–67.

58. Spanish expeditions to the New World:

Place	Expeditions	Viceroyalty	Troops
Vera Cruz	7	New Spain	9,685
Santa Marta	2	New Granada	522
Maracaibo	1	New Granada	214
Guaira	1	New Granada	118
Portobelo	3	New Granada	4,960
Costa Firme	2	New Granada	13,703
Montevideo	5	La Plata	4,524
Lima	5	Peru	6,122
Puerto Rico	1	Santo Domingo	224
Havana	5	Santo Domingo	7,009
Total troops			47,081

See A. Matilla Tascón, "Las expediciones o reemplazos militares enviados desde Cadiz a reprimir el movimiento de independencia de hispanoamerica" *Revista de Archivos Bibliotecas y Museos*, 57: 1; 37–52 (1951), 43.

59. Bonilla, *Gran Bretaña*, 1: 23.

CHAPTER FIVE

1. Miguel Hidalgo (1753–1811) was a *criollo* born near Guanajuato. He enrolled at the College of San Nicolás Obispo in Valladolid, Mexico, in 1767 and for the next 25 years was associated with the school. In 1778 Hidalgo was ordained a priest and in 1803 he became the curate at Dolores. His activities during those years clearly demonstrate that Hidalgo was greatly influenced by the Enlightenment. Prior to the *Grito de Dolores*, Hidalgo took an interest in military literature including that addressing the casting of cannon. Hugh Hamill Jr., *The Hidalgo Revolt* (Gainesville: University of Florida Press, 1966), 115, 142.

2. Alexander von Humboldt, *Political essay on the kingdom of New Spain*, 4 vols. (London: Printed for Longman, Hurst, Rees, Orme, & Brown, 1811–22), 1: 109; Fay Robinson, *Mexico and her Military Chieftains* (Hartford: Silas Andus & Son, 1851), 22.

3. Hidalgo favored independence but did not widely argue for this goal. Hamill, *The Hidalgo Revolt*, 122; José Bravo Ugarte, *Compendio de historia de Mexico* (Mexico: Editorial Jus, 1946), 140–41; Marley, *Wars*, 378.

4. Henry Bamford Parkes, *A History of Mexico* (Boston: Houghton Mifflin Company, 1938), 146–47, 150.

5. Robinson, *Mexico*, 38.

6. Michael C. Meyer and William L. Sherman, *The Course of Mexican History* (New York: Oxford University Press, 1979), 257.

7. Ernest Gruening, *Mexico and Its Heritage* (New York: D. Appleton-Century, 1934), 290.

8. Félix Calleja del Rey (1750–1820), born in Castilla la Vieja, Spain, entered the army at the age of fifteen. He fought in Algiers (1775) and took part in the sieges of Gibraltar (1779–83) and Minorca (1782). In 1789 he accompanied the new viceroy to New Spain. He led the fight against Hidalgo and Morelos and was called "the Butcher" by the Revolutionaries because of his treatment of prisoners. Between March 4, 1813, and 1816 he served as Viceroy of New Spain before returning to Spain. Lucas Alamán, *Historia de Mexico desde los primeros movimientos que prepararon su independencia en el año de 1808 hasta la época presente*, 5 vols. (Mexico: Libros del Bachiller Sansón Carrasco, 1985–86), 4: 281.

9. Bancroft, *History of Mexico*, 4: 159; Christon I. Archer, "New Wars and Old: Félix Calleja and the Independence of Mexico, 1810–1816," in *Military Heretics The Unorthodox in Policy and Strategy*, ed. by B. J. C. McKercher and A. Hamish Ion (Westport, Conn.: Praegar, 1994), 41–42; Christon I. Archer, "'La Causa Buena': The Counterinsurgency Army of New Spain and the Ten Years' War," in *Rank and Privilege The Military and Society in Latin America*, ed. by Linda Alexander Rodríguez (Wilmington, Del.: Scholarly Resources, 1994), 14.

10. In fact the lower classes held the *criollos* and *peninsulares* with common disdain. Hamill, *The Hidalgo Revolt*, 110–14.

11. Bancroft, *History of Mexico*, 4: 110–11; Guillermo Costa Soto, *Historia militar de Mexico* (Mexico: Impreso en los Talleros Graficos de la Nacion, 1947), 5; Guillermo Prieto, *Lecciones de historia patria*, 2 parts (Mexico: Secretaría de la Defensa, 1996), 2: 282–83.

12. Ignacio Allende (1769–1811) was second in command of the rebellion. An excellent horseman, Allende engaged in bullfighting which left his left arm crippled. He was a *criollo* and an aristocrat possessing a narrow education. Allende had no enthusiasm for broadening the rebellion to include the masses. During the battles he could or would not effectively employ the only army available to the revolution—masses of illiterate, poorly armed peasants who potentially were an overwhelming force. Hamill, *The Hidalgo Revolt*, 142–43.

13. Bancroft, *History of Mexico*, 4: 116–19; Prieto, *Lecciones*, 2: 284–85; Guillermo Canales Montejano, *Historia militar de Mexico* (Mexico: Ediciones Ateneo, 1940), 46. Superstitions were a part of the Hispanic culture. Knowing this, people such as Hidalgo could motivate the masses toward rebellion.

14. Hamill, *The Hidalgo Revolt*, 135; Bancroft, *History of Mexico*, 4: 123–28; Prieto, *Lecciones*, 2: 285–86; Canales, *Historia militar*, 46.

15. Hamill, *The Hidalgo Revolt*, 139–40; Bancroft, *History of Mexico*, 4: 134–57; Alamán, *Historia de Mexico*, 1: 276–79; Prieto, *Lecciones*, 2: 286–87.

16. Meyer and Sherman, *The Course*, 289–90; Costa Soto, *Historia Militar*, 6.

17. Prieto, *Lecciones*, 2: 287; Bancroft, *History of Mexico*, 4: 160–62; *Anales gráficos de la historia militar de Mexico 1810–1991* (Mexico: Editorial Gustavo Casasola, S.A., 1991), 6.

18. Prieto, *Lecciones*, 2: 288–89; Bancroft, *History of Mexico*, 4: 175–86; Wilbert H. Timmons, *Morelos Priest Soldier Statesman of Mexico* (El Paso: University of Texas Press, 1963), 57.

19. Alamán, *Historia de Mexico*, 1: 384; Bancroft, *History of Mexico*, 4: 186–89; Canales, *Historia militar*, 53–54.

20. Bancroft, *History of Mexico*, 4: 198–201; Parkes, *A History of Mexico*, 151; *Anales Gráficos*, 8; Marley, *Wars*, 381.

21. Parkes, *A History of Mexico*, 152; Prieto, *Lecciones*, 2: 290–92; Costa Soto, *Historia militar*, 8–9.

22. Hamill, *The Hidalgo Revolt*, 197.

23. By this time Allende was plotting to poison Hidalgo. Hamill, *The Hidalgo Revolt*, 200; Jesús de León Toral, "Antecedentes: del ejército mexicatl hasta la consumación de la independencia," in *El Ejército Mexicano* (Mexico: Secretaria de la Defensa Nacional, 1979), 97; Bancroft, *History of Mexico*, 4: 249–50.

24. Meyer and Sherman, *The Course*, 290; Bancroft, *History of Mexico*, 4: 252–58; Prieto, *Lecciones*, 2: 294.

25. Archer, "New Wars and Old," 45–47.

26. Ignacio López Rayón (1773–1832) born in Tlalpujahua, Michoacan, came from a family of moderate means. With his father's death, Rayón supervised the family's mining interests. He joined Hidalgo in October 1810 and fought at the Battles of Monte de las Cruces (October 30, 1810), Aculco (November 3, 1810), and Calderón (January 17, 1811).

27. Prieto, *Lecciones*, 2: 294–95; Parkes, *A History of Mexico*, 152–53.

28. José María Morelos y Pavón (1765–1815) was born near Apatzingan on a ranch; his parents were poor. He enrolled at San Nicolás College in Valladolid in 1790 where Miguel Hidalgo was then serving as rector. Although no evidence exists to show that the two men had close contact, they did share two and a half years at a small school. Morelos was ordained on December 21, 1797. Beginning in 1799, he served as the curate of Corácuaro for eleven years. He owned few possessions and was frugal. Morelos suffered constantly from headaches and typically wore a kerchief tied tightly about his head.

29. Prieto, *Lecciones*, 2: 292–93.

30. Acapulco was the terminus of the Manilla galleon which carried the riches of China, Japan, and the Philippines to the New World. The defenses of Acapulco had been given special attention by the Spaniards and were formidable.

31. Marley, *Wars*, 382.

32. Timmons, *Morelos*, 45–46; Bancroft, *History of Mexico*, 4: 297–301; Prieto, *Lecciones*, 2: 293, 296; Costa Soto, *Historia militar*, 13–14.

33. Prieto, *Lecciones*, 2: 296–97; Bancroft, *History of Mexico*, 4: 302; Marley, *Wars*, 384–85.

34. Timmons, *Morelos*, 49; *Anales gráficos*, 15–16.

35. Archer, "*La Causa Buena*," 21–32; Bancroft, *History of Mexico*, 4: 317–19.

36. Timmons, *Morelos*, 64; Bancroft, *History of Mexico*, 4: 347–49; Prieto, *Lecciones*, 2: 298–99; *Anales Gráficos*, 18.

37. Had Morelos taken Atlixco, which was the heart of the wheat-growing area, he would have threatened Puebla's food supply. Timmons, *Morelos*, 64; Bancroft, *History of Mexico*, 4: 350–51; Antonio Penafiel, *Ciudades coloniales y capitales de la república mexicana*, 5 vol. (Mexico: Impr. y Fototipia de la Secretaría de Fomento, 1908–14) 3: 79.

38. *Morelos documentos inéditos y poco conocidos*, 3 vols. (Mexico: Secretaría de Educación Pública, 1927), 1: 310; Bancroft, *History of Mexico*, 4: 353–60; Archer, "*La Causa Buena,*" 18; Timmons, *Morelos*, 66–67; Marley, *Wars*, 386.

39. Prieto claims that the Royalist army was "12,000 men perfectly endowed with all that was necessary." Prieto, *Lecciones*, 2: 300; Bancroft, *History of Mexico*, 4: 361–63; Canales, *Historia militar*, 60.

40. Henry G. Ward, *Mexico in 1827*, 2 vols. (London: H. Colburn, 1828), 1: 196.

41. *Morelos documentos*, 1: 357–58.

42. Prieto, *Lecciones*, 2: 301–2; Bancroft, *History of Mexico*, 4: 364–70; Canales, *Historia militar*, 61–72.

43. *Morelos documentos*, 1: 367–68; Bancroft, *History of Mexico*, 4: 370–72; Timmons, *Morelos*, 73; Prieto, *Lecciones*, 2: 302.

44. Bancroft, *History of Mexico*, 4: 481–88; Prieto, *Lecciones*, 2: 302; Parkes, *A History of Mexico*, 159.

45. Bancroft, *History of Mexico*, 4: 495–502; Parkes, *A History of Mexico*, 161; Prieto, *Lecciones*, 2: 303.

46. Timmons, *Morelos*, 80; Bancroft, *History of Mexico*, 4: 545–51. Aguirre Colorado et al. argue that Morelos should have attacked the enemy's supply lines, which they state could have been decisive. Rafael Aguirre Colorado, Ruben García, and Pelagio A. Rodríguez, *Campañas de Morelos sobre Acapulco (1810–1813)* (Mexico: Talleres Gráficos de la Nación, 1933), 93.

47. Timmons, *Morelos*, 82–83; Parkes, *A History of Mexico*, 159; Bravo, *Compendio*, 147; Prieto, *Lecciones*, 2: 306.

48. Parkes, *A History of Mexico*, 160; Bravo, *Compendio*, 145; Prieto, *Lecciones*, 2: 306.

49. Bravo, *Compendio*, 147; *Morelos documentos*, 2: 352.

50. Carlos M. de Bustamante, *Cuadro histórico de la revolución de la América mexicana*, 6 vols. (Mexico: Imprenta de la Agiula, 1822–32), 2: 416–17; William Spence Robertson, *Iturbide of Mexico* (New York: Greenwood Press, Publishers, 1968), 26–27; Bancroft, *History of Mexico*, 4: 569–73; Bravo, *Compendio*, 148.

51. Timmons, *Morelos*, 128; Bancroft, *History of Mexico*, 4: 573–75; Parkes, *A History of Mexico*, 162; *Anales gráficos*, 24.

52. Costa Soto, *Historia militar*, 18; James Jeffrey Roche, *By-Ways of War* (Boston: Small, Maynard & Company, 1901), 11; Parkes, *A History of Mexico*, 164.

53. Bancroft, *History of Mexico*, 4: 595–600.

54. Vicente Guerrero (1783–1831) was born in Tixtla into a poor family. Apparently, his heritage was Indian, white, and black. He joined the Revolutionaries in 1810 and was commissioned by Morelos as a captain to attack Taxco. As the revolution faltered by 1820, Guerrero maintained the only effective rebel fighting force.

55. Guadalupe Victoria—pseudonym for Miguel Fernández Félix (1786–1843)— was born in Villa de Tamazula, Nueva Vizcaya (now Durango). He left the College of San Ildefonso in 1811 to join the Revolutionaries. He fought under Morelos. Victoria was defeated at Palmillos in 1817 and spent the next five years being hunted by the Royalists. He refused to consider a pardon.

56. Archer, "*La Causa Buena*," 12, 19–21; Bravo, *Compendio*, 149.

57. Archer, "*La Causa Buena*," 12; Meyer and Sherman, *The Course*, 293–94.

58. Francisco Javier Mina (1789–1817), born in Navarra, Spain, abandoned his studies in 1808 and fought against the French invaders. By 1810 Mina was the Commandant

General of Navarra and a celebrated guerrilla chief. He was captured and sent to France. Minas returned to Spain in 1814 but soon fled his native land when it was discovered that he was conspiring with those who wanted to establish a constitutional government.

59. Bancroft, *History of Mexico*, 4: 659–81; Marley, *Wars*, 404; Costa Soto, *Historia militar*, 18–20; Roche, *By-Ways*, 13.

60. Agustín de Iturbide (1783–1824) was born in Valladolid (now Morelia) and came from a family of moderate wealth. In 1810 Hidalgo offered Iturbide the rank of lieutenant general if he would join the Revolutionaries; instead, Iturbide volunteered as a member of Trujillo's force which defeated Hidalgo at Monte de las Cruces. From 1810 through 1815 Iturbide zealously fought to suppress the rebellion. Among his more important assignments, he was second in command at Valladolid in 1814 against Morelos. In 1815 Iturbide was retired due to accusations that he extorted money from mine owners in exchange for protection, a matter he was still contesting when appointed to command the Army of the South in 1820. He continually petitioned the Viceroy for monies he claimed were owed to him by the Crown.

61. Bancroft, *History of Mexico*, 4: 697–701.

62. Robertson, *Iturbide*, 54–73; Bancroft, *History of Mexico*, 4: 704–11; Meyer and Sherman, *The Course*, 295; Parkes, *A History of Mexico*, 170–71.

63. Bustamante, *Cuadro histórico*, 5: 107; Costa Soto, *Historia militar*, 21–22.

64. Robertson, *Iturbide*, 86–90.

65. ibid., 95; Bustamante, *Cuadro histórico*, 5: 177–78; *Bancroft, History of Mexico*, 4: 714–15.

66. Parkes, *A History of Mexico*, 170–71; Bancroft, *History of Mexico*, 4: 718; Bravo, *Compendio*, 152–53.

67. *Anales gráficos*, 38; Robertson, *Iturbide*, 97.

68. Robertson, *Iturbide*, 127–33; Bancroft, *History of Mexico*, 4: 728–33; *Anales gráficos*, 39.

69. William A. DePalo Jr., *The Mexican National Army, 1822–1852* (College Station: Texas A & M University Press, 1997), 35–37; Bancroft, *History of Mexico*, 5: 71.

70. Wilfred Hardy Callcott, *Santa Anna* (Hamden: Archon Books, 1964) 73; Miguel A. Sánchez Lamego, "El ejército mexicano de 1821 a 1860," in *El ejército mexicano* (Mexico: Secretaría de la Defensa Nacional, 1979), 130–32; Bancroft, *History of Mexico*, 5: 71–73.

71. Callcott, *Santa Anna*, 71–74; Bancroft, *History of Mexico*, 5: 74; Leonardo Pasquel, *Antonio López de Santa Anna* (Mexico: Instituto de Mexicologia, 1990), 54.

72. Callcott, *Santa Anna*, 74–75.

73. Bancroft, *History of Mexico*, 5: 74–75; Sánchez, "El ejército mexicano de 1821 a 1860," 135–36; Callcott, *Santa Anna*, 75–76; DePalo Jr., *The Mexican National Army*, 38–39; Ann Fears Crawford, ed., *The Eagle: The Autobiography of Santa Anna* (Austin: State House Press, 1988), 21–24.

74. Marley, *Wars*, 468–69.

75. Matilla Tascón, "Las expediciones," 42–43; Maricus André writes that there were 8,448 regular Spanish troops in Mexico in 1821. André, *La fin*, 98.

76. Alfonso Corona del Rosal, *La guerra, el imperialismo, el ejército mexicano* (Mexico: Grijalbo, 1989), 247; Loveman, *For la Patria*, 33.

77. Manuel Rivera Cambas, *Los gobernantes de Mexico*, 2 vols. (Mexico: Imp. de J. M. Aguilar Ortíz, 1872–73), 2: 160–476; Archer, "New Wars and Old," 53; Gruening, *Mexico*, 289.

78. Gruening, *Mexico*, 289.

79. Alfonso Teja Zabre, *Vida de Morles: nueva version* (Mexico: Universidad Nacional Autónoma de Mexico, 1959), 280–83.
80. Parkes, *A History of Mexico*, 144–45.
81. Villanueva, *Fernando VII*, 56–57.
82. Manning, *Dipl. Corrs. of the U.S. concerning*, 3: 1600–1.
83. Loveman, *For la Patria*, 32.

CHAPTER SIX

1. Julián María Rubio, *La infanta Carlotta Joaquina y la política de España en America, 1808–1812* (Madrid: Impr. de E. Maestre, 1920), 4; von Pivka, *Navies*, 192; Carlos Penna Botto, *Campanhas navais Sul-Americanas* (Rio de Janeiro: Imprensa Naval, 1940), 24–25; Marley, *Wars*, 376.
2. Donato, *Dicionário*, 114–15; Botto, *Campanhas navais*, 25.
3. Percy Alvin Martin, "Brazil," in *Argentina, Brazil, and Chile since Independence*, ed. by A. Curtis Wilgus (Washington: George Washington University Press, 1935), 158; Botto, *Campanhas navais*, 25.
4. John Armitage, *The History of Brazil*, 2 vols. (London: Smith, Elder, and Co., Cornhill, 1836), 1: 83.
5. Armitage, *The History of Brazil*, 1: 64–66; Martin, "Brazil," 162; Botto, *Campanhas navais*, 26; Marley, *Wars*, 431.
6. Brian Vale, "The Creation of the Imperial Brazilian Navy, 1822–1823," *The Mariner's Mirror* 57: 1; 63–88 (January 1971), 65.
7. José Honório Rodigues, *Independência: revolução e contrarevolução*, vol. 3: *As forcas armadas* (Rio de Janeiro: Ed. Francisco Alves, 1975), 17–40; Botto, *Campanhas navais*, 26; *História do exército brasileiro*, 2 vols. (Brasília and Rio de Janeiro: Edição do Estado-Maior do Exército, 1972), 2: 416.
8. Armitage, *The History of Brazil*, 1: 7–8; João Carlos Gonçalves Caminha, "A guerra da independência—capitulo II." *Navigator: Subsidios para a História Marítíma do Brasil* (Rio de Janeiro) 14: 28–62 (June 1978), 30.
9. Vale, "The Creation," 69; Arlindo Vianna Filho, *Estratégia naval brasileira: abordagem à história da evolução dos conceitos estratégicos navais brasileiros* (Rio de Janeiro: BIBLIEX, 1995), 19–20.
10. Vale, "The Creation," 69–71, 75.
11. ibid., 71–72, 74, 78–79, 83; Armitage, *The History of Brazil*, 1: 99–100.
12. Armitage, *The History of Brazil*, 1: 5–6, 20–21; *História do exército brasileiro*, 2: 404.
13. Vale, "The Creation," 69; Botto, *Campanhas navais*, 26–27; *História do exército brasileiro*, 2: 420–21.
14. Vale, "The Creation," 69; Caminha, "A Guerra," 30–31; Marley, *Wars*, 432.
15. Vale, "The Creation," 82.
16. The most prominent were John Taylor, Thomas Crasbie, John Pascoe Greenfell (who adopted the Portuguese spelling Grenfell), James Norton, James Sheperd, Samuel Gillet, George Clarence, Raphael Wright, and Charles Jell.
17. Vale, "The Creation," 86; Botto, *Campanhas navais*, 28; Marley, *Wars*, 433.
18. Botto, *Campanhas navais*, 28; Brian Vale, "Lord Cochrane in Brazil, I. The Naval War of Independence, 1823" *The Mariner's Mirror*, 57:4, 415–42 (November 1971), 418–19.

19. Thomas Cochrane, *Narrative of the Services in the Liberation of Chili, Peru, and Brazil*, 2 vols. (London: James Ridgway, 1859), 2: 31; Armitage, *The History of Brazil*, 1: 102; Donato, *Dicionário*, 461; Vale, "Lord Cochrane," 421–22; Botto, *Campanhas navais*, 28–29; Marley, *Wars*, 434.

20. Vale, "Lord Cochrane," 423; Cochrane, *Narrative*, 2:30.

21. Armitage, *The History of Brazil*, 1: 103; Vale, "Cochrane I," 424; Botto, *Campanhas navais*, 29–30.

22. Vale, "Lord Cochrane," 426.

23. ibid., 427.

24. Armitage, *The History of Brazil*, 1: 103–4; Donato, *Dicionário*, 461; Vale, "Lord Cochrane," 427.

25. Armitage, *The History of Brazil*, 1; 104–5; Vale, "Cochrane I," 427–31; Botto, *Campanhas navais*, 30; Marley, *Wars*, 434.

26. Vale, "Lord Cochrane," 431–33; Botto, *Campanhas navais*, 31; Marley, *Wars*, 434.

27. Vale, "Lord Cochrane," 433.

28. Donato, *Dicionário*, 328.

29. *História do exército brasileiro*, 2: 428; Vale, "Lord Cochrane," 434.

30. Botto, *Campanhas navais*, 35; Vale, "Lord Cochrane," 434–35.

31. Cochrane, *Narrative*, 2: 72–73; Vale, "Lord Cochrane," 436–37; Botto, *Campanhas navais*, 35; *História do exército brasileiro*, 2: 428–29; Marley, *Wars*, 435.

32. John Pascoe Grenfell (1800–69) born in Battersea, England, entered the service of the East India Company at the age of eleven. He served under Adm. Thomas Cochrane during the Chilean War for Independence and was severely wounded during the capture of the Spanish frigate *Esmeralda*. In 1823 Grenfell accompanied Cochrane to Brazil and was appointed a lieutenant in the Brazilian navy on March 21, 1823. Grenfell lost an arm at the Battle of Quilmes (July 29, 1826) in a war with the United Provinces (Argentina).

33. Botto, *Campanhas navais*, 35–36; Vale, "Lord Cochrane," 439–41; Armitage, *The History of Brazil*, 1: 106–7; *História do exército brasileiro*, 2: 429.

34. Vale, "Lord Cochrane," 442.

35. In March 1817 a serious uprising favoring independence occurred in Pernambuco. Revolutionaries expelled the Portuguese governor. On May 19 the Portuguese drove the revolutionaries out of Recife, hunted them down, and many were executed. Marley, *Wars*, 403–5, 436.

36. Cochrane, *Narrative*, 2: 10–13.

CHAPTER SEVEN

1. Brian Vale, *A War betwixt Englishmen* (London: I. B. Tauris Publishers, 2000), 12.

2. Suárez, *Atlas*, 153.

3. Levene, *A History of Argentina*, 379–80.

4. Joao Pandia Calogeras, *A History of Brazil*, trans. by Alvin Martin (Chapel Hill: University of North Carolina Press, 1959), 101–2.

5. Vale, *A War*, 1.

6. Kirkpatrick, *Latin America*, 155; Hubert Herring, *A History of Latin America* (New York: Alfred A. Knoff, 1955), 601; Vale, "The Creation," 67.

7. Armitage, *The History of Brazil*, 1: 259–60.

8. W. H. Koebel, *British Exploits in South America* (New York: The Century Company, 1917), 327–29; Armitage, *The History of Brazil*, 1: 260–61; Levene, *A History of Argentina*, 381.

9. Vale, *A War*, 3.

10. Born in Buenos Aires, Juan Gualberto de las Heras (1780–1866) fought the British during the 1806 and 1807 invasions. A member of the Army of the Andes, he commanded the element that used the Uspallata Pass. He is credited with rescuing an important component of the Army of the Andes when it was surprised by the Royalists at the Battle of Cancha Rayada (March 19, 1818). Las Heras fought at Chacabuco (February 12, 1817), Maipú (May 5, 1818), and in southern Chile. Las Heras expected but did not receive command of the army in the war against Brazil. He retired to Chile where he eventually died.

11. Suárez, *Atlas*, 156.

12. Armitage, *The History of Brazil*, 1: 208.

13. Koebel, *British Exploits*, 155; "Adventures of an Officer in the Brazilian Navy," *The United Service Journal* (1834), 78–87, 174–82, 352–60 (Part I), 513–20 (Part II), 487–96 (Part III), (1835) 206–16 (Part II), 78–79; Vale, *A War*, 13–17; Jan Read, *The New Conquistadores* (London: Evans Brothers Limited, 1980), 126.

14. Benjamín Villegas Basavilbaso, *La adquisición de armamentos navales en Chile* (Buenos Aires: Imprenta de la universidad, 1927), 29–32; Vale, *A War* 27; Suárez, *Atlas*, 157.

15. Vale, *A War*, 8–9, 21.

16. Read, *The New Conquistadores*, 126–27; Vale, *A War*, 11.

17. Armitage, *The History of Brazil*, 1: 218–19; Vale, *A War*, 3–4.

18. Vale, *A War*, 35–37; Botto, *Camphanhas*, 46; Suárez, *Atlas*, 157.

19. Botto, *Camphanhas*, 46–47; Vale, *A War*, 45–47; Suárez, *Atlas*, 157; Armitage, *The History of Brazil*, 1: 240–41.

20. Vale, *A War*, 48–49.

21. ibid., 50–52; Botto, *Camphanhas*, 47.

22. Vale, *A War*, 50–57; Botto, *Camphanhas*, 48; Prado Maia, *Através da historia naval brasileira* (São Paulo: Companhia Editora Nacional, 1936), 150–55.

23. Rodrigo Pinto Guedes, Barão de Rio da Prata (1762–1845), born into Portuguese nobility, entered the navy in 1781. Pinto Guedes accompanied the imperial Portuguese family when it fled Europe in 1808. In 1822 he chose to support the independence of Brazil against Portugal. Prior to his appointment in 1826 as the commander of the River Plate forces, Pinto Guedes had held administrative positions for some twenty years.

24. Vale, *A War*, 63–65; Botto, *Camphanhas*, 49–51.

25. James Norton (1789–1835) served in the British navy during the Napoleonic Wars. In 1823 he was commissioned as a commander in the Brazilian navy. Norton took part in the fighting against the republicans during the Pernambuco rebellion in 1824. He died with the rank of *Chefe de Divisão* while on his way to New Zealand.

26. Vale, *A War*, 69–75; Botto, *Camphanhas*, 51; Destéfani, *Manual de historia*, 90–91.

27. Vale, *A War*, 76–82; Maia, *Através*, 157–61; Destefani, *Manual de historia naval Argentina*, 91; Carvalho, *Nossa marinha*, 28.

28. Armitage, *The History of Brazil*, 1: 258–59, 262–63.

29. ibid., 1: 269–70; Vale, *A War*, 113.

30. Caillet-Bois, *Historia naval*, 276–81; Vale, *A War*, 105–15; Carvalho, *Nossa Marinha*, 36.

31. Vale, *A War*, 117–22.

32. Caillet-Bois, *Historia naval*, 282–97; Vale, *A War*, 126–30; Botto, *Camphanhas*, 53; Suárez, *Atlas*, 166.

33. Armitage, *The History of Brazil*, 1: 272.
34. Levene, *A History of Argentina*, 381.
35. Hollander Brandsen (1785–1827) was born into French nobility. He fought under San Martín during the liberation of Chile and Peru.
36. Suárez, *Atlas*, 162–65; H. D. [Hermano Damaceno], *Ensayo de historia patria*, 10th ed., 2 vols. (Montevideo: Barreiro y Ramos, 1955), 1: 489; Marley, *Wars*, 472–73.
37. C. I. Salas, "Bibliografía del coronel Federico de Brandzen," *Renacimiento* (Buenos Aires, December 1909) cited in Levene, *A History of Argentina*, 382.
38. Armitage, *The History of Brazil*, 1: 273–74.
39. James Shepherd (unk.–1827), born in Scotland, served under Cochrane in the Chilean navy and accompanied Cochrane to Brazil in 1823. During the early stage of the war with Argentina, he commanded the frigate *Piranga* (64 guns). Shepherd was a strict disciplinarian.
40. Vale, *A War*, 138–45; Botto, *Camphanhas*, 54; "Adventures of an Officer," (1834) (Part I) 78–85; Marley, *Wars*, 473; Armitage, *The History of Brazil*, 1: 276–77.
41. Francis Drummond (1802–27) was born in Scotland. He served in the Brazilian navy was a sublieutenant during the War for Independence (1822–23) and was a member of the crew of the *Niterói* which pursued the Portuguese squadron across the Atlantic Ocean. While awaiting court-martial for disciplinary reasons, Drummond fled to Buenos Aires and offered his services.
42. Vale, *A War*, 150–55; Carvalho, *Nossa marinha*, 36; Botto, *Camphanhas*, 54; Marley, *Wars*, 473; Read, *The New Conquistadores*, 132–33.
43. Vale, *A War*, 148–49.
44. Suárez, *Atlas*, 167.
45. Vale, *A War*, 98; Read, *The New Conquistadores*, 133–34; Héctor Ratto, *Vida de Brown* (Buenos Aires: Emecé Editores, S.A., 1943), 38.
46. Vale, *A War*, 101–3.
47. George DeKay (1802–49) was born in New York and went to sea at an early age. He joined the Chilean navy in 1824 and took part in the siege of Callao. DeKay offered his services to the Brazilian Empire which turned him down, so he turned to privateering for Buenos Aires.
48. Phillis Wheelock, "An American Commodore in the Argentine Navy," *The American Neptune* 6: 1; 5–18 (January 1946), 9, 12–13; Maia, *Através*, 166–70; Vale, *A War*, 190–93.
49. John Halstead Coe (1806–64) was born in Springfield, Massachusetts. Beginning in 1824 he served in the revolutionary navy in the Pacific on the warship *Protector* and took part in the siege of Callao. Coe fought as a volunteer for Buenos Aires during the Battle of Quilmes (July 29, 1826). He served on board the corvette *Chacabuco* during its late-1826 raid off Brazil.
50. *The British Packet*, May 1827, quoted from Read, *The New Conquistadores*, 134.
51. Levene, *A History of Argentina*, 383; Armitage, *The History of Brazil*, 1: 278–79.
52. Vale, *A War*, 202–6.
53. Suárez, *Atlas*, 169–70.
54. "Formation and Revolt of the Irish Brigade in Brazilian Service, at Rio, in 1828," in *The United Service Journal* (1830) 171–80 (Part II); Frederic von Allendorfer, "An Irish Regiment in Brazil, 1826–28," in *The Irish Sword* 3: 12; 28–31 (Winter 1957), 28–30; Vale, *The War*, 211. In July 1828 1,400 survivors were sent home.

55. Suárez, *Atlas*, 170.
56. Calogeras, *A History of Brazil*, 101.
57. Armitage, *The History of Brazil*, 1: 219, 244–45.
58. ibid., 1: 244.
59. Augusto G. Rodríquez, *Reseña histórica del ejército argentino (1862–1930)* (Buenos Aires: Secretaría de Guerra, 1964), 15.

CHAPTER EIGHT

1. José de la Mar y Contazar (1776–1830) was born in Cuenca, Ecuador, and joined the Spanish army in 1794. He fought in the defense of Zaragoza and Valencia, Spain, in 1812. In 1820 he was in command of the defenses at Callao, Peru, when San Martín invaded the country. On September 21 he surrendered to the Revolutionaries, and he and his forces were incorporated into those of San Martín. For changing sides he was rewarded with the command of a Peruvian division. La Mar fought at Junín (August 6, 1924) and commanded the left wing of the Revolutionary army at Ayacucho (December 9, 1824).

2. Agustín Gamarra (1785–1841) was born in Cuzco, Peru, of humble origin. His father was a Padre Saldivar and his mother an Indian woman. He abandoned his seminary studies and joined the Spanish army at an early age. Between 1809 and 1820 he fought for the King in battles at Salta, Tucumán, Huaquí, and Vilcapuquio. On January 24, 1821, he changed sides, joining the rebels against the King. He fought at the battles of Junín (August 6, 1824) and Ayacucho (December 9, 1824). Following the Battle of Ayacucho he was named *Prefecto* (governor) of Cuzco and was promoted to division general. Apparently, Gamarra loathed Antonio Sucre because Gamarra believed that Sucre had not adequately rewarded him for his services.

3. Carlos Dellepiane, *Historia militar del Peru*, 2 vols. (Lima: Liberia e Imprenta Gil, S.A., 1931), 1: 283–91.

4. ibid., 1: 292.

5. In fact, there were probably more Peruvians fighting for the King at Ayacucho than fighting for the Revolutionaries. Following the battle 2,263 Royalists were captured. Of these 1,512 were Americans, most of whom were probably Peruvians or Bolivians (see chapter 4).

6. N. Andrew N. Cleven, "Dictators Gamarra, Orbegoso, Salaverry, and Santa Cruz," in *South American Dictators*, ed. by A. Curtis Wilgus (Washington: George Washington University Press, 1937), 289–90; Jésus María Henao and Gerardo Arrubla, *History of Colombia*, trans. by J. Fred Rippy (Chapel Hill: University of North Carolina Press, 1958), 394; Ronald Bruce St. John, *The Foreign Policy of Peru* (Boulder: Lynne Rienner, 1992), 23–24; Dellepiane, *Historia militar,* 1: 294–96; Manuel Vegas, *Historia de la marina de guerra del Peru 1821–1924* (Lima: Imprenta de la Marina, 1973), 36.

7. St. John, *The Foreign Policy,* 23–24.

8. Denegri, *Peru*, 74–75.

9. Cleven, "Dictators," 287–88.

10. Dellepiane, *Historia militar*, 1: 297; Del Río, *Bolívar*, 186–87; Ayala, *Nueva historia*, 6: 253; Cleven, "Dictators," 288–89.

11. Dellepiane, *Historia militar*, 1: 300–1; Cleven, "Dictators," 288–90; St. John, *The Foreign Policy*, 24; Denegri, *Peru*, 77–78.

12. St. John, *The Foreign Policy*, 24–25; Valdizán, *Historia naval*, 3: 159–60; Henao and Arrubla, *History of Colombia*, 406–7; Alváro Valencia Tovar, "El ejército en la Gran

Colombia," in *Historia de la fuerzas militares de Colombia*, 6 vols. (Bogotá: Planeta, 1993), 2: 126, 129.

13. Ayala, *Nueva historia*, 6: 132–33; Valdes, *Historia de Chile*, 91; Encina-Castedo, *Resumen*, 3: 2011.

14. Del Río, *Bolívar*, 189.

15. Juan José Flores (1799–1864) was born in Puerto Cabello, Venezuela. His father was a Spaniard and his mother an American. He joined the revolutionary army in 1811 and participated in numerous battles throughout northern South America. He fought at the Battle of Pichincha (May 24, 1822) and in the campaign aground Pasto in 1822. Flores married Mercedes Jijón y Vivanco, the daughter of an Ecuadorian aristocrat and one of the wealthiest men in that area.

16. Del Río, *Bolívar*, 189–90; Valencia, "El ejército," 2: 133; Ayala, *Nueva historia*, 6: 255.

17. Del Río, *Bolívar*, 189–90.

18. Valencia, "El ejército," 2: 129.

19. Martin George Guise [Guisse] (1780–1828) born in Gloucester, England, joined the British navy at an early age. When twenty-five years old, he fought at Trafalgar (October 21, 1805). Guise served under Cochrane in the Liberation Expedition. He was wounded during the capture of the Spanish frigate *Esmeralda*. Following Cochrane's departure, Guise created a Peruvian squadron and was given the rank of rear admiral. Guise had a falling out with Bolívar and was imprisoned for twenty months, regaining his freedom when Bolívar returned to Colombia.

20. Jorge Ortíz Sotelo, *El vicealmirante Martín Jorge Guise Wright (1780–1828)* (Lima: Marina de Guerra del Peru, 1993), 138; Rosendo Melo, *Historia de la marina del Peru*, 2 vols. (Callao: Museo Naval, 1980–81), 1: 163; Vegas, *Historia de la marina*, 35–36.

21. Mariano Sánchez Bravo, *Buques y personajes* (Guayaquil: Instituto de Historia Maritima, 1991), 12.

22. Dellepiane, *Historia militar*, 1: 310–11; Henao and Arrubla, *History of Colombia*, 407; Valencia, "El ejército," 2: 128–29.

23. Dellepiane, *Historia militar*, 1:314; Henao and Arrubla, *History of Colombia*, 407.

24. Melo, *Historia de la marina*, 1: 167–69; Ayala, *Nueva historia*, 6: 254; Ortiz, *El vicealmirante* 149–50; Dellepiane, *Historia militar*, 1: 204–5.

25. Vegas, *Historia de la marina*, 38–39; Fernando Romero, *Notas para una biografía del vice almirante Guise* (Lima: Ministerio de Marina, 1974), 87; Dellepiane, *Historia militar*, 1: 304–5.

26. Valencia, "El ejército," 2: 129–30; Ortiz Sotelo, *El vicealmirante*, 167–69; Romero, *Notas*, 98–99; Valdizán Gamio, *Historia naval*, 3: 168–69.

27. *Fuentes para el estudio de la historia naval del Peru*, 2 vols. (Callao: Talleres Tipográficos de la Escuela Naval del Peru, 1960), 1: 229; Dellepiane, *Historia militar*, 1: 317–18.

28. Capt. José Rufino Echenique, a combatant, wrote, "I have never been able to understand that we gave up the battle for lost." Denegri, *Peru*, 91.

29. Valencia, "El ejército," 2: 133–37; Del Río, *Bolívar*, 190–91; Dellepiane, *Historia militar*, 1: 306, 320–24; Romero, *Notas*, 102–3. *Fuentes para el estudio* 1: 230, places the losses at 800 Colombians and 1,200 Peruvians.

30. Henao and Arrubla, *History of Colombia*, 408; Cleven, "Dictators," 293; Del Río, *Bolívar*, 190.

31. Denegri, *Peru*, 93–94.

32. Valdizán Gamio, *Historia naval*, 3: 177; Dellepiane, *Historia militar*, 1: 324; Del Río, *Bolívar*, 191 places the number of returning Peruvians at 2,000 men which seems less likely.

33. St. John, *The Foreign Policy*, 27–28; Denegri, *Peru*, 94–95.

34. Fredrick Pike, *The Modern History of Peru* (London: Weidenfeld & Nicolson, 1967), 72–73; St. John, *The Foreign Policy*, 25.

35. Cleven, "Dictators," 291–93.

36. Gordon Ireland, *Boundaries, Possessions, and Conflicts in South America* (Cambridge: Harvard University Press, 1938), 187–88; *Fuentes para el studio*, 1: 231–32.

37. Del Río, *Bolívar*, 189; Denegri, *Peru*, 137.

CHAPTER NINE

1. Bruno, *Historia argentina*, 404–6; Comando en Jefe, *Ejército argentine*, 118; Marley, *Wars*, 419.

2. Escuela Superior de Guerra, *Manual*, 2: 307–9.

3. Domingo F. Sarmiento, *Facundo: Civilization and Barbarism* (New York: Hurd and Houghton, 1969), 28.

4. Kirkpatrick, *Latin America*, 134.

5. J. Fred Rippy, "Argentina," in *Argentina, Brazil, and Chile since Independence*, ed. by A. Curtis Wilgus (Washington: George Washington University Press, 1935), 75–80; George I. Blanksten, *Peron's Argentina* (Chicago: The University of Chicago Press, 1953), 22–23.

6. Kirkpatrick, *Latin America*, 136.

7. Mitre, *Historia de San Martín*, 2: 188–204.

8. Bruno, *Historia argentina*, 352–53; Roque Lanús, "Logias en el ejército argentino en el siglo XIX," *La Prensa* 7 (July 1, 1950), 7.

9. Herring, *A History of Latin America*, 601; Rippy, "Argentina," 81.

10. Sarmiento, *Facundo*, 27.

11. Juan Manuel de Rosas (1793–1877) enlisted as a soldier in the 4th Cavalry Squadron at the age of thirteen. He fought in the second defense of Buenos Aires against the British in 1806. Rosas did not fight in the Wars for Independence. Rather, he devoted himself to agriculture on the *pampas* (great plain) and became wealthy. In 1825 Rosas negotiated a new demarcation line with the Indians in the south. He began his political career as one of the wealthiest landholders in the province of Buenos Aires and ended his life possessing modest means. In 1991 Rosas' remains were repatriated to Argentina where they were received with presidential honors.

12. Davis, *History of Latin America*, 407. Prior to the use of this slogan by Rosas, Unitarian Gen. Juan Lavalle used "Death to the *Gauchos*." Cayetano Bruno, *Historia argentina* (Buenos Aires: Editorial Don Bosco, 1877), 492; Aníbal Atilio Röttjer, *Vida del procer argentino brigadier general don Juan Manuel de Rosas* (Buenos Aires: Ediciones Theoría, 1972), 159.

13. Loveman, *For la Patria*, 39.

14. Armin Engelhardt, "The Battle of Caseros—The Dawn of Modern Argentina," *Military Review* 12: 4, 217–25 (Winter 1948), 218–19.

15. Charles Edward Chapman, *Republican Hispanic America* (New York: Macmillan, 1938), 327; Kirkpatrick, *Latin America*, 139–40; Rippy, "Argentina," 93–94. For a more benevolent interpretation of "La Mazorca," see Röttjer, *Vida*, 142–43, 193–94.

16. Andrew Graham-Yooll, *Small Wars You May Have Missed* (London: Junction Books, 1983), 79–80.

17. Kirkpatrick, *Latin America*, 137.

18. Suárez, *Atlas*, 175–77; Chapman, *Republican Hispanic America*, 327; Kirkpatrick, *Latin America*, 138; Marley, *Wars*, 474.

19. James D. Rudolph, ed., *Argentina: A Country Study*, 3d ed. (Washington: Department of the Army, 1986), 24–25; Rippy, "Argentina," 84; Comando en Jefe, *Ejército argentine*, 165.

20. Suárez, *Atlas*, 179; Comando en Jefe, *Ejército argentine*, 165; Meister, *Francisco Solano Lopez*, 33; Marley, *Wars*, 474.

21. Suárez, *Atlas*, 180–83; Córdoba, Mendoza, San Luis, San Juan, Salta, Tucumán, Santiago del Estero, Catamarca, and La Rioja.

22. Bruno, *Historia argentina*, 471–72, 511; Comando en Jefe, *Ejército argentino*, 170; Marley, *Wars*, 475.

23. Bruno, *Historia argentina*, 502; Comando en Jefe, *Ejército argentin*, 180–82.

24. Comando en Jefe, *Ejército argentino*, 182; Marley, *Wars*, 488.

25. Röttjer, *Vida*, 185; Suárez, *Atlas*, 208; Comando en Jefe, *Ejército argentino*, 182.

26. Leon Pomer, *Os confitos da Bacia do Prata* (São Paulo: Editora Brasiliense, 1979), 32–33; Comando en Jefe, *Ejército argentino*, 183; Marley, *Wars*, 488.

27. Justo José de Urquiza (1801–70) was born in Entre Ríos into a landed family. Urquiza served in the Entre Ríos Congress between 1826 and 1827 and championed federalism. He fled to Uruguay following the defeat of Ricardo López Jordán, whom he supported. Urquiza returned to Entre Ríos in 1831 and in 1837 again served in the Provincial Congress. In 1845 he was named the Governor of Entre Ríos. He and two of his sons were assassinated on April 11, 1870.

28. Suárez, *Atlas*, 219–21; Bruno, *Historia argentina*, 504; Röttjer, *Vida*, 173, 235; Comando en Jefe, *Ejército argentino*, 182–83; Rippy, "Argentina," 97; Marley, *Wars*, 489.

29. Bruno, *Historia argentina*, 506; Röttjer, *Vida*, 193.

30. Bruno, *Historia argentina*, 506; Caillet-Bois, *Historia naval*, 391; Suárez, *Atlas*, 220–21.

31. Suárez, *Atlas*, 226–28; Rippy, "Argentina," 97–98.

32. Suárez, *Atlas*, 235–37; Marley, *Wars*, 490; Comando en Jefe, *Ejército argentino*, 188–91; Röttjer, *Vida*, 214.

33. E. A. M. Laing, "The Royal Navy on the River Paraná During the Allied Intervention, 1845–46," *The American Neptune* 36: 2; 125–43 (April 1976), 125; Graham-Yooll, *Small Wars*, 69–71; Suárez, *Atlas*, 209.

34. Kirkpatrick, *A History*, 150.

35. Caillet-Bois, *Historia naval*, 401–2; Suárez, *Atlas*, 210.

36. Caillet-Bois, *Historia naval*, 403–4; Bruno, *Historia argentina*, 515–17; Suárez, *Atlas*, 210.

37. Comando en Jefe, *Ejército argentino*, 190–92; Marley, *Wars*, 491.

38. Röttjer, *Vida*, 235; Bruno, *Historia argentina*, 512; Suárez, *Atlas*, 211; Comando en Jefe, *Ejército argentino*, 196.

39. Kirkpatrick, *A History*, 148–49; Marley, *Wars*, 493.

40. Marley, *Wars*, 493.

41. Suárez, *Atlas*, 213; Marley, *Wars*, 494.

42. Suarez, *Atlas*, 213; Pomer, *Os confitos*, 33.

43. Pierre Jean Honorat Lainé (1796–1875) was promoted to captain in 1831. He participated in the bombardment of San Juan de Ulúa, Mexico, in 1838. Lainé was promoted to rear admiral in 1840 and took command of the La Plata station in 1843.

44. Caillet-Bois, *Historia naval*, 418; Suárez, *Atlas*, 215; Comando en Jefe, *Ejército argentino*, 204.

45. Suárez, *Atlas*, 215; Manley, *Wars*, 494.

46. Francisco Hipólito Uzal, "La batalla de la soberania," *Todo Es Historia* 19, 8–22 (November 1968), 16; Laing, "The Royal Navy," 136–37; Comando en Jefe, *Ejército argentino*, 204–6; Suárez, *Atlas*, 215–16. Upon his death, General José de San Martín willed his saber to Rosas for his firmness against foreign intervention.

47. Bruno, *Historia argentina*, 517; Suárez, *Atlas*, 245; Röttjer, *Vida*, 287; Rippy, "Argentina," 98–99; Manley, *Wars*, 496.

48. Manley, *Wars*, 495–96.

49. Between 1841 and 1851 Grenfell served Brazilian commercial interests in Great Britain. In 1851, he returned to Brazil to take command of the navy in the fight against Rosas. Following the conflict he was promoted to vice admiral and then returned to Great Britain as the Brazilian consul-general in Liverpool.

50. Engelhardt, "The Battle of Caseros," 225; Suárez, *Atlas*, 249–51; Rippy, "Argentina," 100–1; Comando en Jefe, *Ejército argentino*, 220.

51. Kirkpatrick, *Latin America*, 141–42; Escuela Superior de Guerra, *Manual*, 2: 311.

52. Escuela Superior de Guerra, *Manual*, 2: 312–13, 318; Manley, *Wars*, 524.

53. Herring, *A History of Latin America*, 611–12.

54. Manley, *Wars*, 525.

55. Suárez, *Atlas*, 258–61; Escuela Superior de Guerra, *Manual*, 2: 320; Comando en Jefe, *Ejército argentino*, 237–38; Manley, *Wars*, 524.

56. Suárez, *Atlas*, 263–65; Escuela Superior de Guerra, *Manual*, 2: 325–35; Rudolph, *Argentina*, 27.

57. William Dusenberry, "Urquiza's Account of the Battle of Pavón," *Journal of Inter-American Studies* 4: 2, 247–55 (April 1962), 248; Manley, *Wars*, 525.

58. Carlos Ibarguren, *En la penumbra de la historia argentina* (Buenos Aires: Libreria y Editorial "La Facultad," J. Roldán y Cía., 1939), 157–67; Loveman, *For la Patria*, 31.

59. Those who are very critical of Rosas include William Spence Robertson, *History of Latin-American Nations* (New York: D. Appleton, 1923), 232; Nick Caistor, *Argentina In Focus* (London: Latin American Bureau, 1996), 19; Charles Edmond Akers and L. E. Elliot, *A History of South America*, 3d ed. (New York: E. P. Dutton, 1930), 36–37.

60. Those who have been somewhat more sympathetic to Rosas include Rippy, "Argentina," 85–90; Lewis W. Bealer, "The Dictators of Argentina, Paraguay, Uruguay, and Chile," in *South American Dictators*, ed. by A. Curtis Wilgus (Washington: George Washington University Press, 1937), 105.

61. Rippy, "Argentina," 99.

62. Akers and Elliot, *A History*, 38.

CHAPTER TEN

1. Alejandro Marure, *Efemérides de los hechos notables acaecidos en la república de Centro América* (Guatemala: Tipografia Nacional, 1895), 37; Thomas L. Karnes, *The Failure of Union: Central America, 1824–1960* (Chapel Hill: University of North Carolina Press, 1961), 65.

2. Marure, *Efemérides*, 5; Karnes, *The Failure*, 25; Longino Becerra, *Evolución histórica de Honduras* (Tegucigalpa: Baktun Editorial, 1994), 97.

3. Ralph Lee Woodward, "The Aftermath of Independence, 1821–c.1870" from *Central America since Independence*, ed. by Leslie Bethell (New York: Cambridge University Press, 1991), 6; Karnes, *The Failure*, 27; Marure, *Efemérides*, 7.

4. José D. Gámez, *Historia de Nicaragua* (Managua: Tipografica de "El Pasis," 1889), 347–59.

5. Marure, *Efemérides*, 10; Loveman, *For la Patria*, 28. In April 1819 the Scottish adventurer Gregor MacGregor seized Portobelo, Panama, and held it for three weeks. He then sailed north and purchased some liquor and traded this for some 70,000 square miles in Honduras from the Mosquito king. In 1823 and 1824 MacGregor attempted to colonize the region with Scots. These efforts failed and most of the survivors settled in Belize.

6. Marure, *Efemérides*, 13–14; Karnes, *The Failure*, 42–43.

7. Woodward, "The Aftermath," 12.

8. Karnes, *The Failure*, 34–35.

9. Dana Gardner Munro, *The Five Republics of Central America* (New York: Oxford University Press, 1918), 51; Mario Rodríguez, *Central America* (Englewood Cliffs: Prentice-Hall, Inc., 1965), 65, 70–71.

10. Davis, *History of Latin America*, 454; Rippy, *Latin America*, 219; Walter LaFeber, *Inevitable Revolution* (New York: W. W. Norton, 1983), 27.

11. Karnes, *The Failure*, 66–67.

12. Rafael Carrera (1814–65) was born in a barrio of Guatemala City probably of mixed Indian, Negro, and white parentage. He received no formal education. At fourteen he served as a drummer in the Conservative army of Guatemala during the Civil War of 1826–29. Carrera worked as a laborer including muleteer and swine herder. Possessing the qualities of a *caudillo*—toughest of the tough—he was wounded numerous times while leading his fanatical followers. Hubert Howe Bancroft writes, "He could not write a line, but others wrote for him, and printed articles appeared over his name." Hubert Howe Bancroft, *History of Central America*, 3 vols. (San Francisco: A. L. Bancroft, 1883–87), 3: 265.

13. Charles W. Domville-Fife, *Guatemala and the States of Central America* (London: G. Bell & Sons, 1913), 53.

14. Francisco Morazán (1799–1842) was born in Tegucigalpa, Honduras, to a French father and *creole* mother. In 1824 he served as Secretary General of Honduras and then was elected as a provincial senator. He had no military training.

15. Marure, *Efemérides*, 53–54; Becerra, *Evolución histórica*, 106; Karnes, *The Failure*, 70–71.

16. Alfred Barnaby Thomas, *Latin America: A History* (New York: Macmillan, 1956), 591.

17. Karnes, *The Failure*, 76–77.

18. Rodríguez, *Central America*, 65, 70–71.

19. Ralph Lee Woodward Jr., *Central America: A Nation Divided* (New York: Oxford University Press, 1985), 104–5.

20. Karnes, *The Failure*, 82–83.

21. This union included the regions of Quezaltenango, Totolcapán, and Sololá.

22. Woodward, *Central America*, 106–7.

23. Marure, *Efemérides*, 122–23; Becerra, *Evolución histórica*, 108; Woodward, *Central America*, 107–9; Woodward, "The Aftermath," 19.

24. Woodward, *Central America*, 110.
25. Rodríguez, *Central America*, 72–73; Woodward, *Central America*, 110.
26. Miguel R. Ortega, *Morazán Laurel sin ocaso*, 3 vols. (Tegucigalpa: Impreso en Lithopress Industrial, 1988–), 1: 291–306; Marure, *Efemérides*, 115; Becerra, *Evolución histórica*, 108.
27. Domville-Fife, *Guatemala*, 55–56; Marure, *Efemérides*, 123–24; Becerra, *Evolución histórica*, 108; Karnes, *The Failure*, 88.
28. Marure, *Efemérides*, 131–33; Rippy, *Latin America*, 221–22; Becerra, *Evolución histórica*, 108.
29. Davis, *History of Latin America*, 454.
30. Marure, *Efemérides*, 141, 154.
31. Woodward, *Central America*, 111.

CHAPTER ELEVEN

1. Dellepiane, *Historia militar*, 1: 354–55; *Historia militar de Chile*, 3 vols. (Valparaíso: Estado Mayor General del Ejército, 1969), 2: 10–11; Tommie Junior Hillmon, "A History of the Armed Forces of Chile from Independence to 1920" (Ph.D. disseration, Syracuse University, 1963), 61–62; Robert N. Burr, *By Reason or Force* (Berkeley: University of California Press, 1967), 37.
2. Rodrigo Fuenzalida Bade, *La armada de Chile*, 2d ed., 4 vols. (Valparaíso: Talleres Empresa Periodistica, 1978), 2: 403–5; Lane Carter Kendall, "Andrés Santa Cruz and the Peru-Bolivian Confederation," *Hispanic American Historical Review* 16: 1; 29–48 (February 1936), 43–44; Burr, *By Reason*, 37.
3. Andrés de Santa Cruz (1792–1865) was born near La Paz, Bolivia. His father was a minor Spanish official and his mother an Inca princess. Through his mother he inherited wealth and social position. He joined the Spanish Army at the age of fifteen with the rank of captain, thanks to his family's influence; by 1811 he was serving in his father's regiment. Santa Cruz was captured by the Revolutionaries in 1817 and imprisoned near Buenos Aires, but escaped. He was captured again at the Battle of Cerro de Pasco (December 6, 1820). Santa Cruz then changed sides. Both José de San Martín and Simón Bolívar favored him with choice assignments, although he did not hold favor with Andrés de Sucre. Bolívar promoted Santa Cruz to brigadier general as a reward for his valor at the Battle of Pichincha (May 24, 1822) where he commanded the Peruvian Division. Santa Cruz commanded a Revolutionary army which defeated the Royalists at the Battle of Zepita (August 25, 1823) for which he was promoted to marshal. He was elected President of Bolivia on August 12, 1828. He was a very efficient administrator and very thrifty.
4. St. John, *The Foreign Policy*, 28; Cleven, "Dictators," 296–97.
5. Dellepiane, *Historia militar*, 1: 331–32; Clements R. Markham, *A History of Peru* (Chicago: C.H. Sergel & Co., 1892), 297; St. John, *The Foreign Policy*, 29.
6. Pike, *The Modern History*, 74–75; Cleven, "Dictators," 302; Kendall, "Andrés Santa Cruz," 37; Burr, *By Reason*, 33.
7. Felipe Santiago de Salaverry (1806–36) was born in Lima, Peru, to a wealthy *criollo* family. He was well educated. Salaverry joined the revolutionary army at the age of fourteen. He distinguished himself at the battles of Junin (August 6, 1824) and Ayacucho (December 9, 1824). His skill and daring earned him the rank of general by the end of the war. Salaverry was a close friend of Gen. José de La Mar and, therefore, an enemy of Gen. Agustín Gamarra. Salaverry was highly imaginative and possessed a violent temper.

8. Dellepiane, *Historia militar*, 1: 332–34; Pike, *The Modern History*, 78–81; Cleven, "Dictators," 306.

9. Dellepiane, *Historia militar*, 1: 336–37; Fuenzalida, *La armada*, 2: 396; Kendall, "Andrés Santa Cruz," 38–39; Cleven, "Dictators," 308, 314.

10. Dellepiane, *Historia militar*, 1: 340; Vegas, *Historia de la marina*, 47; Graham-Yooll, *Small Wars*, 60–61.

11. Dellepiane, *Historia militar*, 1: 347; Fuenzalida, *La armada*, 2: 395–96; Pike, *The Modern History*, 80–81; Cleven, "Dictators," 314–15.

12. Fuenzalida, *La armada*, 2: 398; Cleven, "Dictators," 304–5; Burr, *By Reason*, 21–23; Graham-Yooll, *Small Wars*, 60–61.

13. Isaac Joslin Cox, "Chile," in *Argentina, Brazil, and Chile since Independence*, ed. by A. Curtis Wilgus (Washington: George Washington University Press, 1935), 306–7; Hillmon, *A History*, 63.

14. Burr, *By Reason*, 47; Suárez, *Atlas*, 195–97.

15. Toro, *Sintesis historico*, 2: 13.

16. López, *Chile: A Brief Naval History*, 35–36; Fuenzalida, *La armada*, 2: 406–7.

17. Discipline was so bad that the officers were even neglecting sanitation. Vegas, *Historia de la marina*, 46, 50; Fuenzalida, *La armada*, 2: 406–8.

18. Luís Uribe Orrego, *Nuestra marina militar, desde la liberación de Chiloé (1826) hasta la guerra con España (1865)* (Valparaíso: Imprenta de la Armada, 1914), 69–70; Fuenzalida, *La armada*, 2: 407, 411; López, *Chile: A Brief Naval History*, 35–36.

19. Toro, *Sintesis historico*, 2: 13; Kendall, "Andrés Santa Cruz," 34; Cleven, "Dictators," 320; Burr, *By Reason*, 33.

20. Seventeen of the mutineers were shot. Hillmon, *A History*, 60–65; Burr, *By Reason*, 47–48; Cox, "Chile," 307–8; *Historia militar de Chile*, 2: 11.

21. Burr, *By Reason*, 33.

22. Toro, *Sintesis historico*, 2: 14–15; *Historia militar de Chile*, 2: 17–18; Dellepiane, *Historia militar*, 1: 359.

23. Dellepiane, *Historia militar*, 1: 361–62; Burr, *By Reason*, 50–51; St. John, *The Foreign Policy*, 35; Hillmon, *A History*, 66–67; Kendall, "Andrés Santa Cruz," 45–46.

24. Dellepiane, *Historia militar*, 1: 365; López, *Chile: A Brief Naval History*, 36; Vegas, *Historia de la marina*, 62.

25. Fuenzalida, *La armada*, 2: 431–35; Vegas, *Historia de la marina*, 64–67.

26. *Historia militar de Chile*, 2: 25; Fuenzalida, *La armada*, 2: 436; Vegas, *Historia de la marina*, 67–68.

27. Suárez, *Atlas*, 142–43; Manley, *Wars*, 485; Burr, *By Reason*, 52–53.

28. Manuel Bulnes Prieto (1799–1866) was born in Concepción in southern Chile. His father was a captain in the Spanish army and his mother a *criollo*. He served in the revolutionary army until the defeat at Rancagua (October 1–2, 1814). He and his brothers were arrested in 1817 for revolutionary activities. He was imprisoned on the island of Quiriquina from which he escaped on a raft. He again joined the revolutionary army and fought at Quechereguas (March 15, 1818), Cancha Rayada (March 19, 1818), Maípo (May 5, 1818), Vegas de Saldías (October 10, 1821), and Gualegüeico (November 26, 1821).

29. Johann Jakob von Tschudi, *Travels in Peru, during the Years 1838–1842, on the Coast, in the Sierra, across the Cordilleras and the Andes, into the Primeval Forrest*, Trans. by Thomasina Ross (London: David Bogue, 1847), 26.

30. Von Tschudi, *Travels,* 28.

31. Dellepiane, *Historia militar,* 1: 373–74; Agustin Edwards, *The Dawn* (London: E. Benn, 1931), 368; Tschudi, *Travels in Peru,* 27; Toro, *Sintesis historico,* 2: 22.

32. St. John, *The Foreign Policy,* 37; Cleven, "Dictators," 328; Burr, *By Reason,* 55.

33. Fuenzalida, *La armada,* 2: 450–51.

34. Toro, *Sintesis historico,* 2: 30; Cleven, "Dictators," 328; Fuenzalida, *La armada,* 2: 462.

35. Privateers were ships armed by private citizens that were granted a license by a nation at war to prey on the commerce of its enemy. In exchange for the license, the government received a percentage of the prize money. The Paris Declaration of 1856, which many countries endorsed, abolished privateering.

36. Frías Valenzuela states the corsairs "were crewed by adventurers of all nations." Vegas states, "The crews were almost exclusively Peruvians." Francisco Frías Valenzuela, *Nuevo manual de historia de Chile,* 10th ed. (Santiago: Zig-Zag, 1990), 278; Vegas, *Historia de la marina,* 74–77; Fuenzalida, *La armada,* 2: 468–72; Isaac G. Strain, *Cordillera and Pampa, Mountain and Plain: Sketches of a Journey in Chili, and the Argentine Provinces in 1849* (New York: Horace H. Moore, 1853), 106.

37. Toro, *Sintesis historico,* 2: 38–39; *Historia militar de Chile,* 2: 40–41.

38. Official Chilean sources place Chilean losses as 229 dead and 435 wounded. However, contemporary accounts state that the losses sustained by the two armies were almost equal. Jordi Fuentes et al., *Diccionario historico de Chile,* 11th ed. (Santiago: Zig-Zag, 1990), 632–33; *Historia militar de Chile,* 2: 41–46.

Eventually Santa Cruz found his way to France where he schemed to install European royalty as monarchs in South America. In 1855 he traveled to Salta, Argentina, to champion his bid for the presidency of Bolivia. However, after losing that election he returned to Europe. Santa Cruz became a confidant of Napoleon III.

39. Humberto Vazquez Machicado, José de Mesa, and Teresa Gisbert, *Manual de historia de Bolivia* (La Paz: Gisbert y Cia., S.A., 1963), 329; Denegri, *Peru and Ecuador,* 121–22; Dellepiane, *Historia militar,* 1: 414–16; Cleven, "Dictators," 332–33.

40. Dellepiane, *Historia militar,* 1: 418–21; William Manning, *Diplomatic Correspondence of the United States Inter-American Affairs 1831–1860,* 12 vols. (Washington: Carnegie Endowment for International Peace, 1932–39), 2: 18; Cleven, "Dictators," 333.

41. Winsor López Videla, *Almanaque historico de Bolivia* (La Paz: Talleres Gráficos Bolivianos, 1960), 11.

42. Juan Bautista Alberti, *Biografía del jeneral don Manuel Bulnes, presidente de la república de Chile* (Santiago: Imprenta Chilena, 1846), 56.

43. This is a persistent theme in the writings of Luis Langlois Vidal.

CHAPTER TWELVE

1. Juan José Flores y Flórez (1801–64), a *mestizo,* was born in Puerto Cabello, Venezuela, into a poor family. He became the servant of a Spanish officer. Flores was captured during an early engagement and entered the revolutionary army as a private. He rose to the rank of general of division in 1830. Flores became an intimate aide to Simón Bolívar and fought in more than twenty battles. Flores married into the Quito elite in 1825. His only serious competitor for the political leadership of Ecuador was Gen. Antonio José de Sucre, who was assassinated on June 4, 1830; some have accused Flores of having been involved. A brave

soldier possessing a seductive manner, Flores was nearly illiterate, possessed poor administrative skills, and was capricious.

2. Special Agent of the United States to Ecuador Delazon Smith writing to Secretary of State John C. Calhoun, August 10, 1845. Manning, *Dipl. Corres. of the U.S. Inter-Amer.*, 6: 253.

See also Alfredo Pareja Diezcanseco, *Ecuador la república de 1830 a nuestros días* (Quito: Editorial Universitaria, 1979), 16; Ireland, *Boundaries*, 177; Alberto Avellan Z., *Historia general, universal y del Ecuador* (n.p., n.d.), 99; Herman G. James and Percy A. Martin, *The Republics of Latin America*, rev. ed. (New York: Harper and Brothers Publishers, 1923), 293.

3. Osvaldo Hurtado, *Political Power in Ecuador*, trans. by Nick D. Mills Jr. (Boulder, Colo.: Westview Press, 1985), 145–49; Davis, *History of Latin America*, 385; Chapman, *Republican Hispanic America*, 386.

4. Davis, *History of Latin America*, 385; Davis, *The Americas*, 445.

5. United States Chargé d' Affaires in Ecuador Courtland Cushing to Secretary of State William L. Marcy, October 31, 1853. Manning, *Dipl. Corres. of the U.S. Inter-Amer.*, 6: 316.

6. Manning, *Dipl. Corres. of the U.S. Inter-Amer.*, 6: 255–56.

7. Robertson, *History*, 386 398, 403; Kirkpatrick, *Latin America*, 239, 246.

8. Manning, *Dipl. Corres. of the U.S. Inter-Amer.*, 6: 255; Gregory J. Kasza, "Regional Conflict in Ecuador: Quito and Guayaquil," *Inter-American Economic Affairs* 35: 2; 3–41 (Autumn 1981), 4–5; Lilo Linke, *Ecuador* (London: Royal Institute of International Affairs, 1954), 6.

9. Hurtado, *Political Power*, 145–46; Herring, *A History of Latin America*, 502.

10. Cleven, "The Dictators," 352; Robertson, *History*, 239; Halperín, *The Contemporary History*, 102.

11. Denegri, *Peru*, 115.

12. Hurtado, *Political Power*, 136.

13. Luis de Urdaneta (1796–1831), a *criollo* born in Maracaibo, Venezuela, joined the Royalist forces in 1810 and served in the *Numancia* Regiment. In 1819 while serving in Peru, he was retired from duty because of his liberal ideas. Urdaneta joined the Revolutionaries and fought at Pichincha (May 24, 1822). Following the wars for independence, he retired to Bogotá. Urdaneta fought for Gran Colombia in the Battle of Tarquí (February 27, 1829) against Peru. He commanded Gran Colombian troops in Guayaquil where he unsuccessfully prevented Ecuador from declaring its independence. Expelled to Panama, Urdaneta became involved in a revolt, was captured, and was shot.

14. Cleven, "The Dictators," 352; Kirkpatrick, *Latin America*, 240–41.

15. Ireland, *Boundaries*, 177; Pareja, *Ecuador*, 22–23.

16. Plazas, "El ejército," 2: 155; Cleven, "The Dictators," 352–53; William Marion Gibson, *The Constitutions of Colombia* (Durham, N.C.: Duke University Press, 1948), 155; Ireland, *Boundaries*, 178.

17. This conflict acquired the name "War of the Chihuahuas" because Ecuadorians knew that the word "Chihuahua" was used by the Mexicans as an exclamation. Pareja, *Ecuador*, 28–29.

18. Pareja, *Ecuador*, 28–31; Kirkpatrick, *Latin America*, 242; Halperín, *The Contemporary History*, 103.

19. Gen. Isiboro Barriga married the widow of Gen. Andrés Sucre who Flores was accused of having assassinated.

20. Pareja, *Ecuador*, 31–32; Denegri, *Peru*, 103–4, 113–14; Kirkpatrick, *Latin America*, 242; Robertson, *History*, 387.

21. Pareja, *Ecuador*, 33–44; George I. Blanksten, *Ecuador: Constitutions and Caudillos* (Berkeley: University of California Press, 1951), 9; Hurtado, *Political Power*, 98; Ireland, *Boundaries*, 179.

22. Denegri, *Peru*, 124.

23. Antonio de Elizalde y La Mar (1795–1862), born into a wealthy family, was an active member of the independence movement by 1820. Antonio rose to the rank of general among the Liberal forces.

24. Blanksten, *Ecuador*, 11.

25. Hurtado, *Political Power*, 133.

26. John Illingworth (1786–1853), born in Stockport, England, fought in the Dutch Campaign (1801–2) as a lieutenant in the British navy and returned to England in poor health. In 1817 he commanded the ship that carried Thomas Cochrane to Vaparaíso. Cochrane chose him to command the corvette *Rosa de los Andes* (36 guns) in the Chilean navy. On May 12, 1820, the *Rosa de los Andes* defeated the Spanish frigate *Prueba* (52 guns). Illingworth served under Sucre during the revolutionary campaign in Ecuador during 1821–22. In 1823 he became a citizen of the republic and returned to private life for two years. Illingworth commanded the revolutionary fleet which blockaded Callao until it surrendered in 1826. He then began organizing a Gran Colombian expedition against Spanish Cuba which was never executed.

27. Pareja, *Ecuador*, 43–44; Kirkpatrick, *Latin America*, 243–44.

28. Ralph W. Haskins, "Juan José Flores and the Proposed Expedition against Ecuador, 1846–47," *Hispanic American Historical Review* 47: 3; 467–95 (August 1947), 471, 476, 490; Pareja, *Ecuador*, 46–47; Cleven, "The Dictators," 358.

29. Pareja, *Ecuador*, 75–76; Robertson, *History*, 389.

30. José María Urbina Viteri (1808–91), born in Ambato, attended the naval school in Guayaquil for a short time. He fought in the siege of Callao, Peru (1824–26), and the Battle of Malpelo (1828). Urbina became the *aide-de-camp* to President Juan José Flores. In 1837 he was banished for plotting against the government. When Flores returned to power, so did Urbina and he was appointed governor of Manabí.

31. Francisco Robles (1811–93), born in Guayaquil, reached the rank of naval captain in 1845. Two years later he was appointed the military commander and governor of Guayas Province.

32. Pareja, *Ecuador,* 77–78; Manning, *Dipl. Corres. of the U.S. Inter-Amer.*, 6: 315; Ireland, *Boundaries*, 179; Thomas, *Latin America*, 470.

33. José de Villamil (1788–1866), born in New Orleans, Louisiana, fought for Ecuadorian independence. He advocated Ecuadorian occupation of the Galapagos Island and became the islands' first governor. Villamil became the Ecuadorian minister to the United States in 1852.

34. Manning, *Dipl. Corres. of the U.S. Inter-Amer.*, 6: 275–89; Pareja, *Ecuador*, 79; Cleven, "The Dictators," 362–63; Denegri, *Peru*, 139–41.

35. Pareja, *Ecuador*, 93–96; Thomas, *Latin America*, 471; Herring, *A History of Latin America*, 503–4; Dennis M. Hanratty, editor, *Ecuador A Country Study*, 3d ed. (Washington: Headquarters, Department of the Army, 1991), 21–22.

36. Robertson, *History*, 392.

37. Mariano Sánchez Bravo, *Buques y Personajes* (Guayaquil: Instituto de Historia Marítima, 1991), 22–24; Robertson, *History*, 392; Hanratty, *Ecuador*, 23.

38. Pareja, *Ecuador*, 144–46; Sánchez, *Buques*, 24; *The American Annual Cyclopaedia 1865* (New York: D. Appleton, 1866), 326.

39. José Ignacio de Veintemilla (1828–1908), born in Quito, served as Minister of War in 1865–67 and narrowly escaped execution by President García Moreno by fleeing into exile. Veintemilla returned from exile in 1875.

40. Pareja, *Ecuador*, 179–81; Akers and Elliot, *A History*, 633.

41. José Eloy Alfaro Delgado (1842–1912) was born into a middle-class family. In 1864 he fought in the uprising against García Moreno's plan to annex Ecuador to France. Exiled, Alfaro went to Panama where he became very successful in business. Returning to Ecuador, in 1875 Alfaro led an unsuccessful expedition to capture Guayaquil. He escaped from prison and returned to Panama. Following 1875 he led numerous expeditions against those who governed in Ecuador.

42. Pareja, *Ecuador*, 188–89.

43. Sánchez, *Buques*, 28–32.

44. Pareja, *Ecuador*, 190–91; Akers and Elliot, *A History*, 634; Robertson, *History*, 394–95.

45. Pareja, *Ecuador*, 204–6; Hanratty, *Ecuador*, 24; Akers and Elliot, *A History*, 635–36.

46. Alfaro also appreciated the value of a formal military education. His sons Eloy, Jaime, and Olmedo attended the U.S. Military Academy, West Point.

47. Pareja, *Ecuador*, 211–13; Linke, *Ecuador*, 24; Robertson, *History*, 395; Akers and Elliot, *A History*, 636.

48. Leónidas Plaza Gutiérrez (1865–1932), born in Charapotó, Manabí Province, began his military career at the age of eighteen. He fought in the failed 1883–84 Liberal uprising in Manabí Province where he rose to the rank of sergeant major. Plaza fled to Central America. While there, he served in administrative positions in El Salvador, Costa Rica, and Nicaragua. While in Costa Rica he became a major general.

49. Hanratty, *Ecuador*, 26–27; Robertson, *History*, 388, 398–99.

50. Kasza, "Regional Conflict," 10–12.

51. Hurtado, *Political Power*, 132–33.

CHAPTER THIRTEEN

1. Martin, "Brazil," 176–77; Armitage, *History of Brazil*, 2: 132–33.

2. Martin, "Brazil," 168–69.

3. Manoel de Oliveira Lima, *O imperio brasileiro 1822–1889* (São Paulo: Comp. Melhoramentos de Sao Paulo, 1927), 14–15; Martin, "Brazil," 169–70.

4. Martin, "Brazil," 174; Read, *The New Conquistadors*, 117–18.

5. Claudio Moreira Bento, *O exército farrapo e os seus chefes*, 2 vols. (Rio de Janeiro: Biblioteca do Exército Editora, 1992–93), 1: 3; Oscar d'Araujo, *L'idée républicaine au Brésil* (Paris: Perrin, 1893), 3–4; Read, *The New Conquistadors*, 118–19; Martin, "Brazil," 170; Botto, *Campanhas navais*, 41–43.

6. Martin, "Brazil," 174–76.

7. Lima, *O imperio brasileiro*, 13–14; Thomas, *Latin America*, 346.

8. Riots erupted throughout the empire: in Bahia on April 7, 1831; in Pernambuco on May 3; in Pará on May 14; in Maranhão on May 25; in Rio de Janeiro on July 15; in Pará and Pernambuco again on August 3; in Ceará on December 14; in Minas Gerais on March

22, 1832; and again in Rio de Janeiro on June 22. d'Araujo, *L'idée républicaine*, 29–32. See also Martin, "Brazil," 176–78.

9. Kirkpatrick, *Latin America*, 295; Martin, "Brazil," 179.

10. Lima, *O imperio brasileiro*, 27–28; Bento, *O exército farrapo*, 2: 55; Calogeras, *A History of Brazil*, 171.

11. The Brazilian army classified all muskets and carbines used during the War for Independence as Model 1822 regardless of time and place of manufacture. Most had a 19mm bore. Only a few parts for their maintenance were manufactured in Brazil. A few 4-pound and 12-pound field guns, 4-pound mountain guns, and small mortars were produced in Brazil. Most artillery was purchased from Europe. Bento, *O exército farrapo*, 2: 67.

12. Botto, *Campanhas Navais*, 62–63; Calogeras, *A History of Brazil*, 124–25.

13. Calogeras, *A History of Brazil*, 126; Marley, *Wars*, 476–77.

14. Following the loss of his right arm, Grenfell had returned to England to regain his health. He returned to Brazil in 1828.

15. Martin, "Brazil," 179–80; Bento, *O exército farrapo*, 1:3, 6; Calogeras, *A History of Brazil*, 126–27.

16. Botto, *Campanhas navais*, 64; Bento, *O exército farrapo*, 1: 8; Calogeras, *A History of Brazil*, 128–29.

17. Calogeras, *A History of Brazil*, 135–36.

18. Estado-Maior do Exército, *História do exército brasileiro*, 2 vols. (Brasília: Impresso no Serviço Gráfico da Fundação IBGE, 1972), 2: 469; Botto, *Campanhas navais*, 64.

19. Lima, *O imperio brasileiro*, 26–27; Botto, *Campanhas navais*, 64; Calogeras, *A History of Brazil*, 128–29.

20. Calogeras, *A History of Brazil*, 129–30.

21. ibid., 130.

22. Giuseppe Garibaldi (1807–82), alias Joseph Borel, fled Italy in the mid-1830s under a death sentence for having participated in a revolt by Giuseppi Mazzini's Young Italy Movement.

23. Botto, *Campanhas navais*, 64–65; Bento, *O exército farrapo*, 1: 11.

24. Estado-Maior do Exército, *História*, 2: 471.

25. Botto, *Campanhas navais*, 65; Bento, *O exército farrapo*, 1: 12; Estado-Maior do Exército, *História*, 2: 473.

26. Calogeras, *A History of Brazil*, 130–32; Lima, *O imperio brasileiro*, 28.

27. Marley, *Wars*, 477.

28. Luis Alves de Lima e Silva (1803–80) became Brazil's most acclaimed soldier. He was the son of General and Senator Francisco de Lima e Silva, one of the regents of the empire between 1831 and 1835. He was one of four hundred officers known as the Sacred Battalion whose members commanded the newly created national guard. Because of his campaigns pacifying rebellious Brazilian provinces and victories over foreign enemies, he was awarded the following titles: 1840 baron; 1843 viscount; 1845 count; 1852 marquis; and 1869 duke. Luis was the only Brazilian duke not to be a member of the royal family.

29. Martin, "Brazil," 180.

30. Calogeras, *A History of Brazil*, 119, 137–40, 162–64.

31. Lima, *O imperio brasileiro*, 28–29.

32. ibid., 29–30.

33. ibid., 30–31.

34. Calogeras, *A History of Brazil*, 169–70.
35. Lima, *O imperio brazileiro*, 31–32; Bento, *O exército farrapo*, 1: 15.
36. Calogeras, *A History of Brazil*, 171–72.
37. Lima, *O imperio brasileiro*, 31–32; Calogeras, *A History of Brazil*, 172–73; Marley, *Wars*, 476–77.
38. Martin, "Brazil," 184–85; Lima, *O imperio brasileiro*, 32–36.

CHAPTER FOURTEEN

1. Mary Deborah Petite, *1836 Facts about the Alamo and the Texas War for Independence* (Mason City, Iowa: Savas, 1999), ii; Bill Groneman, *Battlefields of Texas* (Plano: Republic of Texas Press, 1998), 28–32; Robert A. Calvert and Arnoldo de León, *The History of Texas* (Arlington Heights: Harlan Davidson, 1990), 65–66.
2. Calvert and De León, *The History,* 48–53; Lynn I. Perrigo, *Our Spanish Southwest* (Dallas: Banks Upshaw, 1960), 107.
3. Calvert and De León, *The History*, 53–55.
4. Antonio López de Santa Anna (1794–1876) was born in Jalapa, Vera Cruz. Santa Anna joined the Spanish army in 1810 as a "gentleman cadet" (*caballero cadete*), a position given to children from distinguished families who sought military careers, in the Infantry Regiment of Vera Cruz. In 1815 he fought in Cotaxtla and Sancampuz, Province of Vera Cruz, and took part in the capture of Boquilla de Piedra for which he was awarded a second "badge" for courage. In March 1821 he was given command of the Permanent Lancers of Vera Cruz. Defeating Revolutionary José Miranda, Santa Anna was promoted to lieutenant colonel by the viceroy and on the same day pronounced in favor of the Plan of Iguala, thus earning another promotion for changing sides. Fighting for the Revolutionaries, he captured Jalapa and Perote. In May 1822 Santa Anna was promoted to brigadier general by Iturbide but broke with him in December. In 1824 the new republic made him military governor of the Yucatan. President Guerrero made Santa Anna a general of division, and Santa Anna defeated a Spanish expeditionary force at Tampico (July–September 1829), for which he was proclaimed a national hero. Robert L. Scheina, *Santa Anna: A Curse upon Mexico* (Washington, D.C.: Brassey's, 2002); Richard Hitchman, "Rush to Glory: The U.S. Mexican War 1846–1848," *Strategy & Tactics* 127: 14–26, 60–62 (June–July 1989), 14.
5. Calvert and De León, *The History*, 57.
6. ibid., 57–58.
7. The governor and legislature of Coahuila sought aid from and then refuge in Texas. The Texans did not help these Mexican Federalists out of fear of reprisals from Santa Anna.
8. Callcott, *Santa Anna*, 115–16; Pedro Santoni, *Mexicans at Arms* (Fort Worth: Texas Christian University Press, 1996), 18–19; Petite, *1836 Facts*, ii–iii; Calvert and De León, *The History*, 63–64.
9. Martín Perfecto de Cós (1800–54), born in Vera Cruz, entered the Spanish army as a cadet in February 1820. The following year, he declared for the "Army of the Three Guarantees." He married the sister of Antonio López de Santa Anna in the early 1820s. From that time he held important commands whenever Santa Anna governed even though Cós was not considered an effective leader.
10. Bancroft, *History of Mexico*, 5: 146–47.
11. At that time colonists were divided between "war hawks" and "peace doves." "War hawks" were recent immigrants from the United States and were led by William H. Wharton and Samuel Houston. The "peace doves" were led by Stephen Austin and influential *Tejanos*.

12. Calvert and De León, *The History*, 64–65; Perrigo, *Our Spanish Southwest*, 127.

13. Meyer and Sherman, *The Course*, 336; Petite, *1836 Facts*, 170; Calvert and De León, *The History*, 59–60.

14. The Baker firearms were discontinued from British service in 1838. The rifle weighed 9.5 pounds. *El soldado mexicano, 1837–1847* (Mexico: Ediciones Nieto-Brown-Hefter, 1958), 53–54.

15. Calvert and De León, *The History*, 62.

16. Petite, *1836 Facts*, 13, 23–27.

17. Terry Hooker, *The Revolt in Texas Leading to Its Independence from Mexico 1835–1836* (Cottingham: El Dorado Books, 1993), 10.

18. Petite, *1836 Facts*, 13–14.

19. Calvert and De León, *The History*, 60.

20. Petite, *1836 Facts*, 29–30; Enríque Cardenas de la Peña, *Semblana marítima de Mexico independiente y revoluionario*, 2 vols. (Mexico: Secretaría de Marina, 1970), 1: 94.

21. Groneman, *Battlefields*, 33–35; Marley, *Wars*, 480.

22. Groneman, *Battlefields*, 38–40.

23. Benjamin Rush Milam (1788–1835) was born in Kentucky. Milam joined an expedition to aid the Mexican Revolutionaries in 1819. He was jailed during Iturbide's regime for his republican sympathies; he was released through the efforts of Joel R. Poinsett. On December 7, 1845, Milan was killed during the attack on San Antonio.

24. Groneman, *Battlefields*, 41–43; Calvert and De León, *The History*, 56; Petite, *1836 Facts,* 17–22.

25. José Urrea (1797–1849) was born into a military family in the Presidio of Tucson, province of New Mexico. In 1809 he joined the Spanish army as a cadet of the Presidio Company of San Rafael Buenavista. In 1821 he declared for the Plan of Iguala and took part in the attacks against Castle San Juan de Ulúa in Vera Cruz harbor. In 1827 Urrea was removed from the army for having supported the unsuccessful *coup* led by Nicolás Bravo against Vicente Guerrero. In 1829 he fought as a volunteer against the Spaniards at Tampico and was restored to the army and promoted to lieutenant colonel in 1831. In 1835 Urrea was promoted to brigadier general and fought Comanches in Durango.

26. Samuel Houston (1793–1863) was born in Virginia and moved to Tennessee in 1807 after the death of his father. Houston was twice wounded during the War of 1812 and reached the rank of lieutenant. In 1818 he resigned rather than participate in the forced relocation of the Cherokee. In 1827 he was elected governor of Tennessee. In 1832, after a disastrous marriage, he resigned the governorship and headed west. He lived among the Cherokee in Arkansas and drank heavily. In 1835 he was appointed a major general in the Texas army. Houston served two terms as President of Texas (1836–38 and 1841–44). In 1859 he was elected to the U.S. Senate. Houston refused to take an oath of allegiance to the Confederacy and was removed from office.

27. Groneman, *Battlefields*, 44–45; Herbert Ingram Priestley, *The Mexican Nation: A History* (New York: Cooper Square, 1923), 286–87; José Urrea, "Diary of the Military Operations of the Division which Under His Command Campaigned in Texas," in *The Mexican Side of the Texan Revolution*, trans. by Carlos E. Castañeda (Dallas: P. L. Turner, 1928), 214–16.

28. Antonio López de Santa Anna, "Manifesto Relative to His Operations in the Texas Campaign and His Capture," in *The Mexican Side of the Texan Revolution*, trans. by Carlos

E. Castañeda (Dallas: P. L. Turner, 1928), 11; *El ejército mexicano* (Mexico: Secretaria de la Defensa Nacional, 1979), 148.

29. Frank C. Hanighen, *Santa Anna, the Napoleon of the West* (New York: Coward-McCann, 1934), 81–82; Marley, *Wars*, 480–81.

30. Hooker, *The Revolt*, 24–25; Calvert and De León, *The History*, 56.

31. Ramón Martínez Caro, "A True Account of the First Texas Campaign and the Events Subsequent to the Battle of San Jacinto," in *The Mexican Side of the Texan Revolution*, trans. by Carlos E. Castañeda (Dallas: P. L. Turner, 1928), 100.

32. Petite states, "At least 183 men died defending the Alamo, although evidence suggests that as many as 250 or 260 lost their lives in the tragedy." Petite, *1836 Facts*, 61–83.

33. Philip Haythornthwaite, *The Alamo and the War of Texas Independence 1835–36* (London: Osprey, 1986), 22; Calvert and De León, *The History*, 68–69; Groneman, *Battlefields*, 48–52. Hooker, *The Revolt*, 39, places the Mexican casualties at 521.

34. Urrea, "Diary," 216; Marley, *Wars*, 482.

35. Santa Anna, "Manifesto," 15, 20; Vicente Filísola, "Representation Addressed to the Supreme Government," in *The Mexican Side of the Texan Revolution*, trans. by Carlos E. Castañeda (Dallas: P. L. Turner, 1928), 171.

36. Groneman, *Battlefields*, 59–63; Urrea, "Diary," 222–29.

37. Allen Lee Hamilton, "Pathway to Retreat Ignored," *Military History* 18–25 (October 1988), 18–19; Calvert and De León, *The History*, 69–70.

38. *The Texas Navy* (Washington: Naval History Division, 1968), 7–8; Petite, *1836 Facts*, 31–32.

39. Callcott, *Santa Anna*, 134.

40. Vicente Filísola (ca. 1785–1850), born in Rivoli, Italy, joined the Spanish army in 1804. In early 1814 Filísola was assigned to Agustín Iturbide's command and the two became friends. In 1821 Filísola adhered to the Plan of Iguala and joined the Revolutionaries. Emporer Agustín I (Iturbide) promoted Filísola to brigadier general and knighted him in the "Imperial Order of Guadalupe." Filísola was sent to Central America when various provinces of the Captaincy-General of Guatemala (more or less today's Central America) asked to become part of Mexico. He served as Mexico's Captain-General of Guatemala between June 12, 1822, and July 4, 1823. With the fall of Iturbide and the Central American declaration of independence, Filísola returned to Mexico. He retired in 1833 due to ill health but was recalled in November 1835. Serving as second in command of the army that invaded Texas in 1836, he obeyed Santa Anna's order to withdraw following Santa Anna's capture. He underwent court-martial for his actions following the Battle of San Jacinto. Acquitted in 1841, he retired. Filísola was recalled to duty between 1847 and 1853.

41. Haythornthwaite, *The Alamo*, 22; Groneman, *Battlefields*, 67–71; Calvert and De León, *The History*, 70.

42. Calvert and De León, *The History*, 70–71; Perrigo, *Our Spanish Southwest*, 131.

43. Santa Anna, "Manifesto," 32.

44. DePalo, *The Mexican National Army*, 52–53.

45. Petite, *1836 Facts*, 168–69.

CHAPTER FIFTEEN

1. José María Tornel y Mendivil, "Relations between Texas, the United States of American, and Mexico," in *The Mexican Side of the Texan Revolution*, trans. by Carlos E. Castañeda

(Dallas: P. L. Turner Company, 1928), 356; DePalo, *The Mexican National Army*, 66; Calvert and De León, *The History of Texas*, 48–50.

2. Gabriel Valencia (1799–1848), born in Mexico City, entered the Spanish Army in 1810 as a cadet in the Provincial Cavalry Regiment of Tulancingo. He changed sides in March 1821 when he embraced Agustín de Iturbide's Plan of Iguala. During the 1835–36 Texas campaign he served as General Nicolás Bravo's chief of staff.

3. DePalo, *The Mexican National Army*, 66.

4. Nicholás Bravo (ca. 1786–1854) was born in Chilpancingo, Guerrero, and joined the revolutionary army in 1811. His family fought under Father José Morelos in the south, both his father and brother being killed. Bravo was captured in 1817 and imprisoned until October 1821. He chose to support the Plan of Iguala in 1821 and served in the regency in 1822. Bravo was elected vice president in 1824 and served until 1828. In that year he opposed the presidency of Vicente Guerrero and was exiled to Guayaquil, Ecuador. He returned under an amnesty the following year.

5. Anastasio Bustamante (1780–1853) was born in Jiquilpán, Michoacán, and studied in the seminary at Guadalajara as well as medicine in Mexico City. He joined the Spanish army in 1810 shortly after Hidalgo's *Grito de Dolores*. Bustamante fought in numerous early engagements against the Revolutionaries and was cited for valor. He announced his alliance to the Plan of Iguala in 1821. Bustamante was elected vice president in 1829 and overthrew President Vicente Guerrero in June 1830 and ordered him executed. Bustamante was himself overthrown and exiled. He later returned to Mexico.

6. Perrigo, *Our Spanish Southwest*, 132.

7. Miguel A. Sánchez Lamego, *The Second Mexican-Texas War 1841–1843* (Hillsboro, Texas: Hill Junior College, 1972), 24.

8. Calvert and De León, *The History of Texas*, 76–78, 91.

9. General Mariano Paredes, Lt. Colonel [first name unknown] Ugarte, [first name unknown] Luzardo Lechón (Ugarte's second in command), and Francisco Condelle (rebel governor of the state of San Luís Potosí) each had lost a hand in previous battles.

10. Mariano Paredes y Arrillaga (1797–1849) was born in Mexico City and entered the Spanish Army in 1812. In March 1821 he adhered to the Plan of Iguala.

11. Enrique Cárdenas de la Peña, *Semblanza marítima del Mexico independiente y revolucionario*, 2 vols. (Mexico: Secretaría de Marina, 1970), 1: 95.

12. *Texas Navy*, 9–10.

13. DePalo, *The Mexican National Army*, 70–71.

14. Antonio de la Peña y Reyes, *La primera guerra entre Mexico y Francia* (Mexico: Publicaciones de la Secretaría de Relaciones Exteriores, 1927), 120–41; Nancy Nichols Baker, *The French Experience in Mexico, 1821–1861* (Chapel Hill: University of North Carolina Press, 1979), 73–75.

15. A. du Sein, *Histoire de la marine de tous les peuples depuis les temps les plus reculés jusqu'a nos jours*, 2 vols. (Paris: Fuimin Didot frères, 1863), 2: 691–93; André Reussner and Louis Nicolas, *La puissance navale dans l'histoire*, 3 vols. (Paris: Éditions Maritimes et Coloniales, 1958–63), 2: 26; Joannès Tramond and Andre Reussner, *Elements d'histoire maritime et coloniale, 1815–1914* (Paris: Société d'Éditions Géographiques Maritimes et Coloniales, 1924), 29; René Jouan, *Histoire de la marine française* (Paris: Payot, 1932), 215–16; DePalo, *The Mexican National Army*, 68–69; Eugène Maissin, *The French in Mexico and Texas (1838–1839)*, trans. by James L. Shepherd III (Solado: Anson Jones, 1961), 52.

16. DePalo, *The Mexican National Army*, 67–70.

17. ibid., 70–71; Sánchez, *The Second Mexican-Texas War*, 4–5; David M. Vigness, "La expedición Urrea-Mejía," *Historia Mexicana* 5: 211–19 (July 1955–June 1956), 212–16.

18. Pedro de Ampudia (1805–68) born in Havana, Cuba, joined the Spanish army in 1818. Lieutenant Ampudia arrived in Mexico in 1821 in the retinue of New Spain's last Spanish Viceroy, Juan O'Donojú just prior to Agustín Iturbide's pronouncement of the Plan of Iguala. Ampudia chose to support Mexican independence. In 1829 he fought against the Spanish at the Fortress of San Juan de Ulúa for which he was promoted to brigade general. American Gen. William Worth dubbed Ampudia "the Culinary Knight" for his boiling in oil the head from General Sentmanat's corpse.

19. Sánchez, "El ejército mexicano de 1821 a 1860," 154.

20. Nelson Reed, *The Caste War of Yucatan* (Stanford: Stanford University Press, 1964), 27–28; Leticia Reina, *Las rebeliones campensinas en Mexico (1819–1906)* (Mexico: Siglo Veintiuno, 1980), 363; Marley, *Wars*, 498.

21. *Texas Navy*, 11–12; Perrigo, *Our Spanish Southwest*, 132.

22. Edwin Moore (1810–65) entered the U.S. Navy in 1825 as a midshipman. He advanced to the rank of lieutenant before resigning in 1836 to serve in the Texas navy.

23. *Texas Navy*, 13–14.

24. DePalo, *The Mexican National Army*, 76–77; Marley, *Wars*, 498

25. Perrigo, *Our Spanish Southwest*, 135.

26. Calvert and De León, *The History of Texas*, 91.

27. David S. Weber, *The Mexican Frontier 1821–1846: The American Southwest under Mexico 1821–1846* (Albuquerque: University of New Mexico Press, 1982), 266; Charles R. McClure, "The Texan-Santa Fe Expedition of 1841," *New Mexico Historical Review* 48:1, 45–56 (January 1973), 50–54; Sánchez, *The Second Mexican-Texas War*, 70–71; Calvert and De León, *The History of Texas*, 91; Perrigo, *Our Spanish Southwest*, 156–57.

28. Smith to Jones, March 31, 1843, in Garrison, *Diplomatic Correspondence*, 3: 1429.

29. DePalo, *The Mexican National Army*, 77–78; Marley, *Wars*, 498; Callcott, *Santa Anna*, 172–74.

30. Sánchez, *The Second Mexican-Texas War*, 75–84; George Lockhart Rives, *The United States and Mexico 1821–1848*, 2 vols. (New York: Charles Scribner's Sons, 1913), 1: 485; DePalo, *The Mexican National Army*, 82–83; Calvert and De León, *The History of Texas*, 91.

31. Sánchez, *The Second Mexican-Texas War*, 85–88; Sánchez, "El ejército mexicano de 1821 a 1860," 168–69.

32. Sánchez, *The Second Mexican-Texas War*, 89–91.

33. Adrian Woll (1795–1875) was born in Saint Germain en Laye, France, and fought in the defense of Paris in March 1814 as a private and rapidly rose to the rank of captain. With the fall of Bonaparte, Woll immigrated to the United States. He joined the U.S. Army as a sergeant major and served as Lt. Col. Winfield Scott's field adjutant. In 1816 he joined the revolutionary Francisco Javier Mina as a lieutenant colonel and took part in the landing at Soto la Marina, Mexico, on April 15, 1817. He then commanded the ship *Congreso Mexicano*, cruising against Spanish shipping. In 1823 the Mexican government recognized his revolutionary rank of lieutenant colonel. In 1829 he fought against the Spanish at Tampico. Woll advanced rapidly, being promoted to brigade general in 1832. In 1835 he was the quartermaster of the army that marched into Texas.

34. Sánchez, *The Second Mexican-Texas War*, 92–94.

35. Perrigo, *Our Spanish Southwest*, 137.
36. Sánchez, *The Second Mexican-Texas War*, 95–100; Groneman, *Battlefields*, 106–7.
37. *Texas Navy*, 15–16.
38. Tomás Marín (1805–73) born in Guadalupe Hidalgo (today the Federal District), attended the Tlacotalpan Maritime College where he was among the first of the graduates. Marín participated in the defense of Vera Cruz against the French in 1839.
39. Cardenas de la Peña, *Semblanza maritime*, 1:100; *Texas Navy*, 16–17.
40. DePalo, *The Mexican National Army*, 80.
41. ibid., 83–84.
42. Groneman, *Battlefields*, 108–14; DePalo, *The Mexican National Army*, 85.
43. Sánchez, *The Second Mexican-Texas War*, 101–15.
44. Ralph A. Wooster, "Texas Military Operations Against Mexico, 1841–1843," *The Southwestern Historical Quarterly* 67:4, 465–79 (April 1964), 473–76; Sánchez, *The Second Mexican-Texas War*, 116–20; Sánchez, "El ejército mexicano de 1821 a 1860," 169–70.
45. Wooster, "Texas Military Operations," 476–81; Green, *Journal of the Texan Expedition against Mier*, 479; Calvert and De León, *The History of Texas*, 91.
46. Marley, *Wars*, 499.
47. Wooster, "Texas Military Operations," 481–82.
48. ibid., 482–84; William Campbell Binkley, "The Last Stage of Texan Military Operations against Mexico, 1843," *The Southwestern Historical Quarterly* 260–71 (January 1919), 262; McClure, "Texas-Santa Fe Expedition," 54.
49. *Texas Navy*, 18–25.
50. Cardenas de la Peña, *Semblanza maritime*, 1: 101–3; *Texas Navy*, 18–25.
51. DePalo, *The Mexican National Army*, 80–81.
52. Sánchez, *The Second Mexican-Texas War*, 53–62; DePalo, *The Mexican National Army*, 84–85.
53. Robinson, *Mexico*, 259; DePalo, *The Mexican National Army*, 81.
54. José Joaquín de Herrera (1792–1854) was born in Jalapa, Vera Cruz, and joined the Spanish army in 1809 as a cadet. He fought against both Hidalgo and Morelos during the early years of the War for Independence but joined the Revolutionaries in 1821.
55. Callcott, *Santa Anna*, 206–8; DePalo, *The Mexican National Army*, 86–87.
56. Callcott, *Santa Anna,* 208–19; DePalo, *The Mexican National Army*, 87; Marley, *Wars*, 499.
57. DePalo, *The Mexican National Army*, 72–75.
58. Frances Calderón de la Barca, *Life in Mexico* (Berkeley: University of California Press, 1982), 433.
59. David Montejano, *Anglos and Mexicans in the Making of Texas, 1836–1986* (Austin: University of Texas Press, 1987), 25; Calvert and De León, *The History of Texas*, 79–90; Reubin M. Potter, "The Republic of Texas," *The Magazine of American History* 10; 38–51 (July–December 1883), 51.

CHAPTER SIXTEEN

1. In 1843 the Mexican Secretary of Foreign Relations stated that "the Mexican Government will consider the equivalent to a declaration of war against the Mexican Republic the passage of an act for the incorporation of Texas with the territory of the United States." Justin H. Smith, *The War with Mexico,* 2 vols. (New York: Macmillan, 1919), 1: 84.

2. Hitchman, "Rush to Glory," 15; Canales, *Historia militar*, 86–87; Calvert and Deleon, *The History of Texas,* 94; Groneman, *Battlefields*, 116–18.

3. Philip Shriver Klein, *President James Buchanan* (University Park: Pennsylvania State University Press, 1962), 175; Richard R. Stenburg, "President Polk and California: Additional Documents," *The Pacific Historical Review* 10: 2; 217–19 (June 1941), 217–19; Edward G. Bourne, "The Proposed Absorption of Mexico in 1847–48," *Annual Report of the American Historical Association for the Year 1899*, 2 vols. (Washington: Government Printing Office, 1900), 1: 157.

4. Richard A. Pfost, "War with Mexico!" *Command* 40; 20–32 (November 1996), 20; Hitchman, "Rush to Glory," 15; Calvert and DeLeón, *The History of Texas*, 94; Perrigo, *Our Spanish Southwest*, 140–42.

5. Zachary Taylor (1784–1850), "Old Rough and Ready," was a veteran of numerous Indian campaigns. He was courageous, frequently exposing himself to enemy fire; possessed shrewd common sense; and had an excellent rapport with the common soldier. Taylor was notoriously indifferent to sanitation, lax concerning discipline, sloppy in his own appearance, and uncouth. President Polk chose Taylor to command the army sent to Texas only after failing to find a qualified Democratic general.

On September 5, 1846, President Polk observed of Taylor, "[H]e makes no suggestions as to the plan of campaign, but simply obeys orders and gives no information to aid the administration in directing his movement." James Polk, *Polk: The Diary of a President 1845–1849*, ed. by Allan Nevins (New York: Longmans, Green, 1952), 145.

6. Pfost, "War with Mexico," 21; DePalo, *The Mexican National Army*, 95.

7. Not all Conservatives were Centralists and not all Liberals were Federalists, but in general, this held true. The Liberals were divided into two main factions, the *puros* who favored radical reform and the *moderados* who advocated gradual change.

8. DePalo, *The Mexican National Army*, 94.

9. Callcott, *Santa Anna* 278; Bureau of the Census, *Historical Statistics of the United States* (Washington: Government Printing Office, 1961), 7; DePalo, *The Mexican National Army*, 96–97; Pfost, "War with Mexico," 24.

10. José Fernando Ramírez, *Mexico during the War with the United States*, ed. by Walter V. Scholes, trans. by Elliott B. Scheer (Columbia: University of Missouri Press, 1950), 61.

President James Polk wrote, "[t]he army upon whose support General Paredes depended to uphold him in power, being badly fed and clothed and without pay might and probably would soon desert him, unless money could be obtained to supply their wants." Polk, *The Diary*, 66.

11. Pfost, "War with Mexico," 22–24; G. P. Stokes, "War with Mexico!" *Command* 40; 34–51 (November 1996), 34.

12. Polk, *The Diary*, 91; Hitchman, "Rush to Glory," 14; DePalo, *The Mexican National Army*, 94.

13. Polk wrote, "I gave it as my opinion that the first movement should be to march a competent force into the northern provinces and seize and hold them until peace was made." Polk, *The Diary*, 93; K. Jack Bauer, *Zachary Taylor* (Baton Rouge: Louisiana State University Press, 1985), 167.

The Commanding General of the Army, Winfield Scott, thought both the timing and objective were wrong. Writing in the third person Scott stated, "he doubted whether that was the right season, or the Rio Grande the right basis for *offensive* operations against Mexico;

and suggested the plan of conquering a peace [by capturing the Mexican capital] which he ultimately executed." Winfield Scott, *Memoirs of Lieut.-General Scott, LL.D.* (New York: Sheldon, 1864), 384.

14. Polk, *The Diary*, 105.

15. Pedro Ampudia (1805–68) prematurely attempted to lead the Mexico City garrison into revolt in support of General Paredes on December 27, 1845. Ramírez, *Mexico*, 24, 41, 43.

16. Hitchman, "Rush to Glory," 16; DePalo, *The Mexican National Army*, 96–99.

17. Mariano Arista (1802–55) joined the Royalist militia of San Luís Potosí in 1817. In 1821 he was promoted to lieutenant colonel and in June changed sides declaring in favor of the Plan of Iguala. He was exiled to the United States between 1833 and 1839 for supporting the anti-Federalist rebellion against President Gómez Farías. Arista learned a trade while in the United States, was devoted to agriculture, and admired the accomplishments of the United States. On January 7, 1846, José Fernando Ramírez wrote, "Orders have been issued relieving Arista of his command of the Army of the North. The man has been sullying himself with graft ever since the Texas conflict." Ramírez, *Mexico*, 62.

18. Winfield Scott (1786–1866) was born into a wealthy Virginia family, joined the army in 1809 as a captain, and fought in the War of 1812. Financially independent, Scott visited the European battlefields of the Napoleonic Wars and interviewed participants. He supervised the writing of the first standard set of drill regulations for the army. In 1841 he was appointed the Commanding General of the Army. In 1847 he planned the assault on Vera Cruz, the largest amphibious landing carried out by U.S. forces until that time. Because of his insistence upon strict discipline, Mexican civilians fared better from the forces under his command than those commanded by Zachary Taylor. Scott was fastidious, egotistical, and politically ambitious. His love of military pomp earned him the nickname "Old Fuss and Feathers." Biographer Charles Elliott wrote, "Not even the gorgeously bedizened marshals of Napoleon wore their plumes, sashes, aiguillettes, and glittering uniforms with more complacency than did this republican soldier whose imposing and symmetrical form was so well set off by such martial embellishments." Charles W. Elliott, *Winfield Scott: The Soldier and the Man* (New York: ARNO Press, 1979), 383.

Polk wrote on November 17, 1846, "I have strong objections to General Scott, and after his exceptionable letter in May last [criticizing the administration] nothing but stern necessity and a sense of public duty could induce me to place him at the head of so important an expedition." Polk, *The Diary*, 169.

19. José María Roa Bárcena, *Recuerdos de la invasión norteamericana, 1846–1848*, 3 vols. (Mexico: Editorial Porrua, S.A., 1947), 1: 62; Groneman, *Battlefields*, 116–18.

20. Hitchman, "Rush to Glory," 16; Roa, *Recuerdos*, 1: 63–64.

21. Smith, *The War*, 1: 161–62; Ramón Alcaraz, *The Other Side: Or Notes for the History of the War between Mexico and the United States*, trans. by Albert C. Ramsey (New York: Burt Franklin, 1850), 48.

22. Hitchman, "Rush to Glory," 17; Pfost, "War with Mexico," 22–23; Roa, *Recuerdos*, 1: 66–67; DePalo, *The Mexican National Army*, 100–1.

23. Hitchman, "Rush to Glory," 17; Pfost, "War with Mexico," 24–25; Roa, *Recuerdos*, 1: 82–84; DePalo, *The Mexican National Army*, 101–2.

24. A slang term which most commonly is used by Latin Americans to refer to persons from the United States. In bygone years, most frequently, the term was derogatory. The origin of the term is lost and numerous explanations of its origin have been offered.

25. Parkes, *A History of Mexico*, 214–15; Rives, *The United States*, 2: 119–22; Smith, *The War*, 1: 201–3; DePalo, *The Mexican National Army*, 103.

26. Hitchman, "Rush to Glory," 21; DePalo, *The Mexican National Army*, 104.

27. Parkes, *A History of Mexico*, 214; Hitchman, "Rush to Glory," 18; Perrigo, *Our Spanish Southwest*, 165.

28. Ramírez, *Mexico*, 73; Alcaraz, *The Other Side*, 67–68; "Letters of General López de Santa Anna Related to the War between the United States and Mexico, 1846–1848," ed. by Justin H. Smith in *Annual Report of the American Historical Association for the Year 1917* (Washington: Government Printing Office, 1920), 364.

29. Hitchman, "Rush to Glory," 19; Pfost, "War with Mexico," 25–26; Alcaraz, *The Other Side*, 69.

30. Hitchman, "Rush to Glory," 19; Alcaraz, *The Other Side*, 75–76.

31. Roa, *Recuerdos*, 1: 122; Alcaraz, *The Other Side*, 79–80; Hitchman, "Rush to Glory," 19–20; Pfost, "War with Mexico," 27.

On October 11, 1846, Polk wrote, "In agreeing to the armistice General Taylor violated his express orders and I regret that I cannot approve his course." Polk, *The Diary*, 155–56.

32. Polk, *The Diary*, 154–55, 158–59, 164–65. Taylor's opinion was that the army should seize northern old Mexico, particularly Chihauhua, the commercial center northwest of Monterrey, and should secure the Río Grande Valley. Should this fail to bring about negotiations, Taylor recommended that he lead a 10,000-man army from Saltillo to San Luis Potosí, the capture of which he believed would force the Mexicans to come to terms. Bauer, *Zachary Taylor*, 172.

33. Hitchman, "Rush to Glory," 20; Smith, *The War*, 1: 286–90; Stokes, "War with Mexico," 40; Perrigo, *Our Spanish Southwest*, 168–69.

34. Polk, *The Diary*, 227.

35. Carlos María de Bustamante, *El nuevo Bernal Díaz del Castillo o sea historia de la invasión de los anglo-americanos en Mexico* (Mexico: Secretaría de Educación Pública, 1949), 2: 223–28; Smith, *The War*, 1: 312–13; Perrigo, *Our Spanish Southwest*, 170–71.

36. Hitchman, "Rush to Glory," 20.

37. George Tays, "Frémont Had No Secret Instructions," *The Pacific Historical Review* 9: 2; 157–71 (June 1940), refutes this speculation that Gillespie was carrying secret orders. See also Stenburg, "President Polk," 219.

38. Hitchman, "Rush to Glory," 20–21; Smith, *The War*, 1: 333–39; Perrigo, *Our Spanish Southwest*, 174–76.

39. Hitchman, "Rush to Glory," 21; Perrigo, *Our Spanish Southwest*, 176.

40. Hitchman, "Rush to Glory," 21; Perrigo, *Our Spanish Southwest*, 176. Due to the vagueness of their instructions, Kearny and Stockton argued over who was in charge. Once Stockton departed, Fremont carried on the quarrel with Kearny and was ultimately sent back to Washington under arrest for court-martial.

41. Hitchman, "Rush to Glory," 21; Perrigo, *Our Spanish Southwest*, 165.

42. Manuel Balbontín, *La invasíon americana 1846–1848* (Mexico: Tip. de Gonzalo A. Esteva, 1883), 55; Alcaraz, *The Other Side*, 83–85; Roa, *Recuerdos*, 1: 126–27; Smith, *The War*, 1: 264–66.

43. Canales, *Historia militar*, 91–92; Hanighen, *Santa Anna*, 205.

44. Parkes, *A History of Mexico*, 215–16; Hitchman, "Rush to Glory," 21; Scott, *Memoirs*, 402; Roa, *Recuerdos*, 1: 199–201; Alcaraz, *The Other Side*, 98.

45. Parkes, *A History of Mexico*, 216; Hitchman, "Rush to Glory," 21–22; Canales, *Historia militar*, 97–98; Pfost, "War with Mexico," 30–31.

46. K. Jack Bauer, *The Mexican War 1846–1848* (New York: Macmillan, 1974), 214; Parkes, *A History of Mexico*, 216; Canales, *Historia militar*, 100–1.

47. Jefferson Davis was promoted to brigadier general for his actions at Monterey and Buena Vista.

48. Hitchman, "Rush to Glory," 22–23; Canales, *Historia militar*, 102; Smith, *The War*, 1: 384–98; Roa, *Recuerdos*, 1: 166–74, 185.

49. Santa Anna never explains his decision. DePalo concludes, "But evidently he [Santa Anna] believed his army had reached the point of ineffectuality and elected to break contact rather than risk decisive defeat." DePalo, *The Mexican National Army*, 113.

50. Alcaraz, *The Other Side*, 137.

51. *El Soldado Mexicano*, 78; Alcaraz, *The Other Side*, 137–41; Canales, *Historia militar*, 103–4.

52. Michael P. Costeloe, "The Mexican Church and the Rebellion of the Polkos," *Hispanic American Historical Review* 46: 2; 170–78 (May 1966), 170–73; Roa, *Recuerdos*, 1: 245–48.

53. Hanighen, *Santa Anna*, 206; Stokes, "War with Mexico," 35.

54. Initially, President Polk wanted to give the command of the expedition to Democratic Senator Thomas H. Benton, who was completely inexperienced in military affairs, in order to keep it out of the hands of the politically ambitious Winfield Scott.

55. Stokes, "War with Mexico," 36–38; Scott, *Memoirs*, 422–29; Smith, *The War*, 2: 340; Roa, *Recuerdos*, 1: 312–18.

56. Hitchman, "Rush to Glory," 21–22.

57. Stokes, "War with Mexico," 38–39; Hitchman, "Rush to Glory," 24; Smith, *The War*, 2: 347; Roa, *Recuerdos*, 2: 16–17.

58. Stokes, "War with Mexico," 39; Ramírez, *Mexico*, 118; Roa, *Recuerdos*, 2: 23–48; Alcaraz, *The Other Side*, 208.

59. Ramírez, *Mexico*, 120.

60. Hitchman, "Rush to Glory," 24–25.

61. Ramírez, *Mexico*, 124.

62. DePalo, *The Mexican National Army*, 125.

63. Ramírez, *Mexico*, 134.

64. Among those who returned to the United States was General Pillow, Polk's former law partner. Once home he was promoted to major general in spite of his poor performance at Cerro Gordo.

65. Stokes, "War with Mexico," 41; Parkes, *A History of Mexico*, 219; Hitchman, "Rush to Glory," 25; Smith, *The War*, 2: 69–71.

66. The Duke of Wellington, the patriarch of military strategy, proclaimed, "Scott is lost. He cannot capture the city and he cannot fall back upon his base." Smith, *The War*, 2: 89. President Polk wrote on July 13, "General Scott had undoubtedly committed a great military error by breaking up the post at Jalapa and leaving his whole rear exposed to the enemy." Polk, *The Diary*, 249.

67. Stokes, "War with Mexico," 43.

68. DePalo, *The Mexican National Army*, 126–27; Stokes, "War with Mexico," 43.

69. Alcaraz, *The Other Side*, 261; Roa, *Recuerdos*, 2: 175–83; Smith, *The War*, 2: 87–88.

70. Hitchman, "Rush to Glory," 25; Scott, *Memoirs*, 467–68; Smith, *The War*, 2: 372–73.

71. Stokes, "War with Mexico," 44; Hitchman, "Rush to Glory," 26; Roa, *Recuerdos*, 2: 220–28, 241–42; Alcaraz, *The Other Side*, 279–80.

72. *El Soldado Mexicano*, 78; Hitchman, "Rush to Glory," 26.

73. Hitchman, "Rush to Glory," 26.

74. All were later convicted by court-martials—50 were hanged and 16 were lashed, incarcerated, and branded. Richard Blaine McCornack, "The San Patricio Deserters in the Mexican War," *The Americas* 8: 2; 131–42 (October 1951).

75. *El soldado mexicano*, 54; Ramírez, *Mexico*, 152; Balbontín, *La invasion*, 119–23; Smith, *The War*, 2: 112–18.

76. DePalo, *The Mexican National Army*, 132–33; Stokes, "War with Mexico," 46.

77. Balbontin, *La invasion*, 126–29; Hanighen, *Santa Anna*, 236; Pasquel, *Antonio López de Santa Anna*, 132; Alcaraz, *The Other Side*, 339–43.

78. Stokes, "War with Mexico," 48–49; Alcaraz, *The Other Side*, 356–57; Smith, *The War*, 2: 152–53; DePalo, *The Mexican National Army*, 135–37.

79. Stokes, "War with Mexico," 49–50; Hitchman, "Rush to Glory," 26; DePalo, *The Mexican National Army*, 137–38; Alcaraz, *The Other Side*, 362–63.

80. Stokes, "War with Mexico," 50–51; Parkes, *A History of Mexico*, 220; Hitchman, "Rush to Glory," 26; Smith, *The War*, 2: 415–16.

81. The various U.S. schemes for acquiring territory from Mexico as a consequence of the war are depicted in Charles O. Paullin, *Atlas of the Historical Geography of the United States* (Washington: Carnegie Institution of Washington, 1932), plate 94.

82. Parkes, *A History of Mexico*, 221.

83. Polk, *The Diary*, 270–71.

84. Ramírez wrote, "I believe that poor General S.A. is suffering as much as I am today [3 April 1847], because, brushing aside all polite considerations, he said yesterday that in his profession all the generals, including himself, would hardly make good corporals." Ramírez, *Mexico*, 116.

85. Sometime after the war, Scott said, "I give it as my fixed opinion that but for our graduated cadets [the Military Academy at West Point] the war between the United States and Mexico might, and probably would, have lasted some four or five years." Russell F. Weigley, *History of the United States Army* (New York: Macmillan, 1967), 481.

86. Gen. Gideon Pillow's only qualification was that he had been President Polk's law partner.

87. Bauer, *The Mexican War*, 322.

88. On July 16 Polk wrote, "The protraction of the war may properly be attributed to the folly and ridiculous vanity of General Scott." Polk, *The Diary*, 185, 251.

89. Scott, *Memoirs*, 380.

90. ibid., 403.

91. DePalo, *The Mexican National Army*, 114.

92. ibid., 139.

93. David H. Zook Jr. and Robin Higham, *A Short History of Warfare* (New York: Twayne, 1966), 179; Hitchman, "Rush to Glory," 16.

94. Calvert and DeLeón, *The History of Texas*, 95–96.

95. Hitchman, "Rush to Glory," 14.

96. José Vasconcelos, *Breve historia de Mexico* (Mexico: Editorial Polis, 1944), 462–63; Alfonso Teja Zabre, *Historia de Mexico una moderna interpretacion*, 4th ed. (Mexico: Impresora Juan Pablos, 1961), 335.
97. DePalo, *The Mexican National Army*, 139–40.
98. Stokes, "War with Mexico," 37; Hitchman, "Rush to Glory," 14.
99. Bancroft, *History of Central America*, 3: 312.

CHAPTER SEVENTEEN
1. R. A. Humphreys, "Anglo-American Rivalries in Central America," *Transactions of the Royal Historical Society*, 5th Series; 18; 174–208 (1968), 181–82; J. Fred Rippy, *Latin America in World Politics* (New York: F. S. Crofts, 1938), 99.
2. Humphreys, "Anglo-American Rivalries," 186; Rippy, *Latin America*, 99–100, 104; Rodriguez, *Central America*, 74–75.
3. Mary Wilhelmine Williams, *Anglo-American Isthmian Diplomacy 1815–1915* (Washington: The American Historical Association, 1916), 34–36; Dexter Perkins, *Hands Off: A History of the Monroe Doctrine* (Boston: Little, Brown, 1941), 74; Rippy, *Latin America*, 100.
4. Williams, *Anglo-American Isthmian Diplomacy*, 33.
5. ibid., 37; Robert A. Naylor, "The British Role in Central America Prior to the Clayton-Bulwer Treaty of 1850," *Hispanic American Historical Review* 40: 3, 361–82 (August 1960), 370; John Bigelow, *Breaches of Anglo-American Treaties* (New York: Sturgis & Walton, 1917), 150.
6. Williams, *Anglo-American Isthmian Diplomacy*, 38–39; Bigelow, *Breaches*, 152–53.
7. Williams, *Anglo-American Isthmian Diplomacy*, 41; Bigelow, *Breaches*, 50–53; Peter F. Stout, *Nicaragua: Past, Present and Future* (Philadelphia: John E. Potter, ca. 1880), 169; Gámez, *Historia de Nicaragua*, 743.
8. Humphreys, "Anglo-American Rivalries," 191; Williams, *Anglo-American Isthmian Diplomacy*, 42–44; Naylor, "The British Role," 377; Bigelow, *Breaches*, 53.
9. Bigelow, *Breaches*, 54–55; Gámez, *Historia de Nicaragua*, 744.
10. Humphreys, "Anglo-American Rivalries," 193; Lester D. Langley, *America and the Americas* (Athens: University of Georgia Press, 1989), 75; Williams, *Anglo-American Isthmian Diplomacy*, 48–49; Bigelow, *Breaches*, 56.
11. Bigelow, *Breaches*, 58–59; A. W. Ward and G. P. Gooch, *The Cambridge History of British Foreign Policy 1783–1919*, 3 vols. (Cambridge: Cambridge University Press, 1923–39), 2: 266; Humphreys, "Anglo-American Rivalries," 193; Graham H. Stuart, *Latin America and the United States* (New York: D. Appleton-Century, 1943), 288.
12. In April 1844 James Polk, prior to being a candidate for the presidency, set the tone for his future administration *vis-a-vis* the Monroe Doctrine, "Let the fixed principle of our government be, not to permit Great Britain, or any other foreign power, to plant a colony or hold dominion over any portion of the people or territory of either [continent]." Perkins, *Hands Off*, 78.
13. Stuart, *Latin America*, 288; Williams, *Anglo-American Isthmian Diplomacy*, 57–58; Bigelow, *Breaches*, 64; Humphreys, "Anglo-American Rivalries," 180–81.
14. Williams, *Anglo-American Isthmian Diplomacy*, 59–60; Stuart, *Latin America*, 291.
15. Williams, *Anglo-American Isthmian Diplomacy*, 60–64; Bigelow, *Breaches*, 64–65.
16. Williams, *Anglo-American Isthmian Diplomacy*, 64–66; Langley, *America*, 76.
17. Perkins, *Hands Off*, 96–98; Rippy, *Latin America*, 101; Woodward, *Central America*, 134; Williams, *Anglo-American Isthmian Diplomacy*, 158.

18. David F. Long, *Gold Braid and Foreign Relations* (Annapolis: Naval Institute Press, 1988), 122–23; Bigelow, *Breaches*, 100.

19. Williams, *Anglo-American Isthmian Diplomacy*, 139–67; Ward and Gooch, *The Cambridge History,* 2: 271; Bigelow, *Breaches*, 154–55.

20. Williams, *Anglo-American Isthmian Diplomacy*, 168–71.

21. Long, *Gold Braid*, 123–24; Williams, *Anglo-American Isthmian Diplomacy*, 172.

22. Long, *Gold Braid,* 124–29; Stout, *Nicaragua*, 176–77; Williams, *Anglo-American Isthmian Diplomacy*, 174–80; Bigelow, *Breaches*, 100–1.

23. Williams, *Anglo-American Isthmian Diplomacy*, 176–87.

24. Ward and Gooch, *The Cambridge History*, 2: 275.

25. Rippy, *Latin America*, 104.

26. Bigelow, *Breaches*, 101.

CHAPTER EIGHTEEN

1. In 1846 the former president of Ecuador, Gen. Juan José Flores, unsuccessfully attempted to raise and outfit a filibustering expedition in Europe, the objective of which was to make a Spanish prince the ruler of Ecuador. In 1857 Uruguayan Juan C. Gómez inspired an unsuccessful invasion of his homeland, the objective of which was to unite Uruguay and Argentina into the United States of the Plata.

2. Perrigo, *Our Spanish Southwest*, 101–2. Wilkinson died in Mexico City in 1825.

3. Samuel Flagg Bemis, *A Diplomatic History of the United States*, 5th ed. (New York: Holt, Rinehart and Winston, 1965), 218–19; Julius W. Pratt, *A History of United States Foreign Policy* (Englewood Cliffs: Prentice-Hall, 1955), 156–57.

4. James Long (ca. 1793–1822) was born in North Carolina. He studied medicine and served as a physician under Andrew Jackson at the Battle of New Orleans. Long married Jane H. Wilkinson, the niece of Gen. James Wilkinson.

5. Hubert Howe Bancroft, *History of the Northern Mexican States and Texas*, 2 vols. (San Francisco: The History Company, 1889), 2: 47–48; Calvert and De León, *The History of Texas*, 48.

6. Bancroft, *History of the Northern Mexican States*, 2: 48–49; Perrigo, *Our Spanish Southwest*, 105.

7. Bancroft, *History of the Northern Mexican States*, 2: 50–51; Perrigo, *Our Spanish Southwest*, 106.

8. Perrigo, *Our Spanish Southwest*, 207.

9. Gaston Raoulx de Raousset de Boulbon (1817–57) was born at Avingnon, France, and educated by the Jesuits. He fought as an adventurer in the new French colony in Algeria. His family's wealth was lost in the Revolution of 1848, which he supported. In spite of his heritage, the Count was sympathetic toward liberal causes.

10. Bancroft, *History of the Northern Mexican States*, 2: 676–77.

11. ibid., 678–79.

12. ibid., 679–80; Marley, *Wars*, 522.

13. Bancroft, *History of the Northern Mexican States*, 2: 680–82; J. Fred Rippy, *The United States and Mexico* (New York: F. S. Crofts, 1931), 91–92; W. O. Scroggs, *Filibusters and Financiers* (New York: Macmillan, 1916), 27–28; Rufus Kay Wyllys, "The Republic of Lower California, 1853–54," *Pacific Historical Review* 2: 2; 194–213 (1933), 199–200; Cardenas, *Semblanza maritime*, 2: 142–43; J. Fred Rippy, "Anglo-American Filibusterings and the Gadsden Treaty," *The Hispanic American Historical Review* 5: 2; 155–80 (May 1922), 163–65.

14. Rippy, *The United States*, 93; Rippy, "Anglo-American Filibusterings," 165–66; Wyllys, "The Republic of Lower California," 194–95, 199; Bancroft, *History of the Northern Mexican States*, 2: 721.

15. Wyllys, "The Republic of Lower California," 201–2; Scroggs, *Filibusters*, 35–36; Bancroft, *History of the Northern Mexican States*, 2: 722.

16. Rippy, "Anglo-American Filibusterings," 166; Scroggs, *Filibusters*, 36–37; Wyllys, "The Republic of Lower California," 203–4; Bancroft, *History of the Northern Mexican States*, 2: 722.

17. Rippy, *The United States*, 94; Scroggs, *Filibusters*, 38–39; Bancroft, *History of the Northern Mexican States*, 2: 722–23.

18. Rippy, *The United States*, 95; Rippy, "Anglo-American Filibusterings," 167; Wyllys, "The Republic of Lower California," 207.

19. Wyllys, "The Republic of Lower California," 207; Scroggs, *Filibusters*, 41; Bancroft, *History of the Northern Mexican States*, 2: 723.

20. Roche, *By-Ways*, 44–46; Scroggs, *Filibusters*, 42; Mario Lavalle Arguidín, *Buques de la armada de Mexico*, 2 vols. (Mexico: Secretaria de Marina, 1991–92), 1: 11–12.

21. Scroggs, *Filibusters*, 45; Rippy, *The United States*, 95; Bancroft, *History of the Northern Mexican States*, 2: 723.

22. Roche, *By-Ways*, 47; Scroggs, *Filibusters,* 31–41; Rippy, *The United States*, 95; Bancroft, *History of the Northern Mexican States*, 2: 723.

23. Roche, *By-Ways*, 47–48; Bancroft, *History of the Northern Mexican States*, 2: 724.

24. Roche, *By-Ways*, 49–52; Rippy, "Anglo-American Filibusterings," 168; Scroggs, *Filibusters*, 47–48; Rippy, *The United States*, 96.

25. Bancroft, *History of the Northern Mexican States*, 2: 684–85; Rippy, *The United States*, 169.

26. Bancroft, *History of the Northern Mexican States*, 2: 685–86; Marley, *Wars*, 522.

27. Bancroft, *History of the Northern Mexican States*, 2: 686–92; Scroggs, *Filibusters*, 54; Rippy, *The United States*, 169–70; Alcée Fortier and John Rice Ficklen, *The History of North American*, 20 vols. (Philadelphia: George Barrie, 1903–7), 9: 334; Marley, *Wars*, 522.

28. Henry A. Crabb (1827–57) became a lawyer in 1845 at Vicksburg, Mississippi. Killing a man in an election duel during the campaign of 1848, Crabb traveled to California. Crabb was called as a witness for the defense during William Walker's 1854 filibustering trial. He unsuccessfully endeavored to become the "Know-Nothing" party's candidate for a U.S. Senate seat in 1855. He married into the Ainza family, prominent in Sonoran politics.

29. Rufus Kay Wyllys, "Henry A. Crabb—A Tragedy of the Sonora Frontier," *Pacific Historical Review* 9: 2; 183–94 (June 1940), 187–89; Scroggs, *Filibusters*, 311.

30. Wyllys, "Henry A. Crabb," 189–90; Bancroft, *History of the Northern Mexican States*, 2: 694.

31. Wyllys, "Henry A. Crabb," 191–92; Scroggs, *Filibusters*, 313–15; Rippy, *The United States*, 178–79; Bancroft, *History of the Northern Mexican States*, 2: 694.

32. Scroggs, *Filibusters*, 308–16; Wyllys, "Henry A. Crabb," 192–93; Rippy, *The United States*, 184; Marley, *Wars*, 523.

33. Andrew F. Rolle, "Futile Filibustering in Baja California, 1888–1890," *Pacific Historical Review* 20: 2; 159–66 (May 1951), 160.

34. Rolle, "Futile Filibustering," 161–62.

35. ibid., 162–66.

36. Dwane Hal Dean, "The Last Filibusters," *Journal of the West* 24: 2; 113–14 (April 1985), 113; Lowell L. Blaisdell, "Was It Revolution or Filibustering? The Mystery of the Flores Magón Revolt in Baja California," *Pacific Historical Review* 23: 2; 147–64 (May 1954), 150–51; Daniel Gutíerrez Santos, *História militar de Mexico*, 3 vols. (Ediciones Ateneo, S.A., 1955–61), 3: 86–87; Alfonso Taracena, *La verdadera revolución mexicana*, 12 vols. plus (Mexico: Editorial Jus, 1960–63), 1: 116–17.

37. Gutíerrez, *História militar*, 3: 87.

38. ibid., 3: 88; Taracena, *La verdadera revolución*, 1: 124.

39. Gutíerrez, *História militar*, 3: 89; Taracena, *La verdadera revolución*, 1: 130; Dean, "The Last Filibusters," 114; Blaisdell, "Was It Revolution," 149–50.

40. Gutíerrez, *História militar*, 3: 89; Taracena, *La verdadera revolución*, 1: 132.

41. Gutíerrez, *História militar*, 3: 90; Taracena, *La verdadera revolución*, 1: 142.

42. Gutíerrez, *História militar*, 3: 91.

43. ibid., 3: 91–92; Taracena, *La verdadera revolución*, 1: 143, 147–49; Dean, "The Last Filibusters," 113–14; Blaisdell, "Was It Revolution," 150.

44. Gutíerrez, *História militar*, 3: 92–93; Taracena, *La verdadera revolución*, 1: 154; Dean, "The Last Filibusters," 114; Blaisdell, "Was It Revolution," 149–50.

45. Klein, *President James Buchanan*, 322.

CHAPTER NINETEEN

1. Narciso López (1798–1851) was born in Spanish Venezuela into a family of moderate wealth. Early in the Wars of Independence, López fought with the patriots until captured. He changed sides to avoid execution. López rose to the rank of colonel in the Spanish army by the age of twenty-one. During the collapse of the Spanish empire in South America, López, along with many other Royalists, sought haven in Cuba. Moving to Spain, he fought in the first Carlist War, rising to the rank of major general, and was appointed Governor of Valencia in 1839. He returned to Cuba in 1843 as a protegé of Governor General Gerónimo Valdés. López married into a wealthy Cuban *Criollo* family.

A work that presents López as a patriot is Herminio Portell Vilá, *Narcisco López y su Epoca*, 3 vols. (La Habana: Compaña Editoria de Libros y Folletos, 1930–58). A book that views López as an opportunist is Sergio Aguirre, *Quince objectivos a Narcisco López: anexionismo, esclavitad, mercenarios* (La Habana: Dirección Nacional de Escuelas de Instrucción Revolucionaria, 1961).

2. Basil Rauch, *American Interests in Cuba 1848–1855* (New York: Columbia University Press, 1948), 76–77; Thomas, *Cuba*, 213.

3. Rippy, *Rivalry*, 72–73, 85; Herbert Everett Putnam, *Joel Roberts Poinsett* (Washington: Mimeoform Press, 1935), 87–89; Rauch, *American Interests*, 15, 29; Jane Franklin, *Cuba and the United States* (New York: Ocean Press, 1997), 2–3.

4. Rafael Fermoselle, *The Evolution of the Cuban Military: 1492–1986* (Miami: Ediciones Universal, 1987), 50; Rauch, *American Interests*, 39, 50–52; Portell Vilá, *Narcisco López*, 2: 16.

5. Rauch, *American Interests*, 52.

6. Suspected conspirators were tied to ladders and then lashed in order to obtain confessions. Some 4,000 persons were arrested and 300 tortured to death. Franklin, *Cuba*, 4.

7. Rauch, *American Interests*, 42–45.

8. John L. O'Sullivan (1813–95), according to tradition, was born on a British warship off Gibraltar. He invested heavily in the two López' expeditions and lost his money. Twice

O'Sullivan was indicted for violating the neutrality laws but was not convicted. He worked as a New York journalist. He coined the phrase "Manifest Destiny" which he used for the first time in the *U.S. Magazine and Democratic Review* in 1845.

9. Franklin, *Cuba*, 4; Polk, *The Diary*, 321, 326. Secretary of State James Buchanan to Minister to Spain Romulus Saunders, June 17, 1848, Instructions to American Ministers to Spain, Department of State Correspondence, National Archives; Josef Opatrny, *U.S. Expansionism and Cuban Annexation in the 1850s* (Prague: Charles University, 1990), 167; Hugh Thomas, *Cuba: The Pursuit of Freedom* (New York: Harper & Row, 1971), 213.

10. Opatrny, *U.S. Expansionism*, 181–82; Rauch, *American Interests*, 75–76.

11. Thomas, *Cuba*, 214; Long, *Gold Braid*, 115; Rauch, *American Interests*, 76–81; Franklin, *Cuba*.

12. Rauch, *American Interests*, 114.

13. Thomas, *Cuba*, 214; Rauch, *American Interests*, 112–13.

14. Opatrny, *U.S. Expansionism*, 185–86; Rauch, *American Interests*, 117–20; Anderson C. Quisenberry, *Lopez's Expeditions to Cuba 1850 and 1851* (Louisville: John P. Morton, 1906), 30–31; Portell Vilá, *Narciso López*, 2: 209.

15. John A. Quitman (1799–1858), was born in Natchez, Mississippi. Between 1825 and 1835 Quitman held state political offices. In 1836 he raised and led a group of men into Texas to oppose Mexico. In 1846 he was appointed brigadier general in the U.S. Army. Serving under General Taylor, Quitman fought at Monterrey (September 1846). He was among those transferred to Scott's army in early 1847. He served at the seize of Vera Cruz (March 1847), the expedition against Alvarado (April 1847), and the capture of Puebla (May 15, 1847). He took part in the assault on Mexico City (September 1848) and Scott appointed him governor of that city. Returning to the United States, he was elected governor of Mississippi and nominated for the vice presidency on a losing ticket. While governor, the U.S. government charged him with complicity in the illegal López filibustering expedition but he was acquitted. Between 1854 and 1858 he served in the U.S. Congress.

16. Rauch, *American Interests*, 123–24.

17. Quisenberry, *Lopez's Expeditions*, 33–34; Rauch, *American Interests*, 125–27; Long, *Gold Braid*, 117.

18. Quisenberry, *Lopez's Expeditions*, 50–51; Rauch, *American Interests*, 128; Roche, *By-Ways*, 23–24; Long, *Gold Braid*, 117.

19. Quisenberry, *Lopez's Expeditions*, 52.

20. ibid., 54–64; Roche, *By-Ways*, 24–27; Philip S. Foner, *A History of Cuba and Its Relations with the United States*, 2 vols. (New York: International Publishers, 1962–63), 2: 53; Rauch, *American Interests*, 128–29.

21. Daniel Barringer to Daniel Webster, October 3, 1850, Dispatches to American Ministers to Spain, Department of State Correspondence, National Archives.

22. Rauch, *American Interests*, 151.

23. Opatrny, *U.S. Expansionism*, 197–98; Quisenberry, *Lopez's Expeditions*, 70–71, 80; Rauch, *American Interests*, 155–57.

24. Quisenberry, *Lopez's Expeditions*, 76–77.

25. ibid., 79–81.

26. ibid., 76–85; Rauch, *American Interests*, 157–60; Opatrny, *U.S. Expansionism*, 198–200; Roche, *By-Ways*, 27–28; Fermoselle, *The Evolution*, 52.

27. Quisenberry, *Lopez's Expeditions*, 100; Rauch, *American Interests*, 160–61; Long, *Gold Braid*, 119; *Los primeros movimientos revolucionarios del general Narciso López 1848–50*

(Havana: Oficina del Historiador de la Ciudad de la Habana, 1950), 188; Julio Morales Coello, *La importancia del poder naval positivo y negativo — en el desarrollo y en la independencia de Cuba* (La Habana: Academia de la Historia de Cuba, 1950), 40.

28. Rauch, *American Interests*, 161.

29. Franklin, *Cuba*, 5.

CHAPTER TWENTY

1. William Walker (1824–60) was a native of Tennessee and a graduate of the University of Nashville at the age of fifteen. A small, slight man, Walker at various times was a medical doctor, a law student, and a filibuster.

2. William Walker, *The War in Nicaragua* (Tucson: The University of Arizona Press, 1985), 25.

3. Munro, *The Five Republics*, 75. As early as 1850 Vanderbilt attempted to secure support from British capitalists for the construction of a canal through Nicaragua. The project was eventually scrapped.

4. William Oscar Scroggs, "William Walker and the Steamship Corporation in Nicaragua," *The American Historical Review* 10: 4; 792–811 (July 1905), 793; Eduard S. Wallace, *Destiny and Glory* (New York: Coward-McCann, 1957), 159–60.

5. Laurence Greene, *The Filibuster* (New York: Bobbs-Merrill, 1937), 58–59; Wallace, *Destiny*, 161.

6. Greene, *The Filibuster*, 59.

7. Scroggs, "William Walker," 794–95; Greene, *The Filibuster* 49; Wallace, *Destiny* 163; William V. Wells, *Walker's Expedition to Nicaragua* (New York: Stringer and Townsend, 1856), 41–43; Walker, *The War*, 24–25, 30.

8. Roche, *By-ways*, 75–76.

9. ibid., 71, 89–91.

10. Roche, *By-ways*, 73–74; Albert Z. Carr, *The World and William Walker* (New York: Harper & Row, 1963), 122.

11. Roche, *By-ways*, 76–77; Wallace, *Destiny*, 167.

12. Santos Guardiola (1812–62), a Honduran Conservative, was of Indian-African heritage. His opponents nicknamed him "the tiger of Honduras" and "the butcher."

13. Roche, *By-ways*, 79–80.

14. Wallace, *Destiny*, 168–69; Roche, *By-ways*, 80–81.

15. Walker, *The War*, 88.

16. Roche, *By-ways*, 81–82; Wallace, *Destiny*, 169–70.

17. Walker, *The War*, 127; Scroggs, "William Walker," 795–96; Wallace, *Destiny*, 172.

18. Munro, *The Five Republics*, 81; Roche, *By-ways*, 84–86; Wallace, *Destiny*, 171–72.

19. Wallace, *Destiny*, 176–77.

20. Wells, *Walker's Expedition*, 77–82; Walker, *The War*, 125–34; Munro, *The Five Republics*, 82; Roche, *By-ways*, 87–88.

21. Wallace, *Destiny*, 179–80; Roche, *By-ways*, 89–90.

22. Walker, *The War*, 127–28; Scroggs, *Filibusters*, 125; Wallace, *Destiny*, 180–81; Marley, *Wars*, 522.

23. Fermoselle, *The Evolution*, 54–55.

24. Wallace, *Destiny*, 187–88.

25. Walker, *The War*, 152–55; Wells, *Walker's Expedition*, 203–22; Scroggs, "William Walker," 802–3; Long, *Gold Braid*, 130.

26. Vanderbilt's fury was captured in a note he sent to Morgan and Garrison. "Gentlemen: You have undertaken to cheat me. I won't sue you, for the law is too slow. I'll ruin you." Long, *Gold Braid*, 129; Scroggs, "William Walker," 804.

27. Richardson, *A Compilation*, 10: 388.

28. Criminal charges were pending against French and the New York district attorney issued a warrant for his arrest.

29. Roche, *By-ways*, 98, 103. Costa Rica did not agree to the terms so the arms were never delivered. Williams, *Anglo-American Isthmian Diplomacy*, 211; Becerra, *Evolucíon histórica*, 118–19.

30. U.S. Senate, Executive Document 68, 34th Congress, 1st Session, 6, 57, 74, 131; Williams, *Anglo-American Isthmian Diplomacy*, 212–13.

31. Manuel Medina Castro, *Estados Unidos y America Latina, siglo XIX*, 2d ed. (Guayaquil: Lit. e imp. de la Universidad de Guayaquil, 1987), 348; Ricardo Fernández Guardia, *Cartilla histórica de Costa Rica*, 7th ed. (San José: Librería e Imprenta Lehmann, 1933), 99.

32. Five forty-man companies were organized by origin. A French company was led by Captain [first name unknown] Legaye, a German by [first name unknown] Prange, a New Orleans by [first name unknown] Thorpe, a New York by [first name unknown] Creighton, and a California by Rudler. Walker chose Schlesinger to lead the expedition because he was the only officer who spoke all of the languages. Wallace, *Destiny* 193.

33. Those executed following the Battle of Santa Rosa reveal the international composition of Walker's following: six from the United States, three from Ireland, three from Germany, one from Italy, one from Corfu, one from Samos, one from France, two from Prussia, and one from Panama. Schlesinger was court-martialed for cowardice and sentenced to death. He escaped that fate by breaking parole. Roche, *By-ways*, 100–1; Fernández, *Cartilla histórica*, 88.

34. Fernández, *Cartilla histórica*, 89–90.

35. ibid., 90.

36. Scroggs, *Filibusters*, 214.

37. Charles Frederick Henningsen won notoriety while fighting with the Carlists in Spain and in Russian and Hungarian Revolutionaries.

38. Wallace, *Destiny*, 207–8; Fernández, *Cartilla histórica*, 91.

39. Fernández, *Cartilla histórica*, 93; Wallace, *Destiny*, 215.

40. Callender Irvine Fayssoux served on board the *Pampero* and *Creole* during the López expeditions to Cuba.

41. Wallace, *Destiny*, 214–15; Fernández, *Cartilla histórica*, 93.

42. Charles William Doubleday, *Reminiscences of the "Filibuster" War in Nicaragua* (New York: G. P. Putnam's Sons, 1886), 173; Fernández, *Cartilla histórica*, 93; Scroggs, "William Walker," 806; Marley, *Wars*, 523.

43. Wallace, *Destiny*, 216–18.

44. ibid., 218–26.

45. ibid., 226–29; Fernández, *Cartilla histórica*, 94.

46. Fernández, *Cartilla histórica*, 94; Wallace, *Destiny*, 230–31.

47. Scroggs, *Filibusters*, 300; Scroggs, "William Walker," 807; Wallace, *Destiny*, 237.

48. Fernández, *Cartilla histórica*, 95; Long, *Gold Braid*, 132; Wallace, *Destiny*, 237; Marley, *Wars*, 523.

49. The disagreement was mediated by El Salvador and the respective presidents signed a treaty delineating the boundary on April 15, 1858, which was later ratified by the legislative bodies in both countries. Fernández, *Cartilla histórica*, 97; Munro, *The Five Republics*, 86.

50. Scroggs, "William Walker," 808; Marley, *Wars*, 523.

51. Richardson, *Messages*, 5: 466; Long, *Gold Braid*, 133–34; Marley, *Wars*, 523.

52. Long, *Gold Braid*, 135–36; Fernández, *Cartilla histórica*, 96.

53. Scroggs, "William Walker," 810–11.

54. Stout, *Nicaragua*, 209–10; Scroggs, *Filibusters*, 305; Scroggs, "William Walker," 808; Davis, *The Americas*, 467.

CHAPTER TWENTY-ONE

1. Halperín, *The Contemporary History*, 105.

2. A term used throughout South America, *Godos* or Goths were those individuals who did not actively serve the cause for independence.

3. James Ferguson, *Venezuela in Focus* (London: Latin American Bureau, 1994), 7–9.

4. Gilmore, *Caudillism*, 163–64; Akers, *A History*, 700; Chapman, *Republican Hispanic America*, 289.

5. Pedro Arturo Omaña, *Historia de la artilleria* (Caracas: Congreso de la República, 1978), 192–94; Martín García Villasmíl, *Escuelas para la formación de oficiales del ejército (1810–1964)* (Caracas: Ministerio de la Defensa, 1964), 38–52.

6. Arraíz, *Los días*, 146; Guillermo García Ponce, *Las armas en la guerra federal* (Caracas: Ediciones Muralla, 1968), 14–15; Akers, *A History*, 684.

7. Arraíz, *Los días*, 155–59; García Ponce, *Las armas*, 32–35; Omaña, *Historia*, 194–95.

8. See volume 6, *Presidencia de la Republica, Las fuerzas armadas de Venezuela en el siglo XIX*, 10 vols. (Caracas: Las Prensas Venezolanas de Edoroial Artes, 1963–67).

9. Vargas, *Historia naval*, 4: 55–85; Francisco Alejandro Vargas, *Síntesis histórica de la marina venezolana* (Caracas: Imprenta Naval, 1975), 9–10; Hadélis S. Jiménez L., "La artillería naval en Venezuela (1830–1945)," *Revista de la Armada*, 21: 68–81 (July 24, 1990), 71. In 1811 a naval school had been established but was closed during the War for Independence.

10. Vargas, *Historia naval*, 4: 82; "Unidad táctica de combate 'mariscal Antonio José Sucre,'" *Revista de la Armada* 33: 43–44 (July 24, 1994), 43.

11. Pedro Manuel Arcaya, *The Gómez Régime in Venezuela and Its Background* (Washington: The Sun Press, 1936), 103; Angel Ziems, *El Gomecismo y la formación del ejército nacional* (Caracas: Editorial Ateneo, 1979), 57.

12. Gene E. Bigler, "The Armed Forces and Patterns of Civil-Military Relations," in *Venezuela: The Democratic Experience*, ed. by John D. Martz and David J. Myers (New York: Praeger Publishers, 1977), 114.

13. José Tadeo Monagas (1784–1868), born in Maturín in eastern Venezuela, was of Spanish and *mulatto* descent. He was a fierce fighter, renowned with the machette, and an excellent horseman. He entered the War for Independence in 1813 as a landless second lieutenant and emerged in 1822 as the Civil and Military Governor of Barcelona and Commander of the Orinoco Department as well as one of the nation's richest landholders. R. B. Cunninghame Graham, *José Antonio Páez* (New York: Cooper Square Publishers, 1970), 269.

14. José Gregorio Monagas (1795–1858) was born in the city of Aragua de Barcelona in eastern Venezuela. He fought against Boves, Morales, and Morillo. In 1824 Gregorio

commanded Colombian auxiliaries who were sent to Peru to reinforce Simón Bolívar. By the end of the war Gregorio had reached the rank of general of a brigade.

15. Arraíz, *Los días*, 41; José Antonio Páez, *Autobiografía del general José Antonio Páez*, 2 vols. (Caracas: Academia Nacional de la Historia, 1987), 2: 133–34.

16. Santiago Mariño (1788–1854), a *criollo*, was born in eastern Venezuela. He fought as a Royalist until July 1812 when he changed sides. He frequently attempted to assert his independence from Simón Bolívar but never broke with "The Liberator." Mariño was Bolívar's chief of staff at the Battle of Carabobo and his Vice President of Gran Colombia.

17. Páez, *Autobiografía*, 2: 142.

18. Arraíz, *Los días*, 41–42; Páez, *Autobiografía*, 2: 143–51.

19. Carlos Soublette (1789–1870) was born in La Guaira. He joined the revolutionary army in 1811 and fought in many major engagements. By 1817 he had risen to become Bolívar's chief of staff. In 1821 Bolívar appointed Soublette as Gran Colombia's Secretary of War and Marine. In 1834 Páez appointed him Venezuela's Secretary of War and Marine.

20. Pedro Carujo (1801–35), born in Barcelona in eastern Venezuela, was the son of a Spanish official and a Venezuelan mother. He joined the revolutionary army in 1818. Carujo was convicted of participating in the assassination attempt against Simón Bolívar on September 25, 1828, and condemned to death by a court-marital. He escaped, was recaptured, and jailed in a fortification in Puerto Cabello. There, Carujo launched an aggressive writing campaign professing his innocence. In June 1830 he was liberated and expelled to Curaçao. Carujo returned to Maracaibo under an amnesty. In 1831 he organized a force of 1,000 men, rebelled, was defeated, and pardoned. He was retired from the army in 1831. Four years later he joined the Reformers and plotted against President Vargas.

21. Arraíz, *Los días*, 32, 42–43; Páez, *Autobiografía*, 2: 219–22; Vargas, *Historia naval*, 4: 102–4.

22. Jane Lucas De Grummond, *Renato Beluche Smuggler, Privateer and Patriot 1780–1860* (Baton Rouge: Louisiana State University Press, 1983), 261–63.

23. Páez, *Autobiografía*, 2: 219–22, 241–54; Arraíz, *Los días*, 42–43; Vargas, *Historia naval*, 4: 95–97; De Grummond, *Renato Beluche*, 264–65.

24. Vargas, *Historia naval*, 4: 93–98; Páez, *Autobiografía*, 2: 251.

25. Nicolás Joly (unk–1848) was born in France and began his naval career in the French navy. Next, he served in the Mexican navy under Commodore Luís Aury where he advanced to the rank of captain. In 1818 he joined the revolutionary navy of Venezuela. He married the sister of Gen. Juan Bautista Arismendi. In 1832 Joly was appointed Commander of the Puerto Cabello Naval Station, Venezuela's principal naval base.

26. Renato Beluche (1770–1860) was born in the colony of Louisiana. He began his naval career with the privateer Jean Laffite. In January 1815 he participated in the defense of New Orleans against the British. In 1816 he traveled to Haiti where he volunteered to serve at the orders of Simón Bolívar. Beluche was incorporated into the revolutionary navy with the rank of commander. In 1828 Beluche commanded the two-ship squadron sent from the Caribbean around Cape Horn to fight against Peru; the war ended before the ships arrived off Peru. In 1835 Beluche supported the Reformers and after their defeat was expelled from Venezuela. In 1845 his rank, titles, and decorations were reinstated.

27. Arraíz, *Los días*, 43; Vargas, *Historia naval*, 4: 99, 101–5; Páez, *Autobiografía*, 2: 256–58; De Grummond, *Renato Beluche*, 266–67; Francisco Alejandro Vargas, *Calendario historico naval de Venezuela* (Caracas: Comandancia de la Armada, n.d.), 349. Among those

who surrendered were Commanders Joseph C. Swain and John Clark. They had been among the ten North American officers who sailed the corvette *Bolívar* (ex-*Hercules*) to Venezuela in 1822. They were incorporated into the revolutionary navy as lieutenants. In 1837 they plotted to return to Venezuela as members of an expedition which General Mariño was organizing in Santo Domingo. When this failed, they traveled to Baltimore. In 1845 the Venezuelan government reinstated their ranks and decorations and permitted them to return. Apparently only Clark did so. He died at La Guaira in 1847.

28. These included General Mariño, Gen. Justo Briceno, Col. Francisco María Farías, and naval Commanders Domingo Roman, Joseph Swain, and John Clark.

29. Tomás Pérez Tenreiro, Lo*s presidentes de Venezuela y su actuación militar* (Caracas: Academia Nacional de la Historia, 1981), 199–200; Omaña, *Historia*, 94; Vargas, *Historia naval*, 4: 108.

30. Ziems, *El Gomecismo*, 58; Gilmore, *Caudillism*, 138–41.

31. Gilmore, *Caudillism*, 70–71, 141–42; Morón, *A History*, 154.

32. Arraíz, *Los días*, 35; Arcaya, *The Gómez Régime*, 35; Kirkpatrick, *Latin America*, 275–76; Thomas Rourke, *Gómez: Tyrant of the Andes* (New York: Greenwood Press, 1969), 23.

33. Ezequiel Zamora (1817–59) was born in Cúa to the south of Caracas. By 1846 he was a Liberal leader and lost an unfair election for the state assembly. On September 29, 1846, Zamora was defeated at Lagua de Piedra. He was captured near Villa de Cura on March 27, 1847, and sentenced to death. When the Monagas government came to power, Zamora was freed and incorporated into the army. Following the fall of Monagas in 1858, Zamora and numerous other Liberal *caudillos* were expelled from Venezuela.

34. Manning, *Dipl. Corres. of the U.S. Inter-Amer.*, 12: 555–61; Francis James Dallett, "The Creation of the Venezuelan Naval Squadron 1848–1860," *The American Neptune* 30: 4, 260–78 (October 1970), 262–63; Arraíz, *Los días*, 49–50.

35. Dallett, "The Creation," 264–66; Vargas, *Síntesis histórica*, 11; José Antonio Páez, *Autobiografía*, 2 vols. (Caracas: Ministerio de Educación Nacional), 2: 417–37.

36. Dallett, "The Creation," 267–68; Páez, *Autobiografía*, 420–37; Arraíz, *Los días*, 50.

37. Dallett, "The Creation," 269–70; Vargas, *Síntesis histórica*, 12–13; Páez, *Autobiografía*, 443–44.

38. Vargas, *Síntesis histórica*, 14; Dallett, "The Creation," 270–71; Arraíz, *Los días*, 50–51; Páez, *Autobiografía*, 448–51.

39. Arraíz, *Los días*, 51–52; Graham, *José Antonio Páez*, 290–92; Páez, *Autobiografía*, 2: 488.

40. Arraíz, *Los días*, 52–53.

41. The Constitution of 1830 permitted a four-year presidential term without the possibility for consecutive terms. The Monagas-sponsored constitution allowed for six-year terms and reelection. David R. Moore, *A History of Latin America* (New York: Prentice-Hall, 1947), 373–74.

42. Arraíz, *Los días*, 56–57; Guillermo Morón, *Breve historia contemporánea de Venezuela* (Mexico: Fondo de Cultura Económica, 1994), 210; Arcaya, *The Gómez Régime*, 38.

43. Juan Crisóstomo Falcón (1820–70) was born in the state of Coro (later renamed Falcón) into a wealthy, landholding family. He was influenced by the writings of Victor Hugo and Alphonse Lamartine. He possessed no formal military training but was a natural leader.

44. Jacinto Pérez Arcay, *La guerra federal*, 7th ed. (Caracas: Ministerio de la Defensa, 1989), 98–101.

45. Pérez, *La guerra federal*, 105–9; Arraíz, *Los días*, 65.

46. Pérez, *La guerra federal*, 112–18; Morón, *Breve historia*, 212; Arraíz, *Los días*, 66.

47. Arraíz, *Los días*, 68–69; Pérez, *La guerra federal*, 125–38; Morón, *Breve historia*, 212–13; Vargas, *Calendario*, 16.

48. Morón, *Breve historia*, 213; Pérez, *La guerra federal*, 140–42; Kirkpatrick, *Latin America*, 276–77; Arraíz, *Los días*, 70.

49. Morón, *Breve historia*, 211; Pérez, *La guerra federal*, 143–44; Rourke, *Gómez*, 25.

50. Morón, *Breve historia*, 213.

51. Antonio Guzmán Blanco (1829–99), born in Caracas, received a good education. At the age of eighteen, he followed his father, Antonio Leocadio Guzmán, into exile. When José Tadeo Monagas came to power in 1847, Guzmán's father, Antonio Leocadio Guzmán, returned to Venezuela and held important positions within the government. Antonio, the son, lost favor in 1858 when the Monagas family was overthrown. Antonio, along with other Liberals including his father, was exiled to St. Thomas. In 1859 Antonio joined the Liberal faction led by fellow exile Gen. Juan C. Falcón. Antonio was given the rank of lieutenant colonel and made the Auditor General of the Federal army. Along with other rebels, he landed at Palma Sola in July 1859 and fought at a number of the major battles. In May 1863 he was promoted to General in Chief, the highest rank possible. President Falcón made Guzmán Blanco vice president. He was widely known for his vanity and endowed himself with titles such as "The Illustrious American." During his rule he erected numerous statues of himself only to have them come crashing down when he was deposed.

52. Arraíz, *Los días*, 88–89; Morón, *Breve historia*, 213.

53. Arraíz, *Los días*, 90–91; Morón, *Breve historia*, 211–13; Pérez, *La guerra federal*, 147–49.

54. Arcaya, *The Gómez Régime*, 46–49; Arraíz, *Los días*, 100–1.

55. Robertson, *The History*, 411; Morón, *A History of Venezuela*, 174; *The American Annual Cyclopaedia . . . 1865*, 812; Rourke, *Gómez*, 25.

56. Arcaya, *The Gómez Régime*, 54–55; Arraíz, *Los días*, 101; Morón, *Breve historia*, 214–15; Rourke, *Gómez*, 25.

57. Morón, *Breve historia*, 216–17; Arraíz, *Los días*, 112–13.

58. Rourke, *Gómez*, 27; Arcaya, *The Gómez Régime*, 55; Vargas, *Calendario*, 10, 31.

59. Arraíz, *Los días*, 115–21; Arcaya, *The Gómez Régime*, 61; Vargas, *Síntesis histórica*, 19–20; Vargas, *Calendario*, 21, 336.

60. Joaquín Crespo (1841–98) was the son of a farmer of the *llanos*. He started fighting for the Federal cause at an early age. By 1870 he commanded a large following due to his bravery on the battlefield.

61. Rourke, *Gómez*, 29–30; Arcaya, *The Gómez Régime*, 84–85; Robertson, *The History*, 412–15; J. Fred Rippy, "Dictators of Venezuela," in *South American Dictators*, ed. by A. Curtis Wilgus (Washington: George Washington University Press, 1937), 403; Chapman, *Republican Hispanic America*, 292–93.

62. Arraíz, *Los días*, 124–25; Morón, *Breve historia*, 217; Rourke, *Gómez*, 30, 50, 53; Arcaya, *The Gómez Régime*, 92–93.

63. José Manuel Hernández (1853–1919) born in Caracas, Hernández was a perpetual rebel during his early years. Severely wounded in 1870, he acquired the nickname of "the Maimed."

64. Rourke, *Gómez*, 59–60; Arcaya, *The Gómez Régime*, 101–4.

65. Cipriano Castro (1858–1924), born in Capacho in the Andean highlands of the state of Táchira, received little formal education. In 1892 he supported President Raimundo Andueza Palacio. When he was driven from power, Castro was forced to flee to Colombia. He was vain, notoriously unfaithful to his wife, and an extravagant spender. According to Rourke, "His debaucheries during his time as president were so continuous and so spectacular that they became the most notable part of his whole career and are about the only things the old-timers remember about the man." Rourke, *Gómez*, 86–87.

66. Eleazar López Contreras, *Paginas para la historia militar de Venezuela* (Caracas: Tipografía Americana, 1944), 4–7; Rourke, *Gómez*, 65–66.

67. Rourke, *Gómez*, 67–69; Arraíz, *Los días*, 126; López, *Paginas*, 11–13.

68. Rourke, *Gómez*, 70–71; Arraíz, *Los días*, 126; López, *Paginas*, 13–28.

69. Rourke, *Gómez*, 76–77; Arraíz, *Los días*, 126; López, *Paginas*, 28–33.

70. Juan Vicente Gómez (ca. 1857–1935) was born on July 24 (Simón Bolívar's birthday) in "La Mulera," a *hacienda*, in the state of Táchira in the Andean highlands near the Colombian border. His mother was an Indian and his father an educated *criollo*. He had little or no formal education and probably had not traveled more than a few miles from his home during his first forty-two years. For thirty-five years Gómez remained distant from politics. In 1892 he sided with President Raimundo Andueza Palacio, serving as a quartermaster. When Palacio was driven from office, Gómez fled to Colombia and returned when Cipriano Castro, also an exile, invaded Venezuela. Castro gave Gómez increasing responsibilities. He died on December 17 (the anniversary of Simón Bolívar's death).

71. Rourke, *Gómez*, 77–79; Arraíz, *Los días*, 126–27; López, *Paginas*, 33–34.

72. Rourke, *Gómez*, 91; Morón, *Breve historia*, 220–21; Arcaya, *The Gómez Régime*, 104.

73. "Dictators of Venezuela," 410–11; Robertson, *The History*, 416–17.

74. Carlos Alarico Gómez, *La amarga experiencia (El Bloqueo de 1902)* (Caracas: Ministerio de Educación, 1983), 146–48.

75. Robertson, *The History*, 419; Akers, *A History*, 696–97; Gómez, *La amarga experiencia*, 148–49; Vargas, *Calendario*, 367.

76. Rourke, *Gómez*, 93.

77. ibid., 94.

78. ibid., 94–95.

79. Arcaya, *The Gómez Régime*, 110–11; Rourke, *Gómez*, 95–96; Ziems, *El Gomecismo*, 59–60.

80. Rourke, *Gómez*, 96–97.

81. ibid., 97–98.

82. ibid., 98–99.

83. Arraíz, *Los días*, 130–31; Ziems, *El Gomecismo*, 66–67; Rourke, *Gómez*, 99; Arcaya, *The Gómez Régime*, 104–5.

84. Rourke, *Gómez*, 99–100.

85. ibid., 101–2; Arraíz, *Los días*, 131; López, *Paginas*, 60–61.

86. Rourke, *Gómez*, 102–4; Arraíz, *Los días*, 131–32; López, *Paginas*, 65–67.

87. Rourke, *Gómez*, 105–7; Arraíz, *Los días*, 132.

88. Ziems, *El Gomecismo*, 65; Rourke, *Gómez*, 85–86.

89. Rippy, "Dictators of Venezuela," 415.

90. Ziems, *El Gomecismo*, 68–69; Bigler, "The Armed Forces," 115.

91. Bigler, "The Armed Forces," 115; Arcaya, *The Gómez Régime*, 118.

92. Arraíz, *Los días*, 32; Chapman, *Republican Hispanic America*, 290.

93. Fritz Epstein, "European Military Influence in Latin America," 44. This incomplete manuscript found in the Library of Congress, Washington, D.C., lacks its source notes.

94. Arraíz, *Los días*, 179.

95. Ziems, *El Gomecismo*, 73–246; Halperin, *The Contemporary History*, 140–41.

96. Gilmore, *Caudillism*, 147–48; Rippy, "The Dictators of Venezuela," 393–94; Akers, *A History*, 684.

97. Akers, *A History*, 684.

98. Arraíz, *Los días*, 94, 146; Gilmore, *Caudillism*, 83–84; Howard I. Blutstein et al., *Area Handbook for Venezuela* (Washington: U.S. Government Printing Office, 1977), 35.

CHAPTER TWENTY-TWO

1. Chapman, *Republican Hispanic America*, 246; Kirkpatrick, *Latin America*, 364.

2. Bancroft, *History of Central America*, 3: 186–90, 208–11; Robertson, *History*, 448; Chapman, *Republican Hispanic America*, 245; Munro, *Latin American Republics*, 408.

3. Kirkpatrick, *Latin America*, 364.

4. Davis, *History of Latin America*, 557; Munro, *Latin American Republics*, 416.

5. Lester D. Langley and Thomas Schoonover, *The Banana Men: American Mercenaries & Entrepreneurs in Central America, 1880–1930* (Lexington: University of Kentucky Press, 1995), 65–66.

6. Langley and Schoonover, *The Banana Men*, 63; *Historia de El Salvador*, 2 vols. (San Salvador: Ministro de Educación, 1994), 2: 204.

In 1833, Aquino, a peasant on a Salvadorian indigo plantation, led an unsuccessful uprising against impressment into the army. Typically, the *compesinos* did not resist impressment given the harsh consequence of doing so. Richard A. Haggerty, editor, *El Salvador: A Country Study*, 2d ed. (Washington: Headquarters, Department of the Army, 1990), 11.

7. Russell Fitzgibbon, *Latin America* (New York: Appleton-Century-Crofts, 1971), 120.

Nation	Population	Date
Costa Rica	80,000	1844
	243,205	1892
El Salvador	434,520	1870
	777,895	1891
Guatemala	1,180,000	1865
	1,471,025	1892
Honduras	350,000	1850s
	431,917	1889
Nicaragua	350,000	1873
	312,845	1888

See *Hand Book of the American Republics 1893* (Washington: Bureau of the Americas, n.d.), 114, 135, 158, 183, 216; Fitzgibbon, *Latin America*, 120; Davis, *History of Latin America*, 556; Tim L. Merrill, editor, *Honduras: A Country Study*, 3d ed. (Washington: Headquarters, Department of the Army, 1993), 17; *The Statesman's Year-Book 1873*, 528, 545, 559.

8. Bancroft, *History of Central America*, 3: 266, 645–49; Bailey and Nasatir, *Latin America*, 472; Munro, *The Latin American Republics*, 409.

9. Bancroft, *History of Central America*, 3: 191–93; Gregorio Bustamante Maceo, *Historia militar de El Salvador*, 2d ed. (San Salvador: Imprenta Nacional, 1951), 42.

10. Bancroft, *History of Central America*, 3: 193–200; Bustamante, *Historia militar*, 42–43; *Historia de El Salvador*, 2: 209–10; José D. Gamez, *Historia de Nicaragua* (Managua: Tipografía El País, 1889), 513–16.

11. Bancroft, *History of Central America*, 3: 200–6, 294; Bustamante, *Historia militar*, 43–44; A. Curtis Wilgus, *The Development of Hispanic America* (New York: Farrar & Rinehart, 1941), 559.

12. Merrill, *Honduras*, 15; Thomas, *Latin America*, 608; Davis, *The Americas*, 467.

13. Bancroft, *History of Central America*, 3: 279–80; Bustamante, *Historia militar*, 44–45; *Historia de El Salvador*, 2: 211.

14. Bancroft, *History of Central America*, 3: 256.

15. Becerra, *Evolución histórica*, 118.

16. Bancroft, *History of Central America*, 3: 280–81, 299, 322–23; Becerra, *Evolución histórica*, 118; Merrill, *Honduras*, 15; Keen, *A History of Latin America*, 441.

17. Gerardo Barrios (1813–65) was born in the department of San Miguel, El Salvador, into a wealthy family. He joined the military at the age of fifteen. During the Wars for Central American Union, he fought at the Battles of San Miguelito (February 5, 1829), Mixco (February 15, 1829), Espiritu Santo (April 6, 1839), and Perulapan (September 25, 1839). He fought against William Walker during the mid-1850s. Barrios served as the Salvadorian president between 1858 and 1863. In 1863 Barrios was captured by Carrera, imprisoned, and executed in 1865.

18. Bustamante, *Historia militar*, 52–57.

19. ibid., 58.

20. ibid., 58–66; Bancroft, *History of Central America*, 3: 324–25; Wilgus, *The Development of Hispanic America*, 560.

21. Bancroft, *History of Central America*, 3: 395–97, 456; Bustamante, *Historia militar*, 69–70; Robertson, *History*, 452.

22. Justo Rufino Barrios (1835–85) was born in San Lorenzo, Guatemala, into a prominent ranching family. In 1867 Barrios joined the Liberal revolt against President Vincente Cerna. Following a failed attack on the San Marcos barracks, he fled to Chiapas, Mexico. On June 29, 1871, Barrios routed Cerna's army at the Battle of San Lucas Sacatepéquez outside Guatemala City. In 1873 Barrios was elected president, a position he retained until killed in battle.

23. Herring, *A History*, 438; Rippy, *Latin America*, 224–25.

24. Bustamante, *Historia militar*, 70.

25. Bancroft, *History of Central America*, 3: 398–99, 460–61; Bustamante, *Historia militar*, 70–71; Manuel Zea Carrascosa, *Semblanzas ministros de la guerra y de la defensa nacional de Guatemala* (n.p.: Ministerio de la Defensa Nacional, 1971), 116–17.

26. Seven years later, in 1883, President Soto fell into disfavor with Guatemalan President Barrios and through intimidation he was forced to resign. Bancroft, *History of Central America*, 3: 402, 435–36, 462–63; Merrill, *Honduras*, 16–17; Munro, *The Latin American Republics*, 414; Rippy, *Latin America*, 225.

27. Bustamante, *Historia militar*, 72–76; Bancroft, *History of Central America*, 3: 394–95, 435–36; Rippy, *Latin America*, 225; Fernández, *Cartilla histórica*, 104.

28. Tomás Guardia Gutíerrez (1831–82) was born in Bagaces, Costa Rica, into an important ranching family. In the mid-1850s he distinguished himself during the National War against William Walker. On April 27, 1870, Colonel Guardia and fifteen others seized control of the artillery barracks in San José. This led to a successful *coup d'etat* against Jesus Jiminez. He was a Liberal president between 1870–72, 1872–76, and 1877–82.

29. Fernández, *Cartilla histórica*, 105.

30. Bustamante, *Historia militar*, 76–81; Bancroft, *History of Central America*, 3: 386–87, 390–91, 410–11, 459, 486; Merrill, *Honduras,* 17; Rippy, *Latin America*, 225; Robertson, *History*, 455, 457.

31. Patrick H. Roth, *On Watch Off Central America: The Navy and the Guatemala-Salvador War of 1890* (Burke, Va.: Privately Printed, 1995), 1–6.

32. Bustamante, *Historia militar*, 85–87.

33. Becerra, *Evolución histórica*, 133–34.

34. José Santos Zelaya (1853–1919) was President of Nicaragua between 1893 and 1909. He promoted many civic improvements but was also known for his corruption and brutality toward his enemies. Zelaya resigned in large measure due to the intrigues of the United States.

35. Merrill, *Honduras* 17–18; Benjamin Keen, *A History of Latin America*, 4th ed. (Boston: Houghton Mifflin Company, 1992), 449; Rippy, *Latin America*, 227.

36. Becerra, *Evolución histórica*, 134–35.

37. Robertson, *History*, 458; Becerra, *Evolución histórica*, 135.

38. Becerra, *Evolución histórica*, 135.

39. Bustamante, *Historia militar*, 100–1; Langley and Schoonover, *The Banana Men*, 61–64; Stuart, *Latin America*, 306–7; Merrill, *Honduras*, 20.

40. Becerra, *Evolución histórica*, 136; Langley and Schoonover, *The Banana Men*, 64–65; Stuart, *Latin America*, 308–9; Merrill, *Honduras*, 20.

41. Langley and Schoonover, *The Banana Men*, 64–65.

42. Bustamante, *Historia militar*, 101–3; Langley and Schoonover, *The Banana Men*, 66–67; Becerra, *Evolución histórica*, 136.

43. Becerra, *Evolución histórica*, 136–37; Merrill, *Honduras*, 20–21; Langley and Schoonover, *The Banana Men*, 67.

44. Munro, *Latin American Republics*, 420–21.

45. Bailey and Nasatir, *Latin America*, 680; Chapman, *Republican Hispanic America*, 245–46.; Robertson, *History*, 462–63.

46. Becerra, *Evolución histórica*, 137, Munro, *Latin American Republics,* 421; Merrill, *Honduras*, 21.

47. Harold D. Nelson, ed., *Costa Rica A Country Study*, 2d ed. (Washington: Headquarters, Department of the Army, 1984), 32.

48. Lowell Gudmundson and Héctor Lindo-Fuentes, *Central America, 1821–1871 Liberalism before Liberal Reform* (Tuscaloosa: University of Alabama Press, 1995), 30–31.

CHAPTER TWENTY-THREE

1. Rippy, *Latin America*, 265.

2. Herbert S. Klein, *Bolivia: The Evolution of a Multi-Ethnic Society*, 2d ed. (Oxford: Oxford University Press, 1992), 121–22, 132; Valentin Abecia Baldivieso, *Breve historia de Bolivia* (Caracas: Academia Nacional de la Historia, 1985), 108; Chapman, *Republican Hispanic America*, 372; Robertson, *History of the Latin-American Nations*, 321.

3. Abecia, *Breve Historia*, 108; Munro, *The Latin American Republics*, 273.

4. Abecia, *Breve historia*, 124–25; Rex A. Hudson and Dennis M. Hanratty, eds., *Bolivia: A Country Study*, 3d ed. (Washington: Headquarters, Department of the Army, 1989), 19; Klein, *Bolivia*, 138; Cleven, "Dictators," 336.

5. Chapman, *Republican Hispanic America*, 376: Davis, *History of Latin America*, 519.

6. Klein, *Bolivia*, 121, 134.

7. W. L. Schurz, *Bolivia: A Commerical and Industrial Handbook* (Washington: Government Printing Office, 1921), 152.

8. José Ballivián (1805–52), born in La Paz into an upper-class family, joined the Spanish army at the age of twelve. Later, he switched sides to the revolutionary army. Ballivián was self-educated. He died of yellow fever in poverty while living in Rio de Janeiro.

9. Abecia, *Breve historia*, 127; López, *Almanaque*, 10, 14; Klein, *Bolivia*, 121; Harold Osborne, *Bolivia: A Land Divided* (London: Royal Institute of International Affairs, 1954), 55.

10. López, *Almanaque*, 40, 178.

11. Manuel Isidoro Belzú (1811–65), born into a poor family in La Paz, was educated by the Franciscans. In 1821 he ran away from the monastery and joined the Spanish army. He was called the "Bolivian Mohammed" because of his popularity with the masses.

12. René Canelas López, *Teoría del motín y las sediciones en Bolivia* (La Paz: Editorial Los Amigos del Libro, 1983), 52–54, 66; Vazquez et al., *Manual*, 334, 338.

13. Manning, *Dipl. Corres. of the U.S. Inter-Amer.*, 2: 14–15; Canelas, *Teoria del motín*, 57–61; Vazquez et al., *Manual*, 335.

14. Klein, *Bolivia*, 128–29; Munro, *The Latin American Republics*, 270; Donghi, *The Contemporary History*, 101; Kirkpatrick, *Latin America*, 202.

15. Canelas, *Teoria del motín*, 62–64. On April 16, 1849, Belzú had Col. Carlos Wincendon executed. Wincendon was a soldier of fortune, who received his training in the French army. He held a commission in the Ecuadorian army and was acting as General Ballivián's agent when arrested.

16. José María Linares (1808–61) was born in Tilcala into a wealthy family and was well educated. Once Linares returned to Bolivia he became involved in ceaseless plotting against Belzú. In June 1849 Linares financially supported the short-lived rebellion of the Littoral against Belzú. He spent the entire family's fortune seeking or holding the presidency, and died in poverty in Chile.

17. López, *Almanaque*, 124.

18. Vazquez et al., *Manual*, 342–43; Canelas, *Teoria del motín*, 70–72; López, *Almanaque*, 166, 173–74; Klein, *Bolivia*, 130.

19. Canelas, *Teoria del motín*, 73–74; López, *Almanaque*, 129.

20. Canelas, *Teoria del motín*, 74.

21. Mariano Melgarejo (1820–71), born in Tarata, Cochabamba, was a *cholo* and illegitimate. He ran away from home at the age of nine and soon entered the army as a soldier and rose through the ranks. Melgarejo fought at the battles of Montenegro (June 24, 1838) and Yungay (January 20, 1839), where he was captured. To escape from the prison, he set fire to the barracks to cause confusion. In a pyrrhic success, which enhanced his reputation as a man of daring, Melgarejo and a few survivors escaped. He fought at the Battle of Ingavi (August 14, 1841). Melgarejo rebelled against Belzú in December 1853, was captured on January 26, 1854, condemned to death, and pardoned. He possessed no formal education. Melgarejo was a murderous sot but extraordinarily strong and brave. He taught his horse to drink beer, had his soldiers march through second-story windows, and celebrated his birthday during Holy Week. Melgarejo was killed near Lima, Peru, by his son-in-law and the brother of his favorite mistress.

22. Canelas, *Teoria del motín*, 74–78; López, *Almanaque*, 155, 199–200.

23. Manning, *Dipl. Corres. of the U.S. Inter-Amer.*, 2: 90–91, 112–13; López, *Almanaque*, 167, 174, 195; Vazquez et al., *Manual*, 343; William Carter, *Bolivia: A Profile* (New York: Praeger, 1971), 43.

24. Canelas, *Teoria del motín*, 86–87; López, *Almanaque*, 171.

25. Canelas, *Teoria del motín*, 86–87; López, *Almanaque*, 167.

26. Vazquez et al., *Manual*, 343–44, 350; López, *Almanaque*, 17, 214–15; Robertson, *History of the Latin-American Nations*, 321–22; Donghi, *The Contemporary History*, 149.

27. Canelas, *Teoria del motín*, 96–97.

28. López, *Almanaque*, 171. Canelas states this often-cited quotation "is merely anecdotal." Regardless, it is in character for Melgarejo. Canelas, *Teoria del motín*, 98.

29. López, *Almanaque*, 171.

30. Canelas, *Teoria del motín*, 98–101.

31. Canelas, *Teoria del motín*, 102–4; López, *Almanaque*, 64, 238; Vazquez et al., *Manual*, 353; Robertson, *History of the Latin-American Nations*, 322.

32. Cleven, "Dictators," 341.

33. Charles Edward Chapman, "Melgarejo of Bolivia: An Illustration of Spanish-American Dictatorships," *Pacific Historical Review* 8: 1; 37–45 (March 1939), 38; López, *Almanaque*, 165; Canelas, *Teoria del motín*, 115; Cleven, "Dictators," 336–39.

34. Hilarión Daza (1840–94), born in Sucre, was the illegitimate son of an Italian acrobat. He joined the army as a soldier at an early age and was flogged numerous times for thievery. He rose to the rank of colonel under Melgarejo. In 1879 he concealed the news of war with Chile in order not to interrupt an ongoing party. Daza was a drunken reprobate and exhibited few morals. Following his overthrow he traveled to Europe where he lived extravagantly on money stolen from the Bolivian treasury. Daza returned to Bolivia in 1894 and was assassinated in Uyuni.

35. Canelas, *Teoria del motín*, 119–20; López, *Almanaque*, 228–29.

36. López, *Almanaque*, 18; Vazquez et al., *Manual*, 364, 377.

37. Vazquez et al., *Manual*, 378; López, *Almanaque*, 22, 156–57, 214, 216–17; Chapman, *Republican Hispanic America*, 375.

38. López, *Almanaque*, 20, 63, 235.

39. Vazquez et al., *Manual*, 375; López, *Almanaque*, 13, 36.

40. Canelas, *Teoria del motín*, 130–32; López, *Almanaque*, 89–90.

41. Abecia, *Breve historia*, 140; Vazquez et al., *Manual*, 384–85, 393; Robertson, *History of the Latin-American Nations*, 324–25; Klein, *Bolivia*, 147–48.

42. López, *Almanaque*, 187; Canelas, *Teoria del motín*, 140–41; Carlos D. Mesa Gisbert, *Presidentes de Bolivia: entre urnas y fusiles*, 2d ed. (La Paz: Editionial Gisbert y Cia., S.A., 1990), 442–45.

43. Canelas, *Teoria del motín*, 144–46.

44. José Manuel Pando (1848–1917), born in La Paz, initially studied medicine but then chose a military career. He briefly retired when Daza seized the government. Pando returned to military service, fought, and was wounded in the War of the Pacific. He was promoted to colonel in 1882. Pando founded the Republican Party. He was assassinated in 1917.

45. Hudson and Hanratty, *Bolivia*, 25.

46. Canelas, *Teoria del motín*, 147–49.

47. Canelas, *Teoria del motín*, 148–49; López, *Almanaque*, 25.

48. López, *Almanaque*, 45.

49. ibid., 49.
50. ibid., 62, 70–71; Canelas, *Teoria del motín*, 149.
51. López, *Almanaque*, 72–73; Canelas, *Teoria del motín*, 149–50; Vazquez et al., *Manual*, 401; Robertson, *History of the Latin-American Nations*, 328.
52. Canelas, *Teoria del motín*, 150; Hudson and Hanratty, *Bolivia*, 25; Klein, *Bolivia*, 136.
53. Chapman, *Republican Hispanic America*, 374.
54. Chapman, *Republican Hispanic America*, 375–77; Robertson, *History of the Latin-American Nations*, 322–23; Klein, *Bolivia*, 137–39; Carter, *Bolivia*, 45–46.

CHAPTER TWENTY-FOUR

1. Keen, *A History*, 498; P. L. Bell, *Colombia: A Commercial and Industrial Handbook* (Washington: Government Printing Office, 1921), 401.
2. José Manuel Restrepo, *Diario politico y militar: memorias*, 5 vols. (Bogotá: Imprenta Nacional, 1954–57), 2: 71.
3. Eduardo Caballero Calderón, *Historia privada de los colombianos* (Bogotá: Talleres Antares, 1960), 67.
Halperin writes, "Colombia had effectively exported much of its potentially troublesome officer corps to Ecuador, Peru, and Bolivia during the wars of independence." Halperin, *The Contemporary History*, 104.
4. In 1855 military pensions were abolished, and two years later the entire army totaled 109 officers and men! Typically, between 1858 and 1874 the army averaged 1,200 officers and men.
5. J. Fred Rippy, "The Dictators of Colombia," in *South American Dictators*, ed. by A. Curtis Wilgus (Washington: George Washington University Press, 1937), 367–69; *The Political and Socio-Economic Role of the Military in Latin America*, 5 vols. (Coral Gables: Center for Advanced International Studies, University of Miami, 1972), 2: E10; Fitzgibbon, *Latin America*, 365–66; Adrian English, *Armed Forces of Latin America* (London: Jane's, 1984), 167.
6. The Liberals were referred to as *Gólgotas* because of their frequent reference to Christ as the "Martyr of Golgotha."
7. Keen, *A History*, 500–1; Dennis M. Hanratty and Sandra W. Meditz, eds., 4th ed., *Colombia: A Country Study* (Washington: U.S. Government Printing Office, 1990), xxiii–xxiv, 193; Akers and Elliott, *A History of South America*, 652–53.
8. Guillermo Plazas Olarte, "El ejército y los conflictos del Siglo XIX," *Historia de las fuerzas militares de Colombia*, directed by Alvaro Valencia Tovar, 6 vols. (Bogotá: Planeta, 1993), 2: 218.
9. Francisco de Paula Santander (1792–1840) was born in Cúcuta, Nueva Granada, to a prominent family. He was sent to Bogotá to study law but soon joined the Revolutionary army in 1810. In 1813 when the Revolutionaries split between Centralists and Federalists, he fought as a Federalist against the Royalists in northeastern Nueva Granada. He was captured by the Royalists in January 1813 but exchanged. Santander served under Col. Simón Bolívar later that year. In 1819 he commanded Bolívar's vanguard which crossed the Andes and fought in the decisive battle of Boyacá (August 7, 1819), after which he was promoted to division general. In December 1819 Santander was elected vice president of Gran Colombia and governed in the absence of President Bolívar. Santander was accused of complicity in the failed September 1828 assassination plot against Bolívar. Santander was exiled between 1829 and 1832.

Returning to Colombia in 1832, he was elected president and served until 1837. A very able administrator, Santander was known as "the man of laws" (*el hombre de las leyes*).

10. Plazas, "El Ejército," 2: 156–57; William Marion Gibson, Th*e Constitutions of Colombia* (Durham: Duke University Press, 1948), 156; Herring, *A History of Latin America*, 478.

11. Those who led the rebellion anointed themselves *jefes supremos* (supreme chiefs).

12. José María Obando (1797–1861), born near Popayán, Nueva Granada, gained fame as a guerrilla, fighting for the Royalists. In February 1822 he changed sides, retaining his rank as lieutenant colonel. Obando was the most prominent *caudillo* in the province of Pasto. In June 1839 he unsuccessfully sought to command government forces sent to crush the rebellion in Pasto, forces he would soon oppose. Obando was the individual most commonly accused of Sucre's assassination.

13. Pedro Alcántara Herrán (1800–72) was born in Bogotá to a family of moderate wealth. He joined the Revolutionaries as a private in 1814. He was captured at the Battle of La Cuchilla del Tambo (June 29, 1816) and changed sides. Herrán served as a Royalist until 1820, at which time he again changed sides. As a Revolutionary, he fought at the Battles of Pichincha (May 24, 1822), Junín (August 6, 1824), and Ayacucho (December 9, 1824).

14. Gibson, *The Constitutions*, 155–57; Plazas, "El Ejército," 2: 159–60; Munro, *The Latin American Republics*, 299.

15. José Hilario López (1798–1869) was born in Popayán, Nueva Granada. He joined the Revolutionaries in 1812 and campaigned principally in the province of Pasto. López was captured at the Battle of La Cuchilla del Tambo (June 29, 1816). Condemned to death, he chose to serve in the Royal army. Following the Battle of Boyacá, López rejoined the Revolutionaries. López opposed Bolívar's dictatorship and defeated Col. Tomás Cipriano de Mosquera, winning control of Cauca. In 1830 he was promoted to general.

16. Plazas, "El Ejército," 2: 163–64; Halperin, *The Contemporary History*, 144; Gibson, *The Constitutions*, 192–94; Rippy, *Latin America*, 253–54.

17. José María Melo (1800–60) was born in Chaparral, Tolima, Nueva Granada. He joined the Revolutionaries in 1819. He served in the Venezuela army between 1830 and 1835 before being expelled for his mutinous activities. Melo served at the Bremen Military Academy for three years. He returned to Colombia and achieved the rank of general in 1849. Following his unsuccessful *coup* in 1854, Melo was expelled from Colombia for eight years. Melo was captured by the Mexican Conservatives and shot while serving in the forces of Benito Juárez.

18. Tomás Cipriano de Mosquera, José Hilario López, and Pedro Alcántara Herrán.

19. Plazas, "El ejército," 2: 165–66; Patricia Pinzón de Lewin, *El ejército y Las elecciones* (Bogotá: CEREC, 1994), 28–29; Gibson, *The Constitutions*, 217–19; Rippy, *Latin America*, 254.

20. Gibson, *The Constitutions*, 247–48.

21. Tomás Cipriano de Mosquera (1778–1867) was born in southern Popayán and came from an influential family. He joined the Revolutionary army at age fifteen as a cadet. He was captured by the Royalists at La Cuchilla del Tambo (June 29, 1816) in Cauca. In 1822, as a lieutenant colonel, Mosquera served as *aid-de-camp* to Simón Bolívar. Mosquera was elected president in 1845 as a Conservative and as a Liberal in 1861 and 1866. His brother, José, was the Archbishop of Bogotá. Mosquera was strong-willed and difficult to predict.

22. Plazas, "El ejército," 2: 171–72.

23. ibid., 2: 172–73.

24. ibid., 2: 173–77.
25. ibid., 2: 177–79; Pinzón, *El ejército*, 32–33; Gibson, *The Constitutions*, 248–49.
26. Gibson, *The Constitutions*, 248–49; Hellen Miller Bailey and Abraham P. Nasatir, *Latin America* (Englewood Cliffs, N.J.: Prentice-Hall, 1960), 447.
27. Plazas, "El ejército," 2: 181.
28. ibid., 2: 184–85; Sánchez, *Buques*, 23.
29. Pinzón, *El ejército*, 33–34; Plazas, "El ejército," 2: 186–89; Gibson, *The Constitutions*, 302–3; Bailey and Nasatir, *Latin America*, 447.
30. Keen, *A History*, 502; Halperin, *The Contemporary History*, 145.
31. Plazas, "El ejército," 2: 192–97.
32. ibid., 2: 197–98.
33. ibid., 2: 200.
34. ibid., 2: 201–9.
35. Ultimately, Prestán was captured following the surrender of Calamar on July 21, returned to Colon, and executed on August 17, 1885. Plazas, "El ejército," 2: 212, 216.
36. ibid., 2: 211–12.
37. ibid., 2: 213–14.
38. ibid., 2: 214–15.
39. ibid., 2: 215–17.
40. Gibson, *The Constitutions*, 309–12; Keen, *A History*, 503; Rippy, "The Dictators of Colombia," 381; Robertson, *History of Latin-American Nations*, 369–70.
41. Rafael Reyes (1850–1918) was born in Santa Rosa de Viterbo in Boyacá Province. During the 1870s he and his brothers explored and attempted to economically exploit the Colombian *selva*. He joined the Conservative army, campaigning in the southwest, and by October 1885 he had achieved the rank of general.
42. Plazas, "El ejército," 2: 222–27; Rippy, "The Dictators of Colombia," 386.
43. Plazas, "El ejército," 2: 235–39.
44. ibid., 2: 239–41.
45. ibid., 2: 247–49; Marley, *Wars*, 605.
46. Plazas, "El ejército," 2: 253–54.
47. ibid., 2: 254–64; Marley, *Wars*, 605–6.
48. Plazas, "El ejército," 2: 267.
49. Pinzón, *El ejercito*, 53; Hanratty and Meditz, *Colombia*, 27–28; Henao and Arrubla, *History of Colombia*, 519; Marley, *Wars*, 606.
50. Plazas, "El ejército," 2: 267–69; Moore, *A History of Latin America*, 371; Akers and Elliott, *A History of South America*, 660.
51. The U.S. officer in charge of protecting the Panama Railroad informed the Colombian government that under the Mallarino-Bidlack Treaty (December 12, 1846) he would maintain free transit regardless of the actions of either combatant. Plazas, "El Ejército," 2: 269; Akers and Elliott, *A History of South America*, 660.
52. Plazas, "El ejército," 2: 269–70.
53. ibid., 2: 271.
54. ibid., 2: 272.
55. ibid., 2: 273–77.
56. Chapman, *Republican Hispanic America*, 283–84; Keen, *A History*, 504–5; Hanratty and Meditz, *Colombia*, xxiv, 28; Kirkpatrick, *Latin America*, 261.
57. Hanratty and Meditz, *Colombia*, 255; Halperin, *The Contemporary History*, 204.

58. *Hand Book . . . 1893*, 97; Plazas, "El ejército," 2: 160; Moore, *A History of Latin America*, 367; Rippy, *Latin America*, 253.

59. Henao and Arrubla, *History of Colombia*, 519.

60. *Hand Book . . . 1893*, 99 and 208; Rippy, *Latin America*, 257.

61. Pinzón, *El ejército*, 53–54; Munro, *Latin America*, 304, Thomas, *Latin America*, 497; Bailey and Nasatir, *Latin America*, 448.

CHAPTER TWENTY-FIVE

1. Fructuoso Rivera (ca. 1784–1854) was born near Montevideo into a wealthy, landed *criollo* family. He was one of José Artigas' most trusted lieutenants during the War for Independence (see chapter 7). Between 1816 and 1820 Rivera fought against the invading Portuguese and Brazilians, participating in most of the major battles. Defeated in March 1820, he joined the invaders and accepted a commission in the Portuguese army. In 1822 he sided with the Brazilians against the Portuguese. In 1825 Rivera was captured by members of an independence movement led by Lavalleja and joined that cause. A year later he broke with Lavalleja and went to Santa Fe, Argentina. He was popular among the "have-nots" of Montevideo and the Uruguayan *gauchos*.

2. Juan Antonio Lavalleja (1784–1853) joined the Revolutionaries in 1811. Between 1816 and 1818 he fought against the Portuguese and Brazilians. Lavalleja was captured in 1818 and imprisoned in Rio de Janeiro for three years. Returning to Uruguay, he plotted against the Brazilians. Discovered, Lavalleja fled to Argentina. In 1825 he led the "33 immortals" who landed in Uruguay in 1825 to fight the Brazilians.

3. Halperín, *The Contemporary History*, 111.

4. Herring, *History*, 662; Rippy, *Latin America*, 281–82; Chapman, *Republican Hispanic America*, 343; Kirkpatrick, *Latin America*, 156.

5. Rex A. Hudson and Sandra W. Meditz, eds., *Uruguay: A Country Study*, 2d ed. (Washington: Headquarters, Department of the Army, 1992), 11; Chapman, *Republican Hispanic America*, 342; Graham-Yooll, *Small Wars*, 80–81.

Uruguay population is estimated to have been: 1862—281,500 people; 1883—450,000 people. Kirkpatrick, *Latin America*, 155–57.

6. Herring, *History*, 658; Chapman, *Republican Hispanic America*, 341; Ireland, *Boundaries*, 130–38.

7. Bailey and Nasatir, *Latin America*, 417.

8. Alfredo Traversoni, *Historia del Uruguay*, 3d ed. (Montevideo: Editorial Medina, 1960), 573.

9. Traversoni, *Historia*, 574.

10. Traversoni, *Historia*, 353; H. D., *Ensayo*, 2: 3–4; Robertson, *History*, 258.

11. Eugenio Garzón (1796–1851) joined the Revolutionary army in 1811. He served under José de San Martín during the liberation of the Pacific coast nations. Garzón served in the Argentine army in the 1825–28 war against Brazil. He served as the Uruguayan Minister of War and Marine in 1828 and was promoted to general of the army in 1838.

12. Traversoni, *Historia*, 355; H. D., *Ensayo*, 2: 19–20; Bealer, "The Dictators," 119.

13. H. D., *Ensayo*, 2: 21–22; Bealer, "The Dictators," 120.

14. Manuel Oribe (1792–1857), born in Montevideo into a wealthy family, joined the Revolutionary army and in 1814 took part in the capture of Montevideo. In 1823 he led an unsuccessful revolt in Uruguay and fled to Buenos Aires. Oribe returned to Uruguay as one of the "33 immortals" who landed in 1825 to fight the Brazilians. In 1828 he was sent to

arrest Fructuoso Rivera for having broken a truce with Brazil by invading Misiones. This began a blood feud between the two future *caudillos* which lasted their lifetimes.

15. H. D., *Ensayo*, 2: 29–30; Traversoni, *Historia*, 357–58; Robertson, *History*, 258; Bealer, "The Dictators," 120.

16. Traversoni, *Historia*, 358; Bealer, "The Dictators," 120–21; Robertson, *History*, 258.

17. H. D., *Ensayo*, 2: 27, 31–37; Traversoni, *Historia*, 358–59; Bealer, "The Dictators," 122.

18. H. D., *Ensayo*, 2: 61–63; Traversoni, *Historia*, 394–97; Robertson, *History*, 259; Thomas, *Latin America*, 315. In 1845 Rivera sought refuge in Brazil. He returned to Uruguay but was deposed on October 3, 1847, for starting secret negotiations with Oribe. The Brazilians refused to allow him to return to Uruguay until January 20, 1853, but he died en route.

19. Robertson, *History*, 259–60; Hudson and Meditz, *Uruguay*, 14; Thomas, *Latin America*, 316.

20. Venancio Flores (1808–68), born in the town of Porongos (today Trinidad), fought against the Brazilians between 1825 and 1828. A *Colorado*, he became the most prominent *caudillo* of the department of San José. Throughout much of the War of the Triple Alliance (1864–70), Flores commanded the allies' vanguard and won the Battle of Yatai on August 17, 1865.

21. H. D., *Ensayo*, 2: 141–57; Dana Gardner Munro, *The Latin American Republics*, 3d ed. (New York: Appleton-Century-Crofts, 1960), 202–3; Bailey and Nasatir, *Latin America*, 418–19.

22. Traversoni, *Historia*, 495; Akers, *A History*, 207–8.

23. Traversoni, *Historia*, 495; H. D., *Ensayo*, 2: 219; Akers, *A History*, 208–9; Kirkpatrick, *Latin America*, 157.

24. Traversoni, *Historia*, 501–52; H. D., *Ensayo*, 2: 224–28; Akers, *A History*, 209.

25. Traversoni, *Historia*, 502–3; H. D., *Ensayo*, 2: 230; Akers, *A History*, 210.

26. Akers, *A History*, 211; H. D., *Ensayo*, 2: 230–31.

27. Akers, *A History*, 212; H. D., *Ensayo*, 2: 231.

28. Akers, *A History*, 212.

29. Traversoni, *Historia*, 502–8; Akers, *A History*, 213; H. D., *Ensayo*, 2: 232–33; Robertson, *History*, 261.

30. Lorenzo Latorre (1840–1916), born in Montevideo, was the son of an immigrant. He joined the *Colorado* army in 1863 and was promoted to ensign in 1865. Latorre was seriously wounded at the Battle of Estero Bellaco (May 2, 1866) during the War of the Triple Alliance. By January 1875 he had become the Minister of War and Marine.

31. Akers, *A History*, 214–15; Traversoni, *Historia*, 510–11.

32. Akers, *A History*, 216; Traversoni, *Historia*, 514–15; H. D., *Ensayo*, 2: 246–47.

33. H. D., *Ensayo*, 2: 248–49; Traversoni, *Historia*, 517–18; Akers, *A History*, 217.

34. The rebels adopted the tricolor flag which Lavalleja had used in 1825.

35. Traversoni, *Historia*, 518; Akers, *A History*, 217–18; H. D., *Ensayo*, 2: 250–52.

36. Kirkpatrick, *Latin America*, 158; Traversoni, *Historia*, 525–29; Akers, *A History*, 219; H. D., *Ensayo*, 2: 270.

37. Máximo Tajes (1852–1912) joined the 1st Battalion of *Cazadores* in 1868 and fought in the War of the Triple Alliance (1864–70). He served as Inspector General of Weapons, Political Chief of Duazno, and finally, Minister of War and Marine.

38. H. D., *Ensayo*, 2: 292–93.

39. Traversoni, *Historia*, 536–37; Kirkpatrick, *Latin America*, 158; Hudson and Meditz, *Uruguay*, 19; Akers, *A History*, 222–23.

40. Aparicio Saravia (1856–1904) was born near Santa Clara de Olimar in northern Uruguay; his father was a Brazilian. Saravia fought as a rebel in the Brazilian Intraclass Rebellion of 1893–94 (see chapter 37). He possessed little formal education but was shrewd. He led his first armed demonstration against the *Colorados* in 1896.

41. Diego Lamas (unk–1897) was the son of a prominent *Blanco* officer who emigrated to Argentina when the *Colorados* took control of Uruguay in the 1860s. Lamas was educated in Buenos Aires and entered the Argentine army where by 1897 he earned the rank of major. Joining the rebellious *Blancos*, Lamas was wounded in the arm during the "Nationalistic" Rebellion. Following the armistice, Lamas was thrown from his horse on the outskirts of Montevideo and died from his injuries.

42. Akers, *A History*, 228; Hudson and Meditz, *Uruguay*, 19.

43. Traversoni, *Historia*, 554–55; H. D., *Ensayo*, 2: 341–42.

44. Akers, *A History*, 228–29; Traversoni, *Historia*, 555.

45. Akers, *A History*, 229–30.

46. H. D., *Ensayo* 2: 342–49; Akers, *A History*, 231–33; Traversoni, *Historia*, 555; Robertson, *History*, 264.

47. H. D., *Ensayo*, 2: 349–51; Akers, *A History*, 233.

48. H. D., *Ensayo*, 2: 359–61; Traversoni, *Historia*, 600–1.

49. H. D., *Ensayo*, 2: 362–64; Traversoni, *Historia*, 601–2; Akers, *A History*, 233–34; Hudson and Meditz, *Uruguay*, 21.

50. H. D., *Ensayo*, 2: 366–67; Traversoni, *Historia*, 602–3; Munro, *The Latin American Republics*, 206.

51. Bailey and Nasatir, *Latin America*, 417.

52. Halperín, *The Contemporary History*, 187–88; Robertson, *History*, 270; Bailey and Nasatir, *Latin America*, 419.

53. Martin C. Needler, *Political Systems* (Princeton, N.J.: D. Van Nostrand, 1964), 448.

CHAPTER TWENTY-SIX

1. José María de la Cruz Prieto (1799–1875) was born in Concepción. At the age of fourteen, he joined the Revolutionaries. He fought his first engagement at Chillán in July 1813. During 1813 and 1814 José served as aide to General O'Higgins. Following the Revolutionary disaster at Rancagua, he fled to Mendoza, Argentina. A member of the Army of the Andes, he again served as aide to O'Higgins. De la Cruz fought at numerous engagements including Chacabuco (February 12, 1818), Cancha Rayada (March 19, 1818), Maípo (May 5, 1818), and Pangal (September 1820). Following the exile of O'Higgins in 1823, de la Cruz retired. In 1830 he returned to active service and was promoted to general of a brigade in February 1832. He served as General Bulnes' chief of staff during the second expedition against the Peru-Bolivian Confederation in 1838–39.

2. Gilliss, *The U.S. Naval Astronomical Expedition*, 1: 498, 505; Galdames, *A History of Chile*, 288; Estado Mayor, *Historia del ejército del Chile*, 10 vols. (Santiago: Ejército de Chile, 1980–83), 4: 70–76; Bynum E. Weathers Jr., *The Role of the Military in Chilean Politics, 1810–1980* (Maxwell, Ala.: Air University Library, 1980), 23.

3. Cox, "Chile," 312–13; Galdames, *A History of Chile*, 288; Chapman, *Republican Hispanic America*, 359.

4. Maurice Zeitlin, *The Civil Wars in Chile* (Princeton, N.J.: Princeton University Press, 1984), 13–16, 23–25, 61; Thomas, *Latin America*, 393–94.

5. Estado Mayor, *Historia del ejército del Chile*, 4: 78–79.

6. Zeitlin, *The Civil Wars*, 30–31, 48–54; Rex A. Hudson, ed., *Chile: A Country Study* (Washington: Headquarters, Department of the Army, 1994), 21; Chapman, *Republican Hispanic America*, 358.

7. Gilliss, *The U.S. Naval Astronomical Expedition*, 1: 304, 310–11.

8. ibid., 1: 339.

9. ibid., 1: 312–14.

10. ibid., 1: 315; Estado Mayor, *Historia militar de Chile*, 2: 53; Estado Mayor, *Historia del ejército del Chile*, 4: 84–88; Bealer, "The Dictators," 192–93.

11. Five years after the rebellion, on January 30, 1856, the *Cazador* ran aground on the Rocks of Carranza. Almost 500 persons lost their lives. López, *Historia de la marina*, 197.

12. Gilliss, *The U.S. Naval Astronomical Expedition*, 1: 312–15; Luís Novoa de la Fuente, *Historia naval de Chile*, 2nd ed. (Valparaíso: Imprenta de la Armada, 1944), 63; López Urrutia, *Historia de la marina*, 423.

13. Estado Mayor, *Historia militar de Chile*, 3 vols. (Santiago: Instituto Geográfico Militar, 1969), 2: 54–55; Estado Mayor, *Historia del ejército del Chile*, 4: 88–97; Gilliss, *The U.S. Naval Astronomical Expedition*, 1: 321–25.

14. "Fifty thousand dollars, it was said, had been offered a Colonel [Manuel] Zañartu for himself and the famous Carampangue battalion, if they would abandon General [De la] Cruz; and the temptation proved irresistible." Gilliss, *The U.S. Naval Astronomical Expedition*, 1: 331.

Having so many killed when compared to the number wounded may be attributed to the lethality of new weapons, the poor tactics employed by the cavalry on both sides, and the lack of control exercised by the officers on both sides. Gilliss, *The U.S. Naval Astronomical Expedition*, 1: 328–33; Estado Mayor, *Historia militar de Chile*, 2: 55–56; Cox, "Chile," 314; Chapman, *Republican Hispanic America*, 359.

15. Gilliss, *The U.S. Naval Astronomical Expedition*, 1: 316.

16. ibid., 1: 334.

17. Estado Mayor, *Historia del ejército del Chile*, 4: 101.

18. Estado Mayor, *Historia militar de Chile*, 2: 56–57; Hillmon, "A History of the Armed Forces," 112.

19. Bealer, "The Dictators," 192; Davis, *The Americas*, 440; Herring, *A History*, 550.

20. Estado Mayor, *Historia del ejército del Chile,* 4: 125–26; Chapman, *Republican Hispanic America*, 359; Wilgus, *The Development of Hispanic America*, 378; Herring, *A History*, 550.

21. Estado Mayor, *Historia militar de Chile*, 2: 61–63.

22. Pedro León Gallo Goyenechea (1830–77), born into a wealthy mining family in Copiapó in northern Chile, was active in politics from an early age. He took part in the April 20, 1851, street fighting as a militia member defending the government against the rebels. Gallo became active in local politics, turning against Montt as the decade progressed. Following the failed 1859 rebellion, Gallo returned from exile in 1863. He served in the Chamber of Deputies beginning in 1867 and in 1876 was elected to the Senate.

23. Pablo H. Barrientos Gutíerrez, *Historia de la artillería de Chile* (Santiago: Instituto Geográfico Militar, 1946), 138–39; vol. 16 in the Biblioteca del Oficial, Estado Mayor General del Ejército; Hillmon, "A History of the Armed Forces," 118.

24. Estado Mayor, *Historia militar de Chile*, 2: 62; Estado Mayor, *Historia del ejército del Chile*, 4: 143; Galdames, *A History of Chile*, 298–99; Hillmon, "A History of the Armed Forces," 119–20.

25. Estado Mayor, *Historia militar de Chile*, 2: 62; Estado Mayor, *Historia del ejército del Chile*, 4: 144–45; Barrientos, *Historia*, 142; Galdames, *A History of Chile*, 299.

26. Bealer, "The Dictators," 192, 197; Robertson, *History of Latin-American Nations*, 298.

27. Zeitlin, *The Civil Wars*, 56–57; Bealer, "The Dictators," 196–97; Chapman, *Republican Hispanic America*, 359–60; Weathers, "The Role," 26.

28. Gilliss, *The U.S. Naval Astronomical Expedition*, 1: 339; Zeitlin, *The Civil Wars*, 56; Moore, *A History*, 330–31.

CHAPTER TWENTY-SEVEN

1. Ruth R. Olivera and Liliane Crété, *Life in Mexico under Santa Anna 1822–1855* (Norman: University of Oklahoma Press, 1991), 15–16; Callcott, *Santa Anna*, 281–88.

2. Vasconcelos, *Breve historia*, 468–70; Lilia Díaz, "El liberalismo militante," 819–97 in *Historia general de Mexico*, 2 vols. (Mexico: HARLA, 1988), 2: 830; Hanighen, *Santa Anna*, 280.

3. The Plan of Ayutla called for a temporary dictatorship while a new constitution was drafted.

4. Callcott, *Santa Anna*, 307–9; Hanighen, *Santa Anna*, 279; Parkes, *A History*, 226–27.

5. Díaz, "El liberalismo militante," 2: 831; Marley, *Wars*, 527–28; Parkes, *A History*, 228–29.

6. Benito Juárez (1806–72), born in San Paulo Guelatao, Oaxaca, was the son of Zapotecan Indian peasants. Orphaned at the age of three years, he spent his preteen years as an illiterate shepherd. Juárez was educated for the priesthood by a Franciscan; however, Juárez preferred law. He served as a member of the Oaxaca state legislature (1832–34) and of the National Congress (1847–52), and as the Governor of Oaxaca (1847–52). He was exiled by López de Santa Anna in 1853 to New Orleans where he worked in a cigarette factory. Juárez returned to Mexico to join the Plan of Ayutla and became the Minister of Justice. He already had a reputation of being incorruptible.

7. Vasconcelos, *Breve historia*, 473–74; Priestley, *The Mexican Nation*, 323.

8. Vicente Riva Palacio, ed., *Mexico a través de los siglos*, 4th ed., 5 vols. (Mexico: Editorial Cumbre, 1962), 5: 100–2, 104; José J. Alvarez, *Parte general que sobre la campaña de Puebla* (Mexico: Vicente G. Torres, 1856), iii; Anselmo de Portilla, *Historia de la revolución de Mexico contra la dictadura de General Santa Anna, 1853–1855* (Mexico: V. Garcia Torres, 1856), 265.

9. Sánchez,, "El Ejército mexicano de 1821 a 1860," 202; Portilla, *Historia*, 267–68; Riva Palacio, *Mexico*, 5: 104–5.

10. Díaz, "El liberalismo militante," 2: 838; Portilla, *Historia*, 268–72; Riva Palacio, *Mexico*, 5: 109–10.

11. Ray F. Broussard, "The Puebla Revolt: First Challenge to the Reform," *Journal of the West* 18: 1, 52–57 (January 1979), 54; Alvarez, *Parte general*, iii; Portilla, *Historia*, 273.

12. Broussard, "The Puebla Revolt," 55; Riva Palacio, *Mexico*, 5: 99.

13. Portilla, *Historia*, 285–88; Alvarez, *Parte general*, iii–v, xxii, 1–3, 9–10; Riva Palacio, *Mexico*, 5: 113–15; Broussard, "The Puebla Revolt," 55–56.

14. Díaz, "El liberalismo militante," 2: 838; Riva Palacio, *Mexico*, 5: 116–21; Broussard, "The Puebla Revolt," 57; Scholes, *Mexican Politics*, 7–8.

15. José Manuel Lozano Fuentes and Amalia López Reyes, *Historia del Mexico Contemporáneo* (Mexico: Cia. Editorial Continental, 1988), 99–100; Fortier and Ficklen, *The History of North America*, 9: 335; James Creelman, *Díaz Master of Mexico* (New York: D. Appleton and Company, 1911), 70–71.

16. Sánchez, "El ejército mexicano de 1821 a 1860," 205; Díaz, "El liberalismo militante," 2: 841–42; Scholes, *Mexican Politics*, 23–24; Lozano and López, *Historia del Mexico*, 100; Parkes, *A History*, 240–41.

17. Miguel Miramón (1832–67) studied at the Military Academy at Chapultpec and as a cadet participated in the defense of the Academy against the U.S. attack on September 13, 1847. On April 27, 1857, he was briefly imprisoned for participating in a plot against President Comonfort. With the death of General Luis G. Osollo on June 18, 1858, Miramón became the military leader of the Mexican Conservatives.

18. Costa Soto, *Historia militar*, 55.

19. Broussard, "The Puebla Revolt," 53; Francisco Bulnes, *El verdadero Juárez y La verdad sobre la intervención y el imperio* (Mèxico: Libería de la Vda de Ch. Bouret, 1904), 157–58.

20. Scholes, *Mexican Politics*, 30–31.

21. Parkes, *A History*, 242–43.

22. Díaz, "El liberalismo militante," 2: 843–44; Scholes, *Mexican Politics*, 27–28; Parkes, *A History*, 241; Vasconcelos, *Breve historia*, 478–79.

23. Parkes, *A History*, 242–43.

24. Scholes, *Mexican Politics*, 27–28; Teja Zabre, *Historia de Mexico*, 342; Jesús Romero Flores, *Lic. Benito Juárez, benemerito de las Americas* (Mexico: B. Costa-Amic Editor, 1972), 39, 50–52; Parkes, *A History*, 245–46.

25. Parkes states that the fortifications at Vera Cruz were too strong to be overcome by an attack. This was easily accomplished by Winfield Scott a decade earlier in large measure because he had heavy artillery from the blockading U.S. squadron. Parkes, *A History*, 244.

26. Scholes, *Mexican Politics*, 30; Díaz, "El liberalismo militante," 2: 844–45; Marley, *Wars*, 531; Fortier and Ficklen, *The History of North America*, 9: 337.

27. Vasconcelos, *Breve historia*, 475; Parkes, *A History*, 246.

28. Díaz, "El liberalismo militante," 2: 848; Scholes, *Mexican Politics,* 32.

29. James Morton Callahan, "The Mexican Policy of Southern Leaders under Buchanan's Administration," 135–51 in *Annual Report of the American Historical Association for the Year 1910* (Washington: Government Printing Office, 1912), 146–51; Samuel Flagg Bemis, *The Latin American Policy of the United States* (New York: Harcourt, Brace and Company, 1943), 110; Fortier and Ficklen, *The History of North America*, 9: 338.

30. Marley, *Wars*, 531; Costa Soto, *Historia militar*, 97.

31. Sánchez, "El ejército mexicano de 1821 a 1860," 211; Regis Planchet, *La cuestion religiosa en Mexico*, 3d ed. (El Paso, Tex.: Editorial Revista Catolica, 1927), 154–59; Vasconcelos, *Breve historia*, 485.

32. Sánchez, "El ejército mexicano de 1821 a 1860," 211; Marley, *Wars*, 532; Parkes, *A History*, 248; Costa Soto, *Historia militar*, 62–63.

33. Parkes, *A History*, 248–49.

34. Sánchez, "El ejército mexicano de 1821 a 1860," 211–12; Díaz, "El liberalismo militante," 2: 850–51; Victor Alba, "Reforms," in *Mexico From Independence to Revolution, 1810–1910*, edited by W. Dirk Raat (Lincoln: University of Nebraska Press, 1982), 145; Romero Flores, *Lic. Benito Juárez*, 60.

35. Romero Flores, *Lic. Benito Juárez*, 64–65; Scholes, *Mexican Politics*, 57; Fortier and Ficklen, *The History of North America*, 9: 339.

36. Creelman, *Diaz*, 107; Meyer and Sherman, *The Course*, 383.

37. Lozano and López, *Historia del Mexico*, 101.

CHAPTER TWENTY-EIGHT

1. Ferdinand Maximilian Habsburg (1832–67) was tall and handsome and had a magnificent blonde beard. He was a sailor, traveler, linguist, author, and ruler (governor-general of the Austrian province of the Lomdardo-Venetian) but not a soldier. Maximilian lacked common sense and he was prone to illusions of grandeur—Maximilian wrote a 600-page volume to govern the etiquette of his Mexican court. In 1857 Maximilian married Marie Charlotte Amélie, a Belgian princess who was even more of a romantic than he, if that was possible. Both were very devoted to the arts and sciences.

2. Scholes, *Mexican Politics*, 64–66; Priestley, *The Mexican Nation*, 340–41; Vasconselos, *Breve historia*, 487–88; Marley, *Wars*, 552.

3. Scholes, *Mexican Politics*, 71–72, 82; Parkes, *A History of Mexico*, 251–52; Costa Soto, *Historia militar*, 64.

4. Meyer and Sherman, *The Course*, 388; Priestley, *The Mexican Nation*, 347; Marley, *Wars*, 552.

5. Guillermo Mendoza Vallejo and Luis Garfias Magaña, "El ejército mexicano de 1860 a 1913," in *El ejército mexicano* (Mexico: Secretaría de la Defensa Nacional, 1979), 180; Fortier and Ficklen, *The History of North America*, 9: 343; Marley, *Wars*, 552–53.

The French claimed twelve million pesos in cash and fulfillment of the Jecker bonds, the rights to which they had purchased at a discount to strengthen their position. Parkes, *A History of Mexico*, 253.

6. Scholes, *Mexican Politics*, 76–77; Parkes, *A History of Mexico*, 252–54.

7. Traveling with the French were the exiled Mexican Conservatives General J. N. Almonte, General Miguel Miramón, Father F. J. Miranda, Antonio de Haro y Tamaris, and others. The British commodore threatened to arrest General Miramón, the leader of the Conservatives for much of the War of the *Reforma*, if he landed, for having robbed the British legation in 1860. Therefore, Miramón took a steamer to Havana, Cuba.

8. Mendoza and Garfias, "El ejército mexicano de 1860 a 1913," 221; René Chartrand and Richard Hooker, *The Mexican Adventure 1861–67* (London: Osprey Publishing Ltd., 1994), 19–20.

9. Garfías, *Generales mexicanos*, 190–91; Parkes, *A History of Mexico*, 255–56.

10. Chartrand and Hooker, *The Mexican Adventure*, 12.

11. For Juarez' struggle with his Liberal rivals, see Scholes, *Mexican Politics*, 25–42.

12. Costa Soto, *Historia militar*, 67; *Anales gráficos*, 107.

13. Mendoza and Garfias, "El ejército mexicano de 1860 a 1913," 222–26; Lorano and López, *Historia del Mexico*, 112–13; Díaz, "El liberalismo militante," 866; Fortier and Ficklen, *The History of North America*, 9: 345; Parkes, *A History of Mexico*, 256.

After his defeat at Puebla, General Forey wrote to Napoleon, "We have here nobody who is for us, the moderate party does not exist, and the reactionary party, reduced to nothing, is odious." Georges Pradaliè, 5th ed., *Le second empire* (Paris: Presses universitaires de France, 1974), 110.

14. Fortier and Ficklen, *The History of North America,* 9: 345; Parkes, *A History of Mexico*, 256–57; Costa Soto, *Historia militar*, 68.

15. *Anales gráficos*, 111; Scholes, *Mexican Politics*, 90–91; Parkes, *A History of Mexico*, 256–57.

16. Mendoza and Garfias, "El ejército mexicano de 1860 a 1913," 230–39; Díaz, "El liberalismo militante," 868; Lorano and López, *Historia del Mexico*, 113; Parkes, *A History of Mexico*, 257; Marley, *Wars*, 555–56.

Among those prisoners was General of a Division Ignacio Mejía. He was held in Evreux, France. Twice Napoleon III offered to free Mejía and to restore his rank if he would join the forces of Maximilian, which he refused to do. Finally, on July 1, 1864, Napoleon freed all the Liberal prisoners. The general returned to Mexico, arriving at Paso de Norte in October 1865. On November 30 Juárez named Mejía the Minister of War and Marine.

17. Jonathan Kandell, *La Capital* (New York: Random House, 1988), 339; Marley, *Wars*, 556.

18. Tony Geraghty, *March or Die* (New York: Facts on File, 1987), 67.

19. Captain Danjou's prosthesis left-arm is a relic at the Legion headquarters in Aubagne, France. Marley, *Wars*, 556; Geraghty, *March or Die*, 68–73; Patrick Turnbull, *The Foreign Legion* (London: Heinemann, 1964), 60–64.

20. François-Achille Bazaine (1811–88) is said to have intrigued to become the Emperor of Mexico while he was there. In 1865 he married a fifteen-year-old Mexican girl. After his return to France in 1867, he was deprived of his military privileges for six months, but the reason is unclear.

21. Fortier and Ficklen, Th*e History of North America*, 9: 347; Vasconcelos, *Breve historia*, 497.

22. Mendoza and Garfias, "El ejército mexicano de 1860 a 1913," 245; Díaz, "El liberalismo militante," 870–71; *Anales gráficos*, 120; Fortier and Ficklen, *The History of North America*, 9: 348.

23. Scholes, *Mexican Politics*, 108–9; Parkes, *A History of Mexico*, 258.

24. Chartrand and Hooker, *The Mexican Adventure*, 8, 35–37. Another source places Maximilian's force at 63,800 men (28,000 French, 6,000 Austrian, 1,300 Belgians, and 28,500 Conservative Mexicans including guerrillas). *Anales gráficos*, 127.

25. Reussner and Nicolas, *La puissance navale*, 2: 25–26; René Jouan, *Histoire de la marine française*, 275–76.

26. Napoleon extracted from Maximilian the promise to pay 270 million francs (the amount that Napoleon claimed the French had already spent on the intervention), 1,000 francs a year for each French soldier who remained, and the outstanding debt to the French, British, and Spanish parties that had caused the initial landing, including the Jecker bonds. In exchange, Napoleon promised that French troops would remain until the end of 1867. Fortier and Ficklen, *The History of North America*, 9: 348; Parkes, *A History of Mexico*, 260.

27. Parkes, *A History of Mexico*, 264–65.

28. Díaz' army was somewhere between 4,000 and 7,000 men. The majority, and perhaps most, were guerrillas and poorly armed peasants. Mendoza and Garfias, "El ejército mexicano de 1860 a 1913," 252; Marley, *Wars*, 559.

29. Díaz, "El liberalismo militante," 886–87; Parkes, *A History of Mexico*, 266–67.

30. By comparison, only a few ex-Confederate soldiers fought in Mexico and they had no influence on the outcome.

31. Parkes, *A History of Mexico*, 266–67; Meyer and Sherman, *The Course*, 398; Vasconcelos, *Breve historia*, 498.

32. Fortier and Ficklen, *The History of North America*, 9: 349.
33. ibid.; Parkes, *A History of Mexico*, 268–69.
34. Parkes, *A History of Mexico*, 268–69.
35. Liliane Funcken and Fred Funcken, "The Forgotten Legion," *Campaigns* 6: 32; 27–35 (January/February 1981); Marley, *Wars*, 562.
36. Parkes, *A History of Mexico*, 269.
37. Díaz, "El liberalismo militante," 888–89; Lorano and López, *Historia del Mexico*, 123–24; Parkes, *A History of Mexico*, 270.
38. Kandell, *La Capital*, 350; Parkes, *A History of Mexico*, 271.
39. Díaz, "El liberalismo militante," 893.
40. ibid.; Vasconcelos, *Breve historia*, 499; Parkes, *A History of Mexico*, 272.
41. Lorano and López, *Historia del Mexico*, 124–25; Parkes, *A History of Mexico*, 272; Costa Soto, *Historia militar*, 80.
42. Díaz, "El liberalismo militante," 894–96; Fortier and Ficklen, *The History of North America*, 9: 353–55; Parkes, *A History of Mexico*, 272–73; Marley, *Wars*, 563–65.

The "American Legion" (a unit in the Liberal Army composed of former U.S. soldiers) apparently hatched a plot to rescue Maximilian. However, they were ordered to march to Mexico City the day it was to be executed. "Maximilian and the American Legion," *Overland Monthly* 7: 1st Series, 445–48 (November 1871); Robert Ryal Miller, "The American Legion of Honor," *Pacific Historical Review* 30: 3; 229–241 (August 1961), 238.

43. Teja Zabre, *Historia de Mexico*, 348–49.
44. Ángel Miranda Basurto, *La evolución de Mexico* (Mexico: Ediciones Numancia, S.A., 1992), 229.
45. Lorano and López, *Historia del Mexico*, 126.
46. Previous estimates of the number of deaths vary significantly. One source claims that 65,000 imperialists (Conservative Mexicans, French, Austrians, Belgians, and other European soldiers) died, although this figure seems high. See Miranda, *La evolucion*, 229; Mendoza and Garfias, "El ejército mexicano de 1860 a 1913," 282.

A number of authors claim that 50,000 Mexicans fighting for the Republics died. See Meyer and Sherman, *The Course*, 401; Kandell, *La Capital*, 351.

Sources generally place the French Army losses at about 6,000 or 7,000 individuals. However, this probably does not include the French navy, the French allies, and possibly even the Foreign Legion. See Geraghty, *March or Die*, 66.

CHAPTER TWENTY-NINE

1. Francisco Solano López (1826–70) succeeded his father as president of Paraguay in 1862. Militarily, he received no formal training and had limited experience. In 1845–46 at the age of nineteen, López commanded an army of 4,000 which crossed the Paraná River into Corrientes to support the *caudillo* of that province against the Rosas' government in Buenos Aires. The *Correntinos* were defeated by Justo José Urquíza, then a lieutenant of Rosas', before the Paraguayans could support their effort. López recrossed the river without firing a shot. Four years later, López commanded a second foreign expedition to Misiones against Rosas. López had unbounded confidence in his own abilities.

Since independence Paraguay had been ruled by two successive long-lived dictators, José Gaspar Rodríguez de Francia (1814–40) and Carlos Antonio López (1841–62). See Lewis W. Bealer, "Francisco Solano López, 'A Dictator Run Amuck'" in A. Curtis Wilgus, ed., *South American Dictators* (Washington, D.C.: George Washington University Press, 1937), 154–72.

2. López did not articulate any specific war objectives. Jurg Meister, a student of the conflict, speculates that López may well have dreamed of a La Plata empire built around Paraguay dominating Mato Grosso, Corrientes, Entre Ríos, Rio Grande do Sul, and Uruguay. He may also have had aspirations of marrying the daughter of the Emperor of Brazil, although these suspected ambitions cannot be documented. Meister, *Francisco Solano López*, 24–26.

3. Eliza Lynch (1835–86) became one of the most influential women in Latin American history. Francisco Solano López met her in Paris, and she returned with him to Paraguay as his mistress in 1855. She bore him seven children. She was beautiful, knew how to dress, was an excellent horsewoman, a good mother, and faithful to López. Lynch made no fuss about his other mistresses. She was a typical social climber, greedy and indifferent to other people's problems. Eliza was intelligent, speaking at least English, French, and Spanish, and perhaps some Guaraní, and introduced the theater to Paraguay. She was hated by the López family, by the small upper class of Asunción, and at least by the wives of most of the consuls and diplomats there. Apparently, she did not dominate López, but rather encouraged his mad dreams.

4. The belief that López created a military juggernaut persists to this day. A number of factors helped create this misconception. Francisco Solano López and his father imported a modest amount of the most advanced technology into Paraguay, primarily to improve its military posture. The region's first rail line ran between Asunción and the military post at Cerró Léon. The first telegraph line in South America linked the capital with the fortification at Humaitá. President Francisco Solano López dressed the part of a highly decorated military leader even though the Paraguayan peacetime army was shabbily outfitted and poorly drilled. What may have impressed some foreigners was the obvious show of militarism and devotion to Francisco Solano López.

Edmond Akers' evaluation is typical of the inflated opinion of the Paraguayan army. According to Akers, in 1865 the Paraguayan army consisted of "12,000 troops of six years' service; 6,000 men who had served with the colours and passed to the reserve; 22,000 national guards under the leadership of trained officers; and 20,000 in recently raised levies undergoing instruction. Altogether, the army comprised 45,000 infantry, 10,000 cavalry, and 5,000 artillery." Akers and Elliot, *A History*, 146.

Meister estimates that there were never 60,000 Paraguayans under arms at the same time; at best 40,000, and soon due to losses much less. Most of the time López had between 20,000 and 25,000 all told, of which 15,000 to 20,000 were available for action around Humaitá but at least 10 percent were always sick. Meister observes that the Paraguayan army was not numerically the strongest, nor the best trained, nor the best armed, nor the best led, but certainly possessed iron discipline and were on the whole courageous. Meister, *Francisco Solano López*, 343–44.

5. In early June 1863, Uruguay captured the Argentine steamer *Salto*, which was carrying weapons presumably to the rebels. The crew and ship were released, but the suspected contraband was held at Montevideo. Uruguay asked the Argentine government to claim the property and to prove that it was not intended for Uruguayan rebels. In response, an Argentine warship seized the Uruguayan warship *General Artigas* and blockaded the mouth of the Uruguay River.

6. Brazilian senior naval ranks were: Chefe de Divisão (Commodore), Chefe de Esquadra (Rear Admiral), Vice Almirante, and Almirante.

7. Venancio Flores (1809–68) had little formal military training and led through example. Flores personally led Uruguay's troops in the war against Paraguay and volunteered to command the vanguard once General Urguiza retired from the war. His troops affectionately referred to him as "el cabo viejo" (the old corporal) because of his informal dress and manner. Manual Gálvez, *Humaitá* (Buenos Aires: Libreria y Editorial "La Facultad," 1932), 85.

8. Meister, *Francisco Solano López*, 70.

9. Paraguay had not formally declared war on Brazil. However, a diplomatic note formulated on August 30, 1864, had contained a veiled threat of warlike actions if Brazil continued its military and diplomatic actions against Uruguay. Gregorio Benites, *Anales diplomático y militar de la guerra del Paraguay*, 2 vols. (Asunción: Establecimento Tipográfico de Muñoz Hnos, 1906), 1: 94–96.

10. Jurg Meister, *Francisco Solano López*, 46–47, 60, 73–74, 427–30, 442.

11. Charles Kolinski, *Independence or Death! The Story of the Paraguayan War* (Gainesville: University of Florida Press, 1965), 40–43.

12. Meister, *Francisco Solano López*, 59–62.

13. In a certain sense, there was homogeneity of language and race among the Paraguayans. They were and are rather an almost perfect mixture of two races and all are bilingual.

14. During the nineteenth century Paraguay was the only Latin American country where the *mestizos* controlled the political power. Even European immigrants tended to marry into Paraguayan families. Practically all spoke Guaraní as well as Spanish.

15. Nelson Werneck Sodré, *Formação da sociedade brasileira* (Rio de Janeiro: J. Olympio, 1944), 308.

16. The Brazilian army purchased a small quantity of French Model 1822 percussion cap muskets in 1835. This musket was a converted smoothbore flintlock. In 1852 the army purchased about 900 Dreyse center-fire rifles from Germany and these were used in the campaign against Rosas in that year; these weapons proved unreliable. In 1855 the Brazilian army purchased 2,200 Minié percussion cap muskets. This was followed by additional orders and by the time the War of the Triple Alliance began this was the standard weapon of the army. Two calibers were acquired, 14.66mm (the most common) manufactured in Belgium and 14.80mm manufactured in England. In 1867 the Brazilian army purchased 5,000 Robert rifles; however, these never saw service during the war due to ammunition problems. Also, in 1867 Count d'Eu ordered that some 2,000 Spencer carbines be purchased for the cavalry and these were delivered the following year.

17. Meister, *Francisco Solano López*, 349–50.

18. Prior to the war Paraguay had ordered the double-turret monitors *Bellona* and *Nemesis* (which became the Brazilian *Lima Barros* and *Silvado*), the single-turret monitors *Minerva* and *Bellona* (which became the Brazilian *Bahia* and *Bellona*), and the lightly armored gunboats *Medusa* and *Triton* (which became the Brazilian *Herval* and *Mariz e Barros*) from European yards. Paraguay was unable to take delivery due to the lack of money and the Brazilian blockade. George A. Gratz, "Warships of the War of the Triple Alliance," *Warship International* 35: 2; 210–11 (1998).

19. Trajano Augusto de Carvalho, *Nossa marinha—seus feitos e glórias* (Rio de Janeiro: Odebrecht, S.A., 1986), 58; Kolinski, *Independence or Death*, 49–58, 79.

20. Meister, *Francisco Solano López*, 56; Kolinski, *Independence*, 64–65.

21. Before the declaration of war, López wrote to Mitre unsuccessfully attempting to get permission to march through Argentine territory. He also wrote to Urguiza trying in vain to

obtain his support. In a secret meeting the Paraguayan Congress declared war on Argentina on March 18, 1865, but delayed delivering it until May 3. Benites, *Anales diplomático*, 1: 159–70.

22. Meister, *Francisco Solano López*, 62–63.

23. The *25 de Mayo* and *Gualeguay* constituted just about the entire Argentine navy at that time. When the Paraguayans attacked Corrientes the *Gualeguay* was undergoing repairs. Both were commissioned into the Paraguayan navy.

24. Bartolomé Mitre (1821–1906) served as an artillery lieutenant with the Uruguayan *Colorado* forces of General Rivera at the age of eighteen. He was an exile of the Rosas' government in Montevideo during the long siege of that city. He fought at the Battle of Arroyo Grande and was a lieutenant colonel at the age of twenty-five. In 1852 he commanded an artillery battery against the Rosas' forces at the Battle of Monte Caseros. Mitre commanded the federal army defeated by General Urquíza at Cepeda in October 1859 as well as the one that narrowly defeated Urquíza at Pavon in 1861. On October 12, 1862, Mitre became the first constitutional president of the modern Argentine nation.

25. The Allied landing force consisted of 3,846 men. Paraguay lost 120 dead, 19 taken prisoner, and 83 wounded. It also lost two guns. The allies lost 69 dead and 215 wounded, including 23 officers. Donato, *Dicionário,* 273.

26. Meister, *Francisco Solano López*, 86; Botto, *Campanhas navais,* 85–92; Donato, *Dicionário*, 417–19.

Several days after the battle, López sent steamers to salvage vessels that had grounded. The *Paraguari* was refloated and towed to Asunción. Before the Paraguayans were able to repair this ship, they had to evacuate the naval arsenal in 1868. The hulk was scuttled in an attempt to block the river. Thus she became the fourth steamer lost due to the action at Riachuelo. The *Tacuarí* was towed to Asunción and repaired.

27. George Thompson, *The War in Paraguay* (London: Longmans, Green, 1869), 71–81.

28. The fact that such an important expedition was entrusted to the command of a mere lieutenant colonel and a major is explained by the fact that Francisco Solano López, like his predecessors, held down the number of high-ranking officers for political and financial reasons.

29. Brazilian forces included the armed tug *Uruguay* and the armed boats *São João* and *Garibaldi*. They were later joined by four other craft. The Paraguayans had some twenty canoes with wheels, of which at least six were sunk on July 29, 1865.

30. The Allied force was made up of 4,547 Argentines with 24 guns (whose shells had no fuses), 1,450 Brazilians, and 2,584 Uruguayans with 8 guns.

31. The city had been fortified by the Brazilians who had garrisoned it with about 8,000 men under Gen. David Canabarro. This force retreated without firing a shot on the approach of the Paraguayans.

32. Several hundred *Blancos* did join López and fought in the Paraguayan army. López ultimately executed many whom he did not fully trust.

33. Donato, *Dicionário*, 516, 524–25; Meister, *Francisco Solano López*, 102.

34. López ordered Robles arrested for having failed to obey his order to retreat at once, and six months later had him shot. Meister, *Francisco Solano López*, 82.

35. José Díaz (1833–67) had become Marshal López' most brilliant general. Unfortunately for the Paraguayan cause, he was mortally wounded by a shell from a Brazilian warship in January 1867 while scouting the river in a canoe.

36. Meister, *Francisco Solano López*, 109.

37. This sandbank was also known as Banco de los Purutúes, Isla Redencion, Ilha Redempcao, and Isla Cabrita.

38. Brazilian army general officers' ranks were: Brigadeiro, Marechal de Campo, Tenente General, and Marechal de Exército.

39. Manuel Luis Osório (1808–79), was born at São Pedro, Rio Grande do Sul. He also fought for the central government against separationist movements in the 1830s. Osório commanded the Rio Grande lancers during the campaign against Rosas in 1852. He commanded both the 1st and 3rd Corps during the War of the Triple Alliance. He was shot in the jaw at the Battle of Avaí and returned to Brazil for treatment. Following the war, Osório entered politics. He served as Army Minister in 1878 and 1879. Today, Osório is remembered as the Patron of the Brazilian cavalry.

40. Carvalho, *Nossa marinha*, 66; Botto, *Campanhas navais*, 103–5.

41. The 40th Battalion had been recruited from among the artisans, students, and civil servants from Asunción and even contained some foreigners. When first organized, its strength was about 1,200 men.

42. Meister, *Francisco Solano López*, 129–39.

43. Most of the small quantity of quality rifles, carbines, and accruements were lost during the 1864–65 offensives. A Paraguayan wrote that in 1866 Battalion Six "was armed with machetes that had been captured at Corrientes . . . after which it became some sort of an amphibious or marine unit, serving on board the Paraguayan warships at Richuelo." Luis Vittone, *Las fuerzas armadas paraguayas en sus distintas épocas la infanteria paraguaya y su patrono* (Asunción: Editorial "El Grafico," 1969), 160; Meister, *Francisco Solano López*, 454–55.

The quality of the horses used by the Paraguayans was very poor. Large numbers were lost at the battles of Second Tuyutí (November 3, 1867), Tatayiba (October 1867), and Lomas Valentinas (December 1867). The Paraguayan cavalry was mostly on foot due to the lack of horses. Léon de Palleja, *Diario de la campaña de las fuerzas aliadas contra el Paraguay*, 2 vols. (Montevideo: Ministerio de Instrucción Públic y Previsión Social, 1960), 2: 371.

44. Carvalho, *Nossa marinha*, 62; Botto, *Campanhas navais*, 103–7; Donato, *Dicionário*, 282–83. The 10th Paraguayan Infantry Battalion disintegrated under the shock of battle. López ordered the 10th Battalion stricken from the Army List and the execution of every fifth officer and tenth soldier.

45. Magalhães, *A evolução militar*, 142–43.

46. Carvalho, *Nossa marinha*, 74; Botto, *Campanhas navais*, 106–8; Donato, *Dicionário*, 280–81.

47. Magalhães gives the casualties as 4,093 for the allies of whom 2,011 were Brazilians. He cites the Paraguayan loses as only 250 men. Magalhães, *A evolução militar*, 143.

48. Luis Alves de Lima e Silva (1803–80) was born at Vila de Estrela, Rio de Janeiro. He was successively titled Baron, Count, Marquis, and Duke of Caxias. Caxias completed his military training as an officer in 1821 and fought against the Portuguese at Bahia in 1823. He fought in the War against Argentina (1825–28) and against numerous separatist movements. Caxias fought in the 1852 campaign against Rosas of Argentina. He was Minister of War both before and after the War of the Triple Alliance. In 1861, 1862, and 1878 Caxias served as prime minister.

49. Meister, *Francisco Solano López*, 197–200.

50. Asiatic cholera added to the death and misery already caused by diarrhea, gangrene, smallpox, and the other diseases. Efraim Cardozo, *Hace cien años*, 13 vols. (Asunción: Ediciones EMASA, 1967–82), 5: 238.

51. Thompson, *The War*, 190; see F. Stansbury Haydon, "Documents Relating to the First Military Balloon Corps Organized in South America: The Aeronautic Corps of the Brazilian Army 1867–68," *Hispanic American Historical Review* 19: 4, 504–17 (November 1939).

52. Max von Versen, "História da guerra do Paraguai," *Revista do Instituto Historico e Geográfico Brasileiro*, 76: 2; 1–270 (Rio de Janeiro, 1913), 127–29.

53. General Mitre returned to the front on July 28, but he chose to leave Caxias in command of the campaign.

54. López was temporarily able to restore communications between Humaitá and Asunción by clearing a 54-mile path and stringing telegraph wire through the marshes and forests of the Chaco along the west bank of the Paraguay River.

55. Botto, *Campanhas navais*, 108–19; Meister, *Francisco Solano López*, 208.

56. The Allied casualties were: Brazilian 249 killed, 394 missing, and 1,047 missing; Argentine (which included the Paraguayan Legion) 35 killed, 41 missing, and 51 wounded. Among the Brazilian missing were 11 officers and 203 men of the 4th Artillery Group, which having no guns were used as infantry and taken prisoner.

57. Carvalho, *Nossa marinha*, 78; Donato, *Dicionário* 306–7.

58. Carvalho, *Nossa marinha* 80–82; Botto, *Campanhas navais*, 119–27.

59. This was the third time that the Paraguayans planned such an attack. They had attempted to take the *Alagoas* on February 19 as she was fighting her way past the batteries at Humaitá. They had also planned to attack the Brazilian squadron on February 27 but the men panicked before sighting the enemy.

60. The Paraguayan gunboats *Tacuarí* and *Ygurey* were trapped. The first, scuttled while under the fire of the *Bahia* and the *Para* in the Riacho Guaycurú, was nonetheless able to land her guns before being destroyed. The *Ygurey* was sunk by the Brazilian ironclad *Barroso* and the monitors *Para* and *Rio Grande do Sul*.

61. Meister, *Francisco Solano López*, 246.

62. After López departed, Col. Paulino Alén became the commander of the Humaitá defenses. Once the fate of the complex was sealed, Alén attempted suicide on July 20, 1868, by firing two pistol shots into his head. He only succeeded in blinding himself. Alén was evacuated, survived, and was executed together with many others on December 21, 1868, at Lomas Valentinas. The command now fell to Col. Francisco Martínez. Following his abandoning the defenses, López imprisoned and then executed his wife. Meister, *Francisco Solano López*, 287–88.

63. Among those massacred were the President's brother, "Admiral" Benigno López; Gen. Vicente Barrios, the dictator's brother-in-law; José Berges, Minister of Foreign Affairs; Saturnino Bedoya, another brother-in-law to López and Treasurer; the wife of Col. Francisco Martínez, who had surrendered Humaitá; Bishop Manuel Antonio Palacios; and at least 500 more. George Frederick Masterman, *Seven Eventful Years in Paraguay* (London: Sampson, Low, and Marston, 1869), 308.

64. José de Lima Figueiredo, *Brasil militar* (Rio de Janeiro: n.p., 1944), 75; Botto, *Campanhas navais*, 127–29.

65. Donato, *Dicionário*, 341–43; Affonso de Carvalho, *Caxias* (Rio de Janeiro: Biblioteca do Exército, 1976), 252–54.

66. On his return to Rio de Janeiro, Caxias received the hero's welcome, but he was called before the Senate to explain López' successful escape from the battles at Lomas Valentinas. He did receive the Gran Cruz da Ordem de Pedro, a decoration previously reserved to those of royal blood, and on March 26, 1869, Caxias was made a duke—the only Brazilian to achieve this imperial distinction.

67. Conde d'Eu was a twenty-six-year-old French nobleman and the Orleanist pretender to the French throne. His previous military experience had not included the command of large units. After his marriage to Princess Isabel, d'Eu was incorporated into the Brazilian army as Marecal de Exército. D'Eu badgered his father-in-law, the Emporer, to send him to fight. D'Eu made a brief appearance at the siege of Uruguayana in 1865. After being appointed commander of the army in 1868, a number of authors state that d'Eu was a figurehead and that the real command rested with the subordinate Brazilian generals.

68. Francisco Isidoro Resquín, *Datos historicos de la guerra del Paraguay con la triple alianza* (Buenos Aires: Compañia Sud-Americana de Billetes de Banco, 1896), 117; Masterman, *Seven Eventful Years*, 293.

69. Masterman, *Seven Eventful Years*, 292; Richard F. Burton, *Letters from the Battlefields of Paraguay* (London: Tinsley Brothers, 1870), 449.

70. Meister, *Francisco Solano López*, 351–54. See also the preface, endnote 6. Herrera quotes M. Gonzalez de la Rosa, *Nuevo atlas geográfico universal*, "Its [Paraguay] population, that was in 1857 1,337,431 and 221,079 (of these 28,746 males) in 1873." Luis Alberto de Herrera, *El Uruguay internacional* (Paris: Bernard Grasset, Éditeur, 1912), 69n; Loveman, *For la Patria*, 50.

71. "No one should ignore that the major weight of the war was born by their [the Brazilian] men." Herrera, *El Uruguay*, 100.

72. Meister, *Francisco Solano López*, 351–54; Loveman, *For la Patria*, 51–52.

73. Argentine losses are difficult to estimate. Officially about 4,000 were killed in action against the Paraguayans and about 5,000 during revolts, but to this must be added at least 11,000 who died from sickness. Perhaps 20,000 is the lowest realistic estimate. Meister, *Francisco Solano López*, 351–52; Loveman, *For la Patria*, 50–51.

74. After López' death, Lynch remained silent, except for her pamphlet, concerning anything about or against López, the war, or her role. She tried in vain to recover her and López' fortunes in Paraguay and died a pauper in Paris.

75. At least three of these guns were used in the defense of Humaitá, Angostura, and Asunción. Kolinski, *Independence*, 39.

CHAPTER THIRTY

1. William Columbus Davis, *The Last Conquistadores* (Athens: University of Georgia Press, 1950), 27–29; St. John, *Foreign Policy*, 68–69; Valdizan, *Historia naval*, 3: 290–91.

2. Fuenzalida, *La armada*, 2: 571.

3. Burr, *By Reason*, 90.

4. Galdames, *A History of Chile*, 307; Melo, *Historia de la marina*, 1: 208; St. John, *Foreign Policy*, 69–70.

5. Davis, *The Last Conquistadores*, 52–58; Fuenzalida, *La armada*, 2: 576; Galdames, *A History of Chile*, 307; St. John, *Foreign Policy*, 70.

6. St. John, *Foreign Policy*, 70–75; Davis, *The Last Conquistadores*, 122, 149–60; Burr, *By Reason*, 91; Pike, *The Modern History*, 115–16.

7. Davis, *The Last Conquistadores*, 160–62, 193–95; López, *Historia de la marina*, 205–6 42; Felipe de la Barra, *Objetivo: palacio de gobierno* (Lima: Editorial Juan Mejía Baca, 1967), 78; *El poder naval chileno*, 2 vols. (Valparaíso: Revista de Marina, 1985), 2: 343.

8. Burr, *By Reason*, 91–97; Fuenzalida, *La armada*, 2: 584–87; Galdames, *A History of Chile*, 308; St. John, *Foreign Policy*, 75.

9. On November 25, 1865, the *Triunfo* was accidently destroyed by fire. Davis, *The Last Conquistadores*, 118–19.

10. Fuenzalida, *La armada*, 2: 578; Melo, *Historia de la marina*, 1: 207; Davis, *The Last Conquistadores*, 13–15; Burr, *By Reason*, 98.

11. Fuenzalida, *La armada*, 2: 573, 577–78, 587.

12. The *América* and *Unión* had originally been ordered from France by the Confederate States of America as the *Georgia* and the *Texas*. They were purchased by Peru from the builders. Vegas, *Historia de la marina*, 109; Melo, *Historia de la marina*, 1: 210–11, 217–18, 241; Valdizan, *Historia naval*, 4: 12–13.

13. Fuenzalida, *La Armada*, 2: 582–83; Davis, *The Last Conquistadores*, 231–32, 266–68, 276–77; Burr, *By Reason*, 98.

14. St. John, *Foreign Policy*, 75–76; Davis, *The Last Conquistadores*, 274–75.

15. Colombia intimated that it would probably join in the war against Spain if the conflict proved protracted and Venezuela implied it might as well. St. John, *Foreign Policy* 75–76; Burr, *By Reason* 98.

16. Burr, *By Reason*, 97–99.

17. Fuenzalida, *La armada*, 2: 595–601; López, *Historia de la marina*, 211–12; Davis, *The Last Conquistadores*, 248–54; *El poder naval chileno*, 2: 345.

18. López, *Historia de la marina*, 217–19; Davis, *The Last Conquistadores*, 271–72; Melo, *Historia de la marina*, 1: 224–29; Valdizan, *Historia naval*, 4: 25–29.

19. Vegas, *Historia de la marina*, 114.

20. Scheina, *Latin America*, 30.

21. Davis, *The Last Conquistadores*, 291–310; Fuenzalida, *La armada*, 2: 628–30; López, *Historia de la marina*, 222–23; St. John, *Foreign Policy*, 77; Burr, *By Reason*, 99.

22. Melo, *Historia de la marina*, 1: 236–37; Vegas, *Historia de la marina*, 122–23; Davis, *The Last Conquistadores*, 311–17.

23. Davis, *The Last Conquistadores*, 311–22; Melo, *Historia de la marina*, 1: 236–45; Vegas, *Historia de la marina*, 124–27; López, *Historia de la marina*, 223–25.

24. López, *Chile: A Brief Naval History*, 43; St. John, *Foreign Policy*, 79–81.

25. Davis, *The Last Conquistadores*, 225–26, 268; López, *Historia de la marina*, 207.

26. *El poder naval chileno*, 2: 345; López Urrutia, *Chile*, 44.

27. Vegas, *Historia de la marina*, 117, 130.

CHAPTER THIRTY-ONE

1. Juan Pablo Duarte (1803–76) was the son of a ship chandler. He received his higher education in Europe and was in Paris during the July 1830 revolution. He received no military training.

2. Each of the nine founding members swore an oath "in the name of the most holy, most August, and indivisible Trinity of Almighty God" to work for Dominican independence. Ian Bell, "Santo Domingo's Struggle for Independence from Haiti," *History Today* 31; 42–47 (April 1981), 44.

3. Sumner Welles, *Naboth's Vineyard: The Dominican Republic 1844–1924*, 2 vols. (New York: Payson & Clarke, 1928), 1: 57; J. Marino Inchaustegui, *Historia dominicana*, 2 vols. (Ciudad Trujillo: Impresora Dominicana, 1955), 2: 23; Emilio Rodríguez Demorizi, *La marina de guerra dominicana 1844–1861* (Ciudad Trujillo: Editora Montalvo, 1958), 9.

4. Welles, *Naboth's Vineyard*, 1: 17–18.

5. Rodman, *Quisqueya*, 42–43.

6. Under the Treaty of Paris, May 30, 1814, France re-ceded Santo Domingo back to Spain. Hazard, *Santo Domingo*, 157–58; Rodman, *Quisqueya*, 44–45.

7. Richard A. Haggerty, ed., *Dominican Republic and Haiti* (Washington: Government Printing Office, 1991,) 9; Rodman, *Quisqueya*, 45; Hazard, *Santo Domingo*, 159.

8. Inchaustegui, *Historia dominicana*, 2: 9–11.

9. Rodríguez, *La marina*, 9; Rodman, *Quisqueya*, 45; Bell, "Santo Domingo's Struggle," 43; James G. Leyburn, *The Haitian People* (New Haven, Conn.: Yale University Press, 1966), 64; Inchaustegui, *Historia dominicana*, 2: 11–14.

10. Welles, *Naboth's Vineyard*, 1: 77.

11. Ian Bell, *The Dominican Republic* (Boulder: Westview Press, 1981), 33.

12. Haggerty, *Dominican Republic*, 11; Welles, *Naboth's Vineyard*, 1: 57.

13. Haggerty, *Dominican Republic*, 12; Welles, *Naboth's Vineyard*, 1: 38; Rodríguez, *La marina*, 9; Bell, "Santo Domingo's Struggle," 44.

14. Bell, "Santo Domingo's Struggle," 45.

15. Pedro Santana Familias (1801–64) is described by F. A. Kirkpatrick as "a big uncouth ignorant *caudillo*, in whose countenance the negro element predominated over the European and Indian strains." Santana was known for his great strength and frequently demonstrated bravery on the battlefield, winning for himself a substantial following. Kirkpatrick, *Latin America*, 400.

16. Inchaustegui, *Historia dominicana*, 2: 30; Bell, "Santo Domingo's Struggle," 46.

17. Welles, *Naboth's Vineyard*, 1: 59–60; César A. DeWindt Lavandier, Victor Francisco García Alecont, and Albérico Ventura Dominguez, *La marina en la guerra de independencia dominicana* (Santo Domingo: CENAPEC, 1992), 12.

18. Bell, *The Dominican Republic*, 34; Welles, *Naboth's Vineyard*, 1: 64–65.

19. Welles, *Naboth's Vineyard*, 1: 64–65; Inchaustegui, *Historia dominicana*, 2: 33–34; Rodríguez, *La marina*, 11; Nelson Antonio Arciniegas Valentin, *Historia de la marina de guerra dominicana* (Santo Domingo: Editora Nivar, C. por A.,1984), 25.

20. Welles, *Naboth's Vineyard*, 1: 70–71; DeWindt, *La marina*, 26–36; Rodríguez, *La marina*, 11; Inchaustegui, *Historia dominicana*, 2: 35.

21. Bell, *The Dominican Republic*, 35–37; Haggerty, *Dominican Republic*, 12; Rodríguez, *La marina*, 16–17.

22. Buenaventura Báez Méndez (1812–84), in many respects, was the antithesis of his rival Santana. Báez was born in Azua to a wealthy planter and a black slave. He was educated in Europe and was influenced by its culture.

23. Bell, *The Dominican Republic,* 37–39; Bell, "Santo Domingo's Struggle," 47.

24. Rodríguez, *La marina*, 12–13.

25. ibid., 13–14, 201–20; Inchaustegui, *Historia dominicana,* 2: 39.

26. Rodríguez, *La marina*, 13–14; DeWindt, *La marina,* 19, 41; Inchaustegui, *Historia dominicana*, 2: 39–40.

27. Dispatches from U.S. envoy Jonathan Elliott to Secretary of State James Buchanan indicated that the invading Haitian army was 10,000 men strong. Welles, *Naboth's Vineyard*, 1: 89. Inchaustegui places the number at 18,000 men. Inchaustegui, *Historia dominicana* 2: 42. Other sources have numbers as low as 4,000 men.

28. Philip Evanson, "The Third Dominican-Haitian War and the Return of General Santana: Part of a Long Story," *Caribbean Studies* 4: 1; 13–23 (April 1964), 16.

29. ibid., 16; Rodríguez, *La marina*, 13–14.

30. Inchaustegui, *Historia dominicana*, 2: 42–43; Evanson, "The Third Dominican-Haitian War," 17; DeWindt, *La marina*, 48.

31. Inchaustegui, *Historia dominicana*, 2: 43; Evanson, "The Third Dominican-Haitian War," 17; Bell, *The Dominican Republic*, 40–41; Hazard, *Santo Domingo*, 248–49.

32. Samaná Bay, located south of Hispañola's northeast peninsula, is one of the world's largest natural harbors.

33. Rodman, *Quisqueya*, 66–67.

34. Rodríguez, *La marina*, 16–17; DeWindt, *La marina*, 55–58; Inchaustegui, *Historia dominicana*, 2: 44.

35. Juan Alejandro Acosta Bustamante (1813–86) was born in Bani into a locally prominent family. At the age of sixteen, Acosta became a good friend of Juan Duarte. Acosta became a member of the secret patriotic society, "La Trinitaria." He commanded the brigantine *Leonor*, the first ship to fly the Dominican flag. Acosta commanded various Dominican warships during the fighting against Haiti. He opposed annexation of the Dominican Republic to another nation and was expelled from the Dominican Republic by Buenaventura Bàez. He died in poverty.

36. Rodríguez, *La marina*, 17; DeWindt, *La marina*, 59–61; Inchaustegui, *Historia dominicana*, 2: 44.

37. Rodríguez, *La marina*, 18; Haggerty, *Dominican Republic*, 14.

38. Bell, *The Dominican Republic*, 42–43.

39. Welles, *Naboth's Vineyard*, 1: 157–58; Rodríguez, *La marina*, 20–21; Rodman, *Quisqueya*, 67–70. However, Haiti did not recognize Dominican independence until 1874.

40. Welles, *Naboth's Vineyard*, 1: 224.

41. Rodman, *Quisqueya*, 76–77; Welles, *Naboth's Vineyard*, 1: 238–39; Bell, *The Dominican Republic*, 44–49; Inchaustegui, *Historia dominicana*, 2: 60–61.

42. Gregorio Luperon, *Notas autobiografias y apuntes historicos* 2d ed., 3 vols. (Santo Domingo: Central de Libros C. por A., 1992), 2: 7–8; Bell, *The Dominican Republic*, 49–50.

43. Welles, *Naboth's Vineyard*, 1: 232–33; Inchaustegui, *Historia dominicana*, 2: 61–62; Haggerty, *Dominican Republic*, 16; Hazard, *Santo Domingo*, 429–30.

44. Luperon, *Notas*, 2: 8–9.

45. Welles, *Naboth's Vineyard*, 1: 245–46.

46. ibid., 1: 247–48.

47. Rodman, *Quisqueya*, 79.

48. Inchaustegui, *Historia dominicana*, 2: 64.

49. Welles, *Naboth's Vineyard*, 1: 250. Welles gives the commercial agent's name as Yaeger; Rodman, *Quisqueya*, 79–80; Inchaustegui, *Historia dominicana*, 2: 68.

50. Some authors write that he may have committed suicide. Haggerty, *Dominican Republic*, 16–17; Rodman, *Quisqueya*, 80–81; Welles, *Naboth's Vineyard*, 1: 262–63, 270; Bell, *The Dominican Republic*, 49–51.

51. Welles, *Naboth's Vineyard*, 1: 275.
52. ibid.
53. ibid., 1: 275–77.
54. Rodman, *Quisqueya*, 81.
55. ibid.; Kirkpatrick, *Latin America*, 401; Luperon, *Notas*, 2: 8–9.

CHAPTER THIRTY-TWO

1. Edilberto Marbán and Elio Leiva, *Curso de historia de Cuba*, 2 vols. (La Habana: Impresora Modelo, S.A., 1959), 2: 310–11; Jay Mallin, *History of the Cuban Armed Forces* (Reston, Va.: Ancient Mariners Press, 2000), 9; Hugh Thomas, *Cuba*, 245; Franklin, *Cuba*, 5.

2. Langley, *America*, 50; Carlos A. Villanueva, *Resumen de la historia general de America* (Paris: Casa Editorial Garnier Hermanos, n.d.), 346–47.

3. Julius W. Pratt, *America's Colonial Experiment* (New York: Prentice-Hall, 1951), 41.

4. Fermoselle, *The Evolution*, 59–60.

5. Juan Jiménez Pastrana, *Los chinos en las luchas por la liberación cubana 1848–1930* (La Habana: Instituto de Historia, 1963), 69–82; Marbán and Leiva, *Curso*, 2: 312; Mallin, *History*, 10; Fermoselle, *The Evolution*, 64.

6. Fermoselle, *The Evolution*, 65.

7. ibid., 64; Antonio Pirala, *Anales de la guerra de Cuba*, 3 vols. (Madrid: F. Gonzalez Rojas, 1896), 1: 385; 498–99.

8. John Lawrence Tone, "The Machete and the Liberation of Cuba," *The Journal of Military History* 62: 1; 7–28 (January 1998), 16.

9. Adolfo Jiménez Castellanos, *Sistema para combatir las insurrecciones en Cuba, según lo que aconseja la exeriencia* (Madrid: Establecimiento tipogràfico, 1883), 30; Tone, "The Machete," 13–15, 19–21.

10. Quintin Banderas (1837–1906) was an illiterate black who joined the Revolutionary cause in 1871. He rose to the rank of division general. Following the Wars for Independence, Banderas retired to a farm. He was assassinated in 1906.

11. Tomas Savignon, *Quintín Banderas: el mambí sacrificado y escarnecido* (La Habana: Imp. P. Fernández y Cia, 1948), 22; Mallin, *History*, 11; Fermoselle, *The Evolution*, 64.

12. Jiménez Castellanos, *Sistema*, 96–115.

13. Marbán and Leiva, *Curso*, 2: 312.

14. Máximo Gómez (1836–1905), nicknamed "The Old Chinaman," was born in Bani, Santo Domingo. He possessed a good education and fought against the Haitians during their invasions of Santo Domingo. During the Spanish recolonization of Santo Domingo (1861–65), Gómez served as an officer in the Spanish army.

15. Thomas, *Cuba*, 247.

16. Pirala, *Anales*, 1: 298; Thomas, *Cuba*, 247–48.

17. Thomas, *Cuba*, 250–51.

18. Pirala, *Anales*, 1: 551–54; Marbán and Leiva, *Curso*, 2: 227–28.

19. Thomas, *Cuba*, 255–56.

20. Marbán and Leiva, *Curso*, 2: 330; Michael Blow, "The *Trochas*," *MHQ: The Quarterly Journal of Military History* 10: 4; 46–51 (Summer 1998), 47–48; Thomas, *Cuba*, 256–60.

21. Marbán and Leiva, *Curso*, 2: 334; Tone, "The Machete," 19–21.

22. The *Tornado* had been built as the *Pampero* by Galbraith & Denny of Glasgow, Scotland, for the Confederate States of America. Undelivered, the warship was purchased by Chile,

which was at war with Spain between 1865 and 1866. Renamed the *Tornado*, the steam corvette was captured off Madeira, Spain, on August 22, 1866, by the Spanish screw frigate *Gerona* and taken into the Spanish navy.

23. William D. O'Ryan, "General W. A. C. Ryan: The Cuban Martyr," *The Irish Sword* 8: 31, 115–19 (Winter 1967), 115–19; Marbán and Leiva, *Curso*, 2: 361–70; Thomas, *Cuba*, 262–63.

24. Mallin, *History*, 13.

25. Antonio Maceo (1848–96), a mulatto known as the "Titan of Bronze," joined the Revolutionary army in 1869. He advanced rapidly, reaching the rank of major general by the end of the Ten Years' War. His father and six of his brothers were either killed or seriously wounded during the Cuban Wars for Independence.

26. Fermoselle, *The Evolution*, 68; Thomas, *Cuba*, 264.

27. Not to be confused with Las Guásimas (7 mi SE of Santiago).

28. Marbán and Leiva, *Curso*, 2: 372–73; Mallin, *History*, 13; Fermoselle, *The Evolution*, 68.

29. Thomas, *Cuba*, 264.

30. ibid., 264–65.

31. Arsenio Martínez Campos (1831–1900) was held in high esteem within Spain. He fought in Moroco (1864) and served in Cuba (1869–72). In 1874 he led the revolt that reestablished the monarchy, thus ending ten years of civil war.

32. Marbán and Leiva, *Curso*, 2: 380–81; Mallin, *History*, 15; Fermoselle, *The Evolution*, 69.

33. Fermoselle, *The Evolution*, 70; Thomas, *Cuba*, 266; Marbán and Leiva, *Curso*, 2: 381–82.

34. Thomas, *Cuba*, 269; Fermoselle, *The Evolution*, 70; James D. Rudolph, ed., *Cuba: A Country Study*, 3d ed. (Washington: Headquarters, Department of the Army, 1987), 15.

35. A liberal constitution was promulgated in 1869, and, as a compromise a Conservative, Carlos Manuel de Céspedes, was named president. He was deposed in October 1873 by Salvador Cisneros Betancourt, the leader of the Liberals. Fermoselle, *The Evolution*, 69.

36. Fermoselle, *The Evolution*, 85; Louis A. Pérez Jr., "Class, Property, and Sugar: Conflict and Contradiction in Cuban Separatism, 1895–1898," *Inter-American Economic Affairs* 34 (Summer 1980), 1, 3–26: 11; Thomas, *Cuba*, 103; Luis E. Aguilar, *Cuba 1933: Prologue to Revolution* (New York: W. W. Norton, 1977), 13.

37. Keith Ellis, *Cuba's Nicolas Guillen* (Toronto: University of Toronto Press, 1983), 31.

38. Félix Ojeda Reyes, *Peregrinos de la libertad* (Río Piedras: Editorial de la Universidad de Puerto Rico, 1992), 16–18.

39. Foner, *A History*, 164.

40. Olga Jiménez de Wagenheim, *Puerto Rico's Revolt for Independence* (Princeton: Markus Wiener, 1993); Fermoselle, *The Evolution*, 70–71.

41. Ojeda, *Peregrinos*, 15, 22, 126–29.

42. Mallin, *History*, 15; Thomas, *Cuba*, 266–67.

43. Thomas, *Cuba*, 268–69; Foner, *A History*, 287.

44. Villanueva, *Resumen*, 349–50; Mallin, *History*, 15.

45. José Martí (1853–95) was born in Havana and educated in Cuba. In January 1869 Martí founded the newspaper *Patria Libre*. The following year he was arrested for sedition and sentenced to six years in prison. In 1871 he was deported to Spain on the condition that

he not return to Cuba. Martí returned to Cuba in December 1878 but was expelled in less than a year. In 1881 he moved to New York City.

46. Ojeda, *Peregrinos*, 175, 214; John M. Kirk, *José Martí* (Tampa: University Press of Florida, 1983), 82.

47. José Martí, *Mi tiempo: un mundo Nuevo*, selections by Jaime Labastida (Mexico: SEP/UNAM, 1982), 280.

48. José Martí, *Our America* (New York: Monthly Review Press, 1977), 294.

49. Martí, *Our America*, 301.

50. José Martí, "La guerra de razas," *Pátria* 3 (1 Abril 1893), 3.

51. Foner, *A History*, 347–50, 357; Franklin, *Cuba*, 7.

52. Fermoselle, *The Evolution*, 80; R. L. Bullard, "The Cuban Negro, O," *North American Review* 184 (March 15, 1907), 625; Dorothy Stanhope, "The Negro Race in Cuba: Insular Society Draws No Discriminatory Color Line," *New York Times* 5 (September 16, 1900), 5; Thomas, *Cuba*, 323–24.

53. Thomas, *Cuba*, 319.

54. Warren Zimmermann, "Jingoes, Goo-Goos, and the Rise of America's Empire," *Wilson Quarterly* 22: 2; 42–65 (Spring 1998), 58–59.

55. Pérez, "Class," 10–14.

56. Blow, "The *Trochas*," 47–48.

57. Mallin, *History*, 21–22; Morales C., *La importancia*, 68; Thomas, *Cuba*, 316–19.

58. Hubert Howard, "Five weeks with the Cuban Insurgents," *The United Service* (Philadelphia: L. R. Hamersly, 1896), 14, new series, 127–36: 134.

59. Tone, "The Machete," 11; Pérez, "Class," 13–14.

60. José Miró y Argenter, *Cuba; crónicas de la Guerra*, 4th ed. (Havana: Lex, 1945), 147–49; Blow, "The *Trochas*," 48; Thomas, *Cuba*, 322.

61. Manuel Piedra Martel, *Campañas de Maceo en la última guerra de independenia* (Havana: Editorial Lex, 1946), 68–72; Fermoselle, *The Evolution*, 83.

62. Mallin, *History*, 23–26; Fermoselle, *The Evolution*, 83–84; Blow, "The *Trochas*," 48; Tone, "The Machete," 16.

63. Valeriano Weyler y Nicolau (1838–1930) of Spanish-German descent, he served as the Spanish military attaché to the United States during its civil war (1861–65). Weyler was an admirer of U.S. General William Tecumseh Sherman. A strong, robust man, Weyler seemed unaffected by the tropics. He shared the living conditions and food of his troops. Weyler fought in the Cuban Ten Years' War (1868–78), the Carlist War (1873–76) in Spain, and the Philippine Insurrection (1891). He was ruthless towards men but had a great compassion for horses. The American "yellow press" gave him the nickname "the Butcher."

64. Mallin, *History*, 27; Pratt, *America's Colonial Experiment*, 40–41; Blow, "The *Trochas*," 48; Thomas, *Cuba*, 330.

65. Blow, "The *Trochas*," 48–49; Thomas, *Cuba*, 329–30.

66. Fermoselle, *The Evolution*, 85–86; Marbán and Leiva, *Curso*, 2: 451.

67. Thomas, *Cuba*, 331.

68. Pedro Roig, *La guerra de Martí* (Miami: Ediciones Universal, 1984), 145–47; Thomas, *Cuba*, 334; Fermoselle, *The Evolution*, 86–87.

69. Blow, "The *Trochas*," 50; Thomas, *Cuba*, 335

70. Blow, "The *Trochas*," 50; Thomas, *Cuba*, 339; Franklin, *Cuba*, 8.

71. Thomas, *Cuba*, 346–49; Fermoselle, *The Evolution*, 90.

72. Tone, "The Machete," 12–13; Thomas W. Crouch, *A Yankee guerrillo: Frederick Funston and the Cuban Insurrection, 1896–1897* (Memphis: Memphis State University Press, 1975), 110.

73. Marbán and Leiva, *Curso*, 2: 488; Mallin, *History*, 29–30.

74. Mallin, *History*, 30–31.

75. Fermoselle, *The Evolution*, 90–91.

76. Emily Hatchwell and Simon Calder, *Cuba* (London: Latin American Bureau, 1995) 10.

77. Pratt, *America's Colonial Experiment*, 41, 48; Blow, "The *Trochas*," 51; Thomas, *Cuba*, 324.

78. Pratt, *America's Colonial Experiment*, 41.

CHAPTER THIRTY-THREE

1. Suárez, *Atlas*, 323.

2. Gilliss, *The U.S. Naval Astronomical Expedition*, 1: 325.

3. A major difference in tactics between those used by the Indians and the modern guerrilla is that most modern guerrillas are members of the society they are attacking and most endeavor to hide their identity.

4. Estado Mayor, *Historia del ejército de Chile*, 4: 221; Bailey and Nasatir, *Latin America*, 405; Frederick M. Nunn, *The Military in Chilean History* (Albuquerque: University of New Mexico Press, 1976), 27.

5. Estado Mayor, *Historia del ejército de Chile*, 4: 222–23.

6. ibid., 4: 223–24.

7. ibid., 4: 224–25; Fuentes et al., *Diccionario*, 251–52; Frías, *Nuevo Manual*, 304–5.

8. Bailey and Nasatir, *Latin America*, 410; Galdames, *A History of Chile*, 299–300.

9. Estado Mayor, *Historia del ejército de Chile*, 4: 237–38; Fuentes et al., *Diccionario*, 590.

10. Estado Mayor, *Historia del ejército de Chile*, 4: 279–93.

11. Suárez, *Atlas*, 325–27.

12. ibid., 327–28.

13. P. P. King, Robert Fitzroy, and Charles Darwin, *Narrative of the Surveying Voyages of His Majesty's Ships Adventure and Beagle*, 3 vols. (London: H. Colburn, 1839–40), 3: 83.

14. Davis, *History of Latin America*, 406; Herring, *A History*, 598; Suárez, *Atlas*, 329; Ysabel Rennie, *The Argentine Republic* (New York: Macmillan, 1945), 121.

15. Suárez, *Atlas*, 329–30; Rennie, *The Argentine Republic*, 121.

16. Suárez, *Atlas*, 330–33; Marley, *Wars*, 579.

17. Rennie, *The Argentine Republic*, 124.

18. Suárez, *Atlas*, 333–34; Rennie, *The Argentine Republic*, 125; Herring, *A History of Latin America*, 622; Marley, *Wars*, 581.

19. Leopoldo Lugones, *Historia de Roca* (Buenos Aires: Editorial de Belgrano, 1980), 186.

20. Reed, *The Caste War*, 27–28, 49.

21. ibid., 53–99; Cristobal Molina, "War of the Castes: Indian Uprisings in Chiapas, 1867–70," No. 5, 357–97 in Department of Middle American Research, *Studies in Middle America* (New Orleans: Tulane University, 1934), 359–60; Mario Lavalle Ardudín, *La armada en el Mexico independiente* (Mexico: Secretaría de Marina, 1985), 134; Parkes, *A History of Mexico*, 221.

22. Reed, *The Caste War*, 103–4.
23. ibid., 108–12.
24. ibid., 113–14.
25. ibid., 116–20.
26. ibid., 127, 160–84, 290; Lavalle, *La armada*, 135.
27. *Anales gráficos*, 145.
28. Mendoza and Grafias, "el ejército mexicano de 1860 a 1913," 318; Reed, *The Caste War of Yucatan*, 231; Lavalle, *La armada*, 140–43; Parkes, *A History of Mexico*, 296.
29. Paul J. Vanderwood, *Disorder and Progress* (Lincoln: University of Nebraska Press, 1981), 28.
30. Bancroft, *History of Mexico*, 6: 366; *Anales gráficos*, 60, 146.
31. Mendoza and Grafias, "el ejército mexicano de 1860 a 1913," 316; Vanderwood, *Disorder*, 155; Bancroft, *History of Mexico*, 6: 461–62; Parkes, *A History of Mexico*, 296; Marley, *Wars*, 583.
32. Mendoza and Grafias, "el ejército mexicano de 1860 a 1913," 318; *Anales gráficos*, 159, 162–63; Marley, *Wars*, 607–8; Costa Soto, *Historia militar*, 89–90.
33. Kirkpatrick, *Latin America*, 349.
34. Luís Garfías Magaña, "el ejército mexicano de 1913 a 1938," in *El ejército mexicano* (Mexico: Secretaria de la Defensa Nacional, 1979), 464–66; John W. F. Dulles, *Yesterday in Mexico* (Austin: University of Texas Press, 1961), 311–12; Costa Soto, *Historia militar*, 89–90.

CHAPTER THIRTY-FOUR

1. Toro, *Sintesis*, 2: 48; Cox, "Chile," 339; Loveman, *For la Patria*, 53.
2. Theodorus Mason, *The War on the Pacific Coast of South America between Chile and the Allied Republics of Peru and Bolivia 1879–81* (Washington: Government Printing Office, 1883), 7; United States Hydrographic Office, *The Coast of Chile, Bolivia, and Peru* (Washington: Government Printing Office, 1876), 1; Dellepiane, *Historia militar*, 2: 11–13; Estado Mayor, *Historia militar de Chile*, 2: 68–69; Cox, "Chile," 336–39.
3. Estado Mayor, *Historia militar de Chile*, 2: 77, 93–94; Dellepiane, *Historia militar*, 2: 22–23; Toro, *Sintesis*, 2: 48.
4. Since the winning of independence in the 1820s, Bolivia and Peru had argued over Bolivia's access to the sea. Although Bolivia did possess a coastline in 1878, it was not the most convenient access to the interior. This was through Peruvian territory with Arica and Mollendo as the most convenient seaports. Peru feared that Bolivia might go over to the Chilean side if offered the more accessible Peruvian territory in exchange for their own. Halperín, *The Contemporary History*, 148.

During much of the time Bolivian President Daza camped at Tacna with his Peruvian allies, he listened to secret Chilean proposals that Bolivia change sides. Therefore, Peru's fears that Bolivia might desert the alliance were not without foundation. Richard Snyder Phillips Jr., "Bolivia in the War of the Pacific, 1879–1884" (Ph.D. dissertation, University of Virginia, 1973), 75–146; Pike, *The Modern History*, 142; Dellepiane, *Historia militar*, 2: 27–28.

5. Pike, *The Modern History*, 143.
6. The *Huáscar*, the principal Peruvian warship, was no more than a seagoing monitor with a ram. Completed in 1866 at Laird Birkenhead shipyards in England, the ship had a turret that was trained by manpower. The *Huáscar* could only fire on the beams because the forecastle blocked the field of fire over the bow. It was easier to train the ship than the gun.

The *Huáscar* was faster than most reference books give her credit. Apparently, on builder's trials she made 12.3 knots. According to Samuel MacMahon, her chief engineer, the maximum speed that the *Huáscar* was capable of at Angamos was about eleven knots. Some Peruvian sources credit the *Huáscar* with only nine knots. Jacinto López, *Historia de la guerra del guano y salitre* (Lima: Editorial Milla Batres, 1979), 2: 137–39.

7. Mason, *The War*, 12–21; Dellepiane, *Historia militar*, 2: 33–37. In 1873 the Bolivian President had proposed to the country's Congress that two armored warships of the type purchased by Chile be bought. The Congress replied that Bolivia was "a peaceful nation and La Paz [the capital of Bolivia] does not need nor will it ever need ships of war."

William F. Sater, *Chile and the War of the Pacific* (Lincoln: University of Nebraska Press, 1986), 18, holds a low opinion on the state of the Chilean navy in 1879.

8. Pike, *The Modern History*, 139; Mason, *The War*, 9; Phillips, "Bolivia," 93.

9. Estado Mayor, *Historia militar de Chile*, 2: 80–83, 87; Terry Hooker, *The Pacific War 1879–1884* (Cottingham, England: El Dorado Books, 1993), 2; Dellepiane, *Historia militar*, 2: 89–90.

Sater, *Chile*, 17, offers a very different evaluation. "A careful examination of the Moneda's [Chile's "government house"] army and navy reveals, however, the wretched condition of the nation's armed forces in 1879."

A Mr. Paraf invented a machine that altered captured cartridges so that they could be used in Chilean rifles, thus the origins of the term "Paraf Gold."

10. In an attempt to correct this problem, Juan Crisóstomo Grieve cast field pieces in Lima. However, due to the inexperience of the workmen, these were of poor quality; they were used in the defense of Lima in 1881. By 1880 a few Krupps and Vavasseurs began to arrive from Europe.

11. Hooker, *Pacific War*, 3; Estado Mayor, *Historia militar de Chile*, 2: 89–90; Mason, *The War*, 12; Dellepiane, *Historia militar*, 2: 78, 85–89.

12. Phillips, "Bolivia," 93–94; Dellepiane, *Historia militar*, 2: 89; Estado Mayor, *Historia militar de Chile*, 2: 91–92; Hooker, *Pacific War*, 4.

13. Juan Williams Rebolledo (1826–1910) was the son of an English naval officer who had fought for Chilean independence. He was born in Valparaíso and entered the Chilean navy in 1844. In 1863 he was given command of the steam corvette *Esmeralda* and captured the Spanish gunboat *Covadonga* during the Pacific War with Spain (1865–66). Later in that war, he commanded the combined Chilean-Peruvian fleet.

14. Sater, *Chile*, 19; Estado Mayor, *Historia militar de Chile*, 2: 95–96.

15. Toro, *Sintesis*, 2: 54; Phillips, "Bolivia," 108.

16. Mariano Felipe Paz Soldán, *Narración histórica de la guerra de Chile contra el Perù y Bolivia* (Buenos Aires: Impr. y libr. de Mayo, 1884), 165. Paz Soldán was the Peruvian Minister of Justice when the war broke out.

See also Edmundo H. Civati Bernasconi, *Guerra del Pacifico 1879–1883*, 2 vols. (Buenos Aires: República Argentina, 1946), 1: 161; José Vicente Ochoa, *Diario de la campaña del ejército boliviano en la guerra del Pacifico* (Sucre: Tipografía y Librería Económica, 1899), 10–21.

17. Alfonso Crespo, *Los Aramayo de Chichas* (Barcelona: Editorial Blume, 1981), 119; Ochoa, *Diario*, 317.

18. Miguel Grau (1834–79) was born in Piura and went to sea at the age of nine. Grau entered the Peruvian navy in 1856 as a sublieutenant and served on board practically every

ship in the navy. He first commanded the *Huáscar* in 1868. In 1873 he represented Paita in Congress. Grau earned the reputation as a gentleman.

19. Arturo Prat Chacón (1848–78) had a reputation without equal within the Chilean navy. Born near Quirihue, he spent a few years in a private school in Santiago before entering the Chilean Naval Academy in Valparaíso. He took part in the capture of the *Covadonga* from the Spanish in 1866. Throughout his career, Prat was an ardent student of astronomy, mathematics, law, and diplomacy.

20. Mason, *The War*, 32–35; Estado Mayor, *Historia militar de Chile*, 2: 97–99; Dellepiane, *Historia militar*, 2: 40–42; Toro, *Sintesis*, 2: 56–58.

21. Mason, *The War*, 37; Dellepiane, *Historia militar*, 2: 44; Toro, *Sintesis*, 2: 58; Cox, "Chile," 340.

22. Sater, *Chile*, 20; Dellepiane, *Historia militar*, 2: 45.

23. Galvarino Riveros Cárdenas (1833–92), born in Chiloé, attended the old military academy and entered the Chilean navy in 1848. During the Pacific War with Spain (1865–66) he was the commander of naval arsenals and later commanded the steamer *Concepción*.

24. The speed of a warship was influenced by many factors. Most significant were the condition of her boiler tubes, the quality of the coal she was burning, the cleanliness of her bottom, and the experience of her engine-room crew. Therefore, a difference of a few knots in designed speed could prove insignificant.

25. Mason, *The War*, 40.

26. Patricio Carvajal Prado, "Pudo haber escapado el *Huáscar* el 8 de octubre 1879?" *Revista de Marina* (Valparaíso) 76: 39–46 (1960). The author argues that the *Huáscar* could have escaped.

27. Mason, *The War*, 43–49; Dellepiane, *Historia militar*, 2: 47–56; Estado Mayor, *Historia militar de Chile*, 2: 105–7; Toro, *Sintesis*, 2: 60.

28. Estado Mayor, *Historia militar de Chile*, 2: 109–11; Dellepiane, *Historia militar*, 2: 104–13; Hooker, *Pacific War*, 7; Toro, *Sintesis*, 2: 62–70.

29. Sater, *Chile*, 21.

30. Phillips, "Bolivia," 150–56; Estado Mayor, *Historia militar de Chile*, 2: 112; Dellepiane, *Historia militar*, 2: 132–33; Toro, *Sintesis*, 2: 72.

31. Mason, *The War*, 50–51; Dellepiane, *Historia militar*, 2: 139; Estado Mayor, *Historia militar de Chile*, 2: 114–17; Toro, *Sintesis*, 2: 76–79.

32. Estado Mayor, *Historia militar de Chile*, 2: 118–22; Dellepiane, *Historia militar*, 2: 167–81; Sater, *Chile*, 23.

33. Dellepiane, *Historia militar*, 2: 183–84; Pike, *The Modern History*, 144–45.

34. Narciso Campero (1813–96) born at Tojo, in Upper Peru (later Bolivia), joined the army and fought against the Argentines in 1837 and against Peru in 1840. By 1841 Campero reached the rank of lieutenant colonel. Between 1844 and 1856 he traveled to Europe as part of a commission trying to win Bolivia diplomatic recognition. He joined the French army and attended the General Staff School at St. Cyr. Between the 1850s and 1870s Campero alternated between important military posts and exile.

35. Phillips, "Bolivia" 167–69; Dellepiane, *Historia militar*, 2: 184; Robertson, *History of Latin-American Nations*, 324.

36. Toro, *Sintesis*, 2: 102; Estado Mayor, *Historia militar de Chile*, 2: 135; Dellepiane, *Historia militar*, 2: 219.

37. Sater, *Chile*, 25–26.

38. Manuel Baquedano (1826–97), born in Santiago, sailed as a stowaway at the age of twelve in the second expedition against the Peru-Bolivian Confederation, fighting in the Battles of Portada de Guias (August 21, 1838) and Yungay (January 20, 1839). He also participated in the 1851 Civil War, fighting on the side of the government. Baquedano fought against the Araucanian Indians in 1868 and was a brigadier general when the war broke out with Bolivia and Peru.

39. Toro, *Sintesis*, 2: 92–94, 100–4; Dellepiane, *Historia militar*, 2: 217, 251–52.

40. Phillips, "Bolivia," 183–85; Dellepiane, *Historia militar*, 2: 260; Toro, *Sintesis*, 2: 108.

41. Phillips, "Bolivia," 185; Toro, *Sintesis*, 2: 112.

42. Toro, *Sintesis*, 2: 116; Estado Mayor, *Historia Militar de Chile*, 2: 141–43; Dellepiane, *Historia militar*, 2: 269–84.

43. Hooker, *Pacific War*, 16; Dellepiane, *Historia militar*, 2: 304; Toro, *Sintesis*, 2: 114–16.

44. Dellepiane, *Historia Militar*, 2: 311–25; Toro, *Sintesis*, 2: 120–24; Estado Mayor, *Historia Militar de Chile*, 2: 146–47; Cox, "Chile," 341–42.

45. Callao's defenses included ten 15-inch Rodman smooth bores; one 15-inch Dahlgren smooth bore; three 11-inch Rodman smooth bores; three 11-inch Blakley rifles; two 10-inch Rodman smooth bores; four 10-inch Armstrong rifles; and four 9-inch Vavasseur rifles. All of these guns were muzzle loaders. Letter from Lt. J. B. Briggs, USN, and Surgeon A. C. Heffenger, USN, to Rear Admiral T. R. Stevens, USN, February 1, 1881, in National Archives, Record Group 38. See Dellepiane, *Historia militar*, 2: 365–66.

46. José Gálvez Moreno (1850–94) was the son of the Peruvian Minister of War, who had been killed during the Spanish bombardment of Callao on May 2, 1866. José entered the navy in November 1864 as a midshipman. He was among those who traveled to the United States to retrieve the monitors *Manco Cápac* and *Atahualpa*. Gálvez either volunteered or was recalled during the war. He was wounded in the attack on the *Janequeo*.

47. Mason, *The War*, 66–67; Sater, *Chile*, 30–31.

48. Estado Mayor, *Historia militar de Chile*, 2: 155–56; Dellepiane, *Historia militar*, 2: 336–38; Toro, *Sintesis*, 2: 130.

49. Federico Blume Othon (1831–1901), born on Saint Thomas in the Lesser Antilles, was educated as an engineer in Germany and spent three decades constructing railroads in the United States, Chile, and Peru. Early in his career he was influenced by the work of Robert Fulton and developed an interest in building a ship that could navigate underwater. During the War with Spain, Blume sent plans and specifications for an undersea craft to Gen. Juan Antonio Pezet, President of Peru, but nothing came of them and apparently the details were lost. His interest in submarine design lingered and, using his own money and a railway workshop, he built the *Toro Submarino* in Paita, Peru.

50. Pedro J. Gálvez Velarde, "Submarino, minas y brulotes en la guerra del 79 y sus autores," *Revista del Instituto de Estudios Historicos-Maritimos del Peru* 1: 23–36 (January–June 1979), 27–28.

51. Toro, *Sintesis*, 2: 128; Estado Mayor, *Historia militar de Chile*, 2: 162–63.

52. Some troops carrying Remington .50 caliber rifles were supplied with .45 caliber ammunition for Peabody-Martini rifles and vice-versa.

53. Toro, *Sintesis*, 2: 138–42; Estado Mayor, *Historia militar de Chile*, 2: 165–69; Dellepiane, *Historia militar*, 2: 361–65, 384–98.

54. Carlos Miró Quesada, *Autopsia de los partidos politicos* (Lima: Ediciones "Paginas Peruanas," 1961), 145; Estado Mayor, *Historia militar de Chile*, 2: 169–73; Dellepiane, *Historia militar*, 2: 424–33; Cox, "Chile," 343.

55. Toro, *Sintesis*, 2: 156; Cox, "Chile," 343.

56. Estado Mayor, *Historia militar de Chile*, 2: 179 89.

57. Cox, "Chile," 343–48; Loveman, *For la Patria*, 54–55; Estado Mayor, *Historia militar de Chile*, 2: 189–92.

58. Halperín, *The Contemporary History*, 192; Estado Mayor, *Historia militar de Chile*, 2: 78–80.

59. Medina Castro, *Estados Unidos*, 466.

60. F. A. Kirkpatrick wrote, "[T]he War of the Pacific . . . [was] the greatest war which has divided Latin-American nations." Kirkpatrick, *Latin America*, 189.

CHAPTER THIRTY-FIVE

1. Best, *Historia*, 2: 109–10.

2. Akers and Elliott, *A History*, 78.

3. Best, *Historia*, 2: 110; José Ferrer, "The Armed Forces in Argentine Politics to 1930," (Albuquerque: Ph.D. Dissertation, University of New Mexico, 1965), 70.

4. "Our Sister Republics," *The United Service* 11, New Series, 203–20 and 519–35 (1894), 212.

5. Best, *Historia*, 2: 110.

6. Akers and Elliott, *A History*, 80; Luis Sommi, *La Revolución del 90*, 2nd ed., (Buenos Aires: Ediciones Pueblos de América, 1957), 179–80; Ferrer, "Armed Forces," 80–84.

7. Sommi, *Revolución*, 179–81; Pablo E. Arguindeguy, *Apuntes sobre los buques de la armada Argentina*, 7 vols. (Buenos Aires: Departamento de Estudios Historicos Navales, 1972), 4: 1585; 3: 1280.

8. Akers and Elliott, *A History*, 81–82.

9. Sommi, *Revolución*, 263; "Síntesis histórica de la infantería de marina," *Del Mar* (112) 63–64 (September–December); V. Mario Quartaruolo, "La armada y la revolución de 1890" *Del Mar* (118) 57–64 (January–June 1982), 57–64.

10. Akers and Elliott, *A History*, 82.

11. The foreign warships in Buenos Aires were Britain's steel screw sloop *Beagle* and composite gunboat *Bramble*, Spain's cruiser *Infanta Isabel*, the U.S. sidewheel gunboat *Tallapoosa*, and Uruguay's gunboat *General Rivera*.

12. U.S. National Archives, Record Group 24, log of the *Tallapoosa*, July 28, 1890.

13. Roberto Etchepareborda, *La revolución argentina del 90* (Buenos Aires: Edit. Eudeba, 1966), 60.

14. Akers and Elliott, *A History*, 83–84; Ferrer, "Armed Forces," 83–85.

15. U.S. Department of the Navy, Bureau of Navigation, *International Code of Signals* (Washington: Government Printing Office, 1889), 11.

16. Quartaruolo, "Armada y la revolución de 1890," 63; U.S. National Archives, Record Group 24, log of the *Tallapoosa*, July 29, 1890.

17. Akers and Elliott, *A History*, 83–84; Robertson, *History of the Latin-American Nations*, 244.

18. Sommi, *Revolución*, 300–31.

19. Herring, *History of Latin America*, 625; Robertson, *History of the Latin-American Nations*, 244.

20. Ferrer, "Armed Forces," 84–85.
21. Akers and Elliott, *A History*, 84–85.
22. ibid., 102.
23. ibid., 100–1.
24. *Crónica Argentina*, 5 vols. (Buenos Aires: Editorial Codex, S.A., 1968–69), 5: 109.
25. ibid.
26. ibid., 5: 111; Akers and Elliott, *A History*, 101–2.
27. *Crónica Argentina*, 5: 113–14.
28. ibid., 5: 116.
29. ibid., 5: 117.
30. ibid.
31. Quartaruolo, "Armada y la revolución de 1890," 31–35; Arguindeguy, *Apuntes*, 3: 1213.
32. Warships remaining loyal were the coast-defense ships *Independencia* and *Libertad*, the central battery corvette *Almirante Brown*, the protected cruisers *Nueve de Julio* and *Patagonia*, and the torpedo boats *Espora* and *Pinedo*.
33. Humberto F. Burzio, *Historia de torpedo y sus buques en la armada Argentina 1874–1900* (Buenos Aires: Departamento de Estudios Históricos Navales, 1968), 355–62; Quartaruolo, "Armada y la revolución de 1890," 31–35.
34. Arguindeguy, *Apuntes*, 3: 1213–15.
35. ibid., 3: 1213–14, 4: 1746–47 and 1935; "Combate del *Independencia* y del *Andes*," *Revista General de Marina* (Madrid) 34, 227–30 (1894), 227–28.
36. *Crónica Argentina*, 5:118.
37. Akers and Elliott, *A History*, 102–3.

CHAPTER THIRTY-SIX

1. Jorge Montt Alvarez (1845–1922), born in Casablanca, entered the Chilean Naval Academy in 1858. During the Pacific War with Spain (1865–66), Montt took part in the capture of the *Covadonga*. He was the commanding officer of the *O'Higgins* during the War of the Pacific (1879–83). In 1884 he headed a naval mission to Europe. Three years later Montt was named maritime governor of Valparaíso.
2. Hillmon, "A History," 216.
3. Joaquín Nabuco, *Balmaceda* (Rio de Janeiro: Leuzinger, 1895), 128.
4. Antonio Iniquez, *Golpe de estado y la revolución, primero y siete de enero 1891* (Santiago: Imprenta Victoria, 1891), 50–51; Nabuco, *Balmaceda*, 129.
5. George L. Dyer, "The Recent Revolution in Chile," *The California Illustrated Magazine* 1; 138–53 (February 1892), 145.
6. The *Gobiernista* navy also possessed four small torpedo boats. William Laird Clowes, *Four Modern Naval Campaigns* (London: Unit Library, Limited, 1902), 133–36; Novoa de la Fuenté, *Historia naval*, 137–47.
7. Clowes, *Four Modern Naval Campaigns*, 136.
8. "Chile," *Journal of the American Society of Naval Engineers*, 4: 528–32 (1892) 528–29.
9. Maurice H. Hervey, *Dark Days in Chile: An Account of the Revolution of 1891* (London: E. Arnold, 1892), 192.
10. The U.S. Supreme Court ultimately ruled that the seizure of the Itata was illegal. Clowes, *Four Modern Naval Campaigns*, 150–52.

11. Emil Korner (1846–1920), born in Saxony, fought against Austria in the Austrian-Prussian War (1866). In 1886 the Chilean army contracted Korner as an instructor and he helped found the Chilean Army War College (Academia de Guerra). Korner joined the *Congresionalistas* in May 1891 as the Secretary-General of the Staff (in fact, the chief of staff). The German authorities were at first displeased with Korner's decision to join the *Congresionalistas* but pardoned and congratulated him after they won the civil war.

12. George C. Morant, *Chile and the River Plata in 1891* (London: Waterlow & Sons, 1891), 181.

13. The Russians claim that they sank a Turkish warship by a Whitehead torpedo during the night of January 26, 1878, off Batum. The Turks deny that this occurred.

14. Clowes, *Four Modern Naval Campaigns*, 154–55; López, *Chile,* 69; L. Haffner, *Cent ans de marine de guerre* (Paris: Payot, 1931), 225–28.

15. John H. Sears and B. W. Wells, *Chilean Revolution of 1891* (Washington: Government Printing Office, 1893), 28–29.

16. Francisco Encina, *Historia de Chile desde la prehistoria hasta 1891*, 20 vols. (Santiago: Editorial Nascimento, 1945–52), 20: 237–84: Dyer, "The Recent Revolution," 146–48.

17. Anson Uriel Hancock, *A History of Chile* (Chicago: C. H. Sergel, 1893), 360; Sears and Wells, *Chilean Revolution*, 30.

18. Sears and Wells, *Chilean Revolution*, 35–37; Dyer, "Recent Revolution," 151.

19. In fact, Manuel Blanco Encalada, Argentine born and a naturalized Chilean, briefly served as president of Chile in 1826. Jorge Montt was a dominant figure in the Chilean navy until his death in 1922. Following his retirement from the navy in 1913, he was mayor of Valparaíso.

20. U.S. warships were used to protect a cable ship from the U.S.-owned Central and South America Cable Company while it spliced a bypass around Iquique. With this, the *Congresionalistas* lost their ability to control message traffic between the Balmaceda government and the outside world. Next came the Itata affair described in the text. On August 19 Acting Rear Adm. George Brown, commander of the U.S. squadron, sailed to Quinteros Bay to investigate the rumors concerning a landing by the *Congresionalistas*. He sent a message by commercial cable to Washington detailing the landing in plain language. The *Congresionalistas* charged that this provided the *Gobiernistas* with valuable intelligence and was a violation of neutrality. Overlaying these incidents was the open support by U.S. ambassador Egan for Balmaceda. Following the *Congresionalista* victory, Egan refused to surrender eighty *Gobiernistas* to whom he had granted asylum even after law and order had been restored in Santiago. This was contrary to late-nineteenth-century practices.

See Osgood Hardy, "Was Patrick Egan a Blundering Minister?" *Hispanic American Historical Review* 8: 1; 65–82 (February 1928).

CHAPTER THIRTY-SEVEN

1. Augusto de Castilho, *Portugal e Brazil: conflicto diplomático*, 3 vols. (Losboa: M. Gomes, 1894), 2: 26–28.

2. Amado Luiz Cervo and Clodoaldo Bueno, *História da polítca exterior do Brasil* (São Paulo: Ed. Ática, 1992), 157.

Mello sought to defend the presidentialist Constitution of 1891, while the Revolutionaries in the South originally wanted to remove Júlio de Castilhos from the governorship of Rio Grande do Sul, and replace the positivist-inspired presidential state constitution with a parliamentarist one. See Hélio Leôncio Martins, "Revolta da Armada e Revolução Federalista," *Revista do Exército Brasileiro* 130 (3) 28–34 (October–December 1993).

3. The uprising in Rio Grande do Sul was sparked by the rebellion of General Silva Tavares against Governor Júlio de Castilhos. Numerous signs of unrest followed. Felisbelo Freire, *História da revolta de setembro de 1893* (Brasilia: Editora Universidade de Brasilia, 1982), 23–44; A. Thompson, *Guerra civil do Brasil* (Rio de Janeiro: Editora Ravaro, 1934), 13–25.

4. Freire, *História da revolta*, 10, 52; Thompson, *Guerra civil*, 28–31.

5. Lauro Nogueira Furtado de Mendonça, "O *Aquidaban* e seu trágico destino," *Revista Marítima Brasileira* 114 (7/9) 103–14 (July/September 1994), and Estanislau Façanha Sobrinho, "O lendário *Aquidaban*," *Revista do Exército Brasileiro*, 130 (4) 60–62 (October/December 1993). Both titles use the old-fashioned spelling of the ship's name.

6. Freire, *História da revolta*, 52–53, 76–77; Herbert W. Wilson, *Ironclads in Action: A Sketch of Naval Warfare from 1855 to 1895*, 2 vols. (Boston: Little, Brown, 1896), 2: 35.

7. J. Scott Keltie, *The Statesman's Year-book 1893* (London: Macmillan, 1893), 404.

8. *Rio News* (September 27, 1893), 5.

9. British Naval Intelligence Division, Report on Brazil (1891), Public Record Office, Kent, Richmond, Great Britain.

10. Thompson, *Guerra civil*, 33; Freire, *História da revolta*, 91; Clowes, *Four Modern Naval Campaigns*, 188.

11. Although the *Tamandare* was classified as a cruiser by the Brazilian navy, this ship was only 800 tons and capable of 14 knots.

12. Castilho, *Portugal*, 2: 369.

13. "It is needless to add that all business has been completely suspended." *Rio News* (September 14, 1893), 5.

14. Cervo and Bueno, *História da política exterior*, 157.

15. Freire, *História da revolta*, 92–94, 111–12, 115, 119, 130–32, 150–59; Mario Rubio Muñoz, "La guerra del Brasil y sus enseñanzas navales," *Revista General de Marina* 35: 160–64 (1894), 160–62; Alberto Gonçalves, "Almirante Jerônimo Franciso Gonçalves," vol. 4 of *Subsídios para a história marítima do Brasil* (Rio de Janeiro: Imprensa Naval, 1942), 515–19.

16. Charles R. Flint, *Memories of an Active Life* (New York: G. P. Putnam's Sons, 1923), 89–100.

17. John Ericsson was the most famous U.S. naval architect of his day. He had designed the USS *Princeton* and USS *Monitor* of Civil War fame. The *Destroyer* was an experimental "torpedo" craft built during the 1880s. A non-self-propelled torpedo was fired from an underwater gun mounted in the bow. The craft had been evaluated by the U.S. Navy but not accepted. Cláudio Moreira Bento, "A esquadra Legal ou 'esquadra de papelão': suas vitórias no Rio de Janeiro e em Santa Catarina," *Revista do Exército Brasileiro* 130 (4) 63–68 (October/December 1993).

18. Flint, *Memories*, 89–100.

19. Carlos Miguez Garrido, "Fortificações do Brasil," in vol. 3 of *Subsídios para a história marítima do Brasil* (Rio de Janeiro: Imprensa Naval, 1940), 278–459.

20. Castilho, *Portugal*, 2: 399–407.

21. Thompson, *Guerra civil*, 155–61; James F. Vivian, "United States Policy during the Brazilian Naval Revolt, 1893–94: The Case for American Neutrality," *The American Neptune* 41: 4; 245–61 (October 1981); Cervo and Bueno, *História da política exterior*, 157–59.

22. Castilho, *Portugal*, 3: 217–18; Freire, *História da revolta*, 207–9. The rebel fleet under Admiral da Gama in Rio had been organized into three divisions in early December.

23. Castilho, *Portugal*, 3: 221.

24. Present at Bahia on January 25, 1894, were the *Niterói* (ex-*El Cid*) from the United States, *Gustavo Sampaio* from Great Britain, and the minor Brazilian warships *Parnaíba*, *Primeiro de Março*, *Bracanot*, *Pirajá*, and *Caravelas*. On the twenty-sixth, the *Andrade* (ex-*America*), *Piratini* (ex-*Destroyer*), and torpedo boats *Tamborim* and *Greenhalgh* arrived from the United States. A few days later, five torpedo boats arrived from Europe. Freire, *História da revolta*, 207–9. See also Bento, "A esquadra," 63–68.

25. Castilho, *Portugal*, 3: 221.

26. Wilson, *Ironclads in Action*, 2: 41.

27. Freire, *História da revolta*, 255–56; see also Bento, "A esquadra," 63–68.

28. Clowes, *Four Modern Naval Campaigns*, 209.

29. Admiral da Gama escaped to Buenos Aires with a few of his supporters. They returned to Brazil and again were defeated in battle by government troops. The Admiral was killed.

30. Thompson, *Guerra civil*, 155–61.

31. The government squadron was made up of the armed merchantmen *Niterói*, *Andrada*, *São Salvador*, *Itaipú*, and *Santos*, gunboat *Tiradentes*, and torpedo boats *Gustavo Sampaio*, *Pedro Afonso*, *Pedro Ivo*, and *Silvado*.

32. In his report of the action, Commander Alexandrino de Alencar (who would later become an admiral and Minister of the Navy) emphasized that actually there were no mines available. See Carlos Ramos de Alencar, *Alexandrino, o Grande Marinheiro* (Rio de Janeiro: SDGM, 1989), 83–90. According to Capt. Lauro Nogueira Furtado de Mendonca, the buoys used to simulate mines were improvised from empty oil drums.

33. See Mendonça, "O *Aquidaban*," 103–14.

34. *Rio News* (September 14, 1893), 3.

35. *All the World's Fighting Ships 1860–1905* (London: Conway Maritime Press, 1979), 408.

CHAPTER THIRTY-EIGHT

1. Artist Frederic Remington had earlier cabled William Randolph Hearst, owner of numerous newspapers including the *New York Journal*, "Everything is quiet. There is no trouble here [Cuba]. There will be no war. I wish to return." Hearst's reply is cited at the opening of this chapter. Zimmermann, "Jingoes," 47–48.

2. Zimmermann, "Jingoes," 48; *Dictionary of American Naval Fighting Ships*, 8 vols. (Washington: Naval History Division, 1959–81), 4: 201; John Alden, *The American Steel Navy* (Annapolis: Naval Institute, 1989), 32.

3. The term evolved from a comic strip character, "the Yellow Kid," who first appeared in a New York newspaper in 1895. The "Kid" wore a small hat and a yellow smock. He possessed big ears.

4. Carlos García Barrón, "Enrique Dupuy de Lôme and the Spanish-American War," *The Americas* 36: 1; 39–58 (July 1979), 51; Marbán and Leiva, *Curso*, 2: 496–98.

5. Those working for H. Rickover concluded, "In the light of much greater experience acquired since the court and the board investigated the *Maine* . . . in all probability, the damage between frames 28 and 31 was caused by an internal explosion alone." H. G. Rickover, *How the Maine Was Destroyed* (Annapolis: Naval Institute Press, 1995), 104.

6. "Newspaper War over 'Yellow Journalism,'" *Literary Digest* 16: 367–68 (1898), 367.

7. U.S. Senate, 55th Cong., 2nd Sess., *Congressional Record* (1898) April 15 (3899), April 16 (3988), and April 18 (4012).

8. Even the Spanish battleship *Pelayo* was influenced by the theories of the *jeune école*. She was more closely akin to a coast defense ship than a battleship. She sacrificed endurance for greater protection.

9. Vance von Borries, "The New Empire," *Strategy and Tactics*, 108; 15–24, 41 (July–August 1986) 19–20.

10. John C. Reilly Jr. and Robert L. Scheina, *American Battleships 1886–1923* (Annapolis: Naval Institute Press, 1980), 18–49.

11. Jeffery Michael Dorwart, "A Mongrel Fleet: America Buys a Navy to Fight Spain, 1898," *Warship International* 17: 2; 129–55 (1980), 129–36.

12. Von Borries, "The New Empire," 19–20.

13. ibid., 17; Thomas, *Cuba*, 382.

14. Von Borries, "The New Empire," 17.

15. David C. Clark, ed., *Arms for the Nation* (Greensburg, Pa.: South Greensburg Printing Co., 1994), 34; Von Borries, "The New Empire," 178; "The Military and Naval Power of the United States in 1896 (a Spanish Estimate)," in *Selected Professional Papers Translated from European Military Publications* (Washington: Government Printing Office, 1898), 142.

16. The U.S. Ambassador to Germany, Andrew W. White, reported, "On the Continent there has never been a time, probably, when ill will towards the United States has been so strong as at the present. Nevertheless, I do not believe that a coalition will be formed against us." Orestes Ferrera, *The Last Spanish War* (New York: The Paisley Press, 1937), 97.

17. Senator Henry Cabot Lodge told President McKinley during the war, "If the war in Cuba drags on through the summer with nothing done we [the Republican Party] shall go down in the greatest defeat ever known." Frank Freidel, *The Splendid Little War* (Boston: Little, Brown, 1958), 6.

18. Thomas, *Cuba*, 385.

19. Nelson A. Miles (1839–1925) was educated in Boston. Miles volunteered in the U.S. Army on September 9, 1861, and entered as a lieutenant in the 22nd Massachusetts Infantry. From 1861 through 1865 he participated in practically every major battle fought by the Army of the Potomac. Throughout the 1870s and 1880s, he fought in numerous Indian campaigns. On July 23, 1892, he was awarded the Congressional Medal of Honor "for distinguished gallantry at Chancellorsville" during the U.S. Civil War. On September 29, 1895, Miles was promoted to major general and became the Commander-in-Chief of the U.S. Army.

20. William Shafter (1835–1904) was raised on the frontier and possessed only a common education. During the U.S. Civil War, he rose from a private to a major. He won a Congressional Medal of Honor at the Battle of Fair Oaks (1862). During the 1870s and 1880s, he campaigned against the Indians, earning the nickname "Pecos Bill." Shafter was promoted to brigadier general in 1897. By the beginning of the Spanish-American War, he weighed over 300 pounds and suffered from gout. Shafter was known as a determined, aggressive leader. He opposed racial prejudice and possessed a keen sense of fairness. He was hard to get along with; he drove subordinates by threats; he delegated responsibility only as a last resort; and his personal appearance was sloppy.

21. Von Borries, "The New Empire," 21.

22. "The Military and Naval Power," 158–59; Richard Wainwright, "The Spanish-American War," *The United Service* 1: 3; 1–11 (January 1902), 4–5.

23. Von Borries, "The New Empire," 22.
24. ibid.
25. ibid.
26. Thomas, *Cuba*, 386; Marbán and Leiva, *Curso*, 2: 500.
27. M. Plüddlemann, "Main Features of the Spanish American War," *Journal of the Royal United Service Institute* 43: 654–66 (January–June 1899), 662; Von Borries, "The New Empire," 22–23; Mallin, *History*, 37.
28. Fermoselle, *The Evolution*, 91; Thomas, *Cuba*, 388–89; Marbán and Leiva, *Curso*, 2: 501.
29. Von Borries, "The New Empire," 23.
30. Marbán and Leiva, *Curso*, 2: 504–5; Von Borries, "The New Empire," 23.
31. Fermoselle, *The Evolution*, 92; Henry Cabot Lodge, "The Spanish-American War," *Harper's New Monthly Magazine* 99: 53–77 (June 1899–November 1899), 53; Von Borries, "The New Empire," 23–24; Marbán and Leiva, *Curso*, 2: 505.
32. Von Borries, "The New Empire," 24, 41; Mallin, *History*, 40–41.
33. Thomas, *Cuba*, 398–99.
34. Marbán and Leiva, *Curso*, 2: 507–08; Zimmermann, "Jingoes," 60.
35. Lodge, "The Spanish-American War," 66–77; Fermoselle, *The Evolution*, 92; Zimmermann, "Jingoes," 60.
36. Walter Millis, *The Martial Spirit* (Boston: Houghton Mifflin, 1931), 340.
37. *Treaties, Conventions, International acts, protocols, and agreements between the United States of America and other powers*, 2 vols. (Washington: Government Printing Office, 1910), 2: 1690–95.
38. Thomas A. Bailey and David M. Kennedy, *The American Pageant* (Lexington, Mass.: D. C. Heath, 1983), 581.
39. Louis A. Pérez Jr., "Supervision of a Protectorate: The United States and the Cuban Army, 1898–1908," *Hispanic American Historical Review* 52: 2; 250–72 (May 1972), 250–52; Mallin, *History*, 43–44.
40. Bailey and Kennedy, *The American Pageant*, 577.
41. Zook and Higham, *A Short History*, 254.
42. P. H. Colomb, "The Lessons of the Spanish-American War," *Journal of the Royal United Service Institute* 43: 420–51 (January–June 1899), 433.

POSTSCRIPT
1. Robert Debs Heinl Jr., *Dictionary of Military and Naval Quotations* (Annapolis: United States Naval Institute, 1966), 317.

Index to Full Bibliographical Citations

Latin America's Wars, 1791–1899 drew upon numerous sources. Their short citations, which were used throughout this volume except for the initial citation, are listed below and the page number where the full citation may be found is provided.

Although no general military history of Latin America's nineteenth-century wars exists, a number of very fine survey textbooks written by outstanding scholars were most useful in helping me to create the framework for this book. All of these survey works are included in the books listed below. Of particular importance to me were the writings of Charles Chapman, Harold Davis, Hurbert Herring, J. Fred Rippy, William Spence Robertson, and A. Curtis Wilgus.

Also, two recent works were of great help to me in creating this framework. They were the fine encyclopedia edited by Barbara Tenenbaum and the chronology of David Marley.

Abecia Baldivieso, Valentin *Breve historia,* 493n2
"Adventures of an Officer," 453n13
Aguilar, Luis E., *Cuba, 1933,* 518n36
Aguirre, Sergio, *Quince objetivos,* 482n1
Aguirre Colorado, Rafael, *Campañas,* 449n46
Akers, Charles Edmond, *A History,* 459n59
Alamán, Lucas, *Historia de México,* 447n8
Alba, Victor, "Reforms," 504n34
Alberti, Juan Bautista, *Biografía,* 463n42
Albi, Julio, *Banderas olvidades,* 439n95
Alcaraz, Ramón, *The Other Side,* 475n21
Alden, John, *The American Steel Navy,* 529n2
Alencar, Carlos Ramos de, *Alexandrino,* 529n32
All the World's Fighting Ships, 1860–1905, 529n35
Allendorfer, Frederic von, "An Irish Regiment," 454n54
Alvarez, José J., *Parte general,* 503n8
Anales gráficos, 447n17
André, Marius, *La fin,* 429n2
Arboleda, Gustavo, *Revoluciones,* 429n5
Arcaya, Pedro Manuel, *The Gómez Régime,* 486n11
Archer, Christon I., "'La Causa Buena'," 447n9

Archer, Christon I., "New Wars," 447n9
Arciniegas Valentin, Nelson Antonio, *Historia,* 515n19
Arguindeguy, Pablo E., *Apuntes,* 525n7
Armitage, John, *The History of Brazil,* 451n4
Arráiz, Antonio, *Los días,* 428n8
Arrechea Rodríguez, Elío, *Próceres,* 433n7
Arrubla, Gerardo, *History of Colombia,* 455n6
Avellan Z., Alberto, *Historia,* 464n2
Ayala Mora, Enríque, *Nueva historia,* 428n8
Bailey, Hellen Miller, *Latin America,* 498n26
Bailey, Thomas A., *The American Pageant,* 531n38
Baker, Nancy Nichols, *The French Experience,* 471n14
Balbontín, Manuel, *La invasión Americana,* 476n42
Bancroft, Hubert Howe, *History of Central America,* 460n12
Bancroft, Hubert Howe, *History of Mexico,* 429n1
Bancroft, Hubert Howe, *History of the Northern Mexican States,* 480n5
Barra, Felipe de la, *Objetivo,* 514n7
Barrientos Gutíerrez, Pablo H., *Historia,* 502n23

Bauer, K. Jack, *The Mexican War*, 477n46
Bauer, K. Jack, *Zachary*, 474n13
Bealer, Lewis W., "Francisco Solano López," 507n1
Bealer, Lewis W., "The Dictators," 459n60
Beaucheff, Jorge, *Memorias militares*, 444n24
Becerra, Longino, *Evolución histórica*, 460n2
Belaúde, Víctor Andrés, *Bolívar*, 433n1
Belgrano, Manuel, *Autobiografía*, 440n1
Bell, Ian, "Santo Domingo's Struggle," 514n2
Bell, Ian, *The Dominican Republic*, 515n11
Bell, P. L., *Colombia*, 496n1
Bemis, Samuel Flagg, *A Diplomatic History*, 480n3
Bemis, Samuel Flagg, *The Latin American Policy*, 504n29
Benites, Gregorio, *Anales diplomático*, 509n9
Bento, Cláudio Moreira, "A esquadra," 528n17
Bento, Cláudio Moreira, *O exército farrapo*, 466n5
Best, Félix, *Historia*, 440n2
Bigelow, John, *Breaches*, 479n5
Bigler, Gene E., "The Armed Forces," 486n12
Binkley, William Campbell, "The Last Stage," 473n48
Blaisdell, Lowell L., "Was it Revolution," 482n36
Blanksten, George I., *Ecuador*, 465n21
Blanksten, George I., *Peron's Argentina*, 457n5
Blow, Michael, "The *Trochas*," 517n20
Blutstein, Howard I., *Area Handbook*, 491n98
Bonilla, Heraclio, *Gran Bretaña*, 429n7
Botto, Carlos Penna, *Campanhas navais*, 451n1
Bourne, Edward G., "The Proposed Absorption," 474n3
Bravo Ugarte, José, *Compendio*, 447n3
Broussard, Ray F., "The Puebla Revolt," 503n11
Bruno, Cayetano, *Historia argentina*, 457n12
Bueno, Clodoaldo, *História da polítca*, 527n2
Bullard, R. L., "The Cuban Negro," 519n51
Bulnes, Francisco, *El verdadero Juárez*, 504n19
Bureau of the Census, *Historical Statistics*, 428n7
Burr, Robert N., *By Reason*, 460n1
Burton, Richard F., *Letters*, 513n69
Burzio, Humberto F., *Historia de torpedo*, 526n33
Bustamante, Carlos María de, *Cuadro histórico*, 449n50

Bustamante, Carlos María de, *El nuevo Bernal Díaz*, 476n35
Bustamante Maceo, Gregorio, *Historia militar*, 491n9
Caballero Calderón, Eduardo, *Historia privada*, 496n3
Caillet-Bois, Teodoro, *Historia naval*, 441n22
Caistor, Nick, *Argentina*, 459n59
Calder, Simon, *Cuba*, 520n76
Calderón de la Barca, Frances, *Life in Mexico*, 473n58
Callahan, James Morton, "The Mexican Policy," 504n29
Callcott, Wilfred Hardy, *Santa Anna*, 450n70
Calogeras, João Pandia, *A History of Brazil*, 452n4
Calvert, Robert A., *The History*, 468n1
Caminha, João Carlos Gonçalves, "A guerra," 451n8
Campos Harriet, Fernando, *José Miguel Carrera*, 444n15
Canales Montejano, Guillermo, *Historia militar*, 447n13
Canceco, Aldo N., "La guerra naval," 440n13
Canelas López, René, *Teoria del motín*, 494n12
Cardenas de la Peña, Enríque, *Semblanza marítima*, 469n20
Cardozo, Efraim, *Hace cien años*, 512n50
Carr, Albert Z., *The World*, 484n10
Carranza, Anjel Justiniano, *Campañas Navales*, 444n31
Carrascosa, Manuel Zea, *Semblanzas ministros*, 492n25
Carrera, José Miguel, *Diario militar*, 443n6
Cartas de Bolívar, 434n13
Carter, William, *Bolivia*, 495n23
Carvajal Prado, Patricio, "Pudo haber escapado," 523n26
Carvalho, Affonso de, *Caxias*, 512n65
Carvalho, Trajano Augusto de, *Nossa marinha*, 509n19
Castilho, Augusto de, *Portugal*, 527n1
Cervo, Amado Luiz, *História da polítca*, 527n2
Chapman, Charles Edward, *Colonial Hispanic America*, 429n8
Chapman, Charles Edward, "Melgarejo," 495n33
Chapman, Charles Edward, *Republican Hispanic America*, 457n15
Chartrand, René, *The Mexican Adventure*, 505n8

Christensen, Juan Carlos, *Historia Argentina*, 440n7
Civati Bernasconi, Edmundo H., *Guerra*, 522n16
Clark, David C., *Arms*, 530n15
Cleven, N. Andrew N., "Dictators," 455n6
Clowes, William L., *Four Modern Naval Campaigns*, 526n6
Cochrane, Thomas, *Narrative*, 452n19
Colomb, P. H., "The Lessons," 531n42
Comando en Jefe del Ejército, *Reseña historica*, 440n10
"Combate del *Independencia*," 526n35
Corona del Rosal, Alfonso, *La guerra*, 450n76
Costeloe, Michael P., "The Mexican Church," 477n52
Costa Soto, Guillermo, *Historia militar*, 447n11
Cox, Isaac Joslin, "Chile," 462n13
Crawford, Ann Fears, *The Eagle*, 450n73
Creelman, James, *Díaz*, 504n15
Crespo, Alfonso, *Los Aramayo*, 520n17
Crété, Liliane, *Life in Mexico*, 503n1
Crónica argentina, 526n24
Crouch, Thomas W., *A Yankee guerrillo*, 520n72
Dallett, Francis James, "The Creation," 488n34
d'Araujo, Oscar, *L'idée républicaine*, 466n5
Darwin, Charles, *Narrative*, 520n13
Davis, Harold E., *The Americas*, 428n10
Davis, Harold E., *History of Latin America*, 433n8
Davis, William Columbus, *The Last Conquistadores*, 513n1
De Chair, Somerset, *Napoleon*, 432n37
De Grummond, Jane Lucas, *Renato Beluche*, 487n22
De León, Arnoldo, *The History*, 468n1
Dean, Dwane Hal, "The Last Filibusters," 482n36
Del Río, Daniel A., *Bolívar*, 434n10
Dellepiane, Carlos, *Historia militar*, 455n3
Denegri Luna, Félix, *Perú*, 429n7
DePalo, Jr., William A., *The Mexican National Army*, 449n69
Destéfani, Laurio, *Manual de historia*, 441n22
DeWindt Lavandier, César A., *La marina*, 515n17
Díaz, Lilia, "El liberalismo militante," 503n2
Díaz Venteo, Fernando, *Las campañas*, 434n21
Dictionary of American Naval Fighting Ships, 529n2
Documentos del almirante Brión, 437n53
Domville-Fife, Charles W., *Guatemala*, 460n13
Donato, Hernâni, *Dicionário*, 428n2
Dorwart, Jeffery Michael, "A Mongrel Fleet," 530n11
Doubleday, Charles William, *Reminiscences*, 485n42
Du Sein, A., *Histoire*, 471n15
Duffy, Michael, *Soldiers*, 430n2
Dulles, John W. F., *Yesterday in Mexico*, 521n34
Dusenberry, William, "Urquiza's Account," 459n57
Dyer, George L., "The Recent Revolution," 526n5
Earle, Rebecca, "'A Grave,'" 439n94
Edwards, Agustin, *The Dawn*, 463n31
"El ejército mexicano," 470n28
El poder naval chileno, 514n7
El soldado mexicano, 469n14
Eljuri-Yunez S., Antonio R., "La primera campaña," 432n22
Elliot, L. E., *A History*, 459n59
Elliott, Charles W., *Winfield Scott*, 475n18
Ellis, Keith, *Cuba's Nicolas Guillen*, 518n37
Encina, Francisco, *Historia de Chile*, 527n16
Encina-Castedo, Francisco Antonio, *Resumen*, 443n2
Engelhardt, Armin, "The Battle of Caseros," 457n14
English, Adrian, *Armed Forces*, 496n5
Epstein, Fritz, "European Military Influence," 491n93
Escuela Superior de Guerra, *Manual*, 434n25
Estado Mayor, *Historia del ejército del Chile*, 501n2
Estado Mayor, *Historia militar de Chile*, 502n10
Estado-Maior do Exército, *História*, 467n18
Etchepareborda, Roberto, *La revolución*, 525n13
Evanson, Philip, "The Third Dominican-Haitian War," 516n28
Feliú y Cruz, Guillermo, "La elección," 444n25
Ferguson, James, *Venezuela*, 486n3
Fermoselle, Rafael, *The Evolution*, 482n4
Fernández Guardia, Ricardo, *Cartilla histórica*, 485n31
Ferrer, José, "The Armed Forces," 525n3
Ferrera, Orestes, *The Last Spanish War*, 530n16
Ficklen, John Rice, *The History*, 481n27

Figueiredo, José de Lima, *Brasil militar*, 512n64
Filho, Arlindo Vianna, *Estratégia naval*, 451n9
Filosola, Vicente, "Representation," 470n35
Fitzgibbon, Russell, *Latin America*, 491n7
Fitzroy, Robert, *Narrative*, 520n13
Flint, Charles R., *Memories*, 528n16
Foner, Philip S., *A History*, 483n20
"Formation and Revolt," 454n54
Fortier, Alcee, *The History of North American*, 481n27
Franklin, Jane, *Cuba*, 482n3
Freidel, Frank, *The Splendid Little War*, 530n17
Freire, Felisbelo, *História da revolta*, 528n3
Frías Valenzuela, Francisco, *Nuevo manual*, 463n36
Fuentes, Jordi, *Diccionario*, 463n38
Fuentes para el estudio, 456n27
Fuenzalida Bade, Rodrigo, *La armada*, 461n2
Funcken, Fred, "The Forgotten Legion," 507n35
Funcken, Liliane, "The Forgotten Legion," 507n35
Galdames, Luis, *A History of Chile*, 443n12
Gálvez, Manual, *Humaitá*, 509n7
Gálvez Velarde, Pedro J., "Submarino," 524n50
Gámez, José D., *Historia de Nicaragua*, 460n4
Gandía, Enrique de, "Las guerras," 445n49
García, Manuel R., "Estudios," 440n14
García, Ruben, *Campañas*, 449n46
García Alecont, Victor Francisco, *La marina*, 515n17
García Barrón, Carlos, "Enrique Dupuy de Lôme," 529n4
García Gamba, Andrés, *Memorias*, 446n50
García Ponce, Guillermo, *Las armas*, 486n6
García Villasmíl, Martín, *Escuelas*, 486n5
Garfías, Luís, *Generales mexicanos*, 429n13
Garfias Magaña, Luis, "El ejército de 1860 a 1913," 521n34
Garfias Magaña, Luis, "El ejército de 1913 a 1938," 505n5
Garrido, Carlos Miguez, "Fortificações," 528n19
Garrison, George P., *Diplomatic Correspondence*, 429n9
Geggus, David, *Slavery*, 431n23
Geggus, David, "The Cost," 428n4
Gentiluomo, Federico A., "Los planes," 442n40
Geraghty, Tony, *March or Die*, 506n18

Gibson, William Marion, *The Constitutions*, 464n16
Gíl Fortoul, José, *Historia constitucional*, 433n7
Gilliss, J. M., *The U.S. Naval Astronomical Expedition*, 430n18
Gilmore, Robert L., *Caudillism*, 434n14
Gisbert, Teresa, *Manual*, 463n39
Gómez, Carlos Alarico, *La amarga experiencia*, 490n74
Gonçalves, Alberto, "Almirante," 528n15
Gooch, G. P., *The Cambridge History*, 479n11
Graham, Gerald S., *The Navy*, 441n24
Graham, J., *The Reports*, 440n3
Graham, R. B. Cunninghame, *José Antonio Páez*, 429n13
Graham-Yooll, Andrew, *Small Wars*, 458n16
Gratz, George A., "Warships," 509n18
Greene, Laurence, *The Filibuster*, 484n5
Groneman, Bill, *Battlefields*, 468n1
Gruening, Ernest, *Mexico*, 447n7
Gudmundson, Lowell, *Central America*, 493n48
Gutíerrez Santos, Daniel, *História militar*, 482n36
H. D. [Damaceno, Hermano], *Ensayo*, 454n36
Haffner, L., *Cent ans de marine*, 527n14
Haggerty, Richard A., *Dominican Republic*, 515n7
Haggerty, Richard A., *El Salvador*, 491n6
Halperín Donghi, Tulio, *The Contemporary History*, 429n14
Hamill, Jr., Hugh, *The Hidalgo Revolt*, 446n1
Hamilton, Allen Lee, "Pathway," 470n37
Hancock, Anson Uriel, *A History of Chile*, 527n17
Hand Book . . . , 1893, 491n7
Hanighen, Frank C., *Santa Anna*, 470n29
Hanratty, Dennis M., *Bolivia*, 493n4
Hanratty, Dennis M., *Colombia*, 496n7
Hanratty, Dennis M., *Ecuador*, 465n35
Hardy, Osgood, "Was Patrick Egan," 527n20
Hasbrouck, Alfred, *Foreign Legionaries*, 435n30
Haskins, Ralph W., "Juan José Flores," 465n28
Hatchwell, Emily, *Cuba*, 520n76
Haydon, F. Stansbury, "Documents," 512n51
Haythornthwaite, Philip, *The Alamo*, 470n33
Hazard, Samuel, *Santo Domingo*, 428n4
Heinl, Jr., Robert Debs, *Dictionary*, 531n1
Heinl, Jr., Robert Debs, *Written in Blood*, 428n4

Heinl, Nancy Gordon, *Written in Blood*, 428n4
Henao, Jesús María, *History of Colombia*, 455n6
Henríquez-Ureña, Pedro, *Literary Currents*, 428n10
Herrera, Luis Alberto de, *El Uruguay*, 513n70
Herring, Hubert, *A History*, 452n6
Hervey, Maurice H., *Dark Days*, 526n9
Higham, Robin, *A Short History*, 478n93
Hillmon, Jr., Tommie, *A History*, 461n1
Historia de El Salvador, 491n6
História do exército, 451n12
Historia general del ejército peruano, 446n57
Historia militar de Chile, 461n1
Hitchman, Richard, "Rush to Glory," 468n4
Holt, W. Stull, "The United States," 430n16
Hooker, Richard, *The Mexican Adventure*, 505n8
Hooker, Terry, *The Armies*, 442n53
Hooker, Terry, *The Pacific War*, 522n9
Hooker, Terry, *The Revolt*, 469n17
Howard, Hubert, "Five weeks," 519n58
Hudson, Rex A., *Bolivia*, 493n4
Hudson, Rex A., *Chile*, 502n6
Hudson, Rex A., *Uruguay*, 499n5
Humboldt, Alexander von, *Political essay*, 446n2
Humphreys, R. A., "Anglo-American Rivalries," 479n1
Humphreys, R. A., *The Navy*, 441n24
Hurtado, Osvaldo, *Political Power*, 464n3
Ibarguren, Carlos, *En la penumbra*, 459n58
Inchaustegui, J. Marino, *Historia dominicana*, 515n3
Iniquez, Antonio, *Golpe de estado*, 526n4
Ireland, Gordon, *Boundaries*, 457n36
James, C. L. R., *The black Jacobins*, 432n35
James, Herman G., *The Republics*, 464n2
Jane, Cecil, *Liberty*, 429n3
Jiménez Castellanos, Adolfo, *Sistema*, 517n9
Jiménez Pastrana, Juan, *Los Chinos*, 517n5
Jiménez de Wagenheim, Olga, *Puerto Rico's Revolt*, 518n40
Jiménez L., Hadélis S., "La artillería," 486n9
Jouan, René, *Histoire*, 471n15
Kandell, Jonathan, *La Capital*, 506n17
Karnes, Thomas L., *The Failure*, 459n1
Kasza, Gregory J., "Regional Conflict," 464n8
Keen, Benjamin, *A History*, 493n35
Keltie, J. Scott, *The Statesman's Year-book*, 528n7

Kendall, Lane Carter, "Andrés Santa Cruz," 461n2
Kennedy David M., *The American Pageant*, 531n38
King, P. P., *Narrative*, 520n13
Kirk, John M., *José Martí*, 519n46
Kirkpatrick, Frederick A., *A History*, 445n36
Kirkpatrick, Frederick A., *Latin America*, 434n23
Klein, Herbert S., *Bolivia*, 493n2
Klein, Philip Shriver, *President James Buchanan*, 474n3
Koebel, W. H., *British Exploits*, 452n8
Kolinski, Charles, *Independence*, 509n11
La Peña y Reyes, Antonio de, *La primera guerra*, 471n14
LaFeber, Walter, *Inevitable Revolution*, 460n10
Laing, E. A. M., "The Royal Navy," 458n33
Langley, Lester D., *America*, 479n10
Langley, Lester D., *The Banana Men*, 491n5
Langlois, Luis, *Influencia*, 444n18
Lanús, Roque, "Logias," 457n8
Lavalle Arguidin, Mario, *Buques*, 481n20
Lavalle Arguidin, Mario, *La Armada*, 520n21
Lecuna, Vicente, *Crónica*, 445n43
Léger, J. N., *Haiti*, 430n6
Leiva, Elio, *Curso*, 517n1
León Toral, Jesús de, "Antecedentes," 448n23
"Letters of General López de Santa Anna," 476n28
Levene, Ricardo, *A History of Argentina*, 441n29
Levene, Ricardo, *Historia*, 433n5
Leyburn, James G., *The Haitian People*, 515n9
Lima, Manoel de Oliveira, *O imperio brasileiro*, 466n3
Lindo-Fuentes, Héctor, *Central America*, 493n48
Linke, Lilo, *Ecuador*, 464n8
Lodge, Henry Cabot, "The Spanish-American War," 531n31
Logan, Rayford W., *Haiti*, 430n4
The London *Times*, 431n27
Long, David F., *Gold Braid*, 480n18
López, Jacinto, *Historia de la guerra*, 522n6
López Contreras, Eleazar, *Bolívar*, 435n30
López Contreras, Eleazar, *Paginas*, 490n66
López de Santa Anna, Antonio, "Manifesto," 469n28
López Reyes, Amalia, *Historia del México*, 504n15

López Urrutia, Carlos, *Chile*, 445n33
López Urrutia, Carlos, *La escuadra chilena*, 445n41
López Urrutia, Carlos, *Historia de la marina*, 443n7
López Videla, Winsor, *Almanaque*, 463n41
Los primeros movimientos revolucionarios, 483n27
Loveman, Brian, *For la Patria*, 439n95
Lozano Cleves, Alberto, *Así se hizo*, 435n27
Lozano Funtes, José Manuel, *Historia del México*, 504n15
Lugones, Leopoldo, *Historia de Roca*, 520n19
Luperon, Gregorio, *Notas*, 516n42
Madariaga, Salvador de, *The Fall*, 429n8
Maia, Prado, *Através*, 453n22
Maissin, Eugène, *The French*, 471n15
Mallin, Jay, *History*, 517n1
Manning, William, *Dipl. Corres. of the U.S. concerning*, 428n8
Manning, William, *Dipl. Corres. of the U.S. Inter-Amer.*, 463n40
Marbán, Edilberto, *Curso*, 517n1
Marion Gibson, William, *The Constitutions*, 497n10
Markham, Clements R., *A History*, 461n5
Marley, David, *Wars*, 430n7
Martí, José, "La guerra de razas," 519n50
Martí, José, *Mi tiempo*, 519n47
Martí, José, *Our America*, 519n48
Martin, Percy Alvin, "Brazil," 451n3
Martin, Percy Alvin, *The Republics*, 464n2
Martínez Caro, Ramón, "A True Account," 470n31
Martins, Hélio Leôncio, "Revolta," 528n2
Marure, Alejandro, *Efemérides*, 459n1
Mason, Theodorus, *The War*, 521n2
Masterman, George Frederick, *Seven Eventful Years*, 512n63
Matilla Tascón, A., "Las expediciones," 446n58
"Maximilian and the American Legion," 507n42
McClure, Charles R., "The Texan-Santa Fe Expedition," 472n27
McCornack, Richard Blaine, "The San Patricio Deserters," 478n74
Medina Castro, Manuel, *Estados Unidos*, 485n31
Meditz, Sandra W., *Colombia*, 496n7
Meditz, Sandra W., *Uruguay*, 499n5
Meister, Jurg, *Francisco Solano López*, 428n6

Melo, Rosendo, *Historia de la marina*, 446n52
Mendonça, Lauro Nogueira Furtado de, "O Aquidaban," 528n5
Mendoza Vallejo, Guillermo, "El ejército mexicano de 1860," 505n5
Menendez, R. F., *Las conquistas territoriales*, 443n2
Merrill, Tim L., *Honduras*, 491n7
Mesa, José de, *Manual*, 463n39
Mesa Gisbert, Carlos D., *Presidentes*, 495n42
Meyer, Michael C., *The Course*, 447n6
Mézière, Henri, *Le Général LeClerc*, 430n4
Miller, Robert Ryal, "The American Legion," 507n42
Miller, John, *Memoirs*, 434n19
Millis, Walter, *The Martial Spirit*, 531n36
Miranda Basurto, Ángel, *La evolución*, 507n44
Miró Quesada, Carlos, *Autopsia*, 525n54
Miró y Argenter, José, *Cuba*, 519n60
Mitre, Bartolomé, *Historia de San Martin*, 439n91
Molina, Cristobal, "War," 520n21
Montejano, David, *Anglos and Mexicans*, 473n59
Moore, David R., *A History*, 488n41
Morales Coello, Julio, *La importancia*, 484n27
Morant, George C., *Chile*, 527n12
Morelos documentos, 449n38
Morón, Guillermo, *A History*, 429n12
Morón, Guillermo, *Breve historia*, 488n42
Moses, Bernard, *Spain's Declining Power*, 429n8
Munro, Dana Gardner, *The Five Republics*, 460n9
Munro, Dana Gardner, *The Latin American Republics*, 500n21
Muñoz, Mario Rubio, "La guerra," 528n15
Nabuco, Joaquín, *Balmaceda*, 526n3
Nasatir, Abraham P., *Latin America*, 498n26
Naylor, Robert A., "The British Role," 479n5
Needler, Martin C., *Political Systems*, 501n53
Nelson, Harold D., *Costa Rica*, 493n47
"Newspaper War," 530n6
Nicolas, Louis, *La puissance navale*, 471n15
Novoa de la Fuente, Luís, *Historia naval*, 502n12
Nunn, Frederick M., *The Military*, 520n4
O'Ryan, William D., "General W. A. C. Ryan," 518n23
Ochoa, José Vicente, *Diario*, 522n16
Ojeda Reyes, Félix, *Peregrinos*, 518n38

Olivera, Ruth R., *Life in Mexico*, 503n1
Omaña, Pedro Arturo, *Historia*, 486n5
Opatrny, Josef, *U.S. Expansionism*, 483n9
Orrego, Luís Uribe, *Nuestra marina*, 462n18
Ortega, Miguel R., *Morazán*, 460n26
Ortíz Sotelo, Jorge, *El vicealmirante*, 456n20
Osborne, Harold, *Bolivia*, 494n9
Ott, Thomas O., *Haitian Revolution*, 432n49
"Our Sister Republics," 525n4
Páez, José Antonio, *Autobiografía*, 487n15
Palacio Fajardo, Manuel, *Outline*, 433n9
Palleja, Léon de, *Diario*, 511n43
Palmer, Michael A., *Stoddert's War*, 431n31
Pareja Diezcanseco, Alfredo, *Ecuador*, 464n2
Parkes, Henry Bamford, *A History*, 447n4
Pasquel, Leonardo, *Antonio López de Santa Anna*, 450n71
Patch, Richard W., "Bolivia," 429n12
Paullin, Charles O., *Atlas*, 478n81
Paz, J. M., *Memorias póstumas*, 442n45
Paz Soldán, Mariano Felipe, *Narración histórica*, 522n16
Peckham, Howard H., *The Toll*, 428n3
Penafiel, Antonio, *Ciudades coloniales*, 448n37
Pérez, Jr., Louis A., "Class," 518n36
Pérez, Jr., Louis A., "Supervision," 531n39
Pérez Arcay, Jacinto, *La guerra federal*, 488n44
Pérez Tenreiro, Tomás, *Los presidentes*, 488n29
Perkins, Dexter, *Hands Off*, 479n3
Perrigo, Lynn I., *Our Spanish Southwest*, 468n2
Petite, Mary Deborah, *1836*, 468n1
Pfost, Richard A., "War with Mexico!" 474n4
Phillips, Jr., Richard Snyder, "Bolivia," 521n4
Piedra Martel, Manuel, *Campañas*, 519n61
Pike, Frederick, *The Modern History*, 457n34
Pinzón de Lewin, Patricia, *El ejército*, 497n19
Pirala, Antonio, *Anales*, 517n7
Planchet, Regis, *La cuestion*, 504n31
Plazas Olarte, Guillermo, "El ejército," 496n8
Plüddlemann, M., "Main Features," 531n27
Polk, James, *Polk: The Diary*, 474n5
Pomer, Leon, *Os confitos*, 458n26
Portell Vilá, Herminio, *Narciso López*, 482n1
Portilla, Anselmo de, *Historia*, 503n8
Potter, Reubin M., "The Republic of Texas," 473n59
Poulter, R., *The Armies*, 442n53
Pradaliè, Georges, *Le second empire*, 505n13
Pratt, Julius W., *A History*, 480n3
Pratt, Julius W., *America's Colonial Experiment*, 517n3

Presidencia de la República, *Las fuerzas armada*, 486n8
Priestley, Herbert Ingram, *The Mexican Nation*, 469n27
Prieto, Guillermo, *Lecciones*, 447n11
Putnam, Herbert Everett, *Joel Roberts Poinsett*, 482n3
Quartaruolo, V. Mario, "La armada," 525n9
Quisenberry, Anderson C., *Lopez's Expeditions*, 483n14
Ramírez, José Fernando, *Mexico*, 474n10
Ratto, Héctor, *Vida de Brown*, 454n45
Rauch, Basil, *American Interests*, 482n2
Read, Jan, *The New Conquistadores*, 453n13
Reed, Nelson, *The Caste War*, 472n20
Reilly, Jr., John C., *American Battleships*, 530n10
Reina, Leticia, *Las rebeliones campensinas*, 472n20
Rennie, Ysabel, *The Argentine Republic*, 520n14
Resquín, Francisco, Isidoro *Datos historicos*, 513n68
Restrepo, José Manuel, *Diario politico*, 496n2
Restrepo, José Manuel, *Historia de la revolución*, 434n12
Reussner, Andre, *Elements*, 471n15
Reussner, André, *La puissance navale*, 471n15
Richardson, James Daniel, *A Compilation*, 429n10
Rickover, H. G., *How the Maine*, 529n5
Rio News, 528n8
Rippy, J. Fred, "Anglo-American Filibusterings," 480n13
Rippy, J. Fred, "Argentina," 457n5
Rippy, J. Fred, *Latin America*, 479n1
Rippy, J. Fred, "The Dictators of Colombia," 496n5
Rippy, J. Fred, "The Dictators of Venezuela," 489n61
Rippy, J. Fred, *The United States*, 480n13
Riva Palacio, Vicente, *México*, 503n8
Rivera Cambas, Manuel, *Los gobernantes*, 450n77
Rives, George Lockhart, *The United States*, 472n30
Roa Bárcena, José María, *Recuerdos*, 475n19
Robertson, William Spence, "Francisco de Miranda," 433n4
Robertson, William Spence, *History*, 459n59
Robertson, William Spence, *Iturbide*, 449n50

Robinson, Fay, *Mexico*, 446n2
Roche, James Jeffrey, *By-ways*, 449n52
Rodigues, José Honório, *Independência*, 451n7
Rodman, Selden, *Quisqueya*, 432n54
Rodney, Caesar A., *The Reports*, 440n3
Rodríquez, Augusto G., *Reseña histórica*, 455n59
Rodríguez, Mario, *Central America*, 460n9
Rodríguez, Pelagio A., *Campañas*, 449n46
Rodríguez Ballesteros, José, *Historia*, 445n44
Rodríguez Demorizi, Emilio, *La marina*, 515n3
Roig, Pedro, *La guerra*, 519n68
Rolle, Andrew F., "Futile Filibustering," 481n33
Romero, Fernando, *Notas*, 456n25
Romero Flores, Jesús, *Lic. Benito Juárez*, 504n24
Ros, Martin, *Night of Fire*, 428n4
Rosa, José María, *Historia Argentina*, 440n2
Roth, Patrick H., *On Watch*, 493n31
Röttjer, Aníbal Atilio, *Vida*, 457n12
Rourke, Thomas, *Gómez*, 488n32
Rubio, Julián María, *La infanta*, 451n1
Rudolph, James D., *Argentina*, 458n19
Rudolph, James D., *Cuba*, 518n34
Russell Ybarra, Thomas, *Bolivar*, 435n35
Salas, C. I., "Bibliografía," 454n37
Sánchez Bravo, Mariano, *Buques*, 456n21
Sánchez Lamego, Miguel A., "El ejército mexicano," 450n70
Sánchez Lamego, Miguel A., *The Second Mexican-Texas War*, 471n7
Santander, Francisco de Paula, *Cartas*, 434n18
Santoni, Pedro, *Mexicans at Arms*, 468n8
Saravi, Mario Guillermo, "La misión," 445n43
Sarmiento, Domingo F., *Facundo*, 457n3
Sater, William F., *Chile*, 522n7
Savignon, Tomas, *Quintín Banderas*, 517n11
Scheina, Robert L., *American Battleships*, 530n10
Scheina, Robert L., *Latin America*, 430n17
Scheina, Robert L., *Santa Anna*, 468n4
Scholes, Walter V., *Mexican Politics*, 429n6
Schoonover, Thomas, *The Banana Men*, 491n5
Schurz, W. L., *Bolivia*, 494n7
Scott, Winfield, *Memoirs*, 475n13
Scroggs, William Oscar, *Filibusters*, 480n13
Scroggs, William Oscar, "William Walker," 484n4
Sears, John H., *Chilean Revolution*, 527n15
Sherman, William L., *The Course*, 447n6
"Síntesis histórica," 525n9

Skidmore, Thomas E., *Modern Latin America*, 430n15
Smith, Justin H., *The War*, 473n1
Smith, Peter H., *Modern Latin America*, 430n15
Sobrinho, Estanislau Façanha, "O lendário Aquidaban," 528n5
Sommi, Luis V., *La Revolución*, 525n6
St. John, Ronald Bruce, *The Foreign Policy*, 455n6
Stanhope, Dorothy, "The Negro Race," 519n52
Stenburg, Richard R., "President Polk," 474n3
Stokes, G. P., "War with Mexico!" 474n11
Stout, Peter F., *Nicaragua*, 479n7
Strain, Isaac G., *Cordillera*, 463n36
Stuart, Graham H., *Latin America*, 479n11
Suárez, Martín, *Atlas*, 441n21
Tambs, Lewis A., "Seven Times," 442n55
Taracena, Alfonso, *La verdadera revolución*, 482n36
Tays, George, "Frémont," 476n37
Teja Zabre, Alfonso, *Historia de México*, 479n96
Teja Zabre, Alfonso, *Vida de Morles*, 451n79
Tenenbaum, Barbara A., *Encyclopedia*, 428n1
The American Annual Cyclopaedia, 466n38
"The Military and Naval Power," 530n15
The Political and Socio-Economic Role, 496n5
The Texas Navy, 470n38
Thomas, Alfred Barnaby, *Latin America*, 460n16
Thomas, Hugh, *Cuba*, 483n9
Thompson, A., *Guerra civil*, 528n3
Thompson, George, *The War*, 510n27
Timmons, Wilbert H., *Morelos*, 448n18
Tone, John Lawrence, "The Machete," 517n8
Toribio Medina, José, *La Expedición*, 444n18
Tornel y Mendivil, José María, "Relations," 470n1
Toro Dávila, Agustin, *Sintesis histórico*, 443n6
Torrente, Mariano, *Historia de la revolución*, 429n1
Tramond, Joannès, *Elements*, 471n15
Tramond, Joannès, *Manuel d'histoire maritime*, 432n53
Traversoni, Alfredo, *Historia*, 499n7
Treaties, Conventions, International acts, 531n37
Trend, John B., *Bolivar*, 436n49
Turnbull, Patrick, *The Foreign Legion*, 506n19
Ullrick, Laura F., "Morillo's Attempt," 437n51
"Unidad táctica," 486n10

United States, Dept. of the Navy, *International Code*, 525n15
United States, Hydrographic Office, *The Coast of Chile*, 521n2
United States, Senate. Ex. Doc., 68, 34th Cong. 1st Sess., 485n30
United States Magazine, 483n8
Urrea, José, "Diary," 469n27
Uzal, Francisco Hipólito, "La batalla," 459n46
Valdés Vergara, Francisco, *Historia de Chile*, 443n2
Valdizan Gamio, José, *Historia naval*, 446n52
Vale, Brian, *A War*, 452n1
Vale, Brian, "Lord Cochrane," 451n18
Vale, Brian, "The Creation," 451n6
Valencia Tovar, Alváro, "El ejército," 455n12
Vanderwood, Paul J., *Disorder*, 521n29
Vargas, Francisco Alejandro, *Calendario historico*, 487n27
Vargas, Francisco Alejandro, *Historia naval*, 438n63
Vargas, Francisco Alejandro, *Nuestros próceres navales*, 437n53
Vargas, Francisco Alejandro, *Síntesis histórica*, 486n9
Vasconcelos, José, *Breve historia*, 479n96
Vazquez Machicado, Humberto, *Manual*, 463n39
Vegas, Manuel, *Historia de la marina*, 455n6
Ventura Dominguez, Albérico, *La marina*, 515n17
Versen, Max von, "História da guerra," 512n52
Vicuña Mackenna, Benjamin, *El general*, 441n17
Vigness, David M., "La expedición," 472n17
Villanueva, Carlos A., *Resumen*, 517n2
Villegas Basavilbaso, Benjamín, *La adquisición*, 453n14
Vittone, Luis, *Las fuerzas armadas*, 511n43
Vivian, James, "United States Policy," 528n21
von Borries, Vance, "The New Empire," 530n9
von Pivka, Otto, *Navies*, 440n13
von Tschudi, Johann Jakob, *Travels*, 462n29
Wainwright, Richard, *Spanish-America*, 530n22
Walker, William, *The War*, 484n2
Wallace, Eduard S., *Destiny*, 484n4
Ward, A. W., *The Cambridge History of British Foreign Policy*, 479n11
Ward, Henry G., *Mexico*, 449n40
Weathers, Jr., Bynum E., "The Role," 501n2
Weber, David S., *The Mexican Frontier*, 472n27
Webster's New International Dictionary, 428n11
Weigley, Russell F., *History*, 478n85
Welles, Sumner, *Naboth's Vineyard*, 515n3
Wells, B. W., *Chilean Revolution*, 527n15
Wells, William V., *Walker's Expedition*, 484n7
Werneck Sodré, Nelson, *Formação*, 509n15
Wheelock, Phillis, "An American Commodore," 454n48
Wilgus, A. Curtis, *The Development*, 492n11
Williams, John Hoyt, "Governor Velasco," 441n20
Williams, Mary Wilhelmine, *Anglo-American Isthmian Diplomacy*, 479n3
Wilson, Herbert W., *Ironclads*, 528n6
Woodward, Jr., Ralph Lee, *Central America*, 460n19
Woodward, Jr., Ralph Lee, "The Aftermath," 460n3
Wooster, Ralph A., "Texas Military Operations," 473n44
Worcester, Donald E., *Sea Power*, 445n42
Wyllys, Rufus Kay, "Henry A. Crabb," 481n29
Wyllys, Rufus Kay, "The Republic," 480n13
Zeitlin, Maurice, *The Civil Wars*, 502n4
Ziegler, Philip, "Bolívar's British Legion," 438n71
Ziems, Angel, *El Gomecismo*, 486n11
Zimmermann, Warren, "Jingoes," 519n54
Zook, Jr., David H., *A Short History*, 478n93

INDEX

*Numbers in italics refer to figures or maps.
*Numbers in **bold** indicate biographical sketches.

Abascal y Souza, Fernando de, 25, 44, 47, 55
Abercromby, Ralph, 9
Abreu, José de, 45
Abtao, *336*, 340
Abtao (Chilean warship), 378–79
Acámbaro, 81
Acapulco, 76, 78–79, 81–82, 295, 308, 448n30
Accessory Transit Company, 202, 221, 225, 227–29
Achá, José María de, 265
Acosta Bustamante, Juan Alejandro, 346, **516n35**
Acre, 268
Acre, Aniceto, 267
Acre, José, 252
Activo, (Portuguese warship), 89
Aculco, 74
Acultzingo, 305
Adams, John, 21
Adams, John Quincy, 40, 84, 214, 352
Adela (Colombian warship), 108
Adlercreutz, Friedrich de, 38
Admirable Campaign, 27–28, 435n33, 438n72
affranchis, xiii, xxiii, 2–9, 11–12, 14, 16
Agamonte, Ignacio, 356
Agreda, Sebastián, 138, 264, 266
Agricultural and Mining Association (Central America), 203
Aguapey, 52
Aguascalientes, 158

Agüera, Rosendo, 258
Aguiar, Rafael Tobias de, 154
Aguila (Chilean navy), 62
Aguila (Mexican warship), 176
Aguirre, Atanasio, 314
Aguirre, Miguel, 266
Agustín I, 82. *See also* Iturbide, Agustín de
Ahuachapán, 254, 256
aircraft, use of, 373
AK-47 rifle, *354*
Alacrán Island, 384
Alagoas, 150
Alagoas (Brazilian warship), 327, 512n59
Alajuela (British merchantship), 276
Alamán, Luis, 295
Alamo, 161–62, 164
Alarm (British warship), 200
Albán, Carlos, 279
Albany (American warship), 202, 417
Alcántara, Linares, 249
Alcántara Herrán, Pedro, 273, **497n13**
Alcérreca, José Miguel, 402
Aldao, José Félix, 368
Aldea, Juan de Dios, 378
Alegrete, Marqués de, 52
Alejandro I (Spanish warship), 63
Alem, Leandro, 391, 394, 396
Alén, Paulino, 512n62
Alert (American merchantship), 345
Alfaro, José Eloy, 145–46, 279, **466n41**
Algeria, 308
Allanza (Peruvian warship), 384

Allende, Ignacio, 73–75, **447n12**
Almansa (Spanish warship), 334
Almirante Abreu (Brazilian warship), 417
Almirante Blanco (filibuster), 144
Almirante Brown (Argentine warship), 395
Almirante Cochrane (Chilean warship), 340, 376, 378–79, *380*, 386, 398
Almirante Condell (Chilean warship), 398
Almirante Lynch (Chilean warship), 398, 400
Almirante Padilla (rebel warship), 279–80
Almirante Tamandaré (Brazilian warship), 411, 413
Alonso, Severo, 267–68
Altamira, 83
altiplano, 65, 94, 262, 266–67, 377, 378
Alto Peru, 69. *See also* Upper Peru
Alvarado, Juan Bautista, 167
Alvarado, Rudecindo, 66
Alvares, Joaquim Curado Oliveira, 51
Álvarez, Juan, 158, 193–94, 196, 296, 308
Álvarez de Arenales, Juan, 64–66
Álvarez Condarco, Josè, 58, 63
Alvear, Carlos de, 44, 48, 50, 58, 99–101, **440n16**
Alzaga, Martín, 43
Amarillos (Venezuelans), 236
Amazon River, 151

Amazonas (Brazilian warship), 320, 417
Amazonas (Peruvian warship), 335
Ambato, 142
América (Confederate/Peruvian warship), 335, 337, **514n12**
América (Ecuadorian warship), 145
American Legion, 507n42
American mercenaries. *See* filibustering
American Revolution, xxiv, 3. *See also* United States
Americana (Argentine warship), 45
Amiens, Peace of, 16
Amiraya, 48
Amotape, 143
amphibious landings, 404, *421*
Ampudia, Pedro de, 170, 173, 175, 177, 181–83, 185, 188, **472n18**
Ana Celestina (rebel warship), 239
Anaya, Pedro María, 83, 189, 193–94
Ancón, 137
Andalucia, 23
Anderson, Frank, 232
Andes Mountains, 27, 31, 35–36, 41, 57–58, 60–61, 109, 138, 235, 262, 271, 383
Andrada, José Bonafacio, 149
Andrada, Martim Francisco, 149
Andrade, Ignacio, 244, 278
Andrade, Manuel Paes de, 150
Andreda e Silva, José Bonifacio de, 86
Angamos, 379–80, *380*, 385
Angamos (Chilean warship), 385
Angostura (Paraguay), 329–30
Angostura (Venezuela), 23, 25, 33–37, 243, 247–48
Anna (blockade runner), 356
Anne (British merchantship), 145
Antarctic, 63
Antezana, Leonardo, 266
Antigua, 130
Anita (filibuster), 208

Antioquía, 20, 273, 276
Antofagasta, 268, 376–77, 379, 400
Apa River, 325
Apache Indians, 371
Apaneca, 256
Aponte, José, 352
Apure, 34, 239
Apure River, 34–35
Apurimac (Peruvian warship), 335, 337
Aquidabã (Brazilian warship), 405–7, 409, 411–13, *412*, *423*
Aquiles (Spanish/Chilean warship), 132, 134, 136, 446n52
Aquino, 491n6
Araçatuba (Brazilian warship), 96
Aragua de Barcelona, 237
Aramendi, Francisco, 34
Aranjuez, xxiv
Aranta, 135
Aranzazú (Spanish warship) 44
Araóz, Bernabé, 114
Aráoz de la Madrid, Gregorio, 119
Arapey, 52
Araucanian Indians, 69–70, 135, 137, 139, 290–91, 293, 366–67, 373
Arauco, 366
Arauco (merchantship), 291
Araujo, Sebastião Pinto de, 52
Araure, 29
Arboleda, Julío, 275
Arbolito, 286
Arce, Januel José, 127–29
Arch de Triomphe, *22*, 433n3
Archibald Gracie (merchantship), 207
Arequipa, 47, 66–67, 107, 133. 135
Arequipeño (Peruvian warship/privateer), 107, 132, 136–38
Arequira, 138
Arequito, 114
Aréthuse (French warship), 407
Argentina, xxv, 264, 282–88, 404; Buenos Aires versus the Provinces, xxv, 63, 113–25; relations with Chile, 376; intraclass conflict, 390–96; War against the Peru-Bolivia Confederation, 117; War for Banda Oriental Province, 93–104; War for Independence, 41–53; wars against Indians, 365–73; War of the Triple Alliance, xiv, xxvi, 313–32

Argentina (Argentine warship), 60
Argentine Confederation, 123
Argolo, Gen., 329–30, 332
Argonauta (Spanish warship), 55
Argüedas, Alcides, 262
Arias, Céleo, 255
Arica, 66, 106, 136, 266, 378–79, 381–83, *384*, 388
Arismendi, Juan Bautista, 30–31, 33, 40, **436n50**
Arismendi, Luisa Cáceresde, 436–37n50
Arista, Mariano, 169, 171–72, 181–83, 185, **475n17**
Ariza y Torres, Rafael, 127
Armijo, Manuel, 168, 171, 185
Arminan, Brig. Gen., 357
Armiñán, 80
Armitage, John, 95
Armstrong cannon, *338*, 339
Army of the Andes, 49, 57, 114, 444n20, 453n10
Army of the Three Guarantees, 81–83
Arredondo, José Miguel, 286
Arredondo, Manuel, 25
Arrow (filibuster), 208
Arroyo del Aguila, 96
Arroyo Grande, 120–21, 154
Arroyo Pantanoso, 120
Arrubla, Gerardo, 280
Arrúe, Julio, 286
Arteaga, 292
Artigas, José Gervasio, 46, 48, 50–52, 94, **441n25**
Artigas, Manuel, 93
Aruba Island, 21
Arzú, Manuel, 127
Asia (Spanish warship), 56, 68, 446
Astrada, Berón de, 118

Index

Asunción, xxv, 44–45, 313–14, 319, 321, *322*, 324, 326, 328–32
Atacama Desert, 55, 134, 263, 293, 375, 379, 402
Atahualpa (Peruvian warship), 385
Atlantic and Pacific Ship-Canal Company, 201–2
Atocha, Alejandro, 183
Atotonilco, 73
Auchmuty, Samuel, 42–43
Audaz (Brazilian tug), 410
audiencia (the highest court in the colony), 43, 47
Augusta (American merchantship), 240
Aury, Luis, 205–6
Austin, Moses, 158
Austin, Stephen, 158, 468n11
Austin (Texas warship), 170–71, 176
Austria, foreign mercenaries from, 303, *306*, 308–9, 311
Auxiliary Division (Portuguese army), 86–87
Avani-Garde (Haitian warship), 346
Avay, 329, 330
Avellaneda, Nicolás, 368
Avila (Venezuelan warship), 240
Avilez, Jorge d', 86
Ayacucho, 68–70, 94, 105, 133, 352
Ayala, Rafael, 258
Aymará Indians, 262, 377
Ayoayo, 267
Ayo Ayo, 67
Ayohuma, 49
Ayutla, Plan of, 503n3
Aznar, Miguel, 172
Azopardo, Juan Bautista, 45
Azua, 344–45, 347
Azuay, 140, 143
Azufre, 60

Babahoyo, 39, 143
Bacalar, 370, 371
Báez Méndez, Buenaventura, 344, 346–47
Bage, 99, 101
Bahia, 86–87, 149, 407, 410
Bahia (Brazilian warship), 90, 327–28, 408, 509n18, 512n60
Bahía Honda, 218
Baire, Yell of, 360
Baja California, 207–9, 211, 213
Baker musket, 236, 469
Balbontín, Manuel, 188
Ballivián, Adolfo, 266
Ballivián, José, 136, 138, 263–65, 292, **494n8**
Balmaceda, José Manuel, 397–98, 400, 402, 404
Baltimore, 55, 80
Baltimore (American warship), 404
Banda Oriental, 43, 45–46, 48, 50–53, 85, 93, 114. *See also* Uruguay
Banderas, Quintin, 355, 361, 363, **517n10**
Banright (merchantship), 246
Baptista, Felipe, 238
Baptista, Leopoldo, 245
Baquedano, Manuel, 291, 383, 386, 397, **524n38**
Baraguá, Protest of, 358–59
Barbacena, Marquis de, 87, 99–100
Barbacoas Cliff, 37
Barbados Island, 21
Barbosa, Ruy, 406, 409
Barbula, 29
Barcelona (Venezuela), 29, 33, 247
Barillas, Manuel, 257
Barinas, 27, 242
Barquisimeto, 26, 238, 242, 245, 247
Barradas, Isidro, 82–83
Barranca, 25, 27, 277
Barranquilla, 277–78
Barreiro, José María, 36
Barreto, João Manuel Mena, 325, 331
Barreto, João Paulo dos Santos, 154
Barriga, Isidoro, 143, 464n19
Barrios, Gerardo, 254–55, **492n17**
Barrios, Justo Rufino, xiv, 250–51, 255–57, **492n22**
Barrios, Vicente, 314, 512n63
Barrios, Vinda de, 327
Barroetaveña, Francisco A., 391
Barros Arana, Diego, 54
Barroso (Brazilian warship), 328
Barroso da Silva, Francisco Manoel, 320
Barrundia, José Francisco, 129–30
Basadre, José Ignacio, 83
Basle, Treaty of, 8
Basora, José Francisco, 358
Batallón de Carabineros (Bolivian army), 264
Batlle, Lorenzo, 284–85
Batlle y Ordoñez, José, 287–88
Baudin, Charles, 168–69
Bauzá, Rufino, 52
Bay Islands, 198, 202–3, 232
Bay of San Vicente, 55
Bayamo, 351, 355, 360, 363
Bayonne, 21; Treaty of, xxiv
Bazaine, François-Achille, 307–10, **506n20**
Bazoche, François, 168
Beagle (British warship), 393
Beaumont rifle, 377, 398
Beazley, Thomas, 102
Bedoya, Saturnino, 512n63
Belém, 91, 151
Belén (Spanish warship), 44
Belgium, foreign mercenaries from, 303, *306*, 308–9, 311
Belgrano, Manuel, 41, 45–46, 48–51, 57, 114, 319, **440n1**
Belize, 198, 370
Belle (privateer), 210
Bello, Andrés, 292
Bellona (Brazilian warship), 509n18
Beluche, Renato, 238, **487n26**
Belzú, Francisco de Paula, 264
Belzú, Manuel, 264–66, 268, **494n11**
Benham, Andrew, 410
Benjamin Constant (Brazilian warship), 407
Bentances, Ramón E., 358–59
Berenguela (Spanish warship), 334, 339
Beresford, William Carr, 42
Berges, José, 512n63
Bermejo River, 268

Bermuda (blockade runner), 362
Bermúdez, José Francisco, 33–35, **438n61**
Bermúdez, Pedro Pablo, 133
Bernardino (rebel warship), 145
Berro, Bernardo, 284
Berthold, Simón, 211, 212
Betances, Ramón Emeterio, 358
Biblao, Francisco, 289–90
Bió Bió River, 366–67
Bismarck (rebel warship), 277
Black Bean Incident, 175
blacks, xiii, xxiii–xxiv, 1–19, 24, 33, 62, 83, 288, 341, 343, 351–52, 357, 360–61, 423
Blakely cannon, 339
Blanca (Spanish warship), 334, 337, 348
Blanchet, Jean, 137–38
Blanco, Máximo, 231
Blanco, Miguel, 207
Blanco, Pedro, 268
Blanco, Ramón, 416
Blanco Encalada, Manuel, 62–63, 69–70, 135, **444n30**, 527n19
Blanco Encalada (Chilean warship), 340, 376, 378–79, *380*, 385–86, 398, 400, *401*
Blanco Erenas, Ramón, 363
blancos (Uruguayans), 114, 118, 122, 152, 282–88, 313–14, 319–21
Bligh, William, 11
Bliss, William, 189
Blume Othon, Federico, 385–86, **524n49**
Bobadilla, Tomás, 343
Bogotá, Santa Fé de, 20, 30–31, 33, 36–37, 67, 69, 271–80
Bogotá (Colombian warship), 280
bolas, 95
boleadora, 116–17, 365
Bolívar, Simón, xiii, xxiii–xxiv, 20, 23, 26–27, 29–40, *32*, 65–70, 94, 105–8, 110, 140–42, 235, 273, 342, **433n10**, 439n87, 461n3, 486–87n14
Bolívar (Colombia), 274, 376
Bolívar (rebel warship), 145

Bolívar (Venezuelan warship), 248
Bolivarians, 238, 248
Bolivia: Confederation War with Chile, 132–39; economy of, 263, 375–76; misrule by caudillos, 262–69; War for Independence, 46–51, 53, 65–70; War of the Pacific, xxvii, 375–89; War with Argentina, 117; mentioned, xxiv, 40–41, 52, 105–8, 110, 113, 119, 335, 339, *374*
Boliviana (Venezuelan warship), 240
Bolognesi, Francisco, 382–84
Bombarde, 6–7
Bomboná, 39
Bonachea, Ramón, 359
Bonaparte, Joseph, xxiv, 20, 23
Bonaparte, Napoleon, xxiv, 13, 15–16, 18, 21, 23, 42–43, 52, 71, 332, 427, 432n45, 433n9, 434n10
Bonifacio, 88
Bonilla, Manuel, 258–59
Bonilla, Policarpo, 258–60
Borda, Juan I., 286
Borland, Solon, 202
Borrero, Antonio, 145
Borrero, Eusebio, 273
Bosch, Francisco, 395
Bouët-Willaumez, Louis Edouard, 308
Bouguier, Sebastián, 238
boundary disputes, xxv, xxviii, 93, 105, 113
Bounty (British warship), 11
Bourbon rule, xxv
Boves, José Tomás, xxvii, 28–30, **435n39**
Bowie, James, 160–62
Bowie knife, 223, 228
Boyacá, 36, 276–77
Boyacá (Colombian warship), 279
Boyacá River, 36
Boyer, Jean-Pierre, 342
Bracamonte, Eusebio, 254
Brache, Trinidad, 241
Braga, Fernandez, 152
Bramble (British warship), 393
Brandsen, Hollander, 99

Brant, Felisberto Caldeira, 87, 98
Brasil (Brazilian warship), 321
Bravo, Ignacio, 371
Bravo, Leonardo, 78
Bravo, Miguel, 77
Bravo, Nicolás, 78–79, 82–83, 167, 177, 194–95, **471n4**
Brazil, 43–44, 52, 65, 116, *148*, 281–84, 286; intraclass wars, 405–13; navy, 87, 89; Revolution of 1893–94, xvi, xxvii; separation vs. union, 149–55; War for Cisplatine Province, 93–104; War for Independence, xv, 85–82, 149; War of the Triple Alliance, xiv–xv, xxvi, 313–32
Brazilian Civil War of 1893–94, xxvii, 405–13
Brazilian Revolution. *See* Brazilian Civil War of 1893–94
Briceño, Justo, 238
Briceño Méndez, Pedro, 238
Brión, Luis, 31, 33–35, 37, **437n52**
Briscoe, W. F., 216
Britannia (British merchantship), 35
British Antilles, 21
British Honduras, 199. *See also* Belize
British Legion, 36–38. *See also* Napoleonic Veterans
British intervention, 92
British mercenaries, 89, 141, 143, 230
Brown, Jacob, 182
Brown, Phillip, 260
Brown, William (Guillermo), 50, 60, 96–102, 104, 119–10, **442n48**
Brown Bess musket, 313
Brutus (Texas warship), 163, 168
Bruzual, Ezequiel, 243
bubonic plague, 141
Bucaramanga, 278
Buchanan, James, xxvi, 181, 213, 214–15, 219, 232
Buchivcoa, 242
Buenaventura, 142, 280

Buena Vista, 188–89, 192
Buenavista, Bay of, 356
Buendia, José, 381–82
Buenos Aires, xxv, 30, 41–52, 55, 58, 60–64, 70, 93–102, 104, 113–25, 134, 150, 286–87, 318, 368, 376, 391–96. *See also* Porteños
Buenos Aires (Argentine warship), 95, 123
Bulnes, Manuel, 70, 137–38, 289, 291–92, 366–67, **462n28**
Bunch, W. T., 216
Burke, Edmund, xiv
Burr, Aaron, 205
Burriel, Juan Nepomuceno, 356
Burton, Richard F., 313
Bustamante, Anastasio, 83, 167–69, 171–72, **471n5**
Bustos, Juan Bautista, 117
Butler, William, 185
Bynon, George, 100

Caaguazú, 120
Caamaño, José, 145
caatinga (brushwood), 90
Caballos, 60
Cabañas, José Trinidad, 225, 253–54
Cabañas, Manuel Anastacio, 45
Cabellero, 329, 331
cabildo abierto (town meeting), 20, 41, 43, 52, 64, 433n1
Cabo Rojo, 82
Caboclo (Brazilian warship), 101
Cabral, José María, 346, 347
Cabral (Brazilian warship), 328
Cabrera, José, 348
Cabrera, Manuel Estrada, 259, 260
Cacarajícara, 362
Cáceres, Andrés, 382
Cachirí, 31
Cacique (Brazilian warship), 102–3
Cádiz, 23, 37, 81
Cagua, uprising in, 243
Cajeme. *See* Leyva, José María
Calabozo, 34
Calalán, 52
Calama, 400
Calamar. *See* Barranca

Caldera, 400, 402
Calderón, 75
Calderón, Francisco, 108
Caldwell, Matthew, 174
Calfucurá, 368
California, xxvi, 65, 144, 179, 181, 207–11; fight for, 185–86, 195, 197; gold rush, 290
Calipso (Portuguese warship), 89á
Callao, 54–55, 60–61, 63–69, 106, 108, 132, 134, 136–37, 333–34, *338*, 339, 377–78, 382, 385–87, 524n45
Calleja, Félix, 71–78, **447n8**
Camacho, Eliodoro, 267
Camacua Chico, 101
Camagüey, 355–57
Camagueyanos (Cubans), 358
camalotes, 328–29
Camaquã, 153
Câmara, José Antônio Corrêa de, 331
Camargo, 268
Camba, Andres García, 51
Cambiaso, Juan Bautista, 344
Camero, Facundo, 242
Cameron, Ewen, 175
Campeche, 170, 176, 369, 370
Campechana (Mexican warship), 176
Campero, Gen., 51
Campero, Narciso, 266, 382–83, **523n34**
Campichuelo, 45
Campo Elías, Vicente, 29
Campo Grande, 331
Campos, João Felix Pereira de, 88–89
Campos, Luis María, 396
Campos, Manuel J., 391–94, 396
Camus, Hermogenes, 400
Canal, Leonardo, 276
Canales, Antonio, 170, 173
Canalizo, Valentín, 83, 169, 177
Cañas, José María, 229–30
Canave, Arsenio, 378
Cancha Rayada, 61–62
Candelaria, 319
Canelones, 285
Canning, George, 70, 93, 217
Canoe Paddlers Corps, 328

Cánovas del Castillo, Antonio, 363
Canterac, José, 51, 64–66, 68–69
Cape of Good Hope, 42
Cape Honduras, 200
Cape Horn, 60, 63, 65, 108, 134, 339
Cape San Lucas, 208
Capetown, 42
Cape Verde Islands, 419
Cap François, 7
Cap Haitien, 19
capitalism, xxvii–xxviii
Capriles, Anibal, 268
Captaincy-General of Venezuela, 20–40
Cap Tiburon, 6–7, 11
Capucin Monks, 26
Caraballo, Francisco, 284
Carabaño y Ponce, Francisco, 238
Carabobo, 29, 37–38, 235, 241–43
Caracas, 21, 23, 25–26, 29, 34, 237–39, 241–48
Carampangue Battalion (Chilean army), 292
Carchi, 146
Carchi River, 142
"Cardboard Fleet," 413
Cárdenas (Cuba), 217
Cárdenas Expedition, 216–17
Caribbean, xxiii, 9, 20, 35, 271, 274, 277, 279, 341
Caricari, 267
Carillo, Braulio, 131
Carlos III, xxiv, 43
Carlos IV, xxiv
Carlosama, 275
Carlota (Spanish warship), 44
Carlota (Venezuelan warship), 239
Carlota, Joaquina, 43, 45
Carmen de Patagones, 100
Caro, Miguel Antonio, 277
Caroline (filibuster), 208
Carolines, 416
Carora, 26
Carpintería, 283
Carrera (Chile), 292
Carrera, José Miguel, 55–58, 63, **443n3**
Carrera, Juan Luis, 57, 70

Carrera, Luis, 56
Carrera, Rafael, xxviii, 126, 128–31, 250–55, **460n12**
Carson, "Kit," 185–86
Cartagena, 20, 26–27, 30–31, 37–38, 276–77, 280
Carujo, Pedro, 238
Carumbé, 52
Carvalho, Delfim Carlos de, 327
Carvalho, Manoel de, 94
Casa de Moneda (the royal treasure house), 48
Casa Rosada, 392–93
Casáirs, Ramón, 129
Casanare, 35
Caseros, 123
Casma, 137–38
Caste War, 369–70
Castellanos, Victoriano, 254, 255
Castelli, Juan José, 47
Castellon, Francisco, 221–23, 227
Castilla, Ramón, 197
Castillo, Manuel del, 30
Castillo, Romualdo, 285
Castillo, Severo del, 296
Castillo "Libertador," 245
Castillo Viejo, 231
Castro, Cipriano, xiv, 244–48, 275–76, 427, **490n65**
Castro, Enrique, 285, 286
Castro, Julián, 241
Castro, Rafael de, 215
Catamarca, 119
Catholic Church. *See* Roman Catholic Church
Cauca, 273–76
caudilhos, 153
caudillos, xxvi–xxviii, 34, 40, 51, 94–96, 102, 114–18, 123, 125, 135, 140, 144, 146, 152, 235–37, 242–49, 250–51, 255, 262, 264, 273–75, 281–84, 286, 288, 331, 343–44, 348–49, 426–27, 429n11
Caujaral, 34
causes for war. *See* war, causes for
Cauty, George, 231
Cavada, Federico, 356
Caxias, 90–91

Caxias, Baron/Duque. *See* Lima e Silva
Cazador (merchantship), 291
Ceará, 89–90, 94, 150
Ceja del Negro, 362
Celaya, 73
Celman, Juárez, 391–94
Central America, xxvi–xxvii, 40, 126, *220*, 353; conflicts with Great Britain, 198–203; filibustering against, 221–33, *226*; Mayans in, 369; mini-wars among caudillos, 250–61. *See also* United Provinces
centralism, xxvii, 150
Cepeda, 113–14, 124
Ceres (Argentine warship), 395
Ceres (Spanish warship), 37
Cerro de las Campañas (Hill of the Bells), 310
Cerro Gordo, 190–92, *191*
Cerro Largo (now Melo), 46, 285
Cerro de Pasco, 68
Cerros Blancos, 287
Cerros Colorados, 286–87
Cerruti, Nicolás María, 33
Cervera y Topete, Pascual, 419–20, 422–23, 425
Céspedes, Manuel de, 351–355–56
Cetro (Spanish steamboat), 370
Chacabuco, 61, 63
Chacabuco (Chilean/Argentine warship), 98, 335, 340
Chacabuco (Chilean warship II), 378
Chacabuco (privateer), 100
Chacabuco Regiment (Chilean army), 289, *389*
Chaco, 120, 268
Chalchuapa (El Salvador), 254, 256, 257
Chalchuapa (Honduras), 128
Challenge (British merchantship), 210
Chamorro, Fruto, 222–23
Chapultepec, 194–95, 308
Charcas, 44, 47
Charite (merchantship), 346
Charles IV, 21
Charleston (American warship), 400, 410

Charrúa Indians, 282
Charybdis (British warship), 245
Chascomús, 119
Chassepot rifle, 377
Chatfield, Frederick, 198–99, 201
Chavannes, Jean-Baptiste, 2–3
Chaves, Luis Rodrigues, 90
Chesapeake Bay, 5
Chiapas, 126, 128
Chiaulta, 76
Chihuahua, xxvi, 308
Chilapa, 76
Chile, 42, 44, 49, 98, 114, 117, 137, 146, 267–68, 321, *374*, 425; German immigrants to, 367; intraclass conflicts, xxviii, 289–94, 397–404; navy, 69–70; Pacific War, xxiv–xxv, 333–40; Revolution of 1891, xvi, 397–404; War for Independence, 54–70; wars against Indians, 365–73; War against the Peru-Bolivia Confederation, 132–39; War of the Pacific, xxvii, 375–89
Chilean Revolution of 1891, 397–404
Chili (filibuster), 144
Chillán, 55–56, 291, 366
Chiloé, 55, 69–70, 132, 134, 337
Chilpancingo, 79
Chimborazo (Ecuadorian warship), 145
China, 146; relations with Cuba, 353, 357
Chincha islands, 333
Chiquimula, 253
Chiquitos, 94
Chiriguaná
cholera, 325, 326, 512n15
cholos. See mestizos
Choluteca, 258
Chorrillos, 385–87
Christophe, Henry, 12, 14–15, 342, **432n40**
Chuquisaca (Sucre, Bolivia), 41, 44, 47, 106
Churubusco, 193–94
Cibao, 342, 345, 348

Cienfuegos, 420
científicos, 371
Cincinnati (American warship), 280, 417
Cisne (Spanish warship), 44
Cisneros, 43, 47
Cisneros Betancourt, Salvador, 356
Cisplatine Province, 52, 85, 87, 93, 150. *See also* Uruguay
City of Sidney (American merchantship), 257
Ciudad Bolívar. *See* Angostura
Ciudadela de Tacumán, 117
Clarence, George, 451n16
Clark, John, 488n27
Claro River, 56
class system, xxiii–xxiv
Clayton-Bulwer Treaty, 201–2
Clifton (merchantship), 63
Club of Independent Supporters, 359. *See also* Figueda Fernández, Sotero
Coahuila, 158, 160, 172, 309
Cobija, 264, 266, 376
Cochabamba, 49, 262, 264, 266–68
Coche, Treaty of, 243
Cochrane, Alexander, 21
Cochrane, Thomas, 63–65, 88–91, 94–95, 97, **445n32**
Codazzi, Agustín, 239
Coe, John Halstead, 102, 119, 123, **454n49**
coffee, 1, 3, 8
Coimbra, 314
Cole, Byron, 223, 225
Colima (American merchantship), 257
Collazo, Enrique, 363, 420
Collinsworth, George M., 160
Colo Colo (Chilean warship), 134
Colomb, P. H., 425
Colombia, xxiv, xxviii, 66–70, 140–41; army, 66; interclass conflict, xxv; intraclass wars, 271–80; War against Peru, 105–10; War for Independence, 20, 26–28, 30–32, 35–40
Colombia (Colombian warship), 108, 142, 278
Colón, 276

Colonia, 95–97, 99, 121
colonial rule, 83
"Colorado" Battalion (Bolivian army), 266, 377
Colorado River (Argentina), 368
Colorado River (United States), 163, 209, 211–12
colorados (Uruguayans), 114, 118, 123, 282–88, 313–14, 318–19
colorados (Venezuelans), 239
Colt (merchantship), 56
Colt revolver, 228
Comblain rifle, 377
Comercio de Lima (merchantship), 95
Comercio de Mexico Regiment, 171
Cometa (rebel warship), 277
Commercial Volunteers of Havana, 353
Comonfort, Ignacio, 295–97, 307–8
Concepción (Chile), 54–56, 60–61, 290–91, 293, 366, 367, *389*, 398
Concepción del Uruguay, 95
Concha, José de la, 218
Condessa de Ponte (merchantship), 101
Confederación (Chilean warship), 134, 137
Confederación (Confederation warship), 136
Confederate States of America, xxiv, 514n12, 517n22
Confederation of the Andes, 134
Confederation of the Equator, 94, 150
Confianza (rebel warship), 277
conflict terminology, xv
Congo, 2
Congresionalistas (Chileans), 398–402, *401*, *403*
Congreso (Peruvian warship), 107
Congreso Nacional (Argentine warship), 100
Congress of Panama, 105, 214
Congrêve rocket, 316
Conquistadores, 24
Consecuencia (Spanish merchantship), 60

Conspiracy of the Ladder, 215
Constança (Brazilian warship), 100
Constitução (Portuguese warship), 89
Constitucion (Dominican warship), 346
Constitución (Venezuelan warship), 239, 240
Constitution of 1801 (Haiti), 432n44
Constitution of 1812 (Spain), 23, 30, 37, 64, 67, 81, 342
Constitution of 1824 (Mexico), 158–61, 164
Constitution of 1830 (Venezuela), 236, 488n41
Constitution of 1843 (Bolivia), 263
Constitution of 1843 (Colombia), 273
Constitution of 1857 (Mexico), 297
Constitution of 1858 (Colombia), 274
Constitution of 1886 (Colombia), 277
Constitution of 1891 (Chile), 527n2
Contoy Island, 216
Contreras, 193, 196
Contreras, José, 347
Cooke, Philip St. George, 173
Cooke, William, 171
Copacabana, 265
Copán, 253, 259
Copiapó, 60, 292–93
Coplé, 242
Coquimbo, 290–93, 379, 398, 402
Corales, 96–97
Cordero, Bartolomé, 392
Cordero, Indalecio, 253
Cordero, Luís, 146
Córdoba (Argentina), 42–44, 47–49, 113, 117, 327, 393
Córdoba (Mexico), 82, 307
Córdoba, Joaquín María, 276
Córdoba, José de, 47
Córdoba, José María, 69
"Córdoba Clique," 391, 394
Córdova, Jorge, 264–65, 268
Coro, 23, 26, 29, 242, 249
Corpus Christi, 179

Corral, Ponicano, 223, 225, 227–28
Corrales, 101
Correa, Ramón, 27
Corrêa, Serzedello, 406
Correo de Mejico (Mexican warship), 160
Corrientes, 50–52, 104, 114, 116, 118–21, 123, 283, 318–21, 332, 394–95
Corro, José Justo, 166
Cortés, José María, 265
Cortes (American merchantship), 227
Côrtes (Portuguese congress), 86, 89–92
Cortés (Spanish congress), 23, 30
Cortés de Madariaga, Jose, 20
Corumba, 314
Cós, Martín Perfecto de, 158–59, 160–61, 164, 169–70, **468n9**
Cosmini, 267
Costa, Alvaro da, 93
Costa, Julio, 395
Costa Brava, 120
Costa Firme, 30
Costa Rica, 131, 133, 222, 228–29, 231–33, 250–61, 288; relations with Cuba, 358–60; War for Central American Union, 127–28, 130–31
costeños (Ecuador), 141
Cotagaita, 47, 264, 265
cotton, 1, 86
Courcy, Michael de, 46
Covadonga (Spanish/Chilean warship), 334, 337, 378–79, 385
Covarrubias, Alvaro, 333
Crabb, Henry A., 210–11, **481n28**
Crabb Filibustering Expedition, 213
Cramer [Kramer], Ambrosio, 61
Crasbie, Thomas, 451n16
Craufurd, Robert, 42–43
Creole (filibuster), 216, 217, 485n40
Crespo, Joaquín, xiv, 244, 249
Crimean War, 203, 305, 346

criollos, xxiv, 23–24, 39, 42–45, 47, 51, 64, 68, 71–72, 76, 80–84, 131, 180, 218, 235, 266, 351, 352, 369, 371
Cristóbal Colon (Spanish warship), 417, 419–20
Crittenden, William S., 218
Crockett, David, 162
Croix des Bouquets, 3
Cruz, José de la, 75
Cuajimalpa, 74
Cuautla Amilpas, 77–78
Cuba, xiv, xxiii–xxiv, xxvi, 13, 26, 38, 82–83, 129, *350*; filibustering against, 214–19; relations with Santo Domingo, 341, 346–49; and sugar, 215, 361, 364; and tobacco, 364; wars for independence, 351–64, 415–25, 427
Cuban Revolutionary Party, 359
Cubas, José, 119
Cucalón y Villamayor, Bartolomé, 25
Cúcuta, 27, 38, 278
Cuenca, 39, 108–9, 142–43
Cuestas, Juan, 287
Cul de Sac, 10
Cullen, Domingo, 118
Culta, José, 48
Cumaná, 29–30, 33, 35, 37, 238, 247
Cumberland (merchantship), 63
Cundinamarca, 30, 36, 276–77
Curaçao, 26, 241, 243–45, 248, 344, 358, 420
Curupatí, 324–26, 328–39, 332
Curuzú, 324–25
Curuzú Chica, 313
Cuyo, 49
Cuzco, 66, 68–69, 133
Cyane (American warship), 202

Daiquiri, *421*
Danjou, Jean, 307
Danuzzio, Santiago, 395
d'Aury, Luis, 80
Dardo (Venezuelan warship), 31
Darwin, Charles, 114, 368
Dauntless (blockade runner), 362
Dautant, Pedro, 238

Dautant, Pierre, 100–102
Davidson, George R., 227
Dávila, Miguel R., 260
Davis, Charles H., 231
Davis, Jefferson, 189, 216
Dawson, Frederick, 170
Day of the Youth, 28, 436n43
Daza, Hilarión, 266–68, 378, 381–82, **495n34**
Declaration of Paris (1856), 335, 463n35
Decrés, Duc de, 15
de Faria, Gen., 91
Degollado, Santos, 298–99, 301, 303
degolladores (executioners), 116
DeKay, George, 102–3, **454n47**
Del Espejo, 62
de la Cruz, José María, 289–92, **501n1**
Delamare, Rodrigo, 87–88
Delgado, Emilio, 255
Democracia (Venezuelan warship), 240
Derby, George, 190
Desaguadero River, 47, 106, 133
Desfourneaux, Edmé-Etienne Borne, 9
Dessalines, Jean Jacques, 5, 10, 12–16, 18, *19*, 342, **431n13**
Destroyer (warship), 409
Detroit (American warship), 410
D'Eu, Conde, 330, 331, 513n67
Diana (Venezuelan warship), 240
Díaz, José, 321, 325, **510n35**
Díaz, Porfírio, 211, 212, 305, 307–10, 371, 373
Díaz Canseco, Fermin, 379
Díaz Vélez, Eustaquio, 120
Dieudonné, Pierre, 8
Dillon Irish Regiment, 6
disease, 197, 227. *See also* dysentery, small pox, typhoid, yellow fever
distances, explanation of, xv
ditch. *See la trocha*
Doblado, Santiago, 301
Dolores, 71, 73

Dolores Preza, José, 260
Dom João VI (Portuguese warship), 89
Domínguez, Francisco, 345
Dominican Republic. *See* Santo Domingo
Dona Paula (Brazilian warship), 100
Doniphan, Alexander W., 185
d'Orleans, François Ferdinand, 169
Dorrego, Manuel, 50, 102, 117
Dos de Mayo (Peruvian warship), 384
Doubleday, C. W., 223, 225, 227
Draconianos (Colombians), 272
Drago, Luís, 246
Dragoons of Caracas, 29
Drummond, Francis, 100, **454n41**
Duany, Demetrio Castillo, 421–22
Duarte, Juan Pablo, 341, 343–44, **514n1**
Duarte, Pedro, 320–21
Dueñas, Francisco, 253–55
Dulce, Domingo, 355
Dupuy de Lôme, Enrique, 416
Duqueza de Goias (Brazilian warship), 100
Durango, 165
Dutch Guinea, 11
Dutch mercenaries, 8–9
"Dynamite Fleet," 413
dynamite gun, 409–10, 413
dysentery, 35

Echagüe, Pascual, 118–20
economic causes for war, xxiv–xxv, 42, 54, 335, 364, 375–76, 388. *See also* mercantilism
Ecuador, xvi, xxiv, xxviii, 36, 106–8, 110, 272, 275, 335, 339, *374*; Guayaquil versus Ecuador, 140–46; War for Independence, xiv, 20, 25, 38–40
Edgar Stewart (blockade runner), 356
Edmond (privateer), 137
Egan, Morris P., 404
Eguino, Auturo, 268

El Alamo (Mexico), 212
El banco, 27
El Barro, 246
El Cercado, 347
El Cerrito, 48
El Chucuito (Colombian warship), 279
El Cid (merchantship), 409
El Coco, 257
El Emperador (revolutionary warship), 21
Elias Bonnemaison, Manuel, 386
Elío, Francisco Javier de, 46, 48
Elizalde, Antonio, 143–44, **465n23**
Elizalde, Juan Francisco, 106
Ellaurí, José, 285–86
El Leandro (revolutionary warship), 21
Elliott, Jonathan, 516n27
El Membrillar, 56
El Morro, 384, *384*
Eloisa (merchantship), 238
El Oro, 145
El Pacto de la Cruz, 287
El Pájaro del Océano (Spanish warship), 348
El Palmar, 118
El Penón, 193
El Salvador, 229–32, 250–61; War for Central American Union, 126–31, 201
El Seibo, 344, 345, 348
El Semen, 34
El Socorro, 278
El Venadito, 80
El Vigilante (rebel warship), 277
Embrace of Maquinhuayo, 133
Emerald (British merchantship), 35
Emigration of 1814, 29
Emilia (Portuguese warship), 91
Emperán, Vicente de, 20, 23
Empire of the Rio de la Plata, xxvi
Encarnación, 45, 318
Enciña, Alberto, 395
Enciso, 277
encomienda, 369
Enfield rifle, 313, 358
England. *See* Great Britain
English mercenaries, 50

Enlightenment, 71
Enna, Manuel, 218
Ensenada (Argentina), 42
Ensenada (Mexico), 207, 208, 209, 211, 212–13
Ensenada Spit, 100
Entre Ríos, 48, 50–51, 113–14, 116–20, 123, 125, 283, 318–20, 369, 395
Entrena, Col., 277
Ericsson, John, 409, 528n17
Escala, Erasmo, 383
Escalante River, 240
Escalona, Juan de, 40
Escambray Mountains, 356
Escobedo, Mariano, 310
Escolo Militar, 318
Escoto, Masario, 227
Escudeira (Brazilian warship), 100
Esmeralda (Chilean warship), 146, 335, 337, 378, 402
Esmeralda (Spanish warship), 62, 64
Esmeraldas, 145, 275
Esperança (Brazilian transport), 409, 411
Espiña, Mariano, 395
Espínola, José de, 45
Espinosa, Miguel, 255
Espinosa, Rafael, 208
Espirito Santo, 154
Espora, Tomas, 98
Espora (Argentine warship), 395–96
Esquivel, Aniceto, 257
estacamentos volantes (flying detachments), 80
Estero Bellaco, 323
Estigarribia, Antonio de la Cruz, 320–21
Estrada, Emilio, 146
Estrada, José María, 223
Estrada Palma, Tomás, 359, 363
Estranzuela Convention, 172
Estrella (Venezuelan warship), 240
Estrelleta, 345
Europe, xxiv, xxvii, 8, 34, 54, 67, 85–86, 88
European revolutions of 1848, 121
expansionism, American, , 157, 179, 197, 198. *See also*

filibustering, Manifest Destiny
Eyre, William, 101
Ezéta, Antonio, 258
Ezéta, Carlos, 257–58

factionalism. *See* political reasons for war
Fagalde, Charles J., 346
Falcón, Juan, 241–43, 249, **488n43**
Fama (Venezuelan warship), 240
Famaillá, 119–20
Fanfa, Isle of, 152
Fannie (blockade runner), 356
Fannin, James W., 160, 161, 162–63
Fanny (filibuster), 216
Farfán, Francisco, 239
Faría, Francisco María, 238
farinha (coarse flour), 89
farrapos (mercenaries), 153–54
Fashion (filibuster), 232
Fauna (Spanish warship), 44
Faustin I. *See* Soulouque, Faustin
Fayssoux, Callender Irvine, 230, 485n40
Febres Cordero, León de, 242
Federal War, 242–43, 249
federalism, xxvii
Feijó, Diogo Antonio, 150, 152–53
Feliz Inteligencía (merchantship), 136
Ferdinand VII, xxiv, 20–21, 23, 26, 30, 37, 41, 43, 46–47, 49, 52, 54–55, 64, 67, 72, 80–84, 89, 157, 342, 437n50, 440n14
Fernández, Antonio, 246
Fernández, Ignacio Mejía, xxvii
Fernández, Ruperto, 265
Fernando de Noronha Island, 90
Ferrand, Marie-Louise, 18
Ferrera, Francisco, 131
Ferris, Richard, 213
Fidié, João José da Cunha, 90
Fierro, Vicente, 275
Figueda Fernández, Sotero, 359
Filgueira, Count, 52
filibustering, xxvi, 95–96, 143, 203, 221–33, 291, 415; against Central America, 221–33, *226*; against Cuba, 214–19; against Honduras, 232; against Mexico, 205–13, 295; against Nicaragua, 221–33
Filísola, Vicente, 127, 163, 166–67, **470n40**
Fillmore, Millard, 217–18
Firefly (merchantship), 291
Fisher, S. Rhodes, 168
Fisher, William, 175
Flach, Carlos, 337
Flint, Charles R., 408–9, 411, 413
flintlock musket, 355
Flon, Manuel de, 72, 75
Flor de Avante (Ecuadoran warship), 275
Flor del Mar (Confederation warship), 134
Flora (Spanish warship), 44
Flores, Cirilo, 126–27
Flores, Eduardo, 284
Flores, Fortunato, 284
Flores, José Maria, 186
Flores, Juan José, 107, 110, 140, 142–45, 275, 456n15, **463n1**, 480n1
Flores, Nicanor, 266
Flores, Ramón, 395
Flores, Venancio, 283–84, 314, 318, 320, 324, 327, 332, **500n20**, 509n7
Flores Magón brothers, 212–13
Florida (United States), 157, 206; relations with Cuba, 352, 420
Florida (Uruguay), 93, 285
Florida Regiment (Uruguayan army), 323
"flying artillery," 182, 189, 196. *See also* Taylor, Zachary
Fonseca, Manoel Deodoro da, 406–7
Forbes, Gordon, 8–10
Foreign Enlistment Act of 1819, 120, 438n71
Forey, Elie, 303, 307, 505n13
Forsyth, John, xxvi, 213
Fort Bizothon, 7
Fort Borough, 10
Fort Castillo Viego, 230
Fort Dauphin, 3–5, 14
Fort Escahobe, 10
Fort l'Acul, 6
Fort Leavenworth, 186, 427
Fort Libérté, 5, 14–16
Fort San Carlos, 82, 227, 230
Fort Texas, 182
Fort Yuma, 209, 210
Fourmantine, François, 100–1
France, xv, 1, 23, 34, 66–67, 116, 118–22, 134, 138, 149, 321; foreign mercenaries from, 120, *306*; Haitian War for Independence, 1–19; intervention in Mexico, 303–11; navy, 5, 18, 104; relations with Santo Domingo, *306*, 341–42, 346, 349
Francia, Gaspar Rodríguez de, 507n1
Franco, Guillermo, 144–45
Franco, Manuel María, 273
Frederick, Robert Charles, 200
Freire, Col., 284
Freire, Ramón, 70, 132
French, Parker H., 225, 227–28
French Guiana, 85
French intervention in Mexico, xxvii, 370–71
French National Assembly, 1–4
French navy, 5, 18
French Revolution, xxiii–xxiv, 1, 20, 341
Frías, Tomás, 266
Fry, Joseph, 356
Fuentes, Doroteo, 257
fuero militar (a separate legal system), 83
Fullam, William F., 260
Fundador (Confederation warship), 134, 136
Furor (Spanish warship), 420

Gabilondo, Hilario, 210
gachupines, xxiv. *See also peninsulares*
Gadsden Colonization Company, 211
Gadsden Purchase, 295. *See also* Mesilla Valley
Gaines, Edmund, 160
Gaínza, Gavino, 56–57
Gaitán Obeso, Ricardo, 276
Galarza, Salvador, 254

Index 551

Galbaud, Thomas-François, 4–5
Galeana, Hermenegildo, 77–79
Gallo, Pedro León, 293, **502n22**
Galte, 145
Galveston, 163, 168
Gálvez (Spanish warship), 44
Gálvez, José, 385, **524n46**
Gálvez, Mariano, 129
Gama, Luis Felipe de Saldanha da, 405, 407, 409–11, 413
Gamarra, Agustín, xiv, 66–67, 105–7, 109–10, 132–33, 137–38, **455n2**, 461n7
Gamarra, Francisca Zubiaga de, 133
Gamboa, José Antonio, xxv
Gaona, Antonio, 162
Garáy, Col., 163
Garção, Francisco Salema Freire, 91
García, Albino, 79
García, Basilio, 39
García, Calíxto, *354*, 359, 362, 420–21, 424
García, Francisco, 158
García, Joaquín, 342
García, Manuel, 102
García Calderón, Francisco, 387
García Moreno, Gabriel, xxviii, 144–45, 275
García Robira, Custodio, 31
Garibaldi, Giuseppe, 120–22, , *122*, 153, **467n22**
Garibaldi (Brazilian warship), 510n29
Garibay, Pedro de, 71
Garrapata, 276
Garrido, Victoriano, 132
Garrison, Cornelius K., 225, 227–28, 231
Garza, Catarino, 277, 278
Garzón, Eugenio, 282, **499n11**
Gasset y Mercader, Manuel, 304
Gatazo, 146
Gatling machine gun, 272, 377, 384
gauchos, 46, 48, 50–51, 57, 94–96, 102, 104, 113–14, 116, 123, 151, 281–82, 368–69
Gaulter (Portuguese warship), 89
Gelly y Obes, Juan Andrés, 330, 332

General Artigas (Uruguayan warship), 508n5
General Balcarce (Argentine warship), 95
General Belgrano (Argentine warship), 95–96
General Brandzen (privateer), 102–3
General Bravo (Mexican warship), 160
General Gartán (rebel warship), 279
General Jackson (rebel warship), 240
General Mancilla (privateer), 102
General Miramón (Mexican warship), 301
General Pinto (Argentine warship), 123–24
General Rivera (Uruguayan warship), 393
General Santana (Dominican warship), 346
George III, 8
George Canning (British merchantship), 440n16, 441n17
Georgia (Confederate warship), 514n12
Georgiana (filibuster), 216
Germany, 96, 388, 400; dispute with Venezuela, 245–46; foreign mercenaries from, 95–96, 104, 218, *306*
Gerona (Spanish warship), 518n22
Ghilardi, Luis, 296
Gibraltar, 8–9
Gillespie, Archibald, 186
Gillet, Samuel, 451n16
Gilliss, J. M., xxviii, 292, 366
Gilman, Charles, 227
Giovanni Basan (Italian warship), 407–8
Girardot, Atanasio, 27, **435n33**
Giró, Juan Francisco, 283
Glenelg (filibuster), 144
Gobiernistas (Chileans), 398–404, *401*, *403*
godos, xxiv, 236, 486n2. *See also peninsulares*
Godoy, Manuel, xxiv

Goicouria, D. Domingo de, 228
Gólgotas (Colombians), 272
Goliad, 160–64, 206
Gomensoro, Tomás, 285
Gómez, Francisco (Pancho), 363
Gómez, Juan C., 480n1
Gómez, Juan Vicente, 245–49, **490n70**
Gómez, Leandro, 314, 319
Gómez, Máximo, 353, 355–56, 517n14
Gómez Farías, Valentín, 158, 183, 188–89
Goncaives, 3, 5, 10, 14, 342
Gonçalves, Jerônimo, 408, 410
Gonçalves da Silva, Bento, 152
González, Cecilio, 357
González, Francisco, 38
González, José Antonio, 242, 254
González, Lerdo, 212
González, Santiago, 254, 255
González Moreno, Francisco, 25
González Ortega, Jesús, 301–2, 305
González Pacheco, Rafael, 244
Gorriti Island, 99
Goths, 486n2
Goyeneche, José Manuel de, 47, 49, 70
Gracias, 253, 255
Gramalote, 278
Gran Colombia, 36, 38–39, 60, 68, 105–110, 140–42, 150, 235–38, 248, *270*, 272, 275, 342. *See also* Colombia
Gran Expedición, 81
Granada (Nicaragua), 221, 223, 228–31
Granada (filibuster), 230
Granada (merchantship), 231
Granadine confederation, 272. *See also* Colombia
Granados, Garcia, 256
grand blanc, 2
Grand Bois, 10
Grand Cayman Islands, 199
Grand Gôave, 6, 13
Grande-Anse, 11
Granville, Guillermo, 101

Grão Pará (Portuguese warship), 90
Grant, James, 161, 162
Grant, Ulysses S., 179, 356
"Grass Fight," 161
Grass rifle, 377, 398
Grau, Miguel, 378–79, *380*, 522n18
Great Britain, xiii–xiv, xxvi–xxviii, 5–13, 16, 18, 20–21, 25–26, 31, 34–35, 42, 46, 48, 63, 70, 85, 91, 101–2, 104, 116, 118–23, 134, 141, 145, 150, 228, 232, 321, 479n12; army, 9; conflicts in Central America, 198–203; conflict with Venezuela, 245–46; foreign mercenaries from, 303–4, *306*; navy, 6, 11, 16, 23, 43, 56, 85, 104; relations with Chile, 398–400; relations with Cuba, 352; relations with Santo Domingo, 342, 346
Grenada (Nicaragua), 127
Grenada Island, 33, 35
Grenfell, John Pascoe, 91, 98, 123, 152, 153, 451n16, **452n32**, 459n49
Grey, Charles, 200. *See also* Greytown
Greytown, 200, 202–3, 231, 232
Griggs, John, 153
gringo, 183, 475n24
grito do Ypiranga, 85
Guachi, 38
Guadalajara, 74–75, 177, 298–99, 302, 308
Guadalupe (Mexican warship), 173, 176
Guadalupe Hidalgo (Mexico), 195
Guadalupe-Hidalgo, Treaty of, 195, 197, 207
Gual, Pedro, 242
Gualeguay (Argentine warship), 510n23
Gualeguaychu, 121
Guamal, 27
Guámairo Convention, 355
Guanajuato, 73–74, 80–81, 188, 296, 301, 308

Guanare, 242
guano, 375. *See also* nitrates
Guantanamo, 420, 422
Guarani (Brazilian warship), 88
Guardia, Tomás, 257, **492n28**
Guardiola, José Santos, 252–54
Guardiola, Santos, 225, 227–29, **484n12**
Guárico, uprising in, 243
Guatemala, xxviii, 199, 202–3, 222, 229–32, 250–61; War for Central American Union, 126–31
Guatemala City, 126–27, 129–30, 252–54, 256, 259
Guayabos, 50, 286
Guayana, 25, 29, 33, 236, 238–39, 243
Guayaquil, 25, 38, 60, 65–66, 106, 108–10, 140–46
Guayaquilena (Colombian warship), 108–9
Guayas, 108, 140, 142–43
Guayas (Ecuadorian warship), 145
Guayas (rebel warship), 145
Guayas River, 60, 144–45
Guaymas, 207, 209–10
Guedes, Rodrigo Pinto, 97, 99–101, **453n23**
Güemes, Miguel Martín, 48, 50–51, 114, **442n51**
Guerra, Ramón, 244
Guerrero, Sub-lt., 212
Guerrero, Vicente, 80–81, 83, **449n54**
Guevara, Manuel de, 21
Guevera, Lorenze, 244
Guiana, 241
Guise, Martín, 67–68, 107–8, **456n19**
Guiseppe Garibaldi (Italian warship), 417
Guitia, 34
Gulf of California, 208
Gulf of Cortez, 65
Gulf of Fonseca, 230, 255, 260
Gulf of Mexico, 80
gunpowder, 8
Guruceta, Roque, 446n52
Gustavo Sampaio (Brazilian warship), 411–12
Gutiérrez, Bernardo, 80

Gutiérrez, Dionisio, 259
Gutiérrez, Santos, 275
Gutierrez de la Fuente, Antonio, 132
Guzmán, Antonio Leocadio, 239
Guzman, Joaquín Eufracio, 253
Guzmán Blanco, Antonio, xxvi, 242–44, 249, **489n51**

Habanero (Spanish warship), 216, 218
Hache River, 37
Hague Tribunal, 246
Haiti: War for Independence, xiii–xv, xxiii, 1–19, *17*; Wars with Santo Domingo, 341–49; mentioned, 31, 33, 83, 351, 356, 358
Halcón (Argentine warship) 60
Hamilton, Alexander, 21
Hannah Alexander (American merchantship), 160
Hanoverian mercenaries, 8
Haro y Tamariz, Antonio, 296–97
Harris, James, 100–101
Harrisburg, 163
Haut-de-Cap, 15
Havana, 18, 73, 81, 215, 217–18, 304, 351, 355–57, 360–63, 415–16, 418–20, 424
Hay, John, 424
Hearst, William Randolph, 415–16, 529n1
Hédouville, Gabriel-Theodore-Joseph, 11–12
Henao, Jesús María, 280
Heneken, Stanley Theodore, 344
Henningsen, Charles Frederick, 230, 231, 485n37
Hérard, Charles, 343–44
Heras, Juan de las, 95, **453n10**
Hercelles, Justo, 143
Hércules (Argentine warship), 60
Hércules (Colombian warship), 278
Hernández, Carlos, 420
Hernández, José Manuel, 244, 247, **489n63**
Herrán, Antonio, 274

Herrera, Benjamín, 278, 279
Herrera, Francisco, 252
Herrera, José Joaquin de, 82–83, 177, 180–81, **473n54**
Herval (Brazilian warship), 328, 509n18
Hidalgo, Miguel, xxiv, xxviii, 71–76, 78–80, 83–84, 302, **446n1**, 447n3, 450n60
Hidalgo de Cisneros, Baltasar, 41
Hijo de Mayo (privateer), 101
Hillyar, James, 56
Hise, Elijah, 200–1
Hise-Selva Treaty, 200–1
Hispañola, *xxx*, 8, 13, 341–42, 430n1
Holland, 9; foreign mercenaries from, *306*
Hollins, George N., 202
Honduras, xv, xxvi, 197, 199, 201–3, 222, 225, 229, 231, 250–61; filibustering against, 232; War for Central American Union, 126–31
Honduras Bay, 198. *See also* Bay Islands
Hood, Samuel, 121
Hornby, Phipps, 201
Hornet (blockade runner), 356
Hornos, Manuel, 368
horseshoes, 24
Hotchkiss machine gun, 248
Houston, Samuel, 161, 163–64, 167, 171, 173, 174–76, 468n11, **469n26**
Huachi, 38
Huacho, 64, 137
Huacho (Ecuadorian warship), 145
Huamachuco, 388
Huancavelica, 133
Huancayo, 66
Huaqui, 46–47
Huara, 399
Huáscar (Peruvian/Chilean warship), 335, 337, 339–40, 376, 378–80, *380*, 385, 398, 521n6
Huáscar (rebel warship), 145
Huasco, 136, 292
Huaylas, 138

Huerta, Victoriano, 373
Huidobro, Jose Ruiz, 368
Huigra, 146
Humaitá, 320–21, 323–29, 332
Humboldt, Alexander von, 71
Hungarian mercenaries, 217–18
Hutchinson, Norman, 248

Ibarra, Diego, 25, 238
Iberian Peninsula, 57
Ibicuí, 102
Ibiracahy, 51
Icarus (British warship), 232
Illingworth, John, 108, 143–44, **465n26**
Illinois Regiment (American army), 188–89
Ilo, 66–67, 383
Iman, Santiago, 170
Iman (Mexican warship), 176
Imbert, José María, 344
Imbituba, 153
Imperatriz (Brazilian warship), 97
Imperial (Brazilian warship), 88
Imperial (Chilean merchantship), 398
Independence (Texas warship), 163, 168
independence, ideology of, xxiii–xxv, xxviii
Independencia (Argentine warship), 395–96
Independencia (Chilean/Argentine warship), 64–65, 95, 100–1
Independencia (Mexican warship), 168
Independencia (Peruvian warship), 335, 337, 339–40, 376, 378, 384
Independencia (Venezuelan warship), 240
Indêpendencia ou Morte (Brazilian warship), 101
India Muerta, 52, 120
Indianola (merchantship), 301
Indians, xxiv, xxvi, 24, 47, 55, 72–73, 101, 114, 117, 128, 130–31, 133, 141, 146, 159, 170, 262–63, 265–66, 268–69, 325, 365–73, 377. *See also* Araucanians,

Aymara, Mayans, native Americans, Quechua, Ranqueles, Yaquis
Infanta Isabel (Spanish warship), 393
Infante D. Miguel (Portuguese warship), 90–91
Ingavi, 138, 263
inmortales, 94
International Workers of the World, 211
Interpido (royalist warship), 33
interventions, xxvii–xxviii, 303, 415
intraclass wars, xxvii–xxviii, 125, 271, 281, 289, 295, 303, 391, 397, 405
Intrépida (Venezuelan warship), 240
Invincible (Argentine warship), 45
Invincible (Texas warship), 163, 168
Iquique, 378–81, 399–400, 402, 404
Ireland, 95, 101; foreign mercenaries from, 3, 6, 50, 95, 104, 120, 141, 143, *306*
Iris (Brazilian warship), 411
Iris (merchantship), 279
Irisarri, Antonio José de, 205
Irish Brigade (British), 10
Irois, 10–11
Isabel la Católica (Spanish warship), 348
Isabel Maria (Brazilian warship), 97
Isabela (rebel warship), 277
Isabella (Brazilian warship), 102
Isabella II, 347, 349
Isla de los Estados, 396
Islay, 133, 136
Italy, 122, conflict with Venezuela, 245–46; foreign mercenaries from, 120, *306*
Itaparica (Brazilian warship), 100
Itata (Chilean merchantship), 400, 404
Iturbide (Mexican warship), 168, 208

Iturbide, Agustín de, 79, 81, 127, 158, **450n60**. *See also* Agustin I
Iturrigaray, José, 71
Ituzaingó (Paso del Rosario), 99–101
Izúcar, 77

Jackson, Andrew, xxvi
Jacmel, 3, 7–8, 12–13
Jacuí River, 152
Jaeger, William G. W., 347
Jalapa, 83
Jalisco, 158, 167, 188, 301
Jalón y Dochagavia, Diego, 29
Jamaica, 4–7, 10–11, 13, 30–31, 199, 342, 431n34
Jambelí Channel, 145
Janequeo (Chilean warship), 385
Japan, 146
Jaramillo Alvarado, Pío, 140
Jardim, José Gomes Vasconcellos, 152
Jarvis, Joseph, 301
Jauja, 66
Jean Rabel, 6–7
Jean-François, 4
Jecker, Jean Baptiste, 299
Jefferson, Thomas, 214
Jell, Charles, 451n16
Jenipapo River, 90
Jérémie, 5, 7, 10–11
Jeréz, Maximo, 231
Jesuits, 273, 275
jeune école (the young school), 417
Jimenes, Manuel, 345–46
Jiménez, Col., 109
Jiménez Castellanos, Adolfo, 424
João VI, 44, 85, 87, 91–92, 94, 104, 149–50
Joaquín, Ramírez Sesma, 162
John L. Stevens (American merchantship), 298
Johnson, Francis, 161
Joly, Nicolás, 238, **487n25**
Jones, Thomas A. C., 175
Jordan, S. W., 171
Jordan, Thomas, 353
Jordao, Polidoro da Fonseca Quintanilha, 324, 325

Juan Fernández Island, 57, 60, 136
Juárez, Benito, 296–99, 301–2, 303–5, 307–11, **503n6**
Júcaro, 356
Jujuy, 47, 49, 119
Jumaguayu, 356
Júncal, 33
Junín, 68
Junín (Confederation warship), 134, 136
Júpiter (Brazilian merchantship), 406
Jusacamea, Juan Ignacio, 371

Kearny, Stephen W., 185
Kentucky Regiment, 216–17
Kewen, Achilles, 225
Key West, 217, 420
King George (British armed transport), 7
Kinney, H. L., 203
Koning, Abraham, 388
Korner, Emil, 400, **527n11**
Krag-Jorgeson repeating rifle, 418
Krupp artillery, 248, 260, 268, 282, 327, 377, 383, *387*, 398, 418, 422

La Bahía, 206. *See* also Goliad
La Banda Oriental (Eastern Shore of the Uruguay River), 282
Labatut, Pierre (Pedro), 27, 88
Laborde, Angel, 38, 82
La Ceiba, 258–60
Lackawanna (American warship), 386
La Concepción (Peru), 388–89
La Crête-a-Pierrot fort, 14–15
Lacroix, Pamphile de, 12, 14
La Cruz, 104
La Cruz Prieto, José María, 367
ladinos (*criollos* and *mestizos*), 369–70, 373
La Falange Americana (the American Phalanx), 225, 228
La Filantrópica, 343
La Florida (Argentina), 50
La Fuente, Antonio Gutierrez de, 107, 110, 137

La Gándara y Navarro, José de, 348
Lagos dos Patos, 152–53
Lagos Hilario, 123
La Guayra, 26, 241, 247–48
Laguna, 153
Laguna, Barão de, 87
Laguna Limpia, 121
La Hittes cannon, 313, 321, 325–26
La Humareda, 277
Laine, Francisco Alejandro, 228
Lainé, Pierre Jean Honorat, 121, **459n43**
Laja River, 366
Lake Maracaibo, 38, 238, 242. *See also* Maracaibo
Lake Nicaragua, 221, *222*, 225, 227, 230–32
Lake Titicaca, 66–67, 265, 378
Lake Tramandaí, 153
La Mar, José de, 65, 69, 105–10, **455n1**, 461n7
Lamar, Mirabeau Bonarparte, 167, 171, 176
Lamas, Diego, 286, **501n41**
La Mouche (Haitian warship), 344
lance, 24–25, 31, 94, 116, *124*, 151, 180, 282, 365–66, 369, 427
Lance (French warship), 308
Lane, Joseph, 195
Lantaro (Chilean merchantship), 279
La Paz, 47, 66, 117, 138, 262–68
La Paz, 378, 382
La Plata, 394–95
La Plata River, 49
La Puerta, 29
La Puerta, Luis, 382
Lares, 358
La Rioja, 119
La Rosita (rebel warship), 279
Larrea-Gual Treaty, 110
Las Carreras, 345, 346
Las Cases, Emmanuel Comte de, 18
La Serena, 290–93
La Serna, 64, 66–68
la Serna, José de, 51
Las Guásmas, 422

Las Heras, Juan Gregorio de, 61
Las Matas, 345–46
Las Mercedes (Dominican warship), 346
Las Piedras Mill, 46
lasso, 95
Lastarria, José Victorino, 290
Lastra, Francisco de la, 56
Las Villas, 357, 363
La Tablada, 117
Latacunga, 142
Latin America, *xxii*, *112*; defined, xiii
Latorre, Andrés de, 52
Latorre, Lorenzo, 281, 285–86, **500n30**
La Torre, Miguel de, 34, 37–38
La Tortue, 16
La Trinidad (Honduras), 128
La Trinidad (Nicaragua), 231
La Trinitaria, 341, 343
la trocha (the ditch), 356, 357, 362
Lautaro (Chilean warship), 62–65
Lautaro Lodge, 49, 58
La Union, 253, 256
Lavalle, José Antonio, 376
Lavalle, Juan, 117–19
Lavalle Square, 391
Lavalleja (privateer), 101
Lavalleja, Juan Antonio, 94, 96, 102, 281–83, **499n2**
Laveaux, Etienne-Maynard, 4, 6–7
La Vela de Coro, 22, 241–43, 246–47
La Victoria, *28*, 29, 245, 247
La Virgin (merchantship), 227, 231
La Virgin, 221
Lawton, Henry, 422
Lay torpedo, 379, 386
LeBlanc, Luis, 118
Le Cap, 2–5, 7, 12, 14–16, 342, 430n5
Leclerc, Charles Victor-Emmanuel, 13–16, 18, 342, **432n45**
Lecor, Carlos Federico, 51–52, 93, 98, 100, 104
Lee, Fitzhugh, 416, 424
Lee, Robert E., 190, 216

Legion of Hell, 29
Legión Sagrada (Sacred Legion), 296
Legitimistas (Colombians), 278–80
Leiva, Ponciano, 256, 258
Léogane, 6–9, 11–12
León, 75, 252
Leon (Nicaragua), 221, 223, 225
Leopoldina, Empress, 150
Lerdo de Tejada, Sebastián, 311
Lersundi, Francisco, 355
Les Cayes, 6–7, 13, 15–16, 346
Le Signifie (Haitian warship), 344, 346
letters of marque, 325, 345
Ley Juárez, 295–96
Ley Lerdo, 295–96
Leyva, José María, 211, 212, 371
Liberal (Brazilian warship), 88
Libertad (Argentine warship), 395
Libertad (Chilean warship), 134, 136
Libertad (Peruvian warship), 107–8, 135
Libertad Regiment (Uruguayan army), 284
Libertador (Mexican warship), 168
Libertador (rebel warship), 240, 246
Lima, 41, 54–55, 58, 64–69, 109, 133–34, 137–38, 325–35, 339, 376–77, 382, 386, 388
Lima, Pedro de Araujo, 152
Lima Barros (Brazilian warship), 328, 509n18
Lima e Silva, José Joaquim de, 89
Lima e Silva, Luis Alves de (Baron/Duque of Caxias), 154, 153, 155, **467n28**, 513n66
Limache cannon, 377, *387*
Limeña (Peruvian Confederation warship), 107, 134
Linares, 182, 183
Linares, Arsenio, 422, 424

Linares, José María, 264–65, **494n16**
Lindo Zelaya, Juan, 253
Lines of Rojas, 323–26
Liniers, Santiago, 42–43, 47
Linnes, Arsenio, 362
"Lion of the Andes." *See* Castro, Cipriano
Lira, Ramón, 392
Lircay, Treaty of, 56, 443n9
Lisbon, 44, 87, 90
Little War, 359
Littoral League, 117
Liverpool, 80
Llana, Julián de la, 286
llaneros, 24, 29–31, 34–36, 38, 236–37, 437n56
Llano, Ciriaco de, 77, 79
llanos, 236, 239, 241–42, 244, 246–48, 271, 343
Llave, Ignacio de la, 296, 298
Loa (Chilean transport), 385
Loa (Peruvian warship), 335
Lobo, Rodrigo Ferreira, 96–97
Lobos Island, 99
Lodge, Henry Cabot, 530n17
Loma del Gato, 363
Lomas Valentinas, 329–30
Lombardini, Manuel María, 188
Loncomilla, xxviii, 291–92, 367
London, 42–43, 49–50, 87
Long, James, 206, **480n4**
López, Benigno, 512n63
López, Carlos, 121, **507n1**
López, Estanislao, 102, 113–14, 117–18
López, Francisco de Paula, 176
López, Francisco Solano, xxvi,xxviii, 121, 124, 284, 313–32, *315*, **507n1**, 508n4, 509n8, 509n10, 509n12, 509n17, 509n20, 510n22, 510n22, 510n26, 510n28, 510n32–34, 511n36, 511n42, 511n49, 512n54–55, 512n61–62, 513n66, 513n72–74
López, Horacio E., 213
López, José Felix, 331
López, José Hilario, 142, 144, 273–74, 497n15
López, Miguel, 310
López, Juan Pablo, 118–19

López, Narciso, 214–19, 225, 352, **482n1**, 485n40
López, Panchito, 331
López Rayón, Ignacio, 75, **448n26**
Lorena, Frederico, 408
Lorencez, Guillaume Latrille de, 304–5
Lorraine, Lambton, 356
Los Aguacates, 33
Los Andes (Argentine warship), 393–95
Los Angeles (Chile), 366
Los Angeles (Mexico), 186
Los Altos, 128–30, 253
Los Araguatos, 239
Los Cayos, 31
Los Chancos, 276
Los Loros, 293
Los Patos Pass, 58, 60
Los Pozos, 97–98, 100
Los Pozos Island, 218
Los Remedios, 80
Louisiana, 82; slavery in, 208
Louisiana Regiment, 216
Louisiana Territory, 157
Louverture, Toussaint, 5–15, 18, 342, 351, **430n12**, 432n49
Luna Pizarro, Francisco Javier de, 106, 133
Luperón, Gregorio, 348
Lynch, Eliza, 313, 331–32, **508n3**
Lynch, Patricio, 334, 385

Macdonald, Alexander, 199–200
Maceió (Brazilian warship), 99
Maceo, Antonio, 356–63, **518n25**
MacGregor, Gregor, 205, 460n5
Machado, Alvares, 154
Machado, Eduardo, 357
Machado, Joaquim Nones, 155
Machain, José, 45
Machala, 144–45
Machiavelli, 13
Macias, Juan Manuel, 358
Mackenna O'Reilly, Juan, 56
Madariaga, Joaquin, 121
Madariaga, Juan, 121
Madeira River, 268

Madeira de Melo, Inácio Luiz, 87–88
Madero, Francisco, 212
Madrid, 23, 47
Madrid, Emiliano, 252
Madriñán, Francisco de Paula, 276
Magallanes (Chilean warship), 340, 379, 398
Magdalena, 274, 276
Magdalena River, 27, 37, 271–72, 274, 277–78
Maggiolo, Juan Bautista, 344
Maine (American warship), 354, 363, 415–16, 419, *423*
Maipo (Chilean merchantship), 398
Maipú, 56, 62, 69
Maipú (Argentine warship), 392–93
Maitland, Thomas, 431n18
malaria, 10, 13, 35
Mallarino-Bidlack Treaty, 498n51
Maldonado, 42
Malespín, Francisco, 131, 252
Manabi, 145
Manabí (Ecuadorian warship), 145
Managua, Treaty of, 203
Manantiales, 285
Manco Capac (Peruvian warship), 382, 384–85
Manifest Destiny, xxvi, 104, 157, 205, 214, 352, 483n8
Manila, 81, 420, 448n30
Manizales, 276
Mannlicher repeating rifle, 400, 402
Mansfield, Charles E., 429n7
Manson, George, *103*
Mantecal, 35
Manzanares (Venezuelan warship), 240
Manzanillo, 298, 359, 363, 422
Manzanillo Bay, 348
Manzo, Francisco, 373
Mapasingue, Treaty of, 144
Maquinhuayo, 133
Maracaibo, 23, 26, 29, 37, 236, 238, 240, 243–44
Maranhão, 87, 90, 94, 153

Maranhão (Brazilian warship), 91
Marblehead (American warship), 259
Marceió (Brazilina warship), 101
Marceo, José, 360
Marcilio Dias (Brazilian warship), 408
Marcó del Pont, Francisco Casimiro, 57–58, 61
Marcos, José, 145
Marcy, William L., 179
Margarita Island, 27, 29–31, 33–35, 435n31, 437n50
Maria Chica (Dominican warship), 344
María Emma (rebel warship), 277
Maria da Glória (Brazilian warship), 85
Maria Isabel (Brazilian warship), 102
María Isabel (Spanish warship), 63–64
Marianas, 416, 424
Mariath, Frederick, 99, 153
Maria Theresa (Brazilian warship), 88
Marietta (Honduran warship), 260
Mariluán, Francisco, 366
Marín, Tomás, 173, 176, 301, **473n38**
Marin Shaw, Francisco Gonzalo, 359
Mariño, Santiago, 27, 29–30, 33, 40, 237–38, 239, **435n31**, 487n16
Mariquita, 273
Mariz e Barros (Brazilian warship), 509n18
Marmelade, 6
Maroons, 431n34
Maroto, Rafael, 61
Marques de la Habana (Mexican warship), 301
Marqués de Olinda (Brazilian merchantship), 313–14
Márquez, José Arnaldo, 376
Márquez, José Ignacio de, 273
Márquez, Leonardo, xxvii, 298–99, 302, 303, 305, 309–10

Marroquín, José Manuel, 279
Martí, José, 351, 359–60, 364, **518n45**, 518n47–50
Martín García Island, 49–50, 97, 99, 118–19, 121, 124, 283, 369, 395
Martínez, Francisco, 512n62
Martínez, Tomás, 231, 255
Martínez de Campos, Arsenio, 357–58, 360, 362
Martinique Island, 7, 11, 307
Martins, Gaspar da Silveira, 405
Masaguara, 254
Masaya, 229–31
Masoller, 287
Mason, J. Y., 219
Matamoros, 161, 162, 167, 169–70, 173, 181–83, 308
Matamoros, Mariano, 79
Matanzas, 217
Mataruca, 244
Matias Cousino (Chilean warship), 385
Mato Grosso, 94, 314, 318, 321, 325
Matos, Manuel Antonio, 246–48
Maturín, 29, 249
Maule River, 56, 62, 291
Mauser rifle, 236, 248, 267, 353, 355, 418
Maxim machine gun, 260
Maximilian, Ferdinand, 303–11, *300*, *306*, 353, **505n1**, 506n26, 507n42
Mayans, 365–66, 369–73
Mayo River, 371
Mayol, Miguel, 212
Mayorgo, Mateo, 227–28
Mayz, José Antonio, 37
Maza, Hermogenes, 37
Maza, Ramón, 118
Mazatlan, 308
mazombos, 86
mazorca, 116, 125
McDonald, C. J., 227
McKinley, William, 416, 418, 424, 530n17
McKinstry, Justus, 209
McLane Ocampo Treaty, 301
McLean, Thomas C., 280
McLeod, Hugh, 171
Medellín, 271–72
Medina, Antonio, 83

Medina, José María, 255, 256
Medina, Rosendo, 245
Mejía, Ignacio, 506n16
Mejía, José Antonio, 158, 168–70
Mejía, Tomás, *300*, 303, 310
Mejillones, 263, 376
Melcher, Felix Antonio Clemente, 151
Melgarejo, Mariano, 265–66, 268, 427, **494n21**
Mello, Custódio José de, 405–13
Melo, José María, 273, **497n17**
Mena, Baretto, 332
Méndez, Juan, 309
Méndez, Luis López, 23, 34
Méndez, Nuñez Casto, 337, 339
Méndez, Ramón, 310
Mendieta, Justino, 212
Menéndez, Francisco, 257, 256
Mendoza, 49, 51, 57–58, 60, 64, 68, 368
Mendoza, Luciano, 246, 247
Mercado, José María, 74
mercantilism, xxiv–xxv, 85
Mercedes, 286
mercenaries, 68, 87, 101, 135, 279, 319, 353, 411
Mercurio (Spanish warship), 44
Mérida (Mexico), 170, 369, 371
Mérida (Venezuela), 27
Merlo, 119
Merrimac (Collier), 420
Mesilla Valley, 295
mestizos, xxiv, 24, 30, 33, 40, 128, 131, 141, 159, 262, 264, 369
Meteoro (Brazilian warship), 411
Meteoro (Chilean warship), 291
Mexicali, 211–12
Mexican Land and Colonization Company, 211
Mexican Revolution (1910–1920), 373
Mexicana (privateer), 137
Mexicano (Mexican warship), 176
Mexico, xvi, xxiv, xxvi–xxvii, 30, 40, 65, 67, 121, 127, 129, *156*, 259–60, 273; filibustering against, 205–

13; French interventions, xxvii–xxviii, 303–11; intraclass wars, 295–302; Pastry War, xv; second war with Texas, 166–78; War for Independence, xiv–xv, xxviii, 71–84; wars against Indians, 365–73; War of La Reforma, xxvii, 295–302; War with Texas, 157–65; Wars with United States, xiv–xv
Mexico City, 73–74, 76–77, 79–82, 158–59, 163, 166–72, 181–83, 185, 206–7, 295, 297–99, 301–2, 303–5, 307–11, 369–70, 373
Meza, Pedro Ignacio, 320
Michoacán, 79, 299
Midnight Sun (merchantship), 409
Mier y Benitz, Joaquín de, 37
Mier y Terán, Manuel de, 83, 158
Milam, Ben, 161, **469n23**
Miles, Nelson A., 418, 420–21, 424, **530n19**
Miller, John, 24
Miller, William, 64, 68–69, **445n37**
Mina, Francisco Javier, 80, **449n58**
Miñarica, 143
Minas Gerais, 86, 104, 154
Minatitlan, 308
Mindelo (Portuguese warship), 408
mines, 408, 415–16
Minié rifle, 230, 377
Miragoane, 12
Miramón, Miguel, 298–302, *300*, 303, 309–10, **504n17**
Miranda, Francisco de, 20–21, *22*, 26, 40, 49, **433n3**, 434n26, 435n28
Miranda, Indalecio, 256
Mirebalais, 10
Misiones, 45, 318, 320
Mississippi Regiment, 216
Mistletoe (British warship), 46
Mita, 130
Mitre, Bartolomé, 59, 124–25, 319, 323–25, 327, 331–32, 368, 394, **510n24**

Mitre, Emilio, 330
Mizner, Lansing B., 257
mobile flying columns, 13
Moctezuma (Mexican warship), 173, 176
Moctezuma, Esteban, 167
Model 1822 musket, 467n11
Mojo, 264
molasses, 86
Môle St. Nicolas, 6–7, 10–12, 15–16
Molino del Ray, 194, 196
Mollendo, 378, 383
Mompós, 27
Monagas, José Gregorio, 237, 241, **486n14**
Monagas, José Ruperto, 243
Monagas, José Tadeo, 237–41, 243, 249, **486n13**
Monagas, Julio, 249
Mon-Almonte Treaty, 299
Monarch (filibuster), 144
Monet, Antonio, 67, 69
Monroe, James, 214, 352
Monroe Doctrine, xxviii, 198, 201, 479n12
Monserrat (merchantship), 419
Monte Caseros, 283
Monte de las Cruces, 74
Monte Santiago Bank, 100
Monteagudo (Peruvian/Chilean warship), 107, 132, 136
Montenegro, 117
Monterey (California), 175, 186
Montero, Lizardo, 382, 383
Montero, Pedro, 146
Monterrey (Mexico), 183, 185, 188, 309
Montes, Toribio, 25
Monteverde, Domingo de, 26, 29, **434n24**
Montevideo, xxv, 41–46, 48–50, 52, 63, 87–88, 91, 94–99, 116, 118–123, 154, 281–88, 314, 327, 396, 406–9, 410
Montezuma (French warship), 308
Montilla, Mariano, 37, 238
Montilla, Rafael, 247
Montt, Jorge, xiv, 397, 404, **526n1**, 527n19
Montt Torres, Manuel, 289, 291–92, 294, 367

Moore, Edwin, 170
Moore, John W., 157
Moore, John, 385
Moquegua, 66, 138
Mora, Federico, 257
Mora, José Rafael, 228–31
Morales (Mexico), 296
Morales, Agustín, 264, 266, 268
Morales, Francisco Tomás, 29–31, 34, 38, **435n40**
Morales, José, 296
Morales, Juan, 173–74
Moralitos, 362
Morán, Trinidad, 136
Morazán, Francisco, 128–30, 199, **460n14**
Morción, Benito, 348
Morehead, Joseph C., 206–7
Morelos Batallion (Mexican army), 161
Morelos, José María, xxviii, 74–80, 83–84, **448n28**, 449n46, 450n60
Moreno, Mariano, 41, 48
Moreno, Tomás, 207
Morgan, J. P., 228, 231, 485n26
Morillo, Pablo, 30–35, 37, 40, 50, 434n10, 435n40, **436n47**, 439n87
Morro (British merchantship), 276
Morro do Castelo, 86
Morro de São Paulo, 89
Mosby, Jack, 212, 213
Mosquera, Tomás Cipriano de, 274–75, **497n21**
Mosquito Coast, 198, 200–1, 203
Moyse (Gilles Bréda), 5, 10, 14, **431n14**
mulattes, 2
mulattos, 24, 33, 40, 72, 128
Mulkey, J. K., 211
Muñoz, José Cornelio, 239
Muñoz, José Trinidad, 223, 225, 253
Musitú, Mateo, 76

Nabón, 109
Nacimiento, 366, 367
Nacogdoches, 158, 206
Napoleon. *See* Bonaparte, Napoleon

Napoleon III, 303–5, 308–9, 311, 505n13, 506n16
Napoleonic veterans, 34, 61, 99
Napoleonic wars, 30, 54, 73, 80, 85, 305, 351
Narvarte, Andrés, 238, 239
Nash, Ogden, 426
National Road (Mexico), 190
National War, 81
native Americans, xxvi. *See also* Indians
Navarro, 117
"needle" rifle, 236, 243
Negro River, 95, 98, 100
Negroes, 128
Negrete, 367
Negrete, Pedro Celestino, 83
Neiba, 345
Neill, James, 161
Neiva, 273
Neptune (filibuster), 144
Neto, Coelho, 410
Netos (Uruguayans), 285, 286
Netto, Antônio de Souza, 153
Neuquén River, 369
Neutrality Act (1818), 216, 223
Newark (American warship), 410
New Granada, xxiv, 20, 26–28, 30–31, 35–40, 236, 238, 242, 352. *See also* Colombia
New Orleans, 80, 158, 169, 173, 176–77, 217–18, 232, 298–99, 301
New Orleans (American warship), 417
New Orleans (filibuster), 216
"New Orleans Greys." *See* San Antonio Greys
New Spain: 54. *See also* Mexico
New York, 215–17, 228
New York (American warship), 410
New York City, 21
Nicaragua, xxvi, 130, 146, 200–3, 250–61; filibustering against, 221–33; War for Central American Union, 126–31
Nicaraguan canal, 222
Nieto, Vicente, 47

Niger (privateer), 102
"night of agony," 149
"night of the bottles," 150
Niobe (British warship), 356
Niquitao, 27
Niterói, 407–8, 410
Niterói (Brazilian warship), 88, 90, 97, 410
Nitrate War, xxvii. *See* War of the Pacific
nitrates, importance to Chilean economy, 375, 376, 381. *See also* guano, War of the Pacific
Noailles, Vicomte de (Louis Marie d'Arpajon), 16
Noboa, Diego, 144
Norfolk, 80
North America, xxiv
Northern Light (American merchantship), 202
Norton, James, 97–98, 100, 102, 451n16, **453n25**
Nova Scotia, 431n34
Novella, Francisco, 82
Nueces River, 172, 173, 179
Nueva Granada, 24, 141–44, 272. *See also* New Granada
Nueve de Julio (Argentine warship), 395
Nuevo León, 80, 158, 298, 309
Numancia (Spanish warship), 334, 336–37, *336*
Numancia Battalion (Spanish army), 64
Núñez de Cáceres, José, 342

Oaxaca, 78, 80, 296, 308–9
Obando, José María, 142, 144, 273, **497n12**
Obeso, José María, 71
Obregón, Alvaro, 373
O'Brian, Johny, 362
observation balloons, 326
Ocampo, Melchor, 303
Ocaña, 27
Ocatlán, 297
Ochoa, Felipe, 255
O'Connor, Eduardo, 392–93
Ocotepeque, 252, 254
Ocumare, 21, 33
O'Donnell, Leopoldo, 215
O'Donojú, Juan, 82

Oeiras, 90, 151
Ogazón, Pedro, 298
Ogden, Samuel, 21
Ogé, Vincent, 2–3
O'Hara, Theodore, 216
O'Higgins, Bernardo, 56–58, 61–62, 64, 70, **443n8**, 445n38
O'Higgins (Chilean warship), 64–65, 95, 335, 340
O'Higgins (Chilean warship II), 378, 398, 402
Olañeta, 66–69
Olave, Col., 284
Olimpo (Paraguayan warship), 326
Olive (Haitian warship), 346
Ometepec, 77
Ometepe Island, 231
Omoa, 129, 254, 256
Oncativo, 117
Once de Abril (Costa Rican warship), 230
Oquendo (Spanish warship), 419
Oratorio, 274
Orbegoso, Luis José de, 133, 136–37
Orbegoso (Peruvian warship), 132
Order of the Golden Field, 211
Oregon, 179
Oregon (American warship), 417
Orelie Antoine I, 367
Oribe, Manuel, 118–20, 122–23, 152, 155, 282–83, **499n14**
Oriental Argentina (privateer), 100–1
orientales, 48, 94
Orientales (Cuba), 358
Oriente, 351, 355, 362–63
Orinoco River, 25, 33, 37, 236, 243, 248
Orion (Brazilian warship), 406
Orizaba, 304–5
Orleans Dragoons, 4
Oronoz, Carlos, 297
Ortega, González, 298
Ortega, Jesús G., 307–8
Ortíz de Ocampo, Francisco, 47
Oruro, 47, 67, 262, 264–66, 268

Osório, Manuel Luis, 323, 326, 329–30, 332, **511n39**
Osorio, Mariano, 56–57, 62
Ospina Rodríguez, Mariano, 274
Ostend Manifesto, 219
O'Sullivan, John L., 215, **482n8**
Otamendi, Juan, 142
Ottoni, Teófilo Benedito, 154
Ouinaminthe, 4
Ouro Preto, 154

Pacheco, Francisco, 188
Pacheco, Gregorio, 264
Pacific Ocean, xxvi, 57, 65, 135, 271, 279
Pacific War, xxiv, 60, 333–40, *338*
Pact of El Zanjón, 358–59
Pact of San Nicolás, 123
Pacto de Nico Pérez, 287
Padilla, José Prudéncio, 37–38, **439n81**
Páez, José Antonio, xxvii, 31, 33–35, 38, 40, 235, 237–43, 246, 248–49, **437n56**
Pagayos, 33
Pago Largo, 118
Paipa, 36
Paita, 63
Palacio, Raimundo Andueza, 244
Palacios, Enrique, 257
Palacios, Manuel Antonio, 512n63
Palas (Brazilian warship), 408
Palma, Estrada, 357
Palmar, 283
Palmer, Joseph, 225
Palmerston, Lord, 144, 201
Palmira, 276
Palo Alto, 182–83
Palomas, Battle, of, 286
Palonegro, 278
pampas, 58, 124, 343, 367–69
Pampero (Confederate warship), 517n22
Pampero (filibuster), 218, 485n40
Pamplona, 273
Panama, 39, 109, 126, 130, 142, 145–46, 211, 222, 273–74, 276–78, 280

Panama, Congress of, 105, 214, 352
Panama City, 126
Panama Railroad, 498n51
Pan de Azúcar, 138
Pando, José M., 267–68, **495n44**
Pandora (Haitian warship), 344
Panizo, Juan José, 136
Pantano de Vargas, 36
Pará, 87, 91, 151–52
Para (Brazilian warship), 512n60
Parades, Mariano, 167–68, 172, 177–78
Paraguarí, 45
Paraguay, xxvi, 41, 113, 121; War for Independence, xxv, 41, 43–45, 53; War of the Triple Alliance, xiv, xxvi, 313–32, 428n6
Paraguay River, 45, 268, 313–14, 319, 321–24, *322*, 326, 328–29
Paraguayan Legion, 325
Parahyba, 94
Paraiba (now João Pessoa), 90, 150
Páramo, 35
Paraná, 125
Paraná (Argentine warship), 392
Paraná River, 45, 97, 118, 119, 121, 123–24, 282, 314, 318–19, 321, 323–24, 394, 395, 396
Parapara, 245
Paredes, Mariano, 83, 180–81, 183, 474n10
Pareja, Antonio, 55–56
Pareja, José Manuel, 334–35, 337
Paris, xxvi, 20
París, Joaquín, 274
Parker, Foxhall A., 202
Parnaibo, 90
Parra, Aquileo, 276
Parrodi, Anastasio, 298
Partie de l'Est, 342
Pasaquina, 256
Paso del Norte (now Ciudad Juárez), 308
Paso de Patria, 321

Pasto, 39, 108, 143–44, 272–73
Pastry War, xv, 168–69
Patagonia, 367, 369
Patagonia (Argentine warship), 392–93, 395
patrones, 272
Paucarpata, Treaty of, 135–36
Paulding, Hiram, 232
Paunero, Wenceslao, 319–20, 325, 332
Pavón, 125
Payara, 239
Paynter, James, 201
Paysandú, 284–85, 314, 319
Paz, José M., 100, 117, 120–21
Peabody rifle, 277
Pearl (merchantship), 56
Pedro I, 85–92, 94, 98, 104, 149–50, 151, 155
Pedro II, 149, 155
Pedro Afonso (Brazilian warship), 411–12
Pedro Alcántara (Spanish warship), 30
Pedro Ivo (Brazilian warship), 411–12
Peixoto, Floriano, 320, 405–9, 411, 413
Peña, Lucas de, 348
Peña Blanca, 244
peninsulares, xxiv, 23–24, 33, 39–40, 44, 71–72, 81–82, 127, 351, 352
Peralonso, 278
Peralonso (rebel warship), 279
percussion-cap musket, 236
Pereira, José Clemente, 98–99, 154
Pérez, Albino, 168
Pérez, Francisco, 193
Pérez, Gregorio, 265
Pérez, Ignacio, 206
Pérez, José Joaquín, 294, 337
Pérez, Máximo, 284, 285
Pérez Jiménez, Maros, 249
Perico Flaco, 282
Perit (blockade runner), 356
Perla (Chilean warship), 56, 63
Permanent Central American Court of Justice, 260–61
Pernambuco, 86–87, 91, 94, 102, 150, 155
Perola (Portuguese warship), 89

Perote, 82
Perseverano, 286
Peru, 30, 38–42, 44, 47–48, 130, 140–41, 143–44, 267, 321, *374*, 443n1; Confederation War with Chile, 132–39; and guano trade, 335; navy, 39, 65; Pacific War, xxiv–xxv, 333–40, *338*; War against Gran Colombia, 105–110; War for Independence, 54–70, *338*; War of the Pacific, xxvii, *338*, 375–89
Peru (privateer), 137
Peruviana (Peruvian warship), 107, 132
Pesoa, Juana Pabla, 331
Pétion, Alexandre, 13–15, 31, 33, **432n42**
petit blanc, 2
Petit Canal (rebel warship), 239
Petit Gôave, 13
Petit Riviere de l'Artibonite, 14
Peyton, Balie, 291
Pezet, Juan Antonio, 334
Pezuela, Joaquín de la, 49–50, 64, 70
Philippines, 416–17, 424
Píar, Manuel Carlos, 33, **437n60**
Piauí, 89–90, 150
Pichincha, 39, 143
Pichincha (Colombian warship), 108
Pichincha (rebel warship), 145
Pickett, John T., 217
Pico, Andrés, 186
Picolet (Haitian warship), 346
Pierce, Franklin, 193, 219, 228–29
Piérola, Nicolas de, 382, 386–87
Pierrot, Luis, 344, 345
Pike, Fredrick, 375
Pilcomayo (Chilean warship), 385, 398
Pilcomayo River, 268
Pillow, Gideon, 190, 193, 195, 477n64, 478n86
Piñango, Judas Taber, 239–40, 249
Pinto, Andrés Avelino, 249
Pinto, Aníbal, 377

Pinzón, Luis Hernández, 333–34
Pinzón, Próspero, 278
Piranga (Brazilian warship), 88
Piratini, 155
Piribebuy, 330
Pisagua, 380–81, 399
Pisba Pass, 35
Pisco, 64, 386
Pitt, William, 21, 433n3
Pizzaro, Manuel D., 394
Pizarro (Spanish warship), 216, 217
Plan of Ayutla, 295
Plan of Iguala, 81–82
Plan of Political Regeneration, 172
Planchon Pass, 60
Plate River, 96–99, 101
Plaza de Artillería, 391–93
Plaza Gutiérrez, Leónidas, 109, 146, **466n48**
Plaza Libertad, 393
Plüddenmann, M., 421
Point Arenas (Nicaragua), 202
Pointsett, Gabriel, 56
Polish mercenaries, 217
political power, sources of, xiii–xiv
political reasons for war, 106, 126, 128, 131, 155, 178, 180, 281, 289, 296, 302, 310
Polk, James K., 179, 181, 183, 185–86, 188, 190, 195–96, 200, 215, 474n5, 475n18, 476n32, 476n34, 477n54, 478n83, 478n88, 479n12
Polverel, Etienne, 4
Ponsonby, J., 93
Popayán, 20, 142
Popham, Hume, 21, 42–43
Porlier, Rosendo, 77
Portales, Diego 132, 134–35
Port-au-Prince, 2–3, 5–8, 10–16, 80
Port-de-Paix, 6–7, 12, 14, 16
Porto Alegre, 152–54
Porto Alegre, Conde de. *See* Souza, Manuel
porteños, 42–43, 45, 47–48, 50–53, 60, 62–63, 94–100, 104, 113–114, 116, 394. *See also* Buenos Aires

Portete de Tarqui, 109–110
Portillo (Chilean warship), 56
Portillo Pass, 60
Porto Alegre, 104
Portobelo, 20
Portrero de Vences, 121
Portsmouth (American warship), 208, 209
Portugal, xv, xxv, 46; army, 44; Brazilian War for Independence, 85–92; foreign mercenaries from, 306; marine corps, 44; navy, 44, 85–86; War for Uruguayan Independence, 43–46, 48–53
Posadas, José, 46
Potosí, 41, 47–50, 66, 265–67
Pozo y Sucre, José del, 20
Prado, Mariano Ignacio, xxiv, 334–35, 376, 378, 381–82
Praieira Revolt, 155
Prat, Arturo, 378, **523n19**
Presidente (Peruvian warship), 107–8
presidio (fort), 158
Prestán, Pedro, 276
Priatinim republic, 152
Prieto, Guillermo, 298
Prieto, Joaquín, 135–36
Prim, Juan, 355
Princeza Real (Portuguese warship), 89
Principe (Portuguese warship), 89
Principe Imperial (Brazilian warship), 102
Principistas (Uruguayans), 285, 286
privateering, 60, 65, 100–2, 137, 206, 427, 463n35. *See also* mercenaries, sailors-of-fortune
Prometheus (American merchantship), 201
Prosperina (Spanish warship), 44
Prospero Pinzón (Colombian warship), 279
"Protector of the Peace," 252
Protestants, 129
Prouting, Thomas, 102
Provincianos (Central Americans), 126

Prueba (Spanish warship), 39, 63
Prussia, 309
Prussian mercenaries, 225, 229
Pryce, Carl Rhys, 212–13
Puebla, 76–77, 80, 82, 177–78, 192, 194–95, 296, 297, 309; Battles of, 305–7
Puello, José Joaquín, 345
Puente de Buin, 138
Puerto Cabello, 21, 26, 29, 38, 236, 238, 240–43, 245
Puerto Cartés, 259–60
Puerto Plata, 348
Puerto Rico, 9–10, 416–18, 420, 424; relations with Santo Domingo, 341–42, 347, 349
Puerto Santo, 30
Pueyrredón, Juan Martín de, 42, 48, 51–52, 60, 114
Puig (merchantship), 285
Pulgar, Venancio, 243, 244
Pulido, José Ignacio, 244
Pulitzer, Joseph, 416
Puná Island, 142, 144
Puno, 133, 135, 138, 378
Punta Gorda, 98
Punta Malpelo, 108
Puntas de Soto, 286
Purvis, John, 120
Putato Plata, 344–45
Pyrenees Mountains, 8, 80

Quebracho Herrado, 119
Quechereguas, 56
Quechua Indians, 262, 377
Queen's Cavalry Regiment (Spanish army), 73
Querétaro, 75, 81, 177, 296, 298, 303, 308–10
Quevedo, Quintin, 266
Quezaltenango, 127–28, 130
Quilca, 135
Quillota, 135
Quilmes, 42, 98
Quinones, Agatón, 172
Quintana Roo, 370–71
Quintero, 398, 402, 404
Quintero Bay, *421*
Quinteros prison, 284
Quinto Misiones (Argentine warship), 395
Quiroga, Antonio, 37

Quiroga, Facundo, 117
Quisiro, 240
Quitman, John A., 192, 194–95, 216, **483n15**
Quito, 20, 25, 36, 38–39, 108, 140–43, 145–46
Quito (rebel warship), 145

race war, xxiii, 1–3, 131
railroads, 141, 289, 293, 330, 362, 398, 402
Rainsford, Marcus, 11
Ramsay, Robert, 46
Ramírez, Col., 225
Ramírez, José Fernando, 180, 192
Ramírez, Pedro, 114
Ramírez Arellano, Manuel, 310
Ramírez y Sesma, Joaquín, 163
Ramón, Martínez Caro, 161
Ramos, Pedro, 242
Rancagua, 57, 62
Randolph, Victor M., 216
Ranqueles, 365–69, 373
Raousset de Boulbon, Gaston de, 207, 209–10, **480n9**
Raulet, Pedro, 109
Ravine-a-Couleuvre, 14, 431n27
Rayo (American merchantship), 275
Rayón, 79
Real Carolina (Brazilian warship), 89
Realejo, 223, 225, 252
Real Pedro (Brazilian warship), 96–97
Rebolledo, José Pío, 243, 244
Rebolledo, Juan C., 208
Recife, 91, 150, 155
Reeves, Henry Earl, 353
Refigo Mission, 172
Regalado, Tomás, 259
Regeneração (Portuguese warship), 89
reinols, 86
Reinvindicador (Venezuelan warship), 244
religious wars, xxviii
Remington, Frederic, 415, 529n1
Remington rifle, 255–56, 272, 277, 282, 353, *354*, 361, 377, 395

Remolcador (Venezuelan warship), 244
Rendón, José Manuel, 266
repartimiento, 369
Repúblic Argentina (Argentine warship), 100
Republic of Northern Mexico, 211
República (Brazilian warship), 406–8, 410–11
República (Venezuelan warship), 244
Republican Society of Cuba and Puerto Rico, 358
Resaca de la Palma, 182–83
Resolución (Spanish warship), 334
resource wars, xxvii–xxviii
Resquín, Francisco Isidoro, 314, 321
Restauração (Portuguese warship), 89
Restaurador (Venezuelan warship), 246, 248
Retiro, 393
"retreat of the shrimp," 382
revolution: definition, xv; misuse of term, xv–xvi
Revolutionary Committee of Puerto Rico, 358
Revolutionary Cuban Party, 359. *See also* Marin Shaw, Francisco Gonzalo
Revolutionary Junta of New York, 356
Revolutions of 1848 (Europe), 218, 290
Reyes, Isidro, 172
Reyes, Rafael, 276, 277, **498n41**
Riachuelo (Brazilian warship), 407
Ribas, José Félix, 29, **436n42**
Ribeiro, Bento Manuel, 152, 153, 155
Ricaurte (Venezuelan warship), 244
Richery, Richard de, 9
Richuelo, 320, 332
Ricketts, Charles Milner, 70
Rickover, H., 529n5
Riego, Rafael de, 37, 81
Riera, Gregorio Segundo, 247

Rigaud, André, 3, 6–8, 10–13, **430n8**
Rimac (Chilean transport), 379
Rincón, Manuel, 193
Rincón de las Gallinas, 96
Riobamba, 146
Rio Branco, Barao de, 330
Rio Cuareim, 283
Río Frío, 296, 297
Rio Grande, 167, 170, 172, 175, 179–83, 185, 190, 195
Rio Grande do Norte, 94, 150
Rio Grande, Republic of the, 171
Rio Grande do Sul, 51–52, 98–99, 102, 104, 120, 151–55, 282–83, 287, 314, 316, 321, 323, 405–6, 409, 411
Rio Grande do Sul (Brazilian warship), 328, 512n60
Riohacha, 279
Rioja, 117
Rio de Janeiro, 46, 86–88, 91, 98, 102, 104, 120, 149–55, 314, 316, 325, 405–8, 410–11, 413
Rio de Janeiro (Brazilian warship), 324
Río Negro, 46, 99, 284–85, 369
Rio Pardo, 152–53
Rio Pardo, Conde de, 154
Río de la Plata, 41, 44, 46–47, 49–53, 55, 57, 61–62, 64–65, 67–68, 96, 151. *See also* Argentina, 281, *312*
Río Tacuarí, 45
Rippy, J. Fred, 271
Rita (royalist warship), 33
Riva Agüero, José de la, 66–67
Rivadavia, Bernardino, 101–2
Rivas (Nicaragua), 225–31, *226*
Rivas, Ignacio, 368
Rivas, José, 127
Rivas, José María, 258
Rivas, Patricio, 228–29
Rivas y Salas, Joaquín, 170
Rivera (Uruguay), 287
Rivera, Bernabé, 52
Rivera, Fructuoso, 50, 52, 94, 96, 102, 118–20, 152, 154, 281, 283, **499n1**
Rivera, Primo de, 348
Rivera, Ruis, 358

Rivero y Lemoyne, Felipe, 347
Riveros, Galvarino, 379, 385, **523n23**
Robles, Francisco, 144, **465n31**
Roca, Julio A., 369, 394
Rocafuerte, Vicente, 141–44
Rochambeau, Donatien, 9, 16, 342, 351, **431n27**, 432n52
Rodas, Caballero de, 355
Rodil, José, 69
Rodríguez, Luís, 212
Rodríguez, Manuel (Chilean), 57–58, 62, 70
Rodríguez, Martín, 95, 99
Rodríguez, Santiago, 348
Rodríguez, Victor, 244
Rodríguez Francia, José Gaspar, 45
Rodríguez Peña, Nicolás, 57
Rodríguez del Toro, Fernando, 23, 434n11
Rojas, Pedro Manuel, 243
Rojas Paúl, Juan, 244
Rolando, Nicolás, 247–48
Roman Catholic Church, xxv, xxviii, 24, 28–29, 81, 84, 126, 128–29, 131, 141, 144, 154, 158, 238, 250, 258, 272–77, 292, 295, 297–99, 301–2, 309, 347, 369
Romarate, Jacinto de, 45, 50
Romero, Carlos, 268
Romero, Lino, 268
Rondeau, José, 46, 49–51, 60, 65, 114
Rooke, James, 36
Roosevelt, Theodore, 246, 424
Rosario, 121, 394–96
Rosas, Juan Manuel de, xiv, xxviii, 113–23, *115*, 125, 134, 154, 155, 281–83, 288, 368, **457n11**, 459n49
Rosas, Prudenciode, 119
Rosero, Matías, 275
"Rough Riders," 422
Round Island, 216
Routh (American merchantship), 202
Rouvray, Marquis de, 3, 430n9
Rowan, Andrew, 420
Ruatán Island, 199, 202
Ruiz, José María, 277

Ruiz de Castilla, Comde de, 25
Ruiz Sandoval, Francisco, 279
rum, 8
Russia, 63; foreign mercenaries from, *306*
Ryswick, Peace of, 430n1

Sa, Juan, 327
Saavedra, Cornelio, 41
Sabana de la Cruz, 242
Sabana Larga, 346
Sabina (Spanish warship), 80
Sabina Álvares de Rocha Vieira, Francisco, 153
Sabine River, 206
Sabo, 347
Sacasa, Roberto, 258
Sacramento, 186
Sáenz, José María, 142
Sáenz Peña, Luis, 394–95
sailors of fortune, xxviii, 50, 80, 103. *See also* mercenaries, privateering
Saint Domingue. *See* Haiti
Saint Marc, 6–8, 10, 14–15
"Saint Patrick" Battalion, 193–94
Saint Raphael, 3
Saint Thomas, 80, 358
Salado (Ecuadorian warship), 145
Salamanca, 80
Salas, Manuel José de, 20
Salas, Mariano, 83
Salaverry, Felipe Santiago de, 133, 135, **461n7**
Salazar, Carlos, 130
Salazar, Víctor M., 279
Salazar y Mazarredo, Eusebio de, 333
Salcedo, Francisco Antonio, 345
Salcedo Ramírez, José Antonio, 348
Salmon, Norvell, 232
Salm Salm, Felix von, 310
Salnave, Sylvain, 348
Salta, 44, 48–49, 51–52, 57, 66, 114, 119, 121
Saltillo, 183, 188, 309
Salto (Argentine merchantship), 508n5
Salvador (Brazil), 87–91, 153
Salvadorians, 252–57

Sama Valley, 383
Samaná Bay, 14
Sampson, William T., 419–22
San Antonio (Paraguay), 329
San Antonio (Texas warship), 171
San Antonio de Bejar (now San Antonio, Texas), 80, 136, 157, 159, 161–64
"San Antonio Greys," 160, 161, 162
San Bernard (Texas warship), 170–71
San Blas Bay (Argentina), 101
San Borja, 51
San Bruno, 57, 61
San Carlos (Argentina), 368
San Carlos (Chile), 366, 367
San Carlos (Venezuela), 240, 242
San Carlos de Ancud, 132
San Carlos River, 230–31
Sánchez, Antonio, 265
Sánchez, Francisco, 56
Sánchez, Francisco del Rosario, 347
Sánchez, Limbano, 359
Sánchez, Longino, 257
Sánchez Lagomarsino, José, 385
Sánchez Ramírez, Juan, 342
Sanclemente, Manuel Antonio, 279
San Cosme, 303
San Cristobál, 244, 245
Sancti Spiritus, 357
San Diego, 186, 207, 209, 212, 400, 427
San Diego Convent, 77
San Diego Fortress, 79
San Felipe (Chile), 60, 293
San Felipe (merchantship), 160
San Felipe (Texas), 160
San Felipe Castle (Puerto Cabello), 26
San Félix, 33
San Fernando (Argentina), 42
San Fernando (Paraguay), 329
San Fernando (Venezuela), 29, 35
San Francisco, 186, 207–9, 225, 227–28, 231
San Francisco (American warship), 410

San Francisco (merchantship), 419
San Francisco *Chronicle*, 211
San Francisco Commercial Adventurer, 209, 223
San Gabriel (Brazil), 99
San Inés, 242
San Jacinto (Nicaragua), 254
San Jacinto (Texas), 164, 166–67, 170
San Jacinto (rebel warship), 279
San Jacinto (Texas warship), 171
San Jacinto River, 164
San José (Argentina), 46
San José (Costa Rica), 229
San José (Guatemala), 257
San José (Peruvian warship), 384
San José (Uruguay), 285
San José Heredia y Alhajuela, 131
San Juan (Bolivia), 265
San Juan (Puerto Rico), 418, 420, 424
San Juan (Santo Domingo), 345
San Juan Bautista (now Villahermosa), 171, 177
San Juan de los Lagos, 72
San Juan de Ulúa, Castle of, 82, 169
San Juan del Norte, 200, 203
San Juan del Río, 81
San Juan del Sur, 225, 227, 230
San Juan River, 200, 201, 221, *222*, 223, 227, 230–33
San Lorenzo, 48, 307
San Lorenzo Island, 339
San Luis, 49, 158, 394–95
San Luis Potosí, 72, 161, 167, 169, 181, 183, 185, 188–89, 296, 297–98, 301, 307–8
San Marcos (Honduras), 259
San Martín, (Spanish warship), 63–64
San Martín, José de, 38–39, 41, 44, 48–49, 51, 57–62, *59*, 64–66, 70, 88, 107, 114, **441n17**, 444n20, 445n38, 461n3
San Mateo, Convent of, 193
San Miguel (El Salvador), 256–57

San Miguel (Mexico), 73
San Miguel (New Mexico), 171
San Miguel (Spanish warship), 63
San Miguel de Chimbo, 146
San Miguel del Monte, 368
San Nicolás, 45
San Nicolás College, 75
San Pascual, 186, *187*
San Pedro, 186
San Roque, 117
San Salvador (El Salvador), 127, 129–30, 253–55, 257
Santa Ana, 254–55, 258
Santa Anna (Venezuela), 248
Santa Anna, Antonio López de, xxvi, 82–83, 157–58, 160–65, 166, 169–70, 172, 174, 177–78, 180, 183–84, *184*, 188–97, 209–10, 223, 295–96, 427, **468n4**, 478n84
Santa Anna do Livramento, 99
Santa Bárbara (Colombia), 274
Santa Bárbara (Chile), 366
Santa Catarina, 408, 411
Santa Catharina, 153
Santa Cruz (Bolivia), 262, 267
Santa Cruz (Honduras), 256
Santa Cruz (Peruvian/Chilean warship), 132, 137
Santa Cruz, Andrés de, 39, 66–67, 105–7, 110, 132–39, 263, **461n3**
Santa Elena (now Fernández City), 168
Santa Eulalia, 137
Santa Fé (Argentina), 50–51, 102, 113–14, 118–19, 123, 369, 394–95
Santa Fé (Audiencia), 26
Santa Fé (New Mexico), 168, 171–72, 175–76, 185–86
Santa Fé (Venezuela), 34, 38
Santa Lucia (Ecuadorian warship), 145
Santa María, 52
Santa María River, 99
Santa María, Vicente de, 71
Santamaría, Juan, 229
Santa Marta, 27, 30–31, 37, 274
Santana, Pedro, xiv
Santana Familias, Pedro, 343–49, **515n15**

Santander (Colombia), 274, 276–78
Santander, Francisco de Paula, 24, 31, 35–36, 38, 40, 68, 141, 273, **496n9**
Santa Rosa (Peruvian warship), 384
San Telmo (Spanish warship), 63
Santiago (Chile), 44, 55–58, 60–62, 289–94, 337, 366, 376–77, 398–400, 401–2, 404
Santiago (Cuba), 348, 351, 356, 359–60, 363, 420–24, *423*
Santiago (Santo Domingo), 342, 344, 348
Santiago del Estero, 394
Santo Domingo, xxiv, 4–5, 8–10, 13–14, 21, 353; racial composition of, 341, 343; War for Independence, 341–49. *See also* Dominican Republic
Santo Domingo (city of), 344–45, 347
Santo Domingo Convent, 77
Santomé, 346–47
Santos, 102
Santos, Máximo, 286
Santos Zelaya, José, 258, 279
Santo Tomás, 208, 209
San Vicente (Mexico), 209
São Gonçalo River, 152
São João (Brazilian Warship), 510n29
São Luiz, 90
São Matheos, 89
São Paulo, 154
São Salvador (Brazilian warship), 411–12
Saraguro, 109, 142
Saranac (American warship), 202
Sarandí, 96
Sarandí (Argentine warship), 98, 100
Saratoga (American warship), 232, 301
Saravia, Timoteo Aparicio, 284–86, 288, 501n39
Sardá, José, 273
Sarmiento, Domingo, 114, 369, 428n10

Sarmiento, Siervo, 279
Sarratea, Manuel de, 48
Sarría, Leopoldo, 244
Sauce, 285
Savana, 36
Savannah (Georgia), 217
Schlesinger, Louis, 218, 229
Schley, Winfield Scott, 419–20
Scotland, foreign mercenaries from, 306
Scott, Walter, 114
Scott, Winfield, 181, 188–90, 192–96, 474n13, **475n18**, 476n44, 477n54, 478n85
Scourge (rebel warship), 240
Sea Bird (privateer), 210
Seabra, J. J., 406
Sea Gull (filibuster), 216
Segovia, 274
Segundo Crucero, 268
Seival (rebel craft), 153
selva (jungle), 107, 110, 271
Sensuntepeque, 255
Sentmanat, Francisco, 177
Separación Dominicana (Dominican warship), 344
separation versus union, xxv, xxviii, 53, 113, 126, 132, 140, 146, 149
Seraphin, Gen., 345
Serrano, Francisco, 355
Serrano, Ignacio, 378
Serviles (Central Americans), 126
Severino, 284
Seville, 43
Seward, William, 347
Shafter, William "Pecos Bill," 418, 421–22, 424, **530n20**
Sharps repeater, 228
Shepherd, James, 100, 451n16, **454n39**
Sheridan, Philip, 309
Shields, James, 190
Shrine of Guadalupe, 82
Siboney, 422
Sibún River, 199
Sierra, Miguel, 50
Sierra, Terencio, 259, 260
Sierra Chica, 368
Sierra Gorda, 310
"Silly Spain," 342
Silva Chávez, José María, 293

Silvado (Brazilian warship), 411–12, 509n18
Simcoe, John Graves, 10, **431n29**
Simpson, Roberto, 136, 138, 335
Sin Par (privateer), 101
Sinaloa, 75
Sipe Sipe, 51, 58
Sirius (British warship), 407
slavery, xv, 1–5, 7, 11–13, 18, 24, 55, 58, 83, 86, 160, 199, 214–15, 232, 249, 282, 288, 341, 346, 430n11
Sloat, John, 186
small pox, 512n50. See also disease
Smith, Delazon, 140–41
Smith, T. T., 202
Smith, Walter Gifford, 211
Smith, William S., 21
Smyrk (Ecuadorian warship), 145
Snider rifle, 357
Snively, Jacob, 173
Sobremonte, Rafael, 42–43
Socabaya, 133
Socabaya (Confederation warship), 134, 136–37
Socha, 35
Society of Equality, 289
Society for the Improvement of Economics, 23
Sogamoso River, 36
Solagnie, Amábile, 247
Solar, Estanislao, 61
Solares, Gregorio, 256
Solares, Joaquín, 253
soldiers of fortune, xxviii. See also filibusters, mercenaries
Soledad, 25
Somervell, Alexander, 174
Sonblette, Carlos, 237, 238, 241
Sonoita, 210
Sonora, xxvi, 207–8, 227, 371, 373
Sonthonax, Léger Félicité, 4–6
Sora Sora, 67
Soriano, 285
Sorocaba, 154
Sorondo, 25
Sosa y Lorenzo de Sena, Francisco, 346–47

Sotillo, Juan Antonio, 242
Soto, Enrique, 259
Soto, José M., 400
Soto, Marco Aurelio, 256
Soto la Marina, 80
Sotomayor, Rafael, 383
Soublette, Carlos, 237, 239, 241, **487n19**
Souffront, Gen., 344
Soulé, Pierre, 219
Soulouque, Faustin, 345–46
Sousa, Diogo de, 46
South America, 30, 40, 54–55, 69–70, 83–84, 106, *374*
Souza, Guillermo Xavier de, 330
Souza, Leopoldina, 86
Souza, Manuel Marques de, 155, 224, 326–27
Souza, Maximiano de, 86
Spain, xv, xxiv–xxv, 5–6, 8, 89, 94, 129, 303–4, *306*; army, 37, 44, 49, 57, 83; and Cuban Independence, 351–64; Early Latin American Wars for Independence, 20–84; navy, 24, 38, 44, 49, 55, 65; Pacific War, 333–40; Spanish-American War, 415–25; Wars with Santo Domingo, 341–49
Spanish-American War, 363, 415–25
Spencer, Sylvannius H., 230
Spencer rifle, 310, 313, 377
Springfield rifle, 418
Squier, Ephraim George, 201–2
Stag (American merchantship), 238
St. Augustine, 205
St. Helena Island, 18
St. Louis Island, 11
St Marys (American warship), 231
St. Thomas Island, 240–41, 238
Stirling, Charles, 43
Stockton, Robert, 185–86
Strangford, Percy, 46
Streber, Ricardo, 255
Suárez, José, 284–85
Suárez, José María, 265
Suárez, Manuel, 357
submarines, 337, 415
Sucre (formerly Churquisaca), 262, 264–65, 267

Sucre, Antonio José de, 38–39, 66–68, 70, 105–10, **439n87**, 464n19
Sucre (Venezuelan warship), 244
sugar cane, 1, 3, 8, 86, 215
Suipacha, 47
Susan Loud (filibuster), 216
Swain, Joseph C., 488n27
Switzerland, 431n20

Tabas, Juan, 373
Tabasco, 170, 177
Tabasco River, 171
Táchira, 244–45, 248
Tacna, 66, 138, 263, 267, 378, 381–83, 386, 388
Tacuarembó Chico, 52
Tacurí (Paraguayan warship), 313–14, 317, 512n60
Taguanes, 27
Tagus, 90
Tajes, Máximo, 286, **500n37**
Talambo, 333
Talavera Regiment (Spanish army), 56
Talca, 56–57, 62, 293
Talca (chartered warship), 145
Talcahuano, xxviii, 55–56, 61–63, 136, *380*
Tamandaré, Joaquim, 314, 319–20, 324–25, 332
Tamandaré (Brazilian warship), 321
Tamiahua Lagoon, 83
Tampico, 82–83, 159, 163, 168–70, 173, 185, 188, 190, 308–9
Tarapacá, 381, 388
Taratara, 240
Tarija, 117, 134
Tartar (British warship), 88
Taxco, 77
Tayí, 326, 328
Taylor, John, 90, 451n16
Taylor, Zachary, 179, 181–83, 185, 188–89, 196, 216–17, **474n5**, 475n18, 476n32
Tebicuary, *322*
Tebicuary River, 328–29
technology, 196, 366
Tegucigalpa, 252, 254–56, 258–60
Tehuacán, 79

Tehuantepec, Isthmus of, 301
telegraph, 417
Téllez, José Gabriel, 264
Tenerife, 27
Tennessee Company of Mounted Volunteers, 162
Ten Years War, 352–60, 364
Teresa (Spanish warship), 419
territorial conquests, xxvi, xxviii, 157, 166, 179, 198, 313, 333, 365
Tesalaca, 79
Texas, xxvi, 75, 80, 205–6, 211; annexation of, 179; second war with Mexico, 166–78; and slavery issue, 179; War with Mexico, 157–65
Texas (American warship), *423*
Texas (Confederate warship), 514n12
Texas Rangers, 172, 183, 196
Thames (British merchantship), 408
Thiébaut, Juan, 120
Thompson, George, 324
Tiahuanacu, 267
Tidblon, Cmdr., 101
Tierra Firme, 20, 50
Tierra del Fuego, 396, 400
"Tiger of Tacubaya," 299. *See also* Miramón, Miguel
Tigre, 42, 394, 395
Tijuana, 212–13
Timbó, 328, 329
Tiradentes (Brazilian warship), 407–8
Tobacco, 86
Tobago Island, 11
Tocopilla, 376
Todd, Charles S., 40
Toledo, Alvarez de, 80
Tolima, 276–77
Tolten (Chilean warship), 340
Toltén River, 366
Toluca, 74
Tonosí, 279
Toral, José, 424
Torata, 66
Tornado (Spanish warship), 356, 517n22
Tornel y Mendivil, José María, 166
Toro Submarino (Peruvian submarine), 385–86

torpedoes, 400, *401*, 406, 410–11, *412*
Torre, Miguel de la, 33, **438n65**
Torrejón, Anastasio, 182–83, 189
Torrelio, Mariano, 265
Torres, Gabriel de, 38
Torres, Lorenzo, 371–72
Tortuguero, 344
Tounens, Aurelio Antonio de, 367
Toussaint. *See* Louverture, Toussaint
Traconis, Juan B., 296
Trafalgar, 55
Transcontinental Treaty of 1819, 206
Travis, William Barret, 158, 162
Treaty of Acaguá, 287
Treaty of Alcaraz, 121
Treaty of Ancon, 388
Treaty of Basle, 342
Treaty of Córdoba, 82
Treaty of Girón, 109
Treaty at Guayaquil, 110
Treaty of Paris, 424
Treaty of Pilar, 113–114
Treaty of Piquiza, 106
Treaty of Purapel, 292
Treaty of Rio de Janeiro, 331
Treaty of Ryswick, 341
Treaty of Valparaiso, 267
Tres Acequias, 57
Tres Arboles, 286
Tres Esquinas, 274
Tres Palos, 76
Trinidad (Argentine warship) 60
Trinidad (Spanish transport), 63
Trinidad Island, 9–11, 21, 241, 246
Tristán, Domingo, 65
Tristán, Pío, 49
Triunfo (Spanish warship), 334
Trou du Nord, 3
Trujillo (Colombia), 27, 67–68, 129
Trujillo (Honduras), 232, 256, 258–59
Trujillo (Venezuela), 243
Trujillo, Julián, 276
Trujillo, Torcuato, 74
Tucumán, 48–51, 57–58, 114, 119, 393–95

Tumaco, 279
Tumbes, 143–44
Tumbes (Peruvian warship), 335
Tumusla, 69
Tunja, 27, 30, 36, 273
Tupac Amarú II, 443n5
Tuxpán, 83, 170
Tuy Valley, 237, 247
Tuyutí, 323–24, 325, 326–27, 332
Twiggs, David, 185, 190, 194
Tyler, John, 175
typhoid, 307. *See also* disease

Ucayali River, 268
Ugarte, Alfonso, 385
Ugarte, Ramón, 167
Ugartechea, Domingo de, 159
Unión (Confederate/Peruvian warship), 335, 337, 379, 382, 385, 514n12
Union Argentina (privateer), 102
Unión Civica, 391–92, 394, 396
Unión Civica Radical, 394
Unitarian League, 117
Unitarians (Argentines), 120
United Liberation Army, 66
United Provinces (Argentina), 368
United Provinces against Brazil and Uruguayan Independence, xxviii, 427
United Provinces of Central America, 198–99, 203; Wars for Union, 126–31
United Provinces of Río de la Plata, 51, 58, 60, 93–96, 102–4, 113–16, 123, 125, 134–36, 139
United States, xxvii–xxviii, 1, 8, 20–21, 63, 75, 80, 84, 101, 121, 127, 134, 157, 160–63, 198–203, 259–60, 272, 321, 369–70, 373; Civil War, xiv, 349; Congress, xxvi; filibustering against Mexico, 205–13; filibustering against Central America, 221–34; filibustering against Cuba, 214–19; filibustering against Honduras, 232; intervention in Brazil, 410–11; Navy, 13; relations with Chile, 388, 400, 404, 425; relations with Cuba, 352–53, 355, 362–64; relations with Mexico, 304, *306*, 308–11; relations with Santo Domingo, 346; Revolutionary War, xiii, xxiv; Spanish-American War, 415–25; Wars with Mexico, xxvi
Upper Peru, 41, 43–44, 46–52, 57, 64–70, 94, 106. *See also* Bolivia
Urbieta, Martin, 314
Urbina, José, 144–45, **465n30**
Urdaneta, Luis de, 142, **464n13**
Urdaneta, Rafael, 35, 37, **438n72**
Uribe, Rafael, 278–80
Urica (Venezuelan warship), 239
Urquíza, Justo José de, xxvi, 118, 120–21, 124–25, 283, 319–20, **458n27**
Urrea, José, 162–63, 166, 168–71, **469n25**
Uruguay, 86, 117, 119–20, 122–23, 140, 150, 151; intraclass conflict, 281–88; War for Independence, 41, 43–46, 48–53, 93–104; War of the Triple Alliance, xiv, xxvi, 313–32
Uruguay (Brazilian tug), 510n29
Uruguay River, 45, 48, 52, 94–95, 97–99, 102, 118, 120, 122, 281–82, 314, 318, 320
Uruguayana, 320–21
Uspallata Pass, 57–58, 60

Valdés, Gerónimo, 51, 66, 68–69, 215
Valdivia, 55, 63
Valdivia (Chilean warship), 65
Valdivia Regiment (Chilean army), 289
Valdivieso, Jose Felix, 143
Valencia (Venezuela), 26–27, 29, 34, 37, 238, 245
Valencia, Gabriel, 166, 171–72, 177, 193, 196, 471n2
Valencey Battalion (Spanish army), 38
Valera, Ramón, 172
Valerio, Fernando, 344
Valladolid (now Morelos), 73–76, 79, 81
Valladolid (southern Mexico), 170, 369
Valle, Andrés, 256
Valle, Aristóbulo del, 394
Valle, Leandro, 303
Valle de la Pascua, 237
Vallejo, José María, 145
Vallière, 3
Valotta, Gerardo, 395
Valparaíso, 42, 54–56, 61–64, 132, 134–35, 290, 293, 335, 337, 339, 340, 379, 385, 397–400, 401–2, 404
Valparaíso (Chilean warship), 134, 136, 138, 340
Vanderbilt, Cornelius, 202, 221, 228, 230–32, 485n26
vaqueiros (cowboys), iv
Vara del Rey, Joaquin, 422
Varela, Mariano, xiv
Varela, Pedro, 285
Vargas, Antonio, 294
Vargas, José María, 237, 238, 239
Vargas, Pedro, 268
Vargas Santos, Gabriel, 278
Vasconcelos, Doroteo, 253
Vasconcelos, José, 365
Vásquez, Domingo, 258–59
Vázquez, Rafael, 172
Veeder, P. S., 209
Vega, Celso, 211, 212–13
Veintemilla, José, 145
Vela de Coro, 21
Velasco, Bernardo de, 45
Velasco, José Miguel de, 138, 264
Velasco, Treaties of, 164
Vallé, José María, 225, 227
Venadito, 82
Vencedor del Alamo (Mexican warship), 168
Vencedora (Spanish warship), 334

Venegas, Francisco Javier de, 73, 77–78
Venezuela, xxvi–xxvii, 64, 105, 272, 278–79; development of coffee plantations, 236; race in, 236; struggle among caudillos, 235–49; War for Independence, xiv, 20–40, 235
Venezuelan rifles, 36
Venganza (Spanish warship), 39
Venus (merchantship), 287
Vera Cruz, 72, 79–80, 82, 160, 168–70, 173, 177, 185, 188–90, 192, 195, 296, 298–99, 301, 303–305, 307, 309–10, *421*
Verdeloma, 38
Vesta (merchantship), 225
Viacha, 66, 267
Viceroyalty of New Granada, 20–40, 109, 126. *See also* Colombia
Viceroyalty of New Spain, 71–84. *See also* Mexico
Viceroyalty of Peru, 54–70, 105, 109–10, 132, 139
Viceroyalty of Río de la Plata, 41–54, 113. *See also* Argentina
Victoria (Peruvian warship), 335
Victoria (rebel warship), 145
Victoria, Guadalupe, 80, **449n55**
Victoria R. (Argentine tug), 395, 396
Vidaurre Leal, Juan, 292, 293
Vidaurri, Santiago, 298
Viel, Benjamín, 290
Vienna, Peace of, 151
Vigodet, Gaspar, 48–49
Vijil, Augustín, 228–29
Vilcapugio, 49
Villa, Vicente, 37
Villa de Madrid (Spanish warship), 334, 337, 339
Villa del Saito (Uruguayan warship), 314
Villa de la Unión, 285
Villalobos, Mariscal, 69
Villamil, José de, 144, **465n33**
Villamizar, Vicente, 278

Villar, Manuel, 337
Villarroel, Hipólito, 72
Villate, Blas, 355
Villatte, 7
Villeta, 329
Vinagre, Pedro, 151
Vineta (German warship), 245
Virgin Bay, 228
Virgin of Guadalupe, 73
Virginius (blockade runner), 356
Vivanco, Manuel Ignacio de, 263, 334
Vixen (British warship), 200
Vizcaya (Spanish warship), 419
Voluntários do Pátria, 317
vomitó. *See* yellow fever
von Bismarck, Otto, 425
von Holmberg, Edward Kaillitz, 49
von Natzmer, Bruno, 225, 229
von Tschudi, Johann Jakob, 137
Vuelta de Obligado, 121
Vulture (American merchantship), 55

Wabash (American warship), 232
Walker, Patrick, 200
Walker, William, 203, 207–9, 221–33, *224*, 353, 481n28, **484n1**
Wandenkolk, Eduardo, 406
war, causes for, xxiii–xxviii; and economic power, xv; and social change, xv. *See also* boundary disputes, capitalism, *caudilloism*, intraclass wars, race war, religious wars, resource wars, territorial conquest
War of the Chihuahuas, 142
War of the Confederation, 132–39, 339, 367, 427
War of the Death (Venezuela), 27, 30, 33
War to the Death (Chile), 366
"war hawks" (Texans), 158
War of the Knives (Haiti), 11–13
War of the Pacific, xxvii, 268, *338*, 340, 367, 375–89, 397–98, *403*, 429n14

"War of the Ragamuffins," 151–53
War of the *Reforma*, 295–302, *300*, 303–5, 311, 353, 370
War of a Thousand Days, 278–80
War of the Triple Alliance, xv; xxvi, xxviii, 284, 313–32, 428n6
Ward, Henry G., 77
Warren (American merchantship), 55–56
Wars for Independence, xv, xxiv, xxvii
Warspite (British warship), 399
Washington, 80, 179, 198
Washington (rebel warship), 145
Washington, George, 431n27
Washington Treaty of 1907, 260–61
Waterloo, 290
Waters, John, 231
Wave (merchantship), 301
Webster, R. C., 230
Wellington, Duke of, 477n66
West Africa, 2
West Indies, 8–9, 11, 13, 18
Weyler, Valeriano, 362–63, **519n63**
Wharton (Texas warship), 176
Wharton, William H., xxvi, 468n11
Wheat, Chatham R., 216
Wheeler, John H., 229
White, Andrew H., 530n16
White, E. D., 216
Whitelocke, 43
whites, xiv, 2–5, 9, 12, 14, 86, 352, 357, 361, 367
Whyte, John, 10
Wilcocks, James Smith, 84
Wilcox, Frank A., 213
Wild Geese, 6
Wilhelm II, 246
Wilkinson, James, 205, 214, 480n4
William A. Turner (American merchantship), 177
William Robbins (Texas warship), 160
Williams, Stanley, 212
Williams, Vicente, 258

Index 569

Williams Rebolledo, Juan, 337, 377, 379, **522n13**
Williamson, Adam, 6–8
Wilson, W. H., 397
Winchester rifle, 255, 272, 353, 377
Windham (merchantship), 62
Windward Islands, 7, 9
Windward Passage, 6, 10, 346
Wisconsin (American warship), 280
Witton rifle, 316
Witworth cannon, 314, 318, 320, 326–27
Woll, Adrian, 172, 174–75, 177, **472n33**
Wool, John E., 186, 189
Worth, William, 183, 185, 190, 192–95, 215
Wright, Raphael, 451n16

Xatruch, Florencio, 255, 257

Yagarí River, 331
Yaguachi, 38
Yanacocha, 133
Yanacocha (Confederation warship), 134
Yañez, José María, 210
Yáñez, Plácido, 265
Yaqui River, 371
Yaquis, 371–73, *372*
Yara, 355
Yataí, 320–21
Yataity Corá, 324
Yavi, 51
yellow fever, 6–9, 13, 15–16, 35, 40, 82, 141, 168, 176, 197, 299, 304, 308, 311, 347–48, 361, 418, 424. *See also* disease
yellow jack. *See* yellow fever
yellow press, 416, 519n63

Yeruá, 119
Ygurey (Paraguayan warship), 326, 512n60
Yrigoyen, Hipólito, 395
Yucatan, 167, 170–71, 173–74, 177, 216, 295, 369–71
Yucutujá, 283
Yungay, 138

Zacapoaxtla, 296
Zacatecas, 73, 158, 296
Zacatula, 76
Zaldívar, Rafael, 256
Zamora (Venezuelan warship), 248
Zamora, Ezequiel, 239, 241–42, 249, **488n33**
Zapotlanejo, 302
Zaragoza, Ignacio, 305, 307
Zárate, Pablo, 267
Zárate, Villca, 268
Zelaya, José Santos, 259–60, **493n34**
Zelaya, Juan Lindo, 253
Zepita, 66
Zitácuaro, 76–77
Zulia River, 240
Zuloaga, Félix María, 297–98, 301–2

1st Gran Colombian Division (Colombia), 109
1st Infantry Battalion (Chilean army), 138
1st Mississippi Volunteers (American army), 189
1st Missouri Mounted Volunteers (American army), 189
1st Regiment of *Cazadores* (Uruguayan army), 285
2nd Brigade (Mexican army), 305

2nd Division (Argentine army), 62
2nd Paraguayan Horse Artillery Regiment, 320
3 de Agosto (Venezuelan warship), 244
4th Artillery Regiment (Uruguayan army), 287
5 de Mayo, 305. *See also* Puebla
5th Infantry Regiment (Mexican), 171
7th Colonial Brigade (Haitian), 15
7th Infantry (French), 16
8th Colonial Brigade (Haitian), 15
8th Infantry Battalion (Mexican army), 212
10 de Fevereiro (Portuguese warship), 89
10th Infantry Regiment (Argentine army), 392
11th Light Infantry (French), 16
19th Cavalry Regiment (Paraguayan army), 323
25 de Mayo (Argentine warship), 45, 95–98
25 de Mayo (Argentine/Paraguayan warship), 326, 510n23
27 de Febrero (Dominican warship), 346
28 de Julio (Venezuelan warship), 239
40th Battalion (Paraguayan army), 323, 329, 511n41
40th Regiment (British), 10
66th Regiment (British), 9
69th Regiment (British), 9
71st Infantry (French), 16
96th Foot (British), 8

ABOUT THE AUTHOR

Robert L. Scheina, Ph.D., is a professor of history at the National Defense University and a leading authority on Latin American military history. He has published hundreds of articles and four other books on Latin America, including *Latin America: A Naval History, 1810–1987*, the seminal work on the subject. He is also the author of *Santa Anna: A Curse upon Mexico*, a volume in the Brassey's "Military Profiles" series. He lives in Crofton, Maryland.